Analyzing Moral Issues

THIRD EDITION

JUDITH A. BOSS
Brown University

New York San Francisco St. Louis
...on London Madrid Mexico City
...ngapore Sydney Taipei Toronto

 *To my ethics students at Brown Medical School*

ANALYZING MORAL ISSUES
Published by McGraw-Hill, a business unit of The McGraw-Hill Companies, Inc., 1221 Avenue of the Americas, New York, NY, 10020.

This book is printed on acid-free paper.

5 6 7 8 9 0 FGR/FGR 0 9 8 7

ISBN 978-0-07-287703-8
MHID 0-07-287703-0

Publisher: *Christopher Freitag*
Sponsoring editor: *Jon-David Hague*
Senior marketing manager: *Zina Craft*
Lead project manager: *Jean Hamilton*
Lead production supervisor: *Randy L. Hurst*
Associate designer: *Srjdan Savanovic*
Media project manager: *Meghan Durko*
Permissions editor: *Marty Granahan*
Cover design: *Srdjan Savanovich*
Typeface: *9.5/12 New Baskerville*
Compositor: *G&S Typesetters*
Printer: *Quebecor World Fairfield Inc.*

Library of Congress Control Number: 2004108300

www.mhhe.com

Preface

Although there are several approaches to teaching college ethics, the use of moral issues is probably the most popular as well as the most appealing to students. The moral issues approach, on its own, however, has some drawbacks. It often fails to provide students with the analytical tools necessary for making real-life moral decisions. Students may also come to confuse "ideology," or the holding of certain views on issues, with morality itself. This, in turn, may contribute to "moral passivity" in which

> . . . great numbers of people, the young and educated especially, feel they have an adequate moral identity merely because they hold the "right" views on such matters as ecology, feminism, socialism, and nuclear energy. They may lead narrow, self-indulgent lives . . . yet still feel a moral advantage over those who actively work to help the needy but who are, in their eyes, ideologically unsound.*

Analyzing Moral Issues provides a corrective to these drawbacks by combining the appeal and strengths of the moral issues approach with a solid foundation in moral theory and moral reasoning. In addition to giving an overview of some of the major moral issues in our society, it (1) introduces students to both Western and non-Western moral theories, (2) includes a supplement that gives students the hands-on skills necessary to recognize and analyze moral arguments, and (3) is accompanied by the *Ethics Powerweb* which provides additional readings.

THE ORGANIZATION OF THE BOOK

The Moral Theory Chapter

This chapter covers the major moral theories. It also includes a section on moral development. When grounded in moral theory, the moral issues approach can engage the students' interest and connect abstract moral theory to what is going on in the world around them. Connecting moral theory to real-life moral decisions encourages students to accept personal responsibility for their moral choices rather than substituting ideology

---

*Christiana Sommers, "Where Have All the Good Deeds Gone?" *Hastings Center Report,* August 1982, pp. 13–14.

for character development. This chapter is followed by short readings from nine major world philosophers. More complete selections from some of the key philosophers can be found in the accompanying *Ethics Powerweb.*

The Reading Selections

The reading selections following Chapters 2 to 12 begin with a bridge between moral theory and moral issues by showing students how to apply moral reasoning to an actual philosophical reading on a moral issue—Judith Jarvis Thomson's "A Defense of Abortion." They include readings from traditional Western moral philosophers as well as readings that represent non-Western, multicultural, feminist, religious, and legal perspectives. The readings have been selected to introduce students to diverse and opposing viewpoints regarding the particular issue under discussion.

The Eleven Issues Chapters

Chapters 2–12 each cover a different contemporary moral issue. Each issue is related, when possible, to the students' everyday experience, thus connecting their lives as college students to wider societal issues. While students' lives may not be directly affected by broader issues such as capital punishment, as citizens in a democratic society they will be directly responsible for formulating policy regarding these issues. Bringing in broader social issues also requires students to extend their range of moral concern beyond their immediate community, which is one of the goals of a college education.

The introduction to each chapter includes a historical background of the issue and an overview of the traditional philosophical perspectives on the issue presented. Following is a summary of each of the eleven chapters.

Chapter 2, Abortion: Despite its legalization, abortion remains one of the most divisive moral issues. This chapter looks at the history of the abortion debate and some of the key moral issues underlying this debate, such as women's rights and the moral status of the fetus. It also raises the issue of selective abortion and discrimination.

Chapter 3, Genetic Engineering and Cloning: Cloning entered the ethics spotlight in 1997 with the announcement of the birth of Dolly, the first mammal to be cloned from an adult cell. This chapter explores some of the moral issues raised by new reproductive technologies, cloning, and other forms of genetic engineering. In doing so it also addresses the issue of personhood as well as the morality of trying to control what it means to be a human.

Chapter 4, Euthanasia and Assisted Suicide: Euthanasia has become an important moral issue mainly because of advances in medical technology that permit physicians to extend life. The demand for legalized euthanasia is also a reflection of the emphasis on personal autonomy and freedom in modern society. This chapter focuses primarily on the question of voluntary, active euthanasia and the debate over physician-assisted suicide.

Chapter 5, Punishment and the Death Penalty: The issue of punishment, and in particular capital punishment, touches on the most basic questions of justice and what is meant by the moral value of human life. This chapter looks at both the legal and moral issues involved in the debate over capital punishment. In addition to questions regarding the morality of the death penalty, it also challenges students to think about the more basic question of the morality of punishing wrongdoers.

Chapter 6, Drug and Alcohol Abuse: Drug and alcohol use among college students has increased dramatically since 1990. This chapter looks at some of the moral issues involved in the use of both legal and illegal drugs. It also includes an examination of the disease model and the moral model of addiction.

Chapter 7, Sexual Intimacy and Marriage: Most Americans regard sexual intimacy, especially outside of marriage, as an ethical hotbed. This chapter provides students with the background information as well as the moral issues raised in the debates over cohabitation, same-sex marriages, divorce, prostitution, and rape.

Chapter 8, Freedom of Speech: Rather than being an absolute right, freedom of speech needs to be considered in context and in light of other values that may conflict with it. In this chapter, freedom of speech is analyzed primarily in the context of hate speech, especially on college campuses, pornography, and of restrictions on speech in cyberspace. Also examined are the moral underpinnings of the First Amendment and the implications of the First Amendment for regulating these types of speech.

Chapter 9, Racism and Affirmative Action: Racism, the belief that certain groups of people are morally inferior simply because of their race, is perpetuated and reinforced at both the institutional and the individual level. This chapter examines the roots of racism in Western philosophy and American culture and the policies, such as affirmative action and reparation for slavery, that are designed to overcome the effects of racism.

Chapter 10, Feminism, Motherhood, and the Workplace: Feminism takes many different forms. This chapter gives an overview of the types of feminism (and anti-feminism) and how each addresses issues such as the nature of men and women, motherhood, the division of labor in the home, and special rights for parents in the workplace.

Chapter 11, War and Terrorism: War and terrorism have become a prominent moral issue in the United States following September 11, 2001. This chapter discusses the differences between war and terrorism and examines the question of whether either is morally justified and, if so, under what conditions.

Chapter 12, Nonhuman Animals and the Environment: This chapter explores questions regarding the moral status of nonhuman animals and the environment, as well as our obligations toward other animals and nonhuman nature. In particular, it challenges students to rethink anthropocentrism and to question whether human practices such as meat-eating, animal experimentation, hunting, and deforestation are morally acceptable.

The Critical Reading and Discussion Questions

Analyzing Moral Issues encourages students to apply critical thinking and reading skills to each reading through the use of critical thinking and discussion questions. Each reading is preceded by a short introduction and a set of critical reading questions related to the main points raised in the reading. The discussion questions at the end of each reading require students to think deeper about the arguments and concepts raised in that particular reading. The discussion questions also encourage students to relate these concepts and arguments to the different moral theories and other readings in the book as well as to real-life moral issues in their own lives.

Case Studies

Each moral issues chapter includes, at the end, several case studies related to the particular moral issue. The majority of these case studies are based on real-life events. By placing the issue within a context, students are encouraged to apply theory and moral reasoning to actual situations that they might encounter in their own lives.

Some of the case studies involve moral dilemmas that force students to defend a particular position on a controversial issue. Discussion of real-life moral dilemmas has been shown to enhance a student's ability to engage in effective moral reasoning. On the other hand, exclusive focus on dilemmas runs the danger of leaving students with the impression that there are no right and wrong answers and that morality is all relative. Therefore, other cases focus on issues that are fairly straightforward but which require introspection and reflection.

ACKNOWLEDGMENTS

I thank the reviewers for their helpful suggestions: Renée Smith, Coastal Carolina University; Donald C. Hubin, Ohio State University; Frank Schalow, University of New Orleans; John Beaudoin, University of Nebraska, Omaha; Mike Coste, Front Range Community College; Matthew Lawrence, Long Beach City College; Sara Goering, California State University, Long Beach; Sarah-Vaughan Brakman, Villanova University; and James Hudson, Northern Illinois University.

Thanks to my editor, Jon-David Hague, and his assistant, Allison Rona, for their enthusiastic support and suggestions. Heartfelt thanks also go to Jean Hamilton of McGraw-Hill, for managing the project and keeping me on schedule, and to Carol Rose for her excellent job of editing the third edition. I would also like to express my appreciation to Marty Granahan, permissions editor, for her patience and assistance in obtaining permissions for the new reading selections in this edition. In addition, I am grateful to the many authors who gave me permission to use their writings in this edition. My deepest gratitude also goes out to the many people, including Michael Jackson, reference librarian at Brown University, and my daughter Alyssa Boss, Esq., who assisted me with my research and provided feedback on the manuscript. Thanks also to Michael Simon for his assistance in preparing the third edition. Last, but not least, I would like to thank my former assistant, James Nuzum, for his continuing enthusiasm, his dedication to this project, and his invaluable input and assistance in putting this text together.

Contents

CHAPTER 11 War and Terrorism 629

CHAPTER 12 Nonhuman Animals and the Environment 707

CHAPTER 1

Moral Theory

A favorite theory is a possession for life.
—William Hazlitt, *Characteristics* (1837)

Adolf Hitler once said, "What good fortune for those in power that people do not think." In the early 1960s, Yale psychologist Stanley Milgram conducted an experiment on obedience to determine if Americans would be as ready to blindly follow the orders of an authority figure as were the Nazis.

In Milgram's experiment, subjects, many of whom were college-educated professionals, were led to believe that they were delivering a series of increasingly painful electric shocks as part of an experiment on the effect of punishment on learning. In fact, the person who was playing the role of the learner was an accomplice of the experimenter and was not actually receiving the shocks.

When the subjects balked upon hearing the screams of pain from the learner, they were urged to continue by an experimenter wearing a white lab coat. Despite the feigned protests of the learner, about two-thirds of the subjects obeyed the experimenter and continued delivering what they believed were potentially fatal electric shocks.

The findings of this experiment suggest that people can be persuaded to torture, and perhaps even kill, another person simply at the urging of an authority figure. A film made of the experiment revealed that those who were most likely to give in to the urging of the authority figure knew that what they were doing was wrong but were unable to articulate *why* it was wrong.[1] Those who were able to resist the authority figure, on the other hand, were able to provide justifications, in the form of moral principles and moral theory, for their refusal; they were able to say *why* continuing to deliver the shocks was wrong. Milgram wrote of his findings:

> Ordinary people, simply doing their jobs, and without any particular hostility on their part, can become agents in a terribly destructive process. Moreover, even when the destructive effects of their work become patently clear, and they are asked to carry out actions incompatible with fundamental standards of morality, relatively few people have the resources needed to resist.[2]

Like the subjects in the Milgram experiment, many of us also lack the resources necessary to critically analyze moral issues. For example, in a study of how college students judge social issues, such as abortion, pornography, and homosexuality, researchers found that many students had inconsistent "informational assumptions"; they were unable to offer a well-reasoned justification for their position on an issue, shifting positions depending on the questions asked.[3] Although the outcome of this research may not be as dramatic as the Milgram experiment, this inability hinders many of us from engaging in thoughtful discussions of issues such as euthanasia, abortion, capital punishment, animal rights, and environmental ethics. Like the Milgram subjects, simply deferring to those in authority or refusing to take a stand can contribute to a life-and-death decision for those affected.

MORAL PHILOSOPHY

Moral philosophy is the study of the values and guidelines by which we live, as well as the justification of these values and guidelines. There are two traditional subdivisions in moral philosophy: (1) normative ethics and (2) theoretical ethics.

Normative ethics is concerned with the study of the values and guidelines by which we live. Normative ethics also includes the study of moral issues—the primary focus of this text. *Applied ethics* is the application of normative ethics to actual cases.

Theoretical ethics, also known as *metaethics,* is concerned with the justification of these values and guidelines. These justifications involve skill in *moral reasoning* and critical thinking. In other words, while we can legitimately study theoretical ethics on its own, the study of moral issues and applied or normative ethics is built on an understanding of moral reasoning and theoretical ethics.

It is important to distinguish between descriptive theories or statements and normative prescriptive theories and statements. Prescriptive statements deal with values. They tell us what ought to be; for example, "People ought to keep their promises." Descriptive statements, on the other hand, tell us what is: "Chris broke his promise by not paying back the money he owed Frank."

If we simply begin debating moral issues without first establishing this foundation, our arguments may be weak and can easily collapse like the proverbial house built on the sand. Without the ability to critically analyze or offer theoretical underpinning for our position on a given moral issue, we are unable to effectively defend it or respond to others' arguments.

This inability contributes to the feelings that our position on a moral issue is simply a matter of personal opinion. "Well," we may say with a shrug of the shoulders, "we all have a right to our opinions." Having a right to our own opinion, however, is not the same as saying that all opinions are equally reasonable.

Or, in our frustration, we may resort to using logical fallacies, glaring at our opponents in an attempt to intimidate them, or attacking their character; we may make wild generalizations that we are unable to back up, or we may simply change the topic. We see this especially in highly polarized issues such as the current abortion debate that seems to go nowhere but where emotions run high.

The moral rightness or wrongness of a position or action, such as delivering potentially lethal shocks to another subject in an experiment, is not a matter of personal feeling or opinion but of reason. The study of moral theory and moral reasoning helps us recognize and organize these general principles and moral concerns. It is up to us as critical thinkers to decide which arguments are the strongest and to come up with a well-reasoned position that takes into account the strengths of both sides of the argument.

For students who have not had a course in logic, see the section on "Moral Reasoning" in the Supplement.

WHAT IS THE PURPOSE OF MORAL THEORIES?

Most people, if given a choice, would prefer to skip moral theory and get on with discussions of real-life moral issues. Theory is often contrasted with action. This is a false dichotomy, since it is theory that informs our actions. Knowing how to ground discussions of moral issues in moral theory and good moral reasoning will make us less vulnerable to persuasive, but logically incorrect, thinking.

A theory is a conceptual framework for explaining a set of facts or concepts. In moral philosophy, theory *explains* why a certain action—such as torturing babies—is wrong and why we *ought* to act in certain ways and be a certain type of person. Moral theory also helps us *clarify, critically analyze,* and *rank* the moral concerns raised by particular moral issues.

A good theory should also be able to explain the whole range or scope of morality, not just particular types of actions. For example, the theory that morality is a private choice is inadequate for dealing with choices such as rape, torture, and genocide, since these actions affect other people. In addition, a theory should take into account what we, upon reflection, believe to be right. Aristotle (384–322 B.C.E.), for example, takes as the starting point in developing his moral theory the moral intuitions of ordinary people. Moral theory, however, goes beyond our everyday notions about morality. It requires consistency in our thinking and the weeding out of those commonly held beliefs about morality that are inconsistent or superfluous.

Moral theories can be compared to road maps. A good theory offers *guidance* or signposts for thinking about and resolving moral issues. Although we may just happen to come upon a good solution, a moral theory, like a road map, makes it more likely that we will reach our destination with the least amount of wrong turns and aggravation. By providing guidelines, moral theories help us identify conflicts and contradictions in our thinking and make more satisfactory moral decisions.

Like maps, not all theories are equally good. Some may be good as far as they go, but they leave out too much. In this case we may want to combine them with other theories or "maps." Other moral theories, such as ethical subjectivism, lead us down dead ends. Knowing about the strengths and weaknesses of the different moral theories can save us from heading down these dead ends!

Theories provide us with a framework for discussing real-life moral issues; they also shape our worldviews or interpretations of our experiences. We all approach the world with certain assumptions that, loosely, form our theories about what to expect in the world. In any culture there are certain theories that are so embedded in the cultural worldview that they are uncritically assumed to be true. For example, in Western culture the theory that humans are superior to and separate from other animals (anthropocentrism) is rarely questioned. This is reflected in our language, where the common use of the term *animal* does not include humans. Anthropocentrism is also implicit in the assumption of ethical relativists that humans are the ultimate source of what is right and wrong. Rather than uncritically adopting the prevailing theories of our culture, we need to ask first if their assumptions can be justified or if they embody false views.

THE TYPES OF MORAL THEORIES

There are two main types of moral theories: (1) ethical relativism and (2) universalist or objectivist. *Ethical relativist moral theories* state that morality is different for different people. An ethical relativist claims that morality is invented or created by people; therefore morality, like fashion, can vary from time to time and from person to person. *Universalist* or *objectivist moral theories,* in contrast, state that there are fundamental, objective moral principles and values that are universally true for all people, independent of their personal beliefs or culture.

In his study of moral development, psychologist Lawrence Kohlberg found that when it comes to moral theory, 90 percent of adult Americans, while they may acknowledge universal moral principles such as equality, believe, for the most part, that morality is relative to or created by society.[4] In other words, for the majority of Americans, being morally good means following the norms and values of their society or culture—whether this be their peer culture, their church,[5] their country, or a combination of these. The theory that morality is relative to societal norms is known in moral philosophy as *cultural relativism.*

Many college students, on the other hand, claim that morality is relative to the individual and is different for every person depending on what they feel.[6] This theory is known in philosophy as *ethical subjectivism.* Philosopher Stephen Satris maintains, however, that students' relativism is not a genuine philosophical position but a way of avoiding critical analysis of their opinions. Indeed, critical analysis of these two theories uncovers implications that few people would be willing to accept. Rather than promote tolerance as a universal moral value, ethical relativism breeds suspicion of those who are different and allows exploitation of the weak by the powerful.

Because of this it is important that we learn how to analyze different moral theories. As critical thinkers and students of moral philosophy, we cannot be content with simply accepting the norms of our culture or dismissing morality as a matter of personal opinion. Rather than depend on the opinions of others and risk getting off course, we can use theory as a guide as we make our way through the often bewildering morass of moral issues that confront us in modern life.

EXERCISES

1. What do you mean when you say that something is morally right or morally wrong?
2. Make a list of guidelines and values that you use in making moral decisions. Are your values and guidelines consistent? Where did you get these guidelines and values? Do they give you sufficient guidance in resolving difficult moral issues? Explain.
3. Choose a moral issue that is important to you. Discuss how the guidelines and values you listed in the previous answer help shape your position on that issue.

RELATIVISM IN ETHICS

> *There is one thing a professor can be absolutely certain of: almost every student entering the university believes, or says he believes, that truth is relative . . .*
>
> —Allan Bloom, *The Closing of the American Mind*

The fact of moral disagreement among individuals and between cultures raises the question of whether there are really any objective or universal moral principles. Cultural and individual disagreements, fueled by popular clichés such as "morality is all relative," "do what you feel is right," "don't force your values on me," and "who am I to judge?" create serious doubts in people's minds about whether moral issues can ever be resolved, or whether meaningful dialogue between those holding opposing positions is even possible.

Ethical relativism is one of the most popular moral theories among college students. According to ethical relativists, there are no independent or objective moral standards. Instead, morality is *created* by people. In other words, humans, either individually or collectively, are the ultimate measure of what is right and wrong.

Ethical Subjectivism

> *What I feel is right is right. What I feel is wrong is wrong.*
>
> —Jean-Jacques Rousseau

Ethical relativism can be subdivided into ethical subjectivism and cultural relativism. Ethical subjectivists claim that individual people create their own morality. There are no objective moral truths—only individuals' opinions or preferences. What is right for you may be wrong for me, depending on our respective feelings. You may feel that racism is wrong; I may feel that white supremacy is morally right. You may feel that it is wrong to eat meat; I may feel it is right for me. The rightness or wrongness of our actions depends solely on how each of us *feels* about racism or meat-eating.

Do not confuse ethical subjectivism with the obviously true and descriptive trivial statement that "whatever a person believes is right for him or her is what that person believes is right for him or her." Ethical subjectivism goes beyond this by claiming that sincerely believing or feeling that something is right makes it right for the individual. Because morality is merely a matter of personal opinion, we can never be mistaken about what is right and wrong. In other words, my actions in terrorizing black students on campus are morally commendable and perhaps even morally obligatory, so long as I personally feel that what I am doing is right.

When asked if he thought what he did was wrong, convicted serial killer Craig Price calmly replied, "Morality is a private choice." If morality is simply a matter of personal opinion, there is no point in trying to use rational arguments to convince the racist or the serial killer that what he did was wrong, anymore than it would make sense to try to convince me that I really don't like cashew nuts. Similarly, there would not be any point in proceeding further in a moral-issues course.

If morality is based only on personal feelings or opinion, no one can ever be mistaken about what is morally correct or incorrect. The correct position on a moral issue is simply a matter of personal feeling, rather than reason or shared values. When peoples' views come into conflict, those who are strongest will be able to impose their agenda on others, as Craig Price did. Under ethical subjectivism we do not have to tolerate other people's views or even their lives unless, of course, we feel that tolerance is right for us. Ethical relativism, in other words, provides no guidance for reaching moral decisions when there is a question of what to do. Returned to the metaphor of moral theories as a road map, ethics subjectivism is rather like a map that always says "You're wherever you think you are."

What Would the World Be Like If We Took Ethical Subjectivism Seriously? Ethical subjectivism is one of the weakest moral theories. If taken seriously, it permits people to exploit and hurt others without having to justify their actions. As a theory, it does not provide a correct explanation for why certain actions are wrong. In real life we generally make moral judgments independently of anyone's feelings toward the action. Indeed, the fact that a serial killer enjoys torturing and killing his victims or that a child molester sincerely believes that his young victims enjoyed being raped only makes their actions more horrific. If ethical subjectivism were true, the opposite would be the case: Our moral heroes would be psychopaths—people who act solely on their feelings, without concern for any universal moral principles.

Cultural Relativism

> *We recognize that morality differs in every society, and is a convenient term for socially approved habits.*
>
> —Ruth Benedict (1933)

The modern theory of cultural relativism developed primarily out of late-nineteenth- and early-twentieth–century studies of simple cultures by prominent anthropologists such as Ruth Benedict, Emile Durkheim, William Graham Sumner, and Franz Boas. Like ethical subjectivists, *cultural relativists* maintain that standards of right and wrong are created by people. It is societal norms, however, rather than the opinions of isolated individuals, that form the basis of morality. Public opinion, not private opinion, determines what is right and wrong. There are no objective universal moral standards that hold for all people in all cultures, only different cultural customs.

Cultural relativists are not merely arguing that some moral values are relative to culture. They claim that *all* moral values are nothing more than cultural customs. Because there are no universal moral standards, the moral values of one culture cannot be judged to be any better or worse than those of any other culture. Headhunting, for example, is right or wrong only within a particular cultural context. In some New Guinea cultures, it is morally commendable for a young man to give his sweetheart a shrunken head as a trophy. In our country such an action would be regarded as highly immoral and even evidence of serious mental illness. Similarly, if a culture believes that women should be kept in subjection, women have a moral obligation to be submissive to their fathers or husbands, and men have a moral right, and perhaps even a moral duty, to use brute force should their women deviate from the cultural norm. It is wrong in our culture for men to beat their wives, but, according to a cultural relativist, it is wrong *only* because it goes against cultural norms.

For more on cultural relativism please see "Anthropology and the Abnormal" by Ruth Benedict, in *Ethics PowerWeb.*

Cultural Relativism Is Not the Same as Sociological Relativism Cultural relativism is a moral theory about what *ought to be. Sociological relativism* is a descriptive rather than normative theory. It is simply the observation that there is disagreement among cultures regarding moral values. Unlike cultural relativism, sociological relativism draws no conclusions about the rightness or wrongness of these values. Sociological relativists leave open the possibility that a culture may be mistaken about its moral values (such as Nazi Germany or the headhunting cultures) and that there *may* be universal moral principles that all cultures ought to respect. Cultural relativism, on the other hand, claims that if a culture believes something is morally right, that in itself makes it morally right. Because morality is nothing more than custom, there are no legitimate grounds for criticizing the moral practices of other cultures.

Morality may also change within a culture over time, much like laws and fashions. Slavery is now considered highly immoral in the United States. Two hundred years ago, however, slavery was not only *believed to be* morally acceptable by the majority, it *was,* according to cultural relativists, morally acceptable. If morality is synonymous with conformity to cultural norms, it was the abolitionists, not the slaveholders, who were immoral. Similarly, Martin Luther King Jr. was immoral for protesting the segregation laws of the South.

For cultural relativists, if something is legal or at least culturally acceptable, whether it be slavery, apartheid, abortion, capital punishment, affirmative action, or pornography, it is, by definition, morally acceptable. Things that are illegal—such as recreational drug use, human cloning, assisted suicide, and, in some states, homosexual activity—are, in general, immoral according to the cultural relativist. Of course some laws have nothing to do with morality, while other laws are considered to be immoral by the majority—such as laws forbidding consensual sex between homosexuals. But, in general, cultural relativists tend to be legalistic when it comes to morality.

Cultural Relativism Is Based on Faulty Reasoning Cultural relativism argues from the fact that a culture believes something, such as slavery, *is* moral, to the conclusion that that is the way things *ought to be.* In logic this type of faulty reasoning is known as the naturalist fallacy. The *naturalist fallacy* draws a conclusion about what ought to be, based on what is. As noted earlier, the fact that people believe something to be true, whether it be the flatness of the earth or the morality of slavery, does not make it true or moral. Yet even though the reasoning behind cultural relativism is faulty, the conclusion that it is the correct description of morality may still just happen to be true.

What If Cultural Relativism Is True? Further analysis of cultural relativism, however, reveals that, like ethical subjectivism, it is fraught with problems and contradictions.

Cultural relativism offers no criteria for distinguishing between reformers, such as Martin Luther King Jr. and Susan B. Anthony, who may break the law as an act of conscience, and common criminals. Both the social reformer and the criminal break cultural norms; both, therefore, are immoral. Identifying what is moral with what is legal is problematic, however, since there are some laws—such as laws supporting slavery or prohibiting women from voting—that are clearly unjust and that reasonable people believe should be changed.

Because it identifies morality with maintaining the status quo, cultural relativism cannot explain moral progress. Yet most people believe that the abolition of slavery in the United

States, the civil rights movement, and granting women full rights of citizenship all represented moral progress. Similarly, cultural relativism cannot account for the fact that most people believe that there are ways in which their own society can be improved. Not only does cultural relativism prevent criticism of other cultures, it also rules out the possibility of engaging in a rational critique of one's own cultural customs.

Cultural relativism encourages blind conformity to cultural norms rather than rational analysis of moral issues. Rather than using dialogue, we resolve a moral issue simply by taking a poll or calling a lawyer. But surely this is not an accurate description of how we make moral decisions. We do not resolve moral issues by checking the law books or taking a hand count. Legalizing abortion and capital punishment did not stop moral debate over those two issues; and outlawing the cloning of humans in the United States will not end moral discussion on the matter. Futhermore, the fact that most Americans eat meat is irrelevant to someone who is struggling with the morality of meat-eating.

Cultural relativism does not work in pluralistic cultures. Although it may have been possible a century ago for anthropologists to identify the cultural norms of simple, relatively isolated and static cultures, in the rapidly changing modern world it is becoming more and more difficult to draw sharp distinctions between cultures or even to figure out what our own cultural norms are. Most of us are members of several cultures or subcultures. We may be members of a Catholic, Cambodian, Native American, African American, feminist, or homosexual subculture whose values may conflict with those of the wider culture. Indeed, the so-called dominant cultural values are sometimes simply the values held by a small group of people who happen to hold the power in that culture.

We also cannot assume that simply because the majority holds a certain value that it is desirable. In his essay "On Liberty," at the end of Chapter 8, John Stuart Mill (1806–1873) argues that basing public policy on the will of the people can result in the "tyranny of the majority." Suppression of freedom of speech and religion, censorship of the press, and discrimination against minorities have all, at some time, had the blessing of the majority. Aristotle likewise warns that majority rule is not necessarily in the best interests of the community.

The belief that there are no shared universal moral values can lead to suspicion and mistrust of people from other cultures or subcultures, rather than tolerance and a sense of community. We may feel that "they" do not share our respect for life; that people from other cultures may even have dangerous values. Because cultural relativism rules out the possibility of rational discussion when cross-cultural values come into conflict and persuasion fails, groups may resort to either apathy and isolationism when the values of other cultures are not a threat, or to violence when another culture's values or actions create a threat to one's own way of life.

Most theories, even though they may not stand up under the scrutiny of critical analysis, contain at least a grain of truth. Cultural relativism reminds us that culture and history are important in the moral life. Our traditions, our religious values, and our political and social institutions all shape the way in which we apply moral values. In their concern to disavow ethical relativism, too many philosophers have divorced morality from the actual historical and cultural settings in which we make our moral decisions, but cultural relativism takes this observation too far. Although the *application* of specific moral principles is relative to cultures (as noted in the Eskimo example later in this chapter), this does not imply that these moral principles are the *creation* of cultures.

Cultural relativism is also a reminder of how easily we can confuse custom and tradition with morality. Because of this, we need to be able to critically analyze not just issues that are considered moral controversies, but also customs that society accepts as perfectly moral, such as meat-eating.

Ethical Relativism and Doublethink The simplicity and popularity of the two types of ethical relativism theories make them particularly seductive. Ethical subjectivism absolves people of ever having to deliberate before making a moral judgment, whereas cultural relativism absolves people from moral responsibility so long as they follow the crowd. At the same time, almost everyone wants others to treat them with respect and be held morally culpable for their hurtful actions.

Some people try to hold on to ethical relativism by jumping back and forth between the different theories, depending on what is more expedient in a particular situation. For example, some students may argue that morality is a private choice when it comes to something they are doing, such as binge drinking or cheating on a test or using hate speech. At the same time, they may be morally critical of teachers who break cultural norms by coming to class drunk or who use sexist or racist language in class or play favorites in grading tests. Ethical subjectivism and cultural relativism, however, are mutually exclusive theories. A person cannot consistently believe both that morality is created by individuals and that morality is a cultural creation.

Some people who claim that they are relativists may also bring universal moral principles concerning justice and respect in through the back door. They may argue that sexist and racist language is disrespectful or that playing favorites in grading is unfair. They may even cite the Golden Rule or some form of it. Because the two types of theories are based on contradictory claims regarding the source of morality, however, both forms of ethical relativism are incompatible with universalist theories.

What About Moral Disagreement?

But, you may ask, if ethical relativism is incorrect, how can we explain the lack of agreement among individuals and cultures over moral values? The fact that people disagree does not necessarily mean that there are no objective moral principles. People can disagree for a number of reasons. They may be mistaken about their facts. At one time most people believed that the earth was flat, but it turns out they were mistaken. Physicians used to routinely lie to dying cancer patients, believing that the truth would be so upsetting that it might kill them. It wasn't until the 1970s that studies were carried out that showed physicians to be wrong. There may also be objective moral standards, even though we may have yet to discover them, or at least their exact nature.

Disagreement can also occur because natural conditions and religious beliefs influence the expression of a particular moral value. In 1941 Gontran de Poncins wrote the following about the Kabloona, an Eskimo culture living in the Canadian arctic.

> One observer was told of an Eskimo who was getting ready to move camp and was concerned about what to do with his blind and aged father, who was a burden to the family. One day the old man expressed a desire to go seal hunting again, something he had not done for many years. His son readily assented to this suggestion, and the old man was dressed warmly and given his weapons. He was

> then led out to the seal grounds and was walked into a hole in the ice into which he disappeared.[7]

Is cultural relativism the only way to explain the difference between the Kabloona and modern Americans? Modern Americans can hire caregivers or put their ailing parents or grandparents in nursing homes. The Kabloona, on the other hand, were a nomadic people; there were no nursing homes or hospitals or spare bedrooms in the house for grandparents. As nomadic people their lives depended on following the seal herds. To take a blind and ailing parent on one of these treks could have resulted in starvation, not just of the elderly parent, but of the whole family. In addition, the son, as was the tradition, respected his father's autonomy, waiting until he requested the "hunting" trip.

What was different here, in other words, were not the fundamental moral values of respect for life, family loyalty, and personal autonomy, but different conditions that placed limitations on how these values could best be *applied*. The description is different, not the fundamental moral norms. In other words, the Kabloona practice can be explained as an example of sociological relativism. Saving the lives of many took precedence over prolonging the father's life. The question of when, if ever, it is morally permissible to assist a terminally ill person in taking his or her life is not one limited to the Kabloona culture. The introduction of medical technology that can prolong the lives of the elderly and the dying has brought the issues of death with dignity and assisted suicide to the forefront in our own culture.

People may also disagree about moral issues not because they hold fundamentally different moral values, but because they *rank* or prioritize them differently. Both Aristotle and the Confucians give a high ranking to community and social values. In his article "Law, Morality, and 'Sexual Orientation,'" John Finnis opposes homosexual marriage on the grounds that it is destructive to the common good. Libertarians, on the other hand, like most Americans, place a higher value on individual autonomy and freedom. Michael Nava and Robert Dawidoff defend gay marriage as being a private choice. Moral theory helps us recognize and rank these values and in so doing helps us come to a resolution that honors as many moral values as possible.

Relativism, Personhood, and Moral Community

Variations in cultural norms can also occur because of differences in how cultures define their moral communities. According to anthropologist Clyde Kluckholn, there are universal moral values that are recognized by all cultures. No culture, for example, approves of indiscriminate lying, cheating, or stealing. Random violence is also prohibited universally. Every culture also makes arrangements for the care of its children. These moral values, however, apply only to members of a particular culture's *moral community*, that is, to those who are seen as having moral value. Headhunters, for example, always select their victims from outside their immediate community.

Beings who have moral worth are known in moral philosophy as *persons*. Persons are worthy of respect as valuable in themselves, rather than simply because of their usefulness or value to someone else. The widespread identification of *person* with *human being* in our culture betrays our anthropocentric bias in defining moral community; the use of the term *man* for all humans also shows our patriarchal bias. In coming up with a rational and consistent definition of the moral community, it is important to look beyond culturally biased terms.

Cultural Relativism and Ethnocentrism Cultural relativism defines moral community in ethnocentric terms: Someone, or something, has moral value only because society grants this status. There is no source of moral value other than one's culture. Those who are granted moral status by their culture receive the protection and support of the community. Moreover, those who are closer to the center of the moral community—such as white males in our culture—receive more privileges and protection. Those who are *marginalized*—such as women, homosexuals, blacks, and Hispanics—have less access to economic and social benefits. When members of a marginalized group transgress cultural norms, they are not given the same protection as those in power. For example, in the United States, blacks are more likely to receive the death penalty.[8] Beings who are outside the moral community—such as nonhuman animals, fetuses, and the environment in our culture—on the other hand, can be treated as a "means only" and disposed of, eaten, or exploited solely for the benefit of those within the moral community.

In Buddhist cultures and some of the Native American cultures, the moral community is defined very broadly to include all living beings—human and nonhuman. Other cultures define their moral community more narrowly. For a group of beings to be excluded from the moral community, they first have to be "depersonalized." Before embarking on their "final solution," for example, the German Supreme Court in 1936 ruled that "the Jew is only a rough copy of a human being, with human like facial traits but nonetheless . . . lower than any animal . . . otherwise nothing." In the 1857 *Dred Scott v. Sanford* decision, the United States Supreme Court reaffirmed that the slave was "property in the strictest sense of the word" and an "inferior being that had no rights which the white man was bound to respect." In the 1973 *Roe v. Wade* decision, which legalized abortion, the Court declared that "the word 'person,' as used in the Fourteenth Amendment, does not include the unborn."

Discussions of whether these exclusions were or are morally justified should be based on reason, not cultural or legal tradition. The cultural definition of the moral community is, to a large extent, politically and economically motivated and serves to maintain the status quo. By protecting the interests of those in power and morally sanctioning the marginalization and exploitation of other groups, cultural relativism promotes ethnocentrism and legitimates hatred and discrimination. Problems such as racism and sexism, which are based on long traditions of discrimination against blacks and women, exist in our culture, in part, because the majority of American adults are cultural relativists.

The power of our cultural worldview is much more pervasive in our moral thinking than most of us realize. Many people, while giving lip service to the universal principle of equality, in their everyday lives tacitly adopt the prevailing cultural view of the moral community. In the study mentioned earlier of how college students judge social issues, researchers found that slightly more than half of the students interviewed, for example, evaluated homosexuality in a positive light, stating that it was a personal preference just as heterosexuality was a personal preference.[9] When the same students were presented with a hypothetical example of their own child being homosexual, however, 92 percent shifted their position, stating that this would not be morally acceptable or desirable. In other words, they shifted from a definition of the moral community based on the principle of equality to the cultural definition of the moral community that marginalizes homosexuals. To avoid getting mired in doublethink, it is important to be aware of how the cultural definition of the moral community shapes viewpoints on moral issues.

Unlike cultural relativism, universalist theories of morality require rational criteria for personhood and, most important, that the exclusion of a particular group of people or beings from the moral community be justified. Much of the dissension over abortion, animal rights, and environmental ethics stems from disagreement over the definition of moral community and personhood. Thus, any debate on these issues must be based on a rational and consistent definition of these key terms. Mary Anne Warren in her article on abortion, for example, devotes considerable space to defining personhood. As with slavery, justifying practices such as meat-eating, commodification of the environment, or abortion on the grounds of tradition or legality just won't do.

For a critique of cultural relativism see "The Challenge of Cultural Relativism" by James Rachels in *Ethics PowerWeb.*

EXERCISES

1. Philosopher Stephen Satris argues that the ethical relativism of most college students is intended not as a well-thought-out philosophical theory but as an "invincible suit of armor" to "prevent or close off dialogue and thought."[10] Do you agree? Discuss an instance when you, or someone else, used ethical subjectivism as a means of ending the discussion on a moral issue.
2. Do your views on the issues covered in this chapter coincide, for the most part, with those of your culture or subculture? To what extent do you use widespread agreement as support for the "rightness" of your position on issues such as abortion or capital punishment?
3. In his book *1984,* George Orwell coined the term *doublethink* to describe when people simultaneously hold two contradictory views and believe both to be true. He predicted that doublethink would become more and more prevalent as people lost the ability to think critically. Do you agree with Orwell? What are some instances of doublethink in debates on moral issues?
4. What criteria do you use to decide who or what is included and who or what is excluded from the moral community? Are you satisfied with your criteria? How does your definition of personhood affect your views on the moral issues included in this text?

MOVING BEYOND ETHICAL RELATIVISM

Moral thought, then, seems to behave like all other kinds of thought. Progress through the moral levels and stages is characterized by increasing differentiation and increasing integration, and hence is the same kind of progress that scientific theory represents.

—Lawrence Kohlberg, *The Philosophy of Moral Development* (1971)

French novelist André Gide (1869–1951) once wrote: "Culture, born of life, ultimately kills life." Just as children must one day leave their parents and strike out on their own if they are to continue maturing, so too must we put behind us the dictates of our peer group or culture as the ultimate moral authority and seek a more solid and reliable foundation for everyday moral decisions.

Both types of ethical relativism—ethical subjectivism and cultural relativism—are inadequate as explanations of how we make real-life moral decisions and as guides for what we ought to do. Universalist moral theories offer an alternative to ethical relativism. These theories claim that morality is universal and objective and, as such, exists independently of personal or cultural opinions.

The Stage Theory of Moral Development

According to developmental psychologists, there are innate cognitive structures that are fundamental to all humans. These structures include—among others—causality, time and space, and moral excellence. In his study of moral reasoning, psychologist Lawrence Kohlberg found that humans move through distinct stages of moral development. These stages are universal and cross-cultural and represent "transformations in the organization of thought, rather than increasing knowledge of cultural values." The earlier stages are not so much replaced by higher stages as incorporated into them—much like elementary school arithmetic becomes part of understanding complex statistical analysis. People move on to the next or "higher" stage of moral development only when they find their current type of moral reasoning inadequate. This generally occurs when they encounter a crisis that their current mode of thinking is unable to satisfactorily resolve.

Young children use primarily egoistic or preconventional moral reasoning. Morality is simply a matter of satisfying their own needs. Indeed, sociobiologists such as Edward O. Wilson[11] claim that all human behavior, even altruism, is basically selfish in that it is primarily oriented toward passing on one's genes to future generations.

According to Kohlberg, in the second or conventional stage of moral reasoning, people look to others, whether it be their peers or societal norms, for their moral values. In other words, they reject egoism and adopt cultural relativism. The transition to the conventional stage generally takes place during early adolescence. While egoistic reasoning may be effective in helping the young child get what he or she wants, in high school and college, egoism is more likely to irritate others and alienate the egoist from his or her peers.

Conventional moral reasoners are concerned with pleasing others and respecting social rules. Their position on a moral issue is generally determined by what their peers believe, or, at the higher level of conventional reasoning, what is legal. As a developmental stage, conventional moral reasoning helps to socialize young people and move them beyond egoism to a concern for community values and the needs of others.

The final stage, according to Kohlberg, is that of principled reasoning. In justifying this as a more desirable or higher stage than the previous stages, Kohlberg points out that people at this stage prefer it to their earlier stages of moral reasoning. In addition, most world philosophers have long held that autonomous moral reasoning, universality and impartiality, and compassion and a concern for justice for all are the hallmarks of sound moral reasoning.

Kohlberg used only males in formulating his theory on moral development. Not surprisingly, his stage theory has been criticized for not taking into account the way women think about moral issues. Through her interviews with women and a study of women in literature, Harvard psychologist Carol Gilligan concluded that women's moral development tends to follow a different path than men's: Men tend to be duty- and principle-oriented; women are more context-oriented and tend to view the world in a more emotional and personal way.[12] Women's moral judgment, Gilligan found, is characterized by concern for themselves and others, accepting and maintaining responsibility within relationships, attachment, and self-sacrifice.

Although Gilligan's and Kohlberg's theories emphasize different aspects of moral development, and Kohlberg divides each stage into two levels, their stages are roughly parallel. The preconventional stage in both their theories includes the egoists and ethical subjectivists who put their needs before those of others. Conventional moral reasoners, in both theories, are cultural relativists. The different descriptions of the conventional stage are not surprising given the different ways in which men and women are socialized in our culture. Men, for the most part, are socialized to be the upholders of law and order—whether it be the law of the land or the rules laid down by their fraternity. Women, on the other hand, are taught that being a good woman involves self-sacrifice and placing the welfare of others before her own. As Susan Wolf points out in her article on feminism and euthanasia, this can make women more vulnerable to pressure to choose euthanasia.

In both theories the postconventional stage is represented by autonomous moral reasoning, where a person looks to transcultural universal values—whether these are in the form of abstract principles of justice and respect or sentiments such as compassion and empathy. These two theories or perspectives are not mutually exclusive. Indeed, scores on Kohlberg's Moral Judgment Interview are significantly related to those of the Ethic of Care Interview.[13] Developing an awareness that respect applies to all persons involves being able to empathize with others. Psychopaths, who lack the ability to empathize, also lack any sense of moral duty. In addition, Gilligan's postconventional stage entails that women realize that principles of justice and respect apply to themselves as well as to other people.

Recent research has shown that most people—men and women alike—use both the care and the justice perspective in their moral reasoning. Neither perspective is better than the other; both Gilligan and Kohlberg came to acknowledge that moral maturity involves the development and integration of both perspectives.[14]

The preference for one of the two perspectives can show up in how students debate different moral issues. Women, as well as some men, at the conventional stage of moral reasoning may fail to speak up or challenge someone for fear of offending them. Men, as well as some women, at the conventional stage may conform to the rules of their peer culture or confuse what is moral with what is legal. These stages also influence how students make real-life moral decisions. Studies of drinking on campuses, for example, show that freshmen men are more likely than women to succumb to peer pressure to engage in heavy drinking and drug use. Female freshmen, in contrast, are more likely to refrain from drinking and drug use, because of concern for how it will affect their families.[15]

Being wary of peer pressure and being concerned about the impact of our actions on our relationships are both important in moral decision making. Being aware of your own moral-decision-making style, and the fact that it may differ in emphasis from that of others, can help you cultivate your own strengths and overcome your weaknesses. It will also encourage you to appreciate the strengths and contributions of other perspectives in moral decision making and in group discussions of moral issues.

STAGES OF MORAL REASONING

Stage	Kohlberg[17]	Gilligan[18]
Preconventional	Punishment (avoid punishment) Egoist (satisfy one's own needs; consider the needs of others only if it benefits you)	Self-centered (view one's own needs as all that matters)
Conventional	Good boy/nice girl (please and help others; concern for earning others' approval; conformity to peer norms) Society-maintaining (respect authority and social rules; maintain the existing social order)	Self-sacrificing (view others' needs as more important)
Postconventional	Social contract or legalistic (obey useful social rules; appeal to social consensus and majority rule as long as minimal basic rights are safeguarded) Conscience and universal principles (autonomously recognize universal rules, such as justice and equality; respect for equal human rights and the dignity of each individual)	Mature care ethics (balance one's own needs and the needs of others)

College and Moral Development

When young people begin college, they may discover that what they thought were clear-cut cultural norms and values are not so conventional after all. Their cherished worldviews may come into conflict with those of others, especially people from different cultural backgrounds. This, in turn, leads them to question the morality of some of their own cultural norms. During this transition period, students are torn between the rejection of moral values that are culturally relative and the reluctance to commit to universal moral principles (postconventional moral reasoning). This conflict can manifest itself in hedonistic disregard for any moral values—either relative or universal.[16]

Moral maturity entails making our own well-reasoned moral decisions rather than simply following the dictates of the crowd or going with our selfish desires. At the same time, moral maturity involves integrating into our moral reasoning the strengths of these earlier stages; in particular, a sensitivity to cultural and historical norms in *applying* moral principles and a realization that our desires and needs count as much as anyone else's.

Unfortunately, most college students do not complete the transition to postconventional moral reasoning, but instead move into a higher level of conventional moral reasoning. Although they may become less dependent on the opinions of their peers, the trade-off is that they become more conforming to wider societal norms. Rather than making the transition from cultural relativism to postconventional (principled) moral reasoning, they simply accept the norms and laws of their culture as the final word in what is right or wrong. While this may serve a person well in a just society, blind obedience to cultural norms can lead to disasters like the Holocaust in Nazi Germany, the slave trade, and the massacre of Native Americans.

The Importance of Moral Development and Ethics Education

Could such culturally approved holocausts happen today in the United States? Most people would like to think that they would draw the line at participating in such atrocities. If laws were enacted ordering, let's say, the euthanasia of all people over 65, or mandatory prenatal genetic testing and the destruction of all genetically "imperfect" fetuses, or mandatory "reprogramming" of the brains of racists or sexists, would we go along with these laws? Most of us would like to think that we would draw the line at participating in atrocities such as genocide and mind control. Although these practices may make us feel uncomfortable, if we identify morality with cultural norms, on what grounds are we going to oppose them?

One of the primary purposes of ethics education is to help students make the transition to postconventional moral reasoning by providing them with the resources to make effective moral decisions that they will not come to regret later. Unlike moral indoctrination, ethics education is not about telling people what is right and wrong. Most people, with the exception of psychopaths, "know" right from wrong.[19]

In the Milgram experiment, for example, many of the subjects were openly distressed and "knew" that what they were doing was wrong, but they were unable to say why. Ethics education helps us articulate moral values. It also teaches us how to effectively apply moral theory and moral reasoning to a particular issue or real-life moral decision. Because the majority of subjects in the Milgram experiment could not support their intuition with moral principles and moral reasoning, they instead defaulted to the authority figure.[20]

The study of moral theory and the reasoning underlying moral issues also help motivate people. Research has found that people who are morally mature and better at moral reasoning are more motivated to act on their beliefs.[21] People at the higher stages of moral development not only sympathize with those who are suffering, but take active steps to help alleviate that suffering. They are willing to speak out on behalf of themselves and others when they witness an injustice and will take effective and well-thought-out action to correct the injustice.

The ability to effectively analyze moral issues, such as those addressed in this text, should motivate students to take moral action, also known as *praxis,* rather than simply being content to subscribe to the "correct" ideology. Praxis can take many forms, whether it be engaging in a letter-writing campaign regarding an issue such as capital punishment, assisting women who have unwanted pregnancies, speaking up when confronted with a sexist or racist comment or action, joining an animal rights or environmental group, or working in a campus drug-and-alcohol awareness program.

Moral action involves not only *doing* the right thing, but striving to *be* the best person we can be. Virtuous people, those who regard morality as an important aspect of their self-identity, are more likely to do the right thing and to get involved in social action.[22] Taking a class in ethics helps us on our journey to becoming the best people we can be.

EXERCISES

1. Which perspective—Kohlberg's justice perspective or Gilligan's care perspective—most accurately describes the way you approach discussions of moral issues? To what extent do you draw from both perspectives? Illustrate your answer with specific examples.
2. Has the college experience enhanced your moral development? Has your strategy for making moral decisions changed at all since you started college? If so, are you more satisfied with your current strategy? Explain using specific examples.
3. Have your views on any of the issues covered in this chapter changed or been called into doubt as a result of your college experience? Explain using specific examples.
4. Discuss a time when you went along with others even though you "knew" that what they were doing was morally questionable.
5. Discuss ways in which you are engaged in moral action or praxis. What motivates you to take action? Illustrate your answer with an example.

MORALITY AND RELIGION

> *A list of virtues or duties drawn up by a Buddhist would not differ very greatly from one drawn up by a Christian, a Confucianist, a Muhammadan or a Jew. Formally all of the ethico-religious systems are universalist in scope.*
>
> —Morris Ginsberg, *Reason and Unreason in Society* (1947)

Many people look to religion for moral guidance. The concept of God in the major world religions—Hinduism, Judaism, Christianity, and Islam—is intimately connected with that of moral goodness.[23] People worship God, in part, because God represents perfect goodness. Worshipping reaffirms these moral values. This raises the question of the connection between religion and morality. Is morality dependent on religion or does it exist independently of religion?

The Divine Command Theory

The first position, that something is moral merely because God approves of it, is known as the *divine command theory*. Just as morality for the cultural relativist is relative to cultural norms, for the divine command theorist morality is relative to what God commands or wills. There are no independent, universal moral standards by which to judge God's commands. No other justification is necessary for an action to be right other than God's commanding it. For example, Israeli law student Yigal Amir shot and killed Israeli prime minister Yitshak Rabin as Rabin was leaving a peace rally. When apprehended, Amir told police, "I acted alone on God's orders and I have no regrets." In another case a woman put her baby in a microwave oven and turned it on; she too defended her actions on the grounds that God had commanded her to kill her child. If we respond that God would not have commanded anyone to do something so horrible, we are implying that there are independent moral standards by which we can judge God's commands.

If we accept the divine command theory, the only way to resolve a moral issue such as cloning or affirmative action, or to decide if we should kill someone, would be to wait for God to speak to us. There are no other criteria for deciding right from wrong. If someone claims that God spoke to her and commanded her to oppose cloning, we have no independent criteria for judging whether she, in fact, heard God or not. Under the divine command theory, God's commands are arbitrary; they are based only on divine whim. Most of us, however, including most religious people, believe that actions such as rape or genocide are not arbitrary but a matter of reason.

Natural Law Theory

Natural law theorists disagree with the divine command theory. They maintain that God commands something *because* it is moral, not the other way around. Whereas religious teachings may affirm universal moral principles, morality exists independently of religion and God's commands. Morality is universally binding on everyone, no matter what their religion or lack thereof. According to the natural law theory, morality is grounded in rational human nature rather than in God's commands or personal feelings or cultural norms. We act morally for the same reasons God does. According to Thomas Aquinas (c. 1225–1274), it is through the "light of natural reason," which was given to us by God, that humans discern moral or natural law. These moral laws are very general and exist in the form of guidelines, such as the Golden Rule, the Ten Commandments, or respect for persons. Moral law is also teleological; it directs us toward a particular purpose or goal of the natural order. It is incumbent upon us as rational humans to discern how these moral laws apply at a particular time in history and in a particular case.

Although natural law theory is often identified with the Catholic Church, one need not be Catholic—or even believe in God—to subscribe to this theory. Many, if not most, modern theologians and religious ethicists, including Martin Luther King Jr., subscribe to some form of natural law theory and reject divine command theory. Aristotle believed that, rather than being created by God, the moral law has always been part of the natural order. Variations of natural law theory are also found in non-Western cultures, such as the Akan tribe of Ghana.[24]

Natural law ethicists reject cultural relativism. According to them a human or civil law (legislation) or tradition is moral only to the extent that it is in accord with natural or moral law. If a law is unjust, we may have a moral obligation to disobey it. A human law is unjust if it is degrading to humans, such as laws that permit torture or slavery. Laws that are discriminatory, such as segregation laws and, perhaps, affirmative action, may also be unjust. In engaging in civil disobedience, the dissident can use only moral means and must be nonviolent and open about his or her actions. Civil disobedience, on the grounds of obedience to a higher moral law, has a long history in this country. Members of animal liberation groups break into laboratories and set animals free; anti-abortionists block women from entering abortion clinics; anti-nuclear activists block roads leading to nuclear power plants and military establishments; during the Vietnam War, college students openly burned their draft cards to protest the war; and in the back of his Volkswagen van, Dr. Jack Kevorkian—despite repeated warnings from the courts—continued to assist terminally ill people in ending their lives. In each of these cases, the people engaged in civil disobedience justified their actions on the grounds of a higher moral law.

For more information on Aquinas's natural law theory, his "Treatise on Law" from the *Summa Theologica* is included in the *Ethics PowerWeb.*

UNIVERSALITY AND RELIGIOUS ETHICS

In discussing moral issues, it may be tempting to dismiss a particular position as a religious issue, especially if we are unsure of how to defend our own position. For example, anti-slavery arguments were dismissed for many years as the rantings of fanatic Quakers who were trying to force their religious views on the southerners. Today certain moral positions on abortion and homosexuality are dismissed as religious views. The fact that a specific religion, however, whether it be Quaker or Roman Catholic or Hindu, takes an official stand on a certain moral issue such as slavery, abortion, or homosexuality does not imply that these issues are religious rather than moral issues. In discussing these and similar issues, we must be careful to separate the moral issues involved from specific religious doctrines.

Most theologians and philosophers maintain that morality exists independently of religion—that religious ethics is not fundamentally different from philosophical ethics. Although a moral code is incorporated into the doctrine of most religions, moral issues can be discussed without appealing to religion. When people who are religious use the terms *right* and *wrong,* they generally mean the same thing as someone who is not religious. Religious differences tend to fall away in most serious discussion of moral issues, such as slavery and abortion, not because religion isn't important to the participants but because moral disputes can be discussed and even resolved without bringing religion into the equation.[25]

EXERCISES

1. How, if at all, have your religious beliefs shaped your morality? Is there a difference between religious and secular morality in your life? What happens when your religion and your culture take radically different positions on a particular moral issue? How do you resolve the conflict?
2. Discuss a case in which someone justified a position that most people would consider immoral, such as mandatory euthanasia of a particular group of people, on the grounds that God commanded him or her to take this position. How would you respond to such a person?
3. Choose a controversial topic, such as abortion, euthanasia, or homosexuality, that is sometimes regarded as a religious issue. Can the morality of these practices be discussed without bringing in religious doctrine? Support your answer.

UNIVERSAL MORAL THEORIES

> *Two things fill the mind with ever new and increasing admiration and awe, the oftener and more steadily we reflect on them: the starry heavens above and the moral law within.*
>
> —Immanuel Kant, *Critique of Practical Reason* (1788)

Like natural law theorists, most moral philosophers believe that there are moral principles that are universal and objective. There are several different universalist theories, including natural law theory, utilitarianism, deontology, rights ethics, and virtue ethics. They all agree, however, that there are universal moral principles that are binding on all people regardless of their personal opinions, culture, or religion. These moral principles are *discovered* rather than created by people. Although individual interests or cultural customs, as noted in the example about the Kabloona, can influence how a particular moral principle is applied, fundamental moral principles are universal and transcultural.

Just as scientists disagree about the origin of the universe or the nature of gravity, people may disagree about the source and nature of these principles and sentiments. Some philosophers believe that we intuitively know what is morally right and wrong; others argue that reason is the primary source of moral knowledge. The fact of disagreement, however, does not mean that objective universal moral principles do not exist, anymore than it follows that disagreement about the source of the universe or the nature of gravity means that the universe and gravity do not exist.

There is a great deal of overlap between the different universalist theories. Instead of being mutually exclusive, like ethical subjectivism and cultural relativism, universalist theories, for the most part, emphasize one particular aspect of morality. In addition, almost all ethicists include aspects of more than one of these theories in their moral philosophy.

UTILITARIANISM

> *The happiness of the individuals, of whom a community is composed, that is their pleasures and their security, is the end and the sole end which the legislator ought to have in view.*
>
> —Jeremy Bentham, *Principles of Morals and Legislation* (1789)

Modern utilitarian theory was developed by English jurist, philosopher, and social reformer Jeremy Bentham (1748–1832) in response to the flagrant injustices and the desperate needs of workers. The industrial revolution, coupled with the widespread political unrest that culminated in the American and French revolutions, brought about tremendous changes in Western society. Bentham's goal was to develop a practical ethical theory that could provide a secure, scientific foundation for developing social policy and legislation.

Jeremy Bentham: Father of Modern Utilitarian Theory

Bentham's utilitarian theory was inspired primarily by the theories of Epicurus (341–270 B.C.E.) and David Hume (1711–1776). Hume and Epicurus both argued that certain traits are virtues because of their utility, or usefulness. Those traits that promote happiness have the greatest utility. Bentham took this one step further by arguing that utility provides the *only* source of political obligation for the state; it is utility alone that proved the test of what a law ought to be and which laws ought to be obeyed.

According to utilitarian theory, the morality of an action is determined solely by its consequences. Utilitarians maintain that the desire for happiness is universal and that we intuitively recognize it as the greatest good. Happiness, they argue, is synonymous with pleasure; unhappiness with pain. Actions are right, therefore, to the extent that they tend to promote overall happiness, and wrong to the extent that they tend to promote overall unhappiness. What counts is not just individual or even human happiness, but the sum of the happiness of the whole community of *sentient beings*—that is, those beings who are capable of feeling pleasure and pain.

Readings from both Jeremy Bentham's *An Introduction to the Principles of Morals and Legislation* and David Hume's *Enquiries Concerning the Human Understanding and Concerning the Principles of Morals,* can be found in the accompanying *Ethics PowerWeb.*

The Principle of Utility: Promoting Happiness and Minimizing Pain

In determining which action or policy has the greatest utility (produces the greatest amount of happiness) we cannot rely on a majority vote, since people's choices are not always well informed. The majority, either because of ignorance about the nuances of a particular issue or because of irrational traditions and prejudice, may be mistaken about what is the best course of action. Nor can we rely on feelings alone, such as sympathy, because feelings can also mislead us. Instead we need a rational principle by which to guide our actions and choices. This principle is the *principle of utility,* or the *greatest happiness principle:*

> Actions are right in proportion as they tend to promote happiness, wrong as they tend to produce the reverse of happiness.[26]

In deciding which action is the most morally compelling, we need only measure the total amount of pleasure and the total amount of pain involved in the alternatives, and choose the alternative with the greatest net pleasure. Because the interests of all sentient beings count, the pain caused by human practices to other animals—such as animal agriculture, logging, and research using nonhuman animals—also has to be taken into consideration.

John Stuart Mill's Reformulation of Utilitarianism

Jeremy Bentham advocated equality and impartiality. He argued that all pleasures, whether those of a pig or a human, are equal. Equality, according to him, is not a description of actual equality of ability; rather, it is a moral ideal or prescription of how we ought to treat all sentient beings. The happiness of any one individual is no more or less important than that of any other.

Utilitarian John Stuart Mill disagreed with Bentham regarding the equality of pleasures, arguing instead that some pleasures are higher or more desirable than others. In particular, he claimed that the intellectual pleasures, such as listening to a symphony or reading a great book, are *qualitatively* better than those of the body, such as eating or enjoying a day basking in the sun. In other words, the intellectual pleasures experienced by humans, though they are less intense at times, are morally preferable to the simple pleasures of a pig. This is not to say that the pleasures of the pig should not count at all.

In fact, utilitarians, such as Peter Singer, continue to be in the forefront of the animal-welfare movement.

Utilitarianism and Social Reform

Utilitarian theory has had a profound influence over the past two hundred years on social reform and the shaping of public policy. Jeremy Bentham was an advocate of animal welfare and prison reform. John Stuart Mill spoke out eloquently on behalf of equal opportunities for women, freedom of the press, and the legalization of homosexual acts between consenting adults. Contemporary discussions of capital punishment, euthanasia, animal welfare, genetic engineering, pornography, legalization of drugs, and environmental ethics all have utilitarian components.

Unlike most moral theories, utilitarian theory adopts a practical bottom-up approach. It begins with the actual happiness of the people and other sentient beings rather than imposing morality and social ideals on them from above. The principle of utility requires that we do not take refuge in ideological slogans, cultural traditions, or personal opinion, but that we instead examine our position on moral issues in light of the actual consequences. This entails overcoming our ignorance regarding the extent to which our lifestyle is built upon the suffering of other people or animals.

Utilitarianism requires that we first do our research. For example, is capital punishment, in fact, an effective deterrent? Does viewing pornography and violence, in fact, cause people to behave more violently? Does permitting people who are openly homosexual to teach in schools, in fact, make children more likely to become homosexuals?

We also need to look at possible consequences of our decisions. Would censorship of hate speech and pornography cause more harm than allowing hate speech and access to pornography? Are terrorism or a preemptive attack on another country ever justified if other avenues have failed to remove a leader who inflicts massive suffering on his or neighboring people? Would legalizing recreational drugs result in more or in less drug abuse and drug-related crime? Would condoning voluntary euthanasia put us on the slippery slope toward involuntary euthanasia? The slippery-slope argument applies to issues with large gray areas in which it is difficult to draw a distinct line between what is morally acceptable and what is morally unacceptable. In "The Question of Human Cloning," John Robertson raises the question of whether seemingly valid uses of cloning might open the door to undesirable uses of the technology.

Finally, we need to balance harm and benefit. Is the harm that human activities cause to the environment and to other animals justified by the benefit the products bring to humans? Would permitting parents to genetically engineer their children result in more overall happiness for society, or less?

The Strengths and Limitations of Utilitarianism

Utilitarian theory is a powerful tool for formulating social policies. It is also a reminder that tradition alone cannot serve as a foundation for morality.

One of the greatest strengths of utilitarian theory is that it challenges us to rethink our traditional notions about moral community. If we are going to exclude or marginalize people or other animals, we have to offer a rational justification for our decision. For example, we cannot exclude other animals from moral consideration based on irrational religious doctrines that claim that only humans are created in the image of God. Nor can we jus-

UTILITARIAN GUIDELINES FOR THINKING ABOUT MORAL ISSUES

- **Determine who or what will be affected:** Who will be caused pain or pleasure?
- **Look at the possible consequences:** What are both the long-term and short-term consequences of the different alternatives?
- **Maximize happiness:** Which solution will bring about the greatest net happiness?
- **Minimize pain:** Which solution will cause the least pain and suffering to those affected by the decision?

tify expending expensive limited resources on humans who are no longer sentient simply on the grounds that they are human.

The utilitarian insistence on equality and impartiality is both one of its greatest strengths and one of its weaknesses. Justice as impartiality assumes that people living in a community share a common conception of the good. In reality, however, people have different needs and goals. The capitalist's idea of happiness, for example, is not the same as that of the religious contemplative. John Rawls (b. 1921), a critic of utilitarian theory, also points out that justice demands not only impartiality, but also that we treat people fairly and in proportion to their needs and merits. A person who works hard deserves a raise or reward simply because he has done a good job. Utilitarians, in contrast, are not concerned with what a person deserves, but whether giving rewards based on merit produces the most utility.

There are other desirable goals in life besides pleasure. Another criticism of utilitarian theory is its claim that pleasure is the only intrinsic good. Most people agree that goals such as friendship, spiritual growth, and appreciation of the aesthetic are also desirable. On the other hand, utilitarian theory reminds us that one of the primary purposes of morality is not to make our lives more tedious or to make us feel more guilt-ridden, but to improve the quality of our lives by promoting ideals and behavior that provide optimal conditions for us to flourish, both as individuals and as a community.

By claiming that only consequences count, utilitarianism underplays the importance of individual integrity and personal responsibility. In considering only consequences when determining the rightness and wrongness of an action, utilitarian theory may sometimes require us to act in ways that violate our integrity and our conscience. For example, say that a particularly heinous murder, which the community believes to have been racially motivated, has created racial tension, looting, and killing in that community. The police have been unable to find the murderer. It also seems fairly certain that the community rampage will continue until someone is brought to "justice" and given the death penalty. In desperation the police arrest a man—an unsavory character who has a history of petty crime—whom they know is not guilty of the murder. As a judge, you can bring about more pleasure and restore social harmony by convicting the man and giving him the death penalty. What should you do? The utilitarian would probably have to say: Send the man to the electric chair as a means of restoring social order. But our actions do not happen just as part of a wider context of the general good; each of us is also responsible for what we do as individuals.

Because only pleasure has intrinsic value, utilitarian theory allows us to use people as a means toward that end, rather than requiring us to respect people as ends in themselves. In the previous example, the accused man was used as a means to social harmony, as was the judge. In addition, to pressure the judge into bringing about the death of an innocent person to prevent the death of others is to treat the judge as a means only.

Utilitarian theory is not so much wrong as incomplete. Despite its limitations utilitarian theory provides valuable guidelines for discussions of issues in social ethics. Although other moral philosophers may regard other moral considerations as more fundamental than the principle of utility, as deontologist John Rawls writes: "all ethical doctrines worth our attention take consequences into account in judging rightness. One which did not would simply be irrational, crazy."[27]

EXERCISES

1. Utilitarian theory is frequently used to formulate social policies regarding issues like AIDS testing, going to war, and distribution of social benefits such as scholarships and medical care. Find some examples of utilitarian thinking in current public or college policies. Explain why these policies represent utilitarian thinking.
2. Does social ethics require a different strategy than personal moral decision making? If so, how do the two strategies differ? On what grounds can you justify these differences?
3. Do you agree with Mill that human intellectual pleasures have greater moral value than the pleasures of other animals? Discuss how adopting either Bentham's or Mill's position would influence public policy on the use of nonhuman animals to benefit humans.
4. Both Confucianism and modern care ethics teach that our concern should be strongest for our family and friends. Utilitarian theory, in contrast, teaches that our concern for others' happiness should be impartial. Discuss these two competing concepts of moral obligation. Do we have as strong a moral obligation to benefit or increase the happiness of people we don't know as we do to our own friends and family? Support your answer using examples from your own life.

DEONTOLOGY: THE ETHICS OF DUTY

Look to your own duty; do not tremble before it . . .

—Bhagavad Gita

Deontological theories regard duty as the basis of morality. *Duty,* or doing what is right for its own sake, is the foundation of morality. There are strong strands of deontology in Confucianism and Hindu ethics as well as in many Western philosophies.

Immanuel Kant and the Categorical Imperative

Deontologist Immanuel Kant (1724–1804) believed that we should do our duty purely out of goodwill, not because of rewards or punishment or other consequences. A person of goodwill can be depended on to do what is right, even when other motives are absent. An action that is done out of sympathy or because one enjoys helping others, rather than out of a sense of duty, may be praiseworthy, but according to Kant it has no moral value.

Kant also argued that if there is a universal moral law and if it is to be morally binding, it must be based on reason. According to Kant, the most fundamental moral principle is the *categorical imperative.* He came up with two formulations of the categorical imperative. The first formulation states:

> Act only on that maxim by which you can at the same time will that it should become a universal law.

Kant believed that all rational beings would recognize the categorical imperative as universally binding. Because reason provides the foundation of morality, this makes humans and other rational beings very special in Kant's mind. Whereas rational beings have free will, everything else in nature operates according to physical laws. Because autonomy is essential for dignity, only rational beings have intrinsic worth. Rational beings can therefore never be treated as expendable, but must be treated with dignity as ends in themselves. This ideal is summed up in the second formulation of the categorical imperative:

> So act as to treat humanity, whether in thine own person or in that of any other, in every case as an end in itself, never as a means only.

The categorical imperative is a formal principle that provides a framework for deriving moral maxims or duties, such as "Do not lie" and "Help others in distress," that can be applied in specific situations. When deciding if a particular maxim creates a moral duty, we need only ask, keeping in mind that rational beings must be treated with dignity, whether we would will that it be a universal law.

The *Golden Rule* in Judeo-Christian ethics, and the *law of reciprocity* in Confucian ethics are both similar to the categorical imperative. The Golden Rule states, "Do unto others as you would have them do unto you." Similarly, when Confucius (551–479 B.C.E.) was asked if there was a single principle that can be used as a guide to conduct in our lives, he replied, "Do not impose on others what you yourself do not desire."[28]

Universalization

Universalization is one of the trademarks of morality: Moral maxims or duties, by their very nature, apply to everyone and under all circumstances. It is inconsistent, for example, to argue that it is wrong for others to lie but that it is okay for us. If it is wrong to lie, it is wrong for everyone. If we could make an exception of ourselves whenever it is to our advantage, the moral rule "Do not lie" would be meaningless.

Many people become easily confused in discussions of moral issues because their basic moral assumptions do not meet the standard of universality. They may feel tricked and frustrated when what they believed was a carefully thought-out argument ends up supporting a position they never intended to support.

For example, in the study of how college students judge social issues, 35 percent of students stated that abortion is immoral because life starts at conception; therefore, abortion violates the moral maxim "It is wrong to take an innocent life."[29] When asked whether abortion would be morally permissible for a woman who was raped, however, many students said yes. Others in the pro-life group stated that abortion was morally wrong because the fetus was a person, but at the same time added that abortion should be legal because it is a personal choice. Their inconsistency can be further exposed by asking whether killing children after birth should also be a personal choice.

Twenty-seven percent of students in the study responded that abortion is not immoral because "abortion is a personal choice." Like the pro-life students, however, many of the pro-choice students were inconsistent when it came to universalizing their fundamental moral maxims or assumptions. When asked if abortion was morally acceptable for sex selection, many of the pro-choice students said no. In other words, they were unwilling to universalize their moral maxim "Abortion is a personal choice."

Effective analysis and discussion of moral issues requires that we first examine our basic assumptions about what is a good moral maxim. A good moral maxim must be consistent with the demands of the categorical imperative. Are we willing, in good conscience, to consistently apply our moral maxims? If not, why not? If we are unwilling to universalize a particular moral maxim—that is, apply it consistently in all similar cases—we should either modify the maxim or toss it out.

Unlike the categorical imperative itself, specific moral maxims are open for debate. For example, many people question whether we would want to universalize, as did Kant, a maxim that states, "Do not commit suicide." Kant, of course, was writing in the days before medical technology could artificially extend the dying process. Besides problems with universality, some people believe that refusing to help someone die who is suffering terribly and is unable to carry out his own suicide is disrespectful and, hence, violates the second formulation of the categorical imperative. What moral maxims, then, can we come up with for shaping a policy on euthanasia and assisted suicide? Would we want to universalize a maxim that states, "Physicians have a duty to carry out the requests of their patients"? This may sound good in some situations, but there may be others in which it would not be, such as when a student who is temporarily depressed because she got a poor grade on an exam requests medical assistance in committing suicide. What if a patient demands an expensive and potentially dangerous treatment for a minor illness? In fact, further consideration of this maxim reveals so many exceptions that it proves to be of little use in making moral decisions.

W. D. Ross: Duties Are Prima Facie

Kant argued that universalizing moral maxims requires that they be absolutely binding in all circumstances. If it is wrong to lie, then, according to him, it is *always* wrong to lie, no matter what the circumstance. He also believed that because morality is based on reason, there could never be a conflict between moral duties.

Most moral philosophers, while agreeing with Kant that moral duties or maxims are universal, disagree that they are also absolute. Moral duties are prima facie rather than absolute. *Prima facie* duties are moral duties that may on occasion be overridden by stronger moral claims.

According to W. D. Ross (1877–1971), moral duties cannot be absolute, because there are particular situations in which they come into conflict. The moral duty of nonmaleficence, for example, could conflict with the moral duty to keep a promise when keeping that promise could result in death or injury. Because duties are context-bound, the particular circumstances and possible consequences will affect which moral duties are most important in any given situation.

W. D. ROSS'S SEVEN PRIMA FACIE DUTIES

Future-Looking Duties

Beneficence the duty to do good acts and to promote happiness
Nonmaleficence the duty to do no harm and to prevent harm

Duties Based on Past Obligations

Fidelity duties arising from past commitments and promises
Reparation duties that stem from past harms to others
Gratitude duties based on past favors and unearned services

Ongoing Duties

Self-Improvement the duty to improve our knowledge and virtue
Justice the duty to give each person equal consideration

Unlike Kant, Ross also believed that consequences matter when applying moral principles. Moral duties, however, cannot be overridden by nonmoral duties or considerations such as obeying the law, financial success, or getting good grades in college. When there is a conflict between moral and nonmoral duties, we ought to do what is morally right.

Seven Prima Facie Duties

Ross came up with a list of seven prima facie duties that he claimed we intuitively know. These include duties concerning the consequences of our actions, such as the duty of *nonmaleficence* (do no harm) and the duty of *beneficence* (increase happiness). These two duties are also recognized by utilitarians. *Ahimsa,* or the principle of nonviolence, in Buddhist ethics, is a version of the principle of nonmaleficence and is the most fundamental moral principle in Buddhist ethics. Buddhists oppose meat-eating because it violates this principle.

Although almost all ethicists agree that we have a positive duty to refrain from harming others, they disagree about whether we have a positive duty of beneficence—that is, to perform altruistic actions. Both Judith Jarvis Thomson in her essay "A Defense of Abortion" and Margaret Pabst Battin in "The Case for Euthanasia" discuss the question of whether we have a positive duty of beneficence, and, if so, what the limits of this duty are.

We also have duties that stem from past obligations. The duty of *fidelity* arises from past commitments and promises. We have a commitment to our fellow students, to our parents, and to our children, independent of the pleasure we may get from them at the moment. The duty of fidelity or filial piety is particularly important in Confucian ethics and generally takes precedence over individual liberty rights. Some philosophers argue that part of the physician's commitment to his or her patients is to assist dying patients who request assistance in committing suicide. Others, such as Daniel Callahan, argue that the duty of nonmaleficence is more compelling in this case and that physicians should refuse to carry out actions that cause lethal harm to their patients.

The duty of *gratitude* is evoked when we receive gifts or unearned favors and services from others. Some environmental ethicists argue that we have a duty of gratitude toward the earth which nourishes us.

The duty of *reparation* is also based on past actions. Reparation requires that we make up for past harms we have caused others. Affirmative action is an attempt to make up for past harms to women and minorities. Some philosophers argue that affirmative action is unjust and that justice in this case is a more compelling duty than reparation.

Finally, there are two ongoing duties: self-improvement and justice. *Self-improvement,* as a moral duty, entails striving to improve our moral knowledge and our virtue. Self-improvement requires that we work to overcome our ignorance by becoming well informed about moral issues. It also requires that we be open to new ideas. In addition, being a virtuous person requires that we use our moral knowledge to make this world a better place.

Justice

Justice is the seventh prima facie duty. Many philosophers consider justice to be our most important social duty. The ongoing duty of *justice* requires that we give each person equal consideration. Because laws and social institutions are generally the agencies for balancing conflicting interests, the issue of justice is closely tied with that of "the good society." As noted earlier, however, not all laws are just, nor are all demands for justice addressed by law.

There are two types of justice: retributive justice and distributive justice. *Retributive justice* requires punishment for wrongdoing in proportion to the magnitude of the crime. Both Immanuel Kant and Ernest van den Haag argue that the only suitable punishment for murder is the death penalty. Hugo Adam Bedeau and Helen Prejean, on the other hand, in their readings at the end of Chapter 5 claim that the death penalty is immoral because it violates the underlying moral principle of respect for persons. Buddhist philosophers also oppose the death penalty as being in conflict with the principle of nonviolence (*ahimsa*).

Distributive justice refers to the fair distribution of benefits and burdens in a society. Benefits include education, medical care, police protection, legal representation, and economic opportunities. Taxes, jury duty, and military conscription are examples of shared burdens. Distributive justice becomes a concern when (1) there are conflicts of interest and (2) people have competing claims for certain limited or scarce societal goods. Because there are not enough good jobs, college scholarships, and medical care for everyone, the distribution of these goods is an issue of justice. For example, John Hardwig supports euthanasia on the grounds that it is unjust that those who are dying long, lingering deaths get such a disproportionate share of medical and other resources. He claims that in cases such as these, we have a duty to die.

Distributive justice also requires impartiality. We should treat equals equally and unequals in proportion to their differences. In a just society, we all deserve a fair opportunity to pursue our goals. Charles R. Lawrence III argues that hate speech creates an atmosphere on campuses in which certain groups of people are denied this opportunity. Aristotle, on the other hand, focuses more on merit as the key criterion in distributive justice. He was opposed to democracy, preferring instead an oligarchy, or an elitist political system based on merit. Those who are most talented and most virtuous, and who have contributed most to society, ought to get a greater share of the privileges and opportunities.

John Rawls and Justice as Fairness

In his book *A Theory of Justice,* John Rawls maintains that justice requires not only impartiality but also treating people fairly and in proportion to their needs as well as their merits. There are inequalities of birth and natural endowment (what Rawls calls the "natural lottery") and historic circumstances, such as slavery, that create undeserved disadvantages for certain people. Simply redistributing opportunities or wealth does not solve the root problem as long as the underlying conditions that disadvantage certain people still exist. What is needed, Rawls argues, is a change in the social system so that it does not permit these injustices to occur in the first place.

Rawls's solution is to base justice upon a social contract that is unbiased and impartial. To do this Rawls proposes that we use a conceptual device that he calls the "veil of ignorance," where everyone is ignorant of the advantages or disadvantages he or she will receive in this life. Under these conditions, Rawls argues, all rational people would agree upon the following two principles of justice:

1. Each person is to have an equal right to the most extensive basic liberty compatible with a similar liberty for others.
2. Social and economic inequalities are to be arranged so that both are (a) reasonably expected to be to everyone's advantage and (b) attached to positions and offices open to all.

Rawls's theory of justice has been used to reform social institutions and to develop policy in areas such as health-care reform and education. Sissela Bok, for example, argues that we must first alleviate the extraordinary inequalities in the way medical care is distributed to people at the end of their lives before we can think of moving toward legalizing voluntary euthanasia. While it is, of course, impossible to truly forget our advantages and disadvantages in this life, the "veil of ignorance" provides a powerful conceptual tool for thinking about different moral issues from an impartial point of view.

Moral Dilemmas and Resolving Moral Issues

Any of the above duties can come into conflict with one another. When moral duties and other moral concerns come into conflict, we have a *moral dilemma.* Because moral duties are prima facie, when we have an issue that involves a moral conflict, we must carefully weigh each duty, decide which duties are the most compelling for that particular issue, and try to arrive at a resolution that honors as many duties as possible.

According to Ross, there is no set formula for determining which action we should take in a moral dilemma. Whereas the general duties themselves may be self-evident, judgment about our duties in a particular case is not. Because of this we need to use reason and creativity in making judgments about our duty in a particular case. Ross believed that this lack of clarity is due to the nature of moral decision making, which, he claims, is more like creating a work of art than solving a mathematical problem. When there is a moral dilemma, no solution is going to be completely satisfactory. Different people may come to different solutions because they prioritize duties differently. The purpose of

DEONTOLOGY: CONSIDERATIONS FOR THINKING ABOUT MORAL ISSUES

- **Universality:** Are we willing to universalize our rules and assumptions?
- **Reciprocity:** How would we want to be treated in a similar situation?
- **Respect:** Is our position on an issue respectful of all persons affected, or does it entail treating some as a means only?
- **Impartiality:** Are we treating equals equally?
- **Identify relevant duties:** What are the relevant duties in this particular issue?
- **Prioritize duties:** If there is a conflict of duties, which duties are the most important?

moral deliberation in these cases is to arrive at the *best* solution or, if this doesn't occur, the best possible alternatives.

Strengths and Limitations of Deontology

Kant's deontology, because of its abstractness and lack of specificity, suffered a decline in popularity during the past century. It is currently making a comeback, however, in part because of disillusionment with ethical relativism. Many contemporary philosophers, such as John Rawls and Sissela Bok, while adopting the basic premises of deontology, have revised it or combined it with the strengths of other theories, such as social contract theory and utilitarianism, so it is more useful in everyday moral decision making.

Kantian deontology, with its claim that duties are absolute and that there are no conflicts between moral rules, is unable to provide guidance in situations where there is a moral dilemma. A good moral theory, as noted earlier, should provide guidance for making real-life moral decisions. Although prima facie deontology has overcome this limitation to some extent, it has been criticized for failing to provide a strategy for ranking conflicting duties.

Deontology sacrifices community in the name of individual autonomy. In Kantian deontology in particular, the private life replaces the public life as the sphere of moral actions. According to philosophers such as Confucius and Aristotle, humans are first and foremost social or political beings; humans need the community in order to be virtuous. German philosopher Georg Hegel (1770–1831), Kant's contemporary, also questioned Kant's belief that individual autonomy and rationality are possible prior to membership in an ethical community. Kant's assumption that people are basically autonomous, private units who are free to carry out the moral law fails to take into consideration that we are all part of a wider social network of relationships that places restraints on the actions of some people and bestows privilege on others.

The deontologist's overriding concern with duty and justice fails to take into account the role of sentiment and care in morality. Feminist care ethicists, such as Carol Gilligan and Nel Noddings, in her reading at the end of this chapter, claim that deontology, or what they call the "justice perspective," is a distinctly male approach that ignores caring in relationships. Practical morality, they argue, is constructed dialectically through interaction with others, not merely by an autonomous examination of the dictates of reason. Care ethicists also claim that reason alone is insufficient both to provide us with practical guidance and to motivate us to act morally. Indeed, as studies with psychopaths have shown, reason without the ability to empathize with others seems unable to produce the categorical imperative or to inspire us to respect others.

Deontology ignores consequences. Kant's denial that consequences are morally relevant has been criticized by utilitarians as well as by modern deontologists. Even if we agree that consequences are not as important as duty, most philosophers still believe that they must be taken into consideration. Indeed, John Stuart Mill points out that the categorical imperative by its very nature requires that we take consequences into account when adopting moral rules. According to Mill, rational people would not universalize a moral rule that would harm, rather than benefit, the moral community.

Few philosophers accept Kant's deontology in its entirety; nevertheless, Kantian deontology is one of the most, if not *the* most, influential and fertile moral philosophies in modern history. Despite its shortcomings, the strengths and richness of deontology far outshine its weaknesses.

It would be a mistake to consider any philosophical, or even scientific, theory a finished or complete statement about a particular phenomenon. One of the characteristics of a good theory is that it is open-ended and generates further thought. In this respect deontology has made important contributions to the study of ethics. In particular, with its emphasis on the dignity of the individual, deontology has had a major influence on the development of rights ethics in Western and non-Western philosophies.

EXERCISES

1. List some of the fundamental moral assumptions or maxims that you use in discussing moral issues such as capital punishment, affirmative action, same-sex marriage, war, or animal rights. Examine each of these maxims in light of the imperative of universality.
2. Select a moral issue that involves a moral dilemma. List the duties that support the "pro" side of the issue, then list the moral duties that support the "con" side of the issue. Which duties are the most compelling? Discuss possible solutions that take the most duties into account.
3. Is it morally acceptable to euthanize people who have terminal illnesses and who request physician-assisted suicide? Is it morally acceptable to euthanize people with burdensome illnesses, such as coma or severe brain damage, who are unable to give their consent? Discuss the contributions both utilitarians and deontologists would make to a debate on this issue.
4. In 1997 Ron Fitzsimmons, executive director of the National Coalition of Abortion Providers, confessed that he had lied about the number of late-term abortions performed, which are far more frequent than the public had been led to believe. He and his colleagues also admitted that many of these abortions were being performed on healthy women, not only those who were dying or whose fetuses had severe deformities. Some pro-choice advocates defended Fitzsimmons, arguing that the means—lying—justified the ends—keeping late-term abortions legal and available to all women. How would both Kantian and prima facie deontologists respond to Fitzsimmons's actions? Compare and contrast their responses with that of a utilitarian.

RIGHTS-BASED ETHICS

> *We hold these truths to be self-evident, that all men are created equal, that they are endowed by their Creator with certain inalienable Rights, that among these are Life, Liberty and the Pursuit of Happiness.*
>
> —*United States Declaration of Independence* (July 4, 1776)

Before the eighteenth century, the focus of moral theory was primarily on duty. The language of rights in Western philosophy emerged primarily in the context of the growing confrontation with the principle of absolute sovereignty. Rights ethics enjoyed a revival following World War II and the Holocaust. In 1948 the United Nations issued the Universal Declaration of Human Rights as "a common standard of achievement for all peoples and all nations." Its preamble states that human rights are not simply a Western creation but belong to people everywhere.

Moral rights are not the same as legal rights, although in a just society the two would overlap. Moral rights instead are generally seen as either (1) natural and existing independently or (2) derived from duties.

John Locke's Natural Rights Ethics

The philosophical doctrine of natural rights first appeared in Western philosophy in the seventeenth century as a demand for equality for all people. According to natural rights ethicists such as John Locke (1632–1704), these rights stem from our human nature and are self-evident and God-given. Humans alone have moral rights because of our creation in the image of God. These natural rights include a right to own property, a right to marry and have children, and a right to punish someone who has wronged us. The right of private punishment, which exists in a state of nature, is turned over to the state when we agree to form a civil society. The freedom or right to pursue our interests without interference is limited to legitimate interests; that is, those interests that do not harm other people by violating their similar and equal interests.

The doctrine of natural rights had a profound influence on the thinking of Thomas Jefferson, who drafted the Declaration of Independence. The influence of natural rights in the United States is especially evident in the way that moral rights are generally equated with human rights and are discussed without any reference to correlative duties. For example, freedom of speech, especially in the cases of pornography and hate speech, is sometimes depicted as a natural right that exists independently of any duty of nonmaleficence or concerns for the harm caused to others by the speech.

Whether hate speech constitutes a legitimate interest that should be protected is up for debate. In Chapter 8, Jonathan Rauch argues that hate speech should be protected but Charles R. Lawrence III argues that we do not have a right to use hate speech because it causes harm to those targeted by it.

Ayn Rand and Laissez-Faire Capitalism

Ayn Rand (1905–1982) is one of the foremost contemporary defenders of natural rights ethics. According to her, the doctrine of natural rights created the possibility of free societies. The United States, she argued, has the honor of being the first society created upon natural rights ethics; only through free enterprise and laissez-faire capitalism can individual rights and a free society be sustained.

Like Locke, Rand believed that rights exist independently of duties. Moral rights define and protect our freedoms without imposing obligations on anyone else. For example, the right to property does not entail an obligation to provide people with property; the right to life does not entail an obligation to provide people with the necessities of life.

Although she agreed with John Locke that rights exist prior to and independent of duties, she disagreed with him about the source of these rights. The source of our rights, she argues, is not God, but man's rational nature. Moral rights, according to Rand, define and protect our freedoms without imposing obligations on anybody else. According to Rand, humans are fundamentally solitary individuals, each pursuing his or her own rational self-interests. The ideal society, consequently, is one that protects people's individual liberty rights so they can freely pursue their interests.

Rights and Duties

Most philosophers disagree with natural rights ethics. They maintain that moral rights do not stand on their own but are linked to or even, some deontologists argue, derived from duties. For example, the duty of nonmaleficence requires that people refrain from interfering with other people's rights to pursue their interests. Rights, as noted earlier, are also limited by the duty of nonmaleficence. The duty of fidelity entails a right to expect others to keep their promises and the right of children to receive proper care from their parents. Utilitarians, deontologists, natural law ethicists, and Buddhist ethicists all see rights as entailing duties. According to duty-based rights ethics, rights are something to which we are *entitled.* Rights protect us as persons who ought to be treated with respect. Because we are entitled to certain rights, others have a duty to honor these rights.

Natural rights ethicists like Locke, in contrast, maintain that our possession of a right does not imply that someone else has a duty to honor that right. Under natural rights ethics, being able to actually claim our rights boils down to having the power—generally political or economic power—to assert ourselves. Because the environment and nonhuman animals lack the power of assertion, they lack rights.

Unlike John Locke, philosophers such as Tom Regan argue that rights stem from interests. Regan maintains that because nonhuman animals have interests, such as not being confined or eaten, they also have rights that we have a duty to respect. Similarly, Catharine MacKinnon argues that women have a right not to be raped, molested, and used solely for pleasure and profit; therefore, publishers have a corresponding duty not to produce hard-core pornography. In his article on "Abortion and Fathers' Rights" Steven Hales argues that if a woman has a liberty right to escape future duties to her progeny through abortion then the principle of equality entails that fathers also have a right of refusal to avoid future burdens such as child support.

Liberty and Welfare Rights

Moral rights are generally divided into liberty rights and welfare rights. *Welfare rights* entail the right to receive certain social goods such as education, medical care, and police protection. Welfare rights are important because without a minimal standard of living or education, we cannot pursue our legitimate interests. Socialist and Marxist countries place more emphasis on welfare rights.

Liberty rights, in contrast, entail the right to be left alone to pursue our legitimate interests without interference from the government or other people. Liberty rights include autonomy, privacy, freedom of speech, freedom to own property, freedom from harassment and confinement, and freedom to choose our own career. Our "legitimate interests" are those that do not violate other people's similar and equal interests. For example, a misogynist may have an interest in keeping women out of the workplace, but this does not give him the right to discriminate in hiring, because doing so would violate women's rights to equal opportunity.

In the United States, we tend to place more emphasis on liberty rights. Our privacy rights, freedom of speech, and right to own property, for example, are carefully protected. People, such as Ayn Rand, who emphasize liberty rights are known as *libertarians.* Libertarians believe that personal *autonomy*—the freedom to make our own decisions—is the highest moral value. According to libertarians, respect for others means allowing them freedom to develop and exercise the capacities that are necessary for them to pursue their concept of the good. This includes freedom of speech and privacy as well as freedom from coercive interference from the government. Robertson likewise argues that since cloning does not harm anyone or violate their legitimate interests, it should be permitted.

According to deontologists our liberty rights are limited by our duty to respect ourselves; we do not have a right to harm ourselves or neglect our own welfare. Kant, for example, regarded suicide as "an abomination because it involves the misuse of freedom to destroy oneself and one's freedom."[30] In contrast, Dr. Jack Kevorkian, a libertarian, considers suicide to be one of our most fundamental rights.

The emphasis on liberty rights at the expense of welfare rights, however, tends to handicap those who are unable to assert their liberty rights either because of natural disadvantages or because of traditional roles that limit their options. Supporters of affirmative action, such as Bernard Boxill, point out that merely being granted access to societal goods, such as jobs and education, will not ensure that people will actually be able to purchase the goods they need or pursue an education without facing discrimination or harassment.

Like duties, most rights are prima facie. Rights may come into conflict with one another or with duties. A white man's right to a college education may conflict with a duty of reparation toward African Americans who have been harmed by our public education system. The welfare rights of nonhuman animals, if they have rights, may come into conflict with our search for a cure for cancer using nonhuman animals as subjects.

The Strengths and Limitations of Rights Ethics

Rights ethics is an important component of a comprehensive moral theory. Nevertheless, there are some shortcomings, especially with natural rights ethics, which claims that rights ethics can stand on its own.

The theological basis of natural rights ethics, which privileges humans as a special creation, is difficult, if not impossible, to justify on either rational philosophical or empirical grounds. Natural rights ethics has given a moral blessing to the exploitation of other animals and the en-

RIGHTS ETHICS: CONSIDERATIONS FOR THINKING ABOUT MORAL ISSUES

- **Identify the relevant rights:** What are the liberty rights in the moral issue? What welfare rights are at stake in the issue?
- **Identify the legitimate interests:** Does exercising any of these rights infringe on the equal and similar rights of others?
- **Prioritize rights and duties:** If there is a conflict of rights and/or duties, which ones are most important?

vironment. The reduction of nonhuman animals and the environment to the status of resources for humans has had a devastating effect on the environment.

The separation of rights from duties fails to take into account the limitations placed on marginalized groups by societal traditions. The claim that all people are created equal has too often been treated as a description rather than a moral ideal. Natural rights ethicists such as Rand and Locke assume that in a free society everyone is equally able to pursue their concept of the good life. Not all people are equally capable of asserting their rights, however. Traditional roles, for example, give men and people born into wealthy families greater access to resources, thus disadvantaging women and poorer people in a free marketplace. If the right to accumulate property is not constrained by the duty of distributive justice, the gap between the haves and have-nots will become greater and greater.

The claim that pursuing liberty rights does not impose obligations on others is false. The libertarian model of rights actually depends on the backing of an extensive and expensive legal and police system. Liberty rights to own property and businesses, for example, are protected by tax monies, most of which are forcibly taken from people who are too poor to own property.

The assertion by natural rights ethicists that rights are self-evident leaves us with no criteria for determining which claims are legitimate rights. The belief that rights need no justification has led to a proliferation of demands for certain rights. Former U.S. ambassador to the United Nations Jeane Kirkpatrick (b. 1926) compares the current proliferation of rights declarations with "writing letters to Santa Claus"; they are based on wishful thinking rather than any reasonable expectations.[31] Without any criteria for justifying rights, there is no way to decide which rights are frivolous and which should be taken seriously. For this reason most philosophers argue that rights must be grounded in duties and, in particular, from the fundamental duty of respect for the dignity of others.

Although rights ethics is problematic if it is used as a complete explanation of morality, rights are important because they protect our dignity as persons. If we do not have rights, all our claims to be treated with respect simply amount to requests for favors and privileges. If there are no rights to freedom and equal opportunity, we need to make a case for having our freedom or equal opportunities.

Although few philosophers deny that rights are morally meaningful, the origin and nature of rights have been the focus of considerable debate. The claim that rights are based on the principle of equality has prompted animal rights advocates such as Tom Regan to question why this principle should not also be extended to other animals. Buddhist ethicists go even further and extend the concept of rights to all of nature. The extension of the concept of rights to all humans—and even to nonhumans—has been a difficult endeavor, but one that has been very fruitful in calling our attention to the dignity of those who are different from us.

EXERCISES

1. Are rights self-evident, as natural rights ethicists argue? List some rights that you consider to be important in making moral decisions. On what grounds do you justify these rights?
2. Referring to the list of rights you created in question 1, which are welfare rights? Which are liberty rights?
3. Do you agree with Ayn Rand that capitalism is the only system that can protect our individual freedoms? Does capitalism benefit not only the powerful but also those who have the least power in our society? Or does it merely further empower those who are already privileged? Support your answers.
4. Do we have a moral right to property and inheritance acquired through someone else's forced labor, such as slave labor and the exploitation of people living under conditions of poverty? If not, do we have a duty of reparation to those who were forced to work to provide us with our property? Explain.
5. Select a moral issue that involves a conflict between rights or between rights and duties. List the rights and duties that support the "pro" side of the issue, then list the rights and duties that support the "con" side of the issue. Which rights and/or duties are the most compelling? Discuss possible solutions that take the greatest number of rights into account.

VIRTUE ETHICS

> *The rule of virtue can be compared to the Pole Star which commands the homage of the multitude of Stars without leaving its place.*
>
> —Confucius, *The Analects,* book 4:4

Virtue ethics emphasizes right being over right action. The sort of people we are constitutes the heart of our moral life. More important than the rules or principles we follow is our character. Virtue ethics, however, is not an alternative to ethical theories that stress right conduct, such as utilitarianism and deontological theories. Rather, virtue ethics and theories of right action complement each other.

A *virtue* is an admirable character trait or disposition to habitually act in a manner that benefits ourselves and others. The actions of virtuous people stem from a respect and concern for the well-being of themselves and others. Compassion, courage, generosity, loyalty, and honesty are all examples of virtues.

Virtues are often spoken of as though they were discrete, individual traits; but virtue is more correctly defined as an overarching quality of goodness that gives unity and integrity to a person's character. Because virtuous people are motivated to act in ways that benefit society, the cultivation of a virtuous character is an important aspect of social ethics. For example, generous people are more likely to act in ways that benefit those who are least well-off in society. Honesty is an important social virtue because without

ARISTOTLE'S DOCTRINE OF THE MEAN[33]

Deficit (Vice)	Mean (Virtue)	Excess (Vice)
cowardice	courage	foolhardiness
inhibition	temperance	overindulgence/ intemperance
miserliness	liberality	prodigality/extravagance
shabbiness	magnificence	bad taste/vulgarity
unambitiousness	proper pride	ambitiousness
poor spiritedness	gentleness	irascibility
peevishness/surlyness	friendliness	obsequiousness/flattery
malice	righteous indignation	envy
irony	truthfulness	boastfulness
boorishness	wittiness	buffoonery
shamelessness	modesty	shame

honest communication, society would soon collapse. According to both Aristotle and Confucius, a good social policy or resolution to a social issue is one that encourages the development of virtue among people. "If the will be set on virtue," Confucius taught, "there will be no practice of wickedness."[32]

Buddhism, care ethics, and the moral philosophies of David Hume, Aristotle, and Jesus of Nazareth are often classified as virtue ethics. Confucian ethics has strong strands of both virtue ethics and deontology. The ancient Greek ethicists, like most Eastern ethicists, focused primarily on virtue and character rather than on duty and principles.

Aristotle: Reason and Virtue

Aristotle divided virtues into two broad categories: intellectual virtues and moral virtues. The intellectual virtues are cultivated through growth and experience; the moral virtues through habit. Wisdom is the most important virtue because it makes all other virtues (intellectual and moral) possible. The role of habituation, including repeated exposure to particular types of stimuli and behavior, in the development of virtuous and vicious behavior is one of the questions involved in censorship of pornography and campus restrictions on drinking and drug use.

Aristotle believed that all life has a function that is peculiar to its particular life-form. The function peculiar to human life, he claimed, is the exercise of reason. The function of the excellent man, therefore, "is to exert such activities well." Virtue, which is essential to the good life, involves living according to reason. Only by living in accord with reason, which is our human function, can we achieve happiness and inner harmony.

Aristotle also believed that people by nature are political animals, and that the state is a natural form of society. Humans need community in order to be virtuous. The purpose of the state is to promote the virtuous or good life. Justice is the primary virtue of the state; unless a state is just and encourages the development of virtue in its citizens, it has no power to make its citizens good.

According to Aristotle most virtues entail finding the mean between excess and deficiency. For example, courage is the mean between cowardice (a deficit) and foolhardiness (an excess); truthfulness lies between irony and boastfulness.

This doctrine of the mean should not be misinterpreted as advising us to be wishy-washy or to compromise our moral standards. Aristotle was not suggesting that we seek consensus or take a moderate position on moral issues. The doctrine of the mean is meant to apply to virtues, not to our positions on social issues. By suggesting that we seek the mean, Aristotle was not referring to being lukewarm or a fence-straddler but to seeking what is *reasonable.* Indeed, the most effective moral reformers have taken positions that differed sharply from the status quo. The abolitionists, as well as the early feminists, for example, were considered extremists and fanatics. Instead, Aristotle writes, "virtue discovers the means and deliberately chooses it."

The doctrine of the mean is found in moral philosophies throughout the world. Confucians as well as Buddhist ethicists teach that the mean is that which is consistent with harmony and equilibrium, or the Way (Tao).

Confucian Virtue Ethics

Confucius is one of the most important Chinese philosophers. Although Confucius died one century before the birth of Aristotle, there are remarkable similarities between the ethics of the two men. Both taught that virtue, in general, involves hitting the mean between excess and deficit, both emphasized the role of habituation in the cultivation of virtue, and both believed that virtue was essential for individual and social harmony. A deontologist as well, Confucius also taught that a virtuous person is a person of goodwill who puts duty first.

Like Aristotle, Confucius believed that a virtuous society and individual virtue are inseparable. It is the rulers, therefore, who have the greatest power to promote virtue in society and individuals. People are happiest and most virtuous when they are living in a just and well-ordered society. If the actions and policies of the government are consistent with the Way, the common people will also be good, and there will be no need for the government to use punishment to maintain order.

Buddhist Virtue Ethics

Buddhist ethics affirms the absolute worth of the individual and the community of all living beings. Buddhism rejects individualism as an illusion; we exist only as members of a community. Because we are all part of the same web of being, to be true to ourselves is to extend concern for everything that lies in our path of experience. The virtuous person is motivated not by self-interest, but by a concern to benefit all living beings.

Like Aristotle and Confucius, Buddhists believe that good and evil—virtue and vice—are expressed in our actions. Engaging in destructive actions makes it more likely that we'll repeat that behavior in the future; engaging in virtuous actions makes it more likely that we'll repeat that behavior in the future. A good society encourages the development of moral wisdom and virtue. We cannot resolve the problems that plague modern society by encouraging an individualism, such as that advocated by natural rights ethics, that allows people to pursue their concept of good at the expense of other human and nonhuman beings. Without moral progress, modern Buddhists warn, our rapid technological advances could lead us down the path to disaster.

Nietzsche and the *Übermensch*

Friedrich Nietzsche was an outspoken critic of cultural relativism, what he called herd morality. He was particularly critical of traditional bourgeois Christian morality that, he claimed, forms the basis of modern Western morality. This morality, which extols meekness, unconditional forgiveness, self-sacrifice, and equality as virtues, he argued is destructive to individual integrity and growth.

Humility and meekness play no role as virtues in the life of Nietzsche's *Übermensch,* or superman, just as they are not part of the life of Artistotle's virtuous person or the Confucian superior man. The *Übermensch* is a person of integrity and self-mastery who is able to rise above the morality of the crowd and exercise the "will to power," which entails the will to grow, courage, generosity toward the vanquished, and human nobility. In contrast, weak people extol humility and self-sacrifice as virtues because they lack the virtues of the *Übermensch.* Thus traditional Christian or Western bourgeois morality drags the best and strongest people down to the lowest common denominator.

Nietzsche's ethics have often been misinterpreted as the will to dominate and subjugate others. However, truly strong or virtuous people are not cruel, nor do they desire to subjugate others. While Nietzsche condemned modern Christianity, arguing that it bears little resemblance to that which was promoted by Jesus, he apparently admired Jesus as an example of an *Übermensch.*

A selection from Nietzsche's book *Beyond Good and Evil* is included in the *Ethics PowerWeb.*

Care Ethics

Care ethics emphasizes caring over considerations of justice and impartiality. Care ethics, as a moral theory, developed primarily out of Carol Gilligan's study of women's moral reasoning. It has also been influenced by David Hume's ethics, which emphasize moral sentiment over moral reasoning.

According to Hume, it is sympathy rather than reason that motivates us to act morally. Sympathy opens us up to others by breaking down the "we/them" barriers that impede the development of caring relationships.

Gilligan also stresses the importance of sympathy in moral decision making. In her interviews with women and through her study of women in literature, Gilligan concluded that women's moral development tends to follow a different path than men's. Men, she found, tend to base their moral decisions on duty and principle-oriented moral theories; women are more context-oriented and concerned with relationship.

According to care ethicist Nel Noddings in her reading at the end of this chapter, we are at our moral best when we are "caring and being cared for." Whereas Noddings limits her moral community to humans, arguing that nonhuman animals are incapable of being in a caring relationship, ecofeminist Karen Warren expands care ethics to include all living creatures and all of nature. Unlike abstract moral principles, sympathy joins us to others and breaks down barriers. It is care, not rational calculations or an abstract sense of duty, that creates moral obligations. Caring is also ranked highly in Confucian ethics, where traditional family ties and loyalty are extremely important.

An inclination to care, however, is not enough. When our personal inclination to care is lacking, our commitment to an ideal or principle of caring motivates us to do what is right. On this point care ethicists and deontologists find common ground. A person of goodwill—a person who is truly virtuous and caring—can be counted on to act out of a sense of duty even when the immediate emotional inclination to do so is lacking.

Care ethicists maintain that, rather than being limited to personal relationships, moral sentiments such as compassion and sympathy are forms of knowledge that should be taken seriously in discussing social issues and formulating social policy. Philosopher Virginia Held, for example, disagrees with the traditional division wherein justice as a value belongs to the public sphere and care to the private domain of family, friends, and charity.[34] Just as justice is needed in the family, so is the care perspective badly needed in the public domain. Care ethics plays a central role in the hospice movement's opposition to euthanasia and its belief that we should work on providing a more caring and supportive environment for those who are dying. In her book *Dead Man Walking*, Helen Prejean enjoins her readers to see condemned to death row prisoners from a care perspective as well as a justice perspective.

Care ethicists do not want to dispense with justice; rather, they want to see the two approaches used together in formulating social policy. Care ethics serves as a corrective to our traditional views by demanding that we recognize welfare rights as basic rights. It also requires that we see others in relationship as individuals with their own needs and dignity, rather than adopting a paternalistic attitude toward them.

Although care ethics is often associated with feminism, some feminists reject it on the grounds that it reinforces traditional stereotypes of women's roles in the family and in society.

The Strengths and Limitations of Virtue Ethics

The primary criticism of virtue ethics is that it is incomplete. It has also been criticized for its lack of coherence as a bag-of-virtues approach. This criticism is based on a misunderstanding of the nature of virtue, however. Virtue ethicists do not mean virtue to imply a list of unrelated character traits, but rather a unity of character—a unity that most of us are still striving to achieve.

Virtue ethics does not offer sufficient guidance for making real-life moral decisions. While a virtuous character may be enough to motivate the saint and those at the higher stages of moral development, most of us also need formal guidelines. Indeed, according to Kant, to a person of perfect goodwill (God), the concept of duty no longer applies.

On the other hand, virtue ethicists do not toss out abstract principles regarding duties and rights; instead they give them a personal face. Virtue ethicists are not suggesting that we ignore moral principles; they are saying that virtue ethics is more fundamental than duty ethics. Nor does virtue ethics entail discarding reason and relying solely on our "good" feelings. In the virtuous person, reason and feeling, as Hume himself pointed out, complement and confirm one another.

Virtue ethics goes beyond pure duty and rights-based ethics. They directly challenge the individual to rise above ordinary moral demands and to work toward creating a society in which it is easy for everyone to be virtuous and enjoy the good life.

 VIRTUE ETHICS: CONSIDERATIONS FOR THINKING ABOUT MORAL ISSUES

- **Seeking the mean:** Does the trait we are encouraging represent a balance between excess and deficiency?
- **Social policies and the promotion of virtue:** Does this social policy or resolution to a social issue encourage the development of virtue in the people affected by it?
- **Relationships:** What relationships are involved in this moral issue?
- **Caring and caring for:** How can we best nurture these relationships both as the "ones-caring" and the "ones-cared-for"?

EXERCISES

1. Which motivates you more to take action, a sense of justice or a feeling of sympathy for other persons? Illustrate your answer.
2. Discuss possible social policies for dealing with an issue such as hate speech, pornography, or alcohol and drug use on campus. Which policies are most likely to promote virtue in citizens? Support your answer.
3. Select a specific moral issue that is covered in this text. Discuss ways in which the care perspective might help in coming up with a resolution.
4. Examine the contemporary notion of nation-building in light of the Confucian concept of the virtuous society. Should virtue be imposed on the leadership of other nations, as is happening in Iraq and, if so, do other nations have a moral obligation to impose virtue in government, or at least their concept of a virtuous government, in wayward nations? Support your answer.

CONCLUSION

Moral issues are complex. No one theory offers the complete truth or perfect solution to a moral issue. On the other hand, theories can work together to provide us with more comprehensive tools for effectively analyzing moral issues. Theories help us recognize and prioritize moral principles and concerns. We should not simply discard a theory because it has limitations, but adopt a multidimensional approach that draws from the strengths of each of the theories. Whether the theory is deontological and oriented toward autonomy and the careful delineation of rules and rights; or utilitarian and concerned with consequences and mazimizing benefits; or virtue-based and focused on making us better, more caring people—all theories have the same ultimate goal: to provide a rational basis for making better moral decisions.

It is up to each of us, as critical thinkers, to apply moral theory to real-life moral decisions. In addition, although moral theory offers guidance, theory alone does not offer specific solutions. An understanding of the relevant facts, cultural traditions and conditions, practical wisdom, and sound moral reasoning are all necessary adjuncts to theory.

ARISTOTLE

Nicomachean Ethics

Aristotle was born in Stagira, a Greek colony north of Athens. He spent most of his childhood in Macedonia, where his father, Nicomachus, was a court physician and scholar. Unlike his forerunners Socrates and Plato, Aristotle had a fondness for luxury and wealth, owned several slaves, and hobnobbed with the rich and powerful.

A true Renaissance man, Aristotle was a scientist, philosopher, logician, poet, and psychologist who wrote hundreds of works, including poems, treatises, and books. *Nicomachean Ethics* is one of Aristotle's best-known works. In *Nicomachean Ethics,* Aristotle argues that living the good life—the life of virtue—is our most important human activity. Because the peculiar function of humans is the exercise of reason, virtue involves living according to reason. Only by living in accord with reason can we achieve happiness, inner harmony, and a well-ordered society.

Much of Aristotle's writing on the state is in response to the views of his teacher, Plato. Aristotle joined Plato's academy in Athens as a teenager and remained there for twenty years, until Plato's death at the age of eighty-one.

After the death of Plato, Aristotle took on the education of Alexander the Great, future king of Macedonia. The young ruler took Aristotle's teachings about world political unity to heart and, upon coming to the throne, set out to conquer the world, much to the chagrin of the Greeks. Given Aristotle's close association with the Macedonian conqueror, the Athenians had mixed feelings about him. Alexander the Great's untimely death in 323 B.C.E. unleashed a flood of anti-Macedonian feeling in Athens. Soon after, Aristotle was charged with impiety. Rather than take a chance that "the Athenians should sin a second time against philosophy" (they had put Plato's teacher Socrates to death for impiety in 399 B.C.E.), Aristotle fled to Euboea. He died in Babylon a year later.

Aristotle is sometimes dismissed as being too much of an elitist to be relevant for today's democracies. His critique of democracy, however, is a timely warning against the dangers of relying on majority rule as the criterion for deciding what is just.

Critical Reading Questions

1. How does Aristotle go about analyzing the term *good?*
2. According to Aristotle, what is the most important human activity? What is the final end of human activity?
3. What is the relationship between morality and happiness?
4. What is virtue? What are the two types of virtue?
5. What does Aristotle mean by habituation? What does habituation have to do with becoming virtuous? What is the role of the state in helping citizens become virtuous?

Nicomachean Ethics, from Richard McKeon (ed.), *The Basic Works of Aristotle* (New York: Random House, 1941). Copy of an earlier translation by Benjamin Jowett (1817–1893). Notes have been omitted.

6. What does Aristotle mean when he says that goodness is the quality that hits the mean? Is virtue always a matter of hitting the mean?
7. What are some examples of excesses and deficits? How do we avoid them?

Book I

CHAPTER 1

Every art and every inquiry, and similarly every action and pursuit, is thought to aim at some good; and for this reason the good has rightly been declared to be that at which all things aim. But a certain difference is found among ends; some are activities, others are products apart from the activities that produce them. Where there are ends apart from the actions, it is the nature of the products to be better than the activities. . . .

CHAPTER 7

Let us again return to the good we are seeking, and ask what it can be. It seems different in different actions and arts; it is different in medicine, in strategy, and in the other arts likewise. What then is the good of each? Surely that for whose sake everything else is done. In medicine this is health, in strategy victory, in architecture a house, in any other sphere something else, and in every action and pursuit the end; for it is for the sake of this that all men do whatever else they do. Therefore, if there is an end for all that we do, this will be the good achievable by action, and if there are more than one, these will be the goods achievable by action.

So the argument has by a different course reached the same point; but we must try to state this even more clearly. Since there is evidently more than one end, and we choose some of these (e.g., wealth, flutes, and in general instruments) for the sake of something else, clearly not all ends are final ends; but the chief good is evidently something final. Therefore, if there is only one final end, this will be what we are seeking, and if there are more than one, the most final of these will be what we are seeking. Now we call that which is in itself worthy of pursuit more final than that which is worthy of pursuit for the sake of something else, and that which is never desirable for the sake of something else more final than the things that are desirable both in themselves and for the sake of that other thing, and therefore we call final without qualification that which is always desirable in itself and never for the sake of something else.

Now such a thing happiness, above all else, is held to be; for this we choose always for itself and never for the sake of something else, but honour, pleasure, reason, and every virtue we choose indeed for themselves (for if nothing resulted from them we should still choose each of them), but we choose them also for the sake of happiness, judging that by means of them we shall be happy. Happiness, on the other hand, no one chooses for the sake of these, nor, in general, for anything other than itself. . . .

Presumably, however, to say that happiness is the chief good seems a platitude, and a clearer account of what it is is still desired. This might perhaps be given, if we could first ascertain the function of man. For just as for a flute-player, a sculptor, or any artist, and, in general, for all things that have a function or activity, the good and the "well" is thought to reside in the function, so would it seem to be for man, if he has a function. Have the carpenter, then, and the tanner certain functions or activities, and has man none? Is he born without a function? Or as eye, hand, foot, and in general each of the parts evidently has a function, may one lay it down that man similarly has a function apart from all these? What then can this be? Life seems to be common even to plants, but we are seeking what is peculiar to man. Let us exclude, therefore, the life of nutrition and growth. Next there would be a life of perception, but *it* also seems to be common even to the horse, the ox, and every animal. There remains, then, an active life of the element that has a rational principle; of this, one part has such a principle in the sense of being obedient to one, the other in the sense of possessing one and exercising thought. And, as "life of the rational element" also has two meanings, we must state that life in the sense of activity is what we mean; for this seems to be the more proper sense of the term. Now if the function of man is an activity of soul which follows or implies a rational principle, . . . : if this is the case, [and we state the function of man to be a certain kind of life, and this to be an activity or actions of the soul implying a rational principle, and the function of a good man to be the good and noble performance of these, and if any action is well performed when it is performed in accordance with the appropriate excellence: if this is the case,] human good turns out to be activity of soul in accordance with virtue, and if there are more than one virtue, in accordance with the best and most complete.

But we must add "in a complete life." For one swallow does not make a summer, nor does one day; and so too one day, or a short time, does not make a man blessed and happy. . . .

Book II

CHAPTER 1

Virtue, then, being of two kinds, intellectual and moral, intellectual virtue in the main owes both its birth and its growth to teaching (for which reason it requires experience and time), while moral virtue comes about as a result of habit, whence also its name *ethike* is one that is formed by a slight variation from the word *ethos* (habit). From this it is also plain that none of the moral virtues arises in us by nature, for nothing that exists by nature can form a habit contrary to its nature. For instance the stone which by nature moves downwards cannot be habituated to move upwards, not even if one tries to train it by throwing it up ten thousand times; nor can fire be habituated to move downwards, nor can anything else that by nature behaves in one way be trained to behave in another. Neither by nature, then, nor contrary to nature do the virtues arise in us; rather we are adapted by nature to receive them, and are made perfect by habit.

Again, of all the things that come to us by nature we first acquire the potentiality and later exhibit the activity (this is plain in the case of the senses; for it was not by often seeing or often hearing that we got these senses, but on the contrary we had them before we used them, and did not come to have them by using them); but the virtues we get by first exercising them, as also happens in the case of the arts as well. For the things we have to learn before we can do them, we learn by doing them, e.g. men become builders by building and lyre-players by playing the lyre; so too we become just by doing just acts, temperate by doing temperate acts, brave by doing brave acts.

This is confirmed by what happens in states; for legislators make the citizens good by forming habits in them, and this is the wish of every legislator, and those who do not effect it miss their mark, and it is in this that a good constitution differs from a bad one.

Again, it is from the same causes and by the same means that every virtue is both produced and destroyed, and similarly every art; for it is from playing the lyre that both good and bad lyre-players are produced. And the corresponding statement is true of builders and of all the rest; men will be good or bad builders as a result of building well or badly. For if this were not so, there would have been no need of a teacher, but all men would have been born good or bad at their craft. This, then, is the case with the virtues also; by doing the acts that we do in our transactions with other men we become just or unjust, and by doing the acts that we do in the presence of danger, and being habituated to feel fear or confidence, we become brave or cowardly. The same is true of appetites and feelings of anger; some men become temperate and good-tempered, others self-indulgent and irascible, by behaving in one way or the other in the appropriate circumstances. Thus, in one word, states of character arise out of like activities. This is why the activities we exhibit must be of a certain kind; it is because the states of character correspond to the differences between these. It makes no small difference, then, whether we form habits of one kind or of another from our very youth; it makes a very great difference, or rather *all* the difference.

CHAPTER 2

Since, then, the present inquiry does not aim at theoretical knowledge like the others (for we are inquiring not in order to know what virtue is, but in order to become good, since otherwise our inquiry would have been of no use), we must examine the nature of actions, namely how we ought to do them; for these determine also the nature of the states of character that are produced, as we have said. Now, that we must act according to the right rule is a common principle and must be assumed—it will be discussed later, i.e. both what the right rule is, and how it is related to the other virtues. . . .

First, then, let us consider this, that it is the nature of such things to be destroyed by defect and excess, as we see in the case of strength and health (for to gain light on things imperceptible we must use the evidence of sensible things); both excessive and defective exercise destroys the strength, and similarly drink or food which is above or below a certain amount destroys the health, while that which is proportionate both produces and increases and preserves it. So too is it, then, in the case of temperance and courage and the other virtues. For the man who flies from and fears everything and does not stand his ground against anything becomes a coward, and the man who fears nothing at all but goes to meet every danger becomes rash; and similarly the man who indulges in every pleasure and abstains from none becomes self-indulgent, while the man who shuns every pleasure, as boors do, becomes in a way insensible; temperance and courage, then, are destroyed by excess and defect, and preserved by the mean.

But not only are the sources and causes of their origination and growth the same as those of their destruction, but also the sphere of their actualization will be the same; for this is also true of the things which are more evident to sense, e.g. of strength; it is produced by taking much food and undergoing much exertion, and it is the strong man that will be most able to do these things. So too is it with the virtues; by abstaining from pleasures we become temperate, and it is when we have become so that we are most able to abstain from them; and similarly too in the case of courage; for by being habituated to despise things that are terrible and to stand our ground against them we become brave, and it is when we have become so that we shall be most able to stand our ground against them. . . .

CHAPTER 5

Next we must consider what virtue is. Since things that are found in the soul are of three kinds—passions, faculties, states of character, virtue must be one of these. By passions I mean appetite, anger, fear, confidence, envy, joy, friendly feeling, hatred, longing, emulation, pity, and in general the feelings that are accompanied by pleasure or pain; by faculties the things in virtue of which we are said to be capable of feeling these, e.g. of becoming angry or being pained or feeling pity; by states of character the things in virtue of which we stand well or badly with reference to the passions, e.g. with reference to anger we stand badly if we feel it violently or too weakly, and well if we feel it moderately; and similarly with reference to the other passions.

Now neither the virtues nor the vices are *passions,* because we are not called good or bad on the ground of our passions, but are so called on the ground of our virtues and our vices, and because we are neither praised nor blamed for our passions (for the man who feels fear or anger is not praised, nor is the man who simply feels anger blamed, but the man who feels it in a certain way), but for our virtues and our vices we *are* praised or blamed.

Again, we feel anger and fear without choice, but the virtues are modes of choice or involve choice. . . . Further, in respect of the passions we are said to be moved, but in respect of the virtues and the vices we are said not to be moved but to be disposed in a particular way.

For these reasons also they are not *faculties;* for we are neither called good nor bad, nor praised nor blamed, for the simple capacity of feeling the passions; again, we have the faculties by nature, but we are not made good or bad by nature; we have spoken of this before.

If, then, the virtues are neither passions nor faculties, all that remains is that they should be *states of character.*

Thus we have stated what virtue is in respect of its genus.

CHAPTER 6

We must, however, not only describe virtue as a state of character, but also say what sort of state it is. We may remark, then, that every virtue or excellence both brings into good condition the thing of which it is the excellence and makes the work of that thing be done well; e.g. the excellence of the eye makes both the eye and its work good; for it is by the excellence of the eye that we see well. Similarly the excellence of the horse makes a horse both good in itself and good at running and at carrying its rider and at awaiting the attack of the enemy. Therefore, if this is true in every case, the virtue of man also will be the state of character which makes a man good and which makes him do his own work well. . . .

Virtue, then, is a state of character concerned with choice, lying in a mean, i.e. the mean relative to us, this being determined by a rational principle, and by that principle by which the man of practical wisdom would determine it. Now it is a mean between two vices, that which depends on excess and that which depends on defect; and again it is a mean because the vices respectively fall short of or exceed what is right in both passions and actions, while virtue both finds and chooses that which is intermediate. Hence in respect of its substance and the definition which states its essence virtue is a mean, with regard to what is best and right an extreme.

But not every action nor every passion admits of a mean; for some have names that already imply badness, e.g. spite, shamelessness, envy, and in the case of actions adultery, theft, murder; for all of these and suchlike things imply by their names that they are themselves bad, and not the excesses or deficiencies of them. It is not possible, then, ever to be right with regard to them; one must always be wrong. Nor does goodness or badness with regard to such things depend on committing adultery with the right woman, at the right time, and in the right way, but simply to do any of them is to go wrong. It would be equally absurd, then, to expect that in unjust, cowardly, and voluptuous action there should be a mean, an excess, and a deficiency; for at that rate there would be a mean of excess and of deficiency, an excess of excess, and a deficiency of deficiency. But as there is no excess and deficiency of temperance and courage because what is intermediate is in a sense an extreme, so too of the actions we have mentioned there is no mean nor any excess and deficiency, but however they are done they are wrong; for in general there is neither a mean of excess and deficiency, nor excess and deficiency of a mean.

For a more extensive reading from Aristotle's *Nichomachean Ethics,* use the accompanying *Ethics PowerWeb.*

Discussion Questions

1. Do you agree with Aristotle that every act and inquiry aims at some good (goal)? Is there a single end toward which all human behavior is directed? If so, does this justify the regulation of people's behavior, including restrictions on viewing media violence and pornography, by the government so they are more likely to achieve this end? Use specific examples to support your answer.
2. Do colleges have a duty to help students become virtuous people by creating an atmosphere in which good behavior becomes habitual for them? Support your answer. Should campus administrations prohibit certain excessive behaviors in order to make

it easier for students to become good people? Discuss your answer in light of regulations on hate speech, cheating, and drug and alcohol abuse.

3. Aristotle warned against the rule of the many, arguing that "the many are more corruptible than the few." Is the fact that the United States is a democracy an impediment to getting the United States to comply with international policies regarding environmental protection? Discuss whether important public policies, especially those that affect the international community, should be left up to the experts or to majority rule.

JOHN STUART MILL

Utilitarianism

John Stuart Mill (1806–1873) was educated at home by his father James Mill, with the help of Jeremy Bentham, to carry on the utilitarian tradition. When Mill was about twenty, he experienced a nervous breakdown and sank into a deep depression that lasted for two years. During this time, he began to question some of the tenets of Bentham's utilitarian theory, particularly Bentham's insistence on the equality of pleasures.

Like Bentham, Mill was interested in legislation and social reform. However, unlike Bentham, Mill believed that certain pleasures should count more than others.

Critical Reading Questions

1. What is the principle of utility, and what are the only things that the principle of utility regards as desirable moral ends?
2. Which pleasures does Mill regard as superior?
3. What method does Mill use for determining which pleasures are of a higher quality?
4. Whose interests should be taken into account when determining the utility of an action?
5. What is the relationship between the principle of utility and the golden rule?

The creed which accepts as the foundation of morals, Utility, or the Greatest Happiness Principle, holds that actions are right in proportion as they tend to promote happiness, wrong as they tend to produce the reverse of happiness. By happiness is intended pleasure, and the absence of pain; by unhappiness, pain, and the privation of pleasure. To give a clear view of the moral standard set up by the theory, much more requires to be said; in particular, what things it includes in the ideas of pain and pleasure; and to what extent this is left an open question. But these supplementary explanations do not affect the theory of life on which this theory of morality is grounded—namely, that pleasure, and freedom from pain, are the only things desirable as ends; and that all desirable things (which are as

Originally published in three installments in Fraser's magazine, 1861.

numerous in the utilitarian as in any other scheme) are desirable either for the pleasure inherent in themselves, or as means to the promotion of pleasure and the prevention of pain. . . .

It is quite compatible with the principle of utility to recognise the fact, that some *kinds* of pleasure are more desirable and more valuable than others. It would be absurd that while, in estimating all other things, quality is considered as well as quantity, the estimation of pleasures should be supposed to depend on quantity alone.

If I am asked, what I mean by difference of quality in pleasures, or what makes one pleasure more valuable than another, merely as a pleasure, except its being greater in amount, there is but one possible answer. Of two pleasures, if there be one to which all or almost all who have experience of both give a decided preference, irrespective of any feeling of moral obligation to prefer it, that is the more desirable pleasure. If one of the two is, by those who are competently acquainted with both, placed so far above the other that they prefer it, even though knowing it to be attended with a greater amount of discontent, and would not resign it for any quantity of the other pleasure which their nature is capable of, we are justified in ascribing to the preferred enjoyment a superiority in quality, so far outweighing quantity as to render it, in comparison, of small account.

Now it is an unquestionable fact that those who are equally acquainted with, and equally capable of appreciating and enjoying, both, do give a most marked preference to the manner of existence which employs their higher faculties. Few human creatures would consent to be changed into any of the lower animals, for a promise of the fullest allowance of a beast's pleasures; no intelligent human being would consent to be a fool, no instructed person would be an ignoramus, no person of feeling and conscience would be selfish and base, even though they should be persuaded that the fool, the dunce, or the rascal is better satisfied with his lot than they are with theirs. . . . It is better to be a human being dissatisfied than a pig satisfied; better to be Socrates dissatisfied than a fool satisfied. And if the fool, or the pig, are of a different opinion, it is because they only know their own side of the question. The other party to the comparison knows both sides.

. . .

According to the Greatest Happiness Principle, as above explained, the ultimate end, with reference to and for the sake of which all other things are desirable (whether we are considering our own good or that of other people), is an existence exempt as far as possible from pain, and as rich as possible in enjoyments, both in point of quantity and quality; the test of quality, and the rule for measuring it against quantity, being the preference felt by those who in their opportunities of experience, to which must be added their habits of self-consciousness and self-observation, are best furnished with the means of comparison. This, being, according to the utilitarian opinion, the end of human action, is necessarily also the standard of morality; which may accordingly be defined, the rules and precepts for human conduct, by the observance of which an existence such as has been described might be, to the greatest extent possible, secured to all mankind; and not to them only, but, so far as the nature of things admits, to the whole sentient creation.

. . .

I must again repeat, what the assailants of utilitarianism seldom have the justice to acknowledge, that the happiness which forms the utilitarian standard of what is right in conduct, is not the agent's own happiness, but that of all concerned. As between his own happiness and that of others, utilitarianism requires him to be as strictly impartial as a disinterested and benevolent spectator. In the golden rule of Jesus of Nazareth, we read the complete spirit of the ethics of utility. To do as you would be done by, and to love your neighbour as yourself, constitute the ideal perfection of utilitarian morality. As the means of making the nearest approach to this ideal, utility would enjoin, first, that laws and social arrangements should place the happiness, or (as speaking practically it may be called) the interest, of every individual, as nearly as possible in harmony with the interest of the whole; and secondly, that education and opinion, which have so vast a power over human character, should so use that power as to establish in the mind of every individual an indissoluble association between his own happiness and the good of the whole; especially between his own happiness and the practice of such modes of conduct, negative and positive, as regard for the universal happiness prescribes; so that not only he may be unable to conceive the possibility of happiness to himself, consistently with conduct opposed to the general good, but also that a direct impulse to promote the general good may be in every individual one of habitual motives of action, and the sentiments connected therewith may fill a large and prominent place in every human being's sentient existence. If the impugners of the utilitarian morality represented it to their own minds in this its true character, I know not what recommendation possessed by any other morality they could possibly affirm to be wanting to it; what more beautiful or more exalted developments of human nature any other ethical system can be supposed to foster, or what springs of action, not accessible to the utilitarian, such systems rely on for giving effect to their mandates. . . .

For a more extensive reading from Mill's *Utilitarianism,* use the accompanying *Ethics PowerWeb.* A selection from Mill's *On Liberty* is included after Chapter 8 "Freedom of Speech."

Discussion Questions

1. Do you agree with Mill that the life of an unhappy human is preferable to that of a satisfied pig? On what grounds does Mill make such an assertion? Is this distinction between the different pleasures justified? If so, on what basis?
2. How does Mill's concept of pleasure differ from that of Bentham's? Which definition is most useful? Apply Mill's concept of the quality of pleasures to moral issues involving nonhuman animals, for example, meat-eating versus vegetarianism, keeping animals in zoos, and the use of nonhuman animals in medical experimentation and cosmetic experimentation.
3. What is "sentience"? Why does Mill use sentience as a criterion for determining whose interests should be taken into account? Do you agree with this criterion? Using this criterion what would Mill's position most likely be regarding euthanasia and "partial-birth" abortions?
4. Discuss the legalization of drugs and pornography in light of Mill's theory.

Fundamental Principles of the Metaphysic of Ethics

An intellectual giant, German philosopher Immanuel Kant (1724–1804) stood barely five feet tall as an adult. Born with a deformed chest, Kant was plagued with health problems his entire life. Because of his poor health, Kant maintained a strict regimen; his daily walks were so regular that people could set their watches by the time he walked past their houses.

After completing his studies, Kant worked for several years as a tutor to the children of Prussian aristocrats. In 1755 he got a job as privatdocent at the University of Konigsberg, making Kant the first of the major philosophers to be a professional university teacher. As a privatdocent Kant was licensed to give lectures. He was not paid by the university, however, but by the students. Kant lectured as many as twenty-one hours a week on subjects ranging from fireworks and physical geography to metaphysics. As a lecturer he was witty and inspiring. One of his students later wrote that they "never left a single lecture in his ethics without having become better men." Despite his popularity as a teacher, Kant remained poor for many years.

In 1770, after many years of trying to get a permanent teaching position at the university, Kant was finally appointed professor of logic and metaphysics. He remained at the university as a professor until poor health forced him to retire in 1796. In his later years, Kant gained fame as a sort of oracle, and Konigsberg became a shrine of philosophy. People came from all over to consult Kant on all sorts of issues, including the lawfulness of vaccinations. He died in 1804, having spent his entire life in Konigsberg.

Kant's first great work in philosophy, *Critique of Pure Reason,* was not published until 1781, when he was in his late fifties. It was followed in relatively quick succession by other great works, including the *Fundamental Principles of the Metaphysic of Morals* in 1785.

Unlike the utilitarians, Kant was more concerned with establishing a metaphysical foundation for morality than in coming up with an ethical system that could be used for formulating social policy. He believed that only reason could provide this foundation. If moral law is to be morally compelling, he argued, it must be logically consistent as well as absolutely binding. Kant's concepts of the Good Will and the categorical imperative—the most fundamental moral principle—continue to be two of the most useful concepts in discussion of moral issues.

Critical Reading Questions

1. What is the Good Will? What is the relevance of the Good Will in making decisions regarding social policy?
2. What gives an action moral worth?

Fundamental Principles of the Metaphysic of Ethics, trans. by Thomas Kingsmill Abbott (London: Longmans, Green and Co., Ltd., 1926). Some notes have been omitted.

3. Why does Kant reject utilitarianism as the foundation of morality?
4. What is the source of moral knowledge?
5. Why does Kant argue that moral maxims must be universal rather than relative?
6. What is the categorical imperative? How does it differ from a hypothetical imperative? Give examples of both types of imperatives.
7. What does it mean for a being to be an "end in itself"? What gives a being value as an end in itself?
8. What is the difference between treating a being as an end in itself and treating a being as a means only? Why is it wrong to treat persons as means only?

Nothing can possibly be conceived in the world, or even out of it, which can be called good without qualification, except a Good Will. Intelligence, wit, judgment, and the other *talents* of the mind, however they may be named, or courage, resolution, perseverance, as qualities of temperament, are undoubtedly good and desirable in many respects; but these gifts of nature may also become extremely bad and mischievous if the will which is to make use of them, and which, therefore, constitutes what is called *character*, is not good. It is the same with the *gifts of fortune*. Power, riches, honour, even health, and the general well-being and contentment with one's condition which is called *happiness*, inspire pride, and often presumption, if there is not a Good Will to correct the influence of these on the mind, and with this also to rectify the whole principle of acting, and adapt it to its end. . . .

A Good Will is good not because of what it performs or effects, not by its aptness for the attainment of some proposed end, but simply by virtue of the volition, that is, it is good in itself, and considered by itself is to be esteemed much higher than all that can be brought about by it in favour of any inclination, nay, even of the sum total of all inclinations. Even if it should happen that, owing to special disfavour of fortune, or the niggardly provision of a step-motherly nature, this will should wholly lack power to accomplish its purpose, if with its greatest efforts it should yet achieve nothing, and there should remain only the Good Will (not, to be sure, a mere wish, but the summoning of all means in our power), then, like a jewel, it would still shine by its own light, as a thing which has its whole value in itself. Its usefulness or fruitlessness can neither add to nor take away anything from this value. . . .

To be beneficent when we can is a duty; and besides this, there are many minds so sympathetically constituted that, without any other motive of vanity or self-interest, they find a pleasure in spreading joy around them, and can take delight in the satisfaction of others so far as it is their own work. But I maintain that in such a case an action of this kind, however proper, however amiable it may be, has nevertheless no true moral worth, but is on a level with other inclinations, *e.g.* the inclination to honour, which, if it is happily directed to that which is in fact of public utility and accordant with duty, and consequently honourable, deserves praise and encouragement, but not esteem. For the maxim lacks the moral import, namely, that such actions be done *from duty*, not from inclination. Put the case that the mind of that philanthropist was clouded by sorrow of his own extinguishing all sympathy with the lot of others, and that while he still has the power to benefit others in distress, he is not touched by their trouble because he is absorbed with his own; and now suppose that he tears himself out of his dead insensibility, and performs the action without any inclination to it, but simply from duty, then first has his action its genuine moral worth. . . .

Thus the moral worth of an action does not lie in the effect expended from it, not in any principle of action which requires to borrow its motive from this expected effect. For all these effects—agreeableness of one's condition, and even the promotion of the happiness of others—could have been also brought about by other causes, so that for this there would have been no need of the will of a rational being; whereas it is in this alone that the supreme and unconditional good can be found. The pre-eminent good which we call moral can therefore consist in nothing else than *the conception of law* in itself, *which certainly is only possible in a rational being,* in so far as this conception, and not the expected effect, determines the will. . . .

But what sort of law can that be, the conception of which must determine the will, even without paying any regard to the effect expected from it, in order that this will may be called good absolutely and without qualification? As I have deprived the will of every impulse which could arise to it from obedience to any law, there remains nothing but the universal conformity of its actions to law in general, which alone is to serve the will as a principle, *i.e.* I am never to act otherwise than *so that I could also will that my maxim should become a universal law.* Here now, it is the simple conformity to law in general, without assuming any particular law applicable to certain actions, that serves the will as its principle, and must so serve it, if duty is not to be a vain delusion and a chimerical notion. The common reason of men in its practical judgments perfectly coincides with this, and always has in view the principle here suggested. Let the question be, for example: May I when in distress make a promise with the intention not to keep it? I readily distinguish here between the two significations which the question may have: Whether it is prudent, or whether it is right, to make a false promise. The former may undoubtedly often be the case. . . . The shortest way, however, and an unerring one, to discover the answer to this question whether a lying promise is consistent with duty, is to ask myself, Should I be content that my maxim (to extricate myself from difficulty by a false promise) should hold good as a universal law, for myself as well as for others? and should I be able to say to myself, "Every one may make a deceitful promise when he finds himself in a difficulty from which he cannot otherwise extricate himself"? Then I presently become aware that while I can will the lie, I can by no means will that lying should be a univeral law. For with such a law there would be no promises at all, since it would be in vain to allege my intention in regard to my future actions to those who would not believe this allegation, or if they overhastily did so would pay me back in my own coin. Hence my maxim, as soon as it should be made a universal law, would necessarily destroy itself. . . .

I do not indeed as yet *discern* on what this respect is based (this the philosopher may inquire), but at least I understand this, that it is an estimation of the worth which far outweighs all worth of what is recommended by inclination, and that the necessity of acting from *pure* respect for the practical law is what constitutes duty, to which every other motive must give place, because it is the condition of a will being good *in itself,* and the worth of such a will is above everything. . . .

Everything in nature works according to laws. Rational beings alone have the faculty of acting according *to the conception* of laws, that is according to principles, *i.e.* have a *will.* Since the deduction of actions from principles requires *reason,* the will is nothing but practical reason. . . .

The conception of an objective principle, in so far as it is obligatory for a will, is called a command (of reason), and the formula of the command is called an Imperative.

All imperatives are expressed by the word *ought* [or *shall*], and thereby indicate the relation of an objective law of reason to a will, which from its subjective constitution is not necessarily determined by it (an obligation). They say that something would be good to do or to forbear, but they say it to a will which does not always do a thing because it is conceived to be good to do it. . . .

Now all *imperatives* command either *hypothetically* or *categorically.* The former represent the practical necessity of a possible action as means to something else that is willed (or at least which one might possibly will). The categorical imperative would be that which represented an action as necessary of itself without reference to another end, *i.e.* as objectively necessary.

Since every practical law represents a possible action as good, and on this account, for a subject who is practically determinable by reason, necessary, all imperatives are formulæ determining an action which is necessary according to the principle of a will good in some respects. If now the action is good only as a means *to something else,* then the Imperative is *hypothetical;* if it is conceived as good *in itself* and consequently as being necessarily the principle of a will which of itself conforms to reason, then it is *Categorical*. . . .

An imperative which commands a certain conduct immediately, without having as its condition any other purpose to be attained by it . . . is Categorical. It concerns not the matter of the action, or its intended result, but its form and the principle of which it is itself a result; and what is essentially good in it consists in the mental disposition, let the consequence be what it may. This Imperative may be called that of Morality. . . .

When I conceive a hypothetical imperative in general I do not know beforehand what it will contain until I am given the condition. But when I conceive a Categorical Imperative I know at once what it contains. For as the imperative contains besides the law only the necessity that the maxims* shall conform to this law, while the law contains no conditions restricting it, there remains nothing but the general statement that the maxim of the action should conform to a universal law, and it is this conformity alone that the imperative properly represents as necessary.

There is therefore but one Categorical Imperative, namely this: *Act only on that maxim whereby thou canst at the same time will that it should become a universal law.*

Now if all imperatives of duty can be deduced from this one imperative as from their principle, then, although it should remain undecided whether what is called duty is not merely a vain notion, yet at least we shall be able to show what we understand by it and what this notion means.

Since the universality of the law according to which effects are produced constitutes what is properly called *nature* in the most general sense (as to form), that is, the existence of things so far as it is determined by general laws, the Imperative of duty may be expressed thus: *Act as if the maxim of thy action were to become by thy will a Universal Law of Nature*. . . .

A man reduced to despair by a series of misfortunes feels wearied of life, but is still so far in possession of his reason that he can ask himself whether it would not be contrary to his duty to himself to take his own life. Now he inquires whether the maxim of his action could become a universal law of nature. His maxim is: From self-love I adopt it as a principle to shorten my life when its longer duration is likely to bring more evil than satisfaction. It is asked then simply whether this principle founded on self-love can become a universal law of nature. Now we see at once that a system of nature of which it should be a law to destroy life by means of the very feeling whose special nature it is to impel to the improvement of life would contradict itself, and therefore could not exist as a system of nature; hence that maxim cannot possibly exist as a universal law of nature, and consequently would be wholly inconsistent with the supreme principle of all duty. . . .

We have thus established at least this much, that if duty is a conception which is to have any import and real legislative authority for our actions, it can only be expressed in Categorical, and not at all in hypothetical imperatives. We have also, which is of great importance, exhibited clearly and definitely for every practical application the content of the Categorical Imperative, which must contain the principle of all duty if there is such a thing at all. . . .

If then there is a supreme practical principle or, in respect of the human will, a Categorical Imperative, it must be one which, being drawn from the conception of that which is necessarily an end for every one because it is *an end in itself*, constitutes an *objective* principle of will, and can therefore serve as a universal practical law. The foundation of this principle is: *rational nature exists as an end in itself*. Man necessarily conceives his own existence as being so: so far then this is a *subjective* principle of human actions. But every other rational being regards its existence similarly, just on the same rational principle that holds for me: so that it is at the same time an objective principle, from which as a supreme practical law all laws of the will must be capable of being deduced. Accordingly the practical imperative will be as follows: *So act as to treat humanity,*

---

* A MAXIM is a subjective principle of action, and must be distinguished from the *objective principle*, namely, practical law. The former contains the practical rule set by reason according to the conditions of the subject (often its ignorance or its inclinations), so that it is the principle on which the subject *acts;* but the law is the objective principle valid for every rational being, and is the principle on which it *ought to act,* that is, an imperative.

whether in thine own person or in that of any other, in every case as an end withal, never as means only. We will now inquire whether this can be practically carried out.

To abide by the previous examples:

Firstly, under the head of necessary duty to oneself: He who contemplates suicide should ask himself whether his action can be consistent with the idea of humanity *as an end in itself.* If he destroys himself in order to escape from painful circumstances, he uses a person merely as a *mean* to maintain a tolerable condition up to the end of life. But a man is not a thing, that is to say, something which can be used merely as means, but must in all his actions be always considered as an end in himself. I cannot, therefore, dispose in any way of a man in my own person so as to mutilate him, to damage or kill him. (It belongs to ethics proper to define this principle more precisely so as to avoid all misunderstanding, *e.g.* as to the amputation of the limbs in order to preserve myself; as to exposing my life to danger with a view to preserve it, &c. This question is therefore omitted here.)

Secondly, as regards necessary duties, or those of strict obligation, toward others; he who is thinking of making a lying promise to others will see at once that he would be using another man *merely as a mean,* without the latter containing at the same time the end in himself. For he whom I propose by such a promise to use for my own purposes cannot possibly assent to my mode of acting towards him, and therefore cannot himself contain the end of this action. This violation of the principle of humanity in other men is more obvious if we take in examples of attacks on the freedom and property of others. For then it is clear that he who transgresses the rights of men, intends to use the person of the others merely as means, without considering that as rational beings they ought always to be esteemed also as ends, that is, as beings who must be capable of containing in themselves the end of the very same action.

For a more extensive reading from Kant's *Fundamental Principles of the Metaphysics of Ethics,* use the accompanying *Ethics PowerWeb.*

Discussion Questions

1. Kant formulated his views on suicide long before medical technology was developed that could be used to extend the dying process. What would Kant's position most likely be on physician-assisted suicide? Is physician-assisted suicide always incompatible with the categorical imperative? Support your answers.
2. The categorical imperative requires that we treat persons as ends in themselves and never as means only. Develop a policy on affirmative action for college admissions that is based on the categorical imperative.
3. Can hate speech ever be compatible with the categorical imperative? Why or why not? If not, what is your moral duty, as a person of goodwill, if you witness or are the victim of hate speech? Support your answers.
4. Discuss how Kant's definition of personhood and the moral community would influence his position on vegetarianism or environmental issues such as the destruction of the Amazon rain forests. Although Kant excluded nonhuman animals from the moral community, he was opposed to cruelty to other animals on the grounds that it makes us more likely to be cruel to people. Is enjoying the products of animal agriculture, particularly animals raised on land that used to be rain forest, morally acceptable so long as we are not directly involved or do not witness the pain or extinction of other species? Support your answer.

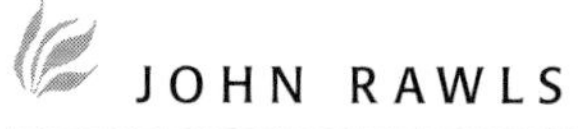

JOHN RAWLS

A Theory of Justice

Harvard philosopher and political theorist John Rawls (b. 1921), like the utilitarians, is primarily concerned with providing a theoretical framework for formulating social policy. Rawls argues that utilitarian theory is too obscure and simplistic to deal with many of the issues facing modern society. In his book *A Theory of Justice,* he offers an alternative to utilitarian social theory by combining deontology with a social contract approach to social ethics.

Social contract theory has its roots in classical Greek philosophy. Elements of social contract theory are also found in the philosophies of John Locke, Jean-Jacques Rousseau, and Immanuel Kant. A social contract is an agreement between individuals and a governing power in which the individuals freely surrender some personal liberties in exchange for the advantages of living in a well-organized society.

According to Rawls, justice as fairness is the most basic requirement of the social contract. This element of justice, he argues, is absent in strict utilitarian theory. In order to determine which principles of justice should govern a society, Rawls came up with a hypothetical device he calls the "veil of ignorance." The veil of ignorance provides an objective and impartial viewpoint from which we can view our place in society and come up with principles of justice that are fair for everyone. Rawls believes that under the veil of ignorance, people in the "original position," the time prior to the founding of the social contract, will come up with two principles of justice outlined in the reading. By applying these two principles, we can resolve disputes in social ethics and formulate social policies that are just.

Rawls's theory of justice has been tremendously influential in discussions of public policy in areas such as health care and welfare reform.

Critical Reading Questions

1. What is "the first virtue of social institutions"?
2. What does Rawls mean by a "social contract" and what is its relevance to resolving moral issues?
3. What is the "original position of equality"? Does this position actually exist or has it ever existed in the past?
4. What is the "veil of ignorance" and what is its purpose?
5. What does Rawls mean by "justice as fairness"?
6. What, according to Rawls, are the two principles of justice that would be chosen in the original position? How are these principles to be applied in resolving social issues?
7. Why does Rawls reject the principle of utility as one that would be chosen in the original position?

A Theory of Justice (Cambridge, Mass.: Harvard University Press, 1971). Notes have been omitted.

8. What are the basic rights, according to Rawls? Does he place more emphasis on liberty rights or on welfare rights?

Justice as Fairness

THE ROLE OF JUSTICE

Justice is the first virtue of social institutions, as truth is of systems of thought. A theory however elegant and economical must be rejected or revised if it is untrue; likewise laws and institutions no matter how efficient and well-arranged must be reformed or abolished if they are unjust. Each person possesses an inviolability founded on justice that even the welfare of society as a whole cannot override. . . .

A society is a more or less self-sufficient association of persons who in their relations to one another recognize certain rules of conduct as binding and who for the most part act in accordance with them. Suppose further that these rules specify a system of cooperation designed to advance the good of those taking part in it. Then, although a society is a cooperative venture for mutual advantage, it is typically marked by a conflict as well as by an identity of interests. There is an identity of interests since social cooperation makes possible a better life for all than any would have if each were to live solely by his own efforts. There is a conflict of interests since persons are not indifferent as to how the greater benefits produced by their collaboration are distributed, for in order to pursue their ends they each prefer a larger to a lesser share. A set of principles is required for choosing among the various social arrangements which determine this division of advantages and for underwriting an agreement on the proper distributive shares. These principles are the principles of social justice: they provide a way of assigning rights and duties in the basic institutions of society and they define the appropriate distribution of the benefits and burdens of social cooperation. . . .

THE MAIN IDEA OF THE THEORY OF JUSTICE

My aim is to present a conception of justice which generalizes and carries to a higher level of abstraction the familiar theory of the social contract as found, say, in Locke, Rousseau, and Kant. In order to do this we are not to think of the original contract as one to enter a particular society or to set up a particular form of government. Rather, the guiding idea is that the principles of justice for the basic structure of society are the object of the original agreement. They are the principles that free and rational persons concerned to further their own interests would accept in an initial position of equality as defining the fundamental terms of their association. These principles are to regulate all further agreements; they specify the kinds of social cooperation that can be entered into and the forms of government that can be established. This way of regarding the principles of justice I shall call justice as fairness.

Thus we are to imagine that those who engage in social cooperation choose together, in one joint act, the principles which are to assign basic rights and duties and to determine the division of social benefits. Men are to decide in advance how they are to regulate their claims against one another and what is to be the foundation charter of their society. . . .

In justice as fairness the original position of equality corresponds to the state of nature in the traditional theory of the social contract. This original position is not, of course, thought of as an actual historical state of affairs, much less as a primitive condition of culture. It is understood as a purely hypothetical situation characterized so as to lead to a certain conception of justice. Among the essential features of this situation is that no one knows his place in society, his class position or social status, nor does any one know his fortune in the distribution of natural assets and abilities, his intelligence, strength, and the like. . . . The principles of justice are chosen behind a veil of ignorance. This ensures that no one is advantaged or disadvantaged in the choice of principles by the outcome of natural chance or the contingency of social circumstances. Since all are similarly situated and no one is able to design principles to favor his particular condition, the principles of justice are the result of a fair agreement or bargain. . . . The original position is, one might say, the appropriate initial status quo, and thus the fundamental agreements reached in it are fair. This explains the propriety of the name "justice as fairness": it conveys the idea that the principles of justice are agreed to in an initial situation that is fair. . . .

In working out the conception of justice as fairness one main task clearly is to determine which principles of justice would be chosen in the original position. To do this we must describe this situation in some detail and formulate with care the problem of choice which it presents. . . . It may be observed, however, that once the principles of justice are thought of as arising from an original agreement in a situation of equality, it is an open question whether the principle of utility would be acknowledged. Offhand it hardly seems likely that persons who view themselves as equals, entitled to press their claims upon one another, would agree to a principle which may require lesser life prospects for some simply for the sake of a greater sum of advantages enjoyed by others. . . .

I shall maintain instead that the persons in the initial situation would choose two rather different principles: the first requires equality in the assignment of basic rights and duties, while the second holds that social and economic inequalities, for example inequalities of wealth and authority, are just only if they result in compensating benefits for everyone, and in particular for the least advantaged members of society. These principles rule out justifying institutions on the grounds that the hardships of some are offset by a greater good in the aggregate. . . .

TWO PRINCIPLES OF JUSTICE

I shall now state in a provisional form the two principles of justice that I believe would be chosen in the original position. . . .

The first statement of the two principles reads as follows.

First: each person is to have an equal right to the most extensive basic liberty compatible with a similar liberty for others.

Second: social and economic inequalities are to be arranged so that they are both (a) reasonably expected to be to everyone's advantage, and (b) attached to positions and offices open to all. . . .

By way of general comment, these principles primarily apply, as I have said, to the basic structure of society. They are to govern the assignment of rights and duties and to regulate the distribution of social and economic advantages. As their formulation suggests, these principles presuppose that the social structure can be divided into two more or less distinct parts, the first principle applying to the one, the second to the other. They distinguish between those aspects of the social system that define and secure the equal liberties of citizenship and those that specify and establish social and economic inequalities. The basic liberties of citizens are, roughly speaking, political liberty (the right to vote and to be eligible for public office) together with freedom of speech and assembly; liberty of conscience and freedom of thought; freedom of the person along with the right to hold (personal) property; and freedom from arbitrary arrest and seizure as defined by the concept of the rule of law. These liberties are all required to be equal by the first principle, since citizens of a just society are to have the same basic rights.

The second principle applies, in the first approximation, to the distribution of income and wealth and to the design of organizations that make use of differences in authority and responsibility, or chains of command. While the distribution of wealth and income need not be equal, it must be to everyone's advantage, and at the same time, positions of authority and offices of command must be accessible to all. One applies the second principle by holding positions open, and then, subject to this constraint, arranges social and economic inequalities so that everyone benefits.

These principles are to be arranged in a serial order with the first principle prior to the second. This ordering means that a departure from the institutions of equal liberty required by the first principle cannot be justified by, or compensated for, by greater social and economic advantages. The distribution of wealth and income, and the hierarchies of authority, must be consistent with both the liberties of equal citizenship and equality of opportunity. . . .

Discussion Questions

1. Is the "veil of ignorance" a useful conceptual device for formulating public policy on issues of social justice? Do you agree with Rawls that people under the veil of ignorance would come up with his two principles of justice? Explain why or why not.
2. How should social benefits, such as a college education, be distributed? Apply Rawls's two principles of justice in developing a public policy on affirmative action in college admissions.
3. Does pornography violate Rawls's first principle of justice? Support your answer.
4. Given that genetic engineering and cloning will probably be an option only for well-off parents, discuss whether it is fair to use public tax money to fund research on cloning and genetic engineering. Support your answer.

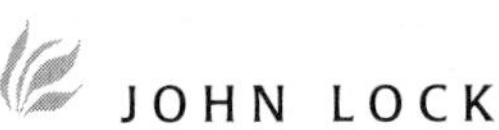

JOHN LOCKE

Two Treatises of Civil Government

British philosopher John Locke (1632–1704) was born into a liberal Puritan family that was heavily involved in political activism. His father, a country attorney, fought on the parliamentary side in the first rebellion against King Charles I.

Locke's theory of natural rights emerged primarily as a protest against the idea that the king possessed divine rights. A deeply religious man, Locke believed that God created the earth as a resource for humans. These natural rights ethics had a profound effect on the founders of the United States, especially Thomas Jefferson. Locke maintained that our natural rights include life, liberty, and property.

In the following selection, from *Two Treatises of Civil Government,* Locke defends our right to own property and explains why people in a state of nature come together to form a political society.

"Natural Rights," from *Two Treatises of Civil Government* (London: A & J Churchill, 1698). Notes have been omitted.

Critical Reading Questions

1. How does Locke define political power?
2. What is the state of nature? What rights do humans have in a state of nature?
3. What is the law of nature?
4. On what grounds does Locke argue that civil society is preferable to a state of nature?
5. According to Locke, why do humans as a group have a right to the resources of the earth?
6. How do humans, as individuals, make these resources their property?
7. What are the limits on what we can claim as our property?
8. According to Locke, why do people come together to form a political society?
9. What are the advantages and disadvantages of living in a political society?

OF THE STATE OF NATURE

4. To understand political power aright, and derive it from its original, we must consider what estate all men are naturally in, and that is, a state of perfect freedom to order their actions, and dispose of their possessions and persons as they think fit, within the bounds of the law of Nature, without asking leave or depending upon the will of any other man.

A state also of equality, wherein all the power and jurisdiction is reciprocal, no one having more than another, there being nothing more evident than that creatures of the same species and rank, promiscuously born to all the same advantages of Nature, and the use of the same faculties, should also be equal one amongst another, without subordination or subjection, unless the lord and master of them all should, by any manifest declaration of his will, set one above another, and confer on him by an evident and clear appointment an undoubted right to dominion and sovereignty.

. . .

6. But though this be a state of liberty, yet it is not a state of license; though man in that state have an uncontrollable liberty to dispose of his person or possessions, yet he has not liberty to destroy himself, or so much as any creature in his possession, but where some nobler use than its bare preservation calls for it. The state of nature has a law of nature to govern it, which obliges everyone; and reason, which is that law, teaches all mankind who will but consult it, that, being all equal and independent, no one ought to harm another in his life, health, liberty, or possessions. For men being all the workmanship of one omnipotent and infinitely wise Maker, they are his property, . . .

. . .

15. . . . "for as much as we are not by ourselves sufficient to furnish ourselves with competent store of things needful for such a life as our Nature doth desire, a life fit for the dignity of man, therefore to supply those defects and imperfections which are in us, as living single and solely by ourselves, we are naturally induced to seek communion and fellowship with others; this was the cause of men uniting themselves as first in politic societies." But I, moreover, affirm that all men are naturally in that state, and remain so till, by their own consents, they make themselves members of some politic society, . . .

OF PROPERTY

. . .

25. God, who hath given the world to men in common, hath also given them reason to make use of it to the best advantage of life and convenience. The earth and all that is therein is given to men for the support and comfort of their being. And though all the fruits it naturally produces, and beasts it feeds, belong to mankind in common, as they are

produced by the spontaneous hand of Nature, and nobody has originally a private dominion exclusive of the rest of mankind in any of them, as they are thus in their natural state, yet being given for the use of men, there must of necessity be a means to appropriate them some way or other before they can be of any use, or at all beneficial, to any particular men. . . .

26. Though the earth and all inferior creatures be common to all men, yet every man has a "property" in his own "person." This nobody has any right to but himself. The "labour" of his body and the "work" of his hands, we may say, are properly his. Whatsoever, then, he removes out of the state that Nature hath provided and left it in, he hath mixed his labour with it, and joined to it something that is his own, and thereby makes it his property. It being by him removed from the common state Nature placed it in, it hath by this labour something annexed to it that excludes the common right of other men. For this "labour" being the unquestionable property of the labourer, no man but he can have a right to what that is once joined to, at least where there is enough, and as good left in common for others.

OF THE BEGINNING OF POLITICAL SOCIETIES

95. Men being, as has been said, by nature all free, equal, and independent, no one can be put out of this estate and subjected to the political power of another without his own consent, which is done by agreeing with other men, to join and unite into a community for their comfortable, safe, and peaceable living, one amongst another, in a secure enjoyment of their properties, and a greater security against any that are not of it. This any number of men may do, because it injures not the freedom of the rest; they are left, as they were, in the liberty of the state of Nature. When any number of men have so consented to make one community or government, they are thereby presently incorporated, and make one body politic, wherein the majority have a right to act and conclude the rest.

96. For, when any number of men have, by the consent of every individual, made a community, they have thereby made that community one body, with a power to act as one body, which is only by the will and determination of the majority.

. . .

99. Whosoever, therefore, out of a state of Nature unite into a community, must be understood to give up all the power necessary to the ends for which they unite into society to the majority of the community, unless they expressly agreed in any number greater than the majority. And this is done by barely agreeing to unite into one political society, which is all the compact that is, or needs be, between the individuals that enter into or make up a commonwealth. And thus, that which begins and actually constitutes any political society is nothing but the consent of any number of freemen capable of majority, to unite and incorporate into such a society. And this is that, and that only, which did or could give beginning to any lawful government in the world. . . .

Discussion Questions

1. Do you agree with Locke that people can exist outside of civil society in a "state of nature"? Support your answer.
2. Do you agree with Locke that there is a law of nature that gives individuals living in a state of nature the right to punish transgressors? Does the lack of an international government mean that nations are living in a state of nature? Discuss whether this justifies, for example, the use of war against nations that violate our property rights.
3. Natural rights ethicists claim that human equality is self-evident. What does this mean? What are the implications of this belief for public policy on gay rights?

4. Discuss how an animal-rights proponent such as Tom Regan might respond to Locke's claim that only humans have moral rights.
5. Ralph Waldo Emerson once said that "people say law but they mean wealth." In the United States 90 percent of the resources are owned by 10 percent of the people. Compare and contrast the capitalist system of property ownership, as supported by Ayn Rand, with Locke's philosophy. Use specific examples to illustrate your answer.

AYN RAND

Man's Rights

Philosopher, novelist, and playwright Ayn Rand (1905–1982) is one of the foremost contemporary defenders of natural rights ethics. Born in St. Petersburg, Russia, Rand immigrated to the United States in 1931. Her rights ethics developed, in part, as a result of her experience living under both the Soviet and the U.S. systems of government. Rand became disillusioned with the demoralizing effects of collectivism and Soviet communism and concluded that the blend of natural rights ethics and ethical egoism underlying laissez-faire capitalism is the only philosophy compatible with respect for the integrity and the reality of the individual human.

The sole purpose of government is the protection of our individual rights. Having the freedom to choose how to use our property, to choose our careers, and to choose where we buy and sell our goods and labor is essential to Rand's concept of the good life. Welfare rights, on the other hand, are not true rights, because they involve forcibly taking goods from people who earned them and giving them to people who have neither earned nor deserve them.

In the selection from her essay "Man's Rights," Rand compares and contrasts her notion of liberty rights with the current notion of economic or welfare rights. Freedom of speech, she argues, has already been curtailed in the name of welfare rights. Affirmative action is another example of welfare rights taking precedence over liberty rights. Rand concludes that the promotion of economic or welfare rights can occur only at the expense of individual freedom.

Critical Reading Questions

1. What, according to Rand, is the relationship between capitalism and individual rights?
2. How does Rand define the term *rights?*
3. What is our most fundamental right? Why?

"Man's Rights," from *The Virtue of Selfishness* (New York: Signet, 1964).

4. Which political/economic system, according to Rand, is the best at promoting and protecting rights? Why?
5. Why does Rand consider the United States to be a great nation? What does she have to say about the Declaration of Independence and the Bill of Rights?
6. What is the distinction between economic rights and political rights?
7. On what grounds does Rand criticize the Democratic platform of 1960?

If one wishes to advocate a free society—that is, capitalism—one must realize that its indispensable foundation is the principle of individual rights. If one wishes to uphold individual rights, one must realize that capitalism is the only system that can uphold and protect them. . . .

"Rights" are a moral concept—the concept that provides a logical transition from the principles guiding an individual's actions to the principles guiding his relationship with others—the concept that preserves and protects individual morality in a social context—the link between the moral code of a man and the legal code of a society, between ethics and politics. *Individual rights are the means of subordinating society to moral law.* . . .

The most profoundly revolutionary achievement of the United States of America was *the subordination of society to moral law.*

The principle of man's individual rights represented the extension of morality into the social system—as a limitation on the power of the state, as man's protection against the brute force of the collective, as the subordination of *might* to *right.* The United States was the first *moral* society in history.

All previous systems had regarded man as a sacrificial means to the ends of others, and society as an end in itself. The United States regarded man as an end in himself, and society as a means to the peaceful, orderly *voluntary* coexistence of individuals. All previous systems had held that man's life belongs to society, that society can dispose of him in any way it pleases, and that any freedom he enjoys is his only by favor, by the *permission* of society, which may be revoked at any time. The United States held that man's life is his by *right* (which means: by moral principle and by his nature), that a right is the property of an individual, that society as such has no rights, and that the only moral purpose of a government is the protection of individual rights.

A "right" is a moral principle defining and sanctioning a man's freedom of action in a social context. There is only *one* fundamental right (all the others are its consequences or corollaries): a man's right to his own life. Life is a process of self-sustaining and self-generated action; the right to life means the right to engage in self-sustaining and self-generated action—which means: the freedom to take all the actions required by the nature of a rational being for the support, the furtherance, the fulfillment and the enjoyment of his own life. (Such is the meaning of the right to life, liberty and the pursuit of happiness.)

The concept of a "right" pertains only to action—specifically, to freedom of action. It means freedom from physical compulsion, coercion or interference by other men.

Thus, for every individual, a right is the moral sanction of a *positive*—of his freedom to act on his own judgment, for his own goals, by his own *voluntary, uncoerced* choice. As to his neighbors, his rights impose no obligations on them except of a *negative* kind: to abstain from violating his rights.

The right to life is the source of all rights—and the right to property is their only implementation. Without property rights, no other rights are possible. Since man has to sustain his life by his own effort, the man who has no right to the product of his effort has no means to sustain his life. The man who produces while others dispose of his product, is a slave.

Bear in mind that the right to property is a right to action, like all the others: it is not the right *to an object,* but to the action and the consequences of producing or earning that object. It is not a guarantee that a man *will* earn any property, but only a guarantee that he will own it if he earns it. It is the right to gain, to keep, to use and to dispose of material values.

The concept of individual rights is so new in human history that most men have not grasped it fully to this day. In accordance with the two theories of ethics, the mystical or the social, some men assert that rights are a gift of God—others, that rights are a gift of society. But, in fact, the source of rights is man's nature. . . .

To violate man's rights means to compel him to act against his own judgment, or to expropriate his values. Basically, there is only one way to do it: by the use of physical force. There are two potential violators of man's rights: the criminals and the government. The great achievement of the United States was to draw a distinction between these two—by forbidding to the second the legalized version of the activities of the first.

The Declaration of Independence laid down the principle that "to secure these rights, governments are instituted among men." This provided the only valid justification of a government and defined its only proper purpose: to protect man's rights by protecting him from physical violence.

Thus the government's function was changed from the role of ruler to the role of servant. The government was set to protect man from criminals—and the Constitution was written to protect man from the government. The Bill of Rights was not directed against private citizens, but against the government—as an explicit declaration that individual rights supersede any public or social power. . . .

Altruism is incompatible with freedom, with capitalism and with individual rights. One cannot combine the pursuit of happiness with the moral status of a sacrificial animal.

It was the concept of individual rights that had given birth to a free society. It was with the destruction of individual rights that the destruction of freedom had to begin. . . .

The Democratic Party platform of 1960 summarizes the switch boldly and explicitly. It declares that a Democratic Administration "will reaffirm the economic bill of rights which Franklin Roosevelt wrote into our national conscience sixteen years ago."

Bear clearly in mind the meaning of the concept of *"rights"* when you read the list which that platform offers:

"1. The right to a useful and remunerative job in the industries or shops or farms or mines of the nation.
2. The right to earn enough to provide adequate food and clothing and recreation.
3. The right of every farmer to raise and sell his products at a return which will give him and his family a decent living.
4. The right of every businessman, large and small, to trade in an atmosphere of freedom from unfair competition and domination by monopolies at home and abroad.
5. The right of every family to a decent home.
6. The right to adequate medical care and the opportunity to achieve and enjoy good health.
7. The right to adequate protection from the economic fears of old age, sickness, accidents and unemployment.
8. The right to a good education."

A single question added to each of the above eight clauses would make the issue clear: *At whose expense?*

Jobs, food, clothing, recreation (!), homes, medical care, education, etc., do not grow in nature. These are man-made values—goods and services produced by men. Who is to provide them?

If some men are entitled *by right* to the products of the work of others, it means that those others are deprived of rights and condemned to slave labor.

Any alleged "right" of one man, which necessitates the violation of the rights of another, is not and cannot be a right.

No man can have a right to impose an unchosen obligation, an unrewarded duty or an involuntary servitude on another man. There can be no such thing as *"the right to enslave."*

A right does not include the material implementation of that right by other men; it includes only the freedom to earn that implementation by one's own effort.

Observe, in this context, the intellectual precision of the Founding Fathers: they spoke of the right to *the pursuit* of happiness—*not* of the right to happiness. It means that a man has the right to take the actions he deems necessary to achieve his happiness; it does *not* mean that others must make him happy. . . .

The right to property means that a man has the right to take the economic actions necessary to earn property, to use it and dispose of it; it does *not* mean that others must provide him with property.

The right of free speech means that a man has the right to express his ideas without danger of suppression, interference or punitive action by the government. It does *not* mean that others must provide him with a lecture hall, a radio station or a printing press through which to express his ideas.

Any undertaking that involves more than one man, requires the *voluntary* consent of every participant. Every one of them has the *right* to make his own decision, but none has the right to force his decision on the others. . . .

And while people are clamoring about "economic rights," the concept of political rights is vanishing. It is forgotten that the right of free speech means the freedom to advocate one's views and to bear the possible consequences, including disagreement with others, opposition, unpopularity and lack of support. The political function of "the right of free speech" is to protect dissenters and unpopular minorities from forcible suppression—*not* to guarantee them the support, advantages and rewards of a popularity they have not gained. . . .

Such is the state of one of today's most crucial issues: *political* rights versus "*economic* rights." It's either-or. One destroys the other. But there are, in fact, no "economic rights," no "collective rights," no "public-interest rights." The term "individual rights" is a redundancy: there is no other kind of rights and no one else to possess them.

Those who advocate *laissez-faire* capitalism are the only advocates of man's rights.

There is also a selection from Ayn Rand's *The Virtue of Selfishness* in the accompanying *Ethics PowerWeb.*

Discussion Questions

1. Discuss how Rand would approach the issue of affirmative action. Explain why. Relate your answer to the concepts of liberty rights and welfare rights.
2. Discuss how Rand might approach the issue of hate speech on campus.
3. What concern\s would Rand have regarding the regulation of violence in children's television programs and hard-core pornography? Would it matter to her if it could be shown that exposure to television violence and hard-core pornography increases violent behavior in viewers?
4. How might Rand reconcile her support for laissez-faire capitalism and free enterprise with the increasing problem of industrial pollution and the destruction of the environment? Develop a policy for dealing with global warming based on Rand's rights ethics. Are you satisfied with this policy? Why or why not?

NEL NODDINGS

Caring: A Feminine Approach to Ethics and Moral Education

American philosopher and virtue ethicist Nel Noddings is a professor at Stanford University. Noddings's care ethics integrates the personal and the analytical. The mother of ten children, five of her own and five that she and her husband adopted, Noddings asked herself how she could bring together her personal life, particularly her life as a mother, and her analytical training in philosophy. This question changed the direction of her work. Shortly after, she published her first article on care ethics.

Care ethics, which expands on Carol Gilligan's studies of women's moral reasoning, is currently one of the most influential feminist theories in moral philosophy. Unlike the analytical approach of most earlier philosophers, care ethics stresses the contextual aspect of morality. Care, according to Noddings, is an active virtue. We are at our moral best when we are caring and being cared for in relationships. It is care, not an abstract sense of duty, that creates moral obligations.

In the selection from her book *Caring: A Feminine Approach to Ethics and Moral Education,* Noddings illustrates the role of feelings or sentiment in morality, using the example of the natural care a mother feels for her child. Ethical caring in relationships builds on and strives to maintain this feeling of natural care. Thus, caring becomes an ethical ideal.

Although Noddings does not altogether reject the use of principled moral reasoning, she believes that as an ideal, care offers us guidance in actual situations and relationships that an abstract ethics of duty cannot provide. Care ethics requires that we consider issues such as abortion, physician-assisted suicide, and gay marriage from within the context of actual caring relationships, rather than simply from the perspective of abstract universal principles.

Critical Reading Questions

1. What does Noddings mean by the term *care?*
2. How do we demonstrate caring for others?
3. What are the limitations on caring? Do we, for example, have a moral obligation to care for people we do not know or people we do not like?
4. What is the difference between natural caring and ethical caring? What are some examples of each type?
5. What, according to Noddings, is the "ethical ideal" or "vision of the best self"?
6. Why does Noddings consider the ethical ideal of caring preferable to moral principles as a guide to moral actions?
7. Why does Noddings reject the principle of universality? In particular, why does she reject the principle of universal love?

Caring: A Feminine Approach to Ethics and Moral Education (Berkeley: University of California Press, 1984).

8. On what grounds does Noddings claim that we do not have moral obligations to other animals?
9. What does Noddings mean when she says that an ethic of care is a "feminine," as opposed to a "masculine," ethic?

From Natural to Ethical Caring

David Hume long ago contended that morality is founded upon and rooted in feeling—that the "final sentence" on matters of morality, "that which renders morality an active virtue"—". . . this final sentence depends on some internal sense or feeling, which nature has made universal in the whole species. For what else can have an influence of this nature?"

What is the nature of this feeling that is "universal in the whole species"? I want to suggest that morality as an "active virtue" requires two feelings and not just one. The first is the sentiment of natural caring. There can be no ethical sentiment without the initial, enabling sentiment. In situations where we act on behalf of the other because we want to do so, we are acting in accord with natural caring. A mother's caretaking efforts in behalf of her child are not usually considered ethical but natural. Even maternal animals take care of their offspring, and we do not credit them with ethical behavior. . . .

Recognizing that ethical caring requires an effort that is not needed in natural caring does not commit us to a position that elevates ethical caring over natural caring. Kant has identified the ethical with that which is done out of duty and not out of love, and that distinction in itself seems right. But an ethic built on caring strives to maintain the caring attitude and is thus dependent upon, and not superior to, natural caring. The source of ethical behavior is, then, in twin sentiments—one that feels directly for the other and one that feels for and with that best self, who may accept and sustain the initial feeling rather than reject it.

We shall discuss the ethical ideal, that vision of best self, in some depth. When we commit ourselves to obey the "I must" even at its weakest and most fleeting, we are under the guidance of this ideal. It is not just any picture. Rather, it is our best picture of ourselves caring and being cared for. . . .

I feel the moral "I must" when I recognize that my response will either enhance or diminish my ethical ideal. It will serve either to increase or decrease the likelihood of genuine caring. My response affects me as one-caring. In a given situation with someone I am not fond of, I may be able to find all sorts of reasons why I should not respond to his need. I may be too busy. He may be undiscerning. The matter may be, on objective analysis, unimportant. But, before I decide, I must turn away from this analytic chain of thought and back to the concrete situation. Here is this person with this perceived need to which is attached this importance. I must put justification aside temporarily. Shall I respond? How do I feel as a duality about the "I" who will not respond?

I am obliged, then, to accept the initial "I must" when it occurs and even to fetch it out of recalcitrant slumber when it fails to awake spontaneously. The source of my obligation is the value I place on the relatedness of caring. This value itself arises as a product of actual caring and being cared-for and my reflection on the goodness of these concrete caring situations. . . .

Let me say here, however, why it seems preferable to place an ethical ideal above principle as a guide to moral action. It has been traditional in moral philosophy to insist that moral principles must be, by their very nature as moral principles, universifiable. If I am obligated to do *X* under certain conditions, then under sufficiently similar conditions you also are obligated to do *X*. But the principle of universifiability seems to depend, as Nietzsche pointed out, on a concept of "sameness." In order to accept the principle, we should have to establish that human predicaments exhibit sufficient sameness, and this we cannot do without abstracting away from concrete situations those qualities that seem to reveal the sameness. In doing this, we often lose the very qualities or factors that gave rise to the moral question in the situation. That condition which makes the situation different and thereby induces genuine moral puzzlement cannot be satisfied by the application of principles developed in situations of sameness.

This does not mean that we cannot receive any guidance from an attempt to discover principles that seem to be universifiable. We can, under this sort of plan, arrive at the doctrine of "prima facie duty" described by W. D. Ross. Ross himself, however, admits that this doctrine yields no real guidance for moral conduct in concrete situations. It guides us in abstract moral thinking; it tells us, theoretically, what to do, "all other things being equal." But other things are rarely if ever equal. . . .

Our obligation is limited and delimited by relation. We are never free, in the human domain, to abandon our preparedness to care; but, practically, if we are meeting those in our inner circles adequately as ones caring and receiving those linked to our inner circles by formal chains of relation, we shall limit the calls upon our obligation quite naturally. We are not obliged to summon the "I must" if there is no possibility of completion in the other. I am not obliged to care for starving children in Africa, because there is no way for this caring to be completed in the other unless I abandon the caring to which I am obligated. I may still choose to do something in the direction of caring, but I am not obliged to do so. When we discuss our obligation to animals, we shall see that this is even more sharply limited by relation. We cannot refuse obligation in human affairs by merely refusing to enter relation; we are, by virtue of our mutual humanity, already and perpetually in potential relation. Instead, we limit our obligation by examining the possibility of completion. In connection with animals, however, we may find it possible to refuse relation itself on the grounds of a species-specific impossibility of any form of reciprocity in caring. . . .

One under the guidance of an ethic of caring is tempted to retreat to a manageable world. Her public life is limited by her insistence upon meeting the other as one-caring. So long as this is possible, she may reach outward and enlarge her circles of caring. When this reaching out destroys or drastically reduces her actual caring, she retreats and renews her contact with those who address her. If the retreat becomes a flight, an avoidance of the call to care, her ethical ideal is diminished. Similarly, if the retreat is away from human beings and toward other objects of caring—ideas, animals, humanity-at-large, God—her ethical ideal is virtually shattered. This is not a judgment, for we can understand and sympathize with one who makes such a choice. It is more in the nature of a perception: we see clearly what has been lost in the choice.

Our ethic of caring—which we might have called a "feminine ethic"—begins to look a bit mean in contrast to the masculine ethics of universal love or universal justice. But universal love is illusion. Under the illusion, some young people retreat to the church to worship that which they cannot actualize; some write lovely poetry extolling universal love; and some, in terrible disillusion, kill to establish the very principles which should have entreated them not to kill. Thus are lost both principles and persons.

For more on care ethics see the selections from Virginia Held's *Women and Moral Theory,* and Rita Manning's *Speaking From the Heart: A Feminist Perspective of Ethics* in the accompanying *Ethics PowerWeb.*

Discussion Questions

1. Compare and contrast the moral philosophies of Nel Noddings and Immanuel Kant. In particular, what is the source and role of duty or moral obligation in care ethics?
2. Do you agree with Noddings that care requires reciprocity in a relationship? Discuss the implications of her ethics for issues such as abortion and euthanasia. If moral

obligation requires reciprocal relationships, does a pregnant woman have a moral obligation to her fetus? Do families have a moral obligation to care for members who are severely retarded or senile, or is euthanasia morally permissible for members of a family who are unable to reciprocate caring?

3. Discuss how a care ethicist might approach issues in environmental ethics such as global warming and preservation of wildlife. Is care ethics adequate for dealing with these issues? Support your answer.
4. Pornography takes women out of relationships and objectifies them. While a care ethicist might be morally opposed to pornography because of this, how would this translate into a public policy regarding pornography in the media? Support your answer.
5. Some judges hear victims' statements before passing sentences. To what extent should a sentence depend on the willingness of the family and friends of the victim to express care for the guilty party? Is capital punishment permissible if no one wants to be in a caring relationship with the guilty party? If so, is it fair that one's moral worth as a person is judged by others' willingness to care? Support your answers.

CONFUCIUS

The Analects

Confucius (551–479 B.C.E.) is the most revered philosopher in China. He lived during the period of the "hundred philosophers" (the late-sixth to the early-third centuries B.C.E.). This period in history was paralleled by the golden age in Greek philosophy; indeed, Confucius died only ten years before the birth of Socrates, the "father of Western philosophy."

As a young man, Confucius had trouble holding on to a job because he was too outspoken about the proper conduct of rulers, so he gave up his dream of becoming a government official and settled for being a teacher. Confucius traveled for many years with his pupils, teaching and trying to influence rulers. Much of the writing in *The Analects* is directed toward the rulers, since it is the rulers who have the most power to advance virtue in society and individuals.

As a teacher Confucius radically changed Chinese philosophy by focusing on our duties to humanity rather than on spiritual concerns. Confucian moral philosophy is a blend of deontology, virtue ethics, and communitarianism; it emphasizes duties over rights, virtue over self-interest, and the well-being of the community over individual interests. Like Aristotle, Confucius believed that humans were happiest and found it easiest to be virtuous when they were living in a just and well-ordered society. Righteousness demands that we do what is right simply because it is our moral duty, not because it benefits us personally.

The Analects, trans. by D. C. Lau (New York: Penguin Books, 1979). Notes have been omitted.

Confucian philosophy is not incompatible with expanding human rights in China; unlike Western natural rights ethics, however, where rights exist independently of our duties, rights exist in Confucian ethics only in the context of, and are derived from, our duty to the wider community. Freedom of speech, for example, should not be extended to the point that it threatens the harmony of the community. Freedom of speech should be extended, however, to permit criticism of the government and demand for social reform.

Critical Reading Questions

1. What does Confucius mean by "benevolence"?
2. Does Confucius think that virtue or benevolence is relative to the individual or culture? Or does he believe that it is the same for all people?
3. What does Confucius mean by the terms *gentleman* and *small man?*
4. Which does Confucius value the most—personal freedom or social harmony?
5. What duties do children have toward their parents?
6. What does Confucius mean when he says that the "gentleman is not invariably for or against anything. He is on the side of what is moral"?
7. Why is trust the most important social virtue?
8. What is the root of injustice?
9. What does Confucius say about punishment?
10. Why do we have crime? What is the role of government and social policy in promoting virtuous behavior?

Book I

. . . 2. Yu Tzu said, "It is rare for a man whose character is such that he is good as a son and obedient as a young man to have the inclination to transgress against his superiors; it is unheard of for one who has no such inclination to be inclined to start a rebellion. The gentleman devotes his efforts to the roots, for once the roots are established, the Way will grow therefrom. Being good as a son and obedient as a young man is, perhaps, the root of a man's character."

3. The Master said, "It is rare, indeed, for a man with cunning words and an ingratiating face to be benevolent."

4. Tseng Tzu said, "Every day I examine myself on three counts. In what I have undertaken on another's behalf, have I failed to do my best? In my dealings with my friends have I failed to be trustworthy in what I say? Have I passed on to others anything that I have not tried out myself?"

5. The Master said, "In guiding a state of a thousand chariots, approach your duties with reverence and be trustworthy in what you say; avoid excesses in expenditure and love your fellow men; employ the labour of the common people only in the right seasons."

6. The Master said, "A young man should be a good son at home and an obedient young man abroad, sparing of speech but trustworthy in what he says, and should love the multitude at large but cultivate the friendship of his fellow men. If he has any energy to spare from such action, let him devote it to making himself cultivated." . . .

8. The Master said, "A gentleman who lacks gravity does not inspire awe. A gentleman who studies is unlikely to be inflexible.

"Make it your guiding principle to do your best for others and to be trustworthy in what you say. Do not accept as a friend anyone who is not as good as you.

"When you make a mistake, do not be afraid of mending your ways." . . .

Book IV

1. The Master said, "Of neighbourhoods benevolence is the most beautiful. How can the man be considered wise who, when he has the choice, does not settle in benevolence?"

2. The Master said, "One who is not benevolent cannot remain long in straitened circumstances, nor can he remain long in easy circumstances.

"The benevolent man is attracted to benevolence because he feels at home in it. The wise man is attracted to benevolence because he finds it to his advantage." . . .

4. The Master said, "If a man sets his heart on benevolence, he will be free from evil."

5. The Master said, . . . "If the gentleman forsakes benevolence, in what way can he make a name for himself? The gentleman never deserts benevolence, not even for as long as it takes to eat a meal. If he hurries and stumbles one may be sure that it is in benevolence that he does so."

6. The Master said, "I have never met a man who finds benevolence attractive or a man who finds unbenevolence repulsive. A man who finds benevolence attractive cannot be surpassed. A man who finds unbenevolence repulsive can, perhaps, be counted as benevolent, for he would not allow what is not benevolent to contaminate his person. . . .

7. The Master said, "In his errors a man is true to type. Observe the errors and you will know the man."

8. The Master said, "He has not lived in vain who dies the day he is told about the Way."

9. The Master said, "There is no point in seeking the views of a Gentleman who, though he sets his heart on the Way, is ashamed of poor food and poor clothes."

10. The Master said, "In his dealings with the world the gentleman is not invariably for or against anything. He is on the side of what is moral."

11. The Master said, "While the gentleman cherishes benign rule, the small man cherishes his native land. While the gentleman cherishes a respect for the law, the small man cherishes generous treatment."

12. The Master said, "If one is guided by profit in one's actions, one will incur much ill will." . . .

13. The Master said, "The gentleman understands what is moral. The small man understands what is profitable." . . .

15. The Master said, "In serving your father and mother you ought to dissuade them from doing wrong in the gentlest way. If you see your advice being ignored, you should not become disobedient but remain reverent. You should not complain even if in so doing you wear yourself out." . . .

Book XII

. . . 2. Chung-kung asked about benevolence. The Master said, "When abroad behave as though you were receiving an important guest. When employing the services of the common people behave as though you were officiating at an important sacrifice. Do not impose on others what you yourself do not desire. In this way you will be free from ill will whether in a state or in a noble family." . . .

7. Tzu-kung asked about government. The Master said, "Give them enough food, give them enough arms, and the common people will have trust in you."

Tzu-kung said, "If one had to give up one of these three, which should one give up first?"

"Give up arms."

Tzu-kung said, "If one had to give up one of the remaining two, which should one give up first?"

"Give up food. Death has always been with us since the beginning of time, but when there is no trust, the common people will have nothing to stand on." . . .

10. Tzu-chang asked about the exaltation of virtue and the recognition of misguided judgement. The Master said, "Make it your guiding principle to do your best for others and to be trustworthy in what you say, and move yourself to where rightness is, then you will be exalting virtue. When you love a man you want him to live and when you hate him you want him to die. . . .

16. The Master said, "The gentleman helps others to realize what is good in them; he does not help them to realize what is bad in them. The small man does the opposite."

17. Chi K'ang Tzu asked Confucius about government. Confucius answered, "To govern (*cheng*) is to correct (*cheng*). If you set an example by being correct, who would dare to remain incorrect?" . . .

19. Chi K'ang Tzu asked Confucius about government, saying, "What would you think if, in order to move closer to those who possess the Way, I were to kill those who do not follow the Way?"

Confucius answered, "In administering your government, what need is there for you to kill? Just desire the good yourself and the common people will be good. The virtue of the gentleman is like wind; the virtue of the small man is like grass. Let the wind blow over the grass and it is sure to bend." . . .

21. Fan Ch'ih was in attendance during an outing to the Rain Altar. He said, "May I ask about the exaltation of virtue, the reformation of the depraved and the recognition of misguided judgement?" The Master said, "What a splendid question! To put service before the reward you get for it, is that not exaltation of virtue? To attack evil as evil and not as evil of a particular man, is that not the way to reform the depraved? To let a sudden fit of anger make you forget the safety of your own person or even that of your parents, is that not misguided judgement?"

22. Fan Ch'ih asked about benevolence. The Master said, "Love your fellow men."

He asked about wisdom. The Master said, "Know your fellow men." Fan Ch'ih failed to grasp his meaning. The Master said, "Raise the straight and set them over the crooked. This can make the crooked straight." . . .

23. Tzu-kung asked about how friends should be treated. The Master said, "Advise them to the best of your ability and guide them properly, but stop when there is no hope of success. Do not ask to be snubbed." . . .

Book XIII

11. The Master said, "How true is the saying that after a state has been ruled for a hundred years by good men it is possible to get the better of cruelty and to do away with killing."

12. The Master said, "Even with a true king it is bound to take a generation for benevolence to become a reality."

13. The Master said, "If a man manages to make himself correct, what difficulty will there be for him to take part in government? If he cannot make himself correct, what business has he with making others correct?" . . .

19. Fan Ch'ih asked about benevolence. The Master said, "While at home hold yourself in a respectful attitude; when serving in an official capacity be reverent; when dealing with others do your best. These are qualities that cannot be put aside, even if you go and live among the barbarians." . . .

Discussion Questions

1. In light of what Confucius says about the relative importance of personal freedom and social harmony, discuss concerns he would have regarding the regulation of hate speech and pornography. Compare and contrast his approach with that of John Stuart Mill.
2. Discuss whether filial duty requires us to carry out a parent's or grandparent's wish for assistance in committing suicide. If so, is the duty to carry out these types of requests absolute or prima facie? Support your answer.
3. Compare the Confucian principle of reciprocity (book XII–2) to Kant's categorical imperative.
4. Why is Confucius opposed to capital punishment? What would he say about why capital punishment is legal in the United States? Discuss alternatives to capital punishment that Confucius might propose.

P. DON PREMASIRI

The Relevance of the Noble Eightfold Path to Contemporary Society

Buddhist moral philosopher P. Don Premasiri is a philosophy professor at the University of Peradeniya in Sri Lanka. In his paper he argues that Buddha's noble eightfold path offers valuable guidance for addressing and resolving contemporary moral issues. He suggests that Buddhist ethics offers a vision of the good society that may have even greater relevance for today's technologically advanced world than it did in Buddha's time.

Indian philosopher Siddhartha Gautama (c. 563–c. 483 B.C.E.), better known as Buddha or the "enlightened one," lived at the same time as Confucius. Buddha was born into a wealthy family in India, near Nepal. At the age of twenty-nine, he left his family and fortune in a quest for truth. After six years of fasting, meditation, and study, he received enlightenment while sitting under a bodhi tree.

Leading a moral and virtuous life is central to Buddhist philosophy. Right livelihood involves above all adopting right view and avoiding behavior that harms others. Only through encouraging the development of virtue through right living and right thinking can we as a society achieve moral progress and a resolution of the many social problems that plague modern society.

"The Relevance of the Noble Eightfold Path to Contemporary Society," from Charles Wei-hsun Fu and Sandra A. Wawrytko (eds.), *Buddhist Ethics and Modern Society* (New York: Greenwood Press, 1991), pp. 134–139. Notes have been omitted.

Unlike Hinduism and most Western ethics, Buddhism is nonhierarchical, emphasizing the interrelatedness and moral value of all living beings. Right living, therefore, includes compassion and an attitude of nonviolence toward all of nature. Buddha's rejection of the Hindu caste system and his imperative that we treat all beings with dignity has brought attention to the dignity of the poor and has inspired great leaders such as Mohandas Gandhi. Buddhism has also played a prominent role in both the animal-rights and environmental ethics movements.

Critical Reading Questions

1. On what grounds does Premasiri claim that the Buddhist eightfold path is relevant in addressing contemporary social issues?
2. How have advances in science and technology contributed to an increase in moral problems?
3. Why is our current approach to morality inadequate for resolving moral issues?
4. What is the noble eightfold path?
5. What does Buddha mean by "moral wisdom"?
6. What is the relationship between an individual's moral development (or lack thereof) and the prevalence of injustice and moral problems in society?
7. What, according to Buddha, is the primary source of suffering and corruption?
8. What is "right view"? Why is it important, in order for moral progress to occur, to embrace "right view"?
9. What does Buddha mean when he says that "evil dispositions are expressed in behavioral terms"?
10. What does Buddha mean by "right livelihood"?
11. How can we cultivate in ourselves an attitude that will contribute to moral progress and a better understanding of social issues?

THE CONTEMPORARY HUMAN CONDITION

In many respects the present age cannot be compared with Buddha's time. Today, human beings have made enormous progress in scientific knowledge. They have increased their knowledge about the nature of their own physical existence and the nature of their physical environment. With this increased theoretical knowledge, their technological capabilities to control and manipulate the physical environment have increased correspondingly. There is no doubt that we are making rapid and ongoing progress in the areas of scientific knowledge and technological skill. However, reflection on another aspect of our contemporary situation makes it evident that no corresponding progress has been achieved in practical wisdom. All the progress humanity has made appears to be endangered by the very technological skills that humans have achieved. We live in an age in which the evils that humans inflict on others have reached unparalleled extremes of barbarism. . . .

According to Buddhism, society can never be totally free of immorality and the resulting tensions and conflicts, for the predominant factors that generally govern human behavior, untutored by spiritual nurture and impelled purely by the baser instincts of human nature, are greed, hatred, and confusion. Buddhism considers these three psychological dispositions to be the roots of evil and human misery. Scientific progress has not made it possible for humanity to overcome these roots. Consequently, we are placed in a more precarious predicament when the discoveries and inventions based on our own intelligence threaten us with destruction. . . .

Technological progress has been utilized to feed human greed, with no limits set for human wants and patterns of consumption. Ecologists and environmental scientists foresee devastating effects from modern technology on the natural environment, as is now becoming apparent.

Associated with the above trends is a growth of other types of social evils, such as the spread of alcoholism and drug addiction. The younger generation, who have moved away from traditional religious values, appears to be seeking a new kind of salvation in the hallucinatory and escapist experiences evoked by alcohol and psychedelic drugs. This has resulted in a dulling of reason and intellect and a debilitation of sound judgment, contributing further to the growing trends of violence, insanity, and irresponsible behavior. . . .

Today, morality is often believed to belong to the sphere of the nonrational. This has given rise to an intellectual climate in which morality is seen as devoid of a rational foundation. It came to be believed that no universally acceptable standards of morality could be rationally discovered. Consequently, the possibility of moral knowledge and moral truth has been denied.

THE NOBLE EIGHTFOLD PATH IN A CONTEMPORARY CONTEXT

Buddhism does not subscribe to this view. It believes that what is indispensable in the life of humanity is moral wisdom. Those who lack moral wisdom are said to be stupid and deluded (*mando, momuho*). Each step in the Noble Eightfold Path of the Buddha is characterized morally and evaluatively as "right" (*sammā*). This path is the quintessence of Buddhist morality. . . .

Social harmony, peace, and justice depend largely on the moral development of the individual members constituting a society. Where this is lacking, we enter the vicious circle of morally degenerate individuals and a corrupt social order. Moral progress must reduce the intensity of the roots of evil. Our contemporary situation amply testifies to the fact that, although we have progressed in material science and technology, there has been no improvement, but rather a regression, in the moral sphere. Technological skill devoid of moral consciousness leads only to more effective expressions of cruelty and viciousness. . . .

RIGHT VIEWS

Right views (*sammā ditthi*) is the first step of the Noble Path, and there is an important reason why. It brings into focus the need for a wholesome ideological orientation or worldview, as a prerequisite for anyone who embarks on the search for the meaning of life and wishes to make intelligent choices regarding the way one ought to conduct oneself. However, the Buddhist notion of right views does not imply a dogmatic clinging to an ideological position. Attachment to a view (*ditthi rāga*) is as much a hindrance to moral progress as attachment to a material thing. The Buddha cautioned his disciples against converting his teachings into a dogma. Dogmatic clinging to an ideology can create conflicts not only among those with a diversity of aims and interests, but also among those whose aims and interests are the same. Fanaticism and intolerance often result from the delusion that, "this alone is the truth and everything else is false" (*idam eva saccam mogham aññam*), causing people to commit atrocities in the name of "truth." This applies to any ideological commitment—religious, moral, or political. . . .

Buddhism believes in personal survival after death, while the moral law of *kamma* is conducive to moral restraint. The materialist worldview is for Buddhism a life devoid of moral, spiritual, or religious concerns (*abrahmacariyāvāsa*). In the age of science it is felt that scientific humanism, which is essentially the adoption of a utilitarian norm coupled with the conviction that individual existence is limited to this life, is sufficient to guide human behavior. There is good reason to question this based on modern day experience. The Buddhist position is that human beings can be motivated to lead a moral life only if they can be urged to act on enlightened self-interest, especially in the initial stages of their spiritual development. The belief in *kamma* and rebirth, and the prudential concept of merit (*puñña*) serves an important role in the moral life of the Buddhist. . . .

Right Thought, Right Speech, and Right Action

Buddhism recognizes three modes in which evil dispositions are expressed in behavioral terms: physical, verbal, and mental acts. Three steps of the Noble Path, right thought (*sammā sankappa*), right speech (*sammā vācā*), and right action (*sammā kammanta*), are specifically meant to prevent these evils. Buddhism attaches great significance to our mental life. Moral progress becomes possible only when a person acquires the ability to bring the mental processes under the direction of the will. . . .

Methods and schemes of moral development recommended by Buddhism appear to be based on an understanding of the mutual relationship between overt behavior and psychological dispositions. . . . Every verbal and bodily act creates a disposition toward repetition, thus contributing to the formation of a general pattern of behavior. Recognizing this fact, Buddhism emphasizes the importance of cultivating right speech and right action. Right speech consists first of avoiding false speech (*musā-vāda*), while cultivating truthfulness and trustworthiness. Second, it involves avoiding slanderous speech (*pisunāvācā*) intent on causing dissension among people, and cultivating speech that heals divisiveness and strengthens the bonds of those already united in bonds of friendship. Third, it involves the avoidance of harsh speech (*pharusāvacā*) and the cultivation of pleasant speech. Fourth, it involves abstention from frivolous or vain talk (*samphappalāpa*) and the cultivation of meaningful, purposeful, useful, and timely speech.

In right action (*sammā kammanta*), one is expected to abstain from injury to life, from violence and acts of terrorism, laying aside all weapons that cause injury to living beings. It also involves the positive cultivation of a mind filled with love and compassion, leading to compassionate action. . . .

Right Livelihood

Another step in the Noble Path that has considerable contemporary relevance is right livelihood (*sammā ājiva*). . . . At the level of the ordinary layperson, *sammā ājiva* draws attention to the necessity of adopting a morally acceptable means of livelihood and avoiding occupations that might be materially productive but morally reprehensible. These occupations include trading in weapons (*satthāvanijjā*), living beings (*sattavanijja*), flesh (*mamsavanijjā*), intoxicants or drugs (*majjavanijjā*) and poisons (*visavanijjā*). Almost all these forms of trade are practiced today on a global scale purely to satisfy commercial interests, without regard for their harmful social consequences. Most destructive of all is the trade in military weapons and addictive drugs. Commercial interests associated with excessive greed hinder responsible people from taking effective measures to prevent the miseries resulting from these social menaces. . . .

Right Effort, Right Mindfulness, and Right Contemplation

The sixth step, right effort (*sammāvāyāma*) recommends initiative and effort to prevent the growth of evil dispositions, cultivate healthy attitudes, and stabilize the wholesome dispositions of character already acquired. The moral agent constantly experiences inner conflict when choosing between what is considered to be the right thing to do and what passions, emotions, instincts, and inclinations prompt us to do. Right effort is considered to be the most effective means of overcoming those natural impulses, [and] is possible only if one does not resign oneself to external causes due to a false belief in fatalism or strict determinism.

The seventh step, right mindfulness (*sammāsati*), stands for watchfulness over the overall functioning of one's personality, both mental and physical. . . .

The eighth step of the path, right contemplation (*sammā samādhi*), stands for the clear and composed mind that is a prerequisite for the understanding that leads to moral perfection. Right contemplation is no doubt much needed by contemporary humanity; we are constantly bombarded by a dizzying variety of sensuous stimuli from our material environment, driving us to the brink of insanity. Those who have had the unsettling experience of sensory overload and excessive sensuous gratification suffer subsequent spells of boredom and depression, leading them to seek solace in psychedelic drugs that promise temporary states of altered consciousness, rapture, or mental ecstasy. Unfortunately, they are forms of false contemplation . . .

Most human suffering, of which human volition itself is the cause, springs from the actions of people whose minds are confused. Confused minds seem to be operative at all levels of contemporary society, from the topmost levels of decision-making to the lowest levels in the social hierarchy. In Buddhist theory, moral corruption or moral growth tends to flow from higher levels of the social hierarchy to the lower levels. It is imperative that we entrust the guidance of the destinies of the world to individuals who have cultivated the kind of right contemplation that Buddhism prescribes in its Noble Path if we are to avert the global annihilation that ominously looms before us.

Discussion Questions

1. Compare and contrast Buddha's beliefs about the role of leaders in moral progress with those of Confucius and Aristotle.
2. Like Aristotle, Buddha believed that engaging in destructive behavior makes us more likely to repeat that behavior in the future. Discuss the implications of his teachings regarding the morality of drug and alcohol use, pornography, and hate speech.
3. If Buddha were giving a speech to freshmen on your campus, what advice would he mostly likely give them for how to achieve moral wisdom and live the virtuous life?
4. Discuss what Buddha would most likely think about the morality of professions that involve animal agriculture, clearing of wildlife habitats for commercial use, or cloning. Apply the concept of "right livelihood" to your own career choice.
5. Many people believe that science is morally neutral and that, therefore, there is no problem in developing technology independent of considerations of the moral implications of such technology. Buddhists, on the other hand, warn against rapid technological advances that are not accompanied by similar progress in practical wisdom. Which position do you find most compelling from a moral point of view? Discuss the proposal a Buddhist ethicist would most likely make regarding the regulation of scientific research in cloning and genetic engineering.

CHAPTER 2

Abortion

There is probably no more controversial issue in bioethics today, or one that touches so many lives, as abortion. An estimated 43 percent of American women will have an abortion by age forty-five.[1] Prior to the early 1960s, however, there was little public debate over the morality of abortion or support for reform of the restrictive abortion laws that had been on the books in the United States since the turn of the century.

In 1962 Sherri Finkbine, the star of a popular Arizona children's show and mother of four small children, discovered much to her horror that the drug thalidomide, which she had taken early in her pregnancy to help her sleep, could cause birth defects such as missing limbs or seal-like flippers, paralysis, and malformed internal organs. After much tortured soul-searching, the Finkbines decided that the best course of action for them was abortion. Because it was not sold in the United States, the devastating effects of thalidomide on unborn children had not received as much coverage in the American press as it had in the European press.

Shortly before the scheduled day for her abortion, Sherri Finkbine decided to go public in order to warn other women about the dangers of thalidomide. Although she requested that her name not be used by the press, the newspaper article made her identity relatively easy to figure out. As a result of the publicity, the hospital, fearful of legal prosecution, withdrew its consent to perform the abortion. Sherri Finkbine eventually obtained an abortion in Sweden. The fetus was severely deformed. Sherri Finkbine's tragic ordeal helped galvanize public support for relaxing laws regulating therapeutic abortions.

BACKGROUND

Abortion was legalized in the United States in January 1973 by the U.S. Supreme Court *Roe v. Wade* ruling. Between 1973, when 760,000 abortions were performed, and 1980, the national abortion rate increased rapidly every year. The abortion rate continued to increase at a slower rate between 1980 and 1990. The abortion rate in the United States began dropping after 1990, when 1,608,600 abortions were reported, to 1,313,000 in 2000 and is continuing to decline.[2] The decline is attributed in part to better contraception use among teenagers and to decreasing public support of abortion, as well as to advances in prenatal technology, such as real-time ultrasound, that allow us to visualize the fetus, and growing concerns over late-term abortions. Nevertheless, the abortion rate in the United States is still higher than that in other industrialized nations. In the United States today, about 25 percent of pregnancies are ended by abortion.[3] Of these, 85 to 90 percent are terminated in the first twelve weeks of pregnancy.[4]

The drop in abortion rates has been attributed to a combination of factors, including changes in sexual practices, reduced access to abortion services with fewer doctors and medical centers willing to perform abortions, changes in attitude toward abortion with more people trying to avoid it, greater acceptance of unmarried mothers, and a decline in the overall number of pregnancies.[5] There is also less acceptability of abortion among younger people. According to the American Council of Education and University of California national college freshman survey, freshman support for legalized abortion has declined steadily since 1993. In 1999 50.9 percent of freshmen supported legalized abortion compared with 53.5 percent in 1997 and 64.9 percent in 1990.[6]

While abortion is declining in the United States, it is increasing worldwide. According to the World Health Organization approximately 45 million abortions were performed in 1998, up from 25 million in 1990. There were 30 million performed in developing countries, with Vietnam having the highest abortion rate in the world. Poverty seems to be one of the factors most closely associated with abortion, in the United States as well as worldwide.

THE HISTORY OF ABORTION IN THE UNITED STATES

Abortion was not uncommon in America during the colonial period up until the late 1800s. When abortion was mentioned, it was not the abortion itself that was usually condemned but the violation of other social taboos, such as sexual relations outside of marriage, that led to the abortion.[7] Many middle- and upper-class women also used abortion as a means of birth control.

During the early 1820s, American physicians began to take an interest in medical law and the legal regulation of abortion.[8] In 1821, Connecticut passed the country's first antiabortion law. Early-nineteenth-century antiabortion laws, for the most part, applied only to women "quick with child." Before the mid-nineteenth century, it was generally believed that the unborn child or fetus did not come to life until "quickening"—the moment, generally between sixteen and eighteen weeks, when the pregnant woman first feels the movement of her fetus. Despite laws against abortion, folk remedies and patented medicines continued to be widely available to women.

In the mid-nineteenth century, the newly founded American Medical Association (AMA) spearheaded a movement to outlaw abortion. In an 1859 resolution, the AMA condemned abortion as an "unwarranted destruction of human life," calling upon state legislators to pass or toughen their existing antiabortion laws.[9]

Although many people, including physicians, blamed the prevalence of abortion on feminist ideas, the early feminists disapproved of abortion, which they considered to be "a revolting outrage against . . . our common humanity" and a form of infanticide.[10] Unlike the physicians, however, the feminists did not think that outlawing abortion without getting to the root cause of abortion—the oppression of women—would have the desired effect. Instead they wanted the *need* for abortion to be eliminated. "We want prevention, not merely punishment," Susan B. Anthony wrote in 1869. "We must reach the root of the evil, and destroy it."[11] Elizabeth Cady Stanton also regarded abortion as just one more result of degradation of women.[12]

Between 1855 and 1880, most states passed antiabortion laws. By 1900 every state had laws prohibiting or restricting abortion; all but six included a "therapeutic exception" in their abortion laws. These laws remained virtually unchanged until the 1960s.

Several events during the 1960s led to an increasing dissatisfaction with the restrictive abortion laws. These included an increase in the number of women in the workforce, a desire for smaller families, increased publicity about the dangers of illegal abortion, improvements in the safety of surgical abortion, and a series of front-page stories chronicling the desperate circumstances of women such as Sherri Finkbine who were denied legal therapeutic abortions. The thalidomide tragedy was closely followed by a German measles epidemic in the United States. Many pregnant women who came down with German measles were unable to obtain legal abortions in the United States. As a result of this outbreak, 15,000 babies were born with birth defects—including blindness, mental retardation, and heart problems—between 1963 and 1966.

Fueled by the publicity generated by the thalidomide and German measles tragedies, the push for legal reform came primarily from the medical and legal professions. Although most people supported more liberal laws regarding the regulation of therapeutic abortions, there was little public support in the late 1960s for nontherapeutic abortions or "abortion on demand"—what later became known as the prochoice position.[13]

In 1969 Planned Parenthood, which had historically been opposed to abortion, reversed its position and came out in support of repealing all antiabortion laws. The following year the AMA followed suit, voting to support a physician's right to perform abortions if the woman's social and economic circumstances would make it difficult for her to have a baby. These changes, together with the first legal acknowledgment of a constitutional "right to privacy" in the 1965 Supreme Court *Griswold v. Connecticut* case, provided lawyers with the grist they needed to turn the wheels of reform by challenging the constitutionality of existing antiabortion laws.

Between 1967 and 1970, twelve states, including California, Hawaii, New York, Alaska, and Washington, repealed their restrictive abortion laws. The failures in liberalizing state abortion laws outnumbered the successes, however, due in part to a lack of public support as well as to the efforts of the fledgling right-to-life movement.

THE U.S. SUPREME COURT *ROE V. WADE* DECISION

A major turning point in the abortion-reform movement came when the battleground moved to the federal courts. In January 1973 the Supreme Court in *Roe v. Wade* ruled that the Texas antiabortion law violated a woman's fundamental constitutional right to privacy as implied in the Fourteenth Amendment. It also ruled that the fetus was not a person according to the Fourteenth Amendment. The effect of this ruling was to legalize abortion, at least prior to viability, throughout the United States. After viability, set at twenty-eight weeks, the state has a legitimate interest in "potential life" and can pass laws to regulate abortion, except for abortions to preserve the life and health of the mother. Selections from the *Roe v. Wade* majority ruling can be found on pages 80–81.

ROE V. WADE: EXCERPTS FROM THE MAJORITY OPINION

[Justice Blackmun delivered the opinion of the Court]

It is . . . apparent that at common law, at the time of the adoption of our Constitution, and throughout the major portion of the nineteenth century, abortion was viewed with less disfavor than under most American statutes currently in effect. Phrasing it another way, a woman enjoyed a substantially broader right to terminate a pregnancy than she does in most states today. . . .

Three reasons have been advanced to explain historically the enactment of criminal abortion laws in the nineteenth century and to justify their continued existence.

[First] It has been argued occasionally that these laws were the product of a Victorian special concern to discourage illicit sexual conduct. . . .

A second reason is concerned with abortion as a medical procedure. When most criminal abortion laws were first enacted, the procedure was a hazardous one for the woman. . . . Modern medical techniques have altered this situation. . . .

The third reason is the state's interest—some phrase it in terms of duty—in protecting prenatal life. Some of the argument for this justification rests on the theory that a new human life is present from the moment of conception. . . . Only when the life of the pregnant mother herself is at stake, balanced against the life she carries within her, should the interest of the embryo or fetus not prevail. Logically, of course, a legitimate state interest in this area need not stand or fall on acceptance of the belief that life begins at conception or at some other point prior to live birth. In assessing the state's interest, recognition may be given to the less rigid claim that as long as at least *potential* life is involved, the state may assert interests beyond the protection of the pregnant woman alone. . . .

The Constitution does not explicitly mention any right of privacy. . . . [Earlier Supreme Court] decisions make it clear that only personal rights that can be deemed "fundamental" or "implicit in the concept of ordered liberty" . . . are included in this guarantee of personal privacy. They also make it clear that the right has some extension to activities relating to marriage . . . [and] procreation. . . .

Rather than settling the abortion question once and for all, *Roe v. Wade* has left Americans deeply divided. Positions regarding the moral permissibility of abortion range from the pro-life view that all abortions are wrong except to save the life of the mother, to the pro-choice view that abortion is morally acceptable for any reason at any time during the pregnancy.

A majority of Americans want legal restrictions on abortion, particularly after the first trimester and for minors.[14] In response to the question "With respect to the abortion issues, would you consider yourself to be pro-choice or pro-life?" in a 1995 and a 2000 Gallup Poll, the number of people who identified with the pro-life position rose from 33 percent to 43 percent over the five years, while support for the pro-choice

We therefore conclude that the right of personal privacy includes the abortion decision, but that this right is not unqualified and must be considered against important state interests in regulation.

. . . [N]o case could be cited that holds that a fetus is a person within the meaning of the Fourteenth Amendment. . . . All this, together with our observation, *supra,* that throughout the majority portion of the nineteenth century prevailing legal abortion practices were far freer than they are today, persuades us that the word "person," as used in the Fourteenth Amendment, does not include the unborn. . . .

There has always been strong support for the view that life does not begin until live birth. . . . Physicians and their scientific colleagues have. . . . tended to focus either upon conception or upon live birth or upon the interim point at which the fetus becomes "viable," that is, potentially able to live outside the mother's womb, albeit with artificial aid. Viability is usually placed at about seven months (28 weeks) but may occur earlier, even at 24 weeks. . . .

With respect to the state's important and legitimate interest in the health of the mother, the compelling point, in the light of present medical knowledge, is at approximately the end of the first trimester. This is so because of the now established medical fact . . . that until the end of the first trimester mortality in abortion is less than mortality in normal childbirth. It follows that, from and after this point, a state may regulate the abortion procedure to the extent that the regulation reasonably relates to the preservation and protection of maternal health. Examples of permissible state regulation in this area are requirements as to the qualifications of the person who is to perform the abortion. . . .

With respect to the state's important and legitimate interest in potential life, the "compelling" point is at viability. This is so because the fetus then presumably has the capability of meaningful life outside the mother's womb. State regulation protective of fetal life after viability thus has both logical and biological justifications. If the state is interested in protecting fetal life after viability, it may go so far as to proscribe abortion during that period except when it is necessary to preserve the life or health of the mother. . . .

position declined from 56 percent to 48 percent. By 2002, support for the statement that abortion was morally acceptable had declined further to 38 percent.[15]

Support for abortion is strongest when the woman's life or physical health is endangered; it is lowest for abortions performed after the first term with 66 percent of those polled opposing the legalization of "partial-birth" abortions, also known as intact dilation and extraction or IDX.[16] (See page 85 for a description of this procedure.) The challenge to *Roe v. Wade* comes not only from the pro-life movement but also from the pro-choice groups who would like to see all restrictions on abortion removed.

Although the percentage of Americans who identify themselves as moderates has remained relatively stable between 1980 and the mid-1990s, nationwide there has been a trend toward wanting more restrictions placed on abortion, particularly abortions after the first trimester and those for social or economic reasons.[17] A 1998 ABC News poll found a marked shift since 1994 away from acceptance of abortion as a woman's right toward wanting more restrictions on abortion. The rise in violence against abortion clinics and abortion providers and the reluctance of younger doctors to perform abortions has also contributed to a decline in the number of facilities providing abortions and the number of doctors who are willing to perform them.[18] The number of providers in 2000 was 37 percent lower than 1982, the all-time high. The number of hospitals that perform abortions also declined by 57 percent.[19]

Since 1973 several states have passed legislation that places restrictions on abortion. Thirty-seven states enacted laws restricting abortion in 1997 alone. These restrictions include parental and spousal notification requirements, mandatory waiting periods, and bans on federal funding for abortions. Several bills for a constitutional amendment that would overturn *Roe v. Wade* have been introduced, including the Human Life Amendment, which would extend "personhood" or legal protection to "all human beings."

In the 1992 *Planned Parenthood v. Casey* case, the U.S. Supreme Court replaced the trimester framework used in *Roe v. Wade* with a floating viability line. Since modern technology keeps pushing back the date of viability, this ruling has the potential of placing further restrictions on a woman's opportunity to obtain an abortion. Forty-four states, as of 2003, also passed laws requiring parental consent or notification prior to a minor's abortion.

In the 2000 *Stenberg v. Carhart* case, the U.S. Supreme Court struck down, in a 5 to 4 ruling, a Nebraska law that banned "partial-birth" abortion. About thirty states at the time had similar laws banning "partial-birth" abortion. The court ruled that the Nebraska law placed an "undue burden" on women since it failed to include an exception in which the health of the pregnant woman was at risk.

The following month the U.S. Supreme Court, in *Hill v. Colorado,* ruled in favor of a Colorado statute that restricted protesters from coming within eight feet of women who were within one hundred feet of an entrance to an abortion clinic. Three years previously the Court had upheld a New York law that established buffer zones around abortion clinics in which antiabortion demonstrations are prohibited.

The fact that abortion is currently legal does not mean that it is moral; nor does believing that abortion is immoral necessarily imply that it ought to be outlawed. On the other hand, the resolution of most moral issues that confront us as a society involves not just discerning right from wrong, but determining how best to embody this moral wisdom in a just public policy. This involves balancing concerns about abortion with other concerns such as equal economic rights for women. As both Confucius and Aristotle maintain, good laws and public policy are important because they make it easier for people to be virtuous.

ABORTION AND RELIGION

Although the pro-life stand is often labeled as the "religious" position, religious views on abortion vary widely. Muslims believe that human life is sacred and that the fetus is a person with rights under the law from the moment of "ensoulment." This is tempered by practical concerns, however, and Islamic law generally permits early abortions on medical and health grounds.[20]

In Hinduism the killing of a conscious fetus carries the same penalty as the murder of a learned Brahman. However, the current emphasis on having sons in many Asian countries, including India, has led to a high rate of selective abortion for gender, despite laws in some countries specifically prohibiting abortion for sex selection.

There is little mention of abortion in the Bible, and what there is is ambiguous. Orthodox Jews emphasize passages in Genesis that teach that, because we are created in the image of God, all human life is inviolable and sacred. Thus abortion is prohibited except to save the life of the mother. Liberal and reform Jews, on the other hand, point out that Adam did not become a living being or fully human until God breathed life into him. Likewise, the infant does not become a *nephesh,* or a person with a soul, until he or she takes the first breath of air. Abortion, therefore, is morally permissible at any time during the pregnancy.

The position of the early Christian Church was similar to that of the Orthodox Jews. The *Didache,* written no later than A.D. 100, contains a prohibition against abortion, calling those who procure abortions "destroyers of God's image." This prohibition was reiterated by the early Christian writers. The only exception to the prohibition was abortion to save the life of the mother.

Unlike the early Church, Thomas Aquinas set the time of ensoulment at forty days for males and eighty days for females. Based on this distinction, for centuries the Church regarded late-term abortions as more sinful than early abortions. The belief that early abortions are less morally problematic is still common today. In the nineteenth century, the Roman Catholic Church changed its position, returning to the early Christian prohibition against abortion at any time of the pregnancy.

Unlike their Catholic contemporaries, who permitted early abortions, both John Calvin (1509–1564) and Martin Luther (1483–1546) were emphatic in their opposition to abortion, believing that one is fully human from the moment of conception. The reaction of modern Protestants to abortion is varied. Most fundamentalist, evangelical, and African American Protestant churches take a position similar to that of the Roman Catholics, whereas most of the mainstream Protestant churches take a moderate stand, supporting abortion prior to viability.

The moral controversy over abortion cannot be resolved simply by uncritically accepting religious dogma. At the same time, the arguments used by the different religions should not be dismissed offhand, because they are generally based on philosophical rather than purely theological arguments. Good ethical analysis, while eschewing arguments based solely on faith, entails being open to, listening to, and subjecting to critical analysis, the moral arguments put forth by the various religions.

STAGES OF FETAL DEVELOPMENT

Discussions on the morality of abortion often focus on the level of development of the fetus. The following are some of the milestones in prenatal human development:

> *Day 1: Conception.* The egg and sperm, each containing twenty-three chromosomes, unite to form one cell with forty-six chromosomes. The newly fertilized egg is known as the zygote.

Day 2 to week 2: Blastocyst. The fertilized egg, or blastocyst, travels down the fallopian tube and implants in the uterus. The blastocyst is composed of an embryonic disk, which will develop into an embryo after implantation, and two cavities, an amniotic cavity and the yolk sac.

Weeks 2 to 8: Embryo. The germ layers of the embryonic disk develop into the principle organ systems. At this stage of development, the cells are rapidly dividing and transforming into specialized cells such as eye, skin, and muscle cells. Brain waves are detectable between six and eight weeks. By eight weeks the embryo is 23 millimeters long.

Week 8 to birth: Fetus. By eight weeks all organs and structural features are in place and the fetus resembles a very small newborn child. Between twenty and twenty-four weeks, the fetus becomes viable and is able to survive outside the womb.

Week 40: Birth.

METHODS OF ABORTION

There are three primary types of abortion: medical abortions, surgical abortions, and medical induction of uterine contractions. The method used depends primarily on the time of gestation.

Medical Abortions

Medical abortions include the morning-after pill and mifepristone, popularly known as RU 486. Medical abortions can be done only early in pregnancy.

The morning-after pill. The morning-after pill is actually a high dose of birth control pills taken at two intervals over the three days following intercourse. The doses prevent the blastocyst from implanting in the uterine wall. This method is 75-percent successful at preventing implantation.

Mifepristone (RU 486). Mifepristone, popularly known as RU 486, was developed in France and approved by the U.S. Food and Drug Administration (FDA) in September 2000 for sale to the public, thus decreasing the need for surgical abortions in early pregnancies. Mifepristone induces menstruation, thus expelling the implanted embryo. It is more than 90 percent effective in terminating pregnancies of less than seven weeks' gestation. In 10 to 20 percent of the cases, it takes more than two weeks for the fetus to be expelled.[21]

Surgical Abortions

Most abortions are performed surgically. The 98- to 99-percent success rate of surgical abortion is much higher than that of medical abortion.

Dilation and curettage (D & C). Dilation and curettage used to be one of the most popular methods of abortion. It involves expanding the cervix of the uterus so a spoon-shaped curette can be inserted to scrape the surface of the uterine wall. This method has since fallen out of favor because of the risk of puncturing the uterus, which, in turn, can cause maternal hemorrhaging and even death.

Vacuum aspiration (D & E). The development in China in the early 1960s of the safer vacuum aspiration method was accompanied by a sharp decline in the death rate in women from abortions. Also known as dilation and evacuation (D & E), vacuum aspiration was first used in the United States in the late 1960s. This method is similar to D & C, but the fetus is suctioned rather than scraped out of the uterus. Today more than 90 percent of abortions in the United States are vacuum aspirations.

Intact dilation and extraction (IDX or "partial-birth" abortion). This method is used only in late-term abortions. After partially delivering an intact fetus feet-first, the doctor punctures the fetus's skull, suctions out the brains, and then crushes the skull so the fetus can fit easily through the woman's birth canal. An estimated five thousand "partial-birth" abortions are performed annually.[22]

Hysterectomy and hysterontomy. Surgical removal of the fetus is generally reserved for late-term abortions. A hysterectomy entails the surgical removal of the whole uterus; a hysterontomy, the removal of the fetus through an incision in the uterus. Because of the large number of fetuses who survive these procedures and the high incidence of maternal complications, these methods are rarely used anymore except in emergencies.

Medical Induction of Uterine Contractions

Abortions between sixteen and twenty weeks can be carried out using either surgical removal of the fetus or medical induction of uterine contractions.

Saline solution. With a saline abortion, about 200 milliliters of amniotic fluid is withdrawn from the amniotic sac and replaced with a similar amount of saline solution. The fetus's heartbeat usually stops within sixty to ninety minutes after the injection, and the fetus is expelled from the womb within seventy-two hours. Although the saline solution is meant to kill the fetus, this method occasionally results in a live birth.

Prostaglandins. This method involves an intramuscular or intravaginal injection of prostaglandins to induce labor. The use of prostaglandins, or a combination of prostaglandins and saline solution, is associated with fewer live births than using just saline solution.

THE MORAL ISSUES

The Moral Status of the Fetus

The question of fetal personhood is important because persons have rights that we ought to respect. Is a fetus ever a person? If so, is there a distinct point when embryos or fetuses achieve personhood, or do they gradually achieve this status based on developmental criteria?

John Noonan maintains that there is no distinction between biological humanhood and personhood. We have moral value simply because we have a human genotype, no matter what our age or stage of development. Therefore, even the zygote is a person with moral standing. Mary Anne Warren, in contrast, argues that at no stage does the fetus meet the criteria of personhood. A fetus does not become a person until sometime after birth, when the infant becomes a "socially responsive member of a human community."

Most definitions of personhood fall between these extremes. According to utilitarians, only sentient beings need to be given moral consideration. Abortion, therefore, becomes a moral issue only after the fetus is able to experience pain. While there is considerable controversy over whether the older embryo and young fetus are able to feel pain or whether they are simply responding reflexively to external stimuli, most physicians agree that by thirteen weeks the fetus is able to experience pain.[23] A related developmental milestone that has been suggested as marking the beginning of personhood is the presence of brainwaves, which occurs at about six weeks.[24] This criterion has the advantage of being symmetrical with definitions of the end of personhood. On the other hand, an adult whose brainwaves have ceased is no longer alive and developing, whereas an embryo, despite lack of a brain, is.

Viability—"the capacity to survive disconnection from the placenta"[25]—replaced quickening after the 1973 *Roe v. Wade* ruling as the most widely accepted point for granting the fetus moral rights. Viability is problematic as a criteria, however, because personhood becomes dependent on medical technology rather than on any characteristic of the fetus. In 1950, viability occurred at about thirty weeks' gestation. When the *Roe v. Wade* decision was handed down in 1973, medical technology had advanced to the point where viability occurred at twenty-four weeks. Now fetuses as young as twenty weeks are surviving. If an artificial womb, or another means for the young fetus to breathe and survive outside the womb, is created, viability could occur much earlier, making *Roe v. Wade* a pro-life ruling.

A final criterion is that of potentiality, according to which the potential to develop into a full-fledged adult confers personhood on a fertilized egg. Noonan's definition of personhood embraces this criterion. Thomson, on the other hand, rejects it in her analogy between human development and the development of an acorn into an oak tree.

The moral status of the fetus is currently being challenged at both ends of the continuum in debates on the morality of embryonic stem cell research, which involves the destruction of embryos, and debates on partial-birth abortion, which involves the destruction of viable fetuses. A federal ban was placed on partial birth abortion in the fall of 2003. The use of federal funds for research into cloning human embryos for stem cell research was outlawed in 2001. For more on the moral issues surrounding cloning human stem cells see Chapter 3 "Genetic Engineering and Cloning."

Some people, frustrated with the lack of consensus on a definition of personhood, argue that it is better left to personal or religious opinion. To say that one's definition of personhood is a matter of opinion, however, is to mire the debate in ethical subjectivism. Not only is abortion morally permissible, if in one's opinion a fetus is not a person, but so is infanticide, slavery, and genocide, so long as the perpetrators of these practices believe, or their religions teach, that their victims are not persons. Because of this, it is important that in discussions of the morality of abortion we give careful consideration to the criteria for personhood and the implications of these criteria, and not uncritically accept cultural definitions or those that are politically and economically expedient, as happened with declaring slaves nonpersons.

In 1999 the U.S. House of Representatives passed legislation making the harming of a fetus during a federal crime a separate, prosecutable crime. The status of the fetus killed during a crime came under public scrutiny again in the 2003 California Laci Peterson case in which her unborn son Connor died as a result of her brutal murder. In addition, some states, such as Rhode Island, which use federal money to subsidize health care to children from low-income families, now include pregnant women in the plans. Some abortion rights advocates oppose these moves, arguing they will weaken a woman's legal right to an abortion. On the other hand, denying the fetus any moral status, pro-life feminists point out, denies the pregnant woman's special status and relationship with her unborn child and limits her options. The moral status and rights of the fetus are also an issue in maternal alcohol and drug use (see case study on page 127).

Even if we grant the fetus some moral status, as Judith Jarvis Thomsom does in her landmark article "A Defense of Abortion," it is still possible to argue that abortion is morally permissible under some circumstances. If a fetus is a person who can feel pain, however, the method used for abortion becomes a moral concern, since it is wrong to cause unnecessary pain. This is currently used as one of the arguments against partial-birth abortion (see case study on page 130).

Don Marquis, in his article "Why Abortion Is Immoral," argues that the killing of human beings who are able to enjoy their future experiences is wrong because it deprives them of the value of their future. Because the fetus, like an adult human, has a future which he or she can value—a future that is destroyed by abortion—abortion, according to Marquis, is immoral.

The Rights and Autonomy of the Mother

Some people think that the emphasis in the abortion debate on the personhood of the fetus has been at the expense of concerns about the rights of the woman. Judith Jarvis Thomson shifts the debate from the moral status of the fetus to the rights of the mother. She agrees that trying to prove that the fetus is not a person is fraught with difficulties; therefore, she gives the fetus the benefit of the doubt. From here she argues that even though the fetus may have moral standing, the rights of the mother, in most cases, outweigh those of the fetus.

Mary Anne Warren likewise maintains that a woman's liberty rights, or autonomy, is paramount; women should have the right to make decisions about their own bodies. To deny women this basic right, according to Warren, is to treat them as a means only. Steven Hales argues that women have a right to abortion as a mechanism to avoid future burdens. Opponents of abortion, in response, argue that autonomy is not an absolute right. While women have a moral right to control their bodies, this right does not extend to abortion, because abortion involves destroying the body of an unborn child.

The extent to which women have a right to control their own bodies is an issue not just in abortion. It also arises in the debate over whether women have a responsibility to refrain from prenatal behaviors, such as drug and alcohol use, that may harm fetuses.

Fetal alcohol syndrome, according to the Center for Disease Control, is the leading cause of mental retardation in the United States. More infants are born with fetal alcohol syndrome than the combined total of Down's syndrome, spina bifida, muscular dystrophy, and HIV. Women who smoke during pregnancy also are at a higher risk for having babies with low birth weight, respiratory problems, and sudden infant death syndrome (SIDS).

Advocates of abortion argue that as long as we have a patriarchal society in which pregnant women and mothers are socially and economically disadvantaged, abortion must remain a legitimate alternative. To have it otherwise is to deny women full and equal participation in society. Because women need to have the option of abortion, justice is also an issue in access to abortion services. Restrictive abortion laws, lack of money to pay for an abortion, unavailability of a clinic in one's area, and the presence of pro-life harassment outside of abortion clinics—all contribute to a situation in which some women, especially poor women, do not have the same access to abortion. For more on contemporary pro-life feminism see Sidney Callahan's "Abortion and The Sexual Agenda: A Case for Prolife Feminism" in the *Ethics PowerWeb.*

It should be noted that a right to have an abortion to avoid future unjust burdens would only apply to burdens caused by the pregnancy and giving birth since adoption provides a mechanism for avoiding the burdens of raising the child after birth. Because adoption is an option, the decision to carry a pregnancy to term and the decision to raise the child should be seen as two separate decisions. This being said, the burdens of pregnancy in terms of discrimination faced in the workplace, and the stigma and pain of giving up a child for adoption are still very real. Whether or not permissive abortion policies are exacerbating this injustice remains to be studied.

Abortion and Father's Rights and Duties

Service providers of contraception and abortion have focused almost exclusively on women. Wayne Pawlowski, who works for Planned Parenthood, notes that "abortion clinics give tremendous lip service to the need to involve male partners, but 99 percent of them won't even talk to the guy . . ."[26] In fact, there isn't even a term for men who are involved in a pregnancy.

In the selection from his article "Abortion and Fathers' Rights," Steven Hales argues that because women have a right to avoid future burdens through abortion, the principle of equality requires that men should also have the right of refusal when it comes to contributing to the support of his child after birth. Women have a similar right through the mechanism of adoption in which the natural parents can terminate their rights and obligations toward their child and the adoptive parents assume these rights and obligations.

Others maintain that it is fair to force fathers to pay child support should the women decide to keep their children, even though women do not have a duty to consult the father in making a decision about whether or not to terminate the pregnancy. This is because men bear some responsibility for the child's conception and birth, and because of the social consequences of the father refusing to support his child. Indeed, studies show that unmarried fathers are far more interested in their children than we generally give them credit for.

Selective Abortion and the Principle of Discrimination

Injustice based on discrimination is one of the key issues in selective abortion. Unlike elective abortion, in which the pregnancy itself is unwanted, in selective abortion it is the particular fetus, rather than the pregnancy, that is unwanted. About 7 percent of infants are born with a physical and/or mental disorder. Prenatal diagnosis provides parents with information about most of these disorders as well as the gender of the fetus. The overwhelming majority of pregnancies in which the fetus is diagnosed as having a genetic disorder are terminated by selective abortion.

In countries where a daughter is considered a greater burden than a son with a handicap, selective abortion is more likely to be used for sex selection than for genetic disorders. Because of this, there is a great discrepancy in some parts of India and China between the number of males and the number of females.[27] In the great majority of cases, including within the United States, where there is a preference for sons as firstborn and only children, selective abortion is used to dispose of unwanted female fetuses. In

South Korea the abortion rate of female fetuses in later pregnancy is as high as 40 percent.[28] According to the *The Economist,* of eight thousand abortions in Bombay in which the sex of the fetus was known, all but one of the aborted fetuses was female.[29] India banned the use of abortion intended for sex selection in 1994 and China followed suit in 2003. However, these laws have been hard to enforce given the strong preference for boys in parts of these countries and the easy availability of ultrasound for determining the gender of the fetus.

In a 1987 study, the United States was one of only three nations in which the majority of geneticists surveyed said they would perform prenatal diagnosis for sex selection.[30] Abortion for sex selection is legal in the United States with American physicians being most supportive worldwide of the practice, citing the woman's autonomy as their reason for performing the procedure. With increasing knowledge of the human genome, geneticists may soon be able to prenatally diagnose tendencies toward obesity, cancer, and homosexuality—to name only a few traits that most Americans consider undesirable in their children.[31]

The principle of nondiscrimination states that humans not be denied benefits or equal treatment for morally irrelevant reasons, such as sex or skin color or physical abilities. Does selective abortion involve discrimination against females, people with handicaps, and other socially unacceptable people? Even if it does involve discrimination, this has to be weighed against women's autonomy as well as against the social consequences of having "undesirable" children who will be a burden on their parents and on society.

Consequentialist Arguments: Abortion as a Benefit to Born Children

Those who favor a permissive public policy on abortion point to the harmful consequences to women, and society in general, of restrictive abortion policies. These include complications and deaths from self-induced and illegal abortions, overpopulation, the burden on women of mandatory motherhood, at least during the nine months of pregnancy, and the burden on society when unwanted children are neglected or abandoned.

The use of consequentialist or utilitarian arguments in the formulation of social policy requires that we base our arguments in experience or fact, rather than conjecture. One of the arguments for abortion, summarized in the slogan Pro-Child/Pro-Choice, is that abortion not only benefits women, but benefits children by ensuring that all born children are wanted children. However, studies have not shown that abortion leads to a decrease in child abuse and improves the quality-of-life of born children.

Indeed, some pro-life feminists maintain that abortion, rather than benefiting children, has lead to a devaluation of children and an increase in child abuse. According to a 1989 study, while the general well-being of the nation remained relatively stable in the 1970s, declining slightly in the first part of the 1980s, the "social health" of children and youth began a steady course of decline beginning in 1974, the year after abortion was legalized.[32] In addition, the rates of child abuse began rising after 1973, increasing 566 percent between 1977 and 1980 alone.[33] This increase cannot be attributed solely to better reporting of child abuse cases because most of the improvement in reporting techniques took place in the early 1980s in response to the alarming increase in child abuse. These abused—and perhaps unwanted—children came from wanted pregnancies since abortion was a legal option. A study conducted at Johns Hopkins Hospital by the Baltimore, Maryland Department of Social Services of 532 abused children found that previous abortions and stillbirths place a family at significantly higher risk for child abuse, independently of other factors such as socioeconomic and marital status.[34] While a positive correlation between child abuse and previous abortions may sound counter-intuitive, psychiatrist Phillip Nye suggests that by legitimating the death of the fetus in utero we have weakened the normal instinctual restraint and social taboo against the use of violence against young children dependent on our care.[35]

On the other hand, the harms to born children may be corrected by creating better support systems for parents and young children. These harms also have to be weighed against the harm to women of depriving them of control over their bodies during pregnancy. In any case we cannot argue in favor of abortion on the grounds that it benefits born children. Instead, we must be willing to examine the morality of abortion, using factually correct premises and consistent arguments.

CONCLUSION

As members of a pluralistic society, can we ever reach a resolution to the current abortion debate? Indeed, should we even bother to try? Why can't we just be tolerant of other people's views: "If you don't believe in abortion, don't have one." Unfortunately, the hands-off approach doesn't work, because those who are opposed to abortion are not merely expressing a personal opinion about abortion; they are saying that abortion is wrong because it goes against universal moral principles. Furthermore, to claim that we should be tolerant of other people's moral opinions is to advocate tolerance not only of abortion but also of other practices. Few of us would be willing to carry a bumper sticker sporting the slogan "If you don't believe in slavery, don't own slaves."

Ethical analysis should not be a matter of personal opinion or majority consensus. It should be logical, consistent, and universal in its application. Until we can approach the moral issue of abortion rationally, the issue is unlikely to be resolved. The following readings are an invitation to rethink the abortion issue with an open and analytical mind.

JUDITH JARVIS THOMSON

A Defense of Abortion*

Judith Jarvis Thomson is a professor of philosophy at the Massachusetts Institute of Technology. Her article "A Defense of Abortion," published two years before *Roe v. Wade,* has become a classic in the abortion debate. Rather than attempt to refute the premises that the fetus is a person and that every person has a right to life, Thomson argues that abortion may be morally permissible even if these premises are true. Using her now-famous violinist analogy, Thomson attempts to show that even if the fetus has a right to life, this right does not entail the right to have whatever one needs—including use of a woman's body—to stay alive.

Critical Reading Questions

1. What is Thomson's position regarding the personhood of the fetus?
2. How does Thomson use the violinist analogy to illustrate the relationship between the fetus and the woman?
3. What conclusion regarding the rights of the fetus, the rights of the mother, and the moral permissibility of abortion does Thomson draw based on the violinist analogy?
4. Why does Thomson reject the "extreme" pro-life view of abortion?
5. Which position on abortion is Thomson addressing when she uses the analogy of a person being trapped in a tiny house with a rapidly growing child?
6. How does Thomson respond to the pro-life argument that if the fetus has a right to life, abortion is unjust killing?
7. What analogy does Thomson use to justify abortion in cases of contraceptive failure?
8. Are there any circumstances, according to Thomson, in which abortion is not morally permissible?
9. What is the difference between a Minimally Decent Samaritan and a Good Samaritan? What is the relevance of this distinction in the abortion debate?
10. On what grounds does Thomson draw a moral distinction between the right to have an abortion and the right to secure the death of an unborn child?

Most opposition to abortion relies on the premise that the fetus is a human being, a person, from the moment of conception. The premise is argued for, but, as I think, not well. Take, for example, the most common argument. We are asked to notice that the development of a human being from conception through birth into childhood is continuous; then it is said that to draw a line, to choose a point in this development and say "before this point the thing is not a person, after this point it is a person" is to make an arbitrary choice, a choice for which in the nature of things no good reason can be given. It is concluded that

CA 1: Fetus is a person

J.T.'s response to CA 1

"A Defense of Abortion," *Philosophy and Public Affairs* 1, no. 1 (1971): 47–66. Notes have been omitted.

*This article has been annotated using the guidelines set out in Chapter 2, "Critical Reading" of the *Reasoning, Reading, Writing, and Debating in Ethics* CD-ROM that comes packaged with this book.

the fetus is, or anyway that we had better say it is, a person from the moment of conception. But this conclusion does not follow. [Similar things might be said about the development of an acorn into an oak tree, and it does not follow that acorns are oak trees, or that we had better say they are.] Arguments of this form are sometimes called "slippery slope arguments"—the phrase is perhaps self-explanatory—and it is dismaying that opponents of abortion rely on them so heavily and uncritically.

Oak tree analogy

J. T.'s response to CA 1

I am inclined to agree, however, that the prospects for "drawing a line" in the development of the fetus look dim. I am inclined to think also that [we shall have to agree that the fetus has already become (a human person) well before birth.] Indeed, it comes as a surprise when one first learns how early in its life it begins to acquire human characteristics. By the tenth week, for example, it already has a face, arms and legs, fingers and toes; it has internal organs, and brain activity is detectable. On the other hand, I think that the premise is false, that the fetus is not a person from the moment of conception. A newly fertilized ovum, a newly implanted clump of cells, is no more a person than an acorn is an oak tree. But I shall not discuss any of this. For it seems to me to be of great interest to ask what happens if, for the sake of argument, we allow the premise. . . .

Definition of key term "person"

Premise #1: Fetus is a person

Explanation of premise #1

I propose, then, that [we grant that the fetus is a person from the moment of conception.] How does the argument go from here? Something like this, I take it. [Every person has a right to life.] So the fetus has a right to life. No doubt the [mother has a right to decide what shall happen in and to her body;] everyone would grant that. But surely a person's right to life is stronger and more stringent than the mother's right to decide what happens in and to her body, and so outweighs it. [So the fetus may not be killed; an abortion may not be performed.]

Premise #1 and premise #2: Fetus has a right to life

Premise #3: The mother has a right to life

CA 2: The fetus may not be killed

It sounds plausible. But let me ask you to imagine this. You wake up in the morning and find yourself back to back in bed with an unconscious violinist. A famous unconscious violinist. He has been found to have a fatal kidney ailment, and the Society of Music Lovers has canvassed all available medical records and found that you alone have the right blood type to help. They have therefore kidnapped you, and last night the violinist's circulatory system was plugged into yours, so that your kidneys can be used to extract poisons from his blood as well as your own. The director of the hospital now tells you, "Look, we're sorry the Society of Music Lovers did this to you—we would have never permitted it if we had known. But still, they did it, and the violinist is now plugged into you. To unplug you would be to kill him. But never mind, it's only for nine months. By then he will have recovered from his ailment, and can be safely unplugged from you." Is it morally incumbent on you to accede to this situation? No doubt it would be very nice of you if you did, a great kindness. But do you *have* to accede to it? What if it were not nine months, but nine years? Or longer still? What if the director of the hospital says, "Tough luck, I agree, but you've now got to stay in bed, with the violinist plugged in to you, for the rest of your life. Because remember this. All persons have a right to life, and violinists are persons. Granted you have a right to decide what happens in and to your body, but a person's right to life outweighs your right to decide what happens in and to your body. So you cannot ever be unplugged from him." I imagine you would regard this as

J. T.'s response to CA 2: violinist analogy

Rejection of CA 2

Rejection of CA 2

outrageous, which suggests that something really is wrong with that plausible-sounding argument I mentioned a moment ago.]

Violinist analogy

In this case, of course, you were kidnapped; you didn't volunteer for the operation that plugged the violinist into your kidneys. Can those who oppose abortion on the ground I mentioned make an exception for a pregnancy due to rape? Certainly. They can say that persons have a right to life only if they didn't come into existence because of rape; or they can say that all persons have a right to life, but that some have less of a right to life than others, in particular, that those who came into existence because of rape have less. But these statements have a rather unpleasant sound. Surely the question of whether you have a right to life at all, or how much of it you have, shouldn't turn on the question of whether or not you are the product of a rape. And in fact the people who oppose abortion on the ground I mentioned do not make this distinction, and hence do not make an exception in case of rape. . . .

Explanation

Some won't even make an exception for a case in which continuation of the pregnancy is likely to shorten the mother's life; they regard abortion as impermissible even to save the mother's life. Such cases are nowadays very rare, and many opponents of abortion do not accept this extreme view. All the same, it is a good place to begin: a number of points of interest come out in respect to it.

CA 3: Extreme pro-life view

1. Let us call the view that abortion is impermissible even to save the mother's life "the extreme view." I want to suggest first that it does not issue from the argument I mentioned earlier without the addition of some fairly powerful premises. Suppose a woman has become pregnant, and now learns that she has a cardiac condition such that she will die if she carries the baby to term. What may be done for her? The fetus, being a person, has a right to life, but as the mother is a person too, so has she a right to life. Presumably they have an equal right to life. How is it supposed to come out that an abortion may not be performed? If mother and child have an equal right to life, shouldn't we perhaps flip a coin? Or should we add to the mother's right to life her right to decide what happens in and to her body, which everybody seems to be ready to grant—the sum of her rights now outweighing the fetus' right to life?

J.T.'s response to extreme view

The most familiar argument here is the following. We are told that performing the abortion would be directly killing the child, whereas doing nothing would not be killing the mother, but only letting her die. Moreover, in killing the child, one would be killing an innocent person, for the child has committed no crime, and is not aiming at his mother's death. . . .

If directly killing an innocent person is murder, and thus is impermissible, then the mother's directly killing the innocent person inside her is murder, and thus is impermissible. But [it cannot seriously be thought to be murder if the mother performs an abortion on herself to save her life. It cannot seriously be said that she *must* refrain, that she *must* sit passively by and wait for her death.] Let us look again at the case of you and the violinist. There you are, in bed with the violinist, and the director of the hospital says to you, "It's all most distressing, and I deeply sympathize, but you see this is putting an additional strain on your kidneys, and you'll be dead within the month. But you *have* to stay where you are all the same. Because unplugging you would be directly killing an

Premise #4: It is not murder to perform an abortion to save your life

Violinist analogy explanation of premise #4

innocent violinist, and that's murder, and that's impermissible." If anything in the world is true, it is that you do not commit murder, you do not do what is impermissible, if you reach around to your back and unplug yourself from that violinist to save your life.

The main focus of attention in writings on abortion has been on what a third party may or may not do in answer to a request from a woman for an abortion. This is in a way understandable. Things being as they are, there isn't much a woman can safely do to abort herself. So the question asked is what a third party may do, and what the mother may do, if it is mentioned at all, is deduced, almost as an afterthought, from what is concluded that third parties may do. But it seems to me that to treat the matter in this way is to refuse to grant to the mother that very status of person which is so firmly insisted on for the fetus. For we cannot simply read off what a person may do from what a third party may do. Suppose you find yourself trapped in a tiny house with a growing child. I mean a very tiny house, and a rapidly growing child—you are already up against the wall of the house and in a few minutes you will be crushed to death. The child on the other hand won't be crushed to death; if nothing is done to stop him from growing he'll be hurt, but in the end he'll simply burst open the house and walk out a free man. Now I could well understand it if a bystander were to say, "There's nothing we can do for you. We cannot choose between your life and his, we cannot be the ones to decide who is to live, we cannot intervene." But it cannot be concluded that you too can do nothing, that you cannot attack it to save your life. However innocent the child may be, you do not have to wait passively while it crushes you to death. Perhaps a pregnant woman is vaguely felt to have the same status of house, to which we don't allow the right of self-defense. But if the woman houses the child, it should be remembered that she is a person who houses it. . . .

Rejection of CA 3: Extreme pro-life position

Explanation of rejection of CA 3 Analogy of house with growing child

Premise #5: A pregnant woman's body is her own

In sum, a woman surely can defend her life against the threat to it posed by the unborn child, even if doing so involves its death. And this shows also that the extreme view of abortion is false, and so we need not canvass any other possible ways of arriving at it from the argument I mentioned at the outset.

Sub conclusion and Premise #6: A woman can defend herself against threats from the unborn child even if it results in child's death

2. The extreme view should of course be weakened to say that while abortion is permissible to save a mother's life, it may not be performed by a third party, but only by the mother herself. But this cannot be right either. For what we have to keep in mind is that the mother and the unborn child are not like two tenants in a small house which has, by an unfortunate mistake, been rented to both: the mother *owns* the house. The fact that she does adds to the offensiveness of deducing that the mother can do nothing from the supposition that third parties can do nothing. But it does nothing more than this: it casts a bright light on the supposition that third parties can do nothing. Certainly it lets us see that a third party who says "I cannot choose between you" is fooling himself if he thinks this is impartiality. If Jones has found and fastened on a certain coat, which he needs to keep from freezing, but which Smith also needs to keep him from freezing, then it is not impartiality that says "I cannot choose between you" when Smith owns the coat. Women have said again and again "This body is *my* body!" and they have reason to feel angry, reason to feel that it has been like shouting in the wind. . . .

CA 4: Self-defense allows only mother to perform abortion

J.T.'s rejection of CA 4: Smith owns the coat

We should really ask what it is that says "no one may choose" in the face of the fact that the body that houses the child is the mother's body. It may be simply a failure to appreciate this fact. But it may be something more interesting, namely the sense that one has a right to refuse to lay hands on people, even where it would be just and fair to do so, even where justice seems to require that somebody do so. This justice might call for somebody to get Smith's coat back from Jones, and yet you have a right to refuse to be the one to lay hands on Jones, a right to refuse to do physical violence to him. This, I think, must be granted. But then what should be said is not "no one may choose," but only "*I* cannot choose," and indeed not even this, but "*I* will not *act,*" leaving it open that somebody else can or should, and in particular that anyone in a position of authority, with the job of securing people's rights, both can and should. So this is no difficulty. I have not been arguing that any given third party must accede to the mother's request that he perform an abortion to save her life, but only that he may. . . .

3. Where the mother's life is not at stake, the argument I mentioned at the outset seems to have a much stronger pull. "Everyone has a right to life, so the unborn person has a right to life." And isn't the child's right to life weightier than anything other than the mother's own right to life, which she might put forward as ground for an abortion?

This argument treats the right to life as if it were unproblematic. It is not, and this seems to me to be precisely the source of the mistake.

For we should now, at long last, ask what it comes to, to have a right to life. In some views having a right to life includes having a right to be given at least the bare minimum one needs for continued life. But suppose that what in fact *is* the bare minimum a man needs for continued life is something he has no right at all to be given? If I am sick unto death, and the only thing that will save my life is the touch of Henry Fonda's cool hand on my fevered brow, then all the same, I have no right to be given the touch of Henry Fonda's cool hand on my fevered brow. It would be frightfully nice of him to fly in from the West Coast to provide it. It would be less nice, though no doubt meant well, if my friends flew out to the West Coast and carried Henry Fonda back with them. But I have no right at all against anybody that he should do this for me. Or again, to return to the story told earlier, the fact that for continued life that violinist needs the continued use of your kidneys does not establish that he has a right to be given the continued use of your kidneys. He certainly has no right against you that *you* should give him continued use of your kidneys. For nobody has any right to use your kidneys unless you give him such a right; and nobody has the right against you that you shall give him this right—if you do allow him to go on using your kidneys, this is a kindness on your part, and not something he can claim from you as his due. . . .

But I would stress that I am not arguing that people do not have the right to life—quite to the contrary, it seems to me that the primary control we must place on the acceptability of an account of rights is that it should turn out in that account to be a truth that all persons have a right to life. I am arguing only that having a right to life does not guarantee having either a right to be given the use of or a right to be allowed continued use of another person's body—even if one needs it for life itself.] So the right to life will not serve the opponents of abortion in the very simple and clear way in which they seem to have thought it would.

4. There is another way to bring out the difficulty. In the most ordinary sort of case, [to deprive someone of what he has a right to is to treat him unjustly.] Suppose a boy and his small brother are jointly given a box of chocolates for Christmas. If the older boy takes the box and refuses to give his brother any of the chocolates, he is unjust to him, for the brother has been given a right to half of them. But suppose that, having learned that otherwise it means nine years in bed with that violinist, you unplug yourself from him. You surely are not being unjust to him, for you gave him no right to use your kidneys, and no one else can have given him any such right. But we have to notice that in unplugging yourself, you are killing him; and violinists, like everybody else, have a right to life, and thus in the view we were considering just now, the right not to be killed. So here you do what he supposedly has a right you shall not do, but you do not act unjustly to him in doing it.

Premise #8: It is unjust to deprive someone of something to which they have a right

Explanation of premise #8

The emendation which may be made at this point is this: [the right to life consists not in the right not to be killed, but rather in the right not to be killed unjustly.] This runs a risk of circularity, but never mind: it would enable us to square the fact that the violinist has a right to life with the fact that you do not act unjustly toward him in unplugging yourself, thereby killing him. For if you do not kill him unjustly, you do not violate his right to life, and it is no wonder you do him no injustice.

Premise #9: The right to life consists only of the right not to be killed unjustly

But if this emendation is accepted, the gap in the argument against abortion stares us plainly in the face: it is no means enough to show that the fetus is a person, and to remind us that all persons have a right to life—we need to be shown also that killing the fetus violates its right to life, i.e., that abortion is unjust killing. And is it?

I suppose we may take it as a datum that in a case of pregnancy due to rape the mother has not given the unborn person a right to the use of her body for food and shelter. Indeed, in what pregnancy could it be supposed that the mother has given the unborn person such a right? It is not as if there were unborn persons drifting about the world, to whom a woman who wants a child says "I invite you in."

But it might be argued that there are other ways one can have acquired a right to the use of another person's body than by having been invited to use it by that person. Suppose a woman voluntarily indulges in intercourse, knowing that the chance it will issue in pregnancy, and then she does become pregnant; is she not in part responsible for the presence, in fact the very existence, of the unborn person inside her? No doubt she did not invite it in. But doesn't her partial responsibility for its being there itself give it a right to the use of her body? If so, then her aborting it would be more like the boy's taking away the chocolates, and less like your unplugging yourself from the violinist—doing so would be depriving it of what it does have a right to, and thus would be doing it an injustice. . . .

CA 6: If mother "invites" fetus to use her body, it is unjust to then kill the fetus

The first thing to be said about this is that it is something new. Opponents of abortion have been so concerned to make out the independence of the fetus, in order to establish that it has a right to life, just as its mother does, that they have tended to overlook the possible support they might gain from making out that the fetus is *dependent* on the mother, in order to establish that she has a special kind of responsibility for it, a responsibility that gives it rights against her which are not possessed by any independent person—such as an ailing violinist who is a stranger to her.

On the other hand, this argument would give the unborn person a right to its mother's body only if her pregnancy resulted from a voluntary act, undertaken in full knowledge of the chance a pregnancy might result from it. It would leave out entirely the unborn person whose existence is due to rape. Pending the availability of some further argument, then, we would be left with the conclusion that unborn persons whose existence is due to rape have no right to the use of their mothers' bodies, and thus that aborting them is not depriving them of anything they have a right to and hence is not unjust killing.

And we should also notice that it is not at all plain that this argument really does not go even as far as it purports to. For there are cases and cases, and the details make a difference. If the room is stuffy, and I therefore open a window to air it, and a burglar climbs in, it would be absurd to say, "Ah, now he can stay, she's given him a right to the use of her house—for she is partially responsible for his presence there, having voluntarily done what enabled him to get in, in full knowledge that there are such things as burglars, and that burglars burgle." It would be still more absurd to say this if I had had bars installed outside my windows, precisely to prevent burglars from getting in, and a burglar got in only because of a defect in the bars. It remains equally absurd if we imagine it is not a burglar who climbs in, but an innocent person who blunders or falls in. Again, suppose it were like this: people-seeds drift about in the air like pollen, and if you open your windows, one may drift in and take root in your carpets or upholstery. You don't want children, so you fix up your windows with fine mesh screens, the very best you can buy. As can happen, however, and on very, very rare occasions does happen, one of the screens is defective; and a seed drifts in and takes root. Does the person-plant who now develops have a right to the use of your house? Surely not—despite the fact that you voluntarily opened your windows, you knowingly kept carpets and upholstered furniture, and you knew that screens were sometimes defective. Someone may argue that you are responsible for its rooting, that it does have a right to your house, because after all you *could* have lived out your life with bare floors and furniture, or with sealed windows and doors. But this won't do—for by the same token anyone can avoid a pregnancy due to rape by having a hysterectomy, or anyway by never leaving home without a (reliable!) army.

It seems to me that the argument we are looking at can establish at most that there are *some* cases in which the unborn person has a right to the use of its mother's body, and therefore *some* cases in which abortion is unjust killing. There is room for much discussion and argument as to precisely which, if any. But I think we should sidestep this issue and leave it open, for at any rate the argument certainly does not establish that all abortion is unjust killing.

5. There is room for yet another argument here, however. We surely must all grant that there may be cases in which it would be morally indecent to detach a

person from your body at the cost of his life. Suppose you learn that what the violinist needs is not nine years of your life, but only one hour: all you need to do to save his life is to spend one hour in that bed with him. Suppose also that letting him use your kidneys for that one hour would not affect your health in the slightest. Admittedly you were kidnapped. Admittedly you did not give anyone permission to plug him into you. Nevertheless it seems to me plain you *ought* to allow him to use your kidneys for that one hour—it would be indecent to refuse.

Explanation of premise #10: The violinist analogy revisited

Again, suppose pregnancy lasted only an hour, and constituted no threat to your life or health. And suppose that a woman becomes pregnant as a result of rape. Admittedly she did not voluntarily do anything to bring about the existence of a child. Admittedly she did nothing at all which would give the unborn person a right to the use of her body. All the same it might well be said, as in the newly emended violinist story, that she *ought* to allow it to remain for that hour—that it would be indecent in her to refuse.

Now some people are inclined to use the term "right" in such a way that it follows from the fact that you ought to allow a person to use your body for the hour he needs, that he has the right to use your body for the hour he needs, even though he has not been given that right by any person or act. They may say that it follows also that if you refuse, you act unjustly toward him. This use of the term is perhaps so common that it cannot be called wrong; nevertheless it seems to me to be an unfortunate loosening of what we would do better to keep a tight rein on. Suppose the box of chocolates I mentioned earlier had not been given to both boys jointly, but was given only to the older boy. There he sits, stolidly eating his way through the box, his small brother watching enviously. Here we are likely to say "You ought not to be so mean. You ought to give your brother some of those chocolates." My own view is that it just does not follow from the truth of this that the brother has any right to any of the chocolates. If the boy refuses to give his brother any, he is greedy, stingy, callous—but not unjust. . . .

Premise #13: Even if there are cases in which the mother ought to allow the unborn child to use her body, this does not mean the child has a right to her body

So my own view is that even though you ought to let the violinist use your kidneys for the one hour he needs, we should not conclude that he has a right to do so—we should say that if you refuse, you are, like the boy who owns all the chocolates and will give none away, self-centered and callous, indecent in fact, but not unjust. And similarly, that even supposing a case in which a woman pregnant due to rape ought to allow the unborn person to use her body for the hour he needs, we should not conclude that he has a right to do so; we should conclude that she is self-centered, callous, indecent, but not unjust, if she refuses. The complaints are no less grave; they are just different. . . .

Key terms: Good Samaritan and Minimally Decent Samaritan

6. We have in fact to distinguish between two kinds of Samaritan: the Good Samaritan and what we might call the Minimally Decent Samaritan. . . . The Good Samaritan went out of his way, at some cost to himself, to help one in need of it. . . . [in Luke 10:30–35]

Explanation of two types of Samaritans

These things are a matter of degree, of course, but there is a difference, and it comes out perhaps most clearly in the story of Kitty Genovese, who, as you will remember, was murdered while thirty-eight people watched or listened, and did nothing at all to help her. A Good Samaritan would have rushed out to give direct assistance against the murderer. Or perhaps we had better allow that

Explanation of two types of Samaritan

it would have been a Splendid Samaritan who did this, on the ground that it would have involved a risk of death for himself. But the thirty-eight not only did not do this, they did not even trouble to pick up a phone to call the police. Minimally Decent Samaritanism would call for doing at least that, and their not having done it was monstrous.

After telling the story of the Good Samaritan, Jesus said "Go, and do thou likewise." Perhaps he meant that we are morally required to act as the Good Samaritan did. Perhaps he was urging people to do more than is morally required of them. At all events it seems plain that [it was not morally required of any of the thirty-eight that he rush out to give direct assistance at the risk of his own life] and that [it is not morally required of anyone that he give long stretches of his life—nine years or nine months—to sustaining that life of a person who has no special right (we were leaving open the possibility of this) to demand it.]

Premise #14: We are only morally required to be Minimally Decent Samaritans

Premise #15: Being a Minimally Decent Samaritan does not require us to give long stretches to sustain the life of someone who has no special rights

Indeed, with one rather striking class of exceptions, no one in any country in the world is *legally* required to do anywhere near as much as this for anyone else. The class of exceptions is obvious. My main concern here is not the state of the law in respect to abortion, but it is worth drawing attention to the fact that in no state in this country is any man compelled by law to be even a Minimally Decent Samaritan to any person; there is no law under which charges could be brought against the thirty-eight who stood by while Kitty Genovese died. . . .

Explanation of premises #14 and #15

I should think, myself, that Minimally Decent Samaritan laws would be one thing, Good Samaritan laws quite another, and in fact highly improper. But we are not here concerned with the law. What we should ask is not whether anybody should be compelled by law to be a Good Samaritan, but whether we must accede to a situation in which somebody is being compelled—by nature, perhaps—to be a Good Samaritan. We have, in other words, to look now at third-party interventions. I have been arguing that no person is morally required to make large sacrifices to sustain the life of another who has no right to demand them, and this even where the sacrifices do not include life itself; we are not morally required to be Good Samaritans or anyway Very Good Samaritans to one another. But what if a man cannot extricate himself from such a situation? What if he appeals to us to extricate him? It seems to me plain that there are cases in which we can, cases in which a Good Samaritan would extricate him. There you are, you were kidnapped, and nine years in bed with that violinist lie ahead of you. You have your own life to lead. You are sorry, but you simply cannot see giving up so much of your life to the sustaining of his. You cannot extricate yourself, and ask us to do so. I should have thought that—in light of his having no right to the use of your body—it was obvious that we do not have to accede to your being forced to give up so much. We can do what you ask. There is no injustice to the violinist in our doing so.

CA 7: The woman has a special kind of obligation toward her fetus because she is the mother

7. Following the lead of opponents of abortion, I have throughout been speaking of the fetus merely as a person, and what I have been asking is whether or not the argument we began with, which proceeds only from the fetus' being a person, really does not establish its conclusion. I have argued that it does not.

But of course there are arguments and arguments, and it may be said that I have simply fastened on the wrong one. It may be said that what is important is not merely the fact that the fetus is a person, but that it is a person for whom the woman has a special kind of responsibility issuing from the fact that she is the mother. And it might be argued that all my analogies are therefore irrelevant—for you do not have that special responsibility for that violinist, Henry Fonda does not have that special kind of responsibility for me. And our attention might be drawn to the fact that men and women both *are* compelled by law to provide support for their children.

J.T.'s response to CA 1

Premise #16: We do not have a responsibility for another person unless we have assumed it

I have in effect dealt (briefly) with this argument in section 4 above; but a (still briefer) recapitulation now may be in order. [Surely we do not have any such "special responsibility" for a person unless we have assumed it, explicitly or implicitly.] If a set of parents do not try to prevent a pregnancy, do not obtain an abortion, and then at the time of birth of the child do not put it out for adoption, but rather take it home with them, then they have assumed responsibility for it, they have given it rights, and they cannot *now* withdraw support from it at the cost of its life because they now find it difficult to go on providing for it. But if they have taken all reasonable precautions against having a child, they do not simply by virtue of their biological relationship to the child who comes into existence have a special responsibility for it. They may wish to assume responsibility for it, or they may not wish to. And I am suggesting that if assuming responsibility for it would require large sacrifices, then they may refuse. . . .

Part 1 of conclusion: Abortion is permissible except in cases where it falls beneath the standard of Minimally Decent Samaritan

8. My argument will be found unsatisfactory on two counts by many of those who want to regard abortion as morally permissible. First, while I do argue that abortion is not impermissible, I do not argue that it is always permissible. There may well be cases in which carrying the child to term requires only Minimally Decent Samaritanism of the mother, and this is a standard we must not fall below. I am inclined to think it a merit of my account precisely that it does *not* give a general yes or a general no. It allows for and supports our sense that, for example, a sick and desperately frightened fourteen-year-old schoolgirl, pregnant due to rape, may *of course* choose abortion, and that any law which rules this out is an insane law. And it also allows for and supports our sense that in other cases resort to abortion is even positively indecent. It would be indecent in the woman to request an abortion, and indecent in a doctor to perform it, if she is in her seventh month, and wants the abortion to avoid the nuisance of postponing a trip abroad. The very fact that the arguments I have been drawing attention to treat all cases of abortion, or even all cases of abortion in which the mother's life is not at stake, as morally on a par ought to have made them suspect at the outset.

Part 2 of conclusion: The woman does not have a right to secure the death of her child, but only to remove it from her body

Secondly, while I am arguing for the permissibility of abortion in some cases, I am not arguing for the right to secure the death of the unborn child. It is easy to confuse these two things in that up to a certain point in the life of the fetus it is not able to survive outside the mother's body; hence removing it from her body guarantees its death. But they are importantly different. I have argued that you are not morally required to spend nine months in bed, sustaining the life of that violinist; but to say this is by no means to say that if, when you unplug yourself, there is a miracle and he survives, you then have to turn around and slit his throat. You may detach yourself even if this costs him his life; you have no right to be guaranteed his death, by some other means, if unplugging yourself does not kill him. There are some people who will feel dissatisfied by this feature of my argument. A woman may be utterly devastated by the thought of a child, a bit of herself, put out for adoption and never seen or heard of again. She may therefore want not merely that the child be detached from her, but more, that it die. Some opponents of abortion are inclined to regard this as beneath contempt—thereby showing insensitivity to what is surely a powerful source of despair. All the same, I agree that the desire for the child's death is not one which anybody may gratify, should it turn out to be possible to detach the child alive.

At this place, however, it should be remembered that we have only been pretending throughout that the fetus is a human being from the moment of conception. A very early abortion is surely not the killing of a person, and so is not dealt with by anything I have said here.

Discussion Questions

1. Do you agree with Thomson that abortion is morally defensible even if the fetus is a person? In her analogies does Thomson take the presumption of the personhood of the fetus as seriously as she does the personhood of the mother? Support your answers.
2. Imagine that you find a baby or toddler in your winter cabin. There is no one else around to help care for the child and, because of heavy snows, no way to get to town for the next eight months. Assuming that you have enough food in the cabin for both of you, do you have a moral obligation, as a Minimally Decent Samaritan, to let the child share your cabin for the next eight months? Would it be morally permissible for you to put the child outside even though you knew she would certainly die of exposure if you did? Discuss the analogy between this case and that of abortion.
3. Using the Aristotelean and Confucian doctrine of the mean, discuss whether being a Minimally Decent Samaritan is sufficient for living the good and virtuous life.
4. Does Thomson's argument that the fetus has no right to the mother's womb justify killing the fetus? Does Thomson do an adequate job of distinguishing between the right of a mother to have an abortion and the moral injunction against taking the life of the fetus? Support your answers.
5. Thomson argues that we have no responsibility for another person unless we have voluntarily assumed it. Do you agree? What are the implications of Thomson's argument for cases in which the woman chose to continue her pregnancy when the father did not want to have the child? Does the father have any moral obligation toward the child in terms of child support and sharing in the care of the child? Support your answers.
6. Discuss how Thomson would most likely stand in the debate over late-term "partial-birth" abortions.

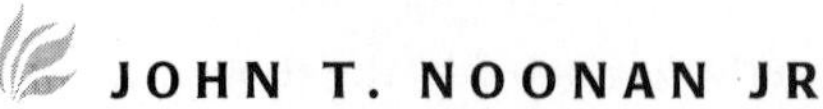

JOHN T. NOONAN JR.

An Almost Absolute Value in History

John Noonan is a professor of law at the University of California in Berkeley. Like Thomson's "A Defense of Abortion," Noonan's 1970 article on abortion remains one of the classics in abortion debates. Both Noonan and Thomson begin with the presumption that the fetus is a person with moral standing. Unlike Thomson, however, Noonan draws the conclusion that abortion is rarely, if ever morally justified. After rejecting the various criteria of personhood used by defenders of abortion, he concludes that anyone conceived by human parents is a person.

Critical Reading Questions

1. What, according to Noonan, is the most fundamental question in the abortion debate?
2. What does Noonan mean by "ensoulment"? Why does he claim that the notion of ensoulment does not require a theological basis?
3. On what grounds does Noonan reject viability as the point that distinguishes persons from nonpersons? What are the implications, according to Noonan, of using independence as a criterion for personhood?
4. On what grounds does Noonan reject experience and the possession of memories as an argument in support of abortion? What are some of the implications of this argument that Noonan finds unacceptable?
5. On what grounds does Noonan reject both parental feelings toward the fetus and social visibility as morally irrelevant to the moral status of the fetus?
6. What criterion does Noonan use to define personhood? What support does he offer for his definition?
7. What analogy does Noonan offer to support his argument that even if we are not sure that the fetus is a person, we should give the fetus the benefit of the doubt?
8. How does Noonan use "biological probabilities" to support his argument that the fetus is a person?
9. How does Noonan suggest that we resolve conflicts between the rights of the fetus and the rights of the mother? Under what conditions does Noonan permit abortion?
10. What philosophical principle is, according to Noonan, equivalent to the scriptural command to "love your neighbor as yourself"? How does this principle apply to the fetus?

"An Almost Absolute Value in History," *The Morality of Abortion: Legal and Historical Perspectives* (Cambridge, Mass.: Harvard University Press, 1970), 51–59. Notes have been omitted.

The most fundamental question involved in the long history of thought on abortion is: how do you determine the humanity of a being? To phrase the question that way is to put in comprehensive humanistic terms what the theologians either dealt with as an explicitly theological question under the heading of "ensoulment" or dealt with implicitly in their treatment of abortion. The Christian position as it originated did not depend on a narrow theological or philosophical concept. . . . The theological notion of ensoulment could easily be translated into humanistic language by substituting "human" for "rational soul"; the problem of knowing when a man is a man is common to theology and humanism.

If one steps outside the specific categories used by the theologians, the answer they gave can be analyzed as a refusal to discriminate among human beings on the basis of their varying potentialities. Once conceived, the being was recognized as man because he had man's potential. The criterion for humanity, thus, was simple and all-embracing: if you are conceived by human parents, you are human.

The strength of this position may be tested by a review of some of the other distinctions offered in the contemporary controversy over legalizing abortion. Perhaps the most popular distinction is in terms of viability. Before an age of so many months, the fetus is not viable, that is, it cannot be removed from the mother's womb and live apart from her. To that extent, the life of the fetus is absolutely dependent on the life of the mother. This dependence is made the basis of denying recognition to its humanity.

There are difficulties with this distinction. One is that the perfection of artificial incubation may make the fetus viable at any time: it may be removed and artificially sustained. Experiments with animals already show that such a procedure is possible. This hypothetical extreme case relates to an actual difficulty: there is considerable elasticity to the idea of viability. Mere length of life is not an exact measure. The viability of the fetus depends on the extent of its anatomical and functional development. . . .

The most important objection to this approach is that dependence is not ended by viability. The fetus is still absolutely dependent on someone's care in order to continue existence; indeed a child of one or three or even five years of age is absolutely dependent on another's care for existence; uncared for, the older fetus or the younger child will die as surely as the early fetus detached from the mother. The unsubstantial lessening in dependence at viability does not seem to signify any special acquisition of humanity.

A second distinction has been attempted in terms of experience. A being who has had experience, has lived and suffered, who possesses memories, is more human than one who has not. Humanity depends on formation by experience. The fetus is thus "unformed" in the most basic human sense. . . .

This distinction is not serviceable for the embryo which is already experiencing and reacting. The embryo is responsive to touch after eight weeks and at least at that point is experiencing. At an earlier stage the zygote is certainly alive and responding to its environment. The distinction may also be challenged by the rare case where aphasia has erased adult memory: has it erased humanity? More fundamentally, this distinction leaves even the older fetus or the younger child to be treated as an unformed inhuman thing. Finally, it is not clear why experience as such confers humanity. It could be argued that certain central experiences such as loving or learning are necessary to make a man human. But then human beings who have failed to love or to learn might be excluded from the class called man.

A third distinction is made by appeal to the sentiments of adults. If a fetus dies, the grief of the parents is not the grief they would have for a living child. The fetus is an unnamed "it" till birth, and is not perceived as personality until at least the fourth month of existence when movements in the womb manifest a vigorous presence demanding joyful recognition by the parents.

Yet feeling is notoriously an unsure guide to the humanity of others. Many groups of humans have had difficulty in feeling that persons of another tongue, color, religion, sex are as human as they. Apart from reactions to alien groups, we mourn the loss of a ten-year-old boy more than the loss of his one-day-old brother or his 90-year-old grandfather. The difference felt and the grief expressed vary with the potentialities extinguished, or the experience wiped out; they do not seem to point to any substantial difference in the humanity of baby, boy, or grandfather.

Distinctions are also made in terms of sensation by the parents. The embryo is felt within the womb only after about the fourth month. The embryo is seen only at birth. What can be neither seen nor felt is different from what is tangible. If the fetus cannot be seen or touched at all, it cannot be perceived as man.

Yet experience shows that sight is even more untrustworthy than feeling in determining humanity. By sight, color became an appropriate index for saying who was a man, and the evil of racial discrimination was given foundation. Nor can touch provide the test; a being confined by sickness, "out of touch" with others, does not thereby seem to lose his humanity. To the extent that touch still has appeal as a criterion, it appears to be a survival of the old English idea of "quickening"—a possible mistranslation of the Latin *animatus* used in the canon law. To that extent touch as a criterion seems to be dependent on the Aristotelian notion of ensoulment, and to fall when this notion is discarded.

Finally, a distinction is sought in social visibility. The fetus is not socially perceived as human. It cannot communicate with others. Thus, both subjectively and objectively, it is not a member of society. As moral rules are rules for the behavior of members of society to each other, they cannot be made for behavior toward what is not yet a member. Excluded from the society of men, the fetus is excluded from the humanity of men.

By force of the argument from the consequences, this distinction is to be rejected. It is more subtle than that founded on an appeal to physical sensation, but it is equally dangerous in its implications. If humanity depends on social recognition, individuals or whole groups may be dehumanized by being denied any status in their society. Such a fate is fictionally portrayed in *1984* and has actually been the lot of many men in many societies. In the Roman empire, for example, condemnation to slavery meant the practical denial of most human rights; in the Chinese Communist world, landlords have been classified as enemies of the people and so treated as nonpersons by the state. Humanity does not depend on social recognition, though often the failure of society to recognize the prisoner, the alien, the heterodox as human has led to the destruction of human beings. Anyone conceived by a man and a woman is human. Recognition of this condition by society follows a real event in the objective order, however imperfect and halting the recognition. Any attempt to limit humanity to exclude some group runs the risk of furnishing authority and precedent for excluding other groups in the name of the consciousness or perception of the controlling group in the society.

A philosopher may reject the appeal to the humanity of the fetus because he views "humanity" as a secular view of the soul and because he doubts the existence of anything real and objective which can be identified as humanity. One answer to such a philosopher is to ask how he reasons about moral questions without supposing that there is a sense in which he and the others of whom he speaks are human. Whatever group is taken as the society which determines who may be killed is thereby taken as human. A second answer is to ask if he does not believe that there is a right and wrong way of deciding moral questions. If there is such a difference, experience may be appealed to: to decide who is human on the basis of the sentiment of a given society has led to consequences which rational men would characterize as monstrous. . . .

There is a kind of continuity in all life, but the earlier stages of the elements of human life possess tiny probabilities of development. Consider for example, the spermatozoa in any normal ejaculate: there are about 200,000,000 in any single ejaculate, of which one has a chance of developing into a zygote. Consider the oocytes which may become ova: there are 100,000 to 1,000,000 oocytes in a female infant, of which a maximum of 390 are ovulated. But once spermatozoon and ovum meet and the conceptus is formed, such studies as have been made show that roughly in only 20 percent of the cases will spontaneous abortion occur. In other words, the chances are about 4 out of 5 that this new being will develop. At this stage in the life of the being there is a sharp shift in probabilities, an immense jump in potentialities. . . .

It may be asked, What does a change in biological probabilities have to do with establishing humanity?

The argument from probabilities is not aimed at establishing humanity but at establishing an objective discontinuity which may be taken into account in moral discourse. As life itself is a matter of probabilities, as most moral reasoning is an estimate of probabilities, so it seems in accord with the structure of reality and the nature of moral thought to found a moral judgment on the change in probabilities at conception. The appeal to probabilities is the most commonsensical of arguments, to a greater or smaller degree all of us base our actions on probabilities, and in morals, as in law, prudence and negligence are often measured by the account one has taken of the probabilities. If the chance is 200,000,000 to 1 that the movement in the bushes into which you shoot is a man's, I doubt if many persons would hold you careless in shooting; but if the chances are 4 out of 5 that the movement is a human being's, few would acquit you of blame. Would the argument be different if only one out of ten children conceived came to term? Of course this argument would be different. This argument is an appeal to probabilities that actually exist, not to any and all states of affairs which may be imagined.

The probabilities as they do exist do not show the humanity of the embryo in the sense of a demonstration in logic any more than the probabilities of the movement in the bush being a man demonstrate beyond all doubt that the being is a man. The appeal is a "buttressing" consideration, showing the plausibility of the standard adopted. The argument focuses on the decisional factor in any moral judgment and assumes that part of the business of a moralist is drawing lines. One evidence of the nonarbitrary character of the line drawn is the difference of probabilities on either side of it. If a spermatozoon is destroyed, one destroys a being which had a chance of far less than 1 in 200 million of developing into a reasoning being, possessed of the genetic code, a heart and other organs, and capable of pain. If a fetus is destroyed, one destroys a being already possessed of the genetic code, organs, and sensitivity to pain, and one which had an 80 percent chance of developing further into a baby outside the womb who, in time, would reason.

The positive argument for conception as the decisive moment of humanization is that at conception the new being receives the genetic code. It is this genetic information which determines his characteristics, which is the biological carrier of the possibility of human wisdom, which makes him a self-evolving being. A being with a human genetic code is man. . . .

Even with the fetus weighed as human, one interest could be weighed as equal or superior: that of the mother in her own life. The casuists between 1450 and 1895 were willing to weigh this interest as superior. Since 1895, that interest was given decisive weight only in the two special cases of the cancerous uterus and the ectopic pregnancy. In both of these cases the fetus itself had little chance of survival even if the abortion were not performed. As the balance was once struck in favor of the mother whenever her life was endangered, it could be so struck again. The balance reached between 1895 and 1930 attempted prudentially and pastorally to forestall a multitude of exceptions for interests less than life.

The perception of the humanity of the fetus and the weighing of fetal rights against other human rights constituted the work of the moral analysts. But what spirit animated their abstract judgments? For the Christian community it was the injunction of Scripture to love your neighbor as yourself. The fetus as human was a neighbor; his life had parity with one's own. The commandment gave life to what otherwise would have been only rational calculation.

The commandment could be put in humanistic as well as theological terms: do not injure your fellow man without reason. In these terms, once the humanity of the fetus is perceived, abortion is never right except in self-defense. When life must be taken to save life, reason alone cannot say that a mother must prefer a child's life to her own. With this exception, now of great rarity, abortion violates the rational humanist tenet of the equality of human lives.

Discussion Questions

1. Noonan argues that parents' feelings toward their fetus are morally irrelevant. Discuss how a care ethicist, such as Nel Noddings, might respond to Noonan's argument.

2. According to Noonan, "anyone conceived by a man and a woman is human [a person]." Do you agree? Critically evaluate the premises that Noonan offers in support of this definition of personhood.
3. Discuss Noonan's criterion of personhood in light of the fact that it is now possible to clone human beings.[36]
4. Imagine a conversation between Noonan and Thomson. How might Noonan respond to Thomson's defense of abortion? How might Thomson respond to Noonan's claim that abortion is never right except in cases of self-defense?
5. While Noonan supports the Catholic position on abortion, he points out that this position can be supported on rational philosophical or humanistic premises. Has Noonan done an adequate job of supporting his position on abortion using only philosophical premises? Support your answer.

MARY ANNE WARREN

The Moral Significance of Birth

Mary Anne Warren is a professor of philosophy at San Francisco State University. Warren defends a pro-choice position on abortion: Women have a fundamental right to make their own decisions about their bodies. After rejecting the traditional criteria of personhood, including that used by Noonan, Warren argues that personhood does not begin until after birth. Because the fetus is not a person, abortion can be justified under any circumstances. Her definition of personhood also permits infanticide under some circumstances.

Critical Reading Questions

1. According to Warren, what is the relationship between moral and legal rights?
2. What are Warren's arguments against the use of the "intrinsic-properties assumption" and the "single-criterion assumption" as the foundation of moral rights?
3. Why does Warren reject both sentience and viability as sufficient conditions for personhood?
4. What arguments does Warren use in support of self-awareness as a condition for personhood?
5. Why does Warren consider early infanticide morally preferable to infanticide after a few weeks, even though the two-week-old infant is not yet a person?
6. What arguments does Warren use to support her claim that, in our society, we should extend protection to human infants even though they are not yet persons? What are

"The Moral Significance of Birth," *Hypatia* 4, no. 3 (Fall 1989): 46–65. Notes have been omitted.

some of the problems involved in extending the same protection to sentient, late-term fetuses?

7. What is the relationship, according to Warren, between personhood and being a member of a community? Does personhood require that one be a member of a social community?
8. What does Warren mean when she says that granting legal personhood to the fetus is "necessarily incompatible" with respect for the personhood of women? How does Warren deal with the conflict between maternal autonomy and protection of the fetus?

Does birth make a difference to the moral right of the fetus/infant? Should it make a difference to its legal rights? Most contemporary philosophers believe that birth cannot make a difference to moral rights. If this is true, then it becomes difficult to justify either a moral or a legal distinction between late abortion and infanticide. I argue that the view that birth is irrelevant to moral rights rests upon two highly questionable assumptions about the theoretical foundations of moral rights. If we reject these assumptions, then we are free to take account of the contrasting biological and social relationships that make even relatively late abortion morally different from infanticide.

English common law treats the moment of live birth as the point at which a legal person comes into existence. Although abortion has often been prohibited, it has almost never been classified as homicide. In contrast, infanticide generally is classified as a form of homicide, even where (as in England) there are statutes designed to mitigate the severity of the crime in certain cases. But many people—including some feminists—now favor the extension of equal legal rights to some or all fetuses (S. Callahan 1984, 1986). The extension of legal personhood to fetuses would not only threaten women's right to choose abortion, but also undermine other fundamental rights. I will argue that because of these dangers, birth remains the most appropriate place to mark the existence of a new legal person. . . .

THE DENIAL OF THE MORAL SIGNIFICANCE OF BIRTH

The view that birth is irrelevant to moral rights is shared by philosophers on all points of the spectrum of moral views about abortion. For the most conservative, birth adds nothing to the infant's moral rights, since all of those rights have been present since conception. Moderates hold that the fetus acquires an equal right to life at some point after conception but before birth. The most popular candidates for this point of moral demarcation are (1) the stage at which the fetus becomes viable (i.e., capable of surviving outside the womb, with or without medical assistance), and (2) the stage at which it becomes sentient (i.e., capable of having experiences, including that of pain). For those who hold a view of this sort, both infanticide and abortion at any time past the critical stage are forms of homicide, and there is little reason to distinguish between them either morally or legally.

Finally, liberals hold that even relatively late abortion is sometimes morally acceptable, and that at no time is abortion the moral equivalent of homicide. However, few liberals wish to hold that infanticide is not—at least sometimes—morally comparable to homicide. Consequently, the presumption that being born makes no difference to one's moral rights creates problems for the liberal view of abortion. Unless the liberal can establish some grounds for a general moral distinction between late abortion and early infanticide, she must either retreat to a moderate position on abortion, or else conclude that infanticide is not so bad after all.

To those who accept the intrinsic-properties assumption, birth can make little difference to the moral standing of the fetus/infant. For birth does not seem to alter any intrinsic property that could reasonably be linked to the possession of a strong right to life. Newborn infants have very nearly the same intrinsic properties as do fetuses shortly before birth. . . .

Prenatal neurophysiology and behavior suggest that human fetuses begin to have rudimentary sensory experiences at some time during the second trimester of pregnancy. . . .

These two theories are worth examining, not only because they illustrate the difficulties generated by the intrinsic-properties and single-criterion assumptions, but also because each includes valid insights that need to be integrated into a more comprehensive account. Both Sumner and Tooley are partially right. Unlike "genetic humanity"—a property possessed by fertilized human ova—sentience and self-awareness are properties that have some general relevance to what we may owe another being in the way of respect and protection. However, neither the sentience criterion nor the self-awareness criterion can explain the moral significance of birth.

THE SENTIENCE CRITERION

Both newborn infants and late-term fetuses show clear signs of sentience. For instance, they are apparently capable of having visual experiences. Infants will often turn away from bright lights, and those who have done intrauterine photography have sometimes observed a similar reaction in the late-term fetus when bright lights are introduced in its vicinity. Both may respond to loud noises, voices, or other sounds, so both can probably have auditory experiences. They are evidently also responsive to touch, taste, motion, and other kinds of sensory stimulation.

The sentience of infants and late-term fetuses makes a difference to how they should be treated, by contrast with fertilized ova or first-trimester fetuses. Sentient beings are usually capable of experiencing painful as well as pleasurable or effectively neutral sensations. . . . Thus, sentient beings may plausibly be said to have a moral right not to be deliberately subjected to pain in the absence of any compelling reason. For those who prefer not to speak of rights, it is still plausible that a capacity for sentience gives an entity some moral standing. . . .

But it is not clear that sentience is a sufficient condition for moral equality, since there are many clearly-sentient creatures (e.g., mice) to which most of us would not be prepared to ascribe equal moral standing. . . .

The 1973 *Roe v. Wade* decision treats the presumed viability of third-trimester fetuses as a basis for permitting states to restrict abortion rights in order to protect fetal life in the third trimester, but not earlier. Yet viability is relative, among other things, to the medical care available to the pregnant woman and her infant. Increasingly sophisticated neonatal intensive care has made it possible to save many more premature infants than before, thus altering the average age of viability. Someday it may be possible to keep even first-trimester fetuses alive and developing normally outside the womb. The viability criterion seems to imply that the advent of total ectogenesis (artificial gestation from conception to birth) would automatically eliminate women's right to abortion, even in the earliest stages of pregnancy. At the very least, it must imply that as many aborted fetuses as possible should be kept alive through artificial gestation. But the mere technological possibility of providing artificial wombs for huge numbers of human fetuses could not establish such a moral obligation. A massive commitment to ectogenesis would probably be ruinously expensive, and might prove contrary to the interests of parents of children. The viability criterion forces us to make a hazardous leap from the technologically possible to the morally mandatory.

The sentience criterion at first appears more promising as a means of defending a moderate view of abortion. It provides an intuitively plausible distinction between early and late abortion. Unlike the viability criterion, it is unlikely to be undermined by new biomedical technologies. . . .

The strong version of the sentience criterion treats sentience as a sufficient condition for having full and equal moral standing. The weak version treats sentience as sufficient for having some moral standing, but not necessarily full and equal moral standing. . . .

[According to the strong version] any being which has even minimal capacities for sensory experience is the moral equal of any person. If we accept this theory, then we must conclude that not only is late abortion the moral equivalent of homicide, but so is the killing of such sentient nonhuman beings as mice. . . . [According to the weak version] all sentient beings have some moral standing, but beings that are more highly sentient have greater moral standing than do less highly sentient beings. This weaker version of the sentience criterion leaves room for a distinction between the moral standing of mice and that of sentient humans—provided, that is, that mice can be shown to be less highly sentient. However, it will not support the moral equality of late-term fetuses, since the relatively undeveloped condition of fetal brains almost certainly means that fetuses are less highly sentient than older human beings. . . .

THE SELF-AWARENESS CRITERION

Although newborn infants are regarded as persons in both law and common moral conviction, they lack certain mental capacities that are typical of persons. They have sensory experiences, but, as Tooley points out, they probably do not yet think, or have a sense of who they are, or a desire to continue to exist. It is not unreasonable to suppose that these facts make some difference to their moral standing. Other things being equal, it is surely worse to kill a self-aware being that wants to go on living than one that has never been self-aware and that has no such preference. If this is true, then it is hard to avoid the conclusion that neither abortion nor infanticide is quite as bad as the killing of older human beings. And indeed many human societies seem to have accepted that conclusion. . . .

But if infanticide is to be considered, it is better that it be done immediately after birth, before the bonds of love and care between the infant and the mother (and other persons) have grown any stronger than they may already be. Postponing the question of the infant's acceptance for weeks or months would be cruel to all concerned. Although an infant may be little more sentient or self-aware at two weeks of age than at birth, its death is apt to be a greater tragedy—not for it, but for those who have come to love it. I suspect that this is why, where infanticide is tolerated, the decision to kill or abandon an infant must usually be made rather quickly. If this consideration is morally relevant—and I think it is—then the self-awareness criterion fails to illuminate some of the morally salient aspects of infanticide. . . .

WHY PROTECT INFANTS?

I have already mentioned some of the reasons for protecting human infants more carefully than we protect most comparably-sentient nonhuman beings. Most people care deeply about infants, particularly—but not exclusively—their own. Normal human adults (and children) are probably "programmed" by their biological nature to respond to human infants with care and concern. For the mother, in particular, that response is apt to begin well before the infant is born. But even for her it is likely to become more intense after the infant's birth. The infant at birth enters the human social world, where, if it lives, it becomes involved in social relationships with others, of kinds that can only be dimly foreshadowed before birth. It begins to be known and cared for, not just as a potential member of the family or community, but as a socially present and responsive individual. . . . The newborn is not yet self-aware, but it is already (rapidly becoming) a social being.

Thus, although the human newborn may have no intrinsic properties that can ground a moral right to life stronger than that of a fetus just before birth, its emergence into the social world makes it appropriate to treat it as if it had such a stronger right. This, in effect, is what the law has done, through the doctrine that a person begins to exist at birth. . . .

Another reason for condemning infanticide is that, at least in relatively privileged nations like our own, infants whose parents cannot raise them can usually be placed with people who will love them and take good care of them. This means that infanticide is rarely in the infant's own best interests, and would often deprive some potential adoptive individual or family of a great benefit. . . .

But have I not left the door open to the claim that infanticide may still be justified in some places, e.g., where there is severe poverty and a lack of accessible adoption agencies or where women face exceptionally harsh penalties for "illegitimate" births? I have, and deliberately. The moral case against the toleration of infanticide is contingent upon the existence of morally preferable options. Where economic hardship, the lack of contraception and abortion, and other forms of sexual and political oppression have eliminated all such options, there will be instances in which infanticide is the least tragic of a tragic set of choices. In such circumstances, the enforcement of extreme sanctions against infanticide can constitute an additional injustice.

WHY BIRTH MATTERS

I have defended what most regard as needing no defense, i.e., the ascription of an equal right to life to human infants. Under reasonably favorable conditions that policy can protect the rights and interests of all concerned, including infants, biological parents, and potential adoptive parents.

But if protecting infants is such a good idea, then why is it not a good idea to extend the same strong protections to sentient fetuses? The question is not whether sentient fetuses ought to be protected: of course they should. Most women readily accept the responsibility of doing whatever they can to ensure that their (voluntarily continued) pregnancies are successful, and that no avoidable harm comes to the fetus. Negligent or malevolent actions by third parties which result in death or injury to pregnant women or their potential children should be subject to moral censure and legal prosecution. A just and caring society would do much more than ours does to protect the health of all its members, including pregnant women. The question is whether the law should accord to late-term fetuses *exactly the same* protections as are accorded to infants and older human beings.

The case for doing so might seem quite strong. . . .

But there is one crucial consideration which this argument leaves out. It is impossible to treat fetuses *in utero* as if they were persons without treating women as if they were something less than persons. The extension of equal rights to sentient fetuses would inevitably license severe violations of women's basic rights to personal autonomy and physical security. In the first place, it would rule out most second-trimester abortions performed to protect the women's life or health. Such abortions might sometimes be construed as a form of self-defense. But the right to self-defense is not usually taken to mean that one may kill innocent persons just because their continued existence poses some threat to one's own life or health. If abortion must be justified as self-defense, then it will rarely be performed until the woman is already in some extreme danger, and perhaps not even then. Such a policy would cost some women their lives, while others would be subjected to needless suffering and permanent physical harm.

Other alarming consequences of the drive to extend more equal rights to fetuses are already apparent in the United States. In the past decade it has become increasingly common for hospitals or physicians to obtain court orders requiring women in labor to undergo Caesarean sections, against their will, for what is thought to be the good of the fetus. . . . Forced Caesareans threaten to reduce women to the status of inanimate objects—containers which may be opened at the will of others in order to get at their contents. . . .

Another danger in extending equal legal protections to sentient fetuses is that women will increasingly be blamed, and sometimes legally prosecuted, when they miscarry or give birth to premature, sick, or abnormal infants. It is reasonable to hold the caretakers of infants legally responsible if their charges are harmed because of their avoidable negligence. But when a woman miscarries or gives birth to an abnormal infant, the cause of harm might be traced to any of an enormous number of actions or circumstances which would not normally constitute any legal offense. She might have gotten too much exercise or too little, eaten the wrong foods or the wrong quantity of the right ones, or taken or failed to take certain drugs. She might have smoked, consumed alcohol, or gotten too little sleep. She might have "permitted" her health to be damaged by hard work, by unsafe employment conditions, by the lack of affordable medical care, by living near a source of industrial pollution, by a physically or mentally abusive partner, or in any number of other ways.

Are such supposed failures on the part of pregnant women potentially to be construed as child abuse or negligent homicide? If sentient fetuses are entitled to the same legal protections as infants, then it would seem so. . . .

Such an approach to the protection of fetuses authorizes the legal regulation of virtually every aspect of women's public and private lives, and thus is incompatible with even the most minimal right to autonomy. Moreover, such laws are apt to prove counterproductive, since the fear of prosecution may deter poor or otherwise vulnerable women from seeking medical care during pregnancy. I am not suggesting that women whose apparent negligence causes prenatal harm to their infants should always be immune from criticism. However, if we want to improve the health of infants we would do better to provide the services women need to protect their health, rather than seeking to use the law to punish those whose prenatal care has been less than ideal. . . .

Such arguments will not persuade those who deeply believe that fetuses are already persons, with equal moral rights. How, they will ask, is denying legal equality to sentient fetuses different from denying it to any other powerless group of human beings? If some human beings are more equal than others, then how can any of us feel safe? The answer is twofold.

First, pregnancy is a relationship different from any other, including that between parents and already-born children. It is not just one of innumerable situations in which the rights of one individual may come into conflict with those of another; it is probably the *only* case in which the legal personhood of one human being is necessarily incompatible with that of another. Only in pregnancy is the organic functioning of one human individual biologically inseparable from that of another. This organic unity makes it impossible for others to provide the fetus with medical care or any other presumed benefit, except by doing something to or for the woman. To try to "protect" the fetus other than through her cooperation and consent is effectively to nullify her right to autonomy, and potentially to expose her to violent physical assaults such as would not be legally condoned in any other type of case. The uniqueness of pregnancy helps to explain why the toleration of abortion does not lead to the disenfranchisement of other groups of human beings, as opponents of abortion often claim. . . .

But, granting the uniqueness of pregnancy, why is it *women's* rights that should be privileged? If women and fetuses cannot both be legal persons then why not favor the fetus, e.g., on the grounds that they are more helpless, or more innocent, or have a longer life expectancy? It is difficult to justify this apparent bias towards women without appealing to the empirical fact that women are already persons in the usual, nonlegal sense—already thinking, self-aware, fully social beings—and fetuses are not. Regardless of whether we stress the intrinsic properties of persons, or the social and relational dimensions of personhood, this distinction remains. Even sentient fetuses do not yet have either the cognitive capacities or the richly interactive social involvements typical of persons.

This "not yet" is morally decisive. It is wrong to treat persons as if they do not have equal basic rights. Other things being equal, it is worse to deprive persons of their most basic moral and legal rights than to refrain from extending such rights to beings that are not persons. This is one important element of truth in the self-awareness criterion. If fetuses were already thinking, self-aware, socially responsive members of communities, then nothing could justify refusing them the equal protection of the law. In that case, we would sometimes be forced to balance the rights of the fetus against those of the woman, and sometimes the scales might be almost equally weighted. However, if women are persons and fetuses are not, then the balance must swing toward women's rights.

CONCLUSION

Birth is morally significant because it marks the end of one relationship and the beginning of others. It marks the end of pregnancy, a relationship so intimate that it is impossible to extend the equal protection of the law to fetuses without severely infringing women's most basic rights. Birth also marks the beginning of the infant's existence as a socially responsive member of a human community. Although the infant is not instantly transformed into a person at the moment of birth, it does become a biologically separate human being. As such, it can be known and cared for as a particular individual. It can also be vigorously protected without negating the basic rights of women. There are circumstances in which infanticide may be the best of a bad set of options. But our own society has both the ability and the desire to protect infants, and there is no reason why we should not do so.

We should not, however, seek to extend the same degree of protection to fetuses. Both late-term fetuses and newborn infants are probably capable of sentience. Both are precious to those who want children; and both need to be protected from a variety of possible harms. All of these factors contribute to the moral standing of the late-term fetus, which is substantial. However, to extend equal legal rights to fetuses is necessarily to deprive pregnant women of the rights to personal autonomy, physical integrity, and sometimes life itself. *There is room for only one person with full and equal rights inside a single human skin.* That is why it is birth, rather than sentience, viability, or some other prenatal milestone that must mark the beginning of legal parenthood.

REFERENCES

Callahan, Sidney. 1984. Value choices in abortion. In *Abortion: Understanding differences.* Sidney Callahan and Daniel Callahan, eds. New York and London: Plenum Press.

Callahan, Sidney. 1986. Abortion and the sexual agenda. *Commonweal,* April 25, 232–238.

Tooley, Michael. 1983. *Abortion and infanticide.* Oxford: Oxford University Press.

Discussion Questions

1. Does Warren confuse cultural norms and legal rights with moral rights? Can she defend her position without reference to cultural norms and legal rights? Use specific examples to support your answers.
2. Discuss Warren's claim that deontology, rights ethics, and care ethics all support abortion and early infanticide. Would a utilitarian also agree with Warren's position on abortion? How would a Buddhist respond to Warren's argument? Support your answers.
3. Do you agree with Warren that self-concept is necessary for personhood? How can we determine if a being has a self-concept and a desire for a future? Support your answers. What are the implications of accepting this criterion for the moral standing of infants and brain-damaged, senile, and comatose humans? Would Warren permit euthanasia for these groups of humans? What are the implications of her criteria for how we should treat adult nonhuman mammals?
4. Massachusetts Institute of Technology psychology professor Steven Pinker claims that the killing of newborn babies is perfectly natural and has been practiced and accepted in most cultures. "To a biologist," he points out, "birth is as arbitrary a milestone as any other . . . so how do you provide grounds for outlawing neonaticide? The facts don't make it easy."[37] Discuss how Warren might respond to Pinker's claim. What is the moral relevance, if any, of their claim that infanticide is natural and, in some cultures, acceptable?
5. The United Nations Population Fund advocates abortion as a means of population control, especially in areas of the world that are already plagued by overpopulation, such as China and India.[38] Discuss what Warren would most likely think of this policy.

DON MARQUIS

Why Abortion Is Immoral

Don Marquis is a professor of philosophy at the University of Kansas. Marquis disagrees with philosophers such as Warren who believe that birth is morally significant in terms of the value of a human's life. He argues instead that the moral presumption against killing a fetus is as strong as the moral presumption against killing an adult human or newborn because both involve the murder of humans after birth, and abortion deprives the victims of the value of the activities, experiences, and enjoyments of their future. He concludes that while abortion may sometimes be morally permissible, it is prima facie seriously immoral.

Critical Reading Questions

1. What is the major presumption of Marquis's argument that abortion is immoral?
2. Why, according to Marquis, is it wrong to kill adult humans?
3. What does Marquis mean by the phrase a "future like ours"?
4. What are the implications of Marquis's argument for the killing of nonhuman animals? What are the implications of Marquis's argument for euthanasia?
5. On what grounds does Marquis dismiss arguments against abortion that depend on the category of personhood?
6. Why is a "future like ours" of value to the fetus? Why is it wrong to deprive a fetus of this future?
7. What are the implications of Marquis's argument for the use of contraception?

The view that abortion is, with rare exceptions, seriously immoral has received little support in the recent philosophical literature. No doubt most philosophers affiliated with secular institutions of higher education believe that the anti-abortion position is either a symptom of irrational religious dogma or a conclusion generated by seriously confused philosophical argument. The purpose of this essay is to undermine this general belief. This essay sets out an argument that purports to show, as well as any argument in ethics can show, that abortion is, except possibly in rare cases, seriously immoral, that it is in the same moral category as killing an innocent adult human being.

The argument is based on a major assumption. Many of the most insightful and careful writers on the ethics of abortion—such as Joel Feinberg, Michael Tooley, Mary Anne Warren, H. Tristram Engelhardt, Jr., L. W. Sumner, John T. Noonan, Jr., and Philip Devine*—believe that whether or not abortion is morally permissible stands or falls on

---

Don Marquis, "Why Abortion is Immoral," *Journal of Philosophy*, vol. 86, April 1989. Some notes have been omitted.

*Feinberg, "Abortion," in *Matters of Life and Death: New Introductory Essays in Moral Philosophy*, Tom Regan, ed. (New York: Random House, 1986), pp. 256–293; Tooley, "Abortion and Infanticide," *Philosophy and Public Affairs*, II, 1 (1972): 37–65, Tooley, *Abortion and Infanticide* (New York: Oxford, 1984); Warren, "On the Moral and Legal Status of Abortion," *The Monist*, LVII, 1 (1973): 43–61; Engelhardt, "The Ontology of Abortion," *Ethics*, LXXXIV, 3 (1974): 217–234; Sumner, *Abortion and Moral Theory* (Princeton: University Press, 1981); Noonan, "An Almost Absolute Value in History," in *The Morality of Abortion: Legal and Historical Perspectives*, Noonan, ed. (Cambridge: Harvard, 1970); and Devine, *The Ethics of Homicide* (Ithaca: Cornell, 1978).

whether or not a fetus is the sort of being whose life it is seriously wrong to end. The argument of this essay will assume, but not argue, that they are correct.

Also, this essay will neglect issues of great importance to a complete ethics of abortion. Some anti-abortionists will allow that certain abortions, such as abortion before implantation or abortion when the life of a woman is threatened by a pregnancy or abortion after rape, may be morally permissible. This essay will not explore the casuistry of these hard cases. The purpose of this essay is to develop a general argument for the claim that the overwhelming majority of deliberate abortions are seriously immoral. . . .

A necessary condition of resolving the abortion controversy is a more theoretical account of the wrongness of killing. After all, if we merely believe, but do not understand, why killing adult human beings such as ourselves is wrong, how could we conceivably show that abortion is either immoral or permissible?

In order to develop such an account, we can start from the following unproblematic assumption concerning our own case: it is wrong to kill *us*. Why is it wrong? Some answers can be easily eliminated. It might be said that what makes killing us wrong is that a killing brutalizes the one who kills. But the brutalization consists of being inured to the performance of an act that is hideously immoral; hence, the brutalization does not explain the immorality. It might be said that what makes killing us wrong is the great loss others would experience due to our absence. Although such hubris is understandable, such an explanation does not account for the wrongness of killing hermits, or those whose lives are relatively independent and whose friends find it easy to make new friends.

A more obvious answer is better. What primarily makes killing wrong is neither its effect on the murderer nor its effect on the victim's friends and relatives, but its effect on the victim. The loss of one's life is one of the greatest losses one can suffer. The loss of one's life deprives one of all the experiences, activities, projects, and enjoyments that would otherwise have constituted one's future. Therefore, killing someone is wrong, primarily because the killing inflicts (one of) the greatest possible losses on the victim. To describe this as the loss of life can be misleading, however. The change in my biological state does not by itself make killing me wrong. The effect of the loss of my biological life is the loss to me of all those activities, projects, experiences, and enjoyments which would otherwise have constituted my future personal life. These activities, projects, experiences, and enjoyments are either valuable for their own sakes or are means to something else that is valuable for its own sake. Some parts of my future are not valued by me now, but will come to be valued by me as I grow older and as my values and capacities change. When I am killed, I am deprived both of what I now value which would have been part of my future personal life, but also what I would come to value. Therefore, when I die, I am deprived of all of the value of my future. Inflicting this loss on me is ultimately what makes killing me wrong. This being the case, it would seem that what makes killing *any* adult human being prima facie seriously wrong is the loss of his or her future. . . .

The view that what makes killing wrong is the loss to the victim of the value of the victim's future gains additional support when some of its implications are examined. In the first place, it is incompatible with the view that it is wrong to kill only beings who are biologically human. It is possible that there exists a different species from another planet whose members have a future like ours. Since having a future like that is what makes killing someone wrong, this theory entails that it would be wrong to kill members of such a species. Hence, this theory is opposed to the claim that only life that is biologically human has great moral worth, a claim which many anti-abortionists have seemed to adopt. This opposition, which this theory has in common with personhood theories, seems to be a merit of the theory.

In the second place, the claim that the loss of one's future is the wrong-making feature of one's being killed entails the possibility that the futures of some actual nonhuman mammals on our own planet are sufficiently like ours that it is seriously wrong to kill them also. Whether some animals do have the same right to life as human beings depends on adding to the account of the wrongness of killing some additional account of just what it is about my future or the futures of other adult human beings which makes it wrong to kill us. No such additional account will be offered in this essay. Undoubtedly, the provision of such an account would be a very difficult matter. Undoubtedly, any such account would be quite controversial. Hence, it surely should not reflect badly on this sketch of an elementary theory of the wrongness of killing that it is indeterminate with respect to some very difficult issues regarding animal rights.

In the third place, the claim that the loss of one's future is the wrong-making feature of one's being killed does not entail, as sanctity of human life theories do, that active euthanasia is wrong. Persons who are severely and incurably ill, who face a future of pain and despair, and who wish to die will not have suffered a loss if they are killed. It is, strictly speaking, the value of a human's future which makes killing wrong in this theory. This being so, killing does not necessarily wrong some persons who are sick and dying. Of course, there may be other reasons for a prohibition of active euthanasia, but that is another matter. Sanctity-of-human-life theories seem to hold that active euthanasia is seriously wrong even in an individual case where there seems to be good reason for it independently of public policy considerations. This consequence is most implausible, and it is a plus for the claim that the loss of a future of value is what makes killing wrong that it does not share this consequence.

In the fourth place, the account of the wrongness of killing defended in this essay does straightforwardly entail that it is prima facie seriously wrong to kill children and infants, for we do presume that they have futures of value. Since we do believe that it is wrong to kill defenseless little babies, it is important that a theory of the wrongness of killing easily account for this. Personhood theories of the wrongness of killing, on the other hand, cannot straightforwardly account for the wrongness of killing infants and young children.* Hence, such theories must add special ad hoc accounts of the wrongness of killing the young. The plausibility of such ad hoc theories seems to be a function of how desperately one wants such theories to work. The claim that the primary wrong-making feature of a killing is the loss to the victim of the value of its future accounts for the wrongness of killing young children and infants directly; it makes the wrongness of such acts as obvious as we actually think it is. . . .

The claim that the primary wrong-making feature of a killing is the loss to the victim of the value of its future has obvious consequences for the ethics of abortion. The future of a standard fetus includes a set of experiences, projects, activities, and such which are identical with the futures of adult human beings and are identical with the futures of young children. Since the reason that is sufficient to explain why it is wrong to kill human beings after the time of birth is a reason that also applies to fetuses, it follows that abortion is prima facie seriously morally wrong.

This argument does not rely on the invalid inference that, since it is wrong to kill persons, it is wrong to kill potential persons also. The category that is morally central to this analysis is the category of having a valuable future like ours; it is not the category of personhood. The argument to the conclusion that abortion is prima facie seriously morally wrong proceeded independently of the notion of person or potential person or any equivalent. . . .

Of course, this value of a future-like-ours argument, if sound, shows only that abortion is prima facie wrong, not that it is wrong in any and all circumstances. Since the loss of the future to a standard fetus, if killed, is, however, at least as great a loss as the loss of the future to a standard adult human being who is killed, abortion, like ordinary killing, could be justified only by the most compelling reasons. The loss of one's life is almost the greatest misfortune that can happen to one. Presumably abortion could be justified in some circumstances, only if the loss consequent on failing to abort would be at least as great. Accordingly, morally permissible abortions will be rare indeed unless, perhaps, they occur so early in pregnancy that a fetus is not yet definitely an individual. Hence, this argument should be taken as showing that abortion is presumptively very seriously wrong, where the presumption is very strong—as strong as the presumption that killing another adult human being is wrong.

*Feinberg, Tooley, Warren, and Engelhardt have all dealt with this problem.

How complete an account of the wrongness of killing does the value of a future-like-ours account have to be in order that the wrongness of abortion is a consequence? This account does not have to be an account of the necessary conditions for the wrongness of killing. Some persons in nursing homes may lack valuable human futures, yet it may be wrong to kill them for other reasons. Furthermore, this account does not obviously have to be the sole reason killing is wrong where the victim did have a valuable future. This analysis claims only that, for any killing where the victim did have a valuable future like ours, having that future by itself is sufficient to create the strong presumption that the killing is seriously wrong. . . .

In this essay, it has been argued that the correct ethic of the wrongness of killing can be extended to fetal life and used to show that there is a strong presumption that any abortion is morally impermissible. If the ethic of killing adopted here entails, however, that contraception is also seriously immoral, then there would appear to be a difficulty with the analysis of this essay.

But this analysis does not entail that contraception is wrong. Of course, contraception prevents the actualization of a possible future of value. Hence, it follows from the claim that futures of value should be maximized that contraception is prima facie immoral. This obligation to maximize does not exist, however; furthermore, nothing in the ethics of killing in this paper entails that it does. The ethics of killing in this essay would entail that contraception is wrong only if something were denied a human future of value by contraception. Nothing at all is denied such a future by contraception, however.

Candidates for a subject of harm by contraception fall into four categories: (1) some sperm or other, (2) some ovum or other, (3) a sperm and an ovum separately, and (4) a sperm and an ovum together. Assigning the harm to some sperm [or ovum] is utterly arbitrary, . . . One might attempt to avoid these problems by insisting that contraception deprives both the sperm and the ovum separately of a valuable future like ours. On this alternative, too many futures are lost. Contraception was supposed to be wrong, because it deprived us of one future of value, not two. One might attempt to avoid this problem by holding that contraception deprives the combination of sperm and ovum of a valuable future like ours. But here the definite article misleads. At the time of contraception, there are hundreds of millions of sperm, one (released) ovum and millions of possible combinations of all of these. There is no actual combination at all. Is the subject of the loss to be a merely possible combination? Which one? This alternative does not yield an actual subject of harm either. Accordingly, the immorality of contraception is not entailed by the loss of a future-like-ours argument simply because there is no nonarbitrarily identifiable subject of the loss in the case of contraception.

The purpose of this essay has been to set out an argument for the serious presumptive wrongness of abortion subject to the assumption that the moral permissibility of abortion stands or falls on the moral status of the fetus. Since a fetus possesses a property, the possession of which in adult human beings is sufficient to make killing an adult human being wrong, abortion is wrong. This way of dealing with the problem of abortion seems superior to other approaches to the ethics of abortion, because it rests on an ethics of killing which is close to self-evident, because the crucial morally relevant property clearly applies to fetuses, and because the argument avoids the usual equivocations on "human life," "human being," or "person." The argument rests neither on religious claims nor on Papal dogma. It is not subject to the objection of "speciesism." Its soundness is compatible with the moral permissibility of euthanasia and contraception. It deals with our intuitions concerning young children.

Finally, this analysis can be viewed as resolving a standard problem—indeed, *the* standard problem—concerning the ethics of abortion. Clearly, it is wrong to kill adult human beings. Clearly, it is not wrong to end the life of some arbitrarily chosen single human cell. Fetuses seem to be like arbitrarily chosen human cells in some respects and like adult humans in other respects. The problem of the ethics of abortion is the problem of determining the fetal property that settles this moral controversy. The thesis of this essay is that the problem of the ethics of abortion, so understood, is solvable.

Discussion Questions

1. Without bringing in the concept of "personhood," discuss why it is wrong to kill newborns and adult humans. Apply your criteria to the killing of fetuses.
2. Break down Marquis's argument into its premises and conclusion. Analyze the argument. Are the premises acceptable? Are the premises complete? Does the conclusion follow from the premises? If not, come up with a counterargument that addresses Marquis's concerns.
3. Apply Marquis's argument to the use of RU 486. Discuss whether his argument against abortion would or would not preclude the use of the early abortion pill.
4. In his essay, Marquis does not address the future of the pregnant woman who wants an abortion. Even if we accept Marquis's claim that abortion is a prima facie wrong because it destroys the future of the fetus, are there circumstances where continuing the pregnancy might damage the value of the woman's future to such an extent that it overrides the value of her fetus's future? How about situations in which the fetus has a severe genetic anomaly associated with a life of suffering and/or death shortly after birth? Role-play a situation where you are discussing these possible exceptions with Marquis.
5. Discuss how both Thomson and Warren might respond to Marquis's argument.

STEVEN D. HALES

Abortion and Fathers' Rights

Steven Hales is a professor of philosophy at Bloomsburg University in Pennsylvania. In the selection from "Abortion and Fathers' Rights," Hales argues that there is a prima facie inconsistency between three widely accepted principles: (1) Women had a moral right to abortion on demand, a right that cannot be vetoed by the father, (2) Men and women have equal moral rights and duties and should have equal legal rights and duties; and (3) Parents have a moral duty to provide support for their children after they are born. He concludes that if a mother can escape the burdens of future duties to her progeny through abortion, then men should also be able to escape future duties to their progeny through the mechanism of refusal.

Critical Reading Questions

1. What are the three widely accepted principles, according to Hales, regarding abortion and parental rights?
2. What is the basis for a woman's right to an abortion?

"Abortion and Fathers' Rights," in *Reproduction, Technology, and Rights,* eds. James M. Humber and Robert F. Almeder (Totowa, NJ: 1996), pp. 5–26. Notes have been omitted.

3. Why does Hales maintain that these three principles are prima facie inconsistent?
4. How does Hales resolve the apparent conflict between the principle of equality, the father's moral duty to his future children, and the woman's right to avoid future child-rearing duties through abortion?
5. What is the fourth "commonly accepted principle" and why does Hales reject it in some cases?
6. What is a right of refusal? How and under what conditions would a father carry it out?
7. How does Hales use Judith Jarvis Thomson's violinist analogy to support his conclusion regarding a father's right of refusal?
8. How does Hales respond to the argument that the father's obligation is to the mother, not the future child?
9. How does Hales respond to the argument that by bearing the burden of pregnancy, a woman receives the "benefit of guaranteed paternal support"?
10. How does Hales respond to the appeal to social welfare arguments that state that it is in the interests of society that a father be compelled to support his children?

THE PROBLEM

In this chapter I argue that three widely accepted principles regarding abortion and parental rights are *prima facie* jointly inconsistent. These principles are probably accepted by most who consider themselves feminists, so the conundrum posed is particularly acute for them. There is one obvious way of resolving the inconsistency. However, as will be made clear, this solution is prevented by a fourth principle—that fathers have an absolute obligation to provide material support for their children. I argue that this principle is false, that fathers have no such absolute obligation, and thereby provide a way of making the first three principles consistent.

These three principles are apparently inconsistent.

1. Women have the moral right to get abortions on demand, at their discretion. They can make unilateral decisions whether or not to abort, and are not morally obligated to consult with the father, or any other person, before reaching a decision to abort. Moreover, neither the father nor any other person can veto or override a mother's decision about the disposition of the unborn fetus. She has first and last say about what happens in, and to, her body.

The principle formulated here is an extreme one. More moderate versions might replace it. . . . Such modifications will not substantially affect what will be said about fathers' rights, given suitable changes, *mutatis mutandis,* in the description of those rights.

2. Men and women have equal moral rights and duties, and should have equal legal rights and duties. . . .

3. Parents have a moral duty to provide support for their children once they are born. Any legal duties of support (e.g., child welfare laws or court-enforced child support) should supervene on this moral duty.

Given both (2) and (3), we can conclude that the mother and father have equal moral obligations toward their child once it is born. Although it is an interesting question as to *why* (3) is true (even granting that it is), the issue before us here is the distribution of rights and duties *before* the child is born, particularly during the pregnancy of the mother. Principle (1) tells us that the mother has the right to an abortion during her pregnancy. Since (2) tells us that men and women have equal moral rights, it seems that we can therefore conclude that men also have a right to an abortion. On the face of it, this seems either absurd or trivial: absurd because men clearly cannot get pregnant, and so it is silly to talk about them having a right to an abortion; and trivial because it may be true that this conditional right is trivially true of men: If one is pregnant, then one may get an abortion. So for a man to insist on his right to an abortion appears pointless. However, it is pointless only if we understand the right to an abortion in a certain way, viz, the right to an abortion is the right to end one's *own* pregnancy.

Why would anyone care about having a right to an abortion? There are a variety of reasons some women no longer want to be pregnant: They cannot afford another child, they are not psychologically prepared to be a parent, a child would hinder the lifestyle they wish to pursue, they do not want to endure the hardship of pregnancy, and so on. All of these reasons have to do with burdens or hardships that the mother faces in the future. For whatever reason, the mother is not (currently) willing to suffer these hardships, and so has an abortion in order to avoid them. Fortunately, the duties and burdens that the mother wants to escape are ones that she can in fact morally escape. She has no obligation to endure the hardship of pregnancy (according to [1]), nor any absolute, inevitable duty to shoulder the burden of an infant. True, these are burdens and duties that she faces if she continues with the pregnancy, but they are ones that she can avoid by having an abortion. Thus, it seems that the motivation for wanting a right to an abortion is because a mechanism is wanted to avoid future duties and burdens. Abortion constitutes just such a mechanism.

If it were immoral to avoid these future duties of childrearing (i.e., if they were absolute and morally inexorable), then clearly there could be no *right* to an abortion. Her right to an abortion is a liberty right; that is, having the right tells us that it is morally permissible for her to have an abortion. . . .

Now consider the case of the father. He, too, is facing future duties; in fact (aside from pregnancy itself), the same ones as the mother, as (2) and (3) specify. However, the father, having participated in conception, cannot escape the future duties he will have toward the child. The father can decide that he cannot afford another child, that he is not psychologically prepared to be a parent, that a child would hinder the lifestyle he wishes to pursue, and so on, to no avail. He is completely subject to the decisions of the mother. If she decides to have the child, she thereby ensures that the father has certain duties; duties that it is impossible for him to avoid. Even more, the mother is solely in charge: If she wants to have an abortion and the father does not want her to, she may anyway. If she does *not* want to have an abortion and the father does want her to, it is permissible for her to refuse to have one. If there is any conflict between the mother and the father here, the mother's wishes win out. . . .

It might be argued that, although true, this is an unavoidable (and hence acceptable) consequence of biology. The mother has some kind of absolute right over the disposition of her body, and in a battle of rights, these rights over one's body trump all other rights in the fray. So the fact that the fetus is in her body ensures that she has final say over it. Not only is this "right over one's body" supposed to guarantee that the mother can abort over the father's objections, but also that she can carry the child to term even if the father insists on an abortion. . . .

The difficulty is that it seems that we might agree to all of this and still argue that the father is ill treated. Even if biology prevents men and women from having *absolutely identical* means to exercise their rights, it remains that what we should do is try to achieve equal opportunity to exercise rights as much as possible. Perhaps we will never attain complete equality (biology may prevent us), but we should try our best.

Another objection is that since the father does *eo ipso* have a right to avoid future duties (he just has no opportunity or mechanism to exercise this right), (2) is satisfied, and (1)–(3) are consistent. However, I think it is plausible that genuine equality insists that not only do persons have various liberty rights, but also that they should have equality of opportunity to exercise these rights. So long as some, but not all, persons are equipped with the means to exercise their rights, we cannot say that people have *really* been provided with equal rights. So, even if fathers do have a right to avoid future duties, without any way of acting on this right, the equality principle (2) has *not* been satisfied. . . .

So, in order for us to satisfy our goal of achieving equality as best we can, we should not only admit that fathers have a right to avoid future duties, but there needs to be some mechanism by which they can, by personal fiat, exercise that right. Mothers have the right and a mechanism—the mechanism of abortion. The mechanism employed by fathers, of course, need not be abortion. The important thing to note is that even if we grant that the father cannot avail himself of *abortion* as a way out, it is a giant step from here to conclude that he cannot avail himself of *any* way out. Perhaps it will do to say that, sometime during the span of time that a mother may permissibly abort, a father may simply declare that he refuses to assume any future obligations. If we are prepared to speak loosely of mothers having the right to an abortion, we might also loosely talk of fathers having the right of refusal. By admitting that fathers have this right, we more closely approximate the ideal of moral parity. The right of refusal is to be designed as a parallel (as demanded by [2]) of the mother's right to an abortion (as specified in [1]). Let us put it this way: A man has the moral right to decide not to become a father (in the social, nonbiological sense) during the time that the woman he has impregnated may permissibly abort. He can make a unilateral decision whether to refuse fatherhood, and is not morally obliged to consult with the mother or any other person before reaching a decision. Moreover, neither the mother nor any other person can veto or override a man's decision about becoming a father. He has first and last say about what he does with his life in this regard.

Suppose that the mother is pregnant and the father tells her during the time that she may permissibly abort, "I think this was a big mistake, we should not have done this, I regret that you are pregnant, and wish you would have an abortion." The mother, according to principle (1), may fairly respond, "Sorry, I want the child, and will carry it to term even though you want me to abort." If the father has the right of refusal, he can justly respond, "OK, if that is your decision, have the child, but it will be solely your responsibility. I want out of the deal, and I do not want to have anything to do with the child or any responsibilities toward it." More than this will be needed, of course. The mother's declared intention to have an abortion does not constitute having one, nor is her declaration as expensive, difficult, and unappealing as the actual abortion. An adequate legal implementation of a father's right of refusal will involve written contracts and sufficient penalties to the father to make the exercise of his right of refusal as costly to him (in the broadest sense) as the mother's exercise of her right to an abortion is to her. Fathers should not find exercising a right of refusal to be more appealing than mothers generally find getting an abortion, but they should not find it less appealing either.

The right of refusal solved the problem of inconsistency among our three moral principles. However, this solution is blocked by a fourth commonly accepted principle:

> 4. Fathers are under an absolute moral obligation to provide for the welfare of their children, despite the intentions or desires of the father before the birth of the child. Something close to this is reflected in the law, and serves to underwrite paternity suits and at least some of the complaints about "deadbeat dads." . . .

Those willing to defend something like (4) often have in mind a case of a longish relationship in which the woman gets pregnant and the father, unwilling to be burdened with a child, ends the relationship, or leaves town. Surely the father should not be allowed to just saddle the mother with the child and get off scot-free. He willingly and voluntarily engaged in sex and knowingly took the risks in full awareness of the possibility of pregnancy. For him just to leave the mother and have no future duties toward the child is to dump 100 percent of the burden on the mother when she only assumed 50 percent of the risk. This, advocates of (4) claim, is manifestly unfair—it means that (ignoring disease and such) sex has no consequences for men, and massive consequences for women. This is why we need a principle like (4) that ensures that there are consequences for men too, and one of the reasons that we must protect a woman's right to an abortion, à la principle (1).

It is important to note that in the discussion of (4) that will follow, I will not be discussing the obligations of fathers to continue to support children that they have already been voluntarily supporting. . . . Principle (4) has solely to do with the connection between paternal obligations and prenatal paternal desires.

Admitting that fathers have the right of refusal provided a way of making principles (1), (2), and (3) consistent. The introduction of (4) rejects this solution, and once again generates inconsistency. The mother has the right to do something that the father does not have the right to do: get out of any future commitment to the (yet unborn) child by personal fiat. The mother can get out of it by terminating the life of the fetus, and the father cannot get out of it in any way, not even by refusal. Again principle (2) is violated.

There seem to be only four options. The first is that we can abandon principle (1). There are two ways of giving up (1). The first is to say that the conservative is right after all, and abortions really are impermissible. The second is to maintain that abortions continue to be permissible, but there must be some sort of mechanism for paternal consent. Mothers will have to consult with fathers before they are allowed to have abortions, and (perhaps) fathers will be allowed to insist that mothers have abortions if the father so decides. Women will no longer have complete control over their bodies, and will be subject (at least in part) to the decisions of men.

We can abandon principle (2). Men and women do not have equal rights and duties, or striving for a balance of powers with respect to the exercising of rights is not a valuable goal. Somehow the biological asymmetry of childbirth gives rise to an insuperable moral asymmetry. I suspect that most who accept all three principles will opt for rejection of (2), the equality principle. However, even though one might (with some plausibility) argue that biology prevents fathers from having a right to procure an abortion or insist that the mother have one, it is *much* harder to argue that biology forbids fathers from having a right of refusal. At the very least, such a right has no obvious connection to biology.

We can reject principle (3). Parents do not have an obligation to provide support for their children. Among other problems with this approach, it will entail the rejection of principle (4), whereas rejecting principle (4) will not require us to jettison (3). Thus, other things being equal, if getting rid of the comparably weaker (4) alone will restore consistency, we are better off doing that than getting rid of both (3) and (4).

The last alternative is that we can abandon principle (4) and grant that fathers have a right of refusal. If a father-to-be declares his refusal to accept fatherhood (with attendant legal details) and skips town, abandoning his pregnant girlfriend, he is perhaps callous and unfeeling, but he has not done anything morally wrong. He is no more unfeeling than if the mother intentionally aborted over his strong objections. Just as she can abort the fetus at her discretion, so too can he exercise the right of refusal at his. She can get out of the deal when she wants, and so can he. To reject (4) and accept a father's right of refusal is a radical change in most people's ordinary beliefs. If taken to heart in a broader social context, I believe it would ultimately result in considerable legal change with respect to paternity suits and court-ordered child support. This is the position for which I will argue.

THE SOLUTION

Since all four of the principles seem plausible, and rejecting any one is distasteful, an argument in favor of rejecting any particular one over the others is needed. I will first marshall the arguments in favor of rejecting (4), and then consider other solutions to the dilemma. I will argue that rejecting (4), counterintuitive as it is, is the most cogent solution available. This is why I claimed above that no line-drawing project is needed to adjudicate the cases seemingly relevant to evaluating (4). Principle (4) is false in every case. There are three arguments that I will develop to support the rejection of (4). Two arguments are suggested by positions taken by Judith Thomson in her well-known "A Defense of Abortion," and the last is an analogy that imports our moral intuitions from a logically parallel case.

Thomson's arguments are meant to support (1), and they do. But they also pave the way for abandoning (4). Thomson writes, "[Unless they implicitly or explicitly accept special responsibility] nobody is morally *required* to make large sacrifices, of health, of all other interests and concerns, of all other duties and commitments, for nine years, or even for nine months, in order to keep another person alive."

It is this dilemma that provides much of the support for principle (1). Without accepting some kind of special responsibility for the gestating fetus, the mother is under no obligation to keep it alive, even if it is a person. It is a direct consequence of (1) that the act of conception alone is insufficient to require of the mother that she make major personal sacrifices—most immediately the sacrifice of pregnancy and childbirth. Yet the father has done no more than participate in conception, and as a result he is required to make major personal sacrifices once the child is born. If conceiving alone does not count as accepting any special responsibility for a person for the mother, then it does not count as accepting any sort of special responsibility for a person for the father either. But (4) seems to deny this.

Another Thomsonian argument also supports this position. Her famous violinist case shows that someone who is the victim of a selfish, unilateral act (such as being kidnapped by the Society of Music Lovers, or being raped) is not obligated to make major personal sacrifices. By "unilateral" here, I mean that the victim had no say in what would happen, or, put another way, was kept out of the decision-making loop. Yet if the mother were to carry on with a pregnancy over the father's strong objections, it seems that her act is a selfish, unilateral one. Continuing with the pregnancy was her personal decision, and executed with regard only for her motives and desires. The father was kept out of the loop entirely. That the mother can do all of this is ensured by (1). So it seems on Thomsonian grounds that the father should then be exempt from having to make major personal sacrifices (such as 18 years of child support). But (4) tells us that he is not exempt. . . .

COMPETITORS AND THEIR PROBLEMS

There are, of course, other ways out. One is to find a way to resolve the inconsistency among the four principles without giving any up. Another is to give up either (1) or (2) while retaining (4). A third approach is to agree that fathers have a right of refusal, and find some way of ensuring that fathers pay child support anyway, in spite of this right. The arguments for rejecting (1) are legion, well-known, and will not be rehashed here. I suspect that (2) will be a likely target of those wishing to keep (4), but I have no idea how an argument against retaining (2) (at least as an ideal) might proceed, and so I cannot evaluate such an argument here. But I have been able to identify two arguments that purport to resolve the inconsistency among the four principles, and one that tries to accommodate my results while keeping the feminist preanalytic data, and will consider these in turn.

The first argument that attempts to resolve the inconsistency is this: It is not that the father especially has a commitment to the future child, but rather he has an obligation toward the mother. This commitment consists in something like a responsibility to help support their progeny. So there are not any future duties toward a child that he could escape by having a right of refusal. His duties are toward the mother.

However, this does not seem right, because the mother has no analogous commitment toward the father. She has no responsibility to help the father support their progeny, since such a responsibility would entail a duty to the fetus that it be carried to term. One cannot support something by killing it. Yet the mother clearly has no such duty toward the fetus, as (1) tells us. . . . The mother can avoid future duties through abortion, and the father can not. And principle (4) rules out the analogous paternal right of refusal. The problem remains.

A second argument that purports to resolve the inconsistency is this: The mother undergoes the burden of pregnancy, and receives the benefit of guaranteed paternal support. The father, by contrast, has the benefit of not having to suffer the burden of pregnancy and childbirth, and instead shoulders the burden of necessarily having to help support the child once it is born. Each party has their respective burdens and benefits, and these benefits and burdens are distributed more or less evenly. Thus, the equality principle (2) is satisfied, and (1), (3), and (4) are retained.

I think that there are several difficulties with this approach. The first is that although pregnancy is undoubtedly a burden of some sort, it is relatively short compared to the legal burden under which the father labors. The mother is pregnant for nine months, and in most cases is not suffering for much of that time. The father, by contrast, is obliged to pay considerable sums of income over a period of 18 years. The father's burden lasts 27 times as long. The distribution of burdens hardly seems equitable. It will not help to say that the mother has the same 18-year burden of support, since she *volunteered* to support the child by having it. The father, we are supposing, would have preferred the mother to have an abortion. Since the mother volunteered to support the child and the father did not, it does not seem right to say that she has the same *burden* as the father. We can appeal to the maxim of *volenti non fit injuria* here.

Another problem is this: If anyone should have more duties toward the child, it ought to be the mother, not the father. After all, she is the one who allowed (or is allowing) the fetus to gestate and mature in her body. Thus, it seems that she is establishing some kind of agreement with the fetus that when it is born she will provide for its well-being. The father, on the other hand, has not allowed the fetus to gestate and continue, and, let us suppose, strongly opposes its existence. Moreover, he explicitly rejects the idea that he has duties or future obligations toward the fetus or the child it will become. It is strange, then, to insist that the duties the father acquires after the child is born are just as strong as the mother's. If anything, it would seem that the mother should have *more* and *stronger* duties than the father.

But these are really just side concerns. The central problem with the argument is that it, too, only sidesteps the real issue. We can grant the burden/benefit argument and still generate inconsistency. The mother can escape her burden of pregnancy by personal decision—having an abortion as guaranteed by (1). The father cannot escape his burden of support, either by abortion or by refusal (as insisted on by [4]). So the mother still has something he lacks—a morally permissible escape from future duties.

The final objection I will consider grants that (4) is false—fathers have a right to avoid future duties, and ought to be legally granted the mechanism of refusal in order to have a means of exercising this right. Nevertheless, the objection goes, society can override the individual rights of fathers if it is in the best interest of society as a whole. Just as society can declare the right of eminent domain, and occasionally override the individual rights of property owners by building a highway through their front lawns, so too can society decide that the general public welfare is benefited by placing strong duties on fathers, and the individual rights of fathers are justifiably outweighed by these policy concerns. Moreover, we are generally prepared to grant that it is morally permissible for social concerns to outweigh the concerns of individuals. Thus, recognizing the falsity of (4) need not give rise to major social change. The intuitions behind (4) can be preserved even if (4) is jettisoned.

There are two main paths this objection can take: The interest of the state in benefiting children, and the interest of the state in benefiting mothers. . . .

Consider, then, the first path of this objection. The state decides that it is in the interest of society at large that children be assured of a certain level of financial security or material comfort. To promote this interest, the state does not distribute the burden evenly across all citizens, but instead levies a special tax on a subset. More specifically, the biological parents of these children are obliged to pay for their upbringing (of course, special provisions will have to built into the law to excuse biological parents when the child is adopted). In the case where the mother voluntarily submits to this (by not exercising her right to an abortion), and the father does not (by actively exercising his right to refusal), the father's rights are overridden, and he is still legally bound to pay child support.

One difficulty specific to this strategy is that we are on thin ice if we are prepared to engage in a wholesale suppression of individual rights for the pecuniary benefit of children. There are many children who would be better off living with adoptive parents than with their natural parents. Children born into poverty will, *ceteris paribus,* have worse life prospects that those children born to well-off parents. It would benefit these children, *ceteris paribus,* to take them from their natural parents and place them with wealthy adoptive parents. But surely this is wrong, and it is wrong because it unjustly usurps the rights of natural parents to keep their children. There are cases (e.g., child abuse) in which we might allow society to take children from their parents, but poverty is not one of them. Yet this case and the case of the father seem parallel: Society overrides the right of a biological parent(s) for the financial benefit of children. If we refuse to allow society to take children away from poor parents, so too should we refuse to allow society to override a father's right of refusal.

Let us consider the second path the social welfare objection might take. The state decides that as a contingent matter of fact, women have unequal standing in our society. They make statistically significantly less amount of money than men doing equal jobs, and they are not proportionately represented in positions of power in the government and in business. One practical result of this is that single mothers raising children have a much more difficult time, and a greater burden, than single fathers raising children. Thus, in order to alleviate this burden, the state decides to override systematically the father's right to refusal. This amounts roughly to an affirmative action program for women: Equal treatment in one domain is temporarily suspended with the intention of addressing inequalities in another domain. Once other social inequities between men and women have been adequately resolved, fathers will be allowed to resume their exercise of a right of refusal.

Again, one should note that this path accepts the main conclusion of this chapter—that fathers have a right of refusal. What the argument rejects is the inference from this right to immediate social and legal change. There are several difficulties with the second path of the social welfare argument, and it is hard to tell *a priori* which of these is the most serious. One is that much more argument is needed to show that overriding the father's right of refusal is the best way to address the issue of unequal burdens in single parenting. Since it is presumably in the *state's* interest, or the interest of society in general, to sponsor such an affirmative action program, it may be that society in general ought to pay for it. Another problem is that even if overriding the father's right of refusal is shown to be the best solution, considerable argument is then needed to demonstrate that it is also fair or just to suppress this right. For example, suppose that the national economy (and hence society as a whole) is best served if slavery were still allowed. This in no way means that we are therefore justified in reinstating slavery. Moreover, the reason that we are not thereby justified in reinstating slavery is because slavery impermissibly violates individual rights.

In addition, there are two wholly general problems with the strategy of appealing to the general social welfare in order to maintain the *status quo.* One is this: Suppose that on the ground of eminent domain, the state decided to build a highway across the front lawns of all and only Jewish citizens, all the while maintaining that Jews have a right to own property unmolested. Clearly this "right" would then amount to nothing but a ruse. So too, by telling fathers that they have a right to get out of future obligations through refusal but then invariably forcing these obligations on them anyway, it is clear that their "right" is an empty one. Granting such a right is mere trickery with words. One might object here that fathers do indeed have the right of refusal, it is just that their right is overridden—and there is nothing unusual or odd about overriding a right. This is true. But if a right is uniformly and consistently overridden, to the point that no one can exercise it except at some vague point in the distant future, one becomes suspicious as to whether there is a real right here. If a woman's right to an abortion is consistently overridden by society throughout her life, with a promise of allowing her to exercise it in the nebulous future, there is legitimate question of whether she really has this right.

The second problem is a danger looming for the partisans of principle (1). If a father's right of refusal can easily be trumped by society, then it might well be that a mother's right to an abortion can also easily be trumped. Society might decide, for example, that mothers do indeed have a right to elective abortion, but that social unrest over the abortion issue would be best alleviated by universally suppressing this right. . . .

So appeal to the general social welfare is a dangerous move at best, and a mere trick at worst. I conclude that it does not provide a plausible alternative to the conclusion for which I have argued—that the intentions and desires of the father before the birth of his child are in fact relevant to his duty to provide for the welfare of his children. If the mother can escape future duties to her progeny via the mechanism of abortion, the father also can escape future duties to his progeny via the mechanism of refusal.

Discussion Questions

1. Break Hales's argument down into its premises and conclusion. Are the premises sound? Are there any important premises he omitted and, if so, what are they? Does the conclusion follow from these premises?
2. Hales uses Judith Jarvis Thomson's argument in "A Defense of Abortion" to support his position that fathers have a right of refusal. Would Thomson agree with Hales's reasoning? Discuss how both Thomson and Marquis might respond to Hales's argument.
3. According to a 2001 Gallup Poll, most women are morally opposed to abortion on demand. In fact, almost half of unwanted pregnancies are not terminated by abortion.[39] Do fathers still have a moral right of refusal in cases where a woman, because of moral objections to the laws permitting abortion, does not excuse her legal right to avoid future obligations to her progeny through an abortion? Support your answer.
4. In a response to Hales's article,[40] James Humber argues that it is not unjust to require reluctant fathers to contribute financially to child support for women who choose to keep their children after birth since both parents contributed to the conception of the child and the mother is already unequally burdened or harmed by parenthood even if the father does contribute child support. Hales responds that the woman freely chose to continue the pregnancy and raise the child so there is no harm and, consequently, she deserves no redress.[41] Discuss the merits of both arguments.
5. Hales argues that women have a right to abortion as a mechanism of avoiding future duties of childrearing. However, birth parents can avoid the duties of childrearing through adoption. Does the mechanism of adoption to avoid future duties weaken Hales's argument that women had a right to abortion? Does the option of adoption, as a mechanism of refusal to take on future burden, further weaken the argument that fathers who did not want the child, have a duty to contribute to the support of their offspring?
6. Discuss how a care ethicist, a utilitarian, or a Confucian would most likely respond to Hales's argument.

CASE STUDIES

1. THE UNWANTED DAUGHTERS

Chandra and Ramdas Malik were poor farmers who lived in a small village outside of Bombay. They had one son and one daughter. Although they would have welcomed the birth of another son, they did not want another daughter, because giving the required dowry to her future husband's family would have been financially crippling for the Maliks. Sons also provided the best social security for elderly parents, because daughters were absorbed into their husbands' families. The Maliks decided that they would have an abortion if the fetus was a female. In India minivans carrying ultrasound equipment cruise the countryside, providing prenatal diagnosis of the sex of fetuses. Although the price of an ultrasound was high, it was worth it to the Maliks.[42] "Better 800 rupees now for an abortion," Ramdas Malik said before the procedure, "than tens of thousands of rupees later for a dowry." The ultrasound operator informed them that the child was a boy. Malik let out a sigh of relief.

Chandra Malik's second cousin, Indira, had emigrated to Canada in 1979. Two years later she married a successful engineer, John Sarava, whose grandparents emmigrated to Canada from India in the 1920s. With her son and daughter now in high school, Indira Sarava decided to return to college to complete her degree in business administration. She had just started her first semester when she found out she was pregnant. Because she was forty, Indira had amniocentesis at sixteen weeks to see if the fetus had any genetic disorders. The following week Dr. Lee called her and said, "Congratulations. You're going to have a healthy baby girl!" Two weeks later Indira called Dr. Lee back and asked him to perform an abortion. She explained that although she would have continued the pregnancy had the fetus been a boy, she is not interested in having another daughter. Her husband is opposed to the abortion. He points out that having another daughter would not be a burden for the family since they are financially secure, and because he is semiretired, he is also willing to do most of the child care.

Discussion Questions

1. Discuss how a cultural relativist would respond to each of the above scenarios. Are you satisfied with the answers? Explain.
2. Would it have made a difference if either the Chandras or Indira Sarava had requested the abortion because amniocentesis revealed that their children had Down syndrome?
3. Although the Maliks did not have an abortion, they intended to if the fetus had been a girl. What is the role of intention in moral responsibility? Discuss what Thomson and Boss would think regarding the morality of the Maliks's actions in seeking prenatal diagnosis for sex selection. If it is morally irresponsible to have prenatal diagnosis for sex selection, does this create a moral obligation on the part of physicians administering prenatal diagnosis to withhold information about the gender of the fetus? Support your answers.
4. Does the father have any rights when it comes to deciding whether a pregnancy should be terminated? Support your answer using the two cases described above. How would Steven Hales most likely respond to this question in light of the Sarava case where the father was willing to take on the majority of the burden of raising the child?
5. Sometimes, because of the position of the fetus or material floating in the amniotic fluid, ultrasound misdiagnoses the sex of the fetus. Imagine, much to the Maliks's dismay, that their son turns out to be a girl. They wrap the newborn in a rag and abandon her in a ditch beside a road. Is their action morally acceptable? Would your answer be different if the Canadian couple had done the same? Support your answers.
6. Although most Americans disapprove of abortion for sex selection, they regard abortion for genetic disorders, such as Down syndrome, as morally permissible. Is this distinction morally justified? Should the principle of equality apply to people born with physical or mental handicaps as well as to females? Support your answers.

2. JENNIFER JOHNSON: MATERNAL DRUG USE AND FETAL RIGHTS

When twenty-three-year-old Jennifer Johnson arrived to give birth to her fourth child, hospital drug tests found traces of cocaine in her blood. It was later revealed that her other children had all been cocaine-affected babies. In 1989 Johnson was arrested in a crack house. A Florida judge found her guilty of delivery (through the umbilical cord) of a controlled substance to a child. Johnson was sentenced to fifteen years' probation, drug treatment, random drug testing, and educational and vocational training. She was also ordered to participate in an intensive prenatal care program if she should ever become pregnant again.[43]

According to the Physicians Committee for Responsible Medicine, an estimated one in five pregnant women use illegal drugs. Cocaine use ranges from 8 to 18 percent and costs the nation an additional $504 million dollars a year in addition to medical expenses for cocaine-exposed infants.[44] In response, several states have passed civil child abuse and neglect laws, which state that taking illicit drugs or alcohol during pregnancy constitutes child abuse. As a result of these laws, thousands of women have lost custody of their children and some have even been jailed.

In February 2000 the U.S. Supreme Court agreed, in the case of *Whitner v. South Carolina,* to review a South Carolina law that allowed public hospitals to test pregnant women for drug use and to then give the results to the police without the woman's consent. So far over thirty women have been arrested under the South Carolina law. As in the case of Jennifer Johnson, addicted women can avoid prison by agreeing to undergo drug treatment.[45]

Discussion Questions

1. Discuss whether hospitals that routinely perform drug tests on any pregnant woman "suspected of being a drug user" are violating the privacy rights of the woman. Discuss how both Ayn Rand and Mary Anne Warren might respond to this question. How might a utilitarian respond?
2. In South Carolina a viable fetus is considered a person under law. Opponents of these laws argue that they are based on the mistaken "image of the fetus as separate from the mother-to-be" and a patriarchal worldview in which women are reduced to a "passive receptacle in reproduction."[46] Do you agree? Discuss whether holding women liable for prenatal conduct that may harm the fetus depends on accepting the premise that the fetus is a separate person with rights that can come into conflict with the rights of the mother.
3. Do pregnant women who plan to carry their fetus to term have a moral obligation to refrain from using substances that are harmful to the fetus? If so, does such an obligation depend on the personhood or moral status of the fetus? If the young fetus is not a person, to whom does the pregnant woman have the obligation? Can we have a duty to refrain from behavior that might harm persons who do not yet exist? If so, what is the moral basis of this duty?
4. Joyce Arthur, spokeswoman for the Pro-Choice Action Network, admits that "The situation with children born with fetal alcohol syndrome is certainly serious and very important, but to legislate any kind of coercion on pregnant women is the wrong way to go. Studies have shown that . . . if women fear some sort of coercive intervention, they will completely forego any prenatal care whatsoever."[47] Instead, her organization

suggests that to reduce the incidence of fetal alcohol syndrome, better "social resources and supports" in terms of money, counseling, etc., be provide for expectant mothers. Others disagree, arguing that this view is degrading to women, and that women who abuse alcohol and drugs while pregnant should be held both legally and morally responsible for actions that hurt their offspring. Discuss the two proposed approaches. How would Kant most likely respond to Arthur's proposal?

5. Should a pregnant woman's behavior that is potentially harmful to the fetus be regulated by law? Discuss how Warren and Boss would each stand on the morality of passing laws to protect the fetus from the mother's use of toxic substances during pregnancy. What would a utilitarian philosopher say?
6. Come up with a public policy for resolving the conflict between maternal and fetal rights. Consider the views of Confucius, Aristotle, rights ethicists, utilitarians, and care ethicists in coming to your solution.

---

3. THE LIMITS OF PROTEST: BOMBING OF ABORTION CLINICS

Between 1977 and 2000, antiabortion activists have committed more than two thousand four hundred acts in at least twenty-eight states and the District of Columbia including bombings, assaults, death threats, and even murders.[48] In 2001, more than half of all abortion providers experienced anti-abortion harassment.[49] On January 16, 1997, a bomb blast ripped through a family-planning clinic in Atlanta, Georgia, sending terrified people scattering in all directions. An hour later a second bomb went off in another part of the building. Six people were injured by the blasts; windows in nearby buildings were blown out, and the clinic was left in ruins. President Clinton condemned the bombing as "a vile and malevolent act" of terrorism. "No one has the right to use violence in America to advance their own convictions over the rights of others."[50]

The same clinic, then in a different location, had reportedly been attacked by a firebomb in 1984. In 1992 and 1993, Rachelle Shannon set fire to and vandalized six abortion clinics in California, Nevada, and Oregon. In 1993 Shannon attempted to kill Wichita, Kansas, gynecologist George Tiller. That same year Dr. David Gunn was shot and killed by another abortion foe outside a Pensacola, Florida, clinic. In 1994 John Salvi killed two receptionists at clinics in Massachusetts, and former Presbyterian minister Paul Hill shot and killed two men outside another Pensacola clinic. During 1995 and 1996, abortion-related crime at clinics declined somewhat only to rise again in 1997. During 1997 alone there were six bombings, sixty-five acts of vandalism, and sixty-two cases of stalking.[51]

Discussion Questions

1. The people who are protesting at the clinics believe that *Roe v. Wade* is unjust and that abortion is murder. They compare the abortion clinics with the death camps in Nazi Germany. Is this analogy accurate? Support your answer.
2. Do people have a right to use violence to advance their own convictions over the rights of others? Is violence, including war against nations such as Nazi Germany, ever justified as a means of achieving an end? Discuss how a utilitarian might answer this question.
3. Paul Hill was executed by the state in 2003 for killing two people at a Pensacola abortion clinic. Hill maintained to the end that what he did was moral since he saved more lives, the lives of the unborn, than he took. He also believed that God condoned his

action and would reward him in the afterlife. Do you agree with Hill's argument? What if you believed that the fetus is indeed a person? Are you morally justified to kill if you believe that what you are doing is morally right for you?

4. What are the limits of protest against what is seen as an unjust law? Discuss the morality of vandalism, harassment, stalking, bombing clinics, and causing injury to abortion providers as forms of protest.
5. About one-third of the approximately 200 clinics offering abortion in the United States now have buffer zones that require protesters to stay a certain distance from the clinic.[52] In 1998 a U.S. district court ruled that antiabortion protesters violated federal racketeering laws; and in 2000 the U.S. Supreme Court upheld as constitutional a state law that created a buffer zone around abortion clinics prohibiting antiabortion protesters from being within one hundred feet of the entrance. Antiabortion activists argue that these laws restrict their freedom of speech, because they prevent them from having a one-on-one conversation with or passing out leaflets to women entering the clinics. Discuss how a rights ethicist would balance the rights of the protesters against those of the people who want to use the services of the clinic.

---

4. TEEN PREGNANCY, RAPE, AND ABORTION

Lisa, an eighteen-year-old high school honor student, attends a fraternity party with her nineteen-year-old boyfriend, Derek, a college sophomore. Although alcohol is forbidden on campus, there is plenty of liquor at the party. Derek and his roommate, a twenty-one-year-old junior and social chair of the fraternity, have already started drinking when Lisa arrives. Lisa says she is not interested in drinking. "Come on," her boyfriend chides her, "don't be such a baby." Lisa reluctantly agrees to join them in a drink. After a few drinks, she becomes so tipsy that she can't stand up, so she lies down on Derek's bed. Derek's roommate winks and tells him to "go for it." Then he leaves the room. Derek then has sex with Lisa, who neither consents nor protests.

The next morning Lisa deeply regrets what has happened. She tells Derek that she is worried she might be pregnant. He gives her the name of an out-of-town doctor and reassures her that the doctor will take care of everything. Lisa goes to the doctor that morning. The doctor gives her the morning-after pill and suggests that, because of the circumstances and because she is so upset, she consider seeing a rape crisis counselor.

Lisa doesn't tell anyone else what has happened, nor does she keep her follow-up appointment with the doctor. When her periods don't return and she begins putting on weight, she dismisses the changes as stress and the effects of the morning-after pill. After all, she reassures herself, she couldn't be pregnant because she took the morning-after pill and she hasn't had sex since the fraternity party.

Six months after the incident, Lisa goes to the doctor for what she thinks are stomach problems or possibly a tumor. After examining her, the doctor tells her that she is six months' pregnant.

Discussion Questions

1. Although the abortion rate among teenagers is declining,[53] a disproportionate number of late-term abortions are performed on teenagers, because many teens do not

recognize the early signs of pregnancy. Would a late-term "partial-birth" abortion be morally justified in Lisa's case? State why or why not.

2. Is using the morning-after pill contraception or abortion? Support your answer. Discuss how Thomson, Noonan, Warren, and Marquis would each answer this question. If the morning-after pill is an abortifacient, is there any difference morally between using the morning-after pill and having a late-term abortion?
3. Is this a case of rape? Support your answer. Is this relevant in regard to whether the abortion is morally permissible?
4. Discuss the responsibility, if any, of the other people involved. Should the boyfriend be punished for having sex with Lisa when she was drunk? Is the fact that he was also drunk morally relevant? Should he have to pay for or share Lisa's medical expenses? Should he be compelled to provide support for the child if she decides not to have a late-term abortion? To what extent is the college or fraternity responsible for what happened? Should they owe Lisa a duty of reparation? Discuss how Steven Hales would most likely respond to these questions.
5. Discuss the responsibility of physicians in cases where the patient is a minor. If Lisa had been under eighteen, should the physician have given her the morning-after pill? Did the doctor have a moral responsibility to follow up when Lisa failed to keep her second appointment?
6. The United States has one of the highest teen pregnancy, birth, and abortion rates in the world. Only Russia has a higher rate of teen pregnancy. The teen pregnancy and abortion rate is well above that of other Western nations which, unlike the United States, promote a "safe-sex or no sex" approach and provide confidential and accessible contraceptive services to the teenagers. Discuss the moral issues involved in policies, including access to confidential abortion services, aimed at discouraging teen pregnancies. Discuss how a utilitarian, a rights ethicist, and a virtue ethicist might respond to these policies.

---

5. PARTIAL BIRTH ABORTION

When a family immigrated from India to a suburb of Detroit, Michigan, in 1997 they moved into a two-bedroom apartment, where the sixteen-year-old son and eleven-year-old daughter shared a bedroom. The following spring the girl, now twelve, began complaining of abdominal pains. At first her physician passed them off as digestion problems. However, the pains were not in her stomach. It turned out that she was 27 weeks pregnant. Furthermore, the father of the baby was the girl's brother. The family requested an abortion. After an anguished court battle, the girl finally obtained a "partial-birth" abortion at a Wichita clinic, even though there is a ban on them in Kansas.

An ultrasound in Vikki Stella's thirty-second week of pregnancy revealed that something was very wrong with her baby. More tests revealed that the fetus had several abnormalities, including a fluid-filled cranium with no brain tissue at all. A diabetic, Stella's pregnancy also put a strain on her health, and she did not wish to continue a pregnancy with a fetus who had no chance of survival after birth. She also had a "partial-birth" abortion.

Discussion Questions

1. What are the moral issues involved in the above two cases? Discuss what you might say to each of the two women if you were on the hospital ethics board and they came to you for advice.
2. Dr. Martin Haskell, who has performed over 1,000 "partial-birth" abortions indicated in a 1995 testimony before the U.S. Senate Judiciary Committee that about 80 percent were purely elective and performed on a healthy woman with a healthy fetus.[54] According to a 1998 *U.S. News and World Report,* only 10 percent of late (post-twenty weeks) abortions were for medical reasons.[55] Most late abortions, including "partial-birth" abortions, were on women who didn't know until late that they were pregnant; including young teenagers who still had irregular menstrual cycles and women in their later years who mistook the missed menstrual cycles for menopause. Discuss the morality of using "partial-birth" abortion in these cases. Are the reasons for the abortion morally relevant? Support your answer. Compare these cases with the two in the above case study as well as to the case of Lisa in the previous case study.
3. Should partial-birth abortion be illegal, as it now is, in all cases except to save the life of the mother? What about cases like the above where a girl does not know she is pregnant until late in her pregnancy? Support your answers.
4. According to the American College of Obstetricians and Gynecologists, after viability, "partial-birth" abortion is rarely, if ever, necessary to save the health and life of the mother. Nevertheless, they oppose a ban on the procedure arguing that the decision regarding a third-term abortion should be made within the context of the patient–physician relationship, not by legislators. Provide a moral analysis of their position.
5. Some ethicists consider "partial-birth" abortion infanticide, or at least well down the slippery slope toward infanticide. They maintain that the right to an abortion provides only for the termination of a pregnancy, not a dead child. Abortion is a right because of the burden of being pregnant, not because having a living child is a burden (since adoption is an option). The most a woman can claim is a severance right to be freed from the excessive burdens of pregnancy, not a right to have someone else kill her child. After viability a woman can be freed of the burden of pregnancy without the death of the child. Discuss the strengths and weaknesses of this position.

CHAPTER 3

Genetic Engineering and Cloning

It was one of the most controversial and startling birth announcements in history: On February 23, 1997, Ian Wilmut and a team of scientists at the Roslin Institute in Edinburgh, Scotland, announced to the world that they had created the first genetic clone of an adult mammal. The new arrival was a lamb called Dolly, reportedly named after Dolly Parton. Dolly looked like any other frolicking lamb; however, unlike any other mammal ever born, Dolly was created asexually from a single cell from her mother's udder. Dolly's genetic makeup is, for all practical purposes, identical to her mother's. The announcement of Dolly's birth set off a flurry of debate over the morality of using cloning on humans. Giving greater urgency to the debate is the recent completion of the Human Genome Project, which is expected to revolutionize both medicine and society.

THE HISTORY OF GENETIC ENGINEERING

Until recently, humans created new offspring the old-fashioned, natural way. Our children may not have been perfect, but we accepted them, for the most part, as they were. The desire to improve humans through genetic engineering, however, goes back at least to the time of Plato (c. 427–347 B.C.E.). In his *Republic,* Plato proposed the use of selective breeding as a means of improving society.[1]

The term *eugenics* was first used by English scientist Francis Galton, a cousin of Charles Darwin, to describe the study of human improvement by genetic means. Eugenics fell out of favor in the mid-twentieth century as a result of the eugenic programs that used sterilization to prevent the reproduction of people who were deemed unfit. Although the eugenics programs in the United States never reached the magnitude and level of coerciveness of those in Nazi Germany, memories of the state-run programs of involuntary sterilization left Americans feeling uneasy with talk of genetic engineering.

In 1962 James Watson and Francis Crick won a Nobel Prize for their discovery of the molecular structure of DNA. Each human cell, with the exception of germ or reproductive cells, contains forty-six chromosomes; each chromosome contains thousands of pairs of four different nucleotides or bases. Altogether, each human cell contains about 3 billion base-pairs of nucleotides, which can be roughly divided into about a hundred thousand sequences known as genes. There are also intervening sequences which, as yet, have an unknown purpose.

During the latter part of the twentieth century, reproductive technology focused primarily on the problem of infertility and prenatal diagnosis of birth defects. The development of amniocentesis in 1966 provided a method for diagnosing chromosomal disorders in the fetus.

The birth of Louise Brown, the first "test-tube baby," in England in 1978 heralded a new era of reproductive technology. Conception was no longer limited to the bedroom, so to speak; it could now take place in a petri dish or test tube in a laboratory without the presence of either parent. *In vitro fertilization* (IVF) ("fertilization in a glass") soon became a popular means of overcoming the problem of infertility. By 2003, one million babies worldwide had been born as a result of IVF.[2]

Surrogate motherhood, in which a woman agrees to bear a child for a couple, hit the front pages in 1986 when surrogate mother Mary Beth Whitehead, who was also the baby's natural mother, went to court to get custody of the child she had contracted to have for William Stern, the biological father, and his wife. For readings on the moral issues surrounding surrogate motherhood see John A. Robertson "Surrogate Mothers: Not So Novel after All," and Herbert T. Krimmel "The Case against Surrogate Parenting," in the accompanying *Ethics PowerWeb.*

The Whitehead/Stern case raised a public outcry over treating children, and women's reproductive capacities, as commercial commodities, an outcry that has gained renewed vigor with the completion of the mapping of the human genome.[3] The ability to genetically engineer and even clone humans has awakened fears of a resurgence of large-scale human eugenics programs. Matt Ridley, author of *Genome: The Autobiography of a Species in 23 Chapters,* addresses this issue later in this chapter in his article entitled "The New Eugenics."

THE HUMAN GENOME PROJECT

More than 900 genetic tests (also known as DNA-based tests) are now available for diagnosing genetic diseases and conditions.[4] This figure increased dramatically since the beginning in 1990 of the Human Genome Project, a worldwide cooperative effort to map the entire human genetic makeup. The complete human genome sequence was released to the public in 2003.

There is a staggering array of reproductive options based on this knowledge. Parents may soon be able to have their fetuses tested for genes that incline the child to obesity, shortness, nearsightedness, depression, alcoholism, Alzheimer's disease, sexual preference, and even "risk-taking behavior." Parents theoretically could seek genetic therapy or enhancement to alter the genetic makeup of their fetus or preimplant embryo by overriding or replacing these "undesirable" genes with more "desirable" ones. Parents may even be able to choose the genetic traits they want in their children or have children who are clones of themselves or some famous person. The downside of genetic testing is the use of tests on healthy individuals who, because of family history, are at risk for developing certain diseases such as Alzheimer's disease and Huntington's disease. While these tests may be welcome by some, many physicians and ethicists feel that they have the potential to provoke anxiety, discrimination, and social stigmatization.

The ability to identify and manipulate a person's genome has raised myriad ethical questions. Is it moral to tamper with our genetic makeup? If so, are there limits that should be placed on the use of genetic engineering and cloning? Do people at risk for carrying certain debilitating genetic diseases, either future parents or those who might have a late-onset genetic disorder, have a right not to know their genetic status? Can information about human DNA be owned? Indeed, what does it mean to be human?

GENETIC ENGINEERING

Genetic engineering includes both gene therapy, in which a new gene is introduced to override a defective gene, and genetic enhancement. Genetic enhancement involves the manipulation of the germ cell—in this case the egg—to improve the genetic code of a being. In this chapter we are concerned only with the second type of genetic engineering.

By the late 1980s, scientists were genetically altering food by taking genetic material from fish, bacteria, viruses, and insects and adding it to fruits, grains, and vegetables to improve durability and quality. *Transgenic* animals and plants are those with introduced genes, sometimes from another species. In 1992 the FDA declared that genetically engineered food is safe and does not need FDA approval before marketing. Scientists also began experimenting in the 1990s with mass-producing drugs by inserting human genes into bacteria. Scientists are also experimenting with chimeras—embryos created from the genetic material of two different species.

In late 1997 the same institute that had produced Dolly announced that by blending the two technologies—cloning and genetic engineering—it had created five almost-identical transgenic lambs with human genes that produce factor IX, a blood-clotting substance used in treating hemophilia.

The possibility of using genetic engineering in conjunction with cloning to produce "perfect" humans raises the ante in the debate.

There are two types of gene therapy: somatic cell therapy and germ line therapy. In *somatic cell therapy,* normal genes are introduced to produce something, such as an enzyme or protein, that is lacking because of a genetic defect. Somatic cell therapy is a treatment; it does not get rid of the defective gene, nor does it change a person's genotype. Therefore, the defective gene can still be passed on to future generations.

Germ line therapy, in contrast, actually alters the genetic structure of germ line cells—the sperm and the ova—so that the genotype of future generations is also altered. It is even possible to synthesize completely *new genes and chromosomes,* thus overriding the human genetic code itself. It may soon be possible to protect offspring against AIDS or certain types of cancer through the use of germ line therapy.

Both of these types of genetic engineering can also be used for genetic enhancement. Geneticists are now able to create artificial genes and even whole chromosomes that can be passed on to offspring.[5] Some computer scientists are even talking of "upgrading" humans by combining genetic engineering with robotics. Dr. Gregory Stock writes that "In the not-too-distant future, it will be looked at as kind of foolhardy to have a child by normal conception."[6]

The capacity to create "designer babies," while good news to some, also raises the thorny moral question of "What is a human?" In his article "Genetics and Human Malleability," W. French Anderson, one of the pioneers of human genetic engineering, argues that gene therapy and genetic engineering should be used only for serious illness because of the associated medical risks and inherent moral problems they pose.

CLONING

Cloning is the process of producing genetically identical individuals through asexual reproduction. There are currently two types of cloning: (1) blastocyst (embryo) splitting and (2) nuclei transfer. Nuclei transfer can be further subdivided into nuclei transfer using embryonic or fetal cells and nuclei transfer using adult cells.

In *blastocyst (embryo) splitting,* the blastocyst, or preembryo, consists of two to eight cells. At this stage in development, cells are not yet specialized into different organ

PROPOSED USES OF GENETIC ENGINEERING AND CLONING TECHNOLOGY

- **A solution to infertility:** Couples who are infertile could clone one of themselves in order to have a child that is genetically related to at least one parent.
- **Replacement children:** Parents can clone a child to replace one that has died or is dying.
- **Replicating desirable genomes:** Nuclei transfer from adult cells could be used to create clones of people of great genius, talent, and beauty, such as Michael Jordan, Bill Gates, Mother Teresa, or Cindy Crawford.
- **Genetic testing and gene therapy:** Genetic tests could predict genetic diseases and gene therapy used to override or replace the defective gene(s).
- **Prolonging human life:** The identification of the genes responsible for aging may help us to expand the average human life span to ninety or even one hundred years or more.
- **Directing our evolution:** Scientists predict that by the year 2040 we will be able to direct our own evolution, as well as that of other species, by replacing selected genes or adding new genes.[7]
- **Agriculture:** Scientists could genetically engineer and clone animals and plants that produce high-quality food.
- **Medicinal animals:** Genetically engineered animals with human genetic material could be cloned to be used as drug factories for humans or as models for human diseases.
- **Genetically guided drugs:** The development of whole-genome scanning allows pharmaceutical manufacturers to custom-tailor drugs to a person's genome.[8]
- **Research tools:** Cloned animals could be infected with diseases such as AIDS or cancer, and different therapies could be tried on them. Because all the animals are genetically identical, the research results would be more accurate.
- **Organ donors:** Nonhuman animals could be genetically altered so their organs would be compatible with human organs. Human clones could also be produced for organ transplants.
- **Endangered and extinct species:** Endangered species could be cloned to ensure their survival. Extinct animals could also be cloned if viable cells (generally frozen) are obtainable.

SELECTIONS FROM *CLONING HUMAN BEINGS: THE REPORT AND RECOMMENDATIONS OF THE NATIONAL BIOETHICS ADVISORY COMMISSION* (NBAC), JUNE 1997

In its deliberation, NBAC reviewed the scientific developments which preceded the Roslin announcement, as well as those likely to follow in its path. It also considered the many moral concerns raised by the possibility that this technique could be used to clone human beings. Much of the initial reaction to this possibility was negative. Careful assessment of that response revealed fears about harms to the children who may be created in this way, particularly psychological harms associated with a possibly diminished sense of individuality and personal autonomy. Others expressed concern about a degradation in the quality of parenting and family life.

In addition to concern about specific harms to children, people have frequently expressed fears that the widespread practice of somatic cell nuclear transfer cloning would undermine important social values by opening the door to a form of eugenics or by tempting some to manipulate others as if they were objects instead of persons. Arrayed against these concerns are other important social values, such as protecting the widest possible sphere of personal choice, particularly in matters pertaining to procreation and child rearing; maintaining privacy and the freedom of scientific inquiry; and encouraging the possible development of new biomedical breakthroughs . . .

Within this overall framework the Commission came to the following conclusions and recommendations:

I. The Commission concludes that at this time it is morally unacceptable for anyone in the public or private sector, whether in a research or clinical setting, to attempt to create a child using somatic cell nuclear transfer cloning. We have reached a consensus on this point because current scientific information indicates that this technique is not safe to use in humans at this time . . . The Commission, therefore, recommends the following for immediate action:
   - A continuation of the current moratorium on the use of federal funding in support of any attempt to create a child by somatic cell nuclear transfer.
   - An immediate request to all firms, clinicians, investigators, and professional societies in the private and non-federally-funded sectors to comply voluntarily with the intent of the federal moratorium . . .

II. The Commission further recommends that:
   - Federal legislation should be enacted to prohibit anyone from attempting, whether in a research or clinical setting, to create a child through somatic cell nuclear cloning . . .

III. The Commission also concludes that:
   - The United States government should cooperate with other nations and international organizations to enforce any common aspects of their respective policies on the cloning of human beings.

systems. Each cell is still capable of reproducing an entire organism, as occurs naturally in the case of identical twins or triplets. In 1993 researchers at George Washington University announced that they had created the first clones of human embryos. This event touched off the first round of debates on the morality of human cloning. John Robertson's article focuses primarily on this type of cloning in humans.

In the type of cloning known as *nuclei transfer using embryonic and fetal cells,* the nucleus from an early embryo is transferred to an unfertilized egg from which the original nucleus has been removed. Nuclei transfer using embryonic cells has also been used in cloning mice, rabbits, sheep, and cattle. The first successful cloning in vertebrate animals (animals with backbones), using nuclei transfer from tadpoles rather than embryonic cells, was accomplished in 1952.

In 1984 Danish embryologist Steen Willadsen succeeded in cloning the first lamb from embryonic cells. In 1997 Don Wolf at the Oregon Regional Primate Research Center created two monkey clones from embryonic cells. Bernie Harford of Monash University in Australia informed the world that his team had created 470 identical cattle embryos, which they planned to use to produce herds of high-quality livestock.[9]

Nuclei transfer using adult cells involves taking the nucleus from the cell of an adult and transferring it into a mature egg from which the nucleus has been removed. Prior to the cloning of Dolly, this type of cloning had never succeeded. Since the birth of Dolly in 1997, mice, cows, pigs, and even human embryos have been cloned using this method. Because the new nucleus has the full complement of forty-six chromosomes, the renucleated egg and the individual who contributed the new nucleus will be virtually genetically identical, with the exception of a very small contribution of DNA material from the mitochondria[10] of the host egg. Unlike blastocyst splitting, which is limited by the number of cells in a blastocyst, using nuclei transfer from adult cells, anyone—man or woman, adult or child—can be cloned in any quantity. With the ability to store cells that outlive their donors, as apparently happened in the case of Dolly's donor, it may someday even be possible to clone the dead.

Shortly after the birth of Dolly, an advertisement appeared on the Internet from a Bahamas-based group called Clonaid, which offered to clone people for $200,000 or to save a person's cells after death for future cloning. Clonaid announced the birth of the first human clone on December 26, 2002. They also claim that four other cloned babies have since been born. However, they refuse to release identities of the mothers and infants. Many scientists are skeptical about Clonaid's claim to have cloned humans.

Putting the Brakes on the Research of Human Cloning

Because technological progress is way ahead of the debate over the morality of cloning, many countries have established temporary bans on human-cloning research. In the weeks that followed the announcement of Dolly's birth, human-cloning research was banned in Spain, Italy, Norway, Germany, Canada, Denmark, Great Britain, and the United States. The European Commission on the Ethical Implications of Biotechnology also came out in 1997 with a statement of "condemnation of human reproductive cloning."[11]

The 1997 Cloning Prohibition Act in the United States banned for a period of five years the use of cloning for the creation of humans. The ban was renewed in 2002. In

2003 the Act was updated through amendments and placed a further five-year ban on human cloning. This law affects only research using federal money, however. The private sector is still able to engage in human-cloning research, as well as human cloning itself. Some legislators are calling for a permanent ban on cloning. In his article, "The Question of Human Cloning," John Robertson concludes that such a ban cannot be morally justified. As of the year 2003, nine states have outlawed human cloning. Several other states prohibit research that harms or destroys human embryos.

Ninety percent of Americans are morally opposed to cloning that results in the birth of a human being, and 61 percent are opposed to cloning human embryos for use in medical research. Sixty-six percent of Americans are also opposed to the cloning of animal. About half of Americans (51 percent) support medical research using stem cells obtained from human embryos.[12]

Most religious organizations are opposed to human cloning. Catholic theologian Reverend Albert Moraczewski of the National Council of Catholic Churches claims that cloning is "intrinsically wrong" because it is an attempt to "play God," and it robs people of their uniqueness. Islam scholar Adculaziz Sachedina adds that cloning violates religious teachings about the family and the traditional role of the father in creating children. Rabbi Richard Address of the Union of American Hebrew Congregations also opposes human cloning because "it violates the mystery of what it means to be human."

Is the current ban on human cloning morally justified? Many of the concerns about human cloning are the same, almost verbatim in some cases, as those once raised against in vitro fertilization, which is now commonly accepted. On the other hand, it took nearly twenty-five years for scientists to discover that there are risks associated with IVF, such as babies born with low birth weight and double the rate of multiple birth defects.[13]

MORAL ISSUES OF GENETIC ENGINEERING AND CLONING

Human Dignity

According to Kant, human dignity requires that humans be treated as ends in themselves. Cloning, in particular, Leon Kass argues, treats humans as means to an end—a commodity—rather than as ends in themselves, since clones are valued only for their desirable genome. Because it is wrong to use a human to carry out someone else's desires, cloning is not morally acceptable. However, the fact that we value our children—whether they are clones or "natural" children—for their desirable genomes does not mean that we do not also respect them for who they are. Robertson points out that the argument that it is undignified for one person to have the same genome as another is questionable, given that we do not consider it an affront to dignity to be one of a set of identical twins. And, clones are merely "delayed" twins. On the other hand, it is argued, cloning may violate human dignity in a way that natural twinning does not, because cloning reduces people to their genetic codes.

In 1672 British philosopher and scientist Robert Boyle (1627–1691) expressed the following view of the human body: "I think the physician is to look upon the patient's body as an engine that is out of order, but yet so constituted that, by his concurrence with . . . the parts of the automaton itself, it may be brought to a better state." The idea that the human body can be reduced to an elaborate machine with parts that can be manipulated and analyzed continues to dominate medicine and medical research to this day. In defense of the Vatican's 1987 statement condemning artificial fertilization and the generation of human life outside the body, Cardinal Joseph Ratzinger told a news conference at the Vatican: "We encourage scientific research, but science is not [an] absolute, to which everything must be subordinated and eventually scarified, including the dignity of man."[14] Reductionism removes the human body from its social and personal context and reduces it to an object to be studied and manipulated. To have someone else define who we are, as occurs in cloning, some argue, removes our sense of self-control over our bodies, which is essential to our self-identity and well-being.

Because cloning involves the destruction of surplus embryos, it also raises the same issues of personhood found in the abortion debate. Some philosophers, such as Robertson, maintain that embryos are not persons and therefore do not deserve our moral concern. Bioethicist Richard McCormick argues that cloning collapses the person into genetic data, thus shattering our "wonder at human diversity and uniqueness."[15] Indeed, it is even suggested that cloning might constitute a "wrongful life."

Genetic enhancement, especially germ line therapy, has also been condemned *as tampering with a child's self-identity and right to choose their own future.* However, other bioethicists point out that parents make environmental interventions—including making the child eat a healthy diet, sending the child to school and dance classes, signing them up for sports, and getting them vaccinated against certain diseases—that benefit the children by modifying their phenotype. If it is laudable on the part of parents to control their child's environment in order to produce the "best" offspring possible, why not also use genetic interventions to attain the same goals? Why are genetic interventions regarded as a violation of the child's dignity or essence while environmental ones are not? Bioethicists Allen Buchanan, Dan Brock, Norman Daniels, and Daniel Wikler write:

> Part of what may disturb us is the (mistaken) belief that genotypic interventions modify the essence of essential features of the individual, whereas environmental interventions only modify accidental features. The idea seems to be that genetic interventions result in a different individual, whereas environmental interventions merely modify the same individual . . . our compunctions about genetic interventions seem to rest on some underlying confusion about genetic determinism (we are essentially what our genes make us).[16]

Thus, the critics of reductionism and genetic engineering are using as a premise the very assumption they reject ("we are essentially our genes") to support their conclusion. There is also concern that clones, because they are human inventions, may be denied the rights of full personhood. Clones could be mass produced to act as drones for the "real" humans. On the other hand, clones, because of their more desirable genomes, might become a new master race, while "natural" humans are relegated to an inferior role.

Gene Patents and Owning Life

Another potential threat to autonomy is the patenting of genetic material, a trend that has been accelerated by the Human Genome Project (HGP). Although the HGP was adamant that data on the human genome remain in the public domain,[17] in the United States, and many other countries, human cells that have been genetically modified can be owned and patented. Several companies have already obtained patents on individual genes as well as on genetically engineered animals such as Harvard's oncomouse, which has a gene for cancer. Can we, or should we, draw the line at patenting genetically engineered humans? Laws against slavery prohibit the ownership of humans, but how great a deviation from the human genome is required before we can legally consider a genetically engineered being a nonhuman, and hence, a nonperson that can be used as a means only?

While corporations may not be able to own us in entirety, they can hold patents on parts of us. Questions have already been raised by lawyers about whether genetically enhanced "designer" children will need permission from the company that owns the patent on their designer genes before they can legally pass the genes on to children of their own.

Scientists and biotech companies are also scouting the globe in search of rare genetic traits that may have future market potential. The Human Genome Diversity Project (HGDP), an offshoot of the Human Genome Project, was established to expand the scope of genome research by collecting blood samples from groups of isolated indigenous people. The project, dubbed the "Vampire Project" and "bio-colonialism" by its critics, has been heavily criticized, especially by indigenous groups, as an extension of white colonialism that treats the bodies of indigenous people as commodities to be exploited. Under heavy criticism from bioethicists and political opponents, the HGDP was disbanded, except for small ad hoc groups, in 2001.[18]

Ethicists Lori Andrews and Dorothy Nelkin in their article, "Whose Body Is It Anyway? Disputes Over Body Tissue in a Biotechnology Age," explore the moral issues surrounding the commercialization of human tissue.

Defining "Perfection" and "Disease"

Then there is the question of what it means to be a "perfect" human. Who determines this? Should we define *perfect* in terms of the consequences for the wider community and the species? Or is what constitutes a "perfect" child a private decision that should be left up to parents? By being allowed to impose their concept of perfection on their offspring, the parent generation will control the destiny of subsequent generations. The world, however, does not sit still. Talents that may be appropriate today may be passé in years to come. The reject of today may be the genius of tomorrow's world.

Like the concepts of "perfection" and "health," the concept of "disease" is difficult to define. In his article on "Genetics and Human Malleability," W. French Anderson asks the question of what distinguishes a disease from discomfort or the suffering caused by the variations that exist in the cultural norms. Is shortness or homosexuality a disease? While recognizing that there is a large gray area, Anderson also maintains that there are some severe disorders that are clearly diseases and, as such, are morally permissible candidates for gene therapy.

We also need to ask if cloning and genetic enhancement are the best uses of our limited medical resources. Genetically engineering animals that can produce valuable drugs and organs for humans may drastically reduce that cost of manufacturing these drugs. On the other hand, a utilitarian would balance this against the pain and suffering caused to these animals.

The Right to Be Unique

President Clinton, in announcing the federal ban on funding for research on human cloning, affirmed that "human life is unique, born of a miracle, a 'profound gift.'"[19] Cloning, in particular, is regarded by many of its opponents as a violation of a purported "right to be unique." Cloning, it is argued, robs the clone of his or her sense of uniqueness. The fact that twins occur naturally does not give us the right to impose sameness on other people. Kass, for example, expresses concern that clones will be burdened with genetic identities—those of their parents—that have already lived, thus creating a serious self-identity problem.

Natural twins, however, have a sense of self-identity. Although genes provide the building blocks for individuals, they do not determine who we are. Who we are is the result of the interaction between our genetic inheritance and our social and cultural environment. Thus the idea that we could clone an army of identical Hitlers, or any group of people, who lack a unique identity has no scientific basis.

Genetic engineering too brings up the issue of uniqueness. Defenders of a right to be unique point out that children are unique individuals rather than projections of their parents' plans and wishes. If it becomes widespread, cloning of genetically engineered humans would allow one generation to makes its descendants as it pleases. All subsequent generations, now cleansed of unacceptable genes, would remain subject to that power.

Interfering with Nature

There are two strands to the argument that genetic engineering is wrong because it interferes with nature. The first states that nature and the right to create new life belongs to God and that we should not encroach on God's domain. This objection is somewhat vague: What exactly do we mean by "creating" as opposed to "reproducing" life? What exactly is included in God's domain? This argument is also irrelevant to those who do not believe in God.

The second strand implicit in this argument is the assumption that "natural" and "good" are invariably linked. However, we are constantly interfering with nature in the name of morality. This argument, which is based on the naturalistic fallacy, is one of the weakest arguments against cloning. What is meant by "unnatural"? Is it unnatural for humans to develop and use technology? Indeed, the primary purpose of medicine is to prevent diseases by interfering with their natural courses.

A related argument is that species have integrity as biological units and we should not disrupt the natural boundaries between species. Again this argument assumes that *natural* and *good* are synonymous. The species-integrity argument is also reminiscent of the racial-purity argument. Just what is the moral value in keeping groups biologically separate? In addition, the distinction between species is not as distinct as biologists once thought. Genetic exchange between species occurs in nature without human interference as well as in cloning combined with genetic engineering.

Proposals are already afoot to use cloning to revive extinct species, such as the woolly mammoth (see Case Study 5 at the end of this chapter) and to preserve endangered species such as the giant panda, which experts predict may be extinct by 2010.[20]

Redefining Parenthood and Family

Kass argues that cloning would wreak havoc with our ideas of parenting and family. In particular, he questions the wisdom of separating reproduction from sexuality and the family, which is the fundamental unit of all societies. Without grounding parenting in the family, the care of children loses its natural grounding. The act of conjugal love, therefore, is the only method of human procreation consistent with the dignity of man.

Clones break this connection between family and children, because a clone comes from a single parent who, unless the child's genome was also genetically engineered, may also be that parent's identical twin. What's more, cloning will make men reproductively superfluous. A woman who wants to clone herself would not need a man. On the other hand, a man who wanted to clone himself would need a woman to provide both the egg and a womb.

Kass's critics maintain that the right to have two parents is an artificial right, not a genuine one. As for making men superfluous, cloning would not make social fatherhood obsolete. Clones could still have two social parents. Also, cloning may be the only chance for some couples to have a child who is genetically related to them. The father could provide the nucleus and the mother the egg. That way the mother would at least contribute some material—the DNA from her mitochondria—to their child.

Autonomy and Reproductive Rights

Randolfe Wicke is head of Clone Rights United Front, a New York City group founded in 1997 in the wake of Dolly's birth. Wicke believes that "human cloning is a reproductive option and should be available to all."[21] Cloning, he says, is not the business of government any more than "a woman's decision to have an abortion is."

According to many people, including Matt Ridley, autonomy is one of the most fundamental human rights. Ridley maintains that the right to procreate, including procreation through genetic engineering and cloning, is part of this fundamental right. The desire of parents to have a child who is "their own genetic child" is already widely accepted. In cases of infertility or serious genetic disorders, cloning may provide a way for parents to realize this dream.

Like Kass, we may find repugnant or arrogant the idea of people cloning themselves, or of parents using genetic engineering to produce the "perfect" child; however, it is argued, these feelings do not, in themselves, make these practices morally wrong so long as the children's interests are protected after birth.

On the other hand, given the high cost of genetic engineering and cloning, making it available could severely curtail reproductive freedom for parents who cannot afford the technology. Parents who had a less-than-perfect child in a society full of perfect children would put their child at risk for failure and discrimination. In the 1980 case *Curlander v. Bio-Science Laboratories,* a California appellate court ruled that a child with a genetic defect could bring a "wrongful life" suit against her parents for not undergoing prenatal screening and aborting her. This case could set a precedent for children who do not meet certain social and physical standards to sue their parents because their parents did not choose to have their genome genetically engineered to remove "flaws."

There is also the danger that medical care and social services would be withheld from families that do not avail themselves of the new reproductive technologies—a trend that has also begun with private medical insurance companies. Thus what began as a reproductive right could turn into a duty to have "perfect" children.

Justice as Fairness

Rejection is the flip side of perfection. What will happen to those people who do not meet certain standards of perfection? Genetic engineering might give children who are products of this technology an unfair advantage. Studies show that there is an association between good-looking executives and business success. Overweight women earn less, on the average, and buyers prefer more attractive salespeople. In another study of university students, the students gave good-looking criminals sentences that were 20 percent lighter than others. And as for the argument that beauty is a cultural construct rather than natural, even little babies prefer to look at what most people would consider beautiful faces.[22] If people should be given equal treatment, then do parents or society have an obligation to provide genetic enhancement for certain children who may suffer a disadvantage because they are not to be as handsome or pretty as their peers?

Denying the opportunity for genetic engineering or enhancement to certain groups of people because of cost constraints could draw even tighter boundaries around membership in privileged classes and further increase the gap between the rich, who can afford such technology, and the poor, who cannot. The fact that technology that nullifies the need to have "inferior" children exists may render policy makers less sympathetic to those who are disadvantaged.

John Rawls acknowledges that eugenics could create a caste system that divides society into separate biological populations. He also points out, however, that justice as fairness entails that the talents of those with greater abilities would have to be used for the common advantage. Whether this would happen in actual practice is another question.

Another related issue is the use of genetic tests to identify harmful genes, such as genes that increase the risk of breast cancer, alcoholism, manic-depressive disorder, or Huntington's disease. Is it fair for potential employers, colleges, and medical insurance companies to use these tests to screen people? Mandatory genetic testing by employers or insurance companies could lead to discrimination against people who carry "flawed" genes and could also constitute a violation of their privacy rights.

Consequentialist Arguments

These arguments weigh the harms of genetic engineering and cloning against the benefits. For example, because we have no experience with human cloning, we have to rely for the most part on speculation in determining whether the harms outweigh the benefits.

Even research to improve our knowledge has its own dangers. In 1999, eighteen-year-old Jesse Glesinger died following a gene therapy experiment at the University of Pennsylvania that was thought by the researchers to be relatively safe. Another blow to genetic therapy research came in 2003 when it was learned that two children being treated in a French gene therapy trial had developed a leukemia-like condition.

Some bioethicists maintain that because the possibility for misuse of cloning is so great, all human cloning ought to be banned. Kass, for example, fears that cloning and genetic engineering may lead to the mass production of children and the breakdown of parent/child relationships. Others point to the benefits of cloning to infertile couples, noting that cloning does not harm the offspring, because the clone owes his or her very existence to the cloning process.

Some biologists are concerned that cloning will undermine human diversity. French philosopher Emmanuel Levinas maintains that diversity is one of the key values in social interaction. The primary challenge in social interaction is accepting other people—including our children—precisely as other, rather than as mirror, images of ourselves.

Diminished genetic diversity may also affect our very survival. Almost all of us carry several recessive genes that are potentially debilitating or even fatal. Will cleaning up the gene pool by getting rid of these harmful genes amount to throwing the baby out with the bathwater? By culling genes that may be harmful today, we become less flexible genetically. This in turn may make us less capable, as a species, of adapting to sudden climate changes or of resisting new diseases. A case in point is the gene for sickle-cell anemia. In this genetic disorder, found primarily in people of African descent, the red blood cells have a tendency to become distorted into a sickle shape. These distortions can precipitate a "sickle-cell crisis," which is characterized by severe pain. On the other hand, sickle-cell anemia also provides a measure of immunity against malaria—a potentially deadly disease. Although malaria is no longer a threat in most parts of the world, the deletion of this gene from the human gene pool could make us less resistant to future diseases. On the other hand, genetic technology is now capable of manufacturing and inserting artificial genes and even an entire chromosome. Thus, as Ridley points out in his article, we now have the potential of creating unlimited biodiversity.

There is also concern about the breeding of cloned herds of agricultural animals and plants—a practice that results in a genetically homogeneous population. In these cases genetic diversity, which is necessary for adaptation, may fall below an acceptable limit and the whole herd or crop could be wiped out by a single disease. In 1970 half of the maize crop in the United States was lost to one disease—the southern corn leaf blight. The loss was attributed to lack of genetic diversity in the plant.

The trend in genetic engineering in agriculture, however, is toward increasingly genetically homogeneous populations of plants and livestock. For example, ProLinia Inc., a biotech company associated with the University of Georgia, was to clone livestock, particularly cattle and hogs, on a large scale using the genes from superior animals—"superior" being defined as having traits most appealing to the human palate. The current process of breeding, says a company spokesman, is "time-consuming" and "unreliable . . . the [superior] genes eventually become diluted through generations of mixing and mating."[23]

Some ethicists fear that this reasoning will some day be applied to the currently "unreliable" method of human breeding. What will happen when we have the technology to be guaranteed to have a "superior" child? Kass maintains that access to genetic engineering may lead to the commodification of children. Ridley, on the other hand, argues that genetic engineering and cloning is unlikely to be used to mass produce superior children.

We also do not yet know the effect of using adult cells to create clones. Although the incidence of death among the fetuses and offspring of clones is higher than normal, this problem may be resolved with better cloning technology. Initially there were also fears that cells cloned from an adult animal would age prematurely.[24] However, a recent study found that cells from clones actually have longer life spans than the original cells.[25] Obviously much more research is needed on the effects of cloning.

We also need to take into account the risks associated with genetic engineering and gene therapy. Because of these risks, Anderson insists that gene therapy should be restricted to the treatment of serious disease.

On the positive side, the use of genetically guided drugs, tailored to a person's particular genome, could greatly decrease drug-related side effects associated with the "one size fits all" approach to drugs, and increase the effectiveness of the treatment. Currently medicines have only a 30 to 40 percent chance of working on a particular patient.[26] Genetically engineering crops also has the potential to greatly increase yield and thereby reduce world hunger.

On the other hand, the Human Genome Project has shown us that all living beings—plants and animals—are closely related and interconnected. It is unrealistic to think that we can genetically engineer some organisms without affecting the rest of the biosphere.

The Rights of Nonhuman Animals

In our belief that humans exist outside and above the natural world, we often forget that we are not just *like* animals—we *are* animals. One of the surprising findings of the Human Genome Project is how much humans are genetically like other animals and even plants. For example, humans and chimpanzees share 98 percent of their genomes in common. There are also more parallels between human development and the development of "lower" animals than was previously assumed.[27] In fact, several animals, including sheep like Dolly and man's best friend the dog, have more chromosomes than humans do.[28]

What are we to make of this? In light of these findings, can we continue to justify the moral wedge between humans and nonhuman animals? Does our animal status lessen the moral value of humans; or does the close relationship of humans to other animals mean that we should extend moral respect to all animals, as Buddhists and animal-rights advocates do?

Currently fewer than one in three people who need a transplant receive one. The use of xenotransplants—organs from another species—may be a solution to this problem. On the other hand, it also raises the problem of the moral status of nonhuman animals, including animals genetically engineered with human genes so that their organs are more compatible with ours. This conflict may eventually be resolved if human stem-cell research finds a method for growing new organs from the recipient's own cloned cells.[29] Some researchers are infusing human DNA with a cow egg, which is used as a cellular incubator for the human embryo, in an attempt to grow human embryonic stem cells.[30] This method, in addition to using another species to benefit humans, raises issues of its own, including the destruction of human embryos in order to use their "spare parts" for transplantation and the possibility of inadvertently introducing viruses from the donor cow egg. If other animals have moral status, can we justify the cloning and genetic engineering of animals as a means to benefit humans?

Another issue is the inclusion of human genetic material in other animals. Do other animals with human genetic material deserve the moral respect now reserved only for humans? What are the moral implications of the breeding of transgenic animals for species integrity? Will the concept of species someday become morally irrelevant? Cloning and genetic engineering may bring an end to the traditional line now drawn between humans and other species of animals; indeed it may even obliterate the concept of species. Whether this is morally desirable remains to be seen.

CONCLUSION

The ability to genetically engineer and clone humans is a milestone in history. How are we, as morally responsible citizens, going to respond to this new technology? We must resist the temptation to use the temporary ban on cloning as an opportunity to sweep the moral issues under the rug or to dismiss cloning offhand as too bizarre to be morally acceptable. Such a head-in-the-sand approach may simply encourage the development of unregulated back-alley cloning clinics.

There are compelling and broad-based arguments on both sides of the cloning and genetic engineering debates. These moral concerns also address issues related to abortion and the use of nonhuman animals in medical experiments. How should we balance the different moral concerns? During the five years of the temporary ban, college students and new college graduates will have an opportunity to actively engage in policy making.

MATT RIDLEY

The New Eugenics

Better than the old

Matt Ridley is former editor of the *Economist* and author of *Genome: The Autobiography of a Species in 23 Chapters.* In his article "The New Eugenics," Ridley explores the use of eugenics in light of its history as well as the successful completion of the Human Genome Project. He concludes that the use of eugenics in genetic engineering will not undermine the fundamental moral principle of respect for persons.

Critical Reading Questions

1. What is the history of eugenics? In light of its history, why do many people have misgivings about eugenics?
2. How are we currently practicing eugenics?
3. What is the difference between medical genetic engineering and cosmetic genetic engineering?
4. Why does "everybody" agree that human genetic engineering is wrong?
5. On what grounds does Ridley disagree with his colleague Tom Shakespeare's objection to genetic engineering to correct preventable disabilities such as dwarfism?
6. What are the similarities, according to Ridley, between historic attitudes toward in vitro fertilization and current attitudes toward genetic engineering?
7. What is Ridley's position on the use of cosmetic engineering by parents? On what grounds does he support his position?

The entire human genome has been read. Even ten years ago, that seemed a distant goal; but last month, scientists announced that they have completed reading a "rough draft" of the complete recipe for a human being. It will soon be available on compact disc for anybody to read: a book 800 times longer than the Bible. This breakthrough will open an amazing world of possibilities for

Matt Ridley, "The New Eugenics," *National Review,* July 31, 2000, Vol. 52, Issue 14, pp. 34–36.

medicine—including the prediction, prevention, and treatment of many diseases, from kidney stones to cancer.

But why stop at disease? Instead of merely eliminating the negative, why not accentuate the positive—by tinkering with the text to improve it? After all, in pursuit of the perfect human being, we have willingly tried every weapon that falls into our hands, from prayer to psychoanalysis to breast implants. Will we—and should we—do the same with genes? . . .

A SAD LEGACY

Discussions of these issues are burdened by a complicated history. A century ago, progressive social reformers were obsessed by the new agenda of "eugenics." There was a sense of urgency in their desire to improve the human race by selective breeding. It had worked well enough in cattle and chickens, but we human beings were not only failing to breed from the best specimens; we were allowing the worst to have the most children.

"Some day," said Theodore Roosevelt in 1910, "we will realize that the prime duty, the inescapable duty, of the good citizen of the right type is to leave his or her blood behind him in the world." In the same year, Winston Churchill lobbied for compulsory sterilization of the mentally handicapped: "I feel that the source from which the stream of madness is fed should be cut off and sealed up before another year has passed."

Britain never did pass such a law, thanks to determined opposition from a libertarian member of parliament named Josiah Wedgwood. In America, however, states began to pass laws allowing mandatory sterilization. In 1927, the Supreme Court upheld Virginia's eugenic-sterilization law in *Buck v. Bell.* Carrie Buck, whom the state wished to sterilize, lived in a colony for "epileptics and the feeble minded" in Lynchburg, with her mother Emma and her daughter Vivian. After a cursory examination, Vivian was declared an imbecile—she was six months old at the time!—and Carrie was ordered sterilized to prevent her from bringing more imbeciles into the world. Supreme Court Justice Oliver Wendell Holmes thundered that "Three generations of imbeciles are enough!" Compulsory-sterilization laws were thenceforth upheld in many states; more than 100,000 Americans were sterilized under them.

The tragedy of that story lies not in the science behind eugenics, but in the politics: It is the *coercion* that was wrong. An individual who volunteers for sterilization is doing no harm, whatever his or her motives; one who orders another to be sterilized against his or her will is doing wrong. It is that simple.

The eugenic movement began with the best of intentions. Many of its most strident advocates were socialists, who saw eugenics as enlightened state planning of reproduction. But what it actually achieved, when translated into policies, was a human-rights catastrophe: the rejection of many immigrants, the sterilization of many people whose only crime was to have below-average intelligence, and eventually, in Germany, the murder of millions of people.

But now, a century later, we are once again practicing a sort of eugenics: We abort fetuses that would be born with Down syndrome or inherited disorders. In New York, Ashkenazi Jews who carry the Tay-Sachs mutation can avoid marrying each other through blood testing organized by the Committee for the Prevention of Jewish Genetic Disease. We also stand on the brink of cosmetic genetic engineering.

Are we simply repeating the mistakes of the past? No. The principal difference is that whereas eugenics, as conceived in the early part of the 20th century, was a public project, modern genetic screening is a private matter. Only China still preaches eugenics for the good of society; everywhere else, modern eugenics is about individuals applying private criteria to improve their own offspring by screening their genes. The benefits are individual, and any drawbacks are social—exactly the opposite of the old eugenics.

Another difference is precision: The selective breeding of the past worked slowly and unpredictably—but today, we can insert a gene into an organism and be all but certain what the effect will be: For example, inserting the genetic phrase "Make insulin!" into a bacterium transforms the life of a diabetic.

Genetic engineering of plants and animals is now routine. Only the genetic engineering of human beings is forbidden.

It would work: Of this, there is no doubt. Take a simple example: the gene on chromosome 4 that is associated with Huntington's disease, a terrible mental affliction of middle age. You could go into the gene in a fertilized egg, find the crucial phrase "CAG"—which, in affected people, is repeated more than 39 times in the middle of the gene—and remove about half of the repeats. It would not be easy, but it could probably be done. The result would be a healthy person with no risk of Huntington's, and no risk of passing it on to her children. . . .

It is not just medical genetic engineering that is feasible; cosmetic genetic engineering could also begin tomorrow, though it would still be very primitive. There is a gene on chromosome 17 called the ACE gene, which comes in two equally common varieties, long and short. On average, people who inherit two long ACE genes (one from each parent) are better athletes than people who inherit two short versions. . . .

It would be comparatively trivial to engineer a human embryo so that it had two long ACE genes. The result would be a child slightly more likely to win long-distance running races. There would be no risk of unpredictable consequences, because about one in four of us have two long ACE genes already; it is not unnatural. It would not be cruel to the child, and it would have no consequences for society. But should it be allowed? . . .

NO NIGHTMARE SCENARIOS

Yet even at this "easy" end of the spectrum, there are uncomfortable questions. Cures might seem uncontroversial, but they are not. My colleague, the sociologist Tom Shakespeare, is achondroplastic, but he regards his inherited short stature as a disability only to the extent that society imposes that prejudice on him. With a first-class degree from Cambridge University and a good career, he does not see his genetic disorder as a reason for eliminating future people like him.

He sees genetic engineering as undermining society's respect for people like him, because it sends the message that disability could be—and therefore perhaps *should* be—eliminated. In a genetically engineered society, the parents of a genetically disabled child would feel social opprobrium for not having "done something about it."

I see his point, but I do not fully agree with it, for the following reason: I see nothing in history to suggest that the ability to cure a condition lessens compassion or respect towards its sufferers. Indeed, society's respect for people with "preventable" disabilities has surely never been greater than now: People with Down syndrome, for example, were once abandoned or shunned; they are now treated with much more respect.

I suspect it will prove impossible in practice to draw a line between cure and enhancement, between medical and cosmetic genetic engineering. One person's cure is another person's enhancement. Is an inherited weight problem a disease? Would it be a cosmetic enhancement to "cure" dyslexia?

Assume that one day, genetic alleles that predict homosexuality are discovered—a wild assumption, but not inconceivable. To a heterosexual couple, disabling the "gay genes" in their potentially homosexual child might seem like a "cure" that prevents an "abnormal" life. But if so, then for a homosexual couple trying to procreate through a surrogate mother, disabling the "straight genes" in their child might also seem to be a "cure."

James Watson famously remarked a few years ago that if a mother, following a prenatal diagnosis, wanted to avoid having a gay child, that was up to her. After all, more than 95 percent of abortions are carried out for the convenience of the mother and are of "normal" fetuses. . . .

Another objection to genetic engineering is that it would drive out diversity, as people converge on the "ideal." Again, I think this argument is mistaken. Far from threatening diversity, genetic engineering may actually increase it. Supposing cosmetic genetic engineering became accepted, musical people might seek out musical genes for their children;

athletes might seek athletic genes; etc. It is very unlikely that everybody would choose the same priority.

If diversity is not threatened by genetic engineering, then another argument—that in a genetically engineered world, there would be an underclass of those who could not afford the procedure—also evaporates. In this scare scenario, the rich might buy themselves an even better start in life with the best genes. But this argument applies only if genetic engineering becomes commonplace, and it is at least partly undermined if everybody is using different criteria of perfection. After all, just by choosing our marriage partners we have been practicing private eugenics ever since we became human: Dark good looks, a slender figure, a winning personality, or a quick mind—in considering these attributes in potential mates, we are, at least partly, selecting genes. Yet diversity is not threatened, because each of us has different criteria. . . .

IVF (in vitro fertilization) is actually an instructive precedent for the current debate: When it was invented in the 1970s, society as a whole largely disapproved, finding the procedure unnatural and abhorrent. It gained acceptance because mild disapproval by the many was matched by fierce demand from the few; it took off because infertile individuals demanded it, not because society as a whole decided they could have it. It was an individual decision, not a collective one.

Just as infertile people demanded access to IVF, even before it had been fully tested for safety, it is possible that people who carry fatal genes will demand access to genetic engineering; but this is not very likely. Unlike infertile people, they already have an alternative: pre-implantation genetic diagnosis, which can spot and discard affected embryos in favor of unaffected ones. And if these people, for whom a "bad" gene is the difference between misery and happiness, do not need genetic engineering, why would anybody else need it? It is true that a few people might wish for a blue-eyed boy, but would they really be prepared to abandon the easy business of natural conception for a painful and exhausting test-tube conception instead?

My point is that cosmetic genetic engineering would attract a very small—and probably half-hearted—clientele, even if it were made legal and safe. I simply cannot think of a single feature of my own children that I would have liked to fix in advance. People do not want particular types of children; they just want their own children, and they want them to be a bit like themselves. . . .

The history of eugenics teaches that nobody should be forced to engineer her children's genes—but, by implication, neither should anyone be forced *not* to. To regulate such decisions with heavy-handed state intervention would be to fall into the very trap that caught the do-gooder eugenicists of 1910. I am not against all regulation: At the very least, governments can step in to ensure standards among practitioners (something they are quite good at). But they would be unwise to try to specify in detail what people can and cannot decide to do for themselves. As Thomas Jefferson said: "I know no safe depository of the ultimate powers of the society but the people themselves; and if we think them not enlightened enough to exercise their control with a wholesome discretion, the remedy is not to take it from them, but to inform their discretion."

Discussion Questions

1. Examine your own reaction toward the term *eugenics*. To what extent are your concerns influenced by historic uses of eugenics? Discuss what fallacies, if any, are involved in your conclusions about eugenics. Discuss also how Matt Ridley would most likely respond to your concerns.
2. Critique Ridley's position on the moral permissibility of cosmetic genetic engineering by parents. Discuss how a natural rights ethicist, a natural law ethicist, and a care ethicist would most likely respond to Ridley's argument.
3. Compare and contrast the positions of Ridley and his colleague Tom Shakespeare on the use of genetic engineering to correct genetic disabilities. Which position do you

find most morally compelling and why? Discuss how Ayn Rand might respond to each of their arguments.

4. Using both utilitarian theory and Rawls's two principles of justice, develop a public policy on the use of eugenics and genetic engineering by both parents and biotech corporations.

W. FRENCH ANDERSON

Genetics and Human Malleability

W. French Anderson is professor of biochemistry and pediatrics at the University of Southern California School of Medicine. Anderson is also one of the pioneers in gene therapy. In the following selection, Anderson supports the use of gene therapy for serious diseases. However, he rejects enhancement genetic engineering as both medically hazardous and morally precarious.

Critical Reading Questions

1. What, according to Anderson, are the key questions that must be answered before we can determine the moral permissibility of genetic engineering?
2. What is the difference between gene therapy and genetic enhancement? According to Anderson, why does gene therapy open the door for the latter?
3. What is the difference between somatic gene therapy and germ line therapy? On what grounds does Anderson draw a moral distinction between these two types of gene therapy?
4. Why does Anderson have stronger misgivings about the use of germ line therapy?
5. On what grounds does Anderson reject the use of genetic enhancement?
6. What is the distinction between a serious disease, a minor disease, and a cultural discomfort?

Just how much can, and should we change human nature . . . by genetic engineering? Our response to that hinges on the answers to three further questions: (1) What *can* we do now? Or more precisely, what *are* we doing now in the area of human genetic engineering? (2) What *will* we be able to do? In other words, what technical advances are we likely to achieve over the next five to ten years? (3) What *should* we do? I will argue that a line can be drawn and should be drawn to use gene transfer only for the treatment of serious disease, and not for any other purpose. Gene transfer should never be undertaken in an attempt to enhance or "improve" human beings. . . .

W. French Anderson, "Genetics and Human Malleability," *Hastings Center Report,* vol. 20, January/February 1990, pp. 21–24. Notes have been omitted.

WHAT WILL WE BE ABLE TO DO?

But successful somatic cell gene therapy opens the door for enhancement genetic engineering, that is, for supplying a specific characteristic that individuals might want for themselves (somatic cell engineering) or their children (germ-line engineering) which would not involve the treatment of a disease. The most obvious example at the moment would be the insertion of a growth hormone gene into a normal child in the hope that this would make the child grow larger. Should parents be allowed to choose (if the science should ever make it possible) whatever useful characteristics they wish for their children?

WHAT SHOULD WE DO?

A line can and should be drawn between somatic cell gene therapy and enhancement genetic engineering. Our society has repeatedly demonstrated that it can draw a line in biomedical research when necessary. . . . Our responsibility is to determine how and where to draw lines with respect to genetic engineering.

Somatic cell gene therapy for the treatment of severe disease is considered ethical because it can be supported by the fundamental moral principle of beneficence: It would relieve human suffering. Gene therapy would be, therefore, a moral good. Under what circumstances would human genetic engineering not be a moral good? In the broadest sense, when it detracts from, rather than contributes to, the dignity of man. . . .

Somatic cell enhancement engineering would threaten important human values in two ways: It could be medically hazardous, in that the risks could exceed the potential benefits and the procedure therefore cause harm. And it would be morally precarious, in that it would require moral decisions our society is not now prepared to make, and it could lead to an increase in inequality and discriminatory practices.

Medicine is a very inexact science. We understand roughly how a simple gene works and that there are many thousands of housekeeping genes, that is, genes that do the job of running a cell. We predict that there are genes which make regulatory messages that are involved in the overall control and regulation of the many housekeeping genes. Yet we have only limited understanding of how a body organ develops into the size and shape it does. . . .

Even though we do not understand how a thinking, loving, interacting organism can be derived from its molecules, we are approaching the time when we can change some of those molecules. Might there be genes that influence the brain's organization or structure or metabolism or circuitry in some way so as to allow abstract thinking, contemplation of good and evil, fear of death, awe of a "God"? What if in our innocent attempts to improve our genetic make-up we alter one or more of those genes? . . . If we caused a problem that would affect the individual or his or her offspring, could we repair the damage? . . .

My concern is that, at this point in the development of our culture's scientific expertise, we might be like the young boy who loves to take things apart. He is bright enough to disassemble a watch, and maybe even bright enough to get it back together again so that it works. But what if he tries to "improve" it? Maybe put on bigger hands so that the time can be read more easily. But if the hands are too heavy for the mechanism, the watch will run slowly, erratically, or not at all. . . . Attempts on his part to improve the watch will probably only harm it. We are now able to provide a new gene so that a property involved in a human life would be changed, for example, a growth hormone gene. If we were to do so simply because we could, I fear we would be like that young boy who changed the watch's hands. We, too, do not really understand what makes the object we are tinkering with tick.

In summary, it could be harmful to insert a gene into humans. In somatic cell gene therapy for an already existing disease the potential benefits could outweigh the risks. In enhancement engineering, however, the risks would be greater while the benefits would be considerably less clear.

Yet even aside from the medical risks, somatic cell enhancement engineering should not be performed because it would be morally precarious. Let us assume that there were no medical risks at all from somatic cell enhancement engineering. There would still be reasons for objecting to this procedure. To illustrate, let us consider some examples. What if a human gene were cloned that could produce a brain chemical resulting in markedly increased memory capacity in monkeys after gene transfer? Should a person be allowed to receive such a gene on request? Should a pubescent adolescent whose parents are both five feet tall be provided with a growth hormone gene on request? Should a worker who is continually exposed to an industrial toxin receive a gene to give him resistance on his, or his employer's request?

These scenarios suggest three problems that would be difficult to resolve: What genes should be provided; who should receive a gene; and, how to prevent discrimination against individuals who do or do not receive a gene.

We allow that it would be ethically appropriate to use somatic cell gene therapy for treatment of serious disease. But what distinguishes a serious disease from a "minor" disease from cultural "discomfort"? What is suffering? What is significant suffering? Does the absence of growth hormone that results in a growth limitation to two feet in height represent a genetic disease? What about a limitation to a height of four feet, to five feet? Each observer might draw the lines between serious disease, minor disease, and genetic variation differently. But all can agree that there are extreme cases that produce significant suffering and premature death. Here then is where an initial line should be drawn for determining what genes should be provided: treatment of serious disease.

If the position is established that only patients suffering from serious diseases are candidates for gene insertion, then the issues of patient selection are no different than in other medical situations: the determination is based on medical need within a supply and demand framework. But if the use of gene transfer extends to allow a normal individual to acquire, for example, a memory-enhancing gene, profound problems would result. On what basis is the decision made to allow one individual to receive the gene but not another[?] . . .

Discrimination can occur in many forms. If individuals are carriers of a disease (for example, sickle cell anemia), would they be pressured to be treated? Would they have difficulty in obtaining health insurance unless they agreed to be treated? These are ethical issues raised also by genetic screening and by the Human Genome Project. But the concerns would become even more troublesome if there were the possibility for "correction" by the use of human genetic engineering.

Finally, we must face the issue of eugenics, the attempt to make hereditary "improvements." The abuse of power that societies have historically demonstrated in the pursuit of eugenic goals is well documented. Might we slide into a new age of eugenic thinking by starting with small "improvements"? It would be difficult, if not impossible, to determine where to draw a line once enhancement engineering had begun. Therefore, gene transfer should be used only for the treatment of serious disease and not for putative improvements.

Our society is comfortable with the use of genetic engineering to treat individuals with serious disease. On medical and ethical grounds we should draw a line excluding any form of enhancement engineering. We should not step over the line that delineates treatment from enhancement.

Discussion Questions

1. Discuss how W. French Anderson addresses the problem of the slippery slope in his endorsement of genetic therapy. Does Anderson do an adequate job in drawing the line between acceptable and nonacceptable uses of genetic therapy? Support your answer.
2. Do you agree with Anderson's moral distinction between germ line and somatic gene therapy? Why? Discuss how a utilitarian might respond to Anderson.
3. What does Anderson mean when he says that enhancement engineering is "morally precarious"? Do you agree with Anderson? Support your answer.

4. Compare and contrast the positions of Anderson with that of Matt Ridley on the morality of genetic enhancement. Which person presents the stronger argument? Support your answer.
5. Define the term *disease.* Is it possible to draw a clear distinction between a "disease" and a "cultural discomfort" and, correspondingly, between gene therapy and genetic enhancement? If not, does this invalidate Anderson's moral distinction between gene therapy and genetic enhancement? Support your answers.
6. Discuss Anderson's concerns about the use of both gene therapy and genetic enhancement on discrimination. Discuss how both Rawls and a rights ethicist might respond to Anderson.

JOHN A. ROBERTSON

The Question of Human Cloning

John A. Robertson is a bioethicist and professor of law at the University of Texas. Robertson considers some of the ethical issues raised by human cloning. After looking at some of the possible applications of human cloning, he concludes that no one who deserves our moral respect is harmed by it, and some people may benefit from it. Cloning, therefore, is a morally acceptable reproductive choice.

Critical Reading Questions

1. What are the two types of cloning? Does Robertson think that the first type is likely to be developed for mammals?
2. What was the study at George Washington University Hospital, and why did it raise public fears and concerns about the morality of cloning?
3. What were some of the concerns raised by religious organizations regarding human cloning?
4. What, according to Robertson, is the most prevalent moral concern regarding cloning? How does he respond to this concern?
5. What are some of the potential applications of human cloning? Which of these applications does Robertson regard as morally acceptable?
6. How does Robertson respond to the objection that cloning is wrong because it involves the destruction of embryos?

"The Question of Human Cloning," *Hastings Center Report* 24, no. 2 (1994): 6–14. Some notes have been omitted.

7. On what grounds does Robertson dismiss the argument that producing identical clones, either at the same time or as later-born twins, is not wrong?
8. Should research on cloning be restricted according to Robertson, and, if so, under what conditions?

Accustomed though we are to advances in medical technology, a 24 October 1993 news report that human embryos had been cloned astonished many persons. A *New York Times* story, "Researcher Clones Embryos of Humans in Fertility Effort," was the feature that Sunday morning in many newspapers throughout the country. Media coverage continued for several days, with debates about cloning on editorial pages, *Nightline,* and *Larry King Live.*

Within a week the issue had faded from media consciousness, aided in part by *Time* and *Newsweek* stories that stressed the huge gap between the reported research and the *Jurassic Park*-type fears of cloned human beings that initially spurred national coverage. Bioethicists and lawmakers, however, must still contend with the ethical and policy issues that even limited cloning of humans presents. Should researchers be free to continue cloning research? May infertile couples and their physicians employ cloning to form families? Or should government prevent cloning research or discourage some or all of its later applications?

As with many biomedical developments, these questions present a mix of issues that need careful sorting. They involve, among others, questions of the propriety of embryo research, the validity of deliberately creating twins, and the importance of nature versus nurture in forming human beings. They also raise slippery slope concerns: should otherwise seemingly valid uses of a new technique be stopped to prevent later undesirable uses from occurring? To address those issues we must first describe the cloning research that has touched off the furor and the concerns that it presents. . . .

The study that generated the recent interest in cloning involved a small but essential step toward cloning human beings by embryo splitting. Researchers at George Washington University Hospital in Washington, D.C., separated cells or blastomeres from seventeen two- to eight-celled preembryos and showed that, to a limited extent, they would divide and grow in culture. . . .

The study thus demonstrated that experimental cloning or twinning of human embryos is potentially feasible as an aid to relieving infertility, though much additional work remains before offspring are produced, and there is uncertainty whether the technique will ever work at all. . . .

FEARS AND CONCERNS

Some commentators saw nothing particularly unethical or disturbing in the George Washington research. This was simply another step toward improving the efficacy and efficiency of IVF (in vitro fertilization), particularly for those couples who produce too few eggs or embryos to initiate pregnancy.

Many news reports, however, highlighted the disturbing or possibly unethical features of cloning and quoted ethicists who found the practice troubling. They described hypothetical scenarios in which embryos would be cloned for sale or to produce organs and tissue for existing children who need transplants. One ethicist termed cloning as "contrary to human values"; others saw it as "an opportunity for mischief" that called for "governmental and societal debate and, perhaps, prohibitions and restraints." The Vatican newspaper termed it a step into "a tunnel of madness," while the United Methodist Church called for an executive order banning cloning in all federally financed institutions. A poll a week after the first story reported that 60 percent of Americans opposed cloning.*

---

* *New York Times,* 1 November 1993. Fifty-eight percent of respondents believe that "it was morally wrong to clone a human being." Sixty-three percent believe cloning was against God's will. Fewer than one in five respondents thought that cloning should be allowed to continue.

The fears and concerns about cloning have several strands. Some of them arise from the artificial nature of assisted laboratory reproduction. Others are tied to discomfort with the manipulation and destruction of embryos that cloning research, if not the procedure itself, will inevitably cause. The most prevalent ethical concern, however, arises from the dangers that intentional creation of identical twins or multiples of one genome might pose to resulting offspring. The fear is that cloning will violate the inherent uniqueness and dignity of individuals, as well as create unrealistic parental expectations for their children. It also opens the door to identical embryos being created and sold because of their genetic desirability, as cattle embryos now are sold to increase animal yield and profitability. A worst-case scenario envisages the mass production of identical embryos to be sold to persons seeking desirable children. Finally, there are fears that embryos will be created to provide organs and tissue for existing children who need transplants. . . .

As micromanipulation of eggs and embryos is a rapidly growing practice, the ability to excise blastomeres from an embryo will easily be within the reach of many IVF physicians and embryologists. If shown to be safe and effective, physicians in many fertility centers will then offer the procedure to patients.

These possibilities engender a recurring disquietude about new reproductive technologies. Scientific zeal and the profit motive combine with the desire of infertile couples for biological offspring to create an enormous power to manipulate the earliest stages of human life in infertility centers across the country. . . .

Some persons would argue that the idea of creating exact replicas of other human beings is so novel that there should be a moratorium on further research and development until a national consultative body evaluates the ethical acceptability of the procedure and develops guidelines for research and use of the technique. At the very least, to prevent abuses there should be strict rules about the circumstances in which cloning by embryo splitting occurs, and about the uses made of cloned embryos. . . .

To assess the ethics of embryo splitting and the need for regulation, we must first ask who would use this technique if it were available and why, and then analyze the ethical issues that the likely demand for cloning would generate. We can then address the need for regulation of the embryo research that is essential if cloning by blastomere separation is to occur, and of the uses to which cloning techniques will be put.

THE DEMAND FOR CLONING

The news accounts of the George Washington University research emphasized many speculative uses of cloning, thereby slighting the most likely uses of the technique. The immediate impetus to develop cloning—and its most likely future use—is to enable infertile couples going through IVF to have a child.

To Increase the Number of Embryos Transferred

Initially the main demand for embryo splitting would come from couples undergoing IVF who cannot produce enough viable embryos to initiate pregnancy. In basic IVF practice, the highest rates of pregnancy occur with transfer of three to four embryos. . . .

If they produce only one embryo and embryo splitting has been shown to be safe and effective, they may opt to divide that embryo. Depending on the embryonic stage at which splitting is most successful, this could produce two embryos (if split at the two-cell stage), four (if split at the four-cell stage), or even eight (if two embryos are both split at the four-cell stage). . . .

If they produce four or more viable embryos by blastomere separation, three or four might then be transferred to the uterus in the hopes of having one child, with the rest frozen for later use. . . .*

---

*However, it is possible that three or even all four embryos transferred will implant. In that case, the couple will face the issue of selective reduction of the pregnancy to twins. Depending on the number of children who are born, cloning by separation could lead to twins or even triplets as a result of intentional cloning.

However, this scenario also opens the door to having "twins" (or even "triplets" or "quadruplets") born several years apart. This would occur if one or two children were born as a result of the first transfer cycle. Three years later, perhaps, the couple wishes to have a second child, and rather than go through IVF again, opts to have the remaining cloned embryos thawed and transferred to the wife's uterus. The period between births of children with the same genome could vary from a year or two to several years. . . .

Embryo Splitting as a Form of Life or Health Insurance

An often-cited though highly unlikely demand for embryo cloning could arise from couples seeking insurance against disaster for any children that they have. That is, a couple might request that one or more blastomeres be split from embryos that will be transferred, so that the resulting clone can be frozen for later use in case the child born from the source embryo later dies or needs an organ or tissue transplant. In that case, embryos that are genetically identical to the child already born can be thawed and implanted in the mother (or a surrogate) to produce a genetically identical child to replace the dead child, or to serve as an organ or tissue donor for an existing child.

This scenario could occur, but it is unlikely for several reasons. First, few couples not otherwise undergoing IVF would choose to do so just to gain the hypothetical protection that identical backup embryos might provide. Second, couples that experience the death of a child may not, because of the sadness that it will engender, want to replace that child with a genetic twin, much less plan even before the first child is born to create a replica for that purpose. Third, couples undergoing IVF who produce enough embryos for transfer may not want to risk their viability by separating blastomeres for hypothetical insurance purposes. Fourth, a genetic replica of an existing child might not be necessary to provide needed organs or tissue, or there may not be sufficient time once organ failure in a child occurs to thaw, implant, and bring to term the cloned embryo to serve as an organ or tissue donor. . . .

Because so few couples—even those otherwise going through IVF—will request embryo splitting for this purpose, the use of cloned embryos as backup protection for existing children is likely to arise only with embryos that were created to enhance the efficiency of IVF. In situations of this kind, where the embryonic clones were *not* produced with the specific intention of insuring against disaster, parents might occasionally be glad of the opportunity to avail themselves to the stored cloned embryos to obtain tissue for transplant for an existing child, or to replace a child who has already died. Such scenarios are not impossible, but for the reasons stated above, they are not likely to be frequent.

Embryo Splitting to Obtain a Desirable Genome

Ethicists have speculated that cloning by embryo splitting might occur to facilitate, or might result in, the selection of stored embryos deemed to be particularly desirable. They envisage scenarios whereby parents will try to sell clones of desirable children to other couples, or where an attractive or successful couple will clone many embryos for later sale or dissemination.

These speculations are highly fanciful. Most couples are not in the market for other peoples' genetic offspring, but prefer to have their own. If so, they can exercise some control over the genetic characteristics of offspring by mate or gamete selection, or by preimplantation or prenatal genetic analysis. Few couples who can have their own children would be so obsessed with having a perfect child that they would eschew their own reproduction in order to obtain a cloned embryo that appears to have a desirable genome. . . .

ETHICAL ISSUES: DESTRUCTION OF EMBRYOS

Cloning by blastomere separation raises a number of ethical issues. Some ethical concerns derive from the stark interference with natural reproduction, or the manipulation and destruction of embryos that cloning necessarily entails. However, those concerns are not unique to cloning and have been voiced about embryo research, freezing, and discard, and about IVF generally. Since they are not deemed sufficient to justify banning or restricting those accepted forms of assisted reproduction, they should not be sufficient to ban cloning either.

Yet persons who believe fertilized eggs and embryos are already persons with rights will object that embryo splitting goes beyond the manipulations ordinarily involved in IVF. In this case a new unique individual will be intentionally split to serve other ends. The very process of blastomere separation could destroy embryos that would have developed normally, thus denigrating and undermining the value of human life. Because human life at all stages is a preeminent value, cloning by blastomere separation is an unethical procedure and should be banned.

There may be no way to answer the objections of persons who think that embryos are themselves persons and must be protected at all costs. . . . One can only point to the prevailing moral and legal consensus that views early embryos as too rudimentary in neurological development to have interests or rights. On this view, splitting embryos can no more harm them than freezing or discarding them can. Nor is splitting embryos to enable one or more of them to implant and come to term inherently degrading or disrespectful of human life. Cloning embryos thus poses no greater harm to embryos than other IVF practices and should be permitted to the same extent that they are.

ETHICAL ISSUES: DELIBERATE TWINNING

Ethical objections that are unique to cloning arise from a concern that the intentional creating of genetic replicas of an existing person denies the uniqueness of resulting offspring. This could occur from causing more than one child with the same genome to be born simultaneously. It could also occur from causing more than one child with the same genome to be born at different points in time.

Is the intentional creation of twins who are born simultaneously morally objectionable? Identical twinning occurs naturally and is not generally thought to be harmful or disadvantageous to twins. If anything, being a twin appears to create close emotional bonds that confer special advantages. If this is true, then having twins as a result of embryo splitting should be no more harmful to offspring than having twins naturally. . . .

ETHICAL ISSUES: LATER BORN TWINS

The second ethical issue unique to cloning by embryo splitting is the possibility of genetically identical siblings being born years apart in the same or different families. Are later born children harmed because a twin or triplet already exists? The claim rests on the notion that the later born child lacks the uniqueness or individuality that we deem essential to human worth and dignity, and that human individuality is largely determined by nature or genome rather than by nurture and environmental factors. Because phenotype and genotype do diverge, and because the environment in which the child will be raised will be different from that of his older twin, the child will still have a unique individuality. Physical characteristics alone do not define individuals, and there is no reason to think that personal identity will be wholly controlled by having an older twin.

Still, there could be special problems faced by such a child. Its path through life might be difficult if the later born child is seen merely as a replica of the first and is expected to develop and show the skills and traits of the first. This might be a special danger if the later born child is used as a replacement for an earlier born child who has died. However, it will be some years before the later born child is even aware of his genetic identity relative to an older sibling and the special expectations his parents might have.

But it is also as likely that the later born child will be loved and wanted for his own sake. His status as a later born twin (or triplet) could be seen as a special status, indeed, a unique or novel status that confers attention and love. It could also lead to close ties with the older twin, if the special bond that twins feel is genetically based. However, it could also lead to unique forms of sibling rivalry. Will the older twin feel that he is deficient because his parents wanted a newer version of him, or will he feel special and proud that his parents wanted another child like him? In any event, it is difficult to conclude that later or earlier born twins or triplets are likely to have such serious psychological problems that they should never be born at all. Even if one did so conclude, this would counsel against implanting cloned embryos only when a twin already exists, not against implanting two cloned embryos simultaneously or splitting embryos at all.

ETHICAL ISSUES: CLONING AS LIFE OR HEALTH INSURANCE

Although cloning for the explicit purpose of providing parents with a replica for a lost child or as a source of organs or tissue for transplant for an earlier born child will not frequently occur, couples who have split embryos to treat infertility might occasionally be faced with thawing a cloned embryo for those purposes. Consider, for example, parents who request cloning to protect against the loss or death of a child, or who wish to thaw a cloned embryo to replace a dead child. Wanting a child to replace one who has died is not itself unethical. Nor does it become so merely because the new child will be a twin of the first. Although the parents may hope that the new child will develop and show the same traits as her deceased twin, they should very rapidly learn that the second child is different in some respects and similar in others, and would ordinarily come to treat and accept her as the individual that she is.

The use of cloned embryos as insurance against organ and tissue failure in an existing child presents a different set of issues. Here the concern is that the cloned embryo will be treated as an instrument or means to serve the needs of an older twin and will not be loved or respected for his own sake. . . .

If this is so, thawing cloned embryos to provide tissue or organs for an existing child should also be ethically acceptable. The key is whether the child will be loved and accepted by the family that brings her into the world, not how or why she was conceived, nor even whether she was cloned for that purpose. As long as the child's interests are protected after birth occurs, it is hard to see how being cloned or thawed to provide organs for a twin is any worse than being conceived for that purpose. . . .

ETHICAL ISSUES: EMBRYO SPLITTING FOR GENETIC SELECTION

. . . It is true that the small subset of infertile couples who are candidates for embryo donation might wish to know the actual characteristics of existing twins or triplets of the embryos they seek to "adopt." However, neither having nor satisfying this wish is itself immoral. Indeed, the right of adoptive parents to receive as full information as possible about the children whom they seek to adopt is increasingly recognized. There is no reason why the same principle should not apply to embryo "adoptions." Even though the couple seeking the embryos will be choosing them on the basis of expected characteristics, such a choice is neither invalid nor immoral. As long as the parents are realistic about what the information signifies, do not have unrealistic expectations about the child's perfection, and love the child for itself, seeking and providing such information prior to embryo donation should be ethically acceptable. If it were not, providing such information could be banned without requiring that embryo splitting to treat infertility also be banned. . . .

THE PERMISSIBILITY OF CLONING

The idea of cloning human beings initially sounds so bizarre and dangerous that one would think that such practices should be closely regulated, if permitted at all. Yet this survey of ethical and policy issues in cloning by embryo splitting suggests that the procedure has fewer risks and more benefits than first appeared and would be ethically permissible in most cases. The most unappealing applications of the technique are highly speculative and could be restricted without also stopping more valid uses.

Cloning by embryo splitting thus presents a regulatory situation that often arises with new reproductive technologies. An immediate step that seems justified to meet the legitimate needs of infertile couples could open the door to future applications that are much less defensible. If we ban the immediate steps in order to prevent potentially harmful future applications, infertile couples lose the benefits of the procedure without clear showing that future harms would necessarily have occurred. . . .

As a result, we are left to elucidate and resolve on a reality basis the ethical dilemmas that each new innovation presents. Cloning by embryo splitting is another example of this policymaking process. Unless there are greater risks from its use than are now apparent, the case for adding the technique to the armamentarium of infertility treatments is a reasonable one. Its novelty will not prevent parents from loving and acting in the best interests of children born in this way.

REFERENCES

Michael Waldholz, "Scientists Halt Research to Duplicate Human Embryos after Furor Erupts," *Wall Street Journal,* 27 October 1993; Gina Kolata, "Cloning Human Embryos: Debate Erupts over Ethics," *New York Times,* 26 October 1993.

Time, 5 November 1993; "Cleric Asks President for a Curb on Cloning," *New York Times,* 30 October 1993.

Judith Thomson, "The Trolley Problem," *Yale Law Journal* 94 (1985): 1395–1415.

American Fertility Society, "Ethical Considerations of the New Reproductive Technologies," special supplement, *Fertility and Sterility* 46 (1986); John A. Robertson, "In the Beginning: The Legal Status of the Early Embryo," *Virginia Law Review* 76 (1990): 437–517, at 440–50.

John A. Robertson, "Embryos, Families, and Procreative Liberty: The Legal Structure of the New Reproduction," *Southern California Law Review* 59 (1986): 939–1041.

American Fertility Society, "Ethical Considerations of the New Reproductive Technologies."

Federal Register 59, no. 10 (14 January 1994): 2414. See also, Joseph Palca, "A Word to the Wise," in this issue (p. 5).

Discussion Questions

1. In his discussion of the two types of cloning, Robertson argues that the first type appears unlikely to be accomplished with mammals "even in the mid-range future." Since he wrote his article, however, this type of cloning has been accomplished. Does Robertson underestimate the power of science? Does his argument for cloning support nuclei transfer cloning as well? Or is he able to support only blastocyst splitting because of its inherent limitations? Support your answers.
2. Discuss Robertson's claim that the interests both of parents and offspring are benefited, or at least not harmed, by cloning.
3. Would John Noonan agree with Robertson regarding the moral status of the embryo? Discuss what Noonan's position would most likely be on the morality of cloning.
4. Robertson assumes that cloning will be used primarily to help parents overcome infertility. Is this assumption realistic? Support your answer.
5. One of the arguments against cloning is that people have a right to a unique identity—a right destroyed by cloning. Are twins or triplets harmed by being identical? If possible, use examples from your experience to illustrate your answer. Would there be a cutoff point at, say, a hundred or a thousand identical clones, where this might be an issue? How would Robertson respond to this scenario?

LEON KASS

The Wisdom of Repugnance: Why We Should Ban the Cloning of Humans

Leon Kass, who has an MD in internal medicine and a PhD in biochemistry, is also head of the President's Council on Bioethics, is Hertog Fellow at the American Enterprise Institute, and is on the Committee on Social Thought at the University of Chicago. Kass was one of the first scholars to openly express concern about the morality of human cloning. He gives reasons why people should trust their initial feeling of repugnance toward cloning. Cloning violates some of the most important human values and turns children into commodities. The manufacture of humans by cloning, therefore, should be prohibited.

Critical Reading Questions

1. What does Kass mean when he says that cloning is "the perfect embodiment of the ruling opinions of our new age"?
2. Why does Kass claim that cloning is dehumanizing?
3. What, according to Kass, is the most common reaction of people regarding the prospect of cloning humans? What is the source of this reaction?
4. According to Kass, what are some of the moral values violated by cloning? What are some of the inherent dangers?
5. Why, in Kass's view, is sexual reproduction morally preferable to cloning? What effects would cloning have on parent/child and husband/wife relationships?
6. On what grounds does Kass claim that the independence of clones would be subverted by their maker?
7. How does "making" differ from "begetting"? What is the moral significance of these differences?
8. Why does Kass reject Robertson's "right to reproduction" as a justification of cloning?
9. Why is Kass concerned about cloning taking us down a "slippery slope"?

TAKING CLONING SERIOUSLY, THEN AND NOW

Cloning first came to public attention roughly thirty years ago, following the successful asexual production, in England, of a clutch of tadpole clones by the technique of nuclear transplantation. . . .

Much has happened in the intervening years. It has become harder, not easier, to discern the true meaning of human cloning. We have in some sense been softened up to the idea—through movies, cartoons, jokes and intermittent commentary in the mass media, some serious, most lighthearted. We have become accustomed to new practices in human reproduction: not just in vitro fertilization, but also embryo manipulation, embryo donation and surrogate pregnancy. Animal biotechnology has yielded transgenic animals and a burgeoning science of

"The Wisdom of Repugnance: Why We Should Ban the Cloning of Humans," *The New Republic* 216, no. 22 (1997): 17–26.

genetic engineering, easily and soon to be transferable to humans.

Even more important, changes in the broader culture make it now vastly more difficult to express a common and respectful understanding of sexuality, procreation, nascent life, family, and the meaning of motherhood, fatherhood and the links between the generations. . . .

Cloning turns out to be the perfect embodiment of the ruling opinions of our new age. Thanks to the sexual revolution, we are able to deny in practice, and increasingly in thought, the inherent procreative teleology of sexuality itself. But, if sex has no intrinsic connection to generating babies, babies need have no necessary connection to sex. Thanks to feminism and the gay rights movement, we are increasingly encouraged to treat natural heterosexual difference and its preeminence as a matter of "cultural construction." But if male and female are not normatively complementary and generatively significant, babies need not come from male and female complementarity. Thanks to the prominence and the acceptability of divorce and out-of-wedlock births, stable, monogamous marriage as the ideal home for procreation is no longer the agreed-upon cultural norm. For this new dispensation, the clone is the ideal emblem: the ultimate "single-parent child."

Thanks to our belief that all children should be *wanted* children (the more high-minded principle we use to justify contraception and abortion), sooner or later only those children who fulfill our wants will be fully acceptable. Through cloning, we can work our wants and wills on the very identity of our children, exercising control as never before. Thanks to modern notions of individualism and the rate of cultural change, we see ourselves not as linked to ancestors and defined by traditions, but as projects for our own self-creation, not only as self-made men but also man-made selves; and self-cloning is simply an extension of such rootless and narcissistic self-re-creation.

Unwilling to acknowledge our debt to the past and unwilling to embrace the uncertainties and the limitations of the future, we have a false relation to both: cloning personifies our desire fully to control the future, while being subject to no controls ourselves. Enchanted and enslaved by the glamour of technology, we have lost our awe and wonder before the deep mysteries of nature and of life. We cheerfully take our own beginnings in our hands and, like the last man, we blink. . . .

Human cloning, though it is in some respects continuous with previous reproductive technologies, also represents something radically new, in itself and in its easily foreseeable consequences. The stakes are very high indeed. I exaggerate, but in the direction of the truth, when I insist that we are faced with having to decide nothing less than whether human procreation is going to remain human, whether children are going to be made rather than begotten, whether it is a good thing, humanly speaking, to say yes in principle to the road which leads (at best) to the dehumanized rationality of *Brave New World*. This is not business as usual, to be fretted about for a while but finally to be given our seal of approval. We must rise to the occasion and make our judgments as if the future of our humanity hangs in the balance. For so it does.

THE STATE OF THE ART

. . . For the tens of thousands of people already sustaining over 200 assisted reproduction clinics in the United States and already availing themselves of in vitro fertilization, intracytoplasmic sperm injection and other techniques of assisted reproduction, cloning would be an option with virtually no added fuss (especially when the success rate improves). Should commercial interests develop in "nucleus-banking," as they have in sperm-banking; should famous athletes or other celebrities decide to market their DNA the way they now market their autographs and just about everything else; should techniques of embryo and germline genetic testing and manipulation arrive as anticipated, increasing the use of laboratory assistance in order to obtain "better" babies—should all this come to pass, then cloning, if it is permitted, could become more than a marginal practice simply on the basis of free reproductive choice, even without any social encouragement to upgrade the gene pool or to replicate superior types. Moreover, if laboratory research on human cloning proceeds, even without any intention to produce cloned humans, the existence of cloned human embryos in the laboratory, created to begin with only for research purposes, would surely pave the way for later baby-making implantations.

In anticipation of human cloning, apologists and proponents have already made clear possible uses of the perfected technology, ranging from the sentimental and compassionate to the grandiose. They include: providing a child for an infertile couple; "replacing" a beloved spouse or child who is dying or who has died; avoiding the risk of genetic disease; permitting reproduction for homosexual men and lesbians who want nothing sexual to do with the opposite sex; securing a genetically identical source of organs or tissues perfectly suitable for transplantation; getting a child with a genotype of one's own choosing, not excluding oneself; replicating individuals of great genius, talent or beauty—having a child who really could "be like Mike"; and creating large sets of genetically identical humans suitable for research on, for instance, the question of nature versus nurture, or for special missions in peace and war (not excluding espionage), in which using identical humans would be an advantage. Most people who envision the cloning of human beings, of course, want none of these scenarios. That they cannot say why is not surprising. What is surprising, and welcome, is that, in our cynical age, they are saying anything at all.

THE WISDOM OF REPUGNANCE

"Offensive." "Grotesque." "Revolting." "Repugnant." "Repulsive." These are the words most commonly heard regarding the prospect of human cloning. Such reactions come both from the man or woman in the street and from the intellectuals, from believers and atheists, from humanists and scientists. Even Dolly's creator has said he "would find it offensive" to clone a human being.

People are repelled by many aspects of human cloning. They recoil from the prospect of mass production of human beings, with large clones of look-alikes, compromised in their individuality; the idea of father-son or mother-daughter twins; the bizarre prospects of a woman giving birth to and rearing a genetic copy of herself, her spouse or even her deceased father or mother; the grotesqueness of conceiving a child as an exact replacement for another who has died; the utilitarian creation of embryonic genetic duplicates of oneself, to be frozen away or created when necessary, in case of need for homologous tissues or organs for transplantation; the narcissism of those who would clone themselves and the arrogance of others who think they know who deserves to be cloned or which genotype any child-to-be should be thrilled to receive; the Frankensteinian hubris to create human life and increasingly to control its destiny; man playing God. Almost no one finds any of the suggested reasons for human cloning compelling; almost everyone anticipates its possible misuses and abuses. Moreover, many people feel oppressed by the sense that there is probably nothing we can do to prevent it from happening. This makes the prospect all the more revolting.

Revulsion is not an argument; and some of yesterday's repugnancies are today calmly accepted—though, one must add, not always for the better. In crucial cases, however, repugnance is the emotional expression of deep wisdom, beyond reason's power fully to articulate it. Can anyone really give an argument fully adequate to the horror which is father-daughter incest (even with consent), or having sex with animals, or mutilating a corpse, or eating human flesh, or even just (just!) raping or murdering another human being? Would anybody's failure to give full rational justification for his or her revulsion at these practices make that revulsion ethically suspect? Not at all. On the contrary, we are suspicious of those who think that they can rationalize away our horror, say, by trying to explain the enormity of incest with arguments only about the genetic risks of inbreeding.

The repugnance of human cloning belongs in this category. We are repelled by the prospect of cloning human beings not because of the strangeness or novelty of the undertaking, but because we intuit and feel, immediately and without argument, the violation of things that we rightfully hold dear. Repugnance, here as elsewhere, revolts against the excesses of human willfulness, warning us not to transgress what is unspeakably profound.

Indeed, in this age in which everything is held to be permissible so long as it is freely done, in which our given human nature no longer commands respect, in which our bodies are regarded as mere instruments of our autonomous rational wills, repugnance may be the only voice left that speaks up to defend the central core of our humanity. Shallow are the souls that have forgotten how to shudder. . . .

THE PROFUNDITY OF SEX

To see cloning in its proper context, we must begin not, as I did before, with laboratory technique, but with the anthropology—natural and social—of sexual reproduction.

Sexual reproduction—by which I mean the generation of new life from (exactly) two complementary elements, one female, one male, (usually) through coitus—is established (if that is the right term) not by human decision, culture or tradition, but by nature; it is the natural way of all mammalian reproduction. By nature, each child has two complementary biological progenitors. Each child thus stems from and unites exactly two lineages. In natural generation, moreover, the precise genetic constitution of the resulting offspring is determined by a combination of nature and chance, not by human design: each human child shares the common natural human species genotype, each child is genetically (equally) kin to each (both) parent(s), yet each child is genetically unique.

These biological truths about our origins foretell deep truths about our identity and about our human condition altogether. Every one of us is at once equally human, equally enmeshed in a particular familial nexus of origin, and equally individuated in our trajectory from birth to death. . . . Though less momentous than our common humanity, our genetic individuality is not humanly trivial. It shows itself forth in our distinctive appearance through which we are everywhere recognized; it is revealed in our "signature" marks of fingerprints and our self-recognizing immune system; it symbolizes and foreshadows exactly the unique, never-to-be-repeated character of each human life.

Human societies virtually everywhere have structured child-rearing responsibilities and systems of identity and relationship on the bases of these deep natural facts of begetting. The mysterious yet ubiquitous "love of one's own" is everywhere culturally exploited, to make sure that children are not just produced but well cared for and to create for everyone clear ties of meaning, belonging and obligation. But it is wrong to treat such naturally rooted social practices as mere cultural constructs (like left- or right-driving, or like burying or cremating the dead) that we can alter with little human cost. What would kinship be without its clear natural grounding? And what would identity be without kinship? We must resist those who have begun to refer to sexual reproduction as the "traditional method of reproduction," who would have us regard as merely traditional, and by implication arbitrary, what is in truth not only natural but most certainly profound.

Asexual reproduction, which produces "single-parent" offspring, is a radical departure from the natural human way, confounding all normal understandings of father, mother, sibling, grandparent, etc., and all moral relations tied thereto. It becomes even more of a radical departure when the resulting offspring is a clone derived not from an embryo, but from a mature adult to whom the clone would be an identical twin; and when the process occurs not by natural accident (as in natural twinning), but by deliberate human design and manipulation; and when the child's (or children's) genetic constitution is preselected by the parent(s) (or scientists). Accordingly, as we will see, cloning is vulnerable to three kinds of concerns and objections, related to these three points: cloning threatens confusion of identity and individuality, even in small-scale cloning; cloning represents a giant step (though not the first one) toward transforming procreation into manufacture, that is, toward the increasing depersonalization of the process of generation and, increasingly, toward the "production" of human children as artifacts, products of human will and design (what others have called the problems of "commodification" of new life); and cloning—like other forms of eugenic engineering of the next generation—represents a form of despotism of the cloners over the cloned, and thus (even in benevolent cases) represents a blatant violation of the inner meaning of parent-child relations, of what it means to have a child, of what it means to say "yes" to our own demise and "replacement."

Human procreation, in sum, is not simply an activity of our rational wills. It is a more complete activity precisely because it engages us bodily, erotically and spiritually, as well as rationally. There is wisdom in the mystery of nature that has joined the pleasure of sex, the inarticulate longing for union, the communication of the loving embrace and the deep-seated and only partly articulate desire for children in the very activity by which we continue the chain of human existence and participate in the renewal of human possibility. Whether or not we know it, the severing of procreation from sex, love and intimacy is inherently dehumanizing, no matter how good the product.

We are now ready for the more specific objections to cloning.

THE PERVERSITIES OF CLONING

First, an important if formal objection: any attempt to clone a human being would constitute an unethical experiment upon the resulting child-to-be. As the animal experiments (frog and sheep) indicate, there are grave risks of mishaps and deformities. Moreover, because of what cloning means, one cannot presume a future cloned child's consent to be a clone, even a healthy one. Thus, ethically speaking, we cannot even get to know whether or not human cloning is feasible.

I understand, of course, the philosophical difficulty of trying to compare a life with defects against nonexistence. Several bioethicists, proud of their philosophical cleverness, use this conundrum to embarrass claims that one can injure a child in its conception, precisely because it is only thanks to that complained-of conception that the child is alive to complain. But common sense tells us that we have no reason to fear such philosophisms. For we surely know that people can harm and even maim children in the very act of conceiving them, say, by paternal transmission of the AIDS virus, maternal transmission of heroin dependence or, arguably, even by bringing them into being as bastards or with no capacity or willingness to look after them properly. And we believe that to do this intentionally, or even negligently, is inexcusable and clearly unethical.

The objection about the impossibility of presuming consent may even go beyond the obvious and sufficient point that a clonant, were he subsequently to be asked, could rightly resent having been made a clone. At issue are not just benefits and harms, but doubts about the very independence needed to give proper (even retroactive) consent, that is, not just the capacity to choose but the disposition and ability to choose freely and well. It is not at all clear to what extent a clone will truly be a moral agent. For, as we shall see, in the very fact of cloning, and of rearing him as a clone, his makers subvert the cloned child's independence, beginning with that aspect that comes from knowing that one was an unbidden surprise, a gift, to the world, rather than the designed result of someone's artful project.

Cloning creates serious issues of identity and individuality. The cloned person may experience concerns about his distinctive identity not only because he will be in genotype and appearance identical to another human being, but, in this case, because he may also be twin to the person who is his "father" or "mother"—if one can still call them that. What would be the psychic burdens of being the "child" or "parent" of your twin? The cloned individual, moreover, will be saddled with a genotype that has already lived. He will not be fully a surprise to the world. People are likely always to compare his performances in life with that of his alter ego. True, his nurture and his circumstances in life will be different; genotype is not exactly destiny. Still, one must also expect parental and other efforts to shape the new life after the original—or at least to view the child with the original version always firmly in mind. Why else did they clone from the star basketball player, mathematician and beauty queen—or even dear old dad—in the first place?

Since the birth of Dolly, there has been a fair amount of doublespeak on this matter of genetic identity. Experts have rushed in to reassure the public that the clone would in no way be the same person, or have any confusions about his or her identity: as previously noted, they are pleased to point out that the clone of Mel Gibson would not be Mel Gibson. Fair enough. But one is shortchanging the truth by emphasizing the additional importance of the intrauterine environment, rearing and social setting: genotype obviously matters plenty. That, after all, is the only reason to clone, whether human beings or sheep. The odds that clones of Wilt Chamberlain will be playing in the NBA are, I submit, infinitely greater than they are for clones of Robert Reich.

Curiously, this conclusion is supported, inadvertently, by the one ethical sticking point insisted on by friends of cloning: no cloning without the donor's consent. Though an orthodox liberal objection, it is in fact quite puzzling when it comes from people who also insist that genotype is not identity or individuality, and who deny that a child could reasonably complain about being made a genetic copy. If the clone of Mel Gibson would not be Mel Gibson, why should Mel Gibson have grounds to object that someone had been made his clone? We already allow researchers to use blood and tissue samples for research purposes of no benefit to their sources: my falling hair, my expectorations, my urine and even my biopsied tissues are "not me" and not mine. Courts have held that the profit gained from uses to which scientists put my discarded tissues do not legally belong to me. Why, then, no cloning without consent—including, I assume, no cloning from the body of someone who just died? What harm is done the donor, if genotype is "not me"? Truth to tell, the only powerful justification for objecting is that genotype really does have something to do with identity, and everybody knows it. If not, on what basis could Michael Jordan object that someone cloned "him," say, from cells taken from a "lost" scraped-off piece of his skin? The insistence on donor consent unwittingly reveals the problem of identity in all cloning.

Genetic distinctiveness not only symbolizes the uniqueness of each human life and the independence of its parents that each human child rightfully attains. It can also be an important support for living a worthy and dignified life. Such arguments apply with great force to any large-scale replication of human individuals. But they are sufficient, in my view, to rebut even the first attempts to clone a human being. One must never forget that these are human beings upon whom our eugenic or merely playful fantasies are to be enacted. . . .

Human cloning would also represent a giant step toward turning begetting into making, procreation into manufacture (literally, something "handmade"), a process already begun with in vitro fertilization and genetic testing of embryos. With cloning, not only is the process in hand, but the total genetic blueprint of the cloned individual is selected and determined by the human artisans. To be sure, subsequent development will take place according to natural processes; and the resulting children will still be recognizably human. But we here would be taking a major step into making man himself simply another one of the man-made things. Human nature becomes merely the last part of nature to succumb to the technological project, which turns all of nature into raw material at human disposal, to be homogenized by our rationalized technique according to the subjective prejudices of the day.

How does begetting differ from making? In natural procreation, human beings come together, complementarily male and female, to give existence to another being who is formed, exactly as we were, *by what we are:* living, hence perishable, hence aspiringly erotic, human beings. In clonal reproduction, by contrast, and in the more advanced forms of manufacture to which it leads, we give existence to a being not by what we are but by what we intend and design. As with any product of our making, no matter how excellent, the artificer stands above it, not as an equal but as a superior, transcending it by his will and creative prowess. Scientists who clone animals make it perfectly clear that they are engaged in instrumental making; the animals are, from the start, designed as means to serve rational human purposes. In human cloning, scientists and prospective "parents" would be adopting the same technocratic mentality to human children: human children would be their artifacts.

Such an arrangement is profoundly dehumanizing, no matter how good the product. Mass-scale cloning of the same individual makes the point vividly; but the violation of human equality, freedom and dignity are present even in a single planned clone. And procreation dehumanized into manufacture is further degraded by commodification, a virtually inescapable result of allowing baby-making to proceed under the banner of commerce. Genetic and reproductive biotechnology companies are already growth industries, but they will go into commercial orbit once the Human Genome Project nears completion. . . .

Finally, and perhaps most important, the practice of human cloning by nuclear transfer—like other anticipated forms of genetic engineering of the next generation—would enshrine and aggravate a profound and mischievous misunderstanding of the meaning of having children and of the parent-child relationship. When a couple now chooses to procreate, the partners are saying yes to the emergence of new life in its novelty, saying yes not only to having a child but also, tacitly, to having whatever child this child turns out to be. In accepting our finitude and opening ourselves to our replacement, we are tacitly confessing the limits of our control. In this ubiquitous way of nature, embracing the future by procreating means precisely that we are relinquishing our grip, in the very activity of taking up our own share in what we hope will be the immortality of human life and the human species. This means that our children are not *our* children: they are not our property, not our possessions. Neither are they supposed to live our lives for us, or anyone else's life but their own. To be sure, we seek to guide them on their way, imparting to them not just life but nurturing, love, and a way of life; to be sure, they bear our hopes that they will live fine and flourishing lives, enabling us in small measure to transcend our own limitations. Still, their genetic distinctiveness and independence are the natural foreshadowing of the deep truth that they have their own and never-before-enacted life to live. They are sprung from a past, but they take an uncharted course into the future.

Much harm is already done by parents who try to live vicariously through their children. Children are sometimes compelled to fulfill the broken dreams of unhappy parents: John Doe Jr. or the III is under the burden of having to live up to his forebear's name. Still, if most parents have hopes for their children, cloning parents will have expectations. In cloning, such overbearing parents take at the start a decisive step which contradicts the entire meaning of the open and forward-looking nature of parent-child relations. The child is given a genotype that has already lived, with full expectation that this blueprint of a past life ought to be controlling of the life that is to come. Cloning is inherently despotic, for it seeks to make one's children (or someone else's children) after one's own image (or an image of one's choosing) and their future according to one's will. In some cases, the despotism may be mild and benevolent. In other cases, it will be mischievous and downright tyrannical. But despotism—the control of another through one's will—it inevitably will be.

MEETING SOME OBJECTIONS

The defenders of cloning, of course, are not wittingly friends of despotism. Indeed, they regard themselves mainly as friends of freedom: the freedom of individuals to reproduce, the freedom of scientists and inventors to discover and devise and to foster "progress" in genetic knowledge and technique. They want large-scale cloning only for animals, but they wish to preserve cloning as a human option for exercising our "right to reproduce"—our right to have children, and children with "desirable genes." As law professor John Robertson points out, under our "right to reproduce" we already practice early forms of unnatural, artificial and extramarital reproduction, and we already practice early forms of eugenic choice. For this reason, he argues, cloning is no big deal.

We have here a perfect example of the logic of the slippery slope, and the slippery way in which it already works in this area. Only a few years ago, slippery slope arguments were used to oppose artificial insemination and in vitro fertilization using unrelated sperm donors. Principles used to justify these practices, it was said, will be used to justify more artificial and more eugenic practices, including cloning. Not so, the defenders retorted, since we can make the necessary distinctions. And now, without even a gesture at making the necessary distinctions, the continuity of practice is held by itself to be justificatory.

The principle of reproductive freedom as currently enunciated by the proponents of cloning logically embraces the ethical acceptability of sliding down the entire rest of the slope—to producing children ectogenetically from sperm to term (should it become feasible) and to producing children whose entire genetic makeup will be the product of parental eugenic planning and choice. If reproductive freedom means the right to have a child of one's own choosing, by whatever means, it knows and accepts no limits.

But, far from being legitimated by a "right to reproduce," the emergence of techniques of assisted reproduction and genetic engineering should compel us to reconsider the meaning and limits of such a putative right. In truth, a "right to reproduce" has always been a peculiar and problematic notion. Rights generally belong to individuals, but this is a right which (before cloning) no one can exercise alone. Does the right then inhere only in couples? Only in married couples? Is it a (woman's) right to carry or deliver or a right (of one or more parents) to nurture and rear? Is it a right to have your own biological child? Is it a right only to attempt reproduction, or a right also to succeed? Is it a right to acquire the baby of one's choice?

The assertion of a negative "right to reproduce" certainly makes sense when it claims protection against state interference with procreative liberty, say, through a program of compulsory sterilization. But surely it cannot be the basis of a tort claim against nature, to be made good by technology, should free efforts at natural procreation fail. Some insist that the right to reproduce embraces also the right against state interference with the free use of all technological means to obtain a child. Yet such a position cannot be sustained: for reasons having to do with the means employed, any community may rightfully prohibit surrogate pregnancy, or polygamy, or the sale of babies to infertile couples, without violating anyone's basic human "right to reproduce." When the exercise of a previously innocuous freedom now involves or impinges on troublesome practices that the original freedom never was intended to reach, the general presumption of liberty needs to be reconsidered. . . .

Though I recognize certain continuities between cloning and, say, in vitro fertilization, I believe that cloning differs in essential and important ways. Yet those who disagree should be reminded that the "continuity" argument cuts both ways. Sometimes we establish bad precedents, and discover that they were bad only when we follow their inexorable logic to places we never meant to go. Can the defenders of cloning show us today how, on their principles, we will be able to see producing babies ("perfect babies") entirely in the laboratory or exercising full control over their genotypes (including so-called enhancement) as ethically different, in any essential way, from present forms of assisted reproduction? Or are they willing to admit, despite their attachment to the principle of continuity, that the complete obliteration of "mother" or "father," the complete depersonalization of procreation, the complete manufacture of human beings and the complete genetic control of one generation over the next would be ethically problematic and essentially different from current forms of assisted reproduction? If so, where and how will they draw the line, and why? I draw it at cloning, for all the reasons given.

BAN THE CLONING OF HUMANS

What, then, should we do? We should declare that human cloning is unethical in itself and dangerous in its likely consequences. In so doing, we shall have the backing of the overwhelming majority of our fellow Americans, and of the human race, and (I believe) of most practicing scientists. Next, we should do all that we can to prevent the cloning of human beings. We should do this by means of an international legal ban if possible, and by a unilateral national ban, at a minimum. . . .

Discussion Questions

1. Feeling repugnance does not, in itself, signal that the object of our repugnance is immoral; repugnance can arise from cultural conditioning as well. For example, people once felt deep repugnance at the thought of interracial marriage. Discuss whether

Kass provides a convincing argument for his claim that our repugnance at the prospect of human cloning is based on "deep wisdom" rather than cultural constructs.

2. One of Kass's objections to cloning is that there are too many risks of mishaps and deformities. Would cloning be morally acceptable if it were perfected to the point where the chances of mishaps and deformities were significantly less than relying on sexual reproduction? How would Kass answer this question? How would a utilitarian philosopher respond?
3. Are Kass's concerns regarding the autonomy and identity of a clone well founded? Discuss how Ridley might respond to Kass's concerns. Who presents the most compelling argument—Kass or Ridley? Support your answer.
4. Kass argues that whereas using preimplantation to create a healthy child may be morally acceptable, the use of cloning to produce a healthy child never is. Is this distinction justified? Support your answer.

LORI ANDREWS AND DOROTHY NELKIN

Whose Body Is It Anyway? Disputes over Body Tissue in a Biotechnology Age

Lori Andrews is a professor of law and director of the Institute of Science, Law and Technology at Chicago–Kent College of Law. Dorothy Nelkin is a professor of sociology and a law professor at New York University. In the following selection, Andrews and Nelkin explore the gap between scientific and social views of the body in the increasing commercialization of bodily tissue. In particular, they raise the question of whether individuals have a right to know what use will be made of their bodily tissue for genetic tests and gene patents.

Critical Reading Questions

1. What are some of the historic precedents for the collection and use of bodily tissues by scientists and physicians?
2. What is the biotechnology age? What are some of the ways interest in the use of bodily tissues has changed in the biotechnology age?
3. Define the scientific view and the social view of the body. What is the basis of each view? What are some examples of these views?
4. Which view of the body, the scientific or the social, prevails in the biotechnology age?

Lori Andrews and Dorothy Nelkin, "Whose Body Is It Anyway? Disputes Over Body Tissue in a Biotechnology Age," *Lancet*, Vol. 352, Issue 9095, January 3, 1998, pp. 53–57. Some notes have been omitted.

5. Why is the Human Genome Diversity Project (HGDP) interested in studying the bodily tissue of indigenous people? In what ways does the HGDP's view of the body conflict with those of many indigenous groups?
6. According to Andrews and Nelkin, what rights are at stake in the use of patients' tissues for genetic testing and patents?
7. What are some of the U.S. court decisions regarding the conflict between the use of bodily tissue by scientists and physicians and the rights of the patients?
8. What policies have been proposed for regulating the commercial use of bodily tissue?

The collection and use of human body tissue—from 18th century practices of dissection to 20th century organ transplantation—have evoked concerns about the use of body parts without consent; the psychological, social, and religious impact of breaking down the integrity of the body; and, especially, the potential exploitation of the individuals who are the sources of organs and tissues. Physicians and scientists have been accused of profiteering, insensitivity to the emotions of patients or family members, and secrecy about unseemly practices as they sought out cadavers and body parts.

Recent disputes—over the taking,[1] use,[2] and distribution[3] of body tissue; the genetic testing of previously collected samples;[4,5] and the patentability of human genes[6]—are taking place in an increasingly commercial context. They are often viewed in terms of a narrow practical question: are individuals entitled to know about, and have a say in, the uses that are made of their body tissue? But the proliferation and diversity of disputes over body tissue are symptomatic of a much larger problem—a growing divide between scientific and social views of the body in the commercial context of the biotechnology age. This gap is the focus of our analysis.

THE GROWTH OF INTEREST IN HUMAN TISSUE

Human tissue has always provided clues to health status. But the body in the biotechnology age is speaking in new ways. DNA analysis of waste tissue such as hair, blood, or saliva can reveal intimate and detailed information about a person. Genetic testing of tissue can indicate an individual's future health, information that may open beneficial therapeutic or remedial options, but also the possibility of employment or insurance discrimination.[7] And, according to recent scientific claims, human tissue can reveal information about behavioral traits,[8] race,[9] or sexual preference.[10]

Human tissue has also become a source of raw material for products (such as cell lines and diagnostic tests). The market for skin, blood, placenta, gametes, biopsied tissue, and genetic material is expanding,[11] driven partly by commercial incentives fostered by legal developments in the 1980s. . . . A landmark US Supreme Court case in 1980 granted a patent on a life-form (a bacterium) setting the stage for the patenting of human genes.[12] . . .

As the market for human tissue has increased, so have disputes in which scientific and commercial ideas about the proper uses of tissue confront social and personal understandings about the body. Whereas scientists seek greater access to bodily materials, others defend their cultural values and individual rights. Scientists need to pay greater heed to such social claims, for they reflect legitimate interests and further other important social values and activities. Indeed, courts and other policy-making bodies are struggling to develop systems to accommodate productive use of bodily materials while respecting cultural associations and individual rights. And they are increasingly incorporating social meanings of the body into their decisions.

THE SCIENTIFIC VIEW OF THE BODY

In 1772, Robert Boyle expressed a view of the body that has characterized much of medical practice: "I think the physician is to look upon the patient's body as an engine that is out of order, but yet so constituted that, by his concurrence with . . . the parts of the automaton itself, it may be brought to a better state."[13] This mechanical view of the body as a set of parts that can be manipulated, analyzed, and enhanced has reached the ultimate in genetics in which the very object manipulated, assessed, turned into a product, and enhanced, is the DNA itself. . . .

Expanding commercial interests in the biotechnology age have reinforced this trend, but not without costs. Biologist Ernest Chargaff warns that the growth of human tissue research can be a slippery slope to social disaster, "an Auschwitz in which valuable enzymes, hormones, and so on will be extracted instead of gold teeth."[14] Others see the search for human tissue as a modern-day form of body snatching. The body is clearly more than an abstract object, a project, a resource to be mined.

THE SOCIAL MEANING OF THE BODY

Just as the scientific view of the body serves certain functions for scientists and for society, so personal and social views of the body serve certain functions for individuals and their communities. A person's control over what is done to his or her body, or its parts, is important to the individual's psychological development and well-being. It is also a means to establish identity and convey values to others. But body tissue has social importance beyond the individual.[15] Social conceptions of the body establish community identification, encourage socially responsible behaviors, and set acceptable priorities for group activities. . . .

Because the body is also a means to express personal values, some people want to place limits on the use of their body parts. Some men who donate sperm only want it used by married couples. Some women will serve as a surrogate mother for women with infertility problems, but not for those who want to avoid pregnancy for career reasons. During the Nazi occupation of the Netherlands, many citizens, as a form of social protest, refused to take part in blood transfusions for Nazi soldiers. Some African-American women, recalling past research abuses, refuse to allow amniotic tissue to be collected for prenatal diagnosis out of concern about the uses that could be made of this tissue.[16] Other people have objected to the use of their tissue in the commercialized setting of biotechnology firms. The decisions people make about the body and its parts convey important messages about identity, values, and interests.

Body tissue also has important social meaning. In some developing world societies, blood, hair, and placenta are important in social rituals, defining community identification and reinforcing the values and rules that govern accepted behavior.[17] But even in contemporary western societies, the treatment of body parts can define community and reinforce social values. People signal their identification with their community by the way they display and manipulate their body. Sensitive questions emerge when genetic analysis of body tissue is used to reveal community identity. Through tissue analysis, a person may (whether that person wishes to or not) be identified according to particular genetic criteria as a member of a certain family, a certain race, a certain culture, or a certain sex. Some patients do not want their tissue used (even without their names attached) for research on race and intelligence, race and crime, or sex and mathematical ability because the findings of the research could label and stigmatize their group. . . .

Control over the use of body tissue is also critical for establishing religious identity and demonstrating religious beliefs. Navajo Indians believe that placenta should be buried, rather than regarded as "waste" that is available for research. Voicing opposition to the patenting of genes, some religious leaders insist that the body be valued as a fulfillment of divine purpose: the body belongs to God.[18] . . .

The norms that guide the disposition of body tissue reflect community ideals; the highest priorities for body use in a social sense are not always the same as those advocated by scientists. Giving blood and body tissue rather than selling it, for example, is a way to encourage altruism and affirm social cohesion by linking donors to strangers and donations to the public good. A dispute over the development of private cord-blood banks and the patenting of the cord-blood stem-cell extraction technique resulted from a conflict between community ideals and the encouragement of commerce. Those who believe that cord-blood should be a public resource, freely available to those in need of therapy, have challenged commercial interests that see patenting and privatization as essential for investment in research.

The wide range of social meanings placed upon the body—in defining community, reinforcing acceptable behavior, and establishing priorities—have converged in disputes surrounding the Human Genome Diversity Project (HGDP). In some cases, the opposition to the Project's collection of blood and tissue for DNA analysis reflects ritual beliefs in the communal importance of body tissue. But the opposition also follows from historically informed resentment of exploitation.

HGDP scientists insist that blood is replenishable, that taking it does no harm. But indigenous groups with little reason to trust western science have other priorities that can be expressed through controlling the use of their bodies: the major threat to their health is not genetic disease, but disorders such as diarrhea.[19] They see the harvesting of genes from people from developing countries as "biocolonialism," providing cures for diseases in the developed world and products affordable only in wealthy countries. They believe that the project might threaten their future. Scientists want to "immortalize" the cell lines of groups that are going to become extinct.[20] But members of indigenous groups fear that preservation of their DNA could eliminate the incentives to improve social conditions that would ensure their survival. They derive little comfort from the reductionist idea that their DNA lives on while their descendants perish. In 1993, the World Council of Indigenous Peoples unanimously voted to "categorically reject and condemn the Human Genome Diversity Project as it applies to our rights, lives and dignity."[21]

SCIENTISTS' RESPONSES

The gap between scientific and social perspectives of the body has been exacerbated by the often dismissive or defensive reactions of scientists. . . .

The most powerful arguments made by scientists seeking unimpeded access to human tissue have to do with contributions to scientific and medical progress. They argue that restraints on their ability to gain access to, manipulate, and commercialize tissue will impede the progress of research and deprive society of useful medical benefits. But that argument is wearing thin. The "advances" in genetic diagnosis of late-onset disorders have meant that many currently healthy people live under the sword of Damocles—of knowing they are at enhanced risk for later illnesses, such as breast cancer or Alzheimer's disease. . . .

Moreover, claims about the potential benefits from unrestricted access to patient-tissue have been exaggerated. A federally appointed committee investigating gene therapy found that, even though 567 Americans had undergone gene therapy, in about 100 different experiments, "there is still little or no evidence of therapeutic benefit [of gene therapy] in patients or even animal models." The panel condemned most of the efforts as "pure hype" and expressed concern that in the rush to undertake gene therapy, the development of other easier-to-achieve conventional treatments for the same disease was likely to be ignored.[22]

INTEGRATED CULTURAL MEANING INTO POLICY

The potential contribution of unfettered research to scientific and medical progress has had significant influence on legal and policy decisions. For example, in *Moore v Regents of the University of California,*[23] a patient sued his physician and a biotechnology company for using his biopsied tissue without his consent and transforming it into a patented commercial cell line, and the court sided with the interests of the defendant. Its reasoning was that giving the patient a property right to his tissue would impede progress and "destroy the economic incentive to conduct important medical research."

However, in recent decisions, the federal government, professional societies, institutional review boards, and courts have begun to apply values other than mere scientific progress. Some institutional review boards, for example, have integrated cultural values into the protocols for tissue retrieval and use, giving patients increased rights to control the uses made of their body material. . . .

The personal feelings of individuals about maintaining body integrity are increasingly recognized by the courts. In one case, a man with a strong fear of fire had his leg amputated.[24] 4 weeks later, he inquired about the disposal of the leg. When he learned that it had been incinerated, he suffered psychological "shock." The court did not allow him to sue the hospital for shock because he did not voice his concerns in a timely manner. But the court did indicate that patients have the right to make specific reservations about demands on, or objections to, a hospital's normal procedures for disposal of tissue.

Even in the *Moore* case, the California Supreme Court held that the physician had violated his fiduciary duty by not telling the patient in advance of surgery that the physician had a commercial interest in the tissue: "A physician who treats a patient in whom he also has a research interest has potentially conflicting loyalties."[25] . . .

Cultural norms, too, are beginning to influence the treatment of body tissue. The North American Advisory Group to the HGDP has emphasized the importance of sensitivity to community values in the collection of tissue from indigenous groups. They would require that the current process be handled in a culturally appropriate way, including the need for consent from a representative or the leader of the group or tribe, not only from the individuals being sampled. . . .

Policies governing the use of patients' tissues for genetic testing, product development, and transplantation are currently being debated. The proliferation of disputes suggest that social conceptions of the body serve important purposes for individuals and society. Ignoring them may be hazardous—to the psychological well-being of individuals, to the maintenance of important social values, and to the future of science itself.

NOTES

1. *Mayfield v Dalton,* 901 F.Supp. 300 (1995); US Court of Appeals, 9th Cir. 95-16626.
2. *Moore v Regents of the University of California,* 793 P.2d 479 (Cal. 1990).
3. Mitchell P. European researchers condemn US firm's cord-blood-storage patent. *Lancet* 1997; **349:** 1232.
4. *Norman-Bloodsaw v Lawrence Berkeley Nat'l Lab,* No. C95-03220 (N.D. Cal. Filed Sept 12, 1995).
5. Clayton EW, Steinberg KK, Khoury MJ, et al. Informed Consent for Genetic Research on Stored Tissue Samples. *JAMA* 1995; **274:** 1786–92.
6. Eisenberg RS. "Patenting the Human Genome," 39 *Emory LJ* 721 (1990).
7. Nelkin D, Tancredi L. Dangerous diagnostics, 2nd ed. Chicago: University of Chicago Press, 1995.
8. Kelner K, Benditt J. Genes and Behaviour. *Science* 1994; **264:** 1685–97.
9. Genes in Black and White. *New Scientist* July 8, 1995: 34–37.
10. Hamer D, Copeland P. The science of desire. New York: Simon and Schuster, 1995.
11. Kimbrell A. The human body shop: the engineering and marketing of life. San Francisco: Harper, 1993.
12. *Diamond v Chakabarty,* 447 US 303 (1980).
13. Robert Boyle, Works, vol 5, 1772 p 236. In: Feher M, ed. Fragments for a History of the Human Body 3. New York: Zone Books, 1989.
14. Quoted in Kimbrell A. The Human Body Shop 284. San Francisco: Harper's 1993.
15. Douglas M. Purity and danger. London: Routledge, 1966 (reprinted 1996).
16. Rapp R. Refusing Pre-natal Diagnosis: The Uneven Meanings of Bioscience in a Multicultural World. *Science, Technology and Human Values.* Fall 1997.
17. Turner V. The forest of symbols. Ithaca, New York: Cornell University Press, 1967.
18. Pope John Paul II. "Address to the Pontifical Academy of Sciences." October 8, 1994, quoted in *Family Resource Center News* (Winter 1996).
19. Lappé M. Broken code 80. San Francisco: Sierra Club Books, 1994.

20. Bowcock A, Cavilli-S Forza L. The study of variation in the human genome. *Genomics* 1991; **11:** 191–98.
21. World Council of Indigenous People's "Resolution on the HGDP." Native Net Archive Page, <http://broc09.uthscsa.edu/natnet/archive/nl/hgdp.html>.
22. "Report and Recommendations of the Panel to Assess the NIH Investment and Research on Gene Therapy" 9, 32 (Stuart H Orkin and Arno G Motulsky, co-chairs, Dec 7, 1995).
23. *Moore v Regents of the University of California,* 271 Cal. Rptr. 146, 151 (Cal 1990).
24. *Browning v Norton Children's Hospital,* 504 S.W.2d 713 (Ky. 1974).
25. *Moore v Regents of the University of California,* 271 Cal. Rptr. 146, 151 (Cal 1990).

Discussion Questions

1. Discuss the social and scientific views of the the human body in light of the concepts of genetic determinism.
2. Discuss the moral implications of the social and scientific views of the body for genetic testing and genetic engineering. Are these the only two ways of viewing the human body, and if not, what are some other ways of viewing the human body? What view of the human body is most compatible with the fundamental moral principles of respect for persons?
3. Gus Stokes has been HIV positive for over twenty years, yet he has developed no symptoms of AIDS. His physician, Dr. Sharma, thinks that Stokes might have a genetic antibody to AIDS. If this gene could be identified, it is possible that it could be reproduced and used in somatic gene therapy, thus possibly saving the lives of millions of people who are HIV positive. When Dr. Sharma asks Stokes for permission to use a sample of his blood for research Stokes refuses. "This body is my own," he says, "and I don't want anyone messing with my genes and giving them to other people."

   Dr. Sharma already has several samples of Stokes's blood left over from routine medical tests. Should she use the samples and not tell Stokes; indeed, does she have a moral obligation to do so? Or does Stokes have a moral right to refuse to let scientists use his tissue for a possible cure for AIDS? What would you do if you were Stokes's physician?

   Discuss how Andrews and Nelkin, as well as a utilitarian and a rights ethicist, might each respond to the above scenario.
4. Discuss how both Ridley and Kass would most likely respond to Andrews's and Nelkin's concerns about the commercialization of the human tissue, including the use of genetic material from indigenous people.
5. Formulate a public policy for the use of patients' tissues for genetic testing, research, and transplantation, as well as for gene patents. Evaluate and revise, when appropriate, your policy in light of the universal moral theories presented in Chapter 1.

CASE STUDIES

1. EVE: THE WORLD'S FIRST CLONED HUMAN?

On December 26, 2002, Clonaid, a Bahamas-based company, announced the birth of Eve—the world's first cloned human. According to Clonaid, they fused over two hundred human eggs with adult cells in order to get ten which appeared normal. The other four cloned children were born in 2003.

After initially agreeing to DNA testing on Eve, Clonaid CEO Brigitte Boisselier told the press that Clonaid would not reveal the identity of the mother and child, or cooperate in performing genetic tests on the child and mother to confirm that they were clones. Clonaid made the decision after a Florida judge apparently threatened to remove the child from her mother. Clonaid was concerned that lawsuits filed in the United States and the Netherlands were making testing impossible because the tests would be used to try and identify the parent and child and take them into custody.

Some people fear that the real reason for Clonaid's refusal is that Eve may have already developed serious medical problems. Others dismiss Clonaid's claims that they cloned a human child as a hoax, called Clonaid a "rogue organization," pointing out that the company was founded by members of a sect who believe that humans were created by extraterrestrials.[31] Meanwhile geneticists in Changsha, China recently announced that they have successfully grown eighty cloned human embryos.[32] Whether the embryos will be implanted remains to be seen.

Discussion Questions

1. If Clonaid was indeed successful in cloning the first human babies, were they acting immorally? Is the fact that the company was formed by members of a sect morally relevant? Discuss how Robertson and Kass might each respond to these questions.
2. Is cloning a liberty right? Would we be interfering with a person's reproductive rights if we denied them the opportunity to be cloned? Discuss how Robertson, Kass, and Ridley might each respond to these questions.
3. An American couple offered Clonaid $500,000 to clone their dead infant. The couple has other children and are not infertile. According to a spokesperson at Clonaid: "They just want to give this particular genome another chance."[33] Is this a morally acceptable reason for using cloning? Discuss your answer in light of some of the arguments for and against cloning put forth in this chapter.
4. Discuss the moral issues involved in the destruction of large numbers of embryos in order to produce a clone. Relate your answers to the debates about personhood.
5. Given the additional health risks associated with cloning, what is the responsibility of the state in this case? Should the courts try to force Clonaid to produce DNA tests and the identity of Eve and her mother? What if the child is found to have serious medical problems—is this sufficient reason for the state to take over custody of her? Do parents have a duty to forgo having children who are genetically related to them (through cloning or by normal means) if doing so puts the future children at risk? How about parents who are carriers of serious genetic disorders, yet still choose to have children the "natural" way knowing that, on average, between 25 percent and 50 percent (depending on the disorder) will have the disorder? Should they be

treated by the courts the same way as parents who choose to have a child of their own through cloning? Support your answers.

---

2. DOLLY AND HER SISTERS: GENETICALLY ENGINEERING ANIMALS WITH HUMAN GENES

In December 1997 the same scientists who brought Dolly into the limelight achieved another breakthrough with the birth of five almost-identical Dorset lambs. The lambs were created by fusing a fetal lamb cell, which was altered by the addition of human genetic material, into the nucleus of a cell from a sheep's ovary. The lambs carry a gene to produce factor IX, a blood-clotting substance used in treating a rare form of hemophilia known as hemophilia B or Christmas disease. People with hemophilia B lack factor IX, a component of blood plasma.

The Edinburgh-based firm PPL Therapeutics, which helped fund the research, announced that it wants to eventually establish herds of sheep carrying human genes to produce proteins and blood products for treating diseases such as hemophilia and osteoporosis.

In 1998 George and Charlie, two Holsteins, were born. They were cloned from genetically engineered fetal cells that included human genes so their milk would contain valuable human proteins such as factor IX.[34]

Two years later five piglets were cloned from an adult female by PPL Therapeutics.[35] PPL plans to use them to develop and clone genetically modified pigs whose organs can be used for transplantation into humans.

Trans Ova Genetics in Iowa is currently genetically engineering cows with human genes, then cloning them and inoculating them against biological agents such as anthrax, smallpox, and botulism in the hope that the transgenic cows will eventually produce human antibodies that can be used as an antidote in case of biological warfare.[36]

Discussion Questions

1. Is it morally acceptable to use other animals as a means only? Given that humans are a lot more like other animals than we previously believed, should moral respect be extended to other animals? Is cloning an affront to the dignity of other animals? Can cloning ever be a benefit to them? Discuss the implications of your answers for the morality of cloning and genetic engineering projects that use nonhuman animals.
2. What does it mean to be human? How many human genes must beings have before they merit the respect accorded to persons? Are the genetically engineered animals mentioned in the above case study part human because they carry human genes? If so, how does that affect the moral respect we should show them?
3. Many countries have banned the use of public money for research involving human cloning. Should this ban also include cloning animals with human genetic material? Should private firms be prohibited from cloning? Support your answers.
4. Discuss how a utilitarian might think about the practice of genetically engineering and cloning lambs to produce factor IX to benefit humans with hemophilia B and genetically engineering pigs so their organs can be used by humans.

---

3. USING CLONES AS ORGAN DONORS

One of the proposed uses of genetic engineering is the creation of human organs for transplantation to use as an alternative to xenoplants. One method of doing this would be to clone a person's own cells and then using the embryonic stem cells to grow the needed tissue or organ.

Jeremy has been waiting for a kidney transplant for two years and despairs of ever getting one.[37] He knows that his odds of getting the kidney he so badly needs from a compatible human donor is probably only about 5 percent. He has heard that physicians have been conducting experiments using xenoplants from pigs with limited success. Jeremy, however, feels uneasy about having a xenoplant, in part because of rumors that those people who have received the transplants have been infected with a potentially deadly virus from the transplanted organs (a rumor vehemently denied by the scientists running the experiments).

His physician tells him of an experiment using embryonic stem cells to grow organs. The process entails creating a clone of Jeremy and then aborting the embryo so that the embryo's stem cells can be harvested. The process, the physician tells him, can be carried out in vitro in a newly created "artificial womb." However, the success rate in getting the stem cells to differentiate into a functional kidney is very low, and it may take many attempts before the procedure is successful, if at all. Jeremy is opposed to abortion but also realizes that this may be his only chance for survival.

Discussion Questions

1. Because Jeremy is opposed to abortion he is faced with a moral dilemma. Role-play a situation in which Jeremy comes to you, an ethics student, for assistance in resolving his moral dilemma. Have one student play the role of Jeremy and the other the role of the ethics student. When you are finished, share your insights with the class.
2. The cloning of embryos for transplantation tissue raises the issue of abortion since the embryo must be aborted before the stem cells can be harvested. Is the abortion of embryos in order to obtain tissue for transplantation morally different than elective abortion for the reason that the woman doesn't want the pregnancy? Support your answer.
3. Discuss whether the use of cloned human embryos for organ transplants and medical research is morally preferable to the current practice of using sentient nonhuman animals for organ transplants and medical experimentation.
4. Many people consider a brain a prerequisite for personhood. Biologists have already succeeded in creating mouse embryos that fail to develop a head. According to British biologist Jonathan Slack we could do the same with human embryos.[38] These headless and, hence, nonsentient humans, he says, could serve as "organ sacs" for organ transplants as well as subjects for medical research. Discuss the moral issues involved in genetically engineering and cloning headless humans for organ transplants and medical research.

---

4. PATENTING GENETICALLY ENGINEERED LIFE FORMS

Patenting living organism life-forms is not new. In 1873 Louis Pasteur received a U.S. patent for the manufacture of a yeast that was free of disease. The first patent in the United States for a genetically engineered life-form was given in 1980 when the

U.S. Supreme Court, in *Diamond v. Chakrabarty,* held that a man-made micro-organism was a new and useful "manufacture" and, hence, patentable. In 1988 the Harvard oncomouse, a genetically modified mouse with a heightened susceptibility to cancer, drew worldwide attention when the U.S. Patent and Trademark Office (USPTO) issued a patent for it. Since then over three million genome-related patents have been filed with the USPTO, some of which pertain to genetically engineering humans. For example, in 2002 the University of Missouri was granted a patent that covers methods of cloning animals—including humans.[39]

Despite the legal status of biopatents, there is still considerable controversy about the morality of the practice. Canada does not permit patents for "higher life-forms," such as the oncomouse. China, India, and Thailand prohibit the patenting of any animals. The European Union, on the other hand, permits such patents "provided the potential benefits of the 'invention' outweigh the ethical and moral considerations, in particular the suffering of animals in developing and/or working the claimed invention."[40] Singapore, Australia, New Zealand and Japan also consider animals as patentable.

People who favor biopatents argue that researchers should be rewarded for their discoveries. People would not put the money and years into genetic research unless they had some mechanism of protecting their inventions and investment through patents. Those who are opposed question the assumption that science will advance faster if researchers can have exclusive rights to their inventions. They also point out that the monopoly on certain products and the high royalty costs owed to patent holders may discourage product development since the high costs would be passed on to the consumer, as is currently happening in the pharmaceutical industry. Finally, there is the question of whether it is moral to patent a part of nature or to own life-forms.

Discussion Questions

1. Humans have long set themselves apart from other animals as morally superior, a special creation. However, as philosopher Mary Midgley once put it, "We are not just like other animals; we are animals." Does the belief that we are creators of life reinforce the view that humans and human activities are outside of and above nature rather than part of it? Analyze the following argument: Humans are not a special creation but simply another species of mammal. It is morally acceptable to patent genetically engineered mammals such as mice. Therefore, it is also morally acceptable to genetically engineer and patent human life-forms.
2. Discuss the arguments for and against patenting life-forms. Working in a group, put together a policy for issuing patents for animals. Which moral theories were most useful in providing guidelines for the policy?
3. The United States does not permit patents on humans since it is a violation of Amendment 13 of the U.S. Constitution, which forbids slavery. If so, should transgenic animals, such as the genetically engineered pigs and cows mentioned in the second case study, be patentable? At what point does an animal genetically engineered with human genes become a human? Indeed, is it relevant, in terms of the morality of owning a patent on a mammal, whether it is a human or nonhuman? Support your answers.
4. One of the current issues under debate is the morality of patenting human/nonhuman animal chimeras. A chimera, named after the mythological fire-breathing

creature that had a lion's head, a goat's body, and a serpent's tail, is an artificially produced being with genes from two or more species. If it is morally acceptable to patent others mammals, such as mice, should human/nonhuman chimeras also be patentable? Support your answer.

5. Religious leaders denounced the 1980 *Diamond v. Chakrabarty* Supreme Court decision, calling for a moratorium on the patenting of life-forms. They argue that genetic engineers are not playing God, nor can they design new organisms from scratch. To grant patents on animal or plant genomes is to usurp the "ownership rights of God." Are human beings "creating" other beings? Do you agree that there should be a moratorium on patenting life-forms? Support your answers.
6. In his *Second Treatise of Government,* John Locke argues that ownership is a consequence of authorship. Locke adds that only God can create a living being. Parents do not create their offspring or own them; rather they are "but occasions of their being." Are genetically engineered animals (or humans for that matter) created by scientists their property; or do the scientists merely serve as "the occasions of their being"? To the extent that they use their own ideas rather than ideas found in nature to design these genetically engineered animals, are the scientists the owners of these animals? Support your answers.
7. Discuss the moral issues raised by giving patents on human genes. How might Ridley as well as Andrews and Nelkin respond to this question? Relate your answers to the above case as well as to the issues raised on pages 139–140.

---

5. *JURASSIC PARK* REVISITED

One of the proposed uses for cloning is to save endangered species by creating multiple clones of the few remaining members of the species. If this is morally acceptable, and even perhaps morally desirable, is it also morally acceptable to clone species that have already passed into extinction?

In his book *Jurassic Park,* author Michael Creighton envisions a world where extinct dinosaur species are resurrected by cloning DNA from fossils. On March 8, 1998, British newspapers announced that the DNA from 8,000-year-old human remains, which had been found in a cave in 1903, had been genetically linked to Adrian Targett, a living descendent of the cave dweller. In the not too distant future, it may be possible to clone DNA from prehistoric human remains or to use DNA fragments to alter the genes of a human or animal cell. Doing so might provide valuable information about human evolution and about other earlier species of humanoids.

In 1999 a team of scientists recovered a 23,000-year-old woolly mammoth that was embedded in 26 tons of permafrost 477 miles north of the Arctic Circle.[41] Scientists hope that some of the cells are well preserved enough to be used for cloning. Although scientists have not yet found viable mammoth spermazoids, in 2003 they found viable cells in mammoth remains frozen in permafrost. Japanese scientists are currently working on cloning a mammoth using DNA from the cells.[42]

While the prospect of bringing back the woolly mammoth is exciting for some, others are concerned that reintroducing extinct species will upset the balance of nature. Some people also fear that cloning programs for preserving endangered species may divert resources from efforts to save the natural habitats of these species.

Discussion Questions

1. If you have read the book or seen the movie *Jurassic Park,* discuss the moral issues it raises about cloning extinct animals such as dinosaurs. Does the knowledge we might acquire from cloning already extinct species justify it? Would it make a difference, morally, if the species under question were human rather than dinosaurs? Support your answers.
2. Analyze the arguments for and against cloning extinct animals. Would it be morally relevant if it could be shown, as some paleontologists believe is the case, that it was prehistoric human hunting that led to the extinction of the woolly mammoth? Support your answer.
3. Is it morally acceptable to use cloning to preserve endangered species? Is there a morally relevant difference between preserving species who are on their way to extinction and resurrecting extinct species?
4. Does Adrian Targett, as a direct descendent of the "cave dweller," have a reproductive right to clone his or her DNA? Support your answer. Discuss how Andrews and Nelkin might respond to this question.
5. Would a clone of an extinct species of humans be harmed by cloning, given that cloning is the only means of resurrecting the species? Does the fact that such a clone would not share the genotype of another living person overcome the objection that cloning violates the right of a person to have his or her own genotype? Support your answers. Discuss how Robertson would respond to these questions.

---

6. MY FATHER, MY SON[43]

Dianne's father was on his deathbed. Her father was an only child, and neither she nor her brother had any children, so Dianne decided she wanted to have her "father" as a baby. She wrote to a British geneticist, asking for information on cloning her father. "My father," she explained, "is a remarkable man and I intend to see that he goes on in the world. . . . I am writing in the hope that you can help me find information on where human cloning may be performed now. There must be organizations that are actively pursuing cloning, and I want to contact them and see if there is a possibility of cloning my father. I have little time left to pursue this venture, and I would greatly appreciate your assistance." Dianne offered to be the host mother for the clone of her father.

Derek, who had an opportunity to read Dianne's correspondence on the Internet, was horrified at her request. "The desire to clone a passed-on loved one," he responded, "seems to me to be grotesque. It brings to mind the Stephen King book *Pet Semetary*. The clone would be a disappointment to the donor's relatives, in that the original personality could never be completely duplicated. Additionally, the clone would not be able to live its own life; it would be forced to live in a predefined, unattainable role."

Discussion Questions

1. Discuss how you might respond to Dianne if she came to you, a geneticist, with her request. Discuss how Robertson might respone to Dianne if she came to him with her request.

2. Discuss Derek's initial reaction to Dianne's request. How might Kass explain Derek's repugnance toward Dianne's request? How would Ridley most likely respond to Dianne's request?
3. Are Derek's misgivings valid? Does the fact that the relative's donors might be disappointed, or the concern that the clone may be deprived of an open future, override Dianne's reproductive autonomy? If so, should this criteria be considered anytime a woman wants to have a child, through sexual procreation, to carry as a replica of herself and the father of the child?
4. Discuss whether the clone of Dianne's father would be harmed by being a clone. Would it make a difference morally if Dianne's father had concurred with her request? Support your answer.

CHAPTER 4

Euthanasia and Assisted Suicide

In 1975 twenty-one-year-old Karen Ann Quinlan went into a coma after having a few drinks at a party. Apparently, she had eaten very little in the days before the party and had also taken some drugs—perhaps tranquilizers. She was rushed to the hospital, where doctors restored her breathing and connected her to a respirator. Unfortunately, by this time the lack of oxygen had caused permanent brain damage. Her parents, convinced that Karen would not have wanted to be kept alive by artificial means, asked the hospital to disconnect her from the respirator machine. The hospital refused.

The resulting controversy and court battles brought the issue of euthanasia to the public's attention. In 1976 the New Jersey Supreme Court ruled that Karen Quinlan's right to privacy had been violated by the hospital. As a result, she was removed from the machine and moved to a nursing home to die in peace. To most people's surprise, she continued to live with the assistance of feeding tubes. She remained there in a vegetative state until she died in 1985.

WHAT IS EUTHANASIA?

The term *euthanasia* comes from the Greek *eu* and *thanatos* meaning "good death." In modern usage euthanasia has come to mean painlessly bringing about the death of a person who is suffering from a terminal or incurable disease or condition.

Euthanasia can be classified as active or passive, voluntary or involuntary:

Voluntary euthanasia: A competent, rational person requests or gives informed consent about a particular action or withholding of treatment that will lead to his or her death.

Involuntary euthanasia: Bringing about a person's death who is unable to give or withdraw his or her consent because of incompetence (e.g., a comatose patient or infant), although the consent of relatives or guardians may be obtained.

Active euthanasia: Taking direct action, such as a lethal injection, to kill a person; also known as "mercy killing."

Passive euthanasia: Allowing patients to die by withholding life support or medical treatment that would prolong their lives.

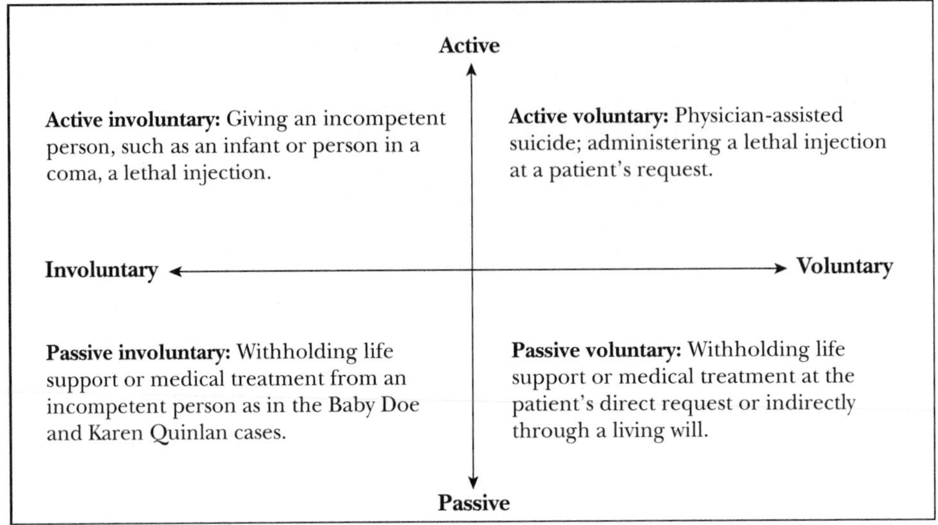

Combining these two continuums, a particular act of euthanasia can fall into one of four categories: active voluntary, passive voluntary, active involuntary, and passive involuntary.

Although physicians in the United States are permitted to withhold treatment for a dying patient, the law prohibits active euthanasia. This position is consistent with both that of the American Medical Association (AMA) and the British Medical Society. In contrast, in the Netherlands, where active, voluntary euthanasia is legal, there is no sharp line drawn between active and passive euthanasia.

> For humane reasons, with informed consent, a physician may do what is medically necessary to alleviate severe pain, or cease or omit treatment to permit a terminally ill patient to die when death is imminent. . . . Even if death is not imminent but a patient is beyond doubt permanently unconscious . . . it is not unethical to discontinue all means of life-prolonging medical treatment . . . [which] includes medication and artificially or technologically supplied respiration, nutrition or hydration.
>
> —AMA Council on Scientific Affairs and Council on Ethical and Judicial Affairs (1990)

It should be noted that the distinction between active and passive euthanasia is sometimes unclear and often depends on the intention of the person carrying out the action.

In his article at the end of this chapter, James Rachels asks whether the distinction between active and passive euthanasia is morally justified. See also Dan Brock's article on "Voluntary Active Euthanasia" and J. Gay-Williams's article on "The Wrongfulness of Euthanasia" in the accompanying *Ethics PowerWeb* for views favoring and opposing active euthanasia.

THE PHILOSOPHERS ON EUTHANASIA

The contemporary philosophical debate on euthanasia has been influenced primarily by ancient Greek and Judeo-Christian views on death.

Greek physicians regarded health as a human ideal par excellence. Because human worth and social usefulness depended on one's state of health, chronically sick people were expendable. Their lives could be terminated with or without their consent. Plato favored euthanasia of deformed and sickly infants because they would be a burden on the polis. The Roman philosopher Seneca (c. 3 B.C.E.–A.D. 65) and the early Stoics taught that humans ought to quit life nobly when they are no longer socially useful.

The Stoic attitude toward dying is reflected in John Hardwig's article "Is There a Duty to Die?" Hardwig answers yes. Old and chronically ill people have a duty to die bravely rather than burden their families and loved ones.

Not all Greek philosophers agreed with the Stoics. Aristotle believed that willful euthanasia was wrong. Virtue, he argued, requires that we face death bravely rather than take the cowardly way out by quitting life in the face of pain and suffering. The Pythagoreans, who wrote the Hippocratic oath, also opposed euthanasia on the grounds that the gods are our keepers and we are the possessions of the gods. To kill ourselves is to sin against the gods:

> Never will I give a deadly drug, not even if I am asked for one, nor will I give any advice tending in that direction.
>
> —HIPPOCRATIC OATH

The theme that humans are owned by God, their creator, is also found in Hebrew scriptures (Gen. 2:2–27). As property of God, no human has the right to destroy his or her life or wantonly take the life of another. This understanding of human life as inherently precious and belonging to God has been immensely influential on the Jewish, Christian, and Islamic views on euthanasia. In the Jewish tradition, death should never be hastened; physicians who kill patients, even if their intention is to relieve pain and suffering, are considered murderers. According to the Islamic religion, illness and suffering are part of God's will. Taking a life interferes with God's will.

In Buddhist philosophy self-willed death, even in cases of suffering and pain, violates the principle of the sanctity of life. It is also wrong because (1) suffering is a means to work out bad karma rather than transferring it to the next life and (2) a person who assists in suicide or performs euthanasia will be negatively affected by that participation. Hinduism also teaches that suffering should be endured, because it allows us to work out negative karma. Those who deliberately shorten their lives will carry their negative karma into a later life. The Dalai Lama teaches that:

> Your suffering is due to your own karma, and you have to bear the fruit of that karma anyway in this life or another, unless you can find some way of purifying it. In that case, it is considered to be better to experience the karma in this life of a human where you have more abilities to bear it in a better way, than, for example, an animal who is helpless and can suffer even more because of that.[1]

Thomas Aquinas incorporated the Aristotelian and biblical prohibition against euthanasia and suicide into his natural law theory, arguing that suicide is unnatural and immoral for three reasons:

> First, everything naturally loves itself, the result being that everything naturally keeps itself in being. . . . Secondly, because every part, as such, belongs to the whole . . . and so, as such, he belongs to the community. Hence by killing himself he injures the community as the Philosopher [Aristotle] declares. Thirdly, because

> life is God's gift to man, and is subject to His power, Who kills and makes to live. Hence whoever takes his own life sins against God. . . . For it belongs to God alone to pronounce sentence of death and life.

Using the model of Jesus on the cross, Christians, like Buddhists, emphasize the redemptive aspect of suffering. Protestant natural rights ethicist John Locke regarded self-killing as cowardly, contrary to nature, and opposed to the commandments of God. His view is echoed in the modern Protestant prohibition of active euthanasia, although most Protestants agree that it is morally acceptable to withhold or discontinue treatment and life support that is merely prolonging the dying process.

Immanuel Kant regarded suicide and voluntary euthanasia as immoral. Suicide does not fulfill the requirements of the categorical imperative because it involves a contradiction—that of exercising our autonomy to destroy our autonomy by destroying ourselves. People who want to end their lives also show a lack of respect for themselves by viewing their lives as a means only rather than an end. The prohibition of euthanasia, bolstered by the Hippocratic oath, Judeo-Christian teachings, and the philosophies of such greats as Aquinas, Locke, and Kant, remained pretty much unchallenged right up to the end of the nineteenth century.[2]

THE CONTEMPORARY DEBATE OVER EUTHANASIA

It was not until the end of the nineteenth century that the public began questioning the prohibition of euthanasia. Public debate over euthanasia turned to horror when it was learned that in Nazi Germany up to a hundred thousand mentally ill and disabled children and adults "considered incurable according to the best available human judgment" were, to use official language, "granted a mercy death."[3] The memory of this terrible event still haunts Germany, which now prohibits euthanasia.

The public debate over euthanasia resumed after the 1950s with the development of new life-sustaining technologies such as the mechanical respirator, which had first been used in the 1930s. Along with these advances came a growing concern over the increasing control of technology over life and death.

In 1957, troubled by the ethical problems involved in resuscitating unconscious individuals, the International Congress of Anesthesiology sought moral guidance from Pope Pius XII. The Pope responded that physicians should not act without the consent of the family. Physicians also have a moral duty to use ordinary, but not "extraordinary," measures to prolong life. The Pope's position was supported by the Church's "principle of double effect." This principle states that if an act has two effects, one intended (in this case to end pain and suffering) and the other unintended (the death of the patient), terminating treatment may be not only morally permissible but morally advisable if it is the only way to bring about the intended effect. This distinction between passive euthanasia, where death is an unintended effect, and active euthanasia, where the intention is to directly bring about the death of the patient, has remained unchallenged for years.

Public opinion began shifting in favor of legalized euthanasia in the early 1970s. Support for physician-assisted suicide began declining in the United States in the 1990s. As of 1996, 69 percent of Americans were in favor of permitting doctors to perform euthanasia if a person has an incurable disease.[4] In the 2002 Gallup Poll only 50 percent of Americans stated that they found the practice morally acceptable.[5]

Support for legalizing euthanasia and physician-assisted suicide tends to be higher in other Western countries. Three-quarters of both Canadians and Australians support active euthanasia, including assisted suicide, for terminal illnesses.[6] Eighty-two percent of the British would like to see euthanasia, although not necessarily assisted suicide, legalized.[7] Support for euthanasia is especially high in France and in the Netherlands where active, voluntary euthanasia has been legal for several years.[8] In China, although euthanasia is illegal, 80 percent of people surveyed in a 1988 poll stated that they were in favor of euthanasia.[9] Although Japanese views on euthanasia have been influenced by the Buddhist repugnance of killing, the influence of the Shinto religion's glorification of self-willed death for the benefit of the country has led to a more permissive attitude toward euthanasia than in other Buddhist countries.

EUTHANASIA LEGISLATION

The 1976 California Natural Death Act became the first law in the United States to address the issue of decision making on the part of incompetent individuals. The act allowed individuals, under certain circumstances, to make decisions in advance about the kind of treatment they would receive at the end of their lives.

Most people, however, do not have a living will. A 1997 study of 4,804 terminally ill patients found that only 14 percent had either prepared written advanced directives regarding their medical care or appointed a durable power of attorney for health care. Of the directives, only 0.5 percent were as detailed as they should have been. Thus it is not surprising that more than 50 percent of patients end up in a "highly undesirable state"—that is, being kept alive despite their apparent wishes or despite family requests to terminate treatment.[10]

In the 1990 landmark case *Cruzan v. Director, Missouri Department of Health*, the U.S. Supreme Court ruled that every competent individual has a constitutional liberty right to be free of unwanted medical treatment if there is "clear and convincing evidence" of the patient's desire to have the medical treatment withdrawn. The Court left it up to the states to decide for incompetent individuals. The following year Washington State's Initiative 119 "Death with Dignity" proposal failed to pass.

In 1994 the citizens of Oregon approved Ballot Measure 16 (the "Oregon Death with Dignity Act"), which would legalize euthanasia under certain conditions. The Oregon Death with Dignity Act took effect in 1997 following a lengthy appeal process in which the appeal court upheld the Act by a 60 to 40 percent vote.[11] By 2001 physicians in Oregon had lawfully prescribed a lethal dose of barbiturates for 139 patients.[12] In 2002 two other states, Hawaii and Ohio, passed death with dignity bills modeled after Oregon's bill. Oregon's Death with Dignity Act was targeted in 2002 by U.S. Attorney General John Ashcroft, who charged that prescribing barbiturates to induce death is illegal under the Controlled Substances Act. The charges raise the question of whether or not prescribing lethal drugs are legitimate medicine. The U.S. District Court ruled in favor of *Oregon v. Ashcroft*. An appeal is pending.

In Australia's Northern Territory of Australia a law became effective in July 2003 permitting terminally ill patients to end their life by pill or lethal injection, and permitting physicians to help anyone who is terminally ill to do so. The law is being challenged by a coalition of churches, physicians, and aboriginal leaders.[13]

CRUZAN V. MISSOURI DEPARTMENT OF HEALTH (1990): EXCERPTS FROM THE MAJORITY OPINION

Chief Justice Rehnquist delivering the opinion of the court:
Petitioner Nancy Beth Cruzan was rendered incompetent as a result of severe injuries sustained during an automobile accident. Copetitioners Lester and Joyce Cruzan, Nancy's parents and coguardians, sought a court order directing the withdrawal of their daughter's artificial feeding and hydration equipment after it became apparent that she had virtually no chance of recovering her cognitive faculties. The Supreme Court of Missouri held that because there was no clear and convincing evidence of Nancy's desire to have life sustaining treatment withdrawn under such circumstances, her parents lacked authority to effectuate such a request. . . .

At common law, even the touching of one person by another without consent and without legal justification was a battery . . . This notion of bodily integrity has been embodied in the requirement that informed consent is generally required for medical treatment. . . . The logical corollary of the doctrine of informed consent is that the patient generally possesses the right not to consent, that is, to refuse treatment. . . .

Whether or not Missouri's clear and convincing evidence requirement comports with the United States Constitution depends in part on what interests the State may properly seek to protect in this situation. . . . As a general matter, the States—indeed, all civilized nations—demonstrate their commitment to life by treating homicide as a serious crime. Moreover, the majority of States in this country have laws imposing criminal penalties on one who assists another to commit suicide. We do not think a State is required to remain neutral in the fact of an informed and voluntary decision by a physically able adult to starve to death. . . . We believe Missouri may legitimately seek to safeguard the personal element of this choice through the imposition of heightened evidentiary requirements. . . .

In our view, Missouri has permissibly sought to advance these interests through the adoption of a "clear and convincing" standard of proof to govern such proceedings. . . .

In sum, we conclude that a State may apply a clear and convincing evidence standard in proceedings where a guardian seeks to discontinue nutrition and hydration of a person diagnosed to be in a persistent vegetative state. We note that many courts which have adopted some sort of substituted judgment procedure in situations like this, whether they limit consideration of evidence to the prior expressed wishes of the incompetent individual, or whether they allow more

The debate over euthanasia is perhaps nowhere so intense as in the Netherlands. Although active euthanasia was only legalized in 2001, it has been tolerated for many years. The new law permits euthanasia only for "medically classified physical or mental diseases and afflictions." Many people are critical of this new law on the grounds that it has too much potential for abuse. Germans, who are adamantly opposed to legalized euthanasia, general proof of what the individual decision would have been, require a clear and convincing standard of proof for such evidence. The Supreme Court of Missouri held that in this case the testimony adduced at trial did not amount to clear and convincing proof of the patient's desire to have hydration and nutrition withdrawn.

The judgment of the Supreme Court of Missouri is Affirmed.

Justice O'Connor concurring. . . The liberty interest in refusing medical treatment flows from decisions involving the States' invasions into the body. Because our notions of liberty are inextricably entwined with our idea of physical freedom and self-determination, the Court has often deemed state incursions into the body repugnant. . . .

The State's artificial provision of nutrition and hydration implicates identical concerns. Artificial feeding cannot readily be distinguished from other forms of medical treatment . . . Feeding a patient by means of a nasogastric tube requires a physician to pass a long flexible tube through the patient's nose, throat, and esophagus and into the stomach. Because of the discomfort such a tube causes, many patients need to be restrained forcibly and their hands put into large mittens to prevent them from removing the tube . . . Requiring a competent adult to endure such procedures against her will burdens the patient's liberty, dignity, and freedom to determine the course of her own treatment.

I . . . also emphasize that the Court does not today decide the issue whether a State must also give effect to the decision of a surrogate decisionmaker. In my view, such a duty may well be constitutionally required to protect the patient's liberty interest in refusing medical treatment. Few individuals [however] provide explicit oral and written instructions regarding their interest to refuse medical treatment should they become incompetent. States which decline to consider any evidence to other than such instructions may frequently fail to honor a patient's intent. Such failures might be avoided if the State considered an equally probative source of evidence: the patient's appointment of a proxy to make health care decisions on her behalf. [Cruzan neither left instructions nor appointed a proxy.]

Today's decision does not preclude a future determination that the Constitution requires the State to implement the decisions of a patient's duly appointed surrogate. Nor does it prevent States from developing other approaches for protecting an incompetent individual's liberty interest in refusing medical treatment. . . . Today we decide only that one State's practice does not violate the Constitution; the more challenging task of crafting appropriate procedures for safeguarding incompetents' liberty interests is entrusted to the "laboratory" of the States. . . .

believe that the Dutch have already begun the slide down the proverbial slippery slope. Indeed, Daniel Callahan points out that an estimated 30 percent of the cases of euthanasia in the Netherlands are involuntary. Active euthanasia is involved in an estimated 3 to 5 percent of deaths in the Netherlands.[14] On the other hand, a European study in 2003 found that demand by patients for physician-assisted suicide death in The Netherlands,

Belgium, Denmark, Italy, Sweden, and Switzerland has not increased since 1995 despite easier access to it.

PHYSICIAN-ASSISTED SUICIDE

Americans are split over whether physician-assisted suicide should be legal.[15] However, public support for physician-assisted suicide is softening. Because of laws against euthanasia, most physicians who help patients die do not go public. One notable exception is Dr. Jack Kevorkian, a retired pathologist and trained physician. In 1990 Kevorkian helped Janet Adkins, an Oregon women who was suffering from the early stages of Alzheimer's disease, to end her life. The vision of Adkins lying dead on the crisp white sheets in the back of Kevorkian's rusting '68 Volkswagen van has become permanently etched onto the American psyche. Since 1990, Kevorkian has presided over the deaths of more than one hundred other people, including one that was televized live on national television in September 1998. In April 1999 a Michigan judge sentenced Kevorkian to ten to twenty-five years in prison for second-degree murder. Kevorkian lost the appeal to have his murder conviction overturned in December 2002 and is still serving time in prison.

The publicity surrounding Kevorkian has sparked intense debate over the morality of physician-assisted suicide. Kevorkian's detractors dubbed him "Dr. Death." Surgeon General C. Everett Koop denounced him as "a serial killer who should be put away."[16] Kevorkian's opponents also point out that he is a pathologist, not a psychiatrist. Unlike health-care workers, who know their patients for a long time, Kevorkian hardly knows his; he knew Janet Adkins only two days before participating in her death. Kevorkian, on the other hand, sees himself as a defender of liberty.

In January 2003, Australian Dr. Philip Nitschke, who conducts workshops for Exit Australia, made public his debreather "COGen" machine which pumps carbon dioxide through a nasal tube and is used with sedatives to assist a person to die. Nitschke plans to begin producing the machine and distributing them to members of the Hemlock Society by the end of 2003.

On June 26, 1997, the U.S. Supreme Court declared that there is no constitutional right to the aid of a physician in dying and that states had the right to outlaw assisted suicide. Echoing the sentiment of most of the jurists, Justice William Rehnquist expressed concern about the slippery slope and "a possible slide towards voluntary and perhaps involuntary euthanasia." While physician-assisted suicide is legal in some states, such as Oregon, over 30 states have outlawed it.

THE HOSPICE MOVEMENT

The number one fear of most people is not fear of dying or of pain, but of loss of control and dignity.[17] The modern hospice movement was founded in 1967 by British physician Cicely Saunders to help people die confidently and with dignity rather than with fear. The first hospice program in the United States opened in 1974. The philosophy behind hospice is to provide palliative care—pain relief, comfort, and compassion—to the dying. As such, hospice has been active in the development of pain control. Hospice also emphasizes attention to the emotional needs of the patient and the patient's family.

According to a survey of 4,000 hospitals conducted by the American Hospital Association, the number of palliative care programs in hospitals is increased by about 20 percent a year. In 1995 there were none. Between 2000 and 2001 the number went from 658 to 806 hospitals with palliative care programs.[18] Despite these improvements in palliative care, proper pain management still remains an issue for the dying.

Hospice is opposed to the legalization of euthanasia. "If one of our patients requests euthanasia," Saunders once wrote, "it means we are not doing our job." Saunders continued:

> We are not so poor a society that we cannot afford time and trouble and money to help people live until they die. We owe it to all those for whom we can kill the pain which traps them in fear and bitterness. To do this we do not have to kill them . . . To make voluntary [active] euthanasia lawful would be an irresponsible act, hindering help, pressuring the vulnerable, abrogating our true respect and responsibility to the frail and the old, the disabled and dying.[19]

Hospice believes that providing terminally ill people with better palliative care allows them to live their last days in relative comfort and dignity.[20] Advocates of euthanasia, on the other hand, maintain that while the hospice program is wonderful for many people, there are still cases in which pain cannot be controlled, and euthanasia should be an option.

THE MORAL ISSUES

The Sanctity of Life

Most Western philosophers believe that human life has intrinsic worth and, therefore, ought to be respected and cherished. Legalizing euthanasia will weaken this respect for life. If life has intrinsic worth, our right not to be killed cannot be overridden, even at our own request.

A variation of this theme is the religious argument that our lives are a gift from God and, therefore, we are not free to end them on our own terms. In their role as healers, however, physicians are continuously working to prevent death and suffering. Does this interfere with God's will?

Furthermore, those who do not believe in God, or God's "ownership" of humans, argue that people are not owned by God, or anyone else for that matter. As beings with intrinsic moral worth, we have inalienable rights that cannot be waived by anyone else—including God. One of the most fundamental of these rights is the right of autonomy.

Autonomy and Self-Determination

Autonomy requires two conditions: freedom from outside control and moral agency. According to Margaret Pabst Battin, autonomy is one of the two key principles in the euthanasia debate. Autonomy requires that, in general, physicians respect a competent person's choices in determining his or her medical treatment, including euthanasia. If euthanasia is a positive right, as Battin claims, physicians may have a duty to assist their patients in dying.

Daniel Callahan, on the other hand, argues that autonomy and self-determination have been given too much weight in the euthanasia debate. People do not have a right to do anything they want to do. He also notes that the leap between claiming that people have a right to end their lives based on autonomy and the claim that it is morally acceptable for physicians to assist in this process is not as self-evident as most advocates of active euthanasia would have us believe.

There is also the danger that making euthanasia available will compromise our autonomy. Some people may feel pressured by circumstances, such as lack of medical insurance or family support, into requesting euthanasia. Susan Wolf, in her article at the end of this chapter, argues that, given the traditional view of women as self-sacrificing, not only are women especially vulnerable to these sorts of pressures, but physicians will be more likely to carry out their requests.

Nonmaleficence and the Principle of *Ahimsa*

The principle of nonmaleficence or "do no harm" is one of the strongest moral principles. In the Buddhist prohibition against euthanasia *ahimsa* is the deciding principle. Battin, on the other hand, argues that the principle of nonmaleficence and the duty to relieve pain and suffering may, at times, require euthanasia.

The Principle of Mercy

The principle of mercy is based on the duty of nonmaleficence. It states that we have a duty both (1) not to cause further pain and suffering and (2) to relieve pain and suffering. Most philosophers agree that the first part of this duty justifies refusal of futile and painful treatment, even though withdrawing or withholding such treatment may result in an earlier death for the patient, but philosophers disagree on the practical implications of the second part of this duty. Both Rachels and Battin agree that pain relief is a universal duty of physicians and that this duty may entail a positive obligation to use active euthanasia when it is the only way to end pain and suffering. Callahan, on the other hand, maintains that the appropriate response to suffering is compassionate care, not conceding to a patient's request to be put to death.

Death with Dignity

The expressions "death with dignity" and the "good death" are often heard in euthanasia debates. Advocates of euthanasia argue that respect for the dignity of life entails allowing a person to *die* with dignity as well, rather than spend the last days of life hooked up to machines and wasting away in agony. Some opponents of euthanasia believe that the good death involves courageously accepting the suffering entailed in dying.

Quality of Life: Pain and Suffering

Human life is more that mere biological existence. Battin points out that the ability to be in relationship with family and friends, to have hopes for the future, and to live without constant pain are all basic goods. When isolation, pain, and suffering outweigh any expectation of enjoying the goods of life, the quality of that life becomes a negative value and death may be preferable.

Pain, however, such as that associated with cancer, can be relieved in up to 90 percent of cases. A 1994 study at Stanford University found that more than half of terminally ill patients spend their last days in agony. A 2002 national survey found that 59 percent of people gave the quality of end-of life care a fair or poor rating, and only 39 percent gave the system a fair or poor grade in making sure patients were comfortable and pain-free as possible at the end of life.[21] This is blamed, in part, not on the lack of effective pain relievers, but on Western society's opiophobia—fear of drug addiction and abuse.[22]

Canadian bioethicist Peter Singer maintains that improving the quality of end-of-life care is a more important issue than euthanasia. According to Singer, "Euthanasia and physician-assisted suicide at best address a very small percentage of the dying population; there are still more than 95 percent of people who die who need to be given quality care and the focus must shift to identifying and addressing their needs."[23] Indeed, one study found that "Substantive palliative interventions lead some—but not all—patients to change their minds about assisted suicide."[24] To address this issue, as well as the finding that technical difficulties occur in almost a fifth of all cases of physician-assisted suicide, the Dutch government spends about US$3 million dollars to train general physicians as "euthanasia consultants."[25] Part of the role of these consultants will be the improvement of the quality of end-of-life care, including better palliative care for pain management.

On the other hand, why should only physical pain count? There are other types of suffering, such as lifelong disability, loneliness, and depression. Should there be a moral distinction between wanting to die because one is depressed or facing chronic illness, as is the case with many of Dr. Kevorkian's patients, and the pain associated with a terminal illness?

Another quality of life issue is determining the quality of life of incompetent patients, such as people in comas and children with disabilities. Who, if anyone, should decide if their lives are worth living? If we answer that euthanasia should be voluntary only, we have to ask ourselves, as Callahan does, if it is fair that incompetent people be doomed to lives of suffering and hopelessness.

Ordinary Versus Extraordinary Treatment

The AMA, while opposing euthanasia, allows the withdrawal of extraordinary treatment. Ordinary medical treatment includes measures that have a reasonable hope of benefiting the patient, whereas extraordinary treatments are measures that provide no reasonable hope of benefiting the patient. They are frequently excessively expensive, as well. This brings up the sticky question of just when treatment becomes extraordinary. How should we draw the line between prolonging life and prolonging the dying process? Is withholding surgery that could save the life of a child with severe disabilities ordinary or extraordinary treatment? Is using chemotherapy on an ailing eighty-five-year-old with cancer ordinary or extraordinary treatment? Also, what counts as a reasonable hope? Is continuing to keep a patient in a coma on artificial life support, even though there is only slight hope of recovery, ordinary or extraordinary treatment?

The Principle of Double Effect: Letting Die Versus Actively Killing

The traditional distinction between active and passive euthanasia rests on intention. According to this argument, in active euthanasia the intention is to cause the death of another person. In the latter case, there is a "double effect": the death of the person is an unintended consequence of the intended effect—the elimination of pain and suffering.

Some philosophers claim that this distinction is hypocritical. Physicians are morally responsible for both intended and foreseen consequences. The double-effect argument is simply a cover for engaging in slow euthanasia. Rachels argues that knowing that high doses of painkillers may hasten a person's death is an action as much as is administering a lethal injection on request. Both involve decision and action on the part of the physician. Indeed, there may be cases in which active euthanasia is the more humane alternative.

The Physician's Role as Healer

Some opponents of physician-assisted suicide and euthanasia argue that expecting physicians to be agents of death runs contrary to their training as healers and comforters and may damage trust in the patient/physician relationship. This argument does not rule out euthanasia. The act of euthanasia could instead be left to others, perhaps people like Dr. Kevorkian or "death technicians," who specialize in it.

Patient Competence

Two of the problems in deciding who should be a candidate for euthanasia are (1) determining if a patient is rational and competent to make such a decision and (2) whether it is a sincere request for death or simply a cry for help. What, in other words, are the patient's real intentions? Furthermore, if the patient is incompetent, how do we determine what is in the patient's best interests? Some people argue that physicians or close family members can usually be counted on to respect a patient's self-determination, whereas others, such as Wolf, question the insidious effect of cultural biases on these decisions. How are we to know that a particular euthanasia decision is based on the doctor's judgment that the request is justified because the patient's life is no longer worth living?

To some the term *assisted suicide* is an oxymoron. They claim that the request, especially in cases in which the patient is able to carry out the suicide without assistance, is often a cloaked request for help. Suicide prevention workers point out that people who are suicidal often feel a sense of depression, hopelessness, and despair. Rather than seeking to end their lives, the request to die is really an expression of that despair and, as such, is a cry for help.

Justice and the Principle of Equality

Some opponents of euthanasia maintain that it is always unjust because it involves the death of an innocent person. Battin, on the other hand, maintains that the duty of justice may require euthanasia, especially in cases in which keeping a person alive is tremendously expensive.

Wolf expresses concern that euthanasia may be unjust because it unfairly targets certain groups. In a society that holds up self-sacrifice as a virtue for women, women are especially vulnerable to gender-biased pressures to put the needs and desires of others before their own. The physician-assisted death of Judith Curren, who was later alleged to have been abused by her husband, is just one case in point.

Another concern is our society's negative view of people who are disabled and the tendency to devalue their lives. While it may be countered that disabled people fall outside the scope of euthanasia because they are not terminally ill, the facts show that infants and children with disabilities, such as Baby Doe, are also vulnerable to euthanasia.

A study of infant deaths at the special-care unit of the Yale–New Haven Hospital between 1970 and 1972 revealed that of 299 deaths, 14 percent were associated with the withholding or withdrawal of treatment in cases of severe congenital disorders.[26]

Burdens to Society

A study published in January 2000 found that a majority of Dutch and American doctors favor physician-assisted suicide for a patient in excruciating pain.[27] However, they differ in their justifications of euthanasia. Dutch doctors are more likely to support physician-assisted suicide in cases in which a patient finds life meaningless; American physicians are more likely to consider a patient's fear of being a burden as a justification for euthanasia.

Both Hardwig and Battin argue that when costly medical resources are needed to sustain a human life, the principle of justice may warrant involuntary, active euthanasia. There are about twenty-five thousand terminally ill Americans annually. In the year 2000, end-of-life costs accounted for 10 percent of the total healthcare spending in the United States and 27 percent of Medicare expense.[28] In contrast, it costs only a few dollars to deliver a lethal injection.

On the other hand, there are cases in which a patient comes out of a coma or makes a miraculous recovery despite a prognosis of imminent death or irreversible brain damage. Jackie Cole, to give one example, suffered a stroke and massive bleeding in her brain. The doctors predicted that without artificial life support she would be dead within a few days. Shortly before slipping into a coma, she had made it clear that she did not want to be kept alive by artificial means. The court, however, refused her husband's petition to have life support withdrawn. Six days later Cole awoke from the coma and slowly began to recover from her stroke.[29] What is a reasonable cost of sustaining hope? Do cases like Jackie Cole's justify spending millions of dollars keeping comatose people alive in hopes that a few of them will come out of it?

The ailing elderly population also puts a strain on medical and social resources. Are these resources well spent? Do the elderly have what Hardwig calls "a duty to die"?

A Duty to Die

While rejecting what he calls a "crass" utilitarian calculus, Hardwig nevertheless argues that burden to family and society creates a duty to die. According to him, there comes a time in life when we have a duty to let go. In a nonegalitarian society, however, where the lives of certain groups are valued less than others, a duty to die might come into conflict with the principle of justice by unfairly targeting certain people, such as women and the disabled.

Slippery Slope Argument

Even if it can be shown that euthanasia, in principle, can be morally justified, there may still be problems when it comes to legalizing it, because of the difficulty of drawing the line between who should and who should not be eligible. If there is no definite line to stop abuses, it will be easy to slip down the slope toward greater and greater acceptance of euthanasia. For example, how do we know if a person's request for euthanasia is genuine and not influenced by outside pressures and cultural biases? Battin argues that evidence that this will happen is weak at best, but a report from the Netherlands states that Dutch physicians "sometimes act without patient requests in performing euthanasia and that there was a sense among some patients that they had a duty to die."[30] The right to euthanasia, in other words, can easily slip into a duty to die. In a society in which euthanasia is an option, it will also be easy to redefine chronic medical conditions as terminal illnesses to justify the euthanasia of people who have Alzheimer's or of children with genetic disorders, a practice that has already begun to some extent.[31]

CONCLUSION

The moral issues surrounding euthanasia are complex. Many of the relevant principles come into conflict with one another and need to be carefully weighed. A further complication is the uncertainty of medical prognoses and the presence of subjective factors in assessing patients' requests for euthanasia. Nevertheless, this does not mean that the issue cannot be resolved.

In addition, public policies on euthanasia need to be drafted within the wider social context. As with abortion, the judgment that euthanasia, or at least certain types of it, is morally acceptable does not imply that the law should permit it.

JAMES RACHELS

Active and Passive Euthanasia

James Rachels is a professor of philosophy at the University of Alabama. In his celebrated article "Active and Passive Euthanasia," which first appeared in the *New England Journal of Medicine* in 1975, Rachels argues that the traditional distinction between active and passive euthanasia cannot be morally justified. He also points out that there are cases in which active euthanasia may be morally preferable to passive euthanasia, especially when passive euthanasia would result in unnecessary suffering and slow and painful, rather than quick and painless, death for terminally ill people.

Critical Reading Questions

1. What is the AMA's position on euthanasia?
2. What is the distinction between active and passive euthanasia? In Rachels's view is this distinction morally relevant?
3. Why is passive euthanasia worse in some cases, according to Rachels, than active euthanasia? What cases does he use to illustrate this?
4. What does Rachels think of the practice of allowing newborns with Down's syndrome to die?

"Active and Passive Euthanasia," *New England Journal of Medicine* (January 9, 1975): 78–81.

5. What point is Rachels illustrating with the analogy of Smith and Jones and the death of their six-year-old cousin?
6. How important, in Rachels's view, is the role of intention in determining if euthanasia is morally justified in a particular case?
7. According to Rachels, what is the crucial issue in euthanasia?
8. Why does Rachels claim that the AMA position as well as the current laws on euthanasia are inconsistent?

The distinction between active and passive euthanasia is thought to be crucial for medical ethics. The idea is that it is permissible, at least in some cases, to withhold treatment and allow a patient to die, but it is never permissible to take any direct action designed to kill the patient. This doctrine seems to be accepted by most doctors, and it is endorsed in a statement adopted by the House of Delegates of the American Medical Association on December 4, 1973:

> The intentional termination of the life of one human being by another—mercy killing—is contrary to that for which the medical profession stands and is contrary to the policy of the American Medical Association.
>
> The cessation of the employment of extraordinary means to prolong the life of the body when there is irrefutable evidence that biological death is imminent is the decision of the patient and/or his immediate family. The advice and judgement of the physician should be freely available to the patient and/or his immediate family.

However, a strong case can be made against this doctrine. In what follows I will set out some of the relevant arguments, and urge doctors to reconsider their views on this matter.

To begin with a familiar type of situation, a patient who is dying of incurable cancer of the throat is in terrible pain, which can no longer be satisfactorily alleviated. He is certain to die within a few days, even if present treatment is continued, but he does not want to go on living for those days since the pain is unbearable. So he asks the doctor for an end to it, and his family joins in the request.

Suppose the doctor agrees to withhold treatment, as the conventional doctrine says he may. The justification for his doing so is that the patient is in terrible agony, and since he is going to die anyway, it would be wrong to prolong his suffering needlessly. But now notice this. If one simply withholds treatment, it may take the patient longer to die, and so he may suffer more than he would if more direct action were taken and a lethal injection given. This fact provides strong reason for thinking that, once the initial decision not to prolong his agony has been made, active euthanasia is actually preferable to passive euthanasia, rather than the reverse. To say otherwise is to endorse the option that leads to more suffering rather than less, and is contrary to the humanitarian impulse that prompts the decision not to prolong his life in the first place.

Part of my point is that the process of being "allowed to die" can be relatively slow and painful, whereas being given a lethal injection is relatively quick and painless. Let me give a different sort of example. In the United States about one in 600 babies is born with Down's syndrome. Most of these babies are otherwise healthy—that is, with only the usual pediatric care, they will proceed to an otherwise normal infancy. Some, however, are born with congenital defects such as intestinal obstructions that require operations if they are to live. Sometimes, the parents and the doctor will decide not to operate, and let the infant die. Anthony Shaw describes what happens then:

> . . . When surgery is denied [the doctor] must try to keep the infant from suffering while natural forces sap the baby's life away. As a surgeon whose natural inclination is to use the scalpel to

> fight off death, standing by and watching a salvageable baby die is the most emotionally exhausting experience I know. It is easy at a conference, in a theoretical discussion, to decide that such infants should be allowed to die. It is altogether different to stand by in the nursery and watch as the dehydration and infection wither a tiny being over hours and days. This is a terrible ordeal for me and the hospital staff—much more so than for the parents who never set foot in the nursery.*

I can understand why some people are opposed to all euthanasia, and insist that such infants must be allowed to live. I think I can also understand why other people favor destroying these babies quickly and painlessly. But why should anyone favor letting "dehydration and infection wither a tiny being over hours and days?" The doctrine that says that a baby may be allowed to dehydrate and wither, but may not be given an injection that would end its life without suffering, seems so patently cruel as to require no further refutation. The strong language is not intended to offend, but only to put the point in the clearest possible way.

My second argument is that the conventional doctrine leads to decisions concerning life and death made on irrelevant grounds.

Consider again the case of the infants with Down's syndrome who need operations for congenital defects unrelated to the syndrome to live. Sometimes, there is no operation, and the baby dies, but when there is no such defect, the baby lives on. Now, an operation such as that to remove an intestinal obstruction is not prohibitively difficult. The reason why such operations are not performed in these cases is, clearly, that the child has Down's syndrome and the parents and doctor judge that because of that fact it is better for the child to die.

But notice that this situation is absurd, no matter what view one takes of the lives and potentials of such babies. If the life of such an infant is worth preserving, what does it matter if it needs a simple operation? Or, if one thinks it better that such a baby should not live on, what difference does it make that it happens to have an unobstructed intestinal tract? In either case, the matter of life and death is being decided on irrelevant grounds. It is the Down's syndrome, and not the intestines, that is the issue. The matter should be decided, if at all, on that basis, and not be allowed to depend on the essentially irrelevant question of whether the intestinal tract is blocked.

What makes this situation possible, of course, is the idea that when there is an intestinal blockage, one can "let the baby die," but when there is no such defect there is nothing that can be done, for one must not "kill" it. The fact that this idea leads to such results as deciding life or death on irrelevant grounds is another good reason why the doctrine should be rejected.

One reason why so many people think that there is an important moral difference between active and passive euthanasia is that they think killing someone is morally worse than letting someone die. But is it? Is killing, in itself, worse than letting die? To investigate this issue, two cases may be considered that are exactly alike except that one involves killing whereas the other involves letting someone die. Then, it can be asked whether this difference makes any difference to the moral assessments. It is important that the cases be exactly alike, except for this one difference, since otherwise one cannot be confident that it is this difference and not some other that accounts for any variation in the assessment of the two cases. So, let us consider this pair of cases:

In the first, Smith stands to gain a large inheritance if anything should happen to his six-year-old cousin. One evening while the child is taking his bath, Smith sneaks into the bathroom and drowns the child, and then arranges things so that it will look like an accident.

In the second, Jones also stands to gain if anything should happen to his six-year-old cousin. Like Smith, Jones sneaks in planning to drown the child in his bath. However, just as he enters the bathroom Jones sees the child slip and hit his head, and fall face down in the water. Jones is delighted; he stands by, ready to push the child's head back under if it is necessary, but it is not necessary. With only a little

---

* Shaw A: "Doctor, Do We Have a Choice?" *The New York Times Magazine*, January 30, 1972, p. 54.

thrashing about, the child drowns all by himself, "accidentally," as Jones watches and does nothing.

Now Smith killed the child, whereas Jones "merely" let the child die. That is the only difference between them. Did either man behave better, from a moral point of view? If the difference between killing and letting die were in itself a morally important matter, one should say that Jones's behavior was less reprehensible than Smith's. But does one really want to say that? I think not. In the first place, both men acted from the same motive, personal gain, and both had exactly the same end in view when they acted. It may be inferred from Smith's conduct that he is a bad man, although that judgment may be withdrawn or modified if certain further facts are learned about him—for example, that he is mentally deranged. But would not the very same thing be inferred about Jones from his conduct? And would not the same further considerations also be relevant to any modification of this judgment? Moreover, suppose Jones pleaded, in his own defense, "After all, I didn't do anything except just stand there and watch the child drown. I didn't kill him; I only let him die." Again, if letting die were in itself less bad than killing, this defense should have at least some weight. But it does not. Such a "defense" can only be regarded as a grotesque perversion of moral reasoning. Morally speaking, it is no defense at all.

Now, it may be pointed out, quite properly, that the cases of euthanasia with which doctors are concerned are not like this at all. They do not involve personal gain or the destruction of normal healthy children. Doctors are concerned only with cases in which the patient's life is of no further use to him, or in which the patient's life has become or will soon become a terrible burden. However, the point is the same in these cases: the bare difference between killing and letting die does not, in itself, make a moral difference. If a doctor lets a patient die, for humane reasons, he is in the same moral position as if he had given the patient a lethal injection for humane reasons. If his decision was wrong—if, for example, the patient's illness was in fact curable—the decision would be equally regrettable no matter which method was used to carry it out. And if the doctor's decision was the right one, the method used is not itself important.

The AMA policy statement isolates the crucial issue very well; the crucial issue is "the intentional termination of the life of one human being by another." But after identifying this issue, and forbidding "mercy killing," the statement goes on to deny that the cessation of treatment is the intentional termination of a life. This is where the mistake comes in, for what is the cessation of treatment, in these circumstances, if it is not "the intentional termination of the life of one human being by another?" Of course it is exactly that, and if it were not, there would be no point to it.

Many people will find this judgment hard to accept. One reason, I think, is that it is very easy to conflate the question of whether killing is, in itself, worse than letting die, with the very different question of whether most actual cases of killing are more reprehensible than most actual cases of letting die. Most actual cases of killing are clearly terrible (think, for example, of all the murders reported in the newspapers), and one hears of such cases every day. On the other hand, one hardly ever hears of a case of letting die, except for the actions of doctors who are motivated by humanitarian reasons. So one learns to think of killing in a much worse light than of letting die. But this does not mean that there is something about killing that makes it in itself worse than letting die, for it is not the bare difference between killing and letting die that makes the difference in these cases. Rather, the other factors—the murderer's motive of personal gain, for example, contrasted with the doctor's humanitarian motivation—account for different reactions to the different cases.

I have argued that killing is not in itself any worse than letting die; if my contention is right, it follows that active euthanasia is not any worse than passive euthanasia. What arguments can be given on the other side? The most common, I believe, is the following:

> The important difference between active and passive euthanasia is that, in passive euthanasia, the doctor does not do anything to bring about the patient's death. The doctor does nothing, and the patient dies of whatever ills already afflict him. In active euthanasia, however, the

doctor does something to bring about the patient's death: he kills him. The doctor who gives the patient with cancer a lethal injection has himself caused the patient's death; whereas if he merely ceases treatment, the cancer is the cause of death.

A number of points need to be made here. The first is that it is not exactly correct to say that in passive euthanasia the doctor does nothing, for he does do one thing that is very important: he lets the patient die. "Letting someone die" is certainly different, in some respects, from other types of action—mainly in that it is a kind of action that one may perform by way of not performing certain other actions. For example, one may let a patient die by way of not giving medication, just as one may insult someone by way of not shaking his hand. But for any purpose of moral assessment, it is a type of action nonetheless. The decision to let a patient die is subject to moral appraisal in the same way that a decision to kill him would be subject to moral appraisal: it may be assessed as wise or unwise, compassionate or sadistic, right or wrong. If a doctor deliberately let a patient die who was suffering from a routinely curable illness, the doctor would certainly be to blame for what he had done, just as he would be to blame if he had needlessly killed the patient. Charges against him would then be appropriate. If so, it would be no defense at all for him to insist that he didn't "do anything." He would have done something very serious indeed, for he let his patient die.

Fixing the cause of death may be very important from a legal point of view, for it may determine whether criminal charges are brought against the doctor. But I do not think that this notion can be used to show a moral difference between active and passive euthanasia. The reason why it is considered bad to be the cause of someone's death is that death is regarded as a great evil—and so it is. However, if it has been decided that euthanasia—even passive euthanasia—is desirable in a given case, it has also been decided that in this instance death is no greater an evil than the patient's continued existence. And if this is true, the usual reason for not wanting to be the cause of someone's death simply does not apply.

Finally, doctors may think that all of this is only of academic interest—the sort of thing that philosophers may worry about but that has no practical bearing on their own work. After all, doctors must be concerned about the legal consequences of what they do, and active euthanasia is clearly forbidden by the law. But even so, doctors should also be concerned with the fact that the law is forcing upon them a moral doctrine that may well be indefensible, and has a considerable effect on their practices. Of course, most doctors are not now in the position of being coerced in this matter, for they do not regard themselves as merely going along with what the law requires. Rather, in statements such as the AMA policy statement that I have quoted, they are endorsing this doctrine as a central point of medical ethics. In that statement, active euthanasia is condemned not merely as illegal but as "contrary to that for which the medical profession stands," whereas passive euthanasia is approved. However, the preceding considerations suggest that there is really no moral difference between the two, considered in themselves (there may be important moral differences in some cases in their *consequences,* but, as I pointed out, these differences may make active euthanasia, and not passive euthanasia, the morally preferable option). So, whereas doctors may have to discriminate between active and passive euthanasia to satisfy the law, they should not do any more than that. In particular, they should not give the distinction any added authority and weight by writing it into official statements of medical ethics.

Discussion Questions

1. Do you agree with Rachels that withholding treatment or assistance is the moral equivalent of intentional termination of life? Discuss whether withholding treatment, as in the case of an infant with Down's syndrome, is the same as causing the patient's death.
2. How would Rachels most likely view the legalization of physician-assisted suicide? Would it matter to him if the person was not terminally ill but requested it?

3. What would Rachels think of the hospice policy of using large doses of morphine to alleviate pain, knowing that it might shorten a patient's life? Is this practice an example of euthanasia? Support your answers.
4. Are we as morally responsible for acts of omission as we are for acts of commission? For example, we can save the lives of dying children in Third World countries through our donations of money and medical supplies. Are we responsible for the deaths of these children because we withhold assistance that we know could have saved their lives? Is the fact that we do not desire their deaths morally relevant, given that the outcome is the same in both cases? Support your answers.

MARGARET PABST BATTIN

The Case for Euthanasia

Margaret Pabst Battin is a professor of philosophy and adjunct professor of internal medicine, Division of Medical Ethics, at the University of Utah. She is also author of the book *The Least Worst Death* (1994). Battin argues that the moral values of mercy, justice, and autonomy support the legalization of euthanasia. The principle of mercy may even impose a positive duty on the physician, in some cases, to assist patients to end their lives.

Critical Reading Questions

1. Why is euthanasia "one of the most acute and uncomfortable problems in medical ethics"?
2. What is the principle of mercy? What two duties does this principle establish for physicians and caregivers? What common medical practices, in Battin's view, go against this principle?
3. According to Battin, does the principle of mercy justify both passive and active euthanasia? What examples does Battin use to illustrate this?
4. What is Battin's response to the argument that euthanasia is no longer necessary because of advances in pain control and palliative care?
5. What is Battin's response to the argument that life itself is a benefit and ought to be preserved? How should we determine when life is no longer a benefit to someone?
6. What is the principle of autonomy, and why is it fundamental to the euthanasia debate? How, according to Battin, is the principle of autonomy conceptually tied to the principle of mercy in the euthanasia debate?
7. What objections to the principle of autonomy does Battin consider? How does she respond to these objections?

"The Case for Euthanasia," from *Health Care Ethics,* ed. by D. VanDeVeer and Tom Regan (Philadelphia, Penn.: Temple University Press, 1987), 58–95. Some notes have been omitted.

8. What is "limited paternalism"? When is it responsible for physicians to deny patient requests for euthanasia? When is it irresponsible?
9. What is the basic premise of "extended paternalism"? Does Battin accept or reject this premise?
10. According to Battin, does patient autonomy create a moral obligation for physicians to perform euthanasia? What examples does Battin use to support her position?
11. How does the principle of justice, according to Battin, support euthanasia?
12. What is Battin's response to those who argue that legalizing euthanasia will take us down the slippery slope to a Nazi-type scenario?
13. What is Battin's position on physician-assisted suicide?

Because it arouses questions about the morality of killing, the effectiveness of consent, the duties of physicians, and equity in the distribution of resources, the problem of euthanasia is one of the most acute and uncomfortable contemporary problems in medical ethics. It is not a new problem; euthanasia has been discussed—and practiced—in both Eastern and Western cultures from the earliest historical times to the present. But because of medicine's new technological capacities to extend life, the problem is much more pressing than it has been in the past, and both the discussion and practice of euthanasia are more widespread. Despite this, much of contemporary Western culture remains strongly opposed to euthanasia: doctors ought not kill people, its public voices maintain, and ought not let them die if it is possible to save life.

I believe that this opposition to euthanasia is in serious moral error—on grounds of mercy, autonomy, and justice. I shall argue for the rightness of granting a person a humane, merciful death, if he or she wants it, even when this can be achieved only by a direct and deliberate killing. . . .

THE CASE FOR EUTHANASIA, PART I: MERCY

The case for euthanasia rests on three fundamental moral principles: mercy, autonomy, and justice.

The principle of mercy asserts that *where possible, one ought to relieve the pain or suffering of another person, when it does not contravene that person's wishes, where one can do so without undue costs to oneself, where one will not violate other moral obligations, where the pain or suffering itself is not necessary for the sufferer's attainment of some overriding good, and where the pain or suffering can be relieved without precluding the sufferer's attainment of some overriding good.* This principle might best be called the principle of medical mercy, to distinguish it from principles concerning mercy in judicial contexts. . . . Contexts that require mercy sometimes require euthanasia as a way of granting mercy—both by direct killing and by letting die. . . .

"Relief of pain is the least disputed and most universal of the moral obligations of the physician," writes one doctor. "Few things a doctor does are more important than relieving pain," says another.[1] These are not simply assertions that the physician ought "do no harm," as the Hippocratic oath is traditionally interpreted, but assertions of positive obligation. . . .

This principle of mercy establishes two component duties:

1. the duty not to cause further pain or suffering; and
2. the duty to act to end pain or suffering already occurring.

Under the first of these, for a physician or other caregiver to extend mercy to a suffering patient may mean to refrain from procedures that cause further suffering—provided, of course, that the treatment offers the patient no overriding benefits. So, for instance, the physician must refrain from ordering painful tests, therapies, or surgical procedures when they cannot alleviate suffering or contribute to a patient's improvement or cure. . . .

Of course, whether a painful test or therapy will actually contribute to some overriding good for the patient is not always clear. Nevertheless, the principle of mercy directs that where such procedures can reasonably be expected to impose suffering on the patient without overriding benefits for him or her, they ought not be done. . . .

In such cases, the principle of mercy demands that the "treatments" no longer be imposed, and that the patient be allowed to die.

But the principle of mercy may also demand "letting die" in a still stronger sense. Under its second component, the principle asserts a duty to act to end suffering that is already occurring. Medicine already honors this duty through its various techniques of pain management. . . . But there are some difficult cases in which pain or suffering is severe but cannot be effectively controlled, at least as long as the patient remains sentient at all. Classical examples include tumors of the throat (where agonizing discomfort is not just a matter of pain but of inability to swallow, "air hunger," or acute shortness of breath), tumors of the brain or bone, and so on. Severe nausea, vomiting, and exhaustion may increase the patient's misery. In these cases, continuing life—or at least continuing consciousness—may mean continuing pain. Consequently, mercy's demand for euthanasia takes hold here: mercy demands that the pain, even if with it the life, be brought to an end.

Ending the pain, though with it the life, may be accomplished through what is usually called "passive euthanasia," withholding or withdrawing treatment that could prolong life. In the most indirect of these cases, the patient is simply not given treatment that might extend his or her life—say, radiation therapy in advanced cancer. . .

But the second component of the principle of mercy may also demand the easing of pain by means more direct than mere allowing to die; it may require *killing.* This is usually called "active euthanasia," and despite borderline cases (for instance, the ancient Greek practice of infanticide by exposure), it can in general be conceptually distinguished from passive euthanasia. In passive euthanasia, treatment is withheld that could support failing bodily functions, either in warding off external threats or in performing its own processes; active euthanasia, in contrast, involves the direct interruption of ongoing bodily processes that otherwise would have been adequate to sustain life. However, although it may be possible to draw a conceptual distinction between passive and active euthanasia, this provides no warrant for the ubiquitous view that killing is morally worse than letting die. Nor does it support the view that withdrawing treatment is worse than withholding it. If the patient's condition is so tragic that continuing life brings only pain, and there is no other way to relieve the pain than by death, then the more merciful act is not one that merely removes support for bodily processes and waits for eventual death to ensue; rather, it is one that brings the pain—and the patient's life—to an end *now*. . . .

But, it may be objected, the cases we have mentioned to illustrate intolerable pain are classical ones; such cases are controllable now. Pain is a thing of the medical past, and euthanasia is no longer necessary, though it once may have been, to relieve pain. . . . Particularly impressive are the huge advances under the hospice program in the amelioration of both the physical and emotional pain of terminal illness, and our culturewide fears of pain in terminal cancer are no longer justified: cancer pain, when it occurs, can now be controlled in virtually all cases. We can now end the pain without also ending the life.

This is a powerful objection, and one very frequently heard in medical circles. Nevertheless, it does not succeed. It is flatly incorrect to say that all pain, including pain in terminal illness, is or can be controlled. Some people still die in unspeakable agony. With superlative care, many kinds of pain can indeed be reduced in many patients, and adequate control of pain in terminal illness is often quite easy to achieve. Nevertheless, complete, universal, fully reliable pain control is a myth. Pain is not yet a "thing of the past," nor are many associated kinds of physical distress. . . . Finally, there are cases in which pain control is theoretically possible but for various extraneous reasons does not occur. Some deaths take place in remote locations where there are no pain-relieving resources. Some patients are unable to communicate the nature or extent of their pain. And some institutions and institutional personnel who have the capacity to control pain do not do so, whether from inattention, malevolence, fears of addiction, or divergent priorities in resources.

In all these cases, of course, the patient can be sedated into unconsciousness; this does indeed end the pain. But in respect of the patient's experience, this is tantamount to causing death: the patient has no further conscious experience and thus can achieve no goods, experience no significant communication, satisfy no goals. Furthermore, adequate sedation, by depressing respiratory function, may hasten death. . . .

The principle of mercy holds that suffering ought to be relieved—unless, among other provisos, the suffering itself will give rise to some overriding benefit or unless the attainment of some benefit would be precluded by relieving the pain. But it might be argued that life itself is a benefit, always an overriding one. Certainly life is usually a benefit, one that we prize. But unless we accept certain metaphysical assumptions, such as "life is a gift from God," we must recognize that life is a benefit because of the experiences and interests associated with it. . . . Philippa Foot treats this as a conceptual point: "Ordinary human lives, even very hard lives, contain a minimum of basic goods, but when these are absent the idea of life is no longer linked to that of good."[2]

Such basic goods, she explains, include not being forced to work far beyond one's capacity; having the support of a family or community; being able to more or less satisfy one's hunger; having hopes for the future; and being able to lie down to rest at night. When these goods are missing, she asserts, the connection between *life* and *good* is broken, and we cannot count it as a benefit to the person whose life it is that his life is preserved.

These basic goods may all be severely compromised or entirely absent in the severely ill or dying patient. . . . Yet even for someone lacking all of what Foot considers to be basic goods, the experiences associated with life may not be unrelievedly negative. We must be very cautious in asserting of someone, even someone in the most abysmal-seeming conditions of the severely ill or dying, that life is no longer a benefit, since the way in which particular experiences, interests, and "basic goods" are valued may vary widely from one person to the next. . . .

It is true that contemporary pain management techniques do make possible the control of pain to a considerable degree. But unless pain and discomforting symptoms are eliminated altogether without loss of function, the underlying problem for the principle of mercy remains: how does *this* patient value life, how does he or she weigh death against pain? We are accustomed to assume that only patients suffering extreme, irremediable pain could be candidates for euthanasia at all and do not consider whether some patients might choose death in preference to comparatively moderate chronic pain, even when the condition is not a terminal one. Of course, a patient's perceptions of pain are extremely subject to stress, anxiety, fear, exhaustion, and other factors, but even though these perceptions may vary, the underlying weighing still demands respect. This is not just a matter of differing sensitivities to pain, but of differing values as well: for some patients, severe pain may be accepted with resignation or even pious joy, whereas for others mild or moderate discomfort is simply not worth enduring. . . .

If the sufferer is the best judge of the relative values of that suffering and other benefits to himself, then his own choices in the matter of mercy ought to be respected. To impose "mercy" on someone who insists that despite his suffering life is still valuable to him would hardly be mercy; to withhold mercy from someone who pleads for it, on the basis that his life could still be worthwhile for him, is insensitive and cruel. Thus, the principle of mercy is conceptually tied to that of autonomy, at least insofar as what guarantees the best application of the principle—and hence, what guarantees the proper response to the ostensive premise in the argument from mercy—is respect for the patient's own wishes concerning the relief of his suffering or pain.

To this issue we now turn.

THE CASE FOR EUTHANASIA, PART II: AUTONOMY

The second principle supporting euthanasia is that of (patient) autonomy: *one ought to respect a competent person's choices, where one can do so without undue costs to oneself, where doing so will not violate other moral obligations, and where these choices do not threaten harm to other persons or parties.* This principle of autonomy, though limited by these provisos, grounds a person's right to have his or her own choices respected in determining the course of medical treatment, including those relevant to euthanasia: whether the patient wishes treatment that will extend life, though perhaps also suffering, or whether he or she wants the suffering relieved, either by being killed or by being allowed to die. It would of course also require respect for the choices of the person whose condition is chronic but not terminal, the person who is disabled though not dying, and the person not yet suffering at all, but facing senility or old age. Indeed, the principle of autonomy would require respect for self-determination in the matter of life and death in any condition at all, provided that the choice is freely and rationally made and does not harm others or violate other moral rules. Thus, the principle of autonomy would protect a much wider range of life-and-death acts than those we call euthanasia, as well as those performed for reasons of mercy. . . .

It is often objected that autonomy in euthanasia choices should not be recognized in practice, whether or not it is accepted in principle, because such choices are often erroneously made. One version of this argument points to physician error. . . . People diagnosed as dying rapidly of inexorable cancers have survived, cancer-free, for dozens of years; people in cardiac failure or long-term irreversible coma have revived and regained full health. . . .

A second argument pointing to the possibility of erroneous choice on the part of the patient asserts the very great likelihood of impairment of the patient's mental processes when seriously ill. Impairing factors include depression, anxiety, pain, fear, intimidation by authoritarian physicians or institutions, and drugs used in medical treatment that affect mental status. Perhaps a person in good health would be capable of calm, objective judgment even in such serious matters as euthanasia, so this view holds, but the person as patient is not. Depression, extremely common in terminal illness, is a particular culprit: it tends to narrow one's view of the possibilities still open; . . . A choice of euthanasia in terminal illness, this view holds, probably reflects largely the gloominess of the depression, not the gravity of the underlying disease or any genuine intention to die.

If this is so, ought not the euthanasia request of a patient be ignored for his or her own sake? According to a limited paternalistic view (sometimes called "soft" or "weak" paternalism), intervention in a person's choices for his or her own sake is justified if the person's thinking is impaired. Under this principle, not every euthanasia request should be honored; such requests should be construed, rather as pleas for more sensitive physical and emotional care.

It is no doubt true that many requests to die are pleas for better care or improved conditions of life. But this still does not establish that all euthanasia requests should be ignored, because the principle of paternalism licenses intervention in a person's choices just *for his or her own good.* Sometimes the choice of euthanasia, though made in an impaired, irrational way, may seem to serve the person's own good better than remaining alive. Thus, since the paternalist, in intervening, must act for the sake of the person in whose liberty he or she interferes, the paternalist must take into account not only the costs for the person of failing to interfere with a euthanasia decision when euthanasia was not warranted (the cost is death, when death was not in this person's interests) but also the costs for that person of interfering in a decision that was warranted (the cost is continuing life—and continuing suffering—when death would have been the better choice). The likelihood of these two undesirable outcomes must then be weighed. To claim that "there's always hope" or to insist that "the diagnosis could be wrong" in a morally responsible way, one must weigh not only the cost of unnecessary death to the patient but also the costs to the patient of dying in agony if the diagnosis is right and the cure does not materialize. . . .

As with limited paternalism, extended "strong" or "hard" paternalism—permitting intervention not merely to counteract impairment but also to avoid great harm—provides a special case when applied to euthanasia situations. The hard paternalist may be tempted to argue that because death is the greatest of harms, euthanasia choices must always be thwarted. But the initial premise of this argument is precisely what is at issue in the euthanasia dispute itself, as we've seen: is death the worst of harms that can befall a person, or is unrelieved, hopeless suffering a still worse harm? The principle of mercy obliges us to relieve suffering when it does not serve some overriding good; but the principle itself cannot tell us whether sheer existence—life—is an overriding good. In the absence of an objectively valid answer, we must appeal to the individual's own preferences and values. . . .

To claim that an incessantly pain-racked but conscious person cannot make a rational choice in matters of life and death is to misconstrue the point: he or she, better than anyone else, can make such a choice, based on intimate acquaintance with pain and his or her own beliefs and fears about death. If the patient wishes to live, despite such suffering, he or she must be allowed to do so; or the patient must be granted help if he or she wishes to die.

But this introduces a further problem. The principle of autonomy, when there are no countervailing considerations on paternalistic grounds or on grounds of harm to others, supports the practice of voluntary euthanasia and, in fact, any form of rational, voluntary suicide. We already recognize a patient's right to refuse any or all medical treatment and hence correlative duties of noninterference on the part of the physician to refrain from treating the patient against his or her will. But does the patient's right of self-determination also give rise to any positive obligation on the part of the physician or other bystander to actively produce death? . . . Although we usually recognize only that the principle of autonomy generates rights to noninterference, in some circumstances a right of self-determination does generate claims to assistance or to the provision of goods. . . .

Some singularly sympathetic cases—like that of the completely paralyzed cerebral palsy victim Elizabeth Bouvier—have brought this issue to public attention. But notice that in euthanasia situations, most persons are handicapped with respect to producing for themselves an easy, "good," merciful death. The handicaps are occasionally physical, but most often involve lack of knowledge of how to bring this about and lack of access to means for so doing. . . . Full autonomy is not achieved until one can both choose and act upon one's choices. It is here, in these cases of "handicap" that afflict many or most patients, that rights to self-determination may generate obligations on the part of physicians (provided, perhaps, that they do not have principled objections to participation in such activities themselves). The physician's obligation is not only to respect the patient's choices but also to make it possible for the patient to act upon his or her choices. This means supplying the knowledge and equipment to enable the person to stay alive, if he or she so chooses; this is an obligation physicians now recognize. But it may also mean providing the knowledge, equipment, and help to enable the patient to die, if that is his or her choice; this is the other part of the physician's obligation, not yet recognized by the medical profession or the law in the United States.

This is not to say that any doctor should be forced to kill any person who asks that: other contravening considerations—particularly that of ascertaining that the request is autonomous and not the product of coerced or irrational choice, and that of controlling abuses by unscrupulous physicians, relatives, or patients—would quickly override. Nor would the physician have an obligation to assist in "euthanasia" for someone not severely ill. But when the physician is sufficiently familiar with the patient to know the seriousness of the condition and the earnestness of the patient's request, when the patient is sufficiently helpless, and when there are no adequate objections on grounds of personal scruples or social welfare, then the principle of autonomy—like the principle of mercy—imposes on the physician the obligation to help the patient in achieving an easy, painless death.

THE CASE FOR EUTHANASIA, PART III: JUSTICE

Although the term "euthanasia" traditionally was employed in cases in which "good death" meant the avoidance of suffering, in recent years use of the term has been extended to cover cases in which the patient is neither suffering nor capable of choosing to die. . . .

This argument from justice is usually employed only to justify the denial of treatment, that is, to justify passive euthanasia; but similar considerations also favor active euthanasia. Passive euthanasia is often practiced upon unsalvageable patients by withholding treatment if a medical crisis occurs: for instance, no-code orders are issued, or pneumonias are not treated, or electrolyte imbalances not corrected if they occur. If justice demands that, despite the prima facie claims of these patients, the resources allocated to their care are better assigned somewhere else, then we must notice that *passive* euthanasia does not provide the most just redistribution of these resources. To "allow" the patient to die may still involve enormous expenditures of money, scarce supplies, or caregiver time. This is most evident in cases of "irretrievably inaccessible" patients, for whom no considerations of mercy or autonomy override the demands of justice in weighing claims. . . . The total cost of maintaining a permanently comatose woman, who was injured in a riding accident in 1956 at age twenty-seven and died eighteen years later, has been estimated at just over $6,000,000; this care provided her with not a single moment of conscious life.[3] The record survival for a coma patient is thirty-seven years and 111 days.[4] The argument from justice demands that these patients, since their claims for care are so weak as to have virtually no force at all, be killed, not simply allowed to die.

OBJECTION TO THE ARGUMENT FROM JUSTICE: THE SLIPPERY SLOPE

But if justice, under the distributive principle employed here, licenses the killing of permanently comatose patients, will it not also license the killing of still-conscious, still-competent dying patients, perhaps still salvageable, close or not so close to death? What extensions of the scope of this principle might be made, should resources become still more scarce? These concerns introduce the "wedge" or "slippery slope" argument, which holds that although some acts of euthanasia may be morally permissible (say, on grounds of mercy or autonomy), to allow them to occur will set a logical precedent for, or will causally result in, consequences that are morally repugnant. Just as Hitler's 1938 "euthanasia" program for mentally defective, senile, and terminally ill Aryans paved the way for the establishment of the extermination camps several years later, it is argued, so permissive euthanasia policies invite irreversible descent down that slippery slope that leads to mass murder. . . .

As it is usually posed, the form of the argument that points to the Nazi experience does not succeed: the forces that brought the mass extermination camps into being were not *caused* by the earlier euthanasia program, and, other things being equal, the extermination camps for Jews would no doubt have been established had there been no euthanasia program at all. To argue that permitting euthanasia now will lead to death camps like Hitler's is to overlook the many other political, social, and psychological factors of the Nazi period. Yet the wedge argument cannot be simply discarded; the factors operating to favor the slide from morally warranted euthanasia to murder are probably much stronger than we realize. They are best seen, I think, as misunderstandings or corruptions of the very principles that favor euthanasia: mercy, autonomy, and perhaps most prominently, justice.

A contemporary version of the wedge argument holds that to permit euthanasia at all—including cases justified on grounds of mercy, autonomy, or justice—will in the presence of strong financial incentives lead to circumstances in which people are killed who are not suffering or who do not wish to die. Furthermore, to permit some doctors to allow their patients to die or to kill them would invite cavalier attitudes concerning the lives of the patients and, in addition to financial incentives, ordinary greed, insensitivity, hastiness, and self-interest, would cause some doctors to let their patients die—or kill them—when there was no moral warrant for doing so. Doctors treating difficult or unresponding patients would find an easy way out. Medical blunders could be more easily covered up, and doctors might use euthanasia as a way of avoiding criticism in cases that were medically difficult to treat. Particularly important, perhaps, are societal and political pressures, most evident in cost-containment policies, to which doctors might respond. After all, to permit earlier, less expensive death would ease the enormous pressures on third-party insurers, public welfare, and the Social Security system: euthanasia is less expensive than continuing medical care. . . .

Is there any reason to think such practices would actually occur? The reasons are closer to hand than one might imagine. Rather than predicting the future, we need simply look to our present practices for evidence that violations of the moral limits to euthanasia can occur. . . .

The wedge argument assumes, without adequate justification, that the rights of those who may become the victims of abuses of a practice outweigh the rights of those who become victims if a practice is prohibited to whose benefits they are morally entitled and urgently need.

To protect those who might wrongly be killed or allowed to die might seem a stronger obligation than to satisfy the wishes of those who desire release from pain, analogous perhaps to the principle in law that "better ten guilty men go free than one be unjustly convicted." . . . But to require the person who chooses to die to stay alive in order to protect those who might unwillingly be killed sometime in the future is to impose an extreme harm—intolerable suffering—on that person, which he or she must bear for the sake of others. Furthermore, since, as we've seen, the question of which is worse, suffering or death, is person-relative, we have no independent, objective basis for protecting the class of persons who might be killed at the expense of those who would suffer intolerable pain; perhaps our protecting ought to be done the other way around. . . .

CONCLUSION: EUTHANASIA AND SUICIDE

It may be objected that requiring the patient to choose between death and life, insofar as the patient must antecedently consider treatment decisions that affect the circumstances and timing of his or her own demise, is equivalent to requiring the patient's consideration of suicide. In a sense, it is; but this is also the more general solution to the euthanasia problem. Although euthanasia is indeed warranted on grounds of mercy, autonomy, and justice, these principles can be more effectively and safely honored by permitting suicide, perhaps assisted by the physician who has care of the patient or a family member under the advice of the physicians, and supplemented by nonvoluntary euthanasia *only* when the patient is permanently comatose or otherwise irretrievably inaccessible. Not only do practical reasons like avoiding greed and manipulation on the part of the physicians or the institutions controlling them speak for preferring physician-assisted suicide to physician-initiated euthanasia, but there are conceptual reasons as well. The conditions that distinguish morally permissible euthanasia from impermissable murder all involve matters that the patient, not the physician, is in a privileged position to know. To extend mercy, the physician must know how the patient weights suffering against death, and at what point *for the patient* death becomes the lesser of two evils. To respect the patient's autonomy, the physician must know what his or her preferences are, given the alternatives available, in the matter of dying. And to exercise justice, the physician must know what treatment the patient realistically desires. . . . Consequently, since the risk of misinterpretation is great and the possibility of manipulation or coercion high, the physician should not be the one to *initiate* the choice. Rather, he or she must be prepared to assist the patient who chooses death, just as he or she is prepared to assist the patient who chooses continuing life. . . .

NOTES

1. Edmund D. Pellegrino, M.D., "The Clinical Ethics of Pain Management in the Terminally Ill," *Hospital Formulary* 17 (November 1982): 1,495–1,496; and Marcia Angell, "The Quality of Mercy," *New England Journal of Medicine* 306 (January 1982): 98–99.
2. Philippa Foot, "Euthanasia," *Philosophy & Public Affairs* 6 (Winter 1977): 95.
3. This case, originally presented in the *Illinois Medical Journal* and reprinted in *Connecticut*

Medicine with commentary from medical, ethical, and legal experts, is summarized in *Concern for Dying* 8 (Summer 1982): 3.

4. President's Commission for the Study of Ethical Problems in Medicine and Biomedical and Behavioral Research, *Defining Death: Medical, Legal, and Ethical Issues in the Determination of Death* (Washington, D.C.: Government Printing Office, 1981), 18, citing the *Guiness Book of World Records* regarding the case of Elaine Esposito.

Discussion Questions

1. Dr. Jack Kevorkian claimed that his mission was one of mercy. He also claimed that by allowing patients to administer the lethal injections themselves, he was respecting their autonomy. Discuss whether Battin would approve of Kevorkian's "mercy killings" given her support of both limited paternalism and physician-assisted suicide.
2. In a note in her article, Battin asks us to try the following thought experiment. Discuss the questions at the end of the experiment.

    > Imagine that you have been captured by a gang of ruthless and superlatively clever criminals, whom you know with certainty will never be caught or change their minds. They plan either to execute you now or to torture you unremittingly for the next twenty years and then put you to death. Which would be worse? Does your view change if the length of the torture period is reduced to twenty days or twenty minutes, and, if so, why? How severe must the torture be?

3. Battin's use of the principles of autonomy and mercy in her support of euthanasia is primarily deontological. Is her claim that life has worth only if it is a benefit and contains "a minimum of basic goods" consistent with the deontological principle that rational beings have intrinsic worth? How has Battin modified the strict Kantian deontological position? Discuss which interpretation of the value of rational human life, Battin's or Kant's, you find most compelling.
4. Are you satisfied with Battin's response to the slippery slope or wedge argument against legalizing euthanasia? Support your answer. Discuss what limits, if any, Battin might place on a public policy regarding euthanasia.
5. David Lewis, an AIDS counselor in Vancouver, British Columbia, revealed in 1990 that he had helped eight friends with AIDS take lethal doses of drugs that had been prescribed earlier by a doctor. The men had begged to die; none of them wanted to suffer anymore, he told a reporter. "To refuse to help them would be criminal."[32] Did Lewis make the morally right decision? Support your answer using the principles of mercy and autonomy as well as Battin's concept of limited paternalism.
6. Discuss Battin's claim that distributive justice supports involuntary, active euthanasia in cases in which costly medical resources are needed to sustain life. Discuss what other considerations might be relevant in a utilitarian calculus regarding euthanasia in cases like these.

DANIEL CALLAHAN

"Aid-in-Dying": The Social Dimensions

Daniel Callahan is co-founder and director of the Hastings Center as well as author of several books and articles in bioethics. Like Hardwig, Callahan argues that euthanasia is not a matter of private self-determination but a social issue; however, Callahan draws a much different conclusion regarding the morality of euthanasia. Euthanasia, Callahan points out, puts absolute power of life and death in the hands of another person, and thus the resulting inequality of power in this relationship is incompatible with respect for human dignity. In addition, the criteria used for euthanasia decisions are necessarily arbitrary and subjective. Therefore, euthanasia should remain illegal.

Critical Reading Questions

1. What, according to Callahan, is one of the greatest fears people have about dying? Does Callahan think that permitting euthanasia is a reasonable response to that fear?
2. On what grounds does Callahan argue that euthanasia and assisted suicide are more than a personal matter of self-determination?
3. Why is Callahan opposed to the legalization of euthanasia?
4. What are the two classic arguments in favor of euthanasia and assisted suicide?
5. How does Callahan respond to the argument that a right to euthanasia is simply an extension of the right to control our own lives and our own bodies?
6. Does John Stuart Mill's principle of freedom support Callahan's position?
7. Why does Callahan claim that there is a contradiction between euthanasia and the principle of autonomy or sovereignty over our lives? What point is Callahan making when he draws a comparison between slavery and euthanasia?
8. What are some of the problems, according to Callahan, of using pain and suffering as a standard for justifying euthanasia?
9. What are some of the problems of requiring patient competence for euthanasia?
10. Do doctors have a duty to relieve suffering by carrying out a patient's request for euthanasia? Why, according to Callahan, is it unfair to burden a physician with the moral decision to end a patient's life?

The fear of dying is powerful. Even more powerful sometimes is the fear of not dying, of being forced to endure destructive pain, or to live out a life of unrelieved, pointless suffering. The movement to legalize euthanasia and assisted suicide is a strong and, seemingly, historically inevitable response to that fear. It draws part of its strength from the failure of modern medicine to reassure us that it can manage our dying with dignity and comfort. It draws another part from the desire to be masters of our fate. Why must we endure that which need not be endured? If medicine cannot always bring us the kind of death we might like through its technical skills, why can it not use them to give us a quick and merciful release? . . .

"'Aid-in-Dying': The Social Dimensions." *Commonweal*, August 9, 1991.

If it should happen to be impossible for us to so easily bring about our own death, would it not be reasonable to ask someone else, specifically a doctor, to help us to die? Would it not, moreover, be an act of mercy for a doctor to give us that kind of a release? Is not the relief of suffering a high moral good?

To say "no" in response to questions of that kind seems both repressive and cruel. They invoke our cherished political values of liberty and self-determination. They draw upon our deep and long-standing moral commitment to the relief of suffering. They bespeak our ancient efforts to triumph over death, to find a way to bring it to heel.

Nonetheless, we should as a society say no, and decisively so, to euthanasia and assisted suicide.... If a death marked by pain or suffering is a nasty death, a natural biological evil of a supreme kind, euthanasia and assisted suicide are wrong and harmful responses to that evil. To directly kill another person in the name of mercy (as I will define "euthanasia" here), or to assist another to commit suicide (which seems to me logically little different from euthanasia), would add to a society already burdened with man-made evils still another.

Euthanasia is mistakenly understood as only a personal matter of self-determination, the control of our own bodies, just a small step beyond the removal of legal prohibitions against suicide. Unlike suicide, euthanasia should be understood as of its nature a social act. It is social because, by definition, it requires the assistance of someone else, as the expression "aid-in-dying" itself makes clear.

Legalization would also provide an important social sanction for euthanasia, affecting many aspects of our society beyond the immediate relief of suffering individuals. The implications of that sanction are profound. . . .

All civilized societies have developed laws to reduce the occasions on which one person is allowed to kill another person. All have resisted the notion that private agreements can be reached allowing one person to take the life of another to serve the interests of one or both parties. Traditionally, only three circumstances have been acceptable for the taking of life: killing in self-defense or to protect another life, killing in the course of a just war, and, in the case of capital punishment, killing by agents of the state. . . .

The proposal for "aid-in-dying" is nothing less than a proposal to add a new category of acceptable killing to those already socially accepted. To do so would be to reverse the long-developing trend to limit the occasions of legally sanctioned killing (most notable in the campaigns to abolish capital punishment and to limit access to firearms). Civilized societies have slowly come to understand how virtually impossible it is to control even legally sanctioned killing. It seems of its nature to invite abuse. Most notably, the proposal would reinstate private killings. By a "private" killing I mean one in which the agreement of one person to kill another is ratified in private by the persons themselves, not by public authorities (even if it is made legal and safeguards are put into effect). Do we want to give one person the right to kill another for the sake of the relief of pain and suffering? That is the question before us. . . .

Yet if we generally accept in our society a right to control our own life and body, why has the extension of that right to private killing been denied? The most obvious reason is a reluctance to give one person absolute and irrevocable power over the life of another, whether there is consent or not. That prohibition is a way of saying that the social stakes in the legitimization of killing are extraordinarily high. It is to recognize that a society should—for the mutual protection of all—be exceedingly parsimonious about conferring a right to kill on anyone, for whatever reason.

John Stuart Mill, in his classic essay *On Liberty,* noted that civilized societies do not grant individuals a legal right to sell themselves into slavery, even though that denial is a limitation on self-determination. "The principle of freedom," he wrote, "cannot require that he should be free not to be free. It is not freedom to be allowed to alienate his freedom."

Yet it is not just the ceding of freedom that is problematic. The absolute power that is put into the hands of another, I would add—the right to be a slaveholder—is not compatible with respect for our human dignity. Both the slaveholder and the enslaved are corrupted by the relationship, even if both have the good of the other as their motive.

The one gives up too much, and the other has too much given him.

A similar consideration applies in the case of killings authorized in the name of mercy: they give one person an absolute power over another. . . .

We cannot, I believe, transfer our sovereignty to another without contradicting it. A sovereignty that can legally and morally be given away is fragile and contingent, not sovereignty at all. To allow another person to kill us is the most radical relinquishment of sovereignty imaginable, not just one more way of exercising it. Our life belongs no longer to us, but to the person into whose power we give it. No person should have that kind of power over another, freely gained or not. . . .

There is another problem. If the person who is to kill is to do so in a responsible fashion, then he or she must have some independent standards for determining when to honor such requests. This becomes all the more important when it is argued, as it sometimes is, that a doctor has not just a right to respond to a request for euthanasia but that, in the name of a duty to relieve suffering, there can be a positive obligation to do so.

We come here to a striking pitfall of the common argument for euthanasia and assisted suicide. Once the key premises of that argument are accepted, there will remain no logical way in the future to: (1) deny euthanasia to anyone who requests it for whatever reason, terminal illness or not; or to (2) deny it to the suffering incompetent, even if they do not request it. . . .

Where are the flaws here? Recall that there are two classical arguments in favor of euthanasia and assisted suicide: our right of self-determination, and our claim upon the mercy of others, especially doctors, to relieve our suffering if they can do so. These two arguments are typically spliced together and presented as a single contention. Yet if they are considered independently—and there is no inherent reason why they must be linked—they display serious problems. Consider, first, the argument for our right of self-determination. It is said that a competent, adult person should have a right to euthanasia for the relief of suffering. But why must the person be suffering? Does not that stipulation already compromise the right of self-determination? How can self-determination have any limits? Why are not the person's desires or motives, whatever they may be, sufficient? How can we satisfy this arbitrary limitation of self-determination? The standard arguments for euthanasia offer no answers to those questions.

Consider next the person who is suffering but not competent, who is perhaps demented or mentally retarded. The standard argument (and the proposed Washington state law) would deny euthanasia to that person. But why? If a person is suffering but not competent, then it would seem grossly unfair to deny relief simply because that person lacks competence. Are the incompetent less entitled to relief from suffering than the competent? Will it only be affluent middle-class people, mentally fit and able, who can qualify? Will those who are incompetent but suffering be denied that which those who are intellectually and emotionally better off can have? Would that be fair? Do they suffer less for being incompetent? . . .

My contention is that the joining of those two requirements is perfectly arbitrary, a jerry-rigged combination if ever there was one. Each has its own logic, and each could be used to justify euthanasia. But in the nature of the case that logic, it seems evident, offers little resistance to denying any competent person the right to be killed, sick or not; and little resistance to killing the incompetent, so long as there is good reason to believe they are suffering. There is no principled reason to reject that logic, and no reason to think it could long remain suppressed by the expedient of arbitrary legal stipulations.

There is a related problem worth considering. If the act of euthanasia, conventionally understood, requires the request and consent of the patient, it no less requires that the person to do the killing have his or her own independent moral standards for acceding to the request. The doctor must act with integrity. How can a doctor who voluntarily brings about, or is instrumental in, the death of another legitimately justify that to herself? Would the mere claim of self-determination on the part of someone be sufficient—"it is my body. Doctor, and, I request that you kill me"? There is a widespread resistance to that kind of claim, and doctors quite rightly have never been willing to do what patients want just because they want it. There is surely a legitimate fear that, if such a claim were sanctioned, there would be no reason to forbid any two competent persons from entering into an agreement for one to kill the other. Perhaps it arises out of a reluctance to put doctors in the role of taking life simply as a means of advancing patient self-determination, quite apart from any medical reasons for doing so.

The most likely reason for resistance to a pure self-determination standard is that we have, traditionally, defined the appropriate role of the physician as someone whose duty it is to relieve suffering. . . . A doctor will not cut off my healthy arm simply because I decide my autonomy and well-being would thereby be enhanced. But the additional requirement that the physician also be relieving suffering carries with it the problem mentioned above. How can a physician determine, much less diagnose in any traditional medical sense, genuine and unrelievable suffering?

The doctor will not be able to use a medical standard. He or she will only be able to use a moral standard. Faced with a patient reporting great suffering, a doctor cannot, therefore, justify euthanasia on purely medical grounds (because suffering is unmeasurable and scientifically undiagnosable). To maintain professional and personal integrity, the doctor will have to justify it on his or her own moral grounds. The doctor must believe that a life of subjectively experienced intense suffering is not worth living. He must believe that himself if he is to be justified in taking the decisive and ultimate step of killing the patient; it must be his moral reason to act, not the patient's reason (even though they may coincide). But if he believes that a life of some forms of suffering is not worth living, then how can he deny the same relief to a person who cannot request it, or who requests it but whose competence is in doubt? This is simply a different way of making the point that there is no self-evident reason why the supposed duty to relieve suffering must be limited to competent patients claiming self-determination. Or why patients who claim death as their right under self-determination must be either suffering or dying.

There is, moreover, the possibility that what begins as a right of doctors to kill under specified conditions will soon become a duty to kill. On what grounds could a doctor deny a request by a competent person for euthanasia? . . .

Our duty to relieve suffering cannot justify the introduction of new evils into society. The risk of doing just that in the legalization of "aid-in-dying" is too great, particularly since the number of people whose pain and suffering could not be relieved would never be a large one (so even most euthanasia advocates recognize). It is too great because it would take a disproportionate social change to bring it about, one whose implications extend far beyond the sick and dying. It is too great because, as the history of the twentieth century should demonstrate, killing is a contagious disease, not easy to stop once unleashed in society. It is too great a risk because it would offer medicine too convenient a way out of its hardest cases, those where there is ample room for further, more benign reforms. We are far from exhausting the known remedies for the relief of pain (frequently, even routinely, underused), and a long way from providing decent psychological support for those who suffer from despair and a sense of futility in continuing life.

Pain and suffering in the critically ill and dying are great evils. The attempt to relieve them by the introduction of euthanasia and assisted suicide is even greater. Those practices threaten the future security of the living. They no less threaten the dying themselves. Once a society allows one person to take the life of another based on their mutual private standards of a life worth living, there can be no safe or sure way to contain the deadly virus thus introduced. It will go where it will thereafter.

Discussion Questions

1. Callahan's argument against euthanasia is based on his definition of euthanasia as "aid-in-dying." Dr. Jack Kevorkian claims that he has overcome this moral objection to euthanasia with the invention of his Mercitron, a device that allows patients to kill themselves with a self-administered lethal injection.[33] Discuss whether the Mercitron

overcomes Callahan's objection to aiding another person in dying. Would Callahan approve of the Mercitron? Support your answer.

2. Callahan argues that linking the criteria of suffering and competence excludes some people who may well be deserving of euthanasia, such as incompetent terminally ill people who are suffering greatly. On the other hand, applying each criterion separately can lead to too many abuses. Because these criteria entail unfairness and can come into conflict with one another, they should be discarded and, therefore, euthanasia should be rejected. Do you agree with Callahan's reasoning? Support your answer. Discuss how both Battin and Hardwig would respond to Callahan's objection.
3. Callahan argues that it is morally unacceptable to make euthanasia decisions based on subjective criteria. Euthanasia, therefore, is morally unacceptable, because there is no way a physician can objectively determine whose requests for euthanasia should be honored. Such a decision ultimately requires subjective moral judgments on the part of the physician. Do you agree with Callahan? Are medical decisions regarding a patient's treatment, especially those based on dialogue between a patient and doctor, always objective, or are such decisions necessarily partly subjective? If decisions regarding a patient's treatment are based, at least in part, on subjective criteria, shouldn't subjective criteria be permitted in euthanasia decisions as well? Support your answers. Discuss how Callahan might respond to this objection.
4. Discuss whether Callahan's argument that legalizing euthanasia would change the role of the doctor sufficiently takes into account the fact that, with modern medical technology, the role of the doctor has already changed.

JOHN HARDWIG

Is There a Duty to Die?

John Hardwig is a professor of philosophy and medical ethics at East Tennessee State University. Hardwig rejects the current emphasis on patient autonomy as the critical issue in euthanasia, because it does not take into account family interests in the care of the patient. Because of modern technology, more and more elderly people are saved from acute illness only to eventually die lingering and costly deaths from chronic illnesses. Adopting a position similar to Plato and the early Stoics, Hardwig argues that when this happens and we become a burden on our family and loved ones, we may have a duty to die.

Critical Reading Questions

1. Why does Hardwig claim that most of us probably do believe in the existence of a duty to die? What examples does he use to support his claim?

"Is There a Duty to Die?" *Hastings Center Report* 27, no. 2 (1997): 34–42. Notes have been omitted.

2. What are some of the developments in modern medicine that have made the duty to die an important issue?
3. According to Hardwig, what "American fantasy" has lead bioethics to see euthanasia as a private decision?
4. How does Hardwig answer the question: Whose life is it, anyway?
5. What are some of the burdens imposed on loved ones who have to care for an old, ailing family member? What obligations, if any, do these families have toward their old and ailing members?
6. What, according to Hardwig, are some of the most serious objections to the idea that there is a duty to die? How does he respond to these objections?
7. What are some of the guidelines Hardwig gives for deciding if someone has a duty to die? Who should make the decision about when a person has a duty to die?
8. According to Hardwig, how does a duty to die affirm rather than compromise our moral agency and human dignity?
9. Why does our fear of death, according to Hardwig, prevent us from finding meaning in death?

When Richard Lamm made the statement that old people have a duty to die, it was generally shouted down or ridiculed. The whole idea is just too preposterous to entertain. Or too threatening. In fact, a fairly common argument against legalizing physician-assisted suicide is that if it were legal, some people might somehow get the idea that they have a duty to die. These people could only be the victims of twisted moral reasoning or vicious social pressure. It goes without saying that there is no duty to die.

But for me the question is real and very important. I feel strongly that I may very well some day have a duty to die. I do not believe that I am idiosyncratic, morbid, mentally ill, or morally perverse in thinking this. I think many of us will eventually face precisely this duty. But I am first of all concerned with my own duty. . . .

CIRCUMSTANCES AND A DUTY TO DIE

Do many of us really believe that no one ever has a duty to die? I suspect not. I think most of us probably believe that there is such a duty, but it is very uncommon. Consider Captain Oates, a member of Admiral Scott's expedition to the South Pole. Oates became too ill to continue. If the rest of the team stayed with him, they would all perish. After this had become clear, Oates left his tent one night, walked out into a raging blizzard, and was never seen again. That may have been a heroic thing to do, but we might be able to agree that it was also no more than his duty. It would have been wrong for him to urge—or even to allow—the rest to stay and care for him.

This is a very unusual circumstance—a "lifeboat case"—and lifeboat cases make for bad ethics. But I expect that most of us would also agree that there have been cultures in which what we would call a duty to die has been fairly common. These are relatively poor, technologically simple, and especially nomadic cultures. In such societies, everyone knows that if you manage to live long enough, you will eventually become old and debilitated. Then you will need to take steps to end your life. The old people in these societies regularly did precisely that. Their cultures prepared and supported them in doing so.

Those cultures could be dismissed as irrelevant to contemporary bioethics; their circumstances are so different from ours. But if that is our response, it is instructive. It suggests that we assume a duty to die is irrelevant to us because our wealth and technological sophistication have purchased exemption for us . . . except under very unusual circumstances like Captain Oates's.

But have wealth and technology really exempted us? Or are they, on the contrary, about to make a duty to die common again? We like to think of modern medicine as all triumph with no dark side. Our medicine saves many lives and enables us to live longer. That is wonderful, indeed. We are all glad to have access to this medicine. But our medicine also delivers most of us over to chronic illnesses and it enables many of us to survive longer than we can take care of ourselves, longer than we know what to do with ourselves, longer than we even are ourselves.

The costs—and these are not merely monetary—of prolonging our lives when we are no longer able to care for ourselves are often staggering. If further medical advances wipe out many of today's "killer diseases"—cancer, heart attacks, strokes, ALS, AIDS, and the rest—then one day most of us will survive long enough to become demented or debilitated. These developments could generate a fairly widespread duty to die. . . .

Let me be clear. I certainly believe that there is a duty to refuse life-prolonging medical treatment and also a duty to complete advance directives refusing life-prolonging treatment. But a duty to die can go well beyond that. There can be a duty to die before one's illnesses would cause death, even if treated only with palliative measures. In fact, there may be a fairly common responsibility to end one's life in the absence of any terminal illness at all. Finally, there can be a duty to die when one would prefer to live. . . .

THE INDIVIDUALISTIC FANTASY

Because a duty to die seems such a real possibility to me, I wonder why contemporary bioethics has dismissed it without serious consideration. I believe that most bioethics still shares in one of our deeply embedded American dreams: the individualistic fantasy. This fantasy leads us to imagine that lives are separate and unconnected, or that they could be so if we chose. . . .

Within a health care context, the individualistic fantasy leads us to assume that the patient is the only one affected by decisions about her medical treatment. If only the patient were affected, the relevant questions when making treatment decisions would be precisely those we ask: What will benefit the patient? Who can best decide that? The pivotal issue would always be simply whether the patient wants to live like this and whether she would consider herself better off dead. "Whose life is it, anyway?" we ask rhetorically.

But this is morally obtuse. We are not a race of hermits. Illness and death do not come only to those who are all alone. Nor is it much better to think in terms of the bald dichotomy between "the interests of the patient" and "the interests of society" (or a third-party payer), as if we were isolated individuals connected only to "society" in the abstract or to the other, faceless members of our health maintenance organization.

Most of us are affiliated with particular others and most deeply, with family and loved ones. Families and loved ones are bound together by ties of care and affection, by legal relations and obligations, by inhabiting shared spaces and living units, by interlocking finances and economic prospects, by common projects and also commitments to support the different life projects of other family members, by shared histories, by ties of loyalty. This life together of family and loved ones is what defines and sustains us; it is what gives meaning to most of our lives. We would not have it any other way. We would not want to be all alone, especially when we are seriously ill, as we age, and when we are dying.

But the fact of deeply interwoven lives debars us from making exclusively self-regarding decisions, as the decisions of one member of a family may dramatically affect the lives of all the rest. The impact of my decisions upon my family and loved ones is the source of many of my strongest obligations and also the most plausible and likeliest basis of a duty to die. "Society," after all, is only very marginally affected by how I live, or by whether I live or die.

A BURDEN TO MY LOVED ONES

Many older people report that their one remaining goal in life is not to be a burden to their loved ones. Young people feel this, too: when I ask my undergraduate students to think about whether their death could come too late, one of their very first responses always is, "Yes, when I become a burden to my family or loved ones." Tragically, there are situations in which my loved ones would be much better off—all things considered, the loss of a loved one notwithstanding—if I were dead.

The lives of our loved ones can be seriously compromised by caring for us. The burdens of providing care or even just supervision twenty-four hours a day, seven days a week are often overwhelming. When this kind of caregiving goes on for years, it leaves the caregiver exhausted, with no time for herself or life of her own. . . .

I am not advocating a crass, quasi-economic conception of burdens and benefits, nor a shallow, hedonistic view of life. Given a suitably rich understanding of benefits, family members sometimes do benefit from suffering through the long illness of a loved one. Caring for the sick or aged can foster growth, even as it makes daily life immeasurably harder and the prospects for the future much bleaker. Chronic illness or drawn-out death can also pull a family together, making the care for each other stronger and more evident. If my loved ones are truly benefiting from coping with my illness or debility, I have no duty to die based on burdens to them.

But it would be irresponsible to blithely assume that this always happens, that it will happen in my family, or that it will be the fault of my family if they cannot manage to turn my illness into a positive experience. Perhaps the opposite is more common: . . .

Our families and loved ones also have obligations, of course—they have the responsibility to stand by us and to support us through debilitating illness and death. They must be prepared to make significant sacrifices to respond to an illness in the family. I am far from denying that. Most of us are aware of this responsibility and most families meet it rather well. . . .

OBJECTIONS TO A DUTY TO DIE

To my mind, the most serious objections to the idea of a duty to die lie in the effects on my loved ones of ending my life. But to most others, the important objections have little or nothing to do with family and loved ones. Perhaps the most common objections are: (1) there is a higher duty that always takes precedence over a duty to die; (2) a duty to end one's own life would be incompatible with a recognition of human dignity or the intrinsic value of a person; and (3) seriously ill, debilitated, or dying people are already bearing the harshest burdens and so it would be wrong to ask them to bear the additional burden of ending their own lives. . . .

An example of the first line of argument would be the claim that a duty to God, the giver of life, forbids that anyone take her own life. It could be argued that this duty always supersedes whatever obligations we might have to our families. But what convinces us that we always have such a religious duty in the first place? And what guarantees that it always supersedes our obligations to try to protect our loved ones? . . .

Secondly, religious considerations aside, the claim could be made that an obligation to end one's own life would be incompatible with human dignity or would embody a failure to recognize the intrinsic value of a person. But I do not see that in thinking I had a duty to die I would necessarily be failing to respect myself or to appreciate my dignity or worth. Nor would I necessarily be failing to respect you in thinking that you had a similar duty. There is surely also a sense in which we fail to respect ourselves if in the face of illness or death, we stoop to choosing just what is best for ourselves. Indeed, Kant held that the very core of human dignity is the ability to act on a self-imposed moral law, regardless of whether it is in our interest to do so. We shall return to the notion of human dignity.

A third objection appeals to the relative weight of burdens and thus, ultimately, to considerations of fairness or justice. The burdens that an illness creates for the family could not possibly be great enough to justify an obligation to end one's life—the sacrifice of life itself would be a far greater burden than any involved in caring for a chronically ill family member.

But is this true? Consider the following case:

> An 87-year-old woman was dying of congestive heart failure. Her APACHE score predicted that

> she had less than a 50 percent chance to live for another six months. She was lucid, assertive, and terrified of death. She very much wanted to live and kept opting for rehospitalization and the most aggressive life-prolonging treatment possible. That treatment successfully prolonged her life (though with increasing debility) for nearly two years. Her 55-year-old daughter was her only remaining family, her caregiver, and the main source of her financial support. The daughter duly cared for her mother. But before her mother died, her illness had cost the daughter all of her savings, her home, her job, and her career.

This is by no means an uncommon sort of case. Thousands of similar cases occur each year. Now, ask yourself which is the greater burden:

a) To lose a 50 percent chance of six more months of life at age 87?

b) To lose all your savings, your home, and your career at age 55?

Which burden would you prefer to bear? Do we really believe the former is the greater burden? . . .

I think most of us would quickly agree that (b) is a greater burden. That is the evil we would more hope to avoid in our lives. . . .

This point does not depend on a utilitarian calculus. Even if death were the greatest burden (thus disposing of any simple utilitarian argument), serious questions would remain about the moral justifiability of choosing to impose crushing burdens on loved ones in order to avoid having to bear this burden oneself. . . .

WHO HAS A DUTY TO DIE?

Suppose, then, that there can be a duty to die. Who has a duty to die? And when? To my mind, these are the right questions, the questions we should be asking. Many of us may one day badly need answers to just these questions. . . .

Some may object that it would be wrong to put a loved one in a position of having to say, in effect, "You should end your life because caring for you is too hard on me and the rest of the family." Not only will it be almost impossible to say something like that to someone you love, it will carry with it a heavy load of guilt. On this view, you should decide by yourself whether you have a duty to die and approach your loved ones only after you have made up your mind to say good-bye to them. Your family could then try to change your mind, but the tremendous weight of moral decision would be lifted from their shoulders.

Perhaps so. But I believe in family decisions. Important decisions for those whose lives are interwoven should be made together, in a family discussion. Granted, a conversation about whether I have a duty to die would be a tremendously difficult conversation. The temptations to be dishonest could be enormous. Nevertheless, if I am contemplating a duty to die, my family and I should, if possible, have just such an agonizing discussion. It will act as a check on the information, perceptions, and reasoning of all of us. But even more importantly, it affirms our connectedness at a critical juncture in our lives and our life together. Honest talk about difficult matters almost always strengthens relationships. . . .

I cannot say when someone has a duty to die. Still, I can suggest a few features of one's illness, history, and circumstances that make it more likely that one has a duty to die. I present them here without much elaboration or explanation.

1. A duty to die is more likely when continuing to live will impose significant burdens—emotional burdens, extensive caregiving, destruction of life plans, and, yes, financial hardship—on your family and loved ones. . . .

2. A duty to die becomes greater as you grow older. As we age, we will be giving up less by giving up our lives, if only because we will sacrifice fewer remaining years of life and a smaller portion of our life plans. . . .

3. A duty to die is more likely when you have already lived a full and rich life. You have already had a full share of the good things life offers.

4. There is greater duty to die if your loved ones' lives have already been difficult or impoverished, if they have had only a small share of the good things

that life has to offer (especially if through no fault of their own).

5. A duty to die is more likely when your loved ones have already made great contributions—perhaps even sacrifices—to make your life a good one. Especially if you have not made similar sacrifices for their well-being or for the well-being of other members of your family.

6. To the extent that you can make a good adjustment to your illness or handicapping condition, there is less likely to be a duty to die. A good adjustment means that smaller sacrifices will be required of loved ones and there is more compensating interaction for them. . . .

7. There is less likely to be a duty to die if you can still make significant contributions to the lives of others, especially your family. . . .

8. A duty to die is more likely when the part of you that is loved will soon be gone or seriously compromised. Or when you soon will no longer be capable of giving love. Part of the horror of dementing disease is that it destroys the capacity to nurture and sustain relationships, taking away a person's agency and the emotions that bind her to others.

9. There is a greater duty to die to the extent that you have lived a relatively lavish lifestyle instead of saving for illness or old age. . . . It is a greater wrong to come to your family for assistance if your need is the result of having chosen leisure or a spendthrift lifestyle. . . .

CAN THE INCOMPETENT HAVE A DUTY TO DIE?

. . . I am tempted to simply bypass the entire question by saying that I am talking only about competent persons. But the idea of a duty to die clearly raises the specter of one person claiming that another—who cannot speak for herself—has such a duty. So I need to say that I can make no sense of the claim that someone has a duty to die if the person has never been able to understand moral obligation at all. To my mind, only those who were formerly capable of making moral decisions could have such a duty.

But the case of formerly competent persons is almost as troubling. Perhaps we should simply stipulate that no incompetent person can have a duty to die, not even if she affirmed belief in such a duty in an advance directive. . . .

But for me personally, very urgent practical matters turn on their resolution. If a formerly competent person can no longer have a duty to die (or if other people are not likely to help her carry out this duty), I believe that my obligation may be to die while I am still competent, before I become unable to make and carry out that decision for myself. Surely it would be irresponsible to evade my moral duties by temporizing until I escape into incompetence. And so I must die sooner than I otherwise would have to. One the other hand, if I could count on others to end my life after I become incompetent, I might be able to fulfill my responsibilities while also living out all my competent or semi-competent days. Given our society's reluctance to permit physicians, let alone family members, to perform aid-in-dying, I believe I may well have a duty to end my life when I can see mental incapacity on the horizon.

There is also the very real problem of sudden incompetence—due to a serious stroke or automobile accident, for example. For me, that is the real nightmare. If I suddenly become incompetent, I will fall into the hands of a medical-legal system that will conscientiously disregard my moral beliefs and do what is best for me, regardless of the consequences for my loved ones. And that is not at all what I would have wanted!

SOCIAL POLICIES AND A DUTY TO DIE

The claim that there is a duty to die will seem to some a misplaced response to social negligence. If our society were providing for the debilitated, the chronically ill, and the elderly as it should be, there would be only very rare cases of a duty to die. . . .

I cannot claim to know whether in some abstract sense a society like ours should provide care for all who are chronically ill or debilitated. But the fact is that we Americans seem to be unwilling to pay for this kind of long-term care, except for ourselves and our own. In fact, we are moving in precisely the opposite direction—we are trying to shift the burdens of caring for the seriously and chronically ill onto families in order to save costs for our health care system. As we shift the burdens of care onto families, we also dramatically increase the number of Americans who will have a duty to die.

I must not, then, live my life and make my plans on the assumption that social institutions will protect my family from my infirmity and debility. To do so would be irresponsible. More likely, it will be up to me to protect my loved ones.

A DUTY TO DIE AND THE MEANING OF LIFE

A duty to die seems very harsh, and often it would be. It is one of the tragedies of our lives that someone who wants very much to live can nevertheless have a duty to die. It is both tragic and ironic that it is precisely the very real good of family and loved ones that gives rise to this duty. Indeed, the genuine love, closeness and supportiveness of family members is a major source of this duty: we could not be such a burden if they did not care for us. Finally, there is deep irony in the fact that the very successes of our life-prolonging medicine help to create a widespread duty to die. . . .

We do not even ask about meaning in death, so busy are we with trying to postpone it. But we will not conquer death by one day developing a technology so magnificent that no one will have to die. Nor can we conquer death by postponing it ever longer. We can conquer death only by finding meaning in it.

Although the existence of a duty to die does not hinge on this, recognizing such a duty would go some way toward recovering meaning in death. . . .

First, recognizing a duty to die affirms my agency and also my moral agency. I can still do things that make an important difference in the lives of my loved ones. Moreover, the fact that I still have responsibilities keeps me within the community of moral agents. My illness or debility has not reduced me to a mere moral patient (to use the language of the philosophers). . . .

To treat me as if I had no moral responsibilities when I am ill or debilitated implies that my condition has rendered me morally incompetent. Only small children, the demented or insane, and those totally lacking in the capacity to act are free from moral duties. There is dignity, then, and a kind of meaning in moral agency, even as it forces extremely difficult decisions upon us.

Second, recovering meaning in death requires an affirmation of connections. If I end my life to spare the futures of my loved ones, I testify in my death that I am connected to them. It is because I love and care for precisely these people (and I know they care for me) that I wish not to be such a burden to them. By contrast, a life in which I am free to choose whatever I want for myself is a life unconnected to others. . . .

This need not be connections with other people. Some people are deeply tied to land (for example, the family farm), to nature, or to a transcendent reality. But for most of us, the connections that sustain us are to other people. . . .

I don't know about others, but these reflections have helped me. I am now more at peace about facing a duty to die. Ending my life if my duty required might still be difficult. But for me, a far greater horror would be dying all alone or stealing the futures of my loved ones in order to buy a little more time for myself. I hope that if the time comes when I have a duty to die, I will recognize it, encourage my loved ones to recognize it too, and carry it out bravely.

Discussion Questions

1. Discuss how Aristotle would reply to Hardwig's argument that there is a duty to die once we have become burdensome. Compare and contrast Aristotle's likely public policy on euthanasia with the one proposed by Hardwig.
2. Hardwig protests that he is "not advocating a crass, quasi-economic conception of burdens and benefits." Much of his argument for a duty to die, however, is based on

utilitarian considerations of consequences. Discuss ways, if any, in which Hardwig's argument differs from, or goes beyond, that of pure utilitarianism.

3. Hardwig draws a comparison between modern society and primitive societies. Looking back at the example of the Kabloona Eskimo in Chapter 1, would Hardwig approve of the practice of walking elderly people into holes in the ice? Compare and contrast this situation with that of an elderly person with a chronic illness in a modern hospital. What would Hardwig suggest had the ailing father refused to walk out on the ice to his death? What would Hardwig suggest if the elderly American on a respirator refused to give permission to be disconnected?
4. Hardwig claims that the duty to die is consistent with Immanuel Kant's claim that "human dignity rests on the capacity for moral agency within a community of those who respect the demands of morality." Kant, however, was opposed to suicide and euthanasia. Discuss how Hardwig might reconcile his claim with Kant's opposition to euthanasia.
5. Discuss whether Noddings would agree with Hardwig that the duty to die is consistent with an ethics of care.
6. Would Battin agree with Hardwig that there are times when we have a duty to die? Discuss your answer using her three principles of autonomy, mercy, and justice.

SUSAN M. WOLF

A Feminist Critique of Physician-Assisted Suicide

Susan Wolf is an associate professor of law and medicine at the University of Minnesota Law School and an associate at the University of Minnesota's Center for Biomedical Ethics. In her essay Wolf argues that euthanasia practices are gender-biased. The traditional view of women as self-sacrificing puts subtle pressures on women to request euthanasia, as well as on doctors to comply with their requests.

Critical Reading Questions

1. What arguments does Wolf use to support her claim that there are gender differences that might contribute to women being more affected than men by the legalization of euthanasia?

"A Feminist Critique of Physician-Assisted Suicide," from Susan M. Wolf, "Gender, Feminism, and Death: Physician-Assisted Suicide and Euthanasia," in *Feminism and Bioethics,* ed. by Susan M. Wolf (New York: Oxford University Press, 1996), 282–317. Copyright 1996 the Hastings Center. Some notes have been omitted.

2. What are some of the implications of the research findings of Lawrence Kohlberg and Carol Gilligan on the euthanasia debate?
3. How does Wolf use the "Debbie" case as well as the Kevorkian cases to support her argument that euthanasia is gender-biased?
4. According to Wolf, why did Kevorkian's female patients request his assistance in their suicides? What is it about the nature of the male-physician/female-patient relationship that makes it both more likely that female patients will request euthanasia and that male doctors will be more likely to comply with their requests?
5. What are some of the traditional female virtues? How, according to Wolf, do these traditional views of women contribute to the greater likelihood that women will request euthanasia?
6. What are the three objections Wolf raises to the rights-based argument for euthanasia?
7. Why does Wolf reject the argument that euthanasia can be based on a physician's duty of beneficence?
8. According to Wolf, why does linking an ethics of justice to an ethics of care require that euthanasia remain illegal?
9. Why does Wolf, despite her opposition to euthanasia, claim that "physicians must honor patients' requests to be free of unwanted life-sustaining treatment"? How does she use care ethics to justify her position?

The debate in the United States over whether to legitimate physician-assisted suicide and active euthanasia has reached new levels of intensity. . . .

Yet the debate over whether to legitimate physician-assisted suicide and euthanasia (by which I mean active euthanasia, as opposed to the termination of life-sustaining treatment) is most often about a patient who does not exist—a patient with no gender, race, or insurance status. This is the same generic patient featured in most bioethics debates. Little discussion has focused on how differences between patients might alter the equation.

Even though the debate has largely ignored this question, there is ample reason to suspect that gender, among other factors, deserves analysis. The cases prominent in the American debate mostly feature women patients. This occurs against a backdrop of a long history of cultural images revering women's sacrifice and self-sacrifice. . . .

What sort of gender effects might we expect? There are four different possibilities. First, we might anticipate a higher incidence of women than men dying by physician-assisted suicide and euthanasia in this country. This is an empirical claim that we cannot yet test; we currently lack good data in the face of the illegality of the practices in most states and the condemnation of the organized medical profession. . . .

There may, however, be a second gender effect. Gender differences may translate into women seeking physician-assisted suicide and euthanasia for somewhat different reasons than men. Problems we know to be correlated with gender—difficulty getting good medical care generally, poor pain relief, a higher incidence of depression, and a higher rate of poverty—may figure more prominently in women's motivation. Society's persisting sexism may figure as well. And the long history of valorizing women's self-sacrifice may be expressed in women's requesting assisted suicide or euthanasia.

The well-recognized gender differences in suicide statistics also suggest that women's requests for physician-assisted suicide and euthanasia may more often than men's requests be an effort to change an oppressive situation rather than a literal request for death. . . .

Third, gender differences may also come to the fore in physicians' decisions about whether to grant or refuse requests for assisted suicide or euthanasia. The same historical valorization of women's self-sacrifice and the same background sexism that may affect women's readiness to request may also affect physicians' responses. Physicians may be susceptible to affirming women's negative self-judgments. This might or might not result in physicians agreeing to assist; other gender-related judgments (such as that women are too emotionally labile, or that their choices would not be taken seriously) may intervene.[1] But the point is that gender may affect not just patient but physician.

Finally, gender may affect the broad public debate. The prominent U.S. cases so far and related historical imagery suggest that in debating physician-assisted suicide and euthanasia, many in our culture may envision a woman patient. . . .

The debate over physician-assisted suicide and euthanasia so starkly raises questions of rights, caring, and context that at this point it would take determination *not* to bring to bear a literature that has been devoted to understanding those notions. Indeed, the work of Lawrence Kohlberg bears witness to what an obvious candidate this debate is for such analysis. It was Kolhberg's work on moral development, of course, that provoked Carol Gilligan's *In A Different Voice,* criticizing Kolhberg's vision of progressive stages of moral maturation as one that was partial and gendered. Gilligan proposed that there were really two different approaches to moral problems, one that emphasized generalized rights and universal principles, and the other that instead emphasized contextualized caring and the maintenance of particular human relationships. She suggested that although women and men could use both approaches, women tended to use the latter and men the former. . . .

The euthanasia debate thus demands analysis along the care, rights, and context axes that the Kolhberg–Gilligan debate has identified. Kolhberg himself used this problem to reveal how well respondents were doing in elevating general principles over the idiosyncrasies of relationship and context. It is no stretch, then, to apply the fruits of more than a decade of feminist critique. . . .

GENDER IN CASES, IMAGES, AND PRACTICE

The tremendous upsurge in American debate over whether to legitimate physician-assisted suicide and euthanasia in recent years has been fueled by a series of cases featuring women. The case that seems to have begun this series is that of Debbie, published in 1988 by the *Journal of the American Medical Association (JAMA).*[2] *JAMA* published this now infamous, first-person, and anonymous account by a resident in obstetrics and gynecology of performing euthanasia. Some subsequently queried whether the account was fiction. Yet it successfully catalyzed an enormous response.

The narrator of the piece tells us that Debbie is a young woman suffering from ovarian cancer. The resident has no prior relationship with her, but is called to her bedside late one night while on call and exhausted. Entering Debbie's room, the resident finds an older woman with her, but never pauses to find out who that second woman is and what relational context Debbie acts within. Instead, the resident responds to the patient's clear discomfort and to her words. Debbie says only one sentence, "Let's get this over with." It is unclear whether she thinks the resident is there to draw blood and wants that over with, or means something else. But on the strength of that one sentence, the resident retreats to the nursing station, prepares a lethal injection, returns to the room, and administers it. The story relates this as an act of mercy under the title, "It's Over, Debbie," as if in caring response to the patient's words.

The lack of relationship to the patient; the failure to attend to her own history, relationships, and resources; the failure to explore beyond the patient's presented words and engage her in conversation; the sense that the cancer diagnosis plus the patient's words demand death; and the construal of that response as an act of mercy are all themes that recur in later cases. The equally infamous Dr. Jack Kevorkian has provided a slew of them.

They begin with Janet Adkins, a 54-year-old Oregon woman diagnosed with Alzheimer's disease. Again, on the basis of almost no relationship with Ms. Adkins, on the basis of a diagnosis by exclusion that Kevorkian could not verify, prompted by a professed desire to die that is a predictable stage in response to a number of dire diagnoses, Kevorkian rigs her up to his "Mercitron" machine in a parking lot outside Detroit in what he presents as an act of mercy.

Then there is Marjorie Wantz, a 58-year-old woman without even a diagnosis. Instead, she has pelvic pain whose source remains undetermined. By the time Kevorkian reaches Ms. Wantz, he is making little pretense of focusing on her needs in the context of a therapeutic relationship. Instead, he tells the press that he is determined to create a new medical specialty of "obitiatry." Ms. Wantz is among the first six potential patients with whom he is conferring. When Kevorkian presides over her death there is another woman who dies as well, Sherry Miller. Miller, 43, has multiple sclerosis. Thus neither woman is terminal.

The subsequent cases reiterate the basic themes. And it is not until the ninth "patient" that Kevorkian finally presides over the death of a man. By this time, published criticism of the predominance of women had begun to appear.

Kevorkian's actions might be dismissed as the bizarre behavior of one man. But the public and press response has been enormous, attesting to the power of these accounts. Many people have treated these cases as important to the debate over physician-assisted suicide and euthanasia. Nor are Kevorkian's cases so aberrant—they pick up all the themes that emerge in "Debbie." . . .

Prevailing values have imbued women's deaths with a specific meaning. Indeed, Carol Gilligan builds on images of women's suicides and sacrifice in novels and drama, as well as on her own data, in finding a psychology and even an ethic of self-sacrifice among women. Gilligan finds one of the "conventions of femininity" to be "the moral equation of goodness with self-sacrifice." "[V]irtue for women lies in self-sacrifice. . . ."[3]

Given this history of images and the valorization of women's self-sacrifice, it should come as no surprise that the early cases dominating the debate about self-sacrifice through physician-assisted suicide and euthanasia have been cases of women. In Greek tragedy only women were ever candidates for sacrifice and self-sacrifice, and to this day self-sacrifice is usually regarded as a feminine not masculine virtue. . . .

Analyzing the early cases against the background of this history also suggests hidden gender dynamics to be discovered by attending to the facts found in the accounts of these cases, or more properly the facts not found. What is most important in these accounts is what is left out, how truncated they are. We see a failure to attend to the patient's context, a readiness on the part of these physicians to facilitate death, a seeming lack of concern over why these women turn to these doctors for deliverance. A clue about why we should be concerned about each of these omissions is telegraphed by data from exit polls on the day Californians defeated a referendum measure to legalize active euthanasia. Those polls showed support for the measure lowest among women, older people, Asians, and African Americans, and highest among younger men with postgraduate education and incomes over $75,000 per year.[4] The *New York Times* analysis was that people from more vulnerable groups were more worried about allowing physicians actively to take life. This may suggest concern not only that physicians may be too ready to take their lives, but also that these patients may be markedly vulnerable to seeking such relief. Why would women, in particular, feel this?

Women are at greater risk for inadequate pain relief.[5] Indeed, fear of pain is one of the reasons most frequently cited by Americans for supporting legislation to legalize euthanasia.[6] Women are also at greater risk for depression.[7] And depression appears to underlie numerous requests for physician-assisted suicide and euthanasia.[8] These factors suggest that women may be differentially driven to consider requesting both practices.

That possibility is further supported by data showing systematic problems for women in relationship to physicians. As an American Medical Association report on gender disparities recounts, women receive more care even for the same illness, but the care is generally worse. Women are less likely to receive dialysis, kidney transplants, cardiac catheterization, and diagnostic testing for lung cancer. The report urges physicians to uproot "social or cultural biases that could affect medical care" and "presumptions about the relative worth of certain social roles."[9]

This all occurs against the background of a deeply flawed health care system that ties health insurance to employment. . . . In the U.S. two-tier health care system, men dominate in the higher-quality tier, women in the lower. . . .

Women may also be driven to consider physician-assisted suicide and euthanasia out of fear of otherwise burdening their families. . . . The history and persistence of family patterns in this country in which women are expected to adopt self-sacrificing behavior for the sake of the family may pave the way too for the patient's request for death. Women requesting death may also be sometimes seeking something other than death. The dominance of women among those attempting but not completing suicide in this country suggests that women may differentially engage in death-seeking behavior with a goal other than death. Instead, they may be seeking to change their relationships or circumstances.

In analyzing why women may request physician-assisted suicide and euthanasia, and why indeed the California polls indicate that women may feel more vulnerable to and wary of making that request, we have insights to bring to bear from other realms. Those insights render suspect an analysis that merely asserts women are choosing physician-assisted suicide and active euthanasia, without asking why they make that choice. The analogy to other forms of violence against women behind closed doors demands that we ask why the woman is there, what features of her context brought her there, and why she may feel there is no better place to be. Finally, an analogy [to domestic violence] counsels us that the patient's consent does not resolve the question of whether the physician acts properly in deliberately taking her life through physician-assisted suicide or active euthanasia. The two people are separate moral and legal agents.

This leads us from consideration of why women patients may feel vulnerable to these practices, to the question of whether physicians may be vulnerable to regarding women's requests for physician-assisted suicide and euthanasia somewhat differently from men's. There may indeed be gender-linked reasons for physicians in this country to say "yes" to women seeking assistance in suicide or active euthanasia. In assessing whether the patient's life has become "meaningless," or a "burden," or otherwise what some might regard as suitable for extinguishing at her request, it would be remarkable if the physician's background views did not come into play on what makes a woman's life meaningful or how much of a burden on her family is too much.[10]

Second, there is a dynamic many have written about operating between the powerful expert physician and the woman surrendering to his care. It is no accident that bioethics has focused on the problem of physician paternalism. Instead of an egalitarianism or what Susan Sherwin calls "amicalism,"[11] we see a vertically hierarchical arrangement built on domination and subordination. When the patient is female and the doctor male, as is true in most medical encounters, the problem is likely to be exacerbated by the background realities and history of male dominance and female subjugation in the broader society. Then a set of psychological dynamics are likely to make the male physician vulnerable to acceding to the woman patient's request for active assistance in dying. . . .

FEMINISM AND THE ARGUMENTS

. . . Advocacy of physician-assisted suicide and euthanasia has hinged to a great extent on rights claims. The argument is that the patient has a right to self-determination or autonomy that entitles her to assistance in suicide or euthanasia. The strategy is to extend the argument that self-determination entitles the patient to refuse unwanted life-sustaining treatment by maintaining that the same rationale supports patient entitlement to more active physician assistance in death. Indeed, it is sometimes argued that there is no principled difference between the termination of life-sustaining treatment and the more active practices.

The narrowness and mechanical quality of this rights thinking, however, is shown by its application to the stories recounted above. That application suggests that the physicians in these stories are dealing with a simple equation: given an eligible rights bearer and her assertion of the right, the correct result is death. What makes a person an eligible rights bearer? Kevorkian seems to require neither a terminal disease nor thorough evaluation of whether the patient has non-fatal alternatives. Indeed, the Wantz case shows he does not even require a diagnosis. Nor does the Oregon physician-assisted suicide statute require evaluation or exhaustion of non-fatal alternatives; a patient could be driven by untreated pain, and still receive physician-assisted suicide. And what counts as an assertion of the right? For Debbie's doctor, merely "Let's get this over with." Disease plus demand requires death. . . .

Feminist critiques suggest three different sorts of problems with the rights equation offered to justify physician-assisted suicide and euthanasia. First, it ignores context, both the patient's present context and her history. The prior and surrounding failures in her intimate relationships, in her resources to cope with illness and pain, and even in the adequacy of care being offered by the very same physician fade into invisibility next to the bright light of a rights bearer and her demand. In fact, her choices may be severely constrained. . . .

Second, in ignoring context and relationship, the rights equation extols the vision of a rights bearer as an isolated monad and denigrates actual dependencies. Thus it may be seen as improper to ask what family, social, economic, and medical supports she is or is not getting; this insults her individual self-governance. Nor may it be seen as proper to investigate alternatives to acceding to her request for death; this too dilutes self-rule. Yet feminists have reminded us of the actual embeddedness of persons and the descriptive falseness of a vision of each as an isolated individual.[12] . . . Indeed, the very meaning of the patient's request for death is socially constructed; that is the point of the prior section's review of the images animating the debate. If we construe the patient's request as a rights bearer's assertion of a right and deem that sufficient grounds on which the physician may proceed, it is because we choose to regard background failures as irrelevant even if they are differentially motivating the requests of the most vulnerable. We thereby avoid real scrutiny of the social arrangements, governmental failures, and health coverage exclusions that may underlie these requests. We also ignore the fact that these patients may be seeking improved circumstances more than death. We elect a myopia that makes the patient's request and death seem proper. We construct a story that clothes the patient's terrible despair in the glorious mantle of "rights." . . .

In fact, there are substantial problems with grounding advocacy for the specific practices of physician-assisted suicide and euthanasia in a rights analysis, even if one accepts the general importance of rights and self-determination. I have elsewhere argued repeatedly for an absolute or near-absolute moral and legal right to be free of unwanted life-sustaining treatment. Yet the negative right to be free of unwanted bodily invasion does not imply an affirmative right to obtain bodily invasion (or assistance with bodily invasion) for the purpose of ending your own life.

Moreover, the former right is clearly grounded in fundamental entitlements to liberty, bodily privacy, and freedom from unconsented touching; in contrast there is no clear "right" to kill yourself or be killed. Suicide has been widely decriminalized, but decriminalizing an act does not mean that you have a positive right to do it and to command the help of others. . . .

There are even less grounds for concluding that there is a right to be killed deliberately on request, that is, for euthanasia. There are reasons why a victim's consent has traditionally been no defense to an accusation of homicide. . . . Similarly, acceding to a patient's request to be killed wipes out the possibility of her future exercise of her liberty. The capacity to command or permit another to take your life deliberately, then, would seem beyond the bounds of those things which you have a right grounded in notions of liberty. . . .

Finally, the rights argument in favor of physician-assisted suicide and euthanasia confuses two separate questions: what the patient may do, and what the physician may do. After all, the real question in these debates is not what patients may request or even do. It is not at all infrequent for patients to talk about suicide and request assurance that the physician will help or actively bring on death when the patient wants; that is an expected part of reaction to serious disease and discomfort. The real question is what the doctor may do in response to this predictable occurrence. That question is not answered by talk of what patients may ask; patients may and should be encouraged to reveal everything on their minds. Nor is it answered by the fact that decriminalization of suicide permits the patient to take her own life. The physician and patient are separate moral agents. Those who assert that what a patient may say or do determines the same for the physician, ignore the physician's separate moral and legal agency. They also ignore the fact that she is a professional, bound to act in keeping with a professional role and obligations. They thereby avoid a necessary argument over whether the historic obligations of the physician to "do no harm" and "give no deadly drug even if asked" should be abandoned. Assertion of what the patient may do does not resolve that argument.

The inadequacy of rights arguments to legitimate physician-assisted suicide and euthanasia has led to a different approach, grounded on physicians' duties of beneficence. This might seem to be quite in keeping with feminists' development of an ethics of care.[13] Yet the beneficence argument in the euthanasia context is a strange one, because it asserts that the physician's obligation to relieve suffering permits or even commands her to annihilate the person who is experiencing the suffering. Indeed, at the end of this act of beneficence, no patient is left to experience its supposed benefits. . . .

What does feminism have to offer these debates? Feminists too have struggled extensively with the question of method, with how to integrate detailed attention to individual cases with rights, justice, and principles. Thus in criticizing Kohlberg and going beyond his vision of moral development, Carol Gilligan argued that human beings should be able to utilize both an ethics of justice and an ethics of care. "To understand how the tension between responsibilities and rights sustains the dialectic of human development is to see the integrity of two disparate modes of experience that are in the end connected. . . . In the representation of maturity, both perspectives converge. . . ."[14] What was less clear was precisely how the two should fit together. And unfortunately for our purposes, Gilligan never took up Kolhberg's mercy killing case to illuminate a care perspective or even more importantly, how the two perspectives might properly be interwoven in that case. . . .

Here we find the beginning of an answer to our dilemma. It appears that we must attend to both context and abstraction, peering through the lens of both care and justice. Yet our approach to each will be affected by its mate. Our apprehension and understanding of context or cases inevitably involves categories, while our categories and principles should be refined over time to apply some contexts and not others. Similarly, our understanding of what caring requires in a particular case will grow in part from our understanding of what sort of case this is and what limits principles set to our expressions of caring; while our principles should be scrutinized and amended according to their impact on real lives, especially the lives of those historically excluded from the process of generating principles. . . .

Against this background, arguments for physician-assisted suicide and euthanasia—whether grounded on rights or beneficence—are automatically suspect when they fail to attend to the vulnerability of women and other groups. . . .

To institute physician-assisted suicide and euthanasia at this point in this country—in which many millions are denied the resources to cope with serious illness, in which pain relief and palliative care are by all accounts woefully mishandled, and in which we have a long way to go to make proclaimed rights to refuse life-sustaining treatment and to use advanced directives working realities in clinical settings—seems, at the very least, to be premature. Were we actually to fix those other problems, we have no idea what demand would remain for these more drastic practices and in what category of patients. . . .

The required interweaving of principles and caring, combined with attention to the heightened vulnerability of women and others, suggests that the right answer to the debate over legitimating these practices is at least "not yet" in this grossly imperfect society and perhaps a flat "no." Beneficence and caring indeed impose positive duties upon physicians, especially with patients who are suffering, despairing, or in pain. Physicians must work with these patients intensively; provide first-rate pain relief, palliative care, and symptomatic relief; and honor patients' exercise of their rights to refuse life-sustaining treatment and use advance directives. Never should the patient's illness, deterioration, or despair occasion physician abandonment. Whatever concerns the patient has should be heard and explored, including thoughts of suicide, or requests for aid or euthanasia.

Such requests should redouble the physician's efforts, prompt consultation with those more expert in pain relief or support care, suggest exploration of the details of the patient's circumstances, and a host of other efforts. What such requests should not do is prompt our collective legitimation of the physician's saying "yes" and actively taking the patient's life. The mandates of caring fail to bless killing the person for whom one cares. Any such practice in the United States will inevitably reflect enormous background inequities and persisting societal biases. And there are special reasons to expect gender bias to play a role. . . .

CONCLUSION

Some will find it puzzling that elsewhere we seek to have women's voices heard and moral agency respected, yet here I am urging that physicians not accede to the request for assisted suicide and euthanasia. Indeed, as noted above, I have elsewhere maintained that physicians must honor patients' requests to be free of unwanted life-sustaining treatment. In fact, attention to gender and feminist argument would urge some caution in both realms. . . . Finally there is a difference between the two domains. As I have argued above, there is a strong right to be free of unwanted bodily invasion. Indeed, for women, a long history of being harmed specifically through unwanted bodily invasion such as rape presents particularly compelling reasons for honoring a woman's refusal of invasion and effort to maintain bodily intactness. When it comes to the question of whether women's suicides should be aided, however, or whether women should be actively killed, there is no right to command physician assistance, the dangers of permitting assistance are immense, and the history of women's subordination cuts the other way. Women have historically been seen as fit objects for bodily invasion, self-sacrifice, and death at the hands of others. The task before us is to challenge all three. . . .

NOTES

1. Compare Jecker, "Physician-Assisted Death," 676, on reasons physicians might differentially refuse women's requests.
2. See "It's Over, Debbie," *Journal of the American Medical Association* 259 (1988): 272.
3. Carol Gilligan, *In a Different Voice,* 70.
4. See Peter Steinfels, "Help for the Helping Hands in Death," *New York Times,* February 14, 1993, sec. 4, pp. 1, 6.
5. See Charles S. Cleeland et al., "Pain and Its Treatment in Outpatients with Metastatic Cancer," *New England Journal of Medicine* 330 (1994): 592–96.
6. See Robert J. Blendon, U. S. Szalay, and R. A. Knox, "Should Physicians Aid Their Patients in Dying?" *Journal of the American Medical Association* 267 (1992): 2658–62.
7. See William Coryell, Jean Endicott, and Martin B. Keller, "Major Depression in a Non-Clinical Sample of Demographic and Clinical Risk Factors for First Onset," *Archives of General Psychiatry* 49 (1992): 117–25.
8. See Susan D. Block and J. Andrew Billings, "Patient Requests to Hasten Death: Evaluation and Management in Terminal Care," *Archives of Internal Medicine* 154 (1994): 2039–47.
9. Council on Ethical and Judicial Affairs, American Medical Association, "Gender Disparities in Clinical Decision Making," *Journal of the American Medical Association* 266 (1991): 559–62, 561–62.
10. As noted above, though, Nancy Jecker speculates that a physician's tendency to discount women's choices may also come into play. See Jecker, "Physician-Assisted Death," 676. Compare Silvia Sara Canetto, "Elderly Women and Suicidal Behavior," in Canetto and Lester, eds., *Women and Suicidal Behavior,* 215–33, 228,

asking whether physicians are more willing to accept women's suicides.

11. Sherwin, *No Longer Patient,* 157.
12. See, for example, Naomi Scheman, "Individualism and the Objects of Psychology," In Sandra Harding and Merrill B. Hintikka, eds., *Discovering Reality: Feminist Perspectives on Epistemology, Metaphysics, Methodology, and the Philosophy of Science* (Boston, MA: D. Reidel, 1983), 225–40, 240.
13. See Leslie Bender, "A Feminist Analysis of Physician-Assisted Dying and Voluntary Active Euthanasia," *Tennessee Law Review* 59 (1992): 519–46, making a "caring" argument in favor of "physician-assisted death."
14. See Gilligan, *In A Different Voice,* 174. Lawrence Blum points out that Kohlberg himself stated that "the final, most mature stage of moral reasoning involves an 'integration of justice and care that forms a single moral principle,'" but that Kohlberg, too, never spelled out what the integration would be. See Lawrence A. Blum, "Gilligan and Kohlberg: Implications for Moral Theory," *Ethics* 98 (1988): 472–91, 482–83.

Discussion Questions

1. Do you agree with Wolf that women are more likely than men to request as well as receive euthanasia? If so, does this necessarily imply that euthanasia is gender-biased? Does the fact that women live longer and may feel freer to seek assistance from others account for at least some of the gender discrepancy? Support your answers.
2. Are the women in your class more likely than the men to say that they would choose euthanasia should they become a burden to their families? If so, how do they justify their decisions? Are women more likely than men to use care ethics to justify their decisions? Which of Gilligan's levels of moral reasoning does the reasoning represent? Does conventional moral reasoning contribute to injustice? Discuss.
3. Discuss how Wolf might reply to Battin's argument that, for the most part, we can trust the physician to serve as a check in preventing "ill-considered" physician-assisted suicide and involuntary euthanasia.
4. Would Wolf support physician-assisted suicide in an egalitarian society? If not, what other conditions would she require? Discuss the specific steps we would have to take in the United States before legalizing euthanasia.
5. Ayn Rand claims that "our right to our own life" is "the one fundamental right." Rand also thinks that the United States is the freest country in the world. Should euthanasia be prohibited simply because some women run into sexist attitudes? Discuss how Rand might respond to this question. Which person, Rand or Wolf, presents the most convincing argument? Support your answers.

CASE STUDIES

1. NANCY CRUZAN: SEVEN YEARS IN A PERSISTENT VEGETATIVE STATE

In 1983 twenty-five-year-old Nancy Cruzan's car crashed after skidding out of control on a patch of ice. She was thrown from the car and landed facedown in a ditch, where she nearly suffocated. Although paramedics restored her breathing, her brain had gone without oxygen for thirteen minutes. When doctors told Nancy's parents that she was in a vegetative state, they requested that the hospital disconnect all life supports, including the feeding tubes in her stomach. They told the doctors that they knew she would not want to be kept alive with machines. Although the hospital complied with the request that Nancy be taken off the respirator, it decided not to remove the feeding tube, arguing that food and water were not medical treatment or artificial life support but merely part of basic care. To not provide food and water would be tantamount to killing Nancy by starvation and dehydration.

The Cruzans turned to the courts for help. In 1990, after Nancy had been in a vegetative state for seven years, the case reached the U.S. Supreme Court *(Cruzan v. Missouri Department of Health)*. The Supreme Court ruled that a person has a constitutional right to refuse life-support treatment, including food and water. The court also ruled, however, that the state could limit that right for incompetent people by requiring that the surrogate decision makers provide "clear and convincing" proof of the "patient's desire to have hydration and nutrition withdrawn." Barred by this requirement from removing their daughter's feeding tube, the Cruzans recruited several of Nancy's co-workers to testify that she had clearly stated that she did not want to be kept alive by artificial means. On December 14, 1990, a Missouri court finally gave the Cruzans permission to remove the feeding tube. Nancy died twelve days later.

Discussion Questions

1. Read the excerpts on pages 186–187 from the United States Supreme Court opinion on *Cruzan v. Missouri Department of Health.* If you had been one of the Supreme Court justices would you have concurred with the ruling or dissented? Explain your position in a paragraph giving your opinion, as a Supreme Court justice, of the case.
2. Does providing food and water to a person in a coma constitute artificial life support? Discuss the statement by the hospital that withholding food and water is the same as killing someone.
3. In Rachels's view, did Nancy Cruzan die in the best possible way, given her condition? Is it morally relevant that Nancy did not seem to be in any pain? Support your answers.
4. Are the principles of autonomy and mercy relevant in this case? Does the physician have a moral obligation to Nancy? If so, do these principles apply to the physician's relationship with the parents?
5. Discuss how Battin's principle of limited paternalism applies to the physician, the parents, and the judge in this case.
6. Compare and contrast the recommendations Battin, Hardwig, and Callahan would each have made in this case. What would you have done had you been Nancy's physician? Support your position.
7. Discuss who should make the decision in cases in which incompetent people have not made their wishes explicitly known in a document such as a living will.

---

2. DR. KEVORKIAN AND THE ASSISTED SUICIDE OF JUDITH CURREN[34]

On August 15, 1996, Judith Curren, a forty-two-year-old mother of two young daughters, committed suicide with the assistance of Dr. Jack Kevorkian. Unlike most of Kevorkian's clients, Curren was not terminally ill; she was suffering from depression, chronic fatigue syndrome, and fibromyalgia—a benign but painful inflammation of fibromuscular tissue.

Curren's husband, psychiatrist Franklin Curren, who was present at his wife's death, was a strong supporter of physician-assisted suicide and his wife's choice to end her life.[35] Kevorkian was surprised when he read a press release a few days later stating that Dr. Curren had been charged with assaulting his wife just three weeks earlier. This was not the first domestic assault charge that had been brought against Curren by his wife.[36]

When questioned about the role that domestic violence may have played in Judith Curren's decision to end her life, Kevorkian replied he had asked the Currens if there had been any trouble in the family and that they had said no. "You can't know what goes on domestically," Kevorkian added in defense of his action.

Kevorkian is currently serving a ten- to twenty-five year jail sentence for assisting in the 1998 suicide of Tom Youk, who was suffering from amyotrophic lateral sclerosis.

Discussion Questions

1. Kevorkian justifies his actions on the grounds that it would be immoral, similar to torture, not to help people in excruciating pain who request his help. How would Battin respond to this argument?
2. Kevorkian claims that he has never caused a death, but merely helped people exercise their last civil right. Kevorkian's supporters claim that he is a "prisoner of conscience," a "martyr to the cause of the right to choose to die." They argue that the assisted suicide of Tom Youk should have been ruled an "act of mercy" rather than murder. Derek Humphry, founder of the Hemlock Society wrote following Kevorkian's conviction: "The severity of the sentence on Kevorkian will drive the practice of voluntary euthanasia and assisted suicide even further underground. It will not stop it . . . Kevorkian's martyrdom—self-imposed as it is—will speed up the day when voluntary euthanasia for the dying is removed from the legal classification of 'murder' and recognized as a justifiable act of compassion."[37] Do you agree with Kevorkian and his supporters? Or did Kevorkian "get what he deserved" in court? Support your answer.
3. Judith Curren was not terminally ill at the time of her death. Should physician-assisted suicide be extended to anyone who desires it? Support your answer. Discuss how you would respond if someone you knew who was depressed and/or suffering from a chronic illness asked you to assist in his or her suicide.
4. Both Callahan and Wolf argue that many people consider euthanasia because they lack adequate pain control medication or medical insurance to seek proper treatment and care, or because they feel they have become a burden to their friends and family and that the world would be better off without them. Discuss these objections to euthanasia in light of the Judith Curren case.
5. According to research, women who adopt traditional views of women as self-sacrificing are more likely to be victims of domestic violence. Discuss this finding in light of the Judith Curren case. Is physician-assisted suicide in these cases simply an extension of violence against women? Discuss how both Wolf and Nel Noddings (Chapter 1) might answer this question.

6. John Stuart Mill argues that security and a safe environment are "the most indispensable of all necessaries after physical nutriment. . . ."[38] Would allowing physicians to assist in the suicide of their terminally ill patients damage this sense of security and safety in a physician/patient relationship? Or would it expand the freedom of the dying patient to choose his or her own destiny? Support your answer.

---

3. "FINAL EXIT": HOW TO COMMIT SUICIDE

In February 2000, "Final Exit," a show on how to commit suicide, was aired on late-night cable television in two Oregon cities. The program, which was produced by Hemlock Society founder Derek Humphry, laid out in detail the tools and drugs needed to end one's life quickly and painlessly. It also offered practical advice on "keeping clear of the law" and, for the friends and family of the deceased, "dealing with the aftermath." The show was also intended to raise public support against proposed federal legislation that would impose sanctions on physicians who prescribe lethal drugs to their terminally ill patients.

Although physician-assisted suicide is legal in Oregon, Barbara Coombs Lee, who led the initiative to get the bill passed, criticized the video as "irresponsible and potentially dangerous for some people . . . There is information about how a person could die using very readily available tools and drugs, and for some people who may be mentally unbalanced or acting impulsively, that could be dangerous information."[39]

In response, the cable station and the producers of the show pointed out that this information is already widely available. The program was based on Humphry's book, *Final Exit,* which has sold over 1 million copies and is available in twelve languages. The book is also available on audiocassette and on Humphry's Internet site. "I feel strongly," says Cindy Noblitt, co-producer of the video, "that if we are truly free, that an individual should have the right to decide when and how to end their lives . . . I think it's a central role of the media to provide complete and accurate information to the public that they may need to make those hard decisions in their lives."[40]

Discussion Questions

1. Analyze the arguments put forth by both Lee and Noblitt. What premises do they use, or could they use, to support their conclusions? Which person presents the stronger argument and why?
2. Should there be limits on freedom of speech when it comes to publicizing methods for killing oneself or others? Should suicide machines such as Kevorkian's Mercitron or Dr. Nitschke's "COGen" machine be made available to the general public? Analyze the case study using Ross's prima facie duties. Present your conclusion in the form of a policy statement for the media.
3. In her article Battin argues that a patient's autonomy may be compromised because of lack of knowledge about humane methods for ending his or her life. Discuss whether the principle of autonomy creates a moral obligation for physicians to provide patients who request it with information on how to die. Role-play a scenario in

which you are a physician and a patient comes to you requesting the video "Final Exit." Would it make a difference if the patient was not terminally ill? If the patient were an adolescent? If the patient seemed depressed? If it was the relative of a comatose patient? Support your answers.
4. Discuss what Kant's position would most likely be regarding the aforementioned case.

---

4. DONALD COWART: "PLEASE, LET ME DIE"

In 1973 twenty-six-year-old jet pilot and sometime rodeo performer Donald Cowart was standing in a field with his father when there was a violent explosion caused by leaking gas. The explosion killed his father and sent Donald, whose body was engulfed in flames, running for half a mile. When a farmer found him, Cowart, who was in excruciating pain from burns covering more than 65 percent of his body, asked for a gun so he could kill himself. The farmer refused his request and called an ambulance. Cowart asked the paramedics not to drive him to the hospital but to leave him in the field to die. They instead administered lifesaving measures and took him to the hospital.

At the hospital Cowart was subjected to daily baths in a chlorine bleach solution to clean his sores. He lost both his eyes and all his fingers and underwent several operations for skin grafts and amputations. After he was released from the hospital, Cowart attempted suicide several times. Eventually, he completed a law degree. Cowart frequently speaks at medical conferences on issues relating to euthanasia. He still insists that the hospital staff who treated him for his burns violated his right to self-determination in keeping him alive.

Discussion Questions

1. Discuss whether the paramedics did the morally right thing in treating Cowart, even though he asked them not to. What moral principles and concerns are relevant to this decision?
2. Imagine that you are Cowart's best friend and that you, rather than the farmer, found him. What is your moral duty as his friend? Discuss whether the fact that you are his friend, rather than a stranger or a medical professional, is relevant in making your decision to end his suffering or call an ambulance. Would your decision have been different if this incident had occurred in a war, or in the wilderness where there was no medical assistance available?
3. Some people argue that suicide attempts are really a cry for help. Does the fact that Cowart never successfully committed suicide, despite repeated attempts, suggest that he was mistaken about his own wishes to end his life? Can people be sincerely mistaken about their desires? How can a physician determine if a request for euthanasia is genuine? If physicians cannot be sure, how should they respond to these requests? How might Battin and Callahan each respond to this question?
4. Many people think that euthanasia is morally acceptable only when a person is dying. Is the fact that Cowart did not have a terminal condition relevant? Support your answer.

---

5. THE DEATH OF "BABY DOE"

When Baby Doe was born in an Indiana hospital in 1982, his parents were at first overjoyed. Their joy turned to dismay, however, when they learned that their son had Down syndrome. It was later found that the baby also had a malformed esophagus, which prevented food from entering his stomach. Whereas a blockage in the esophagus can be easily corrected by surgery, there is no cure for Down syndrome. The parents, believing that their son might be severely retarded, refused to give approval for the surgery. Without the surgery or a feeding tube, the baby would starve to death. The hospital administration took the case to court. The judge who heard the case concluded that Baby Doe's parents had the right to make an informed decision regarding the course of treatment for their child. Baby Doe died, five days after his birth, of starvation and dehydration.

Discussion Questions

1. What are the limits of parental rights? Do parents have a right to make euthanasia decisions for children who are not terminally ill? Is the assumption that parents will act in the best interests of their children justified?
2. Rachels uses the Baby Doe case to illustrate how passive euthanasia can sometimes cause more suffering than active euthanasia. If it is morally permissible for parents to allow their infants to die, should active euthanasia be used instead?
3. The death of Baby Doe created an uproar, especially from people concerned about the rights of the disabled. Columnist George Will, himself the father of a child with Down syndrome, accused the parents of being cruel and treating their child and those like him as less than human. Do you agree with Will? Support your answer. Would the judge have acknowledged the parents' right to refuse lifesaving surgery for the child had Baby Doe been, for example, an unwanted but otherwise perfectly normal baby of the "wrong" gender? What if the parents had refused the surgery because they had not wanted another son? Discuss whether there is a morally relevant difference between refusing lifesaving surgery for a child with a disability and refusing lifesaving surgery for child because he or she is the "wrong" gender.
4. Anencephaly is a congenital disorder in which the brain fails to develop; it is almost always fatal at or very shortly after birth. In 1996 a couple who gave birth to an anencephalic baby had her placed on life support so her organs could be harvested for organ transplants. This way at least some good would come out of their tragedy.

   Proposals have been made recently to the AMA to allow the harvesting of organs from anencephalic infants before death. Should infants who are going to die or be euthanized be harvested for their organs? Whose decision should this be—the parents' or the hospital's? Do parents give up their right to make decisions about their child's future once they request his or her death, as in the Baby Doe case? How would a utilitarian respond to a hospital policy of using these infants for organ transplants? How would Callahan respond to such a policy? Support your answers.

---

6. ROBERT LATIMER: MURDERER OR ANGEL OF MERCY?

In a courtroom in the quiet farming community of Battleford, Saskatchewan, twelve jurors declared Robert Latimer guilty of second-degree murder. Fours years earlier, on October 24, 1993, Latimer, a canola and wheat farmer, had trudged through the snow with his severely disabled twelve-year-old daughter, Tracy, cradled in his arms and placed her gently in the cab of the family pickup truck. He watched through the window as the cab filled with deadly carbon monoxide fumes. Seven minutes later Tracy was dead.

Twelve days earlier Laura Latimer, Tracy's mother, had taken Tracy to the doctor, who recommended the removal of her right thigh bone to ease her pain. She was horrified at the thought of her daughter being mutilated. Both she and Robert broke down and cried as they thought about their daughter's prospects for the future. They had already tried placing her in a group home but she was so unhappy she lost a sixth of her weight. "It would be better for Tracy if she died," Laura told her husband. She was relieved when, twelve days later, she came home and found Tracy dead.

Was this an act of mercy or a cold-blooded murder? As a result of his actions, Latimer received a life sentence with no access to parole for at least ten years.

His supporters argue that Latimer is "a loving man and a decent father" who acted out of compassion; he deserves leniency, not a prison sentence. If the proper legal and social supports for mercy killing had been in place, Latimer would not have taken the law into his own hands.

Many disabled-rights activists see things differently, however. "What that [granting leniency] says is that it's all right to kill your child with a disability because she may encounter some discomfort," says a spokesperson for the Council of Canadians with Disabilities.[41] "What's happened to Tracy Latimer," said Shivawn Wolfe, a severely disabled thirteen-year-old who testified on behalf of the prosecution, "was not an act of love. She was killed the day the love ran out."

Discussion Questions

1. Mercy killing is usually seen as justified only when there is no other way to relieve pain and suffering. According to witnesses at the trial, however, Tracy Latimer experienced no more pain than many other people with disabilities. Six days before Tracy's death, her mother had written in her journal that Tracy had "eaten well" and was "quite cheerful." "You will not find that she was in constant pain or that she had no joy in her last year," the prosecutor told the jury. "Pain is a condition of life, not a reason for death. Must a person like Tracy die because another person cannot bear to watch her fight?"

   How would you respond to the prosecution's position? Should other kinds of suffering besides unremitting pain, including the suffering of the caregivers, be taken into account in justifying mercy killing?
2. Compare and contrast this case with that of the 1982 Baby Doe case. Would it have made a difference if it had been Tracy's physician, rather than her father, who had euthanized her? Would it have made a difference if they had withheld medical treatment rather than actively killed her? Is it morally relevant that Baby Doe was allowed to die, whereas Tracy was actively killed? How would Rachels respond to these two case studies?
3. Two-thirds of Americans support physician-assisted suicide and euthanasia for terminally ill people, but only 37 percent of respondents feel that relatives or friends should be allowed to commit the deed. Is this distinction morally relevant? Discuss in light of the Robert Latimer case study.
4. Discuss what suggestions Daniel Callahan might make to the Latimers regarding their daughter Tracy.

CHAPTER 5

Punishment and the Death Penalty

Fred Simmons and Bob Moore were on their way from Florida to Georgia when they stopped to pick up two hitchhikers, Tony Gregg and Floyd Allen. They later picked up another hitchhiker, Dennis Weaver, whom they dropped off in Atlanta. At a rest stop outside of Atlanta, Gregg told Allen that he was going to rob Simmons and Moore. As Simmons and Moore were returning to the car, Gregg pulled a gun and fired three shots at them. The two men fell into a ditch. Gregg then got out of the car and shot them both point-blank in the head. When Weaver heard about the shootings, he contacted the police and gave them a description of Gregg and Allen as well as of the car they had stolen.

Gregg was found guilty of two counts of armed robbery and two counts of murder and given the death penalty. Gregg appealed his sentence. The death penalty had been ruled unconstitutional in 1972 by the U.S. Supreme Court in *Furman v. Georgia* on the grounds that it had been arbitrarily administered. In response the State of Georgia, as well as Florida and Texas, overhauled their death penalty laws to make them less arbitrary. In 1976 the U.S. Supreme Court in *Gregg v. Georgia* ruled that the revised statutes of Georgia were constitutional, thus overturning the 1972 ruling that had banned the death penalty.

HISTORY OF THE DEATH PENALTY

In the Middle Ages, the purpose of punishment, including the death penalty, was as much to save the criminal's soul as to protect society from harm. Torture instruments, isolation, hard labor, horrendous living conditions, the gallows, and burning at the stake were used to terrorize criminals to the point that they would repent their evil ways and cry out for God's mercy.

During the nineteenth century, public executions were abolished in most of Europe and North America. Citizen participation in the modern democracy depended on people becoming rational participants in public life and restraining their desires for revenge as well as the sadistic and bawdy behavior often displayed at public executions. Rather than abolish the death penalty, however, societies simply moved executions behind the walls of an impersonal penal system. It wasn't until the mid-twentieth century that there was a worldwide movement to abolish the death penalty.

THE DEATH PENALTY TODAY

During the 1980s and 1990s, many countries abolished the death penalty. In 1983 the European Convention of Human Rights was amended to prohibit the death penalty during peacetime. In the decade since 1993, an average of three countries per year abolished the death penalty. As of the end of 2002, 111 countries abolished it in law or practice,[1] including virtually all of Western Europe, as well as Canada, Australia, and most Latin American, South American, and African countries. In fact, admission to the European Union is contingent on abolishing capital punishment.

In 2003, the Council of Europe adopted Protocol No. 13 to the "European Convention on Human Rights," which is a legally binding international treaty abolishing the death penalty under all circumstances. The United Nations High Commission for Human Rights also supports a ban on capital punishment under international law. The United States is the only Western democracy that still retains and practices the death penalty. According to Amnesty International, a human rights organization, recorded executions worldwide hit a peak in 1996 when 4,272 executions were recorded in forty-one countries. In 2002, 1,526 people were executed in thirty-one countries. Three countries—China, Iran, and the United States—accounted for 81 percent of all known executions in 2002. In addition, the United States in 2002 was the only known country to execute juveniles (three in Texas).[2]

Although the death penalty is used in most Islamic countries, the Koran's ancient law of retributive justice or *lex talionis*—"an eye for an eye and a tooth for a tooth"—has been softened to permit the payment of "blood money" in some cases. The imposition of the Islamic penal code and the death penalty on both Muslims and non-Muslims has become a controversial issue in Malaysia and other Asian countries that have both Islamic and non-Islamic populations such as Buddhists, Hindus, and Christians.

Unlike Islamic law, Jewish law interprets the Old Testament law of retributive justice to prohibit capital punishment. According to the Jewish Mishnah, it is murder for the courts to execute a person. The death penalty was a last resort and rarely used in ancient Israel and Judah after A.D. 70.

Most Christian churches likewise regard capital punishment as being inconsistent with the sanctity of human life. Capital punishment is illegal in almost all Protestant and Catholic countries, with the exception of the United States. The papal encyclical *Evangelium Vitae* expressly forbids abortion, capital punishment, and euthanasia. Although the U.S. bishops issued statements in 1973 and again in 1980 opposing the death penalty, the majority of U.S. Catholics support capital punishment.[3]

Whereas, as was just noted, the death penalty has been abolished in all other Western democracies, it is currently being expanded in the United States. Of the thirty-eight states that have the death penalty, Texas has the highest execution rate. The number of inmates on death row has also increased since 1980. In 2002 there were 3,500 inmates on death row, more than in almost any other country.[4]

Prior to the 1970s, there was not much public support for the death penalty in the United States. In a 1971 Roper poll, Americans overwhelmingly responded that society had a duty to reform criminals and give them a second chance.[5] Only 15 percent responded that the primary purpose of prisons was to punish criminals.

The death penalty was ruled unconstitutional in the U.S. Supreme Court 1972 *Furman v. Georgia* case. The Court ruled that the unlimited discretion given to judges

U.S. SUPREME COURT *GREGG V. GEORGIA* (1976): EXCERPTS FROM THE MAJORITY OPINION*

[Justice Potter Stewart delivered the opinion of the Court.]

The issue in this case is whether the imposition of the sentence of death for the crime of murder under the law of Georgia violates the Eighth and Fourteenth Amendments . . .

The Court on a number of occasions has both assumed and asserted the constitutionality of capital punishment. In several cases that assumption provided a necessary foundation for the decision, as the Court was asked to decide whether a particular method of carrying out a capital sentence would be allowed to stand under the Eighth Amendment. But until *Furman v. Georgia,* 408 U.S. 238 (1972), the Court never confronted squarely the fundamental claim that the punishment of death always, regardless of the enormity of the offense or the procedure followed in imposing the sentence, is cruel and unusual punishment in violation of the Constitution. Although this issue was presented and addressed in Furman, it was not resolved by the Court . . . We now hold that the punishment of death does not invariably violate the Constitution.

The phrase ["cruel and unusual" punishment] first appeared in the English Bill of Rights of 1689 . . . The American draftsmen, who adopted the English phrasing in drafting the Eighth Amendment, were primarily concerned with proscribing "tortures" and other "barbarous" methods of punishment . . .

In the earliest cases raising Eighth Amendment claims, the Court focused on particular methods of execution to determine whether they were too cruel to pass constitution muster. The constitutionality of the sentence of death itself was not at issue, and the criterion used to evaluate the mode of the sentence of death itself was not at issue . . .

But the Court has not confined the prohibition embodied in the Eighth Amendment to "barbarous" methods that were generally outlawed in the 18th century. Instead, the Amendment has been interpreted in a flexible and dynamic manner. The Court early recognized that "a principle to be vital must be capable of wider application than the mischief which gave it birth" *Weems v. United States*

and juries to impose the death penalty led to its capricious and arbitrary use. Justice William O. Douglas, in concurring with the opinion of the Court, wrote: "A law which . . . reaches that [discriminatory] result in practice has no more sanctity than a law which in terms provides the same since it is inconsistent with the equal protection of the laws" [provided in the Fourteenth Amendment].

Between 1967 and 1977, there were no executions in the United States. The escalating violent crime rate in the 1970s, however, led to increasing public support for swift and severe punishment, including the death penalty for murder, in place of rehabilitation.

*Footnotes omitted.

(1910). Thus the Clause forbidding "cruel and unusual" punishments "is not fastened to the obsolete but may acquire meaning as public opinion becomes enlightened by a humane justice." . . .

But our cases also make clear that public perceptions of standards of decency with respect to criminal sanctions are not conclusive. A penalty also must accord with "the dignity of man," which is the "basic concept underlying the Eighth Amendment." This means, at least, that the punishment not be "excessive." . . . First, the punishment must not involve the unnecessary and wanton infliction of pain *Furman v. Georgia* (1972) . . .

In the discussion to this point we have sought to identify the principles and considerations that guide a court in addressing an Eighth Amendment claim. We now consider specifically whether the sentence of death for the crime of murder is a per se violation of the Eighth and Fourteenth Amendments to the Constitution. We note first that history and precedent strongly support a negative answer to this question.

The imposition of the death penalty for the crime of murder has a long history of acceptance in the United States and in England.

It is apparent from the text of the Constitution itself that the existence of capital punishment was accepted by the framers. At the time the Eighth Amendment was ratified, capital punishment was a common sanction in every state. Indeed, the first Congress of the United States enacted legislation providing death as the penalty for specified crimes . . .

The death penalty is said to serve two principle social purposes: retribution and deterrence of capital crimes by prospective offenders.

In part, capital punishment is an expression of society's moral outrage at particularly offensive conduct. This function may be unappealing to many, but it is essential in an ordered society that asks its citizens to rely on legal processes rather than self-help to vindicate their wrongs. . . .

Capital punishment may be the appropriate sanction in extreme cases as an expression of the communities' belief that certain crimes are themselves so grievous an affront to humanity that the only adequate response may be the death penalty.

The number of executions more than tripled between 1994 and 1999 when ninety-eight people were executed.[6]

The year 2002, when there were 71 executions, saw the first decrease since 1976 in the number of executions and the number of prisoners under the sentence of death.[7] The rates can be expected to continue declining with so many reprieves, because of DNA evidence and legislation restricting the imposition of the death penalty.

In 1976 the U.S. Supreme Court in *Gregg v. Georgia* reversed the earlier ruling, saying that Georgia's new "guided discretion" laws had removed the arbitrariness of sentencing from the death penalty.

Between 1960 and 1992, the reported rate of violent crime rose by more than 350 percent.[8] The media's extensive coverage of the most brutal and horrific cases, and the onslaught of violent crime on television and in movies, intensified people's fear of and anger over violent crime and their demand for harsher punishment.

By 1994 Americans no longer saw rehabilitation as the goal of prison; instead the majority regarded stricter punishment as the most effective means of dealing with criminals.[9] All but fifteen states had reinstated the death penalty. A decline in violent crime beginning in the late 1990s further convinced many Americans that strict punishment, including capital punishment, was the solution to the nation's crime rate. The number of people in prison and on death row continued to increase in the late 1990s and into the new millennium.

The United States in 2003, with more than two million men, women, and children behind bars, had the largest per capita incarceration rate of any industrialized nation. In fact, in 2003 12 percent of all black men between the ages of 20 and 29 were in prison, more than at any other time in American history.[10]

Support for the death penalty for a person convicted of murder began rising in the 1980s and peaked in 1994 at 80 percent. A June 2000 Gallup poll reported that support dropped to 66 percent with the majority of those stating that they supported it "with reservations."[11] Support for the death penalty began to rise again in 2001. A 2002 Gallup poll found that 72 percent of Americans support the death penalty for a person convicted of murder, although only 52 percent support the death penalty if life imprisonment without the possibility of parole is given as an alternative.[12] Half of those polled in 2002 responded that they thought the "death penalty is applied unfairly in this country today." White people are more likely to believe that the death penalty is being applied fairly.[13]

Despite continuing support for capital punishment, the vast majority of murderers do not receive the death penalty. Of the 20,000 homicides that occur in an average year in the United States, fewer than 300 convicted murderers are sentenced to death.[14] Of the people sentenced to death row, 99 percent are poor and have to rely on public defenders.[15] While blacks make up only 12 percent of the U.S. population, they represent 43 percent of death row inmates.

Race, gender, and education have the most significant effect on a person's position on the death penalty. Men are more likely than women to support capital punishment; and people who have been to college are far more likely to support it than people who did not graduate from high school. The most striking difference is based on race, however, with white people being more than twice as likely as black people to support the death penalty.[16]

THE DEATH PENALTY: JUVENILE AND MENTALLY RETARDED OFFENDERS

In addition to the apparent racial and socioeconomic disparities in the application of the death penalty, violent crime among juveniles has raised the moral issue of whether people under eighteen should be put to death. Violent crime by juveniles (ages twelve to seventeen) peaked in 1993 in the United States when about one-third of all violent offenders were juveniles. Since then the rate of juvenile crime has declined by 75 percent, in contrast to violent crimes by adults which have decreased only 57 percent.[17] Nevertheless, violent juvenile crime is still much higher in the United States than in most countries.[18] A total of 226 death sentences for juveniles have been imposed since 1973. As of June 2003, seventy-eight people who received death sentences as juveniles are still on death row in thirteen states. Twenty-two juvenile offenders had been executed as of April 2003, with two-thirds of the executions carried out in Texas.[19]

Should children who kill be subjected to the same penalties as adults? The United Nations Convention (Article 37(a)) states that "Neither capital punishment nor life imprisonment without possibility of release shall be imposed for offenses committed by persons below eighteen years of age." The United States is the only country in the world that hasn't ratified this agreement. The United States also leads the world in the number of juvenile executions. The last juvenile executions outside the United States occurred in Iran in 2001 and the Democratic Republic of the Congo in 2000.

Despite international pressure to stop the practice, the U.S. Supreme Court in *Stanford v. Kentucky* (1989) reaffirmed that it was not unconstitutional to execute juveniles who were sixteen or seventeen at the time of the crime. This ruling is currently being challenged. There are seven juvenile death penalty cases now pending in the U.S. Supreme Court. At the state level, about half of the states that use the death penalty set eighteen as the minimum age at the time of the crime for being eligible to receive the death penalty, and other states have legislation in progress to raise the age.

Although abolitionists have been unsuccessful to date in having the death penalty for juveniles banned by the U.S. Supreme Court, in June 2003 in *Atkins v. Virginia,* the Supreme Court ruled that executing people who are mentally retarded (an IQ of 70 or lower) violates the Eighth Amendment of the U.S. Constitution which prohibits "cruel and unusual punishments." This decision affects an estimated 5 to 10 percent of people on death row.[20]

Reaction to this decision is mixed. As we all know, intellectual capacity and the ability to act morally are not the same. Justice Scalia, who wrote the dissenting opinion in *Atkins v. Virginia,* was concerned that "if we accept the concept of blanket incapacity, we relegate people with retardation to second-class citizenship, potentially permitting the state to abrogate the exercise of such fundamental interests as the right to marry, to have and rear one's children, to vote or such everyday entitlements as entering into contracts or making a will."

Opponents of capital punishment, on the other hand, welcome the *Atkins v. Virginia* decision as one more step toward the complete abolishment of capital punishment. They feel that this case is one more step toward the complete abolishment of the death penalty and, in particular, opens the door to prohibiting the death penalty for juveniles on the grounds that it violates the Eighth Amendment.

THE MEDICALIZATION OF EXECUTIONS

The gas chamber, firing squads, and hanging have all been used in the past twenty years in the United States and continue to be used in some other countries. Lethal injection and the electric chair, however, are the two most common methods in the United States, accounting for more than 96 percent of the executions since 1977.[21]

The electric chair was first used in the United States in August 1890 as a more humane means of execution. Lethal injection was adopted in Oklahoma and Texas in 1977. Lethal injection involves intravenous injection of a lethal dose of a barbiturate mixture that causes paralysis, suppression of breathing, and death by asphyxiation. Death generally occurs within minutes.

The adoption of lethal injection as the preferred method of execution in most states has led to what some call "medicalized execution."[22] Although it is claimed that lethal injection is more humane than the earlier methods of execution, the use of medical knowledge to kill people has created a conflict between medical professionals and penal officials. In 1980 the American Medical Association (AMA) adopted a resolution that states that "A physician, as a member of a profession dedicated to the preservation of life . . . should not be a participant in a legally authorized execution." In a 2000 resolution the AMA rejected a moratorium on the death penalty, although it reaffirmed its existing policy that precludes physician participation in executions.

Despite consensus on the part of every national and international physicians' organization that physician participation in an execution violates medical ethics, twenty-eight states require the presence of a physician in the death chamber.[23] To protect physicians from censure by their colleagues, some prisons keep the identity of participating physicians secret, even paying them in cash in order to thwart attempts to identify them. In 2003 Illinois passed legislation prohibiting the Department of Corrections from requesting physicians and nurses to participate in executions. The bill is consistent with the Hippocractic oath that enjoins physicians to do everything in their power to relieve suffering and prevent death.

In California, one of the states that requires a physician's presence at executions, a group of physicians is suing the state prison system, charging that requiring physicians to participate in executions forces them to violate their professional code of ethics—"First of all, do no harm."[24] Dr. Janet Kirsch, one of the physicians involved in the suit, points out that "at Nuremberg, the Nazi doctors were found guilty of crimes against humanity for using medical skills to harm by order of the state."

But then who should carry out executions? Dr. Kirsch has an answer: "Anyone can learn to start an IV from a training film. Let Governor [Pete] Wilson do it. He might miss [the vein] and cause a bruise, but he plans to kill that person anyway." Those who support the law requiring physician's presence counter that a physician is needed in case something goes wrong; between 1982 and 1997, states have botched twenty executions.[25] Having a physician present makes it less likely that the condemned prisoner will have to endure extra suffering.

While support among the medical community for physician participation in executions is low, it is likely with the increased use of DNA testing in capital cases that more and more physicians will be called upon to testify in court. This role for physicians is more in line with the Hippocratic oath. Several death row prisoners have already been exonerated and released from prison as the result of post-trial DNA tests.[26] Unfortunately, crime labs are currently backlogged and cannot handle all the requests for DNA testing, a situation that often leads to shoddy work and faulty results. Because of this, Dr. Cyril Wecht, past president of the American Academy of Forensic Sciences, recommends an immediate freeze on all executions until this deficiency can be corrected.[27]

THE PHILOSOPHERS ON THE DEATH PENALTY

The morality of capital punishment became an issue during the Enlightenment Period, with its increasing emphasis on individual rights and the inherent dignity of the individual.

According to natural rights ethicist John Locke, the right to life is the primary human right. This right, however, can be forfeited if we violate another person's right to life. Locke writes in his *Second Treatise of Government:*

> Every Man hath a right to punish the Offender, and be Executioner of the Law of Nature. . . . Thus it is, that every Man in the State of Nature, has a Power to kill a Murderer, both to deter others from doing the like injury, which no Reparation can compensate . . . and also to secure Men from the attempts of a Criminal, who having renounced Reason . . . hath by the unjust Violence and Slaughter he hath committed upon one, declared War against all Mankind, and therefore may be destroyed as a *Lyon* or a *Tyger,* one of those wild Savage Beasts, with whom Men can have no Society nor Security: And upon this is grounded the great Law of Nature, *Who so sheddeth Man's Blood, by Man shall his Blood be shed.*[28]

The right to punish, including the right to administer the death penalty, is transferred to the state when people enter a social contract. Governments assume the prerogative to punish wrongdoers in order to prevent society from degrading into a state of disorder and anarchy, or what Locke refers to as a "state of nature." For more on the social contract see the reading from John Locke at the end of Chapter 1.

The main objection to capital punishment came from social reformers such as Karl Marx and utilitarian Jeremy Bentham. Bentham opposed the death penalty as well as punishment in general, because punishment subtracts from the total happiness of the community. "All punishment is mischief," he wrote. "All punishment is evil." The deliberate infliction of suffering on a person who has committed an evil, such as murder, he argued, merely adds more evil and suffering to the world. Punishment, therefore, can be justified only if it is the *only* way to remove an even greater evil.[29] As an alternative to punishment, Bentham proposed a prison system based on reform and rehabilitation. Although his plan for a model prison was sanctioned by an act of Parliament in 1791, the prison was never built.

Not all utilitarians oppose the death penalty. Unlike Bentham, John Stuart Mill believed that the benefits of capital punishment outweighed the harms. In a 1868 speech delivered in the British House of Commons, Mill called the death penalty appropriate for brutal crimes, arguing that it has a deterrent effect.[30] The deterrent argument is still one of the most popular arguments for the death penalty. Both Ernest van den Haag and Hugo Adam Bedau examine this argument in their readings at the end of this chapter.

Immanuel Kant rejected all consequentialist arguments for capital punishment. A murderer must die, he argued, not because of any social benefits that will accrue as a result of the execution, but because this is the only way to satisfy the requirement of retributive justice. Kant writes:

> The penal law is a categorical imperative; and woe to him who creeps through the serpent-windings of utilitarianism to discover some advantage that may discharge him from the justice of punishment, or even from the due measure of it. . . . For if justice and righteousness perish, human life would no longer have any value in the world . . .
>
> But what is the mode and measure of punishment which public justice takes as its principle and standard? It is just the principle of equality, by which the pointer of the scale of justice is made to incline no more to the one side than the other. It may be rendered by saying that the undeserved evil which any one commits on another, is to be regarded as perpetrated on himself. ". . . if you strike another,

> you strike yourself; if you kill another, you kill yourself." This is the right of retaliation (jus talionis) . . . whoever has committed murder must die.[31]

Kant maintained that not only does the state have a right to punish; wrongdoers also have a right to *be* punished. Punishment, including the death penalty, Kant argued, affirms the criminals' dignity by acknowledging that, unlike children and "animals," they are responsible for their actions. Denying people the right to punishment is to deny that they are rational beings capable of responsibility for their own decisions. Jeffrey Reiman, in his article at the end of this chapter, rejects Kant's conclusion that moral respect and retributivism create a duty for the state to give the death penalty for murder. He argues that there are other types of punishment that can meet these moral requirements.

Marx, likewise, rejected the Kantian justification of capital punishment based on retributive justice. He argued that an abstract theory, like the theory of retributive justice, is unable to take into account the unfair relations among different groups of people in a community, and, especially, in a capitalist society. Capital punishment may work in theory, but in actual practice it is applied unjustly and, hence, is immoral. Helen Prejean addresses this issue in the selection from her book *Dead Man Walking* at the end of this chapter.

Both Buddhist and Confucian philosophers reject the death penalty. Buddhists oppose capital punishment because it violates the principle of *ahimsa,* which requires that both individuals and society refrain from harming living beings. It is through encouraging individuals to cultivate right thinking and embrace the noble eightfold path that society overcomes injustice, not by violent punishment of wrongdoers.

Confucius believed that crime is a symptom of a disordered state, rather than an individual problem. It is the rulers, rather than individual citizens, who have the most power to advance virtue in society and individuals. Because it is easiest for people to be virtuous when they are living in a just and well-ordered society, a state where there is a problem with crime needs to work on developing social policy that is more conducive to individual virtue and social harmony.

The reintroduction of the death penalty in the United States in 1976 after so many years of decline has once again raised questions regarding the morality of capital punishment. Contemporary philosophers are divided over capital punishment. Van den Haag and Christopher Morris both support it. Bedau, Reiman, and Prejean, on the other hand, while believing that criminals ought to be punished, call for the abolition of the death penalty.

MORAL ISSUES

Deterrence

Van den Haag argues that the threat of death is the ultimate deterrent. The deterrence argument is based on the assumption that the more severe the punishment for an action, the less likely people are to engage in it. If the fear of punishment is removed, ordinarily law-abiding citizens may become violent and lawless and ruled by mob mentality.

Not all arguments that appear to be intuitively obvious or logical are true, however. For example, it seems intuitively obvious that if a heavy and a light ball are both dropped from the Tower of Pisa at the same time, the heavy one will hit the ground first. In fact, they both hit the ground at the same time. Similarly, it may seem obvious that the more severe the punishment, the greater the deterrent effect, but this does not mean that the two are logically connected or that the proposition is true. As with dropping the two balls from the tower, we need to examine empirical evidence to see if there really is a causal connection between severity of punishment and deterrence.

Abolitionists of the death penalty point out that studies have not found any connection between the use of capital punishment and the rate of violent crime. Indeed, in Canada, for example, the homicide rate peaked in 1975, the year before the reintroduction of the death penalty, and then continued to decline for the next ten years.[32] In the United States, by contrast, two of the states with the most executions since 1979 have had an increase in murder rates following the reinstitution of the death penalty.[33] Because capital punishment has not been shown to have a deterrent effect, we are not saving innocent lives, but rather adding to the loss of human life.

Incapacitation

Whereas deterrence has a broader social goal of keeping others from committing similar crimes, incapacitation is aimed only at the specific person who was convicted of the crime. This defense of capital punishment is based on an analogy between capital punishment and self-defense. The death penalty, it is argued, is the only way to ensure that a murderer will never kill again. Just as people have the right to use lethal force to protect themselves, so too does the government have the right to use the death penalty to protect society from dangerous criminals.

Opponents of capital punishment, such as Prejean and Bedau, disagree. They maintain that life imprisonment, including the use of restraints and the isolation of those who pose a threat to guards and fellow inmates, is sufficient to incapacitate a would-be repeat murderer. Incapacitation justifies the killing of a wrongdoer only during the commission of a violent crime, such as a police officer or potential murder victim killing to prevent grievous harm from occurring. Several states now have life imprisonment without the possibility of parole as an alternative to the death penalty.

Retributive Justice

Many supporters of the death penalty, including Kant, Locke, and van den Haag state that it doesn't really matter whether capital punishment is a deterrent or if there are other effective ways to incapacitate a murderer. Retributive justice alone justifies the death penalty. Retribution is not the same as revenge. Revenge is based on a personal desire for retaliation; retribution, on the other hand, is the impersonal carrying out of punishment to "cancel out" an evil act. A person who commits a crime creates a debt that must be paid to society. This debt is due regardless of whether the victim desires it.

One of the underlying principles of retributive justice is *proportionality*. Retributive justice requires that the severity of the punishment be proportionate to the crime, what Kant called the "equality of crime and punishment." The only appropriate payment for murder is death of the murderer. The murderer is "getting what he deserves" or "what is coming to him." As long as the debt remains unpaid, there is a sort of imbalance in the community or universe—a state of injustice exists until the debt is paid. Kant also argues that rather than denying the criminal's worth and dignity, retributive justice assumes moral worth and dignity by acknowledging that the criminal is a rational person who can be held morally responsible for his or her actions.

Some philosophers, including Bentham, question whether there really is a moral duty of retribution. How can one act of violence cancel out another evil act? Although both Bedau and Reiman accept the principle of retributive justice, they argue that it does not require an exact fit between the crime and the punishment. We do not rape rapists or burn the homes of arsonists; the deliberate killing of a murderer is also an inappropriate punishment. Instead the appropriate moral response to wrongdoing is to demand that wrongdoers provide restitution to their victims. The goals of restitution are incompatible with capital punishment, because death removes all possibility of victim compensation.

Furthermore, many opponents of capital punishment question Kant's assumption that retributive justice is required on the grounds that murder is based on a rational decision. Evidence indicates that very few murderers engage in any sort of analysis of their actions before committing murder. Rather than being a rational decision, as Kant presumes, evidence suggests that the great majority of murders are carried out impulsively, in the heat of passion, with little deliberation over the possible consequences. If murder is not based on a rational decision, murderers cannot be held morally responsible for their actions. Hence, the requirement of retributive justice that the murderer have a particular state of mind, when applied in practice, rules out capital punishment in most if not all cases.

Human Dignity and the Sanctity of Human Life

Some opponents of capital punishment, including Prejean and the Buddhists, claim that all deliberate taking of human life is wrong. The use of the death penalty diminishes the value of human life and lowers us to the level of the criminal. Prejean rejects the retributivist argument that the death penalty affirms human dignity, arguing instead that it is degrading and inconsistent with respect for the dignity of persons. Because humans have intrinsic moral value, it is wrong to deprive them of their lives.

Human Rights and Moral Standing

Both the United Nations and Amnesty International oppose the death penalty on the grounds that it violates human rights, including the right to life. The human-rights argument has also been used to *support* capital punishment. Like Locke, Morris acknowledges that humans have certain fundamental rights, such as the right to life; but Morris also argues that by intentionally violating the social contract, wrongdoers lose some of their moral standing and, hence, forfeit some of their moral rights. Those who violate other people's right to life by murdering them in turn forfeit their own right to life. Because they have forfeited this right, capital punishment cannot be said to violate it.

Some opponents of capital punishment, such as Prejean, question the logic of this argument, which is known as *reciprocity retributivism,* concluding, like Marx, that it does not take into account unfairness in society. Thus, rather than setting wrongs right, capital punishment can further perpetuate an unfair status quo that denies certain groups of people full rights.

Distributive Justice and the Principle of Equality

There has been considerable concern that capital punishment is unfairly distributed. For example, Tibetans are disproportionately represented on death row in China.

In the United States, blacks are six times more likely than whites to end up on death row. In addition, although less than half of murder victims are white, 80 percent of people executed in the past two decades killed whites.[34] Poorer defendants are also more likely to get the death penalty, because they cannot afford good defense lawyers.[35]

Some opponents of capital punishment argue that it is an extension of the slavery mentality, whereby the death penalty was frequently used on slaves who committed crimes against whites. They point out that all of the states that executed eight or more prisoners in the years since the Supreme Court declared capital punishment to be constitutional were Confederacy states.

Polls find that white people are much more likely to support capital punishment than are black people. In a study of why white Americans support the death penalty, American University researchers found that white support for the death penalty has strong ties to prejudice against blacks and that in some areas of the United States racial prejudice is the strongest predictor of support for the death penalty.[36] Furthermore, although all sixteen states that formed the Confederacy have the death penalty, outside of the former slave-owning states more than half have either abolished it or do not use it even though it is still on the books.

Others disagree with this analysis, maintaining that although racism used to be a problem, the proportion of white and black convicted murderers who get the death penalty is about the same.[37] Furthermore, the distribution-of-justice argument is irrelevant in terms of the morality of capital punishment. Van den Haag maintains that the principle of equality requires not the abolition of the death penalty, but that all those guilty of murder—whether white or black—receive it. Even if the death penalty is applied in a discriminatory manner, this does not mean that capital punishment itself is wrong; it means that too many murderers who deserve the death penalty are getting off.

Some Marxist philosophers argue that capital punishment is inherently unjust. The flaw is not in the way the death penalty is administered, but in the theory of retributive justice itself. Retribution cannot provide a foundation for punishment, because it is unable to take into account the unfair relationships among different groups of people in a community. Justice and equality are also at issue in the handling of cases of terrorism. In November 2001 President George W. Bush created military commissions for trying people accused of "international terrorism." The military commissions, which are composed of seven military officers appointed by the Secretary of Defense, have the power to impose death sentences. There is no jury and no right of appeal.[38]

Utilitarian (Consequentialist) Arguments

The primary purpose of punishment is to harm convicted criminals, whether through incapacitation or depriving them of rights. Because pain is essential to punishment, utilitarians maintain that punishment is permissible only if it leads to an overall decrease in pain and an increase in pleasure for society. Studies have not shown this to be the case, however.

First of all, capital punishment has not been proven to have a deterrent effect. In addition, the cost of the death penalty can be expensive. A 1982 study found that the death penalty costs three to six times as much as life imprisonment.[39] In 2003 Kansas began performing an audit on the cost of the death penalty to the state. Kansas Senator Steven Morris stated, "Overall, we just need to evaluate the whole death penalty issue. If it's going to take millions and millions of dollars per inmate and years before we can execute someone, that's a major policy issue we need to look at."[40] Most of these costs are incurred prior to and during trials, as trials for capital offenses are much more costly and time-consuming.

Capital punishment has also been denounced as cruel and inhumane. Amnesty International, a group opposed to the use of torture on criminals, writes: "International law states that torture or cruel, inhuman, or degrading punishments can never be justified. The cruelty of the death penalty is self-evident." Amnesty International classifies lethal injection, justified by supporters of the death penalty as a more humane method of execution, as a type of deliberate poisoning that is inflicted on people against their will. In *Dead Man Walking,* Prejean also vividly describes the cruelty of the death penalty, both during the actual execution and during the long wait before the final moment. In a 1983 electrocution in Alabama, it took three attempts and fourteen minutes to kill the prisoner. Death from lethal injection can also take several minutes, during which time the prisoner is suffocating.

The suffering of the criminal awaiting execution also has to be considered in a utilitarian calculus. The average time spent on death row before execution in this country is ten years. French writer Albert Camus (1913–1960) once wrote that the moral contradiction inherent in a punishment that imitates the violence that it claims to abhor is only made worse by the premeditated nature of capital punishment:

> Many laws consider a premeditated crime more serious than a crime of pure violence. . . . For there to be equivalence, the death penalty would have to punish a criminal who had warned his victim of the date at which he would inflict a horrible death on him and who, from the moment onward, had confined him at his mercy for months. Such a monster is not encountered in private life.[41]

According to social contract theory, governments are formed because of the need for people to band together to protect themselves against danger. Therefore, one of the primary purposes of capital punishment is to protect society against dangerous people such as murderers. Some opponents of the death penalty, however, argue that it actually reduces public safety by draining public resources that could be used for crime prevention and drug treatment.

The death penalty has repercussions that reach far beyond the death chamber. Not only is the executioner affected by the action; the ripple effect reaches out to the family and friends of both the murder victim and the condemned person, as well as to society in general. Does capital punishment ease the grief of the murder victim's family? What is the effect of participating in an execution on medical professionals, who are sworn to save lives? Does violent punishment reinforce or legitimate violence in society in general?

Finality and the Risk of Errors

In 2003 New York City Mayor Michael Bloomberg expressed his opposition to the death penalty because of the number of innocent people who were incarcerated and even executed. Between 1973 and 2003, 107 people were released from death row because they were later found to be innocent. Some spent ten to twenty years in prisons. Most of these inmates were exonerated on the basis of DNA evidence.[42] However, DNA evidence is not always available in murder cases, and even when available, it is not infallible. The death penalty also removes or ignores the possibility of restitution and repentance, as happened in the case of Karla Faye Tucker, who became a born-again Christian while in prison (see Case Study 1).

Errors can also occur because of flaws in the legal procedure. A Columbia University Law School study released in June 2000 found that between 1973 and 1995 over two-thirds of the death sentences had been overturned in the appeal process because of "procedural flaws or unsound evidence."[43] The report concluded that the American capital punishment system is "fraught with error" mainly due to three factors: incompetent defense lawyers, flawed instructions to jurors, and procedural misconduct such as suppressed evidence. In March 2003, minutes before Delma Banks was to be executed in Texas by lethal injection, the United States Supreme Court halted the execution to consider Banks's latest appeal. Banks had been convicted of murder and robbery in 1980. Banks is just one of many cases that are being reopened because of questions about the defense lawyers' competence.

Flaws in the legal procedure as well as better scientific tests for establishing innocence have led some hard-core supporters of capital punishment to rethink their position. In 2003 Illinois Governor George Ryan commuted the death sentences of 167 death-row inmates to life imprisonment and placed a three-year moratorium on execution after thirteen people awaiting execution were exonerated.[44] Ricky McGinn, who was only eighteen minutes from death by lethal injection in a Texas execution chamber, received word that he had a thirty-day reprieve to prove his innocence through advanced DNA testing. McGinn's case led to demands that all death row inmates who are eligible for DNA testing receive it. Many states now have life imprisonment without the possibility of parole as an alternative to prison, a sentence which allows the possibility of exoneration and release should a person later be found innocent.

Van den Haag dismisses these mistakes as part of the cost of doing justice. He points out that nearly all activities, such as construction work or even driving a car, carry risks and can cost the lives of innocent bystanders. However, we don't give up these activities. Bedau and Prejean, on the other hand, believe that the risk of executing innocent people is morally unacceptable, especially when there is an alternative such as life imprisonment without the possibility of parole.

Care Ethics

Prejean claims that one reason people favor the death penalty is that we don't identify with the condemned persons; we don't see them as humans like us. Before we can discuss the morality of capital punishment, we first have to see those who are condemned from a care perspective rather than a pure justice perspective.

Adopting Jesus Christ as her role model, Prejean maintains that we ought to love and care for people despite what they may have done. We should return compassion and good for evil, rather than evil for evil as the retributivists claim.

Why Punish?

This raises the question of whether punishment is ever morally acceptable. Most discussions of capital punishment begin with the assumption that punishment is the appropriate moral response to wrongdoing. Good moral reasoning, however, requires that we critically examine the premises of an argument as well as the soundness of the reasoning.

This requires asking, "Why punishment?" Does justice require punishment as the retributive justice theorists claim? Or is the punishment paradigm actually counterproductive and harmful to society?

One of the greatest frustrations of our criminal justice system is that criminals often come out in worse shape than when they went in. A 1972 study found that prisoners and guards interacted primarily at the lowest level of moral development—avoiding coercion and punishment. With one another, however, they interacted primarily at Kohlberg's stage two of moral development—mutual benefit. The researchers concluded that prison life tends to mold prisoners into a morality lower than their "private best," that is, their moral development outside the prison environment. In other words, the punishment paradigm, rather than making society safer, may actually be harming society by turning out more-hardened criminals.[45]

CONCLUSION

Although few students will ever be directly faced with decisions involving the death penalty, the moral assumptions underlying both positions affect their daily interaction with one another. Capital punishment raises the issue of the moral value and dignity of humans who, apparently, are at the most despicable end of the spectrum, who have little or no respect for the dignity of those whom they brutally massacre.

The debate over the death penalty also needs to return to the assumption that punishment is justified. We need to question the very punishment paradigm that underlies capital punishment. In addition, even if the death penalty can be morally justified in theory, it does not necessarily follow that it should be used in practice. Creating a just public policy regarding capital punishment requires balancing moral theory with the realities of human nature and society.

ERNEST VAN DEN HAAG

The Ultimate Punishment: A Defense of Capital Punishment

Ernest van den Haag is a retired professor of jurisprudence and public policy at Fordham University. A well-known advocate of the death penalty, van den Haag is author of *Punishment Criminals* and *The Death Penalty: A Debate.* Like Kant, van den Haag argues that the primary purpose of capital punishment is to satisfy the demands of retributive

"The Ultimate Punishment: A Defense of Capital Punishment," *The Harvard Law Review* 99 (1986): 1662–1669. Notes have been omitted.

justice. The often-cited objection that capital punishment is applied in a discriminatory manner, therefore, does not make capital punishment *itself* immoral, but rather the manner in which it is currently meted out. In response to the objection that innocent people are sometimes executed, van den Haag points out that almost all human activities cost the lives of some innocent bystanders. As for lack of proof that it works as a deterrent, the primary purpose of capital punishment, he reminds us, is not deterrence but retribution.

Critical Reading Questions

1. How does van den Haag respond to the argument that capital punishment is morally wrong because it is applied in a discriminatory manner?
2. According to van den Haag, which is the most important value—equality or justice—and why?
3. On what grounds does van den Haag argue that justice requires the death penalty?
4. How does van den Haag respond to the objection that sometimes innocent people are executed?
5. Does van den Haag think that capital punishment is an effective deterrent? Does his argument depend on capital punishment being an effective deterrent?
6. What are some of the "incidental" issues in the capital punishment debate?
7. What is the "rule of retaliation"? What, according to van den Haag, is the relevance of retaliation to the capital punishment debate?
8. How does van den Haag respond to the argument that capital punishment legitimates killing?
9. According to van den Haag, why does the principle of retribution require capital punishment for some crimes?
10. How does van den Haag respond to the argument that capital punishment is degrading to human dignity? Which philosophers does he cite to support his position?

In an average year about 20,000 homicides occur in the United States. Fewer than 300 convicted murderers are sentenced to death. But because no more than thirty murderers have been executed in any recent year, most convicts sentenced to death are likely to die of old age. Nonetheless, the death penalty looms large in discussions: it raises important moral questions independent of the number of executions.

The death penalty is our harshest punishment. It is irrevocable: it ends the existence of those punished, instead of temporarily imprisoning them. Further, although not intended to cause physical pain, execution is the only corporal punishment still applied to adults. These singular characteristics contribute to the perennial, impassioned controversy about capital punishment.

I. DISTRIBUTION

Consideration of the justice, morality, or usefulness of capital punishment is often conflated with objections to its alleged discriminatory or capricious distribution among the guilty. Wrongly so. If capital punishment is immoral *in se,* no distribution among the guilty could make it moral. If capital punishment is moral, no distribution would make it immoral. Improper distribution cannot affect the quality of what is distributed, be it punishments or rewards. Discriminatory or capricious distribution thus could not justify abolition of the death penalty. Further, maldistribution inheres no more in capital punishment than in any other punishment.

Maldistribution between the guilty and the innocent is, by definition, unjust. But the injustice does not lie in the nature of the punishment. Because of the finality of the death penalty, the most grievous maldistribution occurs when it is imposed upon the innocent. However, the frequent allegations of discrimination and capriciousness refer to maldistribution among the guilty and not to the punishment of the innocent.

Maldistribution of any punishment among those who deserve it is irrelevant to its justice or morality. Even if poor or black convicts guilty of capital offenses suffer capital punishment, and other convicts equally guilty of the same crimes do not, a more equal distribution, however desirable, would merely be more equal. It would not be more just to the convicts under sentence of death.

Punishments are imposed on persons, not on racial or economic groups. Guilt is personal. The only relevant question is: does the person to be executed deserve the punishment? Whether or not others who deserve the same punishment, whatever their economic or racial group, have avoided execution is irrelevant. If they have, the guilt of the executed convicts would not be diminished, nor would their punishment be less deserved. To put the issue starkly, if the death penalty were imposed on guilty blacks, but not on guilty whites, or, if it were imposed by a lottery among the guilty, this irrationally discriminatory or capricious distribution would neither make the penalty unjust, nor cause anyone to be unjustly punished, despite the undue impunity bestowed on others.

Equality, in short, seems morally less important than justice. And justice is independent of distributional inequalities. The ideal of equal justice demands that justice be equally distributed, not that it be replaced by equality. Justice requires that as many of the guilty as possible be punished, regardless of whether others have avoided punishment. To let these others escape the deserved punishment does not do justice to them, or to society. But it is not unjust to those who could not escape. . . .

Recent data reveal little direct racial discrimination in the sentencing of those arrested and convicted of murder. The abrogation of the death penalty for rape has eliminated a major source of racial discrimination. Concededly, some discrimination based on the race of murder victims may exist; yet, this discrimination affects criminal victimizers in an unexpected way. Murderers of whites are thought more likely to be executed than murderers of blacks. Black victims, then, are less fully vindicated than white ones. However, because most black murderers kill blacks, black murderers are spared the death penalty more often than are white murderers. They fare better than most white murderers. The motivation behind unequal distribution of the death penalty may well have been to discriminate against blacks, but the result has favored them. Maldistribution is thus a straw man for empirical as well as analytical reasons.

II. MISCARRIAGES OF JUSTICE

In a recent survey Professors Hugo Adam Bedau and Michael Radelet found that 7000 persons were executed in the United States between 1900 and 1985 and that 25 were innocent of capital crimes. Among the innocents they list Sacco and Vanzetti as well as Ethel and Julius Rosenberg. Although their data may be questionable, I do not doubt that, over a long enough period, miscarriages of justice will occur even in capital cases.

Despite precautions, nearly all human activities, such as trucking, lighting, or construction, cost the lives of some innocent bystanders. We do not give up these activities, because the advantages, moral or material, outweigh the unintended losses. Analogously, for those who think the death penalty just, miscarriages of justice are offset by the moral benefits and the usefulness of doing justice. For those who think the death penalty unjust even when it does not miscarry, miscarriages can hardly be decisive.

III. DETERRENCE

Despite much recent work, there has been no conclusive statistical demonstration that the death penalty is a better deterrent than are alternative punishments. However, deterrence is less than decisive for either side. Most abolitionists acknowledge that they would continue to favor abolition even if the death penalty were shown to deter more murders than alternatives could deter. Abolitionists appear to value the life of a convicted murderer or, at least, his non-execution, more highly than they value the lives of innocent victims who might be spared by deterring prospective murderers.

Deterrence is not altogether decisive for me either. I would favor retention of the death penalty as retribution even if it were shown that the threat of execution could not deter prospective murderers not already deterred by the threat of imprisonment. Still, I believe the death penalty, because of its finality, is more feared than imprisonment, and deters some prospective murderers not deterred by the threat of imprisonment. Sparing the lives of even a few prospective victims by deterring their murderers is more important than preserving the lives of convicted murderers because of the possibility, or even the probability, that executing them would not deter others. Whereas the lives of the victims who might be saved are valuable, that of the murderer has only negative value, because of his crime. Surely the criminal law is meant to protect the lives of potential victims in preference to those of actual murderers.

Murder rates are determined by many factors; neither the severity nor the probability of the threatened sanction is always decisive. However, for the long run, I share the view of Sir James Fitzjames Stephen: "Some men, probably, abstain from murder because they fear that if they committed murder they would be hanged. Hundreds of thousands abstain from it because they regard it with horror. One great reason they regard it with horror is that murderers are hanged." Penal sanctions are useful in the long run for the formation of the internal restraints so necessary to control crime. The severity and finality of the death penalty is appropriate to the seriousness and finality of murder.

IV. INCIDENTAL ISSUES: COST, RELATIVE SUFFERING, BRUTALIZATION

Many nondecisive issues are associated with capital punishment. Some believe that the monetary cost of appealing a capital sentence is excessive. Yet most comparisons of the cost of life imprisonment with the cost of execution, apart from their dubious relevance, are flawed at least by the implied assumption that life prisoners will generate no judicial costs during their imprisonment. At any rate, the actual monetary costs are trumped by the importance of doing justice.

Others insist that a person sentenced to death suffers more than his victim suffered, and that this (excess) suffering is undue according to the *lex talionis* (rule of retaliation). We cannot know whether the murderer on death row suffers more than his victim suffered; however, unlike the murderer, the victim deserved none of the suffering inflicted. Further, the limitations of the *lex talionis* were meant to restrain private vengeance, not the social retribution that has taken its place. Punishment—regardless of the motivation—is not intended to revenge, offset, or compensate for the victim's suffering, or to be measured by it. Punishment is to vindicate the law and the social order undermined by the crime. This is why a kidnapper's penal confinement is not limited to the period for which he imprisoned his victim; nor is a burglar's confinement meant merely to offset the suffering or the harm he caused his victim; nor is it meant only to offset the advantage he gained.

Another argument heard at least since Beccaria is that, by killing a murderer, we encourage, endorse, or legitimize unlawful killing. Yet, although all punishments are meant to be unpleasant, it is seldom argued that they legitimize the unlawful imposition of identical unpleasantness. Imprisonment is not thought to legitimize kidnapping; neither are fines thought to legitimize robbery. The difference between murder and execution, or between kidnapping and imprisonment, is that the first is unlawful and undeserved, the second a lawful and deserved punishment for an unlawful act. The physical similarities of the punishment to the crime are irrelevant. The relevant difference is not physical, but social.

V. JUSTICE, EXCESS, DEGRADATION

We threaten punishments in order to deter crime. We impose them not only to make the threats credible but also as retribution (justice) for the crimes that were not deterred. Threats and punishments are necessary to deter and deterrence is a sufficient practical justification for them. Retribution is an independent moral justification. Although penalties can be unwise, repulsive, or inappropriate, and those punished can be pitiable, in a sense the infliction of legal punishment on a guilty person cannot be unjust. By committing the crime, the criminal volunteered to assume the risk of receiving a legal punishment that he could have avoided by not committing the crime. The punishment he suffers is the punishment he voluntarily risked suffering and, therefore, it is no more unjust to him than any other event for which one knowingly volunteers to assume the risk. Thus, the death penalty cannot be unjust to the guilty criminal.

There remain, however, two moral objections. The penalty may be regarded as always excessive as retribution and always morally degrading. To regard the death penalty as always excessive, one must believe that no crime—no matter how heinous—could possibly justify capital punishment. Such a belief can neither be corroborated nor refuted; it is an article of faith.

Alternatively, or concurrently, one may believe that everybody, the murderer no less than the victim, has an imprescriptible (natural?) right to life. The law therefore should not deprive anyone of life. I share Jeremy Bentham's view that any such "natural and imprescriptible rights" are "nonsense upon stilts."

Justice Brennan has insisted that the death penalty is "uncivilized," "inhuman," inconsistent with "human dignity" and with "the sanctity of life," that it "treats members of the human race as nonhumans, as objects to be toyed with and discarded," that it is "uniquely degrading to human dignity" and "by its very nature, [involves] a denial of the executed person's humanity." Justice Brennan does not say why he thinks execution "uncivilized." Hitherto most civilizations have had the death penalty, although it has been discarded in Western Europe, where it is currently unfashionable probably because of its abuse by totalitarian regimes.

By "degrading," Justice Brennan seems to mean that execution degrades the executed convicts. Yet philosophers, such as Immanuel Kant and G. F. W. Hegel, have insisted that, when deserved, execution, far from degrading the executed convict, affirms his humanity by affirming his rationality and his responsibility for his actions. They thought that execution, when deserved, is required for the sake of the convict's dignity. (Does not life imprisonment violate human dignity more than execution, by keeping alive a prisoner deprived of all autonomy?)

Common sense indicates that it cannot be death—our common fate—that is inhuman. Therefore, Justice Brennan must mean that death degrades when it comes not as a natural or accidental event, but as a deliberate social imposition. The murderer learns through his punishment that his fellow men have found him unworthy of living; that because he has murdered, he is being expelled from the community of the living. This degradation is self-inflicted. By murdering, the murderer has so dehumanized himself that he cannot remain among the living. The social recognition of his self-degradation is the punitive essence of execution. To believe, as Justice Brennan appears to, that the degradation is inflicted by the execution reverses the direction of causality.

Execution of those who have committed heinous murders may deter only one murder per year. If it does, it seems quite warranted. It is also the only fitting retribution for murder I can think of.

Discussion Questions

1. Do you agree with van den Haag that retributive justice is more important than equality? Support your answer. Discuss how John Rawls might respond to van den Haag's claim.
2. Discuss how van den Haag would most likely respond to the use of military commissions to try and impose the death penalty on suspected international terrorists.

3. Are you satisfied with van den Haag's argument that miscarriages of justice, in which innocent people are executed, are offset by the moral benefits of retributive justice? Discuss whether his response is consistent with human dignity and the categorical imperative, which state that we should never treat a person as a means only.
4. Clarence Darrow, U.S. lawyer and criminal defense attorney (1857–1938), was renowned for his outspoken opposition to the death penalty. Darrow believed that human behavior is determined by circumstances out of our control and, therefore, does not deserve to be punished. In his "Address to the Prisoners in the Chicago County Jail," Darrow told the inmates:

   > In one sense, everybody is equally good and equally bad. We all do the best we can under the circumstances . . . there were circumstances that drove you to do exactly the thing which you did. You could not help it any more than we outside can help taking the positions we take. . . .
   >
   > I will guarantee to take from this jail, or any jail in the world, five hundred men who have been the worst criminals and law-breakers who ever got into jail, and I will go down to our lowest streets and take five hundred of the most abandoned prostitutes, and go out somewhere where there is plenty of good land, and will give them a chance to make a living, and they will be as good people as the average in the community.[46]

   Do you agree with Darrow? Discuss how van den Haag might respond to Darrow's claim that criminals are simply products of their environments.
5. Discuss how a care ethicist, such as Carol Gilligan or Nel Noddings, might respond to van den Haag's justice-based argument. Is van den Haag's justification of capital punishment consistent with a care ethics approach? Support your answer.

CHRISTOPHER W. MORRIS

Punishment and Loss of Moral Standing

Christopher Morris is a professor of philosophy at Bowling Green University in Ohio. In his article Morris presents a social contract theory of punishment. In social contractarianism, justice is a more compelling moral concern than benevolence. Morris argues that people who intentionally violate the social contract by engaging in wrongdoing lose some moral standing and, hence, forfeit some of their moral rights. Those who murder forfeit their right to life. Because they have forfeited this right, capital punishment cannot be said to violate it.

"Punishment and Loss of Moral Standing," *Canadian Journal of Philosophy* 21, no. 1 (March 1991): 53–80. Some notes have been omitted.

Critical Reading Questions

1. How does Morris answer the question: "By what authority do we punish?"
2. According to Morris, what is the moral status of a wrongdoer? Does wrongdoing affect a person's rights?
3. How does Morris define punishment? What is the purpose of punishment according to Morris?
4. What distinction does Morris make between justice and benevolence? Which of these moral duties is more relevant to the question of punishment?
5. How does Morris define justice? Why, according to him, should we act justly?
6. What is the "doctrine of the circumstances of justice"?
7. According to Morris, what does it mean for someone to have "moral standing"?
8. What are the differences among "moral subjects," "direct moral objects," and "indirect moral objects"?
9. What is the "forfeiture justification of punishment"?
10. According to Morris, why would a rational person choose to be just?
11. What are some of the objections to the forfeiture justification of punishment? How does Morris respond to these objections?

> When any man, even in political society, renders himself by his crimes obnoxious to the public, he is punished by the laws in his goods and person; that is, the ordinary rules of justice are, with regard to him, suspended for a moment, and it becomes equitable to inflict on him, for the *benefit* of society, what otherwise he could not suffer without wrong or injury.[1]

By what authority do we punish? What permits us to deprive people of their liberty or possessions for some wrong that they have committed? Normally we may not do to people what we do when we punish wrongdoers. What exactly allows us to treat the latter as we do? . . .

I. THE MORAL JUSTIFICATION OF PUNISHMENT

. . . I shall argue that wrongdoers do not possess moral rights that stand in the way of their being punished. Thus punishment of wrongdoers will not be unjust.

What is punishment? The matter of the definition of punishment is complicated, as well as controversial. It will suffice for my purposes to have a general characterization of the notion. As such, punishment is the intentional imposition of some pain, unpleasantness, or deprivation for an offense committed by the culprit. It may be imposed so as to teach the offender a lesson, to deter others from similar acts, or to exact retribution. . . .

Criminal penalties are often recommended or defended as effective deterrents, or as appropriate means of retribution for certain offenses or at least of expressing the seriousness with which we view them. It is usually, and quite naturally, assumed that such penalties must consequentially be justified—that is, *morally* justified—if they are to be inflicted. In particular, it is usually thought that a particular kind of moral justification is required in the standard cases of punishment—namely, justification with reference to *justice.*

It is common to think of morality as having different parts or virtues. It is controversial how to understand these parts or even how to distinguish them. But it is widely thought that justice is different from the virtues of friendship, courage, moderation, and the like. More importantly, justice is usually distinguished from charity or benevolence, although there is less agreement here. The standard distinction is to understand justice to pertain to what individuals are *owed,* to what they may *claim,* to what they have a *right.* Benevolence, by contrast, is a virtue that attaches itself directly to the well-being of others. It is exemplified by taking an interest in others' welfare independently of that to which they have a claim. . . .

Typically, infringements of liberty or intentional infliction of pain violate moral rights to be free and not to be harmed. Thus, it would normally be thought that punishment requires a rationale in terms of justice. The state's involvement, it is usually thought, will only strengthen this requirement.

Now the moral rights of criminals do not stand in the way of punishment if we may justifiably *infringe* or *override* them. I do not, however, wish to defend either of these two possibilities. Instead I shall argue that punishment will not be unjust when wrongdoers lose the moral rights that would otherwise protect them against harm or loss. I turn now to the conception of justice that will be the basis of my approach to punishment.

II. JUSTICE BY CONVENTION

Justice is the moral virtue that is concerned with what is *owed* or *due* to individuals. It is that to which individuals appeal when they claim that to which they have a moral *right* (though this is not to say that the domain of rights exhausts that of justice). Recent discussions of justice have focused largely on principles of distributive justice, but this narrow focus should not let us lose sight of the larger virtue.

There is a long western tradition, dating back to Antiphon, Glaucon, and Epicurus, developed by Hobbes, Hume, and Rousseau, and continued in various ways by Rawls, Harsanyi, Mackie, Harman, Scanlon, Gauthier, and Kavka that understands justice to be a type of mutually agreeable convention. According to this tradition, justice consists of principles, rules, and norms that ideally serve to advance the interests and aims of all in certain situations. This tradition is dubbed "contractarian" as it often understands the terms of justice to be the outcome of a hypothetical bargain or "social contract." It might be less misleading to think of contemporary representatives of this tradition as offering a "rational choice" conception of morality after John Rawls's famous remark, "The theory of justice is a part, perhaps the most significant part, of the theory of rational choice."[2]

The account of justice offered by this tradition is designed to answer two traditional questions: what does justice require? and why be just? . . .

The indirect advantages of justice may normally be such that few individuals can wish to forego them. The advantages of injustice may, however, be sufficiently great that individuals are tempted to act unjustly. When then is it rational to be just? The principles of conduct that would emerge from the hypothetical bargain that rational choice ethicists use to determine the requirements of justice are those to which it is rational to agree. For such principles, if complied with, secure everyone's advantage. Without them, life would be nasty, brutish, and short, depending on the efficacy of alternative means of social control (e.g., law, superstition, kinship relations). However, granting that we have a reason to agree to such principles—even to grant that they define what justice is—what reason do we have to comply with their requirements?

We have reason to be just because if we have reason to accept certain principles of conduct, then we have reason to comply with them, provided the conditions under which we accepted the principles remain unchanged. . . .

One of the conditions—one of the "circumstances of justice," to use Rawls's phrase—giving rise to the need for justice is the possibility of mutual benefit. Others are the capacity and willingness of rational beings to impose constraints on their behavior. In the absence of such conditions, one has no reason to abide by the constraints of justice in one's conduct toward others. This is important, for it effectively means that in the absence of (1) mutual benefit or of (2) the capacity or (3) willingness to be just, individuals are not constrained by justice in their behavior toward one another. The answer that contractarian theorists give to the question "why be just?" commits them to the view just expressed, that in the absence of certain conditions there is no reason to act justly; we may call this view "the *doctrine* of the circumstances of justice." This doctrine is crucial to my understanding of the justification of punishment. I turn now to a brief account of *moral standing*.

Let us say that a *moral object* is something that is an object of moral consideration. A *direct* moral object is something *to* which (or to whom) that consideration is paid or owed; an *indirect* moral object is something *about* or *concerning* which moral consideration is paid. The latter is a *beneficiary* of the moral consideration. . . .

To have *moral standing* is to be owed (some) moral consideration, that is, to be a direct moral object. To be a mere indirect moral object is *not* to possess moral standing. In terms of these notions and distinctions, people typically are direct moral objects and have moral standing. Protected natural sites, national monuments, significant works of art might be examples of indirect moral objects. When we destroy the latter, we may be understood to fail in our duties to other people. . . .

We may contrast the notion of a moral object with that of a *moral subject*. The latter is something that has moral duties or may be expected to give moral consideration to direct moral objects. We usually understand adult humans to be moral subjects, while non-human animals and young infants are not so regarded; presumably *agency* would be necessary to being a moral subject.

Supposing that the "circumstances of justice" be satisfied, rational choice or contractarian moral theory understands rational humans, capable and willing to impose moral constraints on their conduct toward others, as moral subjects and direct moral objects. Thus, for this theory, as for most others, in normal circumstances adult humans have moral obligations and are owed certain moral considerations. However, it is important to note that "having moral standing" is a relation; something has moral standing in its relations to some other entity(ies). It should not be assumed that the relation holds universally, as we shall see. . . .

Now contractarian moral theory will imply that in the circumstances of justice all humans capable and willing to impose constraints on their behavior toward others have full moral standing. . . .

III. WRONGDOING AND LOSS OF MORAL STANDING

To have moral standing is to be owed (some) moral consideration. Justice consists in part of a set of moral rights, the most important of which, we may assume, are those to life, liberty, and property. To lose some such rights is to lose some of one's moral standing. I wish to argue that wrongdoers lose some of their rights and some of their moral standing, and that some wrongdoers lose all of their rights (or never possessed the full set) and retain at most what I have called partial moral standing. In other words, I shall defend a type of forfeiture theory, one according to which part (but only part) of the justification for punishment rests in the fact that wrongdoers lack certain rights, the presence of which would normally suffice to block the appropriate punishment. . . .

The first way in which wrongdoers can lose rights is less controversial or novel than the second; so I shall spend less time developing it. We may suppose that the conventions that determine justice, according to the contractarian tradition, have built into them provisions for penalties in the event of violation. Consider a club or organization established for the benefit of its members. It will have rules, respect of which will further the ends of the members. Without supposing duplicity on the part of the latter, it would be reasonable for them to include sanctions, however mild, for the violation of these rules; sanctions may provide assurance that others will not take advantage of one's cooperative behavior. Similarly, we may suppose that the rules of morality have built into them penalties, which may be applied whenever individuals act wrongly, that is, in violation of the rules.

The conception of justice characteristic of the contractarian tradition is that of an "artificial" system—to use the predicate favored by Hobbes and Hume—which ideally serves the interests of members of society. Given the imperfections of human rationality, it would be unwise to desire a system without sanctions for violations of its norms. That is, since we may expect that ordinary humans, without manifesting unwillingness to abide by the constraints of justice, will violate these constraints on occasion, when the temptation proves to be difficult to resist, we build into these constraints penalties for violations. . . .

The normal rights of individuals, then, are suspended whenever they violate the constraints of justice. The *act* of wrongdoing may cause the wrongdoer to lose, if only temporarily, certain rights. . . .

Criminal acts, then, insofar as they manifest the agent's unwillingness to comply with the requirements of justice, lead to (some) loss of moral standing. This is a simple consequence of the conditional nature of contractarian justice. What rights are thus lost? Alan H. Goldman makes the following suggestion:

> if we ask which rights are forfeited in violating rights of others, it is plausible to answer just those rights that one violates (or an equivalent set). One continues to enjoy rights only as long as one respects those rights in others: violation constitutes forfeiture. But one retains those rights which one has continued to respect in others.[3]

Wrongdoers, then, may lose (some of) their rights by their acts. The act alone may cause this loss insofar as the conventions of justice have penalties and the requisite suspension of duties built in. Further, the act, insofar as it manifests an unwillingness to abide by the constraints of justice, will bring about this loss; in some cases, the unwillingness revealed by the act may show that we mistakenly cooperated with the wrongdoer. Inflicting pain or deprivation of property or liberty on wrongdoers as a response to their acts is not unjust for they have lost, through their acts, the moral rights that would otherwise stand in the way of such treatment. Their status is analogous to exile; they are banished, not from a physical space but from a moral space. They have lost, at least in part, their membership in the moral community.

The forfeiture account may be independently appealing for retributive and other reasons. It may be thought that loss of the rights that wrongdoers violate is actually a most appropriate punishment for individuals unwilling to respect the requirements of justice. The intuitive appeal here may be similar to that of *lex talionis* in retributive theories. Further, it might be argued that punishing wrongdoers in ways that emphasize the relation between the rights they have violated and those they have thereby lost best *expresses* the community's outrage or anger at the wrongful act. Insofar as punishment has an expressive function, the criminal's forfeiture of moral rights would be both a consequence of his or her wrong doing and an expression of the moral community's consequent outrage. . . .

IV. THE DEATH PENALTY

The forfeiture account may be illustrated by an application to the death penalty. A discussion of capital punishment in light of the forfeiture thesis may provide a different understanding of the issues than is usually found in the contemporary literature. Consider the cases of contract killers, war criminals, tyrants, and certain terrorists who are unwilling to abide by the constraints of justice in their conduct toward others. . . .

Such people clearly lack full moral standing on a contractarian account of justice. They show by their conduct that they are unwilling to abide by the constraints of justice with most others. With respect to the latter, they themselves lack the protection that justice normally affords people. Suppose that they are apprehended, tried, and convicted of their crimes. Would it be *unjust* to execute them? No, for they lack full moral standing and thus the protection of justice. By their unwillingness to impose the constraints of justice on their conduct toward others, they lose the protection of justice. . . .

[W]e have no moral obligations of justice to contract killers, war criminals, tyrants, and genuine terrorists, or other individuals who place themselves outside the constraints of justice. Were it to be wrong to execute them, we would not be wronging *them* were we to do so; *they* would have no grounds of justice to complain.

We normally possess moral rights to life and to liberty. It is a controversial matter among ethicists exactly how these rights are to be understood, thus the contemporary debates over abortion, euthanasia, nuclear deterrence, and other issues. But at least part of the content of such moral rights is the obligation of others to refrain from intentionally taking one's life or from interfering with one's liberty when such is not necessary in order to protect the equal liberty of others or to serve some other important good. Such characterizations are imprecise, but they will serve my purpose.

Justice gives us our basic moral rights to life and liberty. Most theories of justice, contractarian or other, should have little trouble accounting for these rights, at least as I have characterized them. Thus, normally when we intentionally take another's life or interfere with their liberty, we must justify our actions with reference to justice, given their rights to life and liberty. Since taking or thus restricting another's life or liberty appear to be violations of their moral rights to life or liberty, a moral justification, one which makes reference to justice, seems required. Usually we will seek to show that the rights in question were *overridden* by some moral consideration. . . .

In the cases of the contract killers, war criminals, tyrants, and terrorists, I am suggesting that their moral rights to life or liberty are not overridden. (Indeed, I believe that this is not possible with respect to the moral right to life since I believe that this right is not *defeasible,* though I do not propose to argue this here.) Instead I am arguing that we do not have to give standard *moral* justifications for executing contract killers, war criminals, tyrants, or terrorists because so killing them would neither be a violation nor an overriding of their moral rights to life or liberty. Rather, they no longer have, or never had, such moral rights. Thus we merely need sufficient reason to execute them. To use Hobbes' language, such individuals have only the "right" of nature, that is, mere Hohfeldian liberties that entail no correlative obligations on the part of others. . . .

V. OBJECTIONS

Many will find my account counter-intuitive and will reject the idea that some humans, no matter how amoral, lose their rights and moral standing. And there are many objections that will be, and have been, made. I shall discuss some of these.

Much crime is committed by the destitute in the urban underclass. It may be argued that the account I have offered "does not apply" to them, as "they are *outside* of the circumstances of justice to begin with and have nothing to forfeit." It is unclear what exactly the objection is, for if individuals who commit crimes lack certain rights to begin with, then no rights stand in the way of their being punished for their acts, and the first part of a justification for punishment is complete. This criticism might be the same as that which finds the very idea of someone without full moral standing objectionable. Now there *is* a serious question about the implications of our moral theories for the plight of those in our cities who have no or little stake in the social order. My view is that there are compelling contractarian arguments for some redistribution to the poor and destitute to give them a stake in the social order and bring them into the circumstances of justice. But that would seem to be another matter entirely than the subject of this essay.

It might be argued that the forfeiture account would permit various forms of cruel punishment—for instance, the death penalty—and that this constitutes an objection. If cruelty involves indifference to another's pain or suffering, then punishment as I have characterized it may well be cruel. However, if cruelty involves taking pleasure in another's suffering, then cruelty is not part of the account that I am offering. For on the view that I am defending, the reasons for punishment are independent of the grounds for the permissibility of punishment.

It is a criticism, however, of many of our institutions to point out that our motivations are mixed and include elements of cruelty or malice. Were we to dispose of certain amoral criminals by imprisoning or executing them, accepting the account I have offered, but do so largely from malice and revenge, then our practices would be vulnerable to criticism. Supposing that the criminal in question lacks the moral rights that justice accords, then cruelty will be an objection only insofar as (1) it is contrary to benevolence or some other virtue, (2) it is bad public policy, or (3) we have obligations to others that prohibit us from treating any human cruelly. It is likely that, e.g., torture will virtually always be ruled out for these reasons, though I do not propose to argue this here. . . .

VI. CONCLUSION

Punishment, I have argued, is justified in part because wrongdoers lose the moral rights that would otherwise stand in the way of their being harmed in the manner that we do when we punish. Moral standing is to some degree lost, and moral rights are to some degree forfeited, by wrongdoers.

It might be argued that the position I have put forward does not take justice seriously. I disagree. The forfeiture account I have developed links in a certain way being a direct moral object with being a moral subject. Rational humans who are not willing to impose the constraints of justice on their conduct toward others are not themselves protected by these constraints. In my view, *that* is to take justice seriously.

NOTES

1. David Hume, *Inquiry Concerning the Principles of Morals,* Section III, "Of Justice," Part I, paragraph 10.
2. *A Theory of Justice* (Cambridge, MA: Harvard University Press, 1971), 16; see also 172. It is clear from his most recent writings, if not from some of the elements of *A Theory of Justice,* that Rawls does not really endorse the view of moral theory expressed by his remark.
3. Alan H. Goldman, "The Paradox of Punishment," *Philosophy & Public Affairs* **9** (1979): 44.

Discussion Questions

1. Does Morris make a convincing argument for why it benefits people to behave justly? Consider the story of Gyges's ring recounted by Glaucon in Plato's *Republic.* In a debate with Socrates over justice, Glaucon argues that people are naturally selfish and will behave unjustly whenever they have the opportunity. To illustrate his point, Glaucon tells the story of a shepherd named Gyges. Gyges takes a ring off a dead body, and the ring makes him invisible. Delighted with his discovery, Gyges takes advantage of his invisibility to murder the king and seize the throne. Glaucon argues that everyone would behave unjustly like Gyges if they knew they could get away with it.

   Do people behave justly only to avoid punishment or public censure, as Glaucon claims? Or do people behave justly because it mutually benefits them, as Morris claims? Support your answer. Does the story of Gyges's ring weaken Morris's argument?
2. In a footnote to his article, Morris draws an analogy between forfeiture of rights and exile or banishment of criminals. Someone "violates certain fundamental norms of society (or displeases the rulers) and is stripped of citizenship and banished from the land." Socrates, he notes, was offered the choice of exile or the death penalty; he chose the latter. Most people now believe, however, that the execution of Socrates by the state was not morally justified. Does the death of Socrates and others who question societal norms and laws demonstrate a flaw in the contractual concept of justice? Discuss how Morris might respond to this question.
3. In 1945, following World War II, the tribunal at the United Nations Nuremberg Trials compiled a charter with a list of universal standards of justice. Between 1945 and 1949, almost 200 Nazis were tried under this new charter. Of these 161 were found guilty and 36 sentenced to death. Discuss how a social contractarian such as Morris would respond to the use of the death penalty for the Nazi war criminals. Because the Nazis did not violate their own community's social contract, and the Nuremberg

charter was not written until after the war, did the United Nations act unjustly by punishing the Nazis for being "good" citizens?

4. Inmates on death row are sometimes put on "suicide watch" so they cannot take their own lives. Retributivists claim that the death penalty is not about revenge but about justice, so is there some doublethink inherent in trying to prevent condemned prisoners from taking their own lives? If retribution stems from a respect for the dignity of persons rather than a desire for revenge, wouldn't it be preferable for murderers to voluntarily end their own lives in payment for their crimes rather than be involuntarily executed? Support your answers. Discuss how Kant, Morris, and van den Haag might respond to these questions.

HUGO ADAM BEDAU

Capital Punishment

Hugo Adam Bedau is a professor of philosophy at Tufts University and a well-known opponent of capital punishment. In the following selection, Bedau examines the death penalty in light of important relevant moral values, such as the sanctity of life and the right to life. Bedau rejects Locke's argument that the right to life can be forfeited by murder, arguing that the concept of forfeiture of one's right to life is inconsistent with human dignity. Bedau also rejects Kant's claim that retributive justice requires the death penalty for murder, as well as a utilitarian approach to determining the morality of capital punishment. From here Bedau goes on to question the morality of punishment.

Critical Reading Questions

1. What, according to Bedau, is one of the most important moral values?
2. What is the relationship between the sanctity of human life and the right to life? Why, according to Bedau, is the death penalty inconsistent with these two values?
3. Why does Bedau reject Locke's argument that the right to life is forfeited by murderers?
4. On what grounds does Bedau reject Kant's claim that retributive justice requires capital punishment for murder?
5. According to Kant, in what state of mind must a murderer be to be held morally responsible for his or her actions? Why does Bedau reject Kant's reasoning on this point?
6. On what grounds does Bedau reject utilitarian arguments for capital punishment?
7. What is the nature and purpose of punishment, according to Bedau?

"Capital Punishment," ed. by Tom Regan, *Matters of Life and Death* (New York: McGraw-Hill, 1993), 160–192. Some notes have been omitted.

8. Why does Bedau conclude that the death penalty violates the dignity of persons?
9. On what grounds does Bedau reject the social defense argument for the death penalty?
10. On what grounds does Bedau reject consequentialist arguments, such as deterrence, incapacitation, and crime prevention, for the death penalty?
11. What are the two leading principles that underlie retributive justice?
12. On what grounds does Bedau argue that retributive justice does not require the death penalty for murder?
13. According to Bedau, why does capital punishment demean society as well as the criminal being executed?

INTRODUCTION

When we confront the task of evaluating punishments from the moral point of view, a host of questions immediately arises: Who should be punished? What offenses and harms should be made liable to punishment? What is involved in making the punishment fit the crime? Are some punishments too cruel or barbaric to be tolerated no matter how effective they may be in preventing crime? Are some criminals so depraved or dangerous that no punishment is too severe for them? What moral principles should govern our thinking about crime and punishment?

To give reasonable answers to such questions, we need to appeal to a wide variety of empirical facts. We will want to know, for example, what would happen to the crime rate if no one were punished at all, or if all offenders were punished more leniently or more severely than is now usual. We would want to know whether the system of criminal justice operates with adequate efficiency and fairness when it metes out punishment, or whether the severest punishments tend to fall mainly on some social, racial, or economic classes. But we will want to settle other things besides these matters of fact. Social values, moral ideals, ethical principles are also involved, and we will want to know which values and which ideals they are and how to evaluate them as well. Central among these ethical considerations are the value, worth, and dignity of persons—the victims of crime, the offenders, and the rest of society. How, exactly, does our belief in the value of human life, the worth of each person, our common humanity and our common dignity, bear on the nature and methods of punishment as seen from the moral point of view?

There is no better setting in which to examine these questions than the one provided by the controversy over the morality of capital punishment (the death penalty). From an historical perspective, one of the most important relevant ethical values is the idea of *the sanctity of human life*. . . .

Distinct as the sanctity of human life and the right to life are, they are held together by a common bond. Each expresses the view that it is morally wrong to take a purely instrumental view of human life. By "instrumental view of human life" I mean any view that makes it permissible to kill persons in order to protect some other value (e.g., property) or in order to advance some social or political goal (e.g., national liberation). . . .

So far as the death penalty is concerned, it might seem that once it is granted that human life is sacred or that everyone has an equal right to life, the death penalty is morally indefensible. Such a punishment seems obviously inconsistent with such ideals as human worth and value. The opposite, however, is true if we let history be our guide. Chief among the traditional defenders of capital punishment have been religious and secular thinkers who sincerely believed in these ideals. In fact, these thinkers usually invoked the sanctity of human life and the right to life as part of their defense and justification of death for murderers and other criminals. To see how such a seemingly paradoxical doctrine can be maintained, as well as to begin our examination of the major issues involved in the moral evaluation of the death penalty, we must scrutinize the traditional doctrine of the right to life.

I. THE RIGHT TO LIFE AND CAPITAL PUNISHMENT

The Doctrine of Natural Rights

The general idea shared by many philosophers, beginning in the seventeenth century, was that each person by nature—that is, apart from the laws of the state and simply by virtue of being born a human being—had the right to live. It followed from this that it was a violation of this right to murder another person, and that it was the responsibility of government to protect human rights, prohibit murder, and try to arrest, convict, and punish anyone guilty of this crime. Thus, the right to life can be thought of, first, as underlying the prohibition against murder common to the criminal law of all countries. . . .

The right to life seems to pose a problem for a policy of capital punishment. Even if a person has committed murder (so the argument runs) and has therewith intentionally violated another's right to life, the criminal still has his or her own right to life. Would it not be a violation of the murderer's right for him or her to be put to death as punishment? If so, must not capital punishment be morally wrong? . . .

Forfeiting the Right to Life

Locke argued that although a person's right to life is natural and inalienable, it can be "forfeited" and *is* forfeited whenever one person violates that right in another. [W. D. Ross] has put the point clearly: "The offender, by violating the life, liberty, or property of another, has lost his own right to have his life, liberty, or property respected. . . ."[1] The idea is a familiar one, although there are troubling and unanswered questions: To whom is it forfeited? Can this right, once forfeited, ever be restored? If so, by whom and under what conditions? Thanks to the doctrine of forfeiture, it was possible for Locke to assert without apparent contradiction both that everyone has a natural and inalienable right to life and that the death penalty for a murderer does not violate that right.

Locke's actual reasoning was somewhat more complex and less plausible but more revealing than the account of it so far given. According to Locke, a person forfeits the right to life whenever he or she commits a criminal act that "deserves death."[2] What criterion does Locke use to decide whether a crime deserves death or some lesser penalty? He seems not to have given any thought to the problem. . . .

Difficulties with Locke's Theory

There are various objections to the classic theory of the right to life, two of which deserve to be mentioned here. First, underlying Locke's doctrine of natural rights and wholly independent of it are two important assumptions. One is that punishment under law is necessary for social defense. (By "social defense" is meant the prevention of crime, by means of deterrence and incapacitation, as well as by the reduction of incentives and opportunities for the commission of crimes. Thus, prisons, police forces, controlling the sale of firearms, locks on doors, and threats of punishment can all be regarded as methods of social defense.) The other is that justice requires retribution—criminals deserve to be punished, and the punishment must fit the crime. Such beliefs lead to the conclusion that the punishment for murder and other crimes should be death, and they force Locke to make some accommodation in his theory of natural rights. The device he hit upon, as we have just seen, and one that generations of later thinkers have also adopted, is to declare that the right to life could be forfeited under certain conditions.

Against Locke's doctrine several objections deserve to be considered. First of all, there are other alternatives. . . . [S]uppose it is argued that although punishments typically constitute harms or deprivations to the person who undergoes them, the quality and extent of the deprivations [are] an open question. What is necessary is that the deprivation be imposed on the offender regardless or his or her preferences and choice. On this view, while it would be necessary for the offender to forfeit some rights in order to be punished, it would not be necessary to forfeit the right to life. Yet another possibility is to regard the right to life as an absolute right, one that it is always wrong to violate. Whether any of these alternatives can be better supported than the doctrine of forfeiture need not be resolved here. They do show that forfeiture of rights as Locke presents it is not the only way to permit punishment under a theory of natural rights.

Another difficulty with Locke's doctrine is that it seems to collapse two distinct issues into one. It is one thing to appeal to forfeiting rights in order to permit society to punish the guilty offender in the first place. It is quite another to appeal to forfeiture of rights in order to decide which among the available punishments is the appropriate one. . . . There is no intrinsic feature of any natural right, including the right to life, that makes it subject to loss through forfeiture. The only basis for supposing that any right is forfeited rather than grossly violated by society when it punishes an offender by death is that just retribution and social defense together require the death penalty for offenders guilty of a crime of this sort. If this requirement turns out to be false, unsubstantiated, or doubtful, then the claim that a criminal's right to life has been forfeited turns out to be equally false, unsubstantiated, or doubtful. . . .

Even if it is concluded that a murderer or violent criminal does forfeit the natural right to life, it does not follow that a murderer *must* be put to death. The doctrine of forfeiture does not involve the idea that once a person forfeits a right to *x*, those to whom it is forfeited have a *duty* to take *x* away from that person. This is often overlooked by those who insist that the death penalty is justified because murderers forfeit their lives. Forfeiting one's *right* to life is not identical with forfeiting one's life. . . .

Finally, we should note that Locke's doctrine of forfeiture makes his theory of natural rights vulnerable to utilitarian reasoning, and with devastating effect. The chief attraction of the idea of natural rights is that it provides each of us with moral armor (our rights) to protect us against burdens and deprivations that might be imposed on the ground that they are in the interests of the many or good for society in the long run. . . .

The Dignity of Persons

Although Kant by no means repudiated the doctrine of natural rights, he elevated to primary importance a different idea, the supreme worth or dignity of each person. The most famous single passage in which this doctrine and Kant's views on the punishment of murder are brought together runs as follows:

> If . . . he has committed a murder, he must die. In this case, there is no substitute that will satisfy the requirements of legal justice. There is no sameness of kind between death and remaining alive even under the most miserable conditions, and consequently there is no equality between the crime and the retribution unless the criminal is judicially condemned and put to death. But the death of the criminal must be kept entirely free of any maltreatment that would make an abomination of the humanity residing in the person suffering it.[3] . . .

For Kant, that idea of the dignity of man enters explicitly only to rule out any aggravations and brutality accompanying the sentence of death and its execution. For Kant, the dignity of man underlies the whole idea of society of free and rational persons choosing to submit themselves to a common rule of law that includes the punishment of crimes. Accordingly, in punishment, "a human being can never be manipulated merely as a means to the purposes of someone else. . . . His innate personality protects him against such treatment. . . ."[4] Kant must therefore also reject the idea that a murderer should be punished by death because by doing so we prevent him from killing again and also discourage others from murder. Kant's appeal to the dignity of man requires him to rule out any role for social defense in the justification of capital punishment.

As the above passage also shows, underlying Kant's belief in the appropriateness of punishing murder with death is a principle of just retribution. This is reminiscent of Locke's view. . . . The chief difference between Kant and Locke is that Locke thinks it is proper to take into account not only just retribution but also social defense to determine proper punishments, whereas Kant unequivocally rules out the latter. What Kant has done is to present us with two moral ideas—the dignity or worth of each person as a rational creature, and the principle of retribution—that he regards as inextricably tied together. The latter principle he explained in the following way:

> What kind and what degree of punishment does public legal justice adopt as its principle and standard? None other than the principle of equality . . . , that is, the principle of not treating one side more favorably than the other. Accordingly, any undeserved evil that you inflict on someone else among the people is one that you do to yourself. Only the Law of retribution . . . can determine exactly the kind and degree of punishment.[5] . . .

Kant, as is obvious from his remarks, thought that retribution *required* the death penalty for murder. He is not alone in holding this view; it has widespread appeal even today. . . .

Difficulties with Kant's Theory

In the course of presenting Kant's views, we have already identified three respects in which his theory is vulnerable. One is that, like Locke's, it assumes that just retribution *requires* capital punishment for murder, an assumption that may be unnecessary and in any case is not proved. Another difficulty is that, unlike Locke's theory, Kant's seems to make no room whatever for the role of social defense in the justification of punishment. . . .

Finally, the third objection follows from the fact that Kant's theory is so obviously abstract and unempirical from beginning to end. If we really take seriously the idea of the dignity of the human person, then it may be that we will be led in case after case of actual crime to reject Kant's reasoning on the ground that it is inapplicable in light of the actual facts of the case. Kant's theory tells us what to do only with ideally rational killers; what we need is a theory that tells us how to cope with the actual persons who kill, and how to do that in a way that acknowledges our common humanity with both the victim and the offender, as well as the injustices to which all social systems are prone and the wisdom of self-restraint in the exercise of violence, especially when undertaken deliberately and in the name of justice.

Utilitarianism and the Death Penalty

. . . Just as Kant disregarded considerations of consequences in evaluating the morality of capital punishment, so utilitarians disregard any appeals to natural rights or the dignity of the human person. For them, these ideas at best mask a reference to social benefits, more likely, they are moral standards independent of (and thus potentially in conflict with) the principle of utility. At worst, they are rhetorical phrases of dubious content. The utilitarian, therefore, regards the death penalty as justified by the degree to which it advances the general welfare. Accordingly, its justification proceeds in the following manner: (1) Consider the practice of the death penalty and all its present and future consequences—for the executed offenders, for the victims of crime, their friends and families, and the rest of society. (2) Consider each of the alternative modes of punishment that might be imposed and the consequences of each were it to be employed. (3) Decide in favor of the death penalty rather than any alternative only if, in light of all of the facts, its practice would have the greatest net balance of benefit over burden for everyone affected by it.

Two things are noteworthy about such a pattern of reasoning. First, everything depends on the facts, and diverse issues of fact are always in question. Moreover, these facts are not likely to remain constant in a given society decade after decade, much less from one society to another. The result is that it may be very difficult to reach agreement on all of them, as the unending debate over the deterrent efficacy of executions attests. When that happens, reasonable utilitarians will have to agree to disagree with each other over whether the death penalty should be retained, modified, or abolished for this or that crime. We have, in fact, a perfect illustration of precisely such a disagreement between the two most influential classic utilitarian philosophers. Jeremy Bentham (1748–1832) strongly opposed the death penalty throughout his life and in one of his last essays argued forcefully for its complete abolition in England and France. His student, John Stuart Mill (1806–1873), however, when he was a member of Parliament in the 1860s, argued with comparable firmness against abolition of the death penalty for murder in the England of his day. Thus, within the space of a generation, Bentham and Mill, professing utilitarians, disagreed over the desirability of abolishing the death penalty. . . .

A second point of interest is that the general welfare is an extremely abstract, remote, and elusive end-state to serve as the good to be aimed at in choosing among alternative penal policies. Utilitarians have devoted much energy to trying to give shape and content to this idea, or to what they regard as better-defined alternative conceptions. Still, even the utilitarian may have to be content, as a practical compromise, to rely on some intermediate moral principles less comprehensive in their scope than the principle of utility and more directly applicable to the problem of punishment and the death penalty controversy. . . .

II. THE MORALITY OF PUNISHMENT

As a first step toward providing a fresh setting for the rest of our discussion, it is useful to have a general sketch before us of why it is rational for society to have a system of punishment at all, quite apart from whether the death penalty is used as one of the modes of punishment. We are not likely to assess the morality of capital punishment correctly unless we understand the morality of punishment in general. . . .

The Right to Punish

Society is organized by reference to common norms that forbid anyone and everyone to engage in certain sorts of harmful conduct. When someone deliberately, willfully, and knowingly violates such rules, and therewith harms the innocent, the offender has violated the rights of others and immediately becomes liable to a punitive response. Since the norms were originally designed to provide protection to every person, and since (so we also assume) the culprit knew in advance that his or her conduct was prohibited because it would be injurious to others, and since he or she freely and knowingly chose nevertheless to violate the norm, society cannot simply ignore the violation and continue to treat the offender as if no wrong had been done. It must attempt to bring the offender to judgment. The reason is twofold. First, it is inconsistent for society to establish a set of fair rules, with penalties for their violation, and then to ignore them when actual violations occur. Second, it is unfair for the law-abiding to have to suffer both the undeserved harms inflicted on them by lawbreakers and the inconvenience of complying with laws that they, too, might like to violate, while the criminals indulge their lawless inclinations and suffer nothing in return. . . .

Punishment, therefore, serves the complex function of reinforcing individual compliance with a set of social norms deemed necessary to protect the rights of all the members of society. Once it has been determined that one of these norms has been deliberately violated, then there is no alternative but to set in motion the system of criminal justice that culminates in the punishment of the guilty offender.

Such a system is essentially retributive in at least two respects. Crime must be punished, and the punishment must fit the crime. The theory relied upon here certainly acknowledges the first of these contentions. Punishment by its nature pays back an offender who has inflicted suffering and indignity on an innocent victim by inflicting suffering and indignity on the offender. Justice, more than any other consideration (social defense, reform of the offender), dictates that all crimes be liable to punishment, and that a reasonable portion of social resources (public expenditures) be allocated to the arrest, conviction, and punishment of offenders. . . .

Modes of Punishment

What sorts of punishments are available to society to inflict on offenders? What are the sorts of things any person could be deprived of that would count as punishment? Obviously, one could have one's money or property confiscated, or be deprived of the right to future earnings or an inheritance. But because so much crime against property and against the person is committed by the poor and untalented, by persons with no property and no prospects of any, and because the stolen property is so often disposed of prior to the offender's arrest, it is often point-less to levy punishments in the form of fines or confiscations. . . .

For reasons such as these society has long preferred to take other things of intrinsic value from persons in the name of punishment—notably their freedom and their bodily integrity. Everybody, rich and poor, young and old, male and female, has life and limb and some degree of liberty to lose. Historically, the objection to making punishments mainly a deprivation of liberty was that considerable tax revenues were needed to build and staff prisons. Partly for just such economic reasons the earliest punishments were neither pecuniary nor incarcerative, but corporal: flogging, branding, maiming, and killing. Inexpensive and quick to administer, acutely painful for the offender—it is hardly any wonder that every society today is heir to punitive practices involving widespread and varied use of corporal punishments. . . .

III. THE SEVERITY AND INDIGNITY OF THE DEATH PENALTY

Is Capital Punishment an Untimely and Undignified Death?

Some defenders of capital punishment have complained that opposition to the death penalty entails an overestimation of the value of human life; it tends to ignore that we will all die eventually. All that capital punishment does, according to this objection, is to schedule a person's death at a definite time and place, by a definite mode, and for a definite reason. This raises a new question for us, namely, how the idea of the value, worth, dignity, or sanctity of human life can be made consistent with human mortality.

Even though death is a fact of life, emphasizing the worth of human life is a way of giving sense to the familiar notions of "untimely" death and of an "undignified" death. These terms are admittedly vague and have application in a wide variety of settings, but they also have a place where crime and punishment are concerned. Other things being equal, if a death is brought about by one person killing another, as in murder, then it is an untimely death. If a death is brought about in a way that causes terror during the dying or disfigurement of the body, then it is an undignified death. This, of course, is exactly what murder and capital punishment both typically do. . . .

Why Death Is More Severe than Imprisonment

. . . Roughly, of two punishments, one is more severe than the other depending on its duration and on its interference with things a person so punished might otherwise do. Death is interminable, whereas it is always possible to revoke or interrupt a life sentence. Death also makes compensation impossible, whereas it is possible to compensate a prisoner in some way for wrongful confinement even if it is not possible to give back any of the liberty that was taken away. Of most importance, death permits of no concurrent experiences or activities, whereas even a life-term prisoner can read a book, watch television, perhaps even write a book or repair a television set, and experience various social relations with other people. Death eliminates the presupposition of all experience and activity: life itself. For these reasons, the death penalty is unquestionably the more severe punishment, no matter what a few despondent life-term prisoners or sentimental observers may think they would prefer, and no matter how painless and dignified the mode of execution might be. . . .

The Indignity of Corporal Punishments

In addition to the severity of the death penalty, the killing of persons as punishment shares certain important features with other modes of corporal punishment—maiming, flogging, branding—once widely practiced in our society but now abandoned. All these other methods of corporal punishment have been adandoned in part because they are now seen to violate the dignity of the person being punished. . . .

Why has death as a punishment escaped the nearly universal condemnation visited on all these other punishments with which it is historically and naturally associated? In part, it may be owing to a failure of imagination. Whereas we all know or can easily and vividly imagine the pain and humiliation involved in other corporal punishments, executions today are carried out away from public view, they are quickly over, and the person punished by death is no longer in our midst as a constant reminder. Other factors come into play, too. One is the belief that in some cases there is truly no alternative, because if the criminal were not killed there would be too much risk that he or she would repeat the crime. If so, then neither retribution nor deterrence, but rather incapacitation turns out to be the last line of defense. . . .

IV. CAPITAL PUNISHMENT AND SOCIAL DEFENSE

The Analogy with Self-Defense

Capital punishment, it is sometimes said, is to the body politic what self-defense is to the individual. If the latter is not morally wrong, how can the former be? To assess the strength of this analogy, we need first to inspect the morality of self-defense.

Except for absolute pacifists, who believe it is morally wrong to use violence even to defend themselves or others from undeserved aggression, most of us believe that it is not morally wrong and may even be our moral duty to use violence to prevent aggression directed against either ourselves or innocent third parties. The law has long granted persons the right to defend themselves against the unjust aggressions of others, even to the extent of using lethal force to kill an assailant. . . .

The foregoing account assumes that the person acting in self-defense is innocent of any provocation of the assailant. It also assumes that there is no alternative to victimization except resistance. In actual life, there may be a third alternative: escape, or removing oneself from the scene of the imminent aggression. Hence, the law imposes on us the "duty to retreat." . . . The rule is this: Use of deadly force is justified only to prevent loss of life in immediate jeopardy where a lesser use of force cannot reasonably be expected to save the life that is threatened. . . .

The rationale for self-defense as set out above illustrates two moral principles of great importance to our discussion. One is that if a life is to be risked, then it is better that it be the life of someone who is guilty (in this context, the initial assailant) rather than the life of someone who is not (the innocent potential victim). It is not fair to expect the innocent prospective victim to run the added risk of severe injury or death in order to avoid using violence in self-defense to the extent of possibly killing his or her assailant. Rather, fairness dictates that the guilty aggressor ought to be the one to run the risk.

The other principle is that taking life deliberately is not justified so long as there is any feasible alternative. One does not expect miracles, of course, but in theory, if shooting a burglar through the foot will stop the burglar and enable one to call the police for help, there is no reason to shoot to kill. Likewise, if the burglar is unarmed, there is no reason to shoot at all. . . . In these ways the law shows a tacit regard for the life even of a felon and discourages the use of unnecessary violence even by the innocent; morality can hardly do less.

Deterrence, Incapacitation, and Crime Prevention

The analogy with self-defense leads naturally to the empirical and the conceptual questions surrounding the death penalty as a method of crime prevention. Notice first that crimes can be prevented without recourse to punishment; we do that when we take weapons from offenders, protect targets by bolts and alarms, and educate the public to be less vulnerable to victimization. As for punishment, it prevents crimes by *incapacitation* and by *deterrence.* The two are theoretically independent because they achieve prevention very differently. Executing a murderer prevents crimes by means of *incapacitation* to the extent that the murderer would have committed further crimes if not executed. Incapacitating a murderer will not have any preventative benefits, however, unless the murderer would otherwise have committed some further crimes. (In fact relatively few murderers turn out to be homicidal recidivists.) Nor is killing persons the only way to incapacitate them; isolation and restraints will suffice. Executing a murderer prevents crimes by means of *deterrence* to the extent that others are frightened into not committing any capital crimes by the knowledge that convicted offenders are executed. Thus, successful deterrence is prevention by a psychologically effective threat; incapacitation, if it prevents crimes at all, does so by physically disabling the offender.

The Death Penalty and Incapacitation

Capital punishment is unusual among penalties because its incapacitative effects limit its deterrent effects. The death penalty can never deter an executed person from further crimes. At most, it incapacitates the executed person from committing them. . . . But incapacitation is not identical with prevention. Prevention by means of incapacitation occurs only if the executed criminal would have committed other crimes if he or she had not been executed and had been punished only in some less incapacitative way (e.g., by imprisonment). . . .

This is the nub of the problem. There is no way to know in advance which if any of the incarcerated or released murderers will kill again. It is useful in this connection to remember that the only way to guarantee that no horrible crimes ever occur is to execute *everyone* who might conceivably commit such a crime. Similarly, the only way to guarantee that no convicted murderer ever commits another murder is to execute them all. No modern society has ever done this, and for two hundred years Western societies have been moving steadily in the opposite direction.

These considerations show that our society has implicitly adopted an attitude toward the risk of murder rather like the attitude it has adopted toward the risk of fatality from other causes, such as automobile accidents, lung cancer, or drowning. Since no one knows when or where or upon whom any of these lethal events will fall, it would be too great an invasion of freedom to undertake the severe restrictions that alone would suffice to prevent any such deaths from occurring. It is better to take the risks and keep our freedom than to try to eliminate the risks altogether and lose our freedom in the process. Hence, we have lifeguards at the beach, but swimming is not totally prohibited; smokers are warned, but cigarettes are still legally sold; pedestrians may have the right of way in a crosswalk, but marginally competent drivers are still allowed to operate motor vehicles. Some risk is thereby imposed on the innocent; in the name of our right to freedom, we do not insist on having society protect us at all costs.

The Death Penalty and Deterrence

. . . For half a century, social scientists have studied the questions whether the death penalty is a deterrent and whether it is a better deterrent than the alternative of imprisonment. Their verdict, while not unanimous, is nearly so. Whatever may be true about the deterrence of lesser crimes by other penalties, the deterrence achieved by the death penalty for murder is not measurably any greater than the deterrence achieved by long-term imprisonment. . . .

If the death penalty and long-term imprisonment are equally effective (or ineffective) as deterrents to murder, then the argument for the death penalty on grounds of deterrence is seriously weakened. One of the moral principles identified earlier now comes into play: Unless there is a good reason for choosing a more rather than a less severe punishment for a crime, the less severe penalty is to be preferred. This principle obviously commends itself to anyone who values human life and who concedes that, all other things being equal, less pain and suffering is always better than more. . . .

A Cost/Benefit Analysis of the Death Penalty

A full study of the costs and benefits involved in the practice of capital punishment would not be confined solely to the question of whether it is a better deterrent or preventive of murder than imprisonment. Any thoroughgoing utilitarian approach to the death-penalty controversy would need to examine carefully other costs and benefits as well, because maximizing the balance of all the social benefits over all the social costs is the sole criterion of right and wrong according to utilitarianism. Let us consider, therefore, some of the other costs and benefits to be calculated. Clinical psychologists have presented evidence to suggest that the death penalty actually incites some persons of unstable mind to murder others, either because they are afraid to take their own lives and hope that society will punish them for murder by putting them to death, or because they fancy that they, too, are killing with justification analogously to the lawful and presumably justified killing involved in capital punishment. If such evidence is sound, capital punishment can serve as a counterpreventive or even an incitement to murder; such incited murders become part of its social cost. Imprisonment, however, has not been known to incite any murders or other crimes of violence in a comparable fashion. . . . The risks of executing the innocent are also part of the social cost. The historical record is replete with innocent persons arrested, indicted, convicted, sentenced, and occasionally legally executed for crimes they did not commit. . . . Nor is this all. The high costs of a capital trial and the inevitable appeals, the costly methods of custody most prisons adopt for convicts on "death row," are among the straightforward economic costs that the death penalty incurs. Conducting a valid cost/benefit analysis of capital punishment would be extremely difficult; nevertheless, on the basis of the evidence we have, it is quite possible that such a study would show that abolition of all death penalties is much less costly than their retention. . . .

V. CAPITAL PUNISHMENT AND RETRIBUTIVE JUSTICE

No discussion of the morality of punishment would be complete without taking into account the two leading principles of retributive justice relevant to the capital punishment controversy. One is the principle that crimes ought to be punished. The other is the principle that the severity of a punishment ought to be proportional to the gravity of the offense. These are moral principles of recognized weight. Leaving aside all questions of social defense, how strong a case for capital punishment can be made on their basis? How reliable and persuasive are these principles themselves?

Crime Must Be Punished

. . . Fortunately, this principle need not be in dispute between proponents and opponents of the death penalty. Even defenders of the death penalty must admit that putting a convicted murderer in prison for years is a punishment of that criminal. The principle that crime must be punished is neutral to our controversy, because both sides acknowledge it.

The other principle of retributive justice is the one that seems to be decisive. Under *lex talionis,* it must always have seemed that murderers ought to be put to death. Proponents of the death penalty, with rare exceptions, have insisted on this point, and even opponents of the death penalty must give grudging assent to the seeming fittingness of demanding capital punishment for murder. The strategy for opponents of the death penalty is to argue either that (1) this principle is not really a principle of justice after all, or that (2) to the extent it is, it does not require death for murderers, or that (3) in any case it is not the only principle of punitive justice. As we shall see, all these objections have merit. . . .

Is Death Sufficiently Retributive?

Those who advocate capital punishment for murder on retributive grounds must face the objection that, on their own principles, the death penalty in some cases is morally inadequate. How could death in the electric chair or the gas chamber or before a firing squad or by lethal injection suffice as just retribution, given the savage, brutal, wanton character of so many murders? How can retributive justice be served by anything less than equally savage methods of execution? From a retributive point of view, the oft-heard exclamation, "Death is too good for him!," has a certain truth. Are defenders of the death penalty willing to embrace this consequence of their own doctrine?

If they were, they would be stooping to the squalor of the murderer. Where the quality of the crime sets the limits of just methods of punishment, as it will if we attempt to give exact and literal implementation to *lex talionis,* society will find itself descending to the cruelties and savagery that criminals employ. What is worse, society would be deliberately authorizing such acts, in the cool light of reason, and not (as is usually true of vicious criminals) impulsively or in hatred and anger or with an insane or unbalanced mind. Moral constraints, in short, prohibit us from trying to make executions perfectly retributive. Once we grant that such constraints are proper, it is unreasonable to insist that the principle of "a life for a life" nevertheless by itself justifies the execution of murderers. . . .

As the French writer Albert Camus once remarked:

> For there to be an equivalence, the death penalty would have to punish a criminal who had warned his victim of the date at which he would inflict a horrible death on him and who, from that moment onward, had confined him at his mercy for months. Such a monster is not encountered in private life.[6]

Differential Severity Does Not Require Executions

What, then, emerges from our examination of retributive justice and the death penalty? If retributive justice is thought to consist in *lex talionis,* all one can say is that this principle has never exercised more than a crude and indirect effect on the actual punishments meted out by society. Other moral principles interfere with a literal and single-minded application of this one. Some homicides seem improperly punished by death at all; others would require methods of execution too horrible to inflict. . . .

But retributive justice need not be identified with *lex talionis.* One may reject that principle as too crude and still embrace the retributive principle that the severity of punishments should be graded according to the gravity of the offense. Even though one need not claim that life imprisonment (or any kind of punishment other than death) "fits" the crime of murder, one can claim that this punishment is the proper one for murder. To do this, the schedule of punishments accepted by society must be arranged so that this mode of imprisonment is the most severe penalty used. Opponents of the death penalty can embrace this principle of retributive justice, even though they must reject a literal *lex talionis.*

Equal Justice and Capital Punishment

During the past generation, the strongest practical objection to the death penalty has been the inequity with which it has been applied. As the late Supreme Court Justice William O. Douglas once observed, "One searches our chronicles in vain for the execution of any member of the affluent strata of the society." One does not search our chronicles in vain for the crime of murder committed by the affluent. All the sociological evidence points to the conclusion that the death penalty is the poor man's justice; hence the slogan, "Those without the capital get punishment." The death penalty is also racially sensitive. . . .

Let us suppose that the factual basis for such a criticism is sound. What follows for the morality of capital punishment? Many defenders of the death penalty have been quick to point out that since there is nothing intrinsic about the crime of murder or rape dictating that only the poor or only racial-minority males will commit it, and since there is nothing overtly racist about the statutes that authorize the death penalty for murder or rape, capital punishment itself is hardly at fault if in practice it falls with unfair impact on the poor and the black. There is, in short, nothing in the death penalty that requires it to be applied unfairly and with arbitrary or discriminatory results. At worst such results stem from defects in the system of administering criminal justice. . . .

We can look at these statistics in another way to illustrate the same point. If we could be assured that the nearly four thousand persons executed were the worst of the bad, repeated offenders impossible to incarcerate safely (much less to rehabilitate), the most dangerous murderers in captivity—the ones who had killed more than once and were likely to kill again, and the least likely to be confined in prison without chronic danger to other inmates and the staff—then one might accept half a million murders and a few thousand executions with a sense that rough justice had been done. But the truth is otherwise. Persons are sentenced to death and executed not because they have been found to be uncontrollably violent or hopelessly poor risks for safe confinement and release. Instead, they are executed because at trial they had a poor defense (inexperienced or overworked counsel); they had no funds to bring sympathetic witnesses to court; they are transients or strangers in the community where they are tried; the prosecuting attorney wanted the publicity that goes with "sending a killer to the chair"; there were no funds for an appeal or for a transcript of the trial record; they are members of a despised racial or political minority. In short, the actual study of why particular persons have been sentenced to death and executed does not show any careful winnowing of the worst from the bad. It shows that those executed were usually the unlucky victims of prejudice and discrimination, the losers in an arbitrary lottery that could just as well have spared them, the victims of the disadvantages that almost always go with poverty. A system like this does not enhance human life; it cheapens and degrades it. However heinous murder and other crimes are, the system of capital punishment does not compensate for or erase those crimes. It tends only to add new injuries of its own to the catalogue of human brutality.

VI. CONCLUSION

Our discussion of the death penalty from the moral point of view shows that there is no one moral principle that has paramount validity and that decisively favors one side of the controversy. Rather, we have seen how it is possible to argue either for or against the death penalty, and in each case to be appealing to moral principles that derive from the worth, value, or dignity of human life. . . .

My own view of the controversy is that, given the moral principles identified in the course of our discussion (including the overriding value of human life), and given all the facts about capital punishment, the balance of reasons favors abolition of the death penalty. The alternative to capital punishment that I favor, as things currently stand, is long-term imprisonment. Such a punishment is retributive and can be made more or less severe to reflect the gravity of the crime. It gives adequate (though hardly perfect) protection to the public. It is free of the worst defect to which the death penalty is liable: execution of the innocent. It tacitly acknowledges that there is no way for a criminal, alive or dead, to make complete amends for murder or other grave crimes against the person. Last but not least, long-term imprisonment has symbolic significance. The death penalty, more than any other kind of killing, is done by officials in the name of society and on its behalf. Each of us, therefore, has a hand in such killings. Unless they are absolutely necessary they cannot be justified. Thus, abolishing the death penalty represents extending the hand of life even to those who by their crimes have "forfeited" any right to live. A penal policy limiting the severity of punishment to long-term incarceration acknowledges that we must abandon the folly and pretense of attempting to secure perfect justice in an imperfect world. . . .

NOTES

1. W. D. Ross, *The Right and the Good.* Oxford: Clarendon Press, 1930, pp. 60–61.
2. John Locke, *Second Treatise of Government* (1690), §23, §172.
3. Immanuel Kant, *The Metaphysical Elements of Justice* (1797), Indianapolis, Ind.: Bobbs-Merrill (1965), translated by John Ladd, p. 102.
4. Ibid., p. 100.
5. Ibid., p. 101.
6. Albert Camus, *Resistance, Rebellion, and Death.* New York: Knopf, 1961, p. 199.

Discussion Questions

1. Bedau maintains that the forfeiture-of-rights argument is problematic because it can be used to justify the death penalty for almost any crime. Do you agree with Bedau? Use the execution of Socrates to illustrate your answer.

2. Bedau claims that Kant's criteria for determining a murderer's "state of mind" at the time of the crime are too ambiguous to be of much practical use. Do you agree? Make up a list of criteria that a judge or jury might use in determining if a murderer should be held morally blameworthy. Make a list of criteria that a judge or jury might use in determining if a murderer should get the death penalty. Are the two lists the same? Discuss why or why not.
3. Compare and contrast the arguments of Bedau and van den Haag regarding the morality of capital punishment. Which person presents the most compelling argument? Support your answer.
4. In his *Philosophy of Law,* Kant argues that "even if a civil society were to dissolve itself by common agreement of all its members . . . the last murderer remaining in prison must first be executed, so that everyone will duly receive what his actions are worth . . ." What if a society were dissolved, not by common agreement, but because of a natural disaster that led to the collapse of the government and, with it, the penal system. Discuss whether Bedau would permit the death penalty in situations in which there is no other effective means of incapacitating dangerous criminals.

JEFFREY REIMAN

Why the Death Penalty Should Be Abolished in the United States

Jeffrey Reiman is a professor of philosophy at American University. In this selection from his essay "Why the Death Penalty Should be Abolished," Reiman analyzes the retributivist argument for the death penalty. He concludes that one can accept retributivism, as well as the claim that the murderers deserve to die for their offense, without accepting the claim that murderers ought to receive the death penalty. Instead there are forms of punishment that are both less harsh and less morally questionable that satisfy the requirements of retributivism, justice, and deterrence.

Critical Reading Questions

1. What are the two arguments used by advocates of the death penalty?
2. What does Reiman mean when he says the "desert creates a *right to punish,* not a duty to do so"?
3. What is the standard problem confronting those who justify retributivism?

Jeffrey Reiman, "Why the Death Penalty Should Be Abolished," from Louis P. Pojman and Jeffrey Reiman, *The Death Penalty: For and Against* (Lanham, MD: Rowman & Littlefield Publishers, Inc., 1998), from pages 67, 87–100.

4. What is the "retributivist principle," and how is it related to the justice of *lex talionis*?
5. What is the relationship between *lex talionis* and the Golden Rule?
6. What is the Hegelian approach to retributivism? How does it differ from the utilitarian view of retributivism?
7. What is the Kantian approach to retributivism? What is the role of reason and will in Kant's approach? What is Kant's view of the Golden Rule?
8. What conclusion does Reiman draw about retributive justice from the Hegelian and Kantian approaches?
9. Why is it important to figure out what penalties are equivalent to the crimes?
10. According to Reiman, when is the desire for revenge rational?
11. Why is acceptance of the retributivist principle, and the question of the exacting a particular type of punishment, two different questions?
12. According to Reiman, what types of punishment are monstrous and unacceptable?
13. Who has the right to punish in a civil state?
14. How does Reiman determine the top and the bottom of the range of acceptable punishment? What is the role of deterrence in setting these limits?
15. How does "proportional retributivism" modify the requirements of *lex talionis*? What are the implications of this modification for the use of the death penalty as punishment?

Death penalty advocates commonly press two claims in favor of executing murderers. The first is that the death penalty is a just punishment for murder, a murderer's just deserts. On this line of thought, we do injustice to the victims of murder if we do not execute their murderers. The second claim is that the death penalty is necessary to deter potential murderers. Here, the suggestion is that we do injustice to potential victims of murder if we do not execute actual ones. I accept that the death penalty is a just punishment for some murders—some murderers' just deserts—and that, if the death penalty were needed to deter future murders, it would be unjust to future victims not to impose it. Notice, then, that I accept two of the strongest points urged in favor of the death penalty. If, granting these strong points, I can show that it would still be wrong to impose the death penalty, that should be a strong argument indeed. . . .

DEATH AND DESERT

In this section, I aim to show that execution is justly deserved punishment for some murders, *as a step toward arguing that it is not unjust to punish murder less harshly*. Note, then, that the fact that a punishment is justly deserved does not, in my view, entail that someone has a duty to impose that punishment. Rather, I shall argue in this section that desert creates *a right to punish,* not a duty to do so. To prepare the ground for this argument, I present here three commonplace observations that support the view that desert does not entail a duty to give what is deserved: First, the victim of an offense has the moral right to forgive the offending party rather than punish him though he deserves to be punished; second, we have no duty (not even a prima facie duty) to torture torturers even if they deserve to be tortured; and third, though great benefactors of humanity deserve to be rewarded, no one necessarily has a duty to provide that reward. At most, there is a very weak and easily overridden duty to provide the reward. On the other hand, I will claim that, when the state punishes a criminal, the state has a duty to punish in a way that does not trivialize the harm suffered by the criminal's victim. However, we shall see that this duty is compatible with administering punishment that is less than the full amount deserved. . . .

1. Retributivism, *Lex Talionis,* and Just Desert

There is nothing self-evident about the justice of the *lex talionis* or, for that matter, of retributivism.[1] The standard problem confronting those who would justify retributivism is that of overcoming the suspicion that it does no more than sanctify the victim's desire to hurt the offender back. Since serving that desire amounts to hurting the offender simply for the satisfaction that the victim derives from seeing the offender suffer, and since deriving satisfaction from the suffering of others seems primitive, the policy of imposing suffering on the offender for no other purpose than giving satisfaction to his victim seems primitive as well. Consequently, defending retributivism requires showing that the suffering imposed on the wrongdoer has some worthy point beyond the satisfaction of victims. In what follows, I shall try to identify a proposition—which I call the *retributivist principle*—that I take to be the nerve of retributivism. I think this principle accounts for the justice of the *lex talionis* and indicates the point of the suffering demanded by retributivism. . . .

I think that we can see the justice of the *lex talionis* by focusing on the striking affinity between it and the Golden Rule. The Golden Rule mandates, "Do unto others as you would have others do unto you," while the *lex talionis* counsels, "Do unto others as they have done unto you." It would not be too far-fetched to say that the *lex talionis* is the law enforcement arm of the Golden Rule, at least in the sense that if people were actually treated as they treated others, then everyone would necessarily follow the Golden Rule, because then people could only willingly act toward others as they were willing to have others act toward them. This is not to suggest that the *lex talionis* follows from the Golden Rule, but rather that the two share a common moral inspiration: the equality of persons. Treating others as you *would* have them treat you means treating others as equal to you, because it implies that you count their suffering to be as great a calamity as your own suffering, that you count your right to impose suffering on them as no greater than their right to impose suffering on you, and so on. The notion of the equality of persons leads to the *lex talionis* by two approaches that start from different points and converge.

I call the first approach "Hegelian" because Hegel held (roughly) that crime upsets the equality among persons and that retributive punishment restores that equality by "annulling" the crime.[2] As we have seen, acting according to the Golden Rule implies treating others as your equals. Conversely, violating the Golden Rule implies the reverse: Doing to another what you would *not* have that other do to you violates the equality of persons by asserting a right toward the other that the other does not possess toward you. Doing back to you what you did "annuls" your violation by reasserting that the other has the same right toward you that you assert toward him. Punishment according to the *lex talionis* cannot heal the injury that the other has suffered at your hands; rather, it rectifies the indignity he has suffered, by restoring him to equality with you.

This Hegelian account of retributivism provides us with a nonutilitarian conception of crime and punishment. This is so because "equality of persons" here does not mean equality of concern for their happiness, as it might for a utilitarian. On a utilitarian understanding of equality, imposing suffering on a wrongdoer equivalent to the suffering she has imposed would have little point (unless such suffering were exactly what was needed to deter future would-be offenders). Rather, equality of concern for people's happiness would lead us to impose as little suffering on the wrongdoer as is compatible with promoting the happiness of others. Instead of seeing morality as administering doses of happiness to individual recipients, the Hegelian retributivist envisions morality as maintaining the relations appropriate to equally sovereign individuals.[3] . . . The victim (or his representative, the state) . . . has the right to rectify this loss of standing relative to the criminal by meting out a punishment that reduces the criminal's sovereignty to the degree to which she vaunted it above her victim's. It might be thought that this is a duty, not just a right, but that is surely too much. The victim has the right to forgive the violator without imposing punishment. This suggests that it is by virtue of having the right to punish the violator—having authority over the violator's fate equivalent to the authority over the victim's fate that the violator wrongly took—rather than having the duty to punish the violator, that the victim's equality with the violator is restored.

I call the second approach "Kantian" because Kant held (roughly) that, since reason (like justice) is no respecter of the sheer difference among individuals, when a rational being decides to act in a certain way toward his fellows, he implicitly authorizes similar action by his fellows toward him.[4] A version of the Golden Rule, then, is a requirement of reason: Acting rationally, one always acts as he would have others act toward him.[5] Consequently, to act toward a person as he has acted toward others is to treat him as a rational being, that is, as if his act were the product of a rational decision. From this, it may be concluded that we have a duty to do to offenders what they have done, since this amounts to according them the respect due rational beings. And Kant asserts as much.[6] Here, too, however, the assertion of a duty to punish seems excessive, since, if this duty arose because doing to people what they have done to others is necessary to accord them the respect due rational beings, then we would have a duty to do to all rational persons *everything*—good, bad, or indifferent—that they do to others. The point, rather, is that, by his acts, a rational being *authorizes* others to do the same to him; he doesn't *compel* them to. Here, again, the argument leads to a right, rather than a duty, to exact the *lex talionis*. It should be clear that the Kantian argument, like the Hegelian one, rests on the equality of persons. A rational agent implicitly authorizes having done to him action similar to what he has done to another only if he and the other are similar in the relevant ways.

The Hegelian and Kantian approaches arrive at the same destination from opposite sides. . . . Taken together, these approaches support the following proposition: *The equality and rationality of persons imply that an offender deserves, and his victim has the right to impose on him, suffering equal to that which he imposed on the victim.* This is the proposition I call the *retributivist principle.* This principle provides that the *lex talionis* is the criminal's just desert and the victim's—or, as her representative, the state's—right. . . .

I do not contend that it is easy or even always possible to figure out what penalties are equivalent to the harms imposed by offenders. Hugo Bedau, for example, has observed that, apart from murder and possibly some other crimes against the person, "we have no clear intuitions at all about what such equivalences consist in."[7] Even if this is so, however, it is still worth knowing what the criterion of deserved punishment is. . . . [K]nowing what criminals deserve according to *lex talionis* gives us something at which to aim, a target in light of which we might eventually sharpen our intuitions.

When I say that, with respect to the criminal, the point of retributive punishment is to impress upon him his equality with his victim, I mean to be understood quite literally. If the sentence is just and the criminal rational, then the punishment should normally *force* upon him recognition of his equality with his victim, recognition of their shared vulnerability to suffering and their shared desire to avoid it, as well as recognition of the fact that he counts for no more than his victim in the eyes of their fellows. For this reason, the retributivist requires that the offender be sane not only at the moment of his crime, but also at the moment of his punishment—while this latter requirement would be largely pointless (if not downright malevolent) to a utilitarian. Incidentally, it is, I believe, the desire that the offender be forced by suffering punishment to recognize his equality with his victim, rather than the desire for that suffering itself, that constitutes what is rational in the desire for revenge. . . .

It seems, then, reasonable to take the equality and rationality of persons as implying moral desert in the way asserted in the retributivist principle. I shall assume henceforth that the retributivist principle is true.

2. The Top and the Bottom End of the Range of Just Punishments

The truth of the retributivist principle establishes that *lex talionis* is the offender's just desert; but, since it establishes this as a right of the victim rather than the victim's duty, it does not settle the question of whether or to what extent the victim or the state ought to exercise this right and exact the *lex talionis*. This is a separate moral question because strict adherence to the *lex talionis* amounts to allowing criminals, even the most barbaric of them, to dictate our punishing behavior. . . . It seems certain that there are at least some crimes, such as rape or torture, that we ought not to try to match. And this is not merely a matter of imposing an alternative punishment that produces an equivalent amount of suffering, as, say, some number of years in prison that might "add up" to the harm caused by a rapist or a torturer. Even if no amount of time in prison would add up to the harm caused by a torturer, it still seems that we ought not to torture him even if this were the only way of making him suffer as much as he has made his victim suffer. Or consider someone who has committed several murders in cold blood. On the *lex talionis,* it would seem that such a criminal might justly be brought to within an inch of death and then revived (or to within a moment of execution and then reprieved) as many times as he has killed (minus one), and then finally executed. But surely this is a degree of cruelty that would be monstrous.

Since the retributivist principle establishes the *lex talionis* as the victim's right, it might seem that the question of how far this right should be exercised is "up to the victim." Indeed, this would be the case in the state of nature. But once, for all the good reasons familiar to readers of Locke, the state comes into existence, public punishment replaces private, and the victim's right to punish reposes in the state. With this, the decision as to how far to exercise this right goes to the state as well. . . .

I suspect that it will be widely agreed that the state ought not to administer punishments of the sort described above even if required by the letter of the *lex talionis* and that, thus, even granting the justice of *lex talionis,* there are occasions on which it is morally appropriate to diverge from its requirements. . . .

The implication of the notion that justice permits us to avoid extremely cruel punishments is that there is a range of just punishments that includes some that are just though they exact less than the full measure of the *lex talionis.* What are the top and bottom ends of this range? . . . [A]ll punishments within the range of just punishments must be sufficient to deter rational people generally from the crime in question. Assume, then, for purposes of simplicity, that we are trying to identify the range of just punishments from within a series of punishments of increasing harshness all of which suffice to provide adequate deterrence.

Within this series of punishments, the top end of the range of just punishments is given by *lex talionis,* and the bottom end is, in a way, as well. Based on the argument of the previous section, the top end, the point after which more or harsher punishment is undeserved and thus unjust, is reached when we impose a punishment that is equivalent to the harm caused by the criminal (including both the harm done to his immediate victim and the harm done to the law-abiding by his unfair taking of advantage). As for the bottom end, recall that, if the retributivist principle is true, then denying that the offender deserves suffering equal to that which she imposed amounts to denying the equality and rationality of persons. From this, it follows that we fall below the bottom end of the range of just punishments when we act in ways that are incompatible with the *lex talionis* at the top end. We do injustice to the victim when we treat the offender in a way that is no longer compatible with sincerely believing that she deserves to have done to her what she has done to her victim. In this way, the range of just punishments remains faithful to the victim's right.

This way of understanding just punishment enables us to formulate proportional retributivism so that it is compatible with acknowledging the justice of the *lex talionis.* If we take the *lex talionis* to spell out the offender's just desert, and if other moral considerations require us to refrain from matching the injury caused by the offender while still allowing us to punish justly, then surely we impose just punishment if we impose the closest morally acceptable approximation to the *lex talionis.* Proportional retributivism, then, in requiring that the worst crime be punished by the society's worst punishment and so on, could be understood as translating the offender's just desert into its nearest equivalent in the society's table of morally acceptable punishments. Then, the two versions of retributivism (*lex talionis* and proportional) are related in that the first states what just punishment would be if nothing but the offender's just desert mattered and the second locates just punishment at the meeting point of the offender's just desert and the society's moral scruples.

Inasmuch as proportional retributivism modifies the requirements of the *lex talionis* only in light of other moral considerations, it is compatible with believing that the *lex talionis* spells out the offender's just desert, much in the way that modifying the obligations of promisers in light of other moral considerations is compatible with believing in the binding nature of promises. That a person is justified in failing to keep a promised appointment because she acted to save a life is compatible with still believing that promises are binding. So, too, justifiably doing less than *lex talionis* requires in order to avoid cruelty is compatible with believing that offenders still deserve what *lex talionis* would impose.

Proportional retributivism so formulated preserves the point of retributivism and remains faithful to the victim's right that is its source. Since it punishes with the closest morally acceptable approximation to the *lex talionis,* it effectively says to the offender: You deserved the equivalent of what you did to your victim, and you are getting less only to the degree that our moral scruples limit us from duplicating what you have done. Such punishment, then, affirms the equality of persons by respecting, *as far as seems morally permissible,* the victim's right to impose suffering on the offender equal to what she received, and it affirms the rationality of the offender by treating him as authorizing others to do to him what he has done, though they take him up on it only *as far as it seems to them morally permissible.* Needless to say, the alternative punishments must in some convincing way be comparable in gravity to the crimes that they punish, or else they will trivialize the harms those crimes caused and be no longer compatible with sincerely believing that the offender deserves to have done to him what he has done to his victim and no longer capable of impressing upon the criminal his equality with the victim. . . .

To sum up: When, because we are simply unable to duplicate the criminal's offense, we modify the *lex talionis* to call for imposing on the offender as nearly as possible what he has done, we are still at the top end of punishment justified via *lex talionis,* modifying the *lex talionis* only for reasons of practical possibility. When, because of our own moral scruples, we do less than this, we still act justly as long as we punish in a way that is compatible with sincerely believing that the offender deserves the full measure of the *lex talionis.* If this is true, then it is not unjust to spare murderers as long as they can be punished in some other suitably grave way. For example, a natural life sentence with no chance of parole might be a civilized equivalent of the death penalty—after all, people sentenced to life imprisonment have traditionally been regarded as "civilly dead."[8]

It might be objected that no punishment short of death will serve the point of retributivism with respect to murderers because no punishment short of death is commensurate with the crime of murder. For, while some number of years of imprisonment may add up to the amount of harm done by rapists or assaulters or torturers, no number of years will add up to the harm done to the victim of murder. But justified divergence from the *lex talionis* is not limited only to changing the form of punishment while maintaining equivalent severity. . . . If justice allows us to refrain from these penalties, then justice allows punishments that are not equal in suffering to their crimes. It seems to me that if the objector grants this much, then she must show that a punishment less than death is not merely incommensurate to the harm caused by murder, but so far out of proportion to that harm that it trivializes the harm and thus effectively denies the equality and rationality of persons. . . .

I take it, then, that the justice of the *lex talionis* implies that it is just to execute murderers, but not that it is unjust to spare them as long as they are systematically punished in some other suitably grave way—and as long as the deterrence requirement can be satisfied. . . .

NOTES

1. "[T]o say 'it is fitting' or 'justice demands' that the guilty should suffer is only to affirm that punishment is right, not to give grounds for thinking so" (Stanley I. Benn, "Punishment," *The Encyclopedia of Philosophy,* ed. Paul Edwards [New York: Macmillan, 1967], vol. 7, p. 30).

2. "The sole positive existence which the injury [i.e., the crime] possesses is that it is the particular will of the criminal [i.e., it is the criminal's intention that distinguishes criminal injury from, say, injury due to an accident]. Hence to injure (or penalize) this particular will as a will determinately existent is to annul the crime, which otherwise would have been held valid, and to restore the right" (G. W. F. Hegel, *The Philosophy of Right,* trans. T. M. Knox [Oxford: Clarendon Press, 1962; originally published 1821], 69).
3. For this reason, I think this account of crime and punishment is especially appropriate to a liberal moral theory, and I have defended it as such. See my *Justice and Modern Moral Philosophy* (New Haven, CT: Yale University Press, 1990), 187–99, 306–07; and my *Critical Moral Liberalism: Theory and Practice* (Lanham, MD: Rowman & Littlefield, 1997), 235–70, esp. 240.
4. According to Kant, "any undeserved evil that you inflict on someone else among the people is one that you do to yourself. If you vilify him, you vilify yourself; if you steal from him, you steal from yourself; if you kill him, you kill yourself." Since Kant held that "[i]f what happens to someone is also willed by him, it cannot be a punishment," he took pains to distance himself from the view that the offender *wills* his punishment. "The chief error contained in this sophistry," Kant wrote, "consists in the confusion of the criminal's [i.e., the murderer's] own judgment (which one must necessarily attribute to his reason) that he must forfeit his life with a resolution of the will to take his own life" (Kant, "Metaphysical Elements of Justice," 101, 105–106).
5. Cf. Kant, *Grounding for the Metaphysics of Morals,* 37n. Kant thinks that the Golden Rule, as commonly stated, places too much emphasis on what an agent *wants,* rather than on what he rationally endorses. Nonetheless, Kant affirms that the Golden Rule is derived from his own central moral principle, the categorical imperative.
6. "Even if a civil society were to dissolve itself by common agreement of all its members . . . , the last murderer remaining in prison must first be executed, so that everyone will duly receive what his actions are worth" (Kant, Metaphysical Elements of Justice," 102).
7. Hugo Bedau, personal correspondence to author.
8. I am indebted to my colleague Robert Johnson for this suggestion. Prisoners condemned to spend their entire lives in prison, Johnson writes, "experience a permanent civil death, the death of freedom. The prison is their cemetery, a 6′ by 9′ cell their tomb. Interred in the name of justice, they are consigned to mark the passage of their lives in the prison's peculiar dead time, which serves no larger human purpose and yields few rewards. In effect, they give their civil lives in return for the natural lives they have taken" (Robert Johnson, *Death Work: A Study of the Modern Execution Process* [Belmont, CA: Wadsworth Publishing, 1990], 158).

Discussion Questions

1. Discuss how Morris would most likely respond to Reiman's claim that the principle of retributivism does not require the death penalty for murder. Which person presents the stronger argument? Support your answer.
2. Break down Reiman's article into its premises and conclusion. Are his premises sound? Eliminate any false or weak premises. Does the conclusion logically follow from the remaining premises, or does the conclusion go beyond the premises? Support your answer.

3. Should an exception in the use of the death penalty be made for terrorists who kill hundreds of people? Discuss how Reiman would most likely handle cases of international terrorism.
4. One of Reiman's premises is that all people are moral equals. However, in practice, certain groups of people are denied full and equal rights and have been morally degraded by social practices and attitudes. This inequality is reflected in the greater likelihood that blacks and people from disadvantaged backgrounds will end up in prison. Discuss whether prejudice and lack of social and economic equality should be taken into consideration in determining the top and bottom of the range of punishment in a particular case since the criminal from a disadvantaged background has started from an unequal moral status. How might Reiman most likely respond to this question?
5. Read the quote from lawyer Clarence Darrow in question 4 on page 253. Role-play a conversation between Reiman and Darrow regarding Darrow's claim that criminals are simply products of their environment.
6. Examine how the principle of retributivism, as explicated by Reiman, would apply to children and teenagers that kill. For example, should the boys responsible for the Columbine High School killings, had they lived, received the same punishment as an adult would receive? Support your answer.

HELEN PREJEAN

Dead Man Walking

Helen Prejean is a member of the Sisters of St. Joseph of Medaille in Louisiana. Through her work with inner-city residents in New Orleans, she became involved in ministry to death row inmates at the Louisiana State Prison in Angola. Prejean is also founder of *Survive,* a victims' advocacy group. Prejean, who is opposed to the death penalty, relies primarily on narrative and consciousness-raising to make her argument. Rather than appeal to our sense of justice, as do van den Haag, and Bedau to a lesser extent, Prejean instead appeals to our sense of care and empathy. By inviting us to share in her experiences as a spiritual adviser to prisoners on death row, Prejean seeks to enhance our moral sensitivity to the brutality of capital punishment as well as to raise our collective consciousness about the issue. Her vivid account of the suffering of all the participants as well as her description of an actual execution serves to break down our resistance by forcing us to question our worldviews about capital punishment.

Dead Man Walking (New York: Vintage Books, 1993).

Critical Reading Questions

1. Why does Prejean argue that capital punishment by electrocution is cruel, rather than a painless "euthanasia by electrocution"?
2. What are some types of suffering experienced by prisoners on death row?
3. On what grounds does Prejean argue that rage and grief experienced by the family and friends of a murder victim do not justify the death penalty?
4. Why does Prejean oppose giving the government the power to execute murderers?
5. According to Prejean, why do executioners prefer to remain anonymous?
6. On what grounds does Prejean reject the argument, used by some Christians, that retaliation and the death penalty are consistent with biblical teachings?
7. What is Prejean's position on the use of long-term imprisonment to incapacitate violent criminals?
8. According to Prejean, is the public's fear of crime realistic? What fuels this fear?
9. What utilitarian arguments does Prejean use against capital punishment?
10. Does Prejean believe in retribution and punishment?
11. How does Prejean respond to the grief and desire for retribution felt by the families and friends of murder victims? Does she sympathize with the families, or does she feel they are being unreasonable?
12. Why does Prejean maintain that capital punishment diminishes the crime victim and instead focuses attention on the murderer?
13. What is Gandhi's concept of *satyagraha*? Why were both Mohandas Gandhi and Martin Luther King Jr. opposed to the use of violence in response to violence?
14. In what ways is capital punishment costly to the American people? What are some of the steps proposed by Prejean to make Americans more aware of the violence and costliness of the death penalty?
15. Why is political commentator George Will in favor of capital punishment? How does Prejean respond to his arguments?
16. Why, according to Camus, are executions performed in secret?
17. What were the findings of Bedau and Radelet's study on capital punishment? How did van den Haag respond to these findings?

. . . Death by electrocution was introduced in the United States in 1890 at Auburn Prison in upstate New York, when William Kemmler was killed by the state of New York. The *New York Times* described the new method as "euthanasia by electricity," and the U.S. Supreme Court, upholding the state appellate court's decision that death by electricity was not cruel and unusual punishment, had concluded: "It is in easy reach of the electrical science at this day to so generate and apply to the person of the convict a current of electricity of such known and sufficient force as certainly to produce instantaneous and therefore painless death."

A reporter for the *New World* newspaper who witnessed Kemmler's execution reported:

"The current had been passing through his body for 15 seconds when the electrode at the head was removed. Suddenly the breast heaved. There was a straining at the straps which bound him. A purplish foam covered the lips and was spattered over the leather head band. The man was alive."

"Warden, physician, guards . . . everybody lost their wits. There was a startled cry for the current to be turned on again. . . . An odor of burning flesh and singed hair filled the room, for a moment, a blue flame played about the base of the victim's spine. This time the electricity flowed four minutes. . . ."

That was in 1890.

On October 16, 1985, the electrocution of William Vandiver by the state of Indiana took seventeen minutes, requiring five charges of electricity.

On April 22, 1983, as the state of Alabama electrocuted John Louis Evans, the first electrical charge burned through the electrode on the leg and the electrode fell off. The prison guards repaired it and administered another charge of electricity. Smoke and flame erupted from Evans's temple and leg but the man was still alive. Following the second jolt, Evans's lawyer demanded that Governor George C. Wallace halt the proceedings. The governor refused. Another jolt was administered. It took fourteen minutes for Evans to die. . . .

Later, in the months ahead, Patrick Sonnier will confide his terror to me of the death that awaits him, telling me of a recurring nightmare, always the same: the guards coming for him, dragging him screaming toward the chair, strapping him in with the wide leather straps, covering his face with the hood, and he is screaming, "No, no, no . . ." For him there can never again be restful, unbroken sleep, because the dream can always come. Better, he says, to take short naps and not to sink into deep sleep.

I cannot accept that the state now plans to kill Patrick Sonnier in cold blood. But the thought of the young victims haunts me. Why do I feel guilty when I think of them? Why do I feel as if I have murdered someone myself?

In prayer I sort it out.

I know that if I had been at the scene when the young people were abducted, I would have done all in my power to save them.

I know I feel compassion for their suffering parents and family and would do anything to ease their pain if I knew how. I also know that nothing can ease some pain.

I know I am trying to help people who are desperately poor, and I hope I can prevent some of them from exploding into violence. Here my conscience is clean and light. No heaviness, no guilt.

Then it comes to me. The victims are dead and the killer is alive and I am befriending the killer.

Have I betrayed his victims? Do I have to take sides? I am acutely aware that my beliefs about the death penalty have never been tested by personal loss. Let Mama or my sister, Mary Ann, or my brother, Louie, be brutally murdered and then see how much compassion I have. My magnanimity is gratuitous. No one has shot my loved ones in the back of the head.

If someone I love should be killed, I know I would feel rage, loss, grief, helplessness, perhaps for the rest of my life. It would be arrogant to think I can predict how I would respond to such a disaster. But Jesus Christ, whose way of life I try to follow, refused to meet hate with hate and violence with violence. I pray for the strength to be like him. I cannot believe in a God who metes out hurt for hurt, pain for pain, torture for torture. . . .

In sorting out my feelings and beliefs, there is, however, one piece of moral ground of which I am absolutely certain: if I were to be murdered I would not want my murderer executed. I would not want my death avenged. *Especially by government*—which can't be trusted to control its own bureaucrats or collect taxes equitably or fill a pothole, much less decide which of its citizens to kill.

Albert Camus' "Reflections on the Guillotine" is for me a moral compass on the issue of capital punishment. He wrote this essay in 1957 when the stench of Auschwitz was still in the air, and one of his cardinal points is that no government is ever innocent enough or wise enough or just enough to lay claim to so absolute a power as death.

> Society proceeds sovereignly to eliminate the evil ones from her midst as if she were virtue itself. . . . To assert, in any case, that a man must be absolutely cut off from society because he is absolutely evil amounts to saying that society is absolutely good, and no one in his right mind will believe this today.

I ask [Warden Phelps] to tell me about the execution process that he has designed, and he shows me a copy of Department Regulation Number 10–25, issued April 6, 1981. I glance at the document and notice headings: Purpose, Responsibility, Legal Authority, Incarceration Prior to Execution, Media Access, Time and Place of Execution . . .

"From a personal standpoint it is very, very bizarre to design a process like this," he says, "because you find yourself approaching an execution the same way you approach putting on a rodeo or any other special event." Before designing the process, he says, he made field trips to talk to corrections officials in other states that use the electric chair, and he engaged the services of an electrical engineer—"he worked for free, he refused to be paid"—to devote his attention to "the technical aspects of the apparatus."

Inwardly I translate the terms, *technical aspects of the apparatus,* and I think of how silent it was there in the room as the guard screwed the rubber-coated wire to the top of the metal cap on Pat's shaved head.

Setting up the "process," Phelps explains, involved hiring an executioner.

"We hired a man, an electrician, who filled out a civil service application for the job. Frank Blackburn, the warden at Angola at the time, interviewed the prospective candidate for the job in some depth because we obviously wanted somebody who was screwed down pretty tight and very, very firm in his convictions, not just someone with a morbid interest. We were looking for—this may sound strange—somebody professional. We didn't want a mafia-type executioner." . . . He agreed to be paid $400 per execution. It was a verbal agreement, not written.

I make a mental note of the anonymity of the executioner and the reluctance to sign a contract specifying fee for service. I log it alongside something that Phelps mentioned earlier: that the electrician who wired the chair refused to be paid—the intuitive recognition that this is "blood money," this is "death for hire."

The fact that anonymity is granted to the executioner intrigues me. I've heard that in Utah, when Gary Gilmore was executed by a firing squad, blanks were inserted into one of the rifles so that those firing the guns would not know for certain if they killed the man. No doubt, the uncertainty helps diffuse responsibility.

Phelps says that for him, the most "trouble-some" aspect of the "process" has been the selection of witnesses. With the resumption of executions, some victims' families asked if they might witness, and he says he "pondered" this a long time but "couldn't think of a reason why they shouldn't. Our position in the D.O.C. is that I am not the 'keeper of the morals' but merely the enforcer of the law, and if there is no legal reason barring a victim's family, I see no reason to deny them."

Phelps says that he emphasizes to all witnesses—victims' families included—that during an execution there must be "no emotional outbursts, no obscenities uttered, no undignified behavior of any kind." They have designed a process, he says, that "protects everyone's rights," including those of the one being executed. "They have a family too. A circus atmosphere is not in anyone's interest."

I am listening to all this and I keep picturing Pat's dead body in the chair, the fingers of his right hand curling upward, the doctor's light shining into vacant eyes.

I say that I disagree that the rights of the man being killed are protected because the witnesses to his death are expected to be polite.

"Pat Sonnier was tortured, Mr. Phelps," I say. "I'm not sure what he felt physically when the nineteen hundred volts hit him, but certainly he agonized emotionally and psychologically—preparing to die, anticipating it, dreaming about it. Amnesty International defines torture as an extreme physical and mental assault on a person who has been rendered defenseless. That is what happened to Patrick Sonnier, isn't it, Mr. Phelps? . . .

Yes, I cared for Patrick Sonnier. Despite his terrible crime, he was a human being and deserved to be treated with dignity and, yes, I was emotionally distraught watching him die. "Who wouldn't be," I ask [Warden Blackburn], "watching someone killed in such a cold, calculated way right in front of your eyes? You and the others are part of a process that shields you from natural, human emotions. The raw truth is that you're killing a fellow human being whose hands and feet are tied, and who wants to admit he's doing that?"

There is silence for a short moment, and then Blackburn says, "We can't let feelings dominate our actions or we couldn't carry out our responsibilities. . . .

I challenge him: "But you're a Christian, a minister in your church, a man who professes to follow the way of life that Jesus taught. Yet you are the one who, with a nod of your head, signals the executioner to kill a man. Do you really believe that Jesus, who taught us not to return hate for hate and evil for evil and whose dying words were, 'Father, forgive them,' would participate in these executions? Would Jesus pull the switch?" . . .

"Nope," he says, "I don't experience any contradiction with my Christianity. Never thought about it too much, really. Executions are the law, and Christians are supposed to observe the law, and that's that." And then he adds, "My wife, she's a good Christian woman, and she supports the death penalty, and believe me, you can't find a better Christian woman than my wife."

How is it, I wonder, that the mandate and example of Jesus, so clearly urging compassion and nonviolence, could so quickly become *accommodated?* Over the centuries "lawful authorities"—supposedly in God's name and with God's blessing—have hanged, shot, guillotined, drawn and quartered, burned, gassed, electrocuted, lethally injected—criminals. Over the years the crimes meriting death might change, but, for the most part, the blessing of God on retaliatory punishment has been unquestioned. Of course, those who justify retaliation can cite as authority numerous passages in the Bible, where divine vengeance is meted out to guilty and innocent alike: the Great Flood, the destruction of Sodom and Gomorrah, the slaying of the firstborn sons of the Egyptians (God's "lesson" to a recalcitrant Pharaoh), to mention just a few examples. Even the Pauline injunction "Vengeance is mine, says the Lord, I will repay" can be interpreted as a command and a promise—the command to restrain individual impulses toward revenge in exchange for the assurance that God will be only too pleased to handle the grievance—in spades. That God wants to "get even" like the rest of us does not seem to be in question.

One intractable problem, however, is that divine vengeance (barring natural disasters, so-called acts of God) can only be interpreted and exacted by human beings. *Very* human beings.

I can't accept that.

First, I can't accept that God has fits of rage and goes about trucking in retaliation. Second, I can't accept that any group of human beings is trustworthy enough to mete out so ultimate and irreversible a punishment as death. And, third, I can't accept that it's permissible to kill people provided you "prepare" them with good spiritual counsel to "meet their Maker." . . .

The swath of violence cut by Christians across the centuries is long and wide and bloodstained: inquisitions, crusades, witch burnings, persecutions of Jewish "Christ-killers." Now, in the last decade of the twentieth century, U.S. government officials kill citizens with dispatch with scarcely a murmur of resistance from the Christian citizenry. In fact, surveys of public opinion show that those who profess Christianity tend to favor capital punishment slightly more than the overall population—Catholics more than Protestants. True, in recent years leadership bodies of most Christian denominations have issued formal statements denouncing the death penalty, but generally that opposition has yet to be translated into aggressive pastoral initiatives to educate clergy and membership on capital punishment. And the U.S. Catholic Bishops in their "Statement on Capital Punishment," while strongly condemning the death penalty because of the "unfair and discriminatory" manner in which it is imposed, its continuance of the "cycle of violence," and its fundamental disregard for the "unique worth and dignity of each person," nevertheless uphold the "right" of the state to kill. But if we are to have a society which protects its citizens from torture and murder, then torture and murder must be off-limits to *everyone.* No one, for any reason, may be permitted to torture and kill—and that includes government. Before prisons existed, executions might have been justified as society's only means of defense against crazed, violent killers. But today in the United States, following the example of other modern industrialized countries, we can incapacitate violent criminals through long-term imprisonment. . . .

We know that one of the key issues we must address is the fear of crime which fuels the death penalty. Actually, the public (not by accident) has an exaggerated perception of the risk of felony-type murders (murders which occur in the course of another felony which may be punishable by death). The risk varies, of course, according to one's neighborhood—inner-city residents have *good* reason to fear felony-type murders—but nationwide, according to 1989 statistics, a very small percentage, 2.0 persons in 100,000, die of felony-type murders each year, roughly the same percentage as those who die from drowning or accidental poisoning. In contrast, the probability of dying in an automobile accident is 47.9 per 100,000, and the probability of dying from heart disease is 765.5 per 100,000. But the public's view of crime is largely shaped by the media, which are prone to emphasize death from violence while downplaying more prevalent and commonplace threats to life. . . .

I also point out that execution of a prisoner costs more than life imprisonment. That's because capital trials require more expert witnesses and more investigators, a longer jury-selection process (those who oppose the death penalty must be screened out), the expenses of sequestering a jury, not one but two trials because of the required separate sentencing trial, and appeals in state and federal courts. . . . In Florida, which may be typical, each death sentence is estimated to cost approximately $3.18 million, compared to the cost of life imprisonment (40 years) of about $516,000. Another reason for swollen costs is the added expense of incarcerating prisoners on death row. Most states segregate death-row prisoners in maximum security units and must hire additional security personnel. Nor are most death-row prisoners allowed to work, which prevents them from helping to pay for their upkeep.

Besides the expense there is also a "distortion cost" which capital trials and appellate proceedings impose on the court system. State supreme court judges in some death-penalty jurisdictions report that they spend a disproportionate amount of their judging time tending to capital punishment business.

To these utilitarian arguments I add others in these media interviews—that the death penalty is too selective and capricious to serve as a deterrent, that it is racially biased—but the argument I always save for last is this one: if we believe that murder is wrong and not admissible in our society, then it has to be wrong for everyone, not just individuals but governments as well. And I end by challenging people to ask themselves whether we can continue to allow the government, subject as it is to every imaginable form of inefficiency and corruption, to have such power to kill. . . .

It's my first time meeting people in the media. I notice how friendly many of them are. After the interviews I always shake hands and thank them for coming out, the reporters and the camera people too; and before the walk is over I have quite a collection of their personal cards, which I file so I can call on them in the future. Reflecting back after ten years, I realize now, even more than I did then, just how crucial the media are to public education on this issue, and I am struck by how many reporters and journalists become sympathetic to the cause of abolition once they become knowledgeable about the issue.

We walk in the sunshine. It's October, one of Louisiana's clearest, driest months. The sky is cobalt blue. The trees and grass are still mostly green, but the swamp maples have turned orange-red. It feels good to be walking out on the open road. Bill Quigley is at the head of the line, setting the pace. We'll do twenty-five miles each day. When people drop behind the crowd (people such as me, with short legs), a van picks us up and brings us to the front. That way we keep a brisk pace. Everybody's full of chatter. Some sing. . . .

Many people, barreling along the highway, energetically signal their response to our cause: they put thumbs down; they flip us the middle finger; they shout "Fry the bastards"; they call us "bleeding-heart liberals"; they call us "commies." But every now and then we hear a horn and see a thumb up, and we all wave and cheer. . . .

For three days we walk.

We arrive in Baton Rouge as the sun is setting. The darkness is fast descending and streetlights have come on and give a furry amber glow. As we approach the capitol steps we spot a small group holding up posterboard signs. Supporters coming to join us for the rally? Getting closer, we can make out what the signs say: "What about the victims?" "Justice, *even* for victims." It's a counter-demonstration group. How will we deal with them? Ignore them? Talk to them? The steering committee huddles. We decide to send a couple of people on a "peacekeeping" mission.

We hold the rally. The press gives us good coverage. The "peacekeeping" mission is successful, and we are not interrupted by the counter-demonstrators. . . .

I wonder what will ever be able to heal the Harveys' pain and bring them peace. No, there is no replacing the unique universe of Faith Hathaway. Even if Robert Willie is destroyed, the aching void can never be filled.

I understand the Harveys' desire for retribution. Their lives have been violated by Robert Willie and they want to see him punished. They want to see him made accountable for his actions. They want to see him pay for what he did. So did I. In an ideal world, there would be no need for retribution. But in real societies, punishing the guilty is as integral to the function of law as exonerating the innocent and preventing crime.

Susan Jacoby, in her insightful book *Wild Justice: The Evolution of Revenge,* maintains, and I agree, that the retribution which society metes out should be *measured.* Her objection to capital punishment is that such "eye-for-an-eye" retribution is as excessive as the original crime it punishes. But she also finds it excessive that those convicted of so heinous and irrevocable a crime as murder should be made to serve only a few short years in prison. The Bureau of Justice Statistics reveals that in 1986 the average amount of time served on a life sentence in the United States was six years, nine months.

Jacoby holds that the public's desire to see serious punishment consistently meted out for serious crimes is legitimate and that to ignore it encourages "the boundless outrage that generates demands for boundless retribution." But she says that punishment should be tempered: . . .

Such measured retribution is attained, I believe, by sentencing which requires *nonnegotiable* long-term imprisonment for first-degree murder (also termed *aggravated* or *capital* murder). At least forty states in recent years have revised criminal codes to require life without parole or lengthy mandatory minimum years served for convictions they deem most serious. In a growing number of states—twenty-five as of 1992, including Louisiana—life-without-parole sentences are *true* life sentences. . . .

This evening's encounter with the Harveys has to count as one of the most painful of my life. Never have I met such unrequited grief. What, I wonder, can I possibly do to ease their pain? I am out of my depth. Driving across these dark waters of Lake Pontchartrain, I realize how vulnerable we all are. Faith Hathaway—dead. Loretta Bourque—dead. David LeBlanc—dead. Children snatched from their parents in the night. I think of my sister, Mary Ann. I think of Mama. I think of Mary Ann and Charlie's five children, especially Helen, my namesake. I think of Julie and Marcy, my brother Louie's little girls. When I get home I will telephone Mama. I want to hear that everyone is safe.

This Robert Willie, who is he? I recoil at the thought of him. How dare he calmly read law books and concoct arguments in his defense? He should fall on his knees, weeping, begging forgiveness from these parents. He should spend every moment of his life repenting his heinous deed. But, judging from my first visit, he seems to be in a world of his own, oblivious to the pain he has caused others. . . . *Someone is trying to kill him,* and this must rivet his energies on his own survival, not the pain of others.

My hope for the Harveys is that eventually they will be able to overcome their terrible grief and once again live positive lives. How I can help them I am not sure, but I want to try. And Robert Willie? What can I possibly do for him? I will do what Millard Farmer asked me to do—accompany him, treat him with dignity—but I will also challenge him to take responsibility for his crime and to ask forgiveness of the Harveys.

Emotionally it's confusing to think of the Harveys and their needs alongside Robert Willie and his. Hearing the details of Faith's vicious murder, I find myself sucked into the Harveys' rage. But then I think of the death the state has in store for Robert Willie.

A few days after visiting the Harveys I visit Robert for the second time. I have a notebook on the front seat of the car. I'm not allowed to take it into the prison (only attorneys and news reporters can bring writing materials inside), but afterward I'll jot down notes from our conversation. I'm much more alert now than I was with Pat Sonnier. When the Pardon

Board hearing comes up, facts about Robert's family life and background will be important. I feel that there isn't much time.

Robert comes into the visiting room. He is wearing a black knitted hat. He walks with a little bounce, poising momentarily on the balls of his feet. I dispense with preliminaries.

"I went to visit the Harveys," I say. "They told me about Faith's death. Robert, you raped and stabbed that girl and left her to rot in the woods. Why?" . . .

Unfortunately, the exercise of power practiced by Christians in alliance with the Roman Empire—with its unabashed allegiance to the sword—soon bore no resemblance to the purely moral persuasion that Jesus had taught.

In the fifth century, . . . Augustine provided the theological rationale the church needed to justify the use of violence by church and state governments. Augustine persuaded church authorities that "original sin" so damaged every person's ability to make moral choices that external control by church and state authorities over people's lives was necessary and justified. The "wicked" might be "coerced by the sword" to "protect the innocent," Augustine taught. And thus was legitimated for Christians the authority of secular government to "control" its subjects by coercive and violent means—even punishment by death.

In the latter part of this century, however, two flares of hope—Mohandas K. Gandhi and Martin Luther King—have demonstrated that Jesus' counsel to practice compassion and tolerance even toward one's enemies can effect social change. Susan Jacoby, analyzing the moral power that Gandhi and King unleashed in their campaigns for social justice, finds a unique form of aggression:

"'If everyone took an eye for an eye,' Gandhi said, 'the whole world would be blind.' But Gandhi did not want to take anyone's eye; he wanted to force the British out of India . . ."

> The writings of both men are filled with references to love as a powerful force against oppression, and while the two leaders were not using the term "force" in the military sense, they certainly regarded nonviolence as a tactical weapon as well as an expression of high moral principle. The root meaning of Gandhi's concept of *satyagraha* . . . is "holding on to truth." . . . Gandhi also called *satyagraha* the "love force" or "soul force" and explained that he had discovered "in the earliest stages that pursuit of truth did not permit violence being inflicted on one's opponent, but that he must be weaned from error by patience and sympathy." . . .
>
> King was even more explicit on this point: the purpose of civil disobedience, he explained many times, was to force the defenders of segregation to commit brutal acts in public and thus arouse the conscience of the world on behalf of those wronged by racism. King and Gandhi did not succeed because they changed the hearts and minds of southern sheriffs and British colonial administrators (although they did, in fact, change some minds) but because they *made the price of maintaining control too high for their opponents* [emphasis mine].

That, I believe, is what it's going to take to abolish the death penalty in this country: we must persuade the American people that government killings are too costly for us, not only financially, but— more important—morally.

The death penalty *costs* too much. Allowing our government to kill citizens compromises the deepest moral values upon which this country was conceived: the inviolable dignity of human persons.

I have no doubt that we will one day abolish the death penalty in America. . . . The secrecy surrounding executions makes it possible for executions to continue. I am convinced that if executions were made public, the torture and violence would be unmasked, and we would be shamed into abolishing executions. We would be embarrassed at the brutalization of the crowds that would gather to watch a man or woman be killed. And we would be humiliated to know that visitors from other countries—Japan, Russia, Latin America, Europe—were watching us kill our own citizens—we, who take pride in being the flagship of democracy in the world.

And here I am driving to Baton Rouge from the death house, where tomorrow a man is going to be executed. . . .

As soon as I arrive, a technician, working quickly, hooks the microphone onto the lapel of my coat, hands me a small hearing device to insert into my ear, and in a few short moments I am hooked up to New York. Before we go on the air, Peter Jennings practices saying "Prejean"—"Pray-zshawn." He recognizes that it's French and wants to make sure he pronounces it correctly. To tell you the truth, he tells me, they want my viewpoint because they are featuring the Harveys and they don't want to present only one side of the issue. . . .

The story opens showing the Harveys outside the prison after the execution. Someone is holding a sign that says "Have 'Faith' in the Justice System."

Vernon says he wishes every victim could have the opportunity he had tonight. Lizabeth says that since Robert Willie saw Faith die, her parents should see him die. Warden Blackburn is shown announcing that Robert Willie was pronounced dead at 12:15 A.M. and then Robert's last statement is read. Then they go back to Elizabeth and Vernon Harvey, and Vernon says he feels it was too easy and quick for Willie, "he didn't suffer no pain, and my daughter had to." . . .

Jennings asks if I feel it would be a good thing for people to be exposed to executions, and I say yes, because then they would see the violence unmasked and this would lead them to abolish executions. I say that an execution is a brutal and horrible thing, and that I heard Mr. Harvey say Robert experienced no pain, but that the pain came every time he looked at his watch, knowing that in a few days, a few hours he would die.

Jennings thanks me and turns to George Will, the political commentator, and asks whether he thinks people should be able to witness executions.

George Will says the American people favor capital punishment, not primarily because they believe it's an effective deterrent, but because it satisfies a deeply felt moral intuition that there are some crimes for which death is the only proportionate punishment, and this murder certainly seems to be one of those crimes. That is what the American people feel, he says, and he thinks they're right and that vengeance, far from being shameful, can be noble. . . .

[Walter Burns, a death-penalty advocate], too, fears that public viewing of such events would have a "coarsening" effect upon the populace: "No ordinary person can be required to witness [executions], and it would be better if some people not be permitted to witness them—children, for example, and the sort of persons who would, if permitted, happily join a lynch mob. Executions should not be televised, both because of the unrestricted character of the television audience and the tendency of television to make a vulgar spectacle of the most *dignified event*" [italics mine].

But it's not the presence of television cameras or the composition of the crowd or even whether the crowd acts politely or not that makes the execution of a human being ugly. An execution is ugly because the premeditated killing of a human being is ugly. Torture is ugly. Gassing, hanging, shooting, electrocuting, or lethally injecting a person whose hands and feet are tied is ugly. And hiding the ugliness from view and rationalizing it numbs our minds to the horror of what we are doing. This is what truly "coarsens" us.

I think of the moment when Warden Ross Maggio stood at the microphone to announce the time of Pat Sonnier's execution. His eyes happened to meet mine, and he lowered his eyes. It was instinctive. He had helped kill a man. There was nothing noble about it.

Camus held that executions are performed in secret because they are shameful deeds. State governments, he said, who wish executions to continue, know to keep them hidden from view, not only physically but also symbolically in the euphemistic language used to describe them. . . .

Louisiana became the nineteenth state to use lethal injection to kill prisoners since the state of Oklahoma inaugurated its use in 1977. The method is preferred because it virtually eliminates visible, bodily pain. There is only the "uncomfortableness" of a needle prick into a vein. There remains, however, one dimension of suffering that can never be eliminated when death is imposed on a conscious human being: the horror of being put to death against your will and the agony of anticipation. As if, when they strap you down on the gurney, your arms outstretched, waiting for the silent deadly fluid to flow—the sodium pentothol, which comes first to make you unconscious so you do not feel the pancuronium bromide when it paralyzes your diaphragm and stops your breathing and the potassium chloride which causes cardiac arrest and stops your heart—as if you feel the terror of death any less because chemicals are being used to kill you instead of electricity or bullets or rope?

There is an elaborate ruse going on here, a pitiful disguise. Killing is camouflaged as a medicinal act. The attendant will even swab the "patient's" arm with alcohol before inserting the needle—*to prevent infection*. . . .

A two-year study of capital punishment in the U.S. by Hugo A. Bedau of Tufts University and Michael L. Radelet of the University of Florida documents that in this century 417 people were wrongly convicted of capital offenses and 23 were actually executed. . . .

Ernest van den Haag, a professor of jurisprudence and public policy at Fordham University, when asked to respond to the Bedau-Radelet study showing that innocent people have actually been executed in this country, said: "All human activities—building houses, driving a car, playing golf or football—cause innocent people to suffer wrongful death, but we don't give them up because on the whole we feel there's a net gain. Here [executions], a net gain in justice is being done."

A handful of relatives and friends gather at the Brown-McGeehee Funeral Home in Covington to bury Robert Lee Willie. When I see Elizabeth she holds me tight and cries and I try to comfort her, telling her about the last hours of her son and how bravely he had met his death.

The three boys hover close to their mother, and Junior is here, too. Little Todd keeps taking his mother's hand and holding it.

I walk over to the open casket and look down at what remains of Robert Lee Willie. His body is dressed in blue jeans and a white T-shirt, and I notice a couple of tattoos on his arms that I hadn't noticed before—a peacock and marijuana leaves. It is a shock to see him so quiet and still like this, his eyes closed, his lips not moving.

There is a flutter of commotion and some laughter when word spreads that Robert's aunt Bessie, waving her shoe, just chased away a reporter who tried to enter the funeral home.

When the funeral director announces that the last good-byes are to be said, Elizabeth approaches the casket. "Oh, Robert, Robert, my boy, O God, help me," she says, weeping. "Oh, Robert, how much I loved you." . . .

Discussion Questions

1. Prejean maintains that all humans have intrinsic moral value—"Nobody is disposable human waste." She writes, "Yes, I cared for Patrick Sonnier. Despite his terrible crime, he was a human being and deserved to be treated with dignity."[47] Do you agree with Prejean? Does moral respect require that people be treated with dignity even when they treat others as "disposable human waste"? Support your answers.
2. Discuss the methods Prejean used to protest capital punishment. Is her protest of civil law consistent with natural law ethics? If you believe that capital punishment is immoral, how should you go about protesting it? Explain using specific examples.
3. Prejean argues that capital punishment is contrary to the moral teachings of Jesus of Nazareth, "who taught us not to return hate for hate and evil for evil." Many Christians disagree with this interpretation of Christian ethics. Indeed, in the United States, Christians are more likely to support the death penalty than are non-Christians. Discuss the relative merits of the two interpretations of Christian ethics.
4. According to psychologist Carol Gilligan, moral maturity entails integrating the justice and the care perspectives. Develop a policy on capital punishment that draws from both perspectives.

5. According to care ethicist Nel Noddings, it is being in a caring relationship that gives people moral value. If someone on death row is cared for by others, such as Robert Lee Willie, should that person's life be spared? Is the death penalty more justified if the condemned person is not in a caring relationship of any sort? Support your answers.

CASE STUDIES

1. KARLA FAYE TUCKER: THE REPENTANT MURDERER

There's no question that thirty-eight-year-old Karla Faye Tucker of Texas is guilty of murder. In 1983 while strung out on drugs, Tucker hacked her two helpless victims to death with a pickax. She even boasted afterward that the killing gave her a sexual thrill. So why is she appealing her death sentence?

Tucker has since come to regret her deeds. She has found God, she says, and is a changed person. "God reached down inside of me and literally uprooted all of that stuff and took it out and poured himself in." Tucker is now involved in a prison-run program counseling young people to stay away from crime. "The world per se may not believe I deserve forgiveness," she told the world in an ABC interview, "but God says He's forgiven me."

More than one hundred people gathered outside the Texas prison on February 3, 1998, the day of her scheduled execution, some protesting the death penalty and hoping for a stay of execution, others rallying in support of her execution. Despite pleas for her pardon, Tucker was executed that evening by lethal injection.

Discussion Questions

1. Texas has not executed a woman since the Civil War; only one woman has been executed in the United States since the death penalty was reinstated twenty years ago. Is the fact that the vast majority of violent crime is committed by young men relevant to the practical application of capital punishment? Because women, in general, do not need deterring, can capital punishment be justified in Tucker's case?
2. A 1997 survey of seven hundred death row inmates found that most share certain characteristics. Seven out of ten began their criminal careers as children, going on to commit more and more serious crimes, crimes which often included killing, before the murder that landed them on death row. Nine out of ten also had childhoods marred by poverty, drugs, abuse, alcoholism, broken families, or lack of high school education. Despite their crimes, the survey found that most death row inmates "view themselves as normal people caught up in abnormal circumstances."[48] Like most inmates on death row, Tucker had a rough childhood. A former prostitute, she was using marijuana by age eight and heroin at age eleven. She was on drugs when she committed the murders. Is any of this relevant to her moral responsibility for her action?
3. One of the arguments against the death penalty is that people change, that retributive justice and rehabilitation are, therefore, contradictory goals. Capital punishment denies people the opportunity for growth whereas other types of punishment do not.

It is generally years before a death sentence is finally carried out. Meanwhile some people, like Tucker, go through major changes and moral growth. Should this be taken into consideration? Is it fair to punish people for a crime they committed during a different "stage" in their lives? Support your answers.

4. Discuss how both Kant and van den Haag might respond to the argument that capital punishment and rehabilitation are contradictory goals. Discuss how each would most likely have responded to Tucker's pleas for pardon. Discuss how Morris and Kant might each respond to Tucker's execution.

---

2. THE OKLAHOMA CITY BOMBER AND TERRORISM[49]

Shortly after 9:00 A.M. on April 19, 1995, a fireball ripped through the plate-glass doors of the Oklahoma City Federal Building in Oklahoma City, collapsing all nine floors on the north side.

Patrolman Charlie Hanger was outside of town patrolling for speeders when he heard about the explosion on his police radio. About 10:34 A.M. Hanger stopped a car for having no license plates. When he approached the driver, Hanger noticed a semiautomatic pistol poking out of the driver's shoulder strap. Hanger arrested him for driving an unregistered car and carrying an unregistered handgun and took him to the Noble County Jail. The driver, as it turned out, was twenty-seven-year-old Timothy McVeigh.

The explosion killed 168 people and injured 850. In June 1997 McVeigh was found guilty of murder and conspiracy and sentenced to death for his role in the bombing. McVeigh appealed the conviction claiming that the testimony of a former government militia informer had been excluded from his trial and that the jury was not impartial. His appeal was rejected by a U.S. Court of Appeals in February 1998. McVeigh was executed by lethal injection on June 11, 2001, just three months before the deadly September 11 terrorist attacks on the Twin Towers in New York City.

In November 2001 President George W. Bush created military commissions that have the power to impose the death penalty for people accused of "international terrorism." In 2003 Attorney General John Ashcroft asked lawmakers on Capitol Hill to expand the death penalty to cover people who are accused of perpetrating terrorist activities, even though they may not be directly involved in the actual killings. Over 3000 "foot-soldiers of terror" have been captured since the passage of the U.S. Patriot Act following September 11.[50] The Patriot Act allows illegal immigrants who are suspected of involvement in terrorist activities to be detained indefinitely. So far no international terrorists have been executed under the new laws.

Discussion Questions

1. Prejean argues that capital punishment is inconsistent with the intrinsic value of human life. Nobody, she writes, is disposable human waste . . . Despite their terrible crimes, murderers are human beings and deserve to be treated with dignity. Do you agree? Does morality require that terrorists like McVeigh, who allegedly treat others as "disposable human waste," be treated with dignity?
2. The terrorists who were directly responsible for the destruction of the World Trade Center and the attack on the Pentagon died in the attacks. Should those who assisted

in the planning of the attacks be held responsible for the deaths of the almost 3000 people who died in the attacks? Is it morally acceptable, as Attorney General Ashcroft wants in the case of terrorism, to impose the death penalty on people who are indirectly involved in murders carried out by other people? What are the implications of this for people who may have been involved in, but did not carry out, "ordinary" non-political murders? Should they also be subject to the death penalty? Support your answers. Discuss how Kant and van den Haag would most likely respond to Ashcroft's proposal.

3. French existentialist Albert Camus claimed that there is a moral contradiction in a policy, such as capital punishment, that imitates the violence it is claiming to hate.[51] Do you agree with Camus? Are we as a community made a little less virtuous by executing McVeigh? Support your answers.
4. Kant maintained that if a person makes a rational decision to kill another person, respect for the murderer's dignity and free will requires that we in turn execute him. Although the vast majority of murders are carried out impulsively without previous rational analysis, terrorists seem to be an exception to this rule. Does the fact that McVeigh and the terrorists who destroyed the World Trade Center carefully planned their crimes make them more morally culpable than people who murder on impulse?

---

3. CHILDREN WHO KILL

In 1999, in one of the worst school shootings in history, Eric Harris and Dylan Klebold opened fire on their classmates at Columbine High School in Littleton, Colorado. Thirteen people were killed and twenty-one others wounded before the two boys finally turned the guns on themselves, ending both the rampage and their own lives.

Killings by children are not limited to the school. In 1989, fifteen-year-old Craig Price murdered three of his neighbors. When the police arrived at the Heaton home in Warwick, Rhode Island, they found three mutilated bodies. Joan Heaton, thirty-nine, had been stabbed with a knife eleven times, strangled, and bitten in the face. Her daughter Jennifer, ten, had been stabbed sixty-two times. Melissa, eight, had been stabbed eight times and her skull crushed. "We think of what these little kids went through . . . that screaming . . . that unmerciful attack." Police Captain Kevin Collins shudders recalling that grisly night in September.[52]

Price was arrested shortly after the bodies were found. Police later discovered that two years earlier Price had murdered another neighbor. He also had a record of assaults, burglaries, and other crimes.

Does Price think what he did was immoral? When asked about the murders, Price shrugged his shoulders and responded: "Morality is a private choice." According to Collins, who witnessed Price's confessions to the four murders, "He just loves to kill. There's no doubt . . . that he's going to kill again."[53]

Rhode Island does not have the death penalty. In addition, because Price was fifteen he could not be tried as an adult. Under Rhode Island law, the maximum sentence for juveniles, regardless of their crime, is detention in the training school until they are twenty-one.

Discussion Questions

1. Many societies draw a line at age eighteen, when people are suddenly held to be fully responsible for their actions. Is this practice justifiable? Or should children who kill be treated and punished like adults? Is it a violation of their dignity to deny them an equal "right to punishment"? Support your answers. Discuss how Reiman would most likely respond to these questions.
2. Many schools are tightening up security. While several students have been expelled for bringing weapons to school, others have been expelled simply for making threatening statements to classmates. Critics of this practice maintain that it violates these students' freedom of speech. Discuss ways in which schools and society in general might best respond to the problem of school violence, taking into consideration both utilitarian theory and rights ethics in formulating your policy.
3. People are still searching for an answer to why Harris and Klebold turned killers. One explanation being put forth is that their rage was fueled by vengeance against Columbine High School athletes whose taunting and bullying and harassment of other students at the school, including Harris and Klebold, was generally tolerated. Indeed, Harris and Klebold opened fire on their classmates with the words, "All the jocks stand up." To what extent, if any, do the athletes who engaged in this behavior, bear responsibility for the killings. Should athletes who engage in this type of behavior be punished? How about school officials who generally turned a blind eye to the athletes' behavior. Discuss how a virtue ethicist might respond to these questions.
4. In 1986 there were thirty-seven teenage killers on death row. A 1986 Justice Department study commission recommended that youths fifteen and older be treated as adult killers. Given that most people on death row began their life of crime as children and that most violent acts are committed by men under thirty, wouldn't execution of young killers make more sense as a deterrent than execution of adults? Discuss also how juvenile murderers should be handled in states, such as Rhode Island, that have no death penalty.
5. A 1988 study of fourteen juveniles on death row concluded that they had brain abnormalities, low IQs, and psychiatric problems and had suffered severe head injuries as children. Price, however, did not fit this profile. There is nothing unusual about Price's background: He came from what seemed to be a good family and lived in a middle-class neighborhood. Does the fact that Price did not apparently act out of past conditioning make him more morally blameworthy than if he had grown up amidst poverty and violence? Support your answer.
6. Studies of prisoners' moral development have found that their level of moral reasoning is equivalent to that of thirteen year olds. Should murderers' level of moral development be taken into consideration before sentencing them to death? If not, what is the morally relevant difference between using the death penalty on a thirteen year old and on an adult who operates at a similar low level of moral reasoning? Support your answers.
7. Some psychologists believe that Craig Price, a brutal serial killer, is a psychopath. Psychopaths lack any sense of moral duty or moral right or wrong. Because they lack a conscience, they can maim and murder with impunity. Given that psychopaths lack the ability to distinguish between right and wrong, should they be held morally accountable for their actions? Does their inability mean that the concept of retributive

justice and punishment, including the use of capital punishment, is inapplicable to them? Support your answers. Discuss how van den Haag might respond to these questions.

---

4. IS THERE A CRIMINAL GENE?

The popular science fiction thriller *Alien 3* opens with *Alien* veteran Lieutenant Ripley (Sigourney Weaver) crash-landing on the planet Fiorina "Fury" 161, a decommissioned maximum-security correctional facility for "double-Y-chromosome" offenders.[54] Upon regaining consciousness, Lieutenant Ripley is promptly warned by the prison superintendent not to leave the infirmary without an escort, because these prisoners are presumably unable to control their violent sexual urges in the presence of a woman. As the movie unfolds, it becomes clear that these twenty-five prisoners are a violent and obscene lot—social misfits of the worst sort—"all thieves, rapists, murderers, child molesters—all scum." They are not part of the mainstream human race but, in the words of the prison doctor, "alternative people" set apart from others by their genome and the bar codes indelibly tattooed on their heads. The moviegoer leaves the theater with the uneasy feeling that if these "double-Y-chromosome" men are such a threat, perhaps we ought to be seeking them out and destroying them with the same fervor that the brave Lieutenant Ripley pursued those nasty aliens.

The notion of a criminal gene that will allow us to sort out the chaff from the wheat is not a new one. The observation that young men commit the great majority of violent crimes as well as the finding that 80 percent of youth violence is committed by 7 percent of the youth population suggest that some people may have a genetic predisposition toward violent behavior. In the decade that followed the 1961 discovery of the XYY disorder, researchers found that maximum-security prison hospitals have a much higher than normal incidence of XYY males. They also noted that these men tend to be taller and more aggressive than other prisoners. These findings lead to speculations, which were sensationalized by the press, that there might be a criminal gene.

Although more-recent studies have found that the great majority of XYY males do not engage in any sort of violent criminal activity, interest in a possible genetic basis for violent crime has resurfaced in the wake of the Human Genome Project. Dr. Louis Sullivan, the Bush administration's secretary of Health and Human Services from 1989 to 1993, maintains that violence is a public-health issue. In the early 1990s, philosopher David Wasserman made the observation that genetic research suggests there are "genetic factors in crime." His statement was promptly denounced for fostering prejudice and a "modern-day version of eugenics." Federal funding for research on a genetic basis for crime was withdrawn. Other scientists who have sought to find a genetic link to violence have also been reprimanded.

Discussion Questions

1. Is life imprisonment on a desolate planet preferable to the death penalty? Or should the remaining twenty-five prisoners on planet Fiorina "Fury" 161 be executed? Does the fact that these prisoners have a chromosomal disorder excuse what they did? If so, what is the morally appropriate response to their crimes? Support your answers.

2. Despite the taboo on any suggestion that crime has a genetic link, some scientists have cautiously suggested that genes influencing serotonin production may make certain people, particularly young men, who are most likely to have low levels of serotonin, more susceptible to impulsive and aggressive behavior as well as to alcohol and drug abuse.[55] Should murderers who have an extra Y chromosome, a low level of serotonin, or a genetic predisposition to addictive behavior be held morally responsible for their crimes? Should they be "treated" rather than punished?
3. Being a psychopath seems to be, at least in part, genetically based. There is strong evidence that the frontal-lobe cortex in the brain, which is abnormal in a psychopath, plays a key role in moral decision making.[56] If this is the case, is it fair to hold psychopaths morally responsible for their crimes? Is punishment based on retribution inappropriate even though psychopaths are some of the most dangerous criminals? Support your answers. Role-play a discussion between van den Haag, Morris, and Reiman on these questions.
4. Although researchers say that they expect their findings to be used to screen people who have a predisposition toward violence in order to treat them, there is fear that screening will be used to discriminate against these people or to selectively abort fetuses with genetic predispositions toward violence. Should research on a criminal gene be banned or restricted?

---

5. INSIDE A TEXAS DEATH CHAMBER

Texas has been dubbed "the execution capital of the free world." The frequency of executions in some of the prisons has made them routine. How does participation in capital punishment affect those who carry it out or witness it?

Journalist Michael Graczyk of the Houston bureau of The Associated Press has witnessed about seventy executions. "It's my job," he says. "It's like going to cover a baseball game or a basketball game." Executions are no longer big news in Texas. In the past, executions were scheduled for midnight; now they are held at 6 P.M. for the convenience of those involved. As the prisoner is ushered into the death chamber, guards stand around talking about their kids, Little League, and what they're going to do on their day off. There is no blood, no sense of horror, no scream of anguish as the needle is inserted into the inmate's arm. When the act is over, it just looks like the inmate went to sleep. Graczyk wrote, after the execution of brutal murderer Billy Joe Woods, "It was bizarre to look around and see all these people just doing their job. It was just another day at the office."[57]

Outside was a handful of anti-death penalty advocates crying, "Murderer!"—not at the man about to be executed, but at the gray-shirted guards. Later they chanted into a megaphone, "God bless Billy Woods. God bless Billy Woods."

Discussion Questions

1. Does the death penalty brutalize and numb all those who participate in it, as abolitionists claim? Discuss how van den Haag might respond to this objection to capital punishment.
2. Prejean argues that capital punishment creates sympathy for the murderer, as in the case of Billy Woods. Does it weaken respect for the authority of the law if the state is

seen as the murderer and the death row inmate as the victim? Support your answer. Discuss how a social contractarian would answer this question.

3. Executions involving lethal injection generally require the presence of a physician. Should physicians participate in executions, or does this require them to go against their professional code of ethics, as the AMA claims? Does the principle of nonmaleficence, or "Do no harm," forbid doctors from witnessing or participating in the execution of murderers? If not physicians, who should carry out executions? Does the principle of nonmaleficence forbid anyone from executing another person? Support your answers.
4. Prejean suggests making executions public. It is the secrecy surrounding executions, she maintains, that keeps the public from realizing just how brutal capital punishment really is. Discuss the relative merits of having executions open to the public.

---

6. ADULTERY AND EXECUTION BY STONING

In October 2001 Safiya Yakubu Hussaini, a divorced mother of five children in Nigeria, was sentenced to death by stoning for adultery. The male partner in the alleged adultery was allowed to go free. The gender-discriminatory nature of the sentence created an international furor. Members of the World Women Parliamentarians, which represents 130 countries, adopted a motion calling for amnesty for Safiya Yakubu Hussaini. The Secretary General of the Council of Europe also called on the Nigerian president to give her reprieve.

Safiya Yakubu Hussaini was finally acquitted by the *Sharia* State Court of Appeals in Sokoto state in March 2003 and allowed to go free. However, in the same month another divorced woman, Amina Lawal Kurami, was sentenced to death by stoning by the *Sharia* court in the Nigerian Katsina state for adultery and having a baby out of wedlock. As in the previous case, charges were dropped against the father. There is currently an appeal against her sentence.

Discussion Questions

1. According to cultural relativists moral values are relative to each culture. If sentencing women who commit adultery to death by stoning is considered morally acceptable in a culture then the practice is, by definition, morally acceptable. Do you agree with cultural relativists? If so, is it morally wrong for people from other countries and cultures to condemn and "impose their moral values" on Nigeria in trying to get the sentences overturned? If not, why not?
2. Discuss the moral issues involved in the above case. Is the fact that the women knew that adultery was a capital crime punishable by death morally relevant in holding them responsible for their actions? What about the gender differences in the way the case was handled?
3. The *Sharia* courts in northern Nigeria were set up only for Muslims and are different from courts in the rest of Nigeria. The Nigerian Minister of Justice, Kanu Agabi, sent a letter to the governors of the Muslim Nigerian states saying that they should not imposed punishments more severe than those imposed on other Nigerians, because doing so is "deliberately flouting the Constitution" of Nigeria. Is Kanu Agabi violating

Muslim's religious freedom by holding them to non-Muslim standard of punishment? To what extent should we respect the values of different cultures within a nation, especially those that are religiously based, when it comes to punishment?

4. Relate your answer in discussion question 3 to the use of corporal punishment (spanking, beating, and other physical punishment) for children by religious sects, such as the House of Prayer and the Church of God (Restoration) in the United States. Most of the sects use passages from Proverbs to support the practice. Is the use of corporal punishment on children morally acceptable, if the parents believe it is acceptable? Why or why not? Should the government interfere or punish the parents? Support your answers.

CHAPTER 6

Drug and Alcohol Use

Scott Krueger had graduated near the top of his high school class and was looking forward to balancing the challenging demands of an engineering major at MIT, early-morning crew practice, and an active social life at Phi Gamma Delta, one of the thirty fraternities at MIT. In the fall of 1997, however, the fraternity pledge passed out during a Greek Week celebration after downing sixteen drinks in an hour. Krueger's fraternity brothers carried him back to the fraternity house. When they noticed he was having trouble breathing, they called an ambulance.

When rescue workers arrived, Krueger was already comatose. His blood alcohol level was later found to be more than five times the legal driving limit. A few days later, Krueger's distraught parents had him removed from life support. He died shortly thereafter. Krueger is only one of hundreds of college students whose lives are cut short or devastated every year as a result of drug and alcohol abuse.

In September 2000 Krueger's parents were awarded a $6 million settlement by the university. This unprecedented financial settlement and MIT's declared commitment to change the college conditions that contributed to Krueger's death has spurred other colleges to make similar commitments to create a safer and more secure campus environment for students.

WHAT IS A DRUG?

Drugs, for the purpose of this chapter, are defined as chemicals that enter the bloodstream and are easily transported to the brain, where they alter the way we feel, with predictable results. Alcohol, by this definition, is a type of drug. Drugs can be smoked, injected, snorted, or swallowed.

Drug abuse is defined as "taking a drug or drugs for purposes other than those for which the drug or drugs were intended, and/or the illicit use of a drug or drugs which can cause harm (not necessarily physical) to oneself and/or others."[1] One of the risks of alcohol and drug use is addiction. *Addiction* is "a behavioral pattern of drug use, characterized by overwhelming involvement with the use of a drug [compulsive use], the securing of its supply, and a high tendency to relapse after withdrawal."[2]

DRUG CLASSIFICATIONS

Classification	Drugs	Effects[3]
Stimulants	Amphetamines, cocaine, prescription diet pills, nicotine, caffeine	Alertness; a sense of power; enhanced performance[4]
Depressants	Alcohol, anti-anxiety drugs and sleeping pills containing benzodiazepine and barbiturates	Drowsiness and sedation
Opiates	Prescription painkillers, codeine, heroin, Demerol, methadone, morphine	Diminished or no pain; sense of euphoria
Hallucinogens	LSD, "magic mushrooms," peyote, MDMA ("ecstasy"), mescaline	Intensified perception and sense experience; hallucinations
Cannabinals	All forms of marijuana	Mellowness
Inhalants/ Solvents	Acetone, aerosol gases, glue, paint thinner, correction fluid	Giddiness and confusion
Performance enhancement	Anabolic and androgenic steroids	Increased muscle mass

THE HISTORY OF DRUG AND ALCOHOL USE

Alcohol is the most widely used drug in North America. Wine and beer have been used since ancient times for their pleasurable effects, in medicine, with meals, and in religious ceremonies. Even the *Mayflower* carried a good supply of "bere."

Distilled spirits were first produced in Europe about 1300 and were often referred to as "aqua vitae" because of their purported powers to prolong life. In 1606, alarmed by the increase in drunkenness, the British government made intoxication a statutory offense with the Act of Repression of the Odious and Loathsome Sin of Drunkedness.

Laws in the colonies were relatively lenient and geared primarily toward controlling drunkenness and disorderly conduct. A Connecticut law prohibited drinking for more than one-half hour at a time. A 1760 Virginia law prohibited ministers from "drinking to excess and inciting riots."

There were no large-scale temperance movements in North America until the mid-nineteenth century. The first temperance movement was fired by the sermons of reformers such as the Reverend Lyman Beecher, who denounced all alcohol as inherently evil. For a short period in the mid-1850s, several states as well as the Canadian provinces of Nova Scotia and New Brunswick enacted prohibition laws. Following this, alcohol consumption reached a low point.

Alcohol consumption hit another peak in the United States around the turn of the century. The temperance movement of the late-nineteenth and early-twentieth centuries was spearheaded by groups such as the Women's Christian Temperance Union (WCTU) and the Anti-Saloon League. The WCTU opposed drinking primarily because of its destructive effect on the family. The problem was also blamed on the influx of immigrants from Europe and Ireland, with their decadent European drinking habits.

In 1919 the Eighteenth Amendment to the Constitution outlawed the sale and consumption of alcohol. Despite lack of unanimous support for the amendment, most prohibitionists thought that Americans would not violate their Constitution. They were mistaken. The ratification of the Eighteenth Amendment ushered in an era of organized crime and a vast illegal liquor trade, known as "bootlegging," under the control of such notorious gangsters as Al Capone. Large quantities of alcohol were smuggled in from countries such as Canada and England, which did not have prohibition laws.

Although alcohol consumption declined during the first few years of prohibition, it began to climb again during the 1920s. The cost of trying to stamp out illegal drinking soared into the many millions of dollars. It soon became apparent that prohibition was too unpopular and too expensive to enforce. The Eighteenth Amendment was repealed in 1933 by the Twenty-first Amendment, although some states continued to have local prohibition laws as late as 1966.

Alcohol consumption hit another peak about 1980. Once again the tide of public opinion turned against alcohol. This time it was the medical profession that led the crusade. Rather than denounce alcohol as a moral failing or the work of the devil, as had the early prohibitionists, the medical establishment declared alcoholism to be a disease. The disease model continues to dominate attitudes toward alcohol use in the United States today.

Attitudes toward drug use have followed a similar course. Hallucinogenic drugs have been used since antiquity both for pleasure and religious purposes. Apparently, the techniques of ecstatic trances used by some Hindu yogis involved the use of drugs. The peyote cult of Mexico also used drug-induced ecstasy in mystical and religious rituals. LSD, which was popular in North America in the 1960s, has been similarly credited with helping users get in touch with a deeper mystical wisdom. Western philosophers and psychologists, with their emphasis on reason as the source of knowledge, tend to dismiss these experiences as merely drug induced and, hence, unreal.

Drugs have also been widely used for medicinal purposes. Opium was available in a crude form prior to 1800 and was valued by physicians for its calming effect and as a cure for gastrointestinal illnesses. Noted nineteenth-century physician George Wood wrote that opium produces "an exaltation of our better mental qualities, a warmer glow of benevolence, a disposition to do great things, but nobly and beneficently, a higher devotional spirit, and withal a stronger self-reliance, and consciousness of power."[5]

Morphine, a derivative of opium, became a popular painkiller after 1870. When heroin, a derivative of morphine, was introduced into medical practice in the late 1800s, it was actively promoted by the American Medical Association (AMA) and pharmaceutical companies as a cure for many ailments. The easy availability of these drugs in the late-nineteenth century was accompanied by a substantial increase in the number of drug addicts.[6] This increase, however, could not be attributed solely to easier access to drugs. These same drugs were also widely available in France, Germany, Great Britain, Russia, and Italy, yet these countries did not experience similar increases in numbers of drug addicts.

SECTION 1 OF THE EIGHTEENTH AMENDMENT TO THE UNITED STATES CONSTITUTION

[Adopted January 29, 1919]

Section 1. After one year from the ratification of this article the manufacture, sale, or transportation thereof into, or the exportation thereof from the United States and all territories subject to the jurisdiction thereof for beverage purposes is hereby prohibited.

Cocaine was first isolated from the coca leaf in the mid-nineteenth century. It was popular as a general tonic and for sinusitis and hay fever. Even psychoanalyst Sigmund Freud used cocaine as a tonic. The exhilarating effects of cocaine made it a popular additive in medicine, soda, and wine. In the United States, blacks were blamed by prohibitionists for the "cocaine problem." It was feared that euphoric black cocaine users might forget their place in life and begin attacking white society. Despite the fact that studies at the time failed to confirm the widespread use of cocaine by blacks, the fear of an uprising was used, in part, to justify an era of lynchings and legal segregation.

LEGAL AND ILLEGAL DRUGS

State laws regulating the use of morphine and cocaine were first enacted in the United States in the 1890s. Federal prohibition of drugs was not attempted initially because it was thought to be unconstitutional. Libertarians, physicians, and the major pharmaceutical societies also protested the outlawing in the United States of opiates, cocaine, and cannabis, substances they relied heavily on for symptom relief. Despite support for the medicinal use of drugs, by the mid-1920s the federal government moved to eliminate all heroin use.

The Pure Food and Drug Act of 1906 was the first federal legislation to regulate the use of opium. Blacks were not the only oppressed group in the United States to be scapegoated by drug prohibitionists. Because opium was exported from China, opposition to the recreational use of opium was used to reinforce anti-Chinese sentiment and the persecution of Chinese immigrants.

It is sometimes assumed that the division between legal and illegal drugs is based on rational criteria, but this isn't the case. Alcohol, nicotine (tobacco), and marijuana are currently the three most frequently used drugs in the United States. Yet marijuana, which rarely causes physiological addiction or serious illness, is illegal whereas alcohol and tobacco are not. According to an AMA study, tobacco is the number one "actual cause of death" in the United States; alcohol is number three. Tobacco is responsible for 430,000 deaths a year and alcohol for another 100,000 deaths. Worldwide, tobacco causes about 8.8 percent (4.9 million) of all deaths.[7]

The abuse of legal over-the-counter or prescription drugs, inhalants, or solvents can also lead to addiction, serious health problems, and even death. Heroin, morphine, and cocaine, in contrast, are responsible for fewer than 8,500 deaths a year, while marijuana has yet to be implicated as responsible in anyone's death.[8]

The most recent wave of antidrug laws comes at a time when the public is divided over the wisdom of drug prohibition. Does the state have a right to prohibit or protect adults from using drugs? Is drug abuse a moral, legal, medical, or religious issue? Which drugs should be prohibited and which allowed?

DRUG AND ALCOHOL USE TODAY

When the George H. W. Bush administration declared an official "war on drugs," it had strong public support. Illicit drug use had already begun declining during the 1980s. However, despite tougher laws and some initial victories, the success of the "war" was short-lived. During the mid-1990s, drug use began rising again, especially among young people. The marketing of illicit drugs has also become more sophisticated. In the fall of 1997, the Royal Canadian Mounted Police in Vancouver raided one of the largest and most sophisticated drug-producing operations in North America. The hidden lab, which produced "designer drugs," had computer links to drug networks throughout North America and Europe.[9] The use of illicit drugs by youth peaked in 1981, when 66 percent of American youth under the age of eighteen tried illegal drugs.[10]

By 1994 polls showed that approximately 19 percent of eighth-graders, 36 percent of high school seniors, and 75 percent of people in their twenties had tried illicit drugs.[11] The rate gradually fell to 41 percent until recently when it began to rise again to 54 percent in 2001.[12]

There is growing concern about the high rate of marijuana and tobacco use among young people, because both are regarded by some as "gateway drugs" that may lead to the use of so-called hard drugs. In 2001 an estimated 22.6 percent of adults (people eighteen and older) smoked cigarettes. Smoking declined almost 50 percent between 1963 and 2002, with the largest decline being among men although the smoking rate for men is still 30 percent greater than women.[13] Half of all people who smoke began before their eighteenth birthday. Although teenagers are more likely to smoke cigarettes than adults, with 28.5 percent of high school students and 11 percent of middle school students smoking in 2001, the rate has been declining since 1999. Smoking rates have also declined among college students. People who smoke are also smoking fewer cigarettes, possibly because of the increasing restrictions on where people can smoke (see Case Study 6). On the other hand, 30.7 percent of the adult population uses snuff and pipe smoking is on the increase.[14] In 2003, Canada and forty-one other nations approved an international convention aimed at reducing tobacco use and banning most types of tobacco advertising. The United States is not one of the signatories.

Of Americans age twelve and older, 37 percent have tried marijuana at least once.[15] In 2001 Canada legalized the use of marijuana for medical purposes, and in 2003 decriminalized marijuana possession, so small-time users wouldn't end up with the threat of jail and a criminal record. People caught with 15 grams or less would receive a citation and fine, similar to a traffic ticket. This move has created tension between Canada and the United States, where possession of even a small amount of marijuana is punishable by up to a year in jail (see Case Study 7).

Cocaine, the second most popular illicit drug in the United States, is still regarded by many as primarily a problem among inner-city blacks. In actual fact, white males, at 12 percent, are twice as likely to use cocaine as black, Hispanic, and Native American males. African Americans, on the other hand, are more likely to use heroin. Because heroin-related offenses in the United States receive much more severe legal penalties than cocaine use or alcohol-related crimes such as drunk driving, blacks bear a disproportionate burden with respect to enforcement of drug laws. Blacks are also more likely than whites to receive convictions for similar drug-related offenses.[16] A 2001 study in the state of Washington found that African-Americans, who made up only 3 percent of the state's population, received nearly 20 percent of the drug sentences.[17] This disparity was attributed in part to racial profiling (see Chapter 9 for more on racial profiling).

Both cigarette and alcohol use are substantially higher among white and Native American young people than among blacks and Asian Americans. White and Hispanic college students are almost three times more likely to engage in binge drinking than black students.[18] Men also binge-drink more than women. In a September 1999 Gallup Poll, 36 percent of Americans responded that drinking has been a cause of trouble in their families, up from 14 percent in 1950 and 23 percent in 1990.

DRUG AND ALCOHOL USE AMONG COLLEGE STUDENTS

Drug and alcohol use among college students has risen dramatically since the early 1990s. A 1997 *Time* magazine article described American colleges as "among the nation's most alcohol-drenched institutions."[19] American undergraduates drink 4 billion cans of beer a year and spend an average of $446 on alcoholic beverages—more than they spend on soft drinks and textbooks combined.[20]

Binge drinking is a serious problem on many campuses in both the United States and Canada.[21] A 1994 survey of 140 campuses in the United States revealed that 51 percent of college students are heavy drinkers, with 44 percent of them being binge drinkers.[22] Of these students, those who do not consider themselves to be problem drinkers are the most likely to experience alcohol-related problems as well as to cause problems for others.[23] Indeed, alcohol-related automobile accidents are one of the leading killers of young people. Of the 25,000 annual accidental deaths among teenagers, 40 percent are alcohol-related.

Peer pressure to drink is one of the greatest barriers to giving up binge drinking. Members of fraternities and sororities are at the highest risk of excessive drinking, because intoxication is viewed as an acceptable aspect of Greek life.[24] Of students who live in fraternities and sororities, 84 percent engage in binge drinking, compared with 44 percent of college students overall.[25] White athletes are also at higher risk for binge drinking.[26] Excessive alcohol use in fraternity hazing is once again on the upswing as well. Peer pressure is also a factor in the increased use of steroids by college athletes and young people who want to improve their appearance.[27]

In addition to such problems as poor concentration, lower grade-point average (GPA), and health risks, binge drinking among college students is linked to intentional violence, including assault, homicide, rape, brawls, vandalism, and burglary, as well as being the victim of aggression, in part because being intoxicated makes the person an easier target for a predator.[28]

Of students who do not engage in binge drinking, 87 percent reported problems caused by students who do. These problems ranged from unwanted sexual advances and property damage to having sleep or studying interrupted.[29] About half of all date rapes on campuses are associated with alcohol consumption.[30] Alcohol use is also a causal factor in suicide. Between 1950 and 1990, the suicide rate among 15- to 24-year-old people in the United States tripled. More American youth die from suicide than all other natural causes combined.[31]

In the mid-1980s the drinking age was raised from eighteen to twenty-one throughout the United States in an attempt to curb drunk-driving accidents. However, the drinking-age laws have had little effect on the actual drinking habits of college students. Forty-five percent of students under twenty-one binge-drink compared with only 28 percent of students over twenty-four.[32] In a 1996 study, 46 percent of college students surveyed reported that they used fake IDs to obtain alcohol; fraternity and sorority members were much more likely to use fake IDs.[33] The use of illicit drugs among young people age eighteen to twenty-five has also increased from 14.7 percent in 1997 to 18.8 percent in 1999.[34] Marijuana use in particular is up among college students. In 2001, 35.2 percent of college students used marijuana, a trend some people attribute to tougher restrictions on alcohol on campuses.[35]

College drug use, and binge drinking in particular, takes a huge toll in terms of damage to health and cognitive functioning, violence, property damage, and liability costs to the fraternities and colleges associated with drunken parties.

DRUGS IN SPORTS

Two weeks after the close of the summer Olympics in Sydney, Australia, the International Olympic Committee medical commission recommended that German wrestler Alexander Leipold be stripped of his gold medal. Leipold had tested positive for the steroid nandrolone after defeating American Brandon Slay in freestyle wrestling. Leipold's sample contained 20 nanograms of nandrolone per milliliter of urine, ten times more than the acceptable level of 2 nanograms. He denies taking the steroid and said he had no idea of how he could have tested positive. Leipold is only one of forty-seven athletes who were suspended from the Sydney games for doping offenses, the highest number ever in the history of the Olympics. Apparently mandatory drug testing has been effective. In the 2002 Winter Olympics all the athletes' drug tests came back negative.

Anabolic steroids, such as nandrolone, are testosterone-based drugs that stimulate muscle growth and help athletes recover faster from injuries. However, use of these steroids also increases by fivefold the risk of heart attacks and strokes and may also contribute to the development of liver disease.

Despite the harms associated with performance-enhancement drugs, their use in sports appears to be on the increase. According to one estimate, between 20 and 40 percent of major league baseball players use testosterone-based drugs.[36] Unlike the Olympics, the National Football League, and college athletics policies, random testing of major league baseball players for steroids or other illicit performance-enhancement drugs is forbidden by the current collective bargaining agreement. According to the National Council for the Social Studies, the use of anabolic steroids dropped from

5 percent in 1989 to 1 percent in 2001. Football players (3 percent) are the most likely to use steroids.[37]

The use of performance-enhancing drugs raises several moral issues. Does the duty of self-improvement require that athletes refrain from using drugs that will harm their bodies over the long run? Is it fair that athletes who use these drugs have a competitive advantage? Should drug testing be mandatory; or does mandatory drug testing violate the autonomy of the athlete? Is the use of performance-enhancing drugs in sports inherently coercive since it puts pressure on athletes to use drugs if they want to win? Thomas Murray explores these questions in his article on "Drugs, Sports, and Ethics" at the end of this chapter.

THE DISEASE MODEL OF ADDICTION

The therapeutic revolution in the mid-twentieth century involved relabeling certain behaviors, previously attributed to moral weakness, as diseases. The disease model views addiction primarily as an individual medical problem rather than a social or moral problem. Drug use is discussed in medical terminology; there is a heroin or cocaine "epidemic."

According to this model, it is not lack of willpower or moral character that separates addicts from nonaddicts. Addiction is a pathological state. Addicts abuse drugs or alcohol, not because they are bad people or weak willed, but because they are ill; they are biologically different from nonaddicts. People who harm others or break the law while under the influence of alcohol or drugs should receive treatment or therapy, not punishment, because they were no more in control of what they did when "under the influence" than an epileptic having a seizure.

The disease model of alcoholism was first articulated in the 1940s by Elvine M. Jellinek of the Yale Center of Alcoholic Studies.[38] Since then this view of alcohol and drug addiction has become the official view of both the AMA and the World Health Organization (WHO). In 1956 the AMA recognized drug addiction as a "chemical dependency" and, therefore, a disease like diabetes or cancer. Addicts are not bad people; they are chemically dependent. In 1977 the AMA added alcoholism to its list of illnesses, defining it as "an illness characterized by significant impairment that is directly associated with persistent and excessive use of alcohol. Impairment may involve physiological, psychological, or social dysfunction." Recent advances in genetics lend weight to the disease model of addiction.[39]

Because the cause of the disease lies in the drugs, people with an "addictive personality" will simply substitute one drug for another. And though abstinence may arrest the disease of addiction, the disease itself can never be cured because it is biologically based. Abstinence from all drugs, therefore, is the ideal. This ideal is reflected in laws that seek to ban all addictive drugs because, it is believed, addicts will simply switch to another drug if the one they are using is no longer available.

Alcoholics Anonymous (AA) is based primarily on the disease model of addiction. A fundamental assumption of the AA Twelve Steps program is that healing can occur only when alcoholics admit their powerlessness over addiction and turn the healing process over to a "higher power." The "one disease [addiction], one treatment [abstinence]" approach of AA currently dominates the medical field.

THE MORAL MODEL OF ADDICTION

Many philosophers and bioethicists, such as Thomas Szasz, question the validity of the medical model of addiction and call for a return to the moral model. Addiction, according to the moral model, is a freely chosen vice. Resisting or overcoming addiction is simply a matter of willpower. The religious view that alcoholism is a sin, the prohibition legislation of the early-twentieth century, and the current "Just Say No" campaign are all based on the moral model of addiction.

Most positions on addiction lie somewhere between the two extremes. Although AA is based primarily on the disease model, accepting moral responsibility for one's actions is also part of the recovery process. Similarly, most supporters of the moral model acknowledge that there are social, personal, and genetic factors that make it more likely that certain people will become addicts. They also maintain, however, that a predisposition toward addiction is not the same as a predetermination that one will become addicted. Unlike predispositions to other diseases, such as breast cancer and diabetes, a person who is genetically predisposed to addiction can avoid it altogether by avoiding the substances that may lead to addiction. Therefore, people who harm others while under the influence of alcohol or drugs should be held morally responsible for their choices and actions. Under the moral model, punishment is an appropriate response to drug-related crime.

The disease model has been called into question by scientific studies as well. A Rand Corporation study in the late 1970s and early 1980s suggested that recovering alcoholics can resume moderate or responsible drinking.[40] The claim made by supporters of the disease model that addiction knows no social class, race, gender, or ethnic background also runs contrary to empirical findings. Jews, for example, have one of the lowest, if not *the* lowest, rate of alcoholism.[41]

THE PHILOSOPHERS ON DRUG AND ALCOHOL ABUSE

According to Aristotle, virtue entails acting according to reason. Wisdom is the greatest intellectual virtue and ignorance the greatest vice. People who are drunk are "acting in ignorance." Thus, addicts give up their essential humanity by giving up control of their actions. Aristotle rejects the disease model of addiction, however. We need have no sympathy for a person whose health is destroyed by excessive drinking or drug abuse. Unlike a person whose illness is involuntary, a drunkard is responsible for his ignorance "since it was open to him to refrain from getting drunk."[42]

Although Aristotle would probably not object to the use of drugs and alcohol in moderation, many Buddhists are morally opposed to any use of drugs and alcohol. The eightfold path requires a "clear and composed mind" in order to achieve moral perfection and enlightenment. Seeking solace or distraction in mind-altering drugs is a form of false contemplation. According to Buddha, all human suffering is caused by people whose minds are confused and their reason dulled. Buddhist philosopher Don Premasiri maintains that many of the contemporary social evils, such as violence, irresponsible behavior, and moral corruption, are the result of the spread of alcoholism and drug addiction.

Muslims are also opposed to the use of alcohol and drugs. Alcohol use is a moral failing similar to slander. According to Muslim philosophy, "When a person drinks he becomes intoxicated; when he is intoxicated he raves; and when he raves he falsely accuses."[43]

Libertarians, on the other hand, favor a permissive policy on drug and alcohol use. John Stuart Mill opposed the American prohibition laws of the 1850s as an unjustified interference with people's liberty. He wrote, "Over himself, over his own body and mind, the individual is sovereign."[44] Although Mill acknowledged that drug or alcohol users can harm others by rendering themselves incapable of working, this does not justify prohibiting drugs, because society can afford to absorb these losses for the sake of liberty. The benefits of liberty, in other words, outweigh the harms caused by alcohol and drug use.

MORAL ISSUES

Virtue Ethics and the Good Life

According to virtue ethicists, we have a moral obligation to improve our character through self-examination and the practice of virtuous behavior. The Buddhist virtue of right effort, for example, requires that we live deliberately rather than impulsively. Addiction interferes with our ability to engage in philosophical self-examination and to seek the higher good.

Virtue, in most cases, requires us to seek the mean between excess and deficit. The doctrine of the mean requires that we know ourselves and our limitations and that we use our reason to discern where the mean is, for us, between excess and deficit. According to the disease model, the use of any amount of a drug is an excess for addicts. On the other hand, for other people, moderation may be appropriate and consistent with the good and virtuous life. Recent studies at Harvard University have found that moderate drinkers are healthiest and live the longest. Anti-anxiety drugs can also help people who are depressed by offering them a respite and an opportunity for self-examination; on the other hand, they can also be used as a crutch for avoiding self-analysis. Morphine is another drug where excess for one person may be a deficiency for another. Although morphine can be addictive, to refuse a dying cancer patient morphine because of fear of addiction is to err on the side of deficiency.

Confucius believed that government bears the primary responsibility for promoting virtue in citizens. The purpose of laws and public policy is to make it easier for people to be virtuous. James Q. Wilson argues that if drugs are legal, many people will prefer the pleasure of drug excess over treatment and virtuous behavior. Douglas Husak counters that it is not the place of government to impose on citizens an ideal of human excellence. It is up to each of us to responsibly determine our own concept of the good life.

Human Dignity and the Categorical Imperative

Kant's categorical imperative states that we should never use ourselves as a means only. Addicts debase themselves by using themselves as a means only—to get a fix through the ingestion of drugs or alcohol. Addiction is tempting because it tranquilizes; it "fixes" our disquiet and malaise. We become dependent on this fix. Addiction distracts us from our lives and relieves us of the burden, the frustration, the boredom, and the search for meaning in our lives. Addiction *becomes* the meaning of life. Because drug abuse and addiction prevent us from being fully human, they are incompatible with human dignity.

As rational moral agents, we are responsible for our choices and actions. The disease model is problematic in that it places the burden of "curing" addiction on physicians rather than on the individual using the drugs, thus allowing addicts to abdicate personal responsibility for their behavior. The medical model also invites blaming other people (known as "co-dependents") for the addict's behavior. Passing off responsibility for our destructive and disrespectful behavior is inconsistent with human dignity and freedom.

Autonomy, Liberty Rights, and the Principle of Noninterference

Autonomy involves our ability to make free choices. Autonomous people lead rational and self-critical lives. Our autonomy is violated if we are prevented from doing what we have a moral right to do.

Both Szasz and Husak argue that prohibiting recreational drug use violates our autonomy. Enforcement procedures are not only futile, but an infringement on people's liberty rights. They also reject the disease model of addiction. Drug addicts are autonomous, because any person of "reasonable firmness" can stop using drugs. Szasz likewise argues that the "right of self-medication" is a fundamental right.

Not everyone agrees that adult drug users are acting autonomously, however. Murray, for example, maintains that the use of performance-enhancing drugs in sports is "inherently coercive." In sports, in which one's professional success may ride on using performance-enhancing drugs, the pressure to use these drugs may seriously compromise the athlete's autonomy. The principle of noninterference states that interference with adults' free choice must be justified. Interference in the case of minors may also justify interference in adult drug and alcohol use, because most people become addicted as children, before they are able to make fully informed, rational decisions. In the United States, the average age is twelve for the first alcohol use and thirteen for the first use of illicit drugs.[45] Judges in both Massachusetts and Iowa have upheld a school's right to search students for drugs, ruling in *Iowa v. Marzel Jones (2002)* that the school's interest in maintaining that "a controlled and disciplined environment," overrules a student's right to privacy.

Because those who desire to quit often cannot, addiction is a form of slavery. According to natural rights ethicists such as John Locke, our liberty rights do not permit us to sell ourselves into slavery. Using this analogy, it is also wrong to turn our lives over to drugs, as in doing so we give up ownership of our lives.

Pleasure

Pleasure is by far the most common reason college students give for using alcohol and drugs.[46] According to some utilitarians, the use of drugs for pleasure is not necessarily at odds with the good life and may even contribute to it in some cases. On the other hand, most philosophers, including utilitarians, draw the line at drug use that interferes with living the good life.

Paternalism and Harm to Self

Most people's position on the morality of drug and alcohol use depends primarily on whether they believe that drugs are harmful. Paternalism permits interfering with people's choices for their own good. Drugs and alcohol can be harmful to self. The life of an average alcoholic, for example, is fifteen years shorter than that of a nonalcoholic.[47]

The belief that drug and alcohol abuse is a disease promotes a paternalistic approach toward drug and alcohol regulation. Laws prohibiting alcohol and tobacco use by children are generally based on the principle of paternalism. Given that most untimely adult deaths involve drugs and alcohol abuse, however, shouldn't paternalism extend to adults as well? If prohibition is justified for minors on the grounds that it is harmful and irrational for children to use drugs and alcohol, why is it not the same for adults who abuse drugs? If adults use drugs in a manner that is harmful toward themselves, isn't their "decision" to do so by definition irrational and, hence, not a free and autonomous choice?

Prohibition based on paternalism can come into conflict with the principle of autonomy. The use of coercion—even paternalistic "well-meaning" coercion—in an attempt to regulate another person's character is an affront to human dignity and freedom. Should we prohibit drugs for all because drugs seriously impair the autonomy of some? The belief that people use drugs "against their will" or have "lost control of their lives" or that drug users are "morally deficient" is demeaning. It may be better to let addicts continue harming themselves rather than deny them at least some control over their lives.

Furthermore, because people do not like to be told what to do, paternalism can backfire. There was a dramatic increase in drug use, especially among young people, following Bush's declaration of war on drugs. Studies also suggest that raising the drinking age from eighteen to twenty-one throughout the United States may actually have exacerbated the bingeing problem on campuses. In addition to the lure of forbidden fruit, students are now more likely to drink in private places like their dorms and fraternities or in bars that are lax on checking for proper ID.[48]

"Harm reduction," which attempts to minimize the harms of addictive behavior without engaging in paternalism, is currently a popular approach to controlling such behavior.[49] This alternative to a prohibitionist/criminal approach is used in the Netherlands. Instead of prosecuting drug users, the Dutch policy in general preserves the liberty right to use drugs while minimizing harm by providing sterile needles.

Nonmaleficence and Preventing Harm to Others

One of the most common arguments for drug prohibition is protection of public health and safety. Although restrictions based on paternalism are often considered an affront to personal dignity, most people acknowledge that coercion is justified to prevent people from harming one another.

Wilson argues that the harms of legalizing drugs outweigh those of prohibition. Drug abuse, he points out, is hardly a victimless crime. It is associated with health problems, reduced job productivity, family violence, crime, fetal alcohol syndrome, drug-addicted newborns, and suicide. Many of these costs are passed on to society. Twenty percent of Medicare funds, for example, go to the treatment of problems stemming from alcohol and drug abuse. Indeed, elderly patients are more likely to be hospitalized for conditions related to alcohol abuse than for heart attacks.[50] The cost of treating infants born to cocaine/crack mothers is estimated to be $500 million a year.[51]

In 2002 a U.S. Circuit Court of Appeals in *Ferguson v. City of Charleston* ruled that a public hospital's policy of testing the urine of pregnant women for cocaine and forwarding the results to law enforcement officials violated the Fourth Amendment. Given that cocaine-using mothers are not legally liable for the harms to their offspring, is it fair that others are forced to pick up these costs? Drug-related crimes cost taxpayers more than $30 billion a year. The number of people in prison in the United States for drug-related crimes has dropped since 1994, when about 60 percent of federal prisoners were incarcerated for drug offenses;[52] 81 percent of juvenile offenders are also "substance abusers."[53]

Husak supports legalizing recreational drugs but reminds us that we also have to consider the costs associated with criminalizing drugs. Harm to others is a powerful argument for working toward decreasing drug and alcohol abuse, but it is not obvious that legal prohibition is the best solution; drug education may be more effective. Making drugs illegal forces up the prices of drugs, thus encouraging users to resort to crime to pay for their habits. Much of the street violence in our cities is attributable to the illicit sale of drugs rather than to the actual effects of the drugs themselves. Also, deaths due to overdose reactions and AIDS are in part due to impurities in the street drugs and to contaminated needles. In addition, because street dealers are already criminals, drug prohibition brings young people seeking drugs into contact with the criminal element.

Advocates of more legal restrictions on drugs and alcohol, such as Wilson, counter that the claim that legalizing currently illegal drugs will decrease violence is speculation. Yet, despite the media attention given to the violence associated with illegal drugs, it is legal drugs that are the most deadly. The violence of illegal drugs may be more visible, but there are hidden costs of alcoholism in terms of domestic violence and the breakup of families. In addition, the cost of health care for alcoholics is more than double that of nonalcoholics; much of this cost is borne by taxpayers and employers. Smokers also use more medical resources and have longer hospital stays than nonsmokers. Indeed, lung cancer has now become the leading cause of all cancer deaths in women.[54]

CONCLUSION

Drug and alcohol use raises two concerns. The first relates to virtue ethics: We have a personal responsibility to abstain from harmful drugs or drugs that are addictive to us. If addiction is a disease, virtue dictates that addicts or potential addicts are morally responsible for avoiding drugs and/or alcohol and for seeking a cure, or at least avoiding situations in which they could harm others. On the other hand, the moderate use of certain drugs may actually enhance the good life. Knowing the difference between excess and moderation involves the development of wisdom and character.

The second issue relates to social policy. Some philosophers maintain that drugs should be prohibited. Others, while not supporting drug use, argue that banning drugs is wrong. Sometimes what initially appears to be a moral disagreement turns out to be a factual dispute. This is often the case in debates over appropriate policies on drugs and alcohol. Most people agree that harm to others is a strong justification for restricting drug use; however, they disagree over the best means to achieve the objective of minimizing harm.

THOMAS SZASZ

The Ethics of Addiction

Thomas Szasz is a professor of psychiatry at the State University of New York Upstate Medical Center and author of several books on psychiatry, including *The Myth of Mental Illness* and *The Manufacture of Madness.* In this article Szasz rejects the disease model of addiction and the argument that people who use drugs and/or alcohol lack control over that aspect of their lives. Citing John Stuart Mill's principle of no harm, Szasz argues that drug laws do not respect the right of citizens to exercise control over their own lives. Therefore, all prohibition laws should be repealed, at least for adults.

Critical Reading Questions

1. What is the World Health Organization definition of drug abuse? Why does Szasz maintain that this definition is a moral judgment rather than a medical or technical judgment?
2. According to Szasz, what "propaganda" is used by proponents of the disease model of addiction to justify the prohibition of drug use?
3. Why does Szasz reject the prohibition argument that some drugs are dangerous?
4. According to Szasz, why do people become addicted? Why does Szasz reject the prohibition argument that drug addiction is different from addiction to other substances and stimuli?
5. According to Szasz, what are the primary reasons people take drugs? Which of these reasons is identified with "drug abuse"?
6. Why, according to Szasz, is there so much opposition to the concept of free trade in drugs?
7. What arguments does Szasz use to support his position for the legalization of drugs?
8. On what grounds does Szasz argue that the "right of self-medication" is a fundamental right? Should there be any limitations on this right, and, if so, what are some possible limitations?
9. Why does Szasz support the prohibition of drug and alcohol sales to minors?
10. What are the two principal methods of legitimizing policy in the United States? How have these two methods been used to legitimize the prohibition of drugs?
11. On what grounds does Szasz reject the current medical concept of drug abuse and drug treatment programs?
12. According to Szasz, why are we in need of a "medical reformation"?
13. On what grounds does Szasz argue that we have a constitutional right to use drugs and alcohol?
14. How does Szasz use John Stuart Mill's philosophy to support his position?

"The Ethics of Addiction," *Harper's Magazine* 244, April 1972, 74–79.

AN ARGUMENT IN FAVOR OF LETTING AMERICANS TAKE ANY DRUG THEY WANT TO TAKE

To avoid cliches about "drug abuse," let us analyze its official definition. According to the World Health Organization, "Drug addiction is a state of periodic or chronic intoxication detrimental to the individual and to society, produced by the repeated consumption of a drug (natural or synthetic). Its characteristics include: 1) an overpowering desire or need (compulsion) to continue taking the drug and to obtain it by any means, 2) a tendency to increase the dosage, and 3) a psychic (psychological) and sometimes physical dependence on the effects of the drug."

Since this definition hinges on the harm done to both the individual and society, it is clearly an ethical one. Moreover, by not specifying what is "detrimental," it consigns the problem of addiction to psychiatrists who define the patient's "dangerousness to himself and others."

Next, we come to the effort to obtain the addictive substance "by any means." This suggests that the substance must be prohibited, or is very expensive, and is hence difficult for the ordinary person to obtain (rather than that the person who wants it has an inordinate craving for it). If there were an abundant and inexpensive supply of what the "addict" wants, there would be no reason for him to go to "any means" to obtain it. Thus by the WHO's definition, one can be addicted only to a substance that is illegal or otherwise difficult to obtain. This surely removes the problem of addiction from the realm of medicine and psychiatry, and puts it squarely into that of morals and law.

In short, drug addiction or drug abuse cannot be defined without specifying the proper and improper uses of certain pharmacologically active agents. The regular administration of morphine by a physician to a patient dying of cancer is the paradigm of the proper use of a narcotic; whereas even its occasional self-administration by a physically healthy person for the purpose of "pharmacological pleasure" is the paradigm of drug abuse.

I submit that these judgments have nothing whatever to do with medicine, pharmacology, or psychiatry. They are moral judgments. Indeed, our present views on addiction are astonishingly similar to some of our former views on sex. Until recently, masturbation—or self-abuse, as it was called—was professionally declared, and popularly accepted, as both the cause and the symptom of a variety of illnesses. Even today, homosexuality—called a "sexual perversion"—is regarded as a disease by medical and psychiatric experts as well as by "well-informed" laymen.

To be sure, it is now virtually impossible to cite a contemporary medical authority to support the concept of self-abuse. Medical opinion holds that whether a person masturbates or not is medically irrelevant; and that engaging in the practice or refraining from it is a matter of personal morals or life-style. On the other hand, it is virtually impossible to cite a contemporary medical authority to oppose the concept of drug abuse. Medical opinion holds that drug abuse is a major medical, psychiatric, and public health problem; that drug addiction is a disease similar to diabetes, requiring prolonged (or lifelong) and careful, medically supervised treatment; and that taking or not taking drugs is primarily, if not solely, a matter of medical responsibility.

Thus the man on the street can only believe what he hears from all sides—that drug addiction is a disease, "like any other," which has now reached "epidemic proportions," and whose "medical" containment justifies the limitless expenditure of tax monies and the corresponding aggrandizement and enrichment of noble medical warriors against this "plague."

PROPAGANDA TO JUSTIFY PROHIBITION

Like any social policy, our drug laws may be examined from two entirely different points of view: technical and moral. Our present inclination is either to ignore the moral perspective or to mistake the technical for the moral.

Since most of the propagandists against drug use seek to justify certain repressive policies because of the alleged dangerousness of various drugs, they often falsify the facts about the pharmacological properties of the drugs they seek to prohibit. They do so for two reasons: first, because many substances in daily use are just as harmful as the substances they want to prohibit; second, because they realize that dangerousness alone is never a sufficiently persuasive argument to justify the prohibition of any drug, substance, or artifact. Accordingly, the more they ignore the moral dimensions of the problem, the more they must escalate their fraudulent claims about the dangers of drugs.

To be sure, some drugs are more dangerous than others. It is easier to kill oneself with heroin than with aspirin. But is also easier to kill oneself by jumping off a high building than a low one. In the case of drugs, we regard their potentiality for self-injury as justification for their prohibition; in the case of buildings, we do not.

Furthermore, we systematically blur and confuse the two quite different ways in which narcotics may cause death: by a deliberate act of suicide or by accidental overdosage.

Every individual is capable of injuring or killing himself. This potentiality is a fundamental expression of human freedom. Self-destructive behavior may be regarded as sinful and penalized by means of informal sanctions. But it should not be regarded as a crime or (mental) disease, justifying or warranting the use of the police powers of the state for its control.

Therefore, it is absurd to deprive an adult of a drug (or of anything else) because he might use it to kill himself. To do so is to treat everyone the way institutional psychiatrists treat the so-called suicidal mental patient: they not only imprison such a person but take everything away from him—shoelaces, belts, razor blades, eating utensils, and so forth—until the "patient" lies naked on a mattress in a padded cell—lest he kill himself. The result is degrading tyrannization.

Death by accidental overdose is an altogether different matter. But can anyone doubt that this danger now looms so large precisely because the sale of narcotics and many other drugs is illegal? Those who buy illicit drugs cannot be sure what drug they are getting or how much of it. Free trade in drugs, with governmental action limited to safeguarding the purity of the product and the veracity of the labeling, would reduce the risk of accidental overdose with "dangerous drugs" to the same levels that prevail, and that we find acceptable, with respect to other chemical agents and physical artifacts that abound in our complex technological society.

This essay is not intended as an exposition on the pharmacological properties of narcotics and other mind-affecting drugs. However, I want to make it clear that in my view, *regardless* of their danger, all drugs should be "legalized" (a misleading term I employ reluctantly as a concession to common usage). Although I recognize that some drugs—notably heroin, the amphetamines, and LSD, among those now in vogue—may have undesirable or dangerous consequences, I favor free trade in drugs for the same reason the Founding Fathers favored free trade in ideas. In an open society, it is none of the government's business what idea a man puts into his mind; likewise, it should be none of the government's business what drug he puts into his body.

WITHDRAWAL PAINS FROM TRADITION

It is a fundamental characteristic of human beings that they get used to things: one becomes habituated, or "addicted," not only to narcotics, but to cigarettes, cocktails before dinner, orange juice for breakfast, comic strips, and so forth. It is similarly a fundamental characteristic of living organisms that they acquire increasing tolerance to various chemical agents and physical stimuli: the first cigarette may cause nothing but nausea and headache; a year later, smoking three packs a day may be pure joy. Both alcohol and opiates are "addictive" in the sense that the more regularly they are used, the more the user craves them and the greater his tolerance for them becomes. Yet none of this involves any mysterious process of "getting hooked." It is simply an aspect of the universal biological propensity for *learning*, which is especially well developed in man. The opiate habit, like the cigarette habit or food habit, can be broken—and without any medical assistance—provided the person wants to break it. Often he doesn't. And why, indeed, should he, if he has nothing better to do with his life? Or, as happens to be the case with morphine, if he can live an essentially normal life while under its influence?

Actually, opium is much less toxic than alcohol. Just as it is possible to be an "alcoholic" and work and be productive, so it is (or, rather, it used to be) possible to be an opium addict and work and be productive. . . .

I am not citing this evidence to recommend the opium habit. The point is that we must, in plain honesty, distinguish between pharmacological effects and personal inclinations. Some people take drugs to help them function and conform to social expectations; others take them for the very opposite reason, to ritualize their refusal to function and conform to social expectations. Much of the "drug abuse" we now witness—perhaps nearly all of it—is of the second type. But instead of acknowledging that "addicts" are unfit or unwilling to work and be "normal," we prefer to believe that they act as they do because certain drugs—especially heroin, LSD, and the amphetamines—make them "sick." If only we could get them "well," so runs this comforting view, they would become "productive" and "useful" citizens. To believe this is like believing that if an illiterate cigarette smoker would only stop smoking, he would become an Einstein. With a falsehood like this, one can go far. No wonder that politicians and psychiatrists love it.

The concept of free trade in drugs runs counter to our cherished notion that everyone must work and idleness is acceptable only under special conditions. In general, the obligation to work is greatest for healthy, adult, white men. We tolerate idleness on the part of children, women, Negroes, the aged, and the sick, and even accept the responsibility to support them. But the new wave of drug abuse affects mainly young adults, often white males, who are, in principle at least, capable of working and supporting themselves. But they refuse: they "drop out"; and in doing so, they challenge the most basic values of our society.

The fear that free trade in narcotics would result in vast masses of our population spending their days and nights smoking opium or mainlining heroin, rather than working and taking care of their responsibilities, is a bugaboo that does not deserve to be taken seriously. Habits of work and idleness are deep-seated cultural patterns. Free trade in abortions has not made an industrious people like the Japanese give up work for fornication. Nor would free trade in drugs convert such a people from hustlers to hippies. Indeed, I think the opposite might be the case: it is questionable whether, or for how long, a responsible people can tolerate being treated as totally irresponsible with respect to drugs and drug-taking. In other words, how long can we live with the inconsistency of being expected to be responsible for operating cars and computers, but not for operating our own bodies?

Although my argument about drug-taking is moral and political, and does not depend upon showing that free trade in drugs would also have fiscal advantages over our present policies, let me indicate briefly some of its economic implications.

The war on addiction is not only astronomically expensive; it is also counterproductive. On April 1, 1967, New York State's narcotics addiction control program, hailed as "the most massive ever tried in the nation," went into effect. "The program, which may cost up to $400 million in three years," reported the *New York Times,* "was hailed by Governor Rockefeller as 'the start of an unending war.'" . . . In short, the detection and rehabilitation of addicts is good business. We now know that the spread of witchcraft in the late Middle Ages was due more to the work of witchmongers than to the lure of witchcraft. Is it not possible that the spread of addiction in our day is due more to the work of addictmongers than to the lure of narcotics?

Let us see how far some of the monies spent on the war on addiction could go in supporting people who prefer to drop out of society and drug themselves. Their "habit" itself would cost next to nothing; free trade would bring the price of narcotics down to a negligible amount. . . .

. . . free trade in narcotics would be more economical for those of us who work, even if we had to support legions of addicts, than is our present program of trying to "cure" them. Moreover, I have not even made use, in my economic estimates, of the incalculable sums we would save by reducing crimes now engendered by the illegal traffic in drugs.

THE RIGHT OF SELF-MEDICATION

Clearly, the argument that marijuana—or heroin, methadone, or morphine—is prohibited because it is addictive or dangerous cannot be supported by facts. For one thing, there are many drugs, from insulin to penicillin, that are neither addictive nor dangerous but are nevertheless also prohibited; they can be obtained only through a physician's prescription. For another, there are many things, from dynamite to guns, that are much more dangerous than narcotics (especially to others) but are not prohibited. As everyone knows, it is still possible in the United States to walk into a store and walk out with a shotgun. We enjoy this right not because we believe that guns are safe but because we believe even more strongly that civil liberties are precious. At the same time, it is not possible in the United States to walk into a store and walk out with a bottle of barbiturates, codeine, or other drugs.

I believe that just as we regard freedom of speech and religion as fundamental rights, so we should also regard freedom of self-medication as a fundamental right. Like most rights, the right of self-medication should apply only to adults; and it should not be an unqualified right. Since these are important qualifications, it is necessary to specify their precise range.

John Stuart Mill said (approximately) that a person's right to swing his arm ends where his neighbor's nose begins. And Oliver Wendell Holmes said that no one has a right to shout "Fire!" in a crowded theater. Similarly, the limiting condition with respect to self-medication should be the inflicting of actual (as against symbolic) harm on others.

Our present practices with respect to alcohol embody and reflect this individualistic ethic. We have the right to buy, possess, and consume alcoholic beverages. Regardless of how offensive drunkenness might be to a person, he cannot interfere with another person's "right" to become inebriated so long as that person drinks in the privacy of his own home or at some other appropriate location, and so long as he conducts himself in an otherwise law-abiding manner. In short, we have a right to be intoxicated—in private. Public intoxication is considered an offense to others and is therefore a violation of the criminal law. It makes sense that what is a "right" in one place may become, by virtue of its disruptive or disturbing effect on others, an offense somewhere else.

The right to self-medication should be hedged in by similar limits. Public intoxication, not only with alcohol but with any drug, should be an offense punishable by the criminal law. Furthermore, acts that may injure others—such as driving a car—should, when carried out in a drug-intoxicated state, be punished especially strictly and severely. The right to self-medication must thus entail unqualified responsibility for the effects of one's drug-intoxicated behavior on others. For unless we are willing to hold ourselves responsible for our own behavior, and hold others responsible for theirs, the liberty to use drugs (or to engage in other acts) degenerates into a license to hurt others.

Such, then, would be the situation of adults, if we regarded the freedom to take drugs as a fundamental right similar to the freedom to read and worship. What would be the situation of children? Since many people who are now said to be drug addicts or drug abusers are minors, it is especially important that we think clearly about this aspect of the problem.

I do not believe, and I do not advocate, that children should have a right to ingest, inject, or otherwise use any drug or substance they want. Children do not have the right to drive, drink, vote, marry, or make binding contracts. They acquire these rights at various ages, coming into their full possession at maturity, usually between the ages of eighteen and twenty-one. The right to self-medication should similarly be withheld until maturity.

In short, I suggest that "dangerous" drugs be treated, more or less, as alcohol is treated now. Neither the use of narcotics, nor their possession, should be prohibited, but only their sale to minors. Of course, this would result in the ready availability of all kinds of drugs among minors—though perhaps their availability would be no greater than it is now, but would only be more visible and hence more easily subject to proper controls. This arrangement would place responsibility for the use of all drugs by children where it belongs: on parents and their children. This is where the major responsibility rests for the use of alcohol. It is a tragic symptom of our refusal to take personal liberty and responsibility seriously that there appears to be no public desire to assume a similar stance toward other "dangerous" drugs.

Consider what would happen should a child bring a bottle of gin to school and get drunk there. Would the school authorities blame the local liquor stores as pushers? Or would they blame the parents and the child himself? There is liquor in practically every home in America and yet children rarely bring liquor to school. Whereas marijuana, Dexedrine, and heroin—substances children usually do not find at home and whose very possession is a criminal offense—frequently find their way into the school.

Our attitude toward sexual activity provides another model for our attitude toward drugs. Although we generally discourage children below a certain age from engaging in sexual activities with others, we do not prohibit such activities by law. What we do prohibit by law is the sexual seduction of children by adults. The "pharmacological seduction" of children by adults should be similarly punishable. In other words, adults who give or sell drugs to children should be regarded as offenders. Such a specific and limited prohibition—as against the kinds of generalized prohibitions that we had under the Volstead Act or have now with respect to countless drugs—would be relatively easy to enforce. Moreover, it would probably be rarely violated, for there would be little psychological interest and no economic profit in doing so.

THE TRUE FAITH: SCIENTIFIC MEDICINE

What I am suggesting is that while addiction is ostensibly a medical and pharmacological problem, actually it is a moral and political problem. We ought to know that there is no necessary connection between facts and values, between what is and what ought to be. Thus, objectively quite harmful acts, objects, or persons may be accepted and tolerated—by minimizing their dangerousness. Conversely, objectively quite harmless acts, objects, or persons may be prohibited and persecuted—by exaggerating their dangerousness. It is always necessary to distinguish—and especially so when dealing with social policy—between description and prescription, fact and rhetoric, truth and falsehood.

In our society, there are two principal methods of legitimizing policy: social tradition and scientific judgment. More than anything else, time is the supreme ethical arbiter. Whatever a social practice might be, if people engage in it, generation after generation, that practice becomes acceptable.

Many opponents of illegal drugs admit that nicotine may be more harmful to health than marijuana; nevertheless, they urge that smoking cigarettes should be legal but smoking marijuana should not be, because the former habit is socially accepted while the latter is not. This is a perfectly reasonable argument. But let us understand it for what it is—a plea for legitimizing old and accepted practices, and for illegitimizing novel and unaccepted ones. It is a justification that rests on precedent, not evidence.

The other method of legitimizing policy, ever more important in the modern world, is through the authority of science. In matters of health, a vast and increasingly elastic category, physicians play important roles as legitimizers and illegitimizers. This, in short, is why we regard being medicated by a doctor as drug use, and self-medication (especially with certain classes of drugs) as drug abuse.

This, too, is a perfectly reasonable arrangement. But we must understand that it is a plea for legitimizing what doctors do, because they do it with "good therapeutic" intent; and for illegitimatizing what laymen do, because they do it with bad self-abusive ("masturbatory" or mind-altering) intent. This justification rests on the principles of professionalism, not of pharmacology. Hence we applaud the systematic medical use of methadone and call it "treatment for heroin addiction," but decry the occasional nonmedical use of marijuana and call it "dangerous drug abuse."

Our present concept of drug abuse articulates and symbolizes a fundamental policy of scientific medicine—namely, that a layman should not medicate his own body but should place its medical care under the supervision of a duly accredited physician. Before the Reformation, the practice of True Christianity rested on a similar policy—namely, that a layman should not himself commune with God but should place his spiritual care under the supervision of a duly accredited priest. The self-interests of the church and of medicine in such policies are obvious enough. What might be less obvious is the interest of the laity: by delegating responsibility for the spiritual and medical welfare of the people to a class of authoritatively accredited specialists, these policies—and the practices they ensure—relieve individuals from assuming the burdens of responsibility for themselves. As I see it, our present problems with drug use and drug abuse are just one of the consequences of our pervasive ambivalence about personal autonomy and responsibility.

I propose a medical reformation analogous to the Protestant Reformation: specifically, a "protest" against the systematic mystification of man's relationship to his body and his professionalized separation from it. The immediate aim of this reform would be to remove the physician as intermediary between man and his body and to give the layman direct access to the language and contents of the pharmacopoeia. If man had unencumbered access to his own body and the means of chemically altering it, it would spell the end of medicine, at least as we now know it. This is why, with faith in scientific medicine so strong, there is little interest in this kind of medical reform. Physicians fear the loss of their privileges; laymen, the loss of their protections. . . .

LIFE, LIBERTY, AND THE PURSUIT OF HIGHS

Sooner or later we shall have to confront the basic moral dilemma underlying this problem: does a person have the right to take a drug, any drug—not because he needs it to cure an illness, but because he wants to take it?

The Declaration of Independence speaks of our inalienable right to "life, liberty, and the pursuit of happiness." How are we to interpret this? By asserting that we ought to be free to pursue happiness by playing golf or watching television, but not by drinking alcohol, or smoking marijuana, or ingesting pep pills?

The Constitution and the Bill of Rights are silent on the subject of drugs. This would seem to imply that the adult citizen has, or ought to have, the right to medicate his own body as he sees fit. Were this not the case, why should there have been a need for a Constitutional Amendment to outlaw drinking? But if ingesting alcohol was, and is now again, a Constitutional right, is ingesting opium, or heroin, or barbiturates, or anything else, not also such a right? If it is, then the Harrison Narcotic Act is not only a bad law but is unconstitutional as well, because it prescribes in a legislative act what ought to be promulgated in a Constitutional Amendment.

The questions remain: as American citizens, should we have the right to take narcotics or other drugs? If we take drugs and conduct ourselves as responsible and law-abiding citizens, should we have a right to remain unmolested by the government? Lastly, if we take drugs and break the law, should we have a right to be treated as persons accused of crime, rather than as patients accused of mental illness?

These are fundamental questions that are conspicuous by their absence from all contemporary discussions of problems of drug addiction and drug abuse. The result is that instead of debating the use of drugs in moral and political terms, we define our task as the ostensibly narrow technical problem of protecting people from poisoning themselves with substances for whose use they cannot possibly assume responsibility. This, I think, best explains the frightening national consensus against personal responsibility for taking drugs and for one's conduct while under their influence. . . .

To me, unanimity on an issue as basic and complex as this means a complete evasion of the actual problem and an attempt to master it by attacking and overpowering a scapegoat—"dangerous drugs" and "drug abusers." There is an ominous resemblance between the unanimity with which all "reasonable" men—and especially politicians, physicians, and priests—formerly supported the protective measures of society against witches and Jews, and that with which they now support them against drug addicts and drug abusers.

After all is said and done, the issue comes down to whether we accept or reject the ethical principle John Stuart Mill so clearly enunciated: "The only purpose [he wrote in *On Liberty*] for which power can be rightfully exercised over any member of a civilized community, against his will, is to prevent harm to others. His own good, either physical or moral, is not a sufficient warrant. He cannot rightfully be compelled to do or forbear because it will make him happier, because in the opinions of others, to do so would be wise, or even right. . . . In the part [of his conduct] which merely concerns himself, his independence is, of right, absolute. Over himself, over his own body and mind, the individual is sovereign."

By recognizing the problem of drug abuse for what it is—a moral and political question rather than a medical or therapeutic one—we can choose to maximize the sphere of action of the state at the expense of the individual, or of the individual at the expense of the state. In other words, we could commit ourselves to the view that the state, the representative of many, is more important than the individual; that it therefore has the right, indeed the duty, to regulate the life of the individual in the best interests of the group. Or we could commit ourselves to the view that individual dignity and liberty are the supreme values of life, and that the foremost duty of the state is to protect and promote these values.

In short, we must choose between the ethic of collectivism and individualism, and pay the price of either—or of both.

Discussion Questions

1. What, according to Szasz, are some of the myths surrounding the notion of drug addiction? Would an advocate of the disease model of addiction agree that these are myths? Discuss how Elvine Jellinek, who supported the disease model of addiction (see p. 304), might respond to Szasz. Which person presents the stronger argument? Support your answers.
2. Do you agree with Szasz that people under eighteen or twenty-one are not mature enough to use drugs and alcohol? Is Szasz being logically consistent or is he using doublethink in his rejection of legal access to drugs and alcohol for teenagers? If it is wrong for children to use certain "dangerous" drugs, why isn't it also wrong for adults to use the same drugs? Should "immature" adults who abuse drugs and alcohol also be legally prohibited from using these substances? Support your answers.
3. Szasz rejects appeal to social tradition as a method of legitimizing public policy. Is he also committing the fallacy of appeal to tradition when he argues that we have a constitutional right to use drugs? Or can his argument for a "right of self-medication" stand without appeal to the Constitution? Support your answers.
4. Moonshining—the illegal production and sale of distilled spirits—is an underground art in some rural parts of the Atlantic provinces in Canada. Although moonshiners are not about to put the government liquor stores out of business, the Royal Canadian Mounted Police have been receiving a growing number of tips about the whereabouts of illegal stills, as well as complaints from public-spirited neighbors. Do laws that prohibit moonshining violate the right of citizens to exercise control over their own lives? Support your answer. Discuss how Szasz would respond to this question.

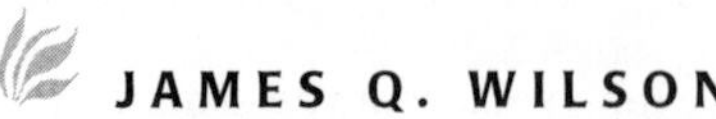

JAMES Q. WILSON

Against the Legalization of Drugs

James Q. Wilson is a professor of management and public policy at the University of California in Los Angeles and chairman of the National Advisory Council for Drug Abuse Prevention. He is also author of *The Moral Sense* and *Crime and Human Nature.* Wilson is particularly interested in the interplay of public policy and morality. In the following article, he rejects the libertarian view that citizens have the right to use drugs and to drink anything they want. Instead, Wilson argues that the harms of legalizing drugs outweigh the harms of prohibition.

Critical Reading Questions

1. What arguments does Wilson use to show that drug prohibition is morally justified?
2. According to Wilson, why are youth less likely to use heroin now than they were in 1972?
3. What is Wilson's view on the disease model of addiction? Has drug therapy been successful in reducing drug use?
4. What evidence does Wilson use to support his position that legalizing drugs would increase their use?
5. Which drugs does Wilson think should be prohibited and why? Is he opposed to the legalization of any drug or only of certain drugs?
6. What are some of the harmful effects of heroin and cocaine that, according to Wilson, justify their prohibition?
7. Why does Wilson reject the concept of drug abuse as a "victimless crime"?
8. Why is Wilson appalled by the argument that drug abusers should be allowed to kill themselves?
9. How does Wilson respond to the anti-prohibition argument that the illegality of drugs increases crime?
10. According to Wilson, what are some of the benefits of making drugs illegal?
11. According to Wilson, why would drug treatment be less successful if drugs were legal?
12. What is Wilson's view on the morality of tobacco use? What are the similarities and differences, according to Wilson, of tobacco use and cocaine use?
13. What is Wilson's view on the morality of alcohol use? What are some of its harms?
14. Why does Wilson dislike the "war on drugs" metaphor? What metaphor does he prefer?
15. According to Wilson, what is the role of science in helping us understand and cope with addiction?

"Against the Legalization of Drugs," *Commentary* 89, no. 2 (February 1990): 21–28.

In 1972, the President appointed me chairman of the National Advisory Council for Drug Abuse Prevention. Created by Congress, the Council was charged with providing guidance on how best to coordinate the national war on drugs. (Yes, we called it a war then, too.) In those days, the drug we were chiefly concerned with was heroin. When I took office, heroin use had been increasing dramatically. Everybody was worried that this increase would continue. Such phrases as "heroin epidemic" were commonplace.

That same year, the eminent economist Milton Friedman published an essay in *Newsweek* in which he called for legalizing heroin. His argument was on two grounds: as a matter of ethics, the government has no right to tell people not to use heroin (or to drink or to commit suicide); as a matter of economics, the prohibition of drug use imposes costs on society that far exceed the benefits. Others, such as the psychoanalyst Thomas Szasz, made the same argument. . . .

That was 1972. Today, we have the same number of heroin addicts that we had then—half a million, give or take a few thousand. Having that many heroin addicts is no trivial matter; these people deserve our attention. But not having had an increase in that number for over fifteen years is also something that deserves our attention. What happened to the "heroin epidemic" that many people once thought would overwhelm us?

The facts are clear: a more or less stable pool of heroin addicts has been getting older, with relatively few new recruits. In 1976 the average age of heroin users who appeared in hospital emergency rooms was about twenty-seven; ten years later it was thirty-two. More than two-thirds of all heroin users appearing in emergency rooms are now over the age of thirty. Back in the early 1970s, when heroin got onto the national political agenda, the typical heroin addict was much younger, often a teenager. . . .

Why did heroin lose its appeal for young people? When the young blacks in Harlem were asked why they stopped, more than half mentioned "trouble with the law" or "high cost" (and high cost is, of course, directly the result of law enforcement). Two-thirds said heroin hurt their health; nearly all said they had had a bad experience with it. We need not rely, however, simply on what they said. In New York City in 1973–75, the street price of heroin rose dramatically and its purity sharply declined, probably as a result of the heroin shortage caused by the success of the Turkish government in reducing the supply of opium base and of the French government in closing down heroin-processing laboratories located in and around Marseilles. These were short-lived gains for, just as Friedman predicted, alternative sources of supply—mostly in Mexico—quickly emerged. But the three-year heroin shortage interrupted the easy recruitment of new users. . . .

RELIVING THE PAST

Suppose we had taken Friedman's advice in 1972. What would have happened? We cannot be entirely certain, but at a minimum we would have placed the young heroin addicts (and, above all, the prospective addicts) in a very different position from the one in which they actually found themselves. Heroin would have been legal. Its price would have been reduced by 95 percent (minus whatever we chose to recover in taxes). Now that it could be sold by the same people who make aspirin, its quality would have been assured—no poisons, no adulterants. Sterile hypodermic needles would have been readily available at the neighborhood drugstore, probably at the same counter where the heroin was sold. No need to travel to big cities or unfamiliar neighborhoods—heroin could have been purchased anywhere, perhaps by mail order.

There would no longer have been any financial or medical reason to avoid heroin use. Anybody could have afforded it. We might have tried to prevent children from buying it, but as we have learned from our efforts to prevent minors from buying alcohol and tobacco, young people have a way of penetrating markets theoretically reserved for adults. Returning Vietnam veterans would have discovered that Omaha and Raleigh had been converted into the pharmaceutical equivalent of Saigon.

Under these circumstances, can we doubt for a moment that heroin use would have grown exponentially? Or that a vastly larger supply of new users would have been recruited? . . .

But we need not rely on speculation, however plausible, that lowered prices and more abundant supplies would have increased heroin usage. Great Britain once followed such a policy and with almost exactly those results. Until the mid-1960s, British physicians were allowed to prescribe heroin to certain classes of addicts. (Possessing these drugs without a doctor's prescription remained a criminal offense.) For many years this policy worked well enough because the addict patients were typically middle-class people who had become dependent on opiate painkillers while undergoing hospital treatment. There was no drug culture. The British system worked for many years, not because it prevented drug abuse, but because there was no problem of drug abuse that would test the system.

All that changed in the 1960s. A few unscrupulous doctors began passing out heroin in wholesale amounts. One doctor prescribed almost 600,000 heroin tablets—that is, over thirteen pounds—in just one year. A youthful drug culture emerged with a demand for drugs far different from that of the older addicts. As a result, the British government required doctors to refer users to government-run clinics to receive their heroin.

But the shift to clinics did not curtail the growth in heroin use. Throughout the 1960s the number of addicts increased—the late John Kaplan of Stanford estimated by fivefold—in part as a result of the diversion of heroin from clinic patients to new users on the streets. An addict would bargain with the clinic doctor over how big a dose he would receive. The patient wanted as much as he could get, the doctor wanted to give as little as was needed. The patient had an advantage in this conflict because the doctor could not be certain how much was really needed. Many patients would use some of their "maintenance" dose and sell the remaining part to friends, thereby recruiting new addicts. As the clinics learned of this, they began to shift their treatment away from heroin and toward methadone, an addictive drug that, when taken orally, does not produce a "high" but will block the withdrawal pains associated with heroin abstinence.

Whether what happened in England in the 1960s was a mini-epidemic or an epidemic depends on whether one looks at numbers or at rates of change. Compared to the United States, the numbers were small. In 1960 there were 68 heroin addicts known to the British government; by 1968 there were 2,000 in treatment and many more who refused treatment. (They would refuse in part because they did not want to get methadone at a clinic if they could get heroin on the street.) Richard Hartnoll estimates that the actual number of addicts in England is five times the number officially registered. At a minimum, the number of British addicts increased by thirtyfold in ten years; the actual increase may have been much larger. . . .

The United States began the 1960s with a much larger number of heroin addicts and probably a bigger at-risk population than was the case in Great Britain. Even though it would be foolhardy to suppose that the British system, if installed here, would have worked the same way or with the same results, it would be equally foolhardy to suppose that a combination of heroin available from leaky clinics and from street dealers who faced only minimal law-enforcement risks would not have produced a much greater increase in heroin use than we actually experienced. My guess is that if we had allowed either doctors or clinics to prescribe heroin, we would have had far worse results than were produced in Britain, if for no other reason than the vastly larger number of addicts with which we began. We would have had to find some way to police thousands (not scores) of physicians and hundreds (not dozens) of clinics. If the British civil service found it difficult to keep heroin in the hands of addicts and out of the hands of recruits when it was dealing with a few hundred people, how well would the American civil service have accomplished the same tasks when dealing with tens of thousands of people?

BACK TO THE FUTURE

Now cocaine, especially in its potent form, crack, is the focus of attention. Now as in 1972 the government is trying to reduce its use. Now as then some people are advocating legalization. Is there any more reason to yield to those arguments today than there was almost two decades ago?*

I think not. If we had yielded in 1972 we almost certainly would have had today a permanent population of several million, not several hundred thousand, heroin addicts. If we yield now we will have a far more serious problem with cocaine.

Crack is worse than heroin by almost any measure. Heroin produces a pleasant drowsiness and, if hygienically administered, has only the physical side effects of constipation and sexual impotence. Regular heroin use incapacitates many users, especially poor ones, for any productive work or social responsibility. They will sit nodding on a street corner, helpless but at least harmless. By contrast, regular cocaine use leaves the user neither helpless nor harmless. When smoked (as with crack) or injected, cocaine produces instant, intense, and short-lived euphoria. The experience generates a powerful desire to repeat it. If the drug is readily available, repeat use will occur. Those people who progress to "bingeing" on cocaine become devoted to the drug and its effects to the exclusion of almost all other considerations—job, family, children, sleep, food, even sex. Dr. Frank Gawin at Yale and Dr. Everett Ellinwood at Duke report that a substantial percentage of all high-dose, binge users become uninhibited, impulsive, hypersexual, compulsive, irritable, and hyperactive. Their moods vacillate dramatically, leading at times to violence and homicide.

Women are much more likely to use crack than heroin, and if they are pregnant, the effects on their babies are tragic. . . . Cocaine harms the fetus and can lead to physical deformities or neurological damage. Some crack babies have for all practical purposes suffered a disabling stroke while still in the womb. The long-term consequences of this brain damage are lowered cognitive ability and the onset of mood disorders. Besharov estimates that about 30,000 to 50,000 such babies are born every year, about 7,000 in New York City alone. There may be ways to treat such infants, but from everything we now know treatment will be long, difficult, and expensive. Worse, the mothers who are most likely to produce crack babies are precisely the ones who, because of poverty or temperament, are least able and willing to obtain such treatment. In fact, anecdotal evidence suggest that crack mothers are likely to abuse their infants.

The notion that abusing drugs such as cocaine is a "victimless crime" is not only absurd but dangerous. Even ignoring the fetal drug syndrome, crack-dependent people are, like heroin addicts, individuals who regularly victimize their children by neglect, their spouses by improvidence, their employers by lethargy, and their coworkers by carelessness. Society is not and could never be a collection of autonomous individuals. We all have a stake in ensuring that each of us displays a minimal level of dignity, responsibility, and empathy. We cannot, of course, coerce people into goodness, but we can and should insist that some standards must be met if society itself—on which the very existence of the human personality depends—is to persist. Drawing the line that defines those standards is difficult and contentious, but if crack and heroin use do not fall below it, what does? . . .

HAVE WE LOST?

Many people who agree that there are risks in legalizing cocaine or heroin still favor it because, they think, we have lost the war on drugs. "Nothing we have done has worked" and the current federal policy is just "more of the same." Whatever the costs of greater drug use, surely they would be less than the costs of our present, failed efforts.

That is exactly what I was told in 1972—and heroin is not quite as bad a drug as cocaine. We did not surrender and we did not lose. We did not win, either. What the nation accomplished then was what most efforts to save people from themselves accomplish: the problem was contained and the number of victims minimized, all at a considerable cost in law enforcement and increased crime. Was the cost worth it? I think so, but others may disagree. What are the lives of would-be addicts worth? I recall

*I do not take up the question of marijuana. For a variety of reasons—its widespread use and its lesser tendency to addict—it presents a different problem from cocaine or heroin.

some people saying to me then, "Let them kill themselves." I was appalled. Happily, such views did not prevail.

Have we lost today? Not at all. High-rate cocaine use is not commonplace. The National Institute of Drug Abuse (NIDA) reports that less than 5 percent of high-school seniors used cocaine within the last thirty days. . . . Medical examiners reported in 1987 that about 1,500 died from cocaine use; hospital emergency rooms reported about 30,000 admissions related to cocaine abuse. . . .

In some neighborhoods, of course, matters have reached crisis proportions. Gangs control the streets, shootings terrorize residents, and drug-dealing occurs in plain view. The police seem barely able to contain matters. But in these neighborhoods—unlike at Palo Alto cocktail parties—the people are not calling for legalization, they are calling for help. And often not much help has come. Many cities are willing to do almost anything about the drug problem except spend more money on it. The federal government cannot change that; only local voters and politicians can. It is not clear that they will.

It took about ten years to contain heroin. We have had experience with crack for only about three or four years. Each year we spend perhaps $11 billion on law enforcement (and some of that goes to deal with marijuana) and perhaps $2 billion on treatment. Large sums, but not sums that should lead anyone to say, "We just can't afford this any more."

The illegality of drugs increases crime, partly because some users turn to crime to pay for their habits, partly because some users are stimulated by certain drugs (such as crack or PCP) to act more violently or ruthlessly than they otherwise would, and partly because criminal organizations seeking to control drug supplies use force to manage their markets. These also are serious costs, but no one knows how much they would be reduced if drugs were legalized. Addicts would no longer steal to pay black-market prices for drugs, a real gain. But some, perhaps a great deal, of that gain would be offset by the great increase in the number of addicts. These people, nodding on heroin or living in the delusion-ridden high of cocaine, would hardly be ideal employees. Many would steal simply to support themselves, since snatch-and-grab, opportunistic crime can be managed even by people unable to hold a regular job or plan an elaborate crime. Those British addicts who get their supplies from government clinics are not models of law-abiding decency. Most are in crime, and though their per-capita rate of criminality may be lower thanks to the cheapness of their drugs, the total volume of crime they produce may be quite large. Of course, society could decide to support all unemployable addicts on welfare, but that would mean that gains from lowered rates of crime would have to be offset by large increases in welfare budgets.

Proponents of legalization claim that the costs of having more addicts around would be largely if not entirely offset by having more money available with which to treat and care for them. The money would come from the taxes levied on the sale of heroin and cocaine.

To obtain this fiscal dividend, however, legalization's supporters must first solve an economic dilemma. If they want to raise a lot of money to pay for welfare and treatment, the tax rate on the drugs will have to be quite high. Even if they themselves do not want a high tax rate, the politicians' love of "sin taxes" would probably guarantee that it would be high anyway. But the higher the tax, the higher the price of the drug, and the higher the price the greater the likelihood that addicts will turn to crime to find the money for it and that criminal organizations will be formed to sell tax-free drugs at below-market rates. If we managed to keep taxes (and thus prices) low, we would get that much less money to pay for welfare and treatment and more people could afford to become addicts. There may be an optimal tax rate for drugs that maximizes revenue while minimizing crime, bootlegging, and the recruitment of new addicts, but our experience with alcohol does not suggest that we know how to find it.

THE BENEFITS OF ILLEGALITY

The advocates of legalization find nothing to be said in favor of the current system except, possibly, that it keeps the number of addicts smaller than it would otherwise be. In fact, the benefits are more substantial than that.

First, treatment. All the talk about providing "treatment on demand" implies that there is a demand for treatment. That is not quite right. There are some drug-dependent people who genuinely want treatment and will remain in it if offered; they should receive it. But there are far more who want only short-term help after a bad crash; once stabilized and bathed, they are back on the street again, hustling. And even many of the addicts who enroll in a program honestly wanting help drop out after a short while when they discover that help takes time and commitment. Drug-dependent people have very short time horizons and a weak capacity for commitment. These two groups—those looking for a quick fix and those unable to stick with a long-term fix—are not easily helped. Even if we increase the number of treatment slots—as we should—we would have to do something to make treatment more effective.

One thing that can often make it more effective is compulsion. Douglas Anglin of UCLA, in common with many other researchers, has found that the longer one stays in a treatment program, the better the chances of a reduction in drug dependency. But he, again like most other researchers, has found that drop-out rates are high. He has also found, however, that patients who enter treatment under legal compulsion stay in the program longer than those not subject to such pressure. . . . If for many addicts compulsion is a useful component of treatment, it is not clear how compulsion could be achieved in a society in which purchasing, possessing, and using the drug were legal. It could be managed, I suppose, but I would not want to have to answer the challenge from the American Civil Liberties Union that it is wrong to compel a person to undergo treatment for consuming a legal commodity.

Next, education. We are now investing substantially in drug-education programs in the schools. Though we do not yet know for certain what will work, there are some promising leads. But I wonder how credible such programs would be if they were aimed at dissuading children from doing something perfectly legal. We could, of course, treat drug education like smoking education: inhaling crack and inhaling tobacco are both legal, but you should not do it because it is bad for you. . . .

Again, it might be possible under a legalized regime to have effective drug-prevention programs, but their effectiveness would depend heavily, I think, on first having decided that cocaine use, like tobacco use, is purely a matter of practical consequences; no fundamental moral significance attaches to either. But if we believe—as I do—that dependency on certain mind-altering drugs is a moral issue and that their illegality rests in part on their immorality, then legalizing them undercuts, if it does not eliminate altogether, the moral message.

That message is at the root of the distinction we now make between nicotine and cocaine. Both are highly addictive; both have harmful physical effects. But we treat the two drugs differently, not simply because nicotine is so widely used as to be beyond the reach of effective prohibition, but because its use does not destroy the user's essential humanity. Tobacco shortens one's life, cocaine debases it. Nicotine alters one's habits, cocaine alters one's soul. The heavy use of crack, unlike the heavy use of tobacco, corrodes those natural sentiments of sympathy and duty that constitute our human nature and make possible our social life. To say, as does Nadelmann, that distinguishing morally between tobacco and cocaine is "little more than a transient prejudice" is close to saying that morality itself is but a prejudice.

THE ALCOHOL PROBLEM

. . . Alcohol, like heroin, cocaine, PCP, and marijuana, is a drug—that is, a mood-altering substance—and consumed to excess it certainly has harmful consequences: auto accidents, barroom fights, bedroom shootings. It is also, for some people, addictive. We cannot confidently compare the addictive powers of these drugs, but the best evidence suggests that crack and heroin are much more addictive than alcohol.

Many people, Nadelmann included, argue that since the health and financial costs of alcohol abuse are so much higher than those of cocaine or heroin abuse, it is hypocritical folly to devote our efforts to preventing cocaine or drug use. But as Mark Kleiman of Harvard has pointed out, this comparison is quite misleading. What Nadelmann is doing is showing that a *legalized* drug (alcohol) produces greater social harm than *illegal* ones (cocaine and heroin). But of course. Suppose that in the 1920s we had made heroin and cocaine legal and alcohol illegal. Can anyone doubt that Nadelmann would now be writing that it is folly to continue our ban on alcohol because cocaine and heroin are so much more harmful?

And let there be no doubt about it—widespread heroin and cocaine use are associated with all manner of ills. Thomas Bewley found that the mortality rate of British heroin addicts in 1968 was 28 times as high as the death rate of the same age group of non-addicts, even though in England at the time an addict could obtain free or low-cost heroin and clean needles from British clinics. Perform the following mental experiment: suppose we legalize heroin and cocaine in this country. In what proportion of auto fatalities would the state police report that the driver was nodding off on heroin or recklessly driving on a coke high? In what proportion of spouse-assault and child-abuse cases would the local police report that crack was involved? In what proportion of industrial accidents would safety investigators report that the forklift or drill-press operator was in a drug-induced stupor or frenzy? We do not know exactly what the proportion would be, but anyone who asserts that it would not be much higher than it is now would have to believe that these drugs have little appeal except when they are illegal. And that is nonsense.

An advocate of legalization might concede that social harm—perhaps harm equivalent to that already produced by alcohol—would follow from making cocaine and heroin generally available. But at least, he might add, we would have the problem "out in the open" where it could be treated as a matter of "public health." That is well and good, *if* we knew how to treat—that is, cure—heroin and cocaine abuse. But we do not know how to do it for all the people who would need such help. We are having only limited success in coping with chronic alcoholics. Addictive behavior is immensely difficult to change, and the best methods for changing it—living in drug-free therapeutic communities, becoming faithful members of Alcoholics Anonymous or Narcotics Anonymous—require great personal commitment, a quality that is, alas, in short supply among the very persons—young people, disadvantaged people—who are often most at risk for addiction.

Suppose that today we had, not 15 million alcohol abusers, but half a million. Suppose that we already knew what we have learned from our long experience with the widespread use of alcohol. Would we make whiskey legal? I do not know, but I suspect there would be a lively debate. The Surgeon General would remind us of the risks alcohol poses to pregnant women. The National Highway Traffic Safety Administration would point to the likelihood of more highway fatalities caused by drunk drivers. The Food and Drug Administration might find that there is a nontrivial increase in cancer associated with alcohol consumption. At the same time the police would report great difficulty in keeping illegal whiskey out of our cities, officers being corrupted by bootleggers, and alcohol addicts often resorting to crime to feed their habit. Libertarians, for their part, would argue that every citizen has a right to drink anything he wishes and that drinking is, in any event, a "victimless crime."

However the debate might turn out, the central fact would be that the problem was still, at that point, a small one. The government cannot legislate away the addictive tendencies in all of us, nor can it remove completely even the most dangerous addictive substances. But it can cope with harms when the harms are still manageable.

SCIENCE AND ADDICTION

One advantage of containing a problem while it is still containable is that it buys time for science to learn more about it and perhaps to discover a cure. Almost unnoticed in the current debate over legalizing drugs is that basic science has made rapid strides in identifying the underlying neurological processes involved in some forms of addiction. Stimulants such as cocaine and amphetamines alter the way certain brain cells communicate with one another. . . .

When dopamine crosses the synapse between two cells, it is in effect carrying a message from the first cell to activate the second one. In certain parts of the brain that message is experienced as pleasure. After the message is delivered, the dopamine returns to the first cell. Cocaine apparently blocks this return, or "reuptake," so that the excited cell and others nearby continue to send pleasure messages. When the exaggerated high produced by cocaine-influenced dopamine finally ends, the brain cells may (in ways that are still a matter of dispute) suffer from an extreme lack of dopamine, thereby making the individual unable to experience any pleasure at all. This would explain why cocaine users often feel so depressed after enjoying the drug. Stimulants may also affect the way in which other neurotransmitters, such as serotonin and noradrenaline, operate. . . .

Tragically, we spend very little on such research, and the agencies funding it have not in the past occupied very influential or visible posts in the federal bureaucracy. If there is one aspect of the "war on drugs" metaphor that I dislike, it is its tendency to focus attention almost exclusively on the troops in the trenches, whether engaged in enforcement or treatment, and away from the research-and-development efforts back on the home front where the war may ultimately be decided.

I believe that the prospects of scientists in controlling addiction will be strongly influenced by the size and character of the problem they face. If the problem is a few hundred thousand chronic, high-dose users of an illegal product, the chances of making a difference at a reasonable cost will be much greater than if the problem is a few million chronic users of legal substances. Once a drug is legal, not only will its use increase but many of those who then use it will prefer the drug to the treatment: they will want the pleasure, whatever the cost to themselves or their families, and they will resist—probably successfully—any efforts to wean them away from experiencing the high that comes from inhaling a legal substance.

Discussion Questions

1. Which model of addiction—the disease model or the moral-failing model—does Wilson adopt? Support your answer.
2. Wilson claims that both tobacco and cocaine corrode our natural sentiments of sympathy and duty. Do you agree? Should tobacco be made illegal across the board for people of all ages? Or is there a relevant moral distinction between cocaine and tobacco? Support your answers.
3. Compare and contrast Wilson's position on the legalization of drugs, for minors and for adults, with that of Thomas Szasz.
4. Discuss how Wilson would most likely react to the Canadian Marijuana Medical Access Regulations (2001) legalizing the use of marijuana for medical purposes.[55]
5. Preemployment drug screening and employee drug testing have become commonplace since the 1980s. The majority of Fortune 500 companies, for example, now have drug-testing programs.[56] Some colleges are also considering mandatory drug-screening programs for undergraduates. Would Wilson approve of mandatory drug testing in the workplace and on college campuses? How would Szasz respond to mandatory drug-testing programs? Support your answers.
6. Weigh the advantages and disadvantages of a drug/alcohol-testing program on your campus. Are there any circumstances in which mandatory drug and alcohol testing is morally justified?

7. Studies show that people under twenty-five are far more likely to binge on drugs and alcohol than people over twenty-five. Are people who engage in excessive drug and alcohol use simply morally immature? Support your answer in light of Lawrence Kohlberg's and Carol Gilligan's stages of moral development. If moral immaturity is a factor in drug and alcohol abuse, how might this knowledge be incorporated into a public or campus policy regarding drug use and drug education? Support your answers.

DOUGLAS N. HUSAK

A Moral Right to Use Drugs

Douglas Husak is a professor of philosophy at Rutgers University. In this article Husak critically analyzes the various arguments against drug use, including those based on harm and the virtue-based argument of James Q. Wilson. After dismissing these arguments, Husak concludes that there is nothing inherently immoral about drug use, apart from any harm it may cause. Therefore, adults have a moral right to use drugs recreationally. Husak concludes by suggesting that, instead of outlawing drugs, drug education programs should be used to combat harmful use.

Critical Reading Questions

1. According to Husak, what is the current status of the "war on drugs"?
2. How does Husak answer the question, Why do so many Americans use recreational drugs?
3. According to Husak, why has a war been declared on illegal drugs?
4. What does Husak mean when he says that "illegal drugs provide the perfect scapegoat"?
5. What is a "drug" and why is this term, as it is commonly used, confusing?
6. What is a "recreational drug"? How does it differ from a "nonrecreational drug"? What are some examples of nonrecreational uses of drugs?
7. What have been some of the consequences of the "get-tough" policy on drugs?
8. What are some of the arguments for the criminalization of drugs? How is paternalism used to support laws against drugs (LAD)? How is legal moralism used to support LAD?
9. On what grounds does Husak reject these arguments?

"A Moral Right to Use Drugs" in *Drugs and Rights* (New York: Cambridge University Press, 1992), 10–22; 44–45; 56–68; 252–256. Some notes have been omitted.

10. Why does Husak reject Wilson's virtue-based argument against the legalization of drugs?
11. What is the difference between maintaining that adults have a right to use drugs and advocating drug use?
12. Why does Husak reject the argument that legalizing drugs will send the wrong message to children?
13. What are the similarities, according to Husak, between his position on drugs and the pro-choice position on abortion?
14. What policy does Husak suggest regarding drug abuse?

Accurate or not, the perception that drug use is out of control has triggered an enormous state response. Illegal drugs have become the single most important concern of our criminal justice system. Although estimates are imprecise, tens of billions of dollars are probably spent to enforce LAD [laws against drugs] every year, and the less direct costs of the war on drugs are several times greater. Ronald Hamowy describes this war as "the most expensive intrusion into the private lives of Americans ever undertaken in the nation's history."

About 750,000 of the 28 million illegal drug users are arrested every year. Between one-quarter and one-third of all felony charges involve drug offenses. . . . As a result, courts have become clogged, and prison overcrowding is legendary. The U.S. Sentencing Commission has estimated that within fifteen years the Anti-Drug Abuse Act passed by Congress in 1986 will cause the proportion of inmates incarcerated for drug violations to rise from one-third to one-half of all defendants sentenced to federal prison. The costs of punishment threaten to drain the treasury, as each prisoner requires expenditures of between $10,000 and $40,000 per year. Since the average punishment for a drug conviction has risen to seventy-seven months in prison, each new inmate will cost taxpayers approximately $109,000 for the duration of the sentence.

Law enforcement officials continue to exercise broad discretion in arresting and prosecuting drug offenders. More than three-quarters of those arrested are eventually charged with possession, typically of marijuana. Many crimes of possession involve amounts that include a presumption of intent to distribute. Sometimes the quantity of drugs that creates this presumption is small. Moreover, the means used to measure the quantity of given drugs can be peculiar. Since statutes typically refer to a "mixture or substance containing a detectable amount" of a drug, the weight of the entire mixture or substance is included when calculating the quantity of a drug. If a tiny dose of LSD has been placed on a tab of paper or a cube of sugar, the weight of the tab or cube is included in the determination of the amount of the drug. The Supreme Court has recently held this practice to be constitutional.

The true extent of the war on drugs cannot be measured in quantities of dollars spent or numbers of defendants punished. The enforcement of drug laws has diminished precious civil liberties, eroding gains for which Americans have made major sacrifices for over two centuries. Increasingly common are evictions, raids, random searches, confiscations of driver's licenses, withdrawals of federal benefits such as education subsidies, and summary forfeitures of property. . . . Governor Douglas Wilder of Virginia proposes mandatory testing of college students for drug use. . . .

First, why do so many Americans use recreational drugs? Or, more specifically, why do so many Americans use the kinds of recreational drugs of which the majority disapproves? The power of drugs per se can only be part of the explanation. Illegal drug use is less prevalent in many countries where drugs are plentiful, inexpensive, and higher in quality than those available in America. A more viable strategy to combat drugs might attempt to identify and change the conditions peculiar to America that have led to widespread use. For present purposes, I am less concerned to attempt to identify these conditions than to ask why this issue has received so little attention from drug prohibitionists. It is hard to see how a long-term solution to the drug problem can be found without knowing why so many Americans are motivated to break the law in the first place. . . .

A second issue is typically neglected in understanding and evaluating the war on drugs: Why has war been declared on illegal drugs? The simplistic answer is that drugs pose a threat to American society comparable to that of an invading enemy. Self-protection requires the mobilization of resources equivalent to those employed in time of war. For reasons that will become clear, I do not believe that this answer can begin to explain the extraordinary efforts of the state in combating drugs. Few wars—and certainly not the war on drugs—can be understood as a purely rational response to a grave social crisis. . . .

The public fears that America is a nation in decline. Crime, poverty, poor education, corporate mismanagement, and an unproductive and unmotivated work force are cited as evidence of this deterioration. Who, or what, should be blamed? The political climate limits the range of acceptable answers. Conservatives will not allow liberals to blame institutional structures for our problems. The difficulty cannot be that government has failed to create the right social programs to help people. Nor will liberals allow conservatives to blame individuals for our problems. The difficulty cannot be that people are lazy, stupid, or egocentric. What alternative explanations remain?

Illegal drugs provide the ideal scapegoat. Drugs are alleged to be so powerful that persons cannot be blamed very much for succumbing to them, as they could be blamed for not studying or working. And drugs are so plentiful and easy to conceal that government cannot be blamed very much for failing to eliminate them. Even better, most drugs are smuggled from abroad, so Americans can attribute our decline to the influence of foreigners. In blaming drugs, politicians need not fear that they will antagonize a powerful lobby that will challenge their allegations and mobilize voters against them. Almost no organized bodies defend the interests of drug users. Illegal drugs represent a "no-lose" issue, the safest of all political crusades.

A scapegoat would be imperfect unless there were at least some plausibility in the accusations of drug prohibitionists. Perhaps illegal drug use *has* increased crime, contributed to poverty, exacerbated the decline of education, and decreased the productivity of workers. Sometimes it may have done so in dramatic ways. The stories of the most decrepit victims of drug abuse lend themselves to biographies and television docudramas that make a deep and lasting impression on viewers. Everyone has seen vivid images of persons who were driven by drugs to commit brutal crimes, abandon their children, steal from their friends, drop out of school, stop going to work, and perhaps even die. In light of these consequences, who can condone illegal drug use? . . .

A third and final issue about the war on drugs raises a matter that I will explore in greater depth: If there is to be a war on drugs, against which drugs should it be waged? . . .

How is "drug" defined by those who make the effort to define it at all? The answer depends on the discipline where an answer is sought. Perhaps the most frequently cited medical definition is "any substance other than food which by its chemical nature affects the structure or function of the living organism." Undoubtedly this definition is too broad. Nonetheless, I tentatively propose to adopt it until a better alternative becomes available.

Notice that this definition refers only to the pharmacological effect of a substance and not to its legal status. For two reasons, "drugs" must not be defined as synonymous with "illegal drugs." First, it would be absurd to suppose that a non-drug could become a drug, or that a drug could become a non-drug, simply by a stroke of the pen. A legislature can change the legal classification of a substance, but not the nature of that substance; it has no more power to decide that a substance is a drug than to decide that a substance is a food. Second, a philosophical study designed to evaluate the moral rights of drug users can hardly afford to rely uncritically on the existing legal status of substances, since the legitimacy of these determinations is part of what is under investigation. To suppose that "drugs" means "illegal drugs" begs important questions and concedes much of what I will challenge. In what follows, I will use the word "drug" to refer to both legal and illegal substances that satisfy the medical definition I cited.

No doubt this usage will create confusion. Despite the desirability of distinguishing "drugs" from "illegal drugs," there is ample evidence that the public tends to equate them. Surveys indicate, for example, that whereas 95 percent of adults recognize heroin as a drug, only 39 percent categorize alcohol as a drug, and a mere 27 percent identify tobacco as a drug. This tendency is pernicious. The widespread premise that only illegal substances are drugs lulls persons into accepting unsound arguments such as the following: Drugs are illegal; whatever is illegal is bad; we drink alcohol; what we do isn't bad; therefore, alcohol is not a drug. Clear thinking about this issue is impossible unless one realizes that whether a substance is a drug is a different question from whether that substance is or should be illegal. . . .

RECREATIONAL DRUG USE

As the examination of the Controlled Substances Act demonstrates, war has not really been declared on *drugs*. War has been declared on persons who make a certain *use* of drugs. I will describe this use as *recreational*.

By "recreational use," I mean consumption that is intended to promote the pleasure, happiness, or euphoria of the user. The more specific purposes that are encompassed under this broad umbrella include sociability, relaxation, alleviation of boredom, conviviality, feelings of harmony, enhancement of sexuality, and the like. Although borderline cases are numerous, paradigm examples of recreational drug use are plentiful. Interviews with users indicate that they are most likely to consume drugs on two general occasions. First, they use drugs to attempt to improve what they anticipate will be a good time. Hence drug use is frequent during parties, concerts, and sex. Second, they use drugs to attempt to make mindless and routine chores less boring. Hence drug use is frequent during house cleaning and cooking. I regard these as paradigm examples of recreational use.

The distinction between recreational and nonrecreational drug use does *not* purport to sort drugs into categories based on their pharmacological properties. Instead, this distinction sorts drug *use* into categories. The claim that a given drug is "recreational" can only mean that it is typically used for a recreational purpose. . . .

The concept of recreational use can be clarified by contrasting it with other purposes for using drugs. The most familiar nonrecreational reason to use drugs is medical. Although most drug use is either recreational or medical, these categories do not begin to exhaust the purposes for which drugs are consumed. Some persons take drugs for the explicit purpose of committing suicide. Others take drugs ceremonially, in the course of religious rituals. Still others take drugs in order to enhance their performance in competitive sports. Undoubtedly this list could be expanded, but I will make no attempt to provide a comprehensive account of the many reasons for using drugs. . . .

Undoubtedly my focus on recreational drug use will give rise to the criticism that my approach is academic, middle-class, and unresponsive to the realities of drug use in impoverished neighborhoods. Drug use in ghettos, it will be said, is not recreational. The less fortunate members of our society do not use drugs to facilitate their enjoyment at concerts but to escape from the harsh realities of their daily lives. Here, at least, gloom and despair play a central role in explaining the high incidence of drug use. . . .

The empirical facts are ambiguous in proving that illegal drug use is a special problem for the black community. Only 20 percent of all illegal drug users are black. Whites are more likely than blacks to have tried illegal drugs, and cocaine in particular, at some time in their lives. The more drug prohibitionists succeed in portraying drug use as a ghetto phenomenon, born of frustration and despair, the easier it is to lose sight of the repudiation of liberal values that LAD entails. As I will emphasize time and time again, too much of our policy about illegal drug use is based on generalizations from worst-case scenarios that do not conform to the reality of typical drug use. I hope to undermine the inaccurate stereotypes of drug use and drug users reinforced by this objection. LAD prohibits drug use by members of all races and classes; a legal policy applicable to all should not be based on the perceived problems of a few.

THE DECRIMINALIZATION MOVEMENT

. . . Courts and jails have become clogged as a result of "get-tough" policies toward drug offenders. The impact of drug offenses has led a number of commentators to speak of a collapse of the criminal justice system. Federal courts have become "drug courts," where narcotics prosecutions now account for 44 percent of all criminal trials, up 229 percent in the past decade. In many jurisdictions, delays in criminal cases not involving drugs or in the adjudication of civil disputes have become intolerable. The number of Americans behind bars has recently exceeded the one million mark and sets new records every day. Prisons cannot be built fast enough to accommodate drug offenders. . . . As a result of overcrowding by nonviolent drug offenders, violent criminals are less likely to serve long prison terms. . . .

Among the more serious effects of prohibition is discrimination against the poor, who increasingly consume a higher and higher percentage of illegal drugs. Although two-thirds of weekly drug users in New York State in 1987 were white, 91 percent of the persons convicted and sentenced to state prison for drug-related offenses were either black or Hispanic. Therapeutic treatment is frequently provided for middle- and upper-class users; prison is the preferred mode of "treatment" for the underprivileged. . . .

The enforcement of LAD has diminished precious civil liberties. Defense lawyers openly acknowledge the "drug exception" to the Bill of Rights. David Evans complains that "martial law has been declared in our inner cities."

Finally and most significantly, the war on drugs is counterproductive in making criminals of tens of millions of Americans whose behavior is otherwise lawful. Most drug users are lucky to escape detection. Others are less fortunate. Countless numbers of offenders have been forced to suffer long terms of imprisonment for violating laws that may not be morally justified. Even those who are eventually acquitted spend tremendous sums of time and money defending themselves in court. . . .

ARGUMENTS FOR CRIMINALIZATION

Defenses of and attacks against arguments for decriminalization have become so familiar that it is easy to forget that the burden of proof should be placed on those who favor the use of criminal penalties. When arguing about criminalization, most philosophers begin with a "presumption of freedom," or liberty, which places the onus of justification on those who would interfere with what a person wants to do. . . .

A second and equally familiar presumption cuts in the opposite direction. A "presumption in favor of the status quo" allocates the burden of proof on those who oppose any change in current laws against the use of recreational drugs. No one has any clear idea about what weight to assign to these "clashing presumptions." For this reason, it is probably unproductive to worry too much about who should bear the burden of proof on this issue. . . .

I assume without much argument that a respectable defense of criminal legislation must demonstrate that it is needed to prevent *harm.* Everyone agrees that persons lack a moral right to cause harm, so criminal laws that prohibit harmful conduct do not violate the basic principles I have described. Punishment of a person who causes harm can be justified by reference to the offender's desert. But in the absence of harm, criminal sanctions are undeserved and unjustified.

The least controversial rationale in favor of criminalization is that the conduct to be prohibited is harmful *to others.* Many legal philosophers, following the lead of [John Stuart] Mill, believe that harm to others is a necessary condition that any criminal law must satisfy in order to be justified. . . . A more controversial rationale in favor of criminalization is that drug use should be prohibited because it is harmful *to users* themselves. Although a number of philosophers are unsympathetic to this rationale, paternalistic arguments in favor of LAD are frequently defended. . . .

One common complaint about my strategy is misguided. Many philosophers are quick to point out that "no man is an island" and that whatever harms oneself also harms others or at least is capable of doing so. Perhaps there are no examples of "pure" or "unmixed" paternalism, that is, of an interference with liberty that is justifiable solely on the ground that the conduct to be prohibited harms the doer. I do not maintain otherwise. I do not suppose that a given activity can harm the doer but not others. The distinction between harm to oneself and harm to others is *not* a distinction between kinds of laws, but rather it is a distinction between *rationales* for laws. Any law might be defended by more than one rationale. I do not treat people as islands in using the distinction between harm to oneself and harm to others as an analytical device to help identify the best reasons for LAD. The paternalistic rationale for LAD may be stronger than the nonpaternalistic rationale, or it may be weaker. In either event, the distinction between harm to oneself and harm to others must be drawn in order to evaluate each of the arguments in support of LAD. . . .

My premise that the use of the criminal sanction should require harm can be questioned. Perhaps arguments can be marshaled in support of LAD that do not depend on harm, either to oneself or to others. According to *legal moralism,* the wrongfulness of conduct per se, apart from its harmful effects, is a sufficient reason to impose criminal punishment.

Many drug prohibitionists resort to legal moralism in support of LAD. Bennett replies to the cost-benefit analyses of decriminalization theorists as follows: "I find no merit in the legalizers' case. The simple fact is that drug use is wrong. And the moral argument, in the end, is the most compelling argument." There can be no doubt that popular objections to illegal recreational drug use are often couched in the strongest possible moral terms. Drug use is frequently portrayed as sinful and wicked. . . .

For two reasons, however, I will have little to say about legal moralism here. First, this principle is extremely problematic. No one has presented a compelling case in favor of legal moralism; responses from philosophers have been almost entirely negative. One recurrent theme of their attack is that legal moralism might be used to enforce community prejudice. The requirement that criminal liability presupposes a *victim* who has been *harmed* helps to assure that persons will not be punished simply for doing what those with political power do not want them to do.

Second, the application of legal moralism to LAD is utterly baffling. Why would anyone believe the drug use per se is immoral, apart from any harm it might cause? . . . As long as moral reservations about drug use are presented as unsupported conclusions—or as feelings—they will prove resistant to criticism. Arguments, not conclusions, are the objects of philosophical evaluation.

What, exactly, do drug prohibitionists believe to be immoral about recreational drug use? Two alternatives are possible. Does the alleged wrong consist in the act of drug use per se, or in the alteration of consciousness that drug use produces? The former alternative seems unlikely. Suppose that the physiology of persons were altered so that a given drug no longer produced any psychological effect. Could anyone continue to believe that the use of that drug would still be immoral? In any event, contemporary Americans widely reject the view that the act of drug use is inherently wrong. Few condemn the moderate use of alcohol. The subdued moral opposition to alcohol heard today is light years away from the level of outrage expressed by zealots during the temperance movement.

The latter alternative seems no more attractive. Why should the alteration of consciousness produced by drug use be immoral, apart from any harm that might result? Some theorists have proposed that practices such as long-distance running and meditation can trigger natural neurological reactions that alter consciousness in respects that are phenomenologically indistinguishable from the effects of drug use. No one has suggested that such practices are immoral, and for good reason. There is ample reason to doubt that harmless experiences are among the kinds of things that *can* be immoral.

Perhaps many Americans share a vague conviction that some but not all ways of altering consciousness, by the use of some but not all drugs, is immoral. If this conviction could be defended, the particular experience of alcohol intoxication might be upheld as morally permissible, whereas the experiences of intoxication produced by various illegal drugs could be condemned. As it stands, however, this conviction is a conclusion in search of an argument. Typically, persons appeal to harm, either to oneself or to others, in attempts to differentiate between intoxication from alcohol and intoxication from illegal drugs. In this guise, the argument should be taken seriously. What is less clear is how to understand a version of this argument that does *not* appeal to harm. . . .

Moral objections to drug use might also be derived from an ideal of human excellence. Drug use might not be conducive to the attainment of a particular conception of virtue. These arguments are frequently endorsed by drug prohibitionists. According to Bennett, "Drug use degrades human character, and a purposeful, self governing society ignores its people's character at great peril." James Q. Wilson confines his virtue-based arguments to illegal drugs: "Tobacco shortens one's life, cocaine debases it. Nicotine alters one's habits, cocaine alters one's soul." What conception of virtue is employed here? . . . According to this tradition, drug use, like any other recreational activity, is suspect. Recreational activities are nonaltruistic and self-indulgent. . . .

The answer is that virtue-based arguments fail to support criminal punishment for recreational drug use. Bennett is correct that a society should not "ignore its people's character." But it does not follow that the protection of character is an appropriate objective of the criminal law. The prohibitions of the criminal law describe the minimum of acceptable behavior beneath which persons are not permitted to sink. Virtue-based considerations cannot be used to show that moderate self-indulgence, as well as any temporary impairment of rationality and autonomy brought about by most incidents of drug use, fall below this permissible level. The criminal law should not enforce a particular conception of human excellence, however attractive it may be. A theory of virtue might be applied to subject drug use to moral criticism. Opponents of LAD need not believe that drug use is beyond moral reproach. But no one should think that persons deserve to be punished as criminals because their behavior falls short of an ideal. . . .

MISINTERPRETATIONS

I have concluded that the arguments in favor of believing that adults have a moral right to use drugs recreationally are more persuasive than the arguments on the other side. This conclusion is easily misinterpreted. . . . The root of each misinterpretation is the supposition that rights exhaust the universe of moral discourse.

First, the conclusion that adults have a moral right to use drugs recreationally does not amount to advocating drug use. . . . This basic distinction is widely appreciated in most other contexts. Adults have the moral right to preach communism or to practice Buddhism. Yet no one who defends this right would be misunderstood to recommend a conversion to communism or Buddhism.

Nonetheless, one of the most widely voiced objections to the proposal to repeal LAD is that it would express the wrong symbolism about drug use, especially among adolescents. John Lawn maintains: "Legalization of drugs would send the wrong message to our nation's youth. At a time when we have urged our young people to 'just say no' to drugs, legalization would suggest that they need only say no until they reach an appropriate age."[1] . . .

In order to dispel the impression that support for a right to use drugs is tantamount to encouraging drug use, those who reject LAD should be described as endorsing a *pro-choice* position on recreational drug use. This label has been carefully crafted by persons who uphold the right of women to terminate their pregnancies. These persons are not "pro-death," or "anti-life," as their critics would like the public to believe. Perhaps many of them would not elect abortion as their own solution to an unwanted pregnancy. Still, they believe that women have the right to make this choice for themselves. Misunderstanding would be avoided if the debate about the decriminalization of recreational drug use borrowed this terminology. The conclusion that adults have a moral right to use drugs recreationally should be described as the pro-choice position on recreational drug use. . . .

Should the rights of adults be infringed in order to ensure that the wrong message is not received by the public (to whom this argument extends very little credit)? The main problem is that this rationale for LAD would not allow the decriminalization of *any* activity that is less than exemplary. At bottom, this argument is simply another utilitarian defense of the status quo. The rights of some adults should not be sacrificed so that others do not misinterpret a message. This injustice is multiplied when the rights of millions of Americans are at stake. . . .

A second related but distinct misunderstanding of my position is as follows. The conclusion that adult use of recreational drugs is protected by a moral right does not entail that drug use is beyond moral reproach. The exercise of a moral right may be subject to criticism. Perhaps all recreational drug use, legal and illegal, is morally tainted. . . . In any event, some instances of recreational drug use are morally objectionable, beyond those in the special circumstances in which users create an impermissible risk of harm to others. These objectionable instances might be described by the pejorative term *drug abuse*. . . .

If the moral right to use drugs recreationally is to be respected, the need to minimize disutility leaves society with little choice but to discourage drug abuse. The process by which this goal is reached might loosely be described as "drug education." But this process differs from drug education as it is usually conceived. Most educational programs are prevention programs. As so designed, education has generally been deemed a failure, largely because it has not been shown to achieve its objective of decreasing drug use. Yet there may be more reason for optimism if the goal of education is to decrease drug abuse.

As so construed, drug education may never have been tried. No existing educational program has attempted either to separate use from abuse or to indicate how abuse might be avoided by means other than abstinence. The introduction of scientifically respectable materials in drug education programs has been politically unacceptable. As Chester Mitchell notes: "Because some parents insist that their children learn the official lies about the drug menace, well-informed teachers are caught in another superstition–science conflict except that the drug conflict has far greater legal repercussions for all involved than the evolution–creation debate."[2] Bruce Alexander adds: "The outrageously exaggerated scare stories about drugs that fill the electronic media are often called 'education' or 'prevention.' These measures are part of the War on Drugs, not alternatives to it."[3] He proposes "domestication: learning to treat drugs with the same pragmatism that society applies to other familiar and sometimes dangerous household articles." . . .[4]

Since I make no attempt to solve America's drug problem as a matter of social policy, I will hazard only one final observation about the prospects for success that drug education as so conceived will minimize drug abuse. To demand that recreational drug users show restraint over the time, place, and quantity of their consumption is not to require the impossible. In fact, virtually every drug user exhibits some degree of control over her consumption. The means by which users manage to avoid abuse deserves careful study and extensive publicity. Perhaps a successful educational program should seek out responsible drug users. . . . To respect the moral right of adults to use recreational drugs may be painful, at least in the short run. But the protection of moral rights has a value to Americans that is not easily expressed in the utilitarian calculus of costs and benefits in which the decriminalization debate is usually cast.

NOTES

1. John Lawn, "The Issue of Legalizing Illicit Drugs," *Hofstra Law Review* 18 (1990): 703, 710.
2. Chester N. Mitchell, *The Drug Solution* (Ottawa: Carlton University Press, 1990), p. 307.
3. Bruce Alexander, *Peaceful Measures: Canada's Way out of the "War on Drugs"* (Toronto: University of Toronto Press, 1990), p. xi.
4. Ibid.

Discussion Questions

1. Virginia's Governor L. Douglas Wilder has proposed mandatory drug testing of all college students. Discuss some of the moral arguments for and against Wilder's proposal. Develop a policy on drug testing for your campus. What might some of the objections be? Discuss how you would defend your policy against objectors.
2. Does Husak present a convincing rebuttal of James Q. Wilson's argument against the legalization of drugs? Support your answer. Discuss how Wilson might respond to Husak's criticism.
3. Do you accept Husak's comparison of the right to use drugs and the pro-choice position in the abortion debate? Support your answer.
4. Do you agree with Husak that drug education, rather than LAD, is the best policy for dealing with drug abuse? Support your answer. Discuss what sort of drug education program would be most effective on your campus.
5. Florida State University in Tallahassee is one of many colleges working with local police and businesses to reduce alcohol abuse by its students. Recently, a bar near the university put on a "Valentine's Day 'No date, get drunk! Free beer all night'." The event was advertised at the college. How should universities, such as Florida State, respond to this type of aggressive advertising aimed at college students? What stance would Wilson and Husak each most likely take? Support your answers.

THOMAS H. MURRAY

Drugs, Sports, and Ethics

Thomas H. Murray is a professor and the director of the Center of Biomedical Ethics at Case Western Reserve University in Cleveland, Ohio. In this paper, Murray argues against the use of performance-enhancing drugs, such as steroids, in sports. He begins by examining studies on the use of these drugs in professional and Olympic sports. After rejecting the standard arguments against the use of drugs in sports, Murray concludes that drug use in sports is still immoral because it restricts the free choice of competing athletes.

Critical Reading Questions

1. What is the difference between pleasure-enhancing and performance-enhancing drugs? What are some examples of the latter?
2. What are some examples of performance-enhancing drug use in sports?

"Drugs, Sports, and Ethics" in *Feeling Good and Doing Better: Ethics and Nontherapeutic Drug Use,* ed. by Thomas H. Murray, Willard Gaylin and Ruth Macklin (Clifton, N.J.: Humana Press, 1984), 107–126. Some notes have been omitted.

3. What are anabolic and androgenic steroids? What are some of the desired effects of these drugs?
4. What are some of the other performance-enhancing drugs used in sports? What are some of the advantages and drawbacks of using high doses of these drugs?
5. Why do athletes take anabolic steroids? What are some of the risks of taking these drugs? Why are some athletes willing to take these risks?
6. According to Murray, what is the "inherent coerciveness" involved in the use of drugs in competitive sports?
7. According to Murray, why are the current policies prohibiting drugs in sports problematic and insufficient?
8. What are the three reasons cited by ethicists that justify restriction of liberties?
9. According to Murray, under what circumstances can restrictions on certain liberties actually work to preserve liberty? Do these circumstances apply to the restriction of performance-enhancing drugs?
10. Why can't restrictions on performance-enhancing drugs be justified on the basis of harm to oneself? What is the relevance of Aristotle's concept of *eudaimonia,* or the good life, to the self-harm argument?
11. What does Murray mean by "free choice under pressure"? How does the use of performance-enhancing drugs violate this free choice?
12. According to Murray, who bears the primary responsibility for drug use among athletes?

Our images of the nonmedical drug user normally include the heroin addict nodding in the doorway, the spaced-out marijuana smoker, and maybe, if we know that alcohol is a drug, the wino sprawled on the curb. We probably do not think of the Olympic gold medalist, the professional baseball player who is a shoo-in for the Hall of Fame, or the National Football League lineman. Yet these athletes and hundreds, perhaps thousands, of others regularly use drugs in the course of their training, performance, or both. I am talking not about recreational drug use—athletes who use drugs for pleasure or relaxation probably no more or less than their contemporaries with comparable incomes—but about a much less discussed type of drug use: taking drugs to enhance performance.

It is a strange idea. . . . Performance-enhancing drug use is so common and so tolerated in some forms that we often fail to think of it as "drug" use. The clearest example is the (caffeinated) coffee pot, which is as much a part of the American workplace as typewriters and timeclocks. We drink coffee (and tea or Coke) for the "lift" it gives us. The source of "that Pepsi feeling" and the "life" added by Coke is no mystery—it is caffeine or some of its close chemical relatives, potent stimulants to the human central nervous system. Anyone who has drunk too much coffee and felt caffeine "jitters," or drunk it too late at night and been unable to sleep can testify to its pharmacological potency. Caffeine and its family, the xanthines, can stave off mental fatigue and help maintain alertness, very important properties when we are working around potentially dangerous machines, fighting through a boring report, or driving a long stretch. In other words, caffeine can enhance our ability to perform tasks that would otherwise be so fatiguing that we might do them badly, or even harm ourselves or others in trying.

But is caffeine a drug? The fact that it is not under the control of doctors is irrelevant. . . .

About the only definition of "drugs" that would exclude things like caffeine and alcohol would be one that arbitrarily excludes them because of their wide availability and long and extensive history of use. Any reasonable definition of "drug" based on its effects on the human organism would have to include these two as well as nicotine and a number of other common substances.

Caffeine, then, is a performance-enhancing drug. . . . What the drug is used for and the intention behind the use—not the substance itself—determines whether we describe it as medical or non-medical; as pleasure- or performance- or health-enhancing.

DRUGS ON THE PLAYING FIELD

The area of human endeavor that has seen the most explosive growth in performance-enhancing drug use is almost certainly sport. At the highest levels of competitive sports, where athletes strain to improve performances already at the limits of human ability, the temptation to use a drug that might provide an edge can be powerful. Is this kind of drug use unethical? Should we think of it as an expression of liberty? Or do the special circumstances of sport affect our moral analysis? In particular, should liberty give way when other important values are threatened, and when no one's good is advanced? These questions frame the discussion that follows. . . .

Drugs did not enter sport in a major way until the 1960s. The 1964 Olympics were probably the first in which steroids were used. A group of steroids related to the masculinizing hormone testosterone was synthesized. These steroids are valued for two principal effects, which they have in varying proportions: androgenic, or masculinizing, and anabolic, or tissue-building. . . .

Those who lift or throw weights appear to have been the first to use steroids, and even today use them most. An informal, confidential survey of weight lifters revealed that between 90 and 100 percent used steroids. A recent study of power-lifters and body builders outside the Olympics, where athletes are a bit less reluctant to talk about their use of performance-enhancing drugs, found almost universal use of steroids as part of training. . . .

At about the same time that steroids were introduced into amateur sports, amphetamines and related stimulants were finding their way into professional sports. We know the most about professional baseball and football. But ignorance about other sports is just that—ignorance—and should not be taken to mean that performance-enhancing drugs are not used in those sports. . . .

WHY ATHLETES TAKE ANABOLIC STEROIDS

Many athletes persist in using performance-enhancing drugs despite official disapproval, possible disqualification, and even risk to their own health. They do so in the face of expert opinion that casts doubt on the effectiveness of the drugs they take. What leads them to jeopardize their futures as athletes, and possibly their very health, for what some medical people claim is an illusory advantage? The best case to illuminate these questions is steroid use among Olympic athletes. Nowhere else are the penalties greater, the efficacy more contended, or the possible health effects more serious. . . .

A recent report in *The Lancet* acknowledged, "Unquestionably, anabolics improve live weight gain, carcass weight, feed efficiency, and percentage meat in some species."[1] Although the report was referring to the practice of mixing steroids with livestock feed, it might have referred equally to humans. Aside from the genitals, the major active site for anabolic–androgenic steroids is skeletal muscles. The action of steroids on muscle tissue is probably related to their effect on nitrogen metabolism—dietary nitrogen is utilized more efficiently in androgenized tissue. There is even suggestive evidence that androgens may act directly on heart tissue; androgen receptors are found in atrial and ventrical myocardial cells.

Athletes also believe that anabolic–androgenic steroids make them more aggressive, and thus enable them to train harder. The case for this, as with most behavioral rather than physiological effects, is more elusive. . . .

AN UNSIGHTLY ARRAY OF RISKS

Along with the effects athletes desire to obtain from steroids come others not so welcome. Again, the lack of careful scientific information on chronic, high-dose usage forces us to rely on anecdotal reports and reasonable inferences. The anecdotes can be frightening. It is important to bear in mind that, despite being billed as "anabolic" steroids, all these drugs are related to testosterone and have a mix of anabolic and androgenic effects. . . . Therefore, any potent anabolic is also going to have a mix of androgenic effects. In male athletes this leads to a well-known decrease in fertility, since the synthetic androgen interferes with the normal feedback loop linking endogenous testosterone with sperm production. Other effects include acne (a real giveaway for steroid use, according to one athlete), and less visibly, cholesterol buildup and altered liver function. Athletes today are likely to have located a doctor who is willing to help them monitor some of the more subtle effects.

The impact on female athletes, like the East German swimmers, is more visible, and potentially catastrophic. Patricia Connelly, former Olympian and now coach, has lamented the use of steroids by women saying it robs them of their womanliness. The obvious changes—lowered voice, increased body hair, masculinized build—are probably reversible. Other changes are less well understood and potentially more dangerous. I have heard reports of two women, world champions in the 1970s, who appeared to age with stunning rapidity. One—in her early thirties—began to grow bald, developed age spots and wrinkles on her skin. . . .

Facing such an unpleasant, poorly understood, and unsightly array of risks, why do athletes persist in using steroids? The answer lies in the nature of international, or for that matter professional, athletic competition. In his Senate testimony, Harold Connelly said ". . . the overwhelming majority of the international track and field athletes I have known would take anything and do anything short of killing themselves to improve their athletic performance." The pressures are almost as intense in professional football. As one former player describes it: "It's hard to get violent every Sunday at 1 PM." Amphetamines permitted athletes to play with the necessary aggressive intensity. . . . The intense competition at the highest levels of sport calls for every effort the athletes can make, and pushes them to seek every possible advantage over their competitors. . . .

In a competitive endeavor, participants will be pressed to use any means available to achieve a competitive advantage. The higher the stakes, the more intense the competition, the more total the commitment, the more likely people are to use exceptional means. For the international amateur or professional athlete this has often come to include drugs. The pressure to use exists when people *believe* that something confers a competitive advantage, whether or not this is objectively true. There is, then, an *inherent coerciveness* present in these situations: when some choose to do what gives them a competitive edge, others will be pressed to do likewise, or resign themselves to either accepting a competitive disadvantage, or leaving the endeavor entirely. . . .

AN ETHICAL ACCOUNT

Now we can confront the fundamental ethical question: May athletes use drugs to enhance their athletic performance? The International Olympic Committee has given an answer of sorts by flatly prohibiting "doping" of any kind. This stance creates at least as many problems as it solves. It requires an expensive and cumbersome detection and enforcement apparatus, turning athletes and officials into mutually suspicious adversaries. It leads Olympic sports medicine authorities to proclaim that drugs like steroids are ineffective, a charge widely discounted by athletes, and thereby decreases the credibility of Olympic officials. Drug use is driven underground, making it difficult to obtain sound medical data on drug side-effects. . . .

Any argument for prohibiting or restricting drug use by Olympic athletes must contend with a very powerful defense of such use based on our concept of individual liberty. We have a strong legal and moral tradition of individual liberty that proclaims the right to pursue our life plans in our own way, to take risks if we so desire and, within very broad limits, to do with our own bodies what we wish. This right in law has been extended unambiguously to competent persons who wish to refuse even life-saving medical care. More recently, it has been extended to marginally competent persons who refuse psychiatric treatment. Surely, competent and well-informed athletes have a right to use whatever means they desire to enhance their performance.

Those who see performance-enhancing drug use as the exercise of individual liberty are unmoved by the prospect of some harm. They believe it should be up to the individual, who is assumed to be a rational, autonomous, and uncoerced agent, to weigh probable harms against benefits, and choose accordingly to his or her own value preferences. It would be a much greater wrong, they would say, to deny people the right to make their own choices. Why should we worry so much about some probabilistic future harm for athletes when many other endeavors pose even greater dangers? High-steel construction work and coal-mining, mountain-climbing, hang-gliding, and auto-racing are almost certainly more dangerous than using steroids or other common performance-enhancing drugs.

Reasons commonly given to limit liberty fall into three classes: those that claim that the practice interferes with capacities for rational choice; those that emphasize harms to self; and those that emphasize harms to others. The case of performance-enhancing drugs and sport illustrates a fourth reason that may justify some interference with liberty, that given the social nature of the enterprise, performance-enhancing drug use in sport is inherently coercive. But first the other three reasons.

There is something paradoxical about our autonomy: we might freely choose to do something that would compromise our future capacity to choose freely. Selling yourself to slavery would be one way to limit liberty, making one's body the property of another person. If surrendering autonomous control over one's body is an evil and something we must refuse to permit, how much worse is it to destroy one's capacity to *think* clearly and independently? Yet that is one thing that might happen to people who abuse certain drugs. We may interfere with someone's desire to do a particular autonomous act if that act is likely to cause a general loss of the capacity to act autonomously. In this sense, forbidding selling yourself into slavery and forbidding the abuse of drugs likely to damage your ability to reason are similar *restrictions* on liberty designed to *preserve* liberty.

This argument applies only to things that do in fact damage our capacity to reason and make autonomous decisions. Although some of the more powerful pleasure-enhancing drugs might qualify, no one claims that performance-enhancing drugs like the steroids have any deleterious impact on reason. This argument, then, is irrelevant to the case of performance-enhancing drugs.

Destroying one's reasoning ability is a special kind of harm to oneself, but there are many other kinds of harm, and they constitute a potential argument in favor of curtailing liberty. Aristotle, in the Nichomachean Ethics, described a conception of *eudaimonia,* or the good life, in which the perfection of natural excellences was a central component. Our physical abilities, character traits, and above all our intellect were all to be perfected. We can infer from this that persons have a duty to do whatever is in their power to perfect their talents, and forsake whatever would interfere with that development. Aristotle might have no hesitation in condemning most or all pleasure-enhancing drug use, but his principle, which paraphrased is "People should develop their natural excellences," stumbles over the case of athletes and performance-enhancing drugs. Athletes use the drugs precisely to perfect their natural excellences. Our objection would have to be that drug use is an improper means to that end, since the end itself is especially commendable in the Aristotelian worldview. We could argue that drug use is wrong because, on balance, it hurts the pursuit of excellence more than it helps it. But then we are reduced to arguing about the facts—improved performances versus side effects. And if it turns out that the drugs work with minimal, reversible side effects, we would say that they are morally justified under the perfection-of-excellence principle.

Another way to put the Aristotelian objection is that we should not use unnatural means—drugs—to perfect natural excellences—athletic abilities. It is difficult to make this stick as a *moral,* and not merely an esthetic, objection. Although we recognize that certain means of perfecting our natural excellences are generally regarded as illegitimate and may be dismissed as "unnatural," the judgments are always with respect to specific ends. A prosthetic hand might be "unnatural" and unfair for the purpose of pitching baseball, but not objectionable if it allowed an injured novelist to operate a typewriter. Even in so narrow a case as drugs in sport, all depends on context. If we would not object to a diabetic athlete using insulin, could we object to a depressed one using an antidepressant, to an exhausted one using a stimulant? We can draw lines, but based on complex practical understandings, rather than solid, simple principles delineating the "natural" from the "unnatural." . . .

A second class of reasons to limit liberty says that we may interfere with some actions when they result in wrong to others. The wrong done may be direct. Lying, cheating, or other forms of deception are unavoidable when steroid use is banned, yet one persists in the practice. Of course, we could lift the ban, and then the steroid use need no longer be deceptive; it could be completely open to the same extent as other training aids. . . .

The wrong we do to others may be indirect. We could make ourselves incapable of fulfilling some duty we have to another person. For example, a male athlete who marries and promises his wife that they will have children makes himself sterile with synthetic anabolic steroids (a probable side effect). He has violated his moral duty to keep a promise. This objection could work, but only where the duty is clearly identifiable and not overly general, and the harm is reasonably foreseeable. . . . Except for cases like the sterile athlete reneging on his promise, instances where athletes make themselves incapable of fulfilling some specific duty to others would probably be rare. In any case, we cannot get a general moral prohibition on drug use in sports from this principle, only judgments in particular cases.

We may also do a moral wrong to others by taking unnecessary risks and becoming a great burden to family, society, or both. The helmetless motorcyclist who suffers severe brain damage in an accident is a prototypical case. Increasingly, people are describing professional boxing in very similar terms. Although this might be a good reason to require motorcyclists to wear helmets or to prohibit professional boxing matches, it is not a sound reason to prohibit steroid use. No one claims that the athletes using steroids are going to harm themselves so grievously that they will end up seriously brain-damaged or otherwise unable to care for themselves. Though the harms they do to themselves may be substantial, they are not disabling.

"FREE CHOICE UNDER PRESSURE"

So far we have not found any wrong done to others that is serious and likely to occur when athletes, at the top of the competitive ladder, commonly use performance-enhancing drugs. Let us look at the problem more closely. Olympic and professional sport, as a social institution, is an intensely competitive endeavor, and there is tremendous pressure to seek a competitive advantage. If some athletes are believed to have found something that gives them an edge, other athletes will feel pressed to do the same, or leave the competition. Unquestionably, coerciveness operates in the case of performance-enhancing drugs and sport. Where improved performance can be measured in fractions of inches, pounds, or seconds, and that fraction is the difference between winning and losing, it is very difficult for athletes to forego using something that they believe improves their competitor's performance. Many athletes do refuse; but many others succumb; and still others undoubtedly leave rather than take drugs or accept a competitive handicap.

Under pressure, decisions to take performance-enhancing drugs are anything but purely "individual" choices. My alleged liberty to take performance-enhancing drugs, which is very hard to oppose from an individualistic conception of morality, is counterbalanced by the pressure I place on my fellow competitors. My "free" choice contains an element of coercion. If enough people like me choose to use performance-enhancing drugs, then the freedom of others not to use them is greatly diminished.

But can we say that "freedom" has actually been diminished because others are using performance-enhancing drugs? I still have a choice whether to participate in the sport at all. In what sense is my freedom impaired by what the other athletes may be doing? If we take freedom or liberty in the very narrow sense of noninterference with my actions, then my freedom has not been violated, because no one is prohibiting me from doing what I want, whether that be throwing the discus, taking steroids, or selling real estate. But if we take freedom to be one of a number of values, whose purpose is to support the efforts of persons to pursue reasonable life plans without being forced into unconscionable choices by the actions of others, then the coerciveness inherent when many athletes use performance-enhancing drugs and compel others to use the same drugs, accept a competitive handicap or leave the competition can be seen as a genuine threat to one's life plan. When a young person has devoted years to reach the highest levels in an event, only to find that to compete successfully he or she must take potentially grave risks to health, we have, I think, as serious a threat to human flourishing as many restrictions on liberty. . . .

My conclusions are complex. First, the athletes who are taking performance-enhancing drugs that have significant health risks are engaging in a morally questionable practice. They have turned a sport into a sophisticated game of "chicken." Most likely, each athlete feels pressed by others to take drugs, and does not feel he or she is making a free choice. The "drug race" is analogous to the arms race.

Second, since the problem is systemic, the solution must be too. The IOC has concentrated on individual athletes, and even then it has been inconsistent. This is the wrong place to look. Athletes do not use drugs because they like them, but because they feel compelled to. Rather than merely punishing those caught in the social trap, why not focus on the system? A good enforcement mechanism should be both ethical and efficient. To be ethical, punishment should come in proportion to culpability and should fall on *all* the guilty parties—not merely the athletes. Coaches, national federations, and political bodies that encourage, or fail to strenuously discourage, drug use, are all guilty. Current policy punishes only the athlete.

To be efficient, sanctions should be applied against those parties who can most effectively control drug use. Ultimately, it is the athlete who takes the pill or injection, so he or she ought to be one target of sanctions. But coaches are in an extraordinary influential position to persuade athletes to take or not to take drugs. Sanctions on coaches whose athletes are caught using drugs could be very effective. Coaches, not wanting to be eliminated from future competitions, might refuse to take on athletes who use performance-enhancing drugs.

Finally, although I am not in a position to elaborate a detailed plan to curtail performance-enhancing drug use in sports, I have tried to establish several points. Despite the claims of individual autonomy, the use of performance-enhancing drugs is ethically undesirable because it is coercive, has significant potential for harm, and advances no social value. Furthermore, any plan for eliminating its use should be just and efficient, in contrast to current policies.

Can we apply this analysis of drug use in sports to other areas of life? One key variable seems to be the social value that the drug use promotes, weighed against the risks it imposes. If we had a drug that steadied a surgeon's hand and improved his or her concentration so that surgical errors were reduced at little or no personal risk, I would not fault its use. If, on the other hand, the drug merely allowed the surgeon to operate more quickly and spend more time on the golf course with no change in surgical risk, its use would be at best a matter of moral indifference. Health, in the first case, is an important social value, one worth spending money and effort to obtain. A marginal addition to leisure time does not carry anywhere near the same moral value.

A careful, case-by-case, practice-by-practice weighing of social value gained against immediate and long-term risks appears to be the ethically responsible way to proceed in deciding the merits of performance-enhancing drugs.

NOTES

1. Editorial: "Anabolics in Meat Production," *Lancet,* March 27, 1982, pp. 721–722.

Discussion Questions

1. Compare and contrast Murray's position on drugs with that of a libertarian such as Thomas Szasz. Does the use of performance-enhancing drugs fall under Szasz's "right of self-medication"? Support your answer.
2. If we reject Aristotle's distinction between natural and unnatural means to perfection, could his virtue ethics and concept of *eudaimonia* be used to support the use of performance-enhancing drugs? If so, under what circumstances? For example, is it morally acceptable to use performance-enhancing drugs—such as caffeine, amphetamines, or other stimulants—before taking an exam, performing on stage, going to a job interview, or driving long distances at night? Support your answers.
3. What type of policy might Murray suggest regarding the use of performance-enhancing drugs in sports? How would it differ from current policies? Who would be penalized most severely by this policy? Who would benefit the most? Explain.

CASE STUDIES

1. FRATERNITIES AND ALCOHOL: THE DEATH OF BENJAMIN WYNNE[57]

Much of the criticism of binge drinking on college campuses is focused on the Greek system. A Harvard study found that 86 percent of fraternity-house residents are binge drinkers. Binge drinking can be deadly.

In August 1997 twenty-year-old Benjamin Wynne of Louisiana State University found out that he had been accepted as a pledge with the Sigma Alpha Epsilon fraternity. To celebrate the happy occasion, Wynne and the other pledges got rip-roaring drunk. The festivities started with an off-campus keg party in which beer was funneled through a rubber hose into the drinker's mouth. Following this, the Sigma Alpha Epsilon brothers headed down to Murphy's Bar, which was only a few hundred yards from the campus, and drank "Three Wise Men," a 151-proof drink made from rum, whiskey, and a liqueur. The festivities ended with the brothers wheeling the pledges back to campus in shopping carts because they were too drunk to walk.

Police were called to the fraternity house several hours later. They found almost two dozen men passed out on the living-room floor. By early morning Wynne was dead of alcohol poisoning, and three other brothers were hospitalized. The autopsy showed that Wynne had consumed the equivalent of twenty-four drinks the night before. When rescue workers arrived, he was already comatose. A few days later, his distraught parents had him removed from life support. This was not an isolated event. Fraternity pledge Scott Krueger died of alcohol poisoning the same semester after a Greek Week celebration at MIT; the previous May five students died in a North Carolina fraternity-house fire because they were too drunk to escape.

Discussion Questions

1. Who bears responsibility for the death of Benjamin Wynne? Did the brothers have a moral responsibility to intervene in order to keep the pledges from drinking in excess? Does the bartender who served Wynne bear part of the responsibility for his death?

Would it make a difference if Wynne had used a fake ID to obtain alcohol? What would you have done had you been at Murphy's Bar that evening? Support your answers.

2. Is it morally acceptable for college students to use fake IDs to obtain alcohol? Support your answer.
3. Studies show that a permissive attitude on campus toward alcohol encourages students to drink more heavily than they otherwise would.[58] In response, several colleges and universities in the United States and Canada have limited or banned alcohol. Bishop's University in Quebec, once famous for its raucous partying, has outlawed all drinking games.

   On the other hand, outright prohibition isn't necessarily the answer. Louisiana State University had a no-alcohol policy in effect the day Wynne died. Create a policy for your campus regarding alcohol use. What moral concerns are most important in the creation of your policy? Given the fact that alcohol abuse is associated primarily with the Greek system, should fraternities and sororities be banned? Support your answers.
4. Some bars rely on college students for most of their business. These bars sometimes distribute handbills to students walking across campus and put fliers under doors in freshman dormitories. Should bars and alcohol companies be prohibited from advertising on college campuses?
5. Rutgers University has a dormitory especially for students who are recovering alcoholics and drug addicts and who wish to stay away from the drug-charged atmosphere of regular dorms. The cost of maintaining the dorm, which includes four people to run a substance-abuse program, is about $300,000 a year. Does the university have a duty to provide rehabilitative services to students who are alcoholics and drug abusers? If so, should these programs be voluntary or mandatory? Support your answers.
6. The primary justification of mandatory drug testing is the utilitarian argument that drug and alcohol use have a negative effect on productivity. Does this justify mandatory drug testing of college students? Support your answer. Discuss how Wilson and Husak might answer this question.
7. In response to the alarming increase in alcohol and drug abuse on college campuses, some police departments use undercover officers on campus. These officers live in dorms and attend classes like regular students in an attempt to gain information about illicit drug and alcohol use on campus and to bring offenders to justice. This approach has been very effective on some campuses in curtailing illicit drug dealing and underage drinking. Is this approach to the drug and alcohol problem morally justified? What would you do if you learned that your roommate or best friend was an undercover police officer? If you knew that another friend was selling drugs in your dorm, and the officer/roommate asked you if this person was selling drugs, what would you say? Support your answers.

   Discuss how both a Kantian and a utilitarian might respond to the morality of this approach.

---

2. BASEBALL STAR MICKEY MANTLE: SHOULD ALCOHOLICS RECEIVE LIVER TRANSPLANTS?

In 1995 sixty-three-year-old Yankee baseball star and Hall-of-Famer Mickey Mantle lay critically ill in a Dallas Hospital, his liver destroyed by forty years of alcohol abuse.

Alcoholism is associated with a liver disease known as alcohol-related end-stage liver disease (ARESLD). In the United States, more than half of all deaths from liver disease are related to chronic alcoholism.[59] Mantle was given two to five weeks to live. The only hope for people with end-stage liver disease is a liver transplant. Livers are very scarce, however, and the waiting list is long. Only a fraction of those who need liver transplants ever get one.

The night after Mantle was hospitalized, a suitable donor was found. Mantle was moved to the top of the recipient list and soon received a new liver. Mantle died shortly after of a failed liver transplant.

Discussion Questions

1. How should scarce resources, such as organs, be allocated? Should it be first come, first served? Is it fair to move to the top of an organ transplant list people who are famous, or who still might make great contributions to society? Should the fact that a person's disease is related to lifestyle be taken into consideration in allocating scarce resources? Given the fact that there are not nearly enough livers even for people who do not have alcohol-related diseases, should alcoholics such as Mickey Mantle even be considered for liver transplants? Support your answer. Discuss how a supporter of the disease model of addiction and a supporter of the moral model of addiction might each answer these questions.
2. In 1991 the American Medical Association proposed as a general guideline that patients with alcohol-related liver disease should not compete equally with other people who need liver transplants.[60] Although they did not say that patients with ARESLD should *never* get liver transplants, they suggested that because livers are a scarce resource, patients with ARESLD be placed lower on the list than patients with nonalcohol-related liver disease. Is this fair? Support your answer. Should ex-alcoholics be treated differently than active alcoholics? Discuss your answer in light of the disease and moral models of addiction.
3. Who should be responsible for the medical costs incurred in Mickey Mantle's liver transplant? Studies show that the medical costs of alcohol and tobacco users are much higher than those of nonusers. Should private and public medical insurance plans cover these costs? Should alcohol and tobacco users have to cover the medical costs that are related to their use of these substances? Should tobacco companies have to foot the bill for diseases caused by tobacco use? Support your answers.
4. Some people argue that insurance companies should not cover the costs of substance-related care, because smokers and alcoholics have much higher medical costs. Others argue that this is unfair: Because smokers and alcoholics die much younger than nonusers, the cost of their health care over a lifetime is not much different than that of nonusers. Discuss how both Aristotle and a utilitarian might respond to these arguments.
5. Libertarian John Taylor argues that people such as Mickey Mantle and rock star Jerry Garcia, who died of a heart attack at age fifty-three, after decades of drug abuse and related health problems, have a right to choose their own ideal of the good life.[61] Abstaining from drugs and alcohol for the sake of longevity, he argues, may be overrated. Taylor writes that both Mantle and Garcia "chose lives that valued recklessness, intensity, sensation, and, in a word, fun over mere longevity. As a result they died at the onset of old age rather than at its outer limits." Do you agree with Taylor? Support

your answer. Discuss how both a supporter and an opponent of the disease model of addiction might respond to Taylor's position.
6. Should the fact that Mantle chose the life he lived mean that he also forfeited his right to a liver transplant? Support your answer.

---

3. WINNING AT ALL COSTS: DRUGS IN SPORTS

You are the captain and star player on your college basketball team, which has made the finals. A wealthy entrepreneur, who is an avid basketball fan and alumnus of your college, has promised to make a $60 million donation to your school *if* your team wins the finals. Your college desperately needs the money. It is currently in serious financial trouble and has been forced to lay off faculty and cut back on academic programs.

A few weeks before the game, the wealthy entrepreneur offers you a banned performance-enhancing substance. He assures you that you will not get caught, because the substance has been slightly altered so that it cannot be detected. He also tells you that he will make a $60 million donation even if your team loses, but only on the condition that you take the drug for the next two weeks. The team you are playing in the finals is better than yours and has won the finals the past two years in a row. According to a noted sports analyst, the odds against your winning are eight to one.[62]

Discussion Questions

1. What should you do? Support your answer.
2. Would your answer be any different if the wealthy entrepreneur had also offered to give *you* $1 million if you agreed to use the drug? Would your answer be any different if you found out that the opposing team was going to be using performance-enhancing drugs? Explain your answers.
3. In a 1995 poll, 198 athletes, most U.S. Olympians or aspiring Olympians, were asked if they would take a banned performance-enhancing drug if the following two guarantees were made: (1) You would not be caught and (2) you will win. One hundred ninety-five of the athletes said yes; three said no. They were then asked if they would take the same drug with these two guarantees: (1) You will not be caught and (2) you will win every competition you enter for the next five years, then you will die from a side-effect of the drug. More than half replied that they would use the drug under these conditions. Does the fact that almost 99 percent of the athletes polled were willing to use drugs under certain circumstances undermine the argument that performance-enhancing drugs should be banned because they violate free choice? Does the prohibition of performance-enhancing drugs interfere more with athletes' free choice? Support your answers.
4. The cozy connection between sports and drugs goes beyond performance-enhancing drug use by athletes. Both the alcohol and the tobacco industries use professional sports to advertise their products. For every hour of professional sports programming, there are 2.4 alcohol commercials, many of which are very appealing to children and young adults.[63] Tobacco companies, such as Virginia Slims, also sponsor women's sporting events, thus encouraging girls to think that there is a connection between smoking and being slim, athletic, and liberated. The large number of teenage girls

who have taken up smoking following its ad campaigns is a testimony to the success of Virginia Slims ads. Should alcohol and tobacco advertisements be more strictly regulated? Should alcohol and tobacco companies be forbidden to advertise? Should the sale of tobacco and alcohol be banned altogether? Support your answers.

5. Is mandatory drug testing of college and professional athletes a violation of their autonomy and privacy rights? Support your answer.

---

4. PROZAC: ENHANCING MORALITY THROUGH DRUGS[64]

Although the role of drugs in lowering inhibitions against immoral behavior is widely acknowledged,[65] there is considerable resistance to the similar idea that certain drugs may actually enhance moral behavior. People who suffer from depression can become self-preoccupied to the point of seeming almost sociopathic in their indifference to the consequences of their actions for others. According to Peter Kramer, author of *Listening to Prozac,* treatment with a drug such as Prozac can in some cases "turn a morally unattractive person into an admirable one."[66] Prozac can also numb feelings, however.

Kramer cites the case of Phillip, an undergraduate who was undergoing psychotherapy because of humiliation he had received from his parents. Initially, Phillip resisted the use of medication. As his depression became more severe, however, Phillip agreed to try Prozac. Although he felt better on the Prozac, he also hated it. He felt phony. Why? Because he had been robbed of his disdain, resentment, and rage without having to first work through it.[67]

Prozac is used not only by people who feel depressed or overwhelmed by the challenges of life; many use it as a means of self-transformation. According to Kramer, using Prozac can increase autonomy and life choices by "lend[ing] people courage and allow[ing] them to choose life's ordinary risky undertakings."[68]

Discussion Questions

1. Wilson argues that morality arises out of our natural sociability. In cases in which our natural sociability is deficient or suppressed by neurosis, would it be morally acceptable, or perhaps even morally obligatory, to use drugs to enhance it?
2. Is it morally admirable to use drugs in our quest to become better people? If we can find a shortcut to self-realization and moral maturity, shouldn't we take it? Support your answers. Discuss how both Aristotle and a Buddhist might respond to this question.
3. The use of mood-altering drugs such as Prozac has been criticized for masking our true personalities or essences, as well as for freeing us from having to "struggle with reality." Do you agree? What is meant by "essence" and "reality"?
4. Prozac use is more prevalent among women than among men. Unlike Valium, however, which made women more compliant, Prozac is described as the "feminist drug" because it seems to transform some people into assertive, self-confident high achievers who are socially adept. Given this, would it be morally desirable for women who put others' needs before their own to take Prozac? Is the assertiveness and self-confidence of women on Prozac morally equivalent to that of women who are at the postconventional stage of moral reasoning? Support your answers. Discuss how Carol Gilligan and care ethicist Nel Noddings might answer this question.

5. Is unhappiness or depression necessarily an indication of a moral failing? Discuss your answer in light of Phillip's experience.
6. Discuss the following statement by Peter Kramer, author of *Listening to Prozac:*

> Working with Prozac has heightened my awareness of the extent to which compulsion is a basis for moral actions. Is it a sound basis? Surely one could make the case that what is compelled is inherently amoral; what characterizes moral action is choice. Still, in addressing this effect of Prozac [tempering compulsive behavior], we face the least irrational, most cogent aspect of pharmacological Calvinism: perhaps diminishing pain can dull the soul.[69]

   How might Szasz respond to Kramer's statement?
7. Apply the doctrine of the mean to the use of Prozac. Discuss when and under what conditions using a mood-altering drug such as Prozac may be a vice and when it may be a virtue.

---

5. THE ALCOHOLICS ANONYMOUS CONFESSION OF A DOUBLE MURDERER[70]

On New Year's Eve 1989, Donald Cox broke into a couples' bedroom and slashed their throats. The murder remained unsolved until Cox confessed his brutal crime at an AA meeting. Following the confession, one of the AA members called the police. Should this confession be admitted as evidence in a court of law?

According to Cox and his lawyers, the rules of AA obligate members to confess their transgressions. Because confession is part of the recovery process in AA, it should remain confidential, like confessions made to a priest or a psychiatrist. "It doesn't seem right," his lawyer Adele Walker argued, "It's like he's being punished for recovering." Furthermore, if confessions made during AA meetings did not remain confidential, AA would not be nearly as effective in helping alcoholics.

On the other hand, it is also an AA principle that alcoholics must accept responsibility for actions performed, even when they are drunk. Although Cox claimed that he was drunk at the time of the murders and tried the "drunken stupor–temporary insanity" defense at his trial, he had no trouble recalling what had happened on that tragic New Year's Eve.

Discussion Questions

1. Should the fact that Cox made his confession as part of his recovery absolve him of responsibility for his actions? Was he "sick," and hence not in control of his actions, when he committed the murders? Support your answers. Discuss how supporters of the disease model of addiction and the moral model of addiction might each respond to these questions.
2. Discuss what moral principles are in conflict when confidential confessions of murder or other horrific crimes—or plans to commit crimes—are made at AA meetings or to priests or psychiatrists. Which principles and moral concerns are most compelling?
3. Discuss what you would have done had you been at the AA meeting the night Cox confessed. Support your position.
4. Both Confucius and Aristotle maintain that a good government helps people to be good. Is the government partly responsible for the deaths of Cox's victims because it permits the sale and consumption of alcohol? Support your answer.

5. Should people who commit crimes under the influence of drugs or alcohol be given stiffer penalties, as in drunk-driving violations? Or should they be treated with greater leniency? Support your answers. Discuss how both a utilitarian as well as supporters of the disease model and the moral model might respond to these questions.

---

6. SMOKING BANS

In 1994 California enacted one of the country's first Smoke-Free Workplace laws. The ban was extended in 1998 to include bars, making California the first state to have smoke-free bars. The tobacco industry opposed the smoke-free legislation, launching an $18 million campaign against the legislation and introducing, unsuccessfully, eight additional bills in an attempt to repeal the ban. The tobacco industry argued that making bars smoke-free would damage business, violate the rights of owners, and deny adults the freedom to smoke.[71] Bar and club owners also opposed the law because of anticipated lost business and revenues, although subsequent studies did not support these fears.

In response, the American Cancer Society released a report showing that 61 percent of voters favored the ban. Health groups also presented evidence that second-hand smoke in the workplace, including bars, was a health hazard to employees, and that smoke-free workplaces were in part responsible for the decline in smoking in California. Indeed, medical research showed that bar workers' respiratory health showed improvement four to eight weeks after the law took effect.[72] The president of the California AFL-CIO stated in an interview, "We believe disease and death should not be a condition of employment."[73]

Discussion Questions

1. Discuss the pros and cons of imposing a smoking ban on workplaces, including bars. Should colleges be included in the ban as well? How about fraternities and sororities?
2. The Montgomery City Council in 2003 tried to pass a bill prohibiting smoking in restaurants and bars but met fierce resistance. One of the arguments against the bill was that the restaurant and bar owners would loose a lot of revenue since, unlike California, smokers could just drive a few miles to a restaurant or bar in another county that allowed smoking. To what extent should the harms to the restaurant and bar owners be taken into account in deciding whether to pass this bill (or to amend it)? How would a utilitarian most likely respond to this bill?
3. Working in groups, and taking into consideration the prima facie moral duties and rights, come up with a smoking policy for your campus.
4. In the United States, where free enterprise is valued, lobbyists from private industry exert a strong influence on legislation. The tobacco industry in 1997–98 contributed an average of $9,829 to legislatures that voted in favor of repealing the smoking bans and an average of $38 to legislatures opposing the repeal. Should private industry be allowed to put pressure on or reward legislators who support their agenda through monetary contributions? How about non-profit groups such as the American Cancer Society or consumer groups? Support your answers. How would Ayn Rand and John Stuart Mill each most likely respond to these questions?

---

7. DECRIMINALIZING MARIJUANA

In March 2003 Jorge Lopez crossed the Canadian border to buy marijuana for his wife, Juanita, who was suffering from unrelenting pain in her joints from a severe form of arthritis. None of the prescription drugs had worked for her. She was bedridden and at her wits end and even contemplating suicide. He did not tell her he was going, fearing that she would try to stop him because of the risks to him. Medical marijuana had been legalized in Canada in 2001 for use by patients with AIDS wasting syndrome, multiple sclerosis, severe pain associated with cancer and chemotherapy, spinal cord injuries, epilepsy, and severe forms of arthritis. In addition, in December 2002 the Canadian Parliament had recommended that marijuana possession be decriminalized, which allowed Mr. Lopez to get some from a friend in Vancouver who grew small amounts for his own personal use. One of the Canadian government's main reasons for decriminalizing marijuana was that small-time users would no longer face threat of jail or a criminal record. Instead violators would be ticketed and receive a fine of $100 to $400.

The United States is moving in the opposite direction of Canada. In 1996 California passed Proposition 215 permitting physicians to prescribe marijuana for medical purposes and the growing and selling of marijuana for these purposes. Since then eight other states have legalized the medical use of marijuana. In 2003 Attorney General John Ashcroft moved to crack down on the marijuana industry, requesting that the Supreme Court take away the medical licenses of physicians who discuss marijuana with their patients.

When Mr. Lopez crossed back over the border into the state of Washington carrying 16 ounces of marijuana for his wife, he was arrested for possession and sentenced to one year in jail. Juanita Lopez pleaded, unsuccessfully, for his release. She died before he was released.[74]

Discussion Questions

1. Should Mr. Lopez have gone to Canada to buy marijuana for his wife? Support your answer. Discuss how a care ethicist might respond to this question.
2. Should marijuana be legalized and, if so, under what conditions? What moral principles and rights are at stake in this debate? Discuss how Wilson and Husak most likely respond to the laws regarding marijuana use in Canada and in the United States.
3. According to a 2002 Seattle survey, 25 percent of whites have used hard drugs, but only 18 percent of blacks and Hispanics have. Yet, blacks and Hispanics are seven times more likely to receive a drug sentence.[75] Would decriminalizing cocaine and marijuana make us a more just society? Or should we be tougher in arresting white people for drug violations? How would John Rawls most likely respond to this question? How would a utilitarian most likely respond? Support your answers.
4. John Walters, director of the United States Office of Drug Control Policy opposes the new Canadian law, arguing that it will exacerbate the illegal marijuana trade from Canada to the United States and that it will allow growers in Canada to produce high-potency marijuana that, like crack, may be more addictive and dangerous. Discuss Walter's concerns. Do countries have a moral obligation to consider the needs and laws of neighboring countries when passing new laws?
5. Discuss the morality of American college students crossing the border to buy or use marijuana in Canada. Do we have a moral obligation to abide by the laws of our society?

C H A P T E R 7

Sexual Intimacy and Marriage

Adam and Brooke, both seniors at Boston University, had been living together in off-campus housing for seven months. The arrangement was initially just a way of saving money since it was cheaper to live off campus and share expenses than to live in a dormitory. Although they did not talk about it, Brooke had come to regard the relationship as a testing ground for marriage. Adam, on the other hand, continued to regard the living arrangement mainly in terms of convenience and believed Brooke thought likewise. One day Brooke discovered that Adam was seeing another woman, Jennifer, a senior at Harvard. When Brooke confronted him, he shrugged it off and told her that he and Jennifer were thinking of renting an apartment together after graduation. Brooke was devastated and accused him of betrayal. "What's the big deal?" he said, genuinely surprised at her reaction. "I haven't done anything wrong. After all, we're not married and haven't made any promises of sexual fidelity or a commitment to a long-term relationship."

RELIGIOUS AND CULTURAL ATTITUDES TOWARD SEXUALITY AND MARRIAGE

The sexual revolution that began in the late 1960s discarded the notion of sexual morality and instead urged people to free themselves from sexual guilt and shame and to freely enjoy the pleasure of sexuality. Was this a desirable move from a moral point of view, or a sign of declining morals in our society?

Sexuality has traditionally been regarded as a necessary but dangerous force that needs to be kept under control by laws and prohibitions. Jewish, Christian, and Islamic attitudes toward sexuality have been shaped by teachings in the *Bible* and *Koran* which regard marriage as the only proper setting for sexual intimacy and which condemn adultery and fornication[1] as well as homosexual relations.[2] Sex outside of heterosexual marriage is considered wrong because it is in conflict with God's natural law. According to Catholic natural law ethics, contraception is also wrong because it interferes with procreation, the natural end of sexuality. Homosexual acts are considered wrong because they undermine the common good, an argument echoed in Finnis's article. The Catholic position on sexual morality is explained in the Vatican's 1973 "Declaration on

Sexual Ethics" found at the end of this chapter. Michael Ruse challenges the belief that procreation is the only moral end to sexuality and that homosexuality is "bad sexuality."

The prohibition against homosexuality, adultery, and fornication has been incorporated into the legal system of most of the Western and Islamic world. State laws punishing homosexual acts have only recently been repealed in the United States. In Iran more than three hundred people were executed between 1990 and 1996 for violation of laws prohibiting homosexuality.[3] In some sub-Saharan Islamic cultures, adulterers, especially women, are still stoned to death.[4]

The use of contraception has also been regulated by laws. Prior to 1976 states could prohibit the sale of contraceptives. In 1969 the U.S. Supreme Court in *Griswold v. Connecticut* ruled that married people should be able to obtain contraception. Seven years later the right to obtain contraceptives was extended to single people. The prohibition against contraception in the United States was based primarily on the scriptural imperative to go forth and multiply, and the belief that the only legitimate end for sexual activity was procreation and that the use of contraception would lead to a decreased sense of responsibility and less restraint.[5] In "Better Sex," Sara Ruddick argues that mutual pleasure is also a natural end of sexual intercourse. Therefore, contraception is morally permissible.

SEXUAL INTIMACY AND LOVE

The romantic view of sex links sex to love. Sexual intimacy entails, at a minimum, consent between two adults. Lois Pineau, in her reading, emphasizes the importance of consent and good communication to sexual intimacy in dating relationships. But does sexual intimacy require love? Is mutual enjoyment and respect sufficient? What about the case of Adam and Brooke—was their relationship one of sexual intimacy? Can one-night encounters count as sexual intimacy? Even if we concede that sexual intimacy requires mutual love, what do we mean by love and what does it add to a sexual relationship?

Alan Goldman, in "Plain Sex," which can be found in the *Ethics PowerWeb,* defines love as "identification with the loved one's interests and an intended long-term commitment to further those interests. It is secondarily self-regarding: a desire for constant companionship with the person, and therefore a pleasant emotion in their presence and a longing in their absence."[6] Romantic erotic love involves a preoccupation with and sexual commitment to one person in which each partner is psychically open to the other.

While love may add value to a sexual relationship, is love required for a sexual relationship to be moral? Ruddick maintains that sex is morally preferable if it involves attempting to secure benefits, not just for oneself, but for the person cared for, a situation that is more likely to occur in a loving, intimate relationship. However, consensual sex outside of a loving relationship may still be morally permissible.

Clearly sexual desire can exist independently from love. Traditional views of sexual desire regard it as debasing and a threat to our personhood and, hence, morally suspect. Sex outside of marriage, according to this view, involves the use of the other as a means only, which is a violation of Kant's categorical imperative. A person who sexually desires another person objectifies the other. Because of this, pornography, prostitution, adultery, and premarital sex are wrong.

 THE DEFENSE OF MARRIAGE ACT

United States Congress
September 21, 1996

No State, territory, or possession of the United States, or Indian tribe, shall be required to give effect to any public act, record, or judicial proceeding of any other State, territory, possession, or tribe respecting a relationship between persons of the same sex that is treated as a marriage under the laws of such other State, territory, possession, or tribe, a right or claim arising from such a relationship.

In determining the meaning of any Act of Congress, or of any ruling, regulation, or interpretation of the various administrative bureaus and agencies of the United States, the word "marriage" means only a legal union between one man and one woman as husband and wife, and the word "spouse" refers only to a person of the opposite sex who is a husband or wife.

However, why must sex affirm one's moral worth or involve an exclusive commitment in order to be morally permissible? Isn't the pleasure gained from consensual sex also a legitimate end? We engage in other bodily activities with others (e.g., contact sports, massage, and surgery) because these activities bring us pleasure or profit without feeling we have to be in an intimate relationship with the other or affirm their moral worth.

MARRIAGE

Marriage between a man and woman is the ideal in almost all cultures. In Islam, as well as Orthodox Judaism, marriage is a holy duty.[7] Others, such as Immanuel Kant, believe that while marriage is morally permissible, a chaste, unmarried life is morally preferable. Because sexuality is associated with sin, a chaste, unmarried life is also held up as an ideal in the Catholic Church; indeed it is required for priests and nuns. Most people, however, regard marriage as morally permissible and even desirable, but not a duty.

Marriage is a social institution, a legal relationship between two people that carries with it certain legal rights and duties. The consent of both parties is a necessary, but not a sufficient, condition for a valid marriage. Some people also believe that the two parties must be of the opposite sex. According to the book of Genesis, God gave man and woman complementary natures. When united in marriage, men and women constitute a unit that is more balanced and greater than the sum of its parts. Husbands and wives are called to "reflect the inner unity of the creator."[8] Because male and female natures complement each other, sex roles are exaggerated in a marriage and bind the couple together. While the *Koran* affirms the primacy of love as the cause of marriage, Islamic authorities, like Catholics, emphasize reproduction and caring for children as the primary purpose of marriage.

Kant defines marriage as "the union of two persons of different sexes for the lifelong possession of each other's sexual attributes."[9] The core expectations of *marriage,* at

GOODRIDGE, ET AL. V. DEPARTMENT OF PUBLIC HEALTH, ET AL.

Suffolk, Massachusetts, March 4, 2003–November 18, 2003

I

The plaintiffs are fourteen individuals from five Massachusetts counties. . . .

In March and April, 2001, each of the plaintiff couples attempted to obtain a marriage license from a city or town clerk's office. As required under G. L. c. 207, they completed notices of intention to marry on forms provided by the registry, and presented these forms to a Massachusetts town or city clerk, together with the required health forms and marriage license fees. In each case, the clerk either refused to accept the notice of intention to marry or denied a marriage license to the couple on the ground that Massachusetts does not recognize same-sex marriage. Because obtaining a marriage license is a necessary prerequisite to civil marriage in Massachusetts, denying marriage licenses to the plaintiffs was tantamount to denying them access to civil marriage itself, with its appurtenant social and legal protections, benefits, and obligations.

On April 11, 2001, the plaintiffs filed suit in the Superior Court against the department and the commissioner seeking a judgment that "the exclusion of the [p]laintiff couples and other qualified same-sex couples from access to marriage licenses, and the legal and social status of civil marriage, as well as the protections, benefits and obligations of marriage, violates Massachusetts law.". . .

We consider next the plaintiffs' request for relief. We preserve as much of the statute as may be preserved in the face of the successful constitutional challenge. . . . We face a problem similar to one that recently confronted the Court of Appeal for

least in modern Western society, are that "it typically involves sexual intimacy, economic domestic cooperation, and a voluntary commitment to sustaining this relationship."[10] Sociologists Carolyn Kapinus and Michael Johnson maintain that in addition to a personal commitment to the relationship, marriage entails a moral commitment—"the feeling that one ought to continue a relationship, that one has a moral obligation to continue," and structural commitments involving joint property and shared friends.[11] In this sense, marriage is different than casual sex and cohabitation.

Marriage is sometimes compared with a contract agreement. Some couples, especially those previously married and older people with considerable assets, insist on premarital agreements, legally binding contracts that detail in advance the allocation of all financial and property assets if the marriage should come to an end. Opponents of premarital agreements argue that marriage is a lifelong commitment between a man and a woman and not a business contract. Premarital agreements indicate a lack of trust and commitment on the part of each partner. A marriage, they argue, is indissoluble or permanent because the two are of one flesh: "What God hath joined together, let no man put asunder."[12] The indissolubility of marriage is also important because the bearing and raising of children are considered by traditionalists to be an essential component of marriage. Divorce not only violates natural law, but harms children.

Ontario, the highest court of that Canadian province, when it considered the constitutionality of the same-sex marriage ban under Canada's Federal Constitution, the Charter of Rights and Freedoms. Canada, like the United States, adopted the common law of England that civil marriage is "the voluntary union for life of one man and one woman, to the exclusion of all others." In holding that the limitation of civil marriage to opposite-sex couples violated the Charter, the Court of Appeal refined the common-law meaning of marriage. We concur with this remedy, which is entirely consonant with established principles of jurisprudence empowering a court to refine a common-law principle in light of evolving constitutional standards.

We construe civil marriage to mean the voluntary union of two persons as spouses, to the exclusion of all others. This reformulation redresses the plaintiffs' constitutional injury and furthers the aim of marriage to promote stable, exclusive relationships. It advances the two legitimate State interests the department has identified: providing a stable setting for child rearing and conserving State resources. It leaves intact the Legislature's broad discretion to regulate marriage.

In their complaint the plaintiffs request only a declaration that their exclusion and the exclusion of other qualified same-sex couples from access to civil marriage violates Massachusetts law. We declare that barring an individual from the protections, benefits, and obligations of civil marriage solely because that person would marry a person of the same sex violates the Massachusetts Constitution. We vacate the summary judgment for the department. We remand this case to the Superior Court for entry of judgment consistent with this opinion.

So ordered.

Some radical feminists maintain that if free consent is a condition for a valid marriage, then most marriages can be annulled since women do not freely choose marriage but are pressured into it because of lack of social and economic equality. Robin West explores "The Harms of Consensual Sex" in her reading in the accompanying *Ethics PowerWeb.*

Almost half of first marriages now end in divorce.[13] Married women's entrance into the paid labor force is credited with much of the increase in divorce, since women with their own incomes are no longer as financially dependent on their husbands and no longer feel compelled to stay in a marriage.[14]

Is divorce morally unacceptable? Does the ease and social acceptability of divorce weaken the institution of marriage as well as harm children? What about cases of loveless marriages, domestic violence, or marriages without sexual intimacy?

HOMOSEXUALITY AND SAME-SEX MARRIAGES

Attitudes toward homosexuality have not changed significantly in the United States in the past few decades. In a 2002 Gallup Poll over half of Americans agreed with the statement that "homosexual behavior is morally wrong" while only 38 percent considered it to be morally acceptable.[15] However, more recent 2004 polls show that Americans may be becoming more sympathetic toward the homosexual community.* Women are more likely than men to regard homosexuality as morally acceptable.

Homosexuality is a modern term, coined in 1869 as a category of scientific investigation. Early researchers reported significant differences between heterosexual and homosexual men in their body type, lisping, and a variety of other physical and psychological traits. Although these stereotypes have been disproved, they remain today.

The belief that homosexuality is a deviation from the norm was reinforced by Sigmund Freud (1856–1939) who wrote that homosexuality resulted from a boy's inability to resolve his Oedipal conflict and sexual attraction to his mother. For many decades the mental health community accepted Freud's definition of homosexuality as a perversion and mental disorder. The high prevalence of HIV/AIDS, which was first diagnosed in 1977 among homosexuals, fueled the public's belief that homosexuality was inherently unhealthy and immoral. It wasn't until 1994 that the American Medical Association revoked the disease model and its position that medical professionals should aim at changing the sexual orientation of homosexuals.

Despite this, the belief that homosexuality is immoral and deviant is still pervasive in American society. Children are bombarded with antihomosexual messages from a young age; 97 percent of public school students report hearing antihomosexual remarks from their peers and 53 percent from their teachers. In addition, 19 percent of gay and lesbian high school students are physically assaulted because of their sexual orientation. Teachers intervene in only 3 percent of the attacks.[16] Coming out, publicly disclosing one's homosexual orientation, increases the risk of hate crimes and assault. Of the hate crimes reported to the FBI in 1995, 13 percent were based on sexual orientation. The perpetrators are generally young, white middle-class males who are bored and intoxicated, and who seek out a gay victim for a sense of adventure and because they believe that society has agreed to dislike homosexuals.[17]

Attitudes against homosexuals on this side of the Atlantic, with the exception of Canada, tend to be more severe than in Europe and non-Islamic Asia. In some Latin American countries homosexuality is punishable by imprisonment. Until 2003, when the U.S. Supreme Court ruled antisodomy laws unconstitutional in *Lawrence v. Texas,* several states had laws that punished homosexuality by up to twenty-five years in prison.

Same-sex marriage is legal in the Netherlands, Belgium, and Canada. In addition, homosexual couples have full legal rights in several European countries.[18] In its 2003 ruling legalizing same-sex marriages, the court in Ontario, Canada stated, "Exclusion perpetuates the view that same-sex relationships are less worth of recognition than opposite-sex relationships." The court also ruled that the government's definition of marriage as being "one man and one woman" was invalid and be changed to "two persons."

The majority of states have laws in place that prohibit same-sex marriages. The U.S. government has made it known that it will not recognize Canadian same-sex marriage licenses. Although same-sex marriage is illegal in all fifty states, a few states, such as Vermont and California, permit civil unions, a legal recognition of the homosexual partnership. Massachusetts in 2003 struck down the ban on same-sex marriages and tried to pass legislation legalizing same-sex marriage. In 2004 same-sex couples were given

---

* "Poll Finds More Acceptance of Gays," *The Providence Sunday Journal* April 11, 2004, p. A5.

marriage licenses in San Francisco. However the Defense of Marriage Act bars the federal government from recognizing same sex-marriages.

The Defense of Marriage Act, signed by President Bill Clinton in 1996, defines marriage as a union between a man and a woman. Some people are pushing to make the Act a Constitutional amendment. The Vatican has also issued a statement condemning the legalization of unions between homosexual persons, a position defended by John Finnis in his reading at the end of this chapter. Michael Nava and Robert Dawidoff examine the arguments both for and against gay marriage in their reading. Unlike Nava and Dawidoff, Cheshire Calhoun has reservations about the desirability of legalizing same-sex marriage. In her reading she argues that traditional heterosexual marriages are inherently oppressive to women.

COHABITATION AND PREMARITAL SEX

In a 2002 Gallup Poll, 42 percent of Americans agreed with the statement that sex between an unmarried man and woman is wrong.[19] Acceptance of casual sex has been declining on college campuses with only 39.6 percent of college freshmen in a 1999 survey agreeing that "if two people really like each other, it's all right for them to have sex even if they've known each other for a very short time." This number is down from 51.9 percent in 1987.

Two-thirds of the women in another study stated that they hoped to meet their future husbands in college. However, the study also found that courtship is no longer part of the college scene. Instead, dating and courtship have been supplanted by "hanging out," and sexual encounters that are usually either casual "hookups" with no emotional commitment, or "joined at the hip" cohabitation.[20]

The Bible condemns all forms of sex outside of marriage. Many people disapprove of premarital sex because they believe it interferes with the deepening of a couple's relationship in other areas. They maintain that premarital chastity is the best way to guarantee marital commitment and faithfulness. Indeed, couples who cohabitate before marriage have a significantly higher divorce rate[21] and rate their marriages less positively than couples who did not cohabitate before marriage.[22]

While acceptance of casual sex is declining, cohabitation is prevalent among college students with between 30 to 40 percent of college students cohabiting at any given time.[23] Cohabitation, formerly called "living together," is defined as people of the opposite sex living together and having sex together on a regular basis and sharing living expenses. Some people prefer cohabitation because there are no legal obligations or restrictions placed on them.

Two of the primary reasons for cohabitation are readily available sex and convenience. Students also cohabitate as a symbol of their emancipation and freedom to make their own decisions. A fourth reason, especially among women, is cohabitation as a testing ground for marriage. However, the great majority of people who cohabitate do not eventually get married. Cohabitation is also associated with significantly higher risk of domestic violence than is marriage.[24] The longer a couple cohabitates the greater the chance they will marry, with 58 percent who have cohabited for at least three years eventually marrying. However, marriages that are preceded by cohabitation have a higher divorce rate.[25] Does this mean that consensual sex outside of marriage is wrong? Ruddick and Goldman explore this question in their readings.

THE PHILOSOPHERS ON SEXUALITY AND MARRIAGE

Like most of the ancient Greek philosophers, Aristotle maintained that there are inherent gender differences and that inequality is an inevitable aspect of marriage. Marriage and the home is the domain of women; the state the primary focus of men. While family is necessary to meet our physical needs, the state is the proper moral sphere. The family contributes to the human good which is participation in the state.

For Augustine and Thomas Aquinas only sexuality within marriage between a man and a woman was morally permissible. Augustine regarded sexual intercourse for the purpose of begetting children as good, and desire simply for intercourse without this purpose as a depravity or a "sin against nature." Homosexual unions cannot be marital since they can never form a "biological unit" and produce children. This philosophy still informs the position of the Catholic Church on sexuality and marriage.

Immanuel Kant wrote that because the sexual impulse treats the other as an object of one's enjoyment rather than as a person, it is a debasement of our humanity and shameful. Sexuality is only compatible with morality in a marriage between a man and a woman since in marriage a person dedicates not only his or her sexuality, but his or her whole person to the other and, in so doing, "constitutes a unity of will."[26] Unlike Aristotle, Kant believed that marriage could be a moral institution. Homosexuality, in Kant's view, is a travesty because it involves the use of the other person as an object and, like masturbation, the misuse of the sexual facilities and "runs counter to the ends of humanity to preserve the species without forfeiture of the person."[27]

Georg Hegel believed that "woman has her substantial destiny in the family." In a marriage the wife cedes rule to the husband on the basis of her natural inferiority. The woman's duty to be subordinate emerges only after marriage. Sex roles are a product of marriage and, according to Hegel, necessary for marital unity.[28] Sexual relations in marriage are not just physical but a manifestation of this spiritual unity. This connection results in the production of children, the physical manifestation of the couple's love for each other. Jean-Jacques Rousseau likewise believed that men and women's duties in a marriage are based on the sexual division of labor as dictated by nature. It is by fulfilling their feminine and maternal duties that women achieve freedom.

It was not until the end of the eighteenth century, in Mary Wollstonecraft's *A Vindication of the Rights of Women,* that the idea emerged of marriage as a union of equals. She envisioned marriage as a union of moral equals, of common humanity united by reason, who had equal rights and autonomy in the public sphere and in marriage. Women should not aim for negative power, power through the dominance of patriarchy, but for equality. The traditional marriage contract, Wollstonecraft argued, is a "fraudulent sexual contract," based on force and domination and resting on women's slavery that denies them access to reason. She believed that if women were better educated and given greater freedom and choices, marriage could become like a friendship of equals.

Wollstonecraft's arguments were expanded by utilitarian John Stuart Mill and Harriet Taylor in the nineteenth century. Like Wollstonecraft, Mill and Taylor regarded marriage as a higher form of friendship based on equality and mutual esteem. This type of marriage, they argued, would bring greater social benefits than one based on inequality.

ADULTERY AND INFIDELITY

In Homer's *Odyssey,* Odysseus was warned of the sirens whose mesmerizing song bewitched men. Blinded by lust, sailors would wreck their ships on the jagged rocks or drown trying to reach the sirens. Odysseus, a happily married man, wisely asked that his men tie him to the mast of the ship and not let him loose no matter how much he begged.

A 2002 Gallup Poll found that 87 percent of Americans thought that it was morally wrong for a married person to have an affair.[29] Despite widespread disapproval, adultery is on the increase, especially among women. Dr. Shirley Glass, a Baltimore psychologist and infidelity researcher, estimates that 25 percent of wives and 44 percent of husbands have extramarital affairs, often with coworkers.[30]

Some married people are also turning to strangers in chat rooms and to Internet pornography sites for companionship. Online forums or "sex-cussion" groups are playing an increasing role in the breakup of marriages. In some cases online relationships can lead to real-life meetings and adultery. But even if they don't is Internet "virtual sex" still immoral or adulterous?

What about couples who aren't married? Do people who are dating or cohabiting have a moral obligation to be sexually faithful to one another, as in the case of Adam and Brooke at the beginning of this chapter?

In the reading "Is Adultery Immoral?," Richard Wasserstrom argues that it is not the extramarital sexual act per se that is immoral, but the deception, the breaking of an implicit promise of sexual loyalty to one's spouse. However, he continues, a commitment to sexual exclusivity is not a necessary condition of marriage. In "open marriages" spouses have agreed to allow extramarital sexual relations. Other philosophers disagree, maintaining that the promise to be sexually loyal to one's spouse is implicit in the marriage vow no matter what the two partners may say to the contrary.

SEX AND VIOLENCE

A disproportionate number of assaults and murders occur within the context of intimate sexual relationships. In 1996, 36 percent of female homicide victims, about 10,000 women, were slain by their husbands or boyfriends. At Kansas State University, 90 percent of all calls to the Crisis Center involve victims of intimate violence.[31] Are these statistics an artifact of gender inequality? Or, does sexual intimacy, with its high emotions and emphasis on exclusivity, promote violence?

Domestic violence (sometimes called intimate violence) is defined as violence within a home or an intimate sexual relationship. The primary purpose of domestic violence is to "gain or maintain power and control over the victim."[32] According to the U.S. Department of Justice Bureau of Statistics, 92 percent of domestic violence is committed by men against women. One-third of women report being physically or sexually abused by a boyfriend or husband at some time in their lives. In October 2000 Congress passed the *Violence against Women Act* that allocated more than $3 billion over five years to programs to prevent domestic violence and to assist women victimized by domestic violence. Of this money, $140 million is earmarked for programs to stop violence against women on college campuses.[33]

In a 2002 study of domestic violence among intimate gay partners, 39 percent reported at least one instance of battering by their partner during the previous five years.[34] In contrast only 11.6 percent of heterosexual women who were married or cohabiting reported being victims of violence during the same five-year period. Violence among lesbian couples is about the same as that among heterosexual couples. Stressors such as harassment, public disapproval, and legal impairments toward making a commitment through marriage, stressors which heterosexual couples do not face, could be contributing to the high incidence of violence in homosexual relationships. Indeed, studies show that cohabitation among heterosexual partners is associated with a "considerably higher risk of domestic violence."[35]

Rape seems to be a uniquely human phenomenon.[36] In her book *Against Our Will: Men, Women and Rape,* Susan Brownmiller argues that rape is a crime of violence—a conscious process of intimidation by men to keep women in a state of fear—rather than an act of sexual passion. Rape is also used in war and in prison among inmates as a form of intimidation and means of maintaining the power structure. Goldman argues that rape is worse than physical assault because it is an attack on a person's personal identity and a violation of the victim's right to privacy.

Rape, as Lois Pineau points out in her reading on date rape, is viewed more ambiguously than most crimes. Women who say they have been raped are often met with suspicion and insinuations that they somehow provoked the rape, as happened in the case of basketball star Kobe Bryant, who was accused of raping a 19-year-old woman at a Colorado luxury resort. Furthermore, many women are reluctant to report rape. Rape shield laws have been passed in some states that shield women from being cross-examined about their sexual pasts.

Most rapists are known by their victims. This has prompted growing concern about rape within marriage and date rape on college campuses. A study of college men found that 34 percent of the men were inclined to rape, as evidenced by their acceptance of rape myths, low empathy for victims of rape, gender stereotypes about women, and the belief that interpersonal violence against women is acceptable.[37] Fraternities in particular have been called "rape-prone contexts." According to trial attorney Fray Tash, fraternity men are involved in more than 90 percent of all gang rapes on campus.[38] Some universities' guidelines, such as those at Antioch College, require students to give explicit verbal consent throughout each step of a sexual activity so there is no misunderstanding.

A survey in *Ms* magazine reported that one-fourth of all college women are victims of rape or attempted rape. However, 75 percent of the women described as rape victims did not define their experience as rape. In her article on date rape at the end of this chapter, Lois Pineau suggests that this is because women have been socialized to see their oppression and violation as normal. While most women believe that force must be used for rape to occur, Robin West maintains that force is not necessary. Rape is sex that is *either* nonconsensual *or* forced, or both. Others, such as Katie Roiphe, in her article at the end of Chapter 10, argue that the problem lies in the definition of date rape used by what she calls "rape crisis" feminists.[39] Instead of helping women overcome oppression, Roiphe argues that the "rape crisis" approach buys into the myth that women are naïve, passive, innocent, and helpless. Another controversial issue is whether rape can occur in the context of marriage. Does the marriage vow or contract ensure sexual access even when one of the partners is not interested?

Pedophilia is often considered a form of rape. Pedophiles seek sexual intimacy with children. Most, though not all, people believe that sex with children, even if it is limited to fondling, is wrong because children cannot consent. Pedophilia also often involves a violation of trust and the duty of fidelity, since most victims of pedophiles know their abuser, who is often a trusted authority figure such as a parent or priest.

Another form of violence associated with sexual intimacy is stalking, an obsessive behavior that causes the victim to fear for her or his safety. Eighty-five percent of stalkers are current or former husbands, cohabiting partners, or boyfriends.[40] Of female students on college campuses, 13.1 percent have been the victims of stalkers.[41] Stalking, however, is not limited to women. In the 1987 film *Fatal Attraction*, Glenn Close portrays an obsessive woman stalking her former lover, played by Michael Douglas.

What are we to make of these findings? Is sexual intimacy and sexual desire inherently fraught with sin and danger? Should they be avoided except in marriage and for procreation? Or is the problem social? In a perfect and just world would intimate violence be nonexistent?

PROSTITUTION

The United States, with the exception of Nevada, is one of the few Western nations where prostitution is illegal. Although prostitution is not, using Ruddick's definition, "complete" or "better sex," is it immoral?

One of the feminist critiques of prostitution is that it legitimates the subordination of women as a class. Debra Satz, in her *Ethics PowerWeb* article "Markets in Women's Sexual Labor," argues that female prostitution is wrong because of the relationship between prostitution and the view that women are men's social inferiors. The very act of prostitution degrades women and reinforces the patriarchal hierarchy. Prostitution also reinforces economic disparities since woman who are poor and who have been sexually abused as children are more likely to become prostitutes. Networks exist that lure impoverished foreign women and children into prostitution rings under the guise of dating and employment agencies or marriage bureaus. Some travel agencies in the United States and Europe cater to pedophiles by booking trips mainly to Southeast Asia and undeveloped countries, but also to cities in the United States and Europe, where the pedophiles are put in contact with child (boys and girls) prostitute rings.[42] Prostitution, whether the prostitutes are minors or adults, is also thought to be harmful to the social good and to public health, since prostitutes are disproportionately afflicted with HIV/AIDS and other sexually transmitted diseases, and for this reason should remain illegal.

Those who favor legalizing prostitution for adult sex workers, including several organizations of sex workers in this country,[43] respond that women gain some benefits from voluntary prostitution since it might be the best employment available to them. Many prostitutes work in terrible conditions, marginalized from the rest of society. Placing prostitutes—sex workers—outside of legal protection puts further burdens on them, making them more vulnerable to predators and pimps who exploit them. Legalizing prostitution and removing the stigma would help overcome many of the degrading aspects of prostitution as it currently exists in the United States. In addition, without regulation, there is no need for prostitutes to get tested and treated for sexually transmitted diseases (STDs) or for clients to use safe-sex practices.

In Canada, where prostitution is legal, full-service, safe-sex work is the accepted norm. Prices are lower because the cost to the sex worker is lower, since there is no need to pay pimps or "protection fees" to organized crime. The right of sex workers to advertise their services in public print is also protected in Canada.

Proponents of legalizing prostitution in the United States maintain that we should not place any significance on the sexual use of the body but leave it up to each individual, as a liberty right. People "sell" their bodily services in many professions; masseurs, athletes, surgeons, dentists, ballroom dancers—however, we do not consider these uses of one's body immoral—why sexuality? Shouldn't it be a woman's right to choose how to use her own body? Goldman argues that rather than prohibiting prostitution we should reform it so it is based on a consensual contract between equal partners. This is only possible if prostitution is a protected legal institution.

MORAL ISSUES

Dignity and Respect for Persons

What is morally good sex? The concept of moral goodness is linked to the well-being and dignity of our fellow human beings. Some philosophers argue that sex outside of heterosexual marriage violates respect for human dignity since it entails using the other merely as an object or tool for one's pleasure. Sex within a marriage, on the other hand, affirms the other's worth and dignity. Goldman acknowledges that sexual acts involve the manipulation of the other's body for one's own pleasure. However, he also believes that sex is morally permissible if you make sure you provide sexual pleasure to your partner. But, if providing sexual pleasure to others is simply a means of attaining your own sexual pleasure, isn't this still treating the other merely as a means rather than as a person? Also, sex within a marriage does not always meet this qualification, while sex outside of marriage may.

Dignity and respect is also an issue in how society treats homosexuals. Denying people the right to be open about their sexual orientation because of fear of retaliation or, in the case of the military, the "Don't Ask, Don't Tell" rule is an affront to a person's integrity. Marriage in particular is an important part of a person's self-identity since it is a public declaration of commitment.

Some radical feminists, in contrast, maintain that traditional marriage violates respect for persons. Rather than affirming the dignity of women, marriage is oppressive to women.

Autonomy and Consent

Mutual consent is an important principle governing good sex. Consensual sex is noncoercive. Imposing our sexual desires on others without their consent is an affront to the other's dignity. It is for this reason that adults having sex with children is considered immoral—not because sex is bad but because it is wrong to violate another person's autonomy. Rape is also immoral because it is imposed upon a person by intimidation or force. However, what about a man "wining and dining" a woman, or using "sweet talk" to get a reluctant woman to agree to have sex with him, or a woman engaging in seductive behavior to entice a man to have sex with her—do these behaviors count as coercion—or are they just part of the "courting" process?

Is consent sufficient for sex to be morally permissible? Kant says no since even with mutual consent sexual acts outside of marriage objectify the other. Also a relationship can be consensual but adulterous. Arguments against prostitution also focus mainly on the socially coercive nature of the institution, especially where the prostitutes' autonomy is severely compromised because they have few other viable options for earning a livelihood.

Radical feminists, such as Catherine MacKinnon, argue that because of the uneven economic and social power, even when women consent to a sexual relationship there is still the problem of coercion. Marriage is viewed as an exchange of sex for money and power, both of which men, in general, have more of. All sexual relationships, even within marriage, unless initiated by the woman, involve lack of consent on the part of women since consent is not possible in an unequal relationship.[44] One of the questionable assumptions underlying this is that women do not enjoy sex and the pleasure it brings for its own sake and would not agree to it unless there was some element of coercion or external benefit attached to the sexual encounter. While this may be true in some cases, it is certainly not true in all cases.

Fidelity and Trust

Although consent may be a necessary condition for sex to be morally acceptable, it is not sufficient. Two people may freely consent to sexual intercourse but the relationship may still be immoral because it is adulterous and violates the principle of fidelity, as least in cases where the marriage is not "open." Some people maintain that couples who are dating steadily or cohabiting have a tacit agreement to remain faithful. Deception can also occur because of pretending we are someone we are not, exaggerating our good qualities, omitting relevant information about our pasts, or using insincere words of love to win the affection of the other person.

Justice and Equality

Some feminists regard the institution of marriage as inherently unjust. The traditional view of marriage, which is tied to sex roles, has been seen as a hindrance to the realization of justice in marriage as well as the recognition of same-sex marriages.

Couples who are homosexual also face discrimination. Discrimination is not inherently wrong; however, unequal treatment must be based on morally relevant differences between two groups. For example, children are not allowed to drive automobiles because of their lack of maturity. Are there similar rational grounds to deny same-sex couples the right to marry?

Unnatural

One of the arguments against homosexuality and same-sex marriage, as well as contraception and masturbation, is that they are unnatural. The assumption underlying this argument is that the sole purpose of sex is procreation of the species. One weakness of this argument is the ambiguity of the term *unnatural.* Does unnatural mean contrary to the "laws of human nature"? Ruse points out in his reading at the end of this chapter that homosexual behavior is found throughout human societies as well as in other species of animals. Or does "unnatural" mean "uncommon"? This definition is also problematic. There are many types of uncommon behavior, such as great genius, beauty, or moral fortitude and compassion that we regard as highly desirable rather than immoral.

Natural can also be defined in terms of function based on the assumption that certain parts of our body were designed, by God or evolution, for specific functions. But why do we have to restrict ourselves to using something only for the function which it was supposedly designed? Isn't part of human creativity the ability to see new possibilities in things? We use our other bodily parts, feet, hands, arms, in many ways.

The modern counterpart to the natural law argument is that homosexuality is a genetic disorder or sickness. If sickness is defined as a pathological condition that interfers with our everyday functioning, it appears on the surface that homosexuality may be a sickness. Many homosexuals have been "disabled" because of their sexual orientation. Advocates of gay and lesbian rights argue that it is not their sexual orientation per se that is disabling, but society's response to their sexual orientation. In this sense, homosexuality is no more a sickness than is having dark skin or being female, two other genetic conditions that can interfere with effective everyday functioning.

Consequentialist Considerations

Many of the arguments against sex outside of marriage are based on beliefs about its harmful consequences. Couples who cohabitate have a higher rate of intimate violence and usually eventually break up. If they marry they have a higher divorce rate. However, do these possible consequences, mean that cohabiting is immoral, or that people should be more discerning, and perhaps even more committed, before getting into such an arrangement?

Adultery and infidelity can be harmful to the third party. However, this is not the only reason adultery may be immoral. If adultery is condemned mainly on the grounds of harm to the third party, then is adultery morally acceptable if the adulterous parties take care that their secret will not be discovered?

Homosexual behavior, it is argued, is wrong because it is offensive to those who are forced to witness public displays of affection. However, a feeling of offense or disgust is not a harm, according to utilitarians, and is not on its own sufficient grounds for declaring certain behaviors to be immoral. It is also argued that homosexuals tend to be child molesters and may seduce young children into adopting a homosexual lifestyle. Homosexuality has also been condemned as promoting promiscuity which, in turn, increases the spread of sexually transmitted diseases. Finally, homosexuality is seen as a threat to the very survival of the human race; if we all became homosexuals, there would be no future generations.

Most consequentialist arguments against homosexuals have proved to be groundless. Homosexuals are no more likely to be child molesters than are heterosexuals. Nor is there any evidence that children's sexual orientation is influenced by contact with homosexuals, or that condoning homosexuality will lead to an increase in the percentage of people who are homosexuals and the demise of the human race.[45] And homosexual men are probably no more promiscuous than heterosexual men.

There is also the issue of harms against homosexuals. In a homophobic society, being gay or lesbian can be dangerous. Disapproval of discrimination and mistreatment of people who are homosexual, however, as Finnis points out, does not entail approval of the practice.

The Common Good

Heterosexual marriage, most philosophers maintain, contributes to the common good of society. Finnis argues that homosexual marriages threaten the stability of the family and of society in general. Laws that prohibit same-sex marriage are justified on the grounds that they preserve the social fabric of the family. Because the primary purpose of marriage is to have children, homosexuals are not significantly harmed by not being able to marry. Other institutions and practices that threaten the stability of marriage, such as prostitution, cohabitation, and adultery, are also immoral. Whether or not legalizing prostitution and same-sex marriages or accommodating cohabitation will weaken the institution of marriage remains to be seen. The institution of marriage does not seem to have been weakened nor the common good damaged in countries where prostitution and same-sex marriages are legal.

CONCLUSION

For sex to be moral it must, at a minimum, be based on mutual and informed consent, and not be coercive or be deceptive. Whether or not marriage or love and sexual intimacy are required for sex to be morally permissible remains open to debate.

THE VATICAN

Declaration on Sexual Ethics

The Declaration on Sexual Ethics was issue by the Vatican on December 29, 1975. In it the writers defend the doctrine, based on natural law ethics and scriptural text, that sexual acts must occur only in the context of marriage. Premarital sex, homosexuality, and masturbation are all condemned.

Critical Reading Questions

1. Why did the Vatican feel the need to issue the *Declaration on Sexual Ethics?*
2. What is the connection between sexuality and human dignity?
3. What is meant by the "essential finality of sexuality"?
4. What is the source of morality?
5. Why is marriage between a man and a woman the only framework where sexual intimacy is moral?
6. What is the moral relationship between sexuality and procreation?
7. Why is premarital sex immoral?
8. Why is homosexuality immoral? How should the church respond to people who are homosexual?
9. What is the Vatican's position on the morality of masturbation?

---

1. According to contemporary scientific research, the human person is so profoundly affected by sexuality that it must be considered as one of the factors which give to each individual's life the principal traits that distinguish it. In fact it is from sex that the human person receives the characteristics which, on the biological, psychological and spiritual levels, make that person a man or a woman, and thereby largely condition his or her progress towards maturity and insertion into society. Hence sexual matters, as is obvious to everyone, today constitute a theme frequently and openly dealt with in books, reviews, magazines, and other means of social communication.

In the present period, the corruption of morals has increased, and one of the most serious indications of this corruption is the unbridled exaltation of sex. . . .

2. The Church cannot remain indifferent to this confusion of minds and relaxation of morals. It is a question, in fact, of a matter which is of the utmost importance both for the personal lives of Christians and for the social life of our time. . . . since the erroneous opinions and resulting deviations are continuing to spread everywhere, the Sacred Congregation for the Doctrine of the Faith, by virtue of its function in the universal Church and by a mandate of the Supreme Pontiff, has judged it necessary to publish the present Declaration.

3. The people of our time are more and more convinced that the human person's dignity and

---

Vatican Statement, "Persona Humana: Declaration on Certain Questions Concerning Sexual Ethics," Given at Rome, at the Sacred Congregation for the Doctrine of the Faith, on December 29, 1975.

vocation demand that they should discover, by the light of their own intelligence, the values innate in their nature, that they should ceaselessly develop these values and realize them in their lives, in order to achieve an ever greater development.

In moral matters man cannot make value judgments according to his personal whim: "In the depths of his conscience, man detects a law which he does not impose on himself, but which holds him to obedience. . . . For man has in his heart a law written by God. To obey it is the very dignity of man; according to it he will be judged."[1]. . .

Therefore there can be no true promotion of man's dignity unless the essential order of his nature is respected. Of course, in the history of civilization many of the concrete conditions and needs of human life have changed and will continue to change. But all evolution of morals and every type of life must be kept within the limits imposed by the immutable principles based upon every human person's constitutive elements and essential relations—elements and relations which transcend historical contingency.

These fundamental principles, which can be grasped by reason, are contained in "the divine law—eternal, objective, and universal—whereby God orders, directs, and governs the entire universe and all the ways of the human community, by a plan conceived in wisdom and love. Man has been made by God to participate in this law, with the result that, under the gentle disposition of divine Providence, he can come to perceive ever increasingly the unchanging truth."[2] This divine law is accessible to our minds.

4. Hence, those many people are in error who today assert that one can find neither in human nature nor in the revealed law any absolute and immutable norm to serve for particular actions other than the one which expresses itself in the general law of charity and respect for human dignity. . . .

But in fact, divine Revelation and, in its own proper order, philosophical wisdom, emphasize the authentic exigencies of human nature. They thereby necessarily manifest the existence of immutable laws inscribed in the constitutive elements of human nature and which are revealed to be identical in all beings endowed with reason.

Furthermore, Christ instituted his Church as "the pillar and bulwark of truth."[3] With the Holy Spirit's assistance, she ceaselessly preserves and transmits without error the truths of the moral order, and she authentically interprets not only the revealed positive law but "also . . . those principles of the moral order which have their origin in human nature itself"[4] and which concern man's full development and sanctification. . . .

5. Since sexual ethics concern certain fundamental values of human and Christian life, this general teaching equally applies to sexual ethics. In this domain there exist principles and norms which the Church has always unhesitatingly transmitted as part of her teaching, however much the opinions and morals of the world may have been opposed to them. These principles and norms in no way owe their origin to a certain type of culture, but rather to knowledge of the divine law and of human nature. They therefore cannot be considered as having become out of date or doubtful under the pretext that a new cultural situation has arisen.

It is these principles which inspired the exhortations and directives given by the Second Vatican Council for an education and an organization of social life taking account of the equal dignity of man and woman while respecting their difference.

Speaking of "the sexual nature of man and the human faculty of procreation," the Council noted that they "wonderfully exceed the dispositions of lower forms of life."[5] It then took particular care to expound the principles and criteria which concern human sexuality in marriage, and which are based upon the finality of the specific function of sexuality.

In this regard the Council declares that the moral goodness of the acts proper to conjugal life, acts which are ordered according to true human dignity, "does not depend solely on sincere intentions or on an evaluation of motives. It must be determined by objective standards. These, based on the nature of the human person and his acts, preserve the full sense of mutual self-giving and human procreation in the context of true love."[6]

These final words briefly sum up the Council's teaching—more fully expounded in an earlier part of the same Constitution—on the finality of the sexual act and on the principal criterion of its morality: it is respect for its finality that ensures the moral goodness of this act.

This same principle, which the Church holds from divine Revelation and from her authentic interpretation of the natural law, is also the basis of her traditional doctrine, which states that the use of the sexual function has its true meaning and moral rectitude only in true marriage.

6. It is not the purpose of the present declaration to deal with all the abuses of the sexual faculty, nor with all the elements involved in the practice of chastity. Its object is rather to repeat the Church's doctrine on certain particular points, in view of the urgent need to oppose serious errors and widespread aberrant modes of behavior.

7. Today there are many who vindicate the right to sexual union before marriage, at least in those cases where a firm intention to marry and an affection which is already in some way conjugal in the psychology of the subjects require this completion, which they judge to be connatural. This is especially the case when the celebration of the marriage is impeded by circumstances or when this intimate relationship seems necessary in order for love to be preserved.

This opinion is contrary to Christian doctrine, which states that every genital act must be within the framework of marriage. However firm the intention of those who practice such premature sexual relations may be, the fact remains that these relations cannot ensure, in sincerity and fidelity, the interpersonal relationship between a man and a woman, nor especially can they protect this relationship from whims and caprices. Now it is a stable union that Jesus willed, and he restored its original requirement, beginning with the sexual difference. "Have you not read that the creator from the beginning made them male and female and that he said: This is why a man must leave father and mother, and cling to his wife, and the two become one body? They are no longer two, therefore, but one body. So then, what God has united, man must not divide."[7] . . . Through marriage, in fact, the love of married people is taken up into that love which Christ irrevocably has for the Church,[8] while dissolute sexual union[9] defiles the temple of the Holy Spirit which the Christian has become. Sexual union therefore is only legitimate if a definitive community of life has been established between the man and the woman. . . .

Experience teaches us that love must find its safeguard in the stability of marriage, if sexual intercourse is truly to respond to the requirements of its own finality and to those of human dignity. These requirements call for a conjugal contract sanctioned and guaranteed by society—a contract which establishes a state of life of capital importance both for the exclusive union of the man and the woman and for the good of their family and of the human community. Most often, in fact, premarital relations exclude the possibility of children. What is represented to be conjugal love is not able, as it absolutely should be, to develop into paternal and maternal love. Or, if it does happen to do so, this will be to the detriment of the children, who will be deprived of the stable environment in which they ought to develop in order to find in it the way and the means of their insertion into society as a whole.

The consent given by people who wish to be united in marriage must therefore be manifested externally and in a manner which makes it valid in the eyes of society. As far as the faithful are concerned, their consent to the setting up of a community of conjugal life must be expressed according to the laws of the Church. It is a consent which makes their marriage a Sacrament of Christ.

8. At the present time there are those who, basing themselves on observations in the psychological order, have begun to judge indulgently, and even to excuse completely, homosexual relations between certain people. This they do in opposition to the constant teaching of the Magisterium and to the moral sense of the Christian people.

A distinction is drawn, and it seems with some reason, between homosexuals whose tendency comes from a false education, from a lack of normal sexual development, from habit, from bad example, or from other similar causes, and is transitory or at least not incurable; and homosexuals who are definitively such because of some kind of innate instinct or a pathological constitution judged to be incurable.

In regard to this second category of subjects, some people conclude that their tendency is so natural that it justifies in their case homosexual relations within a sincere communion of life and love analogous to marriage insofar as such homosexuals feel incapable of enduring a solitary life.

In the pastoral field, these homosexuals must certainly be treated with understanding and sustained in the hope of overcoming their personal difficulties and their inability to fit into society. Their culpability will be judged with prudence. But no pastoral method can be employed which would give moral justification to these acts on the grounds that they would be consonant with the condition of such people. For according to the objective moral order, homosexual relations are acts which lack an essential and indispensable finality. In Sacred Scripture they are condemned as a serious depravity and even presented as the sad consequence of rejecting God.[10] This judgment of Scripture does not of course permit us to conclude that all those who suffer from this anomaly are personally responsible for it, but it does attest to the fact that homosexual acts are intrinsically disordered and can in no case be approved.

9. The traditional Catholic doctrine that masturbation constitutes a grave moral disorder is often called into doubt or expressly denied today. It is said that psychology and sociology show that it is a normal phenomenon of sexual development, especially among the young. . . .

This opinion is contradictory to the teaching and pastoral practice of the Catholic Church. Whatever the force of certain arguments of a biological and philosophical nature, which have sometimes been used by theologians, in fact both the Magisterium of the Church—in the course of a constant tradition—and the moral sense of the faithful have declared without hesitation that masturbation is an intrinsically and seriously disordered act. The main reason is that, whatever the motive for acting in this way, the deliberate use of the sexual faculty outside normal conjugal relations essentially contradicts the finality of the faculty. For it lacks the sexual relationship called for by the moral order, namely the relationship which realizes "the full sense of mutual self-giving and human procreation in the context of true love."[11] All deliberate exercise of sexuality must be reserved to this regular relationship. . . . The frequency of the phenomenon in question is certainly to be linked with man's innate weakness following original sin; but it is also to be linked with the loss of a sense of God, with the corruption of morals engendered by the commercialization of vice, with the unrestrained licentiousness of so many public entertainments and publications, as well as with the neglect of modesty, which is the guardian of chastity. . . .

In the pastoral ministry, in order to form an adequate judgment in concrete cases, the habitual behavior of people will be considered in its totality, not only with regard to the individual's practice of charity and of justice but also with regard to the individual's care in observing the particular precepts of chastity. In particular, one will have to examine whether the individual is using the necessary means, both natural and supernatural, which Christian asceticism from its long experience recommends for overcoming the passions and progressing in virtue. . . .

ENDNOTES

1. *Pastoral Constitution on the Church in the World of Today,* no. 16: *AAS* 58 (1966) 1037 [*TPS* XI, 268].
2. *Declaration on Religious Freedom,* no. 3: *AAS* 58 (1966) 931 [*TPS* XI, 86].
3. 1 *Tm* 3, 15.
4. *Declaration on Religious Freedom,* no. 14: *AAS* 58 (1966) 940 [*TPS* XI, 93].
5. *Pastoral Constitution on the Church in the World of Today,* no. 51: *AAS* 58 (1966) 1072 [*TPS* XI, 293].
6. *Loc. cit.*; see also no. 49: *AAS* 58 (1966) 1069–1070 [*TPS* XI, 291–292].
7. *Mt* 19, 4–6.

8. See *Eph* 5, 25–32.
9. Extramarital intercourse is expressly condemned in 1 *Cor* 5, 1; 6, 9; 7, 2; 10, 8; *Eph* 5, 5–7; 1 *Tm* 1, 10; *Heb* 13, 4; there are explicit arguments given in 1 *Cor* 6, 12–20.
10. *Rom* 1:24–27: . . . See also what St. Paul says of sodomy in 1 *Cor* 6, 9; 1 *Tm* 1, 10.
11. *Pastoral Constitution on the Church in the World of Today*, no. 51: *AAS* 58 (1966) 1072 [*TPS* XI, 293].

Discussion Questions

1. Make a list of the premises used in the declaration. Does their conclusion that sexuality is moral only within a heterosexual marriage follow from these premises?
2. The Vatican argues that procreation is the only proper end of the sexual act. Does this claim logically follow from the fact that procreation occurs as a result of the sexual act? Support your answer.
3. Does the claim that the primary purpose of marriage is the procreation and raising of children reduce marriage to a means to an end? How might the authors of the *Declaration on Sexuality* respond to this question? Support your answers.
4. Examine the Vatican's argument against premarital sex. Is marriage necessarily a more stable and better environment for children than is cohabitation? Support your answer.
5. Discuss the Vatican's condemnation of homosexuality. If the Vatican agrees that homosexuality is innate in some cases, if not most, does this weaken their argument that heterosexual marriage is the only legitimate context for sexual intimacy? Does calling homosexuality a pathological state merely beg the question and avoid the issue? Support your answers.
6. Seventy-five percent of Americans believe that Catholic priests should be allowed to marry and continue to function as priests.[46] How would the authors of the Vatican *Declaration of Sexual Ethics* most likely respond to these views? Is requiring celibacy contrary to natural law or harmful to the social good? Support your answers.

SARA RUDDICK

Better Sex

Sara Ruddick teaches at Eugene Lang College at the New School for Social Research. She is also the author of *Maternal Thinking: Towards a Politics of Peace,* excerpts from which can be found at the end of Chapter 11 on "War and Terrorism." In the following reading Ruddick distinguishes between incomplete and complete or better sex. Better sex,

"Better Sex" in *Philosophy and Sex,* ed. by Robert Baker and Frederick Elliston (Buffalo, NY: Prometheus Books, 1975), 83–104.

she argues, is sex that increases the benefit of the act for the person engaging in it. Better sex is also complete and natural.

Critical Reading Questions

1. What analogy does Ruddick discuss between driving and sexual experiences and why does she reject this analogy?
2. What are the three characteristics which Ruddick maintains have been used to "distinguish some sex acts as better than others"?
3. How does Ruddick define "benefit," "justice," and "virtue"?
4. What is "sexual pleasure"?
5. Upon what does the "completeness of a sexual act" depend?
6. In what ways might a sexual act be incomplete?
7. How, according to Ruddick, do "perverted" sexual acts differ from "natural" sexual acts?
8. What is the conventional distinction between natural and perverted sex acts, and does Ruddick accept this distinction?
9. How does Ruddick respond to the charge that the prima facie benefits of sexual pleasure can appear to be deceptive?
10. According to Ruddick, what is the moral significance of perverted sexual acts?
11. What type(s) of perversion are immoral and on what grounds?
12. What are the dangers of passivity and distancing ourselves from our sexual desires?
13. In what three ways are complete sex acts morally superior to incomplete sex acts?
14. What is the connection between sex and other emotions?

It might be argued that there is no specifically sexual morality. We have, of course, become accustomed to speaking of sexual morality, but the "morality" of which we speak has a good deal to do with property, the division of labor, and male power, and little to do with our sexual lives. Sexual experiences, like experiences in driving automobiles, render us liable to specific moral situations. As drivers we must guard against infantile desires for revenge and excitement. As lovers we must guard against cruelty and betrayal, for we know sexual experiences provide special opportunities for each. We drive soberly because, before we get into a car, we believe that it is wrong to be careless of life. We resist temptations to adultery because we believe it wrong to betray trust, whether it be a parent, a sexual partner, or a political colleague who is betrayed. As lovers and drivers we act on principles that are particular applications of general moral principles. Moreover, given the superstitions from which sexual experience has suffered, it is wise to free ourselves, as lovers, from any moral concerns, other than those we have as human beings. There is no specifically sexual morality, and none should be invented. Or so it might be argued.

When we examine our moral "intuitions," however, the analogy with driving fails us. Unburdened of *sexual* morality, we do not find it easy to apply general moral principles to our sexual lives. The "morally average" lover can be cruel, violate trust, and neglect social duties with less opprobrium precisely *because* he is a lover. . . .

Our intuitions vary but at least they suggest we can use "good" sex as a positive weight on some moral balance. What is that weight? Why do we put it there? How do we, in the first place, evaluate sexual experiences? On reflection, should we endorse these evaluations? These are the questions whose answers should constitute a specifically sexual morality.

In answering them, I will first consider three characteristics that have been used to distinguish some sex acts as better than others—greater pleasure, completeness, and naturalness. Other characteristics may be relevant to evaluating sex acts, but these three are central. If they have *moral* significance, then the sex acts characterized by them will be better than others not so characterized.

After considering those characteristics in virtue of which some sex acts are allegedly better than others, I will ask whether the presence of those characteristics renders the acts *morally* superior. . . .

A characteristic renders a sex act morally preferable to one without that characteristic if it gives, increases, or is instrumental in increasing the "benefit" of the act for the person engaging in it. . . . A benefit may then be described as an experience, relation or object that anyone who properly cares for another is obliged to attempt to secure for him. Criteria for the virtue of care and for benefit are reciprocally determined, the virtue consisting in part in recognizing and attempting to secure benefits for the person cared for, the identification of benefit depending on its recognition by those already seen to be properly caring.

In talking of benefits I shall be looking at our sexual lives from the vantage point of hope, not of fear. The principal interlocutor may be considered to be a child asking what he should rightly and reasonably hope for in living, rather than a potential criminal questioning conventional restraints. The specific question the child may be imagined to ask can now be put: In what way is better sex beneficial or conducive to experiences or relations or objects that are beneficial?

A characteristic renders a sex act morally preferable to one without that characteristic if either the act is thereby more just or the act is thereby likely to make the person engaging in it more just. Justice includes giving others what is due them, taking no more than what is one's own, and giving and taking according to prevailing principles of fairness.

A characteristic renders a sex act morally preferable to one without that characteristic if because of the characteristic the act is more virtuous or more likely to lead to virtue. A virtue is a disposition to attempt, and an ability to succeed in, good acts—acts of justice, acts that express or produce excellence, and acts that yield benefits to oneself or others.

SEXUAL PLEASURE

Sensual experiences give rise to sensations and experiences that are paradigms of what is pleasant. Hedonism, in both its psychological and ethical forms, has blinded us to the nature and to the benefits of sensual pleasure by overextending the word "pleasure" to cover anything enjoyable or even agreeable. The paradigmatic type of pleasure is sensual. Pleasure is a temporally extended, more or less intense quality of particular experiences. Pleasure is enjoyable independent of any function pleasurable activity fulfills. . . .

Sexual pleasure is a species of sensual pleasure with its own conditions of arousal and satisfaction. Sexual acts vary considerably in pleasure, the limiting case being a sexual act where no one experiences pleasure even though someone may experience affection or "relief of tension" through orgasm. Sexual pleasure can be considered either in a context of deprivation and its relief or in a context of satisfaction. Psychological theories have tended to emphasize the frustrated state of sexual desire and to construe sexual pleasure as a relief from that state. There are, however, alternative accounts of sexual pleasure that correspond more closely with our experience. Sexual pleasure is "a primary distinctively poignant pleasure experience that manifests itself from early infancy on. . . . Once experienced it continues to be savored. . . ."[1] Sexual desire is not experienced as frustration but as part of sexual pleasure. Normally, sexual desire transforms itself gradually into the pleasure that appears, misleadingly, to be an aim extrinsic to it. The natural structure of desire, not an inherent quality of frustration, accounts for the pain of an aroused but unsatisfied desire.

Sexual pleasure, like addictive pleasure generally, does not, except very temporarily, result in satiety. Rather, it increases the demand for more of the same while sharply limiting the possibility of substitutes. The experience of sensual pleasures, and particularly of sexual pleasures, has a pervasive effect on our perceptions of the world. We find bodies inviting, social encounters alluring, and smells, tastes, and sights resonant because our perception of them includes their sexual significance. . . . The capacity for sexual pleasure, upon which the erotic structure of perception depends, can be accidentally damaged. The question that this raises is whether it would be desirable to interfere with this capacity in a more systematic way than we now do. With greater biochemical and psychiatric knowledge we shall presumably be able to manipulate it at will. And if that becomes possible, toward what end should we interfere? I shall return to this question after describing the other two characteristics of better sex—completeness and naturalness.

COMPLETE SEX ACTS

The completeness of a sexual act depends upon the *relation* of the participants to their own and each other's *desire*. A sex act is complete if each partner allows himself to be "taken over" by an active desire, which is desire not merely for the other's body but also for his active desire. Completeness is hard to characterize, though complete sex acts are at least as natural as any others—especially, it seems, among those people who take them casually and for granted. The notion of "completeness" (as I shall call it) has figured under various guises in the work of Sartre, Merleau-Ponty, and more recently Thomas Nagel. "The being which desires is consciousness making itself body."[2] "What we try to possess, then, is not just a body, but a body brought to life by consciousness."[3] "It is important that the partner be aroused, and not merely aroused, but aroused by the awareness of one's desire."[4]

The precondition of complete sex acts is the "embodiment" of the participants. Each participant submits to sexual desires that take over consciousness and direct action. It is sexual desire and not a separable satisfaction of it (for example, orgasm) that is important here. . . . Desire is pervasive and "overwhelming," but it does not make its subject its involuntary victim (as it did the Boston Strangler, we are told), nor does it, except at its climax, alter capacities for ordinary perceptions, memories, and inferences. . . .

We may often experience ourselves as relatively disembodied, observing or "using" our bodies to fulfill our intentions. On some occasions, however, such as in physical combat, sport, physical suffering, or danger, we "become" our bodies; our consciousness becomes bodily experience of bodily activity. Sexual acts are occasions for such embodiment; they may, however, fail for a variety of reasons, for example, because of pretense or an excessive need for self-control. If someone is embodied by sexual desire, he submits to its direction. Spontaneous impulses of desire become his movements—some involuntary, like gestures of "courting behavior" or physical expressions of intense pleasure, and some deliberate. His consciousness, or "mind," is taken over by desire and the pursuit of its object, in the way that at other times it may be taken over by an intellectual problem or by obsessive fantasies. But unlike the latter takeovers, this one is bodily. A desiring consciousness is flooded with specifically sexual feelings that eroticize all perception and movement. Consciousness "becomes flesh."

Granted the precondition of embodiment, complete sex acts occur when each partner's embodying desire is active and actively responsive to the other's. This second aspect of complete sex constitutes a "reflexive mutual recognition" of desire by desire.[5]

The partner *actively* desires another person's desire. Active desiring includes more than embodiment, which might be achieved in objectless masturbation. It is more, also, than merely being aroused by and then taken over by desire, though it may come about as a result of deliberate arousal. It commits the actively desiring person to her desire and requires her to identify with it—that is, to recognize herself as a sexual agent as well as respondent. (Active desiring is less encouraged in women, and probably more women than men feel threatened by it.)

The other recognizes and responds to the partner's desire. Merely to recognize the desire as desire, not to reduce it to an itch or to depersonalize it as a "demand," may be threatening. Imperviousness to desire is the deepest defense against it. We have learned from research on families whose members tend to become schizophrenic that such imperviousness, the refusal to recognize a feeling for what it is, can force a vulnerable person to deny or to obscure the real nature of his feelings. Imperviousness tends to deprive even a relatively invulnerable person of his efficacy. The demand that our feelings elicit a response appropriate to them is part of a general demand that *we* be recognized, that our feelings be allowed to make a difference.

There are many ways in which sexual desire may be recognized, countless forms of submission and resistance. In complete sex, desire is recognized by a responding and active desire that commits the other, as it committed the partner. Given responding desire, both people identify themselves as sexually desiring the other. They are neither seducer nor seduced, neither suppliant nor benefactress, neither sadist nor victim, but sexual agents acting sexually out of their recognized desire. Indeed, in complete sex one not only welcomes and recognizes active desire, one desires it. Returned and endorsed desire becomes one of the features of an erotically structured perception. Desiring becomes desirable. (Men are less encouraged to desire the other's active and demanding desire, and such desiring is probably threatening to more men than women.)

In sum, in complete sex two persons embodied by sexual desire actively desire and respond to each other's active desire. Although it is difficult to write of complete sex without suggesting that one of the partners is the initiator, while the other responds, complete sex is reciprocal sex. The partners, whatever the circumstances of their coming together, are equal in activity and responsiveness of desire.

Sexual acts can be partly incomplete. A necrophiliac may be taken over by desire, and a frigid woman may respond to her lover's desire without being embodied by her own. Partners whose sexual activities are accompanied by private fantasies engage in an incomplete sex act. Consciousness is used by desire but remains apart from it, providing it with stimulants and controls. Neither partner responds to the other's desire, though each may appear to. Sartre's "dishonest masturbator," for whom masturbation is the sex act of choice, engages in a paradigmatically incomplete sex act: . . .[6]

Completeness is more difficult to describe than incompleteness, for it turns on precise but subtle ways of responding to a particular person's desire with specific expressions of impulse that are both spontaneous and responsive.

There are many possible sex acts that are pleasurable but not complete. Sartre, Nagel, and Merleau-Ponty each suggest that the desire for the responsive desire of one's partner is the "central impulse" of sexual desire.[7] The desire for a sleeping woman, for example, is possible only "in so far as this sleep appears on the ground of consciousness."[8] This seems much too strong. Some lovers desire that their partners resist, others like them coolly controlled, others prefer them asleep. We would not say that there was anything abnormal or less fully sexual about desire. Whether or not complete sex is preferable to incomplete sex (the question to which I shall turn shortly), incompleteness does not disqualify a sex act from being fully sexual.

SEXUAL PERVERSION

The final characteristic of allegedly better sex acts is that they are "natural" rather than "perverted." The ground for classifying sexual acts as either natural or unnatural is that the former type serve or could serve the evolutionary and biological function of sexuality—namely, reproduction. "Natural" sexual desire has as its "object" living persons of the opposite sex, and in particular their postpubertal genitals. The "aim" of natural sexual desire—that is, the act that "naturally" completes it—is genital intercourse. Perverse sex acts are deviations from the natural object (for example, homosexuality, fetishism) or from the standard aim (for example, voyeurism, sadism). Among the variety of objects and aims of sexual desire, I can see no other ground for selecting some as natural, except that they are of the type that can lead to reproduction.

The connection of sexual desire with reproduction gives us the criterion but not the motive of the classification. The concept of perversion depends on a disjointedness between our experience of sexual desire from infancy on and the function of sexual desire—reproduction. In our collective experience of sexuality, perverse desires are as natural as nonperverse ones. The sexual desire of the polymorphously perverse child has many objects—for example, breasts, anus, mouth, genitals—and many aims—for example, autoerotic or other-directed looking, smelling, touching, hurting. From the social and developmental point of view, natural sex is an achievement, partly biological, partly conventional, consisting in a dominant organization of sexual desires in which perverted aims or objects are subordinate to natural ones. The concept of perversion reflects the vulnerability as much as the evolutionary warrant of this organization.

The connection of sexual desire with reproduction is not sufficient to yield the concept of perversion, but it is surely necessary. Nagel, however, thinks otherwise. There are, he points out, many sexual acts that do not lead to reproduction but that we are not even inclined to call perverse—for example, sexual acts between partners who are sterile. Perversion, according to him, is a psychological concept while reproduction is (only?) a physiological one. (Incidentally, this view of reproduction seems to me the clearest instance of male bias in Nagel's paper.)

Nagel is right about our judgments of particular acts, but he draws the wrong conclusions from those judgments. The perversity of sex acts does not depend upon whether they are intended to achieve reproduction. "Natural" sexual desire is for heterosexual genital activity, not for reproduction. The ground for classifying that desire as natural is that it is so organized that it *could* lead to reproduction in normal physiological circumstances. The reproductive organization of sexual desires gives us a *criterion* of naturalness, but the *virtue* of which it is a criterion is the "naturalness" itself, not reproduction. Our vacillating attitude toward the apparently perverse acts of animals reflects our shifting from criterion to virtue. If, when confronted with a perverse act of animals, we withdraw the label "perverted" from our own similar acts rather than extend it to theirs, we are relinquishing the reproductive criterion of naturalness, while retaining the virtue. Animals cannot be "unnatural." If, on the other hand, we "discover" that animals can be perverts too, we are maintaining our criterion, but giving a somewhat altered sense to the "naturalness" of which it is a criterion.

Nagel's alternative attempt to classify acts as natural or perverted on the basis of their completeness fails. "Perverted" and "complete" are evaluations of an entirely different order. The completeness of a sex act depends upon qualities of the participants' experience and upon qualities of their relation—qualities of which they are the best judge. To say a sex act is perverted is to pass a conventional judgment about characteristics of the act, which could be evident to any observer. As one can pretend to be angry but not to shout, one can pretend to a complete, but not to a natural, sex act (though one may, of course, conceal desires for perverse sex acts or shout in order to mask one's feelings). As Nagel himself sees, judgments about particular sex acts clearly differentiate between perversion and completeness. Unadorned heterosexual intercourse where each partner has private fantasies is clearly "natural" and clearly "incomplete," but there is nothing prima facie incomplete about exclusive oral-genital intercourse or homosexual acts. If many perverse acts are incomplete, as Nagel claims, this is an important fact *about* perversion, but it is not the basis upon which we judge its occurrence.

IS BETTER SEX REALLY BETTER?

Some sex acts are, allegedly, better than others insofar as they are more pleasurable, complete, and natural. What is the moral significance of this evaluation? In answering this question, official sexual morality sometimes appeals to the social consequences of particular types of better sex acts. For example, since dominantly perverse organizations of sexual impulses limit reproduction, the merits of perversion depend upon the need to limit or increase population. Experience of sexual pleasure may be desirable if it promotes relaxation and communication in an acquisitive society, undesirable if it limits the desire to work or, in armies, to kill. The social consequences of complete sex have not received particular attention, because the quality of sexual experience has been of little interest to moralists. It might be found that those who had complete sexual relations were more cooperative, less amenable to political revolt. If so, complete sexual acts would be desirable in just and peaceable societies, undesirable in unjust societies requiring revolution.

The social desirability of types of sexual acts depends on particular social conditions and independent criteria of social desirability. It may be interesting and important to assess particular claims about the social desirability of sex acts, but this is not my concern. What is my concern is the extent to which we will allow our judgments of sexual worth to be influenced by social considerations. But this issue cannot even be raised until we have a better sense of sexual worth.

THE BENEFIT OF SEXUAL PLEASURE

. . . The most eloquent detractors of sexual experience have admitted that it provides sensual pleasures so poignant that once experienced they are repeatedly, almost addictively, sought. Yet, unlike other appetites, such as hunger, sexual desire can be permanently resisted, and resistance has been advocated. How can the prima facie benefits of sexual pleasure appear deceptive?

There are several grounds for complaint. Sexual pleasure is ineradicably mixed, frustration being part of every sexual life. The capacity for sexual pleasure is unevenly distributed, cannot be voluntarily acquired, and diminishes through no fault of its subject. If such a pleasure were an intrinsic benefit, benefit would in this case be independent of moral effort. Then again, sexual pleasures are not serious. Enjoyment of them is one of life's greatest recreations, but none of its business. And finally, sexual desire has the defects of its strengths. Before satisfaction, it is, at the least, distracting; in satisfaction, it "makes one little roome, an everywhere." Like psychosis, sexual desire turns us from "reality"—whether the real be God, social justice, children, or intellectual endeavor. This turning away is more than a social consequence of desire, though it is that. Lovers themselves feel that their sexual desires are separate from their "real" political, domestic, ambitious, social selves. . . .

The mixed, partly frustrated character of any desire is not particularly pronounced for sexual desire, which is in fact especially plastic, or adaptable to changes (provided perverse sex acts have not been ruled out). Inhibition, social deprivation, or disease make our sexual lives unpleasant, but that is because they interfere with sexual desire, not because the desire is by its nature frustrating. More than other well-known desires (for example, desire for knowledge, success, or power), sexual desire is simply and completely satisfied upon attaining its object. Partly for this reason, even if we are overtaken by desire during sexual experience, our sexual experiences do not overtake us. Lovers turn away from the world while loving, but return—sometimes all too easily—when loving is done. The moralist rightly perceives sexual pleasure as a recreation, and those who upon realizing its benefits make a business of its pursuit appear ludicrous. The capacity for recreation, however, is surely a benefit that any human being rightly hopes for who hopes for anything. Indeed, in present social and economic conditions we are more likely to lay waste our powers in work than in play. Thus, though priest, revolutionary, and parent are alike in fearing sexual pleasure, this fear should inspire us to psychological and sociological investigation of the fearing rather than to moral doubt about the benefit of sexual pleasure.

THE MORAL SIGNIFICANCE OF PERVERSION

What is the moral significance of the perversity of a sexual act? Next to none, so far as I can see. Though perverted sex may be "unnatural" both from an evolutionary and developmental perspective, there is no connection, inverse or correlative, between what is natural and what is good. Perverted sex is sometimes said to be less pleasurable than natural sex. We have little reason to believe that this claim is true and no clear idea of the kind of evidence on which it would be based. In any case, to condemn perverse acts for lack of pleasure is to recognize the worth of pleasure, not of naturalness.

There are many other claims about the nature and consequences of perversion. Some merely restate "scientific" facts in morally tinged terminology. Perverse acts are, by definition and according to psychiatric theory, "immature" and "abnormal," since natural sex acts are selected by criteria of "normal" sexual function and "normal" and "mature" psychological development. But there is no greater connection of virtue with maturity and normality than there is of virtue with nature. . . .

If perverted sex acts did rule out normal sex acts, if one were *either* perverted *or* natural, then certain kinds of sexual relations would be denied some perverts—relations that are benefits to those who enjoy them. It seems that sexual relations with the living and the human would be of greater benefit than those with the dead or with animals. But there is no reason to think that heterosexual relations are of greater benefit than homosexual ones. It might be that children can only be raised by heterosexual couples who perform an abundance of natural sex acts. If so (though it seems unlikely), perverts will be denied the happiness of parenthood. This would be an *indirect* consequence of perverted sex and might yield a moral dilemma: How is one to choose between the benefits of children and the benefits of more pleasurable, more complete sex acts?

Some perversions are immoral on independent grounds. Sadism is the obvious example, though sadism practiced with a consenting masochist is far less evil than other, more familiar forms of aggression. Voyeurism may seem immoral because, since it must be secret to be satisfying, it violates others' rights to privacy. Various kinds of rape can constitute perversion if rape, rather than genital intercourse, is the aim of desire. Rape is seriously immoral, a vivid violation of respect for persons. Sometimes doubly perverse rape is doubly evil (the rape of a child), but in other cases (the rape of a pig) its evil is halved. In any case, though rape is always wrong, it is only perverse when raping becomes the aim and not the means of desire. . . .

THE MORAL SIGNIFICANCE OF COMPLETENESS

Complete sex consists in mutually embodied, mutually active, responsive desire. Embodiment, activity, and mutual responsiveness are instrumentally beneficial because they are conducive to our psychological well-being, which is an intrinsic benefit. . . .

The mutual responsiveness of complete sex is also instrumentally beneficial. It satisfies a general desire to be recognized as a particular "real" person and to make a difference to other particular "real" people. The satisfaction of this desire in sexual experience is especially rewarding, its thwarting especially cruel. Vulnerability is increased in complete sex by the active desiring of the partners. When betrayal, or for that matter, tenderness or ecstasy, ensues, one cannot dissociate oneself from the desire with which one identified and out of which one acted. The psychic danger is real, as people who attempt to achieve a distance from their desires could tell us. But the cost of distance is as evident as its gains. Passivity in respect to one's own sexual desire not only limits sexual pleasure but, more seriously, limits the extent to which the experience of sexual pleasure can be included as an experience of a coherent person. With passivity comes a kind of irresponsibility in which one can hide from one's desire, even from one's pleasure, "playing" seducer or victim, tease or savior. Active sexual desiring in complete sex acts affords an especially threatening but also especially happy occasion to relinquish these and similar roles. To the extent that the roles confuse and confound our intimate relations, the benefit from relinquishing them in our sexual acts, or the loss from adhering to them then, is especially poignant.

In addition to being beneficial, complete sex acts are morally superior for three reasons. They tend to resolve tensions fundamental to moral life; they are conducive to emotions that, if they become stable and dominant, are in turn conducive to the virtue of loving; and they involve a preeminently moral virtue—respect for persons. . . .

The connection between sex and certain emotions—particularly love, jealousy, fear, and anger—is as evident as it is obscure. Complete sex acts seem more likely than incomplete pleasurable ones to lead toward affection and away from fear and anger, since any guilt and shame will be extrinsic to the act and meliorated by it. It is clear that we need not feel for someone any affection beyond that required (if any is) simply to participate with him in a complete sex act. However, it is equally clear that sexual pleasure, especially as experienced in complete sex acts, is conducive to many feelings—gratitude, tenderness, pride, appreciation, dependency, and others.

These feelings magnify their object who occasioned them, making him unique among men. When these magnifying feelings become stable and habitual they are conducive to love—not universal love, of course, but love of a particular sexual partner. However, even "selfish" love is a virtue, a disposition to care for someone as her interests and demands would dictate. Neither the best sex nor the best love require each other, but they go together more often than reason would expect—often enough to count the virtue of loving as one of the rewards of the capacity for sexual pleasure exercised in complete sex acts. . . .

Finally, as Sartre has suggested, complete sex acts preserve a respect for persons. Each person remains conscious and responsible, a "subject" rather than a depersonalized, will-less, or manipulated "object." Each actively desires that the other likewise remain a "subject." Respect for persons is a central virtue when matters of justice and obligation are at issue. Insofar as we can speak of respect for persons in complete sex acts, there are different, often contrary requirements of respect. Respect for persons, typically and in sex acts, requires that *actual present* partners participate, partners whose desires are recognized and endorsed. Respect for persons typically requires taking a distance from both one's own demands and those of others. But in sex acts the demands of desire take over, and equal distance is replaced by mutual responsiveness. Respect typically requires refusing to treat another person merely as a means to fulfilling demands. In sex acts, another person is so clearly a means to satisfaction that she is always on the verge of becoming merely a means ("intercourse counterfeits masturbation"). In complete sex acts, instrumentality vanishes only because it is mutual and mutually desired. Respect requires encouraging, or at least protecting, the autonomy of another. In complete sex, autonomy of will is recruited by desire, and freedom from others is replaced by frank dependence on another person's desire. Again the respect consists in the reciprocity of desiring dependence, which bypasses rather than violates autonomy. . . .

While complete sex is morally superior because it involves respect for persons, incomplete sex acts do not necessarily involve immoral disrespect for persons. They may, depending upon the desires and expectations of the partners; but they may involve neither respect nor disrespect. Masturbation, for example, allows only the limited completeness of embodiment and often fails of that. But masturbation only rarely involves disrespect to anyone. Even the respect of the allegedly desirable sleeping woman may not be violated if she is unknowingly involved in a sex act. Disrespect, though likely, may be obviated by her sensibilities and expectations that she has previously expressed and her partner has understood. Sex acts provide one context in which respect for persons can be expressed. That context is important both because our sexual lives are of such importance to us and because they are so liable to injury because of the experience and the fear of the experience of disrespect. But many complete sex acts in which respect is maintained makes other casual and incomplete sex acts unthreatening. In this case a goodly number of swallows can make a summer. . . .

To say that complete sex acts are preferable to incomplete ones is not to court a new puritanism. There are many kinds and degrees of incompleteness. Incomplete sex acts may not involve a disrespect for persons. Complete sex acts only *tend* to be good for us, and the realization of these tendencies depends upon individual lives and circumstances of sexual activity. The proper object of sexual desire is sexual pleasure. It would be a foolish ambition indeed to limit one's sexual acts to those in which completeness was likely. Any sexual act that is pleasurable is prima facie good, though the more incomplete it is—the more private, essentially autoerotic, unresponsive, unembodied, passive, or imposed—the more likely it is to be harmful to someone.

ON SEXUAL MORALITY: CONCLUDING REMARKS

There are many questions we have neglected to consider because we have not been sufficiently attentive to the quality of sexual lives. For example, we know little about the ways of achieving better sex. When we must choose between inferior sex and abstinence, how and when will our choice of inferior sex damage our capacity for better sex?

Does, for example, the repeated experience of controlled sexual disembodiment ("desire which takes over will take you too far") that we urge (or used to urge) on adolescents damage their capacity for complete sex? The answers to this and similar questions are not obvious, though unfounded opinions are always ready at hand.

Some of the traditional sexual vices might be condemned on the ground that they are inimical to better sex. Obscenity, or repeated public exposure to sexual acts, might impair our capacity for pleasure or for respouse to desire. Promiscuity might undercut the tendency of complete sex acts to promote emotions that magnify their object. Other of the traditional sexual vices are neither inimical nor conducive to better sex, but are condemned because of conflicting nonsexual benefits and obligations. For example, infidelity qua infidelity neither secures nor prevents better sex. The obligations of fidelity have many sources, one of which may be a past history of shared complete sex acts, a history that included promises of exclusive intimacy. Such past promises are as apt to conflict with as to accord with a current demand for better sex. I have said nothing about how such a conflict would be settled. I hope I have shown that where the possibility of better sex conflicts with obligations and other benefits, we have a *moral dilemma,* not just an occasion for moral self-discipline.

The pursuit of more pleasurable and more complete sex acts is, among many moral activities, distinguished not for its exigencies but for its rewards. Since our sexual lives are so important to us, and since, whatever our history and our hopes, we are sexual beings, this pursuit rightly engages our moral reflection. It should not be relegated to the immoral, nor to the "merely" prudent.

NOTES

1. George Klein, "Freud's Two Theories of Sexuality," in L. Berger, ed., *Clinical-Cognitive Psychology: Models and Integrations* (Englewood Cliffs, N.J.: Prentice-Hall, 1969), pp. 131–81. This essay gives a clear idea of alternative psychological accounts of sexual pleasure.
2. Jean-Paul Sartre, *Being and Nothingness,* trans. Hazel E. Barnes (New York: Philosophical Library, 1956), p. 389.
3. Merleau-Ponty, *Phenomenology of Perception,* p. 167.
4. Thomas Nagel, "Sexual Perversion," *The Journal of Philosophy* 66, no. 1 (January 16, 1969): 13; herein, pp. 255–56. My original discussion of completeness was both greatly indebted to and confused by Nagel's. I have tried here to dispel some of the confusion.
5. Nagel, "Sexual Perversion," p. 254.
6. Jean-Paul Sartre, *Saint Genet* (New York: Braziller, 1963), p. 398; cited and translated by R. D. Laing, *Self and Others* (New York: Pantheon, 1969), pp. 39–40.
7. Ibid., p. 13.
8. Sartre, *Being and Nothingness,* p. 386.

Discussion Questions

1. Do you agree with Ruddick's three criteria of better sex? If so, why? If not, develop a list of alternative criteria and explain why they are morally preferable.
2. Discuss how the Vatican might respond to Ruddick's definition of complete or better sex acts. Which view do you find more morally acceptable and why?
3. Are sexual acts that enable the possibility of procreation more complete or better sex than those that don't? Support your position.
4. Using Ruddick's criteria, are minors (people under eighteen years of age) capable of engaging in complete sex acts? Discuss the type of policy Ruddick would most likely recommend for a residential high school regarding sexual relationships among the students.

5. Should junior high, high schools, and/or colleges provide free contraception and sex education? Should there be coed dorms and rooms available to college students who wish to cohabit? Support your answers.
6. Using Ruddick's criteria, can prostitution and/or adultery involve better or complete sex? If so, does this mean that prostitution and adultery are morally acceptable in these cases?
7. Is Ruddick promoting a "new Puritanism" by claiming that complete sex acts tend to be morally preferable to incomplete ones? Support your answer.

MICHAEL RUSE

Is Homosexuality Bad Sexuality?

Michael Ruse is a philosophy professor at the University of Guelph in Ontario. Ruse examines the argument that homosexuality is "bad sexuality" because it is unnatural and abnormal. After analyzing the philosophical views on homosexuality in ancient Greece and in the Judeo-Christian tradition, as well as other philosophical views on homosexuality, Ruse concludes that, although some people may see homosexuality as a perversion, it is not immoral. Furthermore, he suggests that if we cannot back up our negative feelings about homosexuality with rational arguments, we have a moral obligation to work on changing those feelings.

Critical Reading Questions

1. What were the conventions regarding homosexuality in ancient Greece?
2. What was Plato's view of homosexuality?
3. Why, according to Ruse, were both Socrates and Plato opposed to the physical consummation of homosexual relationships?
4. What does the Bible say regarding the morality of homosexuality?
5. Why, according to Thomas Aquinas, is homosexuality a violation of natural law?
6. What are the kinds of *crimina carnis*? How does Kant use the concept of *crimina carnis* in his analysis of the morality of homosexuality?
7. What was Jeremy Bentham's position on the morality of homosexuality? On what grounds does Bentham oppose outlawing it?
8. How does Bentham respond to the criticism that homosexuality "runs one down physically"? How does Bentham respond to the criticism that homosexuality among men "deprives women of sex and marriage"?

"Is Homosexuality Bad Sexuality?" In *Homosexuality: A Philosophical Inquiry* (Oxford, England: Basil Blackwell, 1988), 179–192. Some notes have been omitted.

9. What is the source, according to Ruse, of the argument in Western philosophy that homosexuality is unnatural? How does Ruse respond to this argument?
10. According to Ruse, why do so many people regard homosexuality as a perversion? What does Ruse mean when he says that this kind of thinking involves a paradox?
11. On what grounds does Sara Ruddick argue that homosexuality is a perversion? How does Ruse respond to her argument?
12. How does Ruse define "naturalness" for humans? What is the relationship among naturalness, perversion, and morality?
13. Why do people find perversion so disgusting? What type of rules or values does perversion break?
14. What does Ruse mean when he says that the question of the perversity of homosexuality is more of an empirical than a prescriptive matter?
15. What does Ruse mean when he says that perversion, when applied to homosexuality, is a relative concept?
16. What is the difference between moral indignation and disgust?

Is homosexuality, inclination and behavior, an acceptable way for a human being to feel and act, or is it pernicious? Undoubtedly, although there will be less unanimity on this matter today than there would have been (say) a hundred years ago, for a good many people the answer will seem obvious—that homosexuality is aesthetically revolting and morally gross; that in all its aspects it is wrong, and that this is a conclusion not merely confirmed by modern thought but underlined by the whole western religious/philosophical tradition. . . .

The Greeks, so the story would go, accepted and even promoted homosexual relations. Furthermore, this attitude is to be found in the greatest of their philosophers, most especially Plato. The Jews, however, both those of the Old and New Testaments, uniformly and unambiguously condemned all forms of homosexuality. It merited the punishment of man and of God. And it is this latter position which has prevailed ever since, thanks to the rise of Christianity, a religion which has such deep roots in Judaism.

But is this story true? Let us turn to the sources, beginning first with the Greeks. As is so often the case, popular opinion has a very inadequate grasp of the whole. It is indeed true that by the time of "classical Greece" . . . —a time which firmly includes the life span of the philosopher Plato (428–347 BC)—overt homosexuality was a well-established tradition and acceptable part of the Greek life style. But the sexuality of classical Greece was apparently not simply an unrestrained free-for-all, with any two or more people doing whatsoever they liked, to whomsoever they liked. Specifically, the homosexuality one hears about was very much an upper-class phenomenon, strongly associated with the enforced segregation of the sexes, and highly stylized, with emotions rather than actions playing a major role. The central focus was a bond which would be formed between a somewhat older and a somewhat younger man (ideally, a 25-year-old paired with a 15-year-old). It seems to have been rare indeed (and certainly not proper) for two men of exactly the same age to have fallen in love and to have had any kind of physical relationship. Moreover, after marriage the need for (and acceptability of) homosexual relations fell away rapidly. (It is assumed that an analogous story can be told about women, although we know far less about lesbianism. It seems, for some unknown reason, to have been a taboo subject for the male writers.)

The constraint about ages was accompanied also by a constraint about emotions. The older man (the *erastes* or lover) was expected to feel strong sexual emotion for the younger man or boy (the *eromenos* or loved one), admiring his beauty, wanting to get physically close to him, and being prepared to court him with gifts and favors. The boy, however, was not expected to feel the same kind of sexual attraction in response, but rather to admire his older lover, looking upon him as an ideal or model, and wanting to make him happy. This convention about love and ages helped dictate the nature of the physical sexual relations. Officially at least, sodomy was definitely taboo, not to mention things like fellatio. Being sodomized was considered far too degrading . . . Hence, the usual method of intercourse between upper-class lovers was somewhat limited, in a stylized manner. The erastes, the older, would push his penis between the thighs of the eromenos, the younger, and bring himself to ejaculation this way, "intercrurally." The boy was not supposed to ejaculate in return—indeed, he was supposed to find the whole business rather asexual, and to remain unaroused throughout. No doubt there was frequently a gap between the ideal and the actual.

Against this background we can understand Plato's position on homosexuality. . . . Plato, tradition has it, was unmarried and fairly exclusively homosexual in orientation. Be this as it may, [his teacher] Socrates and his (exclusively male) companions lived, thought, and behaved very much in the homosexual milieu described above as being the norm for upper-class Athenians. In Plato's early writings (which report, fairly authentically, on actual Socratic discussions or dialogues), we get repeated, unselfconscious references to the sexual pangs that an older man would feel for a boy or younger man, and the liaisons that would spring up between them. . . .

Although there is much talk of sexual desire, which seems even to be cherished, both Socrates and Plato unambiguously reject and condemn all taking of homosexual attraction to the point of intercourse and orgasm. . . .

Why were Socrates and Plato so strongly against physical homosexual relations? There is an obvious reason, which had nothing to do with homosexuality per se. Both Socrates and Plato were reflecting an important attitude of their society and class, namely a great respect for self-constraint and control. Emotions were seen as things which took control of one, and the man who could withstand them gained stature in his and his colleagues' eyes. . . .

For the mature Plato, therefore, control is essential. To read Plato's early and middle writings as providing a license for homosexual inclination and behavior is not to read them properly. Homosexual attraction is accepted and even venerated, but consummation is condemned. The man who lets his passions thus govern his reason is an object of pity. This, however, is not quite all that there is to Plato's treatment of homosexuality. Towards the end of his life he developed his ideas yet further, and indeed he arrived at a position by a line of argument that was profoundly to influence subsequent thinking on the matter of homosexuality. Simply and categorically Plato condemned homosexual behavior because it is "unnatural." It is not done by the animals, No more should it be done by us.

> Anyone who, in conformity with nature, proposes to re-establish the law as it was before Laios, declaring that it was right not to join with men and boys in sexual intercourse as with females, adducing as evidence the nature of animals and pointing out that [among them] male does not touch male for sexual purposes, since that is not natural, he could, I think, make a very strong case. (Plato, *Laws,* 836c–e, trans. Dover 1978: 166)

The opposition to homosexual acts becomes absolute. . . .

THE JUDAEO/CHRISTIAN TRADITION

Let us turn now to Judaism and its breakaway offspring, Christianity. Here, on the surface at least, popular opinion does seem closer to the truth. The primary source of information about the positions of the Jews and the early Christians is obviously the Bible, Old and New Testaments. In the Old Testament, there are two main sources of information about the positions taken by God and his chosen people on the subject of homosexuality: the story of Sodom and Gomorrah, and various scattered dictates about homosexual practices. Both sources apparently tell the same tale: homosexual behavior is abhorrent in the eyes of the Lord and therefore morally barred to humankind. As it happens, the Sodom and Gomorrah story about the citizens of Sodom, who wanted to have homosexual intercourse with two of God's angels, has been the subject of much Biblical reinterpretation. Most pertinently, it has been argued that the homosexual theme of the Sodom and Gomorrah story is a later interpolation. But the "holiness Code" of Leviticus is unambiguous.

> Thou shalt not lie with mankind, as with womankind: it is abomination. (Leviticus xviii.22)

> If a man also lie with mankind, as he lieth with a woman, both of them have committed an abomination: they shall surely be put to death; their blood shall be upon them. (Leviticus xx.13)

In the New Testament, one likewise finds passages which categorically prohibit homosexual behavior. As is usual on matters of sex, it was not the founder himself who pronounced on these matters, but his chief proselytizer, Paul.

> the men, leaving the natural use of the woman, burned in their lust one toward another, men with men working unseemliness, and receiving in themselves that recompense of their error which was due. (Romans i.27)

> Be not deceived: neither fornicators, nor idolators, nor adulterers, nor effeminate, nor abusers of themselves with men, nor thieves, nor covetous, nor drunkards, nor revilers, nor extortioners, shall inherit the kingdom of God. (I Corinthians vi.9–10)

> law is not made for a righteous man, but for the lawless and unruly . . . for abusers of themselves with men . . . (I Timothy i.9–10)

Nor is lesbian behavior neglected.

> God gave them up unto vile passions: for their women changed the natural use into that which is against nature . . . (Romans i.26)

. . . The most detailed philosophical discussion of homosexuality by a Christian thinker is to be found in the writings of the thirteenth-century theologian St. Thomas Aquinas. Aquinas's treatment of homosexuality, as of most moral issues, depends crucially on the notion of "natural law." . . . Coming to sexuality, Aquinas (who was much influenced by Aristotle) did not ask the straightforward causal question, "How do things work?," but rather the teleological question, "What are things for? What end do they serve?" And the answer he gave is that sex exists for the procreation and raising of children. This is why God made us sexual beings, and this therefore is the end towards which we must strive if we are not to violate natural law, that area of the eternal law where we ourselves must make a contribution.

The consequence of Aquinas's position, as he thought, is that all sex outside marriage is wrong because it is a violation of natural law. Thus, quite apart from homosexuality's prohibition on Biblical grounds, for Aquinas it is necessarily barred as being against natural law: as being in conflict with "right reason." Homosexual encounters do not lead to children, therefore they must be wrong. But there is rather more than this. All lust is immoral, but some acts are doubly to be condemned, because "they are in conflict with the natural pattern of sexuality for the benefit of the species." These are termed 'unnatural vices' (*"vitiae contra naturum"*). . . .

MODERN ETHICAL PHILOSOPHIES

Let us turn now to the modern era, the time after the scientific revolution. There are two major, secular moral philosophies, those of the German thinker, Immanuel Kant, and of the (primarily) British utilitarians. Both groups thought their views threw light on the status of homosexual behavior (again, feelings get short shrift). Let us take them in turn.

Kant thought humans are subject to an overriding and necessary moral law, a supreme directive, the "categorical imperative." It is this law which tells us what we ought to do; wherein lies our duty. . . .

As Kant himself recognized, at a quite general level sex and the categorical imperative have a rather uneasy relationship. The starting point to sex is the sheer desire of a person for the body of another. . . . This gets dangerously close to treating the other as a means to the fulfillment of one's own sexual desire—as an object, rather than as an end. And this, according to the categorical imperative, is immoral. To escape from this dilemma, and one surely must if the end of the human race is not to be advocated on moral grounds, one must go on to treat the object of one's sexual advances as an end. One does this by broadening one's feelings, so that the personhood of the object of one's desire is brought within one's attraction, and by giving oneself reciprocally—by yielding oneself, body and soul, one shows respect for the other as an end, and not just as a means.

But what about a sincere commitment between two people of the same sex, the sort of homosexual equivalent of heterosexual marriage? At this point Kant invokes the notion of a *crimina carnis,* an abuse of one's sexuality. There are two kinds. First, there are acts which are contrary to sound reason, *crimina carnis secundum naturam.* These are immoral acts which go against the moral code imposed upon us as humans, and include such things as adultery. Second, there are acts contrary to our animal nature, *crimina carnis contra naturam.* These include masturbation, sex with animals, and homosexuality. They are the lowest and most disgusting sort of vice, worse in a sense even than suicide, and they are practices that we hesitate to mention. . . .

> A second *crimen carnis contra naturam* is intercourse between *sexus homogenii,* in which the object of sexual impulse is a human being but there is homogeneity instead of heterogeneity of sex, as when a woman satisfies her desire on a woman, or a man on a man. This practice too is contrary to the ends of humanity; for the end of humanity in respect of sexuality is to preserve the species without debasing the person; but in this instance the species is not being preserved (as it can be by a *crimen carnis secundum naturam*), but the person is set aside, the self is degraded below the level of the animals, and humanity is dishonoured.[1]

Contrasting with Kantian ethics is that of the utilitarians, the most prominent of whom were Jeremy Bentham and the two Mills, James (father) and John Stuart (son). For them, the key to ethical theory is happiness: "The creed which accepts as the foundation of morals utility or the greatest happiness principle holds that actions are right in proportion as they tend to promote happiness; wrong as they tend to produce the reverse of happiness." . . .

Bentham thinks homosexual interactions as acceptable morally as Kant finds them pernicious. Such interactions give pleasure to the people engaged in them, and so by the greatest happiness principle they ought to be valued. "As to any primary mischief, it is evident that [a homosexual interaction] produces no pain in anyone. On the contrary it produces pleasure . . .". Bentham is not advocating homosexual behavior for everyone, only for those who want to so indulge. Then, there will be no harm. Nor is there any real problem stemming from the possibility that homosexual practices might incline or influence others into similar behavior. People who indulge homosexual appetites seem to enjoy themselves; so at most one is inclining others to enjoyable practices.

What of the claim that homosexual behavior runs one down physically, thus as it were reducing one's long-term pleasure in life? Bentham's conclusion is that there is no evidence to this effect. In any case, being in line with medical opinion of the time, and accepting that masturbation is physically debilitating, Bentham pointed out the injustice of trying to eliminate homosexuality through the law, when one did (and obviously could) do nothing about self-abuse. What of the claim that homosexuality is a threat to the keeping of population numbers up to an acceptable level? (Bentham had no doubts that a sizeable population is a good thing.) Again Bentham saw no danger on this score. Men's sexual appetites and capabilities far exceed those of females, particularly in the sense that a man can fertilize many more times than a fertilized female can give birth. . . .

IS HOMOSEXUAL BEHAVIOR BIOLOGICALLY UNNATURAL?

. . . Plato, who introduced the argument, has had the greatest influence on western thought about the worth of homosexuality. Plato stated categorically that homosexuality (the behavior at least) is wrong because it is unnatural—it is not something done by the animals. . . .

It is biology which is the strongest plank in the barrier against the permissibility of same-gender sex. But should *we* condemn homosexual behavior as immoral because it is unnatural, in the sense of being against biology? Should we say that animals do not behave homosexually; therefore humans should not behave homosexually? Is it true that genitals were "designed" for heterosexual ends and that all other uses are a wicked corruption? We must try to answer these questions for ourselves, and to this end a number of points must be raised.

First, it is simply not true, if by "unnatural" one means "not performed by animals" or even "not commonly performed by animals," that homosexuality is unnatural. We know that in species after species, right through the animal kingdom, students of animal behavior report unambiguous evidence of homosexual attachments and behavior—in insects, fish, birds, and lower and higher mammals. . . . Whatever the moral implications of homosexuality and naturalness may be, it is false that homosexuality is immoral because it does not exist amongst animals. . . .

Even if it turns out that some kinds of sexual behavior have nothing to do with straight biology, even if it turns out that the homosexual is doing him/herself a biological disservice and perhaps even his/her race or species a similar disservice, this does not as such imply that anything sexual, including homosexual, is immoral. What moral obligation has the individual got to reproduce? What moral obligation has the individual got to help his/her species reproduce? It might be argued that any behavior which is so disruptive of society that society itself fails to reproduce is immoral; . . .

But, in reply, first of all it is obvious that homosexual activity today is not so disruptive of society as to prevent overall reproduction. Second, the moral importance of society's reproduction is not that obvious. We may have an obligation to future generations not so to pollute our planet that life for them becomes depressingly difficult, but do we have an obligation to produce future generations? . . .

My conclusions, therefore, are that once you strike out fallacious arguments about biological naturalness, and bring forward modern realizations of the possibilities for homosexuals of meaningful relationships, the Kantian and utilitarian positions come very much closer together. Certainly, at a minimum, there is moral worth in the close-coupled relationships of the Second Kinsey study, and probably more. . . .

SEXUAL PERVERSION

In theory, this should conclude our discussion at this point. Once you have strained out religious elements, once you have dropped outmoded scientific claims, once you have sorted through the proper relationship between "is" and "ought," once you have discovered a little bit about what homosexuals are really like rather than what you think they might be like, moral conclusions start to fall fairly readily into place. Yet there is something about homosexual activity—and, indeed, the whole overt homosexual life style—that other people find disturbing and threatening; something which drives people to conclude that, for all of the fancy arguments of the philosophers, homosexual activity is a wrong: a moral evil. (The feeling is particularly strong for males, by males—an asymmetry to which I shall return.)

What is it about homosexuality—what is it about male homosexuality in particular—that brings forth such negative judgements? One thing, above all else, comes across. Listen to the eminent theologian Karl Barth (1980):[2] "[Homosexuality] is the physical, psychological and social sickness, the phenomenon of perversion, decadence and decay, which can emerge when man refuses to admit the validity of the divine command in the sense in which we are now considering it" (p. 49). Forget about the sickness part of the complaint. God does not condemn the diabetic. What troubles Barth and his God—what troubles virtually all of those who hate homosexuality—is that they see it as a *perversion*. It is the epitome of wrongdoing, and therefore must be censored in the strongest possible way.

Obviously, from our perspective, we have seen a paradox. Homosexual behavior seems not very morally pernicious; yet, through the notion of perversion, this is precisely how it appears to many people—in our society, at least. How can we resolve it? Fortunately, some help is at hand, for the notion of perversion has been much discussed by analytic philosophers in recent years. Typical in many respects, certainly in that which ties in best with our previous discussion, is an analysis by Sara Ruddick. Trying to capture the concept, she turns to traditional arguments, claiming that what people have been arguing about down through the ages is less a moral question and more one of perversity. She suggests that the natural end of sex is reproduction: that all and only acts which tend to lead to reproduction are natural, and that all unnatural acts are perverted.

> The ground for classifying sexual acts as either natural or unnatural is that the former type serve or could serve the evolutionary and biological function of sexuality—namely, reproduction. "Natural" sexual desire has as its "object" living persons of the opposite sex, and in particular their postpubertal genitals. The "aim" of natural sexual desire—that is, the act that "naturally" completes it—is genital intercourse. Perverse sex acts are deviations . . . (p. 91)[3]

. . . Naturalness keeps coming up. Perhaps the time has come to make it work for us, rather than against us. And indeed, this is a reasonable move, for people like Ruddick are surely right in thinking naturalness important. . . . Yet a biological definition will not do. Perhaps the time has come to make a break. We are human beings: that means we live in a cultural realm, unlike animals who are fundamentally trapped down at the level of pure biology. What I argue, therefore, is that naturalness ought to be defined in terms of culture and not simple biology. What is unnatural, and what is consequently in some important sense perverse, is what goes against or breaks with our culture. It is what violates the ends or aims that human beings think are important or worth striving for. This may include reproduction, but extends to all the things we hold dear, the things that make us happy and make life worth living generally. And this is why perversity is indeed a value laden term, because a perversion puts itself against human norms and values. . . .

This is the key to perversions: what I like to call the "Ugh! factor." A perversion involves a breaking not of a moral rule, but more of an aesthetic rule. We find perversions disgusting, revolting. But why is this? I would suggest the following reason. A perversion involves going against one of culture's values or ends or things considered desirable, and other members of society cannot understand why one would want to go against the value. . . .

We have come back to the original Platonic position—but with crucial shifts. Unnaturalness is connected to culture, not biology. (As a Darwinian, though, I would never deny that the former comes from and is moulded by the latter. That is why many perversions do involve biologically unsavory acts—like eating feces.) And the values involved are not so much moral as aesthetic. So what about homosexuality? Are homosexual acts perverse acts, and is the inclination to such acts a perverse inclination? Acknowledging that I am trying to offer a descriptive rather than prescriptive analysis, I do not think there is any straightforward answer to these questions. But I look upon this as a strength of my analysis, not a weakness! I think the question of the perversity of homosexuality is to a great extent an empirical matter. How do people feel about homosexual behavior? Can they in some sense relate to it, whether or not they want to do it themselves and whether or not they have homosexual inclinations? . . . I suggest that for some people in our society homosexuality is not a perversion and for some it is. Some other societies have seen homosexuality totally as a perversion. Some other societies have not seen it as a perversion at all.

What I am arguing, therefore, is that, faced with divided opinion in our society about the perverted nature of homosexuality (inclination and behavior), neither side is absolutely right and neither side is absolutely wrong. There is a crucial element of subjectivity at work here, as with liking or disliking spinach. Perversion, especially as it applies to homosexuality, is a relative concept. . . . If one agrees that homosexuality is not immoral, then surely one ought to persuade people not to regard homosexuals and their habits with loathing. Certainly, one ought to persuade people not to confuse their disgust at a perversion with moral indignation. . . .

NOTES

1. Immanuel Kant, *Lectures on Ethics,* trans. L. Infield (New York: Harper & Row, 1963), p. 170.

2. Karl Barth, "Church Dogmatics." In E. Batchelor (ed.), *Homosexuality and Ethics* (New York: Pilgrim, 1980), pp. 48–51.

3. Sara Ruddick, "Better Sex." In R. Baker and F. Elliston (eds.), *Philosophy and Sex* (Buffalo: Prometheus, 1975), pp. 83–104.

Discussion Questions

1. Is it morally relevant that homosexuality has been and continues to be regarded as unnatural and morally deviant in many societies? Support your answer.
2. Does Ruse adequately respond to the argument that homosexuality is a disease? Does his concept of perversion allow for "healthy" perversions? Support your answers.
3. What stereotypes come to mind when you hear the terms *gay man, lesbian,* and *bisexual?* (These stereotypes do not have to be ones that you accept; this is just a brainstorming exercise.) Are these stereotypes based on fact? Discuss how these stereotypes affect your perception of gay, lesbian, and bisexual people, and how these stereotypes affect how people who are gay, lesbian, or bisexual feel about themselves. Discuss how these stereotypes limit the opportunities of people who are gay, lesbian, or bisexual. Are these limitations morally justified? Support your answers.
4. Do you agree with Ruse that if we cannot back up our negative feelings about homosexuality with rational arguments, we have a moral obligation to work on changing those feelings? Do we have a moral obligation to try to overcome doublethink? Relate your answer to the study mentioned in Chapter 1, which found that while slightly more than half of college students interviewed evaluated homosexuality in a positive light, stating that it was a personal preference, 92 percent of those same students also stated that it would not be morally acceptable or desirable if their own child was homosexual.[47]
5. Discuss how the authors of the Vatican's "Declaration of Sexual Ethics" would most likely respond to Ruse's arguments regarding the morality of homosexuality. Which arguments do you find the most morally persuasive and why?

JOHN M. FINNIS

Law, Morality, and "Sexual Orientation"

John Finnis is a professor of law and legal philosophy at Oxford University in England. A defender of Colorado Amendment 2 and the Defense of Marriage Act, Finnis argues that homosexuality is intrinsically immoral, not just because it is unnatural but because

"Law, Morality, and 'Sexual Orientation,'" *Notre Dame Law Review* 69 (1994): 1049–1057, 1063–1076. Some notes have been omitted.

it is destructive to the common good. Because a stable family life is of fundamental importance to the community, the state has a compelling interest in denying that homosexual conduct is a valid and humane lifestyle. The high importance of the common good is expressed in sodomy laws that prohibit homosexual activity as well as laws that prohibit same-sex marriage and the adoption of children by homosexual couples.

Critical Reading Questions

1. What are the two components of the standard modern European position on the legal regulation of sexual conduct?
2. Why does the standard modern position reject outlawing discrimination based on sexual orientation?
3. What are the two things implied by the phrase *sexual orientation?* Which of these, according to Finnis, warrants discrimination and which does not?
4. On what grounds does Finnis oppose the adoption of laws that prohibit discrimination based on sexual orientation as a remedy for unjust discrimination against homosexuals?
5. Why did Plato, Aristotle, and Plutarch (c. A.D. 46–120) maintain that homosexual conduct is immoral?
6. What type of good, according to Saint Augustine, is the "good of marital communion"? Why does this good allow marriage of infertile heterosexual couples?
7. What is the position on the morality of extramarital sex in the Catholic encyclical *Veritatis Splendor?* How is this similar to the position of the ancient Greek philosophers?
8. According to Finnis, what are the two aspects of the "real common good" of marriage? Why can't these goods be realized in homosexual relations or in masturbation?
9. On what grounds does Finnis argue that he is not committing the naturalistic fallacy?
10. What is the difference between behavior that is merely offensive and behavior that is immoral? According to Finnis, what is it about homosexual conduct that makes it immoral rather than merely offensive?
11. How, according to Finnis, does the "gay ideology" treat human sexual capacities in a way that is an active threat to the stability of marriage?
12. What does it mean to say that a community has a common good? What are the three types of common goods in an open-ended community?
13. What does Aristotle mean when he speaks of the political community "making" people good? How, according to Finnis, should this be expressed in laws regulating sexual conduct?
14. According to Finnis, why would it be damaging to the common good to decriminalize homosexuality?

I.

During the past thirty years there has emerged in Europe a standard form of legal regulation of sexual conduct. . . . The standard modern European position has two limbs. On the one hand, the state is not authorized to, and does not, make it a punishable offense for adult consenting persons to engage, in private, in immoral sexual acts (for example, homosexual acts). On the other hand, states do have the authority to discourage, say, homosexual conduct and "orientation" (i.e. overtly manifested active willingness to engage in homosexual conduct). And typically, though not universally, they do so. That is to say, they maintain various criminal and administrative laws and policies which have as part of their purpose the discouraging of such conduct. Many of these laws, regulations, and policies discriminate (i.e. distinguish) between heterosexual and homosexual conduct adversely to the latter. . . .

III.

The standard modern position is part of a politico-legal order which systematically outlaws many forms of discrimination. Thus the European Convention on Human Rights (model for several dozen constitutions enacted over the past thirty-five years by the British authorities, for nations gaining independence) provides that the protection of the rights it sets out is to be enjoyed without discrimination on any ground such as "sex, race, colour, language, religion, political or other opinion, national or social origin, association with a national minority, property, birth or other status."

But the standard modern position deliberately rejects proposals to include in such lists the item "sexual orientation." The explanation commonly given (correctly, in my opinion) is this. The phrase "sexual orientation" is radically equivocal. Particularly as used by promoters of "gay rights," the phrase ambiguously assimilates two things which the standard modern position carefully distinguished: (I) a psychological or psychosomatic disposition inwardly orienting one *towards* homosexual activity; (II) the deliberate decision so to orient one's public *behavior* as to express or *manifest* one's active interest in and endorsement of homosexual *conduct* and/or forms of life which presumptively involve such conduct. . . .

It is in fact accepted by almost everyone, on both sides of the political debate, that the adoption of a law framed to prohibit "discrimination on grounds of sexual orientation" would require the prompt abandonment of all attempts by the political community to discourage homosexual conduct by means of educational policies, restrictions on prostitution, non-recognition of homosexual "marriages" and adoptions, and so forth. . . .

IV.

The standard modern position involves a number of explicit or implicit judgments about the proper role of law and the compelling interests of political communities, and about the evil of homosexual conduct. Can these be defended by reflective, critical, publicly intelligible and rational arguments? I believe they can. Since even the advocates of "gay rights" do not seriously assert that the state can never have any compelling interests in public morality or the moral formation of its young people or the moral environment in which parents, other educators, and young people themselves must undertake this formation, I shall in this lecture focus rather on the underlying issue which receives far too little public discussion: What is wrong with homosexual conduct? . . .

Let me begin by noticing a too little noticed fact. All three of the greatest Greek philosophers, Socrates, Plato and Aristotle, regarded homosexual *conduct* as intrinsically shameful, immoral, and indeed depraved or depraving. That is to say, all three rejected the linchpin of modern "gay" ideology and lifestyle. . . .

The same Plato who in his *Symposium* wrote a famous celebration of *romantic* and *spiritual* man-boy erotic relationships, made very clear that all forms of sexual *conduct* outside heterosexual marriage are shameful, wrongful and harmful. This is particularly evident from his treatment of the matter in his last work, the *Laws,* but is also sufficiently clear in the *Republic* and the *Phaedrus,* and even in the *Symposium* itself. . . .

The core of this argument can be clarified by comparing it with Saint Augustine's treatment of marriage in his *De Bono Coniugali.* The good of marital communion is here an instrumental good, in the service of the procreation and education of children so that the intrinsic, non-instrumental good of friendship will be promoted and realized by the propagation of the human race, and the intrinsic good of inner integration be promoted and realized by the "remedying" of the disordered desires of concupiscence.[1] Now, when considering sterile marriage, Augustine had identified a further good of marriage, the natural *societas* (companionship) of the two sexes. Had he truly integrated this into his synthesis, he would have recognized that in sterile and fertile marriages alike, the communion, companionship, *societas* and *amicitia* of the spouses—their being married—*is* the very good of marriage, and is an intrinsic, basic human good, not merely instrumental to any other good. And this communion of married life, this integral amalgamation of the lives of the two persons, has as its intrinsic elements, as essential *parts* of one and the same good, the goods and ends to which the theological tradition, following Augustine, for a long time subordinated that communion. It took a long and gradual process of development of doctrine, . . . to bring the tradition to the position that procreation and children are neither the *end* (whether primary or secondary) to which marriage is instrumental (as Augustine taught), nor instrumental to the good of the spouses (as much secular and "liberal Christian" thought supposes), but rather: Parenthood and children and family are the intrinsic fulfillment of a communion which, because it is not merely instrumental, can exist and fulfill the spouses even if procreation happens to be impossible for them.

Now if, as the recent encyclical on the foundations of morality, *Veritatis Splendor,* teaches, "the communion of persons in marriage" which is violated by every act of adultery is itself a "fundamental human good,"[2]. . . Why cannot non-marital friendship be promoted and expressed by sexual acts? Why is the attempt to express affection by orgasmic non-marital sex the pursuit of an illusion? Why did Plato and Socrates, Xenophon, Aristotle, Musonius Rufus, and Plutarch, right at the heart of their reflections on the homoerotic culture around them, make the very deliberate and careful judgment that homosexual *conduct* (and indeed all extramarital sexual gratification) is radically incapable of participating in, actualizing, the common good of friendship?

Implicit in the philosophical and common-sense rejection of extra-martial sex is the answer: The union of the reproductive organs of husband and wife really unites them biologically (and their biological reality is part of, not merely an instrument of, their *personal* reality); reproduction is one function and so, in respect of that function, the spouses are indeed one reality, and their sexual union therefore can *actualize* and allow them to *experience* their *real common good—their marriage* with the two goods, parenthood and friendship, which (leaving aside the order of grace) are the parts of its wholeness as an intelligible common good even if, independently of what the spouses will, their capacity for biological parenthood will not be fulfilled by that act of genital union. But the common good of friends who are not and cannot be married (for example, man and man, man and boy, woman and woman) has nothing to do with their having children by each other, and their reproductive organs cannot make them a biological (and therefore personal) unit. So their sexual acts together cannot do what they may hope and imagine. Because their activation of one or even each of their reproductive organs cannot be an actualizing and experiencing of the *marital* good—as marital intercourse (intercourse between spouses in a marital way) can, even between spouses who *happen* to be sterile—it can do no more than provide each partner with an individual gratification. For want of a *common good* that could be actualized and experienced *by and in this bodily union,* that conduct involves the partners in treating their bodies as instruments to be used in the service of their consciously experiencing selves; their choice to engage in such conduct thus dis-integrates each of them precisely as acting persons. . . .

In short, sexual acts are not unitive in their significance unless they are marital (actualizing the all-level unity of marriage) and (since the common good of marriage has two aspects) they are not marital unless they have not only the generosity of acts of friendship but also the procreative significance, not necessarily of being intended to generate or capable in the circumstances of generating but at least of being, as human conduct, acts of the reproductive kind—. . .

Does this account seek to "make moral judgments based on natural facts"? Yes and no. No, in the sense that it does not seek to infer normative conclusions or these from non-normative (natural-fact) premises. Nor does it appeal to any norm of the form "Respect natural facts or natural functions." But yes, it does apply the relevant practical reasons (especially that marriage and inner integrity are basic human goods) and moral principles (especially that one may never *intend* to destroy, damage, impede, or violate any basic human good, or prefer an illusory instantiation of a basic human good to a real instantiation of that or some other human good) to facts about the human personal organism.

VI.

. . . Now, as I have said before, "homosexual orientation," in one of the two main senses of that highly equivocal term, is precisely the deliberate willingness to promote and engage in homosexual acts—the state of mind, will, and character whose self-interpretation came to be expressed in the deplorable but helpfully revealing name "gay." So this willingness, and the whole "gay" ideology, treats human sexual capacities in a way which is deeply hostile to the self-understanding of those members of the community who are willing to commit themselves to real marriage.

Homosexual orientation in this sense is, in fact, a standing denial of the intrinsic aptness of sexual intercourse to actualize and in that sense give expression to the exclusiveness and open-ended commitment of marriage as something good in itself. All who accept that homosexual acts can be a humanly appropriate use of sexual capacities must, if consistent, regard sexual capacities, organs and acts as instruments for gratifying the individual "selves" who have them. Such an acceptance is commonly (and in my opinion rightly) judged to be an active threat to the stability of existing and future marriages; it makes nonsense, for example, of the view that adultery is per se (and not merely because it may involve deception), and in an important way, inconsistent with conjugal love. A political community which judges that the stability and protective and educative generosity of family life is of fundamental importance to that community's present and future can rightly judge that it has a compelling interest in denying that homosexual conduct—a "gay lifestyle"—is a valid, humanly acceptable choice and form of life, and in doing whatever it *properly* can, as a community with uniquely wide but still subsidiary functions, to discourage such conduct.

VII.

. . . Every community is constituted by the communication and cooperation between its members. To say that a community has a common good is simply to say that communication and cooperation have a point which the members more or less concur in understanding, valuing and pursuing. There are three types of common good which each provide the constitutive point of a distinctive type of open-ended community and directly instantiate a basic human good: (1) the affectionate mutual help and shared enjoyment of the friendship and *communio* of "real friends"; (2) the sharing of husband and wife in married life, united as complementary, bodily persons whose activities make them apt for parenthood—the *communio* of spouses and, if their marriage is fruitful, their children; (3) the *communio* of religious believers cooperating in the devotion and service called for by what they believe to be the accessible truths about the ultimate source of meaning, value and other realities, and about the ways in which human beings can be in harmony with that ultimate source. . . .

The political community—properly understood as one of the forms of collaboration needed for the sake of the basic goods identified in the first principles of natural law—is a community cooperating in the service of a common good which is instrumental, not itself basic. . . . Its proper range includes the regulation of friendships, marriage, families, and religious associations, as well as of all the many organizations and associations which are dedicated to specific goals or which, like the state itself, have only an instrumental (e.g. an economic) common good. . . . [I]ts purpose must be to carry out the *subsidiary* (i.e. helping, from the Latin *subsidium,* help) function of assisting individuals and groups to co-ordinate their activities for the objectives and commitments they have chosen, and to do so in ways consistent with the other aspects of the common good of this community, uniquely complex, far-reaching and demanding in its rationale, its requirements of cooperation, and its monopolization of force: the political community. . . .

When Aristotle speaks of "making" people good, he constantly uses the word *poiesis* which he has so often contrasted with *praxis* and reserved for techniques ("arts") of manipulating matter.[3] But helping citizens to choose and act in line with integral human fulfillment must involve something which goes beyond any art or technique. For only individual acting persons can by their own choices make themselves good or evil. Not that their life should or can be individualistic; their deliberating and choosing will be shaped, and helped or hindered, by the language of their culture, by their family, their friends, their associates and enemies, the customs of their communities, the laws of their polity, and by the impress of human influences of many kinds from beyond their homeland. . . . And as members of all these communities they have some responsibility to encourage their fellow-members in morally good and discourage them from morally bad conduct.

To be sure, the political community is a cooperation which undertakes the unique tasks of giving coercive protection to all individuals and lawful as associations within its domain, and of securing an economic and cultural environment in which all these persons and groups can pursue their own proper good. To be sure, this common good of the political community makes it far more than a mere arrangement for "preventing mutual injury and exchanging goods." But it is one thing to maintain, as reason requires, that the political community's rationale requires, that its public managing structure, the state, should deliberately and publicly identify, encourage, facilitate and support the truly worth-while (including moral virtue), should deliberately and publicly identify, discourage and hinder the harmful and evil, and should, by its criminal prohibitions and sanctions (as well as its other laws and policies), assist people with parental responsibilities to educate children and young people in virtue and to discourage their vices. It is another thing to maintain that that rationale requires or authorize the state to direct people to virtue and deter them from vice by making even secret and truly consensual adult acts of vice a punishable offence against the state's laws.

So there was a sound and important distinction of principle which the Supreme Court of the United States overlooked in moving from *Griswold v. Connecticut* (private use of contraceptives by *spouses*) to *Eisenstadt v. Baird* (*public distribution* of contraceptives to *unmarried* people). The truth and relevance of that distinction, and its high importance for the common good, would be overlooked again if laws criminalizing private acts of sodomy between adults were to be struck down by the Court on any ground which would also constitutionally require the law to tolerate the advertising or marketing of homosexual services, the maintenance of places of resort for homosexual activity, or the promotion of homosexualist "lifestyles" via education and public media of communication, or to recognize homosexual "marriages" or permit the adoption of children by homosexually active people, and so forth.

NOTES

1. St. Augustine, *De Bono Coniugali,* 9.9.
2. Johan Paul II, *Veritatis Splendor* ¶¶ 13, 48 (1984); *see also id.* at ¶¶, 50, 67, 78, 79.
3. *E.g.* Aristotle, *Nicomachean Ethics,* VI, 5: 1140a2; Aristotle, *Politics,* 1, 2. 1254a5.

Discussion Questions

1. Do you agree with Finnis that the common good and the promotion of virtue in the citizenry require outlawing homosexual activity? Would decriminalizing homosexuality be tantamount to the government promoting a homosexual lifestyle, as Finnis claims? Would decriminalizing homosexuality, in fact, lead to the deterioration of

marriage and society, as Finnis claims? How might Aristotle and Confucius respond to these questions? How might Ruse respond to Finnis's concerns? Support your answers.

2. Does Finnis consider homosexuality a disease? Support your answer. What would Finnis's position most likely be on the use of conversion therapy to change sexual orientation?
3. In 1958, shortly after Mildred "Stringbean" Jetter and Richard Loving returned home to Virginia after their Washington, D.C., wedding, they were awakened by a sheriff flashing a light in their eyes. By living together as husband and wife, they violated the state's segregation laws. The subsequent prosecution of the interracial couple ended in 1967 when the U.S. Supreme Court ruled in *Loving v. Virginia* that Virginia's segregation law violated the equal protection clause of the Constitution. "There can be no doubt that restricting the freedom to marry solely because of racial classifications violates the central meaning of the equal protection clause . . . marriage is one of the 'basic civil rights of man,' fundamental to our very existence and survival." Is this case parallel to the current same-sex marriage? Are people like Finnis, who cite the common good and social stability in their opposition to same-sex marriage, simply betraying a cultural prejudice? Support your answers. Discuss how Finnis would respond to these questions.
4. The formula "Love the sinner, hate the sin" is often promoted by churches regarding homosexuality. Parents, clergy, and others should love the homosexual person while discouraging homosexual acts. Is this approach consistent with Finnis's position on homosexuality? Discuss the morality of this approach. Can we separate the person from the behavior? Is this approach demeaning to homosexuals or an assault on their integrity? Support your answers.
5. Forty percent of Americans believe that homosexuals should not be hired as clergy or as elementary school teachers.[48] Discuss whether Finnis's arguments support a public policy prohibiting homosexuals from entering these professions. Would it make a difference to Finnis if they were not "active" homosexuals? Support your answer. Discuss how Ruse might respond to this prohibition. Which person do you think presents the strongest argument? Support your answer.
6. Would Finnis approve of the current U.S. military policy on homosexuals? Support your answer.
7. In 1994 Finnis was invited to speak at Harvard; not everyone was glad to see him, however. His speech was interrupted by a group of gay-rights advocates who lowered a movie screen behind the podium. Across the screen in large letters was the word *HOMOPHOBE*. Scott Wiener, the student who led the protest, explained that Finnis was a "hate monger" because of his antihomosexual position. Inviting Finnis to campus, he maintained, was similar to inviting a Nazi or Grand Wizard of the Ku Klux Klan. If homophobia is to be stamped out and gay liberation is to become a reality, people such as Finnis must be silenced.[49] Do you agree with Wiener? How would you have responded had you been at the Finnis talk? Support your answers.

MICHAEL NAVA AND ROBERT DAWIDOFF

The Case for Gay Marriage

Michael Nava is a San Francisco lawyer and well-known novelist. Robert Dawidoff is a professor of history at the Claremont Graduate University in Claremont, California. Nava and Dawidoff argue that gay and lesbian couples should have the right to marry. Marriage as a legal and social institution is important to the goals of homosexual couples as well as heterosexual couples. Furthermore, prohibiting same-sex marriage harms not only gay and lesbian couples who wish to marry, but also impedes progress toward sexual equality.

Critical Reading Questions

1. What is the traditional American understanding of marriage? Why is marriage so important in our society?
2. What are some of the government-sponsored incentives that make marriage desirable?
3. Why do gays and lesbians want the right to marry? What are some of the consequences of denying them that right?
4. How do Nava and Dawidoff respond to the objection regarding gays' and lesbians' "inability" to form permanent attachments?
5. What is the significance, for arguments regarding gay and lesbian marriage, of studies showing that extended cohabitation before marriage increases the likelihood of divorce?
6. What evidence do Nava and Dawidoff use to support their argument that same-sex relationships play an important role in promoting "more equal relations between the sexes"?
7. What is the legal argument against gay and lesbian marriage? On what grounds do Nava and Dawidoff reject this argument?
8. How do Nava and Dawidoff respond to the argument that the chief purpose of marriage is procreation? What evidence do they offer for their argument that gays and lesbians make good parents? According to them, why would allowing same-sex marriage be an advantage to the children of these parents?
9. How do Nava and Dawidoff respond to the argument that allowing gays and lesbians to marry would encourage homosexuality and illegal sexual activity?
10. What is the purpose, according to Nava and Dawidoff, of outlawing homosexual activities?
11. According to Nava and Dawidoff, what are the ultimate goals of gays and lesbians? Why is marriage integral to these goals?
12. According to Nava and Dawidoff, who besides homosexuals is harmed by current laws outlawing same-sex marriage?

"The Case for Gay Marriage" in *Created Equal: Why Gay Rights Matter to America* (New York: St. Martin's Press, 1994), 144–157. Some notes have been omitted.

. . . Marriage is how society recognizes the intimate and lasting bond between two people and, in turn, it has become the cornerstone of the American family. Curiously, the American family as we know it is not "traditional" but innovative. Instead of inherited property or bloodlines or unquestioned patriarchal authority, the American family early on developed the view of marriage as a partnership between two consenting adults, not an agreement on their account by their parents or families. The churches that bless the marriage sacrament took their cue from secular, individualist America and, in general, endorse marriage as something entered into by the participants, if they are of age to contract, because they choose to make that commitment.

In the United States marriage is understood to be the decision of two people to live together and be a partnership, a unit, a family. Neither family nor church participates in the legal ceremony, and the religious wedding acquires legal force by the power vested in the officiant by the civil society; the religious ceremony confirms the civil arrangement. Marriage is not conditioned on the intention or the capacity to have children. Nothing in marriage, except custom, mandates partners of different genders. For example, John Boswell notes that in ancient Rome "marriages between males and between females were legal and familiar among the upper classes."[1] The institution of marriage in our society appears to be one that encourages monogamy as the basis for stable personal lives and as one aspect of the family. If we think about what marriage is for, it becomes clear that it is for people to find ways to live ordered, shared lives; it is intended to be the stablest possible unit of family life and a stable structure of intimacy.

Marriage is part of the formal and informal network of extended family, kinship, and friendship, and it is acknowledged in law as society's preferred way for consenting adults to connect their lives. Society recognizes that people have the right and the desire to have those connections solemnized according to their own beliefs; thus, religious ceremonies of all sorts, established or homemade, are encouraged as adjuncts to the civil bond. But it is the civil bond that the law acknowledges and that society encourages in all sorts of ways. No wonder many gay and lesbian Americans see marriage as their equal right. Marriage is society's way of making things easier and better for people who want to form permanent relationships, share their lives and property, and form families.

Marriage is not mere form. Society recognizes its importance not only rhetorically but with such benefits as preferential tax treatment, spousal Social Security and veteran's benefits, favorable immigration laws, property and support rights upon divorce, and intestate succession. In addition, according to Alissa Friedman, "both state and federal governments allocate a great many rights on the basis of marital status and have created powerful incentives for an individual to marry. Furthermore, private entities like insurance companies often provide special benefits and lower rates for married couples and legally recognized couples. Restrictions on the right to marry, therefore, affect both associational rights and a variety of societal entitlements."[2] . . .

Gays and lesbians want the right to marry for the same reasons other Americans do: to gain the moral, legal, social, and spiritual benefits conferred on the marrying couple and especially on their family unit. The material benefits of marriage are considerable, but it is the moral benefit that is especially attractive to many couples, including gay and lesbian ones. Marriage is, or can be, a moral commitment that two people make to one another. The marriage vow enshrines love, honor, respect, and mutual support and gives people access to resources and community acknowledgment that serve to strengthen their bond. Brought up and socialized as most Americans are, gays and lesbians also regard the prospect of marriage as reverently and respectfully as heterosexuals do. To mock and deny them is ultimately to mock and deny the institution of marriage. The impulse to marry, among gays, is essentially the same as it is among heterosexuals, and the capacity to do it well is probably the same. The only real difference is in the identity of the people who want to get married.

What is drastically different, of course, is that gay and lesbian unions get none of the support, encouragement, and benefits society regularly gives to heterosexual unions, however ill-advised. Instead, gays and lesbians are reviled for their "inability" to form permanent attachments. Of course, relationships between people that have to remain clandestine or have no foundation in law or social convention are just that much harder to maintain. Gay relationships can succeed, but always against heavy odds, odds not of the participants' making; heterosexual marriages fail all too often in spite of every conceivable social, familial, legal, and moral support.

The journal *Demography* recently published the results of a twenty-three-year study of the relationship of cohabitation to marriage; they suggest "the possibility that cohabitation weakens commitment to marriage as an institution." The authors of the study concluded that living together before marriage may not strengthen marriage; on the contrary, living together before marriage commonly produces "attitudes and values which increase the probability of divorce."[3]. . . If, as the *Demography* study indicates, marriage is a key ingredient in the longevity and solidity of intimate relationships, then denial of that most important advantage to one class of citizens on account of sexual orientation is cruelly unfair.

One of the ironies of our situation is that the American marriage that is so celebrated actually borrows from the historical character of gay relationships to describe itself. Far from being unnatural, gay and lesbian ways of living have played important roles in every human society. One almost universal function of those relationships has been to pioneer the more equal relations between the sexes. Long-standing relationships between men and between women are well known to history. Antiquity celebrated the bonds of friendship and loyalty between men, bonds that scholars tell us commonly included the sexual. The relationships among Greek soldiers and philosophers, which have played so critical a role in the traditional Western understanding of noble human relations (including the cohesion of the military unit), were modeled on love between men that regularly included sex.

The lifelong partnerships between middle-class or upper-class women in American history—the famous "Boston marriages"—also influenced decisively the understanding of marriage that American women derived from their colleges and their genteel upbringings. Female friendships played a critical role in the creation of the American institution of marriage as a partnership within which the woman was not owned but respected, not a human beast of burden and procreation but an equal source of authority and values for the family that marriage creates. . . .

The distinctive quality of modern American marriage and family is the equal and respectful relations between husband and wife as partners, friends, and co-parents, in the place of the economic, procreative, and kinship unit of traditional societies. Men and women are learning to treat one another as they more habitually treat favored members of their own gender—with confidence, trust, equality, respect, and sensitivity. Gays and lesbians are as capable of forming such relationships and making them work as heterosexual men and women are. . . .

Two main obstacles appear to gay marriage: legal definitions of marriage and the claim that marriage is chiefly for procreation or child-rearing. The legal argument boils down to the following: Marriage is a union of man and woman because it's always been that way. The civil law that governs marriage has its roots in ecclesiastical law, which reflects the biblical proscription of homosexuality. The statutes say that marriage is the union of man and woman, so that is what marriage must be. . . .

Even if we accept parenting as one important reason for the institution of marriage, shifting the model of marriage to include common if untraditional parenting units makes sense. Whatever was the case in the past, it is now common for gays and lesbians to be parents, not just to have fathered or borne children in heterosexual unions, but to be raising children as open gays and lesbians. In a survey of gay couples, Mary Mendola looked at gays and lesbians involved in a "gay marriage relationship," as she put it. She found that a quarter of the women and 17 percent of the men reported that they or their partners had children. Nearly 60 percent of the women reported that their children lived with them and their partners most of the time, while 39 percent reported that their children regularly visited. While only 3 percent of the men reported that their children lived with them and their partners, 53 percent reported that their children regularly visited them.[4] Mendola's report is a dozen years old; if anything the numbers have probably increased as more gays and lesbians are producing children by using artificial insemination (the so-called gayby boom) or adopting them or winning custody of them. If society is serious in its claim that marriage produces the best environment for raising children, then marriage must be extended to gays and lesbians who, in increasing numbers, are becoming parents.

Moreover, the studies available on gay parenting demonstrate that gays and lesbians make good parents; the children of gay families appear to do as well as the children of heterosexual ones. If, as it is sometimes argued, these children face difficulties among their peers because of negative attitudes toward homosexuality, the clear solution is to change those attitudes through education. Allowing same-sex marriage would be an important part of that change and would also promote family stability. If, in fact, that kind of stability is one of the reasons that marriage exists, it makes no sense to promote it in some families but not others by restricting marriage to heterosexuals.

Opponents of gay marriage finally arrive at the bedrock of their argument when they assert that allowing gays and lesbians to marry would encourage illegal sexual activity in the face of sodomy laws. . . . [This] implies a moral judgment against that activity (even in places where there are no sodomy laws), then allowing gays and lesbians to marry is contrary to acceptable morality. Of course, the whole point of gay and lesbian activism is to expose the underlying premise of immorality for the bigotry it is. Making an act illegal doesn't mean the act is inherently criminal. . . .

The quarter century of gay and lesbian political activism and openness has not resulted in a dramatic increase in the homosexual population (although it has dramatically increased the awareness of homosexuality and has also increased the numbers of lesbians and gays living openly). This points to the conclusion that this population is relatively stable and will always be a minority. Thus, punitive laws accomplish nothing but to intimidate a class of American citizens and deny them their constitutional rights. Denying gay and lesbian marriage will not eliminate gay and lesbian relationships; it will just make those relationships harder to sustain. If creating unnecessary suffering in the cause of popular prejudice is a permissible goal of legislation, then not only gay Americans are in for a bad time of it. . . .

Far from harming heterosexuals, gay marriage would give family-inclined gay men and lesbians the chance to fulfill this aspiration in conformity with their own natures. The legitimacy of gay marriage would save lives by creating the kind of respect for gays and lesbians that will work as a counterweight to bigotry and bashing. . . .

WHAT WE WANT

What do gays and lesbians want? What does any person want? Enough to live; basic protections; love, family, freedom, Beyond the basics, in the case of gays and lesbians, would be equal protection of the law, representation along with taxation. And what lies beyond that, it is the individual's place to say. We do not think there is a shared agenda among gays and lesbians that goes much beyond equality and freedom. But there are some other things that we imagine as human counterparts to legal protections.

It would be wonderful if families could see in their children the full range of the affectional possibilities that life in fact holds out. If girlish boys and boyish girls, who do not constitute the full range of homosexuality but who are often the ones targeted, could receive encouragement and praise and the love they deserve instead of derision, intimidation, and disappointment, their lives would be much improved. And it would improve the quality of the culture if these children could grow into adults who, because they were loved and valued, made rich contributions to the culture instead of expending that energy on overcoming the wounds that were inflicted on them.

It would also be wonderful if friends and colleagues of gay people would be as interested in their lives as they are in their company and counsel, if the walls came down and revealed each other's essential humanity. And it would be wonderful to see gay and lesbian judges, mayors, kindergarten teachers, construction workers, actors, fathers, brothers, mothers, sisters, musicians and clerics, all of them acknowledged and honored. In this utopia, little would appear changed, but there would be an addition rather than a diminution of freedom and well-being. . . .

NOTES

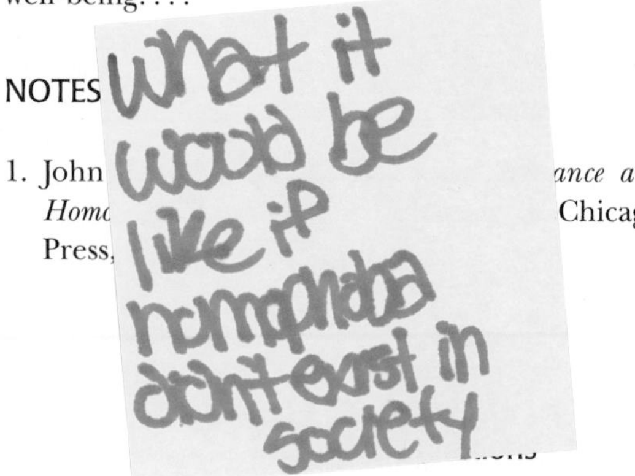

1. John ... *ance and Homo...* ... Chicago Press, ...
2. Alissa Friedman, "The Necessity for State Recognition of Same-Sex Marriage: Constitutional Requirements and Evolving Notions of Family," 3 *Berkeley Women's Law Journal* (1988), pp. 134–70.
3. William G. Axinn and Arland Thorton, "The Relationship Between Cohabitation and Divorce: Selectivity or Casual Influence?" *Demography* 29 (August 1992) 3:357, 361.
4. Mary Mendola, *The Mendola Report: A New Look at Gay Couples* (1980), p. 254.

...IONS

1. Discuss how Finnis would most likely respond to Nava and Dawidoff's arguments for same-sex marriage.
2. Discuss whether natural rights ethicist John Locke would be more likely to agree with Finnis or with Nava and Dawidoff regarding the right of homosexuals to marry.
3. Former U.S. Secretary of Education William Bennett opposes same-sex marriage on the grounds that "broadening the definition of marriage to include same-sex unions would stretch it almost beyond recognition—and new attempts to expand the definition still further would surely follow."[50] Would legalizing same-sex marriage put us on the slippery slope to condoning incestuous marriages between a parent and child or between siblings, as Bennett claims? Can we, or ought we, draw a moral distinction between excluding people with a same-sex orientation from marriage and excluding people with a "same-family" orientation? Should consenting adults be able to marry whomever they want? Support your answers. Discuss how Nava and Dawidoff might respond to Bennett's argument.
4. Representative Bob Barr, the chief sponsor of the Defense of Marriage Act, stated that "America is not ready to change its definition of marriage."[51] Senator Phil Gramm of Texas agrees; he asks, "Are we so wise today that we are ready to reject five thousand years of recorded history? I don't think so."[52] Are these good reasons for supporting the bill, or are they based on fallacious reasoning? How should legislation on moral issues be decided if not by majority rule? Discuss your answers in light of John Stuart Mill's claim that one of the dangers of democracy is "tyranny of the majority."
5. William Bennett argues that marriage is not a blanket right. We do not, for example, allow polygamous, incestuous, or group marriage in the United States. Furthermore, heterosexual marriage is a right because it is the condition of the continuation of society. Discuss how Nava and Dawidoff would respond to Bennett's concerns. Who makes the best argument—Bennett, or Nava and Dawidoff? Support your answers.

CHESHIRE CALHOUN

Family's Outlaws: Rethinking the Connections between Feminism, Lesbianism, and the Family

Cheshire Calhoun is an associate professor of philosophy and the director of women's studies at Colby College in Maine. Whereas many gay and lesbian activists, including Michael Nava and Robert Dawidoff, enthusiastically support same-sex marriage, others such as Calhoun have reservations about marriage itself and buying into "heterosexual norms."[53] Calhoun questions the assumption that marriage is a desirable social institution that should be extended to gay and lesbian couples. She points out that feminists have often raised concerns over the oppressive nature of heterosexual marriage. Instead, lesbians need to be aware of the problems with marriage before attempting to re-create traditional marriage and parenting practices among same-sex partners.

Critical Reading Questions

1. What arguments do feminists offer for the claim that marriage is "a primary site of women's subordination to and dependence on men"?
2. According to Calhoun, why are lesbians uniquely positioned to avoid the problems of the traditional heterosexual family?
3. Why does Calhoun reject liberal efforts to redefine gay and lesbian families as functionally equivalent to heterosexual families?
4. How does lesbian motherhood differ from conventional heterosexual motherhood?
5. On what grounds does Calhoun argue that same-sex marriage does not necessarily revolutionize the traditional oppressive gender structure of marriage?
6. How does Calhoun respond to the argument that gay and lesbian couples lack access to benefits, such as medical insurance, enjoyed by married heterosexual couples?
7. According to Calhoun, what are some of the differences between lesbian and heterosexual relationships, and how would extending marriage to same-sex couples tend to diminish these differences?
8. Why, according to Calhoun, should lesbians resist buying into the traditional model of marriage?
9. How should lesbians and gays respond to laws that deny them the same privileges as heterosexuals?
10. What does Calhoun mean when she refers to lesbians and gays as "familial outlaws"?
11. What does the term *queer family* mean? Why does Calhoun claim that this term is oppressive to gays and lesbians? What does she mean when she says that gay and lesbian families are "real families"?

"Family's Outlaws: Rethinking the Connections Between Feminism, Lesbianism, and the Family" in *Feminism and Families,* ed. by Hilde Lindemann Nelson (New York: Routledge, 1997), 131–150. Some notes have been omitted.

How should we understand lesbians' relation to the family, marriage, and mothering? Part of what makes this a difficult question to answer from a feminist standpoint is that feminism has undertheorized lesbian and gay oppression as an axis of oppression distinct from gender oppression. As a result, lesbians' *difference* from heterosexual women is often not visible—even oddly enough, within explicitly lesbian-feminist thought. . . .

My aim is to suggest that lesbians' distinctive relation to the family, marriage, and mothering is better captured by attending to the social construction of lesbians as familial outlaws than by attending exclusively to the gender structure of family, marriage, and mothering.

FEMINISM AND THE FAMILY

Feminist depictions and analyses of the family, marriage, and mothering have been driven by a deep awareness that the family centered around marriage, procreation, and child-rearing has historically been and continues to be a primary site of women's subordination to and dependence on men, and by an awareness that the gender ideology that rationalizes women's subordinate status is heavily shaped by assumptions about women's natural place within the family as domestic caretakers, as reproductive beings, and as naturally fit for mothering. It has been the task and success of feminism to document the dangers posed to women by family, marriage, and mothering in both their lived and ideological forms.

The ideology of the loving family often masks gender injustice within the family, including battery, rape, and child abuse. Women continue to shoulder primary responsibility for both child-rearing and domestic labor; and they continue to choose occupations compatible with child care, occupations which are often less well paid, more replaceable, and less likely to offer benefits and career-track mobility. The expectation that women within families are first and foremost wives and mothers continues to offer employers a rationale for paying women less. Women's lower wages in the public workforce in turn make it appear economically rational within marriages for women to invest in developing their husband's career assets. . . . Women's custody of children after divorce, their lower earning potential, the unavailability of low-cost child care, the absence of adequate social support for single mothers, and, often, father's failure to pay full child support combine to reduce divorced women's economic position even further, resulting in the feminization of poverty. The ideology of the normal family as the self-sufficient, two-earner, nuclear family is then mobilized to blame single mothers for their poverty, to justify supervisory and psychological intervention into those families, and to rationalize reducing social support for them.

This picture, although generally taken as a picture of women's relation to the family, marriage, and mothering, is not, in fact, a picture of *women's* relation to the family, but is more narrowly a picture of *heterosexual* women's relation to the family, marriage, and mothering. . . . Thus it fails to grasp lesbians' relation to the family.

LESBIAN FEMINISM, THE FAMILY, MOTHERING, AND MARRIAGE

In understanding what lesbians' relation to the family, motherhood, and marriage is and ought to be, lesbian feminists took as their point of departure feminist critiques of heterosexual women's experience of family, motherhood, and marriage. Lesbian feminists were particularly alive to the fact that lesbians are uniquely positioned to evade the ills of the heterosexual, male-dominated family. In particular, they are uniquely positioned to violate the conventional gender expectation that they, as women, would be dependent on men in their personal relations, would fulfill the maternal imperative, would service a husband and children, and would accept confinement to the private sphere of domesticity. Because of their unique position, lesbians could hope to be in the vanguard of the feminist rebellion against the patriarchal family, marriage, and institution of motherhood.

Family

. . . Lesbian-feminist interpretation of lesbians' relation to the family as nonparticipation in *heterosexual,* male-dominated, private families is then translated into nonparticipation in *any* form of family, including lesbian families. In a 1994 essay, for instance, Ruthann Robson argues against recent liberal legal efforts to redefine the family to include lesbian and gay families that are functionally equivalent to heterosexual ones. She argues that, in advocating legal recognition of lesbian families, "we have forgotten the lesbian generated critiques of family as oppressive and often deadly."[1] In particular we have forgotten critiques of the family as an institution of the patriarchal state, of marriage as slavery, and of wives as property within marriage. In her view, the category "family" should be abolished.

Motherhood

Feminist critiques of heterosexual women's experience also supplied the point of departure for lesbian-feminist critiques of lesbian motherhood. Lesbian motherhood, on this view represent a concession to a key element of women's subordination—compulsory motherhood. By refusing to have children, or by giving up custody of their children at divorce, lesbians can refuse to participate in compulsory motherhood. They can thus refuse to accept the myth "that only family and children provide [women] with a purpose and place, bestow upon us honor, respect, love, and comfort."[2] Purpose and place is better found in political activities in a more public community of women. Lesbian feminists thus challenge lesbians contemplating motherhood to reflect more critically on their reasons for doing so and on the political consequences of participating in the present lesbian baby boom. . . .

Marriage

Like lesbian motherhood, lesbian (and gay) marriage seems antithetical to the lesbian-feminist goal of radically challenging conventional gender, sexual, and familial arrangements. Historically, the institution of marriage has been oppressively gender-structured. The historical and cross-cultural record of same-sex marriages does not support the claim that same-sex marriages will revolutionize the gender structure of marriage. On the contrary, same-sex marriages that have been legitimized in other cultures—for instance, African woman-marriage, Native American marriages between a berdache and a same-sex partner, and nineteenth-century Chinese marriage between women—have all been highly gender-structured. Thus there is no reason to believe that "'gender dissent' is inherent in marriage between two men or two women."[3]

Moreover, the attempt to secure legal recognition for lesbian and gay marriages is highly likely to work against efforts to critique the institution of marriage. In particular, by attempting to have specifically *marital* relationships recognized, advocates of marriage rights help to reinforce the assumption that long-term, monogamous relationships are more valuable than any other kind of relationship. As a result, the marriage rights campaign, if successful, will end up privileging those lesbian and gay relationship that most closely approximate the heterosexual norm over more deviant relationships that require a radical rethinking of the nature of families.

Finally, arguments for lesbian and gay marriage rights on the grounds that lesbians and gays lack privileges that heterosexual couples enjoy—such as access to a spouse's health insurance benefits—are insufficiently radical. Distributing basic benefits like health insurance through the middle-class family neglects the interests of poor and some working-class families as well as single individuals in having access to basic social benefits. If access to such benefits is the issue, then universal health insurance, not marriage, is what we should be advocating.

LESBIAN DISAPPEARANCE

The difficulty with the lesbian-feminist viewpoint is that it is one from which lesbian difference from heterosexual women persistently disappears from view.

First, the value of the family and marriage for *lesbians* is judged largely by evaluating the *heterosexual* nuclear family's effects on *heterosexual* women. Lesbians are to resist family and marriage because the family centered around the heterosexual married couple has been gender structured in a way that made marriage a form of slavery where heterosexual women could be treated as property and their labor appropriated by men. But to make this a principal reason for lesbians' not forming families and marriages of their own is to lose sight of the difference between lesbians and heterosexual women. Lesbian families and marriages are not reasonably construed as sites where women can be treated as property and where their productive and reproductive labor can be appropriated by men. It thus does not follow from the fact that heterosexual marriage and family has been oppressive for heterosexual women and a primary structure of patriarchy that *any* form of marriage or family, including lesbian ones, is oppressive for women and a primary structure of patriarchy. . . .

Both lesbians and heterosexual women have reason to resist the construction of mothering as an unpaid, socially unsupported task. Both have reason to reject women's confinement to the domestic sphere and reason to value participation in politically oriented communities of women. Both have reason to resist their gender socialization into the myth of feminine fulfillment through mothering and to assert their deviance from the category of "woman." Both can have justice interests in objecting to a social and legal system that privileges long-term, monogamous relationships over all other forms of relationship and that does not provide universal access to basic benefits like health insurance. All of these are broadly feminist concerns. As a result, the lesbian-feminist perspective does not articulate any distinctively *lesbian* political tasks in relation to the family, marriage, and mothering. Instead, lesbians are submerged in the larger category "feminist."

Finally, the political relation between heterosexuals and nonheterosexuals and the ideologies of sexuality that support the oppression of lesbians and gays simply do not inform the lesbian-feminist analysis of lesbians' relation to the family, marriage, or mothering. What governs the lesbian-feminist perspective is above all the political relations between men and women, and to a lesser extent class relations and the political relations between those in normative long-term, monogamous relations (whether heterosexual or nonheterosexual) and all other human relations. As a result, the radicalness of lesbian and gay family, marriage, and parenting is measured on a scale that looks only at their power (or impotence) to transform gender relations, the privileging of long-term, monogamous relations, and class privilege. Not surprisingly, lesbian and gay families, marriages, and parenting fail to measure up. But this ignores the historical construction of lesbians and gays as outlaws to the natural family, as constitutionally incapable of more than merely sexual relationships, and as dangerous to children.

Within gender ideology, for instance, lesbians have not been and are not constructed as beings whose natural place is within the family as domestic caretakers, as reproductive beings, and as naturally fit mothers. On the contrary, the gender ideology that rationalizes the oppression of both lesbians and gays consists in part precisely in the assumption that both are aliens to the natural family, nonprocreative, incapable of enduring intimate ties, dangerous to children, and ruled by sexual instincts to the exclusion of parenting ones. . . .

Lesbians and gays are, for instance, denied the legal privileges and protections that heterosexuals enjoy with respect to their natural and familial relations. Among the array of rights related to marriage that heterosexuals enjoy but gays and lesbians do not are the rights to legal marriage, to live with one's spouse in neighborhoods zoned "single-family only," and to secure U.S. residency through marriage to a U.S. citizen; the rights to Social Security survivor's benefits, to inherit a spouse's estate in the absence of a will, and to file a wrongful death suit; the rights to give proxy consent, to refuse to testify against one's spouse, and to file joint income taxes.

Lesbians and gays similarly lack access to the privileges and protections that heterosexuals enjoy with respect to biological, adoptive, and foster children. Sexual orientation continues to be an over-riding reason for denying custody to lesbian and gay parents who exit a heterosexual marriage. Gays and lesbians fare equally poorly with respect to adoption and foster parenting. . . .

What comes into view in this picture of the legal inequities that lesbians and gays confront is the fact that the family, marriage, and parenting are a primary site of heterosexual privilege. The family centered around marriage, procreation, and childrearing has historically been and continues to be constructed and institutionalized as the natural domain of heterosexuals only, and thus as a domain from which lesbians and gays are outlawed. . . .

FAMILIAL OUTLAWS

A constitutive feature of lesbian and gay oppression since at least the late nineteenth century has been the reservation of the private sphere for heterosexuals only. Because lesbians and gays are ideologically constructed as beings incapable of genuine romance, marriage, or families of their own, and because those assumptions are institutionalized in the law and social practice, lesbians and gays are displaced from this private sphere.

In what follows, I want to suggest that the historical construction of gays and lesbians as familial outlaws is integrally connected to the history of social anxiety about the failure and potential collapse of the heterosexual nuclear family. In particular, I want to suggest that in periods where there was heightened anxiety about the stability of the heterosexual nuclear family because of changes in gender, sexual, and family composition norms within the family, this anxiety was resolved by targeting a group of persons who could be ideologically constructed as outsiders to the family, identifying the behaviors that most deeply threatened the family with those outsiders, and stigmatizing that group. . . . The construction of gays and lesbians as highly stigmatized outsiders to the family and as displaying the most virulent forms of family-disrupting behavior allayed anxieties about the potential failure of the heterosexual nuclear family in three ways. First, it externalized the threat to the family. As a result, anxiety about the possibility that the family was disintegrating from *within* could be displaced onto the spectre of the hostile outsider to the family. Second, stigma threatening comparisons between misbehaving members of the heterosexual family and the dangerous behavior of gays and lesbians could be used to compel heterosexual family members' compliance with gender, sexual, and family composition norms. Thirdly, by locating the genuinely deviant, abnormal, perverse behavior outside the family, members of heterosexual families were enabled to adjust to new, liberalized norms for acceptable gender roles and sexual behavior within families as well as new, liberalized norms for acceptable family composition. They could, in essence, reassure themselves with the thought: "At least we aren't like them!" . . .

NOT FOR HETEROSEXUALS ONLY

I have argued for the existence of a historical pattern in which anxiety about the stability of the family goes hand in hand with the ideological depiction of gays and lesbians as unfit for marriage, parenting, and family. The construction of lesbians and gays as natural outlaws to the family and the masking of heterosexuals' own family-disrupting behavior results in the reservation of the private sphere for heterosexuals only.

It is because being an outlaw to the family has been so central to the social construction of lesbianism that I think lesbians' relation to the family is better captured by attention to their outlaw status than to the gender structure of marriage and motherhood (as is characteristic of lesbian feminism). Indeed, on the historical backdrop of the various images of family outlaws—the mannish lesbian, the homosexual child molester, and their pretended family relationships—lesbian-feminist resistance to lesbian and gay marriages, lesbian motherhood, and the formation of lesbian and gay families looks suspiciously like a concession to the view of lesbians and gays as family outlaws. Because being denied access to a legitimate and protected private sphere has been and continues to be central to lesbian and gay oppression, the most important scale on which to measure lesbian and gay political strategies is one that assesses their power (or importence) to resist conceding the private sphere to heterosexuals only. On such a scale, the push for marriage rights, parental rights, and recognition as legitimate families measures up.

For similar reasons, it seems to me a mistake to make advocacy of "queer families" *the* political goal for lesbians and gays. By "queer families" I mean ones not centered around marriage or children, but composed instead of chosen, adult, supportive relationships (which would include lesbian-feminist political communities of women).

Equating gay families with queer, nonmarital, and nonparenting families concedes too much to the ideology of gays and lesbians as family outlaws, unfit for genuine marriage and dangerous to children. In addition, describing families that depart substantially from traditional family forms as distinctively gay conceals the queerness of many heterosexual families. . . . Thus claiming that gay and lesbian families are (or should be) distinctively queer and distinctively deviant helps conceal the deviancy in heterosexual families, and thereby helps to sustain the illusion that heterosexuals are specially entitled to access to a protected private sphere because they, unlike their gay and lesbian counterparts, are supporters of the family.

All this is not to say that there is no merit in lesbian feminists' concern that normalizing lesbian motherhood will reinforce the equation of "woman" with "mother." Overcoming the idea that lesbian motherhood is a contradiction in terms may very well result in lesbians' being expected to fulfill the maternal imperative just as heterosexual women are. But this is just to say that the oppression of lesbians and gays is structurally different from gender oppression. Thus, strategies designed to resist *lesbian* oppression (such as pushing for the legal right to coadopt) are not guaranteed to counter *gender* oppression (which might better be achieved by resisting motherhood altogether). In gaining access to a legitimate and protected private sphere of mothering, marriage, and family, lesbians will need to take care that it does not prove to be as constraining as the private sphere has been for heterosexual women.

Nor have I meant to claim that there is no merit in both lesbian feminists' and queer theorists' concern that normalizing lesbian and gay marriage will reinforce the distinction between good, assimilationist gays and bad gay and heterosexual others whose relationships violate familial norms (the permanently single, the polygamous, the sexually non-monogamous, the member of a commune, and so on). Overcoming the idea that lesbian and gay marriages are merely pretended family relationships may very well result in married lesbians and gays being looked upon more favorably than those who remain outside accepted familial forms. But this is just to say that countering lesbians' and gays' family outlaw status is not the same thing as struggling to have a broad array of social relationships recognized as (equally) valuable ones. . . . [L]esbians and gays who resist their construction as family outlaws are not bidding for access to one, highly conventional family form (such as the nuclear, two-parent, self-sufficient, procreative family). They are instead bidding for access to the same privilege that heterosexuals now enjoy, namely the privilege of claiming that *in spite of their multiple deviations* from norms governing the family, their families are nevertheless *real* ones and they are themselves naturally suited for marriage, family, parenting *however* these may be defined and redefined.

NOTES

1. Ruthann Robson, "Resisting the Family: Repositioning Lesbians in Legal Theory," *Signs* 19 (1994), pp. 975–996.
2. Irena Klepfisz, "Women Without Children/ Women Without Families/Women Alone," in *Politics of the Heart: A Lesbian Parenting Anthology*, ed. Sandra Pollack and Jeanne Vaughn (New York: Firebrand Books, 1987), p. 57.
3. Nancy D. Polikoff, "We Will Get What We Ask For: Why Legalizing Gay and Lesbian Marriage Will Not 'Dismantle the Legal Structure of Gender in Every Marriage'," *Virginia Law Review* 79 (1993), 1535–1550, p. 1538.

Discussion Questions

1. Do you agree with Calhoun that lesbians should not buy into traditional models of marriage and family? Support your answer.
2. Is Calhoun's argument compatible with Nava and Dawidoff's argument for the legalization of same-sex marriage? Does her argument imply that gay and lesbian couples

who want to marry should not be allowed to? Support your answers. Discuss how Calhoun and Nava and Dawidoff might respond to each other's arguments.

3. Do you agree with Calhoun that families with same-sex parents are "real families"? Should gay and lesbian couples have the same opportunities as heterosexual couples to adopt children or take in foster children? Support your answers. Discuss how Finnis might respond to Calhoun's argument.
4. Discuss how Calhoun would respond to Finnis's argument that homosexuality is destructive to family stability and the common good.
5. Is marriage inherently oppressive to women? Should the social institution of marriage be dismantled? If so, what should replace marriage as the family unit and the best means for raising children? Support your answers. Discuss how Calhoun and Nava and Dawidoff might answer these questions.

RICHARD WASSERSTROM

Is Adultery Immoral?

Richard Wasserstrom is professor emeritus of philosophy at the University of California at Santa Cruz. He examines the argument that adultery is immoral because it involves breaking promises, as well as the argument that adultery is immoral because it weakens the institution of marriage. Wasserman concludes that although sexual exclusivity is not a necessary condition of marriage, adultery in general is wrong because it involves deception.

Critical Reading Questions

1. What does Wasserstrom mean when he says that deception is prima facie wrong?
2. How does Wasserstrom define adultery?
3. What are the two arguments against adultery based on deception?
4. In what ways might the deception involved in adultery be harmful to the nonparticipating spouse?
5. What is the distinction between active and passive deception?
6. What is the connection between sexual intimacy and the immorality of adultery?
7. What is Wasserstrom's position on the restriction of sexual intimacy to marriage?
8. What does Wasserstrom mean by the "sexual *Weltanschauung* of today's youth"?
9. What are the two positions put forth by advocates of sexual liberation regarding the relationship between sex and love, and what is Wasserstrom's view of these positions?

This article is reprinted from Richard Wasserstrom, ed., *Today's Moral Problems* (New York: Macmillan Co., 1975), with the permission of the author.

10. What is an "open marriage"? Is adultery morally permissible in an open marriage?
11. How does Wasserstrom respond to the claim that "sexual exclusivity is a necessary but not a sufficient condition for the existence of a marriage"?
12. What does Wasserstrom think about the morality of polygamous (plural) marriages?
13. How does Wasserstrom respond to the argument that "a prohibition on extramarital affairs helps maintain the institutions of marriage and the nuclear family"?

. . . Much, if not all, of the recent philosophical literature on the enforcement of morals appears to take for granted the immorality of the sexual behavior in question. The focus of discussion, at least, is on whether such things as homosexuality, prostitution, and adultery ought to be made illegal even if they are immoral, and not on whether they are immoral.

I propose in this paper to consider the latter, more neglected topic, that of sexual morality, and to do so in the following fashion. I shall consider just one kind of behavior that is often taken to be a case of sexual immorality—adultery. I am interested in pursuing at least two questions. First, I want to explore the question of in what respects adulterous behavior falls within the domain of morality at all, for this surely is one of the puzzles one encounters when considering the topic of sexual morality. It is often hard to see on what grounds much of the behavior is deemed to be either moral or immoral, for example, private homosexual behavior between consenting adults. I have purposely selected adultery because it seems a more plausible candidate for moral assessment than many other kinds of sexual behavior. . . .

Before I turn to the arguments themselves, there are two preliminary points that require some clarification. Throughout the paper I shall refer to the immorality of such things as breaking a promise, deceiving someone, and so on. In a very rough way I mean by this that there is something morally wrong in doing the action in question. I mean that the action is, in a strong sense of "prima facie," prima facie wrong or unjustified. I do not mean that it may never be right or justifiable to do the action—just that the fact that it is an action of this description always counts against the rightness of the action. I leave entirely open the question of what it is that makes actions of this kind immoral in this sense of "immoral."

The second preliminary point concerns what is meant or implied by the concept of adultery. I mean by "adultery" any case of extramarital sex, and I want to explore the arguments for and against extramarital sex, undertaken in a variety of morally relevant situations. Someone might claim that the concept of adultery is conceptually connected with the concept of immorality. . . . If extramarital sexual relations are always immoral, this is something that must be shown by argument. If the concept of adultery does in some sense entail or imply immorality, I want to ask whether that connection is a rationally based one. If not all cases of extramarital sex are immoral (again, in the sense described above), then the concept of adultery should either be weakened accordingly or restricted to those classes of extramarital sex for which the predication of immorality is warranted.

One argument for the immorality of adultery might go something like this: What makes adultery immoral is that it involves the breaking of a promise, and what makes adultery seriously wrong is that it involves the breaking of an important promise. For, so the argument might continue, one of the things the two parties promise each other when they get married is that they will abstain from sexual relationships with third parties. Because of this promise both spouses quite reasonably entertain the expectation that the other will behave in conformity with it. Hence, when one of them has sexual intercourse with a third party, he or she breaks that promise about sexual relationships that was made when the marriage was entered into and defeats the reasonable expectations of exclusivity entertained by the spouse.

In many cases the immorality involved in breaching the promise relating to extramarital sex may be a good deal more serious than that involved in the breach of other promises. This is so because adherence to this promise may be of much greater importance to them than is adherence to many of the other promises given or received by them in their lifetime. The breaking of this promise may be much more hurtful and painful than is typically the case.

Why is this so? To begin with, it may have been difficult for the nonadulterous spouse to have kept the promise. Hence that spouse may feel the unfairness of having restrained himself or herself in the absence of reciprocal restraint having been exercised by the adulterous spouse. In addition, the spouse may perceive the breaking of the promise as an indication of a kind of indifference on the part of the adulterous spouse. If you really cared about me and my feelings, the spouse might say, you would not have done this to me. And third, and related to the above, the spouse may see the act of sexual intercourse with another as a sign of affection for the other person and as an additional rejection of the nonadulterous spouse as the one who is loved by the adulterous spouse. It is not just that the adulterous spouse does not take the feelings of the nonadulterous spouse sufficiently into account; the adulterous spouse also indicates through the act of adultery affection for someone other than the nonadulterous spouse. I will return to these points later. For the present it is sufficient to note that a set of arguments can be developed in support of the proposition that certain kinds of adultery are wrong just because they involve the breach of a serious promise that, among other things, leads to the intentional infliction of substantial pain on one spouse by the other.

Another argument for the immorality of adultery focuses not on the existence of a promise of sexual exclusivity but on the connection between adultery and deception. According to this argument adultery involves deception. And because deception is wrong, so is adultery.

Although it is certainly not obviously so, I shall simply assume in this essay that deception is always immoral. Thus, the crucial issue for my purposes is the asserted connection between extramarital sex and deception. Is it plausible to maintain, as this argument does, that adultery always involves deception and is, on that basis, to be condemned?

The most obvious person upon whom deceptions might be practiced is the nonparticipating spouse; and the most obvious thing about which the nonparticipating spouse can be deceived is the existence of the adulterous act. One clear case of deception is that of lying. Instead of saying that the afternoon was spent in bed with A, the adulterous spouse asserts that it was spent in the library with B or on the golf course with C.

There can also be deception even when no lies are told. Suppose, for instance, that a person has sexual intercourse with someone other than his or her spouse and just does not tell the spouse about it. Is that deception? It may not be a case of lying if, for example, he or she is never asked by the spouse about the situation. Still, we might say, it is surely deceptive because of the promises that were exchanged at marriage. As we saw earlier, these promises provide a foundation for the reasonable belief that neither spouse will engage in sexual relationships with any other person. Hence the failure to bring the fact of extramarital sex to the attention of the other spouse deceives that spouse about the present state of the marital relationship.

Adultery, in other words, can involve both active and passive deception. An adulterous spouse may just keep silent or, as is often the case, the spouse may engage in an increasingly complex way of life devoted to the concealment of the facts from the nonparticipating spouse. Lies, half-truths, clandestine meetings, and the like may become a central feature of the adulterous spouse's existence. These are things that can and do happen, and when they do they make the case against adultery an easy one. Still, neither active nor passive deception is inevitably a feature of an extramarital relationship.

It is possible, though, that a more subtle but pervasive kind of deceptiveness is a feature of adultery. It comes about because of the connection in our culture between sexual intimacy and certain feelings of love and affection. The point can be made indirectly by seeing that one way in which we can in our culture mark off our close friends from our mere acquaintances is through the kinds of intimacies that we are prepared to share with them. I may, for instance, be willing to reveal my very private thoughts and emotions to my closest friends or to my wife but to no one else. My sharing of these intimate facts about myself is, from one perspective, a way of making a gift to those who mean the most to me. Revealing these things and sharing them with those who mean the most to me is one means by which I create, maintain, and confirm those interpersonal relationships that are of most importance to me.

In our culture, it might be claimed, sexual intimacy is one of the chief currencies through which gifts of this sort are exchanged. One way to tell someone—particularly someone of the opposite sex—that you have feelings of affection and love for them is by allowing them, or sharing with them, sexual behaviors that one does not share with others. This way of measuring affection was certainly very much a part of the culture in which I matured. It worked something like this: If you were a girl, you showed how much you liked a boy by the degree of sexual intimacy you would allow. If you liked him only a little you never did more than kiss—and even the kiss was not very passionate. If you liked him a lot and if your feeling was reciprocated, necking and, possibly, petting were permissible. If the attachment was still stronger and you thought it might even become a permanent relationship, the sexual activity was correspondingly more intense and intimate, although whether it led to sexual intercourse depended on whether the parties (particularly the girl) accepted fully the prohibition on nonmarital sex. The situation for the boys was related but not exactly the same. The assumption was that males did not naturally link sex with affection in the way in which females did. However, since women did link sex with affection, males had to take that fact into account. That is to say, because a woman would permit sexual intimacies only if she had feelings of affection for the male and only if those feelings were reciprocated, the male had to have and express those feelings too, before sexual intimacies of any sort would occur. . . .

If this sketch is even roughly right, then several things become somewhat clearer. To begin with, a possible rationale for many of the rules of conventional sexual morality can be developed. If, for example, sexual intercourse is associated with the kind of affection and commitment to another that is regarded as characteristic of the marriage relationship, then it is natural that sexual intercourse should be thought properly to take place between persons who are married to each other. And if it is thought that this kind of affection and commitment is only to be found within the marriage relationship, then it is not surprising that sexual intercourse should only be thought to be proper within marriage.

Related to what has just been said is the idea that sexual intercourse ought to be restricted to those who are married to each other, as a means by which to confirm the very special feelings that the spouses have for each other. Because our culture teaches that sexual intercourse means that the strongest of all feelings for each other are shared by the lovers, it is natural that persons who are married to each other should be able to say this to each other in this way. Revealing and confirming verbally that these feelings are present is one thing that helps to sustain the relationship; engaging in sexual intercourse is another. . . .

More to the point, an additional rationale for the prohibition on extramarital sex can now be developed. For given this way of viewing the sexual world, extramarital sex will almost always involve deception of a deeper sort. If the adulterous spouse does not in fact have the appropriate feelings of affection for the extramarital partner, then the adulterous spouse is deceiving that person about the presence of such feelings. If, on the other hand, the adulterous spouse does have the corresponding feelings for the extramarital partner but not toward the nonparticipating spouse, the adulterous spouse is very probably deceiving the nonparticipating spouse about the presence of such feelings toward that spouse. Indeed, it might be argued, whenever there is no longer love between the two persons who are married to each other, there is deception just because being married implies both to the participants and to the world that such a bond exists. Deception is inevitable, the argument might conclude, because the feelings of affection that ought to accompany any act of sexual intercourse can only be held toward one other person at any given time in one's life. And if this is so, then the adulterous spouse always deceives either the partner in adultery or the nonparticipating spouse about the existence of such feelings. Thus extramarital sex involves deception of this sort and is for that reason immoral even if no deception vis-à-vis the occurrence of the act of adultery takes place.

What might be said in response to the foregoing arguments? The first thing that might be said is that the account of the connection between sexual intimacy and feelings of affection is inaccurate—not in the sense that no one thinks of things that way but in the sense that there is substantially more divergence of opinion than the account suggests. For example, the view I have delineated may describe reasonably accurately the concepts of the sexual world in which I grew up, but it does not capture the sexual *Weltanschauung* of today's youth at all. Thus, whether or not adultery implies deception in respect to feelings depends very much on the persons who are involved and the way they look at the "meaning" of sexual intimacy.

Second, the argument leaves unanswered the question of whether it is desirable for sexual intimacy to carry the sorts of messages described above. For those persons for whom sex does have these implications there are special feelings and sensibilities that must be taken into account. But it is another question entirely whether any valuable end—moral or otherwise—is served by investing sexual behavior with such significance. That is something that must be shown and not just assumed. It might, for instance, be the case that substantially more good than harm would come from a kind of demystification of sexual behavior—one that would encourage the enjoyment of sex more for its own sake and one that would reject the centrality both of the association of sex with love and of love with only one other person.

I regard these as two of the more difficult unresolved issues that our culture faces today in respect of thinking sensibly about the attitudes toward sex and love that we should try to develop in ourselves and in our children.

Much of the contemporary literature that advocates sexual liberation of one sort or another embraces one or the other of two different views about the relationship between sex and love. One view holds that sex should be separated from love and affection. To be sure, sex is probably better when the partners genuinely like and enjoy being with each other. But sex is basically an intensive, exciting sensuous activity that can be enjoyed in a variety of suitable settings with a variety of suitable partners. The situation in respect to sexual pleasure is no different from that of the person who knows and appreciates fine food and who can have a satisfying meal in any number of good restaurants with any number of congenial companions. One question that must be settled here is whether sex can be thus demystified; another, more important, question is whether it would be desirable to do so. What might we gain and what might we lose if we all lived in a world in which an act of sexual intercourse was no more or less significant or enjoyable than having a delicious meal in a nice setting with a good friend? The answer to this question lies beyond the scope of this essay.

The second view of the relationship between sex and love seeks to drive the wedge in a different place. On this view it is not the link between sex and love that needs to be broken, but rather the connection between love and exclusivity. For a number of the reasons already given it is desirable, so this argument goes, that sexual intimacy continue to be reserved to and shared with only those for whom one has very great affection. The mistake lies in thinking that any "normal" adult will have those feelings toward only one other adult during his or her lifetime—or even at any time in his or her life. It is the concept of adult love, not ideas about sex, that needs demystification. What are thought to be both unrealistic and unfortunate are the notions of exclusivity and possessiveness that attach to the dominant conception of love between adults in our culture and others. Parents of four, five, six, or even ten children can certainly claim, and sometimes claim correctly, that they love all of their children, that they love them all equally, and that it is simply untrue to their feelings to insist that the numbers involved diminish either the quantity or the quality of their love. If this is readily understandable in the case of parents and children, there is no necessary reason why it is an impossible or undesirable ideal in the case of adults. To be sure, there is probably a limit to the number of intimate, "primary" relationships that any person can maintain at any given time without affecting the quality of the relationship. But one adult ought surely to be able to love two, three, or even six other adults at any one time without that love being different in kind or degree from that of the traditional, monogamous, lifetime marriage. . . . Or is there something about sexual love, whatever that may be, that makes these feelings especially fitting? Once again, the issues are conceptual, empirical, and normative all at once: What is love? How could it be different? Would it be a good thing or a bad thing if it were different?

. . . [Let] us imagine that a husband and wife have what is today sometimes characterized as an "open marriage." Suppose, that is, that they have agreed in advance that extramarital sex is—under certain circumstances—acceptable behavior for each to engage in. Suppose that as a result there is no impulse to deceive each other about the occurrence or nature of any such relationships and that no deception in fact occurs. Suppose, too, that there is no deception in respect to the feelings involved between the adulterous spouse and the extramarital partner. And suppose, finally, that one or the other or both of the spouses then has sexual intercourse in circumstances consistent with these understandings. Under this description, so the argument might conclude, adultery is simply not immoral. At a minimum adultery cannot very plausibly be condemned either on grounds that it involves deception or on grounds that it requires the breaking of a promise.

At least two responses are worth considering. One calls attention to the connection between marriage and adultery; the other looks to more instrumental arguments for the immorality of adultery. Both deserve further exploration.

One way to deal with the case of the "open marriage" is to question whether the two persons involved are still properly to be described as being married to each other. Part of the meaning of what it is for two persons to be married to each other, so this argument would go, is to have committed oneself to have sexual relationships only with one's spouse. Of course, it would be added, we know that that commitment is not always honored. We know that persons who are married to each other often do commit adultery. But there is a difference between being willing to make a commitment to marital fidelity, even though one may fail to honor that commitment, and not making the commitment at all. Whatever the relationship may be between the two individuals in the case just described, the absence of any commitment to sexual exclusivity requires the conclusion that their relationship is not a marital one. For a commitment to sexual exclusivity is a necessary but not a sufficient condition for the existence of a marriage.

Although there may be something to this suggestion, it is too strong as stated to be acceptable. To begin with it is doubtful that there are many, if any, *necessary* conditions for marriage; but even if there are, a commitment to sexual exclusivity is not such a condition.

To see that this is so, consider what might be taken to be some of the essential characteristics of a marriage. We might be tempted to propose that the concept of marriage requires the following: a formal ceremony of some sort in which mutual obligations are undertaken between two persons of the opposite sex; the capacity on the part of the persons involved to have sexual intercourse with each other; the willingness to have sexual intercourse only with each other; and feelings of love and affection between the two persons. The problem is that we can imagine relationships that are clearly marital and yet lack one or more of these features. For example, in our own society it is possible for two persons to be married without going through a formal ceremony, as in the common-law marriages recognized in some jurisdictions. It is also possible for two persons to get married even though one or both lacks the capacity to engage in sexual intercourse. Thus, two very elderly persons who have neither the desire nor the ability to have intercourse can nonetheless get married, as can persons whose sexual organs have been injured so that intercourse is not possible. And we certainly know of marriages in which love was not present at the time of the marriage, as, for instance, in marriages of state and marriages of convenience.

Counterexamples not satisfying the condition relating to the abstention from extramarital sex are even more easily produced. We certainly know of societies and cultures in which polygamy and polyandry are practiced, and we have no difficulty in recognizing these relationships as cases of marriages. It might be objected, though, that these are not counterexamples because they are plural marriages rather than marriages in which sex is permitted with someone other than one of the persons to whom one is married. But we also know of societies in which it is permissible for married persons to have sexual relationships with persons to whom they are not married, for example, temple prostitutes, concubines, and homosexual lovers. And even if we knew of no such societies, the conceptual claim would still, I submit, not be well taken. For suppose all of the other indicia of marriage were present: suppose the two persons were of the opposite sex; suppose they had the capacity and desire to have intercourse with each other; suppose they participated in a formal ceremony in which they understood themselves voluntarily to be entering into a relationship with each other in which substantial mutual commitments were assumed. If all these conditions were satisfied we would not be in any doubt as to whether or not the two persons were married, even though they had not taken on a commitment of sexual exclusivity and even though they had expressly agreed that extramarital sexual intercourse was a permissible behavior for each to engage in.

A commitment to sexual exclusivity is neither a necessary nor a sufficient condition for the existence of a marriage. It does, nonetheless, have this much to do with the nature of marriage—like the other indicia enumerated above, its presence tends to establish the existence of a marriage. Thus, in the absence of a formal ceremony of any sort an explicit commitment to sexual exclusivity would count in favor of regarding the two persons as married. The conceptual role of the commitment to sexual exclusivity can, perhaps, be brought out through the following example. Suppose we found a tribe that had a practice in which all the other indicia of marriage were present but in which the two parties were *prohibited* even from having sexual intercourse with each other. Moreover, suppose that sexual intercourse with others was clearly permitted. In such a case we would, I think, reject the idea that the two persons were married to each other, and we would describe their relationship in other terms, for example, as some kind of formalized, special friendship relation—a kind of heterosexual "blood-brother" bond.

Compare that case with the following one. Again suppose that the tribe had a practice in which all of the other indicia of marriage were present, but instead of a prohibition on sexual intercourse between the persons in the relationship there was no rule at all. Sexual intercourse was permissible with the person with whom one had this ceremonial relationship, but it was no more or less permissible than with a number of other persons to whom one was not so related (for instance, all consenting adults of the opposite sex). While we might be in doubt as to whether we ought to describe the persons as married to each other, we would probably conclude that they were married and that they simply were members of a tribe whose views about sex were quite different from our own.

What all of this shows is that a *prohibition* on sexual intercourse between the two persons involved in a relationship is conceptually incompatible with the claim that the two of them are married. The *permissibility* of intramarital sex is a necessary part of the idea of marriage. But no such incompatibility follows simply from the added permissibility of extramarital sex.

These arguments do not, of course, exhaust the arguments for the prohibition on extramarital sexual relations. The remaining argument that I wish to consider is—as I indicated earlier—a more instrumental one. It seeks to justify the prohibition by virtue of the role that it plays in the development and maintenance of nuclear families. The argument, or set of arguments, might, I believe, go something like this: . . .

It is obvious that one of the more powerful human desires is the desire for sexual gratification. The desire is a natural one, like hunger and thirst, in the sense that it need not be learned in order to be present within us and operative on us. But there is in addition much that we do learn about what the act of sexual intercourse is like. Once we experience sexual intercourse ourselves—and, in particular, once we experience orgasm—we discover that it is among the most intensive, short-term pleasures of the body.

Because this is so it is easy to see how the prohibition on extramarital sex helps to hold marriage together. At least during that period of life when the enjoyment of sexual intercourse is one of the desirable bodily pleasures, persons will wish to enjoy those pleasures. If one consequence of being married is that one is prohibited from having sexual intercourse with anyone but one's spouse, then the spouses in a marriage are in a position to provide an important source of pleasure for each other that is unavailable to them elsewhere in the society.

The point emerges still more clearly if this rule of sexual morality is seen as being of a piece with the other rules of sexual morality. When this prohibition is coupled, for example, with the prohibition on nonmarital sexual intercourse, we are presented with the inducement both to get married and to stay married. For if sexual intercourse is only legitimate within marriage, then persons seeking that gratification that is a feature of sexual intercourse are furnished explicit social directions for its attainment, namely, marriage. . . .

Adultery is wrong, in other words, because a prohibition on extramarital sex is a way to help maintain the institutions of marriage and the nuclear family.

I am frankly not sure what we are to say about an argument such as the preceding one. What I am convinced of is that, like the arguments discussed earlier, this one also reveals something of the difficulty and complexity of the issues that are involved. So what I want now to do in the final portion of this essay is to try to delineate with reasonable precision several of what I take to be the fundamental, unresolved issues.

The first is whether this last argument is an argument for the *immorality* of extramarital sexual intercourse. What does seem clear is that there are differences between this argument and the ones considered earlier. The earlier arguments condemned adulterous behavior because it was behavior that involved breaking a promise, taking unfair advantage of or deceiving another. To the degree to which the prohibition on extramarital sex can be supported by arguments that invoke considerations such as these, there is little question but that violations of the prohibition are properly regarded as immoral. And such a claim could be defended on one or both of two distinct grounds. The first is that action such as promise-breaking and deception are simply wrong. The second is that adultery involving promise-breaking or deception is wrong because it involves the straightforward infliction of harm on another human being—typically the nonadulterous spouse—who has a strong claim not to have that harm so inflicted.

The argument that connects the prohibition on extramarital sex with the maintenance and preservation of the institution of marriage is an argument for the instrumental value of the prohibition. To some degree this counts, I think, against regarding all violations of the prohibition as obvious cases of immorality. . . .

What this should help us see, I think, is the fact that the argument that connects the prohibition on adultery with the preservation of marriage is at best seriously incomplete. Before we ought to be convinced by it, we ought to have reasons for believing that marriage is a morally desirable and just social institution. And such reasons are not quite as easy to find or as obvious as it may seem. For the concept of marriage is, as we have seen, both a loosely structured and a complicated one. There may be all sorts of intimate, interpersonal relationships that will resemble but not be identical with the typical marriage relationship presupposed by the traditional sexual morality. There may be a number of distinguishable sexual and loving arrangements that can all legitimately claim to be called *marriages.* The prohibitions of the traditional sexual morality may be effective ways to maintain some marriages and ineffective ways to promote and preserve others. The prohibitions of the traditional sexual morality may make good psychological sense if certain psychological theories are true, and they may be purveyors of immense psychological mischief if other psychological theories are true. The prohibitions of traditional sexual morality may seem obviously correct if sexual intimacy carries the meaning that the dominant culture has often ascribed to it, and they may seem equally bizarre if sex is viewed through the perspective of the counterculture. Irrespective of whether instrumental arguments of this sort are properly deemed moral arguments, they ought not fully convince anyone until questions such as these are answered.

Discussion Questions

1. Does marriage entail an implicit promise of sexual fidelity to one's spouse? What about "open marriages" where both spouses agree to permit extramarital affairs? Support your answers.
2. Is a commitment to sexual exclusivity a necessary condition for the existence of a marriage? If so, are agreements on the part of spouses to be open to letting the other have extramarital affairs morally invalid? Support your answers.
3. Is there an implicit promise of sexual fidelity in steady dating and cohabitation? Relate your answer to the case of Brooke and Adam at the beginning of this chapter. Discuss how Wasserstrom might answer this question.
4. Discuss whether or not it is morally permissible for a person to have an extramarital affair if they are certain they will not be caught and if they are not emotionally involved with their extramarital partner.
5. Is Internet "sex" adultery? Is it immoral? Why or why not? Discuss how Wasserstrom would most likely answer these questions.
6. Is adultery ever morally permissible in cases where one of the partners is a permanent invalid and unable to have a sexual relationship? Support your answer.
7. Some feminists, such as Catherine MacKinnon and Cheshire Calhoun, argue that marriage is not a desirable social institution because it is oppressive to women and "a primary site of women's subordination to and dependence on men."[54] Do you agree? If so, what are some alternatives that might overcome some of the problems of conventional marriage?

LOIS PINEAU

Date Rape: A Feminist Analysis

Lois Pineau is a professor of philosophy at Kansas State University. Pineau defines date rape as nonconsensual sex that does not involve physical injury. The requirement by courts of evidence of physical injury, she argues, stems from myths that women are sexually provocative and asking for it, and that men's sexual desires are uncontrollable. Pineau rejects these myths as well as the contractual model of sex, arguing instead for a communicative model. According to Pineau, good sex requires communication. When sexuality is not communicative, the man cannot assume consent. To engage in sex without consent is rape.

"Date Rape: A Feminist Analysis," *Law and Philosophy* 8 (1989): 217–243. Some notes have been omitted.

Critical Reading Questions

1. How does Pineau define date rape?
2. Why is physical injury generally required to show that a sexual encounter was rape?
3. Why do courts, according to Pineau, usually shift the burden of proof onto the woman in cases of alleged rape?
4. What is the difference between *actus reas* and *mens reas?* What constitutes *mens reas* in order for a man to be guilty of rape? Why does Pineau find this account of rape unsatisfactory?
5. What are some of the myths underlying the criterion that an alleged rape victim must prove that she vigorously rejected the man's advances?
6. How does Pineau describe a possible date-rape scenario? Why, according to Pineau, do so many women experience paradoxical feelings in cases like these?
7. What are some of the myths about rape and sex in our culture?
8. What assumptions about male and female sexuality enforce the myth that women want to be raped? According to Pineau, why is this a myth?
9. According to Pineau, why is the contract, which supposedly exists when a woman acts provocatively, not binding?
10. Why doesn't a woman's consent given at the beginning of a sexual encounter necessarily establish the legitimacy of the whole encounter?
11. According to Pineau, what is the only way to establish the legitimacy of a sexual encounter?
12. What does Pineau mean by "communicative sexuality"? How does this model differ from the "contract" model? What is the role of consent in both of these models? Why does Pineau reject the contractual model in favor of the communicative model?
13. How would the communicative model change the way the judicial system currently approaches sexuality and the question of date rape?

. . . Date rape is nonaggravated sexual assault, nonconsensual sex that does not involve physical injury, or the explicit threat of physical injury. But because it does not involve physical injury, and because physical injury is often the only criterion that is accepted as evidence that the *actus reas* is nonconsensual, what is really sexual assault is often mistaken for seduction. The replacement of the old rape laws with the new laws on sexual assault have done nothing to resolve this problem. . . .

THE PROBLEM OF THE CRITERION

The reasoning that underlies the present criterion of consent is entangled in a number of mutually supportive mythologies which see sexual assault as masterful seduction, and silent submission as sexual enjoyment. Because the prevailing ideology has so much informed our conceptualization of sexual interaction, it is extraordinarily difficult for us to distinguish between assault and seduction, submission and enjoyment, or so we imagine. . . . I therefore want to begin my argument by providing an example which shows both why it is so difficult to make this distinction, and that it exists. Later, I will identify and attempt to unravel the lines of reasoning that reinforce this difficulty.

> The woman I have in mind agrees to see someone because she feels an initial attraction to him and believes that he feels that same way about her. She goes out with him in the hope that there will be mutual enjoyment and in the course of the day or evening an increase of mutual interest. Unfortunately, these hopes

of *mutual* and *reciprocal* interest are not realized. We do not know how much interest she has in him by the end of their time together, but whatever her feelings she comes under pressure to have sex with him, and she does not want to have the kind of sex he wants. She may desire to hold hands and kiss, to engage in more intense caresses or in some form of foreplay, or she may not want to be touched. She may have reasons unrelated to desire for not wanting to engage in the kind of sex he is demanding. She may have religious reservations, concerns about pregnancy or disease, a disinclination to be just another conquest. She may be engaged in a seduction program of her own which sees abstaining from sexual activity as a means of building an important emotional bond. She feels she is desirable to him, and she knows, and he knows that he will have sex with her if he can. And while she feels she doesn't owe him anything, and that it is her prerogative to refuse him, this feeling is partly a defensive reaction against a deeply held belief that if he is in need, she should provide. If she buys into the myth of insistent male sexuality she may feel he is suffering from sexual frustration and that she is largely to blame.

We do not know how much he desires her, but we do know that his desire for erotic satisfaction can hardly be separated from his desire for conquest. He feels no dating obligation, but has a strong commitment to scoring. He uses the myth of "so hard to control" male desire as a rhetorical tactic, telling her how frustrated she will leave him. He becomes overbearing. She resists, voicing her disinclination. He alternates between telling her how desirable she is and taking a hostile stance, charging her with misleading him, accusing her of wanting him, and being coy, in short of being deceitful, all the time engaging in rather aggressive body contact. It is late at night, she is tired and a bit queasy from too many drinks, and he is reaffirming her suspicion that perhaps she has misled him. She is having trouble disengaging his body from hers, and wishes he would just go away. She does not adopt a strident angry stance, partly because she thinks he is acting normally and does not deserve it, partly because she feels she is partly to blame, and partly because there is always the danger that her anger will make him angry, possibly violent. It seems that the only thing to do, given his aggression, and her queasy fatigue, is to go along with him and get it over with, but this decision is so entangled with the events in process it is hard to know if it is not simply a recognition of what is actually happening. She finds the whole encounter a thoroughly disagreeable experience, but he does not take any notice, and wouldn't have changed course if he had. He congratulates himself on his sexual prowess and is confirmed in his opinion that aggressive tactics pay off. Later she feels that she has been raped, but paradoxically tells herself that she let herself be raped.

The paradoxical feelings of the woman in our example indicate her awareness that what she feels about the incident stands in contradiction to the prevailing cultural assessment of it. She knows that she did not want to have sex with her date. She is not so sure, however, about how much her own desires count, and she is uncertain that she has made her desires clear. Her uncertainty is reinforced by the cultural reading of this incident as an ordinary seduction.

As for us, we assume that the woman did not want to have sex, but just like her, we are unsure whether her mere reluctance, in the presence of high-pressure tactics, constitutes nonconsent. We suspect that submission to an overbearing and insensitive lout is no way to go about attaining sexual enjoyment, and we further suspect that he felt no compunction about providing it, so that on the face of it, from the outside looking in, it looks like a pretty unreasonable proposition for her.

Let us look at this reasoning more closely. Assume that she was not attracted to the kind of sex offered by the sort of person offering it. Then it would be *prima facie* unreasonable for her to agree to have sex, unreasonable, that is, unless she were offered some pay-off for her stoic endurance, money perhaps, or tickets to the opera. The reason is that in sexual matters, agreement is closely connected to attraction. Thus, where the presumption is that she was not attracted, we should at the same time presume that she did not consent. Hence, the burden of proof should be on her alleged assailant to show that she had good reasons for consenting to an unattractive proposition.

This is not, however, the way such situations are interpreted. In the unlikely event that the example I have described should come before the courts, there is little doubt that the law would interpret the woman's eventual acquiescence or "going along with" the sexual encounter as consent. But along with this interpretation would go the implicit understanding that she had consented because when all was said and done, when the "token" resistances to the "masterful advances" had been made she had wanted to after all. Once the courts have constructed this interpretation, they are then forced to conjure up some horror story of feminine revenge in order to explain why she should bring charges against her "seducer."

In the even more unlikely event that the courts agreed that the woman had not consented to the above encounter, there is little chance that her assailant would be convicted of sexual assault. The belief that the man's aggressive tactics are a normal part of seduction means that *mens rea* cannot be established. Her eventual "going along" with his advances constitutes reasonable grounds for his believing in her consent. . . .

The position of the courts is supported by the widespread belief that male aggression and female reluctance are normal parts of seduction. Given their acceptance of this model, the logic of their response must be respected. . . .

RAPE MYTHS

The belief that the natural aggression of men and the natural reluctance of women somehow makes date rape understandable underlies a number of prevalent myths about rape and human sexuality. . . .

The claim that the victim provoked a sexual incident, that "she asked for it," is by far the most common defense given by men who are accused of sexual assault. Feminists, rightly incensed by this response, often treat it as beneath contempt, singling out the defense as an argument against it. . . .

The least sophisticated of the "she asked for it" rationales, and in a sense, the easiest to deal with, appeals to an injunction against sexually provocative behavior on the part of women. If women should not be sexually provocative, then, from this standpoint, a woman who is sexually provocative deserves to suffer the consequences. Now it will not do to respond that women get raped even when they are not sexually provocative, or that it is men who get to interpret (unfairly) what counts as sexually provocative. The question should be: Why shouldn't a woman be sexually provocative? Why should this behavior warrant any kind of aggressive response whatsoever?

Attempts to explain that women have a right to behave in sexually provocative ways without suffering dire consequences still meet with surprisingly tough resistance. Even people who find nothing wrong or sinful with sex itself, in any of its forms, tend to suppose that women must not behave sexually unless they are prepared to carry through on some fuller course of sexual interaction. The logic of this response seems to be that at some point a woman's behavior commits her to following through on the full course of a sexual encounter as it is defined by her assailant. At some point she has made an agreement, or formed a contract, and once that is done, her contractor is entitled to demand that she satisfy the terms of that contract. . . .

The rationale, I believe, comes in the form of a belief in the especially insistent nature of male sexuality, an insistence which lies at the root of natural male aggression, and which is extremely difficult, perhaps impossible to contain. At a certain point in the arousal process, it is thought, a man's rational will gives away to the prerogatives of nature. His sexual need can and does reach a point where it is uncontrollable, and his natural masculine aggression kicks in to assure that this need is met. Women, however, are naturally more contained, and so it is their responsibility not to provoke the irrational in the male. If they do go so far as that, they have both failed in their responsibilities, and subjected themselves to the inevitable. One does not go into the lion's cage and expect not to be eaten. Natural feminine reluctance, it is thought, is no protection against a sexually aroused male.

This belief about the normal aggressiveness of male sexuality is complemented by common knowledge about female gender development. Once, women were taught to deny their sexuality and to aspire to ideals of chastity. Things have not changed so much. . . . The assumption that women both want to indulge sexually, and are inclined to sacrifice this desire for higher ends, gives rise to the myth that they want to be raped. After all, doesn't rape give them the sexual enjoyment that they *really* want, at the same time that it relieves them of the responsibility for admitting to and acting upon what they want? And how then can we blame men, who have been socialized to be aggressively seductive precisely for the purpose of overriding female reserve? If we find fault at all, we are inclined to cast our suspicions on the motives of the woman. . . .

But if women really want sexual pleasure, what inclines us to think that they will get it through rape? This conclusion logically requires a theory about the dynamics of sexual pleasure that sees that pleasure as an emergent property of overwhelming male insistence. For the assumption that a raped female experiences sexual pleasure implies that the person who rapes her knows how to cause that pleasure independently of any information she might convey on that point. Since her ongoing protest is inconsistent with requests to be touched in particular ways in particular places, to have more of this and less of that, then we must believe that the person who touches her knows these particular ways and places instinctively, without any directives from her.

Thus we find, underlying and reinforcing this belief in incommunicative male prowess, a conception of sexual pleasure that springs from wordless interchanges, and of sexual success that occurs in a place of meaningful silence. The language of seduction is accepted as a tacit language: eye contact, smiles, blushes, and faintly discernible gestures. It is, accordingly, imprecise and ambiguous. It would be easy for a man to make mistakes about the message conveyed, understandable that he should mistakenly think that a sexual invitation has been made, and a bargain struck. But honest mistakes, we think, must be excused.

In sum, the belief that women should not be sexually provocative is logically linked to several other beliefs, some normative, some empirical. The normative beliefs are that (1) people should keep the agreements they make, (2) that sexually provocative behavior, taken beyond a certain point, generates agreements, (3) that the peculiar nature of male and female sexuality places such agreements in a special category, one in which the possibility of retracting an agreement is ruled out, or at least made highly unlikely, [and] (4) that women are not to be trusted, in sexual matters at least. The empirical belief, which turns out to be false, is that male sexuality is not subject to rational and moral control.

DISPELLING THE MYTHS

The "she asked for it" justification of sexual assault incorporates a conception of a contract that would be difficult to defend in any other context, and the presumptions about human sexuality which function to reinforce sympathies rooted in the contractual notion of just deserts are not supported by empirical research.

The belief that a woman generates some sort of contractual obligation whenever her behavior is interpreted as seductive is the most indefensible part of the mythology of rape. In law, contracts are not legitimate just because a promise has been made. In particular, the use of pressure tactics to extract agreement is frowned upon. Normally, an agreement is upheld only if the contractors were clear on what they were getting into, and had sufficient time to reflect on the wisdom of their doing so. . . . But whatever the terms of a contract, there is no private right to enforce it. So that if I make a contract with you on which I renege, the only permissible recourse for you is through due legal process. . . .

Thus, even if we assume that a woman has initially agreed to an encounter, her agreement does not automatically make all subsequent sexual activity to which she submits legitimate. If during coitus a woman should experience pain, be suddenly overcome with guilt or fear of pregnancy, or simply lose her initial desire, those are good reasons for her to change her mind. Having changed her mind, neither her partner nor the state has any right to force her to continue. . . .

If the "she asked for it" contractual view of sexual interchange has any validity, it is because there is a point at which there is no stopping a sexual encounter, a point at which that encounter becomes the inexorable outcome of the unfolding of natural events. If a sexual encounter is like a slide on which I cannot stop halfway down, it will be relevant whether I enter the slide of my own free will, or am pushed.

But there is no evidence that the entire sexual act is like a slide. . . . Indeed, the available evidence shows that most of the activity involved in sex has to do with building the requisite level of desire, a task that involves the proper use of foreplay, the possibility of which implies control over the form that foreplay will take. Modern sexual therapy assumes that such control is universally accessible, and so far there has been no reason to question that assumption. Sexologists are unanimous, moreover, in holding that mutual sexual enjoyment requires an atmosphere of comfort and communication, a minimum of pressure, and an ongoing check-up on one's partner's state. . . .

Where the kind of sex involved is not the sort of sex we would expect a woman to like, the burden of proof should not be on the woman to show that she did not consent, but on the defendant to show that contrary to every reasonable expectation she did consent. The defendant should be required to convince the court that the plaintiff persuaded him to have sex with her even though there are no visible reasons why she should.

In conclusion, there are no grounds for the "she asked for it" defense. Sexually provocative behavior does not generate sexual contracts. . . . Secondly, all the evidence suggests that neither women nor men find sexual enjoyment in rape or in any form of noncommunicative sexuality. Thirdly, male sexual desire is containable, and can be subjected to moral and rational control. Fourthly, since there is no reason why women should not be sexually provocative, they do not "deserve" any sex they do not want. . . .

COMMUNICATIVE SEXUALITY: REINTERPRETING THE KANTIAN IMPERATIVE . . .

In thinking about sex we must keep in mind its sensual ends, and the facts show that aggressive high-pressure sex contradicts those ends. Consensual sex in dating situations is presumed to aim at mutual enjoyment. It may not always do this, and when it does, it might not always succeed. There is no logical incompatibility between wanting to continue a sexual encounter, and failing to derive sexual pleasure from it.

But it seems to me that there is a presumption in favor of the connection between sex and sexual enjoyment, and that if a man wants to be sure that he is not forcing himself on a woman, he has an obligation either to ensure that the encounter really is mutually enjoyable, or to know the reasons why she would want to continue the encounter in spite of her lack of enjoyment. A closer investigation of the nature of this obligation will enable us to construct a more rational and a more plausible norm of sexual conduct. . . .

The obligation to promote the sexual ends of one's partner implies the obligation to know what those ends are, and also the obligation to know how those ends are attained. Thus, the problem comes down to a problem of epistemic responsibility, the responsibility to know. The solution, in my view, lies in the practice of a communicative sexuality, one which combines the appropriate knowledge of the other with respect for the dialectics of desire.

So let us, for a moment, conceive of sexual interaction on a communicative rather than a contractual model. . . .

The communicative interaction involved in conversation is concerned with a good deal more than didactic content and argument. Good conversationalists are intuitive, sympathetic, and charitable. Intuition and charity aid the conversationalist in her effort to interpret the words of the other correctly and sympathy enables her to enter into the other's point of view. Her sensitivity alerts her to the tone of the exchange. Has her point been taken good-humoredly or resentfully? Aggressively delivered responses are taken as a sign that *ad hominems* are at work, and that the respondent's self-worth has been called into question. Good conversationalists will know how to suspend further discussion until this sense of self-worth has been reestablished. . . .

Just as communicative conversationalists are concerned with more than didactic content, persons engaged in communicative sexuality will be concerned with more than achieving coitus. They will be sensitive to the responses of their partners. . . . Communicative sexual partners will not overwhelm each other with the barrage of their own desires. They will treat negative, bored, or angry responses, as a sign that the erotic ground needs to be either cleared or abandoned. Their concern with fostering the desire of the other must involve an ongoing state of alertness in interpreting her responses.

Just as a conversationalist's prime concern is for the mutuality of the discussion, a person engaged in communicative sexuality will be most concerned with the mutuality of desire. As such, both will put into practice a regard for their respondent that is guaranteed no place in the contractual language of rights, duties, and consent. . . .

CULTURAL PRESUMPTIONS

The special moral duties we have in certain intimate situations is supported by a conceptual relation between certain kinds of personal relationships and the expectation that it should be a communicative relation. Friendship is a case in point. It is a relation that is greatly underdetermined by what we usually include in our sets of rights and obligations. For the most part, rights and obligations disappear as terms by which friendship is guided. They are still there, to be called upon, in case the relationship breaks down, but insofar as the friendship is a friendship, it is concerned with fostering the quality of the interaction and not with standing on rights. . . .

But is there a similar conceptual relation between the kind of activity that a date is, and the sort of moral practice that it requires? My claim is that there is, and that this connection is easily established once we recognize the cultural presumption that dating is a gesture of friendship and regard. Traditionally, the decision to date indicates that two people have an initial attraction to each other, that they are disposed to like each other, and look forward to enjoying each other's company. . . .

As long as we are operating under the auspices of a dating relationship, it requires that we behave in the mode of friendship and trust. But if a date is more like a friendship than a business contract, then clearly respect for the dialectics of desire is incompatible with the sort of sexual pressure that is inclined to end in date rape. And clearly, also, a conquest mentality which exploits a situation of trust and respect for purely selfish ends is morally pernicious. . . . The proper end of friendship relations is mutual satisfaction. But the requirement of mutuality means that we must take a communicative approach to discovering the ends of the other, and this entails that we respect the dialectics of desire.

But now that we know what communicative sexuality is, and that it is morally required, and that it is the only feasible means to mutual sexual enjoyment, why not take this model as the norm of what is reasonable in sexual interaction. The evidence of sexologists strongly indicates that women whose partners are aggressively uncommunicative have little chance of experiencing sexual pleasure. . . .

Thus, where communicative sexuality does not occur, we lack the main ground for believing that the sex involved was consensual. . . . All that is needed then, in order to provide women with legal protection from "date rape" is to make both reckless indifference and willful ignorance a sufficient condition of *mens rea* and to make communicative sexuality the accepted norm of sex to which a reasonable woman would agree. Thus, the appeal to communicative sexuality as a norm for sexual encounters accomplishes two things. It brings the aggressive sex involved in "date rape" well within the realm of sexual assault, and it locates the guilt of date rapists in the failure to approach sexual relations on a communicative basis. . . .

CONCLUSION

In sum, using communicative sexuality as a model of normal sex has several advantages over the "aggressive-acquiescence" model of seduction. The new model ties the presumption that consensual sex takes place in the expectation of mutual desire much more closely to the facts about how that desire actually functions. Where communicative sex does not occur, this establishes a presumption that there was no consent. The importance of this presumption is that we are able, in criminal proceedings, to shift the burden of proof from the plaintiff, who on the contractual model must show that she resisted or was threatened, to the defendant who must then give some reason why she should consent after all. The communicative model of sexuality also enables us to give a different conceptual content to the concept of consent. It sees consent as something more like an ongoing cooperation than the one-shot agreement which we are inclined to see it as on the contractual model. Moreover, it does not matter, on the communicative model, whether a woman was sexually provocative, what her reputation is, what went on before the sex began. All that matters is the quality of communication with regard to the sex itself.

But most importantly, the communicative model of normal sexuality gives us a handle on a solution to the problem of date rape. If noncommunicative sexuality establishes a presumption of nonconsent, then where there are no overriding reasons for thinking that consent occurred, we have a criterion for a category of sexual assault that does not require evidence of physical violence or threat. If we are serious about date rape, then the next step is to take this criterion as objective grounds for establishing that a date rape has occurred. The proper legislation is the shortest route to establishing this criterion. . . .

Discussion Questions

1. Is Pineau's communicative model of sexuality the only desirable one? Are there times when it is reasonable for a man to believe that a woman has given her consent to sex even though she has not verbally communicated it? Support your answers using examples.
2. Are there times when women might really want to be sexually dominated by men? What about women who prefer not to discuss sex, or who prefer the man to take the initiative—much like patients who prefer to let their doctors make the decisions about their health care? Can there be "good sex" without communicative consensus? Support your answers. Discuss how Pineau might respond to these questions.
3. Catharine MacKinnon maintains that in a society where women are oppressed, communication alone is not sufficient to establish consent to sex. Do you agree? Are there times when a woman might consent out of a feeling of powerlessness, rather than a genuine desire for sexual intimacy? Support your answers using examples. Discuss how Pineau might respond to MacKinnon.
4. Discuss the implications of Pineau's definition of date rape on how such cases should be handled by the courts. Should policies on date rape be instituted on all campuses? Support your answer.
5. In her book *The Morning After: Sex, Fear, and Feminism on Campus* (1993), Katie Roiphe critiques Pineau's approach. Roiphe argues that the fuss over date rape, rather than empowering and liberating women, perpetuates the stereotype of them as vulnerable, naive, and in need of protection. The emphasis on communicative consensus, rather than sexually liberating women, has thrown a damper on relationships and created an atmosphere of suspicion between men and women. Has the current focus on date rape empowered women, or made them more fearful? How has it affected the men on your campus and the heterosexual dating scene? Use examples to illustrate your answer.

6. A woman at a fraternity party gets very drunk. She is dressed in a low-cut blouse and short skirt. A man who is an acquaintance comes over and has a few drinks with her. He then leads her to his room. After making out for a while, he feels she is responding to him and, although no words are actually exchanged, they have intercourse. He then leaves her in the room, asleep or passed out. Is this an example of rape? Did she "ask for it"? Should women who get drunk and/or dress provocatively be expected to accept the consequences of their choices? Is sexual intercourse one of these consequences? Does drinking excuse what happened? If the woman was not responsible for her actions, is it fair that the man be held responsible for his when he had also been drinking? Support your answers. Discuss how Pineau might respond to this scenario.

CASE STUDIES

1. PREMARITAL EDUCATION PROGRAMS

According to the 1999 U.S. Bureau of the Census, 1.8 million couples marry each year in the United States and 1 million get divorces. Another study of newlyweds found that 51 percent had serious doubts that their marriage would last.[55]

There is perhaps no other important aspect of our lives except marriage where we assume a person can be successful without any training, and where a person can get a license without inquiry into the applicant's qualifications. In contrast, trades people and professionals must have an education or extensive training in their field and must pass exams to demonstrate they are competent before being licensed. In addition, many professions now require continuing education credits to make sure they are up-to-date in their field. We take a test to demonstrate competency before we can get a driver's license. But anyone, as long as they are of legal age and opposite gender, can marry in the United States.

Studies show that people who participate in premarital education programs have a 15 to 20 percent lower divorce rate.[56] In 1998, Florida became the first state to pass legislation offering a reduced marriage license fee for those who participate in premarital education programs, which, among other things, help couples work on their communication skills. The Minnesota Premarital Education Bill also provides a $50 reduction on the marriage license fee for couples who take an approved premarital education program of at least twelve hours. The goal of the bill is to strengthen marriage and reduce the divorce rate in the state.

Discussion Questions

1. Should premarital education programs be mandatory for couples applying for marriage licenses? Discuss how a utilitarian and a rights ethicist might each respond to this question.
2. Is the high divorce rate in the United States a cause for concern? Is divorce immoral and, if so, under what circumstances. Are there cases where divorce is morally preferable to marriage? Discuss how the Vatican, Sara Ruddick and Alan Goldman might each answer these questions.

3. Some people argue that divorce laws are too easy and that couples, except in the case of domestic violence, should be required to go through marital counseling before being allowed to divorce. Do you agree? Support your answer.

---

2. GAYS IN THE MILITARY: "DON'T ASK, DON'T TELL"

The U.S. policy on homosexuals in the military is captured in the 1993 statement "Don't ask, don't tell."[57] Under this policy applicants will not be asked about their sexual orientation; they can, however, be discharged for homosexual conduct.[58]

As a protest against this policy, several colleges—including Massachusetts Institute of Technology and Yale University—have demanded that the Reserve Officer Training Corps (ROTC) be banned from their campuses until the military changes its policy. It is discriminatory, they argue, to have different standards for homosexuals and for heterosexuals. In response, in February 1996, Congress passed the ROTC Campus Access Act which cut off all Department of Defense funding to campuses that banned ROTC.[59]

The Young Americans Foundation, who actively worked to get the act passed by Congress, applauds this move. They claim that banning ROTC on campuses unfairly discriminates against ROTC cadets and denies students the right to participate in ROTC programs on their campuses.[60] The ban also discriminates against poorer students, because ROTC has historically assisted economically disadvantaged students in attending college.

Discussion Questions

1. Discuss the arguments for and against banning ROTC. What (and whose) rights are at stake? How might this conflict of rights be resolved? Was the ban the best way to oppose the "Don't ask, don't tell" policy? Discuss what you would have done if you were the president of MIT or Yale.
2. Is the freedom to be open about our sexual orientation essential for ensuring self-respect and a sense of dignity? Discuss how Ruse and Finnis might each respond to this question in the context of the military.
3. In *Meinhold v. U.S. Department of Defense* (1994) the Court upheld the U.S. Navy's action in discharging Keith Meinhold after he said on television, "Yes, I am gay." The court ruled that openly declaring one's homosexual orientation demonstrates "a concrete, fixed, or expressed desire to commit homosexual acts despite their being prohibited."[61] Opponents of the decision argued that it is irrational to assume that because people are open about their homosexuality they will engage in homosexual activities while in the military.[62] Do you agree? Why is it important in a moral debate that arguments be based on rational premises? Use the arguments in the *Meinhold* case to illustrate your answer.
4. Some people argue that allowing gays in the military infringes on the privacy rights of heterosexuals, especially when it comes to housing. Women are housed in separate quarters because they have a right not to have their bodies looked at in a sexual manner by men. Do heterosexual men and women, likewise, have a right not to be looked at in a sexual manner by homosexuals? Does a right to privacy necessarily preclude allowing gay people in the military?

5. Discrimination is morally justified if it is based on rational criteria. Is this the case with the ban on homosexuality in the military? Support your answer. Discuss how both Ruse and Finnis might respond to this question.
6. A 1998 article reports that male students at the U.S. Naval Academy have a strong prejudice against gays as well as women in the military.[63] They justify their exclusionary attitudes on the grounds that group loyalty is paramount in the military and that the presence of gays threatens this cohesion. Does this argument, based on social concerns, justify discrimination against gays in the military? Support your answer. Discuss how Finnis might respond to this question.

---

3. COLLEGE DORMS AND COHABITATION

Grace and Jeffrey met in their sophomore year and have been dating steadily for the past year and a half. At the end of their junior year they got engaged and set their wedding date for August following graduation. During the summer they both took jobs in the same seaside resort and rented a cottage together. When they returned for their senior year they applied to the housing and residential life office to share a double room. However, State University, like most colleges and universities, makes no provision for cohabitation in the undergraduate dorms unless the students are married to each other. Consequently, the school turned down their request. Because State University is in a rural setting and neither Grace nor Jeffrey owns a car, off-campus housing is not an option. Grace and Jeffrey filed a complaint against State University arguing that the housing and residential life office were discriminating against them, pointing out that the university provided housing for married students. They also noted that openly gay and lesbian couples were permitted to share dormitory rooms.

Discussion Questions

1. Should colleges and universities provide accommodation in dormitories for students who wish to cohabitate? Do students have a right to choose their roommate, regardless of gender? If so, what is the basis of that right? If not, why not?
2. Discuss the policy on cohabitation at your college and the justification for the policy.
3. Does it make a difference that Grace and Jeffrey are engaged and intend to marry after graduation? Why or why not?
4. Should the university prohibit, in cases where the couples are open about their sexual orientation and relationship, homosexual couples from sharing a dormitory room? If not, is it fair to deny the same opportunity to heterosexual couples? Support your answers. How would Nava and Dawidoff most likely respond to these questions?

---

4. FACULTY–STUDENT SEXUAL RELATIONSHIPS

Kevin, a junior at Keene State, is having a sexual relationship with his political science professor. As a result, the professor is brought up before the faculty senate disciplinary action committee. However, they had no power to bring disciplinary action against Professor Jones. Aware that this is not an isolated incident, the Keene State administration is considering a policy that will prohibit faculty–student sexual relationships. Many colleges and universities already have such bans.

Those in favor of a ban maintain that faculty–student sexual relationships are sexual harassment and wrong because of the power that the faculty have over students in terms of grading, advising, and their ability to hurt a student's reputation. Furthermore, they believe that the ban should continue even after the class ends because teachers continue to have a duty to students who might at some time need a letter of recommendation from the professor for a job or graduate school. Such a ban would make close friendship easier between faculty and students since everyone would know the limits of the relationship. Opponents of the ban point out that college students are adults and, like other adults, should have the right to make decisions about their own private lives.

Discussion Questions

1. Discuss the pros and cons of a policy prohibiting faculty–student sexual relationships. If you favor such a policy how would you word it? Would there be any exceptions? Would there be a "waiting period" before a faculty member could have a sexual relationship with a former student? How would the ban be enforced? Discuss how a utilitarian and a natural rights ethicist would most likely respond to such a policy.
2. Does your college have a policy prohibiting faculty–student sexual relationships? If so, get a copy of the policy and discuss its merits and weaknesses.
3. Should sexual relationships between employees and employers in the workplace also be prohibited, or at least discouraged? Why or why not?
4. Radical feminists argue that all, or at least most, sexual relationships between men and women, not just those between faculty and students, are coercive because of the unequal economic and social power of women in our society. Would it make a difference, morally, if it was Kevin rather than the professor who initiated the relationship? Is the gender of Professor Jones morally relevant? Is there a difference, morally, between relationships between male faculty and female students, and those between female or male faculty and male students? Support your answer.

---

5. THE RELUCTANT HUSBAND

Joe and Azra have been married fourteen years and have a nine-year-old daughter and a four-year-old son. For the past three years, following his wife's bout with breast cancer and her mastectomy, Joe, once a loving husband, has been uninterested in sex with her and has begun spending many late nights at work as a way of avoiding intimacy with his wife. However, Joe has never been sexually unfaithful because both he and Azra believe strongly that sexual fidelity is important in a marriage. They are also opposed to divorce, believing that couples, even in bad marriages, have a duty to stay together for the sake of the children.

As a result of her husband's neglect, Azra, who valued their moments of sexual intimacy, has become lonely and somewhat depressed. The children are also becoming anxious and wondering what is wrong even though their parents assure them that everything is fine.

One day Azra meets Roberto, an unmarried man, at her writer's group. Roberto and Azra share many common interests, including their love of writing. They strike up a friendship that becomes a great source of companionship and happiness to both of them. After several months Azra tells Roberto about her mastectomy and her strained relationship with her husband. Roberto loves Azra despite her physical scars and the relationship soon becomes sexually intimate.

Discussion Questions

1. Discuss who is being sexually unfaithful to whom in the above case.
2. Was Azra's sexual relationship with Roberto immoral or morally permissible in this case? Support your answer. Discuss how Wasserstrom most likely would answer this question.
3. Discuss whether a promise of sexual exclusivity in a marriage entails a promise of ongoing sexual involvement with each other. What about cases where one spouse is unable to have a sexual relationship because of illness or injury? What about cases where one spouse is uninterested in sex but still has perfunctory sexual relations with his or her spouse? Support your answers. How would a virtue ethicist and a natural law ethicist most likely answer these questions?
4. What is the extent of Roberto's culpability in this situation? Is it immoral for a single person to have sex with a married person and, if so, on what grounds?
5. Joe finds out about Azra's infidelity. In a fit of rage he strikes her, causing bruising on one arm. Was the violence justified in this situation? Support your answer.
6. Joe and Azra agree to seek the assistance of a marriage counselor who works at their church. You are the marriage counselor. How would you advise them?

---

6. GANG RAPE AND COLLEGE FRATERNITIES

Three UCLA undergraduates were arrested in June 1996 on charges for a rape that allegedly occurred during a Zeta Beta Tau fraternity retreat at a Palm Springs hotel.[64] The woman, a member of a UCLA sorority, claimed that she was gang-raped by the three men after she had gone to the hotel room late the previous night.

Although beer kegs at fraternity-sponsored events are a violation of the Interfraternity Council rules, there had been thirty to fifty kegs available that weekend. According to the alleged victim, she and the three men had been drinking alcohol and smoking marijuana in the room while playing a game called Master. During the game the three fraternity brothers began to undress her and then sexually assaulted her. She told them to stop but they ignored her protests. A fourth man watched while they raped her.

Following the rape, the distraught coed returned to her own room, where another student took her to a hospital emergency room. She filed charges with the police early the next morning. The police went to the hotel and arrested the three students. The students claimed in their defense that the sex was consensual. Their fraternity brothers stand by their story. The woman refused to speak to the press about the allegations, and her sorority requested that the media respect her desire for privacy.

Discussion Questions

1. Fraternity violence, including hazing, property destruction, and rape, has long been a problem. Some fraternities use women as bait to attract new members by having

"Little Sisters," attractive undergraduates who attend and serve as hostesses at fraternity parties. Little Sisters are "sexual assets," and fraternities often promise prospective recruits sexual access to these women. The titles *Big Brothers* and *Little Sisters* also reflect the subordinate status of women in fraternity life. The use of women as sexual objects and pawns in a game, some argue, encourage fraternities to see women as objects and rape as a sport.[65] Men are the predators, women their prey. Are fraternities breeding grounds for sexism and violence against women? Should the Little Sister programs be banned? Should fraternities themselves be banned? Support your answers. Discuss how Pineau might answer these questions.

2. Brotherhood and loyalty are highly valued in fraternities as part of male bonding. In the great majority of rape cases, members of a fraternity will refuse to "rat on" or testify against their brothers. They may even make up stories to protect their brothers. Discuss the morality of this type of loyalty. Does the fourth man who watched the rape have a moral obligation to come forth and testify against his fraternity brothers? Is he morally culpable for not trying to stop the rape? Support your answers.
3. Fraternity gang rapes most often occur as part of a game or ritual. During these rituals brothers may "circle dance," during which other drunk and partially naked brothers entertain each other and guests by chanting, mimicking sexual acts, expressing verbal hostility toward women and gay men, and engaging in sexual banter with each other. The selected victim is sometimes referred to as a "nympho," suggesting that she "asked for it." Following fraternity gang rapes, the brothers generally celebrate their masculinity, heterosexual prowess, and group loyalty by drinking heavily together. Discuss how these gang rape rituals and games support gender myths that perpetuate sexism and violence against women. Discuss what policy Pineau might suggest in response to these practices. Do you agree with this policy?
4. In fraternity gang rapes, men generally select women who are socially isolated, psychologically vulnerable, and either too intoxicated or too afraid to resist or complain to the authorities.[66] Discuss the extent, if any, to which our culture, including the college culture, socializes women to be victims of rape or to fear men. Do these norms also encourage or empower women who collaborate with men in the selection of victims? Discuss whether the refusal of the alleged victim and her sorority sisters to discuss the incident with the media perpetuates these norms, or empowers women. What suggestions might virtue ethicists such as Aristotle, Confucius, and Noddings offer for changing attitudes that contribute to rape on college campuses?
5. According to one survey, 26 percent of men who acknowledged committing sexual assault on a date say they were intoxicated at the time.[67] Women who are intoxicated are also less likely to successfully resist assault. According to some college policies such that at Antioch College, people who are intoxicated are unable to give consent to sex. Do you agree with this policy? Does this imply that men who rape while intoxicated are also not responsible for their actions? Discuss your answers in light of the UCLA case study.

---

7. PEDOPHILE PRIESTS

John J. Geoghan, a former Catholic priest accused of sexually molesting nearly 150 boys over three decades, was sentenced in 2002 to ten years in prison for groping a ten-year-old boy. The accusations against Geoghan triggered a sex scandal in the Roman Catholic

Church when it was discovered that the Boston archdiocese had received several complaints over the years against Geoghan. However, they chose to ignore the reports and instead kept transferring him to different parishes. Geoghan was not the only pedophile in the priesthood. Dozens of other priests, including the notorious Paul Shanley and Rev. Joseph Birmingham, were sexually molesting children—both boys and girls—while the archdiocese officials turned a blind eye.

At his request Geoghan was placed in protective custody in a cell block with other pedophiles at the Souza-Baranowski prison outside of Boston. In August 2003 he was beaten and strangled to death in his prison cell by Joseph L. Druce, 37, who was housed only two cells from Geoghan. Druce was serving a life sentence for the 1988 murder of a gay man. When questioned about the murder of Geoghan, Druce, who was molested himself as a child and has a phobia and hatred of homosexuals, stated that he considered Geoghan to be a "prize" and had been carefully planning the attack for over a month.

Discussion Questions

1. Are pedophiles sick or should they be held morally responsible for their actions? Support your answer.
2. Seventy-four percent of Catholics interviewed in a 2002 Gallup Poll thought that the Catholic Church was doing a bad job in dealing with the problem of sexual abuse committed by its priests.[68] How should the hierarchy of the Catholic Church have responded to reports of pedophilia in its midst? Do the archbishops have a duty of fidelity to protect offending priests from exposure? If so, how should this duty be weighed against potential harm to children?
3. Many people think that requiring celibacy is a factor in priest pedophilia and that priests should be allowed to get married. Is celibacy a virtue, as Kant and the Catholic Church claim, or is it a violation of natural law? Support your answer.
4. Most pedophiles claim that the children they victimize wanted or at least enjoyed the encounter. Is a sexual relationship between an adult and a child immoral, even when the child is not physically or emotionally coerced, or are children too young to give their consent? What about sexual relationships between two children or two younger teenagers?
5. Should Druce receive the death penalty for the murder of Geoghan? Support your answer, referring back to the arguments put forth for and against capital punishment in Chapter 5.
6. To what extent was the prison responsible for Geoghan's murder? Do prisons have a moral responsibility to provide additional protective custody to pedophiles? Support your answers.

---

8. JAMES DALE VERSUS THE BOY SCOUTS OF AMERICA

When the Boy Scouts of America (BSA) learned from a 1990 newspaper article that assistant scoutmaster James Dale was gay, they promptly expelled him from the organization. Dale, who had been a scout since childhood and had earned the rank of Eagle Scout, the highest honor given to a scout, decided to fight back. Dale claimed that his expulsion violated a New Jersey law barring sexual orientation-based discrimination in public places. The New Jersey high court agreed, ruling that the BSA was a "public accommodation" and therefore was bound by the antidiscrimination law.

The BSA appealed the decision. Banning gays, they argued, was necessary to maintaining the scout's express message of encouraging youths to lead a "morally straight" and "clean" life. The expression of this message, they further argued, was protected under their First Amendment governing free association and freedom of speech. The United States Supreme Court, in a June 28, 2000 ruling, agreed with the Boy Scouts, ruling that banning homosexuals was consistent with the BSA's right of free expression.

Discussion Questions

1. Discuss the morality of the Supreme Court ruling. Write two paragraphs stating what your ruling would have been if you had been (a) a Supreme Court justice and (b) a member of a specially appointed advisory ethics committee regarding the morality of expelling homosexuals in the Boy Scouts. Compare and contrast your rulings in the two cases. If your rulings differed, what course of action would a cultural relativist and a deontologist each advise you to take?
2. Many people prefer that gays and lesbians keep their identities secret. Do you believe that people who are homosexual, such as James Dale, should keep it to themselves? What about situations in which coming out would be detrimental to a career or would harm a person in other ways as happened in Dale's case. Support your answers. Discuss the question from the perspective of a virtue ethicist.
3. Imagine a scenario in which you learn from your college newspaper that your roommate's sexual orientation is different than you have previously been led to believe. What is your reaction? Discuss the effects of your discovery on concerns such as trust.
4. Imagine that you are Dale's friend and know that he is gay. However, Dale insists on passing as straight because he doesn't want to jeopardize his position in the Scouts. You encouraged Dale to come out because he is living a lie and also because you believe it is contributing to his depression. Also, you feel he would be a positive role model to other young gay men. Does Dale have a moral duty to come out? Discuss the moral issues involved in making a decision as to whether or not to out Dale.
5. Which is most morally compelling in this case: the duty of justice or the liberty right of freedom of speech? What other duties and rights are at stake in this case? Using both prima facie deontology and rights ethics, construct an argument analyzing the case.

CHAPTER 8

Freedom of Speech

When Seth Greenberg, coach of the California State University at Long Beach basketball team, walked into the visitors' locker room in the Pan American Center at New Mexico State University, he was confronted by the greaseboard message, "SETH, GET READY FOR AN ASS-KICKING, YOU JEW BASTARD." The outpouring of hate continued during the game, with some of the fans yelling obscenities and racial epithets such as "Take one of the niggers out." After the game, the visibly upset coach Greenberg told television interviewers that the slurs were "a sad commentary on life and . . . a sad commentary on this university." A few days later, New Mexico State University Executive Vice President Michael Conroy sent a letter to the president of Long Beach State, demanding an apology from Greenberg and castigating him for impugning the reputation of the university and the entire state of New Mexico.

Who was in the wrong? Should Greenberg have been more tolerant of the racial slurs? Should college campuses have speech codes that restrict hate speech, or should hate speech be protected under freedom of speech? The primary focus of this chapter is not whether we ought to engage in hate speech, but whether we are morally justified in restricting the hate speech of others.

WHAT IS "FREEDOM OF SPEECH"?

Freedom of speech is a type of liberty right. We have a right to express our opinions without interference from the government or other people. The primary value of freedom of speech, according to most liberals, is the promotion of truth and expression. John Stuart Mill, in his essay "On Liberty," argues that freedom of speech is at the heart of democracy. Expression of ideas cannot be prohibited simply because people find them offensive or disagreeable.

Not all forms of verbal expression, however, are considered speech. Words can also be used as weapons. Yelling "Fire!" in a crowded theater; "fighting words" intended to inflame someone into committing violent actions; and slanderous, false rumors intended to ruin the reputation and livelihood of someone are not generally protected under freedom of speech. Symbols such as swastikas, armbands, and burning crosses, on the other hand, are protected as freedom of expression in the United States, if they're used in a public place, like a rally or public schools.

Freedom of speech is generally distinguished from discriminatory conduct. Libertarians argue that, although discrimination is wrong, hate speech should be protected because we have a right to express our ideas. Others, such as Charles R. Lawrence III, reject this distinction, arguing that racist speech and discriminatory conduct are part of a totality that is incompatible with equality.

There are many gray areas in the freedom-of-speech debate. Should calls from telemarketers and spam on the Internet be protected speech? What about pornography, or expressions of anti-American sentiment in times of war, flag burning, or speech that condones terrorism? Should cults, or mainstream religion for that matter, be allowed to proselytize on college campuses? The community is even more deeply divided over the moral permissibility of hate speech. *Hate speech* is defined as "epithets conventionally understood to be insulting references to characteristics such as race, gender, nationality, ethnicity, religion, and sexual preference."[1] Should hate speech, which involves treating another person as a moral inferior, be censured?

LIMITATIONS ON FREEDOM OF SPEECH

Like most liberty rights, freedom of speech is not an absolute right but is limited by the rights of others to pursue their equal and similar interests. Freedom of speech does not mean that speech is immune from any sort of regulation, but that "no expression of opinion ought to be suppressed because the opinion itself is considered to be false, heretical, harmful, or subversive."[2]

Every society places limits on speech in order to prevent violence and civil disorder as well as to protect its citizens against fraud, threats, and harassment. Without some rules of order, discussions would degrade into chaos and frustration on the part of those who cannot get a word in edgewise. The question of how far these restrictions should extend is widely debated among ethicists and policy makers.

Liberals such as Jonathan Rauch argue that the government does not have a right to protect citizens from offensive speech; freedom of speech is meaningless if it does not include the right to offend. On the other hand, censorship can occur without legal sanctions. As both Alan M. Dershowitz and John Taylor point out in their articles on political correctness, the censorship of colleagues and political opinion can be just as oppressive. Catharine MacKinnon argues that pornography should be censored because it poses a direct threat to women's equality.

Censorship has traditionally rested on the assumption that people in authority possess the truth and are able to make final judgments about what is right and good. Democracy, with its presumption that the truth is determined by the majority, is not immune from this type of censorship. During other periods in history, censorship was based on the assumption that certain positions were self-evidently true. People who expressed doubts about these truths were labeled heretics, foolish, dangerous, or insane. The oppression of great thinkers like Galileo illustrates how censorship can hold back progress.

Censorship is a normal practice in some parts of the world, such as China, a country that emphasizes social order over individual freedom. The United Nations has sought to combat what it regards as human-rights violations in the international community. The Universal Declaration of Human Rights was adopted by the United Nations in 1948 following World War II as a "common standard of achievement for all peoples and all

 THE FIRST AMENDMENT TO THE UNITED STATES CONSTITUTION

Congress shall make no law respecting an establishment of religion, or prohibiting the free exercise thereof; or abridging the freedom of speech, or of the press; or the right of the people to peaceably assemble, and to petition the Government for a redress of grievances.

nations." Article 19 of the declaration states that "Everyone has the right to freedom of opinion and expression; this right includes freedom to hold opinions without interference and to seek, receive and impart information and ideas through any media and regardless of frontiers."

THE FIRST AMENDMENT TO THE U.S. CONSTITUTION

In the United States, freedom of speech is one of the most highly valued rights.[3] However, it was not until 1931 that the U.S. Supreme Court first recognized freedom of expression as a constitutional right based on the First Amendment.

Before 1789 the only right of free speech was the right to speak in the legislature. The patriots in the Amercian Revolution were no more willing to recognize freedom of speech than the British were and had no qualms about repressing speech that was not favorable to their cause. Indeed, during the American Revolution many loyalists, Quakers, and other political dissenters fled to Canada in fear of their lives.

Nor is there any indication that the Bill of Rights was intended to prevent censorship and regulation of speech. The original purpose of the First Amendment was to delegate the power to restrict freedom of speech to the states; although the federal government could not restrict speech, the state and municipal governments could.

Freedom of speech, in other words, was not regarded as an end in itself, but rather as a means of informing the citizenry and promoting democracy. The most valued type of speech was political speech. "A popular government, without popular information, or the means of acquiring it," wrote James Madison, "is but a Prologue to a Farce or a Tragedy; or perhaps both." Alexander Hamilton, one of the great defenders of free expression, likewise wrote, "The liberty of the press consists in the right to publish, with impunity, truth, with good motives, and for justifiable ends, whether it respects government, magistracy, or individuals." Utterances that abused this liberty (that is, were not made with concern for the truth, or with good motives, or with justifiable ends) could be censored.

Following the Civil War, the power of the states, including their power to regulate speech, was increasingly restricted. World War I gave rise to new concerns about speech that endangered national security. Supreme Court Justices Oliver Wendell Holmes and Louis D. Brandeis were two of the great champions of freedom of speech in the early twentieth century; they believed that freedom of speech was not an absolute value, however. In 1917 Holmes wrote the unanimous opinion of the Court on the constitutionality of the Congressional Espionage Act. It stated that speech is not protected by the First Amendment if it is "of such a nature as to create a clear and present danger" or if it

BOY SCOUTS OF AMERICA V. DALE (2000): EXCERPTS FROM THE MAJORITY OPINION

Chief Justice Rehnquist delivering the opinion of the court:

The forced inclusion of an unwanted person in a group infringes the group's freedom of expressive association if the presence of that person affects in a significant way the group's ability to advocate public or private viewpoints. . . .

The values the Boy Scouts seeks to instill are "based on" those listed in the Scout Oath and Law. The Boy Scouts explains that the Scout Oath and Law provide "a positive moral code for living; . . . The Boy Scouts asserts that homosexual conduct is inconsistent with the values embodied in the Scout Oath and Law, particularly with the values represented by the terms "morally straight" and "clean." . . .

The Boy Scouts asserts that it "teach[es] that homosexual conduct is not morally straight," and that it does "not want to promote homosexual conduct as a legitimate form of behavior." We accept the Boy Scouts assertion. . . .

As we give deference to an association's assertions regarding the nature of its expression, we must also give deference to an association's view of what would impair its expression. That is not to say that an expressive association can erect a shield against antidiscrimination laws simply by asserting that mere acceptance of a member from a particular group would impair its message. But here Dale, by his own admission, is one of a group of gay Scouts who have "become leaders in their community and are open and honest about their sexual orientation." Dale was the copresident of a gay and lesbian organization at college and remains a gay rights activist. Dale's presence in the Boy Scouts would, at the very least, force the organization to send a message, both to the youth members and the world, that the Boy Scouts accepts homosexual conduct as a legitimate form of behavior . . .

"will bring about the substantive evils that Congress has a right to protect." Fear of harm, however, is not sufficient to justify restrictions on freedom of speech. In his dissent in *Abrams v. the United States* (1919) Holmes defended freedom of speech on the grounds that society's ultimate good "is better reached by free trade of ideas—that the best test of truth is the power of the thought to get itself accepted in the competition of the marketplace." Holmes's concept of the free marketplace of ideas, adopted from J. S. Mill's work, has had a major impact on the Supreme Court's thinking about the role of freedom of speech in a democratic society. Supreme Court Justice Brandeis wrote in the 1927 *Whitney v. California decision:* "Fear of serious injury cannot alone justify suppression of free speech and assembly. Men feared witches and burned women. It is the function of speech to free men from the bondage of irrational fears."

In the early 1950s Senator Joseph McCarthy of Wisconsin reported on his investigation of Communist subversion in the United States. His sensationalist report was followed by a series of public hearings in which the careers of many prominent Americans were ruined on the most flimsy, hearsay evidence. Defenders of McCarthyism argued that Communist ideas should be repressed to "protect freedom" and democratic values. According to editor and journalist William F. Buckley Jr., for a free market of ideas to thrive, people out to defraud the public with a defective product (Communism) must be exposed.[4] Restrictions imposed by the 2001 Patriot Act have left some concerned about a repeat of McCarthyism where people, especially people of Arab descent, are fearful of expressing anti-American views for fear of recrimination or even arrest. In a November 2003 speech former Vice President Al Gore challenged the "Bush Administration's implicit assumption that we have to give up many of our traditional freedoms in order to be safe from terrorists."[5]

In 1954 McCarthy was formally censured by the Senate. The demise of McCarthyism was followed by a rapid expansion of the First Amendment. Speech other than political speech—such as sexual speech and pornography, entertainment, commercial speech, nonverbal expressions such as nude dancing and flag burning, and emotional utterances—came to be included under freedom of speech.

More recently, the limits of freedom of speech have been tested in attempts to restrict protesters outside abortion clinics. In the 1997 *Schenck v. Pro-Choice Network* decision, the Supreme Court ruled that abortion protesters may be kept outside a fifteen-foot "bubble zone" protecting those entering and leaving the clinics. In 2000 the United States Supreme Court in *Dale v. Boy Scouts of America* (BSA) ruled that the BSA's policy banning homosexuals from the Boy Scouts was protected under the First Amendment free association and freedom of speech.

FREEDOM OF SPEECH IN CYBERSPACE AND TELEMARKETING

Questions regarding freedom of speech have also arisen in the context of the electronic and telemarketing media. The Telecommunications Act of 1996 amended the Communication Act of 1934. One of the purposes of the large-scale revisions of the 1934 Act was to explicate and strengthen the marketplace of ideas and freedom of speech that have long been, and continue to be, debated in the communications industry. In UCLA's 1998 survey of American freshmen, 43.2 percent agreed that "material on the Internet should be regulated by the government."[6]

In its first ruling on freedom of speech in cyberspace, the United States Supreme Court in 1997 ruled against President Clinton's Communications Decency Act. The Court stated, "The interest in encouraging freedom of expression in a democratic society outweighs any theoretical but unproved benefit of censorship."

By the year 2002, more than 600 million people were Internet users, a thirtyfold increase since 1996.[7,8] Indeed, the 2002 UCLA American freshman survey found that college freshmen were spending more time surfing the web than studying. In addition to spending less time on their homework, high school students' grade average was continuing to climb.[9]

The rapid development of the Internet over the past decade has raised the question of whether the rules surrounding freedom of speech that apply to traditional forms of broadcast technology should apply to Internet speech. Internet technology is distinguished from traditional broadcast technology in that it is more democratic; anyone who has access to a computer can "broadcast" information to people around the world. Because the Internet is so accessible, it has been hailed as "the great equalizer," "the most participatory form of mass speech yet developed," and "the best advancement in democracy since universal suffrage."[10] In China, for example, the Internet gives people complete freedom to talk to people all over the world, a freedom previously denied by the Chinese government. On the other hand, as Chinese film director Zhang Xu points out, there is also a downside to the Internet. Web broadcast TV and radio may homogenize the thinking, interests, and tastes of people around the world.[11]

The ease of access to the Internet also means that children can gain access through home computers. And unlike radio and television, where the hours of broadcast can be regulated, the material on the Internet is available twenty-four hours a day. On the other hand, offensive material on the Internet, unlike that on radio and television, is usually preceded by a title and description of the contents so it is easier for people to avoid being caught by surprise by offensive material.

Reno v. American Civil Liberties Union (1997) was the first United States Supreme Court decision according First Amendment protection to the Internet. The decision also rejected the government's argument that the Internet should be treated like the broadcast industry. The court struck down the Communications Decency Act (CDA) restrictions, which required that online communication be reduced to a "safe for kids" level, stating that in the absence of any effective method for preventing minors from accessing offensive information on the Internet, the restriction of speech on the Internet would apply an undue restriction on adults' access to information.

In June 2000 a U.S. Appellate court supported an injunction by a lower court against the 1998 Child Online Protection Act, which had been passed by Congress following the *Reno v. American Civil Liberties Union* decision. The Appellate court stated that the Act fell short of meeting First Amendment standards of freedom of speech.

The growing number of child pornography sites on the Internet has led to a corresponding proliferation of cyberspace sleuths—adults posing as children in an attempt to expose cyberpedophiles who prey on children. Critics of these self-appointed citizen sleuths point out that their techniques, because they involve deception, border on entrapment. Others who embrace a more utilitarian the-ends-justify-the-means approach applaud the success of these citizen sleuths in catching sex offenders and closing down child pornography sites.

In his article at the end of this chapter on "The First Amendment in Cyberspace" Cass Sunstein addresses some of the moral issues involved in regulating freedom of speech on the Internet. Because the Internet is global, solutions to problems on the Internet will require international cooperation and regulation.

In 2003 the Federal Trade Commission created a Federal Do-Not-Call registry. The registry has been challenged as a violation of commercial telemarketer's freedom of speech. Supporters of the registry argue that unwanted phone calls from telemarketers are a violation of their privacy rights. Another issue is the proliferation of spam, which in 2003 accounted for 48 percent of Internet traffic. Should spam be protected as freedom of speech?[12]

PORNOGRAPHY

The debate over pornography in the past thirty years has moved from arguments over the morality of nonprocreative sex to arguments based on freedom of speech and concerns that pornography may contribute to gender discrimination, rape, and sexual harassment.

This shift is due in part to the proliferation of pornography on the market since the late 1970s. More recently, the use of the Internet to distribute pornography has allowed those inclined to view sexual violence to do so without having to leave the comfort of their homes.

Despite attempts to define pornography, reaching general agreement or establishing precise criteria has been difficult. Appeals to "offensiveness" run the risk of using subjective feelings or majority rule rather than rational criteria. Clearly, not everything that is offensive or repulsive—such as swear words, vomit, or dirty diapers—is harmful or should be legally restricted. Pornography is more about violence than offensiveness or even sexual pleasure. Indeed, the word *pornography* comes from the Greek term *porno* meaning "prostitution" or "female captives." Erotica, in contrast, involves a mutually pleasurable sexual expression; there is no clear conqueror or victim.[13] In 1986 the U.S. Attorney General's Commission on Pornography defined pornography as "the category of material featuring actual or unmistakably immolated or unmistakably threatened violence presented in sexually explicit fashion with a predominant focus on the sexually explicit violence." This definition of pornography is used in this chapter.

Canadians have been relatively consistent in their opposition to pornography. In 1978 the Canadian Standing Committee on Justice and Legal Affairs stated that "the clear and unquestionable danger of this type of material is that it reinforces some unhealthy tendencies in Canadian society [and] male-female stereotypes to the detriment of both sexes."[14]

In the United States, there have been mixed reactions to legal restrictions on pornography. In *Roth v. United States* (1957) the United States Supreme Court ruled that "obscene" material was not constitutionally protected speech. In 1970, however, the Commission on Obscenity and Pornography concluded that pornography was not harmful and recommended that all legal prohibitions against the sale of pornography between consenting adults be removed. In 1986 Attorney General Edwin Meese's Commission on Pornography recommended that pornography be censored, arguing that it contributes to sexual violence and antisocial attitudes.

One of the arguments used by Meese's opponents is the Aristotelian view that pornography acts as a catharsis or release for harmful, pent-up sexual urges.[15] There is no scientific evidence, however, that pornography has a cathartic effect. If anything, studies suggest that pornography provokes greater feelings of sexual aggression. Although the evidence is inconclusive, some studies have found viewing violent pornography to be positively correlated to acts of violence against women.[16]

Catharine MacKinnon argues that pornography is immoral because it poses a substantial threat to women's equality and, therefore, directly harms women. The moral issues surrounding censorship of pornography came into the limelight in 1983, when MacKinnon and Andrea Dworkin drafted an antipornography ordinance for the city of Minneapolis, the first of its kind in the United States. Feminists from around the country traveled to Minneapolis to testify in support of the legislation. Among its supporters was Linda Marchiano, also known as Linda Lovelace, star of *Deep Throat.* Although the ordinance was approved by the city council, it was vetoed by Mayor Donald Fraser.

MacKinnon's position is based on radical feminism which focuses on the oppressive patriarchal hierarchy and its harms to women, rather than autonomy and liberty rights.[17] Danny Scoccia in "Can Liberals Support a Ban on Violent Pornography?," in the *Ethics PowerWeb,* explores the questions from a liberal point of view. He questions the claim that

THE VILLAGE OF SKOKIE V. NATIONAL SOCIALIST PARTY OF AMERICA (1978): EXCERPTS FROM THE MAJORITY OPINION

Honorable Joseph M. Wosik, Judge, Supreme Court of Illinois, delivering the opinion of the court:

Plaintiff, the village of Skokie, filed a complaint in the circuit court of Cook County seeking to enjoin defendants, the National Socialist Party of America (the American Nazi Party) and 10 individuals as "officers and members" of the party, from engaging in certain activities while conducting a demonstration within the village. . . .

It is alleged in plaintiff's complaint that the "uniform of the National Socialist Party of America consists of the storm trooper uniform of the German Nazi Party embellished with the Nazi swastika"; that the plaintiff village has a population of about 70,000 persons of which approximately 40,500 persons are of "Jewish religion or Jewish ancestry" and of this latter number 5,000 to 7,000 are survivors of German concentration camps; that the defendant organization is "dedicated to the incitation of racial and religious hatred directed principally against individuals of Jewish faith or ancestry and non-Caucasians"; and that its members "have patterned their conduct, their uniform, their slogan and their tactics along the pattern of the German Nazi Party." . . .

In defining the constitutional rights of the parties who come before this court, we are, of course, bound by the pronouncements of the United States Supreme Court in its interpretation of the United States Constitution. . . .

"It is firmly settled that under our Constitution the public expression of ideas may not be prohibited merely because the ideas are themselves offensive to some of their hearers" (*Bachellar v. Maryland* (1970) . . . and it is entirely clear that the wearing of distinctive clothing can be symbolic expression of a thought or philosophy. The symbolic expression of thought falls within the free speech clause of the first amendment . . . and the plaintiff village has the heavy burden of justifying the imposition of a prior restraint upon defendants' right to freedom of speech . . .

The village of Skokie seeks to meet this burden by application of the "fighting words" doctrine first enunciated in *Chaplinsky v. New Hampshire* (1942). . . . That

there is sufficient evidence to establish the claim that violent pornography presents a "clear and present danger" to women. He further argues that a ban on violent pornography, such as that proposed by MacKinnon, would have a "chilling effect" on freedom of speech.

HATE SPEECH AS PROTECTED SPEECH

As an Orthodox Jew, radio and television commentator Dr. Laura Schlessinger believes that homosexuals violate scriptural teachings and that homosexual sex is deviant behavior. And she's not afraid to make her views known to her audiences. Her views have incensed many homosexuals who have dubbed Dr. Schlessinger "The Queen of Hate doctrine was designed to permit punishment of extremely hostile personal communication likely to cause immediate physical response, . . .

In *Cohen* the Supreme Court restated the description of fighting words as "those personally abusive epithets which, when addressed to the ordinary citizen, are, as a matter of common knowledge, inherently likely to provoke violent reaction." . . . Plaintiff urges, and the appellate court has held, that the exhibition of the Nazi symbol, the swastika, addresses to ordinary citizens a message which is tantamount to fighting words. . . .

The display of the swastika, as offensive to the principles of a free nation as the memories it recalls may be, is symbolic political speech intended to convey to the public the beliefs of those who display it. It does not, in our opinion, fall within the definition of "fighting words," and that doctrine cannot be used here to overcome the heavy presumption against the constitutional validity of a prior restraint.

Nor can we find that the swastika, while not representing fighting words, is nevertheless so offensive and peace threatening to the public that its display can be enjoined. We do not doubt that the sight of this symbol is abhorrent to the Jewish citizens of Skokie, and that the survivors of the Nazi persecutions, tormented by their recollections, may have strong feelings regarding its display. Yet it is entirely clear that this factor does not justify enjoining defendants' speech.

In summary, as we read the controlling Supreme Court opinions, use of the swastika is a symbolic form of free speech entitled to first amendment protections. Its display on uniforms or banners by those engaged in peaceful demonstrations cannot be totally precluded solely because that display may provoke a violent reaction by those who view it. . . .

We accordingly, albeit reluctantly, conclude that the display of the swastika cannot be enjoined under the fighting-words exception to free speech, nor can anticipation of a hostile audience justify the prior restraint. Furthermore, *Cohen* and *Erznoznik* direct the citizens of Skokie that it is their burden to avoid the offensive symbol if they can do so without unreasonable inconvenience. . . .

Radio." Rather than an adversary whose ideas are to be debated in the free marketplace of ideas, she is viewed as a hateful person, a homophobic and defamer, who should be censored and silenced. The San Francisco Board of Supervisors has officially warned Schlessinger about "making inaccurate statements about gays and lesbians that incite violence and hate."[18] One supervisor compared her speech with yelling fire in a crowded building. However, do her antihomosexual views amount to dangerous hate speech that should be suppressed? Where do we draw the line between hate speech and speech, though offensive and perhaps even inaccurate, that should be tolerated in the name of freedom of speech?

In the United States, there is currently a trend away from laws and codes that ban hate speech. In the 1978 Skokie trial the American Civil Liberties Union (ACLU) defended the right of neo-Nazis to march in Skokie, Illinois, a predominantly Jewish neighborhood in Chicago where a number of Holocaust survivors resided. The ACLU argued that the principle of justice required impartiality or neutrality in deciding whether a particular type of expression should be restricted or protected under freedom of speech. A particular type of expression should not be outlawed simply because some people find the content offensive.

In 1990 Robert A. Viktora and several other white teenagers fashioned a cross out of broken chair legs. They then held a Klan-type cross burning on the lawn of a black family who had just moved into a mostly white neighborhood in St. Paul, Minnesota. Viktora was convicted under the city's hate speech ordinance, which prohibited speech or expressions that were likely to provoke "anger, alarm or resentment in others on the basis of race, color, creed, religion or gender." The prohibition was meant to apply to "fighting words," which the Court had previously ruled in the 1942 *Chaplinsky v. New Hampshire* ruling were not protected speech.

In the 1992 *R.A.V. v. St. Paul* ruling, the first U.S. Supreme Court ruling on hate speech, the Court agreed with Viktora that the St. Paul law violated his freedom of speech. Whereas laws restricting fighting words were constitutional, hate speech laws were not, because they exercised "content-based discrimination"; that is, they were aimed at preventing specific types of hate crimes such as racism. This narrow definition of fighting words has recently been questioned in the context of hate speech.

At the time of the *R.A.V. v. St. Paul* ruling, there were laws against hate speech in forty-six states. The Court declared most of these laws unconstitutional on the grounds that the First Amendment prohibits "laws silencing speech on the basis of its content." In a related ruling, the Wisconsin Supreme Court struck down the state's hate crime law on the grounds that a government "cannot criminalize bigoted thought with which it disagrees."[19]

The neutrality concept is challenged by Charles Lawrence, whose article is included in this chapter. He argues that the social context in which hate speech takes place is morally relevant to whether it should be tolerated. Rather than defending abstract principles such as impartiality, we should be more concerned with defending the real victims.

Canada and Britain also reject the neutrality argument and have laws restricting specific types of hate speech. Recently, the European Union, worried that racists and hate mongers might slip across borders, proposed a rule that would punish the dissemination of racist speech and the public incitement to discrimination or racial hatred.[20] In the United States, Muslims and people of Arab descent are increasingly the victims of hate speech.

SPEECH CODES ON COLLEGE CAMPUSES

In 1992, when the Supreme Court ruling overturned the St. Paul hate speech ordinance, more than a hundred colleges and universities in the United States had speech codes that placed restrictions on some forms of speech, such as hate speech, fighting words, or speech that violates civility codes.[21] Although speech codes are unconstitutional, at least at public colleges, most colleges still censure or punish hate speech.

Campus speech codes evolved primarily out of the campus civil rights movement of the 1960s and 1970s and in response to the escalation of racist incidents on campuses in the 1980s. Sometimes dubbed the "politically correct" movement, these speech codes were intended to restrict offensive and bigoted forms of expression and encourage tolerance of diversity. The University of Wisconsin's speech code, for example, prohibited speech intended to "create a hostile learning environment" by demeaning another person's gender, race, sexual orientation, disability, creed, or ethnic background.

The politically correct movement was the most successful effort in American history to restrict hate speech. It was also one of the first times in history that students asked professors and administrators to place restrictions on offensive speech and conduct. Lawrence was a leader in the movement to curb hate speech on college campuses. His view was shaped by a 1981 boycott of a Harvard Law School course on "Race, Racism and American Law." A group of students demanded that the course be taught by a person of color. When the administration failed to accede to their demands, the students organized their own course. Lawrence was one of the guest lecturers. His ethical and legal expertise provided, in part, the sophisticated arguments needed to convince members of the college community, and in particular other professors, to support speech codes.

Have campus speech codes gone too far? For example, one college has banned thirty offensive words and phrases including "lady," "history," and "slaving over a hot stove."[22] The words "lady" and "gentleman," so the rationale goes, have "class implications," while the word "history" has sexist implications. "Slaving over a hot stove" is considered racist.

The American Civil Liberties Union (ACLU) opposes speech codes. Like John Stuart Mill, the ACLU maintains that more speech, not less, is the best response to offensive and hate speech. Restricting the speech of one group—whether they be Nazis, bigots, antiabortionists, or antiwar protestors—jeopardizes everyone because the laws can be used to silence those who wanted the laws to silence others. For example, under an anti-hate speech code that was in effect at the University of Michigan for eighteen months, twenty black students were charged by white students of offensive speech. The University of Michigan speech code was struck down as unconstitutional in 1987.

Supporters of campus hate speech codes point out that colleges are residential. Because people should be able to feel secure in their own homes, there should be greater protection against hate speech harassment on campuses than might be necessary in a public setting. A college community is also a voluntary association. Agreeing to attend a particular college entails agreeing to abide by a certain set of rules, such as nondrinking rules, restrictions on visiting hours, smoking in dormitories, and restraints on certain forms of offensive speech. Taylor and Dershowitz disagree that campus speech codes are morally justified. They argue that the politically correct movement, which spawned these speech codes, has done more harm than good.

THE PHILOSOPHERS ON FREEDOM OF SPEECH

Although Aristotle did not believe that democracy was the best form of government for ancient Greece, he recognized the importance of liberty and freedom of speech in a democracy. He also believed that expression of violent and hateful thoughts might be cathartic and purge violent urges. Plato disagreed with his esteemed pupil. In his *Republic,* Plato argues that literature, art, verse, and even music that is "impious" and "self-contradictory" should be censored if the republic is to be well ordered. According to Plato, though some of this might appear innocuous in small doses, "lawlessness easily creeps in unobserved . . . in the guise of a pastime, which seems so harmless." A lawless spirit will eventually gain a foothold until it affects all of our dealings, ending by "overthrowing the whole structure of public and private life." The current debate over the morality of pornography and violence in the media depends to a large extent on whether one accepts Aristotle's or Plato's position on the benefits of free expression.

Libertarians maintain that freedom of speech is a necessary condition for other freedoms and, therefore, is a special right. John Locke, whose philosophy had a major influence on the writers of the U. S. Constitution, valued freedom of speech primarily as a political value. He writes, "He who takes away the Freedom [of debate in the legislature], . . . in effect takes away freedom of debate in the legislature, and puts an end to the Government."[23]

Like Locke, Ayn Rand argues that the right of free speech is a fundamental right. A person, she writes, "has the right to express his ideas without danger of suppression, interference or punitive action by the government."[24] John Rawls also regards freedom of speech as "one of the basic liberties of citizens."[25]

John Stuart Mill is probably the most widely quoted—and misquoted—philosopher in the freedom of speech controversy. In his renowned essay "On Liberty," Mill argues that the state does not have the right to interfere with citizens' freedoms except where restriction is necessary to protect the person and property of others. According to him, the harm caused by censorship far outweighs any harm that might result from spreading vicious or false opinions. Truth, he notes, is often found not in the opinion of the status quo nor in the opinion of a dissenter, but in a combination of viewpoints. Therefore, freedom of speech and listening to opposing opinions, no matter how offensive they may be to some people, can allow a fuller truth to emerge.

According to the "marketplace of ideas" metaphor, ideas are like a product on the market. Just as the free market tends to deliver the best consumer goods, if everyone comes to the marketplace of ideas to express her or his opinions, the best opinions will eventually win out. Mill was not suggesting, however, that truth is like a product whose "goodness" is determined by how well it satisfies customer demand. When it comes to expression of ideas, Mill was well aware of the dangers of the tyranny of the majority over the minority. In a democracy, protection against the tyranny of government is not enough; "there needs to be protection also against the tyranny of the prevailing opinion and feeling, against the tendency of society to impose, by other means than civil penalties, its own ideas and practices as rules of conduct on those who dissent from them. . . ."[26] Although freedom of expression is a necessary condition for human progress, it is not a sufficient condition. We cannot assume that true opinions will triumph in a free marketplace of ideas. According to Mill, we must actively encourage the expression of minority viewpoints because of the tendency for the majority to coerce the minority into conforming. "It is the [opinion] which happens at the particular time and place to be in a minority . . . which, for the time being, represents the neglected interests, the side of human well-being which is in danger of obtaining less than its share."[27] Thus, rather than advocating passive tolerance of all forms of speech, Mill placed the highest value on the speech of those who have the least power in society.[28]

The concept of abstract rights that exist independently of a particular context is mostly a Western innovation. Buddhist virtue ethics, in contrast, is concerned with the development of a virtuous disposition, rather than abstract rights or legal prohibitions. Speech is one of the modes in which an evil disposition can be expressed. We have a moral obligation to avoid harsh, slanderous, and divisive speech and to cultivate speech that is truthful and trustworthy and that strengthens the bonds of friendship. Confucianism also emphasizes the virtue of sincerity in our speech and actions.

MORAL ISSUES

Social Order

One reason given for restrictions on the freedom of speech is to preserve public order. Members of a society must share certain core values if the society is to survive. For democracy to thrive, ideas that are subversive to democracy and freedom must be discouraged. Education, by its very nature, reinforces certain ideas over others. In the United States, for example, our schools routinely indoctrinate students in the virtues of democracy.

The Canadian argument for the legal regulation of pornography is based in part on the argument that the community has the right, as well as the duty, to enforce standards of public good. Pornography contributes to unhealthy attitudes and stereotypes and poses a threat to society because it weakens the principle of equality upon which society is founded. On the other hand, this criterion also risks the danger of the "tyranny of the majority"; here the majority in the community impose their values on the minority. Hence, most ethicists in the United States believe that social good, on its own, is not a sufficient justification for outlawing certain types of behavior.

Campus speech codes maintain social order by keeping college campuses from turning into a pandemonium where the advantage goes to those who can shout the loudest and intimidate the most through their persistent expressions of hatred. On the other hand, speech codes can also intimidate and stifle anyone who has an idea that might be offensive to others.

Restrictions on speech in the name of national social order can become overly restrictive. McCarthyism, for example, was carried out in the name of protecting freedom and democratic values against the "clear and present" danger of Communism. Some people fear that the Patriot Act may also place unnecessary restriction on freedom of speech in the name of maintaining social order.

Liberty Rights, Freedom of Speech, and Autonomy

Libertarians focus primarily on abstract liberty rights, whereas radical feminists focus on women's dignity. Radical feminists, such as MacKinnon, accuse libertarians of placing freedom of speech above women's well-being. They also argue that pornography restricts women's freedom of speech and, hence, cannot be defended on the grounds of freedom of speech. Furthermore, pornography has no value in the marketplace of ideas because it presents a distorted view of women and, hence, is based on a lie about women's sexuality. Other feminists, such as Katie Roiphe, disagree. They fear that repression of pornography may impede women's liberation by emphasizing women as victims.

Jonathan Rauch argues that we cannot get rid of racist speech without destroying genuine freedom of speech. We do not have a right to be protected from offensive information. Therefore, we have to learn to live with prejudice. Hate speech is just another idea in the free marketplace of ideas. Some libertarians also believe that allowing hate speech to be freely expressed will contribute to the search for truth. Even racial slurs and hate speech are a type of information because they provide the target with information about the views, including the political views, of the person making the slur. It is better to let false or harmful ideas compete in the marketplace, where they are likely to fade when exposed to the light of truth, than to let the government or others in authority determine what is true and false and what is beneficial and harmful. Restriction of speech, even hate speech, stifles the free exchange of ideas by putting people on guard against making any jokes or statements that might be offensive to others. For example, Alan Dershowitz tapes his lectures on rape statutes, because he fears that someone in the class might interpret what he said as a form of sexual harassment.[29]

Lawrence counters that censoring hate speech is not an infringement on our right to free speech. Hate speech, he maintains, is not really speech because it is not an expression of an idea but an attack, designed to end discussion. Shouting racial slurs is like a slap in the face. Most hate speech is not an invitation to engage in dialogue but an attempt to silence dialogue through intimidation. Proponents of restrictions on hate speech also point out that liberty rights exist to protect the autonomy of persons. One of the conditions of autonomy is rationality. For speech to be a moral right, the speaker must be coming from a position of reason and openness to judgment and rational dialogue. Therefore, hate speech is not morally protected because it oppresses autonomy rather than encouraging it.

Restrictions on telemarketers and spam are claimed to be a violation of the commercial market's liberty rights. Opponents of these practices counter that telemarketers and people that send unwanted spam over the Internet are interfering with people's right to privacy and, with the increasing volume of spam, their ability to pursue their legitimate interests without interference.

Civility and Respect for Human Dignity

According to deontologists, rights stem from duties. A moral right, therefore, must be consistent with a commitment to treating others with dignity and respect and with the creation of conditions under which people can speak openly to each other without feeling threatened. Civility involves recognizing and respecting the dignity of other persons. Disrespect, in contrast, creates an atmosphere of distrust.

Sexism violates Kant's categorical imperative, because it defines women in relation to men, thus treating women as a means only. Pornography dehumanizes women. Rather than being portrayed as autonomous moral beings, women are viewed as instruments of men. Canadians place the dignity of women above freedom of speech in prohibiting pornography; Americans place a higher value on freedom of speech.

Hate speech creates a hostile environment and a message of exclusion. Rather than subjecting themselves to disrespect and assaults on their dignity, members of groups targeted by hate speech are likely to avoid these environments. For example, the rash of racist incidents on campuses in the 1980s was accompanied by a decrease in the college enrollment of black men. Thus hate speech thwarts the aims of education and diversity. Rather than contributing to an open discussion of ideas, hate speech compromises the ability of those targeted by it to respond and to be equal participants in the debate.

Respect for human dignity requires that we as individuals refrain from using hate speech. On the other hand, it is not clear that this justifies legislating civility or placing restrictions on people's speech. There are many ways of treating people as moral inferiors—through ignoring or snubbing them, by interrupting them, or by avoiding them—all acts that few think should be legally banned. Furthermore, people cannot be forced into a subordinate position through hate speech in the way they can through segregation laws or discrimination in hiring. Although hate speech puts down its target as a moral inferior, it does not effect an actual change in the target's moral and legal status. Instead, hate speech essentially leaves the target's status unchanged.

Harm—Nonmaleficence

Most ethicists agree that speech that directly results in physical harm should be prohibited. For example, it is illegal for a prankster to cry "Fire" in a crowded theater. Fraudulent and libelous speech is also restricted because of the harm it causes.

Does the principle of nonmaleficence also justify restrictions on hate speech and pornography? Although Mill uses the harm principle as a limit on freedom of speech, he is not clear on what constitutes harm to others. Is psychological distress sufficiently harmful to override freedom of speech? Lawrence claims that society has a moral duty to protect people from harm. Hate speech harms people by creating unequal opportunity in educational and workplace environments, thus depriving its targets of their freedom of speech by intimidating them into silence.

It is not clear how pornography can directly harm women. Furthermore, even though it may be a "lower" pleasure, pornography *is* pleasurable to those who use it. Unlike domestic violence, where the direct harms to the victims clearly outweigh the pleasure of the perpetrators, the harms of pornography are not as clear. In order to justify censorship it must first be shown that the benefits of outlawing pornography would outweigh the harms of suppressing freedom of speech.

Feminists such as MacKinnon argue that pornography directly harms women by constructing a social environment that is harmful to women and interferes with women's ability to participate fully and equally in social and political life. Scoccia maintains that the possible, and as yet unproven, harms of pornography are not sufficient to justify censorship. Others, such as Aristotle, argue that pornography is actually beneficial because it is cathartic and provides pleasure for millions of consumers. However, there is no solid evidence for this position.

We may agree that pornography and hate speech is wrong because of the harm it imposes on its victims yet also believe that legal restrictions are not the best way to control it. Indeed, laws prohibiting hateful and abusive speech may harm the very groups they are meant to protect. One of the first people convicted under the 1976 British Race Relations Act was a black leader, who was sentenced to twelve months' imprisonment for verbally abusing the white community.[30]

The Slippery Slope

Some ethicists worry that restrictions on pornography, hate speech, and commercial speech in the case of Internet and telemarketing, may become the sled that starts us down the proverbial slippery slope toward more and more restrictions on our freedom of speech. Because it is so difficult to decide what is and what isn't acceptable speech, laws and speech codes prohibiting hate speech might be expanded to embrace speech that is offensive to the powers that be, as happened during the McCarthy period.

Pluralism and Tolerance

Pluralism and multiculturalism require tolerance of individual and group differences. Lawrence maintains that tolerance of hate speech can conflict with pluralism and the elimination of racism. As a moral ideal, pluralism ensures that the most vulnerable groups of people have a place in society. Much of the motivation behind the politically correct movement and campus speech codes is to ensure that people who are not from the mainstream culture will be able to express their views without fear of intimidation.

On the other hand, restricting the freedom of speech of groups whose ideas are at odds with our own is to lay a trap for ourselves as well. Rauch argues that intellectual pluralism requires free exchange of ideas, even those that may be offensive or erroneous.

Impartiality, Equal Justice, and Discrimination

MacKinnon argues that pornography is a form of sex discrimination because it requires the abuse and coercion of women for its manufacture. Pornography is not like hate speech, which does not involve the compliance of its victims for its expression. Pornography does not just convey the idea that women are subordinate; it actually subordinates and silences them by putting them in a position of inferiority. Therefore, according to MacKinnon, legal restrictions on pornography are essential if women are to achieve full equality.

According to Lawrence, tolerance of hate speech conflicts with the elimination of discrimination and racism. He argues that the 1954 United States Supreme Court *Brown v. Board of Education* decision, which outlawed school segregation, was really about freedom of speech. Segregated schools are wrong because they communicate a message of unworthiness to black children. Similarly, prohibiting hate speech is necessary in order to ensure equal protection. Laws against racist speech would reaffirm the conviction that all people are equal. Some feminists also make the same argument: Permitting sexist speech is at odds with the more important goal of egalitarianism.

Those who feel that restrictions on freedom of speech should be content neutral base their argument on the principle of impartiality. Whereas the principle of impartiality in justice may be appropriate in an egalitarian society, in a society where racism and sexism are embedded in the very structure, it only serves to perpetuate inequalities.

Some Marxists argue that freedom of speech in a nonegalitarian society such as the United States can actually perpetuate injustice by empowering the status quo while repressing dissenters.[31] This is happening to some extent in the politically correct movement which, while extolling freedom of speech, oppresses, either through campus codes or through social disapproval, those who do not support the correct ideology.

CONCLUSION

One of the key issues is whether we should restrict pornography and hate speech, as the Canadians do, or continue to have no legal restrictions on it. Should freedom of speech outweigh the welfare rights of others, or does society have a moral obligation to protect people from assaults on their dignity? Regardless of whether we accept the libertarian position that pornography and hate speech should not be legally restricted, a libertarian public policy does not entail the claim that pornography and hate speech are morally acceptable or that we have a right to harm others. Hate speech and violent pornography are clearly inconsistent with respect for persons. We ought not to engage in them. As moral agents we also have a moral obligation to respond to hate speech. Alexander Hamilton once said that the greatest danger to freedom was not in restrictions on freedom of expression but an apathetic citizenry. Freedom of speech is not merely a negative concept of freedom from constraints on speech. Part of freedom of speech is a duty to speak out against hatred, sexism, and bigotry.

JOHN STUART MILL

On Liberty

John Stuart Mill, prominent English utilitarian and defender of liberty rights, wrote *On Liberty* in 1859. In it he argues that while utility is the ultimate appeal on ethical questions, utility must be grounded in the freedom or liberty of people to pursue their own good in their own way, as long as they are not attempting to deprive others of their liberty rights. In particular, freedom of speech and expression are essential in a democracy if we want to avoid the "tyranny of the majority" and intellectual stagnation.

Critical Reading Questions

1. What does Mill mean by the "struggle between liberty and authority?
2. What does Mill mean by "tyranny of the majority?" Why do we need protection against the tyranny of the majority?
3. What is the "appropriate region of human liberty"?
4. Why is liberty of thought essential if we are to be free?
5. Why is it an evil, according to Mill, to silence the expression of an opinion?
6. What is the assumption of those who desire to suppress a particular opinion?
7. Why is liberty of contradicting other's opinions important?
8. How, according to Mill, do wise men acquire wisdom?
9. What happens when a government believes it has a duty to uphold certain beliefs and oppose others to protect the interests of society? How does Mill use Socrates to illustrate his answer?
10. How do we treat dissidents like Socrates today?
11. What is the danger of maintaining "all prevailing opinions outwardly undisturbed"?
12. Why is it so important to be open to challenges even to views that we assume to be true or that are accepted doctrines?
13. What is one of the principle reasons why diversity of opinions should be encouraged?
14. Why is it important, in a democracy, for opposing parties to hold divergent views?
15. Why does Mill oppose restricting freedom of speech even when it is intemperate and presented in a nasty and offensive manner?

INTRODUCTORY

. . . Civil, or Social Liberty: the nature and limits of the power which can be legitimately exercised by society over the individual. . . .

The struggle between Liberty and Authority is the most conspicuous feature in the portions of history with which we are earliest familiar, particularly in that of Greece, Rome, and England. But in old times this contest was between subjects, or some classes of subjects, and the Government. By liberty, was meant protection against the tyranny of the political rulers. . . . In time, however, a democratic republic came to occupy a large portion of the earth's surface,

On Liberty (London: Longman, Roberts & Green, 1869).

and made itself felt as one of the most powerful members of the community of nations; and elective and responsible government became subject to the observations and criticism which wait upon a great existing fact. It was now perceived that such phrases as "self-government," and "the power of the people over themselves," do not express the true state of the case. The "people" who exercise the power are not always the same people with those over whom it is exercised; and the "self-government" spoken of is not the government of each by himself, but of each by all the rest. The will of the people, moreover, practically means the will of the most numerous or the most active *part* of the people; the majority, or those who succeed in making themselves accepted as the majority; the people, consequently *may* desire to oppress a part of their number; and precautions are as much needed against this as against any other abuse of power. . . . in political speculations the tyranny of the majority" is now generally included among the evils against which society requires to be on its guard. . . .

Protection, therefore, against the tyranny of the magistrate is not enough: there needs protection also against the tyranny of the prevailing opinion and feeling; against the tendency of society to impose, by other means than civil penalties, its own ideas and practices as rules of conduct on those who dissent from them; . . .

There is a sphere of action in which society, as distinguished from the individual, has, if any, only an indirect interest; comprehending all that portion of a person's life and conduct which affects only himself, or if it also affects others, only with their free, voluntary, and undeceived consent and participation. . . . This, is the appropriate region of human liberty. It compromises, first, the inward domain of consciousness; demanding liberty of conscience in the most comprehensive sense; liberty of thought and feeling; absolute freedom of opinion and sentiment on all subjects, practical or speculative, scientific, moral, or theological. The liberty of expressing and publishing opinions may seem to fall under a different principle, since it belongs to that part of the conduct of an individual which concerns other people; but, being almost of as much importance as the liberty of thought itself, and resting in great part on the same reasons, is practically inseparable from it. Secondly, the principle requires liberty of tastes and pursuits; of framing the plan of our life to suit our own character; of doing as we like, subject to such consequences as may follow: without impediment from our fellow-creatures, so long as what we do does not harm them, even though they should think our conduct foolish, perverse, or wrong. Thirdly, from this liberty of each individual, follows the liberty, within the same limits, of combination among individuals; freedom to unite, for any purpose not involving harm to others: the persons combining being supposed to be of full age, and not forced or deceived.

No society in which these liberties are not, on the whole, respected, is free, whatever may be its form of government; and none is completely free in which they do not exist absolute and unqualified. The only freedom which deserves the name, is that of pursuing our own good in our own way, so long as we do not attempt to deprive others of theirs, or impede their efforts to obtain it. . . .

OF THE LIBERTY OF THOUGHT AND DISCUSSION

. . . The best government has no more title to [control of expression by government] than the worst. It is as noxious, or more noxious, when exerted in accordance with public opinion, than when in opposition to it. If all mankind minus one were of one opinion, and only one person were of the contrary opinion, mankind would be no more justified in silencing that one person, than he, if he had the power, would be justified in silencing mankind. Were an opinion a personal possession of no value except to the owner; if to be obstructed in the enjoyment of it were simply a private injury, it would make some difference whether the injury was inflicted only on a few persons or on many. But the peculiar evil of silencing the expression of an opinion is, that it is robbing the human race; posterity as well as the existing generation; those who dissent from the opinion, still more than those who hold it. If the opinion is right, they are deprived of the opportunity of exchanging error for truth: if wrong, they lose, what is almost as great a benefit, the clearer perception and livelier impression of truth, produced by its collision with error.

It is necessary to consider separately these two hypotheses, each of which has a distinct branch of the argument corresponding to it. We can never be sure that the opinion we are endeavouring to stifle is a false opinion; and if we were sure, stifling it would be an evil still.

First: the opinion which it is attempted to suppress by authority may possibly be true. Those who desire to suppress it, of course deny its truth; but they are not infallible. They have no authority to decide the question for all mankind, and exclude every other person from the means of judging. To refuse a hearing to an opinion, because they are sure that it is false, is to assume that *their* certainty is the same thing as *absolute* certainty. All silencing of discussion is an assumption of infallibility. Its condemnation may be allowed to rest on this common argument, not the worse for being common. . . . There is no such thing as absolute certainty, but there is assurance sufficient for the purposes of human life. We may, and must, assume our opinion to be true for the guidance of our own conduct: and it is assuming no more when we forbid bad men to pervert society by the propagation of opinions which we regard as false and pernicious. . . . There is the greatest difference between presuming an opinion to be true, because, with every opportunity for contesting it, it has not been refuted, and assuming its truth for the purpose of not permitting its refutation. Complete liberty of contradicting and disproving our opinion is the very condition which justifies us in assuming its truth for purposes of action; and on no other terms can a being with human faculties have any rational assurance of being right. . . . Wrong opinions and practices gradually yield to fact and argument; but facts and arguments, to produce any effect on the mind, must be brought before it. Very few facts are able to tell their own story, without comments to bring out their meaning. The whole strength and value, then, of human judgment, depending on the one property, that it can be set right when it is wrong, reliance can be placed on it only when the means of setting it right are kept constantly at hand. In the case of any person whose judgment is really deserving of confidence, how has it become so? Because he has kept his mind open to criticism of his opinions and conduct. Because it has been his practice to listen to all that could be said against him . . . No wise man ever acquired his wisdom in any mode but this; nor is it in the nature of human intellect to become wise in any other manner. The steady habit of correcting and completing his own opinion by collating it with those of others, so far from causing doubt and hesitation in carrying it into practice, is the only stable foundation for a just reliance on it: . . .

In the present age—which has been described as "destitute of faith, but terrified at scepticism"—in which people feel sure, not so much that their opinions are true, as that they should not know what to do without them—the claims of an opinion to be protected from public attack are rested not so much on its truth, as on its importance to society. There are, it is alleged, certain beliefs so useful, not to say indispensable, to well-being that it is as much the duty of governments to uphold those beliefs, as to protect any other of the interests of society. In a case of such necessity, and so directly in the line of their duty, something less than infallibility may, it is maintained, warrant, and even bind, governments to act on their own opinion, confirmed by the general opinion of mankind. It is also often argued, and still oftener thought, that none but bad men would desire to weaken these salutary beliefs; and there can be nothing wrong, it is thought, in restraining bad men, and prohibiting what only such men would wish to practise. . . .

Mankind can hardly be too often reminded, that there was once a man named Socrates, between whom and the legal authorities and public opinion of his time there took place a memorable collision. . . . This acknowledged master of all the eminent thinkers who have since lived—whose fame, still growing after more than two thousand years, all but outweighs the whole remainder of the names which make his native city illustrious—was put to death by his countrymen, after a judicial conviction, for impiety and immorality. Impiety, in denying the gods recognised by the State; indeed his accuser asserted (see the "Apologia") that he believed in no gods at all. Immorality, in being, by his doctrines and instructions, a "corruptor of youth." Of these charges the tribunal, there is every ground for believing, honestly found him guilty, and condemned the man who probably of all then born had deserved best of mankind to be put to death as a criminal. . . . Men did not merely mistake their benefactor; they mistook him for the exact contrary of what he was, and treated him as that prodigy of impiety which they themselves are now held to be for their treatment of him. The feelings with which mankind now regard these lamentable transactions, especially the later of the two, render them extremely unjust in their judgment of the unhappy actors. These were, to all appearance, not bad men—not worse than men commonly are, but rather the contrary; men who possessed in a full, or somewhat more than a full measure, the religious, moral, and patriotic feelings of their time and people: the very kind of men who, in all times, our own included, have every chance of passing through life blameless and respected. . . . .

It will be said, that we do not now put to death the introducers of new opinions: we are not like our fathers who slew the prophets, we even build sepulchres to them. It is true we no longer put heretics to death; and the amount of penal infliction which modern feeling would probably tolerate, even against the most obnoxious opinions, is not sufficient to extirpate them. But let us not flatter ourselves that we are yet free from the stain even of legal persecution. Penalties for opinion, or at least for its expression, still exist by law; . . .

But though we do not now inflict so much evil on those who think differently from us as it was formerly our custom to do, it may be that we do ourselves as much evil as ever by our treatment of them. Socrates was put to death, but Socratic philosophy rose like the sun in heaven, and spread its illumination over the whole intellectual firmament. Christians were . . . cast to the lions, but the Christian church grew up a stately and spreading tree, overtopping the older and less vigorous growths, and stifling them by its shade. Our merely social intolerance kills no one, roots out no opinions, but induces men to disguise them, or to abstain from any active effort for their diffusion. With us, heretical opinions do not perceptibly gain, or even lose, ground in each decade or generation; they never blaze out far and wide, but continue to smoulder in the narrow circles of thinking and studious persons among whom they originate, without ever lighting up the general affairs of mankind with either a true or a deceptive light. And thus is kept up a state of things very satisfactory to some minds, because, without the unpleasant process of fining or imprisoning anybody, it maintains all prevailing opinions outwardly undisturbed. . . . But the price paid for this sort of intellectual pacification is the sacrifice of the entire moral courage of the human mind. A state of things in which a large portion of the most active and inquiring intellects find it advisable to keep the general principles and grounds of their convictions within their own breasts, and attempt, in what they address to the public, to fit as much as they can of their own conclusions to premises which they have internally renounced, cannot send forth the open, fearless characters, and logical, consistent intellects who once adorned the thinking world. . . . Those who avoid this alternative, do so by narrowing their thoughts and interest to things which can be spoken of without venturing within the region of principles, that is, to small practical matters, which would come right of themselves, if but the minds of mankind were strengthened and enlarged, and which will never be made effectually right until then: while that which would strengthen and enlarge men's minds, free and daring speculation on the highest subjects, is abandoned. . . .

Let us now pass to the second division of the argument, and dismissing the supposition that any of the received opinions may be false, let us assume them to be true, and examine into the worth of the manner in which they are likely to be held, when their truth is not freely and openly canvassed. However unwillingly a person who has a strong opinion may admit the possibility that his opinion may be false, he ought to be moved by the consideration that, however true it may be, if it is not fully, frequently, and fearlessly discussed, it will be held as a dead dogma, not a living truth.

There is a class of persons (happily not quite so numerous as formerly) who think it enough if a person assents undoubtingly to what they think true, though he has no knowledge whatever of the grounds of the opinion, and could not make a tenable defence of it against the most superficial objections. Such persons, if they can once get their creed taught from authority, naturally think that no good, and some harm, comes of its being allowed to be questioned. Where their influence prevails, they make it nearly impossible for the received opinion to be rejected wisely and considerately, though it may still be rejected rashly and ignorantly; for to shut out discussion entirely is seldom possible, and when it once gets in, beliefs not grounded on conviction are apt to give way before the slightest semblance of an argument. Waiving, however, this possibility—assuming that the true opinion abides in the mind, but abides as a prejudice, a belief independent of, and proof against, argument—this is not the way in which truth ought to be held by a rational being. This is not knowing the truth. Truth, thus held, is but one superstition the more, accidentally clinging to the words which enunciate a truth. . . .

To abate the force of these considerations, an enemy of free discussion may be supposed to say, that there is no necessity for mankind in general to know and understand all that can be said against or for their opinions by philosophers and theologians. That it is not needful for common men to be able to expose all the misstatements or fallacies of an ingenious opponent. That it is enough if there is always somebody capable of answering them, so that nothing likely to mislead uninstructed persons remains unrefuted. That simple minds, having been taught the obvious grounds of the truths inculcated on them, may trust to authority for the rest, and being aware that they have neither knowledge nor talent to resolve every difficulty which can be raised, may repose in the assurance that all those which have been raised have been or can be answered, by those who are specially trained to the task.

Conceding to this view of the subject the utmost that can be claimed for it by those most easily satisfied with the amount of understanding of truth which ought to accompany the belief of it; even so, the argument for free discussion is no way weakened. For even this doctrine acknowledges that mankind ought to have a rational assurance that all objections have been satisfactorily answered; and how are they to be answered if that which requires to be answered is not spoken? or how can the answer be known to be satisfactory, if the objectors have no opportunity of showing that it is unsatisfactory?. . . .

If, however, the mischievous operation of the absence of free discussion, when the received opinions are true, were confined to leaving men ignorant of the grounds of those opinions, it might be thought that this, if an intellectual, is no moral evil, and does not affect the worth of the opinions, regarded in their influence on the character. The fact, however, is, that not only the grounds of the opinion are forgotten in the absence of discussion, but too often the meaning of the opinion itself. The words which convey it cease to suggest ideas, or suggest only a small portion of those they were originally employed to communicate. Instead of a vivid conception and a living belief, there remain only a few phrases retained by rote; or, if any part, the shell and husk only of the meaning is retained, the finer essence being lost. The great chapter in human history which this fact occupies and fills, cannot be too earnestly studied and meditated on.

It is illustrated in the experience of almost all ethical doctrines and religious creeds. They are all full of meaning and vitality to those who originate them, and to the direct disciples of the originators. Their meaning continues to be felt in undiminished strength, and is perhaps brought out into even fuller consciousness, so long as the struggle lasts to give the doctrine or creed an ascendancy over other creeds. At last it either prevails, and becomes the general opinion, or its progress stops; it keeps possession of the ground it has gained, but ceases to spread further. When either of these results has become apparent, controversy on the subject flags, and gradually dies away. The doctrine has taken its place, if not as a received opinion, as one of the admitted sects or divisions of opinion: those who hold it have generally inherited, not adopted it; and conversion from one of these doctrines to another, being now an exceptional fact, occupies little place in the thoughts of their professors. Instead of being, as at first, constantly on the alert either to defend themselves against the world, or to bring the world over to them, they have subsided into acquiescence, and neither listen, when they can help it, to arguments against their creed, nor trouble dissentients (if there be such) with arguments in its favour. From this time may usually be dated the decline in the living power of the doctrine. . . . Then are seen the cases, so frequent in this age of the world as almost to form the majority, in which the creed remains as it were outside the mind, incrusting and petrifying it against all other influences addressed to the higher parts of our nature; manifesting its power by not suffering any fresh and living conviction to get in, but itself doing nothing for the mind or heart, except standing sentinel over them to keep them vacant. . . .

The fatal tendency of mankind to leave off thinking about a thing when it is no longer doubtful, is the cause of half their errors. A contemporary author has well spoken of "the deep slumber of a decided opinion." . . .

It still remains to speak of one of the principal causes which make diversity of opinion advantageous, and will continue to do so until mankind shall have entered a stage of intellectual advancement which at present seems at an incalculable distance. We have hitherto considered only two possibilities: that the received opinion may be false, and some other opinion, consequently, true; or that, the received opinion being true, a conflict with the opposite error is essential to a clear apprehension and deep feeling of its truth. But there is a commoner case than either of these; when the conflicting doctrines, instead of being one true and the other false, share the truth between them; and the nonconforming opinion is needed to supply the remainder of the truth, of which the received doctrine embodies only a part. Popular opinions, on subjects not palpable to sense, are often true, but seldom or never the whole truth. They are a part of the truth; sometimes a greater, sometimes a smaller part, but exaggerated, distorted, and disjointed from the truths by which they ought to be accompanied and limited. Heretical opinions, on the other hand, are generally some of these suppressed and neglected truths, bursting the bonds which kept them down, and either seeking reconciliation with the truth contained in the common opinion, or fronting it as enemies, and setting themselves up, with similar exclusiveness, as the whole truth. The latter case is hitherto the most frequent, as, in the human mind, one-sidedness has always been the rule, and many-sidedness the exception. Hence, even in revolutions of opinion, one part of the truth usually sets while another rises. Even progress, which ought to superadd, for the most part only substitutes, one partial and incomplete truth for another; . . .

In politics, again, it is almost a commonplace, that a party of order or stability, and a party of progress or reform, are both necessary elements of a healthy state of political life; until the one or the other shall have so enlarged its mental grasp as to be a party equally of order and of progress, knowing and distinguishing what is fit to be preserved from what ought to be swept away. Each of these modes of thinking derives its utility from the deficiencies of the other; but it is in a great measure the opposition of the other that keeps each within the limits of reason and sanity. Unless opinions favourable to democracy and to aristocracy, to property and to equality, to co-operation and to competition, to luxury and to abstinence, to sociality and individuality, to liberty and discipline, and all the other standing antagonisms of practical life, are expressed with equal freedom, and enforced and defended with equal talent and energy, there is no chance of both elements obtaining their due; . . .

We have now recognised the necessity to the mental well-being of mankind (on which all their other well-being depends) of freedom of opinion, and freedom of the expression of opinion, on four distinct grounds; which we will now briefly recapitulate.

First, if any opinion is compelled to silence, that opinion may, for aught we can certainly know, be true. To deny this is to assume our own infallibility.

Secondly, though the silenced opinion be an error, it may, and very commonly does, contain a portion of truth; and since the general or prevailing opinion on any subject is rarely or never the whole truth, it is only by the collision of adverse opinions that the remainder of the truth has any chance of being supplied.

Thirdly, even if the received opinion be not only true, but the whole truth, unless it is suffered to be, and actually is, vigorously and earnestly contested, it will, by most of those who receive it, be held in the manner of a prejudice, with little comprehension or feeling of its rational grounds. And not only this, but, fourthly, the meaning of the doctrine itself will be in danger of being lost, or enfeebled, and deprived of its vital effect on the character and conduct: the dogma becoming a mere formal profession, inefficacious for good, but cumbering the ground, and preventing the growth of any real and heartfelt conviction, from reason or personal experience.

Before quitting the subject of freedom of opinion, it is fit to take some notice of those who say that the free expression of all opinions should be permitted, on condition that the manner be temperate, and do not pass the bounds of fair discussion. Much might be said on the impossibility of fixing where these supposed bounds are to be placed; for if the test be offence to those whose opinions are attacked, I think experience testifies that this offence is given whenever the attack is telling and powerful, and that every opponent who pushes them hard, and whom they find it difficult to answer, appears to them, if he shows any strong feeling on the subject, an intemperate opponent. But this, though an important consideration in a practical point of view, merges in a more fundamental objection. Undoubtedly the manner of asserting an opinion, even though it be a true one, may be very objectionable, and may justly incur severe censure. But the principal offences of the kind are such as it is mostly impossible, unless by accidental self-betrayal, to bring home to conviction. The gravest of them is, to argue sophisitically, to suppress facts or arguments, to misstate the elements of the case, or misrepresent the opposite opinion. But all this even to the most aggravated degree, is so continually done in perfect good faith, by persons who are not considered, and in many other respects may not deserve to be considered, ignorant or incompetent, that it is rarely possible, on adequate grounds, conscientiously to stamp the misrepresentation as morally culpable; and still less could law presume to interfere with this kind of controversial misconduct. With regard to what is commonly meant by intemperate discussion, namely invective, sarcasm, personality, and the like, the denunciation of these weapons would deserve more sympathy if it were ever proposed to interdict them equally to both sides; but it is only desired to restrain the employment of them against the prevailing opinion: against the unprevailing they may not only be used without general disapproval, but will be likely to obtain for him who uses them the praise of honest zeal and righteous indignation. Yet whatever mischief arises from their use is greatest when they are employed against the comparatively defenceless; and whatever unfair advantage can be derived by any opinion from this mode of asserting it, accrues almost exclusively to received opinions. The worst offence of this kind which can be committed by a polemic is to stigmatise those who hold the contrary opinion as bad and immoral men. To calumny of this sort, those who hold any unpopular opinion are peculiarly exposed, because they are in general few and uninfluential, and nobody but themselves feels much interested in seeing justice done them; but this weapon is, from the nature of the case, denied to those who attack a prevailing opinion: they can neither use it with safety to themselves, nor, if they could, would it do anything but recoil on their own cause. In general, opinions contrary to those commonly received can only obtain a hearing by studied moderation of language, and the most cautious avoidance of unnecessary offence, from which they hardly ever deviate even in a slight degree without losing ground: while unmeasured vituperation employed on the side of the prevailing opinion really does deter people from professing contrary opinions, and from listening to those who profess them. For the interest, therefore, of truth and justice, it is far more important to restrain this employment of vituperative language than the other; and, for example, if it were necessary to choose, there would be much more need to discourage offensive attacks on infidelity than on religion. It is, however, obvious that law and authority have no business with restraining either, while opinion ought, in every instance, to determine its verdict by the circumstances of the individual case; condemning every one, on whichever side of the argument he places himself, in whose mode of advocacy either want of candour, or malignity, bigotry, or intolerance of feeling manifest themselves; but not inferring these vices from the side which a person takes, though it be the contrary side of the question to our own; and giving merited honour to every one, whatever opinion he may hold, who has calmness to see and honesty to state what his opponents and their opinions really are, exaggerating nothing to their discredit, keeping nothing back which tells, or can be supposed to tell, in their favour. This is the real morality of public discussion: and if often violated, I am happy to think that there are many controversialists who to a great extent observe it, and a still greater number who conscientiously strive towards it.

Discussion Questions

1. To what extent do college campuses and American politics fall prey to the "tyranny of the majority"? Illustrate your answer with specific examples. Do you agree with Mill's solution to the tyranny of the majority? What solution(s) does the United States have in place to protect citizens from the "tyranny of the majority"?
2. Given democracy's proneness to "tyranny of the majority," discuss whether or not democracy is the best form of government. What safeguard(s) does the United States have in place to protect citizens against the "tyranny of the majority"? Are these safeguard(s) effective? Support your answer using specific examples.
3. Discuss what Mill would most likely think of campus speech codes or efforts by colleges to prevent hate speech in order to promote diversity. To what extent should offensive, sexist and/or bigoted speech be allowed on campuses in order to promote the search for truth and wisdom?
4. Discuss what solution Mill would most likely support when it comes to restricting, or not restricting, telemarketing and Internet spam.
5. Mill maintains that it is important for political parties in a healthy democracy to hold widely divergent views in order for freedom of expression to flourish. Is this the case in the United States with the Republican and Democratic parties? Do you agree with Mill?
6. Discuss Mill's philosophy in light of the U.S. Patriot Act, which allows FBI agents to search library, business, and bookstore records during terrorist investigations. What would Mill's response most likely have been to the Patriot Act? What solution, regarding freedom of speech and expression, would Mill most likely propose for keeping the United States safe from terrorism? Do you agree with Mill? Why or why not?

CATHARINE A. MACKINNON

Pornography, Civil Rights, and Speech

Catharine MacKinnon is a professor of law at the University of Michigan. MacKinnon argues that some pornography should be legally restricted. According to her, the harm of pornography outweighs the benefit of freedom of speech. The primary harm of

"Pornography, Civil Rights, and Speech," *Feminism Unmodified: Discourse on Life and Law* (Cambridge, Mass.: Harvard University Press, 1987), pp. 168–179, 193–195. Some notes have been omitted.

pornography is not that it is offensive, but that it is a type of sexual discrimination. Pornography subordinates women. Rather than being harmless fantasy, pornography is a political practice that institutionalizes the sexuality of male supremacy. The end served by pornography is not pleasure but power. Pornography also contributes indirectly to violence against women and to their social and economic inequality.

Critical Reading Questions

1. What is the feminist "discovery" regarding the basic assumption of equality in our society?
2. What does the world look like from the feminist point of view?
3. According to MacKinnon, why don't very many people, including women, believe the feminist view of the world?
4. What is pornography? What view of women does pornography construct?
5. What does MacKinnon mean when she says, "What pornography *does* goes beyond its content"?
6. How does pornography harm women, according to MacKinnon?
7. What does MacKinnon mean when she calls sexuality and gender a "social construct"?
8. According to MacKinnon, why can't we consistently defend both pornography and the equality of the sexes?
9. How does pornography differ from obscenity?
10. What does MacKinnon mean when she says that pornography is a political practice?
11. What definition of pornography did MacKinnon and Dworkin use in drafting an antipornography ordinance for the city of Minneapolis?
12. On what grounds does MacKinnon argue that pornography is a type of sex discrimination that violates the guarantee of equal rights?
13. How does pornography harm women? According to MacKinnon, what is the connection between pornography, rape, and sexual harassment? What evidence does MacKinnon cite to support her claim?
14. What was the primary reason some people opposed MacKinnon and Dworkin's antipornography ordinance? How does MacKinnon respond to their concerns?
15. On what grounds does MacKinnon argue that antipornography laws do not violate, but rather promote, freedom of speech?

There is a belief that this is a society in which women and men are basically equals. Room for marginal corrections is conceded, flaws are known to exist, attempts are made to correct what are conceived as occasional lapses from the basic condition of sex equality. Sex discrimination law has concentrated most of its focus on these occasional lapses. It is difficult to overestimate the extent to which this belief in equality is an article of faith for most people, including most women, who wish to live in self-respect in an internal universe, even (perhaps especially) if not in the world. It is also partly an expression of natural law thinking: if we are inalienably equal, we can't "really" be degraded.

This is a world in which it is worth trying. In this world of presumptive equality, people make money based on their training or abilities or diligence or qualifications. They are employed and advanced on the basis of merit. In this world of just deserts, if someone is abused, it is thought to violate the basic rules of the community. If it doesn't, victims are seen to have done something they could have chosen to do differently, by exercise of will or better judgment. Maybe such people have placed themselves in a situation of vulnerability to physical abuse. Maybe they have done something provocative. Or maybe they were just unusually unlucky. In such a world, if such a person has an experience, there are words for it. When they speak and say it, they are listened to. If they write about it, they will be published. If certain experiences are never spoken about, if certain people or issues are seldom heard from, it is supposed that silence has been chosen. The law, including much of the law of sex discrimination and the First Amendment, operates largely within the realm of these beliefs.

Feminism is the discovery that women do not live in this world, that the person occupying this realm is a man, so much more a man if he is white and wealthy. This world of potential credibility, authority, security, and just rewards, recognition of one's identity and capacity, is a world that some people do inhabit as a condition of birth, with variations among them. It is not a basic condition accorded humanity in this society, but a prerogative of status, a privilege, among other things, of gender.

I call this a discovery because it has not been an assumption. Feminism is the first theory, the first practice, the first movement, to take seriously the situation of all women from the point of view of all women, both on our situation and on social life as a whole. The discovery has therefore been made that the implicit social content of humanism, as well as the standpoint from which legal method has been designed and injuries have been defined, has not been women's standpoint. Defining feminism in a way that connects epistemology with power as the politics of women's point of view, this discovery can be summed up by saying that women live in another world: specifically, a world of *not* equality, a world of inequality.

Looking at the world from this point of view, a whole shadow world of previously invisible silent abuse has been discerned. Rape, battery, sexual harassment, forced prostitution, and the sexual abuse of children emerge as common and systematic. We find that rape happens to women in all contexts, from the family, including rape of girls and babies, to students and women in the workplace, on the streets, at home, in their own bedrooms by men they do not know and by men they do know, by men they are married to, men they have had a social conversation with, and, least often, men they have never seen before. Overwhelmingly, rape is something that men do or attempt to do to women (44 percent of American women according to a recent study) at some point in our lives. Sexual harassment of women by men is common in workplaces and educational institutions. Based on reports in one study of the federal workforce, up to 85 percent of women will experience it, many in physical forms. Between a quarter and a third of women are battered in their homes by men. Thirty-eight percent of little girls are sexually molested inside or outside the family. Until women listened to women, this world of sexual abuse was *not spoken* of. It was the unspeakable. What I am saying is, if you *are* the tree falling in the epistemological forest, your demise doesn't make a sound if no one is listening. Women did not "report" these events, and overwhelmingly do not today, because no one is listening, because no one believes us. This silence does not mean nothing happened, and it does not mean consent. It is the silence of women of which Adrienne Rich has written, "Do not confuse it with any kind of absence."[1]

Believing women who say we are sexually violated has been a radical departure, both methodologically and legally. The extent and nature of rape, marital rape, and sexual harassment itself, were discovered in this way. Domestic battery as a syndrome, almost a habit, was discovered through refusing to believe that when a woman is assaulted by a man to whom she is connected, that it is not an assault. The sexual abuse of children was uncovered, Freud notwithstanding, by believing that children were not making up all this sexual abuse. Now what is striking is that when each discovery is made, and somehow made real in the world, the response has been: it happens to men too. If women are hurt, men are hurt. If women are raped, men are raped. If women are sexually harassed, men are sexually harassed. If women are battered, men are battered. Symmetry must be reasserted. Neutrality must be reclaimed. Equality must be reestablished.

The only areas where the available evidence supports this, where anything like what happens to women also happens to men, involve children—little boys are sexually abused—and prison. The liberty of prisoners is restricted, their freedom restrained, their humanity systematically diminished, their bodies and emotions confined, defined, and regulated. If paid at all, they are paid starvation wages. They can be tortured at will, and it is passed off as discipline or as means to a just end. They become compliant. They can be raped at will, at any moment, and nothing will be done about it. When they scream, nobody hears. To be a prisoner means to be defined as a member of a group for whom the rules of what can be done to you, of what is seen as abuse of you, are reduced as part of the definition of your status. To be a woman is that kind of definition and has that kind of meaning. . . .

What women do is seen as not worth much, or what is not worth much is seen as something for women to do. *Women* are seen as not worth much, is the thing. Now why are these basic realities of the subordination of women to men, for example, that only 7.8 percent of women have never been sexually assaulted, not effectively believed, not perceived as real in the face of all this evidence? Why don't *women* believe our own experiences? In the face of all this evidence, especially of systematic sexual abuse—subjection to violence with impunity is one extreme expression, although not the only expression, of a degraded status—the view that basically the sexes are equal in this society remains unchallenged and unchanged. The day I got this was the day I understood its real message, its real coherence: *This is equality for us.*

I could describe this, but I couldn't explain it until I started studying a lot of pornography. In pornography, there it is, in one place, all of the abuses that women had to struggle so long even to begin to articulate, all the *unspeakable* abuse: the rape, the battery, the sexual harassment, the prostitution, and the sexual abuse of children. Only in the pornography it is called something else: sex, sex, sex, sex, and sex, respectively. Pornography sexualizes rape, battery, sexual harassment, prostitution, and child sexual abuse; it thereby celebrates, promotes, authorizes, and legitimizes them. More generally, it eroticizes the dominance and submission that is the dynamic common to them all. It makes hierarchy sexy and calls that "the truth about sex" or just a mirror of reality. Through this process pornography constructs what a woman is as what men want from sex. This is what the pornography means.

Pornography constructs what a woman is in terms of its view of what men want sexually, such that acts of rape, battery, sexual harassment, prostitution, and sexual abuse of children become acts of sexual equality. Pornography's world of equality is a harmonious and balanced place. Men and women are perfectly complementary and perfectly bipolar. Women's desire to be fucked by men is equal to men's desire to fuck women. All the ways men love to take and violate women, women love to be taken and violated. The women who most love this are most men's equals, the most liberated; the most participatory child is the most grown-up, the most equal to an adult. Their consent merely expresses or ratifies these preexisting facts.

The content of pornography is one thing. There, women substantively desire dispossession and cruelty. We desperately want to be bound, battered, tortured, humiliated, and killed. Or, to be fair to the soft core, merely taken and used. This is erotic to the male point of view. Subjection itself, with self-determination ecstatically relinquished, is the content of women's sexual desire and desirability. Women are there to be violated and possessed, men to violate and possess us, either on screen or by camera or pen on behalf of the consumer. On a simple descriptive level, the inequality of hierarchy, of which gender is the primary one, seems necessary for sexual arousal to work. Other added inequalities identify various pornographic genres or subthemes, although they are always added through gender: age, disability, homosexuality, animals, objects, race (including anti-Semitism), and so on. Gender is never irrelevant.

What pornography *does* goes beyond its content: it eroticizes hierarchy, it sexualizes inequality. It makes dominance and submission into sex. Inequality is its central dynamic; the illusion of freedom coming together with the reality of force is central to its working. Perhaps because this is a bourgeois culture, the victim must look free, appear to be freely acting. Choice is how she got there. Willing is what she is when she is being equal. It seems equally important that then and there she actually be forced and that forcing be communicated on some level, even if only through still photos of her in postures of receptivity and access, available for penetration. Pornography in this view is a form of forced sex, a practice of sexual politics, an institution of gender inequality.

From this perspective, pornography is neither harmless fantasy nor a corrupt and confused misrepresentation of an otherwise natural and healthy sexual situation. It institutionalizes the sexuality of male supremacy, fusing the erotization of dominance and submission with the social construction of male and female. To the extent that gender is sexual, pornography is part of constituting the meaning of that sexuality. Men treat women as who they see women as being. Pornography constructs who that is. Men's power over women means that the way men see women defines who women can be. Pornography is that way. Pornography is not imagery in some relation to a reality elsewhere constructed. It is not a distortion, reflection, projection, expression, fantasy, representation, or symbol either. It is a sexual reality.

In Andrea Dworkin's definitive work, *Pornography: Men Possessing Women,* sexuality itself is a social construct gendered to the ground. Male dominance here is not an artificial overlay upon an underlying inalterable substratum of uncorrupted essential sexual being. Dworkin presents a sexual theory of gender inequality of which pornography is a constitutive practice. The way pornography produces its meaning constructs and defines men and women as such. Gender has no basis in anything other than the social reality its hegemony constructs. Gender is what gender means. The process that gives sexuality its male supremacist meaning is the same process through which gender inequality becomes socially real.

In this approach, the experience of the (overwhelmingly) male audiences who consume pornography is therefore not fantasy or simulation or catharsis but sexual reality, the level of reality on which sex itself largely operates. Understanding this dimension of the problem does not require noticing that pornography models are real women to whom, in most cases, something real is being done; nor does it even require inquiring into the systematic infliction of pornography and its sexuality upon women, although it helps. What matters is the way in which the pornography itself provides what those who consume it want. Pornography *participates* in its audience's eroticism through creating an accessible sexual object, the possession and consumption of which *is* male sexuality, as socially constructed; to be consumed and possessed as which, *is* female sexuality, as socially constructed; pornography is a process that constructs it that way.

The object world is constructed according to how it looks with respect to its possible uses. Pornography defines women by how we look according to how we can be sexually used. Pornography codes how to look at women, so you know what you can do with one when you see one. Gender is an assignment made visually, both originally and in everyday life. A sex object is defined on the basis of its looks, in terms of its usability for sexual pleasure, such that both the looking—the quality of the gaze, including its point of view—and the definition according to use become eroticized as part of the sex itself. This is what the feminist concept "sex object" means. In this sense, sex in life is no less mediated than it is in art. Men have sex with their image of a woman. It is not that life and art imitate each other; in this sexuality, they *are* each other. . . .

To defend pornography as consistent with the equality of the sexes is to defend the subordination of women to men as sexual equality. What in the pornographic view is love and romance looks a great deal like hatred and torture to the feminist. Pleasure and eroticism become violation. Desire appears as lust for dominance and submission. The vulnerability of women's projected sexual availability, that acting we are allowed (that is, asking to be acted upon), is victimization. Play conforms to scripted roles. Fantasy expresses ideology, is not exempt from it. Admiration of natural physical beauty becomes objectification. Harmlessness becomes harm. Pornography is a harm of male supremacy made difficult to see because of its pervasiveness, potency, and, principally, because of its success in making the world a pornographic place. Specifically, its harm cannot be discerned, and will not be addressed, if viewed and approached neutrally, because it *is* so much of "what is." In other words, to the extent pornography succeeds in constructing social reality, it becomes invisible as harm. If we live in a world that pornography creates through the power of men in a male-dominated situation, the issue is not what the harm of pornography is, but how that harm is to become visible.

Obscenity law provides a very different analysis and conception of the problem of pornography. In 1973 the legal definition of obscenity became that which the average person, applying contemporary community standards, would find that, taken as a whole, appeals to the prurient interest; that which depicts or describes in a patently offensive way—you feel like you're a cop reading someone's *Miranda* rights—sexual conduct specifically defined by the applicable state law; and that which, taken as a whole, lacks serious literary, artistic, political or scientific value. Feminism doubts whether the average person gender-neutral exists; has more questions about the content and process of defining what community standards are than it does about deviations from them; wonders why prurience counts but powerlessness does not and why sensibilities are better protected from offense than women are from exploitation; defines sexuality, and thus its violation and expropriation, more broadly than does state law; and questions why a body of law that has not in practice been able to tell rape from intercourse should, without further guidance, be entrusted with telling pornography from anything less. Taking the work "as a whole" ignores that which the victims of pornography have long known: legitimate settings diminish the perception of injury done to those whose trivialization and objectification they contextualize. Besides, and this is a heavy one, if a woman is subjected, why should it matter that the work has other value? Maybe what redeems the work's value is what enhances its injury to women, not to mention that existing standards of literature, art, science, and politics, examined in a feminist light, are remarkably consonant with pornography's mode, meaning, and message. And finally—first and foremost, actually—although the subject of these materials is overwhelmingly women, their contents almost entirely made up of women's bodies, our invisibility has been such, our equation as a sex *with* sex has been such, that the law of obscenity has never even considered pornography a women's issue.

Obscenity, in this light, is a moral idea, an idea about judgments of good and bad. Pornography, by contrast, is a political practice, a practice of power and powerlessness. Obscenity is ideational and abstract; pornography is concrete and substantive. The two concepts represent two entirely different things. Nudity, excess of candor, arousal or excitement, prurient appeal, illegality of the acts depicted, unnaturalness or perversion are all qualities that bother obscenity law when sex is depicted or portrayed. Sex forced on real women so that it can be sold at a profit and forced on other real women; women's bodies trussed and maimed and raped and made into things to be hurt and obtained and accessed, and this presented as the nature of women in a way that is acted on and acted out, over and over; the coercion that is visible and the coercion that has become invisible—this and more bothers feminists about pornography. Obscenity as such probably does little harm. Pornography is integral to attitudes and behaviors of violence and discrimination that define the treatment and status of half the population.

At the request of the city of Minneapolis, Andrea Dworkin and I conceived and designed a local human rights ordinance in accordance with our approach to the pornography issue. We define pornography as a practice of sex discrimination, a violation of women's civil rights, the opposite of sexual equality. Its point is to hold those who profit from and benefit from that injury accountable to those who are injured. It means that women's injury—our damage, our pain, our enforced inferiority—should outweigh their pleasure and their profits, or sex equality is meaningless.

We define pornography as the graphic sexually explicit subordination of women through pictures or words that also includes women dehumanized as sexual objects, things, or commodities; enjoying pain or humiliation or rape; being tied up, cut up, mutilated, bruised, or physically hurt; in postures of sexual submission or servility or display; reduced to body parts, penetrated by objects or animals, or presented in scenarios of degradation, injury, torture; shown as filthy or inferior; bleeding, bruised, or hurt in a context that makes these conditions sexual. Erotica, defined by distinction as not this, might be sexually explicit materials premised on equality. . . .

To define pornography as a practice of sex discrimination combines a mode of portrayal that has a legal history—the sexually explicit—with an active term that is central to the inequality of the sexes—subordination. Among other things, subordination means to be in a position of inferiority or loss of power, or to be demeaned or denigrated. To be someone's subordinate is the opposite of being their equal. The definition does not include all sexually explicit depictions *of* the subordination of women. That is not what it says. It says, this which *does* that: the sexually explicit that subordinates women. To these active terms to capture what the pornography *does,* the definition adds a list of what it must also contain. This list, from our analysis, is an exhaustive description of what must be in the pornography for it to do what it does behaviorally. Each item in the definition is supported by experimental, testimonial, social, and clinical evidence. We made a legislative choice to be exhaustive and specific and concrete rather than conceptual and general, to minimize problems of chilling effect, making it hard to guess wrong, thus making self-censorship less likely, but encouraging (to use a phrase from discrimination law) voluntary compliance, knowing that if something turns up that is not on the list, the law will not be expansively interpreted.

The list in the definition, by itself, would be a content regulation. But together with the first part, the definition is not simply a content regulation. It is a medium-message combination that resembles many other such exceptions to First Amendment guarantees. . . .

This law aspires to guarantee women's rights consistent with the First Amendment by making visible a conflict of rights between the equality guaranteed to all women and what, in some legal sense, is now the freedom of the pornographers to make and sell, and their consumers to have access to, the materials this ordinance defines. Judicial resolution of this conflict, if the judges do for women what they have done for others, is likely to entail a balancing of the rights of women arguing that our lives and opportunities, including our freedom of speech and action, are constrained by—and in many cases flatly precluded by, in, and through—pornography, against those who argue that the pornography is harmless, or harmful only in part but not in the whole of the definition; or that it is more important to preserve the pornography than it is to prevent or remedy of whatever harm it does. . . .

The harm of pornography, broadly speaking, is the harm of the civil inequality of the sexes made invisible as harm because it has become accepted as the sex difference. Consider this analogy with race: if you see Black people as different, there is no harm to segregation; it is merely a recognition of that difference. To neutral principles, separate but equal was equal. The injury of racial separation to Blacks arises "solely because [they] choose to put that construction upon it." Epistemologically translated: how you see it is not the way it is. Similarly, if you see women as just different, even or especially if you don't know that you do, subordination will not look like subordination at all, much less like harm. It will merely look like an appropriate recognition of the sex difference.

Pornography does treat the sexes differently, so the case for sex differentiation can be made here. But men as a group do not tend to be (although some individuals may be) treated the way women are treated in pornography. As a social group, men are not hurt by pornography the way women as a social group are. Their social status is not defined as *less* by it. So the major argument does not turn on mistaken differentiation, particularly since the treatment of women according to pornography's dictates makes it all too often accurate. The salient quality of a distinction between the top and the bottom in a hierarchy is not difference, although top is certainly different. . . .

Free speech only enhances the power of the pornographers while doing nothing substantively to guarantee the free speech of women, for which we need civil equality. The situation in which women presently find ourselves with respect to the pornography is one in which more *pornography* is inconsistent with rectifying or even counterbalancing its damage through speech, because so long as the pornography exists in the way it does there *will not be more speech by women.* Pornography strips and devastates women of credibility, from our accounts of sexual assault to our everyday reality of sexual subordination. We are stripped of authority and reduced and devalidated and silenced. Silenced here means that the purposes of the First Amendment, premised upon conditions presumed and promoted by protecting free speech, do not pertain to women because they are not our conditions. Consider them: individual self-fulfillment—how does pornography promote our individual self-fulfillment? How does sexual inequality even permit it? Even if she can form words, who listens to a woman with a penis in her mouth? Facilitating consensus—to the extent pornography does so, it does so one-sidedly by silencing protest over the injustice of sexual subordination. Participation in civic life—central to Professor Meiklejohn's theory—how does pornography enhance women's participation in civic life? Anyone who cannot walk down the street or even lie down in her own bed without keeping her eyes cast down and her body clenched against assault is unlikely to have much to say about the issues of the day, still less will she become Tolstoy. Facilitating change—*this law* facilitates the change that existing First Amendment theory had been used to throttle. Any system of freedom of expression that does not address a problem where the free speech of men silences the free speech of women, a real conflict between speech interests as well as between people, is not serious about securing freedom of expression in this country.

For those of you who still think pornography is only an idea, consider the possibility that obscenity law got one thing right. Pornography is more actlike than thoughtlike. The fact that pornography, in a feminist view, furthers the idea of the sexual inferiority of women, which is a political idea, doesn't make the pornography itself into a political idea. One can express the idea a practice embodies. That does not make that practice into an idea. Segregation expresses the idea of the inferiority of one group to another on the basis of race. That does not make segregation an idea. A sign that says "Whites Only" is only words. Is it therefore protected by the First Amendment? Is it not an act, a practice, of segregation because what it means is inseparable from what it does? *Law* is only words.

The issue here is whether the fact that words and pictures are the central link in the cycle of abuse will immunize that entire cycle, about which we cannot do anything without doing something about the pornography. As Justice Stewart said in *Ginsburg,* "When expression occurs in a setting where the capacity to make a choice is absent, government regulation of that expression may coexist with and *even implement* First Amendment guarantees."[2] I would even go so far as to say that the pattern of evidence we have closely approaches Justice Douglas' requirement that "freedom of expression can be suppressed if, and to the extent that, it is so closely brigaded with illegal action as to be an inseparable part of it."[3] Those of you who have been trying to separate the acts from the speech—that's an act, that's an act, there's a law against that act, regulate that act, don't touch the speech—notice here that the illegality of the acts involved doesn't mean that the speech that is "brigaded with" it *cannot* be regulated. This is when it *can* be.

I take one of two penultimate points from Andrea Dworkin, who has often said that pornography is not speech for women, it is the silence of women. Remember the mouth taped, the woman gagged, "Smile, I can get a lot of money for that." The smile is not her expression, it is her silence. . . .

Classically, opposition to censorship has involved keeping government off the backs of people. Our law is about getting some people off the backs of other people. The risks that it will be misused have to be measured against the risks of the status quo. Women will never have that dignity, security, compensation that is the promise of equality so long as the pornography exists as it does now. The situation of women suggests that the urgent issue of our freedom of speech is not primarily the avoidance of state intervention as such, but getting affirmative access to speech for those to whom it has been denied.

NOTES

1. Adrienne Rich, "Cartographies of Silence," in *The Dream of a Common Language* 16, 17 (1978).
2. *Ginsburg v. New York,* 390 U.S. 629, 649 (1968) (Stewart, J., concurring in result) (emphasis added).
3. *Roth v. United States,* 354 U.S. 476, 514 (Douglas, J., dissenting) (citing *Giboney v. Empire Storage & Ice Co.,* 336 U.S. 490, 498 [1949]); *Labor Board v. Virginia Power Co.,* 314 U.S. 469, 477–78 (1941).

Discussion Questions

1. Discuss MacKinnon's argument that censorship of pornography does not violate our freedom of speech. Has she successfully demonstrated that pornography violates Mill's harm principle? Discuss how Mill might respond to MacKinnon's argument.
2. Discuss MacKinnon's claim that pornography is a type of sex discrimination that directly harms women. Discuss how MacKinnon might respond to the lack of evidence of a causal link between pornography and violence against women. Can her argument stand without it?
3. Political analysts George F. Will and Ellen Willis warn that "if feminists define pornography per se as the enemy, the result will be to make a lot of women ashamed of their sexual feelings and afraid to be honest about them."[32] Do you agree? Support your answer. Discuss how MacKinnon might respond to this concern.
4. Sexist attitudes also flourish in many religious groups, in advertisements, and in television shows. Indeed, this type of sexist message may be more pervasive and harmful than that of pornography. If so, should sexist religious doctrines, ads, and televisions shows that demean women be censored? Does the MacKinnon argument risk sending us down the slippery slope of all-out censorship? Support your answer. Discuss how MacKinnon might respond to this concern.
5. In 1990 Fort Lauderdale record-store owner Charles Freeman was arrested for selling to an undercover policeman a copy of 2 Live Crew's *As Nasty as They Wanna Be,* an album that had been deemed obscene by a federal court. After listening to it, the all-white jury decided that it was indeed obscene and convicted Freeman. Freeman was outraged. "They don't know nothing about the goddam ghetto, . . ." he fumed as he left the court. "The verdict does not reflect my community standards as a black man in Broward County."[33] Do you agree with Freeman? Does MacKinnon's proposed antipornography law demonstrate a white, upper-middle-class cultural bias? Or is pornography wrong no matter what the cultural context?

CHARLES R. LAWRENCE III

If He Hollers Let Him Go: Regulating Racist Speech on Campus

Charles Lawrence III is a professor at the Georgetown University School of Law. In the following article, Lawrence examines the morality of regulating racist hate speech on college campuses. He concludes that the protection of racist speech is incompatible with

"If He Hollers Let Him Go: Regulating Racist Speech on Campus," *Duke Law Journal* 431 (1990): 431–480. Notes have been omitted.

the elimination of racism. Lawrence charges civil libertarians who invoke the First Amendment in defense of hate speech with fanning the flames of racism by protecting racist speech. Rather than encouraging the free exchange of ideas, the tolerance of hate speech silences and devalues the ideas of minorities.

Critical Reading Questions

1. What does Lawrence mean by the "double consciousness" shared by minorities?
2. According to Lawrence, who is harmed more by oppressive speech: minorities who are targets of the speech, or those using hate speech?
3. On what grounds does Lawrence claim that many civil libertarians are actually fanning the flames of racism?
4. According to Lawrence, what is the relevance of the United States Supreme Court *Brown v. Board of Education* ruling to the regulation of racist speech?
5. Why does Lawrence insist that we view individual racist remarks as part of a totality rather than as discrete events?
6. According to Lawrence, why should the *Brown v. Board of Education* decision overrule the First Amendment when it comes to racist speech?
7. Why does Lawrence reject the distinction drawn by many libertarians between conduct and speech?
8. On what grounds does Lawrence claim that racist speech is the functional equivalent of fighting words?
9. What three types of injury does Lawrence argue are caused by racist speech?
10. Why don't blacks have as much faith in free speech as do whites?
11. According to Lawrence, what are some of the effects of racist speech on the marketplace of ideas?
12. On what grounds does Lawrence attack traditional civil libertarians?

NEWSREEL*

Racist incidents at the University of Michigan, University of Massachusetts-Amherst, University of Wisconsin, University of New Mexico, Columbia University, Wellesley College, Duke University, and University of California-Los Angeles.

The campus ought to be the last place to legislate tampering with the edges of First Amendment protections.

University of Michigan:
"Greek Rites of Exclusion": Racist leaflets in dorms, white students paint themselves black and place rings in their noses at "jungle parties."

Silencing a few creeps is no victory if the price is an abrogation of free speech. Remember censorship is an ugly word too.

Northwest Missouri State University:
White Supremacists distribute flyers stating, "The Knights of the Ku Klux Klan are Watching You."

Temple University:
White Student Union formed.

Memphis State University:
Bomb Threats at Jewish Student Union.

*The events that appear in this newsreel are gathered from newspaper and magazine reports of racist incidents on campuses. Each of them is followed by a statement, appearing in italics, criticizing proposals to regulate racism on campus. The latter have been garnered from conversations, debates, and panel discussions at which I have been present. Some I managed to record verbatim and are exact quotes; others paraphrase the sentiment expressed. I have heard some version of each of these arguments many times over.

The harm that censors allege will result unless speech is forbidden rarely occurs.

Dartmouth College:

Black professor called "a cross between a welfare queen and a bathroom attendant" and the Dartmouth Review purported to quote a black student, "Dese boys be sayin' that we be comin' here to Dartmut an' not takin' the classics. . . ."

Yes, speech is sometimes painful. Sometimes it is abusive. That is one of the prices of a free society.

Purdue University:

Counselor finds "Death Nigger" scratched on her door.

More speech, not less, is the proper cure for offensive speech.

Smith College:

African student finds message slipped under her door that reads, "African Nigger do you want some bananas? Go back to the Jungle."

Speech cannot be banned simply because it is offensive.

University of Michigan:

Campus radio station broadcasts a call from a student who "joked": "Who are the most famous black women in history? Aunt Jemima and Mother Fucker."

Those who don't like what they are hearing or seeing should try to change the atmosphere through education. That is what they will have to do in the real world after they graduate.

University of Michigan:

A student walks into class and sees this written on the blackboard: "A mind is a terrible thing to waste—especially on a nigger." . . .

INTRODUCTION

In recent years, American campuses have seen a resurgence of racial violence and a corresponding rise in the incidence of verbal and symbolic assault and harassment to which blacks and other traditionally subjugated groups are subjected. There is a heated debate in the civil liberties community concerning the proper response to incidents of racist speech on campus. Strong disagreements have arisen between those individuals who believe that racist speech, such as that contained in the Newsreel that opens this Article, should be regulated by the university or some public body and those individuals who believe that racist expression should be protected from all public regulation. At the center of the controversy is a tension between the constitutional values of free speech and equality. . . .

The "double consciousness" of groups outside the ethnic mainstream is particularly apparent in the context of this controversy. Blacks know and value the protection the First Amendment affords those of us who must rely on our voices to petition both government and our neighbors for redress of grievances. Our political tradition has looked to "the word," to the moral power of ideas, to change a system when neither the power of the vote nor that of the gun are available. This part of us has known the experience of belonging and recognizes our common and inseparable interest in preserving the right of free speech for all. But we also know the experience of the outsider. The Framers excluded us from the protection of the First Amendment. The same Constitution that established rights for others endorsed a story that proclaimed our inferiority. It is a story that remains deeply ingrained in the American psyche.

We see a different world than that which is seen by Americans who do not share this historical experience. We often hear racist speech when our white neighbors are not aware of its presence.

It is not my purpose to belittle or trivialize the importance of defending unpopular speech against the tyranny of the majority. There are very strong reasons for protecting even racist speech. Perhaps the most important reasons are that it reinforces our society's commitment to the value of tolerance, and that, by shielding racist speech from government regulation, we will be forced to combat it as a community. These reasons for protecting racist speech should not be set aside hastily, and I will not argue that we should be less vigilant in protecting the speech and associational rights of speakers with whom most of us would disagree.

But I am deeply concerned about the role that many civil libertarians have played, or the roles we have failed to play, in the continuing, real-life struggle through which we define the community in which we live. I fear that by framing the debate as we have—as one in which the liberty of free speech is in conflict with the elimination of racism—we have advanced the cause of racial oppression and have placed the bigot on the moral high ground, fanning the rising flames of racism. Above all, I am troubled that we have not listened to the real victims, that we have shown so little empathy or understanding for their injury, and that we have abandoned those individuals whose race, gender, or sexual orientation provokes others to regard them as second class citizens. These individuals' civil liberties are most directly at stake in the debate. . . .

BROWN V. BOARD OF EDUCATION: A CASE ABOUT REGULATING RACIST SPEECH

The landmark case of *Brown v. Board of Education* is not a case we normally think of as a case about speech. As read most narrowly, the case is about the rights of black children to equal educational opportunity. But *Brown* can also be read more broadly to articulate a principle central to any substantive understanding of the equal protection clause, the foundation on which all anti-discrimination law rests. This is the principle of equal citizenship. . . .

The key to this understanding of *Brown* is that the practice of segregation, the practice the Court held inherently unconstitutional, was *speech. Brown* held that segregation is unconstitutional not simply because the physical separation of black and white children is bad or because resources were distributed unequally among black and white schools. *Brown* held that segregated schools were unconstitutional primarily because of the *message* segregation conveys—the message that black children are an untouchable caste, unfit to be educated with white children. Segregation serves its purpose by conveying an idea. It stamps a badge of inferiority upon blacks, and this badge communicates a message to others in the community, as well as to blacks wearing the badge, that is injurious to blacks. Therefore, *Brown* may be read as regulating the content of racist speech. As a regulation of racist speech, the decision is an exception to the usual rule that regulation of speech content is presumed unconstitutional.

The Conduct/Speech Distinction

Some civil libertarians argue that my analysis of *Brown* conflates speech and conduct. They maintain that the segregation outlawed in *Brown* was discriminatory conduct, not speech, and the defamatory message conveyed by segregation simply was an incidental by-product of that conduct. . . . This objection to my reading of *Brown* misperceives the central point of the argument. . . .

Racism is both 100% speech and 100% conduct. Discriminatory conduct is not racist unless it also conveys the message of white supremacy—unless it is interpreted within the culture to advance the structure and ideology of white supremacy. Likewise, all racist speech constructs the social reality that constrains the liberty of non-whites because of their race. By limiting the life opportunities of others, this act of constructing meaning also makes racist speech conduct. . . .

RACIST SPEECH AS THE FUNCTIONAL EQUIVALENT OF FIGHTING WORDS

Much recent debate of the efficacy of regulating racist speech has focused on the efforts by colleges and universities to respond to the burgeoning incidents of racial harassment on their campuses. At Stanford, where I teach, there has been considerable controversy over the questions of whether racist and other discriminatory verbal harassment should be regulated and what form that regulation should take. Proponents of regulation have been sensitive to the danger of inhibiting expression, and the current regulation . . . manifests that sensitivity. It is drafted somewhat more narrowly than I would have preferred, leaving unregulated hate speech that occurs in settings where there is a captive audience, speech that I would regulate. But I largely agree with this regulation's substance and approach. I include it here as one example of a regulation of racist speech that I would argue violates neither First Amendment precedent nor principle. The regulation reads as follows:

> Fundamental Standard Interpretation: Free Expression and Discriminatory Harassment
>
> 1. Stanford is committed to the principles of free inquiry and free expression. Students have the right to hold and vigorously defend and promote their opinions, thus entering them into the life of the University, there to flourish or wither according to their merits. Respect for this right requires that students tolerate even expression of opinions which they find abhorrent. Intimidation of students by other students in their exercise of this right, by violence or threat of violence, is therefore considered to be a violation of the Fundamental Standard.
>
> 2. Stanford is also committed to principles of equal opportunity and non-discrimination. Each student has the right to equal access to a Stanford education, without discrimination on the basis of sex, race, color, handicap, religion, sexual orientation, or national and ethnic origin. Harassment of students on the basis of any of these characteristics contributes to a hostile environment that makes access to education for those subjected to it less than equal. Such discriminatory harassment is therefore considered to be a violation of the Fundamental Standard.
>
> 3. This interpretation of the Fundamental Standard is intended to clarify the point at which protected free expression ends and prohibited discriminatory harassment begins. Prohibited harassment includes discriminatory intimidation by threats of violence, and also includes personal vilification of students on the basis of their sex, race, color, handicap, religion, sexual orientation, or national and ethnic origin.
>
> 4. Speech or other expression constitutes harassment by personal vilification if it:
>
> a) is intended to insult or stigmatize an individual or a small number of individuals on the basis of their sex, race, color, handicap, religion, sexual orientation, or national and ethnic origin; and
>
> b) is addressed directly to the individual or individuals whom it insults or stigmatizes; and
>
> c) makes use of insulting or "fighting" words or non-verbal symbols.
>
> In the context of discriminatory harassment by personal vilification, insulting or "fighting" words or non-verbal symbols are those "which by their very utterance inflict injury or tend to incite to an immediate breach of the peace," and which are commonly understood to convey direct and visceral hatred or contempt for human beings on the basis of their sex, race, color, handicap, religion, sexual orientation, or national and ethnic origin.

This regulation and others like it have been characterized in the press as the work of "thought police," but it does nothing more than prohibit intentional face-to-face insults, a form of speech that is unprotected by the First Amendment. When racist speech takes the form of face-to-face insults, catcalls, or other assaultive speech aimed at an individual or small group of persons, then it falls within the "fighting words" exception to First Amendment protection. The Supreme Court has held that words that "by their very utterance inflict injury or tend to incite to an immediate breach of the peace" are not constitutionally protected.

Face-to-face racial insults, like fighting words, are undeserving of First Amendment protection for two reasons. The first reason is the immediacy of the injurious impact of racial insults. The experience of being called "nigger," "spic," "Jap," or "kike" is like receiving a slap in the face. The injury is instantaneous. There is neither an opportunity for intermediary reflection on the idea conveyed nor an opportunity for responsive speech. The harm to be avoided is both clear and present. The second reason that racial insults should not fall under protected speech relates to the purpose underlying the First Amendment. If the purpose of the First Amendment is to foster the greatest amount of speech, then racial insults disserve that purpose. Assaultive racist speech functions as a preemptive strike. The racial invective is experienced as a blow, not a proffered idea, and once the blow is struck, it is unlikely that dialogue will follow. Racial insults are undeserving of First Amendment protection because the perpetrator's intention is not to discover truth or initiate dialogue but to injure the victim.

The fighting words doctrine anticipates that the verbal "slap in the face" of insulting words will provoke a violent response with a resulting breach of the peace. When racial insults are hurled at minorities, the response may be silence or flight rather than fight, but the preemptive effect on further speech is just as complete as with fighting words. Women and minorities often report that they find themselves speechless in the face of discriminatory verbal attacks. This inability to respond is not the result of oversensitivity among these groups, as some individuals who oppose protective regulation have argued. Rather, it is the product of several factors, all of which reveal the non-speech character of the initial preemptive verbal assault. The first factor is that the visceral emotional response to personal attack precludes speech. Attack produces an instinctive, defensive psychological reaction. Fear, rage, shock, and flight all interfere with any reasoned response. Words like "nigger," "kike," and "faggot" produce physical symptoms that temporarily disable the victim, and the perpetrators often use these words with the intention of producing this effect. Many victims do not find words of response until well after the assault when the cowardly assaulter has departed.

A second factor that distinguishes racial insults from protected speech is the preemptive nature of such insults—the words by which to respond to such verbal attacks may never be forthcoming because speech is usually an inadequate response. . . .

The subordinated victim of fighting words also is silenced by her relatively powerless position in society. Because of the significance of power and position, the categorization of racial epithets as "fighting words" provides an inadequate paradigm; instead one must speak of their "functional equivalent." The fighting words doctrine presupposes an encounter between two persons of relatively equal power who have been acculturated to respond to face-to-face insults with violence. The fighting words doctrine is a paradigm based on a white male point of view. In most situations, minorities correctly perceive that a violent response to fighting words will result in a risk to their own life and limb. Since minorities are likely to lose the fight, they are forced to remain silent and submissive. This response is most obvious when women submit to sexually assaultive speech or when the racist name-caller is in a more powerful position—the boss on the job or the mob. . . .

The proposed Stanford regulation, and indeed regulations with considerably broader reach, can be justified as necessary to protect a captive audience from offensive or injurious speech. Courts have held that offensive speech may not be regulated in public forums such as streets and parks where a listener may avoid the speech by moving on or averting his eyes, but the regulation of otherwise protected speech has been permitted when the speech invades the privacy of the unwilling listener's home or when the unwilling listener cannot avoid the speech. Racist posters, flyers, and graffiti in dorms, classrooms, bathrooms, and other common living spaces would fall within the reasoning of these cases. Minority students should not be required to remain in their rooms to avoid racial assault. Minimally, they should find a safe haven in their dorms and other common rooms that are a part of their daily routine. I would argue that the university's responsibility for ensuring these students received an equal educational opportunity provides a compelling justification for regulations that ensure them safe passage in all common areas. . . .

Understanding the Injury Inflicted by Racist Speech

There can be no meaningful discussion about how to reconcile our commitment to equality and our commitment to free speech until we acknowledge that racist speech inflicts real harm and that this harm is far from trivial. I should state that more strongly: To engage in a debate about the First Amendment and racist speech without a full understanding of the nature and extent of the harm of racist speech risks making the First Amendment an instrument of domination rather than a vehicle of liberation. Not everyone has known the experience of being victimized by racist, misogynist, and homophobic speech, and we do not share equally the burden of the societal harm it inflicts. Often we are too quick to say we have heard the victims' cries when we have not; we are too eager to assure ourselves we have experienced the same injury, and therefore we can make the constitutional balance without danger of mismeasurement. For many of us who have fought for the rights of oppressed minorities, it is difficult to accept that—by underestimating the injury from racist speech—we too might be implicated in the vicious words we would never utter. Until we have eradicated racism and sexism and no longer share in the fruits of those forms of domination, we cannot justly strike the balance over the protest of those who are dominated. My plea is simply that we listen to the victims. . . .

Again, *Brown v. Board of Education* is a useful case for our analysis. *Brown* is helpful because it articulates the nature of the injury inflicted by the racist message of segregation. When one considers the injuries identified in the *Brown* decision, it is clear that racist speech causes tangible injury, and it is the kind of injury for which the law commonly provides, and even requires, redress.

Psychic injury is no less an injury than being struck in the face, and is often far more severe. *Brown* speaks directly to the psychic injury inflicted by racist speech in noting that the symbolic message of segregation affected "the hearts and minds" of Negro children "in a way unlikely ever to be undone." Racial epithets and harassment often cause deep emotional scarring, and feelings of anxiety and fear that pervade every aspect of a victim's life. Many victims of hate propaganda have experienced physiological and emotional symptoms ranging from rapid pulse rate and difficulty in breathing, to nightmares, post-traumatic stress disorder, psychosis and suicide.

A second injury identified in *Brown* . . . is reputational injury. "[L]ibelous speech was long regarded as a form of personal assault . . . that government could vindicate . . . without running afoul of the Constitution." . . .

Brown is a case about group defamation. The message of segregation was stigmatizing to black children. To be labeled unfit to attend school with white children injured the reputation of black children, thereby foreclosing employment opportunities and the right to be regarded as respected members of the body politic. . . . *Brown* reflects that racism is a form of subordination that achieves its purpose through group defamation.

The third injury identified in *Brown* is the denial of equal educational opportunity. *Brown* recognized that black children did not have an equal opportunity to learn and participate in the school community if they bore the additional burden of being subjected to the humiliation and psychic assault that accompanies the message of segregation. University students bear an analogous burden when they are forced to live and work in an environment where, at any moment, they may be subjected to denigrating verbal harassment and assault. . . .

All three of these very tangible, continuing, and often irreparable forms of injury—psychic, reputational, and the denial of equal educational opportunity—must be recognized, accounted for, and balanced against the claim that a regulation aimed at the prevention of these injuries may lead to restrictions on important First Amendment liberties.

The Other Side of the Balance: Does the Suppression of Racial Epithets Weigh for or Against Speech?

In striking a balance, we also must think about what we are weighing on the side of speech. Most blacks—unlike many white civil libertarians—do not have faith in free speech as the most important vehicle for liberation. The First Amendment coexisted with slavery, and we still are not sure it will protect us to the same extent that it protects whites. It often is argued that minorities have benefited greatly from First Amendment protection and therefore should guard it jealously. We are aware that the struggle for racial equality has relied heavily on the persuasion of peaceful protest protected by the First Amendment, but experience also teaches us that our petitions often go unanswered until they disrupt business as usual and require the self-interested attention of those persons in power. . . .

Blacks and other people of color are equally skeptical about the absolutist argument that even the most injurious speech must remain unregulated because in an unregulated marketplace of ideas the best ideas will rise to the top and gain acceptance. Our experience tells us the opposite. We have seen too many demagogues elected by appealing to America's racism. We have seen too many good, liberal politicians shy away from the issues that might brand them as too closely allied with us. The American marketplace of ideas was founded with the idea of the racial inferiority of non-whites as one of its chief commodities, and ever since the market opened, racism has remained its most active item in trade.

But it is not just the prevalence and strength of the idea of racism that makes the unregulated marketplace of ideas an untenable paradigm for those individuals who seek full and equal personhood for all. The real problem is that the idea of the racial inferiority of non-whites infects, skews, and disables the operation of the market (like a computer virus, sick cattle, or diseased wheat). Racism is irrational and often unconscious. Our belief in the inferiority of non-whites trumps good ideas that contend with it in the market, often without our even knowing it. In addition, racism makes the words and ideas of blacks and other despised minorities less saleable, regardless of their intrinsic value, in the marketplace of ideas. It also decreases the total amount of speech that enters the market by coercively silencing members of those groups who are its targets.

Racism is an epidemic infecting the marketplace of ideas and rendering it dysfunctional. Racism is ubiquitous. We are all racists. Racism is also irrational. Individuals do not embrace or reject racist beliefs as the result of reasoned deliberation. For the most part, we do not recognize the myriad ways in which the racism pervading our history and culture influences our beliefs. In other words, most of our racism is unconscious. . . .

[John Stuart] Mill's vision of truth emerging through competition in the marketplace of ideas relies on the ability of members of the body politic to recognize "truth" as serving their interest and to act on that recognition. . . .

Prejudice that is unconscious or unacknowledged causes even more distortions in the market. When racism operates at a conscious level, opposing ideas may prevail in open competition for the rational or moral sensibilities of the market participant. But when an individual is unaware of his prejudice, neither reason nor moral persuasion will likely succeed.

Racist speech also distorts the marketplace of ideas by muting or devaluing the speech of blacks and other non-whites. An idea that would be embraced by large numbers of individuals if it were offered by a white individual will be rejected or given less credence because its author belongs to a group demeaned and stigmatized by racist beliefs. . . .

Finally, racist speech decreases the total amount of speech that reaches the market. I noted earlier in this Article the ways in which racist speech is inextricably linked with racist conduct. The primary purpose and effect of the speech/conduct that constitutes white supremacy is the exclusion of non-whites from full participation in the body politic. Sometimes the speech/conduct of racism is direct and obvious. When the Klan burns a cross on the lawn of a black person who joined the NAACP or exercised his right to move to a formerly all-white neighborhood, the effect of this speech does not result from the persuasive power of an idea operating freely in the market. It is a threat, a threat made in the context of a history of lynchings, beatings, and economic reprisals that made good on earlier threats, a threat that silences a potential speaker. The black student who is subjected to racial epithets is likewise threatened and silenced. Certainly she, like the victim of a cross-burning, may be uncommonly brave or foolhardy and ignore the system of violence in which this abusive speech is only a bit player. But it is more likely that we, as a community, will be denied the benefit of many of her thoughts and ideas. . . .

"WHICH SIDE ARE (WE) ON?"

. . . There is much about the way many civil libertarians have participated in the debate over the regulation of racist speech that causes the victims of that speech to wonder which side they are on. Those who raise their voices in protest against public sanctions of racist speech have not organized private protests against the voices of racism. It has been people of color, women, and gays who have held vigils at offending fraternity houses, staged candlelight marches, counter-demonstrations and distributed flyers calling upon their classmates and colleagues to express their outrage at pervasive racism, sexism, and homophobia in their midst and show their solidarity with its victims.

Traditional civil libertarians have been conspicuous largely in their absence from these group expressions of condemnation. Their failure to participate in this marketplace response to speech with more speech is often justified, paradoxically, as concern for the principle of free speech. When racial minorities or other victims of hate speech hold counter-demonstrations or engage in picketing, leafleting, heckling, or booing of racist speakers, civil libertarians often accuse them of private censorship, of seeking to silence opposing points of view. When both public and private responses to racist speech are rejected by First Amendment absolutists as contrary to the principle of free speech, it is no wonder that the victims of racism do not consider them allies. . . .

There is also a propensity among some civil libertarians to minimalize the injury to the victims of racist speech and distance themselves from it by characterizing individual acts of racial harassment as aberrations, as isolated incidents in a community that is otherwise free of racism. When those persons who argue against the regulation of racist speech speak of "silencing a few creeps" or argue that "the harm that censors allege will result unless speech is forbidden rarely occurs," they demonstrate an unwillingness even to acknowledge the injury. Moreover, they disclaim any responsibility for its occurrence.

The recent outbreak of racism on our campuses in its most obvious manifestations provides an opportunity to examine the presence of less overt forms of racism within our educational institutions. But the debate that has followed these incidents has focused on the First Amendment freedoms of the perpetrator rather than the university community's responsibility for creating an environment where such acts occur. The resurgence of flagrant racist acts has not occurred in a vacuum. It is evidence of more widespread resistance to change by those holding positions of dominance and privilege in institutions, which until recently were exclusively white. Those who continue to be marginalized in these institutions—by their token inclusion on faculties and administrations, by the exclusion of their cultures from core curricula, and by commitment to diversity and multi-culturalism that seems to require assimilation more than any real change in the university—cannot help but see their colleagues' attention to free speech as an avoidance of these larger issues of equality.

When the ACLU enters the debate by challenging the University of Michigan's efforts to provide a safe harbor for its black, Hispanic, and Asian students (a climate that a colleague of mine compared unfavorably with Mississippi in the 1960s), we should not be surprised that non-white students feel abandoned. When we respond to Stanford students' pleas for protection by accusing them of seeking to silence all who disagree with them, we paint the harassing bigot as a martyred defender of democracy. When we valorize bigotry we must assume some responsibility for the fact that bigots are encouraged by their newfound status as "defenders of the faith." We must find ways to engage actively in speech and action that resists and counters the racist ideas the First Amendment protects. If we fail in this duty, the victims of hate speech rightly assume we are aligned with their oppressors.

Discussion Questions

1. What welfare rights, according to Lawrence, are violated by hate speech? Are you satisfied with Lawrence's suggestions for resolving the moral dilemma between welfare rights and liberty rights? Support your answers. Create a policy for your campus for resolving this conflict.
2. Lawrence argues that John Stuart Mill's so-called marketplace of ideas does not include hate speech. Instead, Lawrence maintains that racist speech needs to be regulated because it has a "disruptive and disabling effect on the market of an idea [racism]

that is ubiquitous and irrational." Do you agree with Lawrence? Given that one of the goals of colleges is to be a marketplace of ideas, discuss which would contribute more toward this goal—the tolerance of hate speech on your campus, or the regulation of hate speech.

3. Discuss how Mill might respond to Lawrence's position on the regulation of racist speech.
4. Lawrence argues that the 1954 United States Supreme Court *Brown v. Board of Education* decision, which outlawed school segregation, was really about freedom of speech. Segregated schools are wrong because they communicate a message of unworthiness to black children. Similarly, prohibiting hate speech is necessary to ensure equal protection. Do you agree with Lawrence that the moral duty to promote equal justice outweighs the right to engage in hate speech? Support your answer.
5. Lawrence claims that "in most situations members of minority groups realize that they are likely to lose if they fight back, and are forced to remain silent and submissive." Do you agree with Lawrence that this justifies restrictions on hate speech? Or do members of minority groups, as well as others who hear hate speech being used, have a moral duty to stand up to it? Support your answers. Discuss how virtue ethicists, such as Aristotle and the Buddha, would answer these questions.
6. Do you agree with Lawrence that placing a higher value on freedom of speech than on the elimination of racism puts the bigot on the moral high ground? Support your answer.

JONATHAN RAUCH

In Defense of Prejudice: Why Incendiary Speech Must Be Protected

Jonathan Rauch is author of *Kindly Inquisitors: The New Attacks of Free Thought* (1993). Rauch disagrees with the equation Lawrence draws between hate speech and physical violence and his call to censor hate speech. Instead, Rauch argues that we cannot get rid of racist speech without destroying genuine freedom of speech. We cannot protect some minorities by suppressing the opinions of other minorities. Instead we have to learn how to live with prejudice and hate speech. The way to cope with prejudice and hate speech is not to suppress it, but to openly correct and criticize it.

"In Defense of Prejudice: Why Incendiary Speech Must Be Protected," *Harper's Magazine,* May 1995, pp. 37–46.

Critical Reading Questions

1. According to Rauch, why will there always be bigoted speech where there is freedom of speech?
2. What does Rauch think we should do about bigoted speech?
3. What does Rauch mean when he says that bigoted speech is integral to intellectual pluralism?
4. What is "purism"?
5. Why, according to Rauch, is the purist aim to eliminate prejudicial words and phrases futile?
6. What contribution does Rauch claim that modern feminism has made to the purist position?
7. What arguments does Rauch use to support his claim that purism poses a threat to education?
8. According to Rauch, why does purism pose a threat to minorities?
9. Why does Rauch reject the argument that oppressive speech is a form of violence?
10. What suggestions does Rauch make for dealing with violence that do not involve outlawing oppressive speech?

The war on prejudice is now, in all likelihood, the most uncontroversial social movement in America. Opposition to "hate speech," formerly identified with the liberal left, has become a bipartisan piety. In the past year, groups and factions that agree on nothing else have agreed that the public expression of any and all prejudices must be forbidden. On the left, protesters and editorialists have insisted that Francis L. Lawrence resign as president of Rutgers University for describing blacks as "a disadvantaged population that doesn't have that genetic, hereditary background to have a higher average." On the other side of the ideological divide, Ralph Reed, the executive director of the Christian Coalition, responded to criticism of the religious right by calling a press conference to denounce a supposed outbreak of "name-calling, scapegoating, and religious bigotry." Craig Rogers, an evangelical Christian student at California State University, recently filed a $2.5 million sexual-harassment suit against a lesbian professor of psychology, claiming that anti-male bias in one of her lectures violated campus rules and left him feeling "raped and trapped."

In universities and on Capitol Hill, in work-places and newsrooms, authorities are declaring that there is no place for racism, sexism, homophobia, Christian-bashing, and other forms of prejudice in public debate or even in private thought. "Only when racism and other forms of prejudice are expunged," say the crusaders for sweetness and light, "can minorities be safe and society be fair." So sweet, this dream of a world without prejudice. But the very last thing society should do is seek to utterly eradicate racism and other forms of prejudice.

I suppose I should say, in the customary I-hope-I-don't-sound-too-defensive tone, that I am not a racist and that this is not an article favoring racism or any other particular prejudice. It is an article favoring intellectual pluralism, which permits the expression of various forms of bigotry and always will. Although we like to hope that a time will come when no one will believe that people come in types and that each type belongs with its own kind, I doubt such a day will ever arrive. By all indications, *Homo sapiens* is a tribal species for whom "us versus them" comes naturally and must be continually pushed back. When there is genuine freedom of expression, there will be racist expression. There will also be people who believe that homosexuals are sick or threaten children or—especially among teenagers—are rightful targets of manly savagery. Homosexuality will always be incomprehensible to most people, and what is incomprehensible is feared. As for anti-Semitism, it appears to be a hardier virus than influenza. If you want pluralism, then you get racism and sexism and homophobia, and communism and fascism and xenophobia and tribalism, and that is just for a start. If you want to believe in intellectual freedom and the progress of knowledge and the advancement of science and all those other good things, then you must swallow hard and accept this: for as thickheaded and wayward an animal as us, the realistic question is how to make the best of prejudice, not how to eradicate it.

Indeed, "eradicating prejudice" is so vague a proposition as to be meaningless. Distinguishing prejudice reliably and nonpolitically from non-prejudice, or even defining it crisply, is quite hopeless. We all feel we know prejudice when we see it. But do we? At the University of Michigan, a student said in a classroom discussion that he considered homosexuality a disease treatable with therapy. He was summoned to a formal disciplinary hearing for violating the school's policy against speech that "victimizes" people based on "sexual orientation." Now, the evidence is abundant that this particular hypothesis is wrong, and any American homosexual can attest to the harm that the student's hypothesis has inflicted on many real people. But was it a statement of prejudice or of misguided belief? Hate speech or hypothesis? Many Americans who do not regard themselves as bigots or haters believe that homosexuality is a treatable disease. They may be wrong, but are they all bigots? I am unwilling to say so, and if you are willing, beware. The line between prejudiced belief and a merely controversial one is elusive, and the harder you look the more elusive it becomes. . . .

An enlightened and efficient intellectual regime lets a million prejudices bloom, including many that you or I may regard as hateful or grotesque. It avoids any attempt to stamp out prejudice, because stamping out prejudice really means forcing everyone to share the same prejudice, namely that of whoever is in authority. The great American philosopher Charles Sanders Peirce wrote in 1877: "When complete agreement could not be otherwise be reached, a general massacre of all who have not thought in a certain way has proved a very effective means of settling opinion in a country." . . . "Let all men who reject the established belief be terrified into silence," wrote Peirce, describing this system. "This method has, from the earliest times, been one of the chief means of upholding correct theological and political doctrines."

Intellectual pluralism substitutes a radically different doctrine: we kill our mistakes rather than each other. Here I draw on another great philosopher, the late Karl Popper, who pointed out that the critical method of science "consists in letting our hypotheses die in our stead." Those who are in error are not (or are not supposed to be) banished or excommunicated or forced to sign a renunciation or required to submit to "rehabilitation" or sent for psychological counseling. It is the error we punish, not the errant. By letting people make errors—even mischievous, spiteful errors (as, for instance, Galileo's insistence on Copernicanism was taken to be in 1633)—pluralism creates room to challenge orthodoxy, think imaginatively, experiment boldly. Brilliance and bigotry are empowered in the same stroke.

Pluralism is the principle that protects and makes a place in human company for that loneliest and most vulnerable of all minorities, the minority who is hounded and despised among blacks and whites, gays and straights, who is suspect or criminal among every tribe and in every nation in the world, and yet on whom progress depends: the dissident. I am not saying that dissent is always or even usually enlightened. Most of the time it is foolish and self-serving. No dissident has the right to be taken seriously, and the fact that Aryan Nation racists or Nation of Islam anti-Semites are unorthodox does not entitle them to respect. But what goes around comes around. As a supporter of gay marriage, for example, I reject the majority's view of family, and as a Jew I reject its view of God. I try to be civil, but the fact is that most Americans regard my views on marriage as a reckless assault on the most fundamental of all institutions, and many people are more than a little discomfited by the statement "Jesus Christ was no more divine than anybody else" (which is why so few people ever say it). Trap the racists and anti-Semites, and you lay a trap for me too. Hunt for them with eradication in your mind, and you have brought dissent itself within your sights.

The new crusade against prejudice waves aside such warnings. Like earlier crusades against antisocial ideas, the mission is fueled by good (if cocksure) intentions and a genuine sense of urgency. Some kinds of error are held to be intolerable, like pollutants that even in small traces poison the water for a whole town. Some errors are so pernicious as to damage real people's lives, so wrongheaded that no person of right mind or goodwill could support them. Like their forebears of other stripe—the Church in its campaigns against heretics, the McCarthyites in their campaigns against Communists—the modern anti-racist and anti-sexist and anti-homophobic campaigners are totalists, demanding not that misguided ideas and ugly expressions be corrected or criticized but that they be eradicated. They make war not on errors but on error, and like other totalists they act in the name of public safety—the safety, especially, of minorities.

The sweeping implications of this challenge to pluralism are not, I think, well enough understood by the public at large. Indeed, the new brand of totalism has yet even to be properly named. "Multiculturalism," for instance, is much too broad. "Political correctness" comes closer but is too trendy and snide. For lack of anything else, I will call the new anti-pluralism "purism," since its major tenet is that society cannot be just until the last traces of invidious prejudice have been scrubbed away. Whatever you call it, the purists' way of seeing things has spread through American intellectual life with remarkable speed, so much so that many people will blink at you uncomprehendingly or even call you a racist (or sexist or homophobe, etc.) if you suggest that expressions of racism should be tolerated or that prejudice has its part to play.

The new purism sets out, to begin with, on a campaign against words, for words are the currency of prejudice, and if prejudice is hurtful then so must be prejudiced words. "We are not safe when these violent words are among us," wrote Mari Matsuda, then a UCLA law professor. Here one imagines gangs of racist words swinging chains and smashing heads in back alleys. To suppress bigoted language seems, at first blush, reasonable, but it quickly leads to a curious result. A peculiar kind of verbal shamanism takes root, as though certain expressions, like curses or magical incantations, carry in themselves the power to hurt or heal—as though words were bigoted rather than people. . . .

Faced with escalating demands of verbal absolutism, newspapers issue lists of forbidden words. The expressions "gyp" (derived from "Gypsy") and "Dutch treat" were among the dozens of terms stricken as "offensive" in a much-ridiculed (and later withdrawn) *Los Angeles Times* speech code. The University of Missouri journalism school issued a *Dictionary of Cautionary Words and Phrases,* which included "*Buxom:* Offensive reference to a woman's chest. Do not use. See 'Woman.' *Codger:* Offensive reference to a senior citizen."

As was bound to happen, purists soon discovered that chasing around after words like "gyp" and "buxom" hardly goes to the roots of the problem. As long as they remain bigoted, bigots will simply find other words. If they can't call you a kike then they will say Jewboy, Judas, or Hebe, and when all those are banned they will press words like "oven" and "lampshade" into their service. The vocabulary of hate is potentially as rich as your dictionary, and all you do by banning language used by cretins is to let them decide what the rest of us may say. The problem, some purists have concluded, must therefore go much deeper than laws: it must go to the deeper level of ideas. Racism, sexism, homophobia, and the rest must be built into the very structure of American society and American patterns of thought, so pervasive yet so insidious that, like water to a fish, they are both omnipresent and unseen. The mere existence of prejudice constructs a society whose very nature is prejudiced.

This line of thinking was pioneered by feminists, who argued that pornography, more than just being expressive, is an act by which men construct an oppressive society. Racial activists quickly picked up the argument. Racist expressions are themselves acts of oppression, they said. "All racist speech constructs the social reality that constrains the liberty of nonwhites because of their race," wrote Charles R. Lawrence III, then a law professor at Stanford. From the purist point of view, a society with even one racist is a racist society, because the idea itself threatens and demeans its targets. They cannot feel wholly safe or wholly welcome as long as racism is present. Pluralism says: There will always be some racists. Marginalize them, ignore them, exploit them, ridicule them, take pains to make their policies illegal, but otherwise leave them alone. Purists say: That's not enough. Society cannot be just until these pervasive and oppressive ideas are searched out and eradicated.

And so what is now under way is a growing drive to eliminate prejudice from every corner of society. I doubt that many people have noticed how far-reaching this anti-pluralist movement is becoming.

In universities: Dozens of universities have adopted codes proscribing speech or other expression that (this is from Stanford's policy, which is more or less representative) "is intended to insult or stigmatize an individual or small number of individuals on the basis of their sex, race, color, handicap, religion, sexual orientation or national and ethnic origin." Some codes punish only persistent harassment of a targeted individual, but many, following the purist doctrine that even one racist is too many, go much further. At Penn, an administrator declared: "We at the University of Pennsylvania have guaranteed students and the community that they can live in a community free of sexism, racism, and homophobia." Here is the purism that gives "political correctness" its distinctive combination of puffy high-mindedness and authoritarian zeal.

In school curricula: "More fundamental than eliminating racial segregation has to be the removal of racist thinking, assumptions, symbols, and materials from the curriculum," writes theorist Molefi Kete Asante. In practice, the effort to "remove racist thinking" goes well beyond striking egregious references from textbooks. In many cases it becomes a kind of mental engineering in which students are encouraged to see prejudice everywhere; it includes teaching identity politics as an antidote to internalized racism; it rejects mainstream science as "white male" thinking; and it tampers with history, installing such dubious notions as that the ancient Greeks stole their culture from Africa or that an ancient carving of a bird is an example of "African experimental aeronautics." . . .

Ah, but the task of scouring minds clean is Augean. "Nobody escapes," said a Rutgers University report on campus prejudice. Bias and prejudice, it found, cross every conceivable line, from sex to race to politics: "No matter who you are, no matter what the color of your skin, no matter what your gender or sexual orientation, no matter what you believe, no matter how you behave, there is somebody out there who doesn't like people of your kind." Charles Lawrence writes: "Racism is ubiquitous. We are all racists." If he means that most of us think racist thoughts of some sort at one time or another, he is right. If we are going to "eliminate prejudices and biases from our society," then the work of the prejudice police is unending. They are doomed to hunt and hunt and hunt, scour and scour and scour.

What is especially dismaying is that the purists pursue prejudice in the name of protecting minorities. In order to protect people like me (homosexual), they must pursue people like me (dissident). In order to bolster minority self-esteem, they suppress minority opinion. There are, of course, all kinds of practical and legal problems with the purists' campaign: the incursions against the First Amendment; the inevitable abuses by prosecutors and activists who define as "hateful" or "violent" whatever speech they dislike or can score points off of: the lack of any evidence that repressing prejudice eliminates rather than inflames it. But minorities, of all people, ought to remember that by definition we cannot prevail by numbers, and we generally cannot prevail by force. Against the power of ignorant mass opinion and group prejudice and superstition, we have only our voices. If you doubt that minorities' voices are powerful weapons, think of the lengths to which Southern officials went to silence the Reverend Martin Luther King Jr. (recall that the city commissioner of Montgomery, Alabama, won a $500,000 libel suit, later overturned in *New York Times v. Sullivan* [1964], regarding an advertisement in the *Times* placed by civil-rights leaders who denounced the Montgomery police). Think of how much gay people have improved their lot over twenty-five years simply by refusing to remain silent. Recall the Michigan student who was prosecuted for saying that homosexuality is a treatable disease, and notice that he was black. Under that Michigan speech code, more than twenty blacks were charged with racist speech, while no instance of racist speech by whites was punished. In Florida, the hate-speech law was invoked against a black man who called a policeman a "white cracker"; not so surprisingly, in the first hate-crimes case to reach the Supreme Court, the victim was white and the defendant black. . . .

Here is the ultimate irony of the new purism: words, which pluralists hope can be substituted for violence, are redefined by purists *as* violence. "The experience of being called 'nigger,' 'spic,' 'Jap,' or 'kike' is like receiving a slap in the face," Charles Lawrence wrote in 1990. "Psychic injury is no less an injury than being struck in the face, and is often far more severe." This kind of talk is commonplace today. Epithets, insults, often even polite expressions of what's taken to be prejudice are called by purists "assaultive speech," "words that wound," "verbal violence." "To me, racial epithets are not speech," one University of Michigan law professor said. "They are bullets." In her speech accepting the 1993 Nobel Prize for Literature in Stockholm, Sweden, the author Toni Morrison said this: "Oppressive language does more than represent violence; it is violence."

It is not violence. I am thinking back to the moment on the subway in Washington, a little thing. I was riding home late one night and a squad of noisy kids, maybe seventeen or eighteen years old, noisily piled into the car. They yelled across the car and a girl said, "Where do we get off?"

> A boy said, "Farragut North."
> The girl: "*Faggot* North!"
> The boy: "Yeah! Faggot North!"
> General hilarity.

First, before the intellect resumes control, there is a moment of fear, an animal moment. Who are they? How many of them? How dangerous? Where is the way out? All of these things are noted preverbally and assessed by the gut. Then the brain begins an assessment: they are sober, this is probably too public a place for them to do it, there are more girls than boys, they were just talking, it is probably nothing.

They didn't notice me and there was no incident. The teenage babble flowed on, leaving me to think. I became interested in my own reaction: the jump of fear out of nowhere like an alert animal, the sense for a brief time that one is naked and alone and should hide or run away. For a time, one ceases to be a human being and becomes instead a faggot.

The fear engendered by these words is real. The remedy is as clear and as imperfect as ever: protect citizens against violence. This, I grant, is something that American society has never done very well and now does quite poorly. It is no solution to define words as violence or prejudice as oppression, and then by cracking down on words or thoughts pretend that we are doing something about violence and oppression. No doubt it is easier to pass a speech code or hate-crimes law and proclaim the streets safer than actually to make the streets safer, but the one must never be confused with the other. Every cop or prosecutor chasing words is one fewer chasing criminals. In a world rife with real violence and oppression, full of Rwandas and Bosnias and eleven-year-olds spraying bullets at children in Chicago and in turn being executed by gang lords, it is odious of Toni Morrison to say that words are violence.

Indeed, equating "verbal violence" with physical violence is a treacherous, mischievous business. Not long ago a writer was charged with viciously and gratuitously wounding the feelings and dignity of millions of people. He was charged, in effect, with exhibiting flagrant prejudice against Muslims and outrageously slandering their beliefs. "What is freedom of expression?" mused Salman Rushdie a year after the ayatollahs sentenced him to death and put a price on his head. "Without the freedom to offend, it ceases to exist." I can think of nothing sadder than that minority activists, in their haste to make the world better, should be the ones to forget the lesson of Rushdie's plight: for minorities, pluralism, not purism, is the answer. The campaigns to eradicate prejudice—all of them, the speech codes and workplace restrictions and mandatory therapy for accused bigots and all the rest—should stop, now. The whole objective of eradicating prejudice, as opposed to correcting and criticizing it, should be repudiated as a fool's errand. Salman Rushdie is right, Toni Morrison wrong, and minorities belong at his side, not hers.

Discussion Questions

1. Discuss how Lawrence would most likely respond to Rauch's argument that we should tolerate rather than censor hate speech. Which person presents the more morally compelling argument? Support your answer.
2. According to Rauch, if all forms of hate speech were eliminated, freedom of expression in general would be severely limited. Describe what your campus would be like if hate speech were successfully eliminated by campus speech codes. Would it be a place of peace and harmony? Would it be a place of greater diversity and tolerance? Or would it be a place of tyranny and oppression? Support your answers.
3. Rauch claims that our goal should be to make the best of prejudice "rather than eradicate it." What does he mean by this? How can we make anything good out of prejudice? In terms of public policy, how could you implement Rauch's goal?
4. Unlike in the United States, Canadian criminal code makes the willful promotion of hatred against an identifiable group a crime. Has the outlawing of hate speech in Canada created a society, as Rauch envisions, where freedom of speech is severely limited? Or is the freedom of speech of minority groups more limited in the United States, as Lawrence claims? Canadians have traditionally placed less emphasis than Americans on liberty rights and more on welfare rights. Is this relevant to the type of public policy that might work best, from a moral point of view, in each country? Support your answers using specific examples.
5. Do you agree with Rauch that "the line between a prejudiced belief and a merely controversial one is elusive"? Even if the line between the two is elusive, does this necessarily mean that there are not cases of clearly prejudiced hate speech? If so, would censorship be permissible for these extreme cases? Support your answers.
6. Discuss Rauch's claim that "brilliance and bigotry are empowered in the same stroke." Do you agree with Rauch? Use specific examples to illustrate your answer.

JOHN TAYLOR

Are You Politically Correct?

Journalist John Taylor disagrees with people who argue that diversity is enhanced by restricting racist and other undesirable speech. He maintains that the politically correct movement on college campuses is reminiscent of the McCarthy era of the 1950s. Rather than encouraging diversity and free exchange of ideas, it is eroding our education system. The ultimate irony, he notes, is that the people who advocated free speech during the civil rights era are the very same people who are now trying to restrict speech on campus.

"Are You Politically Correct?" *New York Magazine,* January 21, 1991, pp. 32–40.

Critical Reading Questions

1. Why were Professors Thernstrom and Bailyn accused of being racists? How did students respond to what they regarded as racist speech on the part of these professors? Were the accusations justified, according to Taylor?
2. Who are the "new fundamentalists" on college campuses? Why does Taylor call them fundamentalists? What are some of the methods they use to restrict freedom of speech?
3. Why do the "new fundamentalists" believe that the doctrine of individual liberties is inherently oppressive? Does Taylor agree with them?
4. What does it mean to be "politically correct"? What is "false consciousness"? How do those who are politically correct invoke the concept of false consciousness to support censorship?
5. How does Taylor support his argument that the climate on today's college campus is similar to McCarthyism in the 1950s?
6. What does Taylor mean by "thought reform"? What are some of the examples of thought reform used by Taylor?
7. According to Taylor, why are the humanities a hotbed for political correctness and controversy?
8. What groups are assigned ethnic status by the "new fundamentalists"? What groups are assigned oppressed status? On what grounds does Taylor argue that these assignments are arbitrary?
9. What is the New Age caste system? Who is oppressed under this system?
10. Why does Paglia call gender feminism a "form of psychosis"?
11. How do gender feminists use the concept of false consciousness to attack heterosexuality?
12. On what grounds does Taylor reject the goals and ideologies of gender feminists?
13. Why is Taylor suspicious of reports on the prevalence of rape?
14. What group on campus is most involved in trying to restrict freedom of speech? Why do they want such restrictions?
15. In Taylor's view, how is political correctness eroding rationalism and education?

"Racist."

"Racist!"

"The man is a racist!"

"A *racist!*"

Such denunciations, hissed in tones of self-righteousness and contempt, vicious and vengeful, furious, smoking with hatred—such denunciations haunted Stephan Thernstrom for weeks. Whenever he walked through the campus that spring, down Harvard's brick paths, under the arched gates, past the fluttering elms, he found it hard not to imagine the pointing fingers, the whispers. Racist. There goes *the racist.* It was hellish, this persecution. Thernstrom couldn't sleep. His nerves were frayed, his temper raw. He was making his family miserable. And the worst thing was that he didn't know who was calling him a racist, or why.

Thernstrom, 56, a professor at Harvard University for 25 years, is considered one of the preeminent scholars of the history of race relations in America. He has tenure. He has won prizes and published numerous articles and four books and edited the *Harvard Encyclopedia of American Ethnic Groups.* For several years, Thernstrom and another professor, Bernard Bailyn, taught an undergraduate lecture course on the history of race relations in the United

States called "Peopling of America." Bailyn covered the Colonial era. Thernstrom took the class up to the present.

Both professors are regarded as very much in the academic mainstream, their views grounded in extensive research on their subject, and both have solid liberal democratic credentials. But all of a sudden, in the fall of 1987, articles began to appear in the *Harvard Crimson* accusing Thernstrom and Bailyn of "racial insensitivity" in "Peopling of America." The sources for the articles were anonymous, the charges vague, but they continued to be repeated, these ringing indictments.

Finally, through the intervention of another professor, two students from the lecture course came forward and identified themselves as the sources for the articles. When asked to explain their grievances, they presented the professors with a six-page letter. Bailyn's crime had been to read from the diary of a southern planter without giving equal time to the recollections of a slave. This, to the students, amounted to a covert defense of slavery. Bailyn, who has won two Pulitzer Prizes, had pointed out during the lecture that no journals, diaries, or letters written by slaves had ever been found. He had explained to the class that all they could do was read the planter's diary and use it to speculate about the experience of slaves. But that failed to satisfy the complaining students. Since it was impossible to give equal representation to the slaves, Bailyn ought to have dispensed with the planter's diary altogether.

Thernstrom's failures, according to the students, were almost systematic. He had, to begin with, used the word *Indians* instead of *Native Americans*. Thernstrom tried to point out that he had said very clearly in class that *Indian* was the word most Indians themselves use, but that was irrelevant to the students. They considered the word racist. . . .

Even worse, they continued, Thernstrom had assigned a book to the class that mentioned that some people regarded affirmative action as preferential treatment. That was a racist opinion. But most egregiously, Thernstrom had endorsed, in class, Patrick Moynihan's emphasis on the breakup of the black family as a cause of persistent black poverty. That was a racist idea.

All of these words and opinions and ideas and historical approaches were racist. *Racist!* They would not be tolerated.

The semester was pretty much over by then. But during the spring, when Thernstrom sat down to plan the course for the following year, he had to think about how he would combat charges of racism should they crop up again. And they assuredly would. . . . And a charge of racism, however unsubstantiated, leaves a lasting impression. "It's like being called a Commie in the fifties," Thernstrom says. "Whatever explanation you offer, once accused, you're always suspect."

He decided that to protect himself in case he was misquoted or had comments taken out of context, he would need to tape all his lectures. Then he decided he would have to tape his talks with students in his office. He would, in fact, have to tape everything he said on the subject of race. It would require a tape-recording system worthy of the Nixon White House. Microphones everywhere, the reels turning constantly. That was plainly ridiculous. Thernstrom instead decided it would be easier just to drop the course altogether. "Peopling of America" is no longer offered at Harvard.

THE NEW FUNDAMENTALISM

When the Christian-Fundamentalist uprising began in the late seventies, Americans on the left sneered at the Bible thumpers who tried to ban the teaching of evolution in public schools, at the troglodytes who wanted to remove *The Catcher in the Rye* from public libraries. They heaped scorn on the evangelists who railed against secular humanism and the pious hypocrites who tried to legislate patriotism and Christianity through school prayer and the Pledge of Allegiance. This last effort was considered particularly heinous. Those right-wing demagogues were interfering with individual liberties! They were trying to indoctrinate the children! It was scandalous and outrageous, and unconstitutional too.

But curiously enough, in the past few years, a new sort of fundamentalism has arisen precisely among those people who were the most appalled by Christian fundamentalism. And it is just as demagogic and fanatical. The new fundamentalists are an eclectic group; they include multiculturalists, feminists, radical homosexuals, Marxists, New Historicists. What unites them—as firmly as the Christian fundamentalists are united in the belief that the Bible is the revealed word of God—is their conviction that Western culture and American society are thoroughly and hopelessly racist, sexist, oppressive. . . .

One of the marvels of the new fundamentalism is the rationale it has concocted for dismissing all dissent. Just as Christian fundamentalists attack nonbelievers as agents of Satan, so the politically correct dismiss their critics as victims of, to use the famous Marxist phrase, "false consciousness." Anyone who disagrees is simply too soaked in the oppressors' propaganda to see the truth. . . . "we are all the progeny of a racist and sexist society."

This circular reasoning enables the new fundamentalists to attack not just the opinions of their critics but the right of their critics to disagree. Alternate viewpoints are simply not allowed. Though there was little visible protest when Louis Farrakhan was invited to speak at the University of Wisconsin, students at the University of Northern Colorado practically rioted when Linda Chavez, a Hispanic member of the Reagan administration who opposes affirmative action and believes immigrants should be encouraged to learn English, was asked to talk. The invitation was withdrawn. Last February, Patrick Moynihan declared during a lecture at Vassar that America was "a model of a reasonably successful multiethnic society." Afterward, he got into an argument with a black woman who disagreed with him, and when she claimed the senator had insulted her, militant students occupied a school building until Moynihan returned his lecture fee. "The disturbing factor in the success of totalitarianism is . . . the true selflessness of its adherents," Hannah Arendt wrote in *The Origins of Totalitarianism.* "The fanaticized members can be reached by neither experience nor argument."

It is this sort of demand for intellectual conformity, enforced with harassment and intimidation, that has led some people to compare the atmosphere in universities today to that of Germany in the thirties. "It's fascism of the left," says Camille Paglia, a professor at the University of the Arts in Philadelphia and the author of *Sexual Personae.* "These people behave like the Hitler Youth."

It reminds others of America in the fifties. "This sort of atmosphere, where a few highly mobilized radical students can intimidate everyone else, is quite new," Thernstrom says. "This is a new McCarthyism. It's more frightening than the old McCarthyism, which had no support in the academy. Now the enemy is within. There are students and faculty who have no belief in freedom of speech." . . .

Many schools—including Stanford, Pennsylvania, and the University of Wisconsin—have adopted codes of conduct that require students who deviate from politically correct thinking to undergo thought reform. When a student at the University of Michigan read a limerick that speculated jokingly about the homosexuality of a famous athlete, he was required to attend gay-sensitivity sessions and publish a piece of self-criticism in the student newspaper called "Learned My Lesson."

But is any of this so awful? In the minds of its advocates, thought reform is merely a well-intentioned effort to help stop the spread of the racial tensions that have proliferated in universities in recent years. "I don't know of any institution that is saying you have to adore everyone else," says Catharine Stimpson, dean of the graduate school at Rutgers. "They are saying you have to learn to live with everyone. They are taking insulting language seriously. That's a good thing. They're not laughing off anti-Semitic and homophobic graffiti."

After all, it is said, political indoctrination of one sort or another has always taken place at universities. Now that process is simply being overt. . . .

EVERYTHING IS POLITICAL

If the debate over what students should be taught has become an openly political power struggle, that is only because, to the politically correct, *everything* is political. And nothing is more political, in their view, than the humanities, where much of the recent controversy has been centered.

For most of the twentieth century, professors in the humanities modeled themselves on their counterparts in the natural sciences. They thought of themselves as specialists in the disinterested pursuit of the truth. . . .

That common sense of purpose began to fracture in the sixties. The generation of professors now acquiring prominence and power at universities . . . came of age during that period. They witnessed its upheavals and absorbed its political commitments. . . .

In the view of such activists, the universities were hardly the havens of academic independence they pretended to be. They had hopelessly compromised their integrity by accepting contracts from the Pentagon, but those alliances with the reviled "military-industrial Establishment" were seen as merely one symptom of a larger conspiracy by white males. Less obviously, but more insidiously, they had appointed themselves guardians of the culture and compiled the list of so-called Great Books as a propaganda exercise to reinforce the notion of white-male superiority. "The canon of great literature was created by high-Anglican ass——s to underwrite their social class," Stanley Hauerwas, a professor at Duke's Divinity School, put it recently. . . .

That being the case, any attempt to assign meaning to art, literature, or thought, to interpret it and evaluate it, was nothing more than an exercise in political power by the individual with the authority to impose his or her view. It then followed that the only reason to require students to read certain books is not to "correct taste" or because the books were "the best that has been thought or written" but because they promoted politically correct viewpoints. That ideological emphasis also applied to scholarship generally. . . .

ETHNIC AND IDEOLOGICAL PURITY

The multicultural and ethnic-studies programs now in place at most universities tend to divide humanity into five groups—whites, blacks, Native Americans, Hispanics, and Asians. (Homosexuals and feminists are usually included on the grounds that, though they are not a distinct ethnic group, they, too, have been oppressed by the "white-male" . . . and prevented from expressing their "otherness.") These are somewhat arbitrary categories, and, in fact, the new fundamentalists have two contradictory views about just what constitutes an ethnic group and who can belong. . . .

This obsessive tendency to see oppression everywhere is creating a sort of New Age caste system. The Smith handout listed various categories of oppression that ranged from "classism" and "ageism" to "ableism" (identified as "oppression of the differently abled by the temporarily able") and "lookism," which was revealed to be "the construction of a standard for beauty/attractiveness; and oppression through stereotypes and generalizations of both those who do not fit that standard and those who do." Heightism may be next. In a joke now making the rounds, short people are demanding to be known as "the vertically challenged."

But joking isn't allowed! Even the most harmless, lighthearted remarks can lead to virulent denunciations. In October, Roderick Nash, a professor at the University of California at Santa Barbara, pointed out during a lecture on environmental ethics that there is a movement to start referring to pets as animal companions. (Apparently, domesticated animals are offended by the word *pet.*) Nash then made some sort of off-the-cuff observation about how women who pose for *Penthouse* are still called Pets (and not *Penthouse* Animal Companions). Inevitably, several female students filed a formal sexual-harassment complaint against him. Susan Rode, one of the signers, said, "Maybe this will make more people aware in other classes and make other faculty watch what they say."

Indeed, making people *watch what they say* is the central preoccupation of politically correct students. Stephan Thernstrom is not the only professor who has been forced to give up a course on race relations. . . .

THE GENDER FEMINISTS AND DATE RAPE

"Misogynist!"

"Patriarchal!"

"Gynophobic!"

"Phallocentric!"

Last fall, Camille Paglia attended a lecture by a "feminist theorist" from a large Ivy League university who had set out to "decode" the subliminal sexual oppressiveness in fashion photography. The feminist theorist stood at the front of the room showing slides of fashion photography and cosmetics ads and exposing, in the style of Lacanian psychoanalysis, their violent sexism. She had selected a Revlon ad of a woman with a heavily made-up face who was standing up to her chin in a pool of water. When it came up on the screen, she exclaimed, "Decapitation!"

She showed a picture of a black woman who was wearing aviator goggles and had the collar of her turtleneck sweater pulled up. "Strangulation!" she shouted. "Bondage!"

It went on like this for the entire lecture. When it was over, Paglia, who considers herself a feminist, stood up and made an impassioned speech. She declared that the fashion photography of the past 40 years is great art, that instead of decapitation she saw the birth of Venus, instead of strangulation she saw references to King Tut. But political correctness has achieved a kind of exquisitely perfect rigidity among the group known as the gender feminists, and she was greeted, she says, "with gasps of horror and angry murmuring. It's a form of psychosis, this slogan-filled machinery. The radical feminists have contempt for values other than their own, and they're inspiring in students a resentful attitude toward the world."

Indeed, the central tenet of gender feminism is that Western society is organized around a "sex/gender system." What defines the system, according to Sandra Harding, a professor of philosophy at the University of Delaware and one of its exponents, is "male dominance made possible by men's control of women's productive and reproductive labor."

The primary arena for this dominance is, of course, the family, which Alison Jaggar, a professor at the University of Cincinnati and the head of the American Philosophical Association's Committee on the Status of Women in Philosophy, sees as "a cornerstone of women's oppression." The family, in Jaggar's view, "enforces heterosexuality" and "imposes the prevailing masculine and feminine character structures on the next generation." . . .

Women who have decided to get married and raise families, women who want to become mothers, are, naturally, victims of false consciousness. The radical feminists are fond of quoting Simone de Beauvoir, who said, "No woman should be authorized to stay at home and raise children . . . precisely because if there is such a choice, too many women will make that one." . . .

Unlike the pre-Copernican view that the Earth was at the center of the universe, androcentricity is not, in the view of the gender feminists, merely a flawed theory. It is a moral evil, dedicated to the enslavement of women. And since most of Western culture, according to this view, has been a testament to "male power and transcendence," it is similarly evil and must be discarded. This includes not only patriarchal books like the Bible and sexist subjects like traditional history, with its emphasis on great men and great deeds, but also the natural sciences and even the very process of analytical thinking itself. . . .

But it is not just the coldly analytical and dualistic structures of male thinking that the gender feminists find so contemptible. It is males themselves, or at least heterosexual males. After all, heterosexuality is responsible for the subjugation of women, and so, in the oppressive culture of the West, any woman who goes on a date with a man is a prostitute. "Both man and woman might be outraged at the description of their candlelight dinner as prostitution," Jaggar has written. "But the radical feminist argues this outrage is simply due to the participants' failure or refusal to perceive the social context in which the dinner occurs." In other words, they are victims of—what else?—false consciousness.

This eagerness to see all women as victims, to describe all male behavior with images of rape and violation, may shed some light on the phenomenon of date rape, a legitimate issue that has been exaggerated and distorted by a small group with a specific political agenda. . . .

Much of this discussion starts off with the claim that one in four female students is raped by a date. The figure seems staggeringly high, and debate tends to focus on whether actual rape or merely the reporting of rape is on the rise. But the journalist Stephanie Gutmann has pointed out in *Reason* magazine the gross statistical flaws in the survey of date rape that produced this figure. According to Gutmann, "the real story about campus date rape is not that there's been any significant increase of rape on college campuses, at least of the acquaintance type, but that the word *rape* is being stretched to encompass any type of sexual interaction."

In fact, rape under the new definition does not have to involve physical assault at all. . . .

It is no surprise then that Catherine Nye, a University of Chicago psychologist interviewed by Gutmann, found that 43 percent of the women in a widely cited rape study "had not realized they had been raped." In other words, they were victims of, yes, false consciousness. But by the definition of the radical feminists, all sexual encounters that involve any confusion or ambivalence constitute rape. "Ordinary bungled sex—the kind you regret in the morning or even during—is being classified as rape," Gutmann says. "Bad or confused feelings after sex becomes someone else's fault." Which is fine with the feminists. "In terms of making men nervous or worried about overstepping their bounds, I don't think that's a bad thing," [Andrea] Parrot said. Indeed, since it encourages a general suspicion of all men, it's a good thing. As Parrot has put it, "Since you can't tell who has the potential for rape simply by looking, be on your guard with every man." . . .

MOONIES IN THE CLASSROOM

The supreme irony of the new fundamentalism is that the generation that produced the free-speech movement in Berkeley and rebelled against the idea of *in loco parentis*—that university administrators should act as surrogate parents—is now trying to restrict speech and control the behavior of a new generation of students. The enterprise is undertaken to combat racism, of course, and it is an article of faith among the politically correct that the current climate of racial hostility can be traced to the Reagan and Bush presidencies, to conservative-Republican efforts to gut civil-rights legislation and affirmative-action programs. However true that may be, scholars like Shelby Steele, a black essayist and English professor, have also argued that the separatist movements at universities—black dorms, Native American student centers, gay-studies programs, the relentless harping on "otherness"—have heightened tensions and contributed to the culture of victimization. "If you sensitize people from day one to look at everything in terms of race and sex, eventually they will see racism and sexism at the root of everything," says Alan Kors. "But not all the problems and frustrations in life are due to race and gender."

Furthermore, they say, instead of increasing self-esteem, schools that offer an Afrocentric education will only turn out students who are more resentful, and incompetent, than ever. Indeed, while the more rabid Afrocentrics have claimed that crack and AIDS are conspiracies by whites to eliminate blacks, it could just as easily be argued that white indulgence of Afrocentric education represents a conspiracy to provide blacks with a useless education that will keep them out of the job market.

Of course, to make such a statement is invariably to provoke a charge of racism. But part of the problem with this reaction is that it trivializes the debate. In fact, it makes debate impossible. But that is just as well, according to the new fundamentalists. Debate, and the analytic thinking it requires, is oppressive. It's logocentric. It favors the articulate at the expense of the inarticulate. It forces people to make distinctions, and since racism is the result of distinctions, they should be discouraged. "I have students tell me they don't need to study philosophy because it's patriarchal and logocentric," says Christina Sommers. "They're unteachable and scary. It's like having a Moonie in the classroom."

Resistance to this sort of robotic sloganeering is beginning. "Today, routinized righteous indignation has been substituted for rigorous criticism,"[34] Henry Louis Gates, a black English professor at Duke, recently declared. . . .

A few emboldened administrators are actually suggesting that it is not unreasonable for Western culture to enjoy a certain prominence at American colleges. In an address to incoming Yale students in September, Donald Kagan, dean of the college, encouraged them to center their undergraduate studies around Western culture. He argued that the West "has asserted the claims of the individual against those of the state, limiting its power and creating a realm of privacy into which it cannot penetrate." The West's tradition of civil liberties has produced a "tolerance and respect for diversity unknown in most cultures."

But many of the Yale freshmen—or "freshpeople," as the *Yale Daily News* puts it—considered the dean's statements "quite disturbing." And the dean was denounced with the obligatory mind-numbing litany.

"Paternalistic!"

"Racist!"

"Fascist!"

Discussion Questions

1. Were the "racially insensitive" comments made by Professors Thernstrom and Bailyn examples of hate speech? Should people who use politically incorrect terms such as *Indian* instead of *Native American* be censured or reprimanded? If so, how should this be carried out; for example, should it be through exposés in student newspapers, as happened in this case, through speech codes, through laws, or through boycotts of classes? Support your answers.
2. What are some examples of "red flag" phrases and hate speech on your college campus? On what grounds do you consider them to be so? Discuss whether professors should censure students who use "red flag" phrases in their papers or who engage in hate speech in class.
3. Discuss Taylor's claim that the politically correct climate on today's campus is reminiscent of the McCarthyism of the 1950s. Would Lawrence agree with Taylor? Explain.
4. Do you find that you have to be careful of what you say on campus? Is it necessarily an undesirable thing that we should stop and think of the effects of our words before speaking? Support your answers.
5. Are multiculturalism and gender feminism divisive, as Taylor claims? Support your answer using examples from your own experience.

ALAN M. DERSHOWITZ

Political Correctness, Speech Codes, and Diversity

Alan Dershowitz is a law professor at Harvard University as well as one of the foremost defense lawyers and civil libertarians in the United States. His books include *Taking Liberties: A Decade of Hard Cases, Bad Laws, and Bum Raps,* and *The Abuse Excuse* (1994). In this article, Dershowitz examines the motives behind the political correctness movement. Like Taylor, he concludes that the speech codes promoted by the political correctness movement, while claiming to promote greater diversity, in fact limit diversity of expression.

"Political Correctness, Speech Codes, and Diversity," *Harvard Law Record,* September 20, 1991.

Critical Reading Questions

1. According to Dershowitz, what are two of the basic tenets of the political correctness movement?
2. What is the primary purpose of campus speech codes? Is this purpose, according to Dershowitz, compatible with diversity of expression?
3. Why does Dershowitz question the real motives of the political correctness movement?
4. According to Dershowitz, what is the real motive behind the demand for more diversity on college campuses?
5. What group of people is pushing hardest for political correctness and speech codes?
6. What is the effect of speech codes on political speech?
7. How does Dershowitz respond to students who defend speech codes on the grounds that certain types of speech contribute to "bigotry, harassment and intolerance, and that it makes it difficult for them to learn"?
8. What has been the right-wing reaction to speech codes?
9. According to Dershowitz, what has been the effect of political correctness and speech codes on discussions and learning in the classroom?

There is now a debate among the pundits over whether the "political correctness" [P.C.] movement on college and university campuses constitutes a real threat to intellectual freedom or merely provides conservatives with a highly publicized opportunity to bash the left for the kind of intolerance of which the right has often been accused.

My own sense, as a civil libertarian whose views lean to the left, is that the "P.C." movement is dangerous and that it is also being exploited by hypocritical right wingers.

In addition to being intellectually stifling, the P.C. movement is often internally inconsistent. Among its most basic tenets are (1) the demand for "greater diversity" among students and faculty members; and (2) the need for "speech codes," so that racist, sexist and homophobic ideas, attitudes and language do not "offend" sensitive students.

Is it really possible that the bright and well-intentioned students (and faculty) who are pressing the "politically correct" agenda do not realize how inherently self-contradictory these two basic tenets really are? Can they be blind to the obvious reality that true diversity of viewpoints is incompatible with speech codes that limit certain diverse expressions and attitudes?

I wonder if most of those who are pressing for diversity really want it. What many on the extreme left seem to want is simply more of their own: more students and faculty who think like they do, vote like they do and speak like they do. The last thing they want is a truly diverse campus community with views that are broadly reflective of the multiplicity of attitudes in the big, bad world outside of the ivory towers.

How many politically correct students are demanding—in the name of diversity—an increase in the number of Evangelical Christians, National Rifle Association members, and Right to Life advocates? Where is the call for more anti-communist refugees from the Soviet Union, Afro-Americans who oppose race-specific quotas, and women who are antifeminist?

Let's be honest: the demand for diversity is at least in part a cover for a political power grab by the left. Most of those who are recruited to provide politically correct diversity—Afro-Americans, women, gays—are thought to be supporters of the left. And historically, the left—like the right—has not been a bastion of diversity.

Now the left—certainly the extreme left that has been pushing hardest for political correctness—is behind the demands for speech codes. And if they were to get their way, these codes would not be limited to racist, sexist, or homophobic *epithets*. They would apply as well to politically incorrect *ideas* that are deemed offensive by those who would enforce the codes. Such ideas would include criticism of affirmative action programs, opposition to rape-shield laws, advocacy of the criminalization of homosexuality and defense of pornography.

I have heard students argue that the expression of such ideas—both in and out of class, both by students and professors—contributes to an atmosphere of bigotry, harassment and intolerance, and that it makes it difficult for them to learn.

The same students who insist that they be treated as adults when it comes to their sexuality, drinking and school work, beg to be treated like children when it comes to politics, speech and controversy. They whine to Big Father and Mother—the president or provost of the University—to "protect" them from offensive speech, instead of themselves trying to combat it in the marketplace of ideas.

Does this movement for political correctness—this intolerance of verbal and intellectual diversity—really affect college and university students today? Or is it, as some argue, merely a passing fad, exaggerated by the political right and the media?

It has certainly given the political right—not known for its great tolerance of different ideas—a hey day. Many hypocrites of the right, who would gladly impose their own speech codes if *they* had the power to enforce *their* way, are selectively wrapping themselves in the same First Amendment they willingly trash when it serves their political interest to do so.

But hypocrisy aside—since there is more than enough on both sides—the media is not exaggerating the problem of political correctness. It is a serious issue on college and university campuses. As a teacher, I can feel a palpable reluctance on the part of many students—particularly those with views in neither extreme and those who are anxious for peer acceptance—to experiment with unorthodox ideas, to make playful comments on serious subjects, to challenge politically correct views and to disagree with minority, feminist or gay perspectives.

I feel this problem quite personally, since I happen to agree—as a matter of substance—with most "politically correct" positions. But I am appalled at the intolerance of many who share my substantive views. And I worry about the impact of politically correct intolerance on the generation of leaders we are currently educating.

Discussion Questions

1. List some examples of politically correct ideology. Discuss the criteria you used for deciding whether a particular ideology was politically correct or politically incorrect. Are these criteria based on rational moral principles? Support your answer.
2. Some students confound morality with subscribing to the politically correct ideology. What is the difference between being a moral person and being politically correct? Does the politically correct movement encourage substituting ideology for true moral development? Support your answers.
3. What does diversity mean to you? Discuss whether diversity and freedom of speech are most likely to flourish on a college campus with, or without, speech codes. Use specific examples to illustrate your answer.
4. Ernst Zundel was brought before the Canadian Human Rights Tribunal in October 1997 on charges that he was printing lies about the Holocaust on his Web site.[35] He was accused of propagating hate by denying that the Nazis killed millions of Jews. Should Zundel be prohibited from printing lies about the Holocaust? Support your answer. How would Mill and Dershowitz each most likely respond to this question?
5. Discuss how Lawrence might respond to Dershowitz's objection to campus speech codes. Who makes the strongest argument—Dershowitz or Lawrence? Support your answer.

CASS R. SUNSTEIN

The First Amendment in Cyberspace

Cass Sunstein is a professor of jurisprudence in the law school and the department of political science at the University of Chicago. In the following selection from his book *Free Markets and Social Justice,* Professor Cass explores the impact of the different interpretations of First Amendment freedom of speech on the regulation of cyberspace speech. He concludes that constitutionally based regulations on cyberspace speech should aim to foster democratic ends, including public debate, political equality, and even virtue.

Critical Reading Questions

1. What are the two models of the First Amendment free speech tradition?
2. What are the implications of these two models for the government regulation of speech?
3. Why does Sunstein prefer the Madisonian model over the marketplace model?
4. What are some of the new possibilities opened up by the new communication technology?
5. What are some of the dangers associated with the new communication technology?
6. According to Sunstein, why is universal access to the information superhighway important in a democracy?
7. According to Sunstein, what criteria should be used in deciding whether it is permissible for government to regulate cyberspace speech?
8. What is Sunstein's view on the regulation of obscene, indecent, and sexually explicit material on the Internet? How have the courts handled this in the past?
9. What analogy does Sunstein use in holding electronic mail servers liable for the distribution of unprotected speech?
10. According to Sunstein, what end(s) justify regulating speech in cyberspace?

. . . The existence of technological change promises to test the system of free expression in dramatic ways. What should be expected with respect to the First Amendment?

MARKETS AND MADISON

There have been in the United States two models of the First Amendment, corresponding to two free speech traditions.[1] The first emphasizes well-functioning speech markets. It can be traced to Justice Holmes's great *Abrams* dissent,[2] where the notion of a "market in ideas" received its preeminent exposition. . . .

The second tradition, and the second model, focuses on public deliberation. The second model can be traced from its origins in the work of James Madison, with his attack on the idea of seditious libel, to Justice Louis Brandeis, with his suggestion

Cass R. Sustein, "The First Amendment in Cyberspace," *from Free Markets and Social Justice* (New York: Oxford University Press, 1997), pp. 168–169, 172, 183, 187–191, 196–198, 200.

that "the greatest menace to freedom is an inert people,"[3] . . .

Under the marketplace metaphor, the First Amendment requires—at least as a presumption—a system of unrestricted economic markets in speech. Government must respect the forces of supply and demand. At the very least, it may not regulate the content of speech so as to push the speech market in its preferred directions. Certainly it must be neutral with respect to viewpoint. A key point for marketplace advocates is that great distrust of government is especially appropriate when speech is at issue. . . .

Those who endorse the marketplace model do not claim that government may not do anything at all. Of course, government may set up the basic rules of property and contract; it is these rules that make markets feasible. . . .

The law of free speech will ultimately have to make some hard choices about the marketplace and democratic models. It is also safe to say that the changing nature of the information market will test the two models in new ways. . . .

SPEECH, EMERGING MEDIA, AND CYBERSPACE

New Possibilities and New Problems: Referenda in Cyberspace and Related Issues

It should be unnecessary to emphasize that the explosion of new technologies opens up extraordinary new possibilities. As the Department of Commerce's predictions suggest, ordinary people are starting to be able to participate in a communications network in which hundreds of millions of people, or more, can communicate with each other and indeed with all sorts of service providers—libraries, doctors, accountants, lawyers, legislators, shopkeepers, pharmacies, grocery stores, museums, Internal Revenue Service employees, restaurants, and more. If you need an answer to a medical question, you may be able to push a few buttons and receive a reliable answer. If you want to order food for delivery, you may be able to do so in a matter of seconds. If you have a question about sports, music, or clothing, or about the eighteenth century, you can get an instant answer. People can now purchase many goods on their credit cards without leaving home. It may now be possible to receive a college education without leaving home. . . .

SOME POLICY DILEMMAS

A large question for both constitutional law and public policy has yet to receive a full democratic or judicial answer: To what extent, if any, do Madisonian ideals have a place in the world of new technologies or in cyberspace? Some people think that the absence of scarcity eliminates the argument for governmental regulation, at least if it is designed to promote attention to public issues, to increase diversity, or to raise the quality of public debate. If outlets are unlimited, why is regulation of any value? In the future, people will be able to listen to whatever they want, perhaps to speak to whomever they choose. Ought this not to be a constitutional ideal?

The question is meant to answer itself, but perhaps enough has been said to show that it hardly does that. Recall first that structural regulation, assigning property rights and making agreements possible, is a precondition for well-functioning markets. Laissez-faire is a hopeless misdescription of free markets. A large government role, with coercive features, is required to maintain markets. Part of the role also requires steps to prevent monopoly and monopolistic practices.

Moreover, Madisonian goals need not be thought anachronistic in a period of infinite outlets. In a system of infinite outlets, the goal of consumer sovereignty may well be adequately promoted. That goal has a distinguished place in both law and public policy, but it should not be identified with the Constitution's free speech guarantee. The Constitution does not require consumer sovereignty; for the most part, the decision whether to qualify or replace that goal with Madisonian aspirations should be made democratically rather than judicially. A democratic citizenry armed with a constitutional guarantee of free speech need not see consumer sovereignty as its fundamental aspiration. Certainly it may choose consumer sovereignty if it likes. But instead it may seek to ensure high-quality fare for children, even if this approach departs from consumer satisfaction. It may seek more generally to promote educational and public-affairs programming. . . .

Analogies

An important issue for the future involves the use of old analogies in novel settings. The new technologies will greatly increase the opportunities for intrusive, fraudulent, harassing, threatening, libelous, or obscene speech. With a few brief touches of a finger, a speaker is now able to communicate to thousands or even millions of people—or to pinpoint a message, perhaps a commercial, harassing, threatening, invasive message, to a particular person. A libelous message, or grotesque invasions of privacy, can be sent almost costlessly. Perhaps reputations and lives will be easily ruined or at least damaged. There are difficult questions about the extent to which an owner of a computer service might be held liable for what appears on that service.

At this stage, it remains unclear whether the conventional legal standards should be altered to meet such problems. For the most part, those standards seem an adequate start and must simply be adapted to new settings. For purposes of assessing cyberspace, there are often apt analogies on which to draw. In fact, the legal culture has no way to think about the new problems except via analogies. The analogies are built into our very langauge: e-mail, electronic bulletin boards, cyberspace, cyberspaces, and much more. . . .

Access

The government has said that "universal access" is one of its goals for the information superhighway. The question of access has several dimensions. To some extent, it is designed to ensure access to broadcasting options for viewers and listeners. Here a particular concern is that poor people should not be deprived of access to a valuable good. Currently, the expense of Internet connections is prohibitively high for many families. This may entail a form of disenfranchisement. There is an additional problem of ensuring access for certain speakers who want to reach part of the viewing or listening public. In cyberspace, of course, people are both listeners and speakers.

Perhaps the goal of universal viewer or listener access should be viewed with skepticism. The government does not guarantee universal access to cars, housing, food, or even health care. It may seem puzzling to suggest that universal access to information technologies is an important social goal. But the suggestion is less puzzling than it appears. Suppose, for example, that a certain technology becomes a principal means by which people communicate with their elected representatives; suppose that such communications become a principle part of public deliberation and in that way ancillary to the right to vote. . . . Universal access could be seen to be part of the goal of political equality. More generally, universal access might be necessary if the network is to serve its intended function of promoting broad discussion between citizens and representatives. . . .

Protecting Against Obscene, Libelous, Violent, Commercial, or Harassing Broadcasting or Messages

New technologies have greatly expanded the opportunity to communicate obscene, libelous, violent, or harassing messages—perhaps to general groups via stations on (for example) cable television, perhaps to particular people via electronic mail. Invasions of privacy are far more likely. The Internet poses special problems on these counts. As a general rule, any restrictions should be treated like those governing ordinary speech, with ordinary mail providing the best analogy. If restrictions are narrowly tailored and supported by a sufficiently strong record, they should be upheld.

Consider in this regard a highly publicized case involving "cyberporn" at the University of Michigan. A student is alleged to have distributed a fictional story involving a fellow student, explicitly named, who was, in the story, raped, tortured, and finally killed. The first question raised here is whether state or federal law provides a cause of action for conduct of this sort. Perhaps the story amounts to a threat, or a form of libel, or perhaps the most plausible state law claim would be based on intentional infliction of emotional distress. The next question is whether, if a state law claim is available, the award of damages would violate the First Amendment. At first glance, it seems that the question should be resolved in the same way as any case in which a writer uses a real person's name in fiction of this sort. . . .

What of a regulatory regime designed to prevent invasion of privacy, libel, unwanted commercial messages, obscenity, harassment, or infliction of emotional distress? Some such regulatory regime will ultimately make a great deal of sense. The principal obstacles are that the regulations should be both clear and narrow. It is easy to imagine a broad or vague regulation, one that would seize on the sexually explicit or violent nature of communication to justify regulation that is far broader than necessary. Moreover, it is possible to imagine a situation in which liability was extended to any owner or operator who could have no knowledge of the particular materials being sent. The underlying question, having to do with efficient risk allocation, involves the extent to which a carrier might be expected to find and to stop unlawful messages; that question depends on the relevant technology.

Consider, more particularly, possible efforts to control the distribution of sexually explicit materials on the Internet. Insofar as the government seeks to ban materials that are technically obscene and imposes civil or criminal liability on someone with specific intent to distribute such materials, there should be no constitutional problem. . . . On the other hand, many actual and imaginable bills would extend beyond the technically obscene, to include (for example) materials that are "indecent," "lewd," or "filthy." Terms of this sort create a serious risk of unconstitutional vagueness or overbreadth. At least at first glance, they appear unconstitutional for that reason.

The best justification for expansive terms of this kind would be to protect children from harmful materials. It is true that the Internet contains pornography accessible to children, some of it coming from adults explicitly seeking sexual relations with children. There is in fact material on the Internet containing requests to children for their home addresses. Solicitations to engage in unlawful activity are unprotected by the First Amendment, whether they occur on the Internet or anywhere else. . . .

But when government goes beyond solicitation and bans "indecent" or "filthy" material in general, the question is quite different. Here a central issue is whether the government has chosen the least restrictive means of preventing the relevant harms to children. In a case involving "dial-a-porn," for example, the Court struck down a ban on "indecent" materials on the ground that children could be protected in other ways.[4] . . . Under existing law, it seems clear that in order to support an extension beyond obscenity, Congress would have to show that less restrictive alternatives would be ineffectual. The question then becomes a factual one: What sorts of technological options exist by which parents or others can provide the relevant protection? To answer this question, it would be necessary to explore the possibility of creating "locks" within the Internet, for use by parents, or perhaps for use by those who write certain sorts of materials.

Different questions would be raised by the imposition of civil or criminal liability, not on the distributors having specific intent to distribute, but on carriers who have no knowledge of the specific materials at issue and could not obtain such knowledge without considerable difficulty and expense. It might be thought that the carrier should be treated like a publisher, and a publisher can of course be held liable for obscene or libelous materials, even if the publisher has no specific knowledge of the offending material. But in light of the relatively low costs of search in the world of magazine and book publishing, it is reasonable to think that a publisher should be charged with having control over the content of its publications. Perhaps the same cannot be said for the owner of an electronic mail service. Here the proper analogy might instead be the carriage of mail, in which owners of services are not held criminally or civilly liable for obscene or libelous materials. The underlying theory is that it would be unreasonable to expect such owners to inspect all the materials they transport, and the imposition of criminal liability, at least, would have an unacceptably harmful effect on a desirable service involving the distribution of a great deal of protected speech. If carriers were held liable for distributing unprotected speech, there would inevitably be an adverse effect on the dissemination of protected speech too. In other words, the prob-lem with carrier liability in this context is that it would interfere with protected as well as unprotected speech. . . .

MADISON IN CYBERSPACE?

Do Madisonian ideals have an enduring role in American thought about freedom of speech? The Supreme Court has not said for certain; its signals are quite mixed; and the existence of new technologies makes the question different and far more complex than it once was. It is conceivable that in a world of newly emerging and countless options, the market will prove literally unstoppable, as novel possibilities outstrip even well-motivated government controls.

If so, this result should not be entirely lamented. A world in which consumers can select from limitless choices has many advantages. . . . If choices are limitless, people interested in politics can see and listen to politics; perhaps they can even participate in politics and in ways that were impossible just a decade ago. But that world would be far from perfect. It may increase social balkanization. It may not promote deliberation, but foster instead a series of referenda in cyberspace that betray constitutional goals.

My central point here has been that the system of free expression is not an aimless abstraction. . . . Rooted in a remarkable conception of political sovereignty, the goals of the First Amendment are closely connected with the founding commitment to a particular kind of polity: a deliberative democracy among informed citizens who are political equals. It follows that instead of allowing new technologies to use democratic processes for their own purposes, constitutional law should be concerned with harnessing those technologies for democratic ends—including the founding aspirations to public deliberation, citizenship, political equality, and even a certain kind of virtue. If the new technologies offer risks on these scores, they hold out enormous promise as well. . . .

Discussion Questions

1. Which of the two models of the First Amendment free speech tradition do you prefer and why? Discuss the moral principles and concerns, as well as other assumptions or premises, underlying the models. Discuss which model a rights ethicist, a utilitarian, and a Confucian philosopher would most likely support.
2. Discuss the moral issues raised by the University of Michigan "cyberporn" case. Imagine that you are the president of the University of Michigan. What action, if any, would you have taken if the case was brought to you by the fellow student who was the target of the offending message. Discuss how Charles Lawrence and Jonathan Rauch would most likely have responded had they been the president of the University of Michigan.
3. Analyze Sunstein's argument that electronic mail carriers should not be held liable for the distribution of libelous and obscene unprotected speech. Should this same protection apply to Internet service providers? Support your answer.
4. What position would Sunstein most likely take regarding the regulation of Internet spam and telemarketing? Support your answer.
5. Do you agree with Sunstein that it may be permissible to regulate speech for democratic ends? Support your answer. Discuss how Ayn Rand and John Locke might respond to this question.

CASE STUDIES

1. *HUSTLER* PUBLISHER LARRY FLYNT: "FREE-SPEECH HERO"

The hard-core porn magazine *Hustler,* which has a monthy circulation of more than a million, is a popular source of sex education and socialization among teenage boys. In the world according to *Hustler,* rape is a normal part of male nature. One *Hustler* journalist instucts readers that men are "basically rapists, because we're created that way. We're irrational, sexually completely crazy. Our sexuality is more promiscuous, more immediate, and more fleeting, possibly less deep. We're like stud bulls that want to mount everything in sight."[36] *Hustler* also helps readers select vulnerable targets. For example, one issue had an article titled "Good Sex with Retarded Girls." *Hustler* also used to run a regular kiddie corner called "Chester the Molester."

In the 1996 film *The People vs. Larry Flynt,* producer Oliver Stone portrays *Hustler* magazine publisher Larry Flynt as a free-speech hero. *USA Today* called the movie "a civics lesson that will still be regaling film enthusiasts four decades hence."[37] The controversial film is about Flynt's legal battles against those who want pornography to be censored. Challenging the local obscenity law in Cincinnatti and rural Georgia, Flynt comes face-to-face in the Supreme Court with Jerry Falwell and the "religious right." The Supreme Court ruled that Flynt does indeed have a right to publish and sell pornography. Flynt has been declared by libertarians a free-speech hero and defender of civil liberties. Not everyone thinks so highly of the king of porn. Flynt's daughter, Tonya Flynt, whose father describes her as a "lying little wacko who I don't even know," claims that her father molested her as a child. This, however, was not addressed in the film.

Discussion Questions

1. Does freedom of speech apply to pornography? If so, does freedom of speech override the possible harms of pornography? Discuss the moral issues on both sides of the debate in light of this case study.
2. To what extent, if at all, do the "lessons" in pornography magazines such as *Hustler* harm and subordinate women? To what extent, if at all, do they harm men by socializing them to be sexually violent? Do these harms justify the legal regulation of pornography? Support your answers. Discuss how MacKinnon and Scoccia might respond to these questions.
3. In response to the Supreme Court ruling, Jerry Falwell said, "Larry didn't save the First Amendment. The First Amendment saved him." What do you think Falwell meant by this? Do you agree with him? Support your answers. Discuss whether the First Amendment is consistent with "morality" in the Flynt ruling.
4. Discuss whether or not Mill would consider Larry Flynt to be a "free-speech hero."

---

2. BROWN STUDENTS DESTROY OFFENDING NEWSPAPERS

When *The Brown Daily Herald* at Brown University decided to run an ad from David Horowitz entitled "Ten Reasons Why Reparations for Slavery is a Bad Idea—and Racist Too," a coalition of student groups stole nearly 4,000 copies of the newspaper from campus distribution points. Defendants of the action stated that Horowitz's ad was "an attempt to inject blatantly revisionist and, yes, racist arguments into a legitimate debate about black reparations . . . [In] denying the central role of blacks in demanding their own freedom, Horowitz does more than lie. He reveals his true conception of whites as the bestowers of humanity and his contempt for blacks who ask for too much humanity . . . Outrage is perhaps the only appropriate response [to Horowitz]."[38] They also argued that because Horowitz had the $750 to pay for the full-page ad, the issue was not about freedom of speech but about who can afford to print their views.

The Herald released a statement condemning the action of the students who stole the newspapers, stating "We cannot condone the actions our critics have taken against us. The recent theft of thousands of copies of *The Herald* from Brown's campus was an unacceptable attempt to silence our voice." The University administration released a statement supporting *The Herald.*

Discussion Questions

1. Did the coalition of students do the right thing in destroying the newspapers? Discuss their arguments. Does so-called "freedom of speech" favor those who have the power and money to disseminate their views? How would Mill and Lawrence each most likely respond to the arguments for and against the stealing of the newspapers?
2. The purpose of free speech, in the words of Supreme Court Justice Brandeis, is "to free men from the bondage of irrational fears. A speaker who attempts to monopolize the forum and prevent or intimidate others from speaking is not coming from a position of rationality." How would the students who supported the coalition's actions most likely respond to this statement?
3. One of the professors who supported the students' actions maintained that we have to take a stand "against those who either actively or passively perpetuate oppression by claiming that all acts of speech are equally entitled to level protection. We should deny freedom of speech to the oppressor." Discuss.
4. In a separate incident Brown students disrupted a talk by Richard Perle who supported the war in Iraq. Do we have a right based on freedom of expression to interrupt or jeer people whose views we find offensive? Is interrupting speech a legitimate form of protest? Support your answer.

---

3. *DOE VS. UNIVERSITY OF MICHIGAN*

The University of Michigan had one of the most restrictive campus speech codes. Its policy forbade all conduct that "stigmatizes or victimizes" students on the basis of "race, ethnicity, religion, sex and sexual orientation."[39] The University of Michigan code was created to cut down on the increasing frequency of racist, sexist, and other forms of hate speech.

Fearful that he would be charged as being sexist under the new speech code, a psychology teaching assistant who wanted to discuss mental differences between men and women and how these differences might influence career choices brought suit against the university. Known only as John Doe, he argued that the speech code violated his First

Amendment right to freedom of speech. History Professor C. Vann Woodward supported Doe. Woodward noted:

> It simply seems unnatural to make a fuss about the rights of a speaker who offends the moral or political convictions passionately held by a majority. The far more natural impulse is to stop the nonsense, shut it up, punish it—anything but defend it. But to give rein to that inclination would be to make the majority the arbiters of truth for all. Furthermore, it would put the universities into the business of censorship.[40]

John Doe won his suit against the University of Michigan. The federal district court concluded that while it was "sympathetic to the University's obligation to ensure equal educational opportunities for all of its students, such efforts must not be at the expense of free speech."

Discussion Questions

1. Freedom of speech is highly valued in our society. Are there any moral limits to it? Discuss the nature of these limits.
2. Do we have a right not to be offended? How might Lawrence and Rauch each respond to this question?
3. How should "offensive" be defined? If there is a right not to be offended, how do we know when we have trampled on this right? Is there an objective criterion, or should we rely on people's subjective feelings? Are people's statements that they feel offended by, say, the use of *he* rather than *he or she* in a textbook sufficient to create a duty for a professor not to use that text? Support your answers.
4. Discuss how you could redraft the University of Michigan's speech code so that it did not infringe on freedom of speech.
5. Scholar Stanley Fish writes that "nowadays the First Amendment is the First Refuge of Scoundrels."[41] Do you agree with him? Discuss your answers using the different incidents cited in this case study.

---

4. THE *DARTMOUTH REVIEW*[42]

Dartmouth College in Hanover, New Hampshire, is a member of the Ivy League and one of America's most prestigious colleges. In 1972 this traditionally white, male, liberal arts college decided to admit women and encourage more diversity in the student population. The curriculum was also changed to reflect the new mission. Not everyone was pleased. The conservative independent school paper, the *Dartmouth Review,* vociferously opposed the affirmative action program and criticized the new nontraditional departments as "political indoctrination centers" making personal attacks on certain members of the college community.

In 1983 the *Dartmouth Review* published an article in which it attacked Professor William Cole's music class, calling it the most "outrageous gut" course on campus. They also made personal attacks on Cole. Cole, one of the few black professors on campus, viewed the attacks as racist and demanded an apology. When this was not forthcoming, he filed a libel suit in U.S. district court. Cole charged that the *Dartmouth Review* was trying to interfere with his right to teach in whatever manner he chose. The *Dartmouth*

Review, in turn, accused the college of being hostile to its ideas and of trying to restrict its freedom of speech; it had a right to publish whatever it wanted to publish. The case was eventually settled out of court.

Discussion Questions

1. Did the staff members of the *Dartmouth Review* do anything morally wrong? Support your answer.
2. Supporters of campus speech codes argue that hate speech interferes with the learning environment. Critics of speech codes, on the other hand, argue that such codes stifle professors and students who have ideas they fear may be offensive to others on campus. Discuss these two opposing views in light of the foregoing case study. If you were president of Dartmouth College, how would you resolve this case? Should restrictions be placed on what school newspapers can print? Support your answers.
3. Should classrooms be open forums for the discussion of ideas? Do professors have a right to teach however they see fit even if it is racist or sexist in the opinion of the students and administration? Discuss how Mill would most likely respond to these questions.
4. Discuss what sort of policy Lawrence, Rauch, and Taylor might each suggest for dealing with the *Dartmouth Review.* Which policy do you think is best from a moral perspective? Support your answer.
5. What is the ideal classroom atmosphere? Is it a class where students can express any sort of opinions? Or is it one where only "rational" discussion of ideas occurs? Support your answers using specific examples.

---

5. THE SMOKING GUN: FREEDOM OF SPEECH AND COMMERCIAL ADVERTISING

Commercial speech is protected because of its value in imparting accurate information to consumers about products. Marketing professor Jerry Kirkpatrick argues that advertising is one of the most effective means of combating ignorance and error. According to him, advertising provides us with important knowledge and guides us toward continuous economic progress. "Nothing, as far as I am concerned," Kirkpatrick writes, "could be more benevolent than advertising, beacon of free society."[43]

Not all advertising has such a benevolent goal, however. Some advertising, such as for cigarettes, does not convey information, but uses logical fallacies to make children and other potential consumers associate smoking with things they already desire, such as attractiveness, independence, economic success, and popularity.

In 1995 President Clinton initiated a campaign to prevent children from taking up smoking by severely restricting cigarette advertising on billboards, at sporting events, in magazines, and on promotional items. Clinton's proposal also sought to ban tobacco advertising within 1,000 feet of schools and to require that tobacco companies pay for a $150 million advertising campaign aimed at convincing children and young people to stop smoking. Other countries, such as Brazil, have enacted similar laws against tobacco advertising. In the Czech Republic all cigarette advertising was banned by April 2001, with Poland following suit in 2002. The European Union has also issued a directive phasing out tobacco ads beginning in July 2001.

The tobacco companies, including such giants as Philip Morris and R. J. Reynolds, have protested the U.S. government's restrictions on tobacco advertising as McCarthyism and an assault on their freedom of speech. Furthermore, they claim that the proposed restrictions would interfere with advertising for adults.

Telemarketing and advertising over the Internet have been increasing dramatically. While people can now opt out of receiving calls from telemarketing, spam and pop-up advertisements continue to be legal. Some of these are pornographic and offensive and are imposed on children as well as adults. In addition, sorting through the spam is time-consuming and, some argue, imposes on their privacy.

Discussion Questions

1. Does commercial speech deserve the same protection as political speech? Support your answer.
2. Natural rights ethicist and laissez-faire capitalist Ayn Rand opposes restrictions on the freedom of speech in the name of welfare rights. What policy, if any, would Rand most likely suggest regarding the regulation of tobacco advertising? Support your answer.
3. Do you agree with Kirkpatrick? Does cigarette advertising aimed at children combat ignorance and error? Should restrictions be placed on advertisements that are based on logical fallacies or that mislead customers? Or should the "buyer beware"? Support your answers. How would Mill most likely answer these questions?
4. Does paternalism and the protection of children (as well as adults) from potential harm justify restrictions on cigarette advertising, or is freedom of speech a more compelling moral concern in this case? Support your answer.
5. What moral principles and concerns are involved in the regulation of telemarketing and Internet spam? Working in groups, come up with a policy for dealing with telemarketing and Internet spam. Discuss what policy Mill would most likely propose.

---

6. THE "MEAN WORLD SYNDROME" AND VIOLENCE IN THE MEDIA

Oscar Wilde once said that life imitates art. Perhaps he was right. Epidemiologist Brandon Centerwall of the University of Washington suggests that violence in the media has made us mean people—a situation he labels the "Mean World Syndrome."

In 1995 fourteen-year-old Sandy Charles of La Ronge, Saskatchewan, watched the movie *Warlock* at least ten times in the days leading up to the kidnapping and murder of seven-year-old Jonathan Thimpsen. The 1991 film depicted a satanic murder in which the victim's skull was crushed with a rock and then strips of flesh were peeled off the victim and boiled in liquid fat—the same method used in the murder of Thimpsen. In 1995, three days after the opening of the movie *Money Train,* in which a New York subway token clerk was doused with a flammable liquid and set on fire, two men who had seen the movie carried out a copycat crime, leaving token booth clerk Harry Kaufman in critical condition with burns over 75 percent of his body. In the next few days, two more token booth clerks were attacked or threatened in a similar manner. Copycat crimes have also been carried out based on Oliver Stone's blood-and-guts movie *Natural Born Killers.* A suit against his movie was recently dismissed by the courts.

Murders have also been inspired by printed matter. In 1993 James Perry murdered Mildred Horn, her eight-year-old son, and the son's nurse. When they went through Perry's belongings police found two copies of books from Paladin Press, a Colorado publishing company specializing in the macabre. One of these books was entitled *Hitman: How to Make a Disposable Silencer,* which contained in-depth information on the techniques of professional murder. There were twenty-two instances in which the book's "recommendations" matched actual details in the Perry murders.

The families of the murder victims brought a wrongful-death suit against the publisher, Paul Lind, who responded that the information they publish is protected under freedom of speech and that they are not responsible for how people use that information.[44]

Discussion Questions

1. Media violence disproportionately portrays minorities and women as victims, and young, lower-class Latino or foreign males as perpetrators. To what extent do you think these negative images fuel hate speech? If there is a connection, would this justify the regulation of media on your campus? Support your answers. Discuss how Mill, Lawrence, and Rauch might each respond to these questions.
2. Should the media be held responsible if some people become violent after watching or reading violence? Or should the people who commit the crimes be held solely responsible? What if the killer is a child? How should the pain and death of the victims of copycat murders be weighed against freedom of speech?
3. There was a dramatic increase in violent crime in the United States not long after the introduction of television. A 1992 study in the *Journal of the American Medical Association* found that the average child in the United States will have watched 10,000 murders and 200,000 acts of violence by the age of eighteen. Epidemiologist Brandon Centerwall of the University of Washington hypothesizes that the sharp increase in murder rates in the United States beginning in 1955 is the result of viewing television. Reed Hundt, chairman of the Federal Communications Commission, estimated that without television there would be 10,000 fewer murders, 70,000 fewer rapes, and 700,000 fewer assaults in the United States every year.[45] Similar findings have been found in studies in Canada and Poland. Many scholars believe that there is a causal connection between viewing violence and acting out hatred and aggression.[46] Are these findings relevant to a decision about whether violence in the media, including the Internet, should be regulated? Support your answer.
4. Does the correlation between media and real-life violence justify limiting the freedom of speech of those who produce these shows? If the programming is harmful to children, would this justify regulating such programming for adults as well? Support your answers.

---

7. JOHN ROCKER: PITCHING HATE SPEECH

When Atlanta Braves pitcher John Rocker stated on a June 2000 television show that taking a train to Shea Stadium in New York was like "[riding through] Beirut next to some kid with purple hair next to some queer with AIDS right next to some dude who just got out of jail for the fourth time right next to some 20-year-old mom with four kids"[47]

New Yorkers were outraged. Rocker later apologized saying, "I will put this situation behind me." He asked for others to do the same. However, the people of New York felt the apology was insincere and were not appeased.

When Rocker went in as a relief pitcher in the eighth inning, the crowd of 47,000 responded with deafening booing. Despite the presence of 600 riot police in the stands at least two projectile objects were hurled at the pitcher. The crowd did not calm down until Rocker left the field.

Discussion Questions

1. Was John Rocker exercising his freedom of speech in making the comments he did on the television show? Discuss your answer in light of the concept of liberty rights and legitimate interests.
2. Discuss how you would have responded to Rocker's statements. Examine the moral appropriateness of your response in light of the various moral theories, including virtue ethics, deontology, and utilitarian theory. Using role-playing, with students in the roles of Rocker, the manager of the Braves, and the spectators at the baseball game, come up with a response that is most consistent with moral principles and concerns. Discuss why this response was most morally appropriate.
3. Was the fact that Rocker did not intend to offend others by his comments on the television show morally relevant? Does he owe New Yorkers a duty of reparation? If so, how should he carry out this duty? Do those who booed him in the stadium owe him an apology? Is the fact that the baseball fans may have acted badly relevant to your decision about what Rocker ought to do? Support your answer.
4. Moral opposition to hate speech does not necessarily translate into support for laws banning hate speech. In keeping with the belief that a free marketplace of ideas is the best way to expose hatred for what it is, some maintain that public reaction is a sufficient deterrent. Discuss this statement, in light of the previous case, as well as how Mill, Lawrence, and Rauch would most likely respond to the case.

---

8. HATE AND SEXUAL PREDATION ON THE INTERNET

Hate groups are proliferating on the Internet. Racist groups have discovered that the Internet is an inexpensive way to get their message out to a large audience and to recruit new members.

Alt.support.loneliness was a popular twenty-four-hour Usenet newsgroup for people who were lonely or depressed; that is, until the South Carolina racist group Carolinian Lords of the Caucasus (CLOC) discovered the site. CLOC regularly surfs the Internet searching for new members. After using the site to recruit new members, the CLOC postings on *alt.support.loneliness* turned nasty and threatening. Jay Dyson, who used to post messages on *alt.support.loneliness,* is concerned that such groups can invade a site so easily. "It's frightening because these [lonely] people are at their lowest point in their life," he points out, "and a drowning man will grasp at anything to keep from going under." A CLOC member with the screen name "racial theorist," says that his organization means no harm. "What this thing is about is having fun. And shock value." Besides, they have just as much a right to air their views on the Internet as anyone else, he says.

Child pornography sites are also proliferating on the Internet. Cyberspace sleuth Nancy Casey, mother of two teenage daughters, spends up to eighteen hours a day at home on the Internet posing as young girls in an attempt to attract pedophiles cruising for teenagers and young girls on online-game rooms and chat rooms. Her undercover work has led to the conviction of seven male offenders.[48] While many people applaud her efforts and those of other citizen sleuths like her, others feel it is wrong for people to take the law into their own hands.

Discussion Questions

1. Defenders of the CLOC argue that the point of the Internet is that, unlike traditional media, a wide spectrum of viewpoints, even those that most people find offensive, is tolerated and even encouraged. Do you agree? How might Sunstein and Mill each respond to defenders of CLOC? Support your answers.
2. Discuss the morality of the tactics used by cyberspace sleuths in tracking down online pedophiles.[49] In particular, discuss what Kant and Mill would most likely think of their tactics, particularly the use of deception in posing as children.

   Some of the pedophiles who are arrested by the police as a result of a sleuth's efforts argue in court that they have not committed a crime since they were merely engaging in fantasy, not an actual sex act. Do you agree? Support your answer.
3. People who want the Internet regulated argue that freedom of speech is not an absolute value and it may well destroy the very environment that promotes it. People will stop using the Internet because of badgering by hate groups and sexual predators; also, many schools do not allow students direct access to the Internet because so much of the material there is deemed unsuitable for them. Should there be a code of ethics that prohibits websites promoting hatred and sexual predation?
4. In October 1997 Boston University sued eight companies that sell term papers on the Internet,[50] claiming that the companies encourage student plagiarism. In response the companies argued that the suit, which would close down their businesses, violated their First Amendment right to freedom of speech. They have a right to print what they want. Would Mill agree?

   Do these companies have a moral right to publish term papers on the Internet even though they know how students will most likely use them? Or do the students bear moral responsibility for how they use the information from these companies? Do the colleges and the professors have a moral responsibility for making sure that students are not plagiarizing? Support your answers.

---

9. PUBLIC PRAYER

University of Colorado men's basketball coach, Richardo Patton, had been saying team prayers at the end of practice and after games for years. In February 2000 the American Civil Liberties Union filed a complaint against the coach, stating that saying the prayers at a public university violated the constitutional separation of church and state.

Coach Patton countered that prohibiting his team from saying prayers violated their First Amendment Freedom of Speech. He pointed out that participation in the prayer is voluntary. To prevent the teams from praying is a direct violation of their First Amendment Freedom of Speech. Patton's critics responded that there is an implied coercion when a coach prays with his players. However, when the players were interviewed all of them supported the prayer ritual, supporting Patton's claim that the prayers were voluntary.[51]

In June 2000 the United States Supreme Court, in the case of *Santa Fe (Texas) Independent school districts vs. Jane Doe,* sided with those who want prayer out of public schools. The Supreme Court ruled that student prayers over loudspeakers before public school home football games violated the separation of church and state.

Most Americans disagree with the Supreme Court's decision. In a 1999 Gallup poll 83 percent of Americans agreed that students should be allowed to say prayers as part of graduation ceremonies. Not surprisingly, despite the Supreme Court ruling banning prayer, very few college administrators have plans to police their students and coaches or reprimand them for saying prayers at athletic events.

Discussion Questions

1. Is the fact that the majority of Americans oppose the Supreme Court ruling on prayer morally relevant? Support your answer. Discuss how a cultural relativist and John Stuart Mill would each most likely answer this question.
2. Discuss how a court justice who was a natural law ethicist would most likely have ruled on the issue of prayer in public schools.
3. Patton maintains that "It's not just a coach's job to help these men run better and block better. It's our job to help them grow socially and spiritually." Discuss whether coaches and other educators have a moral right, or even obligation to help their students "grow socially and spiritually." Discuss the implications of your answer on the freedom of speech debate.
4. Identify and analyze the relevant moral principles and concerns in the above case study. Come to a conclusion on the morality of Coach Patton's actions.

CHAPTER 9

Racism and Affirmative Action

In October 1995 black celebrity O. J. Simpson was found not guilty of charges of murdering his white ex-wife Nicole Brown Simpson and her friend Ronald Goldman. Simpson's highly publicized trial focused public attention on the depth of the racial divide in the United States. Critics accused Simpson's defense team of playing the "race card" by capitalizing on the distrust many blacks feel toward the police. Indeed, polls consistently showed that the majority of blacks believed Simpson to be innocent, whereas the majority of whites thought he was guilty. Most people also thought that race influenced the decision of the jury and that the trial had harmed race relations in the United States. Almost half of those polled believed that Simpson would have been found guilty by the jury had he been white.[1] Following the verdict, *Newsweek* ran a story that asked if the United States was, in fact, one nation or two?[2] Is the United States more racially divided than it was twenty years ago?

DEFINING THE KEY TERMS

Race is a loose classification of groups of people based on physical characteristics. Race is more than just a set of physical characteristics, however; it is how people define themselves and others. As such, race is also a social construct. For example, although Jews were singled out as a distinct, inferior race in Nazi Germany, in the United States Jews are generally regarded as white. Hispanics, on the other hand, despite their physical and cultural diversity, are sometimes classified as a race in the United States.

Racism is an ideology or worldview that makes race one of the key defining characteristics of a person. Two fundamental premises of racism are (1) humans can be divided into distinct biological groups and (2) some of these groups are morally inferior to others. The Nazi worldview of Aryan superiority was based on an elaborate pseudo-scientific description of Jewish biological inferiority. Slavery was also bolstered by scientific theories of biological inferiority. Dr. W. H. Holcombe of Virginia wrote in 1861: "The Negro is not a white man with a black skin, but of a different species, . . . the hopeless physical and mental inferior [of the white, and] organically constituted to be an agricultural laborer in tropical climates—a strong animal machine."[3]

Because racial groups are seen as radically different, racism leads to an "us/other" mentality, thereby justifying granting privileges to certain groups while denigrating others. The "other" is also seen as contaminated and to be avoided. The "one drop" of blood criterion, which designates anyone as black who has even one black ancestor, and the scrutinizing of the pasts of Germans for Jewish ancestry illustrate this fear of racial contamination.

Racism implies prejudice. *Prejudice* is based on negative feelings and stereotypes rather than reason. *Racists* categorize people in such a way that they do not see the "other" as a person, but as an object of contempt. Racism is often supported and reinforced by other "isms" such as sexism and classism. Black women, for example, have been stereotyped since slavery as "mammies" or "breeders." This prejudice is perpetuated to this day in the stereotype of the black "welfare queen" who collects welfare checks and passes on her legacy of laziness and pathology to her many children. Another racist stereotype is that of the servile Asian woman who is satisfied being subservient to men. Stereotypes can also be used to justify war and police action, as in the stereotype of the "yellow peril" and the violent young black man.

Discrimination occurs when we treat people differently based on their group membership. Unjust discrimination occurs when we base our actions on prejudices rather than relevant differences. Racial discrimination can take many forms, from racially motivated hate speech to the use of Asian mail-order bride services by middle-aged American men who blame their problems with women on feminism.

Racism occurs on two levels—the personal and the institutional. *Multiculturalists* believe that racism is based primarily on individual ignorance and that education is the solution. *Antiracists,* on the other hand, define racism primarily in terms of power and institutions. Critical race theorists such as Mari Matsuda and Charles R. Lawrence III, for example, emphasize the political and social aspects of racism that privilege certain interpretations of history and everyday experience.[4] According to them, to dismantle racism we need to confront and oppose the dominant societal and institutional structures that maintain it. Economic systems, education, the family, religious organizations, and legal and political structures are all examples of social institutions.

Institutional racism, or enforced discrimination, occurs when the law or a social system is set up to provide advantages to one group of people at the expense of another. Institutional racism exists because of the actions of many individuals who either have the power to make and carry out discriminatory policies, or allow them to continue. Slavery and Jim Crow laws are two obvious examples of institutional racism. Schools also act as agents in perpetuating racism.[5] The myth that schools promote upward mobility among immigrant and minority groups is directly contradicted by the finding that the social mobility of second- and third-generation Hispanics is strictly downward.[6]

Institutional racism affects foreign as well as domestic policy. The use of people in Third World nations for cheap labor sources as well as nonwhite immigrants for cheap labor in this country reflects institutional racism. Indeed the very term *Third World* reflects the Western belief in the inferiority of non-Western countries.

Sometimes institutional racism is indirect. For example, the funding of schools with local, rather than state or federal, taxes means that children from poorer neighborhoods, which may be predominantly black, receive an inferior education. Patterns of environmental use, such as the destruction of American Indian lands by mining companies and the placement of toxic waste sites near minority communities, also reflect institutional racism.

Institutional racism is supported and perpetuated by the media as well as by legal and religious institutions. The 1915 film *The Birth of a Nation,* which is based on the best-selling book *The Clansman,* viciously degraded blacks and glorified the Ku Klux Klan. The movie was an instant hit, at least with some white people. When President Wilson saw the movie, he remarked, "It is like writing history with lightning and my only regret is that it is all so terribly true."

Like sexism, racism is embedded in our everyday language. The term *American* is assumed to mean white, usually white male. Other groups of Americans are distinguished from "real" Americans by the use of qualifying terms as in *African American, Asian American,* or *Native American.* In contrast, one rarely hears the term *European American.* Thus, language is used to perpetuate the colonial discourse, described by Uma Narayan in her article, that these "other" people are not true red-blooded Americans but rather exist as outsiders in American society. The issues surrounding colonialism have resurfaced in the debate over the morality of the American occupation of Iraq.

THE PHILOSOPHERS ON RACISM

Although the ancient Greek philosophers did not directly address the issue, the elitist theories of Aristotle and Plato have been used—or, more correctly, misused—to justify racism. In his *Republic,* Plato argued that those with the greatest inherited capacity for moral and intellectual attainment should be educated to become the rulers. According to Aristotle's moral theory of perfection, certain humans are more highly developed or perfect in terms of virtue and reason. Those humans who are more perfected deserve more of what is good than those who are less perfected. Carrying this line of reasoning one step further, Aristotle concluded that those who are less perfected exist for the sake of and to serve those who are more perfected. Although Aristotle believed that some humans are "slaves by nature" and exist to serve the common good, he did not associate slavery with any particular race.

As with their complicity in endorsing sexism, philosophers are not immune to becoming servants of the status quo. During the seventeenth and eighteenth centuries, racism was incorporated into Western philosophy in part as a response to the need to morally justify European colonialism. John Locke's natural rights ethics, for example, while promoting a doctrine of equal human rights at the same time assumes the superiority of the white Europeans and the inferiority of the American Indians. Locke's version of natural rights theory became the basis of colonial rights discourse.

Swedish botanist Carolus Linnaeus (1707–1778), in *Systema Naturae* (1735), classified humans into varieties, or races, based on physical and psychological characteristics. According to his classification, Europeans are "light, active, ingenious"; Asians are "severe, haughty, miserly"; and Africans are "crafty, lazy, negligent . . . governed by whim." Most Western philosophers accepted Linnaeus's classifications without question. In his essay "National Character" (1748), David Hume alleged that all Negroes were of low intelligence.

In the early nineteenth century, the Lamarkian theory of the inheritance of acquired traits was used by scientists, theologians, and philosophers to explain the superiority of the white European race. It was generally agreed that the fair-skinned northern Europeans ("Aryans") were the superior race and that the dark-skinned Africans were the most inferior race. Indians and Asians were only slightly above Africans. Jean-Jacques Rousseau speculated that the great apes were really humans whose evolution toward civilization had been stunted by adverse environmental conditions. The people of Africa, because they shared a similar environment, were only slightly ahead of the great apes in their evolution. "Primitive" people, such as the African Bushmen and the Australian Aborigines, were studied by anthropologists in order to gain insight into the thinking and culture of prehistoric white men.

The Lamarkian theory was used to support the notion of the perfectibility of humans, which, in turn, justified both colonialization and slavery as a means of assisting "primitive" people in their evolution toward perfection and civilization. This racist worldview was incorporated into the ideals of colonial America. Like Hume and Locke, Thomas Jefferson (1743–1826) accepted the inequality of hereditary endowment in the different human races. The moral principle of equal respect for all persons was thus drowned out by the racist norms of cultural relativism. It was on the basis of these assumptions that the Europeans continued to exercise their "divine and natural right" to conquer, divide up, and exploit the rest of the world for the next two hundred years.

Modern Marxists link racism to capitalism and class exploitation. The Marxist analysis of racism is problematic in that racism is also found in non-Western, noncapitalist economies. Racism is found in the Hindu caste system as well as in the nationalist Shinto religion of Japan. On the other hand, racism is inconsistent with Buddhism, which stresses the moral equality of all humans and the cultivation of the virtue of compassion or "true friendliness."

Perhaps one of the most insidious moral theories is cultural relativism, with its identification of morality with cultural norms. The incompatibility of cultural relativism with the moral condemnation of racism led to the rejection of cultural relativism by all but a few moral philosophers. The majority of Americans, however, still base their moral decisions on cultural relativism. In addition, the current popularity of ethical subjectivism, especially among college students, justifies racism and hatred as a personal choice.

THE ROOTS OF AMERICAN RACISM

Jesse Jackson once said, "America has never come to grips with slavery. It is a hole in the American soul." Although racism is found in many, if not most, cultures, this chapter focuses primarily on racism in the United States.

Racism in the United States is rooted in colonialism, slavery, and the systematic attempted extermination of the Americans Indians. In her article, Narayan explores the roots of racism in colonialism. The first record of African slaves arriving in the American colonies was in Jamestown, Virginia, in 1619. Although the slave trade was outlawed in 1808, the law was widely ignored. About 13 million slaves were brought from Africa to the Americas. Many who landed in the West Indies, Cuba, and Haiti were sold to slaveholders in the United States. The slave trade was both lucrative and brutal. About 10 to 15 percent of the 13 million slaves sent from Africa died en route to the New World.[7]

The American colonies eagerly took part in the slave trade. Although the framers of the Declaration of Independence and the U.S. Constitution briefly considered outlawing the African slave trade (although not slavery itself), the idea was soon dropped because several of them were slaveholders, including Thomas Jefferson, who owned hundreds of slaves.

During the early 1800s, more than a hundred thousand slaves escaped to northern states or found refuge among the Indians. Frustrated at the Native Americans' refusal to comply with orders to return the runaway slaves, southerners sought help from the federal government to pass laws that would make it easier for them to retrieve slaves who had fled to free states. One of these laws, the Fugitive Slave Law of 1850, allowed any black person, even people who had been freed, to be returned to slavery. There was little protest in the North over the law, as even freed blacks were not particularly welcomed and were regarded by the whites as "a dangerous and useless element."

The number of white abolitionists in the United States was never very large. Most people either supported slavery or were indifferent to it. Many of those who were opposed to slavery in principle hated and feared blacks. Frustrated and angry, the northern blacks, with the help of abolitionist groups such as the Quakers, set up the Underground Railroad that smuggled slaves from the United States over the border to Canada.

In 1857 Dred Scott, a slave who had moved with his master in the 1830s to a free territory, sued for his freedom. The Supreme Court ruled against Scott, arguing that blacks were strictly property and had no rights. The Court also ruled that the Missouri Compromise, which made the territory free, was unconstitutional because it deprived white people of their right to enjoy their human property.

When the Civil War broke out in 1861, the conflict was primarily over economic issues rather than slavery. In his 1861 inaugural address, Abraham Lincoln reassured the southern voters: "I have no purpose, directly or indirectly, to interfere with the institution of slavery in the States where it exists. I believe I have no lawful right to do so, and I have no inclination to do so." The 1863 Emancipation Proclamation that freed the slaves, rather than being based on moral repugnance toward slavery, was more of a political move calculated to weaken the Confederate forces and bring an end to the war. Two years later the Thirteenth Amendment to the Constitution guaranteed that "neither slavery nor involuntary servitude . . . shall exist."

Institutional racism did not end with the Thirteenth Amendment, however. The Ku Klux Klan (KKK) was formed in 1866 by a group of Tennessee Confederate veterans. They were soon joined by some of the South's leading businessmen and professionals. During the thirty years following the Civil War, the southern states passed "Jim Crow laws" reminiscent of the old "slave codes." These laws prevented blacks from owning property in certain areas, allowed employers to hunt down and whip troublesome black workers, and enforced segregation in restaurants, theaters, schools, public transportation, hospitals, and even graveyards.

In 1896 the U.S. Supreme Court ruled in *Plessy v. Ferguson* that "separate but equal" segregation was constitutional. According to the Court, the Fourteenth Amendment, while guaranteeing political equality, does not guarantee social equality. The *Plessy v. Ferguson* ruling provided the legal justification for institutional racism for the next sixty years, until 1954, when the Supreme Court overturned the "separate but equal" ruling in *Brown v. Board of Education.*

During the late-nineteenth and early-twentieth centuries, thousands of blacks were raped, beaten, and brutally murdered. By 1880 alone, an estimated 130,000 people had been killed in the South either because they were black or because they sympathized

 EXCERPTS FROM U.S. SUPREME COURT *DRED SCOTT V. SANFORD* (1857)

In the opinion of the court, the legislation and histories of the times, and the language used in the Declaration of Independence, show, that neither the class of person that have been imported as slaves, nor their descendants, whether they had become free or not, were then acknowledged as part of the people, nor intended to be included in the general words used in the memorable instrument. . . .

They had for more than a century before been regarded as beings of an inferior order; and altogether unfit to associate with the white race, either in social or political relations; and so far inferior that they had no rights which the white man was bound to respect; and that the negro might be lawfully reduced to slavery for his own benefit. . . .

This opinion was at that time fixed and universal in the civilized portion of the white race. It was regarded as an axiom in morals as well as in politics which no one thought of disputing, or supposed to be open to dispute. . . . The state of public opinion has undergone no change [from] when the Constitution was adopted. . . .

Now the right of property in a slave is distinctly and expressly affirmed in the Constitution. . . . He is himself property in the strictest sense of the term. And the Government in express terms is pledged to protect it in all future time, if the slave escapes from his owner.

with blacks. Unofficial "lynch laws" in the South allowed white mobs to torture and lynch blacks who couldn't be humbled and controlled by the other laws. The lynchings were advertised in the newspapers and became festive family outings for many white southerners. Even as late as the 1950s, black men could be beaten, jailed, or even lynched for the "reckless eyeballing" of white women.

Race riots followed the migration of southern blacks to the northern cities during the early twentieth century. Up to two hundred blacks were killed and six thousand driven from their homes in a 1917 race riot in East St. Louis, Illinois. With the increase in blacks living in the North, KKK activities spread northward as well. By 1924 the KKK had 4 million members.

Racial segregation continued to be the norm in the United States. There were separate professional leagues for black and white athletes. In Hollywood black actors performed in all-black shows. Although segregated neighborhoods had been ruled unconstitutional by the Supreme Court in 1917, "gentlemen's agreements" among realtors and landlords ensured that neighborhoods—and schools—remained segregated.

During the 1920s the growing "nativist" sentiment made it almost impossible for anyone but people from northern Europe to immigrate to the United States. Racial hatred and Klan activities expanded their targets to include Jews, Puerto Ricans, southern Europeans, Asians, Mexicans, and Native Americans. Following the Japanese attack on Pearl Harbor during World War II, thousands of Japanese Americans were removed from their homes and placed in federal internment camps, even though not a single case of sabotage involving Japanese Americans was ever discovered.

The 1950s ushered in what is called the Second Reconstruction. In 1954 the U.S. Supreme Court, in *Brown v. Board of Education of Topeka, Kansas,* ruled that school

EXCERPTS FROM U.S. SUPREME COURT *BROWN V. BOARD OF EDUCATION OF TOPEKA* (1952)

OPINION: MR. CHIEF JUSTICE WARREN delivered the opinion of the Court.

. . . Minors of the Negro race, through their legal representatives, seek the aid of the courts in obtaining admission to the public schools of their community on a nonsegregated basis. In each instance, they had been denied admission to schools attended by white children under laws requiring or permitting segregation according to race. This segregation was alleged to deprive the plaintiffs of the equal protection of the laws under the Fourteenth Amendment. In each of the cases . . . [the] court[s] denied relief to the plaintiffs on the so-called "separate but equal" doctrine announced by this Court in *Plessy v. Ferguson,* 163 U.S. 537. Under that doctrine, equality of treatment is accorded when the races are provided substantially equal facilities, even though these facilities be separate. . . .

The plaintiffs contend that segregated public schools are not "equal" and cannot be made "equal," and that hence they are deprived of the equal protection of the laws. . . .

Today, education is perhaps the most important function of state and local governments. Compulsory school attendance laws and the great expenditures for education both demonstrate our recognition of the importance of education to our democratic society. It is required in the performance of our most basic public responsibilities, even service in the armed forces. It is the very foundation of good citizenship. Today it is a principal instrument in awakening the child to cultural values, in preparing him for later professional training, and in helping him to adjust normally to his environment. . . . these days, it is doubtful that any child may reasonably be expected to succeed in life if he is denied the opportunity of an

segregation was unconstitutional. The following year Rosa Parks of Montgomery, Alabama, refused to give up her seat on a bus to a white man as required by law. She was promptly arrested. Her act of nonviolent civil disobedience sparked a citywide bus boycott and the civil rights movement. In 1957 Congress created a Civil Rights Commission, which was followed by the passage of civil rights laws.

Martin Luther King Jr. (1929–1968) and Malcolm X (1925–1965) emerged as leaders of the movement. Both were assassinated because of their views. In 1963 Martin Luther King Jr. led the March on Washington. In his famous "I Have a Dream" speech, King emphasized community between blacks and whites. The destiny of whites and blacks in the United States, he told the crowds, could not be separated.

The "Indian problem" was resolved primarily through genocide. By 1675, only fifty-five years after the Pilgrims landed at Plymouth, the Native Americans of New England, who once numbered in the thousands, were almost exterminated. During the early and mid-1800s, the U.S. government undertook the systematic removal of the Indians from education. Such an opportunity, where the state has undertaken to provide it, is a right which must be made available to all on equal terms.

We come then to the question presented: Does segregation of children in public schools solely on the basis of race, even though the physical facilities and other "tangible" factors may be equal, deprive the children of the minority group of equal educational opportunities? We believe that it does.

To separate them from others of similar age and qualifications solely because of their race generates a feeling of inferiority as to their status in the community that may affect their hearts and minds in a way unlikely ever to be undone. The effect of this separation on their educational opportunities was well stated by a finding in the Kansas case by a court which nevertheless felt compelled to rule against the Negro plaintiffs:

> Segregation of white and colored children in public schools has a detrimental effect upon the colored children. The impact is greater when it has the sanction of the law; for the policy of separating the races is usually interpreted as denoting the inferiority of the negro group. A sense of inferiority affects the motivation of a child to learn. Segregation with the sanction of law, therefore, has a tendency to [retard] the educational and mental development of negro children and to deprive them of some of the benefits they would receive in a racial[ly] integrated school system.

. . . We conclude that in the field of public education the doctrine of "separate but equal" has no place. Separate educational facilities are inherently unequal. Therefore, we hold that the plaintiffs and others similarly situated for whom the actions have been brought are, by reason of the segregation complained of, deprived of the equal protection of the laws guaranteed by the Fourteenth Amendment. . . .

their lands. The Bureau of Indian Affairs was created by Congress in 1824. Instead of being advocates for the Indians, however, the bureau was used to legitimate the takeover of their lands. The Cherokee, Choctaw, Chickasaw, Creek, and Seminole tribes in the South owned large tracts of fertile land. In addition to making the land available to the wealthy slaveowners in the South, the removal of the Indians would make it harder for slaves to escape, since the Indians regularly provided refuge for runaway slaves.

In 1830 Congress passed the Indian Removal Act. Although the law required the tribes' consent in order to be relocated, many were forced to move without consent. One-fourth of the Cherokee and half of the Creek died of starvation, exposure, and disease during the forced removal from their homes in the South to reservations in the West.

The near extermination of Native American populations by European settlers was justified as the fulfillment of Manifest Destiny—a divine plan for the expansion of the United States from coast to coast. The massacre of more than two hundred Sioux at Wounded Knee, South Dakota, in 1890 marked the final step in the conquest of Indians' homelands and their removal to reservations administered by the Bureau of Indian Affairs. The ultimate goal of the bureau was assimilation, and schools were set up on reservations so that Native American children could learn English and get a proper "white man's" education.

The American Indians were not the only group in the West to suffer from the slings and arrows of racism. During the mid-1800s thousands of Chinese came to the United States to work on the transcontinental railroad. Once the railroad was completed, they were no longer welcome by the whites. In 1882 Congress passed the Chinese Exclusion Act as a solution to the "Chinese problem" by stopping Chinese immigration and preventing resident Chinese from becoming U.S. citizens. Some of the Chinese returned to China; others, however, sought protection from anti-Chinese violence in segregated areas known as Chinatowns. The Chinese Exclusion Act remained in effect until 1943, when it was repealed by Congress as a gesture of friendship to China during World War II. Although Mexicans and Hispanics are an ethnic rather than a racial group, their treatment in the United States has followed a similar course of discrimination.

Federal initiatives to combat social problems are relatively recent. Under the banner of the Great Society, the Johnson administration in the mid-1960s declared war on poverty. Congress allocated $950 billion for the expansion of existing social services and the establishment of new programs such as Medicare, subsidized housing, and job training to help people break the cycle of poverty.

Following his election in 1980, President Ronald Reagan dismantled much of the Great Society legislation. Instead of viewing poverty as a result of institutional racism, the Reagan administration blamed the behavior and values of the poor. With the dismantling of legislation aimed at overcoming the social problems associated with institutional racism, the social conditions of blacks and other people of color also began to decline. By the late 1980s, black males were worse off than they were in the late 1960s on almost every socioeconomic measure, including employment rate and life expectancy.[8] Black Americans in 2003 had only eight cents for every dollar of wealth that white Americans had. A significant aspect of this disparity is related to residential segregation.[9]

RACISM TODAY

Despite government initiatives to combat racism, 46 percent of blacks interviewed in a 2002 Gallup poll believed "that white hostility towards blacks is fairly widespread."[10] Since the late 1980s, many of the positive gains of the civil rights era have been reversed. Blacks and whites continue to segregate themselves by race in their everyday decisions about housing, church attendance, vacations, and on college campuses. In 1992 housing was more segregated than in the mid-1960s.[11]

Most of the schools in the United States are more segregated and unequal today than they were in 1954 at the time of the *Brown v. Board of Education* ruling.[12] Although segregation is now illegal, tracking, in which students are grouped according to performance on standardized tests, has had the effect of re-creating segregation within schools and holding black children to a lower educational level. There is currently a trend away from increasing efforts to integrating schools and toward increasing minority school funding instead.[13]

The percentage of blacks attending college began falling in 1980.[14] Indeed, young black men were more likely to go to prison than to college. In 1990, 25 percent of all young black men ended up in the criminal justice system, compared with 10 percent of Hispanic men and 6 percent of white men.[15] This trend began reversing in 1990.[16] More than twice as many minorities are enrolled in colleges as in 1980. Forty percent of black high school graduates and 34 percent of Hispanic high school graduates now attend college.[17] The percent of faculty who are minorities, on the other hand, has remained relatively stable with 87 percent of faculty being white.[18]

In the reading "I'm Black, You're White, Who's Innocent?" Shelby Steele examines the current trend to label whites as racist and blacks as innocent victims of racism. He also argues that many of the policies intending to combat racism have instead aggravated it.

Hate Crimes

A hate crime is any crime motivated by hostility to the victim as a member of a group based on color, creed, gender, ethnicity, or sexual orientation. As of June 2000, forty-one states had passed laws against hate crimes.

There has been a rise in racially motivated hate crimes since the mid-1980s. Between 1987 and 1989, hate crimes increased 41 percent in Los Angeles, 33 percent in Boston, and more than 100 percent in New York City. The majority of hate crimes are racially motivated, with antiblack crimes being by far the most common type.[19] In a February 2000 Gallup poll, 28 percent of non-white respondents said that they worried about becoming a victim of hate crime. The number of hate groups in the United States increased by 25 percent between 1996 and 2000.[20] Fewer than one-third of these groups are Klan affiliated, and most are not based in the South. In 1995 and 1996, there was a rash of fires at black churches—seventy-five in eighteen months, more than double the number in the previous five years.[21] Hate crimes against Muslims and Arab immigrants increased sixteen-fold following the September 11, 2001 terrorist attacks.[22] Jews, however, are still more likely than Muslims to be the targets of religiously motivated hate crimes.[23]

The number of racial incidents on college campuses has also been increasing since the mid-1980s. At the turn of the millennium a rash of hate mail was sent to more than a dozen historically black colleges. The letters warned black students of their impending destruction stating that in 2000 there would be all-out war against blacks.[24] College faculty in Middle East studies have also been subject to harassment and threats. Some have had to give up their e-mail addresses because of the deluge of hate e-mail.

Racial and Ethnic Profiling

During the late 1990s another type of insidious racism known as racial profiling made the headlines. *Racial profiling* is the routine, and often unconscious, practice by police and other law enforcement agents, such as the FBI and airport security personnel, of targeting suspects on the basis of their race or ethnicity.[25] In a 1999 Gallup poll, 42 percent of blacks answered "yes" to the question: "Have you ever felt that you were stopped by the police just because of your race or ethnic background?" Only 6 percent of whites polled answered "yes" to the same question.[26]

Studies indicate that racial profiling is a common practice. A study by the New York Attorney General's office found that 50 percent of all police stops were of black New Yorkers, even though blacks make up only 25 percent of New York's population.

Law enforcement agencies claim that since blacks commit crimes at higher rates than whites, racial profiling is justified. However, whether blacks actually commit more crimes or are just more likely to be arrested and sentenced to jail for their alleged crimes remains under debate.[27] An April 2000 study on juvenile justice found that minorities were twice as likely as whites to be sentenced to prison, even when the youths had similar criminal histories.[28] Another study of U.S. Customs services practices found that black women were nine times more likely than white women to be x-rayed after a frisk or pat down, even though they "were less than half as likely to be found carrying contraband as white women."[29]

Since the September 11 attacks, Arab-Americans and Muslim visitors to the United States have also been subject to ethnic profiling both by police and at airports, despite airports' official policy of not using ethnic profiling.[30] Hundreds of Muslims and Americans of Arab descent have also been detained and imprisoned under the U.S. Patriot Act.

Asian Americans have also been the victims of racial profiling. For example, a U.S. Energy Department's inquiry has been accused of singling out Chinese Americans for investigation of security breaches. Both Edward T. Fei, one of the department's top experts on nuclear proliferation, and Wen Ho Lee, a Los Alamos scientist, have been aggressively investigated for security breaches despite lack of solid evidence to support the charges.[31]

Michael Levin in his article at the end of this chapter argues that practices such as racial profiling of African Americans are morally justified because of biological differences between the races. Bernard Boxill, in contrast, argues that color-conscious policies like this violate the principle of distributive justice. Color-conscious policies are justified only when they work toward creating more egalitarian public policy. Opponents of racial profiling also point out that it hurts not only its direct targets but leads to an erosion of trust in the government, especially in the justice system and the police, the very branches of government that are entrusted to protect citizens from injustice.

Affirmative Action

The first affirmative action legislation was passed in 1959. Affirmative action legislation was expanded in the 1960s during the civil rights era. In 1965 President Lyndon B. Johnson delivered a commencement speech at Howard University in which he drew his famous analogy between an American Negro and a shackled runner and called for justice for the American Negro. Excerpts from his speech are found at the beginning of this chapter.

There are several ways to carry out affirmative action. A company or college may simply cast its net farther by advertising in minority newspapers to increase the pool of minority applicants. Another form of affirmative action involves giving preference to a minority person or a woman if that individual is equally qualified with a white male. A more controversial type, known as strong affirmative action, involves giving preference to minorities and women who are less qualified than white male applicants.

Some affirmative action programs set goals in terms of percentage of minority and female employees. These goals are usually ideals rather than requirements. Quotas, on the other hand, are fixed percentages or numbers set by a company or college for the hiring or admission of minorities and women.

A basic assumption of affirmative action is that positive steps need to be taken to correct certain injustices against groups such as minorities and women, as Johnson pointed out. Because racism is institutional, it will not suffice to simply stop discriminating. Affirmative action benefits minorities by breaking the cycle of discrimination and racism. In addition, affirmative action programs bring together people from diverse racial backgrounds, thus creating a more tolerant and multicultural society.

While Gallup polls show that slightly more than half of blacks support it, affirmative action has never enjoyed popular support among whites in the United States.[32] Opponents of affirmative action point out that the most disadvantaged are not in a position to benefit from it. Affirmative action also creates resentment, especially among white males who are harmed by reverse discrimination, and suspicion among white students that minority students are only there because of affirmative action programs.

In 1978 Allan Bakke, a white man, sued the University of California at Davis Medical School because his application was rejected while minorities with lower test scores were admitted. The Supreme Court agreed with Bakke, ruling that reverse discrimination was unconstitutional.

In November 1996, with the passage of Proposition 209, California became the first state to ban affirmative action in the public sector. Washington and Texas have also passed referendums banning affirmative action in college admissions.

Despite initial concerns that minorities needed affirmative action programs to make up for past injustices, the enrollment of minorities at the University of California rebounded significantly in 2000.[33] However, the increase was primarily at the satellite campuses.

In June 2003, in its first affirmative action case since Bakke in 1978, the Supreme Court found the admissions policy of the University of Michigan Law School, which awarded points to applicants based on race, to be flawed. However, the Court in their final ruling permitted race to be considered as one among many factors in admissions when considering individual applicants, stating that the Constitution "does not prohibit the Law School's narrowly tailored use of race in admission decisions to further a compelling interest in obtaining the educational benefits that flow from a diverse student body." This ruling was hailed as a major victory for advocates of affirmative action.

Bernard Boxill defends affirmative action and other policies based on race in his reading on "The Color-Blind Principle" in the middle of this chapter and in his reading on "Affirmative Action" in the *Ethics PowerWeb.* Lisa Newton in her article "Reverse Discrimination is Unjustified," also in the *Ethics PowerWeb,* argues against certain affirmative action policies.

Reparation

Reparations are payments made to a group of people for past harms. Affirmative action has been justified as one way of making reparations for such harms. Blacks, Native Americans, and Japanese Americans have all sought direct reparation from the U.S. government. In 1988 Congress passed the Civil Liberties Act authorizing the government to pay $20,000 to every living Japanese American who was interned in federal camps during World War II. No official apology, however, has been offered to blacks or American Indians.

SUPREME COURT OF UNITED STATES (2003) *BARBARA GRUTTER, V. LEE BOLLINGER, JEFFREY LEHMAN, DENNIS SHIELDS, AND THE BOARD OF REGENTS OF THE UNIVERSITY OF MICHIGAN, ET AL.*

Statement of the Case

This case presents questions about what constitutes a compelling interest that may justify race-based preferences in student admissions at a state law school to applicants from certain racial or ethnic groups. The Sixth Circuit resolved this issue by concluding that the opinion of Justice Powell in *Regents of the Univ. of Cal. v. Bakke,* 438 U.S. 265 (1978), constituted binding precedent establishing "diversity" as such a compelling governmental interest. . . .

Even assuming "diversity" to be a compelling interest, this case presents additional questions concerning what constitutes appropriate "narrow tailoring" of an admissions policy designed to achieve diversity. . . .

I. Factual Background

A. Plaintiff

Plaintiff Barbara Grutter is a white resident of the state of Michigan who applied at the age of 43 in December 1996 for admission into the fall 1997 first-year class of the University of Michigan Law School . . . The Law School first placed Ms. Grutter on the "waitlist," and subsequently denied her admission. . . .

The Law School admits that Ms. Grutter probably would have been admitted had she been a member of one of the racial minority groups to which the Law School gives a preference.

B. Law School Admissions Policies and Practices

Defendants admit that they use race as a factor in making admissions decisions and that the race of plaintiff Grutter was not a factor that "enhanced" the consideration of her application.

Defendants justify the use of race as a factor in the admissions process on one ground only: that it serves a "compelling interest in achieving diversity among its student body." With respect to the consideration of race, the Policy states that the Law School has a "commitment to racial and ethnic diversity with special reference to the inclusion of students from groups which have been historically discriminated against, like African Americans, Hispanics, and Native Americans, who without this commitment might not be represented in the student body in meaningful numbers."

Reasons for Granting The Writ

There can be no serious doubt that the use of racial preferences in university admissions presents an issue of great national importance. . . .

In *Bakke,* this Court found that the admissions program of the University of California Medical School at Davis, which set aside 16 percent of the places in the class for educationally or economically disadvantaged minorities, violated Title VI of the Civil Rights Act of 1964, 42 U.S.C.§ 2000d.

This case does indeed present "a straightforward instance of racial discrimination by a state institution."

Although the case presents specific legal issues, at the most fundamental level the question it raises is whether our Nation's principles of equal protection and non-discrimination mean the same thing for all races. . . . [T]he proposition is tested again by this case, and especially by the justifications for unequal treatment put forth by the Law School and intervenors.

This Court has rejected as compelling certain interests that indisputably are good and important, like remedying the lingering effects of societal discrimination and promoting role models for school children. . . . There may be many reasons why an interest is not sufficiently compelling to withstand the strict scrutiny to which all racial classifications must be subjected, . . .

The diversity rationale articulated by the Law School . . . is a rationale that gives essentially unchecked authority to admissions officers to define what "diversity" or "critical mass" mean; which racial and ethnic groups, among many, are to be considered "underrepresented" or are to receive preferences; the size of the preferences or "plus"; and their duration. The only limitation would be a meaningless one, easily evaded—that the preferences must avoid the express form of a "fixed quota." . . . By accepting such a rationale as a compelling interest, "[t]he dream of a Nation of equal citizens in a society where race is irrelevant to personal opportunity and achievement would be lost in a mosaic of shifting preferences."

There is also a qualitative difference between using race to remedy past, identified instances of governmental discrimination and using it instead to achieve "diversity." When race is used in a narrowly-tailored manner to remedy past, identified discrimination, it is arguably done to right a specific wrong; to *further* the principle of equality by correcting injury done to the principle in defined instances. When, however, race is used to pursue an open-ended objective like "diversity," it is used in *spite* of the principle of equality to further an interest in—diversity. Covering the diversity rationale with arguments about "academic freedom" does not offer it legitimacy under the Constitution or the Nation's civil rights laws: This Court has never held that educational institutions have a First Amendment right to practice race discrimination in admissions. Such a conclusion would be anathema to the outcome and principles articulated in cases like *Brown v. Board of Educ.,* 347 U.S. 483 (1954).

Conclusion

For the foregoing reasons, Barbara Grutter respectfully requests the Court to grant her petition for certiorari.

What do we owe to blacks and Native Americans, if anything, for a legacy of slavery, genocide, and degradation? Is an apology enough? Should descendants of slaves be compensated monetarily, as were the Japanese Americans for their loss of freedom during World War II? Or do we owe only an indirect debt to contemporary blacks, since it was their ancestors, not them, who were brought to this country against their will? How about Arab-Americans and Muslims who have been unjustly detained under the Patriot Act? Should the U.S. government return Indian lands or monetarily compensate Indians for the loss of their lands? Or is it now time to make peace with the past and just put it behind us?

In his controversial anti-reparations ad, David Horowitz argues that the United States does not owe reparation to blacks. Among his reasons are that blacks who are alive today were not enslaved and because American slavery actually benefited contemporary American blacks, since they have a much higher standard of living than they would have had if they were living in the African countries from which their ancestors were kidnapped into the slave trade.[34] His ad has been censored by several college newspapers and student groups (see Chapter 8).

Boxill agrees that the claim made by Horowitz that compensation to blacks for harm to their slave ancestors is a weak argument. However, he maintains that blacks living now have a claim for compensation for harms from current injustices. "It is this injustice," he writes, "the injustice of prevention of the slaves and their descendants from recovering from the harms that slavery caused the slaves, not the injustice of slavery, that is the cause of the harms that entitles the recent black population to reparation."[35]

MORAL ISSUES

Human Dignity and Individual Moral Worth

Racism, by definition, denies the moral worth of certain people based simply on their race. Jorge Garcia, in the reading "The Heart of Racism," defines racism in terms of ill will and a disregard for the dignity and welfare of certain people based on their assigned race. He also argues that individual racism precedes and reinforces institutional racism. One of the problems in overcoming institutional racism is how to restore the dignity of groups that have suffered discrimination without violating the equal moral worth of members of groups who have historically benefited from that discrimination.

Justice and Equality

According to the principle of equality, "it is unjust to treat people differently in ways that deny them some significant social benefits unless we can show that there is a difference between them that is relevant to the differential treatment."[36] The principle of equality requires that differential treatment be based only on real and relevant differences.

Michael Levin in "Race, Biology, and Justice" argues that discrimination against blacks is justified based on, what he claims, are real differences between whites and blacks in terms of intelligence and aggressiveness. Ayn Rand, on the other hand, argues that even if it can be shown that members of one race are, on the average, more intelligent or more aggressive than members of another, this tells us nothing about a particular individual. The principle of equality requires that people be judged on their individual merits, not on their membership in a particular group.[37] Bernard R. Boxill questions whether color-conscious programs, such as affirmative action, are necessarily unjust. He maintains that there are times when race, like talent, is relevant in creating public policy.

Utilitarian Considerations

Racism hurts. In the 1954 *Brown v. Board of Education* ruling, the U.S. Supreme Court spoke of the irrevocable damage to the "hearts and minds" of black children who were compelled to attend segregated schools.

Affirmative action programs are both defended and opposed on utilitarian grounds. Some people argue that preferential treatment of minorities has actually worked against their best interests by fostering social tension and resentment against minorities. It also creates the impression that minorities can't make it on their own merits. Shelby Steele points out that in their enthusiasm to diversify, many universities have admitted minority students who are poorly qualified academically, thus setting them up for failure. Furthermore, it is argued, strong affirmative action programs waste the talents of those who are most qualified. Defenders of preferential hiring, in response, maintain that it helps minorities who are less qualified because of racism to develop their talents, thus creating a greater pool of qualified workers.

One of the problems of relying on a utilitarian calculus is the uncertainty of cause-and-effect relationships as well as the differing values people place on different outcomes. Utilitarian solutions can also run counter to considerations of human dignity and justice. Utilitarian cost/benefit analysis, for example, was used to justify slavery. Indeed, with the demise of slavery the economy of the South collapsed, leaving it the most economically backward region in the United States until after World War II.

Care Ethics

The analytical utilitarian approach is often contrasted with care ethics with its emphasis on sentiment and human relationships. Racism prevents the development of caring relationships between people of different races. Although caring is important, one of the weaknesses of care ethics is that it does not provide a strategy for overcoming racism in a segregated society. When a commitment to caring is absent, it is our commitment to an ideal or principle that must motivate us to do what is right. Care ethics, as Narayan points out, can also be used to justify paternalistic caring and colonialism.

CONCLUSION

Because racism is woven into the very fabric of society and reinforced by personal prejudices, it is difficult to eliminate. We need to look past cultural interpretations and carefully analyze ways in which society today normalizes racism. The racism of the Jim Crow era seemed normal and rational to the great majority of white Americans, just as slavery was once regarded as part of the natural order, at least by those who benefited from it.

Some people argue that those affected by racist policies should take responsibility for changing the system. The problem of racism, however, is not a "black problem," or whatever group is seen as problematic; the problem is white racism. The people who created and maintain racism bear the main responsibility for eradicating it. Those who have the most power to change institutional racism are the very people who have the power to perpetuate it. In addition, all of us, whatever our race, need to resist the temptation to play the role of the innocent victim or to become racists ourselves by scapegoating members of other racial groups.

Racism needs to be addressed at all levels. Being "tolerant" or "color-blind" is not enough. The majority of whites state that they strongly believe in the ideal of racial equality; but, even though we may not personally feel racial hatred, our actions can be infected by the hatred of others. It is not enough to simply change our own personal attitudes. We cannot substitute a politically correct ideology for action. Action or behavior provides the link between personal attitudes and institutional racism. Unless we actively work toward eliminating racism, we are still part of the problem. Martin Luther King Jr. once said that "the choice is ours, and though we might prefer it otherwise, we *must* choose."

To Fulfill These Rights

Lyndon B. Johnson served as president of the United States from 1963, following the assassination of President John F. Kennedy, to 1969. During his presidency Johnson was a tireless advocate of civil rights for blacks. Legislation passed under Johnson's administration included the 1964 Civil Rights Act and several federal initiatives to combat poverty. Following are excerpts from his commencement address delivered at Howard University on June 4, 1965.

Critical Reading Questions

1. According to Johnson, in what ways have American Negroes been another nation?
2. Why isn't freedom enough to bring equal opportunity to the American Negro?
3. What does Johnson mean when he says that "ability is not just the product of birth"?
4. What are some of the causes of inequality?
5. What is the difference between white poverty and Negro poverty?
6. What are the roots of the injustice experienced by the American Negro?
7. What, according to Johnson, is the answer to these problems?
8. What does Johnson mean when he says that "American justice is a very special thing" and what does this mean for the American Negro?

Commencement Address at Howard University, June 4, 1965

. . . In far too many ways American Negroes have been another nation: deprived of freedom, crippled by hatred, the doors of opportunity closed to hope.

In our time change has come to this Nation, too. The American Negro, acting with impressive restraint, has peacefully protested and marched, entered the courtrooms and the seats of government, demanding a justice that has long been denied. The voice of the Negro was the call to action. But it is a tribute to America that, once aroused, the courts and the Congress, the President and most of the people, have been the allies of progress. . . .

That beginning is freedom; and the barriers to that freedom are tumbling down. Freedom is the right to share, share fully and equally, in American society—to vote, to hold a job, to enter a public place, to go to school. It is the right to be treated in every part of our national life as a person equal in dignity and promise to all others.

But freedom is not enough. You do not wipe away the scars of centuries by saying: Now you are free to go where you want, and do as you desire, and choose the leaders you please.

You do not take a person who, for years, has been hobbled by chains and liberate him, bring him up to the starting line of a race and then say, "you are free to compete with all the others," and still justly believe that you have been completely fair.

"To Fulfill These Rights," *Public Papers of the Presidents of the United States: Lyndon B. Johnson, 1965.* Volume II, no. 301 (Washington, D.C.: Government Printing Office, 1966), pp. 635–640.

Thus it is not enough just to open the gates of opportunity. All our citizens must have the ability to walk through those gates.

This is the next and the more profound stage of the battle for civil rights. We seek not just freedom but opportunity. We seek not just legal equity but human ability, not just equality as a right and a theory but equality as a fact and equality as a result.

For the task is to give 20 million Negroes the same chance as every other American to learn and grow, to work and share in society, to develop their abilities—physical, mental and spiritual, and to pursue their individual happiness.

To this end equal opportunity is essential, but not enough, not enough. Men and women of all races are born with the same range of abilities. But ability is not just the product of birth. Ability is stretched or stunted by the family that you live with, and the neighborhood you live in—by the school you go to and the poverty or the richness of your surroundings. It is the product of a hundred unseen forces playing upon the little infant, the child, and finally the man. . . .

For the great majority of Negro Americans—the poor, the unemployed, the uprooted, and the dispossessed—there is a much grimmer story. They still, as we meet here tonight, are another nation. Despite the court orders and the laws, despite the legislative victories and the speeches, for them the walls are rising and the gulf is widening. . . .

We are not completely sure why this is. We know the causes are complex and subtle. But we do know the two broad basic reasons. And we do know that we have to act.

First, Negroes are trapped—as many whites are trapped—in inherited, gateless poverty. They lack training and skills. They are shut in, in slums, without decent medical care. Private and public poverty combine to cripple their capacities.

We are trying to attack these evils through our poverty program, through our education program, through our medical care and our other health programs, and a dozen more of the Great Society programs that are aimed at the root causes of this poverty.

We will increase, and we will accelerate, and we will broaden this attack in years to come until this most enduring of foes finally yields to our unyielding will.

But there is a second cause—much more difficult to explain, more deeply grounded, more desperate in its force. It is the devastating heritage of long years of slavery; and a century of oppression, hatred, and injustice.

For Negro poverty is not white poverty. Many of its causes and many of its cures are the same. But there are differences—deep, corrosive, obstinate differences—radiating painful roots into the community, and into the family, and the nature of the individual.

These differences are not racial differences. They are solely and simply the consequence of ancient brutality, past injustice, and present prejudice. They are anguishing to observe. For the Negro they are a constant reminder of oppression. For the white they are a constant reminder of guilt. But they must be faced and they must be dealt with and they must be overcome, if we are ever to reach the time when the only difference between Negroes and whites is the color of their skin. . . .

Men are shaped by their world. When it is a world of decay, ringed by an invisible wall, when escape is arduous and uncertain, and the saving pressures of a more hopeful society are unknown, it can cripple the youth and it can desolate the men.

There is also the burden that a dark skin can add to the search for a productive place in our society. Unemployment strikes most swiftly and broadly at the Negro, and this burden erodes hope. Blighted hope breeds despair. Despair brings indifferences to the learning which offers a way out. And despair, coupled with indifferences, is often the source of destructive rebellion against the fabric of society.

There is also the lacerating hurt of early collision with white hatred or prejudice, distaste or condescension. Other groups have felt similar intolerance. But success and achievement could wipe it away. They do not change the color of a man's skin. I have seen this uncomprehending pain in the eyes of the little, young Mexican-American schoolchildren that I taught many years ago. But it can be overcome. But, for many, the wounds are always open.

Perhaps most important—its influence radiating to every part of life—is the breakdown of the Negro family structure. For this, most of all, white

America must accept responsibility. It flows from centuries of oppression and persecution of the Negro man. It flows from the long years of degradation and discrimination, which have attacked his dignity and assaulted his ability to produce for his family. . . .

There is no single easy answer to all of these problems.

Jobs are part of the answer. They bring the income which permits a man to provide for his family.

Decent homes in decent surroundings and a chance to learn—an equal chance to learn—are part of the answer.

Welfare and social programs better designed to hold families together are part of the answer.

Care for the sick is part of the answer.

An understanding heart by all Americans is another big part of the answer. . . . American justice is a very special thing. For, from the first, this has been a land of towering expectations. It was to be a nation where each man could be ruled by the common consent of all—enshrined in law, given life by institutions, guided by men themselves subject to its rule. And all—all of every station and origin—would be touched equally in obligation and in liberty.

Beyond the law lay the land. It was a rich land, glowing with more abundant promise than man had ever seen. Here, unlike any place yet known, all were to share the harvest.

And beyond this was the dignity of man. Each could become whatever his qualities of mind and spirit would permit—to strive, to seek, and, if he could, to find his happiness.

This is American justice. We have pursued it faithfully to the edge of our imperfections, and we have failed to find it for the American Negro.

So, it is the glorious opportunity of this generation to end the one huge wrong of the American Nation and, in so doing, to find America for ourselves, with the same immense thrill of discovery which gripped those who first began to realize that here, at last, was a home for freedom. . . .

Discussion Questions

1. Do you agree with Johnson that ability isn't enough to bring equal opportunity to American blacks? If so, what policy do you suggest to ensure equal opportunity for people of all races?
2. Organize a debate between Johnson and Levin on the causes and solutions to racism. Discuss the shortcomings and merits of each position.
3. If Johnson were still president, how would he most likely approach the issue of profiling and detention of Muslims and Arab-Americans as possible terrorists? Support your answer.
4. Discuss how Johnson would most likely respond to both the *Bakke* and the more recent University of Michigan Law School Supreme Court cases.

SHELBY STEELE

I'm Black, You're White, Who's Innocent?

Shelby Steele is a writer and professor of English at San Jose State University in California. Steele examines the origins of racism and conflict in race relations today. According to Steele, both black and white Americans have become trapped in placing color above character. Both have a deep sense of "racial vulnerability." Whites are charged with being racist, blacks with being inferior. Both have found a means of escape by retreating into "innocence" rather than adopting a true moral consciousness. Because of this, many contemporary social policies that were intended to decrease racism have only aggravated it.

Critical Reading Questions

1. According to Steele, why do blacks badger or provoke whites about race? Why did Steele have a hard time overcoming the impulse to do this to white liberals and even his own students?
2. What does Steele mean when he says that "black anger always, in a way, flatters white power"?
3. According to Steele, why is racism a power issue? How is innocence related to power and the feeling of entitlement?
4. On what grounds does Steele claim that both blacks and whites have a "hidden investment in racism"?
5. How do blacks lay claim to their racial "innocence"? What is problematic about claiming innocence through victim status? Why, according to Steele, is this form of power inconsistent with individual responsibility?
6. What explanation does Steele give for the deterioration in the conditions of blacks in America over the past twenty years?
7. What does Steele mean when he says that victimization and poverty have been the source of black power? Why is this type of power useless for overcoming poverty?
8. According to Steele, how should people try to gain real power in America?
9. How does Steele account for the high dropout rate of black college students?
10. Why is "seeing for innocence" more costly for blacks than for whites?
11. What is the difference, morally, between genuine and presumed innocence? What is the basis of genuine innocence? Which type of innocence characterized the early civil rights years?
12. What is the difference, according to Steele, between the racial consciousness that began in the mid-1960s and the moral consciousness of the early civil rights movement?

"I'm Black, You're White, Who's Innocent?" in *The Content of Our Character: A New Vision of Race in America* (New York: HarperCollins, 1991), 1–6; 14–20.

It is a warm, windless California evening, and the dying light that covers the redbrick patio is tinted pale orange by the day's smog. Eight of us, not close friends, sit in lawn chairs sipping chardonnay. A black engineer and I (we had never met before) integrate the group. A psychologist is also among us, and her presence encourages a surprising openness. But not until well after the lovely twilight dinner has been served, when the sky has turned to deep black and the drinks have long since changed to scotch, does the subject of race spring awkwardly upon us. Out of nowhere the engineer announces, with a coloring of accusation in his voice, that it bothers him to send his daughter to a school where she is one of only three black children. "I didn't realize my ambition to get ahead would pull me into a world where my daughter would lose touch with her blackness," he says.

Over the course of the evening we have talked about money, past and present addictions, child abuse, even politics. Intimacies have been revealed, fears named. But this subject, race, sinks us into one of those shaming silences where eye contact terrorizes. . . . Finally, the psychologist seems to gather herself for a challenge, but it is too late. "Oh, I'm sure she'll be just fine," says our hostess, rising from her chair. When she excuses herself to get the coffee, the psychologist and two sky gazers offer to help.

With four of us now gone, I am surprised to see the engineer still silently holding his ground. There is a willfulness in his eyes, an inner pride. He knows he has said something awkward, but he is determined not to give a damn. His unwavering eyes intimidate even me. At last the host's head snaps erect. He has an idea. "The hell with coffee," he says. "How about some of the smoothest brandy you've ever tasted?" An idea made exciting by the escape it offers. Gratefully, we follow him back into the house, quickly drink his brandy, and say our good-byes.

An autopsy of this party might read: death induced by an abrupt and lethal injection of the American race issue. An accurate if superficial assessment. Since it has been my fate to live a rather integrated life, I have often witnessed sudden deaths like this. The threat of them, if not the reality, is a part of the texture of integration. In the late 1960s, when I was just out of college, I took a delinquent's delight in playing the engineer's role, and actually developed a small reputation for playing it well. Those were the days of flagellatory white guilt; it was such great fun to pinion some professor or housewife or, best of all, a large group of remorseful whites, with the knowledge of both their racism and their denial of it. The adolescent impulse to sneer at convention, to startle the middle-aged with doubt, could be indulged under the guise of racial indignation. And how could I lose? . . .

About a year of this was enough: the guilt that follows most cheap thrills caught up to me, and I put myself in check. But the impulse to do it faded more slowly. It was one of those petty talents that is tied to vanity, and when there were ebbs in my self-esteem the impulse to use it would come alive again. . . .

In the literature classes I teach I often see how the presence of whites all but seduces some black students into provocation. When we come to a novel by a black writer, say Toni Morrison, the white students can easily discuss the human motivations of the black character. But, inevitably, a black student, as if by reflex, will begin to set in relief the various racial problems that are the background of these characters' lives. This student's tone will carry a reprimand: the class is afraid to confront the reality of racism. Classes cannot be allowed to die like dinner parties, however. My latest strategy is to thank that student for his or her moral vigilance and then appoint the young man or woman as the class's official racism monitor. But even if I get a laugh—I usually do, but sometimes the student is particularly indignant, and it gets uncomfortable—the strategy never quite works. Our racial division is suddenly drawn in neon. Overcaution spreads like spilled paint. And, in fact, the black student who started it all does become a kind of monitor. The very presence of this student imposes new accountability on the class.

I think those who provoke this sort of awkwardness are operating out of a black identity that obliges them to badger white people about race almost on principle. . . . Race indeed remains a source of white shame; the goal of these provocations is to put whites, no matter how indirectly, in touch with this collective guilt. In other words, these provocations I speak of are *power* moves, little shows of power that try to freeze the "enemy" in self-consciousness. They gratify and inflate the provocateur. They are the underdog's bite. And whites, far more secure in their power, respond with a self-contained and tolerant silence that is itself a show of power. What greater power than that of nonresponse, the power to let a small enemy sizzle in his own juices, to even feel a little sad at his frustration just as one is also complimented by it. Black anger always, in a way, flatters white power. In America, to know that one is not black is to feel an extra grace, a little boost of impunity.

I think the real trouble between the races in America is that the races are not just races but competing power groups—a fact that is easily minimized, perhaps because it is so obvious. What is not so obvious is that this is true quite apart from the issue of class. Even the well-situated middle-class (or wealthy) black is never completely immune to that peculiar contest of power that his skin color subjects him to. Race is a separate reality in American society, an entity that carries its own potential for power, a mark of fate that class can soften considerably but not eradicate. . . .

But the human animal almost never pursues power without first convincing himself that he is *entitled* to it. And this feeling of entitlement has its own precondition: to be entitled one must first believe in one's innocence, at least in the area where one wishes to be entitled. By innocence I mean a feeling of essential goodness in relation to others and, therefore, superiority to others. Our innocence always inflates us and deflates those we seek power over. Once inflated we are entitled; we are in fact licensed to go after the power our innocence tells us we deserve. In this sense, *innocence is power.* Of course, innocence need not be genuine or real in any objective sense, as the Nazis demonstrated not long ago. Its only test is whether or not we can convince ourselves of it.

I think the racial struggle in America has always been primarily a struggle for innocence. White racism from the beginning has been a claim of white innocence and therefore of white entitlement to subjugate blacks. And in the sixties, as went innocence so went power. Blacks used the innocence that grew out of their long subjugation to seize more power, while whites lost some of their innocence and so lost a degree of power over blacks. Both races instinctively understand that to lose innocence is to lose power (in relation to each other). To be innocent someone else must be guilty, a natural law that leads the races to forge their innocence on each other's backs. The inferiority of the black always makes the white man superior; the evil might of whites makes blacks good. This pattern means that both races have a hidden investment in racism and racial disharmony despite their good intentions to the contrary. Power defines their relations, and power requires innocence, which, in turn, requires racism and racial division.

I believe it was his hidden investment that the engineer was protecting when he made his remark—the white "evil" he saw in a white school "depriving" his daughter of her black heritage confirmed his innocence. . . . What none of us saw was the underlying game of power and innocence we were trapped in, or how much we need a racial impasse to play the game. . . .

Now the other side of America's racial impasse: How do blacks lay claim to their racial innocence?

The most obvious and unarguable source of black innocence is the victimization that blacks endured for centuries at the hands of a race that insisted on black inferiority as a means to its own innocence and power. Like all victims, what blacks lost in power they gained in innocence—innocence that, in turn, entitled them to pursue power. This was the innocence that fueled the civil rights movement of the sixties and that gave blacks their first real power in American life—victimization metamorphosed into power via innocence. But this formula carries a drawback that I believe is virtually as devastating to blacks today as victimization once was. It is a formula that binds the victim to his victimization by linking his power to his status as a victim. And this, I'm convinced, is the tragedy of black power in America today. It is primarily a victim's power, grounded too deeply in the entitlement derived from past injustice and in the innocence that Western/Christian tradition has always associated with poverty.

Whatever gains this power brings in the short run through political action, it undermines in the long run. Social victims may be collectively entitled, but they are all too often individually demoralized. Since the social victim has been oppressed by society, he comes to feel that his individual life will be improved more by changes in society than by his own initiative. Without realizing it, he makes society rather than himself the agent of change. The power he finds in his victimization may lead him to collective action against society, but it also encourages passivity within the sphere of his personal life.

Not long ago, I saw a television documentary that examined life in Detroit's inner city on the twentieth anniversary of the riots there in which forty-three people were killed. A comparison of the inner city then and now showed a decline in the quality of life. Residents feel less safe, drug trafficking is far worse, crimes by blacks against blacks are more frequent, housing remains substandard, and the teenage pregnancy rate has skyrocketed. Twenty years of decline and demoralization, even as opportunities for blacks to better themselves have increased. This paradox is not peculiar to Detroit. By many measures, the majority of blacks—those not yet in the middle class—are further behind whites today than before the victories of the civil rights movement. But there is a reluctance among blacks to examine this paradox, I think, because it suggests that racial victimization is not our real problem. If conditions have worsened for most of us as racism had receded, then much of the problem must be of our own making. To admit this fully would cause us to lose the innocence we derive from our victimization. And we would jeopardize the entitlement we've always had to challenge society. We are in the odd and self-defeating position in which taking responsibility for bettering ourselves feels like a surrender to white power.

So we have a hidden investment in victimization and poverty. These distressing conditions have been the source of our only real power, and there is an unconscious sort of gravitation toward them, a complaining celebration of them. One sees evidence of this in the near happiness with which certain black leaders recount the horror of Howard Beach, Bensonhurst, and other recent instances of racial tension. As one is saddened by these tragic events, one is also repelled at the way some of the black leaders—agitated to near hysteria by the scent of victim power inherent in them—leap forward to exploit them as evidence of black innocence and white guilt. . . .

Seeing for innocence pressures blacks to focus on racism and to neglect the individual initiative that would deliver them from poverty—the only thing that finally delivers *anyone* from poverty. With our eyes on innocence we see racism everywhere and miss opportunity even as we stumble over it. About 70 percent of black students at my university drop out before graduation—a flight from opportunity that racism cannot explain. It is an injustice that whites can see for innocence with more impunity than blacks can. The price whites pay is a certain blindness to themselves. Moreover, for whites seeing for innocence continues to engender the bad faith of a long-disgruntled minority. But the price blacks pay is an ever-escalating poverty that threatens to make the worst off a permanent underclass. Not fair, but real. . . .

"Innocence is ignorance," Kierkegaard says, and if this is so, the claim of innocence amounts to an insistence on ignorance, a refusal to know. In their assertions of innocence both races carve out very functional areas of ignorance for themselves—territories of blindness that license a misguided pursuit of power. Whites gain superiority by not knowing blacks; blacks gain entitlement by not seeing their own responsibility for bettering themselves. The power each race seeks in relation to the other is grounded in a double-edged ignorance of the self as well as of the other. . . .

I think the civil rights movement in its early and middle years offered the best way out of America's racial impasse: in this society, race must not be a source of advantage or disadvantage for anyone. This is fundamentally a *moral* position, one that seeks to breach the corrupt union of race and power with principles of fairness and human equality: if all men are created equal, then racial difference cannot sanction power. The civil rights movement was conceived for no other reason than to redress that corrupt union, and its guiding insight was that only a moral power based on enduring principles of justice, equality, and freedom could offset the lower impulse in man to exploit race as a means to power. Three hundred years of suffering had driven the point home, and in Montgomery, Little Rock, and Selma, racial power was the enemy and moral power the weapon.

An important difference between genuine and presumed innocence, I believe, is that the former must be earned through sacrifice while the latter is unearned and only veils the quest for privilege. And there was much sacrifice in the early civil rights movement. The Gandhian principle of nonviolent resistance that gave the movement a spiritual center as well as a method of protest demanded sacrifice, a passive offering of the self in the name of justice. A price was paid in terror and lost life, and from this sacrifice came a hard-earned innocence and a credible moral power.

Nonviolent passive resistance is a bargainer's strategy. It assumes the power that is the object of the protest has the genuine innocence to respond morally, and puts the protesters at the mercy of that innocence. I think this movement won so many concessions precisely because of its belief in the capacity of whites to be moral. It did not so much demand that whites change as offer them relentlessly the opportunity to live by their own morality—to attain a true innocence based on the sacrifice of their racial privilege, rather than a false innocence based on presumed racial superiority. Blacks always bargain with or challenge the larger society; but I believe that in the early civil rights years, these forms of negotiation achieved a degree of integrity and genuineness never seen before or since.

In the mid-sixties all this changed. Suddenly a sharp *racial* consciousness emerged to compete with the moral consciousness that had defined the movement up to that point. Whites were no longer welcome in the movement, and a vocal "black power" minority gained dramatic visibility. Now suddenly the movement itself was using race as a means to power and thereby affirming the very union of race and power it was born to redress. In the end, black power can claim no higher moral standing than white power. . . .

You hear it asked, why are there no Martin Luther Kings around today? I think one reason is that there are no black leaders willing to resist the seductions of racial power, or to make the sacrifices moral power requires. King understood that racial power subverts moral power, and he pushed the principles of fairness and equality rather than black power because he believed those principles would bring blacks their most complete liberation. He sacrificed race for morality, and his innocence was made genuine by that sacrifice. What made King the most powerful and extraordinary black leader of this century was not his race but his morality.

Black power is a challenge. It grants whites no innocence; it denies their moral capacity and then demands that they be moral. No power can long insist on itself without evoking an opposing power. Doesn't an insistence on black power call up white power? (And could this have something to do with what many are now calling a resurgence of white racism?) I believe that what divided the races at the dinner party I attended, and what divides them in the nation, can only be bridged by an adherence to those moral principles that disallow race as a source of power, privilege, status, or entitlement of any kind. In our age, principles like fairness and equality are ill-defined and all but drowned in relativity. But this is the fault of people, not principles. . . .

What both black and white Americans fear are the sacrifices and risks that true racial harmony demands. This fear is the measure of our racial chasm. And though fear always seeks a thousand justifications, none is ever good enough, and the problems we run from only remain to haunt us. It would be right to suggest courage as an antidote to fear, but the glory of the word might only intimidate us into more fear. I prefer the word effort—relentless effort, moral effort. What I like most about this word are its connotations of everyday-ness, earnestness, and practical sacrifice. No matter how badly it might have gone for us that warm summer night, we should have talked. We should have made the effort.

Discussion Questions

1. Steele starts by describing an incident at a party in which race comes up in the conversation. Why did the topic of race make people uncomfortable? Think of a similar incident in your own life. How did people respond?
2. Discuss Steele's claim that innocence is being used as a tool of power by both whites and blacks. To what extent do you, or others you know, engage in this type of power play? Give specific examples. Discuss steps you might take to replace presumed innocence with genuine innocence.
3. Discuss how former President Johnson would most likely respond to Shelby Steele's argument that both blacks and whites, when it comes to racism, retreat into a position of "innocence" rather than adopting a true moral consciousness.
4. Mohandas ("Mahatma") Gandhi was once asked what he thought about Western civilization. He replied that he thought that it would be a good idea. Discuss why Gandhi might have thought that Western society was not truly civilized. What does it mean to be a civilization? Can a racist society be civilized? Support your answers.
5. Thirteen days after the O.J. Simpson verdict, Louis Farrakhan, a Nation of Islam minister, led the Million Man March in Washington, D.C. Several days before the rally, Farrakhan denounced Jews as "bloodsuckers"; a believer in black superiority, he regularly demonizes "blue-eyed devils." Farrakhan also believes in separatism and economic individualism and encourages black men to take personal responsibility for their actions. Discuss how Steele might respond to Farrakhan's teachings. Relate your answer to Steele's contrast of racial consciousness and moral consciousness.
6. Discuss ways in which you use "innocence" to maintain a position of moral superiority and to deny your complicity in racism.

JORGE GARCIA

The Heart of Racism

Jorge Garcia is a professor of philosophy at Rutgers University. Garcia argues that the heart of racism is ill will and disregard for members of certain groups. Racism is rooted in intention rather than in action or simple belief. Garcia argues that his virtue-based definition of racism is not only more consistent with common usage than other definitions, but is better at accounting for interracial hostility. It also accounts for both individual and institutional racism, as well as the connection between the two. Garcia uses several examples to illustrate his concept of racism.

"The Heart of Racism," *Journal of Social Philosophy* 27, no. 1 (1996): 5–45. Some notes have been omitted.

Critical Reading Questions

1. How does Garcia define racism? What is the essence of racism?
2. How does Garcia respond to the claim that because there are no races, there cannot be racism?
3. Can someone disapprove of a culture without being racist?
4. What is "higher order discrimination"?
5. Why does Garcia believe that racism is rooted in the heart rather than in action?
6. According to Garcia, why is racism always immoral? What moral duties and virtues does racism violate?
7. What is the relationship between individual racism and institutional racism? Which type does Garcia claim is of greater moral importance and why?
8. What is the connection between good intentions and racism? What does Garcia mean when he says that individual racism fundamentally lies in volition rather than in action or belief?
9. According to Garcia, can a person be a racist without ever acting on racist attitudes in a way that harms members of another race?
10. Does preferential treatment necessarily imply racism?
11. Is racial discrimination always conscious? What are some examples of unconscious racism?
12. How does Garcia's concept of racism apply to hate speech? What is the difference between hate speech and "racially offensive speech"?
13. On what grounds does Garcia find the gentle but paternal aristocracy of the antebellum period racist?
14. What is the "Kiplingesque" view? Why is the notion of the "white man's burden" racist?
15. Does Garcia think it is wrong for a white woman to avoid black teenagers on the street? How does his answer differ from that of Judith Lichtenberg?
16. Why does Garcia find it necessary to restrict the definition of institutional racism? How do the analogies of the "old boy network" and the alien missile attack on Africa support Garcia's position?
17. What point is Garcia making in the Smythe-Brown analogy?
18. Under what circumstance does Garcia find preferential hiring based on race morally justified?
19. According to Garcia, in what ways do individual and institutional racism reinforce each other? What does Garcia mean when he claims that institutional racism can continue even after individual racism has died out?

A VOLITIONAL CONCEPTION OF RACISM

Kwame Anthony Appiah rightly complains that, although people frequently voice their abhorrence of racism, "rarely does anyone stop to say what it is, or what is wrong with it" (Appiah, 1990: 3). This way of stating the program of inquiry we need is promising, because, although racism is not essentially "a moral doctrine," *pace* Appiah, it is always a moral evil (Appiah, 1990: 13). No account of what racism is can be adequate unless it at the same time makes clear what is wrong with it. How should we conceive racism, then, if we follow Appiah's advice "to take our ordinary ways of thinking about race and racism and point up some of their presuppositions"? (Appiah, 1990: 4). My proposal is that we conceive of racism as fundamentally a vicious kind of racially based disregard for the welfare of certain people. In its central and most vicious form, it is a hatred, ill-will, directed against a person or persons on account of their assigned race. In a derivative form, one is a racist when one either does not care at all or does not care enough (i. e., as much as morality requires) or does not care in the right ways about people assigned to a certain racial group, where this disregard is based on racial classification. Racism, then, is something that essentially involves not our beliefs and their rationality or irrationality, but our wants, intentions, likes, and dislikes and their distance from the moral virtues. Such a view helps explain racism's conceptual ties to various forms of *hatred* and contempt. (Note that "contempt" derives from "to contemn"—not to care [about someone's needs and rights].)

It might be objected that there can be no such thing as racism because, as many now affirm, "there are no races." This objection fails. First, that "race" is partially a social construction does not entail that there are no races. One might even maintain, though I would not, that race-terms, like "person," "preference," "choice," "welfare," etc., and, more controversially, such terms as "reason for action," "immoral," "morally obligatory," etc. may be terms that, while neither included within nor translatable into, the language of physics, nevertheless arise in such a way and at such a fundamental level of social or anthropological discourse that they should be counted as real, at least, for purposes of political and ethical theory. Second, as many racial anti-realists concede, even if it were true that race is unreal, what we call racism could still be real (Appiah, 1992: p. 45). What my account of racism requires is not that there be races, but that people make distinctions in their hearts, whether consciously or not, on the basis of their (or others') racial classifications. That implies nothing about the truth of those classifications.

Lawrence Blum [1991] raises a puzzling question about this. We can properly classify person S as a racist even if *we* do not believe in races. But what if S herself does not believe in them? Suppose S is a White person who hates Black people, but picks them out by African origin, attachment to African cultures, residence or rearing in certain U.S. neighborhoods, and so on. Should we call S racist if she does not hate Black people *as* such (i. e., on the basis of her assigning them to a Black race), but hates all people she thinks have been corrupted by their internalizing [of] undesirable cultural elements from Harlem or Watts, or from Nairobi, or the Bunyoro? I think the case underdescribed. Surely, a person can disapprove of a culture or a family of cultures without being racist. However, cultural criticism can be a mask for a deeper (even unconscious) dislike that is defined by racial classifications. If the person transfers her disapproval of the group's culture to contempt or disregard for those designated as the group's members, then she is already doing something morally vicious. When she assigns all the groups disliked to the same racial classification, then we are entitled to suspect racism, because we have good grounds to suspect that her disavowals of underlying racial classifications are false. If S hates the cultures of various Black groups for having a certain feature, but does not extend that disapproval to other cultures with similar features, then that strongly indicates racism.

Even if she is more consistent, there may still be racism, but of a different sort. Adrian Piper [1990] suggests that, in the phenomenon she calls "higher order discrimination," a person may claim to dislike members of a group because she thinks they have a certain feature, but really disapprove of the feature because she associates it with the despised group. This "higher order discrimination" would, of course, still count as racist in my account because the subject's distaste for the cultural element derives from and is morally infected by race-based disregard.

We should also consider an additional possibility. A person may falsely attribute an undesirable feature to people she assigns to a racial group because of her disregard for those in the group. This will often take the forms of exaggeration, seeing another in the worst light, and withholding from someone the benefit of the doubt. So, an anti-Semite may interpret a Jew's reasonable frugality as greed; a White racist may see indolence in a Black person's legitimate resistance to unfair expectations of her, and so on.

Thinking of racism as thus rooted in the heart fits common sense and ordinary usage in a number of ways. It is instructive that contemptuous, White racists have sometimes called certain of their enemies "Nigger-lovers." When we seek to uncover the implied contrast-term for this epithet, it surely suggests that enemies of those who "love" Black people, as manifested in their efforts to combat segregation, and so forth, are those who hate Black people or who have little or no human feelings toward us at all. This is surely born out by the behavior and rhetoric of paradigmatic White racists.

This account makes racism similar to other familiar forms of intergroup animosity. Activists in favor of Israel and of what they perceive as Jewish interests sometimes call anti-Semites "Jew-haters." . . . What is important for us is to note that *hostility* toward Jews is the heart of anti-Semitism.

Racism is always immoral. As Stephen Nathanson says, "Racism, as we ordinarily speak of it, . . . implies . . . a special disregard for other groups. Hence, there is a sense in which racism is necessarily immoral" (Nathanson, 1992: p. 9). Its immorality stems from its being opposed to the virtues of benevolence and justice. Racism is a form of morally insufficient (i.e., vicious) concern or respect for some others. It infects actions in which one (a) tries to injure people assigned to a racial group because of their XXXXX, or (b) objectionably fails to take care *not* to injure them (where the agent accepts harm to R1s because she disregards the interests and needs of R1s because they are R1s). We can also allow that an action is racist in a derivative and weaker sense when it is less directly connected to racist disregard, for example, when someone (c) does something that (regardless of its intended, probable, or actual effects) stems in significant part from a belief or apprehension about other people, that one has (in significant part) because of one's disaffection toward them because of (what one thinks to be their) race. Racism, thus, will often offend against justice, not just against benevolence, because one sort of injury to another is withholding from her the respect she is owed and the deference and trust that properly express that respect. Certain forms of paternalism, while benevolent in some of their goals, may be vicious in the means employed. The paternalist may deliberately choose to deprive another of some goods, such as those of (licit) freedom and (limited) self-determination in order to obtain other goods for her. Here, as elsewhere, the good end need not justify the unjust means. Extreme paternalism constitutes an instrumentally malevolent benevolence: one harms A to help her. . . .

My account of racism suggests a new understanding of racist behavior and of its immorality. This view allows for the existence of both individual racism and institutional racism. Moreover, it makes clear the connection between the two, and enables us better to understand racism's nature and limits. . . .

Some say that institutional racism is what is of central importance; individual racism, then, matters only inasmuch as it perpetuates institutional racism. I think that claim reverses the order of moral importance, and I shall maintain that the individual level has more explanatory importance.

At the individual level, it is in desires, wishes, intentions, and the like that racism fundamentally lies, not in actions or beliefs. Actions and beliefs are racist by virtue of their *coming from* racism in the desires, wishes, and intentions of individuals, not by virtue of their *leading to* these or other undesirable effects. . . .

How is institutional racism connected to racism within the individual? Let us contrast two pictures. On the first, institutional racism is of prime moral and explanatory importance. Individual racism, then, matters (and, perhaps, occurs) only insofar as it contributes to the institutional racism which subjugates a racial group. On the second, opposed view, racism within individual persons is of prime moral and explanatory import, and institutional racism occurs and matters because racist attitudes (desires, aims, hopes, fears, plans) infect the reasoning, decision-making, and action of individuals not only in their private behavior, but also when they make and execute the policies of those institutions in which they operate. I take the second view. Institutional racism, in the central sense of the term, occurs when institutional behavior stems from (a) or (b) above or, in an extended sense, when it stems from (c). Obvious examples would be the infamous Jim Crow laws that originated in the former Confederacy after Reconstruction. Personal racism exists when and insofar as a person is racist in her desires, plans, aims, etc., most notably when this racism informs her conduct. In the same way, institutional racism exists when and insofar as an institution is racist in the aims, plans, etc., that people give it, especially when their racism informs its behavior. Institutional racism begins when racism extends from the hearts of individual people to become institutionalized. What matters is that racist attitudes contaminate the operation of the institution; it is irrelevant what its original point may have been, what its designers meant it to do. . . .

Not only is individual racism of greater explanatory import, I think it is also more important morally. Those of us who see morality primarily as a matter of suitability responding to other people and to the opportunities they present for us to pursue value will understand racism as an offense against the virtues of benevolence and justice in that it is an undue restriction on the respect and goodwill owed people. (Ourselves as well as others; racism, we must remember, can take the form of self-hate.) Indeed, as follows from what I have elsewhere argued, it is hard to render coherent the view that racist hate is bad mainly for its bad effects. The sense in which an action's effects are bad is that they are undesirable. But that it is to say that these effects are evil things to want and thus things the desire for which is evil, vicious. Thus, any claim that racial disadvantage is a bad thing presupposes a more basic claim that race-hatred is vicious. What is more basic morally is also morally more important in at least one sense of that term. Of course, we should bear in mind that morality is not the same as politics. What is morally most important may not be the problem whose rectification is of greatest political urgency.

IMPLICATIONS AND ADVANTAGES

There are some noteworthy implications and advantages of the proposed way of conceiving of racism.

First it suggests that prejudice, in its strict sense of "pre-judgment," is not essential to racism, and that some racial prejudice may not be racist, strictly speaking. . . .

A person may hold prejudices about people assigned to a race without herself being racist and without it being racist of her to hold those prejudices. The beliefs themselves can be called "racist" in an extended sense because they are characteristically racist. However, just as one may make a wise move without acting wisely (as when one makes a sound investment for stupid reasons), so one may hold a racist belief without holding it for racist reasons. One holds such a belief for racist reasons when it is duly connected to racial disregard: when it is held in order to rationalize that disaffection or when contempt inclines one to attribute undesirable features to people assigned to a racial group. One whose racist beliefs have no such connection to any racial disregard in her heart does not hold them in a racist way and if she has no such disregard, she is not herself a racist, irrespective of her prejudices.

Second, when racism is so conceived, the person with racist feelings, desires, hopes, fears, and dispositions is racist even if she never acts on these attitudes in such a way as to harm people designated as members of the hated race. (This is not true when racism is conceived as consisting in a system of social oppression.) It is important to know that racism can exist in (and even pervade) societies in which there is no systematic oppression, if only because the attempts to oppress fail. Even those who think racism important primarily because of its effects should find this possibility of inactive racism worrisome for, so long as this latent racism persists, there is constant threat of oppressive behavior.

Third, on this view, race-based preference (favoritism) need not be racist. *Preferential* treatment in affirmative action, while race-based, is not normally based on any racial disregard. This is a crucial difference between James Meredith's complaint against the University of Mississippi and Allan Bakke's complaint against the University of California at Davis Medical School (see Appiah, 1990: p. 15). Appiah says that what he calls "Extrinsic racism has usually been the basis [1] for treating people worse than we otherwise might, [2] for giving them less than their humanity entitles them to" (Appiah, 1992: 18). What is important to note here is that (1) and (2) are not at all morally equivalent. Giving someone less than her humanity entitles her to is morally wrong. To give someone less than we could give her, and even to give her less than we would if she (or we, or things) were different is to treat her "worse [in the sense of 'less well'] than we otherwise might." However, the latter is not normally morally objectionable. Of course, we may not deny people even gratuitous favors out of hatred or contempt, whether or not race-based, but that does not entail that we may not licitly choose to bestow favors instead on those to whom we feel more warmly. That I feel closer to A than I do to B does not mean that I feel hatred or callousness toward B. I may give A more than A has a claim to get from me and more than I give B, while nevertheless giving B everything to which she is entitled (and even more). Thus, race-based favoritism does not have to involve (2) and need not violate morality. . . .

As racist discrimination need not always be conscious, so it need not always be intended to harm. Some of what is called "environmental racism," especially the location of waste dumps so as disproportionally to burden Black people, is normally not intended to harm anyone at all. Nevertheless, it is racist if, for example, the dumpers regard it as less important if it is "only," say, Black people who suffer. However, it will usually be the case that intentional discrimination based on racist attitudes will be more objectionable morally, and harder to justify, than is unintentional, unconscious racist discrimination. Rac*ial* discrimination is not always rac*ist* discrimination. The latter is always immoral, because racism is inherently vicious and it corrupts any differentiation that it infects. The former—racial discrimination—is not inherently immoral. Its moral status will depend on the usual factors—intent, knowledge, motive, and so on—to which we turn to determine what is vicious.

This understanding of racism also offers a new perspective on the controversy over efforts to restrict racist "hate speech." Unlike racially *offensive* speech, which is defined by its (actual or probable) effects, racist *hate* speech is defined by its origins, i.e., by whether it expresses (and is thus an act of) racially directed hate. So we cannot classify a remark as racist hate speech simply on the basis of *what* was said, we need to look to *why* the speaker said it. Speech laden with racial slurs and epithets is presumptively hateful, of course, but merely voicing an opinion that members of R1 are inferior (in some germane way) will count as racist (in any of the term's chief senses, at least) only if, for example, it expresses an opinion held from the operation of some predisposition to believe bad things about R1s, which predisposition itself stems in part from racial disregard. This understanding of racist hate speech should allay the fears of those who think that racial oversensitivity and the fear of offending the oversensitive will stifle the discussion of delicate and important matters beneath a blanket of what is called "political correctness." Racist hate speech is defined by its motive forces and, given a fair presumption of innocence, it will be difficult to give convincing evidence of ugly motive behind controversial opinions whose statement is free of racial insults.

SOME DIFFICULTIES

It may seem that my view fails to meet the test of accommodating clear cases of racism from history. Consider some members of the southern White aristocracy in the antebellum or Jim Crow periods of American history—people who would never permit racial epithets to escape their lips, and who were solicitous and even protective of those they considered "their Negroes" (especially Black servants and their kin), but who not only acquiesced in, but actively and strongly supported the social system of racial separatism, hierarchy, and oppression. These people strongly opposed Black equality in the social, economic, and political realms, but they appear to have been free of any vehement racial hatred. It appears that we should call such people racist. The question is: Does the account offered here allow them to be so classified?

This presents a nice difficulty, I think, and one it will be illuminating to grapple with. There is, plainly, a kind of hatred that consists in opposition to a person's (or group's) welfare. Hatred is the opposite of love and, as to love someone is to wish her well (i.e., to want and will that she enjoy life and its benefits), so one kind of hatred for her is to wish her ill (i.e., to want and will that she not enjoy them). It is important to remember, however, that not all hatred is wishing another ill for its own sake. When I take revenge, for example, I act from hate, but I also want to do my enemy ill for a purpose (to get even). So too when I act from envy. (I want to deprive the other of goods in order to keep her from being better off than I, or from being better off than I wish her to be.) I have sometimes talked here about racial "antipathy" ("animosity," "aversion," "hostility," etc.), but I do not mean that the attitude in question has to be especially negative or passionate. Nor need it be notably ill-mannered or crude in its expression. What is essential is that it consists in either opposition to the well-being of people classified as members of the targeted racial group or in a racially based callousness to the needs and interests of such people.

This, I think, gives us what we need in order to see part of what makes our patricians racists, for all their well-bred dispassion and good manners. They stand against the advancement of Black people (as a group, even if they make an exception for "their Negroes"). They are averse to it as such, not merely doing things that have the *side* effect of setting back the interests of Black people. Rather, they *mean* to retard those interests, to keep Black people "in their place" relative to White people. They may adopt this stance of active, conscious, and deliberate hostility to Black welfare either simply to benefit themselves at the expense of Black people or out of the contemptuous belief that, because they are Black, they merit no better. In any event, these aristocrats and their behavior can properly be classified as racist. . . .

It may not be clear how the understanding of racism offered here accommodates the commonsense view that the attitudes, rhetoric, behavior, and representatives of the mindset we might characterize as the "white man's burden" view count as racist. One who holds such a Kiplingesque view (let's call her K) thinks non-Whites ignorant, backward, undisciplined, and generally in need of a tough dose of European "civilizing" in important aspects of their lives. This training in civilization may sometimes be harsh, but it is supposed to be for the good of the "primitive" people. Moreover, it is important, for our purposes, to remember that K may think that, for all their ignorance, lack of discipline and other intellectual and moral failings, individuals within the purportedly primitive people may in certain respects, and even on the whole, be moral superiors to certain of their European "civilizers." Thus, Kipling's notorious coda to "Gunga Din."

The matter is a complex one, of course, but I think that, at least in extreme instances, such an approach can be seen to fit the model of racism whose adoption I have urged. What is needed is to attend to and apply our earlier remarks about breaches of respect and the vice of injustice. An important part of respect is recognizing the other as a human like oneself, including treating her like one. There can be extremes of condescension so inordinate they constitute degradation. In such cases, a subject goes beyond more familiar forms of paternalism to demean the other, treating her as utterly irresponsible. Plainly, those who take it upon themselves to conscript mature, responsible, healthy, socialized (and innocent) adults into a regimen of education designed to strip them of all authority over their own lives and make them into "civilized" folk condescend in just this way. This abusive paternalism borders on contempt and it can violate the rights of the subjugated people by denying them the respect and deference to which their status entitles them. By willfully depriving the oppressed people of the goods of freedom even as part of an ultimately well-meant project of "improving" them, the colonizers act with the kind of instrumentally malevolent benevolence we discussed above. The colonizers stunt and maim in order to help, and therein plainly will certain evils to the victims they think of as beneficiaries. Thus, their conduct counts as a kind of malevolence insofar as we take the term literally to mean willing evils.

Of course, the Kiplinesque agent will not think of herself as depriving responsible, socialized people of their rights over their lives; she does not see them that way and thinks them too immature to have such rights. However, we need to ask why she regards Third World peoples as she does. Here, I suspect, the answer is likely to be that her view of them is influenced, quite possibly without her being conscious of it, by her interest in maintaining the social and economic advantages of having her group wield control over its subjects. If so, her beliefs are relevantly motivated and affected by (instrumental) ill-will, her desire to gain by harming others. When this is so, then her beliefs are racist not just in the weak sense that their content is the sort that characteristically is tied to racial disaffection, but in the stronger and morally more important sense that her own acceptance of these beliefs is partially motivated by racial disaffection. She is *being* racist in thinking as she does. I conclude that the account of racism offered here can allow that, and help explain why, many people who hold the "white man's burden" mentality are racist, indeed, why they may be racist in several different (but connected) ways. . . .

SOME CASES . . .

What should we say of some different cases . . . in which a person who herself harbors no racial disregard or disrespect, nonetheless accedes to others' racism by refusing to hire, promote, or serve those assigned to a targeted racial group? Here the agent's action is infected, poisoned by racial hatred. It has such hate in its motivational structure, and that is the usual hallmark of racist behavior. I think what crucially distinguishes this agent's behavior is that it is not *the agent's own* hatred. I suggest that in addition to the two forms of racial disaffection we have already identified—the core concept of racial malevolence and the derivative concept of a race-based insufficiency of good-will—we can allow that an action may be called racist in an extended sense of the term when it is poisoned by racism, even where the racial disaffection that corrupts it does not lie in the agent's own heart but in those to whom the agent accedes. Thus, the agent in our example, while not herself a racist, performs an action that is in an important way infected by other people's racism. I doubt we should simply say without qualification that her own action is racist, but it is surely morally objectionable. . . . Consider a person who denies service, or promotion, or admission, or employment to people assigned to group G1 in order to appease people with a racial disaffection directed against them. Now suppose further that she herself cooperates in the latter's malevolence by *trying* to harm those classified as G1s in order to placate their enemies. (This would be a form of what moral theologians have called "formal cooperation.") When the agent goes that far, she has internalized racist malice into her own intentions, and thus corrupted her actions in a more grievous way than has the person who merely goes along with neighboring racists in her external actions. This is so whether or not her *feelings* toward people assigned to G1 are hostile.

What should we say of a case Judith Lichtenberg raises, in which, acting from racial fear, a White person crosses the street to avoid Black pedestrians she perceives as possible dangers? Lichtenberg thinks it acceptable for the fearful (and prejudiced?) White person to cross the street in order to avoid proximity with the Black teenagers who approach her at night ([1992] p. 4). She sensibly suggests that this is not racist if the person would respond in the same way with White teenagers. "She might well do the same if the teenagers were white. In that case her behavior does not constitute racial discrimination." (Of course, her behavior now raises a question of age discrimination, but, like Lichtenberg, I will not pursue that topic.) Helpfully, Lichtenberg cites several factors she thinks relevant to deciding when it is unjust to take race into account. How much harm does the victim suffer? How much does the agent stand to suffer if she does not discriminate? Is the person who discriminates acting in a public or official capacity?

Lichtenberg maintains that the Black teenagers suffer "a minimal slight—if it's even noticed." She even suggests that the White person might spare their feelings "by a display of ulterior motivation, like [pretending to] inspect the rosebushes on the other side" of the street in order to make it look as if it were her admiration for the flowers, and not her fear of Black people, that motivated her to cross the street. The latter pretense is, in my judgment, insulting and unlikely to succeed. More important, this appears to be a guilty response, as if the person is trying to cover up something she knows is wrong. I think that fact should cause Lichtenberg and her imagined agent to reconsider the claim that the action is unobjectionable. It is also quite wrong-headed to think that the harm of insult is entirely a matter of whether a person has hurt feelings. Does it make a difference that the victims suffer little direct and tangible harm? Some, but not much. After all, by that criterion, egregiously racist behavior such as engaging in caricatures or telling jokes that mock Black people would be justified if done in an all-White setting.

According to Lichtenberg, it is acceptable for the White woman to try to avoid the Black teenager on the street, but much harder to justify her racially discriminating when he applies for a job. It will be difficult to maintain this position, however. How is this woman—so terrified of contact with young Black males that she will not walk on the same side of the street with them—simply to turn off this uneasiness when the time comes for her to decide whether to offer a job to the Black male? Suppose that the job is to help out in her family's grocery store, and that this is likely to mean that the woman and the teenager will be alone in the store some evenings? Lichtenberg's advice that the woman indulge her prejudice in her private life but rigorously exclude it from their official conduct, seems unstable. Indeed, Lichtenberg seems to assume that the woman can take refuge in bureaucracy, that she will be the personnel officer who does the hiring, while it is other people who will actually have to work in proximity with the new employee. It is the worst of liberal bad faith, however, for this woman to practice her tolerance in official decision-making, but only on the condition that it is other people who will have to bear the burden of adjusting to the pluralistic environment those decisions create and of making that environment work. (Compare the liberal politician who boldly integrates the public schools while taking care to "protect" her own kids in all-White private schools.)

Lichtenberg assumes that private discrimination is less serious morally, but this is doubtful. The heart is where racism, like all immorality, begins and dwells. Even if some moral *virtue*-traits were differentially distributed along racial lines (and even if that were for genetic rather than historical reasons), each individual would still retain the right to be given the benefit of the probability that she is *not* herself specially inclined toward vice. Of course, this sort of racial discrimination need not be racist, since it can be entirely unconnected to any racial disaffection, just as it may not be irrational if it is a response to a genuine statistical disparity in risk. (Similarly, there need be nothing immoral in age-based discrimination should the woman seek to avoid being on dark streets alone with teenagers but not with the elderly.) Nevertheless, such conduct runs substantial risk of reinforcing some of the ugly racial stereotypes that are used to rationalize racial antipathy, and there is reason to avoid relying upon it.

Our view of institutional racism is both narrower and wider than some others that have been offered. To see how it is narrower, that is, less inclusive, let us consider the practice of "word-of-mouth" job-recruitment, in which people assigned to a privileged racial group, who tend to socialize only with one another, distribute special access to employment benefits to social acquaintances similarly assigned. Some deem this institutional racism, because of its adverse impact on those considered members of the disadvantaged group. . . .

Consider . . . the so-called "old boy network." Person F, upon hearing of an opening at his place of employment, tells the people he thinks of (who are all White males like himself) about the job and recommends one of them (Person G) to the boss, who hires him. Ignoring the exaggeration in calling anything so informal an "institution," let us explore whether this "institution" of the "old boy network" is racist. Is F (or F's behavior) racist? Is G (or G's behavior) racist? Some are ready to offer affirmative answers. What should we say? First, G cannot be racist just for receiving the job; that's not sufficiently active. What about G's act of *accepting* the job? That can be racist. I think, however, that it is racist only in the exceptional circumstance where the institutions are so corrupt that G should have nothing to do with them. Second, F may be racist insofar as his mental process skips over some possible candidates simply because the stereotypes he uses (perhaps to mask his racial disaffection from himself and others) keep him from thinking of them as possible job candidates. Third, one needs some further reason not yet given to label racist the practice of the "old boy network." It may work "systematically" to the detriment of Black people. That, however, merely shows that, in our society, with our history of racism, Black people can be disadvantaged by many things other than race-based factors. . . . What is important to note is that it is misleading to call all these things racist, because that terminology fails to differentiate the very different ways in which and reasons for which they disadvantage people. This classification and broad use of the term, then, fails adequately to inform us and, of more practical importance, it fails to direct our attention (and efforts) to the source of the difficulty. It doesn't identify for us *how* things are going wrong and thus *what* needs to be changed.

Some accounts of institutional racism threaten to be excessively broad in other ways. Some implicitly restrict institutional racism to operations *within* a society—they see it as one group maintaining its social control over the other. This is too narrow, since it would exclude, for example, what seem to be some clear cases of institutional racism, such as discrimination in immigration and in foreign assistance policies. However, if this restriction to intra-group behavior is simply removed from these accounts, then they will have to count as instances of institutional racism some actions which do not properly fall within the class. Suppose, for example, the government of a hostile planet, free of any bigotry toward any Earthling racial group, but unenamored of all Earthlings, launches a missile to destroy the Earth. Suppose it lands in Africa. This institutional (governmental) action has a disproportionally adverse impact on Black people, but it is silly to describe it as racist. (It remains silly even if the aliens decide to target *all* their attacks on the same continent—say, because of size or subterranean mineral deposits make it easier for their tracking systems to locate—and the effect thus becomes "systematic.") Talk of racism here is inane because the action, its motivation, and its agents are entirely untainted by any racial disaffection or prejudice. By the same token, however, although the agents of many earthly institutions *are* tainted by racism (e.g., in the U.S. government), that fact cannot suffice, even in combination with adverse impacts, to make its actions institutionally racist. The racism has first to *get into* the institutional conduct somehow by informing the conduct of individual agents. In contrast, proponents of expansive accounts of institutional racism, by focusing on the action's effects, end up in the untenable position of claiming that racism somehow *comes out of* institutional behavior, while simultaneously denying that it must ever even get into the action at the action's source in the aims, beliefs, desires, hopes, fears, and so on of the agents who execute institutional policy.

We can also profitably turn our account to an interesting case Skillen offers. He writes:

> Suppose Dr. Smythe-Browne's surgery has been ticking over happily for years until it is realized that few of the many local Asians visit him. It turns out that they travel some distance to Dr. Patel's surgery. Dr. Smythe-Browne and his staff are upset. Then they realize that, stupidly, he has never taken the trouble to make himself understood by or to understand the Asians in his area. His surgery practices have had the effect of excluding or at least discouraging Asians. Newly aware, he sets out to fix the situation.
>
> By the same token as his practices have been "consequentially," not "constitutively" discriminatory, they have been "blind," lacking in awareness.
>
> The example shows the possibility of a certain sort of "racism" that, if we must attribute blame, is a function of a lack of thought (energy, resources, etc.). If that lack of thought is itself to be described as "discriminatory" it would need to be shown Dr. Smythe-Browne showed no such lack of attention when one of the local streets became gentrified. . . . In such cases, it is not racial sets as such that are the focus of attention, but race as culturally 'inscribed'. In other words, one is concerned with people in respect of how they identify themselves and are identified by others (for example, intimidating institutions or outright racists). (Skillen [1993], p. 81)

Despite what Skillen implies, that an institution intimidates some racial groups ("sets") does not make it racist. Flew is right about the insufficiency (even the irrelevance) of mere effects to establish racism, as he is right about the sufficiency of racism to establish immorality. Otherwise, the interplanetary attacks in our earlier example would count as instances of institutional racism. Moreover, that Smythe-Browne was thoughtless about what might be needed to attract Asians in no way shows his conduct was racist, not even if he was more sensitive and interested in how to attract "yuppies" brought close by local gentrification. Insensitivity to certain race-related differences is not racist, even if one is sensitive to class-related differences or to differences associated with other racial differences. Smythe-Browne does not so much "discourage" Asians as fail to encourage them. Psychologically and ontologically, that is a very different matter, and those differences are likely to correlate with moral differences as well. (Failure to encourage is likely merely to be at worst an offense of *non*benevolence rather of *male*volence.) *Perhaps* the Asians were "invisible" to Smythe-Browne in a way that he is culpable for. To show this, however, more would need to be said about why he did not notice them, their absence, and their special interests. Is it that he cares so little about Asians and their well-being? If there is nothing like this involved, then there is no racism in Smythe-Browne's professional behavior, I say. And if there is something like this involved, then Smythe-Browne's conduct is not purely "'consequentially' . . . discriminatory." It is corrupted by its motivation in racial disaffection. . . .

Skillen . . . adds further detail to his case, asking us to suppose that Dr. Smythe-Browne "decides that the only way to cope with the situation is to get an Asian doctor, preferably female, onto the staff. He advertises the job and, finding a good person of the sort he needs, she joins the practice, whereas a number of, in other respects at least, equally good applicants (white, male for the most part) do not. Is this 'racism'?" Skillen thinks not, and I think he argues his point well. . . . "Dr. Smythe-Browne's criteria remain medical. His selection is legitimate insofar as we accept that medicine is a human and communicative 'art' in respect of which socially significant variables are relevant. In that sense it is simply not the case that bypassed candidates with better degree results were necessarily 'better candidates'" (Skillen [1993], p. 82).

With this understanding and assessment, I agree wholeheartedly. Dr. Smythe-Browne's hiring preference here seems to me to exemplify the sort of race-based distinction that is in its nature and its morality quite different from racist discrimination. . . .

Skillen is correct to observe that oftentimes institutions shape individual intentions and actions. Institutional racism will often exist in reciprocal relation to individual racism. The racism of some individual (or individuals) first infects the institution, and the institution's resultant racism then reinforces racism in that individual or breeds it in others. Once individual racism exists, institutional racism can be a powerful instrument of its perpetuation. This reciprocity of casual influence, however, should not blind us to the question of origins. Individual racism can come into the world without depending on some prior institutionalization. (It could come to be, say, as a result of some twist in one person's temperament.) The converse is not true. Institutional racism can reinforce and perpetuate individual racism. Unless an institution is corrupted (in its ends, means, priorities, or assumptions) by a prior and independent racism in some individual's heart, however, institutional racism can never come to exist.

Nevertheless, we should take care not to overstate the dependence of institutional racism upon individuals. Institutional racism appears to be capable of continuing after individual racism has largely died out. Think of a case where, for example, officials continue, uncomprehendingly, to implement policies originally designed, and still functioning, to disadvantage those assigned to a certain racial group. Indeed, I strongly doubt that the qualifier "and still functioning" is necessary. Institutional racism can exist without actually functioning to harm anyone. Suppose, a few generations back, some R1s designed a certain institutional procedure P specifically to harm R2s, an oppressed racial group, though the designers were never explicit about this aim. Later, anti-R2 feeling among R1s faded away, and in time real social equality was achieved. The R1s, however, are a traditionalist lot, and they continue faithfully to execute P out of deference to custom and their ancestors. P no longer specially harms R2s. (Perhaps it excludes from various privileges those who come from some specific, traditionally poor R2 neighborhoods, and R2s are no longer disproportionally represented in those neighborhoods, which, perhaps, are also no longer disproportionally poor.)

In that case, it appears that the racism of the earlier generation persists in the institutional procedure P, even though P no longer specially harms R2s. This indicates that institutional racism, no less than individual racism, can be either effective or ineffective, either harmful or innocuous. Institutional racism, then, is a bad thing; but it is a bad thing not because of its actual effects, but sometimes merely because of its aims. The study of people's aims directs the social theorist's attention to their hearts, to what they care about, to what they have set themselves on having, or being, or making, or doing. Such is the stuff of the moral virtues, of course. Neither the social theorist nor the moral theorist can continue to neglect them if she wishes to understand the world. Or to change it.

CONCLUSION

These reflections suggest that an improved understanding of racism and its immorality calls for a comprehensive rethinking of racial discrimination, of the preferential treatment programs sometimes disparaged as "reverse discrimination," and of institutional conduct as well. They also indicate the direction such a rethinking should take, and its dependence on the virtues and other concepts from moral psychology. That may require a significant change in the way social philosophers have recently treated these and related topics.

REFERENCES

Appiah, Anthony. "Racisms." In *Anatomy of Racism*, pp. 3–17. Ed. D. T. Goldberg. Minneapolis: University of Minnesota Press, 1990.

——. *In My Father's House: Africa in the Philosophy of Culture.* Oxford: Oxford University Press, 1992.

Blum, Lawrence. "Antiracism, Multiculturalism, and Interracial Community: Three Educational Values for a Multicultural Society." Office of Graduate Studies and Research, University of Massachusetts at Boston, 1991.

Lichtenberg, Judith. "Racism in the Head, Racism in the World." *Philosophy and Public Policy* (Newsletter of the Institute for Philosophy and Public Policy, University of Maryland), Vol. 12 (1992).

Nathanson, Stephen. "Is Patriotism Like Racism?" *APA Newsletter on Philosophy and the Black Experience* 91 (1992): 9–11.

Piper, Adrian M. "Higher Order Discrimination." In *Identity, Character, & Morality*, pp. 285–309. Ed. Owen Flanagan and Amelie Rorty. Cambridge: MIT Press, 1990.

Skillen, Anthony. "Racism: Flew's Three Concepts of Racism." *Journal of Applied Philosophy*. vol. 10 (1993): 73–89.

Discussion Questions

1. Do you agree with Garcia's definition of a racist? According to Garcia's definition, does being a nonracist necessarily entail white people lowering the standards for their children's educations so that nonwhite children can get a better education? Are white people who take advantage of better schools in affluent white neighborhoods racist by definition? Are people who oppose state or federal (instead of local) funding for schools racists? Support your answers.
2. According to Garcia, people who act in ways that retard the interests of blacks, even though they claim to feel no ill will toward them, are racist. Do you agree? Illustrate your answer using affirmative action as an example.
3. Discuss ways in which your actions may be infected by racism even though you yourself may bear no ill will or racial hatred. Use specific examples to illustrate your answer.
4. Do you agree with Lichtenberg that private discrimination is less serious than public discrimination? Compare and contrast Lichtenberg's and Garcia's analyses of the

white woman crossing the street to avoid the black teenager. Which person do you think provides the best analysis? Support your answers.

5. Discuss ways in which the "old boy network" advantages whites and disadvantages blacks and other minorities on your campus. Use specific examples to illustrate your answer.
6. In the Smythe-Browne case study, Garcia argues that the fact that some racial groups are intimidated by an institution does not necessarily make it a racist institution. Do you agree? Discuss your answer in light of Steele's description of minority experience and in light of certain college institutions such as the Greek system.
7. Discuss the implications of Garcia's analysis of racism for affirmative action. What type of affirmative action, if any, might Garcia support? Discuss, in particular, how Garcia might respond to affirmative action in college admissions.
8. Garcia claims that his definition of racism is better than others at explaining interracial antagonism. In the United States, there is often antagonism among minority groups. Following the 1992 Rodney King verdict, riots broke out in Los Angeles among blacks, Hispanics, and Koreans. More than twelve thousand arrests were made in one week. Property damage was estimated at $400 million. Koreans suffered the most damage at the hands of rioters, with more than a thousand Korean-owned businesses burned or looted. Discuss whether Garcia's definition of racism accounts for this type of violence among minorities.

BERNARD R. BOXILL

The Color-Blind Principle

Bernard Boxill is a philosophy professor at the University of North Carolina in Chapel Hill. Boxill rejects the assumption that law and morality should always be color-blind. Whereas some color-conscious policies, such as Jim Crow laws, are clearly unjust, there are other times, he argues, when it is morally justified to base public policy on color-conscious principles. Discrimination is not necessarily unjust. As with differences in talent, differences in color can sometimes justly be considered in circumstances such as hiring.

Critical Reading Questions

1. Who was Homer Plessy and why was he arrested in 1892? On what grounds did Plessy defend his actions? What was the U.S. Supreme Court ruling on the Plessy case?

"The Color-Blind Principle," in *Blacks and Social Justice* (Totowa, N.J.: Rowman & Allanheld, 1984), 9–18. Some notes have been omitted.

2. What did Justice John Marshall Harlan mean when he said, "Our Constitution is color-blind"?
3. Why do some liberals maintain that the "I didn't notice" kind of color-blindness is a worthy ideal?
4. What is the essence of a color-conscious policy and what are some examples of such policies?
5. What are the main arguments used by advocates of the color-blind principle?
6. What is the difference between the racist's and the black nationalist's view on the importance of color? Why, as Boxill notes, do some people say that the slogan *Black is beautiful* rings hollow?
7. What is the "responsibility criterion" and how is it used to support legal color-blind policies? Why does Boxill claim that this can be a false and confusing criterion for creating egalitarian public policies?
8. According to Boxill, why does the fact that race is arbitrary and not freely chosen make color-blind policies unjust?
9. Why does racial discrimination subordinate the best interests of minority communities?
10. According to Boxill, why are color-conscious principles no less discriminatory than the principles of meritocracy?
11. On what grounds does Boxill argue that "adopting a color-blind principle entails adopting a talent-blind principle"? How does Boxill use this argument to support his conclusion that color-conscious policies can be just?
12. How does Boxill respond to the objection that affirmative action leads to reverse discrimination against whites?

PLESSY

In 1892, Homer Plessy, an octoroon, was arrested in Louisiana for taking a seat in a train car reserved for whites. He was testing a state law which required the "white and colored races" to ride in "equal but separate" accommodations, and his case eventually reached the Supreme Court.

Part of Plessy's defense, though it must be considered mainly a snare for the opposition, was that he was "seven-eighths Caucasian and one-eighth African blood," and that the "mixture of colored blood was not discernible in him." The bulwark of his argument was, however, that he was "entitled to every right, privilege and immunity secured to citizens of the white race," and that the law violated the Fourteenth Amendment's prohibition against unequal protection of the laws. Cannily, the court refused the snare. Perhaps it feared—and with reason—that the ancestry of too many white Louisianans held dark secrets. But it attacked boldly enough Plessy's main argument that the Louisiana law was unconstitutional. That argument, Justice Henry Billings Brown wrote for the majority, was unsound. "Its underlying fallacy," he averred, was its "assumption that the enforced separation of the two races stamps the colored race with a badge of inferiority." "If this be so," Brown concluded, "it is not by reason of anything found in the act, but solely because the colored race chooses to put that construction upon it."

Only one judge dissented from the court majority—Justice John Marshall Harlan. It was the occasion on which he pronounced his famous maxim: "Our Constitution is color-blind." In opposition to Justice Brown, Justice Harlan found that the "separation of citizens on the basis of race [was a] badge of servitude . . . wholly inconsistent [with] equality before the law."

Plessy's is the kind of case which makes the color-blind principle seem indubitably right as a basis for action and policy, and its contemporary opponents appear unprincipled, motivated by expediency, and opportunistic. This impression is only strengthened by a reading of Justice Brown's tortuously preposterous defense of the "equal but separate" doctrine. It should make every advocate of color-conscious policy wary of the power of arguments of expediency to beguile moral sense and subvert logic. Yet I argue that color-conscious policy can still be justified. The belief that it cannot is the result of a mistaken generalization from *Plessy*. There is no warrant for the idea that the color-blind principle should hold in some general and absolute way.

"I DIDN'T NOTICE" LIBERALS

In his book *Second Wind,* Bill Russell recalls how amazed he used to be by the behavior of what he called "I didn't notice" liberals. These were individuals who claimed not to notice people's color. If they mentioned someone Russell could not place, and Russell asked whether she was black or white, they would answer, "I didn't notice." "Sweet and innocent," Russell recalls, "sometimes a little proud." Now, the kind of color-blindness the "I didn't notice" liberals claim to have may be a worthy ideal—Richard Wasserstrom, for example, argues that society should aim toward it—but it is absolutely different from the color-blind principle which functions as a basis for policy. Thus, while Wasserstrom supports color-conscious policies to secure the ideal of people not noticing each others' color, the principle of color-blindness in the law opposes color-conscious policies and does not necessarily involve any hope that people will not notice each others' color. Its thesis is simple: that no *law* or *public policy* be designed to treat people differently because they are of a different color.

COLOR-BLIND AND COLOR-CONSCIOUS POLICIES

The essential thing about a color-conscious policy is that it is designed to treat people differently because of their race. But there are many different kinds of color-conscious policies. Some, for example the Jim Crow policies now in the main abolished, aim to subordinate blacks, while others, such as busing and preferential treatment, aim at elevating blacks.

Some color-conscious policies explicitly state that persons should be treated differently because of their race, for example the segregation laws at issue in *Plessy;* others make no mention of race, but are still designed so that blacks and whites are treated differently, for example, the "grandfather clauses" in voting laws that many states adopted at the turn of the century. . . .

Advocates of the belief that the law should be color-blind often argue that this would the best means to an ideal state in which people are color-blind. They appeal to the notion that, only if people notice each other's color can they discriminate on the basis of color and, with considerable plausibility, they argue that color-conscious laws and policies can only heighten people's awareness of each other's color, and exacerbate racial conflict. They maintain that only if the law, with all its weight and influence, sets the example of color-blindness, can there be a realistic hope that people will see through the superficial distinctions of color and become themselves color-blind.

But this argument is not the main thesis of the advocates of legal color-blindness. Generally, they eschew it because of its dependency on the empirical. Their favorite argument, one that is more direct and intuitively appealing, is simply that it is wicked, unfair, and unreasonable to penalize a person for what he cannot help being. Not only does this seem undeniably true, but it can be immediately applied to the issue of race. No one can help being white or being black, and so it seems to follow that it is wicked, unfair, and unreasonable to disqualify a person from any consideration just because he is white or black. This, the advocates of color-blindness declare, is what made Jim Crow laws heinous, and it is what makes affirmative action just as heinous.

The force of this consideration is enhanced because it seems to account for one peculiar harmfulness of racial discrimination—its effect on self-respect and self-esteem. For racial discrimination makes some black people hate their color, and succeeds in doing so because color cannot be changed. Furthermore, a racially conscious society has made color seem an important part of the individual's very essence, and since color is immutable it is easily susceptible to this approach. As a result, the black individual may come, in the end, to hate even himself. . . . The black nationalist agrees with the racists' view that his color is an important and integral part of his self, but affirms, in opposition to the racists, that it has value. This strategy, which is exemplified by the slogans "black is beautiful" and "black and proud," has the obvious advantage of stimulating pride and self-confidence. Nevertheless, it is no panacea. For one thing, it has to contend with the powerful propaganda stating that black is *not* beautiful. And there is a more subtle problem. Since the black cannot choose *not* to be black, he cannot be altogether confident that he would choose to *be* black, nor, consequently, does he really place a special value in being black. Thus, some people, black and white, have expressed the suspicion that the slogan "black is beautiful" rings hollow, like the words of the man who protests too loudly that he loves the chains he cannot escape. In this respect the black who can pass as white has an advantage over the black who cannot. For, though he cannot choose not to be black, he can choose not to be *known* to be black.

THE RESPONSIBILITY CRITERION

A final argument in favor of legal color-blindness is related to, and further develops, the point that people do not choose to be, and cannot avoid being, black or white. This links the question of color-blindness to the protean idea of individual responsibility. Thus, William Frankena writes, that to use color as a fundamental basis for distributing "opportunities, offices, etc." to persons is "unjust in itself," because it is to distribute goods on the basis of a feature "which the individual has not done, and can do nothing about; we are treating people differently in ways that profoundly affect their lives because of differences for which they have no responsibility."[1] Since this argument requires that people be treated differently in ways which profoundly affect their lives only on the basis of features for which they are responsible, I call it the responsibility criterion.

The responsibility criterion also seems to make the principle of color-blindness follow from principles of equal opportunity. Joel Feinberg takes it to be equivalent to the claim that "properties can be the grounds of just discrimination between persons only if those persons had a fair opportunity to acquire or avoid them."[2] This implies that to discriminate between persons on the basis of a feature for which they can have no responsibility is to violate the principle of fair opportunity. But color (or sex) is a feature of persons for which they can have no responsibility.

The responsibility criterion may seem innocuous because, though, strictly interpreted it supports the case for color-blindness, loosely interpreted it leaves open the possibility that color-conscious policies are justifiable. Thus, Frankena himself allows that color could be an important basis of distribution of goods and offices if it served "as [a] reliable sign[s] of some Q, like ability or merit, which is more justly employed as a touchstone for the treatment of individuals."[3] This sounds like a reasonable compromise and is enough to support some arguments for color-conscious policies. For example, it could support the argument that black and white children should go to the same schools because being white is a reliable sign of being middle-class, and black children, who are often lower-class, learn better when their peers are middle-class. Similarly, it might support the argument that preferential hiring is compensation for the harm of being discriminated against on the basis of color, and that being black is a reliable sign of having been harmed by that discrimination.

But however loosely it is interpreted, the responsibility criterion cannot be adduced in support of all reasons behind color-conscious policies. It cannot, for example, sustain the following argument, sketched by Ronald Dworkin, for preferential admission of blacks to medical school. "If quick hands count as 'merit' in the case of a prospective surgeon this is because quick hands will enable him to serve the public better and for no other reason. If a black skin will, as a matter of regrettable fact, enable another doctor to do a different medical job better, then that black skin is by the same token 'merit' as well."[4] What is proposed here is not that a black skin is a justifiable basis of discrimination because it is a reliable sign of merit or some other factor Q. A closely related argument does make such a proposal, viz., that blacks should be preferentially admitted to medical school because being black is a reliable sign of a desire to serve the black community. But this is not the argument that Dworkin poses. In the example quoted above what he suggests is that being black is in *itself* merit, or, at least, something very like merit.

According to the responsibility criterion, we ought not to give A a job in surgery rather than B, if A is a better surgeon than B only because he was born with quicker hands. For if we do, we treat A and B "differently in ways that profoundly affect their lives because of differences for which they have no responsibility." This is the kind of result which puts egalitarianism in disrepute. It entails the idea that we might be required to let fumblers do surgery and in general give jobs and offices to incompetents, and this is surely intolerable. But, as I plan to show, true egalitarianism has no such consequences. They are the result of applying the responsibility criterion, not egalitarian principles. Indeed, egalitarianism must scout the responsibility criterion as false and confused.

Egalitarians should notice first, that, while it invalidates the merit-based theories of distribution that they oppose, it also invalidates the need-based theories of distribution they favor. For, if people are born with special talents for which they are not responsible, they are also born with special needs for which they are not responsible. Consequently, if the responsibility criterion forbids choosing A over B to do surgery because A is a better surgeon because he was born with quicker hands, it also forbids choosing C rather than D for remedial education because C needs it more than D only because he was born with a learning disability and D was not.

At this point there may be objections. First, that the responsibility criterion was intended to govern only the distribution of income, not jobs and offices—in Feinberg's discussion, for example, this is made explicit. Second, that it does not mean that people should not be treated differently because of differences, good or bad, which they cannot help, but rather that people should not get less just because they are born without the qualities their society prizes or finds useful. This seems to be implied in Frankena's claim that justice should make the "same proportionate contribution to the best life for everyone" and that this may require spending more on those who are "harder to help"—probably the untalented—than on others. Qualified in these ways, the responsibility criterion becomes more plausible. It no longer implies, for example, that fumblers should be allowed to practice surgery, or that the blind be treated just like the sighted. But with these qualifications it also becomes almost irrelevant to the color-blind issue. For that issue is not only about how income should be distributed. It is also about how jobs and offices should be distributed.

Most jobs and offices are distributed to people in order to produce goods and services to a larger public. To that end, the responsibility criterion is irrelevant. For example, the purpose of admitting people to medical schools and law schools is to provide the community with good medical and legal service. It does not matter whether those who provide them are responsible for having the skills by virtue of which they provide the goods, or whether the positions they occupy are "goods" to them. No just society makes a person a surgeon just because he is responsible for his skills or because making him a surgeon will be good for him. It makes him a surgeon because he will do good surgery.

Accordingly, it may be perfectly just to discriminate between persons on the basis of distinctions they are not responsible for having. It depends on whether or not the discrimination serves a worthy end. It may be permissible for the admissions policies of professional schools to give preference to those with higher scores, even if their scores are higher than others only because they have higher native ability (for which they cannot, of course, be considered responsible), if the object is to provide the community with good professional service. And, given the same object, if for some reason a black skin, whether or not it can be defined as merit, helps a black lawyer or doctor to provide good legal or medical service to black people who would otherwise not have access to it, or avail themselves of it, it is difficult to see how there can be a principled objection to admissions policies which prefer people with black skins—though, again, they are not responsible for the quality by virtue of which they are preferred.

JUSTICE AND THE RESPONSIBILITY CRITERION

A further point needs to be made in order to vindicate color-conscious policies. The principles of justice are distributive: Justice is concerned not only with increasing the total amount of a good a society enjoys, but also with how that good should be distributed among individuals. Generally, judicial principles dictate that people who are similar in ways deemed relevant to the issue of justice, such as in needs or rights, should get equal amounts of a good, and people who are dissimilar in these regards should get unequal amounts of the good. In terms of these principles certain laws and rules must be considered unjust which would not otherwise be thought unjust. Consider, for example, a policy for admitting persons to medical school which resulted in better and better medical service for white people, but worse and worse medical service for black people. This policy would be unjust, however great the medical expertise—certainly a good—it produced, unless color is relevant to the receiving of good medical attention.

In a case like this, where it is not, the theoretical circumstance outlined by Dworkin, in which black skin might be considered a "merit," becomes viable. It is true, of course, that color is not, precisely, merit. But to insist on strict definition in this context is to cavil. The point is that if black clients tend to trust and confide more in black lawyers and doctors, then color—functioning as merit—enables a good to be produced and distributed according to some principle of justice.

If these considerations are sound, then the responsibility criterion thoroughly misconstrues the reasons for which racial discrimination is unjust. Racial discrimination against blacks is unjust because it does not enable goods to be produced and distributed according to principles of justice. It is not unjust because black people do not choose to be black, cannot *not* be black, or are not responsible for being black. This is completely irrelevant. For example, a policy denying university admission to people who parted their hair on the right side would be unjust because the way in which people part their hair is irrelevant to a just policy of school admission. It does not matter in the least, in relation to the nature and object of education, that they choose how they part their hair. Similarly, even if black people could choose to become white, or could all easily pass as white, a law school or medical school that excluded blacks because they were black would still act unjustly. Nothing would have changed.

The arguments in support of color-blindness tend to make the harmfulness of discrimination depend on the difficulty of avoiding it. This is misleading. It diverts attention from the potential harmfulness of discrimination that *can* be avoided and brings the specious responsibility criterion into play. Suppose again, for example, that a person is denied admission to law school because he parts his hair on the right side. Though he, far more easily than the black person, can avoid being unfairly discriminated *against,* he does not thereby more easily avoid being the object, indeed, in a deeper sense, the victim, of unfair discrimination. If he parts his hair on the left side he will presumably be admitted to law school. But then he will have knowingly complied with a foolish and unjust rule and this may well make him expedient and servile. Of course, he will not be harmed to the same extent and in the same way as the victim of racial discrimination. For example, he probably will not hate himself. Unlike color, the cause of his ill-treatment is too easily changed for him to conceive of it as essential to himself. Moreover, if he chooses to keep his hair parted on the right side and thus to forego law school, he *knows* that he is not going to law school because he freely chose to place a greater value on his integrity or on his taste in hairstyles than on a legal education. He knows this because he knows he could have chosen to change his hairstyle. As I noted earlier, this opportunity for self-assertion, and thus for self-knowledge and self-confidence, is denied the black who is discriminated against on the basis of his color.

Nevertheless, as I stated earlier, the considerations that stem from applying the responsibility criterion to a judgment of racial discrimination are secondary to understanding its peculiar harmfulness. Suppose, for example, that a person is not admitted to medical school to train to be a surgeon because he was born without fingers. If all the things he wants require that he have fingers, he may conceivably come to suffer the same self-hatred and self-doubt as the victim of racial discrimination. Yet his case is different, and if he attends to the difference, he will not suffer as the victim of racial discrimination suffers. The discrimination that excludes him from the practice of surgery is not denigrating his interests because they are his. It is a policy that takes into account a just object—the needs of others in the community for competent surgery. Allowing him to be a surgeon would rate other, equally important, interests below his. But racial discrimination excludes its victims from opportunities on the basis of a belief that their interests are ipso facto less important than the interests of whites. The man without fingers may regret not being born differently, but he cannot resent how he is treated. Though his ambitions may be thwarted, he himself is still treated as a moral equal. There is no attack on his self-respect. Racial discrimination, however, undermines its victims' self-respect through their awareness that they are considered morally inferior. The fact that racial discrimination, or any color-conscious policy, is difficult to avoid through personal choice merely adds to its basic harmfulness if it is in the first place unjust, but is not the *reason* for its being unjust.

It remains to consider Feinberg's claim that if people are discriminated for or against on the basis of factors for which they are not responsible the equal opportunity principle is contravened. This I concede. In particular, I concede that color-conscious policies giving preference to blacks place an insurmountable obstacle in the path of whites, and since such obstacles reduce opportunities, such policies may make opportunities unequal. But this gives no advantage to the advocates of color-blind policies. For giving preference to the competent has exactly the same implications as giving preference to blacks. It, too, places obstacles in the paths of some people, this time the untalented, and just as surely makes opportunities unequal. Consequently, an advocate of color-blindness cannot consistently oppose color-conscious policies on the grounds that they contravene equal opportunity and at the same time support talent-conscious policies. Nor, finally, does my concession raise any further difficulty with the issue of equal opportunity. As I argue later, equal opportunity is not a fundamental principle of justice, but is derived from its basic principles. Often these basic principles require that opportunities be made more equal. Invariably, however, these same principles require that the process of equalization stop before a condition of perfect equality of opportunity is reached.

To conclude, adopting a color-blind principle entails adopting a talent-blind principle, and since the latter is absurd, so also is the former. Or, in other words, differences in talent, and differences in color, are, from the point of view of justice, on a par. Either, with equal propriety, can be the basis of a just discrimination. Consequently, the color-blind principle is not as simple, straightforward, or self-evident as many of its advocates seem to feel it is. Color-conscious policies can conceivably be just, just as talent-conscious policies can conceivably be—and often are—just. It depends on the circumstances.

NOTES

1. William Frankena, "Some Beliefs About Justice," in *Justice,* ed. Joel Feinberg and Hyman Gross (Encino, Calif.: Dickenson, 1977), 49.
2. Joel Feinberg, *Social Philosophy* (Englewood Cliffs, N.J.: Prentice-Hall, 1973), 49.
3. Frankena, "Some Beliefs About Justice," 49.
4. Ronald Dworkin, "Why Bakke Has No Case," *New York Review of Books,* 10 Nov. 1977, 14.

Discussion Questions

1. Does Boxill's argument support affirmative action policies in college admissions? What would Boxill most likely think about the 2003 *Grutter v. Bollinger et al.* Supreme Court ruling on affirmative action? Support your answers.
2. Discuss what Boxill would most likely think of the current trend to create minority curriculums in colleges.
3. Alan Bloom in *The Closing of the American Mind* (1987) writes: "The black [college] student who wishes to be just a student and to avoid allegiance to the black group has to pay a terrific price, because he is judged negatively by his black peers and because his behavior is atypical in the eyes of whites."[38] Do you agree with Bloom? Support your answer using examples from your own college experience. Discuss whether color-conscious policies like those advocated by Boxill encourage stereotyping as well as the isolation of students who prefer a color-blind environment.
4. Several civil rights and Native American groups have protested the use of Indian mascots and symbols by professional sports teams such as the Washington Redskins and the Atlanta Braves. Is this practice morally justified under the color-blind principle? Support your answer. Discuss what Boxill would most likely think of this practice.
5. Discuss how Boxill might respond to Louis Farrakhan's color-conscious philosophy.
6. Discuss what Boxill would most likely think of the policy of detaining Muslim and Arab-Americans as possible terrorist threats under the Patriot Act.
7. Koreans, like other Asian immigrants, are sometimes referred to as "model minorities"—a term they don't particularly like. Despite the fact that most Koreans living in the United States are relative newcomers, nearly 40 percent of them own businesses. During the 1992 Los Angeles riots, more than a thousand Korean stores were burned or ransacked; black resentment of Koreans was cited as the one of the reasons for that. Blacks say they have a harder time getting bank loans, a claim that appears to be true, and that the schools in black neighborhoods are worse. Why might this be the case? Discuss how Boxill might answer this question. What does it mean to be called a "model minority," and why do some Asians dislike this designation?

MICHAEL LEVIN

Race, Biology, and Justice

Michael Levin was a professor of philosophy at City College of New York. Levin argues that the attainment gap between whites and blacks is due not to racism but to genetic differences between the races. Levin cites various studies to support his claim of racial

"Race, Biology, and Justice," *Public Affairs Quarterly* 8, no. 3 (1994): 267–282. Some notes have been omitted.

differences in intelligence and temperament. He argues that affirmative action and other compensatory programs are wrong because, rather than advancing blacks, they annul the natural advantage whites have over blacks.

Critical Reading Questions

1. Why aren't possible biological differences between races openly discussed? Why do some people who say that there are differences between races deny that such differences would matter? Does Levin think genetic differences matter?
2. What are some documented differences between whites and blacks?
3. What does the Smith/Jones analogy illustrate? What is compensatory justice? In what ways is affirmative action compensatory?
4. What is the "bias-fighting rationale" behind affirmative action? What assumption is integral to this argument?
5. On what grounds does Levin reject Boxill's position on affirmative action?
6. How does Levin account for the attainment gap between blacks and whites?
7. What evidence does Levin use to argue that racism isn't a plausible explanation for the attainment?
8. What is the relationship between IQ and job attainment? According to Levin, how do differences in IQ between whites and blacks undermine the claim that racism is the cause of the attainment gap? How do racial IQ differences affect educational attainment?
9. According to Levin, what temperamental characteristics of blacks lead to a propensity toward poverty?
10. On what grounds does Levin discount the role that environment plays in IQ?
11. Why, according to Levin, must the burden of proof be shifted onto blacks who claim that racism has brought about their failure?
12. How does Levin answer the charge that distributive justice requires greater racial equality?
13. How does Levin respond to the argument that slavery and segregation have left blacks disadvantaged?
14. On what grounds does Levin reject Rawls's "natural lottery" as irrelevant to racial differences?
15. How does Levin use Rawls's difference principle, as well as utilitarian considerations, to support his position?

Genetic black/white differences have played almost no role in recent discussions of interracial justice. This paper explores the relevance of these differences to issues of compensation and distribution.

One reason for the neglect of group differences, of course, is the belief that any talk of them is "racist." Obviously, though, the wickedness of mentioning a phenomenon does not diminish its logical bearing on any issue that may present itself.

At the same time, many writers who do admit the possibility of genetic race differences deny that they would matter if found. One of two reasons is usually offered for this conclusion: 1) it might prove possible to suppress genetic differences by manipulating the environment, or 2) moral principles such as a right to equal treatment are independent of the empirical traits of individuals and groups. . . .

RACE DIFFERENCES

The most thoroughly documented race difference is that in intelligence. It is accepted by every competent student of the subject that blacks score about one standard deviation (SD) below whites on all tests of intelligence; under the conventional scaling of IQ, the mean IQ of whites is 100 and that of blacks a bit below 85.[1] A literature survey by the National Academy of Science concluded "The largest difference in group averages [exists] between blacks and whites on all given tests and at all grade levels." . . . The idea that IQ measures immersion in white culture is contradicted by the performance of Japanese and Chinese on IQ tests, which exceeds that of whites and blacks. Finally, IQ associates with numerous variables unrelated to socialization. . . .

It would be hasty to suppose that blacks and whites differ in intelligence only. Many writers[2] claim that blacks are on average less inclined to defer gratification, a conjecture consistent with psychometric data. Black self-esteem is higher than white,[3] a common assumption to the contrary notwithstanding, and black scores on the Minnesota Multiphasic Personality Inventory are elevated in the direction of greater impulsivity.[4] Because they are more conjectural, however, race differences in temperament play only a minor role in what follows.

COMPENSATORY JUSTICE

When Jones limps into court to demand compensation from Smith for his broken leg, there are a number of defenses Smith should avoid. Denial that anyone can put a price-tag on a sound leg is pettifogging; appeal to the statute of limitations—the claim that Jones was harmed too long ago to deserve anything now—is legalistic; complaints about the cost of compensation are beside the point, the point being Jones' entitlement. Concentrating too heavily on the immediate cause of injury may be misdirection; Smith is still guilty if Jones broke his leg slipping on ice after being stranded by Smith on a frozen lake. Finally, concern that a large settlement may blunt Jones' zeal for rehabilitation sounds disingenuous coming from Smith.

Smith's best defense is to challenge the factual claim that he directly or indirectly broke Jones' leg. If Jones' lameness is not his doing, Smith is off the hook, morally and legally. No one is liable for what he did not do. . . .

The parallel with race is patent. Blacks limp behind whites at virtually all prestigious and remunerative tasks. This deficit is blamed on whites; blacks are said to fail because discrimination and racism have stifled their competitive ability. Given the principle of compensation—a person damaged by a wrong deserves what he lost, and is owed it by the wrong-doer—whites owe blacks the positions blacks would have occupied but for discrimination. In practical terms, redress means preferring blacks over whites when they compete.

Many defenders of preference deny they are demanding compensation. They are often the first to agree that the whites being asked to step aside now never discriminated against anyone, and that blacks receiving preference now never experienced discrimination. Yet the arguments intended to fill the resulting void are often compensatory in character. For instance, many preference advocates insist that innocent contemporary whites still benefit from past wrongs, and that anyone better off because of a wrong must surrender his illicit advantage to those the wrong has left worse off. So this new rationale for preference, like the original one, represents preference as putting blacks and whites where they would have been but for the misdeeds of (other) whites. Whether this new argument is called "compensatory," it too assumes that the black attainment deficit is the fault of (some) whites.

Or consider the argument that affirmative action provides role models for young blacks. The obvious question is, what is wrong with the present number of role models? Why not let role models distribute themselves race neutrally? Because, role-model theorists usually reply, blacks have fewer role models and lower aspirations than they would have had but for oppression. Whites should step aside for blacks so that young blacks may have hopes they should have developed. So understood, the role-model argument is patently compensatory.

Affirmative action is sometimes deemed necessary to counteract present discrimination, as revealed by the continued statistical underrepresentation of blacks in desirable positions. . . . [T]he bias-fighting rationale, while not compensatory, also assumes black ability is roughly equal to that of whites.

Now, just as Smith should not defend himself against Jones with technicalities and subterfuges, critics of affirmative action should not dodge their issue either. . . .

Smith retains the moral high ground only by showing that he did not break Jones' leg. So too, critics of quotas can retain the high ground only by showing that "racism" did not cause the attainment gap. Enter the race difference in intelligence (and, perhaps, motivation), which explains black failure better than "racism."

RACE DIFFERENCES AND THE ATTAINMENT GAP

Quite apart from the plausibility of its rivals, "racism" as a catch-all hypothesis has been eroded by the sheer passage of time. Slavery ended 130 years ago, school segregation 40 years ago; blacks have enjoyed full civil rights protection since 1964 and the ever-expanding privileges of quotas since 1970. Yet blacks are not doing appreciably better now than in 1954, and by some measures, such as marital stability, far worse. To take one of many striking examples, the National Science Foundation has spent over $1.5 billion on programs reserved for blacks since 1972, yet "20 years later, matters have barely improved" with regard to blacks in science.[5]

It is difficult to argue that blacks were too heavily burdened for gains to appear in thirty or forty years. Equally burdened groups, notably Chinese in the US and Jews in many places, have made longer strides in less time. The Germans and Japanese, whose countries lay destroyed in 1945, were again world economic powers by 1970. To explain differential responses to adversity by attributing to some groups a "tradition of hard work" begs the question of black failure to develop that tradition. Post-war Europe did receive Marshal Plan aid, and it has become something of a clichè that American blacks need a domestic Marshal Plan, but in fact the net transfer of resources to blacks under Aid to Families with Dependent Children and other subsidies already amounts to a Marshal Plan every three years.

Given the weakness of "racism" as an explanation, one turns naturally to endogenous black traits, such as lower levels of intelligence and self-restraint, to account for the attainment gap. . . .

Compensation theorists might reply that talk of *the* cause of the attainment gap is an oversimplification. The proper question is *how much* of the gap is explained by race differences, for whatever portion of the gap is left unexplained by race differences might be due to compensable racism. . . .

The reader should think of IQ in the black and white populations as represented by overlapping bell curves, with the mean of the black curve lying one SD to the left of the white mean. . . . Thus, assuming the black SD equals the white SD, about 16% of all blacks have IQs of 100 or more, while about 50% of whites do, so there are about 1/3 as many blacks as whites whose IQs exceed 100. As the normal distribution is nonlinear, this ratio varies with IQ. There is 1 black for every 8 whites whose IQs exceed 115, and 1 black for every 18 whites whose IQs exceed 130. . . .

The recruitment gap is explained by the IQ difference alone, without reference to slavery or segregation. More generally, discrimination apparently explained a minute proportion at most of black vocational failure in 1970, and by 1980 has ceased to be a factor altogether. On the evidence, black representation caught up with ability some time after World War II and before affirmative action, by which point the effects of slavery and discrimination—whatever they may once have been—had been attenuated to non-existence. If so, the present competitive abilities of blacks are what they would have been had slavery and discrimination never happened, and no white enjoys any significant wrongful advantage over his black competitors because of them. Hence, no white is required by compensatory justice to forego any of his competitive advantage.

Black academic failure, usually blamed wholly on whites, is also explicable by the race difference in IQ. The correlation between IQ and academic performance exceeds .6 in the lower grades, where the population is most diverse and the race difference most pronounced.[6] The correlation, along with the variance, decreases as one ascends the academic hierarchy, but it still suffices to explain the absence of blacks from graduate education. In 1990, 838 blacks earned the Ph.D.[7] Jensen cites an IQ of 130 as predicting the ability to earn a Ph.D.,[8] and, if the mean IQ in a population is 100, 2.3% of its members have IQs ≥ 130. As there are about 420,000 blacks in any one-year cohort, proportionality requires that .023 × 420,000 = 9600 blacks earn the Ph.D. annually. In fact, however, only .13% of blacks have IQs ≥ 130, leading to a prediction of .013 × 420,000 = 575 blacks annually capable of earning a Ph.D., close to the actual figure. . . .

The high rejection rate for blacks in the NIH competition is actually one instance of a general tendency for whites to outperform blacks when credentials are held constant—whites outearn blacks when occupation and years of schooling are controlled for.[9] This discrepancy strongly suggests bias, but it too can be explained as a statistical artifact. . . . Since wages correlate with IQ within as well as between occupations, the average income of whites exceeds that of blacks in the same jobs and with the same schooling. Proportionately fewer black scientists are outstanding scientists, capable, for instance, of conceiving research projects which win grants in blind competition.

I know of no study like Gottesman's of the relation of black temperament to poverty, but many commentators—including some preference advocates—see a link.[10] Banfield (op. cit.) blames most of the problems of the slums on preference for immediate payoffs. Boxill, who supports quotas, acknowledges that black "chronic tardiness" and other "habits or cultural traits which are debilitating and unproductive" (op. cit.). Black sociologist William J. Wilson has consistently found that ghetto males look down on jobs which don't produce a lot of money for relatively little effort.[11] Richard J. Hernstein and James Q. Wilson report that a pervasive attitude in black slums is that "Straight jobs" are for "suckers." "Every boy interviewed [in a study cited] had been employed at one time, but the turnover was very high. When asked why they left a job, they typically answered that they found it monotonous or low paying . . . [B]eing able to 'make it' while avoiding the 'work game' is a strong, pervasive, and consistent goal."[12] Such attitudes obviously impede attainment.

AN OBJECTION

There is an objection so likely to be raised at this point that it seems less an objection than a decisive refutation of my entire argument. Virtually everyone with whom I have ever discussed race differences has raised it, and it has probably occurred to the reader. Perhaps the *immediate* cause of low black attainment is lower intelligence (and greater impulsiveness), but if this difference is itself a result of racism, whites are still responsible at one remove for black failure, and the competitive edge enjoyed by whites today remains illicit. (Smith was not exonerated because he merely left Jones on the slippery ice without actually tripping him.) While some writers do not take overt or "institutional" discrimination to be the immediate cause of black failure, more thoughtful compensation theorists recognize that blacks are now objectively less able than whites. In Lyndon Johnson's famous comparison of blacks to a once-shackled runner, no one is restraining the shackled runner. He is slower than his competitors. But he is slower *because* of what has been done to him, and so deserves a head start. Likewise, if blacks are less intelligent than whites because of past discrimination, or denial of proper nutrition, or because racism discourages blacks from stimulating their children, they would still deserve a head start of some sort. It may be superior mental ability that gives whites their advantage over blacks, but the advantage should be annulled if the cause of this advantaging factor was a wrong. . . .

The only environmental factor that does seem capable of explaining the systematic character of black failure are disadvantages imposed on blacks by the majority society. . . .

GENETIC DIFFERENTIATION

The evidence strongly suggests that the race difference in intelligence is due significantly, perhaps primarily, to genetic differences. To begin with, the interindividual heritability of intelligence is quite high, between .5 and .7.[13] Operationally, this means that if everyone were raised in the same environment, the average difference between the IQs of different individuals would be almost as large as it is at present. . . . The difference between Africa and Alaska, great as it may be, does not explain the difference in height between Masai and Eskimos; no one expects a Masai baby raised by Eskimos in Alaska to grow up short and stocky. Mathematically speaking, the higher the heritability of a phenotype, the greater the difference must be between the mean environments of two groups for environment to explain completely a fixed mean group phenotypic difference. . . . I know of no scalable environmental variable on which blacks and whites differ that widely, and the worlds of American blacks and whites—the language they speak, the movies and television shows they see, the school subjects they are exposed to, the technology available to them—appear quite similar. Black slums are admittedly less stimulating than white suburbs, but, as a neighborhood is the work of its inhabitants, the slum/suburb difference must count as an effect, not a cause, of race differences.

There are three sources of direct evidence of genetic influences on the race difference in intelligence. The first is the performance of African blacks on the most culture-free IQ tests, which averages about 70 to 75.[14] The second is transracial adoption. Were blacks genetically identical to whites with respect to intelligence, black adoptees raised from infancy in upper-middle class white families should develop the mean IQ of whites. The Minnesota Transracial Adoption Study[15] found the reverse in a sample of about 100 such adoptees. By late adolescence, their mean IQ was 89. By contrast the mean IQ of whites adopted by the same families was 105, and that of the natural children of these families was 109. In a reanalysis of this study, I estimate that genetic variation explains 60% to 70% of the between-race variance in intelligence.[16] . . .

BURDENS OF PROOF

It cannot be proven beyond a shadow of a doubt that intelligence is a valid construct, or that IQ measures it. A genetic explanation of race differences is inherently more conjectural still than the race differences themselves. . . . Yet these uncertainties weaken my argument less than might be supposed.

Claims of damage must be *sustained*. Jones cannot simply storm into court, accuse Smith of breaking his leg, and expect to collect. He must *show* that Smith broke his leg. As this is a civil action, the standard he must meet is the relatively undemanding one of the preponderance of the evidence; he need only show it is more likely than not that Smith broke his leg. But show it he must—which means that, to defend himself successfully, Smith need not *prove* that he did not break Jones' leg. Smith need only show it is more likely that he did not break Jones' leg than that he did. Just so, white failure to prove the accusations against them false does not by itself leave them liable to compensatory damages. Since those who demand compensation are obliged to show that their accusations are plausible, whites are vindicated by a showing that black failure is *less likely* to be due to racism than to phenotypic race differences due in turn to genetic factors. The hereditarian analysis need not be certain, just more probable than "racism"—as I believe any disinterested examination of the evidence will find it to be.

Lest it seem legalistic in its own right to force the accuser of whites to carry the burden of proof, the reader should reflect that over the last quarter-century a great many whites have watched jobs and resources go to less qualified blacks because of the "racism" theory. It is only fair to ask that this theory be shown to be more likely than its rivals before more sacrifices from whites are demanded in its name.

DISTRIBUTIVE JUSTICE

It might be argued that greater racial equality is a requirement, not of compensatory, but of distributive justice, understood as what is obligatory in the initial distribution of goods. Many contemporary social philosophers seem to treat equality as the inertial distributive state, deviation from which needs justifying. Black and white shares are plainly unequal, hence prima facie wrong.

. . . Rather than repeat that the effects of these [past] inequalities have lingered, it is more pertinent to distribution to remark that past inequalities almost certainly did not leave blacks with smaller shares than they would have had in Africa. Slavery was common in Africa—white slavers bought blacks from tribal chiefs who had captured them—and no indigenous black society developed democracy, which blacks at least witnessed in the antebellum South. It is unlikely that blacks left on their own would shape conditions more conducive to mental growth than the ones they have been exposed to, for no indigenous black society ever developed an educational system remotely comparable in quality to the segregated schools of the Jim Crow era or the de facto segregated public schools of today. . . .

It may be replied that the benchmark of equality is not what would have been available for blacks in Africa, but what is available where they are, the US. This might be true when "what is available" refers to natural resources, but schools, housing and wealth—the goods blacks are commonly said to have too little of—are produced by human effort. The work of human hands should presumably go to the hands that did the work. By that standard, black holdings in the US seem less like inequity than white generosity.

Rawls cites the arbitrariness of the "natural lottery" to divorce an individual's contribution to wealth from his distributive share in it. The exceptional individual is said to have no right to the fruits of his talents because those talents, having been caused by fortuitous circumstances, are undeserved. His talents belong to everyone,[17] and he should keep only as much of what he produces as is needed as an incentive to keep him active. Rawls' argument has not to my knowledge been applied explicitly to race, probably out of reluctance to admit race differences in talent, but the obviousness of the application may help explain the popularity of *A Theory of Justice.*

At one level Rawls' inference from determinism to socialism collapses without a shove from empirical data, for it patently confuses *entitlement* with *entitlement to entitlement.* I may not deserve to spot a gold nugget in a stream, but this hardly implies that I do not deserve the nugget once I do spot it. Perhaps I deserve to be a finder of nuggets only by cultivating habits of alertness, but all I have to do to deserve the *nugget* is find it. I don't have to be entitled to find it.

At a deeper but still logical level, Rawls confuses the contradictory of "The natural lottery is required by justice" with one of its contraries. From the clear truth that "The natural distribution [of ability] is neither just nor unjust" (op. cit.) Rawls infers the wrongness of capitalizing on natural abilities. But the fact that a situation is "not just," in the sense of not *required* by justice, does not leave it *forbidden* by justice. Precisely as Rawls says, the natural lottery is neither just *nor unjust.* So, while whites may not *deserve* to have been made cleverer than blacks by the processes of evolution, it hardly follows that there is any *unfairness* in evolution having done this. If there is no positive reason to accept the consequences of evolution, there is also—unless equality is already assumed desirable—no positive reason to resist them. . . .

Second, Rawls' system is far from egalitarian: his difference principle, that the lot of the better off can be improved only when doing so helps the worst off, accords the worst off a veto power denied to other groups. Assuming blacks among the worst off in American society, the difference principle would seem to give priority to helping them. The ghetto has first claim on the next dollar spent on education. . . . Yet given the relevant facts, the difference principle may imply quite another conclusion. Technical innovations, which originate from the high tail of the bell curve, have historically benefited the worst off more than anyone else. The computer, the latest product of Caucasoid ingenuity, most dramatically boosts the productivity and with it the marketability of workers whose talents confine them to routine clerical tasks. Vacuum cleaners most benefited those women unable to afford domestic help.[18] If giving that next dollar to the—almost entirely white and Asian—gifted would benefit blacks more than giving it to blacks, the difference principle says give it to the gifted.

The findings of the best-known enrichment programs for black children[19] do not settle the issue. The Milwaukee Project produced short-term gains in the IQ of black children at a cost of $23,000 per point. The net benefit of the Perry Preschool Program, as measured by such factors as increased chances of employment, was $250 per IQ point in the first year (and negative thereafter). . . . Yet what the Rawlsian needs to know is whether these programs did more for blacks than would have been done for blacks by investing the same resources in the—mostly non-black—gifted. Utilitarians need similar data, since for them the disposition of that next dollar hinges on a straight bang-for-the-buck comparison of the educability of black and non-black children. The studies needed to apply maximin and utilitarian criteria have not been done, and it is far from clear what their outcome would be.

THE FINAL REMARK

Having returned to reasons for studying race differences, I would repeat the main one.

The right to cite truths in one's own defense is very nearly absolute. This right emphatically includes the marshaling of truths that embarrass one's accuser. A man asked to pay for a wrong he did not commit may repel the accusation even if to do so raises questions his accuser would rather not answer. Jones may wish to avoid thinking about his misshapen leg. He may be ashamed that this deformity runs in his family. He may not want anyone to call attention to it. *But if he accuses Smith of having broken it, Smith is entitled to talk about Jones' leg all day long.* If Jones isn't prepared to have his leg talked about, he shouldn't open the topic by hurling accusations. If racial egalitarians hurl immoderate charges at whites, they open the topic of race differences by forcing whites to defend themselves.

NOTES

1. See A. Shuey, *The Testing of Negro Intelligence* (New York: Social Science Press, 1966); J. S. Coleman, et al., *Equality of Educational Opportunity*. Washington, D.C.: U.S. Department of Health, Education, and Welfare, 1966. A. Jensen, and R. Figueroa, "Forward and Backward Digit-Span Interaction with Race and IQ: Predictions from Jensen's Theory." *Journal of Educational Psychology,* vol. 67 (1975), pp. 882–93. Entry for "Negro Intelligence," in R. J. Sternberg, ed., *Encyclopedia of Intelligence* (New York: Macmillan, 1993).
2. E.g., E. Banfield, *The Unheavenly City Revisited* (Boston: Little Brown, 1974).
3. A. Tashakkori, "Race, Gender and pre-Adolescent Self-Structure: A Test of Construct-Specificity Hypothesis [sic]." *Personality and Individual Differences,* vol. 14 (1993).
4. W. Dahlstrom, et al., *MMPI Patterns of American Minorities* (Minneapolis: University of Minnesota Press, 1986).
5. E. Culotta, "What Went Wrong: Why Programs Failed," *Science,* vol. 258 (1992), pp. 1185–190.
6. A. Jensen, *Bias in Mental Testing* (New York: The Free Press, 1980), p. 343.
7. A. DePalma, "Drop in Black Ph.D.'s Brings Debate on Aid to Foreigners," *New York Times,* April 21, 1992, p. A18.
8. *Bias in Mental Testing,* p. 112.
9. See G. Jaynes, and R. Williams, eds., *A Common Destiny: Blacks in American Society* (Washington, D.C.: National Academy Press, 1989), pp. 288, 301.
10. I. I. Gottesman, "Biogenetics of Race and Class," in M. Deutch, I. Katz, and A. R. Jensen (eds.), *Social Class, Race, and Psychological Development* (New York: Holt, Rinehart, and Winston, 1968).
11. William J. Wilson, *The Truly Disadvantaged: The Inner City, the Underclass and Public Policy* (Chicago: University of Chicago Press, 1987).
12. R. Hernstein, and J. Wilson, *Crime and Human Nature* (New York: Simon and Schuster, 1985), pp. 304, 335.
13. Plomin favors .5, see R. Plomin, *Nature and Nurture* (Belmont, CA: Wadsworth, 1990), and "The Role of Inheritance in Behavior," *Science,*

vol. 248 (1990), pp. 183–88. T. J. Bouchard, Jr., et al., "Sources of Human Psychological Differences: The Minnesota Study of Twins Reared Apart," *Science,* vol. 250 (1990), favor .7. The heritabilities of traits of temperament are generally .4–.6.

14. See e.g., K. Owen, "The Suitability of Raven's Standard Progressive Matrices for Various Groups in South Africa," *Personality and Individual Differences,* vol. 13 (1992), pp. 149–59.
15. R. Weinberg, S. Scarr, and I. Waldman, "The Minnesota Transracial Adoption Study: A Follow-up of IQ Test Performance at Adolescence," *Intelligence,* vol. 16 (1992).
16. M. Levin, "Comment on the Minnesota Transracial Adoption Study," *Intelligence,* vol. 19 (1994).
17. J. Rawls, *A Theory of Justice* (Cambridge, MA: Harvard University Press, 1971), pp. 101–102.
18. See J. Fulda, *Are There Too Many Lawyers?* (Irvington, NY: The Foundation for Economic Education, 1993), pp. 1–3.
19. See H. Spitz, *The Raising of Intelligence* (Hillsdale, NJ: Erlbaum, 1986).

Discussion Questions

1. Is Levin a racist? Support your answer. Discuss how Garcia might answer this question.
2. Has Levin adequately demonstrated that there is empirical support for differences between the races? If so, do these differences justify differential treatment? Does Levin support a color-blind or a color-conscious approach?
3. Discuss how Shelby Steele would most likely respond to Levin's claim that the attainment gap between whites and blacks is primarily due to genetic differences between the races. Which person presents the stronger argument? Support your answer.
4. Levin disagrees with Boxill's support of affirmative action. Discuss how Boxill might respond to Levin's criticism of his position.
5. In his article "Response to Race Differences in Crime,"[39] Levin argues that because there is a one-in-four chance that a young black male is a felon, a jogger who sees a black male on the path in front of him is justified in turning around and running away. He also believes that police are justified in racial profiling even on campuses. Do you agree with Levin that this differential treatment of black men is morally justified? Discuss how Garcia and Boxill would each answer this question.
6. When Levin tried to find a publisher for his controversial manuscript *Why Race Matters: Race Differences and Their Implications,* dozen of publishers rejected it, including several academic publishers. Other authors, who have attempted to publish "politically incorrect" views on race differences, such as Arthur Jensen, a preeminent psychometrician, have met similar obstacles in finding publishers.[40] Do publishers have a moral obligation to publish books that they find objectionable? Or does freedom of the press give publishers the right to choose not to publish certain material? Does publishing controversial ideas on alleged differences between the races work to diminish or increase racism? What is the relationship, if any, between freedom of the press, and the perpetuation of the status quo and institutional racism? Support your answers. Discuss how John Stuart Mill might answer these questions.

UMA NARAYAN

Colonialism and Its Others: Considerations on Rights and Care Discourses

Uma Narayan is a professor of philosophy at Vassar College. Narayan shows how colonial care discourse and rights discourse were used to enable colonizers to justify themselves in relationship to "inferior" colonized subjects. She concludes that improvements in both justice and care discourse are needed to make this a world more conducive to human flourishing.

Critical Reading Questions

1. What were the primary elements in the colonial rights discourse and care discourse?
2. How was paternalism and its rhetoric of responsibility and care used by colonists to justify their practices? How did colonists sustain the paternalistic moral vision of colonialism?
3. Why did colonists feel the need to justify colonialism?
4. According to Narayan, what does colonialism teach us about rights discourse? What does it teach us about care discourse?
5. What is the "the white man's burden"? How was this notion used to morally justify colonialism?
6. How did liberal political theory use rights discourse to support colonialism?
7. What views of moral agency are embedded in colonial discourse? How is the "colonialized Other" defined in terms of relationship to the colonizer? How has the "Other" challenged this definition and the colonists' worldview?
8. In what ways have some anticolonal movements reinforced other relationships of power?
9. What is the "doctrine of disqualification" and how is it used to maintain unequal social relationships?
10. Why is Joan Tronto concerned about the widespread adoption of a theory of care? How does Narayan respond to her concerns?
11. What does Narayan mean when she states that we need improvements along the dimensions of both justice and care in order to provide "enabling conditions" for the provision of care? In what ways, according to her, can greater attention to justice foster more-adequate forms of care?

"Colonialism and Its Others: Considerations on Rights and Care Discourses," *Hypatia* 10, no. 2 (1995), 138–140. Some notes have been omitted.

I wish to think about certain aspects of the roles played by rights and care discourses in colonial times. I shall start with the following question: How did the vast majority of people in the colonizing countries motivate themselves to participate in the large-scale phenomena of slavery and colonialism, not only embracing the idea that distant lands and peoples should be subjugated, but managing to conceive of imperialism as an *obligation,* an obligation taken so seriously that by 1914 Europe "held a grand total of roughly 85 percent of the earth as colonies, protectorates, dependencies, dominions, and commonwealths"? (Said 1993, 8).

The answer to this question forces us to attend to the self-serving collaboration between elements of colonial rights discourse and care discourse. Pervasive racist stereotypes about the negative and inferior status of enslaved or colonized Others were used both to justify denial of the rights enjoyed by the colonizers, and to construct the colonized as childish and inferior subjects, in need of the paternalistic guidance and rule of their superiors. In general terms, the colonizing project was seen as being *in the interests of, for the good of,* and as *promoting the welfare of* the colonized—notions that draw our attention to the existence of a *colonialist* care discourse whose terms have some resonance with those of some contemporary strands of the ethic of care. Particular colonial practices were seen as concrete attempts to achieve these paternalistic ends. Coercive religious conversion was seen as promoting the *spiritual* welfare of the "heathen." Inducting the colonized into the economic infrastructures of colonialism was seen as conferring the *material* benefits of western science, technology and economic progress, the *cultural* benefits of western education, and the *moral* benefits of the work ethic. There were often marked gender dimensions to these projects—colonial attempts to get "native women" to conform to Victorian/Christian norms of respectable dress, sexuality, and family life were regarded as in the moral interests of the women.

I am not denying there were powerful economic motivations underlying colonialism and slavery. However, justifications for colonialism and slavery in terms of crude self-interest alone seem to have been rare. These enterprises were made morally palatable by the rhetoric of responsibility and care for enslaved and colonized Others. Though such justifications have often been seen as attempts to convince the dominated of the appropriateness of their domination, I would argue that the central purpose of such arguments often is to make domination morally palatable to those engaged in the infliction of domination. While much of the contemporary discourse on an ethics of care focuses on the import of one's relationships to *particular others,* thinking about care-discourse in the colonial context highlights, in contrast, the roles it has historically played in justifying relationships of power and domination between *groups of people,* such as colonizers and colonized. The paternalistic moral vision of colonialism was sustained by the discourses of religion, philosophy, science, and art—cultural practices that collaborated to make a sense of western superiority part of the collective world-view of people in the colonizing countries. . . .

What does attending to the colonial context teach us about discourses of rights and care? Among the more obvious lessons is that rights discourse was only seemingly universal, not extending to the colonized, among others. Another lesson is that care discourse can sometimes function ideologically, to justify or conceal relationships of power and domination. While it has been pointed out that much of the responsibility for informal as well as institutionalized caring falls on subordinate and relatively powerless members of society—often working class and minority women—I want to add that "paternalistic caring" of the sort found in colonial discourse can also be wielded as a form of control and domination by the powerful and privileged. The colonial notion of "the white man's burden" included both a sense of obligation to confer the benefits of western civilization on the colonized, and a sense of being burdened with the responsibility for doing so—an obligation and responsibility rooted in a sense of being agents who had a world-historic mission to bring the light of civilization and progress to others inhabiting "areas of darkness"! . . .

[T]he contractual focus on relationships between equals, and on agents as independent, separate and mutually disinterested was only *part* of the liberal story. Another part of the story was that these same subjects had paternalistic obligations and responsibilities to "inferior Others," whether women in their own families or distant colonial peoples. Rights-discourse was constructed during the historical time when western countries were becoming increasingly interdependent with, unseparate from, and anything but disinterested in their unfree and unequal colonies, and most liberal political theorists had no difficulty endorsing colonialism. We would be mistaken if we read liberal rights-theorists as concerned only with contractual relationships between equals, or if we focus only on notions of agency pertinent to that side of their thought, since we would be ignoring their support for colonialism, and the more "missionary" notions of agency embedded in that facet of their worldview. If we recognize that the agent of liberal rights theory was also the agent of the colonial project, its independence, separateness and disinterestedness appear to be more qualified properties than the picture of the same agent that emerge if we ignore the colonial dimensions of liberal theory. . . .

Many aspects of the self-perceptions of the colonizers seem to have depended heavily on their relationship to the colonized. The world-view of colonialism, as well as the moral and socio-political world-views of many colonized cultures, subscribed to a picture where several large groups of people were normatively defined in terms of their relationships as inferiors and subordinates vis-a-vis members of dominant groups. To be a slave, a colonized Other, an untouchable, a woman, has often been meant as having one's entire existence defined in terms of one's "proper place" with respect to those with power, which entailed obligations to acquiesce to relationships of domination.

This suggests that strands in contemporary care discourse that stress that we are all essentially interdependent and in relationship, while important, do not go far enough if they fail to worry about the *accounts* that are given of these interdependencies and relationships. The colonizers and the colonized, for example, while both acutely conscious of their relationship to each other, had very different accounts of what the relationship and its interdependencies amounted to, and whether they were morally justified. Many social movements and struggles on the part of subordinate groups, though often couched in terms of individual rights, were also attempts to renegotiate and change the prevailing relationships between social groups.

While I do not endorse reducing the value of any moral theory to its ideological uses, I would argue that we must attend to the ideological functions served by various moral theories. Pervasive structural relationships of power and powerlessness between groups, such as those between colonizers and the colonized, tend to foster ideological justifications for the maintenance of such relationships. While aspects of care discourse have the potential virtue of calling attention to vulnerabilities that mark relationships between differently situated persons, care discourse also runs the risk of being used to ideological ends where these "differences" are defined in self-serving ways by the dominant and powerful. Notions of differences in vulnerabilities and capabilities should be recognized as *contested terrain,* requiring critical attention to who defines these differences as well as their practical implications. . . .

Two broad strategies were used both by western women and by the colonized in these contestations: (a) there were frequent assertions that western women or the colonized possessed the capacities and capabilities that entitled them to the same rights as white male colonizers, and (b) there were frequent redescriptions of the "paternalistic protective project" as one based instead on force and exploitation, inflicting misery on the powerless, and brutalizing those with power. The powerful role played by rights discourse in these emancipatory movements should not lead us to ignore their concurrent critique of the paternalistic colonial care-discourses that operated as justifications for their domination.

The alternative moral visions of the agency of women or of the colonized that developed in such political contestations, though they challenge the moral picture of the world held by the powerful, are not themselves immune to creating or reinforcing other relationships of power. A great deal has been written on how, for instance, the contemporary feminist movement has tended to be focused on the interests of middle-class white women, and about how drawing attention to the problems of women of color remains an ongoing problem. Anticolonial nationalist movements often displayed similar problems—in that nationalist discourses often constructed issues in a manner that marginalized colonized women. Several strands of Indian nationalism, for instance, associated Indian women with the preservation of Indian traditions, culture, and spirituality—a function that simultaneously gave them an *imagined function* in the nationalist agenda, but excluded them from *real participation* in many areas of work, politics, and public culture (Chatterjee 1990, 243). Thus, though I believe large-scale political movements have been historically crucial in bringing about certain forms of moral change and progress, these movements too generate problematic moral narratives. I would conclude that moral theories need to be evaluated not only in terms of their theoretical adequacy in accounting for the range of phenomena in our moral lives but also with regard to the instrumental political uses to which they lend themselves at concrete historical junctures.

I shall end with a few reflections on the relationship between rights and care discourses. The perspectives of colonialism, as well as those of many colonized cultures, and of many contemporary societies, provide several examples of what John Ladd refers to as the "Doctrine of Moral Disqualification," whereby groups with social power define members of other groups in ways that disqualify them for full membership in the moral community (Ladd 1991, 40). These definitions have been repeatedly used to justify the denial of rights to members of "disqualified" groups. These definitions have also been used to justify the failure to be genuinely attentive and responsive to the needs, interests, and welfare of the members of these groups. Dominant social definitions of what an untouchable or a slave was, did not encourage the powerful to care for the less powerful; and the same definitions were in fact inimical to the well-being of the less powerful, who were not, by these definitions, entitled to the means and opportunities for flourishing.

Justice concerns have been central to many social and political movements because asserting and gaining rights have been instrumental in transforming certain groups of people, however imperfectly, into fellow citizens whose concerns mattered, into people whose human worth mattered. However, as many slave-narratives well illustrate, much of the moral and political work that was necessary to change the "moral disqualification" inflicted on powerless groups consisted not only of claims to rights, but of attempts to call attention to the *suffering* inflicted on the powerless by the status quo. These political depictions of suffering can be seen as attempts to elicit the attentiveness and moral responsiveness of those with power, by redescribing the life situations of the powerless in ways that challenged the rationalizations of the powerful. The discourses of slave narratives, for example, make it difficult for members of dominant groups to continue to believe in the myth of happy slaves, content with their lot.

Joan Tronto may well be right in arguing that "one of the practical effects of the widespread adoption of a theory of care may be to make our concerns for justice less central" (Tronto 1995). I would like to add the converse claim, that a more serious commitment to and enforcement of the claims of justice might, at least in some cases, be a precondition for the possibility of adequately caring for and about some people. Tronto herself acknowledges that "*until* we care about something, the care process cannot begin" (Tronto 1995). Social relationships of domination often operate so as to make many who have power unable to *genuinely* care about the marginalized and powerless.

Although I am very sympathetic to the idea of a politics and of public policies that are more sensitive to *needs*, I am not sure we can arrive at what Tronto calls "a full account of human needs" without serious attention to considerations of justice that would enable the powerless to seriously participate in the social and political discourse where such needs are contested and defined. Once again, adequate attention to justice may, in some instances, be a precondition for adequately caring policies. . . .

Carol Gilligan's work suggests that rights and care perspectives provide alternative accounts of moral problems and decisions, and that shifting to a care perspective foregrounds moral issues of preserving and maintaining relationships that are often not well illuminated by a rights perspective. . . .

I would like to suggest yet another possibility. Improvements along dimensions of justice and rights might, in some cases such as the issue of fatal neglect of female children, provide what I shall call "enabling conditions" for the provision of adequate care. In other cases, improvements along care dimensions, such as attentiveness to and concern for human needs and human suffering, might provide the "enabling conditions" for more adequate forms of justice. For instance, attention to the needs, predicaments and suffering of the impoverished and destitute in affluent western societies might result in social policies that institutionalize welfare rights, rights to adequate medical care, and so forth.

I suggest that this is one possible dimension of the relationships between care and justice considerations, and not an over-arching account of their relationship. I am suggesting that, in particular contexts, struggles for greater justice may foster more adequate or richer forms of care and that in others, the cultivation of a care perspective might foster enhanced forms of justice. In some situations at least, justice and care perspectives might be seen less as contenders for theoretical primacy or moral and political adequacy and more as collaborators and allies in our practical and political efforts to make our world more conducive to human flourishing.

REFERENCES

Chatterjee, Partha. 1990. The nationalist resolution of the women's question. In *Recasting women: Essays in Indian colonial history,* ed. Kumkum Sangari and Suresh Vaid. New Brunswick: Rutgers University Press.

Ladd, John. 1991. The idea of collective violence. In *Justice, law and violence,* ed. James A. Brady and Newton Garver. Philadelphia: Temple University Press.

Said, Edward. 1993. *Culture and imperialism.* New York: Alfred A. Knopf.

Tronto, Joan. 1995. Care as a basis for radical political judgements. *Hypatia* 10(2): pp. 141–149.

Discussion Questions

1. Discuss ways in which colonial care discourse has contributed to contemporary institutional racism, citing examples from the previous readings.
2. Narayan points out that both rights discourse and care discourse can be used to justify racism and conceal relationships of power and domination. Discuss examples of situations in which contemporary institutional racism is currently being justified on the grounds of "paternalistic caring."
3. The brutal government removal of Native Americans from their lands in the 1800s was justified as being in their best interest. Examine ways in which colonial care discourse and colonial rights discourse are still embedded in U.S. public policy.
4. Shelby Steele maintains that because many well-meaning whites are fearful of being labeled racists, they try to establish their innocence of this charge by becoming "angels of mercy" and embracing policies such as affirmative action that help blacks overcome their victimization. Discuss the extent, if any, to which this strategy re-creates a colonial care discourse similar to the old concept of the "white man's burden."
5. Examine the American occupation of Iraq in light of Narayan's analysis of colonial care discourse. Is the occupation based on the same thinking as colonialism? Is the occupation and goal of democratizing Iraq morally justified? Support your answers.

6. Compare and contrast Narayan's concept of colonial care discourse with Garcia's analysis of paternalistic racism.
7. Princeton political scientist John DiIulio suggests that certain current social policies, promoted as solutions to racial problems by both conservatives and liberals, are in fact manifestations of ongoing institutional racism. He questions whether the war on drugs and high rate of imprisonment of young black men is a rational response to urban crime and disorder. Antipoverty programs that treat the inner city as an island, he claims, also isolate inner-city blacks and downplay the strategic economic location of inner-city neighborhoods and their connection to the wider community. In addition, DiIulio questions whether making publicly funded abortions more widely available to poor black women is really "an act of enlightened social compassion" or "an unspeakably ugly act of kill-now-rather-than-help-later social control."[41] Do you agree or disagree with DiIulio? How might Narayan respond to DiIulio? Support your answers.

CASE STUDIES

1. *BARABARA GRUTTER V. THE UNIVERSITY OF MICHIGAN LAW SCHOOL*

In 1996 Barbara Grutter, a 43-year-old white resident of Michigan, applied for admission to the University of Michigan Law School. At that time the law school, in order to achieve its "compelling interest in achieving diversity among its student body,"[42] gave additional points to applicants who were members of groups that were historically discriminated against, including African Americans, Hispanics, and Native Americans. In the Supreme Court case the law school conceded that Grutter probably would have been admitted had she been a member of one of the racial minority groups to which the law school gave preference. As plaintiff in the case Grutter maintained that the law school's use of racial preferences in student admission violated the equal protection clause of the Fourteenth Amendement.

The Supreme Court ruled in favor of Grutter. However, while it rejected the use of points as a means of achieving diversity, it did allow race to be used as a criterion in considering individual applications.

Discussion Questions

1. What is "diversity"? Discuss whether or not diversity is a legitimate and desirable educational goal for colleges and universities.
2. In its ruling the Supreme Court stated that while diversity may be a worthwhile goal the use of racial group preferences, such as quotas or point systems, undermines the notion of equality "where race is irrelevant to personal opportunity and achievement." Do you agree? How should justice as reparation, in terms of making up for past discrimination suffered by certain groups, be weighed against the principle of equality in the job market and in accepting applicants for college? Discuss your answers in light of Ross's concept of prima facie duties and Rawls's two principles of justice.

3. In 1992 the application of Cheryl Hopwood, a white student from a poor family, to the University of Texas Law School was turned down despite the fact that she had better grades and LSAT scores than many of the minority students who were admitted.[43] Is it fair that minorities who came from middle-class families be given preferential treatment over whites from economically disadvantaged families? How might President Johnson and Boxill each respond to this question? Support your answers.
4. Compare and contrast the equal protection clause of the Fourteenth Amendment with Kant's categorical imperative. Discuss whether the affirmative action policy of the University of Michigan violated the categorical imperative.
5. Did Grutter have a moral duty to protest her rejection by the University of Michigan? If so, what is the source of this duty?
6. Former senator Bob Dole is opposed to affirmative action. "We ought to do away with preferences," he stated in a 1996 speech. "This is America. It ought to be based on merit." Discuss Dole's position. How might Garcia respond to Dole?
7. Many colleges already extend preferences to athletes. Compare and contrast this policy with affirmative action policies.

---

2. WEARING THE CONFEDERATE FLAG

The Confederate flag had been banned at the mostly white Robert E. Lee high school in Tyler, Texas, in 1971 following a race riot. Undeterred, a sophomore wore a T-shirt to school that featured a Confederate flag with the slogan *It's a white thing, you wouldn't understand.* Other students had been wearing T-shirts with the same slogan but without the flag. The T-shirts had been allowed because they were regarded as a takeoff on a T-shirt, which was popular among blacks as well as some whites, that showed two black youths dressed in fashionable baggy clothes with the slogan *It's a black thing, you wouldn't understand.*

When the rebellious sophomore was told by principal Eddie Milham to change his shirt, he refused, arguing that it was his right to self-expression. A television news crew that happened to be at the school was quick to jump on the story, which appeared on the evening news. Although classes were disrupted for the next few days, students were not sorry that this incident had occurred. They said there was already a lot of racial stuff under the surface and this just helped bring it to light.

Discussion Questions

1. Is wearing the Confederate flag a racist action? Discuss whether the wearing of racist symbols should be protected as freedom of speech or prohibited as promoting racism. Support your answer.
2. Many of the students claimed that they got their racist attitudes from their parents and other adults in their lives and that education has done little to resolve it. Indeed, the principal has a picture of Robert E. Lee in his office in full Confederate regalia. Is this inconsistent with the intent of the ban of the Confederate flag in the school? Should everyone in the school community, and perhaps even in the town, be held to the same standards as the students? Support your answers.

3. Should symbols and names associated with slavery be removed from public schools? Several schools in the South that are named after slaveholders, such as Thomas Jefferson and George Washington, are changing their names. Do you agree with this policy? Compare and contrast this policy to one forbidding swastikas and Nazi symbolism in schools.
4. At the University of Mississippi, several students and alumni insist on their right to wave the Confederate flag at the Ole Miss football games. College officials have asked them to stop. Do they have the right? Support your answer.
5. The flag of Mississippi, with its Confederate emblem, has recently come under fire from civil rights groups who want the state to remove the emblem which, the groups argue, symbolizes oppression of blacks. Defenders of the flag maintain that the Confederate symbol is part of the state's heritage and, as such, should remain on the flag. Discuss which moral principles and concerns are most relevant in deciding whether or not the state has a moral obligation to remove the Confederate emblem.

---

3. COLIN FERGUSON AND THE "BLACK-RAGE" DEFENSE

Maryanne Philips was one of hundreds of commuters who took the Long Island Railroad to and from work in New York City. On December 7, 1993, she watched in horror as Colin Ferguson came down the aisle of her train car, pulled out a semiautomatic handgun, and shot twenty-five people, killing six. At the time of his arrest, Ferguson, a Jamaican immigrant, had notes in his pockets that expressed hatred of whites, Asians, and "Uncle Tom Negroes." Ferguson, who had a long history of angry encounters with whites, had earlier been involved in an incident in which he shouted at his perceived enemies: "Black rage will get you!"

Ferguson's lawyers decided to use black rage in their client's defense. The term *black rage* stems from a 1968 study by two psychiatrists who argued that racism has made blacks mistrustful and suspicious of outsiders. Rage is a response to racism. According to Ronald Kuby, one of Ferguson's lawyers, "Being exposed to racist treatment over a long period of time drove Ferguson to violence."[44] "If you treat people as second-class citizens, they're going to snap," added Kuby's law partner William Kunstler.[45] Ferguson is not responsible for his actions. Like the people he killed, Ferguson is also a victim—a victim of white racism.

A survey of eight hundred people before Ferguson's trial found that 68 percent of blacks and 45 percent of whites believed that a compelling defense could be made on rage stemming from long-term racism. The jury, however, didn't buy the black-rage defense. Ferguson received two hundred years in prison for the murders.

Discussion Questions

1. Should the black-rage defense be taken into consideration in sentencing Ferguson? If so, is long-term imprisonment the appropriate response, or should Ferguson have received counseling?
2. Is Ferguson a victim? Discuss how Shelby Steele might respond to Ferguson's black-rage defense. Relate your answer to Steele's notion of innocence.

3. Journalist Jonathan Alter once asked, "Where does acknowledgment of pain stop and excuse-making begin?" Discuss this question in light of the Ferguson case. Is the lack of rage a sign of servility? Compare and contrast the black-rage defense with the battered-woman defense.
4. Attorney Alan Dershowitz argues that the black-rage excuse is an "insult to millions of law-abiding black Americans." The vast majority of African Americans, he points out, do not use "the mistreatment they have suffered as an excuse to mistreat others."[46] Do you agree with Dershowitz? How should people respond to mistreatment?
5. Dershowitz also suggests that the argument that blacks as a group have more rage than other people, and hence are more prone to violence, instead of helping blacks overcome racism merely reaffirms racism and the fear of many white Americans that crime is a "black problem." Do you agree with Dershowitz? Discuss how Michael Levin and Bernard Boxill might each respond to Dershowitz's concerns.
6. Compare and contrast how libertarian Ayn Rand and a Marxist might each respond to Ferguson's case and his black-rage defense. Which analysis of the case—the libertarian or the Marxist—do you find more compelling from a moral point of view?

---

4. AMADOU DIALLO: A DEADLY CASE OF RACIAL PROFILING

Amadou Diallo, a twenty-two-year-old unarmed West African immigrant with no criminal record, was standing in the doorway of his Bronx apartment building when police approached him. What began as a routine patrol ended in tragedy when the police shot and killed Diallo, hitting him with nineteen of the forty-one shots they fired at him, after mistaking the wallet he pulled from his pocket for a gun. The police were members of an aggressive Street Crimes Unit that conducted stop-and-frisk searches of persons whom they suspected of carrying guns.

When the case went to trial the jury ruled that the police were guilty of making a tragic mistake, but not murder. The National Association for the Advancement of Colored People disagreed, calling the incident "excessive force at its worst."

Discussion Questions

1. Should the police in this case be held morally responsible for their actions and, if so, to what extent? Support your answer. Is the fact that the police were acting on the belief that Diallo was pulling a gun from his pocket morally relevant? Discuss how both Kant and Aristotle might respond to these questions.
2. Discuss what a utilitarian would most likely think of racial profiling.
3. A study in 2000 found that the Street Crimes Unit disproportionately targeted blacks and Hispanics, even when the higher crime rates in minority neighborhoods were taken into account. Less than a third of their searches were conducted in response to victim identification. Discuss how Levin and Boxill might each respond to this practice of racial profiling.
4. Using Rawls's principles of justice, develop a policy for reducing crime in high-crime neighborhoods. What criteria should police in Street Crimes Units use in determining whether to stop-and-frisk a particular person? Or should they only respond to actual crimes in the act of commission? Support your answers.

---

5. KKK GRAND WIZARD DAVID DUKE: POLITICS AND RACISM

In a democratic society, where the majority rules, minorities have the deck stacked against them. In 1984 and 1988, Jesse Jackson became the first black person to run for president, although neither the Republican nor the Democratic Party supported his candidacy. Jackson lost the election by a huge margin. Racists, on the other hand, seem to have better luck.

In 1988 David Duke was elected to the Louisiana House of Representatives. Unlike Jackson, who calls for racial unity, Duke is openly racist. Duke, a former grand wizard of the KKK, believes that blacks have "inherited tendencies . . . to act in anti-social ways." A defender of Nazi ideology as well, Duke expressed great admiration for Nazi war criminals Rudolf Hess and Dr. Josef Mengele. After his election, Duke continued to maintain ties with white supremacist organizations. In 1990 Duke ran for the U.S. Senate with a campaign based on "affirmative action for whites" and "upholding Western European, Christian values." Unlike Jackson, who lost by a huge margin, Duke lost by only a few percentage points. David Duke is now focusing his efforts on spreading his message over the Internet. His name appears on hundreds of websites. He also has a radio program that is broadcast around the world twenty-four hours a day.[47]

Duke is not the only racist with political power. During a trip to the Soviet Union in 1988, President Reagan was asked about the American Indians. He responded that the United States may have "made a mistake" in allowing Indians to retain their own cultures. "Maybe we should not have humored them in that, wanting to stay in that kind of primitive lifestyle," Reagan told a Soviet audience. "Maybe we should have said: 'No, come join us. Be citizens with the rest of us.'" He also claimed that American Indians had become rich because of oil on some of the reservations.

Discussion Questions

1. Does democracy reinforce racism and cultural relativism? How can the "tyranny of the majority" be counteracted in the United States? Would a meritocracy, as promoted by Aristotle and Plato, less likely be racist?
2. *Apartheid* is an Afrikaan word meaning "apartness." Does the United States have apartheid? Does democracy institutionalize apartheid? Is apartheid desirable? Support your answers. Discuss Levin's response to these questions.
3. Political analyst George Will writes that, as a true believer, Duke's "reputation is supposedly redeemed, at least a little bit, by 'sincerity,' considered inherently virtuous in an age so committed to subjectivism that it firmly believes only in believing."[48] Does the fact that Duke sincerely believed in racism morally justify his racist actions? If not, why not? Support your answers. Discuss how an ethical subjectivist would respond to these questions.
4. Were Reagan's remarks about American Indians racist? Is it morally acceptable, or even morally required, for a president to be racist if the majority of the electorate supports racism? Discuss how a cultural relativist and a deontologist would answer these questions.
5. During his trip to Africa in the spring of 1998, President Clinton made an unofficial apology for American slavery and for complicity in apartheid, as well as for U.S. inaction in the face of the genocide in Rwanda. Should President Clinton have apologized? Is an apology sufficient reparation? Support your answers.

6. Many people regard the United States as a "melting pot." Multiculturalists, on the other hand, think of the United States as a stew where different groups of people have their own customs, experiences, and even languages. What does *melting pot* imply? Is the concept racist? Is multiculturalism consistent with democratic ideals? Should minorities in the United States be encouraged to assimilate by adopting the values of the majority? Support your answers.

---

6. "NOT IN MY BACKYARD": FIGHTING A TOXIC-WASTE INCINERATOR[49]

The poor and minorities, like everyone else, don't want a toxic-waste dump in their back yards. So why does toxic waste more often than not end up in their neighborhoods? In 1991 Chemical Waste Management (Chem Waste), the country's largest hazardous-waste company, received approval to build California's first commercial toxic-waste incinerator at its Kettleman Hills dump site in the San Joaquin Valley.

Weeks after receiving approval, Chem Waste, the state, and the county were slapped with a lawsuit claiming discrimination and violation of the residents' civil rights. The suit alleged that the decision to place the toxic-waste incinerator in the almost entirely Hispanic community was part of a national pattern of situating hazardous-waste facilities near minority areas. Chem Waste admitted that most of its toxic-waste sites were in largely minority areas but nevertheless claimed that it didn't engage in discriminatory siting, because the sites it uses already had incinerators or landfills when it acquired them.

Minority activists, in response, maintained that minorities bear the burden of the nation's toxic waste disposal because minorities lack the clout to keep it out of their neighborhoods. Indeed, Chem Waste's other three incinerators are located in poor, black neighborhoods in Chicago; Sauget, Illinois; and Port Arthur, Texas. In December 1991 the people of Kettleman City won their civil rights lawsuit against Chem Waste.

Twelve years later the Community Health Council of Chaparral, New Mexico, one of thousands of *colonias*—Third-World trailer park settlements—along the U.S–Mexican border, filed a similar appeal against a landfill permit and lost. The Council plans to go to the state Supreme Court.

Discussion Questions

1. Discuss whether this case study is an illustration of institutional racism.
2. According to University of California professor Robert Bullard, minority and poor communities are the least likely to fight back against toxic-waste sites. Indeed, some poor communities welcome waste sites in their areas, because they create much needed jobs and tax revenue. Would the placement of toxic-waste sites in poor areas be justified under utilitarianism? Would it be justified under John Rawls's two principles of justice? Support your answers.
3. Discuss whether toxic-waste disposal should be regulated by government or left to private enterprise. Discuss how Ayn Rand might respond to this question. Develop a public policy for toxic-waste disposal.
4. Some philosophers suggest that racism, patriarchy, and the domination of nature are all interconnected. Furthermore, the judgment by those in power that certain racial

groups are "socially polluted" is used to justify environmental pollution of minority communities. Discuss this explanation of environmental racism.

5. Using a utilitarian calculus, decide whose "backyards" companies should use as toxic-waste dumps. Should the people who contribute the most to society also recieve the most protection from toxic waste? Discuss how Levin would answer this question.
6. Is there a connection between the use of Hispanic and Native American neighborhoods for toxic-waste dumps and landfill and a colonial mentality as described by Narayan? Support your answer.

CHAPTER 10

Feminism, Motherhood, and the Workplace

Eight women, all Princeton graduates, sat around a fireplace discussing books in an Atlanta, Georgia home. Some of the women also had earned law degrees from Harvard and Columbia. Most of them were no longer working full-time and had voluntarily left the fast track to stay at home with their children. "Women today, if we think about feminism at all," says one of the women, a former publisher, "see it as a battle fought for 'the choice.' For us, the freedom to choose work if we want to work is the feminist strain in our lives." "I've had women tell me," replied a former lawyer, "that it's women like me that are ruining the workplace because it makes employers suspicious. I don't want to take on the mantle of all womanhood and fight for some sister who isn't really my sister because I don't even know her." Have these women failed the feminist movement?

FEMINISM

Many women entering college today think that feminism is no longer relevant to their lives—that women are liberated, that the days of discrimination in the workplace, home, and classroom are over. This belief that equality has been achieved is perpetuated by the media and other major institutions. However, in reality, women still earn only a fraction of what men earn. Women in families where both spouses are working are still burdened with the great majority of housework and child care. And sexual harassment in the workplace and classroom is still all too common.

Although there are several schools of feminist thought, feminists are united in their commitment to improving women's position in society. They analyze the causes of women's oppression as well as seek solutions for ending it.

British philosopher Mary Wollstonecraft's 1792 book *A Vindication of the Rights of Woman,* was the forerunner of the first wave of feminism in the United States, which ran from the early-nineteenth to the early-twentieth centuries. She argued that biological differences are not a relevant ground for denying women equal rights. Women and men have the same rational nature, the same capacity for reason, and are governed by the same moral standards. John Stuart Mill took up the same arguments in his essay "Subjection of Women." The first wave of feminists, which in the United States included Elizabeth Cady

Stanton, Margaret Sanger, and Susan B. Anthony, focused on civil rights campaigns, access to contraception, and universal suffrage (the right to vote).

Liberal feminists, such as Wollstonecraft, Mill, and the other early feminists, began with the assumption that there is a common rational human nature that transcends gender differences. The purpose of the state is to provide a sphere of liberty where citizens can exercise their rights and freely determine their own lives. Social structures and institutions that limit the rational choices of women are morally wrong because they limit the autonomy and choices of women. The solution is to demand equal access to opportunities and privileges enjoyed by men.

The second wave of liberal feminism, popularly know as the women's liberation movement, began in the United States in the 1960s following the publication of Betty Friedan's controversial book *The Feminine Mystique.* Friedan wrote, "for women to have full identity and freedom, they must have economic independence. Equality and human dignity are not possible for women if they are not able to earn. Only economic independence can free a woman to marry for love, not for status or financial support, or to leave a loveless, intolerable, humiliating marriage . . ."[1] The movement, which was composed of primarily white, middle-class women, focused on equal employment opportunities and abortion rights. Judith Jarvis Thomson's 1971 article, "A Defense of Abortion" (see Chapter 2), emerged from the liberal feminist movement.

Feminists reject conservatism, which regards the roles and capacities of men and women as biologically determined and unchangeable and seeks to retain patriarchy and traditional gender roles. The sexual division in the workplace and home are natural expressions of these biological differences. Rather than providing a critical analysis of women's oppression, conservatism provides a justification for it. In his reading at the end of this chapter on "Male Aggression and the Attainment of Power, Authority, and Status," Steven Goldberg argues that male dominance is rooted in biological differences.

In the reading "Essentialist Challenges to Liberal Feminism," Ruth Groenhout examines gender-essentialist theories, including Sigmund Freud's theory about female inferiority being based on penis envy, and sociobiologist E. O. Wilson's theory that sex differences are central to human biology and evolved to create genetic diversity.[2] She also looks at the radical feminist theory, which states that differences between men and women are cultural, and concludes that liberal feminist theory offers a more powerful tool for securing the rights and freedom of women.

In 1968 the liberal feminist National Organization of Women (NOW), published its *Bill of Rights.* Many, if not most, of their demands still are not realized. Most critiques of liberal feminism center on the claim that there is a common human nature or essence. The radical feminist movement, which emerged in the late 1960s, rejects the liberal feminist claim that there is a common human nature or essence and claims instead that gender is a cultural construct used to sustain a patriarchy.[3] Liberty rights are a male notion, something generated by masculine reason for relationships among men. Men are socialized to be both protectors and sexual predators; women are socialized to be weak and to be sexual prey. According to radical feminists such as Catharine MacKinnon (see her reading on "Pornography, Civil Rights, and Speech" at the end of Chapter 8) one cannot be a woman without being objectified by men as objects for sexual violence. To use a well-known slogan of radical feminists, the most important difference between men and women is that "men fuck and women get fucked." Although women are taught to value connectedness, in reality, women want individuation and liberation from the shackles of

BILL OF RIGHTS: NATIONAL ORGANIZATION FOR WOMEN (NOW)

We Demand

I. That the United States Congress immediately pass the Equal Rights Amendment to the Constitution to prove that "Equality of rights under the law shall not be denied or abridged by the United States or by any state on account of sex" . . .

II. That equal employment opportunity be guaranteed to all women as well as men, by insisting the Equal Employment Opportunity Commission enforces the prohibitions against sex discrimination in employment . . .

III. That women be protected by law to ensure their rights to return to their jobs within a reasonable time after childbirth without loss of seniority or other accrued benefits, and be paid maternity leave as a form of social security and/or employee benefit.

IV. Immediate revision of tax laws to permit the deduction of home and child care expenses for working parents.

V. That child care facilities be established by law on the same basis as parks, libraries and public schools, adequate to the needs of children from the preschool years through adolescence, as a community resource to be used by all citizens from all income levels.

VI. That the right of women to be educated to their full potential equally with men be secured by federal and state legislation, eliminating all discrimination and segregation by sex, written and unwritten, at all levels of education . . .

VII. The right of women in poverty to secure job training, housing, and family allowances on equal terms with men, but without prejudice to a parent's right to remain at home to care for his or her children; revision of welfare legislation and poverty programs when they deny women dignity, privacy and self-respect.

VIII. The right of women to control their own reproductive lives by removing from penal code laws limiting access to contraceptive information and devices and laws governing abortion.

intimacy. Women who want motherhood and marriage are operating under "false consciousness."

Unlike liberal feminists, radical feminists do not place much stock in political or legal reform. If government and other social institutions, such as capitalism and religion, are patriarchal, then participation in a patriarchal system isn't going to help women. For example, protecting pornographers' freedom of speech to make and sell pornography harms women. Some radical feminists call for lesbianism, although not necessarily in sexual terms, but in terms of women working and living together without men and celebrating "gynergy"—the woman spirit/strength.

Other schools of feminism include Marxist and socialist feminism. Marxist feminists believe that the capitalist class system is the cause of oppression for women. French feminist Simone de Beauvoir is a Marxist feminist, although she is sometimes considered a radical feminist as well. Socialist feminism grew out of Marxist feminism in the 1970s. While Marxist feminists are concerned primarily with the public realm, socialist feminists look at both the public and private realms. They believe that sexism is rooted in the sexual division of labor between the private home (the woman's realm) and the outside public workplace (man's realm). They maintain that this split is a product of capitalism. Nancy Dowd's reading on "Work and Family," incorporates socialist feminist ideals and appears in the middle of this chapter.

Some feminists believe that there are essential, innate differences between men and women. However, unlike conservatives, they do not see this as justifying men's dominance of women. Instead women's distinctive nature is to be valued and liberated, primarily through consciousness-raising groups like the one in the scenario at the beginning of this chapter. In 1982 psychologist Carol Gilligan published her landmark book *In A Different Voice,* in which she argues that the liberal emphasis on autonomy and separateness from others is a male value and not the way women interact with the world. Unlike radical feminists, Gilligan maintains that women are fundamentally connected to life and value connection over individuation. Women's moral reasoning and interaction with the world is based on responsibility, intimacy, and care; not on autonomy, justice, and rights reasoning as used by men—and liberal feminists. The readings by Virginia Held and Rita Manning in the *Ethics PowerWeb* look at the connection between feminism and care ethics. Christina Hoff Sommers also represents this view in her reading "Philosophers Against the Family," found toward the beginning of this chapter. The liberal goal of androgyny, the sameness of men and women, is that of striving not toward true equality but toward androgyny—the male ideal in dress, behavior, and career ambitions and the rejection of traditional female roles—such as motherhood and social service.

In the 1980s feminism began moving away from its roots as a radical political movement. In the current postfeminist period, feminist dialogue and gender analysis occurs in the universities.

Support for the feminist movement declined during the past decade. In the mid-1990s, over 60 percent of American women identified themselves as feminists or part of the women's movement.[4] In a 2001 Gallup poll, only 25 percent of women and 20 percent of men considered themselves feminists.[5] Part of the decline may be caused by modern feminism's primary focus on middle-class working women; the marginalization of poor women and stay-at-home mothers; and disillusionment with the lack of progress made for women in the workplace, in politics, and at home. Also, the assertion by academic feminists that one must support abortion-on-demand to be a true feminist has alienated many women (see Sidney Callahan, "Abortion and the Sexual Agenda: A Case for Pro-life Feminism" in the *Ethics PowerWeb*).[6] The rigid classification of feminist theories has also led to a fragmentation of the movement.

THE PHILOSOPHERS ON WOMEN

Philosophers bear part of the responsibility for perpetuating sexism. Plato taught that man is the true humanity and that woman is a deviation. Woman exists as the result of evil and failure to control one's passions. Men's destinies are to use their rational human faculties. If a man fails to control his emotions, he lives unrighteously and will be reincarnated as a woman.

Aristotle continued the philosophical tradition of misogyny. According to him, heat is the fundamental principle of perfection in animals. Women are colder than men and, therefore, less perfect than men. Because nature always aims toward perfection, a female must be a deviation from nature. Aristotle concluded that a female embryo results when there is a deficiency in generative heat. A female, in other words, is a misbegotten male, a "monstrosity," a "mutilated male." Like Aristotle, Steven Goldberg in his article at the end of this chapter maintains that patriarchy has a basis in biology. Although not arguing that women are inferior, Goldberg does maintain that patriarchy is inevitable. Women are not biologically equipped to achieve equality with men in positions of power, authority, and status.

The early Christian philosophers embraced the Platonic doctrine that women are inherently inferior to men. According to Augustine (354–430 A.D.), God created woman to be "in sex subjected to the masculine sex." The second creation story in Genesis, in which Eve was created from the rib of Adam, is used to reinforce the subservient role of women.

The philosophical view that privileges reason and equates male thinking with rationality continues to dominate much of Western philosophy. According to the Enlightenment philosophers, it is through reason that humanity progresses, socially and morally. Like his contemporary, French philosopher Jean-Jacques Rousseau, Immanuel Kant believed that women are deficient in reason. Rousseau maintained that men and women have different duties, based on a natural sexual division of labor. Women can be forced to be free by compelling them to fulfill their duties as mothers and wives. Rousseau writes:

> Woman was made especially to please man. . . . This is the law of nature. If woman is formed to please and to live in subjection, she must render herself agreeable to man instead of provoking his wrath; her strength lies in her charms.

British philosopher and liberal feminist Mary Wollstonecraft (1759–1797), wrote *A Vindication of the Rights of Woman* primarily as a response to Rousseau. Wollstonecraft argued that woman's nature is essentially the same as man's. Moral truths, such as equality, are universal and the same for both men and women.

In the essay "The Subjection of Women," co-authored by Harriet Taylor, John Stuart Mill also denounced patriarchal power, arguing that women need to be freed from subjection to men. The injustices perpetuated on women by an "almost despotic power of husbands over wives" need to be corrected by giving women the same rights and the same protection under the law as men.[7]

Friedrich Engels, in his Marxist analysis of women's oppression, notes that the "husband is obliged to earn a living and support his family, and that in itself gives him a position of supremacy . . . Within the family he is the bourgeois, and the wife represents the proletariat . . . Equality will be achieved only when the special legal privileges of the capitalist class have been abolished . . . and both [men and women] possess legally complete equality of rights. Then it will be plain that the first condition for the liberation of the wife is to bring the whole female sex back into public industry, and that this in turn demands that the characteristic of the monogamous family as the economic unit of society be abolished."[8]

Freud was developing his theory of psychoanalysis at about the same time that the first wave of feminists were fighting for equal rights for women. Freud believed that such a project was doomed to failure. The problem of women's inferior status in society isn't political. Instead, Freud believed that girls feel wronged because they don't have a penis like boys and fall victim to penis envy and resentment. As the girl grows up "the wish for a penis is replaced by one for a baby, in particular a son, from her father." Freud also maintained that the reason women have so little sense of justice, and have a weaker social interest, is because of the prominent role envy plays in their lives. He wrote in 1933, "A man of thirty strikes us as a youthful, somewhat unformed individual, whom we expect to make powerful use of the possibilities for development. . . . A woman of the same age, however, often frightens us by her psychical rigidity and unchangeability . . . There are no paths open to further development."[9]

Modern feminists reject theories claiming that women are inherently inferior to men. In *The Second Sex,* French philosopher Simone de Beauvoir (1908–1986) accuses the philosophical tradition of propagating the view of women as the "other," as deviant human beings. She argues that gender inequalities are primarily the result of upbringing.

PORNOGRAPHY[10]

The debate over pornography in the past thirty years has moved from arguments over the morality of nonprocreative sex to arguments based on freedom of speech and concerns that pornography may contribute to gender discrimination, rape, and sexual harassment. This shift is due in part to the proliferation of pornography on the market since the late 1970s. More recently, the use of the Internet to distribute pornography has allowed those inclined to view sexual violence to do so without having to leave the comfort of their homes. For more on the issue of pornography see pages 432–434.

MOTHERHOOD

The experience of motherhood is central to many women's lives. Most modern feminists view motherhood as an oppressive patriarchal institution. Radical feminists believe that motherhood is a social construct, rather than something women naturally want, and focus on the pathological nature of mother/child relationships. In her 1949 book *The Second Sex,* Simone de Beauvoir wrote that woman's "misfortune is to have been biologically destined for the repetition of life." Women's connection to others, including pregnancy and motherhood, according to radical feminists, is a source of misery and oppression, not celebration and joy.[11] Like sexual intercourse, pregnancy blurs the line between self and other and, hence, is objectionable and debasing. Pregnancy, especially an unwanted pregnancy, is "dangerous, psychically consuming, existentially intrusive, and a physically invasive assault upon the body which in turn leads to a dangerous, consuming, intrusive, invasive assault on the mother's identity."[12] The solution to this "misfortune" is legalized abortion, which is the focus of many feminists. Motherhood, like marriage, should be based on a voluntary commitment. To force a relationship on a woman is oppressive. Indeed, radical feminists maintain that women who claim to enjoy motherhood are operating from a false consciousness and fail to recognize their own oppression in accepting the burdens of motherhood.

Christina Hoff Sommers disagrees, arguing that biological family relationships are not voluntary, nor should they be. This attitude, Sommers contends, is contributing to the disintegration of the family. Sommers also points out the importance of fatherhood, a topic that has only recently been addressed by feminists.

Adrienne Rich, in her book *Of Woman Born* (1976), was one of the first of the contemporary feminists to write at any length about motherhood as an institution and her experiences as a mother, and the patriarchal notion of motherhood as a "sacred calling." Carol Gilligan in *A Different Voice* (1982) and Sara Ruddick in *Maternal Thinking: Towards a Politics of Peace* (1989) further broke down the barrier between feminist theory and discussion of women as mothers and caring nurturers. Ruddick regards maternal thinking as "one kind of discipline among many [such as engineering or political science] each with identifying questions, methods and aims." In her reading "Mothers and Men's Wars," found at the end of Chapter 11, Ruddick suggests that "maternal practice is 'natural resource' for peace politics."[13]

Other feminists, while not rejecting motherhood outright, challenge the idea that motherhood is a biological imperative. They believe that motherhood is a cultural construct of the white middle class. They also reject the myth that all women want and need children, as well as the belief that there is some sort of mystical bond between children and their biological mothers that should only be broken in the most extreme circumstances. This belief is reflected in the social policy of always trying to reunite foster children with their biological mothers, as well as the unease about surrogate motherhood and adoption.

Socialist feminists claim that the capitalist relegation of home and motherhood to the private realm has hurt both mothers and children. Nancy Dowd, in the reading "Work and Family: The Gender Paradox" represents this perspective. Because the home is considered outside the public realm in a capitalist society, the contributions of pregnant women and mothers are not valued or compensated. According to the International Labor Organization, women do two-thirds of the world's work and earn five percent of the income.[14] The United Nations in 1995 estimated that "women's unpaid labor was worth $11 trillion worldwide, and $1.4 trillion in the United States alone."[15] As it stands now, unfair labor practices, where women shoulder the great majority of housework and child care, cannot be protested in public courts.

Liberal feminists are wary of making motherhood the foundation of womanhood because most of the disadvantage imposed on women in the workplace—and at home—is based on women's ability to become pregnant. Liberal feminists' primary concern with motherhood has been how it interferes with the workplace. One solution proposed by liberal feminists is for men and women to share equally in the care of the children. They also support the establishment of twenty-four-hour day-care centers for working mothers and parental leave that would free mothers, as well as fathers, to compete in the job market.

WOMEN IN THE WORKPLACE

The lack of fair opportunities in the workplace has been a major concern of feminists for almost two centuries. There has been little change in the discrepancy between men's and women's salaries in the past twenty-five years. In 1996 the median weekly pay of full-time working women was only 75 percent of the median pay for men.[16] Studies have found that gender is the "best single predictor of the compensation for that job, surpassing in importance education, experience, or unionization."[17] This discrepancy is compounded by gender segregation in the workplace. Despite the entry of more women into traditionally male occupations, most women have jobs, not careers. One-third of women in 1990 were employed in 10 of 503 occupations listed by the U.S. Census Bureau, including secretary, cashier, food preparation, nursing, and elementary school teacher.[18]

Liberal feminists believe that women's lower status in the workplace and the public sphere is the result of discrimination rather than autonomous choices made by women. They also maintain that physical differences between men and women are irrelevant in the workplace and support gender-blind policies, working through the legislative and court system to achieve equality.

Radical feminists claim that the oppression of women is sexual rather than economic. Female occupations are devalued in the workplace because women in general are devalued and sexually objectified. To overcome oppression some radical feminists advocate women living and working in all-female communities.

Like liberal feminists, Marxists believe that women achieve liberation and fulfillment through participation in the workplace. However, unlike liberals they equate oppression of women in the workplace with class oppression. Consequently, Marxist feminists challenge the capitalist market-based system of wages and instead support a comparative worth policy which involves "job reclassification to raise wages in female-dominated occupations to the level paid to men in occupations of comparable worth."[19]

Socialist feminists likewise acknowledge that women's productive work differs from men's and is generally lower paying. However, they argue that the primary cause of women's oppression is not class but capitalist assumptions about the value of women's work and men's work and the relegation of work to the public sphere, and of home and family to the private sphere. By keeping women's wages low in the workplace, men keep women dependent so that women will continue doing the majority of work in the home. Like the home, the workplace is a gendered institution. It is geared toward the needs of a man who has no or minimal home and family obligations. The traditional, inflexible work schedule is hostile to working mothers who are often forced to compromise their careers. In addition, working mothers are now burdened with two full-time jobs—a career and caring for the children and home.

Nancy Dowd maintains that legislation prohibiting discrimination in the workplace does not go far enough. According to the United Nations, the gap between men and women in both the developed and the undeveloped world, increased between 1990 and 2000, a phenomenon known as the "feminization of poverty." [20] Worldwide, women earn a little more than 50 percent of what men earn. Globalization of the market economy, which is linked to a reduction in spending on social programs, has contributed to the feminization of poverty. Since families must pick up the costs, single mothers are especially impacted by globalization.[21] In order to combat the feminization of poverty both in the United States and worldwide, alternative strategies are needed to restructure work–family relationships.

Although conflicts between commitment to work and family affect mainly women, men who are or would like to be more involved in their families also experience this work–home conflict. Socialist feminists also dispute the claim of liberal and Marxist feminists that women achieve a sense of fulfillment through the workplace rather than the home and family. In a 2002 Gallup poll, 45 percent of women and 24 percent of men stated that they'd "prefer to stay at home and take care of the house and family" than "have a job outside the home."[22] Part of this could be because of the discrimination women face in the workplace and the rigid work schedule.

THE FAMILY AND MEDICAL LEAVE ACT OF 1993

Section 102 (a1) ENTITLEMENT TO LEAVE.—Subject to section 103, an eligible employee shall be entitled to a total of 12 workweeks of [unpaid] leave during any 12-month period for one or more of the following:

(A) Because of the birth of a son or daughter of the employee and in order to care for such son or daughter.

(B) Because of the placement of a son or daughter with the employee for adoption or foster care.

(C) In order to care for the spouse, or a son, daughter, or parent, of the employee, if such spouse, son, daughter, or parent has a serious health condition.

(D) Because of a serious health condition that makes the employee unable to perform the functions of the position of such employee.

Critics of liberal feminism charge that while professing to be gender-neutral, liberal feminists define success by the male standard of power, professional achievement, and money. Liberal feminists encourage women to achieve equality by moving into higher-paying, traditionally male professions. And women are attending college and professional schools in record numbers. However, the glass ceiling seems to be impermeable to all but a few women. Studies show that even in the same profession, such as law, there are "steep inequalities of pay, promotion, and opportunities."[23] In universities, female faculty earn only 85 to 90 percent of the income of male faculty at the same rank.[24] This inequity is actually greater since male faculty are more likely to be promoted than female faculty.

While many women are frustrated because of workplace discrimination that prevents them from advancing, other professional women, such as the women mentioned in the opening scenario, no longer find the top so attractive. Professional women are suffering from burnout, stress disorders, and fertility problems. A recent survey found that 26 percent of women at the most senior levels of management who have a chance to advance don't want promotions. Of the 108 women who appear on *Fortune* magazine's list of the most powerful women over the past several years, at least 20 have left their high-powered jobs voluntarily for a more fulfilling life.[25] It is unclear whether this frustration is due to discrimination and sexism at work or a genuine preference for home and family.

Probably nowhere has the conflict between the liberal "equal treatment" model and the "special treatment" model been so controversial as in work policies related to pregnancy. Liberal feminists argue that treating pregnancy as special demeans women.[26] Instead they regard pregnancy as a temporary disability, like any other temporary disability, that takes women away from work for a period of time.

Until the early 1970s employers could fire or refuse to hire a woman because of pregnancy. In 1978 Congress passed the Pregnancy Discrimination Act that prohibited discrimination and denial of benefits to women because of pregnancy. If she is able to work, a pregnant woman must be treated like any other employee.

The Family and Medical Leave Act was passed in 1993. Under the Act, a woman's job may be protected for a total of twelve weeks, including time taken off before and after birth. In line with the liberal feminist gender-neutral approach, employers are under no obligation to make it easier for a pregnant woman to do her job. The law does not distinguish between mothers and fathers.

It has been forty years since Betty Friedan wrote in her *Feminine Mystique* that equality and human dignity are not possible for women if they are not able to earn. Today women make up the majority of the workforce. Are women better off and more fulfilled than they were forty years ago? Or have women been duped by feminism, as some conservatives claim? Is the fast-track superwoman, so glorified by feminists, actually "dehumanized by her career," and "uncertain of her gender identity"?[27] Or is the problem the gendered structure of the workplace that prevents many, if not most, women from finding equality and dignity in their work?

SEXUAL HARASSMENT

Sexual harassment continues to be a problem in both the workplace and schools. The allegations of Anita Hill against Supreme Court Justice Clarence Thomas in 1991 and the Tailhook scandal in the military brought the problem of sexual harassment into the headlines.

According to the National Organization for Women (NOW), 50 to 75 percent of employed women experience sexual harassment on the job,[28] in the great majority of cases by a man in a more powerful position.[29] Seventeen percent of female college students report being sexually harassed by an instructor.[30] The law has been slow to recognize sexual harassment as a form of discrimination against women. Although an amendment was added in 1972 to the Civil Rights Act specifically prohibiting sexual harassment, women are still reluctant to complain or sue because the costs of doing so are high, and in many cases courts have ruled against them.

The Protection from Harassment Act of 1997 gives employees legal power to claim damages and to obtain an injunction against further sexual harassment outside the workplace. In 1999, the United States Supreme Court, in *Davis v. Monroe County Board of Education,* further recognized the potential economic impact of sexual harassment as well as the responsibility of employers, in this case school authorities, to take steps to stop harassment by ruling that public schools can be required to pay damages for failing to stop student-on-student sexual harassment.

In June 2001, seven California women who were former Wal-Mart employees filed a suit alleging that female workers received lower wages, were denied promotions, and were constantly subjected to sexual harassment. As of May 2004 the case of *Dukes v. Wal-Mart Stores, Inc.* was still in litigation.

Many people believe that charges of sexual harassment are simply instances of miscommunication between men and women, or cultural differences, rather than a misuse of power.[31] They also believe that sexual harassment is a "woman's problem," or that women use charges to get back at men, or that it is an attempt to desexualize the workplace, or that women are just being too sexually repressed.

While not denying that sexual harassment can be a means of oppressing women, Katie Roiphe, in the reading "Reckless Eyeballing: Sexual Harassment on Campus," questions the current definitions of sexual harassment. She argues that these definitions, like the "rape crisis" definitions of date rape, are so broad that they create distrust and suspicion among men and women by implying that men are sexual predators and that women are their helpless victims. While some types of sexual harassment should be curtailed, Roiphe argues that in many cases women just have to stand up to their harassers instead of playing the role of victim.

MORAL ISSUES

Autonomy and Liberty Rights

Discrimination and oppression of women by patriarchal institutions violate Kant's categorical imperative because they define women in relation to men. Women's autonomy and liberty right to pursue their legitimate interests is compromised by discrimination and limited choices in the workplace. The traditional family structure also restricts women's autonomy. Liberal and radical feminists, in particular, emphasize autonomy and choice when it comes to motherhood. Sommers disagrees, arguing that motherhood is a special obligation rather than a voluntary undertaking.

Human Nature

Feminist theory is grounded in certain assumptions about human nature and, in particular, the nature of women and men. Assumptions about the nature of women and men have a profound effect on what solutions different feminist, and nonfeminist, theories propose for overcoming the oppression of women. Conservatives such as Aristotle, Augustine, and Freud believe that women are, by nature, inferior and subservient. Patriarchy is natural and society, including the family and workplace, is structured to reflect this reality. Feminist demands for equality are not only unreasonable but harmful to women. These views are still embedded in gender stereotypes that degrade women and justify division of labor based on gender.

Liberal feminists such as Wollstonecraft and Mill disagree with the conservatives, arguing that men and women share the same rational nature. Marxist feminists believe that the division of labor based on gender is a result of the capitalist class system rather than innate differences. Gender essentialists, in contrast, believe that men and women have different natures. However, unlike conservatives, feminist gender essentialists do not believe the differences between men and women justify the oppression of women. Radical feminists such as MacKinnon claim that women and men are different, with men being objectifiers and women being sexually objectified. Other feminists believe that women and men have different natures, with women being more caring and nurturing and men being more oriented toward abstract principles, such as justice and equality.

Some critics maintain that radical feminists have gone too far by promoting a false view of men as sexual oppressors of women. Others criticize liberal feminists for adopting what they regard as a male model of human nature.

Justice, Discrimination, and Gender Equality

At home women still perform the majority of housework and child care. At work women suffer from job discrimination and earn significantly less than what men earn. Conservatives claim that this discrepancy is just based on a natural division of labor. This view has been challenged by the dissatisfaction of women with their treatment in the workplace and the home, as well as men's reluctance to give up their advantage.

Liberal feminists maintain that because men and women share the same nature, justice demands that they be treated the same. Liberals promote gender-neutral policies such as the Family and Medical Leave Act to achieve gender equality in the workplace. Other feminists maintain that women and men have different natures and preferences. However, this does not justify unequal wages or unjust distributions of labor in the home. Some Marxist and socialist feminists recommend a policy of comparable worth to raise the wages in female-dominated occupations to the level paid to men in occupations of comparable worth. Socialist feminists also believe that much of the injustice in the home as well as the workplace is due to the relegation of the home to the private sphere and work to the public sphere. To correct these inequities, they recommend restructuring the work environment so it has flexible work schedules to accommodate the needs of working mothers and fathers.

Utilitarian Considerations: Harms and Benefits

Utilitarian theory entails maximizing pleasure and minimizing pain for the greatest number. While conservatives argue that traditional gender roles benefit both men and women, women clearly are getting the short end of the stick. Discrimination in the workplace not only harms women, but harms society by depriving society of the talents and valuable contributions of women. Women who are mothers are especially vulnerable. Women and children from economically disadvantaged families in particular suffer from the "feminization of poverty" as a result of lower wages paid to women and lack of adequate child-care facilities. The creation of more flexible work schedules, reasonable family leave policies, and twenty-four-hour day-care centers have all been proposed by feminists as means of improving the situation of working mothers. Some radical feminists, such as Simone de Beauvoir, on the other hand, believe that motherhood itself is a harm and should be rejected by women. Sexual harassment also harms women by creating a work or school environment that interferes with women's ability to participate fully and equally. Sommers maintains that the liberal ideal of motherhood as voluntary has also hurt the family and children by contributing to the breakup of the family.

CONCLUSION

Discrimination and oppression of women permeates our society. Lower wages for working women and sexual harassment are just two symptoms of a patriarchal society. Different feminist theories propose different solutions for overcoming the problems of oppression. These solutions, which range from rejection of motherhood and male institutions altogether to enforcing gender-neutral policies in the workplace, are based primarily on differing views of women and men's nature as well as economic institutions. While liberal feminists believe that equality can be achieved within the existing capitalist structure, Marxist and socialist feminists maintain that in order to achieve equality for women we first need to replace the capitalist economic system, which is based on a patriarchal model.

SIMONE DE BEAUVOIR

The Second Sex

French philosopher and author Simone de Beauvoir (1908–1986) wrote *The Second Sex* in 1949, years before the beginning of the modern women's liberation movement. Her book is considered one of the classics in feminist literature. Beauvoir's feminism contains elements of both radical feminism and Marxist feminism. She regards sexuality and motherhood as a key aspect of women's oppression and argues that sexual self-determination is essential for women's liberation. She also maintains that "One is not born, but rather becomes, a woman." In this selection Beauvoir explores what it means to be a woman and to be a mother.

Critical Reading Questions

1. How does Beauvoir answer the question "What is woman"?
2. What does Beauvoir mean when she says that woman is defined as the Other?
3. Why don't women submit to male authority rather than reject the definition of their selves as Other?
4. Why does Beauvoir reject the analogy drawn between women and slaves?
5. In what ways do religions support the subordinate position of women?
6. What was the effect of the Industrial Revolution on women's liberation?
7. Why does the "equal but separate" formula result in discrimination?
8. What parallels does Beauvoir draw between racism and sexism?
9. How do men profit from the Otherness of women?
10. On what grounds does Beauvoir reject motherhood as woman's natural "calling"?
11. What is Beauvoir's view of pregnancy?
12. How does Beauvoir respond to the claim that pregnancy is a creative act?
13. How does Beauvoir respond to the preconception that maternity is the crown of a woman's life?
14. According to Beauvoir, what is the curse that lies upon marriage?
15. How does Beauvoir respond to the preconception that "the child is sure of being happy in its mother's arms"?
16. What is Beauvoir's view of mothers having careers?

INTRODUCTION

. . . [W]hat is a woman? *"Tota mulier in utero,"* says one, "woman is a womb." But in speaking of certain women, connoisseurs declare that they are not women, although they are equipped with a uterus like the rest. All agree in recognizing the fact that females exist in the human species; today as always they make up about one half of humanity. And yet we are told that femininity is in danger; we are exhorted to be women, remain women, become women. It would appear, then, that every female

The Second Sex, trans by H. M. Parshley (New York: Alfred A. Knopf, 1983).

human being is not necessarily a woman; to be so considered she must share in that mysterious and threatened reality known as femininity. . . .

The biological and social sciences no longer admit the existence of unchangeably fixed entities that determine given characteristics, such as those ascribed to woman, the Jew, or the Negro. Science regards any characteristic as a reaction dependent in part upon a *situation*. If today femininity no longer exists, then it never existed. But does the word *woman*, then, have no specific content? . . .

If her functioning as a female is not enough to define woman, if we decline also to explain her through "the eternal feminine," and if nevertheless we admit, provisionally, that women do exist, then we must face the question: what is a woman?

To state the question is, to me, to suggest, at once, a preliminary answer. The fact that I ask it is in itself significant. A man would never get the notion of writing a book on the peculiar situation of the human male. But if I wish to define myself, I must first of all say: "I am a woman"; on this truth must be based all further discussion. A man never begins by presenting himself as an individual of a certain sex; it goes without saying that he is a man. The terms *masculine* and *feminine* are used symmetrically only as a matter of form, as on legal papers. In actuality the relation of the two sexes is not quite like that of two electrical poles, for man represents both the positive and the neutral, as is indicated by the common use of *man* to designate human beings in general; whereas woman represents only the negative, defined by limiting criteria, without reciprocity. . . . Woman has ovaries, a uterus; these peculiarities imprison her in her subjectivity, circumscribe her within the limits of her own nature. It is often said that she thinks with her glands. Man superbly ignores the fact that his anatomy also includes glands, such as the testicles, and that they secrete hormones. He thinks of his body as a direct and normal connection with the world, which he believes he apprehends objectively, whereas he regards the body of woman as a hindrance, a prison, weighed down by everything peculiar to it. "The female is a female by virtue of a certain *lack* of qualities," said Aristotle; "we should regard the female nature as afflicted with a natural defectiveness." And St. Thomas for his part pronounced woman to be an "imperfect man," an "incidental" being. This is symbolized in Genesis where Eve is depicted as made from what Bossuet called "a supernumerary bone" of Adam.

Thus humanity is male and man defines woman not in herself but as relative to him; she is not regarded as an autonomous being. . . . He is the Subject, he is the Absolute—she is the Other. . . .

Why is it that women do not dispute male sovereignty? No subject will readily volunteer to become the object, the inessential; it is not the Other who, in defining himself as the Other, establishes the One. The Other is posed as such by the One in defining himself as the One. But if the Other is not to regain the status of being the One, he must be submissive enough to accept this alien point of view. Whence comes this submission in the case of woman?. . .

Here is to be found the basic trait of woman: she is the Other in a totality of which the two components are necessary to one another. . . .

Master and slave, also, are united by a reciprocal need, in this case economic, which does not liberate the slave. In the relation of master to slave the master does not make a point of the need that he has for the other; he has in his grasp the power of satisfying this need through his own action; whereas the slave, in his dependent condition, his hope and fear, is quite conscious of the need he has for his master. Even if the need is at bottom equally urgent for both, it always works in favor of the oppressor and against the oppressed. That is why the liberation of the working class, for example, has been slow.

Now, woman has always been man's dependent, if not his slave; the two sexes have never shared the world in equality. And even today woman is heavily handicapped, though her situation is beginning to change. Almost nowhere is her legal status the same as man's, and frequently it is much to her disadvantage. Even when her rights are legally recognized in the abstract, long-standing custom prevents their full expression in the mores. In the economic sphere men and women can almost be said to make up two castes; other things being equal, the former hold the better jobs, get higher wages, and have more opportunity for success than their new competitors. In industry and politics men have a great many more positions and they monopolize the most important posts. In addition to all this, they enjoy a traditional prestige that the education of children tends in every way to support, for the present enshrines the past—and in the past all history has been made by men. At the present time, when women are beginning to take part in the affairs of the world, it is still a world that belongs to men—they have no doubt of it at all and women have scarcely any. To decline to be the Other, to refuse to be a party to the deal—this would be for women to renounce all the advantages conferred upon them by their alliance with the superior caste. Man-the-sovereign will provide woman-the-liege with material protection and will undertake the moral justification of her existence; thus she can evade at once both economic risk and the metaphysical risk of a liberty in which ends and aims must be contrived without assistance. Indeed, along with the ethical urge of each individual to affirm his subjective existence, there is also the temptation to forgo liberty and become a thing. This is an inauspicious road, for he who takes it—passive, lost, ruined—becomes henceforth the creature of another's will, frustrated in his transcendence and deprived of every value. But it is an easy road; on it one avoids the strain involved in undertaking an authentic existence. When man makes of woman the *Other,* he may, then, expect her to manifest deep-seated tendencies toward complicity. Thus, woman may fail to lay claim to the status of subject because she lacks definite resources, because she feels the necessary bond that ties her to man regardless of reciprocity, and because she is often very well pleased with her role as the *Other.* . . .

Legislators, priests, philosophers, writers, and scientists have striven to show that the subordinate position of woman is willed in heaven and advantageous on earth. The religions invented by men reflect this wish for domination. In the legends of Eve and Pandora men have taken up arms against women. They have made use of philosophy and theology, as the quotations from Aristotle and St. Thomas have shown. Since ancient times satirists and moralists have delighted in showing up the weaknesses of women. . . .

It was only later, in the eighteenth century, that genuinely democratic men began to view the matter objectively. Diderot, among others, strove to show that woman is, like man, a human being. Later John Stuart Mill came fervently to her defense. But these philosophers displayed unusual impartiality. In the nineteenth century the feminist quarrel became again a quarrel of partisans. One of the consequences of the industrial revolution was the entrance of women into productive labor, and it was just here that the claims of the feminists emerged from the realm of theory and acquired an economic basis, while their opponents became the more aggressive. Although landed property lost power to some extent, the bourgeoisie clung to the old morality that found the guarantee of private property in the solidity of the family. Woman was ordered back into the home the more harshly as her emancipation became a real menace. Even within the working class the men endeavored to restrain woman's liberation, because they began to see the women as dangerous competitors—the more so because they were accustomed to work for lower wages.

In proving woman's inferiority, the antifeminists then began to draw not only upon religion, philosophy, and theology, as before, but also upon science—biology, experimental psychology, etc. At most they were willing to grant "equality in difference" to the *other* sex. That profitable formula is most significant; it is precisely like the "equal but separate" formula of the Jim Crow laws aimed at the North American Negroes. As is well known, this so-called equalitarian segregation has resulted only in the most extreme discrimination. The similarity just noted is in no way due to chance, for whether it is a race, a caste, a class, or a sex that is reduced to a position of inferiority, the methods of justification are the same. . . .

But men profit in many more subtle ways from the otherness, the alterity of woman. Here is miraculous balm for those afflicted with an inferiority complex, and indeed no one is more arrogant toward women, more aggressive or scornful, than the man who is anxious about his virility. Those who are not fear-ridden in the presence of their fellow men are much more disposed to recognize a fellow creature in woman; but even to these the myth of Woman, the Other, is precious for many reasons. They cannot be blamed for not cheerfully relinquishing all the benefits they derive from the myth, for they realize what they would lose in relinquishing woman as they fancy her to be, while they fail to realize what they have to gain from the woman of tomorrow. Refusal to pose oneself as the Subject, unique and absolute, requires great self-denial. Furthermore, the vast majority of men make no such claim explicitly. They do not *postulate* woman as inferior, for today they are too thoroughly imbued with the ideal of democracy not to recognize all human beings as equals.

In the bosom of the family, woman seems in the eyes of childhood and youth to be clothed in the same social dignity as the adult males. Later on, the young man, desiring and loving, experiences the resistance, the independence of the woman desired and loved; in marriage, he respects woman as wife and mother, and in the concrete events of conjugal life she stands there before him as a free being. He can therefore feel that social subordination as between the sexes no longer exists and that on the whole, in spite of differences, woman is an equal. As, however, he observes some points of inferiority—the most important being unfitness for the professions—he attributes these to natural causes. When he is in a co-operative and benevolent relation with woman, his theme is the principle of abstract equality, and he does not base his attitude upon such inequality as may exist. But when he is in conflict with her, the situation is reversed: his theme will be the existing inequality, and he will even take it as justification for denying abstract equality.

So it is that many men will affirm as if in good faith that women *are* the equals of man and that they have nothing to clamor for, while *at the same time* they will say that women can never be the equals of man and that their demands are in vain. It is, in point of fact, a difficult matter for man to realize the extreme importance of social discriminations which seem outwardly insignificant but which produce in woman moral and intellectual effects so profound that they appear to spring from her original nature. The most sympathetic of men never fully comprehend woman's concrete situation. . . . If the "woman question" seems trivial, it is because masculine arrogance has made of it a "quarrel"; and when quarreling one no longer reasons well. . . .

Now, what peculiarly signalizes the situation of woman is that she—a free and autonomous being like all human creatures—nevertheless finds herself living in a world where men compel her to assume the status of the Other. . . . How can a human being in woman's situation attain fulfillment? What roads are open to her? Which are blocked? How can independence be recovered in a state of dependency? What circumstances limit woman's liberty and how can they be overcome? These are the fundamental questions on which I would fain throw some light. This means that I am interested in the fortunes of the individual as defined not in terms of happiness but in terms of liberty.

Quite evidently this problem would be without significance if we were to believe that woman's destiny is inevitably determined by physiological, psychological, or economic forces. . . .

THE MOTHER

It is in maternity that woman fulfills her physiological destiny; it is her natural "calling," since her whole organic structure is adapted for the perpetuation of the species. But we have seen already that human society is never abandoned wholly to nature. And for about a century the reproductive function in particular has no longer been at the mercy solely of biological chance; it has come under the voluntary control of human beings. . . .

Pregnancy is above all a drama that is acted out within the woman herself. She feels it as at once an enrichment and an injury; the fetus is a part of her body, and it is a parasite that feeds on it; she possesses it, and she is possessed by it; it represents the future and, carrying it, she feels herself vast as the world; but this very opulence annihilates her, she feels that she herself is no longer anything. A new life is going to manifest itself and justify its own separate existence, she is proud of it; but she also feels herself tossed and driven, the plaything of obscure forces. It is especially noteworthy that the pregnant woman feels the immanence of her body at just the time when it is in transcendence: it turns upon itself in nausea and discomfort; it has ceased to exist for itself and thereupon becomes more sizable than ever before. . . . Ensnared by nature, the pregnant woman is plant and animal, a stock-pile of colloids, an incubator, an egg; she scares children proud of their young, straight bodies and makes young people titter contemptuously because she is a human being, a conscious and free individual, who has become life's passive instrument.

Ordinarily life is but a condition of existence; in gestation it appears as creative; but that is a strange kind of creation which is accomplished in a contingent and passive manner. There are women who enjoy the pleasures of pregnancy and suckling so much that they desire their indefinite repetitions; as soon as a baby is weaned these mothers feel frustrated. Such women are not so much mothers as fertile organisms, like fowls with high egg-production. And they seek eagerly to sacrifice their liberty of action to the functioning of their flesh: it seems to them that their existence is tranquilly justified in the passive fecundity of their bodies. If the flesh is purely passive and inert, it cannot embody transcendence, even in a degraded form; it is sluggish and tiresome; but when the reproductive process begins, the flesh becomes root-stock, source, and blossom, it assumes transcendence, a stirring toward the future, the while it remains a gross and present reality. The disjunction previously suffered by the woman in the weaning of an earlier child is compensated for; she is plunged anew into the mainstream of life, reunited with the wholeness of things, a link in the endless chain of generations, flesh that exists by and for another fleshly being. The fusion sought in masculine arms—and no sooner granted than withdrawn—is realized by the mother when she feels her child heavy within her or when she clasps it to her swelling breasts. She is no longer an object subservient to a subject; she is no longer a subject afflicted with the anxiety that accompanies liberty, she is one with that equivocal reality: life. Her body is at last her own, since it exists for the child who belongs to her. Society recognizes her right of possession and invests it, moreover, with a sacred character. . . . With her ego surrendered, alienated in her body and in her social dignity, the mother enjoys the comforting illusion of feeling that she is a human being *in herself*, a *value*.

But this is only an illusion. For she does not really make the baby, it makes itself within her; her flesh engenders flesh only, and she is quite incapable of establishing an existence that will have to establish itself. Creative acts originating in liberty establish the object as value and give it the quality of the essential; whereas the child in the maternal body is not thus justified; it is still only a gratuitous cellular growth, a brute fact of nature as contingent on circumstances as death and corresponding philosophically with it. . . . The dangerous falsity of two currently accepted preconceptions is clearly evident. . . .

The first of these preconceptions is that maternity is enough in all cases to crown a woman's life. It is nothing of the kind. There are a great many mothers who are unhappy, embittered, unsatisfied. Tolstoy's wife is a significant example; she was brought to childbed more than twelve times and yet writes constantly in her journal about the emptiness and uselessness of everything, including herself. . . .

As we have seen, the curse which lies upon marriage is that too often the individuals are joined in their weakness rather than in their strength—each asking from the other instead of finding pleasure in giving. It is even more deceptive to dream of gaining through the child a plenitude, a warmth, a value, which one is unable to create for oneself; the child brings joy only to the woman who is capable of disinterestedly desiring the happiness of another, to one who without being wrapped up in self seeks to transcend her own existence. To be sure, the child is an enterprise to which one can validly devote oneself; but it represents a ready-made justification no more than any other enterprise does; and it must be desired for its own sake, not for hypothetical benefits. . . .

There is nothing *natural* in such an obligation: nature can never dictate a moral choice; this implies an engagement, a promise to be carried out. To have a child is to undertake a solemn obligation; if the mother shirks this duty subsequently, she commits an offense against an existent, an independent human being; but no one can impose the engagement upon her. The relation between parent and offspring, like that between husband and wife, ought to be freely willed. . . . A social and artificial morality is hidden beneath this pseudo-naturalism.

That the child is the supreme aim of woman is a statement having precisely the value of an advertising slogan.

The second false preconception, directly implied by the first, is that the child is sure of being happy in its mother's arms. There is no such thing as an "unnatural mother," to be sure, since there is nothing natural about maternal love; but, precisely for that reason, there are bad mothers. And one of the major truths proclaimed by psychoanalysis is the danger to the child that may lie in parents who are themselves "normal." The complexes, obsessions, and neuroses of adults have their roots in the early family life of those adults; parents who are themselves in conflict, with their quarrels and their tragic scenes, are bad company for the child. . . .

We have seen that woman's inferiority originated in her being at first limited to repeating life, . . .

In a properly organized society, where children would be largely taken in charge by the community and the mother cared for and helped, maternity would not be wholly incompatible with careers for women. On the contrary, the woman who works—farmer, chemist, or writer—is the one who undergoes pregnancy most easily because she is not absorbed in her own person; the woman who enjoys the richest individual life will have the most to give her children and will demand the least from them; she who acquires in effort and struggle a sense of true human values will be best able to bring them up properly. If too often, today, woman can hardly reconcile with the best interests of her children an occupation that keeps her away from home for hours and takes all her strength, it is, on the one hand, because feminine employment is still too often a kind of slavery, and, on the other, because no effort has been made to provide for the care, protection, and education of children outside the home. This is a matter of negligence on the part of society; but it is false to justify it on the pretense that some law of nature, God, or man requires that mother and child belong exclusively to one another; this restriction constitutes in fact only a double and baneful oppression. . . .

Discussion Questions

1. Beauvoir regards religion as an institution that supports the oppression of women. Do you agree? Support your answer. If religion does contribute to the oppression of women, how should feminists respond to religion? Since religion is part of society, is it fair to excuse religion from complying with equal opportunity legislation? Discuss whether or not legislation should be passed, as it was for the workplace, which would require religious institutions to treat women equitably.
2. Discuss Beauvoir's observation that many men are engaged in doublethink by affirming in good faith that women are their equals while at the same time saying that women cannot be men's equals and that their demands are in vain. If you are a male student, examine ways in which you might unintentionally be doing this. If you are a female student, examine ways in which you might both want the benefits associated with being the Other and at the same time want equality with men.
3. Discuss Beauvoir's analysis of pregnancy and motherhood. Do you agree with her? Support your answer.
4. Discuss what reforms Beauvoir would most likely suggest for making the workplace more compatible with motherhood.

RUTH GROENHOUT

Essentialist Challenges to Liberal Feminism

Ruth Groenhout teaches philosophy at Calvin College. Groenhout begins by summarizing the basic assumptions of liberal feminist theory regarding human nature. She then contrasts these assumptions with those of gender essentialists such as Catherine MacKinnon and sociobiologist E. O. Wilson. Groenhout concludes that liberal theory provides a more powerful political tool than gender essentialism in the fight against sexual subordination.

Critical Reading Questions

1. What is the basic assumption of liberal political theory?
2. How do evolutionary ethics differ from liberal theory?
3. Why, according to Groenhout, are liberalism and feminism a natural alliance?
4. What is the role of government in liberal theory?
5. What does Groenhout mean when she says that "the notion of individual rights has been a politically powerful tool in the fight against sexual oppression"?
6. Why does Groenhout reject communitarianism?
7. What are the four reasons put forth by Groenhout for why feminism should not give up the liberal tradition?
8. What is a gender essentialist and how do they differ from liberal feminists?
9. On what grounds do feminists such as Catherine MacKinnon challenge liberal feminism? How does Groenhout respond to MacKinnon's theory?
10. How does the sociobiology view of gender, as put forth by E.O. Wilson, differ from that of liberal feminism and the "gender essentialism" of MacKinnon?
11. Why does Groenhout reject sociobiology as a foundation for feminist theory?
12. What are some of the problems, according to Groenhout, with both types of gender essentialism?
13. How does Groenhout respond to the claim by gender essentialists that men are more aggressive than women?
14. How does Groenhout respond to the critics of liberalism?
15. On what grounds does Groenhout conclude that feminism should not give up liberalism?

ESSENTIALIST CHALLENGES TO LIBERAL FEMINISM

Liberal political theory begins with rights, autonomy, and reason. Humans have rights, and their freedom to exercise those rights is properly limited by others' rights. This view of the basic shape of the political terrain is based on certain assumptions about humans. The most basic is the assumption that humans, whatever their other differences,

Social Theory and Practice 28, no. 1, 2002, pp. 51–75. Some notes have been omitted.

share some basic qualities that make them properly bearers of rights. . . .

Because liberal political thought bases rights on what would seem to be a gender-neutral concept such as rationality, it has been a traditional resource for feminist thinkers, from early thinkers such as Mary Wolstonecraft [sic] and Harriet Taylor Mill, to contemporary thinkers . . .

This easy and obvious association of liberal political thought with feminist theory has been challenged from two directions. On the one hand, some feminist theorists have challenged the tight connection between liberalism and feminism, because, they have argued, the notion of rationality on which liberal rights are based is not as gender-neutral as it seems. So in her critique of objective rationality, Catharine MacKinnon argues that traditional notions of objectivity that underlie claims about rationality are inherently tied to the objectification of women.[1] If rationality/objectivity is inherently connected to the objectification of women, then the "rationality" of women becomes problematic. On this view, women must either deny their nature as women (become honorary men) and objectify other women in order to be rational, or they must accept their status as objectified (not objectifiers) and so be incapable of rationality. In either case, rationality cannot be exercised by women as women. If this account of rationality is accepted, the standard liberal assumption that men and women equally share in rationality must be given up. . . .

In more recent years the rise of evolutionary ethics, or sociobiological accounts of human nature, have also contributed to a general skepticism about an account of human nature as either rational, or autonomous, or gender-neutral. . . .

The aspect of evolutionary ethics that has proved most effective in distancing liberal thought from feminist thought is the assumption, deeply imbedded in evolutionary ethics, that men and women are genetically coded for different behavior due to their differing roles in the reproductive process and the different reproductive strategies these roles require. What counts as "rational" from the perspective of genes that find themselves in a male body is, we are told, profoundly different from what counts as "rational" for genes that find themselves in a female body. Strategies that lead to success in propagation for men are different from strategies that lead to success in propagation for women. These differences, further, have been selected for over millennia of evolutionary processes, and are now ineradicably a part of what it is to be a man or a woman. It follows from this that even if one wanted to continue the liberal project of grounding rights in (say) rationality, one could no longer assume that male rationality is the same as female rationality, and the easy connection between liberalism and feminism is again severed. . . .

1. Liberalism and Feminism: A Natural Alliance?

. . .The first thing to note is that the term "liberal political thought" can be used to cover an extremely broad range of thinkers, from Mill to Rousseau, from Wollstonecraft to Hegel. . . . I am assuming that the notion of rationality that undergirds liberal thought is an extensive notion, including the ability to reflect on and choose among conceptions of the good life. This account of rationality is needed to make sense of the moral and political claims of liberal thought.

Liberalism grounds its basic rights in human nature, a nature characterized by rationality and autonomy. There are really two separable aspects to this claim. We might call the first the individualism thesis and the second the rights thesis. Both rely on the notion that there is something morally significant to human capacities for rational deliberation. The first notes that humans are properly thought of first as individuals, not as units in a larger whole. The respect that liberalism accords humans is accorded prior to and independently of membership in any particular community or class. . . .

The rights thesis entails that the respect individuals should be accorded is best articulated in terms of rights, politically protected liberties or entitlements. . . . Which rights need to be protected is, of course, a contested issue in liberal thought. Libertarians defend a rather minimalist notion of protection, limited largely to protection of negative rights such as the right to own property. Rawlsian liberals and others defend a more expansive notion of rights, including rights to education and welfare, because these provide the basic necessities for exercising one's rational capacities. But in either case, the rights being protected are justified on the basis of the individual's capacity to exercise rational judgment and so act freely and be held responsible for his or her choices. This notion of rights naturally leads to a third thesis of liberal thought, that of a necessary, but limited state.

Individual rights cannot be protected without some form of governmental structures that protect them against both other individuals and governmental structures themselves. The liberal political theorist is committed to the notion that one cannot dispense with the state. Liberalism operates with a view of human nature that assumes that some political structures are needed to prevent humans from mistreating each other. This is not the only role the state can play, but it is a fundamental one. . . .

So the state is necessary, but the state must also be limited. Just as humans, left unrestricted by the state, choose on occasion to mistreat others, so the state, left unchecked, will mistreat its citizens. The power of the state must be limited to protect a sphere of liberty for its citizens and for the non-governmental social structures that they create. . . . The notion of individual rights has been a politically powerful tool in the fight against sexual subordination. The history of the struggle against women's oppression has shown that women need to be able to make decisions for and about their lives as individuals. The right to make decisions that determine the course of one's life, in fact, has been a central right in the fight for women's liberation. There is a deep disagreement between feminism and certain versions of communitarianism, both because women know too well the dangers of being treated as a member of the class or social role of Woman and because traditional values have frequently been the source of women's oppression. The struggle to be recognized as an individual in one's own right, and the respect accorded that individuality in law and in society has been too hard won to be given up lightly. Further, the individual is not valued, in liberal thought, because of a specific role that she or he is required to play in society, but instead is valued as an autonomous, that is, self-determining being. . . . These are core feminist values as well; feminism's goal is a world in which women are free to determine the course of their own lives and to play a significant role in political and social decision-making. As long as these remain central feminist values, feminists have reason to place themselves in the liberal tradition.

The second reason feminists should be reluctant to give liberalism up is that rights have been and continue to be important conceptual tropes for understanding the wrongness of gender oppression. There may be other moral frameworks for conceptualizing the moral wrong done to women when they are denied their rights, but few that explain that wrong so clearly, so straightforwardly, or so incontrovertibly. As an example, consider the arguments by Islamic feminists, or similar arguments made by Christians for Biblical Equality. In both cases, there are good reasons given for new interpretations of both religious traditions, arguments that support women's autonomy and independence. But in both cases one faces an uphill battle to convince conservative interpreters of the tradition to change their minds. In contrast, Wollstonecraft's arguments are relatively straightforward. No new interpretation of the notion of a right is needed to recognize that if rational agents deserve the rights intrinsic to autonomy, women must deserve those rights. . . .

A third reason why feminism has good reason to continue to locate itself in the liberal tradition is that the basic analysis of power that is central to feminism finds its historical roots in liberal thought. Power analyses are central to feminist theory, and a basic understanding of how power affects human interactions has been a staple of feminist analyses . . . some of the more perspicuous analyses were offered by Harriet Taylor Mill and John Stuart Mill in the nineteenth century. It is no accident that one finds a careful analysis of how power affects relationships between men and women in these thinkers; their liberal commitments provided a natural location from which to analyze the ways in which power affects individual relationships.

Finally, liberal political thought is based on a respect for the rational capacity of the individual. On this view, humans are more than stimulus response machines. They are capable of making decisions that are the result of critical reflection, and critical self-reflection, and are not purely determined in their actions by the biological and social forces that act on them. Both biological and social determinism truncate moral analysis in ways that make the wrongs done to women by sexism too limited. . . .

The liberal picture of human nature, as more than either biologically or socially determined, is a crucial aspect of the feminist analysis of the wrongness of sexist oppression. Sexual oppression, and social systems that perpetuate sexual oppression, are morally evil because they limit or deny women's capacity to reflect on and determine their own lives. . . .

The basic assumption on which a feminist liberalism is based is the notion of a common human nature. Critics who reject such a conception of human nature offer a critique that is, if correct, devastating to feminist liberalism. I would like to begin by presenting the critique, then argue that, carefully examined, it is not correct, and does not provide grounds for a rejection of feminist liberalism.

2. Against Liberalism: The Challenge from Feminism

Potentially the most devastating feminist critique of liberal thought arises from a denial of the most basic claim in liberalism: the claim that there is some essential human nature that is the source of moral rights. One feminist challenge to this claim arises from the belief that there is no neutral human nature, but rather there are men's natures and women's natures, and the two are radically different. . . .

One theoretical vantage point from which such an attack on liberalism has been made is that of Catharine MacKinnon's account of rationality, objectivity, and legal structures. I should state at the outset that MacKinnon does not consider herself a gender essentialist, since she believes that "man" and "woman" are socially constructed categories. That said, however, she offers no alternative account of what it would be like to be male or female in any other way than as they are currently constructed in terms of men and women. Since she also believes that an oppressive gender hierarchy is a universal feature of human societies,[9] what she describes seems very close to an essentialist picture of men's and women's natures. Men and women are radically different in nature, they are shaped that way by their culture and cannot simply choose to be otherwise, and the very nature of our perceived reality is determined by these differences. . . .

On MacKinnon's view, women's and men's natures are determined by, respectively, their objectification as objects of sexualized violence or their objectification of others as objects of sexualized violence. What it is to be a woman is to be turned into an object that is an appropriate locus for sex and for sexualized violence; to be a woman is to be sexually vulnerable. What it is to be a man is to be one who can sexually objectify another, either through words or actions, and to be capable of sexual predation. Not all men are sexual predators, of course. Some see themselves as protectors of women rather than predators on women. But both of these roles, protector and predator, assume the same things about women—that women are weak and incapable of self-protection, that women are appropriate objects of sexual violence, and that it is men who control sexual access to women, not the women themselves.

On this view, then, women's nature is essentially one of sexual prey. Women are defined in terms of their sexual accessibility and status. Likewise the essence of being a man is being a sexual predator/objectifier. While neither of these roles is, for MacKinnon, biologically or genetically essential, both are essential to the nature of being a man or a woman—the only way to be otherwise is to cease to be a man or a woman, and become we know not what.

MacKinnon offers one version of a sort of gender essentialism, but other feminists have offered other varieties. Others do not rest, as MacKinnon's does, on a sexualized predator/prey relationship, but instead on a sharp dichotomy between male and female natures in terms of value hierarchies. Females, on this view, are primarily oriented toward life-giving, cooperative, nurturing activities, while males are primarily oriented toward death-dealing, aggressive, controlling activities. Sometimes these different orientations are simply assumed to be the case without explanation, sometimes they are explained as a result of a deep Jungian imaginary, or as a result of women's ability to give birth and men's envy of that ability.[13] . . . For the purposes of this paper, however, I would like to focus on MacKinnon's account, because she is concerned directly with the issue of women's participation in a liberal society, and so she addresses precisely the issues with which I am concerned.

If men and women are fundamentally, essentially, different in the ways MacKinnon argues, then the liberal project of identifying basic human rights is misguided. If gender essentialism is correct, then there is no basic human nature, shared rationality, or fundamental similarity among people. There are two different sorts of beings that are lumped together under the rubric "human," but these two sorts of beings think differently, see the world differently, and have completely opposed value systems.

Liberal rights, from this perspective, are rights that are valued by men, generated by masculine reason, and appropriate (if at all) only for relationships among men. MacKinnon writes:

> The rule of law and the rule of men are one thing, indivisible, at once official and unofficial. . . . State power, embodied in law, exists throughout society as male power at the same time as the power of men over women throughout society is organized as the power of the state.[14]

. . . But MacKinnon's critique does not end with the historical record. In addition to noting that rights have, as a matter of historical fact, been the prerogative of men, she also charges that the very notion of rights is an intrinsically masculine construction. Freedom of speech, for example, has functioned, MacKinnon argues, to protect male "speech" in the form of the violent pornographic portrayal of women. Such speech, as she sees it, makes true freedom of speech for women inaccessible, since anything a woman says in the public sphere is undercut by the definition of women as sexual objects in pornographic portrayals. So the legal notion of freedom of speech functions, she claims, to protect male speech and prohibit female speech.[16] In similar manner, abortion rights, framed as privacy rights, function to protect male sexual access to women. Laws against sexual harassment, likewise, have not served to protect working women adequately because of their reliance on the "reasonable man" standard for judging harassment. . . .

This perspectival bias indicates, according to MacKinnon, that these rights really are "basic" only from a male perspective. From the perspective of lived female experience, she argues, rights are the legal structures that both maintain and hide from view male dominance. This offers a serious challenge to any attempt to maintain a feminist liberalism. If liberalism, viewed accurately, is simply male dominance writ large, feminist liberalism is an oxymoron, which makes those who defend it perhaps just morons.

3. Gender and Genes: The Challenge from Sociobiology

A similarly serious challenge to feminist liberalism comes from a very different group of theorists. Like MacKinnon, sociobiologists assert that men and women are essentially different.

Sociobiologists argue that the two sexes are shaped by a long history of evolutionary change. That evolutionary change is driven by success in breeding—those traits that lead to reproductive success are genetically passed on to future generations. Men and women play different roles in the reproductive process. Men's reproductive role is one that can be accomplished relatively quickly and does not involve a great deal of investment. Women's reproductive role, on the other hand, involves an extensive investment in terms of time and energy, first in the nine months of pregnancy, and subsequently in the two to five years of breastfeeding and care-giving.

. . . The assumption in sociobiology is that the differential success of these two different strategies has led to genetically based differences in men and women's behavior. Cultural and social differences, then, between men and women are not so much reflections of differing social roles and expectations as they are reflections of basic genetic differences between men and women.[19]

Men, on this view, are genetically programmed for promiscuity and minimal investment in their children. Some have even argued that men are predisposed to rape as a part of their impulse to procreate. Women are programmed for monogamy and heavy investment in their children. . . .

Sociobiologists have argued that male and female tendencies to exhibit traits such as aggression and empathy are likewise tied to reproductive success, and so men are, by nature, more prone to aggression in all areas of life while women are more prone to docility and empathetic nurturing.

As I mentioned above, the picture sociobiologists have drawn is not wildly different from the view of masculine and feminine nature offered by feminists such as MacKinnon. On both views, men are inherently more aggressive, sexually promiscuous, prone to violence, and oriented toward dominating women sexually. Women are inherently more nurturing, more submissive, (particularly to men), sexually less promiscuous, and less driven by sexual urges, while more concerned about care for children and infants. . . . In contrast to MacKinnon, whose writing is motivated by political concerns, sociobiologists see their work as having bearing on, but not directly dictating, social policy. They do, generally, imply that the differences between men and women will have social effects. Men's natural aggression and sexual dominance will naturally make men the dominant sex in social settings. Women's natural deference and nurturance will generally prevent them from acquiring social power, but will serve the continuance of the human race quite efficiently. . . . Rather than offering social criticism, then, there is a tendency in this literature to offer explanations for why the status quo is what it is. Underlying this explanatory technique, however, there is sometimes the assumption that since the way things are is dictated by the differing natures of men and women, social policy that attempts to change or modify the existing situation is fighting an uphill battle. This is problematic because of the implicit approval it offers to sexist hierarchies. . . . [T]he more problematic version of sociobiology denies that there are any truths about humans not captured by evolutionary science. Humans, on this view, are nothing more than the sum of their evolutionary heritage, and so all accounts of human nature, human rationality, and human morality must be based in evolutionary studies. . . .

If one accepts this view of rationality, then one is forced to reject the notion that men and women share a common rational nature. . . . There may be a fundamental rational principle ("Propagate effectively!") but at the level of evaluation of actions or of social policy there is no shared conception of rationality. What is rational for men is irrational for women, and vice versa.

On this view, liberal rights are merely a thin veneer of illusion over the biological reality of genetics. . . . [F]urther, there is a deep and abiding conviction that hierarchies, particularly hierarchies of gender, are ineluctably written into the human genetic code. So E.O. Wilson famously comments that ". . . a schedule of sex- and age-dependent ethics can impart higher genetic fitness than a single moral code which is applied uniformly to all sex-age groups."[25] And, more recently, Matt Ridley describes the sexual division of labor as "an economic institution that is a vital part of all human societies."[26] Rights and a concern for justice for individuals are all very nice in philosophical treatises, the implication is, but in the real world it is reproductive success that counts.

4. Problems with Gender Essentialisms

If either feminist gender essentialism or sociobiological gender essentialism is correct, then feminist liberalism is incoherent. Feminist liberalism assumes that one can speak of a common human nature, but both sorts of gender essentialists hold that men and women have different natures. . . .

There are problems with both forms of gender essentialism, however, that defuse part of their challenge to liberal thought. The first problem is a matter of over-emphasis on difference. The second problem is an overstatement of determinism, in the one case cultural, in the second case genetic. I would like to deal with each of these in turn.

First, the over-emphasis on difference. Both gender-essentialist feminists and sociobiologists focus so heavily on gender difference that they lose sight of the huge areas of similarity between men and women. Two areas where this is particularly obvious are those of aggression and sexual promiscuity. According to both sorts of gender essentialists, men are more aggressive than women. In both cases theorists move from the statement that men are more aggressive than women to the assumption that aggression is a masculine trait. But the second claim is not entailed by the first. Both men and women are aggressive, though their aggression may show itself in different ways and be elicited by different occasions. . . .

Moreover, sweeping generalizations about the aggressiveness of men frequently ignore the complexity of the notion of aggression itself. It often is used as a synonym for violence, and there are innumerable statistics that show that men engage in more violence against both men and women than do women. But aggression involves more than just "committing murders and making weapons"—the research definition used in one study.[28] Aggression is a complex set of behavioral patterns, . . . If those studying aggression begin with the assumption that aggression is a masculine trait, they will interpret behavior by males as aggressive. Research bias is a well documented problem, and a glance at contemporary discussions of primate research indicates that it is not easily overcome.

But, setting aside for the moment the question of research bias and the difficulty of defining aggression, let us imagine that males can be demonstrated, as a class, to have a tendency to exhibit aggression at a higher level than women. What follows from that with respect to men's and women's natures? It certainly does not follow that women are not aggressive. The fact that men are taller than women does not entail the claim that women don't have height, and the same absurdity occurs when a higher level of aggression in males is equated with a female lack of aggression. Women are aggressive; aggression is a necessary attribute for survival in human life. So from the fact that, as a class, men are more aggressive than women, one surely cannot conclude that women are not aggressive. Nor can one conclude that all men are more aggressive than all women—the statistics would clearly not bear that claim out either. . . .

The second criticism of gender-essentialist thought involves a rejection of the deterministic assumptions such essentialism rests on. One can recognize that sex differences matter in life without moving to the further assumption that they entirely determine every aspect of one's life. . . . We are constrained by the social setting within which we are born and socialized, and we are constrained by our physical nature. . . . But nothing warrants the move from constraint to determinism.

On MacKinnon's account, one cannot be a man without being an objectifier, and one cannot be a woman without being objectified. Further, one cannot choose to opt out of being a man or a woman. Similarly, some sociobiological accounts of human nature assume that being male or female is absolutely determinative of personality. . . . In some cases, in fact, biologically based behavior is more amenable to change than is culturally constructed behavior. Medication can diminish the symptoms of obsessive compulsive disorder, but no medication is likely to change a Westerner's deeply ingrained food taboos against, say, eating grubs. Asserting the "naturalness" of certain sorts of behavior, however implies the opposite. It implies that biological features of our characters and personalities are fixed and determined in ways that are clearly false when we consider the issue carefully.

MacKinnon's own commitment to making legal changes in the way U.S. law deals with pornography suggests, in fact, that she herself has no trouble seeing herself as an agent rather than a sexualized object. Her legal successes suggest that the judicial system is capable of seeing women as more than sexualized objects. Likewise, the dedication to their research that scientists may display suggests that any account of human rationality as determined by the drive to procreate is seriously defective. . . .

5. Liberalism and Critics

While I think that the essentialist case is overstated, I also think that there are valuable lessons to be learned from the critics of liberalism. . . . The first area concerns autonomy. MacKinnon rightly pushes us to recognize that autonomy is not something one either has or does not have. Autonomy occurs along a continuum, and one of the things that makes one more or less autonomous is one's enculturation and socialization into a way of life that may enhance or diminish one's capacity to make and act on choices. MacKinnon is right to point out that women's life choices are diminished when the culture they grow up in defines them as appropriate objects for sexualized violence. She is less concerned with the fact that men's lives, likewise, are diminished when they receive a cultural image of manliness as requiring mindless aggression and the sexual subordination of women. These definitions create a culture that is destructive of human lives and human autonomy. . . .

Likewise, criticisms from sociobiology are healthy for liberal political thought as well. Humans are not disembodied rational intellects. We are embodied, physical beings, whose lives and choices occur always in the context of our physical needs, our evolutionary heritage, and our hormonal present. This does not, in and of itself, negate our freedom and responsibility, but it does situate it in important ways. Careful thinkers have always realized that human freedom and responsibility do not merely occur in an embodied context: they require an embodied context for their exercise. Without a physical existence, it is hard to know what respect for another's needs or rights would even be.

Sociobiologists also help us to avoid the tendency to utopian thinking that can be tempting for moral and political theorists. Humans will always need some form of social safeguards, to prevent them from exploiting others and from being exploited in turn. . . .

Knowing that humans may have natural predispositions to act in certain ways is valuable information for moral reasoning. But it can never substitute for moral reasoning, since from the fact that humans naturally do something we cannot conclude that they ought to do that.

Further, both the feminist and the sociobiological critiques keep liberalism more honest about what it can and cannot do. . . . While both views encourage liberalism to remain humble about its limitations, however, a similar caution is needed in each of their respective cases as well. Sociobiology cannot tell us what the good human life must be, and MacKinnon is quite frank about her own inability to offer a determinate picture of a nonsexually objectified woman. Ultimately, each individual needs to be the one who decides what sort of life she will pursue, but in stating this I find myself back on familiar, liberal, terrain.

6. Conclusion

. . . The belief that women, as women, can fight and win legal battles is one worth holding on to. It seems to be one that MacKinnon herself holds. But it is in rather serious tension with the notion that women are defined, as women, in terms of their sexual violability. The two ideas do not sit well together. A liberal notion that women, oppressed though they may be, are still more than the sum of that oppression is, I think, exactly what is needed to make sense of the many ways in which women have exercised their agency to bring about political change. And it is a belief that is situated squarely in liberal theory.

Liberalism does have its weaknesses. Among them are the tendencies to erase differences among people and to overlook how culture and physical circumstances affect the very meaning of terms such as rights and autonomy. But having recognized these tendencies, is liberalism to be rejected? Not until a better alternative comes along, and that is what often seems missing from the critics of liberalism. . . . If we are not willing to give up the protection of basic rights, and if we think that individual autonomy is worth defending, then what is called for is a new and improved liberalism, not the rejection of liberal theory.

NOTES

1. Catharine MacKinnon, *Toward a Feminist Theory of the State* (Cambridge, Mass.: Harvard University Press, 1989), pp. 162–63.
9. MacKinnon, *Toward a Feminist Theory of the State,* p. 94.
13. There is some aspect of this in both Virginia Held, *Feminist Morality: Transforming Culture, Society, and Politics* (Chicago: University of Chicago Press, 1993), and Sara Ruddick, *Maternal Thinking: Toward a Politics of Peace* (Boston: Beacon Press, 1989).
14. MacKinnon, *Toward a Feminist Theory of the State,* p. 170.
16. MacKinnon's extended argument for this is given in *Only Words* (Cambridge, Mass.: Harvard University Press, 1993).

19. Douglas Kenrick and Melanie Trost, "The Evolutionary Perspective," in Anne Beall and Robert Sternberg (eds.), *The Psychology of Gender* (New York: Guilford Press, 1993), pp. 148–172; see p. 168.
25. E.O. Wilson, "The Morality of the Gene," excerpts from *Sociobiology: The New Synthesis,* in Paul Thompson (ed.), *Issues in Evolutionary Ethics* (Albany: State University of New York Press, 1995), pp. 153–64; see p. 163.
26. Matt Ridley, *On the Origins of Virtue* (New York: Viking, 1996), p. 92. As is frustratingly often the case, Ridley here ignores primate evidence that the human sexual division of labor is far more extreme than any such division among closely related primates. This would seem relevant to an evolutionary ethics, as it suggests that human practices are not "hard wired" in a strong sense.
28. Cited in Kenrick and Trost, "The Evolutionary Perspective," p. 152.

Discussion Questions

1. Make a list of the premises and conclusions regarding human nature in the arguments put forth by radical feminism (MacKinnon), sociobiology, and liberal feminism. Analyze each argument. Do the premises support their conclusions? Have any premises been omitted or are any overstated?
2. Does Groenhout present a convincing argument against gender essentialism? Discuss how MacKinnon (see her reading in Chapter 8) might respond to Groenhout's critique of radical feminist gender essentialism. Discuss how a sociobiologist such as E. O. Wilson might respond to Groenhout's argument.
3. Which view of gender do you find most convincing? Support your answer.
4. Does liberal theory, as explicated by Groenhout, provide an adequate analysis of motherhood? Support your answer.
5. Has Groenhout's claim that liberalism is a more powerful tool for social reform been demonstrated in reality? Discuss your answer in light of some of the legislation and policies based on liberal theory that were designed to overcome the oppression of women in society.

CHRISTINA HOFF SOMMERS

Philosophers Against the Family

Christina Hoff Sommers, a former professor of philosophy at Clark University, is a fellow at the American Enterprise Institute in Washington, D.C. Sometimes described as an antifeminist, Sommers argues that contemporary feminist moral theory fails to consider

From *Person to Person,* ed. by George Graham and Hugh Lafollette (Philadelphia: Temple University Press, 1989), pp. 82–105.

the special nature of the relationship and duty between mothers and children. Radical feminism in particular, she believes, is contributing to the disintegration of the family.

Critical Reading Questions

1. What, according to Sommers, is the focus of contemporary moral theory?
2. Why is the contemporary moral philosopher "unsympathetic to the idea that we have any duties defined by relationships"?
3. How do Aristotelian and Platonic theorists differ in their approach to social criticism?
4. What does Sommers mean when she says that "the prevailing attitude toward the family is radical and not liberal"?
5. What is Simone de Beauvoir's view of marriage and family, and why does Sommers reject this view and that of other philosophers like de Beauvoir?
6. What is Sommers's view of the assimilationist ideal in feminist theory?
7. Why does Sommers reject the comparison between mothers and wives and slaves?
8. What does Sommers mean when she says that "radical feminism creates a false dichotomy between sexism and assimilation"?
9. What is Sommers's view of nonassimilationist feminists such as Carol Gilligan?
10. On what grounds does Sommers reject Judith Thomson's argument for abortion?
11. Why does Sommers reject the volunteerist theory that family relationships are based on voluntary duties? What does Sommers propose as an alternative?
12. According to Sommers, how have philosophers contributed to the breakup of the family?

Much of what commonly counts as personal morality is measured by how well we behave within family relationships. We live our moral lives as son or daughter to this mother and that father, as brother or sister to that sister or brother, as father or mother, grandfather, granddaughter to that boy or girl or that man or woman. These relationships and the moral duties defined by them were once popular topics of moral casuistry; but when we turn to the literature of recent moral philosophy, we find little discussion on what it means to be a good son or daughter, a good mother or father, a good husband or wife, a good brother or sister.

Modern ethical theory concentrates on more general topics. Perhaps the majority of us who do ethics accept some version of Kantianism or utilitarianism, and these mainstream doctrines are better designed for telling us about what we should do as persons in general than about our special duties as parents or children or siblings. We believe, perhaps, that these universal theories can fully account for the morality of special relations. In any case, modern ethics is singularly silent on the bread and butter issues of personal morality in daily life. But silence is only part of it. With the exception of marriage itself, the relationships in the family are biologically given. The contemporary philosopher is, on the whole, actively unsympathetic to the idea that we have *any* duties defined by relationships that we have not voluntarily entered into. . . . The practical result is that philosophers are to be found among those who are contributing to an ongoing disintegration of the traditional family. In what follows I expose some of the philosophical roots of the current hostility to family morality. . . .

THE MORAL VANTAGE

Social criticism is a heady pastime to which philosophers are professionally addicted. One approach is Aristotelian in method and temperament. It is antiradical, though it may be liberal, and it approaches the task of needed reform with a prima facie respect for the norms of established morality. It is conservationist and cautious in its recommendations for change. It is therefore not given to such proposals as abolishing the family or abolishing private property and, indeed, does not look kindly on such proposals from other philosophers. The antiradicals I am concerned about are not those who would be called Burkean. I call them liberal but this use of the term is somewhat perverse since, in my stipulative use, a liberal is a philosopher who advocates social reform but always in a conservative spirit. My liberals share with Aristotle the conviction that the traditional arrangements have great moral weight and that common opinion is a primary source of moral truth. A good modern example is Henry Sidgwick with his constant appeal to common sense. But philosophers like John Stuart Mill, William James, and Bertrand Russell can also be cited. . . .

The more exciting genre of social criticism is not liberal-Aristotelian but radical and Platonist in spirit. Its vantage is external or even supernal to the social institutions it has placed under moral scrutiny. Plato was as aware as anyone could be that what he called the cave was social reality. One reason for calling it a cave was to emphasize the need, as he saw it, for an external, objective perspective on established morality. . . . In our own day much social criticism of a Marxist variety has taken this radical approach to social change. And of course, much of contemporary feminist philosophy is radical.

. . . In particular, I suggest that the prevailing attitude toward the family is radical and not liberal. And the inability of mainstream ethical theory to come to grips with the special obligations that family members bear to one another contributes to the current disregard of the common-sense morality of the family cave. We find, indeed, that family obligations are criticized and discounted precisely because they do not fit the standard theories of obligation. If I am right, contemporary ethics is at a loss when it comes to dealing with parochial morality; but few have acknowledged this as a defect to be repaired. Instead the common reaction has been: If the family does not fit my model of autonomy, rights, or obligations, then so much the worse for the family. . . .

FEMINISM AND THE FAMILY

I have said that the morality of the family has been relatively neglected. The glaring exception to this is of course the feminist movement. This movement is complex, but I am primarily confined to its moral philosophers, of whom the most influential is Simone de Beauvoir. For de Beauvoir, a social arrangement that does not allow all its participants the scope and liberty of a human subjectivity is to be condemned. De Beauvoir criticizes the family as an unacceptable arrangement since, for women, marriage and childbearing are essentially incompatible with their subjectivity and freedom:

> The tragedy of marriage is not that it fails to assure woman the promised happiness . . . but that it mutilates her: it dooms her to repetition and routine. . . . At twenty or thereabouts mistress of a home, bound permanently to a man, a child in her arms, she stands with her life virtually finished forever (1952, 534).

For de Beauvoir the tragedy goes deeper than marriage. The loss of subjectivity is unavoidable as long as human reproduction requires the woman's womb. De Beauvoir starkly describes the pregnant woman who ought to be a "free individual" as a "stockpile of colloids, an incubator of an egg" (p. 553). And as recently as 1977 she compared childbearing and nurturing to slavery (p. 2).

It would be a mistake to say that de Beauvoir's criticism of the family is outside the mainstream of Anglo-American philosophy. Her criterion of moral adequacy may be formulated in continental existentialist terms, but its central contention is generally accepted: Who would deny that an arrangement that systematically thwarts the freedom and autonomy of the individual is *eo ipso* defective? . . . Implicit in her critique is the ideal of a society in which sexual differences are minimal or nonexistent. This ideal is shared by many contemporary feminist philosophers. . . . The ideal society is nonsexist and "assimilationist": "In the assimilationist society in respect to sex, persons would not be socialized so as to see or understand themselves or others as essentially or significantly who they were or what their lives would be like because they were either male or female" (1980, 26). Social reality is scrutinized for its approximation to this ideal, and criticism is directed against all existing norms. . . .

Thus the supernal light shines on the cave revealing its moral defects. *There*, in the ideal society, gender in the choice of lover or spouse would be of no more significance than eye color. *There* the family would consist of adults but not necessarily of different sexes and not necessarily in pairs. *There* we find equality ensured by a kind of affirmative action which compensates for disabilities. . . . Male-dominated sports such as wrestling and football will there be eliminated, and marriage as we know it will not exist.

Other feminist philosophers are equally confident about the need for sweeping change. Ann Ferguson (1977) wants a "radical reorganization of child rearing" (p. 51). She recommends communal living and a deemphasis on biological parenting. In the ideal society "love relationships would be based on the meshing together of androgynous human beings" (p. 66). Carol Gould (1983) argues for androgyny and for abolishing legal marriage. She favors single parenting, co-parenting, and communal parenting. The only arrangement she emphatically opposes is the traditional one where the mother provides primary care for the children. . . .

Though they differ in detail, these feminists hold to a common social ideal that is broadly assimilationist in character and inimical to the traditional family. Sometimes it seems as if the radical feminist simply takes the classical Marxist eschatology of the *Communist Manifesto* and substitutes "gender" for "class." Indeed, the feminist and the old-fashioned Marxist do have much in common. Both see their caves as politically divided into two warring factions: one oppressing, the other oppressed. Both see the need of raising the consciousness of the oppressed group to its predicament and to the possibility of removing its shackles. Both look forward to the day of a classless or genderless society. And both are zealots, paying little attention to the tragic personal costs to be paid for the revolution they wish to bring about. . . .

Any social arrangement that falls short of the assimilationist ideal is labeled sexist. It should be noted that this characteristically feminist use of the term differs significantly from the popular or literal sense. Literally, and popularly, sexism connotes unfair discrimination. . . . But to be antisexist in the technical, radical philosophical sense is not merely to be opposed to discrimination against women; it is to be *for* the assimilationist ideal. The philosopher antisexist opposes any social policy that is nonandrogynous, objecting, for example, to legislation that allows for maternity leave. As Allison Jagger remarks: "We do not, after all, elevate 'prostate leave' into a special right of men" (1977, 102). From being liberally opposed to sexism, one may in this way insensibly be led to a radical critique of the family whose ideal is assimilationist and androgynous. For it is very clear that the realization of the androgynous ideal is incompatible with the survival of the family as we know it.

The neological extension of labels such as "sexism," "slavery," and "prostitution" is a feature of radical discourse. The liberal too will sometimes call for radical solutions to social problems. Some institutions are essentially unjust. To reform slavery or totalitarian systems of government is to eliminate them. . . .

Comparing mothers and wives to slaves is a common radical criticism of the family. Presumably most slaves do not want to be slaves. In fact, the majority of wives and mothers want to be wives and mothers. Calling these women slaves is therefore a pejorative extension of the term. To be slaves in the literal sense these women would have to be too dispirited and oppressed or too corrupt even to want freedom from slavery. Yet that is how some feminist philosophers look upon women who opt for the traditional family. It does seem fanciful and not a little condescending to see them so, but let us suppose that it is in fact a correct and profound description of the plight of married women and mothers. Would it now follow that the term "slave" literally applies to them? Not quite yet. Before we could call these women slaves, we should have to have made a further assumption. Even timorous slaves too fearful of taking any step to freedom are under no illusion that they are not slaves. Yet it is a fact that most women and mothers do not *think* of themselves as slaves, so we must assume that the majority of women have been systematically deluded into thinking they are free. And that assumption, too, is often explicitly made. Here the radical feminist will typically explain that, existentially, women, being treated by men as sex objects, are especially prone to bad faith and false consciousness. Marxist feminists will see them as part of an unawakened and oppressed economic class. Clearly we cannot call on a deluded woman to cast off her bonds before we have made her *aware* of her bondage. So the first task of freeing the slave woman is dispelling the thrall of a false and deceptive consciousness. One must raise her consciousness to the reality of her situation. . . .

The dismissive feminist attitude to the widespread preferences of women takes its human toll. Most women, for example, prefer to have children, and few of those who have them regret having them. It is no more than sensible, from a utilitarian standpoint, to take note of the widespread preference and to take it seriously in planning one's own life. But a significant number of women discount this general verdict as benighted, taking more seriously the idea that the reported joys of motherhood are exaggerated and fleeting, if not altogether illusory. These women tell themselves and others that having babies is a trap to be avoided. But for many women childlessness has become a trap of its own, somewhat lonelier than the more conventional traps of marriage and babies. . . .

It is a serious defect of American feminism that it concentrates its zeal on impugning femininity and feminine culture at the expense of the grass root fight against economic and social injustices to which women are subjected. As we have seen, the radical feminist attitude to the woman who enjoys her femininity is condescending or even contemptuous. Indeed, the contempt for femininity reminds one of misogynist biases in philosophers such as Kant, Rousseau, and Schopenhauer, who believed that femininity was charming but incompatible with full personhood and reasonableness. The feminists deny the charm, but they too accept the verdict that femininity is weakness. It goes without saying that an essential connection between femininity and powerlessness has not been established by *either* party.

By denigrating conventional feminine roles and holding to an assimilationist ideal in social policy, the feminist movement has lost its natural constituency. The actual concerns, beliefs, and aspirations of the majority of women are not taken seriously *except* as illustrations of bad faith, false consciousness, and successful brainwashing. What women actually want is discounted and reinterpreted as to what they have been led to *think* they want (a man, children). What most women *enjoy* (male gallantry, candlelit dinners, sexy clothes, makeup) is treated as an obscenity (prostitution). . . .

Radical feminism creates a false dichotomy between sexism and assimilation, as if there were nothing in between. This is to ignore completely the middle ground in which it could be recognized that a woman can be free of oppression and nevertheless feminine in the sense abhorred by many feminists. For women are simply not waiting to be freed from the particular chains the radical feminists are trying to sunder. The average woman enjoys her femininity. She wants a man, not a roommate. She wants fair economic opportunities, and she wants children and the time to care for them. These are the goals that women actually have, and they are not easily attainable. But they will never be furthered by an elitist radical movement that views the actual aspirations of women as the product of a false consciousness. There is room for a liberal feminism that would work for reforms that would give women equal opportunity in the workplace and in politics, but would leave untouched and unimpugned the basic institutions that women want and support: marriage and motherhood. Such a feminism is already in operation in some European countries. But it has been obstructed here in the United States by the ideologues who now hold the seat of power in the feminist movement.

In characterizing and criticizing American feminism, I have not taken into account the latest revisions and qualifications of a lively and variegated movement. . . . I have in mind the recent literature on the idea that there is a specific female ethic that is more concrete, less rule-oriented, more empathetic and caring, and more attentive to the demands of a particular context. The kind of feminism that accepts the idea that women differ from men in approaching ethical dilemmas and social problems from a care perspective is not oriented to androgyny as an ideal. Rather it seeks to develop this special female ethic and to give it greater practical scope.

The stress on context might lead one to think these feminists are more sympathetic to the family as the social arrangement that shapes the moral development of women and is the context for many of the moral dilemmas that women actually face. However, one sees as yet no attention being paid to the fact that feminism itself is a force working against the preservation of the family. Psychologists like Carol Gilligan and philosophers like Lawrence Blum concentrate their attention on the moral quality of the caring relationships, but these relationships are themselves not viewed in their concrete embeddedness in any formal social arrangement.

It should also be said that some feminists are moving away from the earlier hostility to motherhood (Trebilcot, 1984). Here, too, one sees the weakening of the assimilationist ideal in the acknowledgment of a primary gender role. However, childrearing is not primarily seen within the context of the family but as a special relationship between mother and daughter or—more awkwardly—between mother and son, a relationship that effectively excludes the male parent. And the often cultist celebration of motherhood remains largely hostile to traditional familial arrangements.

It is too early to say whether a new style of nonassimilationist feminism will lead to a mitigation of the assault on the family or even on femininity. In any case, the recognition of a female ethic of care and responsibility is hardly inconsistent with a social ethic that values the family as a vital, perhaps indispensable, institution. And the recognition that women have their own moral style may well be followed by a more accepting attitude to the kind of feminity that the more assimilationist feminists reject.

THE INDIRECT ATTACK

Unlike the feminists, the philosophers do not directly criticize the family. In some cases, they do not even mention it; but each one holds a view that subverts, ignores, or denies the special moral relations that characterize the family and are responsible for its functioning. And if they are right, family morality is a vacuous subject.

Judith Thomson (1971) maintains that an abortion may be permissible even if the fetus is deemed a person from the moment of conception. For in that case being pregnant would be like having an adult surgically attached to one's body; and it is arguable that if we find ourselves attached to another person we have the right to free ourselves, even if this freedom is obtained at the price of the other person's death by, say, kidney failure. For the sake of this discussion I refer to the fetus as a prenatal child. I myself do not think the fetus is a person from the moment of conception. Nor does Thomson. But here we are interested in her argument for the proposition that abortion of a prenatal child/person should be permissible.

Now, many have been repelled by Thomson's comparing pregnancy to arbitrary attachment. Thomson herself is well aware that the comparison may seem bizarre. She says: "It may be said that what is important is not merely the fact that the fetus is a person, but that it is a person for whom the mother has a special kind of responsibility issuing from the fact that she is its mother" (p. 64).

To this Thomson replies that we do not have any such "special responsibility for a person unless we have assumed it, explicitly or implicitly." If the mother does not try to prevent pregnancy, does not obtain an abortion, but instead gives birth and then takes the child home with her, then she has at least implicitly assumed responsibility for it.

One might object that although pregnancy is a state into which many women do not enter voluntarily, it is nevertheless a state in which one is *socially* expected to care for the prenatal child. Many pregnant women do feel such a responsibility to it, and they take measure to assure its survival and future health. But here one must be grateful to Professor Thomson for her clarity. A mother who has not deliberately sought pregnancy bears *no* special responsibility to her prenatal child. For she has neither implicitly nor explicitly taken on the responsibility of caring for it. . . . On the other hand, the postnatal act of taking the child home is at least implicitly an assumption of responsibility: By choosing to take it with her, the mother is undertaking to care for the infant, and she no longer has a right to free herself of the burden of motherhood at the cost of the life of the child.

Note too that Thomson describes the relationship of the prenatal child-person to its mother as *biological.* This is consistent with giving no moral weight whatever to what might be called a sociological/normative relationship in which the child could be thought to have a right against its mother to prenatal care and protection. Here, too, Thomson is clear and uncompromising; there is no such right, either prenatally or postnatally, unless it be implicitly or voluntarily *conferred* on the child by the mother.

The assumption, then, is that there are no noncontractual obligations or special duties defined by the kinship of mother to child. As for social expectations, none are legitimate in the morally binding sense unless they have the backing of an implicit or explicit contract freely entered into. If that assumption is correct, sociological arrangements and norms have no moral force unless they are voluntarily accepted by the moral agent who is bound by them. I call this the volunteer theory of moral obligation. It is a thesis that is so widely accepted today that Thomson did not see the need to argue for it.

Michael Tooley's arguments in defense of infanticide provide another good example of how a contemporary philosopher sidetracks and ultimately subverts the special relations that bind the family. Tooley (1972) holds that being sentient confers the prima facie right not to be treated cruelly, and that possession of those characteristics that make one a person confers the *additional* right to life. Tooley then argues that infants lack these characteristics and so may be painlessly killed. In reaching this conclusion, Tooley's sole consideration is whether the infant intrinsically possesses the relevant "right-to-life-making characteristic" of personality. But this is to abstract from any right to care and protection that the infant's relation to its parents confers on it causally and institutionally. For Tooley, as for Thomson, the relations of family or motherhood are morally irrelevant. . . .

[These] philosophers are typical in holding that any moral requirement is either a general duty or else a specific obligation voluntarily assumed. Let us call a requirement a *duty* if it devolves on the moral agent whether or not it was voluntarily assumed. It is, for example, a duty to refrain from murder. And let us call a requirement an *obligation* only if it devolves on certain moral agents but not necessarily on all moral agents. One is, for example, morally obligated to keep one's promises. According to our philosophers, all duties are general in the sense of being requirements on all moral agents. Any moral requirement that is *specific* to a given moral agent must be grounded in a voluntary commitment. Thus there is no room for any special requirement on a moral agent that has not been voluntarily assumed by that agent. In other words, there are no special duties. This is what I am calling the volunteer theory of obligation. According to the volunteerist thesis, all duties are general and only those who volunteer for them have any obligations. . . .

What I am calling the volunteerist thesis is confidently held by many contemporary Anglo-American philosophers. . . . For it means that there is no such thing as filial duty per se, no such thing as the special duty of mother to child, and generally no such thing as a morality of special family or kinship relations. And this is contrary to what most people think. For most people think we do owe special debts to our parents even though we have not voluntarily assumed our obligations to them. Most people think that what we owe to our own children does not have its origin in any voluntary undertaking, explicit or implicit, that we have made to them, or to society at large, to care for them. . . .

The idea that to be committed to an individual is to have voluntarily made an implicit or explicit commitment to that individual is generally fatal to family morality. For it looks upon the network of felt obligation and expectation that binds family members as a sociological phenomenon without presumptive moral force. The social critics who hold this view of family obligation are usually aware that promoting it in public policy must further the disintegration of the traditional family unit as an institution. But whether they deplore the disintegration or welcome it, they are in principle bound to abet it.

THE SPECIAL DUTIES

I am suggesting that radical disrespect for the morality of the family cave is today rationalized in a strong philosophical thesis about moral rights and moral requirements, a thesis that excludes requirements that would have the status of special duties and their correlative rights against particular individuals. I think it is clear that the special duties cannot be put into the procrustean bed of voluntary undertakings implicitly assumed by the individuals who must discharge them. Thomson's confident assertion that the mother has no special obligation to the child-person she is carrying in her womb must be looked upon as a dogmatic expression of the rejection of special duties and, moreover, as a dogma that violates our basic intuitions about what counts as a moral obligation. It may be that so many philosophers have accepted this dogma because of an uncritical use of the model of promises as the paradigm for obligations. If all obligations are like the obligation to keep a promise, then indeed they could not be incumbent on anyone who did not undertake to perform in a specified way. But there is no reason to take promises as paradigmatic of obligation. Indeed, the moral force of the norm of promise keeping has itself to be grounded in a theory of obligations that moral philosophers have yet to work out (Sommers, 1986).

Once we reject the doctrine that a voluntary act by the person concerned is a necessary condition of special obligation, we are free to respect the common-sense views that attribute moral force to many obligations associated with kinship and other family relationships. We may then accept the family as an institution that defines many special duties but is nevertheless imperfect in many respects. And we still face the choice of how, as social philosophers, we are to deal with these imperfections. That is, we have the choice of being liberal or conservative in our attitude toward reform.

The conservative would change little or nothing, believing that the historical development of an institution has its own wisdom. This person is opposed to utopian social engineering, considering it to be altogether immoral in the profound sense of destroying the very foundations of the special duties. . . .

The liberal is more optimistic about the consequences of reform. Like the conservative, the liberal believes that the norms of any tradition or institution that is not essentially unjust have prima facie moral force. And that means we can rely on our common-sense beliefs that the system of expectations within the family is legitimate and should be respected. The liberal will acknowledge that a brother has the right to expect more help from his brother than from a stranger and not just because of what the one has done for the other lately. And the case is the same for all the traditional expectations that characterize the family members. On the other hand, there may be practices within the family that are systematically discriminatory and unfair to certain members. Unlike the conservative, the liberal is prepared to do some piecemeal social engineering to remove injustice in the family.

A better defense of the special duties would require much more space than I can give it here (Sommers, 1986). I believe it can be made far more plausible than the rival theory that rejects the special duties. My main objective has been to raise the strong suspicion that the volunteer theory of obligation is a dogma very probably wrong and misconceived, and certainly at odds with common opinion.

The space that remains is largely devoted to a survey of some of the social consequences of applying radical theory to family obligation. I have suggested that, insofar as moral philosophers have any influence on the course of social history, their influence has recently been in aid of institutional disintegration. Here now is some indication of how the principled philosophical disrespect for common sense in the area of family morality has weakened the family and how this affects the happiness of its members. . . .

THE BROKEN FAMILY

The most dramatic evidence of the progressive weakening of the family is to be found in the statistics on divorce. Almost all divorce is painful and most divorce affects children. Although a divorce does not end but merely disrupts the life of the child, the life it disrupts is uncontroversially the life of a person who can be directly wronged by the actions of a moral agent. One might therefore expect that philosophers who are carefully examining the morality of abortion would also be carefully examining the moral grounds for divorce. But here, too, the contemporary reluctance of philosophers to deal with the special casuistry of family relations is in evidence. . . . There is very persuasive evidence that children of divorced parents are seriously and adversely affected. Compared with children from intact families, they are more often referred to school psychologists, are more likely to have lower IQ and achievement test scores, are more likely to be arrested, and need more remedial classes (Weitzman, 1985). . . .

One major cause for the difference between children from broken and intact families is the effective loss of the father. In the *majority* of cases the child has not seen its father within the past year. . . .

It would be hard to show that the dismissive attitude of most contemporary moral philosophers to the moral force of kinship ties and conventional family roles has been a serious factor in contributing to the growth in the divorce rate. But that is only because it is so hard in general to show how much bread is baked by the dissemination of philosophical ideas. It is surely fair to say that the emphasis on autonomy and equality, when combined with the philosophical denigration of family ties, has helped to make divorce both easy and respectable, thereby facilitating the rapid change from fault-based to no-fault divorce. If contemporary moralists have not caused the tide of family disintegration, they are avidly riding it. On the other side, it is not hard to show that there is very little in recent moral philosophy that could be cited as possibly contributing to *stemming* the tide. . . .

These philosophers set aside special duties, replacing them with an emphasis on friendship, compatibility, and interpersonal love among family members. This has a disintegrative effect. For if what one owes to members of one's family is largely to be understood in terms of feelings of personal commitment, definite limits are placed on what one owes. For as feelings change, so may one's commitments, and the structure of responsibility within the family is permanently unstable. . . .

I have, in this final section, been illustrating the indifference of contemporary philosophers to the family by dwelling on their indifference to the children affected by divorce. I hope it is clear that nothing I have said is meant to convey that I am opposed to divorce. I am not. . . . [But] moralists who are doing their job must insist that the system of family obligations is only partially severed by a divorce that cuts the marital tie. Morally, as well as legally, the obligations to the children remain as they were. Legally, this is still recognized. But in a moral climate where the system of family obligation is given no more weight than can be justified in terms of popular theories of deontic volunteerism, the obligatory ties are too fragile to survive the personal estrangements that result from divorce. It is therefore to be expected that the parents (and especially the fathers) will be off and away doing their own thing. And the law is largely helpless. . . . I do not know how to make fathers ashamed of their neglect and inadvertent cruelty. What I do know is that moral philosophers ought to be paying far more attention to the social consequences of their views than they are. It is as concrete as taking care that what one says will not adversely affect the students whom one is addressing. If what students learn from us encourages social disintegration, then we are responsible for the effects that this may have on their lives and the lives of their children. It is a grave responsibility, even graver than the responsibility we take in being for or against something like euthanasia or capital punishment, since most of our students will not face that question in a practical way in their own lives. . . .

A moral philosophy that does not give proper weight to the customs and opinions of the community is presumptuous in its attitude and pernicious in its consequences. In an important sense it is not a moral philosophy at all. For it is humanly irrelevant.

REFERENCES

Blum, Lawrence. 1980. *Friendship, Altruism, and Morality*. London: Routledge and Kegan Paul.

Blustein, Jeffrey. 1982. *Parents and Children: The Ethics of the Family*. New York: Oxford University Press.

De Beauvoir, Simone. 1952. *The Second Sex*. H. M. Parshley, trans. New York: Random House.

———. 1977. "Talking to De Beauvoir." In *Spare Rib*.

Ferguson, Ann. 1977. "Androgyny as an Ideal for Human Development." In M. Vetterling-Braggin, F. Elliston, and J. English, eds. *Feminism and Philosophy*, pp. 45–69. Totowa, N.J.: Rowman and Littlefield.

Gilligan, Carol. 1982. *In a Different Voice: Psychological Theory and Women's Development*. Cambridge: Harvard University Press.

Gould, Carol 1983. "Private Rights and Public Virtues: Woman, the Family and Democracy." In Carol Gould, ed. *Beyond Domination*, pp. 3–18. Totowa, N.J.: Rowman and Allanheld.

Grimshaw, Jean. 1986. *Philosophy and Feminist Thinking*. Minneapolis: University of Minnesota Press.

Hewlett, Sylvia Ann. 1986. *A Lesser Life: The Myth of Woman's Liberation in America*. New York: Morrow.

Jagger, Allison. 1977. "On Sex Equality." In Jane English, ed. *Sex Equality*, Englewood Cliffs, N.J.: Prentice-Hall.

———. 1983. "Human Biology in Feminist Theory: Sexual Equality Reconsidered." In Gould, ed. *Beyond Domination*.

———. 1986. "Prostitution." In Marilyn Pearsell, ed. *Women and Values: Readings in Recent Feminist Philosophy*, pp. 108–21. Belmont, Calif.: Wadsworth.

Kittay, Eva, and Diana Meyers, eds. 1987. *Women and Moral Theory*. Totowa, N.J.: Rowman and Littlefield.

Melden, A. I. 1977. *Rights and Persons*. Los Angeles: University of California Press.

Noddings, Nel. 1984. *Caring: A Feminine Approach to Ethics and Moral Education*. Berkeley: University of California Press.

Nolan, R., and F. Kirkpatrick, eds. 1983. *Living Issues in Ethics*. Belmont, Calif.: Wadsworth.

Russell, Bertrand. 1929. *Marriage and Morals*. New York: Liveright.

Sommers, Christina Hoff. 1986. "Filial Morality." *Journal of Philosophy*, 8.

Thomson, Judith. 1971. "A Defense of Abortion." *Philosophy and Public Affairs*, 1.

Tooley, Michael. 1972. "Abortion and Infanticide." *Philosophy and Public Affairs*, 2.

Trebilcot, Joyce, ed. 1984. *Mothering: Essays in Feminist Theory*. Totowa, N.J.: Rowman and Allanheld.

Wasserstrom, Richard. 1980. *Philosophy and Social Issues*. Notre Dame, Ind.: University of Notre Dame Press.

Weitzman, Lenore. 1985. *The Divorce Revolution: The Unexpected Social and Economic Consequences for Women and Children in America*. New York: Free Press.

West, Rebecca. 1930. "Divorce." *London Daily Express*.

Discussion Questions

1. Discuss how Simone de Beauvoir would most likely respond to Sommers's charge that she, and feminists like her, has a distorted view of women and what women value. Which person presents the most accurate picture of the realities of motherhood? Support your answer.
2. Do you agree or disagree with Sommers that feminists don't take the real concerns of women seriously? Discuss Sommers's claim that American feminism has alienated women by denigrating motherhood and conventional feminine roles.
3. Analyze Sommers's argument that the feminist view of motherhood as a voluntary relationship, such as Judith Jarvis Thomson's (Chapter 2) contention that a pregnant woman does not bear any special responsibility toward her fetus unless she voluntarily assumes it, has lead to the progressive weakening of the family.

4. In what ways, according to Sommers, do women and men have different natures? What is your view of human nature and, in particular, the nature of women and men? Give reasons for why you accept this position.
5. Identify and analyze your own assumptions regarding gender roles at home and in the workplace. What is the source of your assumptions? Are these assumptions consistent with your view of women's and men's nature?

NANCY E. DOWD

Work and Family: The Gender Paradox and the Limitations of Discrimination Analysis in Restructuring the Workplace

Nancy Dowd is a professor of law at the University of Florida College of Law. In this reading she examines the nature and causes of the work–family conflict. Much of the conflict is based on a male work pattern which presumes that a worker has few or no family responsibilities. Dowd also discusses the effect of the liberal rhetoric of discrimination and equality on women, and working mothers in particular. She then explores the limitations of current legislation, which are intended to resolve the conflicts between family and the workplace. She concludes by suggesting that we need to seek alternative solutions to restructuring the work–family relationship.

Critical Reading Questions

1. What is the nature of the conflict between work and family? Why does this conflict exist and why does it mainly affect women?
2. What are the two levels of role conflict?
3. Why do women often report greater satisfaction from family than from work?
4. Why is Dowd critical of the "rhetoric of equality"?
5. What are the benefits and costs for both men and women of adopting egalitarian roles?
6. How does management contribute to the conflict between work and family?
7. How does the cultural assumption that work–family issues are private matters contribute to the conflict between work and family?

From *Harvard Civil Rights Civil Liberties Review,* vol. 79, 1989. Some notes have been omitted.

8. Which structural features of the workplace contribute to the work–family conflict?
9. Why does workplace reform require breaching the public/private line between work and family?
10. What does Dowd mean by the "gender paradox and the discrimination framework"?
11. How does Dowd respond to employers who defend discrimination in the workplace?
12. On what grounds does Dowd find the principle of equality and the discrimination model inadequate for reforming the workplace?
13. What steps does Dowd propose for reforming the workplace and resolving the work–family conflict?

Talk about work and family is assumed to be women's talk. It is talk about women's lives, our feelings. Talk about work and family is tied to women's entry into the workforce and the concomitant redefinition of ourselves and our roles. It is also talk about responsibility and conflict, the conflict between work and family. . . .

But talk about work and family ought not to be assumed to be only women's talk. Men are harmed and affected by the existing work–family structure. . . .

Moreover, if we accept the circumscription of "women's talk," we not only limit our perspective, but also obscure the powerful impact of factors other than gender on the structure of work and family. . . .

THE CONTEXT: THE NATURE OF WORK–FAMILY CONFLICT

The conflict between work and family responsibilities is pervasive and serious. Between one-third and one-half of working parents report nearly daily conflict between their work and family roles; this translates into one-quarter or more of the workforce. The manifestations of that conflict are complex and multi-layered. . . .

A. Levels of Conflicts

At the simplest level, the conflict between work and family is expressed as conflicts of time. While they are the easiest to identify and potentially resolve, time conflicts include some of the most intractable work–family problems. Due to the number of hours committed to work and the scheduling of work, many men and women do not have enough time for both family and wage work. . . .

For women, the time conflict is exacerbated by an overload of family and childcare work. Women's entry into the paid workforce has not led to equitable redistribution of work. Rather, the predominant pattern has been the addition of wage work to women's existing unpaid household and childcare work. While men are doing more, they are not doing much more. As one researcher observed, "Under optimal conditions, we note the wife doing five times as much domestic work as her spouse and usually more." Even if the inequity in the distribution of family work responsibilities were resolved, however, it would not alleviate the conflict in the time demands of work and family roles; it would only more equally distribute the stress. The workplace structure presumes a worker with minimal or no family work responsibilities. . . .

Even more fundamentally, family time and work time conflict due to the clash between the occupational cycle of the workplace and the life cycle of the family and individual family members. Our occupational patterns are in many respects geared to the family life of a single individual or a worker who is supported by a non-working wife. The demands are greatest and the stakes are highest at the earlier stages of one's worklife, both in professional and blue-collar occupations. . . .

This clash between occupational and family life cycles has produced starkly different patterns of labor force attachment for men and women. Women continue to fit work to families, and men vice versa. While there has been a marked decline in the stereotypical pattern of women leaving the workforce for childbearing, the presence of children nevertheless has a very strong impact on women's career patterns, even more so than marriage. In contrast to a linear, uninterrupted, upward progression which characterizes the work pattern of most men (tapering off more quickly for blue-collar men) women's career patterns have varied from the typical male pattern to patterns of interrupted and second careers. Women most often make their strongest work contribution in mid-life, whereas men hit the high point in their careers or occupations much earlier in their lives.

This clash between occupational and family life cycles is also reflected in highly gendered occupational patterns. . . .

Work–family conflict arises not only from time and life cycle clashes, but also from deep psychological stress intimately tied to views of appropriate roles. . . . The source and perpetuation of this conflict lies in the social stereotypes of appropriate roles which are embedded in institutional structures.

Role conflict operates on at least two levels. First, there is the conflict arising from the ideal roles or stereotypes for men and women, which construct very different gendered paradigms of the work–family relationship. Those roles conflict with changing concepts of marriage and parenting, and with the workplace. Second, there is the conflict arising out of the role of parent and the role of worker. The workplace culture denies that both roles can exist simultaneously, requiring any conflict between them to be buried or resolved in favor of the worker role. The workplace and the family also demand and reward different sets of values and priorities.

For each sex, the ideal relation between work and family is constructed differently, and the sense of conflict between the ideal and changing social mores is experienced differently. For women, the primary role is one of family and childrearing. It is a role that presumes dependence on a male provider. Women perceive work as presenting a conflict with parenting and family. This is so not only because it conflicts with their family role, but also because women perceive that they are judged at work not simply on their achievement, but also on their gender. Women's perception of conflict is strongly affected by social context and role models. Thus, women often report greater satisfaction from family than from work, but that is only logical, since women have largely been confined to the family sphere, and have felt more conflict with the workplace.

For men, concepts of masculinity support an entirely different work–family relationship. Men are socialized to define themselves by work and to measure their life success occupationally, as epitomized by the breadwinner or good provider role. Men feel entitled to receive emotional support for their career efforts, while they commonly fail to provide that support for their partner; some men even feel hostile or competitive with their career-oriented spouses. Despite professions of equality, men still view their career as primary.

This highly gendered construction of marital work–family roles is mirrored in the gendered construction of parenting roles. Many authors have examined our complex images of motherhood and its disfunction from reality.[15] The role of mother encourages nurturing and caregiving, but at the price of economic dependence and domination. . . .

Conversely, the image of fatherhood lacks social support for nurturing, involved parenting. The role of father is viewed almost entirely as economic. Both legal and social policies make it difficult for men to parent. Employers are less tolerant of work–family conflicts in men than women, and continue to see men as primarily breadwinners in relation to their families, an image that continues to be reinforced by women's lower earnings. . . .

This disfunction between the rhetoric of equality and the persistence of inequality is the source of role overload and role frustration. This is experienced very differently by men and women. Women most frequently experience role overload. Women see the assumption of a paid work role as a positive role expansion, but feel compelled to *add* this role to their primary family role. The attempt to be "superwoman" reflects an attempt to preserve a concept of femininity tied to dependency, not strength, that is associated with the primary family role. It also reflects women's struggle to maintain the value of nurturance within a workplace structure which does not recognize its worth and which continues to evaluate women's work role from a strongly gendered perspective. At the same time, the rhetoric of equality pushes women to adopt the male work role as a neutral role, silencing women from criticizing that role.

Men feel that they have little to gain by changing gender roles and adopting more egalitarian marital roles. While the benefits for women to enter the workforce seem clear (after all, they are simply adopting the valued male breadwinner role), the benefits of sharing family responsibilities are less clear both individually and societally. Furthermore, in order for men to truly achieve the egalitarian model, they must undergo nothing less than a reconstruction of self: "Because male power over women is central to extant views of masculinity and because wives traditionally sustained husbands" personal and work life, men in dual-career families also need to revise their sense of self. This is not a one-time task, and it is not easily accomplished."[20]

The struggle to attain less gendered, more egalitarian roles is closely related to the development of alternative role models and social supports. The choice of role models is strongly affected by so-called "environmental" factors, which include the workplace structure. "A still basic question is how men (and women) surrounded by patriarchal institutions and attitudes can survive, grow, and develop in an egalitarian . . . lifestyle."[21]. . .

A source of much work–family conflict for many employees is the attitude of their supervisors, as well as of management in general. Supervisors develop their perception of appropriate work–family roles from their own socialization, experience and the content of the workplace culture. One of the ironies of the workplace is that management reflects a work–family pattern at odds with the bulk of the workforce. The management pattern is disproportionately one of a male single-earner married to a nonworking spouse, while the predominant workforce pattern is one of dual-earners or single head of household earners. . . . It also reflects a social/cultural assumption that the work–family issues are private, not public, issues.

This ideology of work and family separation and individual responsibility means that work–family conflict is strongly felt as individual conflict. Inability to handle work and family responsibilities is viewed as an individual failure, not as a societal problem. This discourages connecting individual work–family issues to broader structural issues or to values that create or magnify the conflict. Public policy toward families has emphasized limited intervention. Such a policy stance promotes values of autonomy and self-sufficiency. Additionally, social policy has reinforced the idea that home and workplace should be treated as functionally separate and has supported a sexual division of labor.

The struggle to think of work and family *together* requires overcoming the tendency to separate the two and conceive of them as opposites, in contradiction and conflict with each other. . . .

B. Structural Features

The various levels of work–family conflict are not surprising in view of several structural features of the workplace. . . .

First, the workplace is premised upon a singular male stereotype of the employee as an economic parent and the work–family relation as one of separation. This stereotype is a standard that denies the existence of work–family conflict or presumes the accommodation of family to work. Thus, not surprisingly, the workplace is remarkably rigid and inflexible. With respect to time and schedules, most jobs require an eight hour day, a five day week, with a uniform starting and quitting time. Barely fifteen percent of all workers have the option of working a flexible schedule. . . .

That conception is one of a patriarchal family: a male wage earner in the paid workforce married to a stay-at-home female spouse who performs the unpaid housework and childcare. However, only a small minority of families, fewer than ten percent, conform to this pattern and are served by the existing benefit structure.

The great majority of families are characterized by enormous diversity and fluidity. The diversity includes single parent, blended, unmarried and homosexual families. The dominant earner patterns in the workforce are now dual-earner and single-parent/single-earner families. . . .

Yet, the workplace structure makes no allowance for this diversity, and unduly burdens the majority of families. The families most hurt by the maintenance of the patriarchal family model in the workplace are those families headed by women and minorities, and all families that are poor, which disproportionately are the families of women and minorities. . . .

BEYOND THE PARADOX: A PRELIMINARY AGENDA

Gender is one of the primary determinants of the existing work–family structure. The content and assignment of work–family roles are divided on gender lines, and limited, gendered roles of mothering, fathering and parenting are widely accepted. Gender is also present in the perpetuation of a myth of care that belies the reality of the undervaluation of care. Recognition of this mandates an agenda of reform that will take work–family restructuring beyond the paradox. The agenda must include both women's issues and gender issues: improving the status of women and exposing, analyzing and reconstructuring concepts of gender.

Getting beyond the paradox requires real equality for women in the workplace structure. We must eliminate the disadvantages based on biological difference without sacrificing the health, safety or potential for procreation of either sex. Where biological difference has been ignored by the workplace structure, resulting in disadvantage to women, the structure must change to accommodate difference. Where difference has been used as a basis to exclude women, such exclusion must not be permitted. Both insensitivity to biological difference and discriminatory attention to biological difference must be eliminated. . . .

Achieving economic equality for women will require sexual desegregation of the workplace and revaluation of women's work in conformity with its true worth. It may also require the guarantee of a minimal level of sustenance to ensure survival and choice, and a reevaluation of home and family work in market/economic terms.

Sexual desegregation of the occupational structure and within occupational structures is a particularly complex task. It requires elimination of the gender stereotypes in hiring and promotion that steer women into particular occupations and infect the evaluation process. It also requires consideration of the underlying assumptions in particular occupational progressions, which may betray male bias or other assumptions about work and family roles. . . .

The elimination of gender stereotypes and the preference for the traditional male work–family role also requires that we rethink the traditional female work–family role. At least a part of this task is to recognize and provide room for alternative work–family roles without tying them to economic devaluation or patriarchal domination. For example, the workplace structure may need to be reformed to permit women or men to follow the traditional female work–family role without the consequence of occupational limitation and economic impoverishment. An individual would be free to choose that role, with the choice not framed by learned gender constructs, but rather by factors not tied to sex or gender.

Getting beyond the paradox may also involve an entire reconstruction of the relation between work and family, a redefinition of the relationship and the creation of some new role-models or models. . . .

Essential to that exposure and analysis is revealing the pattern of dominance and hierarchy in the division of roles. The gendered structure of work and family as it currently exists is not simply a division of work and family tasks into gender complements; rather, it is a division infused with patriarchy, by the domination of the male role over the female role, by the valuing of the work role over the family role, thereby preserving male power and dominance even in the female sphere of the home. The pattern of patriarchy is accomplished by simultaneous devaluation and elevation of the female work–family role, while also requiring the separation and limitation of the male work–family role. It is essential to eliminate patriarchy if we are to have any meaningful sense of equality and liberty, freedom and choice.

Exposing and eliminating patriarchal power points to one of the greatest difficulties in getting beyond the paradox. Dealing with gender in work and family roles as they are manifested in the workplace structure is a difficult task, but it is further complicated if it is separated from the family structure. If we limit ourselves to the workplace, then arguably, it can at best be reflective of the needs of the existing family structure. There would be only partial, limited and ineffective change. To reach the family structure, however, requires breaching public/private lines, intruding into the individual and private in the name of the state. We must confront the concept of public and private, and consider individual privacy and choice.

Part of the challenge is to conceive of public policy as supportive rather than coercive or intrusive. Such a supportive public policy might encourage diversity in the rethinking and reconstruction of work–family roles, as long as those roles do not reconstitute patriarchy. Furthermore, the public/private distinction might be transcended by supporting work–family roles beyond the workplace. For example, if part of our analysis is the recognition of the devaluation of nurturing, caregiving work by separating it from the valued public sphere of work (making it difficult for those who perform such work to participate in the paid workplace while simultaneously relegating them to a position of economic and social powerlessness), then perhaps we should not merely value and permit nurturing work in the workplace, or provide flexibility to perform paid work and nurturing work at home, but rather develop a support structure for nurturing and caregiving functions that is not limited to the workplace. . . .

[C]an the project of resolving the gender paradox be accomplished through the use of discrimination law? I argue in the next section that discrimination analysis is an extremely limited tool for the project. . . .

THE GENDER PARADOX AND THE DISCRIMINATION FRAMEWORK

Existing discrimination analysis is divided between intentional or disparate treatment discrimination, and unintended or disparate impact discrimination. Very few of the conflicts between work and family responsibilities can be ascribed to conduct which would fall within intentional discrimination analysis. . . . Identifying and eliminating work–family conflict, particularly degenderization of work–family conflict, is not, then, a process of determining blame or guilt, but rather is a process of uncovering the impact of structural factors on work and family roles.

If such structural discrimination, or "unconscious" discrimination, can be reached, therefore, it is only under Title VII disparate impact analysis. Stated in its classic *Griggs*[33] formulation, disparate impact analysis provides that policies fair in form but sexually discriminatory in operation, which cannot be justified as a business necessity, are illegally discriminatory. To what extent can disparate impact analysis contribute to the resolution of the gender paradox?

One way to try to answer that question is to try to fit particular sex/gender aspects of work–family conflict within the disparate impact framework. The attempt to do so reveals the limited reach of this analysis. . . . It refracts complex work–family issues into a single image of women and biological sex, and away from the social construction of gender and the political and power issues of patriarchy.

Consider, for example, trying to deal with the assertion that the existing workplace structure incorporates a male standard by its assumption of a masculine ideal and therefore discriminates against those who do not conform to that ideal, who are disproportionately female. At the same time, try to argue that the singular male standard, based on a particular male stereotype, disadvantages both men and women who do not conform to the ideal or stereotype. Or consider the assertion that any aspect of the employment structure which imposes a hardship on parents (lack of parenting leave, lack of sick leave to care for a sick child, required overtime, required travel, long hours, etc.) disproportionately impacts on women because women disproportionately bear total or primary care responsibility for children. At the same time, try to argue that the structure reinforces gender roles for both men and women (by restraining men from being parents and women from being workers), and perhaps falls even more harshly on men (by disallowing nonconformity with gender role stereotypes). Or try to argue that the structure is discriminatory if it fails to provide an individual who is a primary caretaker with the means to meet job performance standards without detriment to the individual's parenting role or employment opportunities.

Where claims of discrimination identify disproportionate impact based on sex, they appear to fit within the disparate impact framework. . . . Yet the basis of each claim is inextricably intertwined with gender roles, not with biological determinism. At the same time, if the claim expressly raises gender issues by attempting to demonstrate the concurrent harm to both sexes from a structure premised on a single gender standard, the claim will be frustrated by the very duality of the sex/gender system. That duality is the harm to both men and women by the constrictions of gender roles reinforced by the workplace structure. Disparate impact analysis, however, rests upon demonstrating the comparative disadvantage of one sex to the other. It does not comprehend mutual disadvantage.

As a defense to a discrimination claim, an employer might argue that the disproportionate pattern results from the plaintiff's individual choice, not the employer's policy. The employer might further argue that there is no discrimination because of sex, but at best a differential employment pattern based on a different pattern of choices by the sexes. The "maleness" in the structure is tied to gender, not sex, so it is social/cultural discrimination, not sex discrimination, a value choice which is sex-linked but not sex-determined. Women are not precluded from participating in the structure except because of their socialization in and acceptance of "female" social/cultural roles. Finally, the employer would argue that the male standard disadvantages all parents, whether the parent is male or female, and therefore is not discriminatory on the basis of sex. . . .

A. Inability to Reach Structural Change

. . . Discrimination analysis is geared to providing the same opportunity for all, not the best opportunity for all. Equality as a principle has no substance or content. It merely requires that likes be treated alike but does not judge the content of the like treatment nor the nature of the structure within which treatment is given or received. It basically accepts the existing structure as a given, and accomplishes the goal of equal opportunity by minor tinkering and adjustment, removing unnecessary pieces of the structure if they have a disproportionate discriminatory effect. It can, at best, eliminate unjustified barriers; it cannot mandate a fundamental change in the structure. . . .

Since the concept of equality in discrimination analysis accepts the basic workplace structure, it also implicitly accepts the moral choices underlying that structure. It accepts the existing structure as legitimate, rather than asserting a new structure of rights or a new structure not based on rights. Also, by focusing on individual rights and the opportunity to exercise those rights, discrimination analysis obscures the potential for discrimination based upon one's group identification.

The limited structural reach of discrimination analysis is exemplified by the permit/require distinction. Under that distinction, affirmative efforts to restructure the workplace, most commonly compensatory affirmative action (which is really a bridging mechanism, not a type of permanent restructuring), are permitted as long as equality goals are justified and the extraordinary means chosen are narrowly confined. . . .

In California Federal Savings & Loan v. Guerra (*Cal. Fed.*),[34] the Court upheld the validity of the California maternity leave statute against the claim that the statute's sex-specific benefit discriminated against men. The Court reasoned that it was *permissible* for the state to enact legislation which furthered equal opportunity by ensuring that the consequences of procreation were equal between women and men by taking into account and providing for pregnancy-related disability. One week later, the Court decided in Wimberly v. Labor and Industrial Relations Commission of Missouri (*Wimberly*)[35] that a prohibition against pregnancy discrimination in the award of unemployment benefits did not *require* taking pregnancy into account in the design of benefit denials for voluntary termination of employment. The Court upheld the denial of benefits where all employees disabled by a non–work-related disability were denied benefits. The sex-specific impact of a structure based on this "gender-neutral" standard was ignored. Moreover, the recognition in

Cal. Fed. of the inequality in employment opportunity that results if the workplace structure fails to recognize both female and male reproductive roles is totally absent in *Wimberly*. . . .

As many feminist critics have noted, the effect of these analytical limitations is to preserve structures built on a "male" image or standard. The male standard is objectified as neutral and universal. All that is required is that women have the same opportunity under that standard. Similarly, if the presence of women in the workplace generates the creation of new benefits based on a female standard, it requires extending the same benefits to men. The only justification for sex-specific benefits is biological uniqueness and the necessity of minimal benefits to ensure equal opportunity. This permits the continuation of the existing structure as long as its impact is equally felt, positively or negatively, on both sexes as their biological selves.

Yet simply treating women "the same" as men means stifling any change in the concept of parenting; it also suggests that non-support is acceptable. . . .

B. Sex vs. Gender

Discrimination analysis focuses on biological sex, not socially constructed gender. The heart of work–family conflict, however, arises from the way in which the workplace is structured around powerful gender constructs. The assumption and adoption of a male standard is at the core of that structure. While discrimination analysis attacks some issues of gender, it seems profoundly ill-suited for a frontal assault on the gendered structure of the workplace.

Discrimination analysis identifies as most offensive the denial of access or opportunity on the basis of immutable attributes of biology. Accordingly, discrimination analysis is preoccupied with generalizations related to biological sex (i.e., assumptions about consequences of biology: that women are weaker, slower, etc.). Such generalizations are either untrue for all or most women; or are untrue for individual members of the class of women. . . .

While most persons agree that biological difference should not be the basis for work–family distinctions, we are not sure whether to condemn or support roles that have become associated with gender. Analytically, we have difficulty identifying the evil: is it that since there is no biological basis for the division of work and family responsibilities, any characteristic of the structure which reinforces a sexual division of those responsibilities is discriminatory? Or is it that any structure which only incorporates the male standard is discriminatory because it fails to permit the female role to exist on an equal basis, with equal consequences? It is not clear whether we can, or should, attack socially constructed concepts of male and female roles, masculinity and femininity.

This debate is related to the question of whether employers should be held responsible for societal discrimination. Specifically, to what extent should an employer be held responsible for individuals' perception of their range of employment opportunities, or for the extent to which that perception is constrained by a structure that incorporates a gendered view of who belongs in the workplace.

When discrimination analysis *has* focused on gender, it has done so primarily through an analysis of sex stereotypes. Discrimination analysis has focused on the extent to which stereotypes are "anti-individual," i.e., the fact that some individuals don't fit the stereotype (they aren't like other women or they have managed to be like men). But it is unclear how employers should treat specific men or women who fit the stereotype or gender construct. Should employers be allowed to discriminate on that basis when the effect is to adopt a sex-specific model (male) for the workplace? Should such decisions be condemned because they adopt a "male" structure, because they exclude certain individuals on the basis of socially constructed gender?

Alternatively, what is the consequence of "choosing" a gendered role, or "voluntarily" adopting such a role? For example, what is the consequence of choosing the traditional female work–family role, or of choosing traditionally female work, or the consequence of a reluctance to apply for traditionally male positions? The *Sears* case exemplifies a number of these difficulties.[39] In that case, "choice" became a defense to a statistical pattern of discrimination, while the underlying stereotype, the gendered construction of the job and the gendered constraint on choice, was not addressed. The focus of the case shifted from the employment structure and the definition of particular jobs according to a male standard to the reasons why particular employees made their choices, independent of any consideration of the structural or cultural discouragement of making those choices.

C. Issues of Power and Patriarchy

Existing discrimination analysis also fails to deal effectively with problems of power. With the possible exception of sexual harassment, discrimination analysis has not been a means to attack patriarchy. It may be a means to prevent the recreation of patriarchy if any affirmative restructuring occurs, but it seems inadequate to mandate redistribution of existing power or to change the pattern of power relations. This is tied to the structural and gender limitations of the analysis. . . .

Another limitation of discrimination analysis in reaching power issues is its individualistic emphasis. As Fran Olsen points out:

> Antidiscrimination law promotes market individualism and promises each individual woman that she can win success in the market if only she chooses to apply herself. It obscures for women the actual causes of their oppression and treats discrimination against women as an irrational and capricious departure from the normal objective operation of the market, instead of recognizing such discrimination as a pervasive aspect of our dichotomized system. The reforms reinforce free market ideology and encourage women to seek individualistic, inward-looking solutions to social problems.[40]

Rather than empowering, the discrimination framework can disempower. It puts the victim off by requiring that the individual identify as a victim, who must pinpoint the aberration from an otherwise presumably non-discriminatory structure. It ignores the relational constraints that pull against the assertion of rights. The value of the equality framework then becomes largely symbolic, . . . It does not, however, affirmatively expand the choices of potential victims.

Furthermore, commentators have argued that discrimination analysis disempowers when it is used to strike down protectionist legislation under the banner of the equality principle. The practical result of this equality approach (dropping barriers to the workplace without attacking the male bias of the structure) has been, at best, a minor improvement in the lot of most women, and at worst a sanction of the decline of women's status. Employers have gained by being able to treat women like men, rather than "as people with different needs." . . .

A final problem of discrimination analysis is the limited reach of the statutory structure across family/work and public/private divisions. The discrimination framework reinforces the work/family split by leaving family out of the analysis. There is no parallel "family discrimination" alongside employment discrimination; such a concept would breach the sphere of "private" activity. In addition, use of existing discrimination analysis ties the solutions of work–family issues to employment-related benefits, leaving other nurturers unprotected and unsupported. Finally, it reinforces the definition of work as including only paid work; discrimination analysis does not value, empower, or provide economic independence for caregivers.

THE ROLE OF DISCRIMINATION ANALYSIS

. . . The issues raised by work and family go beyond discrimination analysis, requiring not only equalizing treatment, opportunity, and access to the workplace, but also changing the structure of the workplace to include room for parenting. Even in its most expansive form, discrimination analysis is an inadequate, limited tool for restructuring the workplace, a task that requires a deconstruction of gender roles and an attack on patriarchy within family and work and within the relationship between work and family. The restructuring also reaches beyond gender issues: it is not simply a matter of adding women to work and men to family, or integrating the values of each sphere to reflect the other, but requires rethinking and changing work and family and their relationship to each other by imagining that relationship without the framework of gender.

The difficulty in envisioning a non-gendered ideal of work and family attests to the depth of gendered thinking and conceptualization of self, work, family and society. It also demonstrates the need to take gender into account in order to eliminate its predominance in work and family and prevent its reinstitutionalization. Resolving issues of work and family are essential to women's equality, in a real and meaningful sense (as opposed to the sense of formal rights and privileges), and to liberating both women and men from the limited universe of gender-prescribed roles. Work and family is also more than that—it challenges us to reexamine workers and the relation between work and family, the nature and necessity for workplace hierarchy, and the economic consequences of post-industrial capitalism.

Discrimination analysis is at best a partial means to address women's issues and gender issues, and is inadequate to define the restructuring of the workplace that work–family conflict exposes as necessary. Feminist thought contributes to both the project of resolving the gender paradox and the project of transformation: to improving women's position and exposing the anti-female, anti-family bias of the existing work–family structure. It also encourages us to promote values devalued as merely "female" in transforming the workplace and providing support for the functions of families. It begins and is grounded in the inter-woven paradoxes of work and family that are the premises which we must get beyond in order to transform the structure of work and family.

NOTES

15. A. Rich, Of Woman Born (1986); see also A. Daly, Inventing Motherhood (1983); Ruddick, Maternal Thinking, 6 Feminist Stud. 342 (1980).
20. *Id.* at 19. . . .
21. *Id.* at 16.
33. Griggs v. Duke Power Co., 401 U.S. 424 (1971).
34. 479 U.S. 272 (1987).
35. *Id.* at 511.
39. EEOC v. Sears, Roebuck & Co., 839 F.2d 302 (7th Cir. 1988).
40. Olsen, Family and Market, *supra* note 24, at 1547.

Discussion Questions

1. Discuss how a liberal feminist, such as Ruth Goenhout, would most likely respond to Dowd's claim that the principle of equality is not sufficient for reforming the workplace.
2. Compare and contrast Dowd's, Goenhout's, and Beauvoir's approach to workplace reforms for working mothers.
3. Dowd's approach represents the socialist feminist view which rejects the public/private dichotomy between work and family. Discuss whether or not Dowd does an adequate job in showing that family considerations are relevant to policy and legislation regarding the workplace.
4. Dowd maintains that both men and women are harmed by the liberal discrimination analysis based on equality and gender-neutral policies. Do you agree? Support your answer using examples.
5. Dowd's article was written before the Family Leave Act was passed. Does the Family Leave Act adequately address Dowd's concerns about the work–family conflict? Support your answer.

KATIE ROIPHE

Reckless Eyeballing: Sexual Harassment on Campus

Katie Roiphe is an author and a journalist. She argues that the current fear of rape and sexual harassment has been fueled by exaggerations of their actual incidence on campuses as well as by the rhetoric of "rape crisis feminists" such as MacKinnon and Pineau. The current broad definitions of sexual harassment and date rape used on college campuses, rather than empowering women, perpetuate stereotypes of women as both sexless and as powerless victims of male oppression.

Critical Reading Questions

1. What is the standard definition of sexual harassment? Why does Roiphe have concerns about this definition?
2. What is MacKinnon's view on sexual harassment, and what are its political implications?
3. Why does Roiphe maintain that the idea that a male student can sexually harass a female professor is insulting to women?
4. What view of men and women, according to Roiphe, is implied by the current rhetoric against sexual harassment?
5. According to Roiphe, why does such rhetoric create an atmosphere of suspicion and mistrust and reduce the number of meaningful contacts between students and faculty?
6. What does Roiphe mean by the "zookeeper school of feminism"?
7. How, according to Roiphe, do people from other countries view the concern with sexual harassment in the United States?
8. How does Roiphe explain the high incidence of sexual harassment in the United States?
9. What does Roiphe suggest women do instead of focusing so much on the dangers of sexual harassment?
10. On what grounds does Roiphe argue that "people have a right to leer" or, as she puts it, "engage in reckless eyeballing"? What, according to Roiphe, are appropriate moral responses to being leered at?
11. Where does Roiphe draw the line between harmless "harassment" and harassment that is a genuine abuse of power?
12. According to Roiphe, why might telling a woman who did not feel victimized that in fact she *was* a victim of date rape or sexual harassment actually harm rather than empower her?

"Reckless Eyeballing: Sexual Harassment on Campus," in *The Morning After: Sex, Fear, and Feminism on Campus* (Boston: Little, Brown and Co., 1993), 85–112. Some notes have been omitted.

For generations, women have talked and written and theorized about their problems with men. But theories about patriarchy tumble from abstraction when you wake up next to it in the morning. Denouncing male oppression clashes with wanting him anyhow. From playgrounds to consciousness-raising groups, from suffragette marches to pro-choice marches, women have been talking their way through this contradiction for a long time.

Sometimes my younger sister and I go out for coffee and talk about our relationships. We analyze everything: why he acts that way, how unfair this is, how we shouldn't be waiting for his call, and how we have better things to do with our time anyway. How men are always like that, and we are always like this, and our conversation goes on, endless, pleasurable, interesting, over many refills, until we go home and wait for their calls.

Heterosexual desire inevitably raises conflicts for the passionate feminist, and it's not an issue easily evaded. Sooner or later feminism has to address "the man question." But this is more than just a practical question of procreation, more than the well-worn translation of personal into political. It's also a question for the abstract, the ideological, the furthest reaches of the feminist imagination.

Charlotte Perkins Gilman, a prominent feminist writing at the turn of the century, found a fictional solution to the conflict between sex and feminism in her utopian novel, *Herland*. Her solution is simple: there is no sexual desire. . . .

Many of today's feminists, in their focus on sexual harassment, share Gilman's sexual politics. In their videos, literature, and workshops, these feminists are creating their own utopian visions of human sexuality. They imagine a world where all expressions of sexual appreciation are appreciated. They imagine a totally symmetrical universe, where people aren't stilly, rude, awkward, excessive, or confused. And if they are, they are violating the rules and are subject to disciplinary proceedings.

A Princeton pamphlet declares that "sexual harassment is unwanted sexual attention that makes a person feel uncomfortable or causes problems in school or at work, or in social settings."[1] The word "uncomfortable" echoes through all the literature on sexual harassment. The feminists concerned with this issue, then, propose the right to be comfortable as a feminist principle.

The difficulty with these rules is that, although it may infringe on the right to comfort, unwanted sexual attention is part of nature. To find wanted sexual attention, you have to give and receive a certain amount of unwanted sexual attention. Clearly, the truth is that if no one was ever allowed to risk offering unsolicited sexual attention, we would all be solitary creatures.

The category of sexual harassment, according to current campus definitions, is not confined to relationships involving power inequity. Echoing many other common definitions of sexual harassment, Princeton's pamphlet warns that "sexual harassment can occur between two people regardless of whether or not one has power over the other."[2] The weight of this definition of sexual harassment, then, falls on gender instead of status.

In current definitions of sexual harassment, there is an implication that gender is so important that it eclipses all other forms of power. The driving idea behind these rules is that gender itself is a sufficient source of power to constitute sexual harassment. Catharine MacKinnon, an early theorist of sexual harassment, writes that "situations of co-equal power—among co-workers or students or teachers—are difficult to see as examples of sexual harassment unless you have a notion of male power. I think we lie to women when we call it not power when a woman is come on to by a man who is not her employer, not her teacher."[3] With this description, MacKinnon extends the province of male power beyond that of tangible social power. She proposes using the words "sexual harassment" as a way to name what she sees as a fundamental social and political inequity between men and women. Following in this line of thought, Elizabeth Grauerholz, a sociology professor, conducted a study about instances of male students harassing their female professors, a phenomenon she calls "contrapower harassment."[4]

Recently, at the University of Michigan, a female teaching assistant almost brought a male student up on charges of sexual harassment. She was offended by an example he used in a paper about polls—a few sentences about "Dave Stud" entertaining ladies in his apartment when he receives a call from a pollster—and she showed the paper to the professor of the class. He apparently encouraged her to see the offending example as an instance of sexual harassment. She decided not to press charges, although she warned the student that the next time anything else like this happened, in writing or in person, she would not hesitate. The student wisely dropped the course. To understand how this student's paragraph about Dave Stud might sexually harass his teacher, when he has much more to lose than she does, one must recognize the deeply sexist assumptions about male-female relations behind the teaching assistant's charge.

The idea that a male student can sexually harass a female professor, overturning social and institutional hierarchy, solely on the basis of some primal or socially conditioned male power over women is insulting. The mere fact of being a man doesn't give the male student so much power that he can plow through social hierarchies, grabbing what he wants, intimidating all the cowering female faculty in his path. The assumption that female students or faculty must be protected from the sexual harassment of male peers or inferiors promotes the regrettable idea that men are natively more powerful than women.

Even if you argue, as many do, that *in this society* men are simply much more powerful than women, this is still a dangerous train of thought. It carries us someplace we don't want to be. Rules and laws based on the premise that all women need protection from all men, because they are so much weaker, serve only to reinforce the image of women as powerless.

Our female professors and high-ranking executives, our congresswomen and editors, are every bit as strong as their male counterparts. They have earned their position of authority. To declare that their authority is vulnerable to a dirty joke from someone of inferior status just because that person happens to be a man is to undermine their position. Female authority is not (and should not be seen as) so fragile that it shatters at the first sign of male sexuality. Any rules saying otherwise strip women, in the public eye, of their hard-earned authority.

Since common definitions of sexual harassment include harassment between peers, the emphasis is not on external power structures, but on inner landscapes. The boundaries are subjective, the maps subject to mood. According to the Equal Employment Opportunity Commission's definition, any conduct may be deemed sexual harassment if it "has the purpose or effect of unreasonably interfering with an individual's work or academic performance or creating an intimidating, hostile or offensive working or academic environment." The hostility or offensiveness of a working environment is naturally hard to measure by objective standards. Such vague categorization opens the issue up to the individual psyche.

The clarity of the definition of sexual harassment as a "hostile work environment" depends on a universal code of conduct, a shared idea of acceptable behavior that we just don't have. Something that makes one person feel uncomfortable may make another person feel great. At Princeton, counselors reportedly tell students, If you feel sexually harassed then chances are you were. At the university's Terrace Club, the refuge of fashionable, left-leaning, black-clad undergraduates, there is a sign supporting this view. It is downstairs, on a post next to the counter where the beer is served, often partially obscured by students talking, cigarettes in hand: "What constitutes sexual harassment or intimidating, hostile or offensive environment is to be defined by the person harassed and his/her own feelings of being threatened or compromised." This relatively common definition of sexual harassment crosses the line between being supportive and obliterating the idea of external reality.

The categories become especially complicated and slippery when sexual harassment enters the realm of the subconscious. The Princeton guide explains that "sexual harassment may result from a conscious or unconscious action, and can be subtle or blatant." Once we move into the area of the subtle and unconscious, we are no longer talking about a professor systematically exploiting power for sex. We are no longer talking about Hey, baby, sleep with me or I'll fail you. To hold people responsible for their subtle, unconscious action is to legislate thought, an ominous, not to mention difficult, prospect.

The idea of sexual harassment—and clearly when you are talking about the subtle and unconscious, you are talking about an idea—provides a blank canvas on which students can express all of the insecurities, fears and confusions about the relative sexual freedom of the college experience. Sexual harassment is everywhere: it crops up in dinner conversations and advertisements on television, all over women's magazines and editorial pages. No one can claim that Anita Hill is an unsung heroine. It makes sense that teenagers get caught up in the Anita Hill fury; they are particularly susceptible to feeling uncomfortable about sexuality, and sexual harassment offers an ideology that explains "uncomfortable" in political terms. The idea of sexual harassment displaces adolescent uneasiness onto the environment, onto professors, onto older men.

The heightened awareness of the potential for sexual encroachment creates an atmosphere of suspicion and distrust between faculty and students. Many professors follow an unwritten rule: never close the door to your office when you and a female student are inside. One professor told a male teaching assistant I know that closing the door to his office with a student inside is an invitation to charges of sexual harassment. . . .

The inflamed rhetoric against harassment implies that all women are potential victims and all men are potential harassers. "Men in the Academy," an essay in the book *Ivory Power,* vilifies the male academic so effectively that the author is forced to acknowledge that "nonetheless, not all male professors harass female students."[5] That this need even be said is evidence that this perspective is spiraling out of control.

The irony is that these open doors, and all that they symbolize, threaten to create barriers between faculty and students. In the present hypersensitive environment, caution and better judgment can lead professors to keep female students at a distance. It may be easier not to pursue friendships with female students than to risk charges of sexual harassment and misunderstood intentions. The rhetoric surrounding sexual harassment encourages a return to formal relations between faculty and students.

The university, with its emphasis on intellectual exchange, on the passionate pursuit of knowledge, with its strange hours and unworldly citizens, is theoretically an ideal space for close friendships. The flexible hours combined with the intensity of the academic world would appear to be fertile ground for connections, arguments over coffee. Recently, reading a biography of the poet John Berryman, who was also a professor at Princeton in the forties, I was struck by stories about his students crowding into his house late into the night to talk about poetry. These days, an informal invitation to a professor's house till all hours would be a breach of propriety. . . .

Feminists concerned with sexual harassment must fight for an immutable hierarchy, for interactions so cleansed of personal interest there can be no possibility of borders crossed. Although this approach to education may reduce the number of harmful connections between teachers and students, it may also reduce the number of meaningful connections. The problem with the chasm solution to faculty-student relations is that for graduate students, and even for undergraduates, connections with professors are intellectually as well as professionally important.

In an early survey of sexual harassment, a law student at Berkeley wrote that in response to fears of sexual harassment charges, "the male law school teachers ignore female students . . . this means that we are afforded [fewer] academic opportunities than male students."[6] Many male professors have confirmed that they feel more uncomfortable with female students than with male students, because of all the attention given to sexual harassment. They may not "ignore" their female students, but they keep them at arm's length. They feel freer to forge friendships with male students.

The overstringent attention given to sexual harassment on campuses breeds suspicion; it creates an environment where imaginations run wild, charges can seem to materialize out of thin air, and both faculty and students worry about a friendly lunch. The repercussions for the academic community, let alone the confused freshman, can be many and serious.

In an excessive effort to purge the university of sexual corruption, many institutions have violated the rights of the professors involved by neglecting to follow standard procedures. Since sexual harassment is a relatively recent priority, "standard procedures" are themselves new, shrouded, and shaky. Charges of sexual harassment are uncharted territory, and fairness is not necessarily the compass. . . .

The university has become so saturated with the idea of sexual harassment that it has begun to affect minute levels of communication. Like "date rape," the phrase "sexual harassment" is frequently used, and it does not apply only to extremes of human behavior. Suddenly everyday experience is filtered through the strict lens of a new sexual politics. Under fierce political scrutiny, behavior that once seemed neutral or natural enough now takes on ominous meanings. You may not even realize that you are a survivor of sexual harassment.

A student tells me that she first experienced sexual harassment when she came to college. She was at a crowded party, leaning against a wall, and a big jock came up to her, placed his hands at either side of her head, and pretended to lean against her, saying, So, baby, when are we going out? All right, he didn't touch me, she says, but he invaded my space. He had no right to do that.

She has carried this first instance of sexual harassment around in her head for six years. It is the beginning of a long list. A serious feminist now, an inhabitant of the official feminist house on campus, she recognizes this experience for what it was. She knows there is no way to punish the anonymous offender or everyone would be behind bars, but she thinks the solution is education. Like many feminists, she argues that discipline is clumsy, bureaucracy lumbering, and there is no hope for perfect justice in the university. She is more concerned with getting the message across, delineating acceptable behaviors to faculty and students alike, than in beheading professors. She subscribes to a sort of zookeeper school of feminism—training the beasts to behave within "acceptable" parameters.

Many foreigners think that concern with sexual harassment is as American as baseball, New England Puritans, and apple pie. Many feminists in other countries look on our preoccupation with sexual harassment as another sign of the self-indulgence and repression in American society. Veronique Neiertz, France's secretary of state for women's rights, has said that in the United States "the slightest wink can be misinterpreted." Her ministry's commonsense advice to women who feel harassed by coworkers is to respond with "a good slap in the face."[7]

Once sexual harassment includes someone glancing down your shirt, the meaning of the phrase has been stretched beyond recognition. The rules about unwanted sexual attention begin to seem more like etiquette than rules. Of course it would be nicer if people didn't brush against other people in a way that makes them uncomfortable. It would also be nicer if bankers didn't bang their briefcases into people on the subway at rush hour. But not nice is a different thing than against the rules, or the law. It is a different thing than oppressing women. Etiquette and politics aren't synonyms.

Susan Teres of SHARE said, at the 1992 Take Back the Night march, that 88 percent of Princeton's female students had experienced some form of sexual harassment on campus. Catharine MacKinnon writes that "only 7.8% of women in the United States are not sexually assaulted or harassed in their lifetimes."[8] No wonder. Once you cast the net so wide as to include everyone's everyday experience, identifying sexual harassment becomes a way of interpreting the sexual texture of daily life, instead of isolating individual events. Sensitivity to sexual harassment becomes a way of seeing the world, rather than a way of targeting specific contemptible behaviors. In an essay attempting to profile the quintessential sexual harasser, two feminists warn in conclusion (and in all seriousness) that "the harasser is similar, perhaps disturbingly so, to the 'average man.'"[9]

As one peruses guidelines on sexual harassment, it's clear where the average man comes in. Like most common definitions, Princeton's definition of sexual harassment includes "leering and ogling, whistling, sexual innuendo, and other suggestive or offensive or derogatory comments, humor and jokes about sex."[10] MacKinnon's statistic includes obscene phone calls. These definitions of sexual harassment sterilize the environment. They propose classrooms that are cleaner than Sesame Street and Mr. Rogers's neighborhood. Like the rhetoric about date rape, this extreme inclusiveness forces women into old roles. What message are we sending if we say We can't work if you tell dirty jokes, it upsets us, it offends us? With this severe a conception of sexual harassment, sex itself gets pushed into a dark, seamy, male domain. If we can't look at his dirty pictures because his dirty pictures upset us, it doesn't mean they vanish. It means he looks at them with a new sense of their power, their underground, forbidden, male-only value.

Instead of learning that men have no right to do these terrible things to us, we should be learning to deal with individuals with strength and confidence. If someone bothers us, we should be able to put him in his place without crying into our pillow or screaming for help or counseling. If someone stares at us, or talks dirty, or charges neutral conversation with sexual innuendo, we should not be pushed to the verge of a nervous breakdown. . . .

I would even go so far as to say that people have the right to leer at whomever they want to leer at. By offering protection to the woman against the leer, the movement against sexual harassment is curtailing her personal power. This protection implies the need to be protected. It paints her as defenseless against even the most trivial of male attentions. This protection assumes that she never ogles, leers, or makes sexual innuendos herself.

Interpreting leers and leer-type behavior as a violation is a choice. My mother tells me about the time she was walking down the street in the sixties, when skirts were short, with my older sister, who was then three. A construction worker made a comment to my mother, and my three-year-old sister leaned out of her carriage and said, "Hey, mister, leave my mother alone." My mother, never the conventional sort of feminist, told my sister that the construction worker wasn't hurting her, he was giving her a compliment.

Although my mother's reaction may not be everyone's, this is a parable about individual responses. There is spectrum of reactions to something like a leer. Some may be flattered, others distressed; some won't notice, and still others, according to some feminist literature, will be enraged and incapacitated. In its propaganda the movement against sexual harassment places absolute value on the leer. According to its rules, whatever that construction worker said to my mother was violating, harmful, and demeaning. According to its rules, my three-year-old sister was right. By rallying institutional authority behind its point of view, by distributing these pamphlets that say leering always makes women feel violated, this movement propels women backward to a time when sexual attention was universally thought to offend. They are saying, as Catharine MacKinnon neatly summarizes it, that "all women live in sexual objectification the way fish live in water."[11] But I think it depends on where you learned to swim.

History offers an example of another time when looks could be crimes, but today feminists don't talk much about what happened to black men accused of "reckless eyeballing," that is, directing sexual glances at white women. Black men were lynched for a previous incarnation of "sexual harassment." As late as 1955, a black man was lynched for whistling at a white woman. Beneath the Jim Crow law about reckless eyeballing was the assumption that white women were the property of white men, and a look too hard or too long in their direction was a flouting of white power. Reckless eyeballing was a symbolic violation of white women's virtue. That virtue, that division between white women and black men, was important to the southern hierarchy. While of course lynchings and Jim Crow are not the current danger, it's important to remember that protecting women against the stray male gaze has not always served a social good. We should learn the lessons: looks can't kill, and we are nobody's property.

All of this is not to suggest that abuses of power are not wrong. They are. Any professor who trades grades for sex and uses this power as a forceful tool of seduction deserves to face charges. The same would be true if he traded grades for a thousand dollars. I'm not opposed to stamping out corruption; I only think it's important to look before you stamp. Rules about harassment should be less vague, and inclusive. They should sharply target serious offenses and abuses of power rather than environments that are "uncomfortable," rather than a stray professor looking down a shirt. The university's rules should not be based on the idea of female students who are pure and naïve, who don't harbor sexualities of their own, who don't seduce, or who can't defend themselves against the nonconditional sexual interests of male faculty and students. . . .

As feminists interested in the issue themselves argue, "Many have difficulty recognizing their experience as victimization. It is helpful to use the words that fit the experience, validating the depths of the survivor's feelings and allowing her to feel her experience was serious."[12] In other words, these feminists recognize that if you don't tell the victim that she's a victim, she may sail through the experience without fully grasping the gravity of her humiliation. She may get through without all that trauma and counseling. Buried within this description of helping students overcome the problem of "recognizing their experience as victimization" is the nagging concern that the problem may pass unnoticed, may dissolve without political scrutiny. To create awareness is sometimes to create a problem.

Education about sexual harassment is not confined to the space of freshman week. As sexual harassment is absorbed into public discussion, it enters grade schools as easily as colleges. An article in *New York* magazine documents the trickle-down effect: "After her first week at a reputable private school in Manhattan, 8-year-old Alexandra didn't want to go back. A 9-year-old boy had been harassing her: 'He said he wanted to hump me.' She wasn't sure what 'hump' meant."[13]

The article describes what happened when Alexandra discovered the name for her traumatic experience. She was listening to Anita Hill's testimony on the radio when she suddenly exclaimed: "'That's what happened to me! He didn't touch me, but his words upset me!'" The article concludes that "Alexandra's first lesson in sexual harassment may not be her last, but thanks to her parents, who listened to her, believed her and supported her, she'll at least be better prepared to deal with sexual abuse than the women and men of Anita Hill's generation."[14] As Alexandra grows up, will she be better able to deal with sexual abuse, or will she just see it everywhere she looks? Will she blur the line between childish teasing and sexual abuse for the rest of her life? The prospect of a maturing generation of Alexandras, sensitized from childhood to the issue of sexual harassment, is not necessarily desirable from the feminist point of view. As Joan Didion wrote in the sixties, certain segments of the women's movement can breed "women too sensitive for the difficulties of adult life, women unequipped for reality, and grasping at the movement as a rationale for denying that reality."[15]

Responding to sexual harassment in its most expansive definition purges the environment of the difficult, the uncomfortable, and the even mildly distasteful. Feminists concerned with sexual harassment reproduce their own version of Charlotte Perkins Gilman's *Herland,* based on the absence of messy sexual desire. Although it takes some imaginative leaps to get there, their version of Herland is a land without dirty jokes, leers, and other instances of "unwanted sexual attention." Whether or not visions of a universe free from "sexual harassment" are practical, the question becomes whether they're even desirable.

Mary Koss, author of the *Ms.* magazine survey of rape, writes that "experiencing sexual harassment transforms women into victims and changes their lives."[16] Koss sees this transformation into victimhood as something caused by sexual harassment, an external event. In Koss's paradigm, after the student has been harassed, her confidence is perilously shaken, her ability to function and trust men disrupted forever. She sees the "lecherous professor" as the agent of transformation. She does not see that it is her entire conceptual framework—her kind of rhetoric, her kind of interpretation—that transforms perfectly stable women into hysterical, sobbing victims. If there is any transforming to be done, it is to transform everyday experience back into everyday experience.

NOTES

1. "What You Should Know About Sexual Harassment." Princeton, N.J.: SHARE.
2. Ibid.
3. Catharine MacKinnon, *Feminism Unmodified* (Cambridge: Harvard University Press, 1987), 89.
4. *Chronicle of Higher Education,* 24 April 1991.
5. Sue Rosenberg Zalk, "Men in the Academy." In M. Paludi (ed.), *Ivory Power: Sexual Harassment*

on Campus (Albany, NY: State University of New York, 1990), pp. 142–175.

6. "Sexual Harassment: A Hidden Issue." Washington, D.C.: Project on the Status and Education of Women, 1978.
7. *New York Times,* 3 May 1992.
8. MacKinnon, *Toward a Feminist Theory of the State* (Cambridge: Harvard University Press, 1989), 127.
9. Louise Fitzgerald and Lauren Weitzman, "Men Who Harass: Speculation and Data," in Paludi, 139.
10. Princeton, N.J.: SHARE.
11. MacKinnon, *Toward a Feminist Theory of the State,* 149.
12. Kathryn Quina, "The Victimization of Women," in Paludi, ed., 99.
13. *New York,* 16 November 1992.
14. Ibid.
15. Joan Didion, *The White Album* (New York: Farrar, Straus and Giroux, 1979), 116.
16. Mary Koss, "Changed Lives: The Psychological Impact of Sexual Harassment," in Paludi, ed., 73.

Discussion Questions

1. Discuss whether Roiphe believes that the current rhetoric on sexual harassment does more harm than good.
2. What does Roiphe mean when she says that broad definitions of sexual harassment "sterilize the environment"? Do you agree? Support your answers using examples from your campus.
3. Do you agree with the definition of sexual harassment now in common use? If so, explain why. If not, come up with a definition of sexual harassment that overcomes some of the problems in the current definition cited by Roiphe.
4. Do you agree with Roiphe that people have a right to leer? What are some of the pros and cons of including leering under the definition of sexual harassment? Support your answers. Discuss how a liberal feminist might respond. Discuss how Beauvoir might respond to these questions.
5. Discuss Roiphe's claim that feminists such as Pineau who tell victims of date rape that they have been "traumatized" are actually perpetuating the old ethos of female victimhood and contributing to the institutionalization of female weakness.
6. Discuss whether Roiphe adequately addresses the problem of sexual harassment as sexual discrimination and a violation of the right to equal opportunity. Does sexual harassment, even though it may not directly harm a particular woman, create a hostile working or academic environment which, in turn, limits women's opportunities and freedom? Support your answer.
7. Does sexual harassment violate Kant's categorical imperative? Support your answer. If so, discuss what policy should be adopted on your campus for dealing with it.

STEVEN GOLDBERG

Male Aggression and the Attainment of Power, Authority, and Status

Steven Goldberg is chairman of the department of sociology of City College at the City University of New York (CUNY). Goldberg rejects the feminist argument that male dominance oppresses women. Male dominance and female submissiveness, Goldberg argues, are not simply the product of socialization and discrimination, but are rooted in inherent biological differences. Women are doomed by their biology to fail in their attempt to attain equality with men in achieving positions of power, authority, and status.

Critical Reading Questions

1. According to Goldberg, what are some of the inherent differences between men and women? What is the significance of these differences for society?
2. What is the primary difference between men and women, according to Goldberg?
3. What explanation does Goldberg give for patriarchy and higher-status roles for men?
4. According to Goldberg, in what sort of society are the biological differences between men and women most likely to be given free play? How does Goldberg support his argument?
5. How does Goldberg respond to the feminist argument that men's greater power and status is a product of socialization rather than biological differences?
6. How does Goldberg support his argument that society should socialize women for maternal and nurturing roles and away from the roles that men attain through aggression? Why would socializing both girls and boys to compete in the job market or for positions of authority disadvantage women?
7. Would it be desirable, in Goldberg's view, if men and women achieved equality in positions of high authority?
8. How does Goldberg explain the discrepancy between women holding 51 percent of the vote and men holding almost all the positions of high authority in government? How does his explanation differ from that of feminists?
9. How does Goldberg explain what feminists view as the oppression of women?
10. According to Goldberg, why are men more successful than women in attaining desirable positions and roles in society? Why is it difficult for even aggressive women to achieve the same goals as men?
11. Why, according to Goldberg, is patriarchy inevitable?

"Male Aggression and the Attainment of Power, Authority, and Status," in *The Inevitability of Patriarchy* (New York: William Morrow & Co., 1973), 103–114. Notes have been omitted.

IF MALE AGGRESSION WERE THE ONLY DIFFERENCE . . .

Having discussed the universality of patriarchy, male dominance, and male attainment of high-status roles and the biological factors that are relevant to these universals, we are now prepared to examine the mechanisms that *require* these biological factors to be manifested in these social institutions. In discussing these mechanisms we shall proceed as if the only inherent difference between men and women were their different hormonal systems, which leads to an inherent aggression advantage for the male. This does not imply that I doubt that there are positive female biological forces underlying the woman's extraordinary sensitivity and emotional powers or the mother's attentiveness to her infant and her protective reaction to her infant's vulnerability. . . . Such biological imperatives would have enormous significance in the development of male and female roles. Every society must care for its young and, if the need to care for and protect the young is greater in the female than the male, this would be reflected in the social expectations of men and women. If one accepts this female biological factor, he could utilize it to explain the universal sex-role differences I explain by differences in aggression and could use the same lines of reasoning I do without mentioning aggression. Likewise it is not unlikely that the neural factors underlying the male's sexual dominance come into play in social contacts between men and women; there may even be a female desire for men to dominate ("take the lead") that is a secondary manifestation of the neural factors directly relevant to female sexuality. Biological evidence indicates that there is a strong possibility that such dominance and submission factors exist in male and female physiologies, but, since such factors need not exist for the theory presented here to be correct, we will assume that they do not exist. If they do exist, of course, the theory presented here can be only strengthened.

Quite possibly all of these factors lead to the universal institutions we have discussed. *Aggression, however, is the only sexual difference that we can explain with direct (as opposed to convincing, but hypothetical) biological evidence.* Nothing is lost because the inevitable social manifestations of sexual differences in aggression are sufficient to explain the inevitability of patriarchy, male dominance, and male attainment of high-status roles. If the other biological directives do exist we have an example of a situation in which a factor (hormonal aggression) is *sufficient* to describe a reality (institutionalized sex differences), but not *necessary*. Maternal attentiveness, a male need to dominate, or a female desire for male political dominance would be sufficient even if there were no hormonal aggression differences, but none of these need exist for the theory proposed here to be correct.

Therefore, *we are assuming throughout this chapter that there are no differences between men and women except in the hormonal system that renders the man more aggressive.* This alone would explain patriarchy, male dominance, and male attainment of high-status roles; for the male hormonal system gives men an insuperable "head start" toward attaining those roles which any society associates with leadership or high status as long as the roles are not ones that males are biologically incapable of filling.

AGGRESSION AND ATTAINMENT . . .

As we shall see, this aggression "advantage" can be most manifested and can most enable men to reap status rewards *not* in those relatively homogeneous, collectivist primitive societies in which both male and female must play similar economic roles if the society is to survive or in the monarchy (which guarantees an occasional female leader); this biological factor will be given freest play in the complex, relatively individualistic, bureaucratic, democratic society which, of necessity, must emphasize organizational authority and in which social mobility is relatively free of traditional barriers to advancement. There were more female heads of state in the first two-thirds of the sixteenth century than in the first two-thirds of the twentieth.

The mechanisms involved here are easily seen if we examine any roles that males have attained by channeling their aggression toward such attainment. We will assume for now that equivalent women could *perform* the tasks of roles as well as men if they could attain the roles. Here we can speak of the corporation president, the union leader, the governor, the chairman of an association, or any other role or position for which aggression is a precondition for attainment. Now the environmentalist and the feminist will say that the fact that all such roles are nearly always filled by men is attributable not to male aggression but to the fact that women have not been allowed to enter the competitive race to attain these positions, that they have been told that these positions are in male areas, and that girls are socialized away from competing with boys in general. Women *are* socialized in this way, but again we must ask why. If innate male aggression has nothing to do with male attainment of positions of authority and status in the political, academic, scientific, or financial spheres, if aggression has nothing to do with the reasons why *every* society socializes girls away from those areas which are given high status and away from competition in general, then why is it never the *girls* in any society who are socialized toward these areas, why is it never the nonbiological roles played by women that have high status, why is it always boys who are told to compete, and why do women never "force" men into the low-status, nonmaternal roles that women play in every society?

These questions pose no problem if we acknowledge a male aggression that enables men to attain any nonbiological role given high status by any society. . . . Now I have no doubt that there is a biological factor that gives women the desire to emphasize maternal and nurturance roles, but the point here is that we can accept the feminist assumption that there is no female propensity of this sort and still see that a society must socialize women away from roles that men will attain through their aggression. For if women did not develop an alternative set of criteria for success their sense of their own competence would suffer intolerably. It is undeniable that the resulting different values and expectations that are attached to men and women will tend to work against the aggressive woman while they work for the man who is no more aggressive. But this is the unavoidable result of the fact that most men are more aggressive than most women so that this woman, who is as aggressive as the average man, but more aggressive than most women, is an exception. Furthermore, even if the sense of competence of each sex did not necessitate society's attaching to each sex values and expectations based on those qualities possessed by each sex, observation of the majority of each sex by the population would "automatically" lead to these values and expectations being attached to men and women.

SOCIALIZATION'S CONFORMATION TO BIOLOGICAL REALITY

Socialization is the process by which society prepares children for adulthood. The way in which its goals conform to the reality of biology is seen quite clearly when we consider the method in which testosterone generates male aggression (testosterone's serially developing nature). . . . The fetal alteration of the boy's brain by the testosterone that was generated by his testes has probably left him far more sensitive to the aggression-related properties of the testosterone that is present during boyhood than the girl, who did not receive such alteration. But let us for the moment assume that this is not the case. This does not at all reduce the importance of the hormonal factor. For even if the boy is more aggressive than the girl only because the society allows him to be, the boy's socialization still flows from society's acknowledging biological reality. Let us consider what would happen if girls have the same innate aggression as boys and if a society did not socialize girls away from aggressive competitions. Perhaps half of the third-grade baseball team would be female. As many girls as boys would frame their expectations in masculine values and girls would develop not their feminine abilities but their masculine ones. During adolescence, however, the same assertion of the male chromosomal program that causes the boys to grow beards raises their testosterone level, and their potential for aggression, to a level far above that of the adolescent woman. If society did not teach young girls that beating boys at competitions was unfeminine (behavior inappropriate for a woman), if it did not socialize them away from the political and economic areas in which aggression leads to attainment, these girls would grow into adulthood with self-images based not on succeeding in areas for which biology has left them better prepared than men, but on competitions that most women could not win. If women did not develop feminine qualities as girls (assuming that such qualities do not spring automatically from female biology) then they would be forced to deal with the world in the aggressive terms of men. They would lose every source of power their feminine abilities now give them and they would gain nothing. . . .

DISCRIMINATION OF A SORT

If one is convinced that sexual biology gives the male an advantage in aggression, competitiveness, and dominance, but he does not believe that it engenders in men and women different propensities, cognitive aptitudes, and modes of perception, and if he considers it discrimination when male aggression leads to attainment of position even when aggression is not relevant to the task to be performed, then the unavoidable conclusion is that discrimination so defined is unavoidable. Even if one is convinced . . . that the differing biological substrates that underlie the mental apparatus of men and women *do* engender different propensities, cognitive aptitudes, and modes of perception, he will probably agree that the relevance of this to male attainment of male roles is small when compared to the importance of male biological aggression to attainment. Innate tendencies to specific aptitudes *would* indicate that at any given level of competence there will be more men than women or vice versa (depending on the qualities relevant to the task) and that the very best will, in all probability, come from the sex whose potentials are relevant to the task. Nonetheless, drastic sexual differences in occupational and authority roles reflect male aggression and society's acknowledgment of it far more than they do differences in aptitudes, yet they are still inevitable.

In addition, even if artificial means were used to place large numbers of women in authority positions, it is doubtful that stability could be maintained. Even in our present male bureaucracies problems arise whenever a subordinate is more aggressive than his superior and, if the more aggressive executive is not allowed to rise in the bureaucracy, delicate psychological adjustments must be made. Such adjustments are also necessary when a male bureaucrat has a female superior. When such situations are rare exceptions adjustments can be made without any great instability occurring, particularly if the woman in the superior position complements her aggression with sensitivity and femininity. It would seem likely, however, that if women shared equally in power at each level of the bureaucracy, chaos would result for two reasons. Even if we consider the bureaucracy as a closed system, the excess of male aggression would soon manifest itself either in men moving quickly up the hierarchy or in a male refusal to acknowledge female authority. But a bureaucracy is not a closed system, and the discrepancy between male dominance in private life and bureaucratic female dominance (from the point of view of the male whose superior is a woman) would soon engender chaos. Consider that even the present minute minority of women in high authority positions expend enormous amounts of energy trying *not* to project the commanding authority that is seen as the mark of a good male executive. It is true that the manner in which aggression is manifested will be affected by the values of the society in general and the nature of the field of competition in particular; aggression in an academic environment is camouflaged far more than in the executive arena. While a desire for control and power and a single-mindedness of purpose are no doubt relevant, here aggression is not easily defined. One might inject the theoretical argument that women could attain positions of authority and leadership by countering the male's advantage in aggression with feminine abilities. Perhaps, but the equivalents of the executive positions in every area of suprafamilial life in every society have been attained by men, and there seems no reason to believe that, suddenly, feminine means will be capable of neutralizing male aggression in these areas. And, in any case, an emphasis on feminine abilities is hardly what the feminists desire. All of this can be seen in a considerably more optimistic light, from the point of view of most women, if one considers that the biological abilities possessed only by women are complemented by biologically generated propensities directing women to roles that can be filled only by women. But it is still the same picture.

FIFTY-ONE PERCENT OF THE VOTE

Likewise, one who predicates political action on a belief that a society is oppressive until half of the positions of authority are filled by women faces the insuperable task of overcoming a male dominance that has forced every political and economic system to conform to it and that may be maintained as much by the refusal of women to elect widespread female leadership as by male aggression and ability. No doubt an exceptional configuration of factors will someday result in a woman's being elected president, but if one considers a society "sexist" until it no longer associates authority primarily with men and until a woman leader is no longer an exception, then he must resign himself to the certainty that all societies will be "sexist" forever. Feminists make much of the fact that women constitute a slight majority of voters but in doing so make the assumption that it is possible to convince the women who constitute this majority to elect equal female leadership. This is a dubious assumption since the members of a society will inevitably associate authority with males if patriarchy and male dominance are biologically inevitable. It would be even more dubious if there is an innate tendency for women to favor men who "take the lead." However, proceeding from this assumption and assuming that the feminists were successful, it is a sure bet that democracy—which obviously is not biologically inevitable (not patriarchy, which is)—would be eliminated as large numbers of males battled for the relatively small numbers of positions of power from which the rules that govern the battle are made. In any real society, of course, women can have the crucial effect of mobilizing political power to achieve particular goals and of electing those men who are motivated by relatively more life-sustaining values than other men just as mothers have the crucial effect of coloring and humanizing the values of future male leaders.

"OPPRESSION"

All of this indicates that the theoretical model that conceives of male success in attaining positions of status, authority, and leadership as *oppression* of the female is incorrect if only because it sees male aggressive energies as *directed toward* females and sees the institutional mechanisms that flow from the fact of male aggression as *directed toward* "oppressing" women. In reality these male energies are directed toward attainment of desired positions and toward succeeding in whatever areas a particular society considers important. The fact that women lose out in these competitions, so that the sex-role expectations of a society would have to become different for men and women even if they were not different for other reasons, is an inevitable byproduct of the reality of the male's aggression advantage and not the cause, purpose, or primary function of it. In other words, men who attain the more desired roles and positions do so because they channel their aggression advantage toward such attainment; whether the losers in such competitions are other men or women is important only in that—because so few women succeed in these competitions—the society will attach different expectations to men and women (making it more difficult for the exceptional, aggressive, woman to attain such positions even when her aggression is equal to that of the average man). Perhaps one could at least begin to defend a model that stressed "oppression" if he dealt only with male dominance in dyadic relationships; here male energies are directed toward the female, but to call that which is inevitable "oppression" would seem to confuse more than clarify and, if one feels that male dominance is "oppressive," this model offers an illusory hope of change where there is no possibility of change. Male dominance is the emotional resolution (felt by both the man and the woman) of the difference between a man and a woman in the biological factors relevant to aggression; male authority in dyadic relationships, and the socialization of boys and girls toward this male authority, is societal conformation to this biological difference and a result of society's attempting to most smoothly and effectively utilize this difference. Note that all that I say in this paragraph—indeed, in this book—accepts the feminist assumption that women do not follow their own biologically generated imperatives, which are eternally different from those of men. I do this in an attempt to show the inadequacy of the feminist model and not because it is less than ludicrous to suppose that women do not hear their own drummer. This book does not pretend to explain female behavior, but merely to show that women would have to behave as they do if they were nothing more than less aggressive men. If one reversed the feminist model he could view the desire of the vast majority of women to have children as oppressing men by succeeding in an area in which men are doomed by their biology to fail. Such a theoretical model leaves much to be desired.

Discussion Questions

1. Do you agree with Goldberg that patriarchy is inevitable? Does civilization require patriarchy? Support your answers. Discuss how Dowd might respond to Goldberg's argument.
2. Goldberg assumes that civilization depends on aggressive competition for positions of status and power. Do you agree that civilization is incompatible with feminist goals? If so, is civilization, as we now know it, desirable? Can civilization be grounded in cooperation rather than competition? Support your answers.
3. Even if men are naturally aggressive and dominating, as Goldberg claims, does this justify patriarchy, or should this "instinct" be rechanneled toward "objects" other than women or even repressed? Discuss whether pornography and/or prostitution are morally acceptable means for rechanneling it? Support your answers.
4. Discuss how Goldberg would explain the prevalence of date rape and sexual harassment on college campuses. What solution might he offer to these problems? Do you agree with this solution? Support your answers.
5. Discuss what Goldberg's position would most likely be on affirmative action for women as well as what sort of college curriculum and admissions program he might propose. Would he be in favor of coed colleges or would he recommend gender-segregated colleges? Should men and women be funneled into different majors?
6. Nicholas Davidson, author of *The Failure of Feminism,* maintains "Feminism is a failure as an explanation for male psychology and behavior . . . feminism makes all relations with men difficult, and good relations virtually impossible."[32] Do you agree? Would Goldberg? Support your answers. Discuss how Beauvoir, Groenhout, and Roiphe might each respond to Davidson's criticism of modern feminism.

CASE STUDIES

1. LIFE IMITATING ART: SEX-STEREOTYPES IN THE MEDIA

When it comes to the regulation of media that objectifies women and portrays them as subordinate, feminists focus primarily on adult pornography. However, their efforts may be coming too late. Research shows that children have already formed their sex-role stereotypes by the age of seven. Television and movies, in particular, exert a strong influence on children's perception of gender roles.[33] There is significantly lower sex-role stereotyping in children who are exposed to nontraditional gender roles in the media.[34]

However, these shows are the exception. In most children's shows females are portrayed in passive roles, such as housewives, waitresses, and secretaries. Males are portrayed in active roles such as doctor, detective, or commanders. Even television shows for very young children promote sex stereotyping. *Teletubbies* and *Barney & Friends,* for example, while opening up the range of acceptable behavior for boys, reinforce sex stereotypes for girls.[35]

Discussion Questions

1. Are children's shows that portray females in passive, subordinate roles, and males as active problem-solvers, a type of sex discrimination that harms girls and women? Should these shows be censored or regulated and, if so, by whom? Or do television producers have a liberty right to televise children's shows as they see fit? How would a utilitarian and liberal feminist such as John Stuart Mill most likely answer these questions? Support your answers.
2. Discuss how Catherine MacKinnon (Chapter 8) would most likely approach the issue of children's programming if she were responsible for regulating it.
3. What would Simone de Beauvoir most likely think of the portrayal of women in the media, if she were alive today? Does the media reinforce the role of women as Other and, if so, how? Support your answers.
4. Feminist Mary Daly contends that the Madonna, which is presented as the ideal woman by the Church, demeans women by portraying the ideal as passive and only in relation to men (son and father).[36] But what about women heroines in the contemporary media? When women play a lead role, they are generally gorgeous, thin, and young. Discuss the effects of this image of successful women on women's sense of self as well as their views on aging.
5. Magazine covers often show women who fit our cultural stereotypes. For example, in the 1910s, when feminists were demanding suffrage, magazine covers portrayed women as "bad" and a threat to men and the social structure. In the politically conservative 1950s images of Doris Day were popular.[37] What stereotypes of women are portrayed in contemporary magazines? How do these stereotypes shape the way women think of themselves and men think of women? Do magazine publishers have a moral obligation to present a fair view of women and to avoid the use of stereotypes? How would a radical feminist most likely answer this question? Support your answers.

---

2. MOTHERHOOD, SURROGACY, AND SAME-SEX PARENTS

Lesbian and gay parenting are changing our ideas about motherhood and sex roles. Ellen and Lisha Karpay-Brody of Sacramento, California had been partners for two years when they decided they wanted a baby. The great majority of lesbian couples who have babies use artificial insemination. However, in these cases only the woman who carries the baby is legally the parent. The Karpay-Brodys wanted the child to belong to both of them, biologically and legally. One of Lisha's eggs was removed and fertilized with donor sperm, and then implanted in Ellen. Ellen gave birth to a daughter, Sadie Margaret. A Superior Court judge ruled that both women were the "natural" parents to the child.[38]

Gay men who want to father a child have the option of using a surrogate mother. Juan and Michael, who were living in a civil union for several years, made an agreement through a lawyer to pay a woman, Melissa, $20,000 to be a surrogate mother. Both men donated their sperm so neither would know (unless they had the child genetically tested) who the father was. Nine months later Melissa, the surrogate mother, gave birth to a boy. When Juan and Michael went to pick up the baby at the hospital she refused to turn over the child. Juan and Michael took the case to court.

Discussion Questions

1. Psychologist Peggy Drexler contends that same-sex parenting, donor insemination, and surrogate pregnancies show that the terms "mother" and "father" are often archaic.[39] Do you agree? Support your answer.
2. Randy Thomasson, executive director of Campaigning for California Families, opposes parental rights for same-sex parents, arguing that "We have children who are being used as guinea pigs for those who want to blow apart the institutions of marriage and parenthood, institutions that have been respected for centuries." Discuss his response in light of the two above scenarios.
3. Studies of homosexual parents show that rather than adopting the traditional sex roles of heterosexual couples, they create their own parenting roles and distribute "responsibilities based on what suits their characters and temperaments, and what's best for their kids."[40] Is it important for children to have an actual mother and father and, if so, why? Discuss how Sommers would most likely respond to these studies.
4. Who in the case of Melissa, Juan, and Michael is/are the parent(s)? Who should get custody of the baby? Support your reasoning.
5. In 1987 William Stern was given custody of Baby M over the protest of the surrogate mother Mary Beth Whitehead, who had been paid $10,000 to bear Mr. Stern's child. Some feminists protested the court's decision to give preference to the biological father (Stern) over the biological and gestational mother (Whitehead). Surrogate arrangements, they argued, reduce women to wombs for rent. In addition, they do not take into consideration the strong bond a birth mother might feel for her child. Other feminists maintain that Whitehead had signed a contract to give up the child at birth and should have stuck to it. Discuss the merits of both arguments. What position would Beauvoir most likely support? How about a liberal feminist?

---

3. LILLIAN GARLAND: PREGNANCY LEAVE AND THE WORKPLACE

Lillian Garland was employed as a receptionist by the California Savings and Loan Co. in Los Angeles. Her difficult pregnancy required that she take several months of leave in 1982. When she tried to return to work after four months leave she expected her job to have been protected by a California law that granted unpaid pregnancy disability leave. However, there was no job awaiting her. She sued her employer for not giving her maternity leave. Her employer argued that unpaid job-protection maternity laws discriminated against men.

Feminist groups such as NOW and the National Women's Political Caucus filed amicus briefs siding with the employer in the court hearing, arguing for "equal treatment" as opposed to "special treatment" for pregnancy. They contended that pregnancy should be treated just like any other disability. Since men are not given disability leave for pregnancy, neither should pregnant women get disability leave. The federal court ruled with the employer and struck down the California law.

The case was taken to the U.S. Supreme Court where in 1987 in *California Savings and Loan v. Guerra* (1987), the U.S. Supreme Court overturned the earlier ruling and upheld the California law granting unpaid pregnancy disability leave.

Discussion Questions

1. Discuss the liberal feminist position that equality requires that laws be gender-neutral and that maternity leave laws violate the principle of equality.
2. Liberal feminists maintain that "special treatment" for women demeans women. However, there are longstanding laws that require employees to give leave to military reservists and people called for military duty. At the time the laws were enacted only men could serve in the military. Analyze the arguments for and against special treatment in light of this example and special treatment for pregnant women.
3. The current Family and Medical Leave Act applies equally to fathers and mothers. Is this fair, given that many women need to use part of their twelve-week leave prior to the birth of the child?
4. Does the Family and Medical Leave Act discriminate against poor people and single mothers, given that unpaid maternity leave is out of the question for many of them? If so, how should pregnancy and parental leave be structured?
5. Liberal feminists maintain that treating women as "special" demeans women and impedes equal employment opportunities for them. Others regard the gender-neutral approach and the classification of pregnancy as a disability offensive. Women are not just like men. Pregnancy, they argue, is a natural, normal role performed only by women. This difference should be taken into account in laws affecting the workplace. Do you agree? Support your answer. Discuss the merits of the "equal treatment" and the "special treatment" approaches.
6. The level of support in the United States for pregnancy and childrearing is sharply below that of world standards. Almost all industrialized nations provide medical coverage and paid job leave, sometimes up to twelve months, for maternity and parenting. Discuss the merits of the two approaches.

---

4. PAULA JONES VERSUS THE PRESIDENT

In 1994 Paula Jones filed three civil charges against President Clinton alleging sexual harassment during a 1991 encounter at a hotel in Little Rock, Arkansas. At the time of the alleged incident, Clinton was governor of Arkansas and Jones a state employee. Although Jones claimed that the harassment affected her civil rights by affecting her job, her employment records show that she received the usual promotions and raises following the alleged incident. Jones also claimed that Clinton's behavior was so outrageous that it caused her serious emotional harm.

On April 1, 1998, U.S. District Judge Susan Wright Webber dismissed Jones's charges. Judge Webber based her decision on Jones's inability to prove that Clinton exposed himself and asked for oral sex. Judge Webber stated, "Although the governor's alleged conduct, if true, may certainly be characterized as boorish and offensive, even a most charitable reading of the record in the case fails to reveal a basis for a claim of sexual assault."[41]

The dismissal followed months of sensational charges of sexual misconduct by the president. Jones's lawyers appealed the decision. In December 1998, while the appeal was being heard, Clinton agreed to make a cash settlement to Jones, who then dropped the appeal.

Discussion Questions

1. Do you agree with Judge Webber's ruling? Support your answer. Discuss how MacKinnon and Roiphe might each respond to the ruling.
2. In the early 1990s a Massachusetts judge ruled that an election campaign collage, in which a male candidate distributed photocopies of the female opponent's face pasted on top of photographs of nude and seminude women in lewd positions, constitued sexual harassment and, therefore, could be legally prohibited. Do you agree with the judge's ruling that this was a case of sexual harassment? Is the ruling a violation of freedom of speech? If not, should all attempts to degrade opponents in election campaigns be prohibited, or only those based on gender stereotypes? Support your answers. How might Groenhout and MacKinnon respond to these questions?
3. A group of women who worked at Stroh's Beer brought a lawsuit against the company, claiming sexual harassment on the basis of the sexist television ads used by Stroh's to sell its product. They argued that the sexist ads and the behavior of the male employees are connected, creating a hostile work environment for female employees. Do advertisements, calendars, and other graphic material that portray women as sex objects constitute sexual harassment? Support your answers. Discuss how Roiphe would respond to this question.
4. Is sexual harassment a problem on your campus? If so, why? How should women such as Paula Jones respond to sexual harassment in the workplace or on college campuses? Use specific examples to illustrate your answers.
5. Is sexual harassment inevitable if women insist on competing with men in schools and in the workplace? Discuss how Goldberg might respond to this question. What solution would he most likely propose to the problem of sexual harassment?

---

5. THE MILITARY CULTURE OF SEXUAL HARASSMENT

Only since 1976 have women integrated into the once all-male bastion of the military academy. However, many women drop out of the academies and the military because of sexual harassment. For example, Private Sarah Tolaro and four other enlisted women from the Army base at Fort Mead, one of whom had wanted to make the Army her career, all left the Army because of sexual harassment. When Tolaro told someone about the harassment she was told to drop it and "not to make waves." In fact, one of the other women from Fort Mead, rather than make an issue of sexual harassment, accepted the Army's claim—"inability to cope with military life"—as the official reason for her leaving the Army.[42]

Most female cadets who are sexually harassed and assaulted do not report the incident because of fear of reprisal, of not being taken seriously, or of being blamed for the assault. Male cadets sometimes use sexual blackmail or "lesbian bating" to force a women to go along with his sexual demands. Women who refuse to comply are reported to the authorities as being lesbians. Charges of lesbianism, whether substantiated or not, are the single most effective weapon is driving women out of the military. In 1989 the discharge rate, based on charges of homosexuality, was ten times greater for women than it was for men.[43]

In 2003 six former cadets from the United States Air Force Academy at Colorado Springs decided to go public with their stories of sexual harassment and assault. The Air Force officials initially played down the complaints as the result of a few "bad apples." However, a survey administrated by the Defense Department to check the validity of the women's claims of widespread sexual harassment in the academy revealed that 70 percent of the 579 women surveyed had been sexually harassed, and nearly 12 percent of the women who graduated from the Air Force Academy in 2003 were the victims of rape or attempted rape during their four years.[44] The same situation has since been documented in the Navy and Army.

Discussion Questions

1. Female and male cadets are housed together in the same barracks. One of the changes the Air Force Academy is doing to cut down on the incidence of sexual harassment and assault is to move women so their rooms are clustered near the women's bathrooms. Discuss moral issues raised by this policy. What would a liberal feminist and a radical feminist most likely think about this policy?
2. Discuss what type of policy would Katie Roiphe most likely recommend for dealing with sexual harassment in the military.
3. Women in the military are expected to dress like men and act like men. What would Ruddick most likely think about women, especially mothers, in the military?
4. In the military and in war masculinity is defined in part by sexual performance and conquest. Discuss how Goldberg and Roiphe might each address this phenomenon and what each would think about women as soldiers in combat.
5. Seventeen percent of female college students report being subjected to sexual harassment by an instructor.[45] Does this reinforce women's sense of powerless? Discuss the implications of this finding on the quality of women's education and self-confidence.

---

6. ANOREXIA NERVOSA AND BULIMIA: THE TYRANNY OF THINNESS

The myths that the female body and female sexuality are evil contributes to another type of violence against women's bodies: anorexia nervosa and bulimia. These two disorders, which were rare twenty-five years ago, have reached epidemic proportions today. According to the National Eating Disorders Screening Program, in 2001 more than five million Americans had eating disorders, including 15 percent of young women. About one hundred women die each year of anorexia nervosa.[46] In addition, an estimated 12 to 33 percent of college women are bulimic.[47]

Anorectics and bulimics strive to avoid all bodily contact. Both hunger and sexuality are disgusting and dirty. Anorectics and bulimics associate staying thin with being androgynous and, hence, not being a "temptation" to men. In fact, many victims of anorexia have been sexually abused as children.

In her book *Starving for Attention* (1982) Cherry Boone O'Neill describes her battle with bulimia. After her first romantic involvement, which never went beyond kissing, O'Neill wrote: "I feel secretive, deceptive, and . . . tainted by the ongoing relationship." Because sexuality and hunger are psychically connected, romantic encounters can bring on bingeing. O'Neill describes a late binge, eating scraps of leftovers from the dog's dish after spending the evening with her boyfriend:

> I started slowly, relishing the flavor and texture of each marvelous bite. Soon I was ripping the meager remains from the bones, stuffing the meat into my mouth as fast as I could detach it.
>
> [Her boyfriend surprises her, with a look of "total disgust" on his face.]
>
> I had been caught red-handed . . . in an animalistic orgy on the floor, in the dark, alone. Here was the horrid truth for Dan to see. I felt so evil, so tainted, pagan. . . . In Dan's mind that day, I had been whoring after food.[48]

Whereas men are associated with the mind, women are associated with the body. In a society that degrades women, the body becomes alien—a cage or prison. The body is the enemy and an impediment to reason. Thinness is the triumph of mind over body. The ultimate goal of anorectics is to become completely free from their bodies by never having to eat again.

Discussion Questions

1. Discuss how myths about women contribute to anorexia and bulimia. Are these myths generally accepted on your campus? If so, discuss what steps might be taken to counteract these myths.
2. Philosophical views, rather than being merely abstract ideas, have real-life consequences. Philosophers have traditionally associated women with the body and men with the mind. Discuss how this division, along with a degraded view of women, has contributed to women's negative views about their bodies.
3. In the scenario described by O'Neill, her boyfriend reacts with disgust to her gorging. She, in turn, perceives what she has done as "whoring after food." Discuss how these reactions reflect and reinforce negative societal views about women and their supposedly seductive and out-of-control sexuality.
4. The greatest fear of women today is not of a nuclear holocaust or environmental catastrophe, but of getting fat. In a recent survey, adults were asked what they feared most in the world; almost 40 percent replied, "Getting fat." Discuss how, if at all, sexism in the media contributes to this fear.
5. Do you have a moral obligation to try to help friends who are anorexic or bulimic? If so, what is the basis of this obligation? Imagine a situation in which a friend who is anorexic or bulimic comes to you for help. Discuss what you might say to her.

CHAPTER 11

War and Terrorism

On the morning of September 11, 2001 the world watched in stunned horror the televised terrorist attacks on the World Trade Center in New York. Approximately 3,000 people died in the attacks on the World Trade Center, 184 in the attack on the Pentagon, and 40 passengers and crew members in the hijacked plane that went down in Shanksville, Pennsylvania. In addition, nineteen hijackers were killed in the four plane crashes. Following the attacks, President George W. Bush declared war on terrorism and launched a military campaign against Afghanistan's Taliban government and the Afghan-based terrorist organization *al Qaida,* which was held responsible for the attacks on the World Trade Center.

BACKGROUND

The September 11 attack and our response to it raise several moral issues. Is terrorism ever morally justified? Is it morally acceptable to target noncombatants? What is the morally proper response to terrorism? Are preemptive wars or wars of aggression ever morally acceptable? What means should a government use to protect its citizens from attack or threats of attack? Do the benefits accrued by war outweigh the harms of war?

Although there are apparently some societies, such as the Eskimos, who have no term for war and have never engaged in warfare, the human resort to war has been a fact of life in most organized states (including tribal states). Indeed, some philosophers, such as Thomas Hobbes and Elizabeth Anscombe, argue that war is necessary for the survival of a civil society.

The advent of the modern state and nationalism following the European Renaissance increased the scale of war. The nineteenth century witnessed efforts to put an end to war through international peace movements and plans to organize nations to ensure peace. After World War I further abolitionists sought to control war through the formation of the League of Nations. Despite some initial hope for international peace and cooperation, the wars of the twentieth century dwarfed all previous wars in terms of their destructiveness and the number of people involved in the wars. In the twentieth century 191 million people were killed either directly or indirectly by war. Half of these people were civilians. World War I claimed 15 million lives, and World War II another 27 million lives. The United Nations (UN) was established in 1945 to promote world peace and justice. However, this objective was not achieved, possibly because of the UN's lack of judicial and enforcement power. Since the end of World War II there were more than 400 wars. Worldwide, wars now kill about 1.6 million people a year. In addition, many millions more die of starvation and other war-related causes, or are maimed or forced to relocate.[1]

War involves the use of armed violence between nations or between competing political factions within a nation to achieve a political purpose. *Guerrilla war* involves ambush and surprise and is generally carried out against an occupying force, as in the American Revolution and the Vietnam War.

Motives for war include self-defense against aggression or threat of aggression, the desire to expand one's territory either directly or indirectly in terms of control of markets and resources, and ideological/religious motives. The concept of a holy war emerged in the Christian tradition during the Crusades and is found today among certain Islamic groups. Most wars have mixed motives. For example, the current war on terrorism is a war in response to the threat of aggression that also has ideological/religious undertones in it that are portrayed by both sides as a war of good against evil with each side claiming to be doing God's will.

Terrorism involves the use of politically motivated violence to target noncombatants and create intimidation. In his reading, Robinson Grover discusses the issues associated with the increase in international high-tech terrorism. Terrorism can be sponsored by non-state groups, such as the PLO-sponsored suicide bombings in Israel and the September 11 terrorists, or it can be state sponsored as in the Israeli bombing of Palestinian refugee camps. The line between war and terrorism is imprecise. Terrorism can be used as a strategy in the context of a war, such as when the United States dropped nuclear bombs on Hiroshima and Nagasaki during World War II. Terrorism can be domestic, as was the case in the 1995 bombing of the Federal Building in Oklahoma City. Or it can be international as in the case of September 11, 2001. Terrorism is most often used by groups that lack the power to engage in conventional warfare. It is usually indirect and avoids direct confrontation with enemy military forces.

The Islamic term *jihad,* often defined as a holy war, is more broadly defined as an "effort." This effort includes first of all the notion of the "greater *jihad*" or the struggle against one's own internal problems or inner evil, and secondly the struggle against injustice in society or the world. As with the Christian interpretation of Jesus's teachings, some Muslims understand *jihad* as peaceful and nonviolent, whereas other Muslims interpret it as permitting, and perhaps even requiring, war against external enemies. Islamic views on war and peace are discussed in greater detail in the reading by Sohail H. Hashmi.

THE PHILOSOPHERS ON WAR AND TERRORISM

Christian natural law theory has had a major impact on contemporary thinking about the morality of war. In his *Summa Theologica,* Thomas Aquinas (1225–1274) argues that while we should strive toward peace, monarchs have a duty to defend the state. He lists three conditions that must be met for a war to be just: The war must be waged by a legitimate authority, the cause should be just, and the belligerents should have the right intentions. The just-war tradition is discussed in more detail in the following section.

Italian renaissance political thinker Niccolò Machiavelli (1469–1527) maintained that a powerful military was essential for political independence. His position on the ethics of war is often referred to as "realism" in military circles. In his work *The Prince,* Machiavelli counsels rulers to disregard whether their actions will be considered virtuous or vicious, and instead to do whatever is necessary to achieve success in battle quickly and efficiently. Not surprisingly, *The Prince* has been called a handbook for tyrants. Machiavelli was part of the ethical debate on war up until World War II, when the rise of tyrants like Hitler and the advent of nuclear weapons that could obliterate life on this planet made his by-any-means-necessary ideas too dangerous as guidelines for war. In the reading on "Peace and Security," found at the end of this chapter, Jonathan Granoff argues that this Machiavellian philosophy of war is still part of our national security policy and poses a threat to global survival.

Like Aquinas, Dutch statesman and philosopher Hugo Grotius (1583–1645) believed that there should be limits on war. War should only be fought to enforce rights and it should be fought within the limits of law and good faith. Grotius's belief that war should only be fought in the cause of international interests, such as human rights and maintenance of peace, is found in the Charter of the United Nations.

English philosopher Thomas Hobbes (1588–1679) was born prematurely when his mother heard about the approaching Spanish Armada. "Fear and I were born twins," he said to emphasize his conviction that fear of death and the need for security are the psychological underpinnings of civilization. Hobbes believed that although humans have the ability to reason, we are naturally selfish. In a state of nature violence would be the norm and life would be "mean, brutish, and short." The answer to this unpleasant situation is the formation of a civil society to contain human violence. In civil society the authority to use violence is transferred to the sovereign whose power is absolute. "The Sovereign," writes Hobbes in the *Leviathan,* "[has] the Right of making Warre and Peace with other Nations, and Commonwealths; that is to say, of Judging when it is for the publique good."[2]

Although Hobbes argued for absolute sovereigns as a hedge against war, in fact, nations with totalitarian governments seem more susceptible to civil war than democratic governments. Furthermore, even though the formation of commonwealths resolves the problem of constant violence within societies, without an international government the collection of commonwealths still exist in a state of nature. Indeed Hobbes himself believed that nothing short of a world government with a monopoly of power over all nations would be sufficient to ensure peace. In his reading, Grover points out that with globalization we now live in a state of international anarchy.

Prominent Arab historian and philosopher Ibn Khaldun (1332–1406) likewise believed that war is a universal and inevitable part of human existence. This view is also found in the *Koran* and the *sunna* (the practice of Muhammad), both of which hold a prominent place in Muslim ethical/legal discussions about the ethics of war and peace. According to the *Koran,* man's nature is to live in a state of harmony and peace with other living beings. True peace is not just the absence of war, but surrendering to Allah's will and living in accord with his laws. Similar to Christian just-war theory, the prophet Muhammad (c.570–632) taught that the use of force should be avoided except as a last resort. However, given human capacity for choice we are all capable of being tempted by evil and disobeying Allah's will. Consequently the *Koran* gives permission to Muslims to fight against a wrongful aggressor.

THE SUMMA THEOLOGICA, PART II, QUESTION 40

Of War . . .
First Article

Whether It Is Always Sinful to Wage War?

. . . In order for a war to be just, three things are necessary. First, the authority of the sovereign by whose command the war is to be waged. For it is not the business of a private individual to declare war, because he can seek for redress of his rights from the tribunal of his superior. . . . And as the care of the common weal is committed to those who are in authority, it is their business to watch over the common weal of the city, kingdom or province subject to them. And just as it is lawful for them to have recourse to the sword in defending that common weal against internal disturbances, when they punish evil-doers, according to the words of the Apostle (Rom. xiii, 4): *He heareth not the sword in vain: for he is God's minister, an avenger to execute wrath upon him that doth evil;* so too, it is their business to have recourse to the sword of war in defending the common weal against external enemies. Hence it is said to those who are in authority (Ps. lxxxi. 4): *Rescue the poor: and deliver the needy out of the hand of the sinner;* and for this reason Augustine says (*Contra Faust.* xxii. 75): *The natural order conducive to peace among mortals demands that the power to declare and counsel war should be in the hands of those who hold the supreme authority.*

Secondly, a just cause is required, namely that those who are attacked, should be attacked because they deserve it on account of some fault. Wherefore Augustine says (*QQ. in Hept.*, qu. x, *super Jos.*): *A just war is wont to be described as one that avenges wrongs, when a nation or state has to be punished, for refusing to make amends for the wrongs inflicted by its subjects, or to restore what it has seized unjustly.*

Thirdly, it is necessary that the belligerents should have a rightful intention, so that they intend the advancement of good, or the avoidance of evil. Hence Augustine says (*De Verb. Dom.*): *True religion looks upon as peaceful those wars that are waged not for motives of aggrandizement, or cruelty, but with the object of securing peace, of punishing evil-doers, and of uplifting the good.* For it may happen that the war is declared by the legitimate authority, and for a just cause, and yet be rendered unlawful through a wicked intention. Hence Augustine says (*Contra Faust.* xxii. 74): *The passion for inflicting harm, the cruel thirst for vengeance, an unpacific and relentless spirit, the fever of revolt, the lust of power, and such like things, all these are rightly condemned in war.*

In his essay "Perpetual Peace" Immanuel Kant (1724–1804) writes that although "the desire of every nation is to establish an enduring peace [nature] uses two means to prevent people from intermingling and to separate them, differences in languages and differences in religion, which do indeed dispose men to mutual hatred and to pretexts for war." He proposed the creation of a European confederation of states and also believed that the maintenance of peace requires the establishment of constitutional government, rather than autocracy.

Unlike Kant, Friedrich Nietzsche (1844–1900) glorified war and the dangerous life. "A good war hallows every cause," wrote Nietzsche in *Thus Spake Zarathustra.* War, he believed, is a natural activity for the *ubermensch* or "superman." Nietzsche despised Christian morality that makes a virtue out of submissiveness and turning the other cheek. Nietzsche's philosophy was adopted by some Nazi intellectuals to justify Adolph Hitler's war on the Jews.

Utilitarians such as Jeremy Bentham and John Stuart Mill provided much of the philosophical background for the peace movement in the nineteenth century. War is immoral because it causes pain and diminishes happiness. Because of this, another means must be found for resolving international conflicts.

British philosopher and mathematician Bertrand Russell (1872–1970) maintained that the utter destructiveness of modern war, including the threat of nuclear war, was one of the best arguments against war. Russell also believed that a world state, which would be imposed on all nations, was the only measure that would ensure lasting peace.

THE JUST-WAR TRADITION

Just-war theories provide an alternative to total war. Just-war theory is not a single theory but an evolving framework that seeks to define what is meant by a just war. Theories of just war are found in both Western and non-Western, religious, and secular ethics. In their readings in this chapter Coady and Hashmi both examine the just-war tradition, Coady from a Western philosophical tradition and Hashmi from the perspective of Islamic ethics. The just-war tradition addresses the questions of *jus ad bellum* (the right to go to war), and *jus in bello* (the just conduct of war).

Jus ad bellum

Jus ad bellum states that the following conditions should be met before going to war:

1. War must be declared and waged by a legitimate authority.
2. There must be a just cause for going to war.
3. War must be the last resort.
4. There must be a reasonable prospect of success.
5. The violence used must be proportional to the wrong being resisted.[3]

While these conditions seem to be reasonable in theory, it can be difficult to determine if they are being satisfied. For example, what is meant by a legitimate authority? The Hobbesian belief that the only legitimate authority is an absolute sovereignty is no longer accepted. Today people are more likely to question the legitimacy of an absolute sovereign and regard democratically elected governments as more legitimate. The idea of legitimate authority also raises the question of whether governments are the only legitimate authorities. The United Nations recognizes the right of self-determination of groups of people as well as states. Do groups of disenfranchised people, such as the American colonists who waged war against the British, constitute a legitimate authority?

Also, what constitutes a just cause? Does a perceived threat from another country justify a preemptive strike against that country? President Bush reserved the right to make

CHARTER OF THE UNITED NATIONS

Chapter I, Purposes and Principles

Article 1

The Purposes of the United Nations are:

1. To maintain international peace and security, and to that end: to take effective collective measures for the prevention and removal of threats to the peace, and for the suppression of acts of aggression or other breaches of the peace, and to bring about by peaceful means, and in conformity with the principles of justice and international law, adjustment or settlement of international disputes or situations which might lead to a breach of the peace;
2. To develop friendly relations among nations based on respect for the principle of equal rights and self-determination of peoples, and to take other appropriate measures to strengthen universal peace;
3. To achieve international co-operation in solving international problems of an economic, social, cultural, or humanitarian character, and in promoting and encouraging respect for human rights and for fundamental freedoms for all without distinction as to race, sex, language, or religion; and
4. To be a centre for harmonizing the actions of nations in the attainment of these common ends.

Article 2

The Organization and its Members, in pursuit of the Purposes stated in Article 1, shall act in accordance with the following Principles. . . .

3. All Members shall settle their international disputes by peaceful means in such a manner that international peace and security, and justice, are not endangered.
4. All Members shall refrain in their international relations from the threat or use of force against the territorial integrity or political independence of any state, or in any other manner inconsistent with the Purposes of the United Nations.

a preemptive strike against any nation he perceived as a threat, even though that nation had not taken any aggressive action against us. This type of preemptive strike is sometimes called a preventative strike. Is this consistent with the requirements of *jus ad bellum?* If so, would India be justified in a preventative strike against Pakistan (or visa versa), or would the Arab nations be justified attacking Israel and perhaps the United States?

How does one know that we have tried all other options before going to war? According to pacifists, there are always nonviolent alternatives to war, including nonviolent resistance toward an occupying force. And how does one determine if the prospect for

Chapter VII, Action With Respect to Threats to the Peace, Breaches of the Peace, and Acts of Aggression

Article 39

The Security Council shall determine the existence of any threat to the peace, breach of the peace, or act of aggression and shall make recommendations, or decide what measures shall be taken in accordance with Articles 41 and 42, to maintain or restore international peace and security.

Article 41

The Security Council may decide what measures not involving the use of armed force are to be employed to give effect to its decisions, and it may call upon the Members of the United Nations to apply such measures. These may include complete or partial interruption of economic relations and of rail, sea, air, postal, telegraphic, radio, and other means of communication, and the severance of diplomatic relations.

Article 42

Should the Security Council consider that measures provided for in Article 41 would be inadequate or have proved to be inadequate, it may take such action by air, sea, or land forces as may be necessary to maintain or restore international peace and security. Such action may include demonstrations, blockade, and other operations by air, sea, or land forces of Members of the United Nations.

Article 51

Nothing in the present Charter shall impair the inherent right of individual or collective self-defence if an armed attack occurs against a Member of the United Nations, until the Security Council has taken measures necessary to maintain international peace and security. Measures taken by Members in the exercise of this right of self-defence shall be immediately reported to the Security Council and shall not in any way affect the authority and responsibility of the Security Council under the present Charter to take at any time such action as it deems necessary in order to maintain or restore international peace and security.

success is reasonable? When the U.S. and British forces invaded Iraq in March 2002 they felt confident that they had an excellent prospect of quick success. Yet more than two years later the war, despite Coalition occupation of Iraq, was still going on. Remember that few reasonable people thought the American colonists could win a war against the British Empire.

Finally, how do we determine what is proportional? Was the destruction of thousands of civilian lives in the atomic bombings of Hiroshima and Nagasaki worth the possible loss of American military lives in an invasion of Japan? What about the scatter bombing of German cities by the Allied forces in World War II?

Jus in bello

For a war to be conducted justly the following two conditions should be met:

1. Noncombatants should not be intentionally targeted.
2. The tactics used must be a proportional response to the injury being redressed.

It is possible for a justly waged war to be fought unjustly. For example, even though World War II was a just war from the perspective of the Allies, some people maintain that the scatter bombing of German cities by the Allies and the dropping of nuclear bombs on Japan violated both principles of *jus in bello.* The My Lai Massacre in the Vietnam War also violated the principle of noncombatant immunity. In this incident American soldiers entered a Vietnam village and found only women, children, and old men. Frustrated that the male combatants had managed to escape, Lieutenant William Calley ordered his soldiers to open fire on the villagers.

Noncombatants include those who are not agents in directing aggression or carrying it out. However, in modern warfare the line between noncombatants and combatants tends to be blurred. Even children can be drawn into war as combatants, as happened in Vietnam and is currently happening in some of the civil wars in Africa. Also, is it fair to hold individual soldiers responsible in countries where young people are forcibly conscripted into military service? Indeed, the politicians who launch the wars rarely serve on the front lines. Furthermore, is it just to kill enemy combatants who do not pose a direct threat to our lives, as in the case of the bombing of retreating Iraqi soldiers during the First Gulf War? What about the manufacturers of weapons? Should we treat those who work in weapons factories as enemy combatants?

Just-war tradition does not give adequate guidance on who should serve as combatants. Is conscription, or the draft, morally acceptable? What about the conscription of women, especially mothers (and fathers) of young children? The just-war tradition also does not give sufficient guidance on what constitutes acceptable treatment of prisoners of war or enemy combatants, an issue addressed by David Luban in his reading in this chapter.

In addition, the just-war tradition does not adequately address *jus ante bellum,* or justice after war. Is occupation of a defeated nation or territory morally acceptable and, if so, under what circumstances? To what extent is it just for the victor to attempt to change the political system and culture of the occupied country? Do countries have a moral obligation following a war to make restitution to civilians harmed by war?

WEAPONS OF MASS DESTRUCTION

Unlike conventional weapons, weapons of mass destruction (WMD), such as nuclear, chemical, and biological weapons, indiscriminately target both combatants and noncombatants. In the years following World War II nuclear weapons were used as a deterrent by the United States and the Soviet Union. The reasoning behind deterrence is that the consequences of retaliation would be so catastrophic that neither side would risk a first strike with nuclear weapons.

With the end of the cold war, instead of disarming, the threat of global nuclear war between the two superpowers was replaced by the proliferation of nuclear weapons throughout the world and concerns about the use of nuclear weapons by terrorist groups. Between 1940 and 1996 the United States spent nearly $5.5 trillion on nuclear weapons and weapons-related programs.[4] In 1996 the Clinton administration issued a directive making nuclear weapons the cornerstone of the U.S. strategic defense. This was later expanded to include biological weapons. In 2002 President Bush rejected the long-standing commitment of the United States not to use nuclear weapons in a first strike or against non-nuclear nations.

The United States currently has more than 10,000 fully deliverable nuclear bombs. In addition, the number of countries and possibly international terrorist groups as well, who have nuclear weapons or the capacity to produce them is increasing. In an interview with a Pakistani journalist in November 2001, Osama bin Laden stated, "if America used chemical or nuclear weapons against us, then we may retort with chemical and nuclear weapons. We have the weapons as deterrent." It is estimated that Israel has at least 100 nuclear warheads, while India and Pakistan have about 20 warheads each. Arab nations are particularly concerned about Israel's arsenal of nuclear weapons, whereas Israel is concerned about the possibility that Iran and other Arab nations may be producing nuclear weapons and other WMD.[5]

Chemical and biological weapons have been around much longer than nuclear weapons. During the French and Indian War the British gave small-pox-infected blankets to the Delaware Indians. Anthrax and mustard gas were both used by the Germans in World War I. The use, though not the production and possession, of chemical and biological weapons was prohibited by the 1925 Geneva Convention. Despite the prohibition, thousands of people died as a result of Soviet chemical and biological weapons that were used in Afghanistan, Laos, and Cambodia. Saddam Hussein also used chemical weapons against the Kurds in Northern Iraq. In 1995 sarin, a nerve gas, was released in a Tokyo subway.

Today more countries have biological weapons programs than at any other time in history. Unlike the production of nuclear weapons which requires expensive facilities and highly enriched uranium, biological agents for use in terrorism can be obtained from natural outbreaks or laboratories. Also, the same technology can have both peacetime and military applications.

Biological and chemical weapons are sometimes called "the poor man's atomic bomb" because their construction is much cheaper and their effects can be just as devastating. In addition, recent developments in biotechnology and genetic engineering have made it possible to produce biological agents that have greater resistance to detection and treatment. More that 140,000,000 people fly into the United States from foreign countries every year.[6] It takes up to two weeks for the symptoms of a contagious disease contracted in another country or on a plane to appear, which gives potential terrorists ample time to go into hiding. Even now the perpetrators of the deadly mail anthrax attacks on Washington and elsewhere in the United States are still unknown.

PACIFISM AND CONSCRIPTION

There are different types of pacifism. *Absolute pacifists* believe that all violence is wrong, even for self-defense. This position has been criticized for being contradictory since it assumes a right not to be attacked, but not the right of self-defense in order to defend that right.[7] In addition, critics argue, it is immoral and irresponsible not to allow countries to defend their citizens against aggression. Some pacifists get around these objections by maintaining that while they have a duty not to meet force with force, this is a *supererogatory duty* (morality that goes beyond what is normally required) and not one that is binding on all people. Other pacifists oppose violence except for self-defense and may even participate, though generally not as combatants, in a war of self-defense.

The absolute pacifist maintains that pacifism is not about rights, but about respect for persons, including the enemy, and the recognition of a common humanity.[8] Pacifists, consequently, actively seek peaceful alternatives to war. Indian political activist Mohandas "Mahatma" Gandhi (1869–1948) opposed all war and advocated nonviolent resistance (*satyagraha*) as a response to violence and oppression. *Satyagraha* is not passive "nonviolence," but a skill. It is a method of unconditional love (*ahimsa*) in action. Peace in not simply the absence of war but the presence of justice and the practice of *ahimsa.* Although Islamic ethics do not support pacifism, the prophet Muhammad encouraged the use of nonviolent responses to aggression when appropriate. In her article, Elizabeth Anscombe rejects pacifism as a morally untenable position and argues that the *Bible* does permit and even requires war in some instances. She also notes that it is in the context of conscription that pacifism becomes a public issue.

Conscription, or enforced military service, raises issues of justice as well as freedom of conscience. The first national draft in the United States was during the Civil War. However, there was a proviso that allowed a person drafted to buy a substitute for $300 (about a year's wages). The burden this placed on poorer families set off one of the worst riots in U.S. history. The draft was reinstated in World War I. Sixteen million young American men were conscripted between 1917 and the end of the Vietnam War in 1973. In World War II there were an estimated 37,000 conscientious objectors and 200,000 in the Vietnam War.[9]

The military defines *conscientious objection* (CO) as "opposition to war, in any form, based on a moral, religious, or ethical code." In addition to proving they are sincere in their opposition to all wars (no easy task), a conscientious objector still must go through boot camp, although not weapons training, and then be assigned to some sort of civilian duty after the training. Only a small percentage of people who apply for CO status receive it. Some objectors choose to engage in civil disobedience and go to prison. In Israel, which has conscription, more than 250 conscientious objectors have served time in prison since September 2000 for refusing to serve in the army. These figures include members of the *Yesh Gvul,* a group of Israeli soldiers who refused to fight in the occupied territories in Palestine.

Other conscientious objectors choose to leave the country or go into the military but refuse to fire on the enemy. Sometimes people become conscientious objectors after joining the military and experiencing war. According to a survey conducted by the U.S. military at the end of World War II, up to 75 percent of soldiers in some of the units refused to fire on the enemy or fired their weapons into the air.[10]

Although the Selective Service System still exists and young men are required to register with it within a month of their eighteenth birthday, conscription was abolished in the United States after the Vietnam War. Although a bill was introduced in Congress in December 2001 to reinstate the draft, there is currently little support for it from the Pentagon or the private sector.

The primary moral argument against conscription or the draft is based on autonomy. The draft, which puts the draftee at risk for death or permanent disability, is a violation of a person's liberty rights. In addition, conscription is too expensive in terms of money and damage to the morale of young people. On the other hand, the voluntary army is made up disproportionately of poorer people and people of color. Indeed, one of the complaints of the current voluntary system is that military recruiters tend to target poor youth in urban centers—the so-called "poverty draft."[11]

Arguments for the draft focus on social justice and equality. A draft without deferments would contribute to social equality. Opponents of the draft disagree, noting that equality was not promoted when the draft existed. They claim that a universal draft will accomplish only the indoctrination of draftees into nationalistic and militaristic attitudes. In addition, the draft discriminates against men. To be fair, women would also be required to register with the Selective Service System and be eligible for conscription.

MORAL ISSUES

Respect for Persons

Pacifists argue that war is incompatible with the moral imperative to treat persons as ends-in-themselves, never as a means only. War, by dividing groups of people into us and the enemy, dehumanizes the so-called enemy and creates an us versus them/good versus evil mentality. Depersonalization diminishes respect for enemy combatants as well as civilians. For example, despite our claim that civilians in enemy countries are innocent, their deaths as "collateral damages" are not given the moral weight of deaths of American combatants. Jonathan Granoff also notes that war violates the principle of reciprocity or Golden Rule, which is based on respect for persons. On the other hand those who support the just-war theory, such as Thomas Aquinas, Elizabeth Anscombe, and C.A.J. Coady, point out that for a government to stand by and not defend its citizens against an aggressive attack involves not taking the personhood and security of their citizens seriously.

Rights

In the military, autonomy is restricted for the sake of the greater good. This is particularly evident in conscription, where one's duty of fidelity to one's country is seen as overriding a person's liberty rights. War raises the issue of the rights of political communities as well. Hobbes regarded the right to security and freedom from violence as one of the most basic rights of citizens and the primary purpose of the social contract. This right entails the right of a state to defend itself against attack. Whether or not this can be achieved through nonviolent means, as absolute pacifists claim, is open to debate. The right to a preemptive strike is generally regarded as an extension of the right to self-defense. However, how great and how imminent does the threat need to be to justify a preemptive strike? Was the 2002 invasion of Iraq morally justified on the grounds of self-defense?

The Universal Declaration of Human Rights, which was adopted by the General Assembly of the United Nations in 1948, and subsequent international human rights laws protect the rights of all people. Noncombatants have a right to life and a basic standard of living. The rights of noncombatants are also acknowledged in just-war theories. In addition, prisoners of war have a right to decent treatment under international law. However, many nations continue to violate these basic human rights.

The United States refused to adopt international human rights law, based on the belief that U.S. law provides adequate protection of human rights. The rights of more than 600 "enemy combatants" being held by the United States government at Guantanamo Bay in Cuba as part of President Bush's war on terrorism raises questions about the adequacy of this policy. The U.S. Supreme Court in 2004 will hear cases on behalf of some of the Guantanamo prisoners. The U.S.A. Patriot Act, which was passed soon after September 11, and the targeting of over 5,000 Arabs and Muslims for detention and questioning also has serious implications for the protection of human rights. The U.S. government justifies these policies on the grounds of national security, arguing that the positive right of U.S. citizens to security outweighs the liberty rights of potential terrorists. In contrast, two-thirds of Americans feel that it is important to preserve civil liberties in the fight against terrorism.[12] In his reading, Luban argues that the war on terrorism may be seriously eroding international human rights.

Consequentialism and Nonmaleficence

The restriction on rights and the harms associated with war are generally justified as a means of preserving the greater good of society. However, is war the most utilitarian means to preserve beneficial ends such as our freedom, culture, and standard of living? Some pacifists regard occupation and passive resistance to the occupying force as morally preferable to war. However, one can't count on an occupying force to be minimally decent Samaritans.

Utilitarians such as Bentham and Mill, although not pacifists, were opposed to war because of the grievous harms associated with war. According to the World Health Organization, war is one of the leading public health issues of our time.[13] Fifteen million people died in World War I and another 27 million in World War II. In the four decades following World War II there were over 300 wars in which 105 million people were killed during the war, with millions more dying of starvation and disease related to the war.[14] In addition millions of people lost their homes and sometimes even their homeland as a result of war. More than six million people were displaced, most internally, in Sudan and Sierra Leone alone as a result of civil wars. There are also three million Palestinian refugees, almost half of whom live in the Israeli-occupied West Bank and Gaza Strip, which were taken over by Israel in 1967 during the six-day war.

Is war the most utilitarian means of preserving beneficial ends such as our freedom and way of life? Was World War II the best means, from a utilitarian point of view, of defeating Hitler? What about the war in Iraq? While most people agreed that Iraq would be better off without Saddam Hussein's regime, many disagreed that an American invasion of Iraq was the best means of achieving this end. The means in this case may have caused more harm than other alternatives such as international intervention.

Principle of Double Effect

The principle of double effect is found primarily in Catholic just-war theory. According to this principle if a course of action, such as bombing a town, is likely to have two quite different effects, one legitimate and the other not, the action may still be permissible if the legitimate effect was intended (e.g., the disabling of a military installation or the bringing of a war to an end) and the illicit effect (e.g., the killing of civilians) unintended. The principle of double effect, for example, was used to justify the unintended killing of civilians in Hiroshima and Nagasaki.

One of the problems with this principle is that unintentional harms are still harms. Killing civilians unintentionally with another end in mind does not justify knowingly killing them, especially if the unintended harms of the action outweigh the intended benefits. The principle of double effect also reduces people being unintentionally harmed to a means only, and thus violates Kant's categorical imperative.

Justice

The condition of proportionality in the just-war tradition is based on the principle of justice. This principle states that the violence used must be in proportion to the injury being redressed. Justice is also a concern surrounding conscription and in treatment of citizens in an occupied or conquered country.

In "Nuclear Weapons, Ethics, Morals and Law," Jonathan Granoff argues that allowing some nations to possess nuclear weapons while forbidding others to do so violates the principle of equality, which is the foundation of international law. Justice is also an issue in the treatment of prisoners of war and civilians in occupied countries. For example, local Iraqi police are paid much less by the occupying Coalition than are American police in Iraq. Is this just?

Self-Determination

The United Nations recognizes the right of groups other than the state to "self-determination, freedom and independence." The efforts of a victorious country to impose its form of government, its concept of freedom, and its cultural and economic values on another country has been criticized as a violation of a people's right to self-determination.

John Stuart Mill likewise argued that self-determination and political freedom are not the same. A state has the right to self-determination even if its citizens are struggling for political freedom. Self-help, not occupation and liberation by another country, is the best way for citizens to develop the virtues necessary for self-governance.

On the other hand, assisting people in their struggle for freedom does not always violate their right to self-determination. For example, the French assisted the American colonists in the American Revolution. Knowing where to draw the line between interference and assistance in one's struggle for self-determination has always been difficult for nations.

Duty of Fidelity

In October 2002 American citizen John Walker Lindh was sentenced to twenty years in a federal prison for his association with the anti-American terrorist group *al Qaida*. Treason is considered worse than betrayal by a noncitizen since treason violates the duty of fidelity. Living in a country of one's own volition and benefiting from its protection and advantages creates a prima facie duty of fidelity or loyalty to that country. There is considerable debate, however, about what this duty entails. Do we have a duty to fight for our country or at least not to undermine our country's war efforts? Does the prima facie duty of fidelity justify conscription or universal service, or does it merely prohibit treason and terrorist acts against one's own government? What about instances where one's own government is unjust?

Soldiers and others involved in the war effort also have a prima facie duty of fidelity to their commanders. However, this duty must be weighed against other moral duties. The argument by Nazi war criminals that they were just obeying the orders of their superiors was found unacceptable in International Courts and in the 2004 Abu Ghraib prison abuse scandal in Iraq. People need to take personal responsibility for their choices.

Personal Responsibility

Soldiers are not merely passive instruments of war. In the My Lai Massacre in Vietnam, while most of the soldiers followed orders to "waste" the villagers, others refused to obey. One junior officer even stood between the soldiers and the villagers in an attempt to stop the slaughter.

Conscientious objection in the face of conscription also entails taking personal responsibility for one's decision. During the Vietnam War many conscientious objectors chose to leave the United States and take up residence in another country. Others, rather than abandoning their country, engaged in civil disobedience and willingly accepted the punishment for their actions as a means of raising public awareness. *Civil disobedience* is a "public, nonviolent, conscientious yet political act contrary to the law usually done with the aim of bringing about a change in the law or policies of government."[15] Civil disobedience does not require that one break the law that is being protested. For example, people engaged in indirect civil disobedience against a war or war preparation may break laws against trespassing or refuse to pay federal income taxes that support the military.

The people who design and produce weapons also must accept responsibility for their actions. Science was once considered morally neutral. However, people now view scientists as having responsibility for being aware of the broader social and moral consequences of their work. Because much of the technology used in the production and delivery of weapons of mass destruction can have both peacetime and military applications, researchers need to be aware how the technology they are developing might be used.

CONCLUSION

Internationally the world exists in a state of nature or anarchy. Weapons of mass destruction, globalization, and the development of new technologies make war and terrorism a greater threat than ever before to humankind. What is the solution? If the formation of a state under a social contract is the best means for controlling violence between individuals, is international government the answer for controlling violence between nations? Or, is war just a natural part of life and is the solution to develop and enforce ethics for war, such as the just-war tradition? In the end the responsibility lies with each of us as individuals to critically examine the justifications given for war, and to work toward making this world more peaceful, whether that means taking up arms or becoming a conscientious objector.

ELIZABETH ANSCOMBE

War and Murder

British philosopher Elizabeth Anscombe (1919–2001) was a professor of philosophy at Cambridge University in England. "War and Murder" first appeared in a collection of essays written by five Catholic academics who were concerned about the possibility of nuclear war. In her essay she distinguishes between war and murder, which involves the deliberate killing of an innocent person. Using both moral and biblical arguments, she concludes that war, including preemptive strikes, is justified under limited conditions.

Critical Reading Questions

1. What are the two attitudes regarding the exercise of violent coercive power by rulers?
2. According to Anscombe, why is the use of coercive power essential?
3. Why have wars been mostly unjust and "mere wickedness on both sides"?
4. What does it mean to be "innocent"?
5. What is the difference between war and murder?
6. What is "pacifism" and on what grounds does Anscombe reject it?
7. What, according to Anscombe, does the *Bible* say about the permissibility of war?
8. What is the "principle of double effect" and how does Anscombe apply this principle to the killing of innocent people in war?
9. How does Anscombe respond to critics who say that the just-war theory is no longer relevant in the modern world?

THE USE OF VIOLENCE BY RULERS

Since there are always thieves and frauds and men who commit violent attacks on their neighbours and murderers, and since without law backed by adequate force there are usually gangs of bandits; and since there are in most places laws administered by people who command violence to enforce the laws against law-breakers; the question arises: what is a just attitude to this exercise of violent coercive power on the part of rulers and their subordinate officers?

Two attitudes are possible: one, that the world is an absolute jungle and that the exercise of coercive power by rulers is only a manifestation of this; and the other, that it is both necessary and right that there should be this exercise of power, that through it the world is much less of a jungle than it could possibly be without it, so that one should in principle be glad of the existence of such power, and only take exception to its unjust exercise.

It is so clear that the world is less of a jungle because of rulers and laws, and that the exercise of coercive power is essential to these institutions as they are now—all this is so obvious, that probably only Tennysonian conceptions of progress enable people who do not wish to separate themselves from the world to think that nevertheless such violence is

"War and Murder," in *Nuclear Weapons: A Catholic Response,* ed. by Walter Stein (New York: Sheed and Ward Inc., 1961), 45–62.

objectionable, that some day, in this present dispensation, we shall do without it, and that the pacifist is the man who sees and tries to follow the ideal course, which future civilization must one day pursue. It is an illusion, which would be fantastic if it were not so familiar.

In a peaceful and law abiding country such as England, it may not be immediately obvious that the rulers need to command violence to the point of fighting to the death those that would oppose it; but brief reflection shews that this is so. For those who oppose the force that backs law will not always stop short of fighting to the death and cannot always be put down short of fighting to the death.

Then only if it is in itself evil violently to coerce resistant wills, can the exercise of coercive power by rulers be bad as such. . . .

Society is essential to human good; and society without coercive power is generally impossible.

The same authority which puts down internal dissension, which promulgates laws and restrains those who break them if it can, must equally oppose external enemies. These do not merely comprise those who attack the borders of the people ruled by the authority; but also, for example, pirates and desert bandits, and, generally, those beyond the confines of the country ruled whose activities are viciously harmful to it. . . . Further, there being such a thing as the common good of mankind, and visible criminality against it, how can we doubt the excellence of such a proceeding as that violent suppression of the man-stealing business which the British government took it into its head to engage in under Palmerston? The present-day conception of "aggression," like so many strongly influential conceptions, is a bad one. Why *must* it be wrong to strike the first blow in a struggle? The only question is, who is in the right.

Here, however, human pride, malice and cruelty are so usual that it is true to say that wars have mostly been mere wickedness on both sides. Just as an individual will constantly think himself in the right, whatever he does, and yet there is still such a thing as being in the right, so nations will constantly wrongly think themselves to be in the right—and yet there is still such a thing as their being in the right. Palmerston doubtless had no doubts in prosecuting the opium war against China, which was diabolical; just as he exulted in putting down the slavers. But there is no question but that he was a monster in the one thing, and a just man in the other.

The probability is that warfare is injustice, that a life of military service is a bad life "militia or rather malitia," as St. Anselm called it. This probability is greater than the probability (which also exists) that membership of a police force will involve malice, because of the character of warfare: the extraordinary occasions it offers for viciously unjust proceedings on the part of military commanders and warring governments, which at the time attract praise and not blame from their people. It is equally the case that the life of a ruler is usually a vicious life: but that does not shew that ruling is as such a vicious activity.

The principal wickedness which is a temptation to those engaged in warfare is the killing of the innocent, which may often be done with impunity and even to the glory of those who do it. In many places and times it has been taken for granted as a natural part of waging war: the commander, and especially the conqueror, massacres people by the thousand, either because this is part of his glory, or as a terrorizing measure, or as part of his tactics.

INNOCENCE AND THE RIGHT TO KILL INTENTIONALLY

It is necessary to dwell on the notion of non-innocence here employed. Innocence is a legal notion; but here, the accused is not pronounced guilty under an existing code of law, under which he has been tried by an impartial judge, and therefore made the target of attack. There is hardly a possibility of this; for the administration of justice is something that takes place under the aegis of a sovereign authority; but in warfare—or the putting down by violence of civil disturbance—the sovereign authority is itself engaged as a party to the dispute and is not subject to a further earthly and temporal authority which can judge the issue and pronounce against the accused. . . . What is required, for the people attacked to be non-innocent in the relevant sense, is that they should themselves be engaged in an objectively unjust proceeding which the attacker has the right to make his concern; or—the commonest case—should be unjustly attacking him. Then he can attack them with a view to stopping them; and also their supply lines and armament factories. But people whose mere existence and activity supporting existence by growing crops, making clothes, etc. constitute an impediment to him—such people are innocent and it is murderous to attack them, or make them a target for an attack which he judges will help him towards victory. For murder is the deliberate killing of the innocent, whether for its own sake or as a means to some further end.

The right to attack with a view to killing is something that belongs only to rulers and those whom they command to do it. I have argued that it does belong to rulers precisely because of that threat of violent coercion exercised by those in authority which is essential to the existence of human societies. . . .

When a private man struggles with an enemy he has no right to aim to kill him, unless in the circumstances of the attack on him he can be considered as endowed with the authority of the law and the struggle comes to that point. By a "private" man, I mean a man in a society; I am not speaking of men on their own, without government, in remote places; for such men are neither public servants nor "private." The plea of self-defence (or the defence of someone else) made by a private man who has killed someone else must in conscience—even if not in law—be a plea that the death of the other was not intended, but was a side effect of the measures taken to ward off the attack. . . . The deliberate choice of inflicting death in a struggle is the right only of ruling authorities and their subordinates.

In saying that a private man may not choose to kill, we are touching on the principle of "double effect." . . . Thus, if I push a man over a cliff when he is menacing my life, his death is considered as intended by me, but the intention to be justifiable for the sake of self-defence. Yet the lawyers would hardly find the laying of poison tolerable as an act of self-defence, but only killing by a violent action in a moment of violence. Christian moral theologians have taught that even here one may not seek the death of the assailant, but may in default of other ways of self-defence use such violence as will in fact result in his death. The distinction is evidently a fine one in some cases: what, it may be asked, can the intention be, if it can be said to be absent in this case, except a mere wish or desire? . . . [T]he principle of double effect has more important applications in warfare, and I shall return to it later.

THE INFLUENCE OF PACIFISM

Pacifism has existed as a considerable movement in English speaking countries ever since the first world war. I take the doctrine of pacifism to be that it is *eo ipso* wrong to fight in wars, not the doctrine that it is wrong to be compelled to, or that any man, or some men, may refuse; and I think it false for the reasons that I have given. But I now want to consider the very remarkable effects it has had: for I believe its influence to have been enormous, far exceeding its influence on its own adherents.

We should note first that pacifism has as its background conscription and enforced military service for all men. Without conscription, pacifism is a private opinion that will keep those who hold it out of armies, which they are in any case not obliged to join. Now universal conscription, except for the most extraordinary reasons, i.e. as a regular habit among most nations, is such a horrid evil that the refusal of it automatically commands a certain amount of respect and sympathy. . . .

A powerful ingredient in this pacifism is the prevailing image of Christianity. This image commands a sentimental respect among people who have no belief in Christianity, that is to say, in Christian dogmas; yet do have a certain belief in an ideal which they conceive to be part of "true Christianity." It is therefore important to understand this image of Christianity and to know how false it is. Such understanding is relevant, not merely to those who wish to believe Christianity, but to all who, without the least wish to believe, are yet profoundly influenced by this image of it.

According to this image, Christianity is an ideal and beautiful religion, impracticable except for a few rare characters. It preaches a God of love whom there is no reason to fear; it marks an escape from the conception presented in the Old Testament, of a vindictive and jealous God who will terribly punish his enemies. The "Christian" God is a *roi fainéant,* whose only triumph is in the Cross; his appeal is to goodness and unselfishness, and to follow him is to act according to the Sermon on the Mount—to turn the other cheek and to offer no resistance to evil. In this account some of the evangelical counsels are chosen as containing the whole of Christian ethics: that is, they are made into precepts. (Only some of them; it is not likely that someone who deduces the *duty* of pacifism from the Sermon on the Mount and the rebuke to Peter, will agree to take "Give to him that asks of you" equally as a universally binding precept.)

The turning of counsels into precepts results in high-sounding principles. Principles that are mistakenly high and strict are a trap; they may easily lead in the end directly or indirectly to the justification of monstrous things. Thus if the evangelical counsel about poverty were turned into a precept forbidding property owning, people would pay lip service to it as the ideal, while in practice they went in for swindling. "Absolute honesty!" it would be said: "I can respect that—but of course that means having no property; and while I respect those who follow that course, I have to compromise with the sordid world myself." If then one must "compromise with evil" by owning property and engaging in trade, then the amount of swindling one does will depend on convenience. This imaginary case is paralleled by what is so commonly said: absolute pacifism is an ideal; unable to follow that, and committed to "compromise with evil," one must go the whole hog and wage war *à outrance.*

The truth about Christianity is that it is a severe and practicable religion, not a beautifully ideal but impracticable one. Its moral precepts, . . . are those of the Old Testament; and its God is the God of Israel.

It is ignorance of the New Testament that hides this from people. It is characteristic of pacifism to denigrate the Old Testament and exalt the New: something quite contrary to the teaching of the New Testament itself, which always looks back to and leans upon the Old. How typical it is that the words of Christ "You have heard it said, an eye for an eye and a tooth for a tooth, but I say to you . . ." are taken as a repudiation of the ethic of the Old Testament! People seldom look up the occurrence of this phrase in the juridical code of the Old Testament, where it belongs, and is the admirable principle of law for the punishment of certain crimes, such as procuring the wrongful punishment of another by perjury. People often enough *now* cite the phrase to justify private revenge; no doubt this was as often "heard said" when Christ spoke of it. But no justification for this exists in the personal ethic taught by the Old Testament. On the contrary. What do we find? "Seek no revenge," (Leviticus xix, 18), and "If you find your enemy's ox or ass going astray, take it back to him; if you see the ass of someone who hates you lying under his burden, and would forbear to help him; you must help him" (Exodus xxiii, 4–5). And "If your enemy is hungry, give him food, if thirsty, give him drink" (Proverbs xxv, 21).

This is only one example; given space, it would be easy to shew how false is the conception of Christ's teaching as *correcting* the religion of the ancient Israelites, and substituting a higher and more "spiritual" religion for theirs. Now the false picture I have described plays an important part in the pacifist ethic and in the ethic of the many people who are not pacifists but are influenced by pacifism.

To extract a pacifist doctrine—i.e. a condemnation of the use of force by the ruling authorities, and of soldiering as a profession—from the evangelical counsels and the rebuke to Peter, is to disregard what else is in the New Testament. . . . A centurion was the first Gentile to be baptized; there is no suggestion in the New Testament that soldiering was regarded as incompatible with Christianity. The martyrology contains many names of soldiers whose occasion for martyrdom was not any objection to soldiering, but a refusal to perform idolatrous acts.

Now, it is one of the most vehement and repeated teachings of the Judaeo-Christian tradition that the shedding of innocent blood is forbidden by the divine law. No man may be punished except for his own crime, and those "whose feet are swift to shed innocent blood" are always represented as God's enemies.

For a long time the main outlines of this teaching have seemed to be merely obvious morality: . . . And indeed, that it is terrible to kill the innocent is very obvious; the morality that so stringently forbids it must make a great appeal to mankind, especially to the poor threatened victims. Why should it need the thunder of Sinai and the suffering and preaching of the prophets to promulgate such a law? But human pride and malice are everywhere so strong that now, with the fading of Christianity from the mind of the West, this morality once more stands out as a demand which strikes pride- and fear-ridden people as too intransigent. . . .

Now pacifism teaches people to make no distinction between the shedding of innocent blood and the shedding of any human blood. And in this way pacifism has corrupted enormous numbers of people who will not act according to its tenets. They become convinced that a number of things are wicked which are not; hence, seeing no way of avoiding "wickedness," they set no limits to it. How endlessly pacifists argue that all war must be *à outrance!* that those who wage war must go as far as technological advance permits in the destruction of the enemy's people. As if the Napoleonic wars were perforce fuller of massacres than the French war of Henry V of England. It is not true: the reverse took place. Nor is technological advance particularly relevant; it is mere squeamishness that deters people who would consent to area bombing from the enormous massacres *by hand* that used once to be committed.

The policy of obliterating cities was adopted by the Allies in the last war; they need not have taken that step, and it was taken largely out of a villainous hatred, and as corollary to the policy, now universally denigrated, of seeking "unconditional surrender." (That policy itself was visibly wicked, and could be and was judged so at the time; it is not surprising that it led to disastrous consequences, even if no one was clever and detached enough to foresee this at the time.)

Pacifism and the respect for pacifism is not the only thing that has led to a universal forgetfulness of the law against killing the innocent; but it has had a great share in it.

THE PRINCIPLE OF DOUBLE EFFECT

Catholics, however, can hardly avoid paying at least lip-service to that law. So we must ask: how is it that there has been so comparatively little conscience exercised on the subject among them? The answer is: double-think about double effect.

The distinction between the intended, and the merely foreseen, effects of a voluntary action is indeed absolutely essential to Christian ethics. For Christianity forbids a number of things as being bad in themselves. But if I am answerable for the foreseen consequences of an action or refusal, as much as for the action itself, then these prohibitions will break down. If someone innocent will die unless I do a wicked thing, then on this view I am his murderer in refusing: so all that is left to me is to weigh up evils. Here the theologian steps in with the principle of double effect and says: "No, you are no murderer, if the man's death was neither your aim nor your chosen means, and if you had to act in the way that led to it or else do something absolutely forbidden." Without understanding of this principle, anything can be—and is wont to be—justified, and the Christian teaching that in no circumstances may one commit murder, adultery, apostasy (to give a few examples) goes by the board. These absolute prohibitions of Christianity by no means exhaust its ethic; there is a large area where what is just is determined partly by a prudent weighing up of consequences. But the prohibitions are bedrock, and without them the Christian ethic goes to pieces. Hence the necessity of the notion of double effect.

At the same time, the principle has been repeatedly abused from the seventeenth century up till now. The causes lie in the history of philosophy. From the seventeenth century till now what may be called Cartesian psychology has dominated the thought of philosophers and theologians. According to this psychology, an intention was an interior act of the mind which could be produced at will. Now if intention is all important—as it is—in determining the goodness or badness of an action, then, on this theory of what intention is, a marvellous way offered itself of making any action lawful. You only had to "direct your intention" in a suitable way. In practice, this means making a little speech to yourself: "What I mean to be doing is. . . ."

This same doctrine is used to prevent any doubts about the obliteration bombing of a city. The devout Catholic bomber secures by a "direction of intention" that any shedding of innocent blood that occurs is "accidental." I know a Catholic boy who was puzzled at being told by his schoolmaster that it was an *accident* that the people of Hiroshima and Nagasaki were there to be killed; in fact, however absurd it seems, such thoughts are common among priests who know that they are forbidden by the divine law to justify the direct killing of the innocent.

It is nonsense to pretend that you do not intend to do what is the means you take to your chosen end. Otherwise there is absolutely no substance to the Pauline teaching that we may not do evil that good may come.

SOME COMMONLY HEARD ARGUMENTS

There are a number of sophistical arguments, often or sometimes used on these topics, which need answering.

Where do you draw the line? As Dr. Johnson said, the fact of twilight does not mean you cannot tell day from night. There are borderline cases, where it is difficult to distinguish, in what is done, between means and what is incidental to, yet in the circumstances inseparable from, those means. The obliteration bombing of a city is not a borderline case.

The old "conditions for a just war" are irrelevant to the conditions of modern warfare, so that must be condemned out of hand. People who say this always envisage only major wars between the Great Powers, which Powers are indeed now "in blood stepp'd in so far" that it is unimaginable for there to be a war between them which is not a set of enormous massacres of civil populations. But these are not the only wars. Why is Finland so far free? At least partly because of the "posture of military preparedness" which, considering the character of the country, would have made subjugating the Finns a difficult and unrewarding task. The offensive of the Israelis against the Egyptians in 1956 involved no plan of making civil populations the target of military attack.

In a modern war the distinction between combatants and noncombatants is meaningless, so an attack on anyone on the enemy side is justified. This is pure nonsense; even in war, a very large number of the enemy population are just engaged in maintaining the life of the country, or are sick, or aged, or children. . . .

Whether a war is just or not is not for the private man to judge: he must obey his government. Sometimes, this may be, especially as far as concerns causes of war. But the individual who joins in destroying a city, like a Nazi massacring the inhabitants of a village, is too obviously marked out as an enemy of the human race, to shelter behind such a plea.

Finally, horrible as it is to have to notice this, we must notice that even the arguments about double effect—which at least show that a man is not willing openly to justify the killing of the innocent—are now beginning to look old-fashioned. Some Catholics are not scrupling to say that *anything* is justified in defence of the continued existence and liberty of the Church in the West. A terrible fear of communism drives people to say this sort of thing. "Our Lord told us to fear those who can destroy body and soul, not to fear the destruction of the body" was blasphemously said to a friend of mine; meaning: "so, we must fear Russian domination more than the destruction of people's bodies by obliteration bombing."

But whom did Our Lord tell us to fear, when he said: "I will tell you whom you shall fear" and "Fear not them that can destroy the body, but fear him who can destroy body and soul in hell"? He told us to fear God the Father, who can and will destroy the unrepentant disobedient, body and soul, in hell.

. . . So we have to fear God and keep his commandments, and calculate what is for the best only within the limits of that obedience, knowing that the future is in God's power and that no one can snatch away those whom the Father has given to Christ.

It is not a vague faith in the triumph of "the spirit" over force (there is little enough warrant for that), but a definite faith in the divine promises, that makes us believe that the Church cannot fail. Those, therefore, who think they must be prepared to wage a war with Russia involving the deliberate massacre of cities, must be prepared to say to God: "We had to break your law, lest your Church fail. We could not obey your commandments, for we did not believe your promises."

Discussion Questions

1. Anscombe supports preemptive strikes under certain conditions. What are these conditions? Discuss whether she would support the United States's preemptive strikes against Iraq.
2. Anscombe argues that the *Bible* supports war, while Christian pacifists claim that war is inconsistent with the teachings of Jesus. Discuss the merits of both positions.
3. Like Anscombe, President George W. Bush believes that evil exists and that God permits governments to limit the power of evil through the use of violence. However, the Islamic terrorists also believe that God is on their side and it is the United States that is evil. Referring to just-war theory, discuss the legitimacy of the use of religious ideology to morally justify war.
4. In March 2001 a Palestinian detonated explosives next to a bus in Jerusalem, killing himself and injuring 30 Israelis. While some Muslims regard suicide bombers as merely suicide and a violation of God's law, other Muslims regard suicide bombers as martyrs. Martyrdom operations are tactics used by Palestinians. Discuss the use of suicide bombers in light of the *jus in bello.*

C.A.J. COADY

War and Terrorism

C. A. J. Coady is senior research fellow and deputy director of the Centre for Applied Philosophy and Public Ethics at the University of Melbourne, Australia. Coady begins his reading by summarizing Hobbes's position on war and how it mirrors the just-war theory. He then examines and critiques the just-war theory and the conditions it puts forth for (1) when is it right to go to war (*jus ad bellum*) and (2) how one should conduct oneself in war (*jus in bello*). Finally, Coady applies the principles of the just-war theory to the morality of terrorism.

Critical Reading Questions

1. According to Coady, what are some of the problems with Hobbes's political philosophy?
2. In what way does Hobbes's position on war mirror the division in the just-war theory?
3. What is *jus ad bellum* and what are the five rules of *jus ad bellum?*
4. What is the requirement for proportionality?

"War and Terrorism," in *A Companion to Applied Ethics,* ed. by R. G. Frey and Christopher Health Wellman (Oxford, UK: Blackwell Publishing, 2003), 254–265.

5. What are some of the problems with the condition of "reasonable success"?
6. What is the *jus ad bellum* position on the use of war as self-defense?
7. Under the just-war theory, does the threat of aggression ever justify a preemptive strike?
8. What is a "humanitarian war" and what is Coady's position on the permissibility of "humanitarian wars"?
9. What are the two primary rules of *jus in bello?*
10. What is the distinction between a combatant and a noncombatant?
11. What are "collateral damages" in war and how does this relate to the principle of non-combatant immunity and the principle of double-effect?
12. What is "terrorism" and is it ever justified under the just-war theory?

Our discussion can best begin with Thomas Hobbes since for Hobbes civil society primarily exists to solve the problems posed by the endemic role of violence in human life. Hobbes thought that violence created such miseries in pre-civil or non-civil conditions (his "state of nature") that reason required men to alienate, almost entirely, their natural right to self-protection in order to set up a sovereign with the sole right of the sword. His solution to the problem posed by the widespread violence of the state of nature is to monopolize the potentiality for violence in one agency.

The phenomena of war and terrorism, in their different ways, challenge this solution. Hobbes's political philosophy faces certain notorious problems, but even were it to provide a local solution to the problem of violence, it would do so at the cost of establishing a proliferation of (almost) absolute sovereign powers. They would very probably confront each other (as Hobbes realized) in a stance of permanent hostility akin to the war of all against all with which his problematic begins. This "anarchy" of the international order thus poses almost intractable difficulties for the peace that Hobbes took to be a primary objective of the laws of nature and for which sovereign power was to provide the guarantee. . . .

For Hobbes, not only is the sovereign power virtually absolute, but it also defines the contours of justice, inasmuch as nothing the sovereign does can be unjust. . . . The sovereign cannot be accused of injustice but may violate the laws of nature and be answerable to God for what Hobbes calls iniquity. Thus the sovereign has certain obligations as a ruler to preserve the peace, and is bound before God to conform to the tenets of natural law. Consequently, many resorts to war would be ruled out on prudential and moral grounds.

Nor are Hobbes's qualifications restricted to the morality of beginning war, for his brief discussions of honor, cruelty, and necessity in war allow some minimal room for moral restrictions on how a war is conducted (Hobbes, 1969: 78). Hobbes's qualifications mirror the twofold division of discussion within the just-war tradition, the first concerned with the morality appropriate to resort to war at all, and the second with the morality that should govern the way a war is fought. The former is often called *jus ad bellum* and the latter *jus in bello.* The Hobbesian mirroring is reductive: the fulsome shape of the *jus ad bellum* appears in the thin form of "providence" (i.e., prudent foresight) and the demanding conditions of the *jus in bello* are reflected as the (largely unspecified) requirements of honor. . . .

THE JUST WAR: *JUS AD BELLUM*

Although it is common to talk of "just-war theory," the mode of thinking thereby indicated is more a broad tradition than a precisely specified intellectual construction. It is less like the theory of the categorical imperative and more like commonsense morality. None the less, certain rules and maxims are invoked and I will begin with a digest of those that are most central to the argument about when it is right to go to war: the *jus ad bellum.*

1. War must be declared and waged by legitimate authority.
2. There must be a just cause for going to war.
3. War must be a last resort.
4. There must be reasonable prospect of success.
5. The violence used must be proportional to the wrong being resisted.

Each of these conditions raises problems. We shall briefly review some of the difficulties with conditions (3)–(5) and then comment more fully on condition (2). Conditions (3) and (5) are specifications of a commonsense understanding of the rational limits to self-defense. Given the ambiguous benefits and definite risks of most uses of violence, and the inherent tendency it has to move beyond control, the idea of "last resort" registers the desirability of a cautious approach to warfare. None the less, the condition cannot require that a nation must resort to war only after it has tried *every* other option. Some of these will be too absurd or counterproductive; others may delay the inevitable to the grave disadvantage of a just cause. Last resort requires the use of imagination and some degree of risk-taking in the search for reasonable alternatives to war, but it does not counsel peace at any price. Hence it will be a matter of practical judgment whether the relevant alternatives to war have been exhausted. Moreover, it should not be forgotten that some of the alternatives to war may have their own serious moral costs, as is illustrated by growing disenchantment with the human costs of certain sorts of sanctions.

The requirement of proportionality spans the *jus ad bellum* and the *jus in bello* and insists that lethal violence should not be employed without consideration of the balance between the evil it brings and the good to be achieved in resisting evil. There is here an element of calculating consequences, but the appeal to proportionality is not full-bloodedly consequentialist. This is because its focus is narrower. We are not asked to consider whether going to war is the best thing for the universe, all things considered, but whether the foreseeable costs of this resort to violence are out of kilter with the criminal behavior it seeks to redress. . . .

Condition 4 is also a reflection of common sense, but at an even more basic level, since it is merely an application to warfare of an apparently fundamental condition of rational action. Normally one is irrational to engage in a plan with little or no perceived prospect of success. Yet there are desperate circumstances in which one may need to act against the odds. The mountain climber who faces disaster from an avalanche may be rational to attempt the leap across a ravine even where he thinks it unlikely he can make it. In the case of war, a fight against the odds may be justifiable where the stakes are very high, as when a powerful enemy is determined not only to conquer but enslave. This seems plausible, but it does not refute condition 4 so much as require a more subtle interpretation of "reasonable." . . . Some would argue that there are circumstances in which a flight to the death is preferable to mere capitulation. This has most plausibility where the enemy is bent upon enslavement or extermination. But some would extend the circumstances further to encompass the symbolic assertion of national honor, as Michael Walzer seems to do in his discussion of Finland's "futile" war of defense against the Soviet Union in 1939–40. What these arguments show is that the concept of "success" is open to complex interpretations. At first blush, one naturally takes it to mean winning the war, but the counterexamples suggest other purposes. None the less, enough crimes have been committed in the name of national honor to warrant a note of caution about self-immolation for its sake.

Condition 2 concerning just cause also has its origins in commonsense intuitions but again its interpretation raises problems. There are differences between the older tradition and much contemporary theory. The medieval tradition of the just war stems primarily from St Augustine and was generally more permissive, . . . Although the ground of self-defense had always loomed large in legitimating resort to war. Aquinas and others had also allowed various "injuries" of a religious nature. Hence, in some circumstances, a war to return heretical peoples to orthodoxy or, even, to conquer heathens was a candidate for a just war. Both Vitoria and Suarez and later Grotius are anxious to limit further such recourse, so it is plausible to see them as standing at the beginning of a move toward a more restrictive attitude to just cause (Grotius, 1925: 516–17, 553–4; Suarez, 1944; Vitoria, 1991). The current ban on "aggressive war" can be seen, for all its obscurity, as the outcome of such a development.

The strength of this ban is also, of course, connected with the rise of the modern state and the doctrine of sovereignty that has accompained it. . . .

Admittedly, the contemporary abhorrence of "aggression" has critics; moreover, the exact meaning of "aggression" is elusive and open to exploitation. None the less, the moral power of the idea of defense against aggression comes from the moral significance of self-preservation and particularly self-defense. It is not a uniquely modern concept, as Anscombe (1970), for instance, seems to believe since it may be found virtually at any time or place where questions about the legitimacy of war are raised. . . . Moreover, ancient Chinese discussions of the morality of war are specifically concerned to reject the legitimacy of aggressive war, and, although the concept of aggression at work is somewhat different from that enshrined in the UN Charter, it is a recognizable relation (Tzu et al., 1964).

The basic moral intuition draws much of its appeal from the legitimacy of personal resort to self-defense. Hobbes, for instance, treats the legitimacy of self-preservation as the fundamental right of nature. There are certainly problems in extrapolating from the case of an individual to that of a nation-state and in elucidating concepts of national rights, but where the state is clearly defending its people rather than its honor or the power of an elite, then the extension has palpable force. Moreover, it is easy to see the point of some other extensions that have had a place in traditional discussions. If a nation is sometimes entitled to the use of violence in its own defense, then surely other nations may come to its aid as long as their objective is to help repel the attack and no more. This parallels what seems allowed with regard to aid in the case of individuals. Of course, in both the domestic and the international cases, what is abstractly morally permissible is not the whole story. There may be powerful prudential reasons for not helping others defend themselves. When the Soviet Union invaded Hungary and later Czechoslovakia the world stood by, principally because of fear of nuclear war, and those fears were realistic enough at least to make a reasonable case for such agonizing inaction.

Another extension is the idea that a nation may defend against aggression before it has begun. The pre-emptive war is sometimes defended on the ground that when aggression is genuinely imminent it is rational to strike against the enemy before he gets the advantage of the first blow. There seems to be logical space for this, but it remains worrying. As Sidgwick pointed out, the legitimate pre-emption "easily passes over into anticipation of a blow that is merely feared, not really threatened. Indeed this enlarged right of self-protection against mere danger has often been further extended to justify hostile interference to prevent a neighbour growing strong merely through expansion or coalescence with other states" (Sidgwick, 1898: 101). . . .

How then should we understand "aggression"? The UN Charter defines it as follows: "Aggression is the use of armed force by a State against the sovereignty, territorial integrity or political independence of another State or in any other manner inconsistent with the Charter of the United Nations" (United Nations 1974). . . . There are three broad types of criticism of the defense against aggression model of just cause . . .

The first complains that the appeal to aggression is too strong. Sometimes aggression is made to seem as if it obliges those attacked, or their sympathizers, to give a military response. . . . But such insistence ignores the rule of proportionality as illustrated and discussed above, and may well conflict with conditions 3 and 4. At most, defense against aggression satisfies the condition of just cause, but it will only license war if the other conditions are fulfilled.

A second complaint is that the aggression appeal is, in another respect, too weak. This questions modern just-war theory's emphasis upon the central, even unique, role of self-defense, and argues that there are other legitimate causes for war. The basic line of criticism here is that restriction of just wars to *defense against aggression* (even allowing for the extensions discussed above) leaves evils undealt with in the international order. The criticism is put trenchantly by Anscombe: "The present day conception of 'aggression', like so many strongly influential conceptions, is a bad one. Why *must* it be wrong to strike the first blow in a struggle? The only question is, who is in the right?" (Anscombe, 1970: 43–4). As stated, this criticism would not seem to jettison the concept of aggression as dramatically as she supposes since her argument seems to presume the existence of a struggle in which actual blows have not yet been struck, though they or something like them have been extensively prepared for. So some form of aggression (different from the UN model) may have occurred already, or we may be in the area of legitimate preemption discussed earlier.

But a more interesting construal of "the first blow in the struggle" would refer to the aggressive blow that initiates armed conflict. . . . It would encompass the idea of military intervention in another state's affairs in order to remove an awful government or remedy some great internal evil, such as persecution of a minority group. Following current fashion, let us call these many diverse situations "humanitarian wars." These are not philosophers' fantasies, as wars in Uganda, Cambodia, Somalia, and Kosovo have recently shown.

Support for humanitarian warfare strengthened amongst philosophers and other theorists at the end of the twentieth century, though politicians were generally less enthusiastic. Some humanitarian wars are harder than others for the aggression model to handle, but the tendency to return to a more permissive attitude to the just war needs to be treated with wariness. There is a presumption against the moral validity of resort to war given what we know of the history of warfare, of the vast devastation it commonly causes and the dubious motives that have so often fueled it. For these reasons, the development of just-war theory has been progressively away from altruistic legitimations of war. Our experience of wars of religion, of trade and imperialist wars, and of what tends to happen when one nation conquers another "for its own good" speak against allowing expansive accounts of "just cause."

This provides a powerful objection to humanitarian war, but the fact remains that there can be extreme cases that challenge the objection. Walzer treats the Indian invasion of Bangladesh in 1971 as such a case where the intervention was to prevent the massacre of a population by what was nominally its own government. The Vietnamese invasion of Cambodia may be a similar case or the Tanzanian of Uganda, though the histories of those nations since then has been less than happy. Anscombe's example of the use of violence against "the man-stealing business" is another case that has good claims to exception from the ban, though the example is complex because it sometimes involved armed action against criminal groups disowned by their own governments. . . .

A third, related problem with the aggression model is that it sanctifies existing national-state arrangements. Critics ask: why should *these* boundaries and *these* states be given such respect? The question is given added force by the ways in which colonization and decolonization have created states with whimsical boundaries. This is not the place to engage in a full-scale discussion of sovereignty, national determination, nationalism, and the justification for state authority, but we can note two things. One is that any idea of sovereignty that requires absolute immunity from outside involvement has never made much sense and makes even less in the contemporary world; the second is that sovereignty, however qualified, is still usually perceived as having profoundly positive significance by those subject to it. Hence, outside intrusions, no matter how well intentioned, will often face deep moral and political problems. The case for humanitarian war needs to be very conscious of these drawbacks. . . .

THE *JUS IN BELLO*

Moral restrictions on how one conducts oneself in war are apt to be met with incredulity. "You do what needs to be done to win" is a common response. There is a certain appeal in this pragmatic outlook, but it flies in the face not only of just-war thinking but of many common human responses to war. The concept of an atrocity, for instance, has a deep place in our thinking. Even that very tough warrior, the US war ace General Chuck Yeager suffered genuine moral revulsion at orders to commit "atrocities" that he was given and complied with in World War II. He was especially "not proud" of his part in the indiscriminate strafing of a 50-square-mile area of Germany.

The idea that there are non-legitimate targets amongst "the enemy" is the basis of one of the two primary rules of the *jus in bello:* the principle of discrimination. The other is the principle of proportionality, the operation of which parallels its work in the *jus ad bellum,* for there are questions to be raised both about whether the resort to war is a proportional response to some injury, and whether some tactic or means is proportionate to its projected effect.

A major part of the discrimination principle concerns the immunity of non-combatants from direct attack. This is a key point at which utilitarian approaches to the justification of war tend to part company with the classical just-war tradition. Either they deny that the principle obtains at all, or, more commonly, they argue that it applies in virtue of its utility. The former move is associated with the idea that war is such "hell" and victory so important that everything must be subordinated to that end, but even in utilitarian terms it is unclear that this form of ruthlessness has the best outcomes, especially when it is shared by the opposing sides. Hence, the more common move is to argue that the immunity of non-combatants is a useful rule for restricting the damage wrought by wars. Non-utilitarians (I shall call them "intrinsicalists" because they believe that there are intrinsic wrongs, other than failing to maximize goods) can agree that there are such extrinsic reasons for the immunity rule, but they will see this fact as a significant additional reason to conform to the principle. Intrinsicalists will argue that the principle's validity springs directly from the reasoning that licenses resort to war in the first place. This resort is allowed by the need to resist perpetrators of aggression (or, on the broader view, to deal with wrongdoers) and hence it licenses violence only against those agents. This is the point behind distinguishing combatants from noncombatants, or, in another terminology, wrongdoers and innocents. In this context, when we classify people as noncombatants or innocents we do not mean that they have no evil in their hearts, or lack enthusiasm for their country's policies, nor do we mean that the combatants have such evil or enthusiasm. The classification is concerned with the role the individual plays in the chain of agency directing the aggression or wrongdoing. . . .

But even when these distinctions are made, there seems room not only for doubt about the application of the distinction to various difficult categories of person, such as slave laborers coerced to work in munitions factories, but also its applicability at all to the highly integrated citizenry of modern states. It is surely anachronistic to think of contemporary war as waged between armies; it is really nation against nation, economy against economy, peoples against peoples. But although modern war has many unusual features, its "total" nature is more an imposed construction than a necessary reflection of a changed reality. Even in World War II not every enemy citizen was a combatant. In any war, there remain millions of people who are not plausibly seen as involved in the enemy's lethal chain of agency. There are, for instance, infants, young children, the elderly and infirm, lots of tradespeople and workers, not to mention dissidents and conscientious objectors. Moreover, the model of total war that underpins this objection is itself outdated. . . .

In fact, there has been a remarkable change on this issue in the strategic doctrine and military outlook of many major powers since the end of the Cold War. It is now common to pay at least lip service to the principle, as evidenced by certain restraint shown during the Gulf War and the bombing of Serbia, and by the widespread condemnation of Russian brutality in Chechnya. The real question is not so much whether it is immoral to target noncombatants (it is), but how "collateral" damage and death to noncombatants can be defended. This was always a problem in just-war theory, often solved by resort to some form of the principle of double effect. This allowed for the harming of noncombatants in some circumstances as a foreseen but unintended side-effect of an otherwise legitimate act of war. The "circumstances" included the proportionality of the side-effect to the intended outcome. Not everyone agrees with the principle (and this is not the place to discuss it in detail) but the conduct of war in contemporary circumstances is morally impossible unless the activities of warriors are allowed to put noncombatants at risk in certain circumstances. Some modification to the immunity principle to allow indirect harming seems to be in line with commonsense morality in other areas of life, and to be necessitated by the circumstances of war. If it is not available, then pacifism, as Holmes (1989: esp. 193–203) has argued, seems the only moral option.

TERRORISM

For a phenomenon that arouses such widespread anxiety, anger, and dismay, terrorism is surprisingly difficult to define. . . . Rather than extensively reviewing the varieties of definition. I propose to concentrate on one key element in common responses to and fears about terrorism, namely the idea that it involves "innocent" victims. This provides a point of connection with the moral apparatus of just-war theory, specifically the principle of discrimination and its requirement of noncombatant immunity. Of course, terrorism does not always take place in the context of all-out international war, but it usually has a war-like dimension. I will define it as follows: "the use of violence to target noncombatants ('innocents' in the *jus in bello* sense) for political purposes."

This definition has several contentious consequences. One is that states can themselves use terrorism, another is that much political violence by non-state agents will not be terrorist. As to the former, there is a tendency, especially amongst the representatives of states, to restrict the possibility of terrorist acts to non-state agents. But if we think of terrorism, in the light of the definition above, as a tactic rather than an ideology, this tendency should be resisted since states can and do use the tactic of attacking the innocent. Some theorists who think terrorism cannot be perpetrated by governments are not so much confused, as operating with a different definition. They define terrorism, somewhat in the spirit of Hobbes, as the use of political violence by non-state agents against the state. Some would restrict it to violence against a democratic state. This is the way many political scientists view terrorism, and, at least in the case of a democratic state, they see it as morally wrong. Call this the political definition to contrast with the tactical definition.

A further consequence of the tactical definition is that it implies a degree of purposiveness that terrorism is thought to lack. Some theorists have claimed that terrorism is essentially "random," others that it is essentially "expressive." In both cases, the claim is that a reference to political purposes is inappropriate. In reply, it can be argued that talk of terrorism as random is generated by the genuine perception that it does not restrict its targets to the obvious military ones, but this does not mean that it is wild and purposeless. Indeed, most terrorists think that the best way to get certain political effects is to aim at "soft" noncombatant targets. Similarly, there can be no doubt that many terrorist attacks are expressive and symbolic, involving the affirmation of the attitude: "We are still here; take notice of us." Yet the expressive need not exclude the purposive, or even the assertive. "That's a rattle-snake" may express horror, be designed to warn an audience, and state a fact. So terrorist acts can be, and are, both expressive and politically purposive. . . .

The tactical definition faces the problems already discussed concerning the meaning of the term "noncombatant," but even more acutely. In guerilla war, insurgents may not be easily identifiable as combatants and will seek to enlist or involve the villagers and local inhabitants in the campaign thereby blurring their status as noncombatants. On the other hand, many state officials who are not directly prosecuting the campaign against the insurgents may be plausibly viewed as implicated in the grievances the revolutionaries are seeking to redress. There are certainly problems here, but they do not seem insurmountable. In the heat and confusion of battle, it may be difficult and dangerous to treat even children as noncombatants, especially where children are coerced or seduced into combatant roles (as is common in many contemporary conflicts). None the less, a premeditated campaign of bombing regional hospitals to induce civilian lack of cooperation with rebels is in palpable violation of the *jus in bello*. So are the murder of infants and the targeting of state officials, such as water authorities or traffic police, whose roles are usually tangentially related to the causes of the conflict. It is true that some ideologies purport to have enemies so comprehensive as to make even small children and helpless adults into "combatants." Western advocates of "total-war" strategic bombing of cities share with the Islamic fanatics, who incorporate American air travellers and sundry citizens of Manhattan into their holy targets, a simplistic and Manichaean vision of the world that is at odds with the just-war tradition's attempt to bring moral sanity to bear upon the use of political violence.

Is terrorism wrong? Given just-war theory and the tactical definition, the answer is clearly yes. And if one takes the principle of noncombatant immunity to invoke an absolute moral prohibition, as just-war thinkers have commonly done, then it is always wrong. Yet many contemporary moral philosophers, sympathetic to just-war thinking, are wary of moral absolutes. They would treat the prohibition as expressing a very strong moral presumption against terrorism and the targeting of noncombatants, but allow for exceptions in extreme circumstances. So, Michael Walzer thinks that in conditions of "supreme emergency" the violation of the normal immunity is permissible in warfare though only with a heavy burden of remorse (extending even to scapegoating). He thinks the Allied terror bombing of German cities in World War II (in the early stages) was legitimated by the enormity of the Nazi threat. John Rawls has recently endorsed this view while condemning the bombings of Hiroshima and Nagasaki (Walzer, 1992; Rawls, 1999). If this concession is allowed to states, it seems mere consistency to allow it to non-state agents on the same terms. The general reluctance to do so suggests that such categories as "supreme emergency" may mask contestable political judgments.

REFERENCES

Anscombe, G. E. M. (1970) War and murder. In R. Wasserstrom (ed.), *War and Morality*. Belmont, CA: Wadsworth.

Grotius, H. (1925) *The Rights of War and Peace (De jure belli ac pacis libri tres)*, vol. 2, ed. Francis W. Kelsey (orig. pub. 1682). Oxford: Clarendon Press.

Hobbes, T. (1969) *The Elements of Law: Natural and Political*, 2nd edn, ed. Ferdinand Tönnies, with new intro. by M. M. Goldsmith. London: Cass.

Holmes, R. (1989) *On War and Morality*. Princeton, NJ: Princeton University Press.

Rawls, J. (1999) Fifty years after Hiroshima. In S. Freeman (ed.), *Collected Papers*, pp. 565–72. Cambridge, MA: Harvard University Press.

Suarez, F. (1944) *Selections from Three Works of Francisco Suarez*, vol. 2, ed. J. Scott. Oxford: Clarendon Press.

Tzu, H., Tzu, H. F. and Tzu, M. (1964) *Basic Writings of Mo Tzu, Hsun Tzu, and Han Fei Tzu*, trans. B. Watson. New York: Columbia University Press.

United Nations (1974) *General Assembly Ruling 3314*. New York: United Nations.

de Vitoria, F. (1991) *Political Writings: Francesco de Vitoria*, ed. A. Pagden and J. Lawrance. Cambridge: Cambridge University Press.

Walzer, M. (1992) *Just and Unjust Wars*, 2nd edn. New York: Basic Books.

Yeager, C. and Janos, L. (1986) *Yeager*. London: Arrow Books.

Discussion Questions

1. Critique the just-war theory. Is it still applicable in modern society? Support your answer.
2. Is the just-war theory, as explicated by Coady, morally justifiable? Analyze the theory in light of the prima facie moral duties and rights discussed in Chapter 1.
3. Discuss whether the United States's preemptive strike against Iraq, and the attacks by Iraqis on the occupying coalition forces, are justified under the just-war theory.

4. Apply the just-war theory to the Israeli/Palestinian conflict. Are the terrorist attacks by the Palestinians justified under the just-war theory? Support your answer.
5. Discuss whether a policy of nuclear deterrence is justified under the just-war theory.
6. Applying the *jus in bello* reasoning, discuss whether the use of chemical and biological weapons in self-defense is justified if a country is invaded by another country that has greatly superior military strength.
7. In the September 11 attacks, the terrorists chose targets that symbolized what they regarded as the heresy of globalization and the destruction of traditional ways of living, and exploitation of the poor of the world by the rich. Discuss whether targeting symbols of "evil" by groups that lack the power to directly attack the military of a superior force is ever legitimate. How would Coady and a utilitarian each most likely answer this question?
8. On the other hand, President George Bush attacked Iraq as one member of the "axis of evil." What does it mean to be "evil" in the context of the just-war theory? Is being "evil," at least in the eyes of the attacker, ever a just cause for going to war? Support your answers.

SOHAIL H. HASHMI

Interpreting the Islamic Ethics of War and Peace

Sohail H. Hashmi is an associate professor in the International Relations Program at Mt. Holyoke College. In this reading, Hashmi reviews the origins of Islamic ethics of war and peace and the concept of *jihad,* and points out some of the disagreements and ambiguities in the Islamic position on war. He then discusses *jihad* in the context of the just-war tradition. Finally he applies Islamic ethics of *jihad* to current issues such as the killing of civilians during the Iraq/Iran war and the first Gulf War, and the possession and use of weapons of mass destruction.

Critical Reading Questions

1. What is the source of the controversy regarding the concept of *jihad?*
2. What are the primary sources of the ethical discourse in Islam?
3. Who is Ibn Khaldun and what are his views on war and peace?
4. According to the *Koran* (*Qur'an*) why is humanity prone to war?
5. What is peace (*salam*)?

From *The Ethics of War and Peace,* Terry Nardin, ed. (Princeton: Princeton University Press, 1996), pp. 146–166.

6. Under what conditions is the use of force sanctioned by Muslim ethics?
7. Is pacifism an acceptable response to oppression in Islamic ethics?
8. What is the *sunna* and what is its relation to the *Koran?*
9. What was the prophet Muhammed's view on the use of war and violence?
10. When is nonviolent resistance preferable to armed conflict?
11. What are the four types of war distinguished by Ibn Khaldun? Which wars are legitimate and which ones are illegitimate?
12. What is the Islamic view on the use of war or force to convert nonbelievers?
13. What is the medieval distinction between *dar al-harb* and *dar al-Islam* and how does it influence contemporary Islamic views on international relations?
14. What is the modern fundamentalist Islamic view of the role of *jihad* on an international level?
15. What is the basis for *jus in bello* (just conduct of war) and *jus ad bellum* (just waging of a war) in the *Koran* (*Qur'an*) and Islamic ethics?
16. On what grounds did the Iraqis protest the Coalition bombings of cities and industrial facilities during the first Gulf War, as well as the killing of Iraqi troops fleeing Kuwait?
17. What is the Islamic position on the use of weapons of mass destruction?

Muslim writers of many intellectual persuasions have long argued that Westerners hold an inaccurate, even deliberately distorted, conception of *jihad.* In fact, however, the idea of *jihad* (and the ethics of war and peace generally) has been the subject of an intense and multifaceted debate among Muslims themselves. So diffusely defined and inconsistently applied has the idea become in Islamic discourse that a number of religious opposition groups have felt compelled to differentiate their cause from competing "false" causes by naming themselves, tautologically, "Islamic" *jihad.*

Nevertheless, when the contemporary Islamic discourse on war and peace is studied in the context of recent historical events, including decolonization and the many conflicts in which Muslims have been involved, one can discern an emerging consensus among Muslim intellectuals on the current meaning of *jihad.* This consensus is by no means universal, and given the diffuse nature of religious authority in the Islamic tradition, debate on the ethics of war and peace is likely to continue. But as I hope to demonstrate, the concept of *jihad* in contemporary Islam is one that is still adapting to the radical changes in international relations that have occurred since the medieval theory was first elaborated. We are witnessing a period of reinterpretation and redefinition, one characterized by controversy and confusion about how the concept should be applied to contemporary events, but also by movement toward wider agreement on the essential points of an Islamic ethics of war and peace. . . .

Much of the controversy surrounding the concept of *Jihad* among Muslims today emerges from the tension between its legal and ethical dimensions. This tension arises because it is the juristic, and not the philosophical or ethical, literature that has historically defined Muslim discourse on war and peace. With the rise of the legalistic tradition, ethical inquiry became a narrow and secondary concern of Islamic scholarship. What we find from the medieval period are legal treatises propounding the rules of *Jihad* and discussing related issues, but few ethical works outlining a framework of principles derived from the Qur'an and sunna upon which these rules could be based. . . .

CONCEPTIONS OF WAR AND PEACE IN THE QUR'AN

Ibn Khaldun observes in the *Muqaddima,* his celebrated introduction to a history of the world composed at the end of the fourteenth century, that "wars and different kinds of fighting have always occurred in the world since God created it." "War is endemic to human existence," he writes, "something natural among human beings. No nation, and no race is free from it."[2] Ibn Khaldun's brief comment summarizes rather well the traditional Islamic understanding of war as a universal and inevitable aspect of human existence. It is a feature of human society sanctioned, if not willed, by God Himself. The issues of war and peace thus fall within the purview of divine legislation for humanity. Islam, Muslims like to say, is a complete code of life, given the centrality of war to human existence, the moral evaluation of war holds a significant place in Muslim ethical/legal discussion. The Islamic ethics of war and peace is therefore derived from the same general sources upon which Islamic law is based.

The first of these sources, of course, is the Qur'an, which is held by Muslims to be God's final and definitive revelation to humanity. The Qur'anic text, like other revealed scriptures, is not a systematic treatise on ethics or law. It is a discursive commentary on the actions and experiences of the prophet Muhammad, his followers, and his opponents over the course of twenty-three years. But as the Qur'an itself argues in several verses, God's message is not limited to the time and place of its revelation; it is, rather, "a message to all the worlds" (81:27) propounding a moral code with universal applicability (39:41). From this commentary emerge broadly defined ethical principles that have been elaborated throughout Islamic history into what may be termed an Islamic conception of divine creation and man's place in it. In other words, although the Qur'an does not present a systematic ethical argument, it is possible to derive a consistent ethical system from it.

Why is humanity prone to war? The Qur'anic answer unfolds in the course of several verses revealed at various times, the essential points of which may be summarized as follows:

First, man's fundamental nature (*fitra*) is one of moral innocence, that is, freedom from sin. In other words, there is no Islamic equivalent to the notion of "original sin." Moreover, each individual is born with a knowledge of God's commandments, that is, with the essential aspects of righteous behavior. But this moral awareness is eroded as each individual encounters the corrupting influences of human society (30:30).

Second, man's nature is to live on the earth in a state of harmony, and peace with other living things. This is the ultimate import of the responsibility assigned by God to man as His vicegerent (*khalifa*) on this planet (2:30). True peace (*salam*) is therefore not merely an absence of war; it is the elimination of the grounds for strife or conflict, and the resulting waste and corruption (*fasad*) they create. Peace, not war or violence, is God's true purpose for humanity (2:208).

Third, given man's capacity for wrongdoing, there will always be some who *choose* to violate their nature and transgress against God's commandments. Adam becomes fully human only when he chooses to heed Iblis's (Satan's) temptation and disobeys God. As a result of this initial act of disobedience, human beings are expelled from the Garden to dwell on earth as "enemies to each other" (2:36, 7:24). Thus, wars and the evils that stem from them, the Qur'an suggests, are the inevitable consequences of the uniquely human capacity for moral choice.

The Qur'an does not present the fall of man as irrevocable, however, for God quickly returns to Adam to support and guide him. (2:37). This, according to Islamic belief, is the beginning of continuous divine revelation to humanity through a series of prophets ending with Muhammad. God's reminders of the laws imprinted upon each human consciousness through His prophets are a manifestation of His endless mercy to His creation, because all human beings are potential victims of Iblis's guile, that is, potential evildoers, and most human beings are actually quite far from God's laws (36:45–46). When people form social units, they become all the more prone to disobey God's laws through the obstinate persistence in wrongdoing caused by custom and social pressures (2:1.3-1:4, 37:69, 43:22). In this way, the individual drive for power, wealth, prestige, and all the other innumerable human goals becomes amplified. Violence is the inevitable result of the human desire for self-aggrandizement.

Fourth, each prophet encounters opposition from those (always a majority) who persist in their rebellion against God, justifying their actions through various self-delusions. One of the principal characteristics of rejection of God (*kufr*) is the inclination toward violence and oppression, encapsulated by the broad concept *zulm.* When individuals choose to reject divine guidance, either by transgressing against specific divine injunctions or by losing faith altogether, they violate (commit zulm against) their own nature (fitra).... When an entire society rejects God, oppression and violence become the norm throughout the society and in relation with other societies as well the moral anarchy that prevails when human beings abandon the higher moral code derived from faith in a supreme and just Creator, the Qur'an suggests, is fraught with potential and actual violence . . .

Fifth, peace (salam) is attainable only when beings surrender to God's will and live according to God's laws. This is the condition of *islam,* the conscious decision to acknowledge in faith and conduct the presence and power of God. Because human nature is not sufficiently strong to resist the temptation to evil, it is necessary for man to establish a human agency, that is, a state, to mitigate the effects of anarchy and enforce divine law.

Sixth, because it is unlikely that individuals or societies will ever conform fully to the precepts of Islam, Muslims must always be prepared to fight to preserve the Muslim faith and Muslim principles (8:60, 73). The use of force by the Muslim community is, therefore, sanctioned by God as a necessary response to the existence of evil in the world. As the Qur'an elaborates in an early revelation, the believers are those "who, whenever tyranny afflicts them, defend themselves" (42:39). This theme of the just, God-ordained use of force for legitimate purposes is continued in several other verses. In the first verse that explicitly permits the Muslim community to use armed force against its enemies, the Qur'an makes clear that fighting is a burden imposed upon all believers (not only Muslims) as a result of the enmity harbored by the unbelievers.

Permission [to fight] is given to those against whom War is being wrongfully waged . . . those who have been driven from their homelands against all right for no other reason than their saying: "Our Sustainer is God!" . . .

A subsequent verse converts this permission to fight into an injunction: The rationale given for using armed force is quite explicit "Tumult and oppression (*fitna*) is worse than killing" (2:191). These two verses clearly undermine the possibility of an Islamic pacifism. One verse in particular offers an implicit challenge to an ethical position based on the renunciation of all violence: "Fighting is prescribed for you, even though it be hateful to you; but it may well be that you hate something that is in fact good for you, and that you love a thing that is in fact bad for you: and God knows, whereas you do not" (2:216). There is, thus, no equivalent in the Islamic tradition of the continuing debate within Christianity of the possibility of just war: There is no analogue in Islamic texts to Aquinas's Question 40: "Are some wars permissible?" The Islamic discourse on war and peace begins from the a priori assumption that some types of war are permissible—indeed, required by God—and that all other forms of violence are, therefore, forbidden. In short, the Qur'an's attitude toward war and peace may be described as an idealistic realism. Human existence is characterized neither by incessant warfare nor by real peace, but by a continuous tension between the two; Societies exist forever in a precarious balance between them. The unending human challenge *jihad fi sabit Allah* (struggle in the way of God) to mitigate the possibility of war to strengthen the grounds for peace....

CONCEPTIONS OF WAR AND PEACE IN THE SUNNA

The second source for the Islamic ethics of war and peace is the practice (sunna) of the prophet Muhammad. It is impossible to comprehend the Qur'an without understanding the life of the Prophet and impossible to comprehend the life of the Prophet without understanding the Qur'an. As the Prophet's wife, Aisha bint Abi Bakr, is reported to have said: "His character (*khuluqhu*) was the Qur'an.[4]

Muhammad was born into a milieu characterized by internecine skirmishes (*ghazwa*) among rival robes. These were seldom more than raids undertaken for petty plunder of a neighboring tribe's flocks. If the conflict had any "higher" purpose, it was usually collective reprisal for an injury or affront suffered by a single member of the tribe: according to the prevailing *lex talionis*. Larger confrontations for higher stakes, such as the actual conquest of territory, were rare, although not unknown. . . . Naturally, tribal loyalty was the cornerstone of this society's ethos, and virtue was often equated with martial valor. It would, however, be incorrect to view pre-Islamic' Arab culture as glorifying war. . . . [T]he ghazw'a was often viewed by its participants as a sort of ongoing game, a struggle to outwit the opponent with a minimum of bloodshed. The aim was not to vanquish the foe but to demonstrate the qualities of courage, loyalty, and magnanimity-all components of masculine nobility included in the term *muruwwa*. Implicit in the Arab martial code were "rules of the game" that prohibited, among other things, fighting during certain months, the killing of noncombatants, and unnecessary spoliation. . . .

We can construct an outline of the Prophet's approach to the ethics of war and peace not only by referring to the Qur'an, but also by making use of the large body of literature comprising the Prophet's sayings and actions (*hadith*) and biography (*sira*) compiled between the second and fourth Islamic centuries. It is clear from these records that from an early age, Muhammad was averse to many aspects of the tribal culture in which he was born. In particular, there is no indication that he ever showed any interest in affairs of tribal honor, particularly in the ghazwa. [T]hroughout the Meccan period of his prophetic mission (610-22 C.E.), he showed no inclination toward the use of force in any form, even for self-defense—on the contrary, his policy can only be described as nonviolent resistance. . . . The Prophet insisted throughout this period on the virtues of patience and steadfastness in the face of their opponents' attacks. When the persecution of the most vulnerable Muslims (former slaves and members of Mecca's poorer families) became intense, he directed them to seek refuge in the realm of a Christian king, Abyssinia. The Prophet's rejection of armed struggle during the Meccan period was more than mere prudence based on the Muslims' military weakness. It was, rather, derived from the Qur'an's still unfolding conception that the use of force should be avoided unless it is, in just war parlance, a "last resort." . . .

The requital of evil is an evil similar to it hence, whoever pardons [his enemy] and makes peace, his reward rests with God—for, verily; He does not love evildoers. Yet indeed, as for any who defend themselves after having been wronged—no blame whatever attaches to them: blame attaches but to those who oppress [other] people and behave outrageously on earth, offending against all right: for them is grievous suffering in store! But if one is patient in adversity and forgives, this is indeed the best resolution of affairs (42:40–43).

The main result of these early verses is not to reaffirm the pre-Islamic custom of lex talionis but the exact opposite: to establish the moral superiority of forgiveness over revenge. The permission of self-defense is not a call to arms; military force is not mentioned, although neither is it proscribed. Instead, it should be seen as a rejection of quietism, of abnegation of moral responsibility in the face of oppression. Active nonviolent resistance and open defiance of pagan persecution is the proper Muslim response, according to these verses, and was, in fact, the Prophet's own practice during this period. . . .

THE GROUNDS FOR WAR

Ibn Khaldun continues his discussion of war in the *Muqaddima* by distinguishing four types of war: One arises from petty squabbles among rival foes or neighboring tribes, another from the desire for plunder found among "savage peoples." These two types he labels "illegitimate wars." Then, reflecting the prevailing medieval approach, he divides legitimate wars into two types: *jihad* and wars to suppress internal rebellion.[14] This latter division of legitimate wars is the logical outgrowth of the medieval juristic bifurcation of the world into two spheres, *dar al-Islam* (the realm where Islamic law applied), and *dar al-harb* (the realm of war). According to the Sunni legal schools, *jihad* properly speaking was war waged against unbelievers. Because all Muslims were understood to constitute a single community of believers, wars between Muslim parties were usually classed in a separate category, *fitna* (literally, a "trial" or "test"). Like Plato, who has Socrates declare that Greeks do not make war on one another,[15] the Muslim jurists viewed intra-Muslim disputes as internal strife that should be resolved quickly by the ruling authorities. This approach to war among Muslims, important in medieval theory, has assumed greater significance in modern controversies about the definition of *jihad*.

The descriptions of *jihad* in the medieval texts reflect the historical context in which legal theory was elaborated. Because the medieval juristic conception of *jihad* provided legal justification for the rapid expansion of the Islamic empire that occurred in the decades following the Prophet's death, its connotations are offensive rather than defensive. Relatively little consideration was given to *jihad* defined as "defensive struggle," that is, war undertaken strictly to safeguard Muslim lives and property from external aggression. It was considered obvious that Muslims may wage war in self-defense, according to the Qur'anic verses cited earlier. This defensive war was *fard 'ayn,* a moral duty of each able-bodied Muslim, male or female.

More detailed discussion of *jihad* comes in the context of offensive struggles aimed at expansion of Islamic hegemony, an expansion aimed ultimately at the universal propagation of Islam. In the twelfth century, Ibn Rushd (Averroes) wrote a legal treatise that deals at some length with the conditions of *jihad*.[16] . . .

Because the ultimate end of *jihad* is the propagation of the Islamic faith, not material gain or territorial conquest, Ibn Rushd; like other medieval writers, implicitly, if not always explicitly, separates the grounds for *jihad* from the grounds for war (harb or qitai). Because Islam is viewed as a universal mission to all humanity, *jihad* is the perpetual condition that prevails between dar al-Islam and dar, al-harb. Participation in the *jihad* to overcome dar al-harb was, a *fard kifaya,* a moral obligation only for those capable of assuming it, namely able-bodied and financially secure adult males. Actual war arose only as the final step in a "ladder of escalation." The first step in any contact between the Muslim state and a foreign power was an invitation to allow the peaceful preaching of Islam. This was consonant with the practice of the Prophet, who allegedly had sent letters to the rulers of Byzantium, Iran, and Egypt for precisely this purpose. If a foreign ruler refused this invitation, he was to be offered the incorporation of his people into the Islamic realm as a protected non-Muslim community governed by its own religious laws, but obliged to pay a tax, the *jizya,* in lieu of performing military service. Only if the non-Muslims refused these conditions were there grounds for active hostilities. At this point, the Muslim ruler was not only permitted but required to wage war against them. . . .

As Ibn Rushd's discussion makes apparent, the medieval juristic literature is characterized by fundamental disagreements on the grounds for war. But most of the legal scholars agree that the object of *jihad* is not the forcible conversion of unbelievers to the Islamic faith. This object would contradict several clear Qur'anic statements enjoining freedom of worship, including "Let there be no compulsion in religion; the truth stands out clearly from error" (2:256), and "If your Lord had so willed, all those who are on earth would have believed: you then compel mankind, against their will, to believe?" (10:99). . . . The object of *jihad* is generally held by these writers to be the subjugation of hostile powers who refuse to permit the preaching of Islam, not forcible conversion. Once under Muslim rule, they reason, non-Muslims will be free to consider the merits of Islam. The medieval theory of an ongoing *jihad*, and the bifurcation of the world into dar al-Islam and dar al-harb upon which it was predicated, became a fiction soon after it was elaborated by medieval writers. . . . Nevertheless, the idea that "Islam" and the "West" represented monolithic and mutually antagonistic civilizations underlay much Muslim and European writing, particularly during the heyday of European imperialism in the eighteenth and nineteenth centuries. Shades of this viewpoint are very much apparent in our own day.

In his discussion of recent Muslim thinking on the grounds for *jihad*, Bassam ubi outlines two contending approaches, the "conformist" and the "fundamentalist." He suggests that the reinterpretation of the medieval theory of *jihad* 'by modernists (as the conformists are more commonly known) is half-hearted and that, in the end, it is the fundamentalists' resurrection of the medieval dar al-harb/dar al-Islam distinction that best characterizes the current Muslim view of international relations generally and issues of war and peace in particular. . . . Although the Qur'an's division of mankind into believers and unbelievers lends support for such a view, modernist writers argue that the Qur'anic verses cannot be interpreted to suggest a perpetual state of war between the two, nor any territoriality to the "house of Islam," when these verses are taken in the full context of the Qur'anic message. In one of the leading modernist expositions of Islam international law, Mohammad Talaat al-Ghunaimi, dismisses the dir al-Islam/dar al-harb distinction as an idea introduced by certain medieval legal thinkers in response to their own historical circumstances, but having no basis in Islamic ethics. . . .

With the emergence of postcolonial Muslim states, political legitimacy and the rights of the people in the face of oppressive regimes have emerged as central issues in Islamic discourse. These issues figure prominently, of course, in all fundamentalist literature. Fundamentalists view themselves as a vanguard of the righteous, preparing the way for the elimination of jahili values from their societies and the establishment of a Just "Islamic" order. . . . What is clear from these works is the view, supported by experience, that the secular, nationalist regimes ruling most Muslim countries today, backed by their Western supporters, will not willingly cede power, even if the majority of the population does not support them. They will maintain power by any means, including the violent repression of dissent. In other words, it is argued that these regimes have declared war on Islam within their countries, and that it is incumbent upon all true believers to respond by whatever means are necessary, including violence, to overthrow them. The fundamentalist writings are therefore focused on combating the social and international oppression that they believe face the Muslim community (*umma*) everywhere. *Jihad* is for the fundamentalists an instrument for the realization of political and social justice in their own societies, a powerful tool for internal reform and one required by the Qur'an's command that Muslims "enjoin the right and forbid the wrong" (3:104). The thrust of the modern *jihad* is thus very much inward. Warfare on the international level is considered only to the extent that Western governments are viewed as archenemies who impose corrupt and authoritarian regimes upon Muslims. *Jihad* as an instrument for the imposition of Islamic rule in non-Muslim states today hardly figures in fundamentalist works. That goal has been postponed indefinitely, given the fundamentalist position, which they share with many other Muslim writers, that most of the Muslim countries themselves do not at present have Islamic governments.

One area in which modernists and fundamentalists are tending to converge is upon the argument that *jihad* is an instrument for enforcing human rights. For example, the Iranian revolutionary leader Ayatollah Murtaza Mutahhari argues that "the most sacred form of *jihad* and war is that which is fought in defense of humanity and of human rights."[20] Similarly, the Indian/Pakistani scholar Maulana Abu al-A'la Mawdudi writes that *jihad* is obligatory for Muslims when hostile forces threaten their human rights, which in his analysis includes forcibly evicting them from their homes, tampering with their social order, and obstructing religious life.[21] To some extent these arguments are a response to Western writings on the international protection of human rights. But it is interesting to note that whereas there is continuing debate in the West on the legality of humanitarian intervention against sovereign states, continuing ambivalence toward the territorial state in Islamic thought lends weight to the argument in favor of such intervention among a broad range of Muslim writers.[22]

THE CONDUCT OF WAR

Because the goal of *jihad* is the call to Islam, not territorial conquest or plunder, the right conduct of Muslim armies has traditionally been an important concern within Islam. The Qur'an provides the basis for *ius in bello* considerations: "And fight in God's cause against those who wage war against you, but do not transgress limits, for God loves not the transgressors" (2:190). The "limits" are enumerated in the practice of the Prophet and the first four caliphs. According to authoritative traditions, whenever the Prophet sent out a military force, he would instruct its commander to adhere to certain restraints. . . .

Do not act treacherously; do not act disloyally; do not act neglectfully. Do not mutilate; do not kill little children or old men, or women; do not cut off the heads of the palm-trees or bum them; do not cut down the fruit trees; do not slaughter a sheep or a cow or a camel, except for food. You will pass by people who devote their lives in cloisters; leave them and their devotions alone. You will come upon people who bring you platters in which are various sorts of food; if you eat any of it, mention the name of God over it.

Thus, the Qur'an and the actions of the Prophet and his successors established the principles of discrimination and proportionality of means. . . . In addition, the jurists also dealt with the traditional concerns of ius in bello: the definition and protection of noncombatants and restrictions on certain types of weapon. The legal discussions address three issues: Who is subject to damage in war? What types of damage may be inflicted upon persons? What types of damage may be inflicted upon their property? Underlying the differing opinions on these issues once again are the apparent contradictions between the peace verses and the sword verses. . . .

In current Muslim discourse on war and peace, ius in bello issues receive very little attention. This is true despite the vast changes that have occurred in both the international law and the technology of warfare. The discussion that does occur is usually undertaken by modernists seeking to reinterpret the Qur'an and sunna so that Islamic injunctions correspond to current international practice.[27] . . . More contemporary issues, such as the definition of noncombatant immunity and the use of terrorist methods by some Islamic groups have yet to be treated systematically.

Far more relevant arid [sic] interesting discussion or [sic] right conduct in war occurs in the context of specific conflicts. During the "war of the cities" toward the end of the Iran-Iraq War, for example, Mehdi Bazargan and the Liberation Movement of Iran (LMI) repeatedly protested that Khomeini was violating Islamic prohibitions against targeting civilians when he authorized missile strikes against Baghdad in retaliation for Iraq's Scud missile attacks against Teheran. In one "open letter" to Khomeini, the IMI wrote:

According to Islam, it is justifiable retribution only if we, with our own missiles, hit the commanders or senders of the Iraqi missiles rather than hitting civilian areas and killing innocent people and turning their homes and communities into ghost towns and hills of rubble, all in the name of striking military targets.

. . . ius in bello rather than ius ad bellum concerns dominated Muslim debates on the ethics of the conflict. Among the points raised by opponents of the anti-Iraq coalition's policies was that the conflict should be treated as fitna, that is, a dispute among Muslims. The rules concerning fitna developed by medieval jurists do not permit Muslims to ally themselves with non-Muslims, particularly when military decision-making is in non-Muslim hands. The prohibition was based on the belief that unbelievers would not apply the stricter code of conduct incumbent upon Muslims when fighting other Muslims. Critics of the Gulf War have: argued that the conduct of the war by the coalition validates the medieval jurists' concerns. The massive air bombardment of Iraq's governmental and industrial facilities, they charge, was disproportionate to the Iraqi provocation and insufficiently discriminated between military and civilian targets. Moreover, the slaughter of Iraqi troops fleeing Kuwait City on the "highway of death" directly contravened one of the central points of Islamic law, namely that the goal of all military campaigns against other Muslims should be to rehabilitate and not to annihilate the transgressing party.

The most glaring area of neglect in contemporary Islamic analyses of ius in bello concerns weapons of mass destruction. So far, no systematic work has been done by Muslim scholars on how nuclear chemical, and biological weapons relate to the Islamic ethics of war. This is an astonishing fact in light of the development of nuclear technology by several Muslim countries and the repeated use of chemical weapons by Iraq. In discussing the issue with several leading Muslim specialists in international law, I have found a great deal of ambivalence on the subject. Most scholars cite the Qur'anic verse "Hence, make ready against them whatever force and war mounts you are able to muster, so that you might deter thereby the enemies of God" (8:60) as justification for developing nuclear weaponry. Muslims must acquire nuclear weapons, I have been repeatedly told, because their enemies have introduced such weapons into their arsenals. There is unanimous agreement that Muslims should think of nuclear weapons only as a deterrent and that they should be used only as a second strike weapon. But Islamic discussion of this topic remains at a very superficial level. There is little appreciation of the logistics of nuclear deterrence and of the moral difficulties to which a deterrence strategy gives rise.

CONCLUSION

Is the Islamic *jihad* the same as the Western just war? The answer, of course, depends upon who is defining the concepts. But after this brief survey of the debates that have historically surrounded the Islamic approach to war and peace and the controversies that are continuing to this day, I think it is safe to conclude that even though *jihad* may not be identical to the just war as it has evolved in the West, the similarities between Western and Islamic thinking on war and peace are far more numerous than the differences.

. . . *Jihad,* like just war, is grounded in the belief that intersocietal relations should be peaceful, not marred by constant and destructive warfare. The surest way for human beings to realize this peace is for them to obey the divine law that is imprinted on the human conscience and therefore accessible to everyone, believers and unbelievers. . . . No war was *jihad* unless it was undertaken with right intent and as a last resort, and declared by right authority. Most Muslims today disavow the duty to propagate Islam by force and limit *jihad* to self-defense. And finally, *jihad,* like just war, places strict limitations on legitimate targets during war and demands that belligerents use the least amount of force necessary to achieve the swift cessation of hostilities. Both *jihad* and just war are dynamic concepts, still evolving and adapting to changing international realities. As Muslims continue to interpret the Islamic ethics of war and peace, their debates on *jihad* will, I believe, increasingly parallel the Western debates on just war. And as Muslims and non-Muslims continue their recently begun dialogue on the just international order, they may well find a level of agreement on the ethics of war and peace that will ultimately be reflected in a revised and more universal law of war and peace.

NOTES

2. Ibn Khaldun, *The Muqaddimah: An Introduction to History,* trans. Franz Rosenthal (Princeton: Princeton University Press, 1967), 2:73.
4. Ahmad b. 'Abdallah Abu Nu'aim al-Isfahani, *Dala 'il al-nubuwwa* (Hyderabad: Da'irat al-Ma'arif al-Uthmaniyya, 1977), 139.
14. Ibn Khaldun, Muqaddimah, 224.
15. Plato, *The Republic,* trans. Allan Bloom (New York: Basic Books, 1968), 150.
16. Ibn Rushd, *Bidayat al-mujtahid,* in Rudolph Peters, ed. and trans., Jihad, in *Medieval and Modern Islam* (Leiden: E. J. Brill, 1977), 9–25.
20. Ayatollah Murtaza Mutahhari, "Defense: The Essence of Jihad," in Mehdi Abedi and Gary Legenhausen, eds., *Jihad and Shahadat: Struggle and Martyrdom in Islam* (Houston: Institute for Research and Islamic Studies, 1986), 105.
21. Abu al-A'la Mawdudi, *Al-Jihad fi'l-Islam* (Lahore: Idara Tarjuman al-Qur'an, 1988), 55–56.
22. For a more detailed discussion of this issue, see Sohail H. Hashmi, "Is There an Islamic Ethic of Humanitarian Intervention?" *Ethics and International Affairs* 7 (1993), 55–73.
27. Two important modernist discussions of the means of war are Abu Zahra, *Concept of War in Islam;* 44–68, and Muhammad Hamidullah, *The Muslim Conduct of State,* 7th ed. (Lahore: Sh. Muhammad Ashraf, 1977), 202–54.

Discussion Questions

1. Compare and contrast the Islamic ethics of war and peace with the Judeo-Christian tradition. Do the differences between the two ethics systems support ethical relativism? Discuss what a cultural relativist, a natural law ethicist, and/or a deontologist would each make of the similarities and differences.
2. Discuss Islamic views of when it is just to wage war and the Islamic rules for conducting war, in light of the Western just-war tradition.
3. What is the difference between nonviolent resistance and pacifism, and why is the first justified under Islamic ethics, but not the second?
4. In March 2001 a Palestinian detonated an explosive next to a bus in Jerusalem, killing himself and injuring thirty Israelis. Six months later Islamic terrorists crashed two airplanes into the World Trade Center, killing thousands, including themselves. Many Muslims regard suicide bombers as contrary to God's law and Muhammed's teachings. Others regard suicide bombers as martyrs and suicide bombing as a legitimate form of self-defense.[16] Discuss the moral validity of these two positions in light of the Islamic teaching on war.
5. Imagine that you, as an ethicist who is knowledgeable about both Islamic and Judeo-Christian ethical views of war and peace, are chosen to negotiate a peace agreement or settlement between Israel and the Palestinians. How would you proceed? Choose other students in the class to play the roles of the Israeli and Palestinian delegates at the negotiation table.
6. You did such a good job with the Palestinian/Israeli negotiations that you are invited to advise President Bush and his staff on how to proceed with their goal of nation-building and turning Iraq into a modern democratic society. As an ethicist, what advice would you give Bush and his staff?
7. Discuss what course of action an Islamic ethicist would most likely suggest for the Muslim world to take in response to Hitler's program of exterminating the Jews during World War II. Support your answer.

ROBINSON A. GROVER

The New State of Nature and the New Terrorism

Robinson Grover, from the University of Connecticut, argues that modern technology has created a new form of Hobbes's state of nature. This technological state of nature has made terrorism a greater threat than in the past. He concludes his article by making suggestions for dealing with the risk of high-tech terrorism.

"The New State of Nature and the New Terrorism," *Public Affairs Quarterly,* vol. 16, no. 2 (April 2002), 125–141. Notes have been omitted.

Critical Reading Questions

1. What does Grover mean when he says that "Hobbes's concept of the state of nature is still relevant"?
2. What is Hobbes's view of human nature?
3. What is Hobbes's "state of nature" and why is life brutish and short in the state of nature?
4. According to Hobbes, what is the basis of an effective sovereign? Why is a sovereign necessary to prevent war and why is it important that a sovereign have absolute power?
5. What is Grover's view of Hobbes's philosophy?
6. What does Grover mean when he says that "modern technology has created a new form of the state of nature"?
7. What are some of the implications of our "technological state of nature" and how has this made terrorism a greater threat?
8. How can the Internet be used to support terrorism?
9. How is biotechnology in a scientific state of nature?
10. What is the difference between low-tech and high-tech forms of the state of nature?
11. According to Grover, what motivates most modern terrorists, include suicidal terrorists? How does this fit with Hobbes's account of human motivation?
12. In what ways do the September 11 attacks represent the new terrorism?
13. What suggestions does Grover make for combating the new high-tech terrorism and what are some of the problems with these solutions?

THOMAS HOBBES AND THE GLOBAL STATE OF NATURE

This paper is about terrorism and the new global state of nature. The concept of a primitive state of nature as a bleak form of anarchy is usually associated with Thomas Hobbes's writings from the middle of the seventeenth century. According to Hobbes, all culture and production would be impossible in this primitive state and life would become a war of all against all. Today, our universal assumption is that, because of global communications, production, and transport, we live in a high technology world totally removed from the anarchic state of nature Hobbes described. I believe that this is quite wrong and that we are now closer to the state of nature than we have been at any time in the last fifty years. Furthermore, I believe that this state of nature exists because of, not in spite of, modern technology. Hobbes's original concept of the state of nature is indeed out of date. . . . Much of the phenomenon of globalization should be understood as a high-tech, global state of nature, quite different from Hobbes's seventeenth-century image, but still a true state of nature and one that is every bit as threatening as the original version. In this context, Hobbes's account of human greed and reason, human fear and power is crucial to our understanding of global technology and terrorism.

I. HOBBES'S PRIMITIVE STATE OF NATURE

Hobbes begins by imagining a society with no sovereign, in which *men live without a common Power to keep them all in awe* (*Leviathan,* chap. 13, par. 8). In modern terms, Hobbes is picturing a society without any centralized hegemonic power. If we were naturally social animals without any critical intelligence or sense of self, this would not be a problem. We would need no central authority, and would be genetically programmed to preserve our common genes. We would be and would behave like ants, operating on instinct and sacrificing ourselves unthinkingly for the sake of the community. Hobbes, breaking with the Aristotelian tradition, argued that we are not naturally suited to live in civil society. Fortunately or unfortunately, we are complex creatures with strong, selfish passions and also with the ability to reason and to learn from experience. Hobbes calls these selfish passions *competition, diffidence, and glory;* we call them greed, fear, and pride. . . . Unfortunately, a pattern of decisions based on the selfish passions produces civil war and anarchy, while reason and prudence are necessary for life in a civil society. The result is that Hobbes's state of nature is always a state of war and anarchy:

> In such a condition there is no place for industry, because the fruit thereof is uncertain: and consequently no culture of the earth; no navigation nor use of commodities that may be imported by sea; no commodious building; no instruments of moving and removing such things as require much force; no knowledge of the face of the earth; no account of time; no arts; no letters; no society; and, which is worst of all, continual fear and the danger of violent death; and the life of man solitary, poor, nasty, mean, brutish, and short (*Leviathan*, chap. 13).

Worse, our reasoning ability allows us to look ahead and foresee possible harmful conduct by others and therefore gives us additional motives to act selfishly toward others and so preempt their possible selfish actions. According to Hobbes, our reasoning ability, coupled with our selfish passions, often makes life without a sovereign less stable, not more. In modern language, Hobbes is claiming that, in the state of nature, the world-view of the paranoid is basically correct. Unfortunately, living near an intelligent paranoid and far away from effective police power can be very dangerous. . . .

In Hobbes's argument . . . the meaning of "state of nature" is "not having an effective sovereign." Whereas a state of war "*consisteth not in actuall fighting; but in the known disposition thereto, during all the time there is no assurance to the contrary.*" Hobbes claims this always happens when there is no effective sovereign. For Hobbes the "state of nature" and "the state of war" mean different things, but in practice they always occur together. . . . Finally, the anarchy found in the state of nature is the causal result of the lack of a sovereign and our emotional make-up. Without a sovereign and with our selfish passions many of us will be inclined to attack others. Given this state of war, cooperation and trust will be very hard to sustain. But cooperation and trust are essential to producing the goods we need for a commodious life. Hobbes asserts over and over that the state of nature will always and everywhere be a state of war, which will in turn cause a state of primitive anarchy.

Hobbes goes on to argue that this outcome is utterly unacceptable and that autocracy is preferable to anarchy. If he could use modern terminology, he would say that most people are highly risk-averse, and therefore will choose any outcome that avoids anarchy.

Hobbes proposes creating a sovereign which will have effective power to prevent anarchy. This sovereign can be a person such as a king, or a small group such as an oligarchy, or a large group such as a democracy, but whatever the make-up of the sovereign, it must have absolute power and authority. Finally, he argues that the way to get an effective sovereign is to make a contract which gives the sovereign absolute authority and power to maintain the peace and prevent anarchy. Hobbes does not build civil authority on habit or custom; nor does he use traditional natural law or right reason, nor does he invoke the will of god as revealed in holy scripture or church tradition. Instead, he argues for sovereignty based on the rational self-interest of individuals and expressed by tacit contractual agreements between them.

In Hobbes's defense, he lived through the English civil wars, and was a refugee for eleven years in France, which was having its own civil and religious wars at this time. He had good reasons to detest the loss of effective sovereignty and the resulting anarchy. In this century we have suffered at least as much from the despotism of absolute rulers as from the anarchy of the state of nature. Often the two seem to meet each other in some horrible parody of government in which the despotic mis-rule of some President-for-Life in some failed state is both autocratic and anarchic. Most of us do not believe that absolutism is always to be preferred to anarchy. Nevertheless, the thrust of Hobbes's argument is clear and powerful. Even if we do not agree, we must consider his arguments carefully. . . .

II. OUR TECHNOLOGICAL STATE OF NATURE

Contrary to all recent expectations, modern technology has created a new form of the state of nature. This is because of three interlocking effects of modern technology. This new state of nature is much larger than Hobbes's seventeenth century version. It is also much less stable. It is also truly decentralized. As a result, large parts of our society and economy have no effective sovereign.

The first problem is the greatly increased size of the state of nature. In a primitive society with no sovereign, I have just cause to fear—whom? Obviously, the people who can harm me. For practical purposes this means my neighbors far and near, but only my neighbors. For farmers in Malmesbury in the seventeenth century this meant effectively the people in their part of England. Let us be very generous (or paranoid) and include all of the British Isles and those foreign rulers who could invade England, some very powerful religious figures, and a very few international bankers. All the rest of the world's population knew nothing of Malmesbury, and could not threaten people living there if they did. . . .

Compare that situation with today's global economy. Our decentralized transportation system moves people and goods about the entire globe cheaply and quickly. One result is cheaper food, fuel, and clothing. Another result is that contaminated food in Europe effects markets in the Americas, Asia, Africa and Australia—think of mad cow disease. Another result is that people with infectious diseases can fly from their homes to anywhere in the world and give the disease to others. They may not even know they are sick. In both cases, utter strangers may harm us without intending to or even knowing that they are doing so. In addition, many others now have the ability to harm us deliberately to further their own purposes. In its worst manifestation, globalization may give rise to a new form of international bio-terrorism.

Similarly with communications. At mid-century we were used to being able to write a letter to almost anyone anywhere in the world. We can now talk to anyone anywhere in the world and see a fair number of them via video-conferencing. That is, we can transmit and receive very complex information globally and with great speed. The web opens up a whole new level of contact partly because it is so fast and so widespread, but mostly because it is interactive. I can call up your site and leave a message, and because text and commands have similar formats, I can also order your machine to do things such as give me specific information from your web site, or even function differently. This new ability to do something at a distance (send commands) as well as to learn something from a distant source (receive information) also carries with it the ability to alter the commands and data on other machines. I can act at a distance without having to rely on a human agent. So I have the ability to give orders, buy things, look up obscure data, add new data into my system or yours and generally use the Internet for commerce. But I also have the ability to perpetrate fraud, steal confidential information, and spread computer viruses.

International finance is a third example of the mixed uses of this new technology. Again, it is enormously useful to be able to buy and sell currencies and stocks and bonds and derivatives rapidly worldwide. High speed communication coupled with a sophisticated global financial market gives people with capital enormous opportunities to make money and/or avoid loss. However, people who need to borrow capital are now competing with the whole rest of the globe and are often subject to disastrous capital flight. Moreover, the easy transfer of funds across international borders makes it easy for terrorists to move money and themselves around the globe. This makes it easier for them to hide in different countries, to acquire weapons and explosives, and to meet and plot unobserved.

There are many more examples of this explosive growth, but transport, communications and finance will do to call attention to the problems. The most obvious of these problems is the vast increase in the number of people and institutions that can effect us for good or ill. If my seventeenth century English farmers lived in a little world with a short event-horizon, we live in a huge world that includes most of the population of the earth and has a very long event-horizon. And if social control should break down in some serious way, the global state of nature would be huge. We would not have a small, nasty, backward state of nature in and around Malmesbury. We would have a large, nasty, technological state of nature everywhere.

Moreover, the interactive nature of the world-wide web raises a second problem. The web greatly increases our ability to form loose interest-based groups. The individuals in these groups usually receive both practical and psychological support from other members of the group. Unfortunately, some of these groups have malevolent purposes.

Hobbes argued that in the state of nature even the strongest individuals have reason to fear others:

> For as to the strength of body, the weakest has strength enough to kill the strongest, either by secret machination or by confederacy with others that are in the same danger as himself (*Leviathan,* chap. 13).

The Internet now provides a new meeting place for people to form confederacies. Usually these groups are benign, such as chess players, genealogists, sports trivia fans, or even philosophers. But the net can and does serve as a meeting place of a sort for pedophiles, and bomb-makers, and violent racists and homo-phobes. Alone, most of these individuals would probably remain unsavory but isolated and incapable of action. Emboldened, if not empowered, by meeting other like-minded individuals in chat rooms, they become more confirmed in their beliefs and more likely to act. In short, the Internet makes it easier to find like-minded individuals, and such individuals, having formed groups, are more likely to act. This probably makes effective conspiracies more frequent; it certainly increases the fear of such conspiracies in the targeted groups. Thus the very existence of these hate web-sites makes potential victims and their friends and parents understandably fearful. This perfectly justified, rational fear may provoke violent counter measures to forestall attacks. This creates a downward spiral of anger and conspiracy on one side with fear and preemptive strikes on the other side. It is a slippery slope leading to the state of war and anarchy.

The third aspect of this new technology is that it is structurally decentralized. The Internet is the best, but certainly not the only example of this. As long as computers are relatively cheap and can talk to each other—exchange information and commands—anyone can buy a computer and join. The only central authority on the web confines itself to overseeing web addresses and domain names. There is no central controlling authority to decide who gets on the Internet and what they can do once on there. In Hobbesian terms, the Internet has no sovereign. So far this has been a benefit. Indeed, it is hard to imagine how the Internet as we know it could have a sovereign. Most people attribute the growth and usefulness of the Internet to the fact that it is radically decentralized. However, the lack of a centralized controlling authority has allowed greedy individuals to commit fraud, violent individuals to plan violence, and psychotic individuals to stalk victims. Of course, some people do all of these things without touching a computer, but the computer and the Internet allow them to act with speed and anonymity. And, anonymity empowers evil.

What is even more interesting is the phenomenon of hackers and viruses. Some hacking and some viruses may be the product of greed or fear: the result of the temptation to get into a lightly secured place and steal something of value, or the result of fear that others may do something injurious and the resolve to strike preemptively at their computer. However, most hackers and creators of viruses do it out of pride. I am smarter than you, and to prove it I will defeat your security system and leave a message behind. Better yet, I will create a virus that will destroy the data on hundreds of thousands of computers, thus proving that I—the "heroic" lone individual—am smarter that all the rest of you and your corporations. This is exactly what Hobbes meant when he wrote about *glory* as one of the three *principall causes of quarrell.* Glory makes people fight *for trifles, as a word, a smile, a different opinion, or any other signs of undervalue.* A generation earlier in his *Discourse on War* Sir Walter Raleigh wrote in a similar way about pride being the basis of arbitrary and unnecessary wars. Raleigh thought that this sort of pride was common to princes and aristocrats and was a major cause of duels and wars. So today our self-designated intellectual elite, motivated by pride, choose combat by computer. We have a new phenomenon—computer combat by dueling nerds. Unhappily, innocent computer users can be badly damaged by these viral wars.

The global financial system uses its own communication systems as well as the Internet, and it too is highly decentralized. The finance ministers of the major countries have huge resources, but they are vastly out-numbered and out-weighted by the individual and corporate traders, and these traders operate openly on egoistic principles. They are all in it for profit. There are few if any controls on who participates in the market. A number of individuals and companies have the financial resources of small and not so small countries. The result is a close approximation of Hobbes's state of nature. Perhaps the only difference is that some of these traders are individuals with few resources while others are huge multi-national companies. The difference in strength is much greater than it is between individual humans. But even so, the differences in strength are not so great that any of these traders is immune to harm from the global financial market. All members of the system have desires and fears. All hope for gain. All fear loss. Most have large egos as well. Again, we have a situation of egoistic individuals operating in a world with no centralized authority, and motivated by greed, fear, and pride. We have a financial state of nature.

Modern biology provides a different, interesting example. Different because genetic research is not essentially linked to the Internet the way e-commerce and e-communication are. Interesting because we can see the same play of passions here as in the Internet.

Bio-technology and DNA research are proving to be relatively inexpensive to develop and potentially very rewarding. In this they differ from other areas of science and technology. Anyone who wants to build a ballistic missile with an atomic warhead needs the engineering and technological resources of a good sized country. New drugs usually need the resources of a large pharmaceutical company. However, genetic modification takes a few Ph.D.'s, a few assistants, and a medium-sized lab. The technology is relatively inexpensive and unobtrusive. Therefore; it can be done by many and done secretly. And, of course the results may be tremendous. The discovery of the right genetic modification, if it can be patented and the patent enforced, will make some individuals and companies rich. Failure to have the right technology may leave some countries open to biological blackmail. . . . Again we are living on the edge of a scientific state of nature.

Most of us are risk-averse, as Hobbes pointed out 350 years ago. Modern technology provides us with the opportunity to do many things that were impossible or very difficult only a few years ago. But opportunity to do is also risk to be done to. Perhaps that is why the last few years have seemed so unexpectedly unpleasant to most of us. Despite the end of the cold war, the world seems to be a threatening place. In fact, many of us are reacting to all this new technology with apprehension rather than enthusiasm. This is not just because it is new and rapidly changing, but because it appears to be creating an unstable and uncontrollable state of nature.

III. HIGH-TECH TERRORISM

Our concept of terrorism exactly mirrors the distinction between the low-tech and the high-tech forms of the state of nature. In the form of robbery, extortion, kidnapping, assassination, and guerrilla warfare, low-tech terrorism has been with us for centuries. In the form of ideologically motivated attacks by an individual or small group it has been with us for most of the nineteenth and twentieth centuries. In the West we seem [sic] to have thought of terrorism as a form of low-intensity war endemic to backward areas, and accepted it as part of the cost of doing business in those areas. If we think of terrorism this way, we get a concept of terrorism that is very similar to Hobbes's original concept of the state of nature. Terrorism is seen as a phenomenon of backward areas where civil control is weak or entirely absent. It is seen as motivated by individual greed, fear, and pride. Terrorists are thought of as individuals or small groups sharing a similar ideology or background. In all this they are more like an in-bred family than a civil society. They are assumed to be incapable of organizing themselves into large groups operating on bureaucratic principles. In short, we imagine them as the final product of life in Hobbes's state of nature.

This concept of terrorism does not explain the kind of organization that killed more than three thousand people on September 11.

This new terrorism is a global, high-tech terrorism. It is an extreme example of the global, high-tech state of nature I have been discussing. It is global in two senses: first, because it operates in countries around the globe, second, because it uses the advanced technologies of the global economy to carry out its plans. Sometimes this use is direct, such as plotting via the Internet or transferring cash via the global banking system. Sometimes the use is opportunistic: attacking airliners because they are hard to defend and very deadly when used as flying bombs. . . .

High-tech terrorists are no longer isolated and locally based; they can and do cooperate globally with other groups having different but equally extreme ideologies. What is more important is that this new form of terrorism uses resources from one part of the globe to act in other parts, and it can do this thanks to the global high-tech economy. There is an obvious irony here. This new terrorism seeks to destroy the global economy in all its forms, but it can hope do so only by operating through the global economy. . . .

One possible objection to treating high-tech terrorism as a Hobbesian state of nature is that most terrorists seem to be motivated by religious or ethnic hatreds that do not fit into Hobbes's "greed-fear-pride" account of human motivation. Perhaps Hobbes's term "glory" and my rendering of it as "pride" is too restrictive. What Hobbes seems to have had in mind is a set of emotions that we now think of as "self-esteem." Harm to our self-esteem can be very damaging, and produce either anger or depression. Since most of us internalize aspects of our culture and society, especially aspects of our religion and our ethnic identity, any attack that devalues these aspects of our culture—even inadvertent attacks—are going to be felt as attacks on our self-esteem, and will produce either anger or depression. The terrorists' ethnic and religious anger seems to be the product of just such a perceived attack. After all, most terrorists seem to come from the parts of their society that are most affected by western influences, not the most backward, rural parts. They receive the direct effect of advanced western culture, they feel diminished in some way, they respond by getting angry. Others respond with depression.

Thinking of terrorist's motivation as an attempt to preserve or bolster their self-esteem rather than just asserting their pride answers another objection as well. Hobbes is famous for building his political theory around the fear of death. He claims we all fear death, and, finally, it is this fear of death that causes us to contract with each other to create and maintain the civil society. Obviously the suicidal terrorist is not afraid of death, or, at the very least, the fear of death motivates him less than the glory of his sacrifice. The cult of martyrdom becomes more powerful than the fear of death. This makes no sense if we think of suicidal terrorists in terms of Hobbes's egoistic individuals; it makes better sense if we think of them as individuals trying to preserve their self esteem and sense of worth in a society that is threatened with change, is very afraid of chance, and values the changeless society above the individual. A terrorist's suicide can make sense if we adopt a post-Hobbesian psychology in which physical death is less frightening to the terrorist than societal change or personal dishonor.

On September 11 this new terrorism proved that it can be frighteningly effective and in a peculiarly frightening way. There was vast loss of life and vast economic damage. In addition, the terrorists used airliners flying from US airports to achieve their ends. They used the stuff of "our" global economy to attack us at home. Months later this shock still lingers. In this one aspect we are like the terrorists: we identify ourselves, in part, with our culture and when that culture is shown to be vulnerable and also used to attack us, we suffer a loss of self esteem and react by becoming angry or depressed.

It is not easy to see how we can combat this high-tech, high-motivated terrorism. Going back to a simpler, low-tech world is not a realistic option. The answer to dangerously bad technology is not low technology, but better, safer technology. Nevertheless, it is hard to see what that better, safer technology can be. . . . To combat this new terrorism we will have to put checks and controls and identification markers into much of our global communications, transportation, and financial network. Possibly transponders with ID's on vehicles and shipping containers. Possibly a national (voluntary?) identity card. Possibly complex protocols on all e-mail messages to identify the original sender and sender's location.

But these controls will damage the speed and flexibility of the global economy. They may also pose threats to our privacy and our civil liberties. The trade-off is between the cost and danger of continuing to run our current low-cost, high-risk technology and switching to a higher, more expensive technology with a lower risk factor. Before September 11 such a switch seemed undesirable, now it seems necessary. But even at best, the new technological and social solutions will come slowly. They will have to be fitted into our existing technology and society carefully. What will work well in one area will be dangerous or costly in another. There will be no cost-free, simple solutions. There will be no universal solutions. . . .

IV. HOBBES'S UNACCEPTABLE ANSWER

What conclusions should we draw about this global state of nature? Well, what conclusions did Hobbes draw about his state of nature? Hobbes believed that human beings could not tolerate the uncertainty of the state of nature, and the one alternative to the state of nature was a society ruled by an absolute sovereign. There can only be anarchy (in the state of nature) or an absolute, authoritative and authoritarian sovereign (in a civil society.) There can be nothing in between. Therefore, he concluded that we must choose that alternative and accept autocracy. . . .

Therefore, Hobbes's basic position is that sovereignty is indivisible and must be absolute as a logical and as a practical matter. He does temper his picture of the absolute sovereign with admonitions to the sovereign to follow custom and refrain from interfering in individual lives as much as possible. However, these comments are precatory only. If the sovereign behaves badly, but still keeps control, he is still the sovereign.

Obviously, this will not do for us. The history of the twentieth century has taught us that a truly evil sovereign is every bit as bad as any anarchy. We have no stomach for any unitary global order that is centralized and coercive, especially if the sovereign is, as it is for Hobbes, above the law.

V. ON BEYOND HOBBES

If we take the dual threats of anarchy and autocracy seriously, we must find some middle ground that will give us a powerful but limited sovereignty. We need a political system in which the sovereign will be effective and non-threatening. Much of western political theory since Hobbes has been an attempt to articulate just such a system. A full discussion of the attempts to do this would be a multi-volume summary of liberal political philosophy from the seventeenth century to the present.

There have been three main strands in this remedial discourse. The first and best known is to limit the sovereign by invoking a natural right which all individuals will accept and which will serve as the basis for political cohesion. Another is to turn to non-political forces, such as markets, to induce voluntary, self-interested cooperation. A third is to turn to moral virtues such as trust or benevolence or tolerance as the basis of civil cooperation. All three have obvious strengths and weaknesses.

The usual natural rights tactic has been to imagine a tacit contract in which all inhabitants of an area turn over their rights to some sovereign in exchange for security and protection. This is exactly what Hobbes himself does, as does Locke, as do many others. However, the natural right theorist qualifies this argument by claiming that prior to the contract there exist certain natural rights, such as the right to life or property, that may not be given up under any circumstances. In particular, they can not be alienated by contract. Therefore, contracts that involve the sovereign's unrestricted taking of a natural right, such as life or property, are invalid or are not contracts. . . . The United Nations Charter uses this approach in its assertion of Universal Human Rights.

The natural rights argument has great popular appeal, partly because of its simplicity, and partly because it invokes concepts like right and duty that are familiar from our experience with the legal system. In spite of this, it has great weaknesses too. First, there is the problem of getting agreement on what rights are really natural rights. Getting almost universal acceptance on the right to life is easy, until we get to discussing fetuses. Toleration for other people's way of life also seems like a non-controversial idea, until we get to pedophiles or sadists. On closer inspection every purported natural right has hard cases in which it conflicts with other, equally important natural rights. . . .

The third strategy to avoid Hobbes's anarchy or autocracy analysis is to turn to virtues like benevolence or trust. The moral sense theorists did precisely that in the eighteenth century. . . . In the nineteenth century Mill's *On Liberty* preaches the need for restraint and the toleration of different opinions. The interesting point is that he did not argue for laws against the tyranny of the majority, but rather for personal restraint by the individual members of the majority. He did not follow the model of the US Constitution, which seeks to avoid the majority's tyranny by constitutional provisions for the separation of powers and for checks and balances. Instead, he calls for individuals to cultivate the virtue of tolerance. In contemporary political thought we have Francis Fukuyama writing *Trust,* and in general, a series of political commentators arguing that in order to have a democratic society, especially racially or culturally diverse democratic polity, we must first have numerous mechanisms, which they often call "social capital," that will produce a broad basis of trust. The events between 1990 and 2000 in Serbia and Bosnia show what can happen when there is not trust and no tolerance. These same Balkan events show us how difficult it is to avoid anarchy or autocracy by appeal to individual virtues alone.

Therefore, it seems that the original dilemma remains. Our new technology is forcing us toward a new version of Hobbes's state of nature. Even if we live in a high technology world, it is still a dangerous thing to be in a state of nature, because it pushes us toward anarchy or toward some sort of absolute autocracy. We can not live with anarchy. We can not live with autocracy. None of the strategies that seek to avoid this pair of dismal alternatives can guarantee effectiveness over the long run.

VI. CONCLUDING PESSIMISTIC POSTSCRIPT

So what stance should we take toward the possibility of a global Hobbesian state of nature? Should we all start stock-piling food and ammunition against the once and future state of nature? No, I do not really think we should. For one thing, the coming anarchy, if it is really coming, will not be defeated by such simple, short-term solutions. However, I do think that there is a real threat out there between our desires "*for gain or for glory*" (*De Cive,* chap. 1) and our new technology.

The threat will come in the form of increasing instability and uncertainty in communications, finance and science. One immediate effect will be higher transaction costs to deal with the instability and uncertainty. The devastating effects of infectious animal diseases on farming and food distribution is a perfect example of this kind of trouble. Another effect will be a loss of confidence in many of our institutions, with all the anxiety and depression and anger that this psychological uncertainity entails. Recent instabilities in the world's major financial systems seem to be problems of this sort. The result will probably be some degree of local stability and trust whenever institutions can be observed and held accountable, coupled with enormous instability and mistrust whenever institutions get too big or too powerful to be observed and controlled. For example, local travel, shopping, and recreation has been relatively unaffected by the September 11th attack, but international travel has been severely disrupted all across the globe. Unfortunately, the anarchism inherent in the global state of nature will work its way down to the local level in unpredictable ways. Consider the different effects of hoof and mouth disease and mad cow disease. Sometimes the anarchy at the global level results in severe disruptions in a particular area, as in the effects of hoof and mouth disease in England. Sometimes the effect is spotted across the whole globe, as in the effects of mad cow disease.

Being prepared for the global state of nature will have to start with an understanding of the problem and with a flexible imagination to consider unlikely mechanisms that will mitigate the individual effect of high-tech anarchy.

In the twentieth century we have seen amazing human progress and terrible evil. At the very end of the century a non-confrontational global society seemed—briefly—to be possible. Perhaps it still is possible but, at the beginning of the twenty-first century, it seems more likely that we will see instead a new form of Hobbes's state of nature. The worldwide technology of modern communications, transportation, finance, and science has produced wonderful benefits, but it has also opened the way for a global state of nature and global terrorism. Tragically, these great global beasts are, even now, slouching toward Malmesbury to be born.

Discussion Questions

1. Hobbes claims that a sovereign should have absolute power and that people prefer autocracy to anarchy. Does Robinson agree? Do you agree? Use examples from current events to support your answer.
2. Given that the Internet has made it easier for international terrorist groups to recruit members and stay in communication, should Internet websites and chat rooms be more closely monitored by a centralized authority or "sovereign"? Discuss how John Stuart Mill and/or Cass Sunstein, whose readings can be found at the end of Chapter 8 on "Freedom of Speech," might answer this question.
3. The United States Constitution vests in Congress the sole and exclusive authority to initiate hostilities on behalf of the American people. Should this power belong to Congress? What would Hobbes most likely think of this clause in the Constitution? Support your answers.
4. Following the September 11 attacks the United States adopted a policy that permits preemptive war as self-defense. "It's a different world," argued Colin Powell in favor of the policy. "It's a new kind of threat." Weapons of mass destruction, new technology, and the ease with which global terrorist groups can network have increased the likelihood of surprise attacks. Discuss whether advances in technology and biotechnology, such as those described by Robinson, justify preemptive strikes as self-defense under the just-war tradition. If so, under what conditions would a preemptive strike be morally justified?

JONATHAN GRANOFF

Nuclear Weapons, Ethics, Morals and Law

Attorney Jonathan Granoff is a member of the Lawyers Alliance for World Security and president of the Global Security Institute. This article was presented at the Nuclear Non-Proliferation Treaty Prepcom of 1999 and The Hague Appeal for Peace addressing nuclear weapons, morals, ethics, spiritual values, the culture of peace, and law. In the article, Granoff argues that the possession of nuclear weapons by several modern states not only violates the principle of equality, but also shows a lack of respect for human life. Citing international court rulings regarding the legitimacy of nuclear weapons for the purpose of deterrence, he concludes that we should work toward the elimination of nuclear weapons.

Critical Reading Questions

1. According to Granoff, what is the foundation of ethical norms?
2. What are some universal moral norms that are relevant to the debate on nuclear weapons?
3. What is the relationship between ethical values and law?
4. How do nuclear weapons run contrary to the rules of humanitarian law?
5. What is the policy of nuclear deterrence and how do proponents justify it?
6. On what moral grounds do Judge Weeramantry and other members of the international court reject the reasoning behind nuclear deterrence?
7. What solution does Granoff propose for the elimination of nuclear weapons?

ETHICAL AND MORAL FRAMEWORK FOR ADDRESSING THE ISSUE

In his concurrence with the historic opinion of the International Court of Justice (ICJ) issued July 8, 1996, addressing the legal status of the threat or use of nuclear weapons,[1] Judge Ranjeva stated, "On the great issues of mankind the requirements of positive law and of ethics make common cause, and nuclear weapons, because of their destructive effects, are one such issue."[2] Human society has ethical and moral norms based on wisdom, conscience and practicality. Many norms are universal and have withstood the test of human experience over long periods of time. One such principle is that of reciprocity. It is often called the Golden Rule: "Treat others as you wish to be treated." It is an ethical and moral foundation for all the world's major religions.[3]

Several modern states sincerely believe that this principle can be abrogated and security obtained by the threat of massive destruction. The Canberra Commission highlighted the impracticality of this posture: "Nuclear weapons are held by a handful of

"Nuclear Weapons, Ethics, Morals and Law," Presented to the *Nuclear Non Proliferation Prepcom of 1999* and *The Hague Appeal for Peace,* May 1999. Some notes have been omitted.

states which insist that these weapons provide unique security benefits, and yet reserve uniquely to themselves the right to own them. This situation is highly discriminatory and thus unstable; it cannot be sustained. The possession of nuclear weapons by any state is a constant stimulus to other states to acquire them."

The solution can be stated simply: "States should treat others as they wish to be treated in return."[4]

It is inconsistent with moral wisdom and practical common sense for a few states to violate this ancient and universally valid principle of reciprocity. Such moral myopia has a corrosive effect on the law which gains its respect largely through moral coherence. Can global security be obtained while rejecting wisdom universally recognized for thousands of years?

Judge Weeramantry said, "(E)quality of all those who are subject to a legal system is central to its integrity and legitimacy. So it is with the body of principles constituting the corpus of international law. Least of all can there be one law for the powerful and another law for the rest. No domestic system would accept such a principle, nor can any international system which is premised on a concept of equality."[5]

LAW AND VALUES

Law is the articulation of values. Values must be based on moral foundations to have credibility. The recognition of the intrinsic sacredness of life and the duty of states and individuals to protect life is a fundamental characteristic of all human civilized values. Such civilized values are expressed in humanitarian law and custom which has an ancient lineage reaching back thousands of years. "They were worked out in many civilizations—Chinese, Indian, Greek, Roman, Japanese, Islamic, modern European among others." Humanitarian law "is an ever continuous development. . . . (and) grows as the sufferings of war keep escalating. With a nuclear weapon, those sufferings reach a limit situation, beyond which all else is academic."[6] . . .

We must never forget the awesome destructive power of these devices. "Nuclear weapons have the potential to destroy the entire eco system of the planet. Those already in the world's arsenals have the potential of destroying life on the planet several times over."[8]

Not only are they destructive in magnitude but in horror as well.[9]

Notwithstanding this knowledge we permit ourselves to continue to live in a "kind of suspended sentence. For half a century now these terrifying weapons of mass destruction have formed part of the human condition. Nuclear weapons have entered into all calculations, all scenarios, all plans. Since Hiroshima, on the morning of 6 August, 1945, fear has gradually become man's first nature. His life on earth has taken on the aspect of what the Qur'an calls 'long nocturnal journey', a nightmare whose end he cannot yet foresee."[10]

Attempting to obtain ultimate security through the ultimate weapon, we have failed for, "the proliferation of nuclear weapons has still not been brought under control, despite the existence of the Non-Proliferation Treaty. Fear and folly may still link hands at any moment to perform a final dance of death. Humanity is all the more vulnerable today for being capable of mass producing nuclear missiles."[11] . . .

A five megaton weapon represents greater explosive power than all the bombs used in World War II and a twenty megaton bomb more than all the explosives used in all the wars in history. Several states are currently poised ready to deliver weapons that render those used in Hiroshima and Nagasaki small. One megaton bomb represents the explosive force of approximately seventy Hiroshimas while a fifteen megaton bomb a thousand Hiroshimas. Judge Weeramantry emphasized that "the unprecedented magnitude of its destructive power is only one of the unique features of the bomb. It is unique in its uncontainability in both space and time. It is unique as a source of peril to the human future. It is unique as a source of continuing danger to human health, even long after its use. Its infringement of humanitarian law goes beyond its being a weapon of mass destruction, to reasons which penetrate far deeper into the core of humanitarian law."[12]

We are challenged as never before: technology continues to slip away from moral guidance and law chases after common sense.

INTERNATIONAL COURT OF JUSTICE

When the International Court of Justice addressed the legal status of threat or use of nuclear weapons members of the nuclear club, which has since grown, asserted a principled reliance on nuclear weapons. The Court held that "the threat or use of nuclear weapons would generally be contrary to the rules of international law applicable to armed conflict, and in particular the principles and rules of humanitarian law" and that states are obligated to bring to a conclusion negotiations on nuclear disarmament in all its aspects. . . .

The Court stated unequivocally that the rules of armed conflict, including humanitarian law, prohibits the use of any weapon that is likely to cause unnecessary suffering to combatants; that is incapable of distinguishing between civilian and military targets; that violates principles protecting neutral states (such as through fall out or nuclear winter); that is not a proportional response to an attack; or that does permanent damage to the environment.

Under no circumstance may states make civilians the object of attack nor can they use weapons that are incapable of distinguishing between civilian and military targets. Regardless of whether the survival of a state acting in self defense is at stake, these limitations continue to hold.

For this reason the President Judge stated in forceful terms that the Court's inability to go beyond its statement "can in no manner be interpreted to mean that it is leaving the door ajar to the recognition of the legality of the threat or use of nuclear weapons."[23] He emphasized his point by stating that nuclear weapons are "the ultimate evil, destabilize humanitarian law which is the law of the lesser evil. Thus the very existence of nuclear weapons is a great challenge to humanitarian law itself." . . .

The Court said, "(M)ethods and means of warfare, which would preclude any distinction between civilian and military targets, or which would result in unnecessary suffering to combatants, are prohibited. In view of the unique characteristics of nuclear weapons . . . the use of such weapons in fact seems scarcely reconcilable with respect to such requirements."

Discordance between the incompatibility of these devices with the requirements of humanitarian law, the assertion that there could be possible instances in which their use could be legal and the reliance on the doctrine of deterrence compelled the Court to seek a resolution: "the long promised complete nuclear disarmament appears to be the most appropriate means of achieving that result." The requirements of moral coherence and ethical conduct and the need for "international law, and with it the stability of international order which it is intended to govern," drive the imperative of nuclear disarmament.

ONGOING PROBLEM

Legal and moral questions continue to loom before us. We are not faced with nuclear policies founded on a strategy of dropping depth charges in mid-ocean or bombs in the desert. What the world faces is nuclear deterrence with its reliance on the horrific destruction of vast numbers of innocent people, destruction of the environment rendering it hostile to generations yet to be blessed with life.

Deterrence proponents claim that nuclear weapons are not so much instruments for the waging of war but political instruments "intended to prevent war by depriving it of any possible rationale."[31] The United States has boldly argued that because deterrence is believed to be essential to its international security that the threat or use of nuclear weapons must therefore be legal. The United States representative stated: "If these weapons could not lawfully be used in individual or collective self defense under any circumstances there would be no credible threat of such use in response to aggression and deterrent policies would be futile and meaningless. In this sense, it is impossible to separate the policy of deterrence from the legality of the use of the means of deterrence. Accordingly, any affirmation of a general prohibition on the use of nuclear weapons would be directly contrary to one of the fundamental premises of the national security policy of each of these many states."[32]

It is clear that deterrence is designed to threaten massive destruction which would most certainly violate numerous principles of humanitarian law. Additionally, it strikes at generations yet unborn.

Even in the instance of retaliation the moral absurdity challenges us. As Mexico's Ambassador Sergio Gonzalez Galvez told the Court, "Torture is not a permissible response to torture. Nor is mass rape acceptable retaliation to mass rape. Just as unacceptable is retaliatory deterrence—'You burnt my city, I will burn yours.'"[33]

Professor Eric David, on behalf of the Solomon Islands, stated, "If the dispatch of a nuclear weapon causes a million deaths, retaliation with another nuclear weapon which will also cause a million deaths will perhaps protect the sovereignty of the state suffering the first strike, and will perhaps satisfy the victim's desire for revenge, but it will not satisfy humanitarian law, which will have been breached not once but twice; and two wrongs do not make a right."[34]

Judge Weeramantry rigorously analyzed deterrence theory:

1. Intention: "Deterrence needs to carry the conviction to other parties that there is a real intention to use those weapons in the event of an attack by that other party. A game of bluff does not convey that intention, for it is difficult to persuade another of one's intention unless one really has that intention. Deterrence thus consists in a real intention to use such weapons. If deterrence is to operate, it leaves the world of make believe and enters the field of seriously intended military threats."[35]
2. Deterrence and Mere Possession: "Deterrence is more than the mere accumulation of weapons in a storehouse. It means the possession of weapons in a state of readiness for actual use. This means the linkage of weapons ready for immediate take off, with a command and control system geared for immediate action. It means that weapons are attached to delivery vehicles. It means that personnel are ready night and day to render them operational at a moment's notice. There is clearly a vast difference between weapons stocked in a warehouse and weapons so ready for immediate action. Mere possession and deterrence are thus concepts which are clearly distinguishable from each other."[36]

For deterrence to work one must have the resolve to cause the resulting damage and devastation. . . .

While deterrence continues to place all life on the planet in a precarious position of high risk, one must wonder whether it provides any possible security against accidental or unauthorized launches, computer error, irrational rogue actions, terrorist attack, criminal syndicate utilization of weapons and other irrational and unpredictable, but likely, scenarios.

Did the Court undermine the continued legitimacy of deterrence? The Court stated clearly that "if the use of force itself in a given case is illegal—for whatever reason—the threat to use such force will likewise be illegal."[37]

The moral position of the nuclear weapons states is essentially that the threat to commit an illegal act—massive destruction of innocent people—is legal because it is so horrible to contemplate that it ensures the peace. Thus the argument is that the threat of committing that which is patently illegal is made legal by its own intrinsic illogic. . . .

An unambiguous political commitment by the nuclear weapon states to the elimination of nuclear weapons evidenced by unambiguous immediate pledges never to use them first as well as placing the weapons in a de-alerted posture pending their ultimate elimination will promptly evidence the good faith efforts by the nuclear weapon states to reduce our collective risks. These steps increase our collective security, but are hardly enough to meet the clear decision of the court and the dictates of reason. Only commencement in good faith of multilateral negotiations leading to elimination of these devices will bring law, morals, ethics and reason into coherence. Only then will we be able to tell our children that ultimate violence will not bring ultimate security, a culture of peace based on law, reason and values will. . . .

NOTES

1. Legality of the Threat or Use of Nuclear Weapons, General List No. 95 (Advisory

Opinion of the International Court of Justice of July 8, 1996). Unless otherwise noted, references are to this opinion, which was requested by the General Assembly. The historic importance of this decision cannot be overemphasized for it is the first judicial analysis of the issue by this international tribunal even though the first General Assembly Resolution, unanimously adopted January 24, 1946 at the London session, called for elimination of atomic weapons.

2. Opinion of Judge Ranjeva, para. 105(2)E1.
3. Buddhism: "Hurt not others in ways that you yourself would find hurtful." Udana-Varga, 5:18; Christianity: "All things whatsoever you would that men should do to you, do you even so to them." Matthew 7:12; Confucianism: "Do not unto others what you would not have them do unto you." Analects 15:23; Hinduism: "This is the sum of duty: do not unto others which would cause you pain if done to you." Mahabharata 5:1517; Islam: "No one of you is a believer until he desires for his brother that which he desires for himself." Hadith; Jainism: "In happiness and suffering, in joy and grief, we should regard all creatures as we regard our own self." Lord Mahavir 24th Tirthankara; Judaism: "What is hateful to you, do not do to your fellow man. That is the law; all the rest is commentary." Talmud, Shabbat 31a; Zoroastrianism: "That nature only is good when it shall not do unto another whatsoever is not good for its own self." Dadistan-I-Dinik, 94:5.
4. See, excellent analysis, "Ethics of Abolition" in Douglas Roche's *Unacceptable Risk,* Nuclear Age Peace Foundation, 1995, p. 90.
5. Opinion of Judge Weeramantry, V4.
6. Ibid. I 5.
8. Opinion of Judge Weeramantry, II 3(a).
9. "Nuclear weapons cause death and destruction; induced cancers, leukemia, keloids and related afflictions; cause gastrointestinal, cardiovascular and related afflictions; continued for decades after their use to induce the health related problems mentioned above; damage the environmental rights of future generations; cause congenital deformities, mental retardation and genetic damage; carry the potential to cause a nuclear winter; contaminate and destroy the food chain; imperil the eco system; produce lethal levels of heat and blast; produce radiation and radioactive fallout; produce a disruptive electromagnetic pulse; produce social disintegration; imperil all civilizations; threaten human survival; wreak cultural devastation; span a time range of thousands of years; threaten all life on the planet; irreversibly damage the rights of future generations; exterminate civilian population; damage neighboring states; produce psychological stress and fear syndromes—as no other weapons do" Opinion of J, Ibid. para. II 4.
10. Opinion of President Judge Bedjaoui, para. 2.
11. Ibid. para. 5.
12. Opinion of Judge Weeramantry II para. 3.
23. Opinion of President Judge Badjaoui, para. 20.
31. Marc Perrinde Brichambaut, France, Verbatim record (trans.) 1 November, 1995, page 33.
32. Michael Matheson, US, Verbatim record, 15 November, 1995, p. 78.
33. Verbatim record, 3 November 1995, p. 64.
34. Verbatim record, (trans.), 14 November, 1995, p. 45.
35. Opinion of Judge Weeramantry, VII 2(v).
36. Ibid.
37. Para. 47.

Discussion Questions

1. Discuss whether the possession of nuclear weapons and the strategy of deterrence can be justified under just-war theory as explicated by Aquinas and Coady.
2. Since the September 11 attacks, the U.S. policy on nuclear weapons has shifted from deterrence to a first-strike policy, while at the same time demanding that other

nations disarm, nations which Bush believes harbor "the world's most dangerous regimes." Can the American policy of nuclear exceptionalism, given that it violates the principle of equality and humanitarian law, be morally justified on other grounds? If not, what strategy should the United States use instead to lessen the global threat of nuclear terrorism or war?

3. Kim Jong II, leader of North Korea, claims that his country needs nuclear weapons as a deterrent against attacks from South Korea and the United States. How would you respond to his argument?
4. India and Pakistan, both nations with nuclear weapons, have more than once been on the brink of war over Kashmir, a disputed territory. Discuss how the United Nations and the United States should respond, if at all, to the threat of nuclear war between the two nations.
5. Discuss whether the mere possession (or suspicion) of weapons of mass destruction by a country that is a potential threat to another country justifies a preemptive strike. Support your answer using specific examples.
6. Was the dropping of nuclear bombs on Hiroshima and Nagasaki in World War II an example of war or of terrorism? Was the bombing of these two cities justified? Discuss how Granoff and a just-war theorist would each answer this question.

DAVID LUBAN

The War on Terrorism and the End of Human Rights

David Luban is a professor of law and philosophy at Georgetown University Law Center. In his reading he notes that the United States government, in its war on terrorism, has blurred the line between the law model and the war model approaches and has instead adopted a hybrid model that denies terrorist suspects the protections of either model. Also, most wars have a clear ending with defeat or surrender. However, the war on terrorism can last indefinitely because it targets any individuals who might commit terrorist acts in the future. Luban concludes that because of this the war on terrorism may seriously erode international human rights.

Critical Reading Questions

1. What is the model of war and the model of law? What are the advantages and disadvantages of each model?

"The War on Terrorism and the End of Human Rights," *Philosophy and Public Policy Quarterly,* vol. 22, no. 3 (Summer 2002), 9–13.

2. What is the hybrid war–law approach and why, according to Luban, has Washington adopted it?
3. What is the legal status of terrorist suspects imprisoned at Guantanamo Bay and what rights do they have under the hybrid war–law model?
4. What is the source of the term "enemy combatant" and how does the hybrid war–law model go beyond the original meaning of the term?
5. What justification is used for the hybrid war–law model approach?
6. What is the argument against the hybrid war–law model?
7. On what grounds does Luban reject the hybrid war–law model?
8. According to Luban, how does the war on terrorism threaten international human rights?
9. How does the war on terrorism differ from other kinds of wars?
10. According to Luban, how has the war on terrorism been used by governments as a model to justify attacks on insurgents?

In the immediate aftermath of September 11, President Bush stated that the perpetrators of the deed would be brought to justice. Soon afterwards, the President announced that the United States would engage in a war on terrorism. The first of these statements adopts the familiar language of criminal law and criminal justice. It treats the September 11 attacks as horrific crimes—mass murders—and the government's mission as apprehending and punishing the surviving planners and conspirators for their roles in the crimes. The War on Terrorism is a different proposition, however, and a different model of governmental action—not law but war. Most obviously, it dramatically broadens the scope of action, because now terrorists who knew nothing about September 11 have been earmarked as enemies. But that is only the beginning.

THE HYBRID WAR–LAW APPROACH

The model of war offers much freer rein than that of law, and therein lies its appeal in the wake of 9/11. First, in war but not in law it is permissible to use lethal force on enemy troops regardless of their degree of personal involvement with the adversary. The conscripted cook is as legitimate a target as the enemy general. Second, in war but not in law "collateral damage," that is, foreseen but unintended killing of non-combatants, is permissible. (Police cannot blow up an apartment building full of people because a murderer is inside, but an air force can bomb the building if it contains a military target.) Third, the requirements of evidence and proof are drastically weaker in war than in criminal justice. Soldiers do not need proof beyond a reasonable doubt, or even proof by a preponderance of evidence, that someone is an enemy soldier before firing on him or capturing and imprisoning him. They don't need proof at all, merely plausible intelligence. Thus, the U.S. military remains regretful but unapologetic about its January 2002 attack on the Afghani town of Uruzgan, in which 21 innocent civilians were killed, based on faulty intelligence that they were al Qaeda fighters. Fourth, in war one can attack an enemy without concern over whether he has done anything. Legitimate targets are those who in the course of combat *might* harm us, not those who *have* harmed us. No doubt there are other significant differences as well. But the basic point should be clear: given Washington's mandate to eliminate the danger of future 9/11s, so far as humanly possible, the model of war offers important advantages over the model of law.

There are disadvantages as well. Most obviously, in war but not in law, fighting back is a *legitimate* response of the enemy. Second, when nations fight a war, other nations may opt for neutrality. Third, because fighting back is legitimate, in war the enemy soldier deserves special regard once he is rendered harmless through injury or surrender. It is impermissible to punish him for his role in fighting the war. Nor can he be harshly interrogated after he is captured. The Third Geneva Convention provides: "Prisoners of war who refuse to answer [questions] may not be threatened, insulted, or exposed to unpleasant or disadvantageous treatment of any kind." And, when the war concludes, the enemy soldier must be repatriated.

Here, however, Washington has different ideas, designed to eliminate these tactical disadvantages in the traditional war model. Washington regards international terrorism not only as a military adversary, but also as a criminal activity and criminal conspiracy. In the law model, criminals don't get to shoot back, and their acts of violence subject them to legitimate punishment. That is what we see in Washington's prosecution of the War on Terrorism. Captured terrorists may be tried before military or civilian tribunals, and shooting back at Americans, including American troops, is a federal crime (for a statute under which John Walker Lindh was indicted criminalizes anyone regardless of nationality, who "outside the United States attempts to kill, or engages in a conspiracy to kill, a national of the United States" or "engages in physical violence with intent to cause serious bodily injury to a national of the United States; or with the result that serious bodily injury is caused to a national of the United States"). Furthermore, the U.S. may rightly demand that other countries not be neutral about murder and terrorism. Unlike the war model, a nation may insist that those who are not with us in fighting murder and terror are against us, because by not joining our operations they are providing a safe haven for terrorists or their bank accounts. By selectively combining elements of the war model and elements of the law model, Washington is able to maximize its own ability to mobilize lethal force against terrorists while eliminating most traditional rights of a military adversary, as well as the rights of innocent bystanders caught in the crossfire.

A LIMBO OF RIGHTLESSNESS

The legal status of al Qaeda suspects imprisoned at the Guantanamo Bay Naval Base in Cuba is emblematic of this hybrid war–law approach to the threat of terrorism. In line with the war model, they lack the usual rights of criminal suspects—the presumption of innocence, the right to a hearing to determine guilt, the opportunity to prove that the authorities have grabbed the wrong man. But, in line with the law model, they are considered *unlawful* combatants. Because they are not uniformed forces, they lack the rights of prisoners of war and are liable to criminal punishment. Initially, the American government declared that the Guantanamo Bay prisoners have no rights under the Geneva Conventions. In the face of international protests, Washington quickly backpedaled and announced that the Guantanamo Bay prisoners would indeed be treated as decently as POWs—but it also made clear that the prisoners have no right to such treatment. Neither criminal suspects nor POWs, neither fish nor fowl, they inhabit a limbo of rightlessness. Secretary of Defense Rumsfeld's assertion that the U.S. may continue to detain them even if they are acquitted by a military tribunal dramatizes the point.

To understand how extraordinary their status is, consider an analogy. Suppose that Washington declares a War on Organized Crime. Troops are dispatched to Sicily, and a number of Mafiosi are seized, brought to Guantanamo Bay, and imprisoned without a hearing for the indefinite future, maybe the rest of their lives. They are accused of no crimes, because their capture is based not on what they have done but on what they might do. After all, to become "made" they took oaths of obedience to the bad guys. Seizing them accords with the war model: they are enemy foot soldiers. But they are foot soldiers out of uniform; they lack a "fixed distinctive emblem," in the words of The Hague Convention. That makes them unlawful combatants, so they lack the rights of POWs. They may object that it is only a unilateral declaration by the American President that has turned them into combatants in the first place—he called it a war, they didn't—and that, since they do not regard themselves as literal foot soldiers it never occurred to them to wear a fixed distinctive emblem. They have a point. It seems too easy for the President to divest anyone in the world of rights and liberty simply by announcing that the U.S. is at war with them and then declaring them unlawful combatants if they resist. But, in the hybrid war–law model, they protest in vain.

Consider another example. In January 2002, U.S. forces in Bosnia seized five Algerians and a Yemeni suspected of al Qaeda connections and took them to Guantanamo Bay. The six had been jailed in Bosnia, but a Bosnian court released them for lack of evidence, and the Bosnian Human Rights Chamber issued an injunction that four of them be allowed to remain in the country pending further legal proceedings. The Human Rights Chamber, ironically, was created under U.S. auspices in the Dayton peace accords, and it was designed specifically to protect against treatment like this. Ruth Wedgwood, a well-known international law scholar at Yale and a member of the Council on Foreign Relations, defended the Bosnian seizure in war-model terms. "I think we would simply argue this was a matter of self-defense. One of the fundamental rules of military law is that you have a right ultimately to act in self-defense. And if these folks were actively plotting to blow up the U.S. embassy, they should be considered combatants and captured as combatants in a war." Notice that Professor Wedgwood argues in terms of what the men seized in Bosnia were *planning to do,* not what they *did;* notice as well that the decision of the Bosnian court that there was insufficient evidence does not matter. These are characteristics of the war model.

More recently, two American citizens alleged to be al Qaeda operatives (Jose Padilla, a.k.a. Abdullah al Muhajir, and Yasser Esam Hamdi) have been held in American military prisons, with no crimes charged, no opportunity to consult counsel, and no hearing. The President described Padilla as "a bad man" who aimed to build a nuclear "dirty" bomb and use it against America; and the Justice Department has classified both men as "enemy combatants" who may be held indefinitely. Yet, as military law expert Gary Solis points out, "Until now, as used by the attorney general, the term 'enemy combatant' appeared nowhere in U.S. criminal law, international law or in the law of war." The phrase comes from the 1942 Supreme Court case *Ex parte Quirin,* but all the Court says there is that "an enemy combatant who without uniform comes secretly through the lines for the purpose of waging war by destruction of life or property" would "not . . . be entitled to the status of prisoner of war, but . . . [they would] be offenders against the law of war subject to trial and punishment by military tribunals." For the Court, in other words, the status of a person as a non-uniformed enemy combatant makes him a criminal rather than a warrior, and determines *where* he is tried (in a military, rather than a civilian, tribunal) but not *whether* he is tried. Far from authorizing open-ended confinement, *Ex parte Quirin* presupposes that criminals are entitled to hearings: without a hearing how can suspects prove that the government made a mistake? *Quirin* embeds the concept of "enemy combatant" firmly in the law model. In the war model, by contrast, POWs may be detained without a hearing until hostilities are over. But POWs were captured in uniform, and only their undoubted identity as enemy soldiers justifies such open-ended custody. Apparently, Hamdi and Padilla will get the worst of both models—open-ended custody with no trial, like POWs, but no certainty beyond the U.S. government's say-so that they really are "bad men." This is the hybrid war–law model. It combines the *Quirin* category of "enemy combatant without uniform," used in the law model to justify a military trial, with the war model's practice of indefinite confinement with no trial at all.

THE CASE FOR THE HYBRID APPROACH

Is there any justification for the hybrid war–law model, which so drastically diminishes the rights of the enemy? An argument can be offered along the following lines. In ordinary cases of war among states, enemy soldiers may well be morally and politically innocent. Many of them are conscripts, and those who aren't do not necessarily endorse the state policies they are fighting to defend. But enemy soldiers in the War on Terrorism are, by definition, those who have embarked on a path of terrorism. They are neither morally nor politically innocent. Their sworn aim—"Death to America!"—is to create more 9/11s. In this respect, they are much more akin to criminal conspirators than to conscript soldiers. Terrorists will fight as soldiers when they must, and metamorphose into mass murderers when they can.

Furthermore, suicide terrorists pose a special, unique danger. Ordinary criminals do not target innocent bystanders. They may be willing to kill them if necessary, but bystanders enjoy at least some measure of security because they are not primary targets. Not so with terrorists, who aim to kill as many innocent people as possible. Likewise, innocent bystanders are protected from ordinary criminals by whatever deterrent force the threat of punishment and the risk of getting killed in the act of committing a crime offer. For a suicide bomber, neither of these threats is a deterrent at all—after all, for the suicide bomber one of the hallmarks of a *successful* operation is that he winds up dead at day's end. Given the unique and heightened danger that suicide terrorists pose, a stronger response that grants potential terrorists fewer rights may be justified. Add to this the danger that terrorists may come to possess weapons of mass destruction, including nuclear devices in suitcases. Under circumstances of such dire menace, it is appropriate to treat terrorists as though they embody the most dangerous aspects of both warriors and criminals. That is the basis of the hybrid war–law model.

THE CASE AGAINST EXPEDIENCY

The argument against the hybrid war–law model is equally clear. The U.S. has simply chosen the bits of the law model and the bits of the war model that are most convenient for American interests, and ignored the rest. The model abolishes the rights of potential enemies (and their innocent shields) by fiat—not for reasons of moral or legal principle, but solely because the U.S. does not want them to have rights. The more rights they have, the more risk they pose. But Americans' urgent desire to minimize our risks doesn't make other people's rights disappear. Calling our policy a War on Terrorism obscures this point.

The theoretical basis of the objection is that the law model and the war model each comes as a package, with a kind of intellectual integrity. The law model grows out of relationships within states, while the war model arises from relationships between states. The law model imputes a ground-level community of values to those subject to the law—paradigmatically, citizens of a state, but also visitors and foreigners who choose to engage in conduct that affects a state. Only because law imputes shared basic values to the community can a state condemn the conduct of criminals and inflict punishment on them. Criminals deserve condemnation and punishment because their conduct violates norms that we are entitled to count on their sharing. But, for the same reason—the imputed community of values—those subject to the law ordinarily enjoy a presumption of innocence and an expectation of safety. The government cannot simply grab them and confine them without making sure they have broken the law, nor can it condemn them without due process for ensuring that it has the right person, nor can it knowingly place bystanders in mortal peril in the course of fighting crime. They are our fellows, and the community should protect them just as it protects us. The same imputed community of values that justifies condemnation and punishment creates rights to due care and due process.

War is different. War is the ultimate acknowledgement that human beings do not live in a single community with shared norms. If their norms conflict enough, communities pose a physical danger to each other, and nothing can safeguard a community against its enemies except force of arms. That makes enemy soldiers legitimate targets; but it makes our soldiers legitimate targets as well, and, once the enemy no longer poses a danger, he should be immune from punishment, because if he has fought cleanly he has violated no norms that we are entitled to presume he honors. Our norms are, after all, *our* norms, not his.

Because the law model and war model come as conceptual packages, it is unprincipled to wrench them apart and recombine them simply because it is in America's interest to do so. To declare that Americans can fight enemies with the latitude of warriors, but if the enemies fight back they are not warriors but criminals, amounts to a kind of heads-I-win-tails-you-lose international morality in which whatever it takes to reduce American risk, no matter what the cost to others, turns out to be justified. This, in brief, is the criticism of the hybrid war–law model.

To be sure, the law model could be made to incorporate the war model merely by rewriting a handful of statutes. Congress could enact laws permitting imprisonment or execution of persons who pose a significant threat of terrorism whether or not they have already done anything wrong. The standard of evidence could be set low and the requirement of a hearing eliminated. Finally, Congress could authorize the use of lethal force against terrorists regardless of the danger to innocent bystanders, and it could immunize officials from lawsuits or prosecution by victims of collateral damage. Such statutes would violate the Constitution, but the Constitution could be amended to incorporate anti-terrorist exceptions to the Fourth, Fifth, and Sixth Amendments. In the end, we would have a system of law that includes all the essential features of the war model.

It would, however, be a system that imprisons people for their intentions rather than their actions, and that offers the innocent few protections against mistaken detention or inadvertent death through collateral damage. Gone are the principles that people should never be punished for their thoughts, only for their deeds, and that innocent people must be protected rather than injured by their own government. In that sense, at any rate, repackaging war as law seems merely cosmetic, because it replaces the ideal of law as a protector of rights with the more problematic goal of protecting some innocent people by sacrificing others. The hypothetical legislation incorporates war into law only by making law as partisan and ruthless as war. It no longer resembles law as Americans generally understand it.

THE THREAT TO INTERNATIONAL HUMAN RIGHTS

In the War on Terrorism, what becomes of international human rights? It seems beyond dispute that the war model poses a threat to international human rights, because honoring human rights is neither practically possible nor theoretically required during war. Combatants are legitimate targets; noncombatants maimed by accident or mistake are regarded as collateral damage rather than victims of atrocities; cases of mistaken identity get killed or confined without a hearing because combat conditions preclude due process. To be sure, the laws of war specify minimum human rights, but these are far less robust than rights in peacetime—and the hybrid war–law model reduces this schedule of rights even further by classifying the enemy as unlawful combatants.

One striking example of the erosion of human rights is tolerance of torture. It should be recalled that a 1995 al Qaeda plot to bomb eleven U.S. airliners was thwarted by information tortured out of a Pakistani suspect by the Philippine police—an eerie real-life version of the familiar philosophical thought-experiment. The *Washington Post* reports that since September 11 the U.S. has engaged in the summary transfer of dozens of terrorism suspects to countries where they will be interrogated under torture. But it isn't just the United States that has proven willing to tolerate torture for security reasons. Last December, the Swedish government snatched a suspected Islamic extremist to whom it had previously granted political asylum, and the same day had him transferred to Egypt, where Amnesty International reports that he has been tortured to the point where he walks only with difficulty. Sweden is not, to say the least, a traditionally hard-line nation on human rights issues. None of this international transportation is lawful—indeed, it violates international treaty obligations under the Convention against Torture that in the U.S. have constitutional status as "supreme Law of the Land"—but that may not matter under the war model, in which even constitutional rights may be abrogated.

It is natural to suggest that this suspension of human rights is an exceptional emergency measure to deal with an unprecedented threat. This raises the question of how long human rights will remain suspended. When will the war be over?

Here, the chief problem is that the War on Terrorism is not like any other kind of war. The enemy, Terrorism, is not a territorial state or nation or government. There is no opposite number to negotiate with. There is no one on the other side to call a truce or declare a ceasefire, no one among the enemy authorized to surrender. In traditional wars among states, the war aim is, as Clausewitz argued, to impose one state's political will on another's. The *aim* of the war is not to kill the enemy—killing the enemy is the *means* used to achieve the real end, which is to force capitulation. In the War on Terrorism, no capitulation is possible. That means that the real aim of the war is, quite simply, to kill or capture all of the terrorists—to keep on killing and killing, capturing and capturing, until they are all gone.

Of course, no one expects that terrorism will ever disappear completely. Everyone understands that new anti-American extremists, new terrorists, will always arise and always be available for recruitment and deployment. Everyone understands that even if al Qaeda is destroyed or decapitated, other groups, with other leaders, will arise in its place. It follows, then, that the War on Terrorism will be a war that can only be abandoned, never concluded. The War has no natural resting point, no moment of victory or finality. It requires a mission of killing and capturing, in territories all over the globe, that will go on in perpetuity. It follows as well that the suspension of human rights implicit in the hybrid war–law model is not temporary but permanent.

Perhaps with this fear in mind, Congressional authorization of President Bush's military campaign limits its scope to those responsible for September 11 and their sponsors. But the War on Terrorism has taken on a life of its own that makes the Congressional authorization little more than a technicality. Because of the threat of nuclear terror, the American leadership actively debates a war on Iraq regardless of whether Iraq was implicated in September 11; and the President's yoking of Iraq, Iran, and North Korea into a single axis of evil because they back terror suggests that the War on Terrorism might eventually encompass all these nations. If the U.S. ever unearths tangible evidence that any of these countries is harboring or abetting terrorists with weapons of mass destruction, there can be little doubt that Congress will support military action. So too, Russia invokes the American War on Terrorism to justify its attacks on Chechen rebels, China uses it to deflect criticisms of its campaign against Uighur separatists, and Israeli Prime Minister Sharon explicitly links military actions against Palestinian insurgents to the American War on Terrorism. No doubt there is political opportunism at work in some or all of these efforts to piggy-back onto America's campaign, but the opportunity would not exist if "War on Terrorism" were merely the code-name of a discrete, neatly-boxed American operation. Instead, the War on Terrorism has become a model of politics, a world-view with its own distinctive premises and consequences. As I have argued, it includes a new model of state action, the hybrid war–law model, which depresses human rights from their peace-time standard to the war-time standard, and indeed even further. So long as it continues, the War on Terrorism means the end of human rights, at least for those near enough to be touched by the fire of battle.

Discussion Questions

1. Apply the just-war theory to the war on terrorism. Can the U.S. hybrid war–law model be justified under just-law theory?
2. In December 2003 a U.S. Circuit Court of Appeals in San Francisco ruled, on behalf of the 660 enemy combatants from 44 different countries being held by the U.S. military at Guantanamo Bay, that the United States cannot indefinitely detain captured

foreigners without giving them the opportunity to challenge their imprisonment. Overturning a lower court decision that supported the Bush administration's argument that the prisoners are "enemy combatants" being held on foreign soil and hence have no rights to a lawyer under U.S. law, the Court of Appeals ruled that the naval base in Cuba is under U.S. rule and consequently the captives are entitled to due process in the American legal system. Discuss this ruling in light of Luban's distinction between the war model and the law model.

3. Some of the prisoners who have since been released from Guantanamo Bay describe how they were kept in two-meter long cages and interrogated up to 60 times a day. Should the captives who were released receive restitution from the United States government for wrongful imprisonment? Support your answers.
4. Discuss what a rights ethicist, such as John Locke or Ayn Rand, would most likely think about the morality of the U.S. hybrid war–law model.

SARA RUDDICK

Mothers and Men's Wars

Sara Ruddick teaches at the Eugene Lang College at the New School for Social Research. Ruddick maintains that maternal thinking, which forms the basis of maternal practice, is one kind of disciplined reflection among others such as engineer, scientist, and historian. "Preservation love" or keeping a child alive and healthy in an indifferent or hostile world is the basic goal of mothering. In this selection from her book *Maternal Thinking: Toward a Politics of Peace,* Ruddick analyzes the myths of the masculinity of war and women's peacefulness. She concludes that although mothers are not inherently peaceful, maternal practice is a natural resource for peace politics because mothers want to prevent harm to their children.

Critical Reading Questions

1. In what ways is militarist thinking set against maternal thinking?
2. What is the myth of the "masculinity of war" and how is misogyny used to support this myth?
3. Why do soldiers both need women and hold women in contempt?
4. What is the conceptual connection in traditional philosophy between reason, war, and masculinity?
5. What is the *mater dolorosa* and how has this image been used to support the myth of maternal peacefulness?

"Mothers and Men's Wars," from *Maternal Thinking: Toward a Politics of Peace* (Boston, MA: Beacon Press, 1989), 141–159.

6. What roles have women traditionally played during times of war and how has this been used to support the myth of women's peacefulness?
7. Does Ruddick believe that mothers are more inclined to be peaceful than men?
8. What does Ruddick mean when she says that "maternal practice is a 'natural resource' for peace politics"?

The rhetoric that pervades dominant understandings of war and peace is dichotomous and split along gender lines—a perfect illustration of standpoint theory. Within militarist thinking, as well as within larger militarist cultures, a warrior's death—and murder—is set against a child's birth; male violence against feminine connection; military destruction against preservative love.

The soldier* male wears a double face. He is a victim . . .[and] a monster killer . . .

Whether victim or killer, War is his. A woman's name is on his weapon, her body is riddled by his bullets; it is her life, sleep, and care from which he has "fallen." But she cannot share the war he makes and which makes him. And although he counts on her to preserve a place that survives his madness, he also has contempt for what he sees as her innocence and safety:

> We soldiers are in the habit of respecting only those who have stood their ground under fire. That is why so many of us inwardly turn away from women, even when outwardly we can't do without them.[4]

The representative heroine of maternal peacefulness is the *mater dolorosa* ("mother of sorrows"), familiar from the lithographs of Käthe Kollwitz. Scrounging for food to keep her children alive, weeping over the body of her son, nursing survivors, sadly rebuilding her home, reweaving the connections that war has destroyed—as she grieves over her particular loss, she mourns war itself. Where she gives birth and sustains life, his war only hurts and destroys. . . .

*To avoid clumsy repetition, I use the term "soldier" to stand for anyone in the military. I mean no insult to the air force, navy, marine corps, coast guard, or any other branch of the service.

THE MYTH: THE MASCULINITY OF WAR AND WOMEN'S PEACEFULNESS

Even from the soberest perspective, there is much to be said for dividing the world between men's wars and the women's world which they threaten. War certainly seems to be men's business. It is mostly men who make civil and foreign battle plans, who invent weapons and supervise their construction. Men predominate among the spies, police chiefs, judges, and governors who construct a peacetime order guaranteed by the threat of violence. The world's generals and negotiators, bombardiers and captains, chiefs of staff, and defense secretaries have been and still are mostly men. More men than women shoot the pistol and work the missiles; certainly more men than women command them.

Traditionally, in most cultures, it has been men's lot to fight while women watch, suffer, applaud, ameliorate, and forgive. In war men become "warriors." If they are killed, they are killed in action. Their deaths represent a sacrifice that is in part chosen and thus is a testament to courage. A man makes war partly for the woman whom he protects, who is his audience. "She loved me for the dangers I had passed/And I loved her that she did pity them."[6] Her admiring tears make his fighting possible; her danger from his enemy makes his fighting necessary. Raped or killed, her possessions plundered, "his" woman is the last prize and the sweetest revenge his enemy exacts from him.

Militarists use the myth of war's manliness to define soldierly behavior and to reward soldiers.

Boot camp recruits are "ladies" until, trained in obedient killing, they become men. Misogyny is a useful element in the making of a soldier, as boys are goaded into turning on and grinding down whatever in themselves is "womanly." "Women are dinks. Women are villains."[7] Sexist language for women and—almost the same—their bodies is common in military discipline, as many battle chants reveal. Even where misogyny and lust are absent, the warrior embodies a peculiarly masculine ideal of camaraderie and lonely heroism . . .

Erotic male friendship is actually feared in most militaries, while erotic "male bonding" is celebrated. This bonding becomes a condition of fighting, as men's love for each other is wound into their capacity to kill . . .

Virtually no one denies that military thinking is imbued with masculine values. Yet a boy is not born, but rather becomes, a soldier. Becoming a soldier means learning to control fears and domestic longings that are explicitly labeled "feminine." The soldier earns the right to violence and sex; to fail is to remain "womanly" while losing the right to women. This much has long been familiar. What is increasingly clear is that becoming a militarist means acquiring a distinctive way of thinking that has also been associated with masculinity. As feminist critics have noticed, philosophers often honor, even as they construct, conceptual connections between reason, war, and masculinity. As Plato warned, the struggle to become reasonable "mustn't be useless to warlike men"; on the contrary, philosophers see to it that those men and (sometimes) women who are called "reasonable" have "proved best [both] in philosophy and with respect to war."[12] Both philosophy and war require transcending the particular affections and concrete complexities of "womanly" material and domestic life.

As the tendency to define reason in opposition to the feminine takes different historical and philosophical forms, so too the masculinity and abstractness of military thinking change with the changing economic and technological contexts of war. In nuclear defense establishments, a "language of warriors," a "techno-strategic rationality,"[13] is shared by armers and disarmers, chiefs of staff and chief negotiators. This rationality exhibits in near caricature the kinds of dichotomization and abstraction that, in other contexts, have been characterized as male. As Jean Bethke Elshtain points out, military theorists

> portray themselves as clear-sighted, unsentimental analysts describing the world as it is . . . a world of self-confirming theorems invites fantasies of control over events that we do not have. . . . Through abstracted models and logic, hyper-rationalism reduces states and their relations to games which can be simulated. . . . One of the legacies of war is a "habit of simple distinction, simplification, and opposition." . . . One basic task of a state at war is to portray the enemy in terms as absolute and abstract as possible in order to distinguish as sharply as possible the act of killing from the act of murder. . . . It is always "*the enemy,*" a "pseudo-concrete universal."[14] . . .

Techno-strategic rationality is only an extension, albeit a stunning one, of the abstractness that characterizes military discourse as a whole. In militarist thinking, human bodies are subordinated to abstract causes, different bodies are organized around abstract labels of civilian or solider, "the enemy" or ally, us or them. Weapons, positions, and targets have always been the primary referents of military strategy. . . .

If war is "masculine" and "abstract," peace seems "feminine" in exactly the way standpoint theorists predict. Women's peacefulness often begins in negation; alienated women insist that they stand outside men's wars and are repelled by otherwise respectworthy men who have been transformed by war's rhetoric. Virginia Woolf's *Three Guineas,* a feminist antimilitarist tract from the fascist thirties, has assumed a central place in contemporary feminist peace politics:

> Inevitably, we look upon societies as conspiracies that sink the private brother, whom many of us have reason to respect, and inflate in his stead a monstrous male, loud of voice, hard of fist, childishly intent upon scoring the floor of the earth with chalk marks, within whose mystic boundaries human beings are penned, rigidly, separately, artificially. . . .

> Therefore if you insist upon fighting to protect me, or "our" country, let it be understood soberly and rationally between us that you are fighting to gratify a sex instinct which I cannot share; to procure benefits which I have not shared and probably will not share; but not to gratify my instincts, or to protect myself or my country. . . . As a woman I have no country, as a woman I want no country, my country is the whole world.[18]

For many women, a more or less conscious alienation from "men's wars" is positively grounded in a history of caring labor. Patriotic East German women declare their political identities maternally as they address their government:

> We women do not regard military service for women as an expression of our equality, but as standing in contradiction to our existence as women. We regard our equality as consisting *not* in standing together with *those* men who take up arms, but in solidarity with *those* men who have like us recognized that the abstract term "enemy" in practice means destroying human beings. . . . We feel that as women we have a particular mission to preserve life and to give our support to the old, the infirm and the weak.[19] . . .

The Australian physician Helen Caldicott has made a similar maternalist position well known in the United States:

> Women all over the world are mobilizing for disarmament. . . . As mothers we must make sure the world is safe for our babies. . . . Look at one child, one baby. . . . I have three children, and I'm a doctor who treats children. I live with grieving parents. I understand the value of every human life. . . . I appeal especially to the women to do this [peace] work because we understand the genesis of life. Our bodies are built to nurture life.[21]

The same point has been reiterated by so many women from so many nations over so many years that it is hard to hear it afresh. Nor is it only women who expect peacefulness from mothers. Some men attribute to mothers a romantic peacefulness that few who know them would dare to match. . . .

There is a sober basis for this rhetoric. All of women's work—sheltering, nursing, feeding, kin work, teaching of the very young, tending the frail elderly—is threatened by violence. When maternal thinking takes upon itself the critical perspective of a feminist standpoint, it reveals a contradiction between mothering and war. Mothering begins in birth and promises life; military thinking justifies organized, deliberate deaths. A mother preserves the bodies, nurtures the psychic growth, and disciplines the conscience of children; although the military trains its soldiers to survive the situations it puts them in, it also deliberately endangers their bodies, minds, and consciences in the name of victory and abstract causes. Mothers protect children who are at risk; the military risks the children mothers protect . . .

Mothers need not wait for war to become antimilitarist. . . . I believe that everyday maternal thinking contrasts as a whole with military thinking. Just-war theories control our perceptions of war, turning our attention from bodies and their fate to abstract causes and rules for achieving them. . . . The analytic fictions of just-war theory require a closure of moral issues final enough to justify killing and "enemies" abstract enough to be killable. In learning to welcome their own and their children's changes, mothers become accustomed to open-ended, concrete reflection on intricate and unpredictable spirits. Maternal attentive love, restrained and clear-sighted, is ill adapted to intrusive, let alone murderous, judgments of others' lives. If they have made training a work of conscience and proper trust a virtue, if they have resisted the temptation to dominate their children and abrogate their authority, then mothers have been preparing themselves for patient and conscientious nonviolence, not for the obedience and excessive trust in authority on which military adventures thrive.

. . . [I]f military endeavors seem a betrayal of maternal practice, nonviolent action can seem a natural extension. Maternal "peacefulness" is not a sweet, appeasing gentleness that gives peace a bad name and has little to do with living peacefully in the world. When mothers fight with their children or on their behalf, when they teach their children ways of fighting safely, without being trampled on or trampling others, they engage in nonviolent action. Since children are vulnerable and the vulnerable are subject to abuse and neglect, mothers may be more than usually tempted by sadism, self-indulgent aggression, and self-protective indifference to the real needs of others. If mothers refuse to abandon or assault their children but, whatever their disappointment and anger, learn ways to live without giving up on the connections they have fostered or the lives they have tended, they exemplify the commitments of nonviolence.

In the glare of war's destruction and the light of women's hope, what mother would hesitate to "cast her lot" with peacemakers? As suffragist Anna Shaw asked several wars ago:

> Looking into the face of . . . one dead man we see two dead, the man and the life of the woman who gave him birth; the life she wrought into his life! And looking into his dead face someone asks a woman, what does a woman know about war? What, what friends, in the face of a crime like that does a man know about war?[27]

COMPLICATIONS

Men's wars, women's peace; a warrior's murder, a child's birth. "It's up to women to change the world." "Put women in charge, I say!" Both the rhetoric and the theory run up against two facts: men are not so warlike and women are certainly not peaceful.

Consider first the "masculinity" of war. There is, undeniably, a disproportionate male presence in defense councils and on battlefields as well as a masculinist military ideology to justify it. The manliness of war is an outcome of many factors. Considered as a biological class, men *may* have a greater propensity toward aggressiveness than women, and this aggressiveness, which is given license in wars, *may* also motivate some of the men who engage in them. On the other hand, warfare, especially in its contemporary forms, seems to require, as much as physical aggression, a tolerance of boredom or the ability to operate a computer under stress, characteristics that are neither distinctly "masculine" nor heroic. . . . A legend of heroically violent manliness is taught in patriotic homes, neighborhood movies, schools, and boot camps. There is, too, the sheer weight of history, of Fathers and Fathers before them who marched away, fought, and, if they returned, were set apart by their knowledge of the mysteries of danger and death. I would not deny that cumulatively, biological, psychological, and historical conditions provide partial and modest explanations of men's greater propensity for war. The problem is that men's compliance in war or active pleasure in battle has been confidently explained in so many ways that we are likely to forget that the masculinity of war is in large part a myth that sustains both women and men in their support for violence.

Very few of the men who take part in war can be said to "make war." Most are foot soldiers and workers in the service of grand campaigns they did not design, about which they were not consulted, and which they rarely comprehend. Even within the military, the proportion of suppliers and bureaucrats to active fighters is high. Those soldiers who do engage in combat are usually very young men. Many are conscripted for battle; others fight only to escape intolerable civilian life. Some boys fight eagerly; many of the eager boys are as deluded by patriotic fervor and duty to others as they are by masculinist myths. That they often fight for "national interests" and "causes" from which they derive no benefit and which they barely understand should not detract from the principles and loyalty that motivate them.

If men were so eager to be fighters, we would not need drafts, training in misogyny, and macho heroes, nor would we have to entice the morally sensitive with myths of patriotic duty and just cause. Indeed, history suggests that men have an even more ambivalent relation to the fighting expected of them than women do to the mothering work for which they are said to be "naturally suited." . . .

It would be ironic if women were to accept a central, heroic image from military mythology: the male soldier on the battlefield of soldiers, a killer who can be killed. If the soldier is an executioner, he is also victim. As he makes war, war makes and often maddens him. . . .

Women's peacefulness is at least as mythical as men's violence. Women have never absented themselves from war. Wherever battles are fought and justified, whether in the vilest or noblest of causes, women on both sides of the battle lines support the military engagements of their sons, lovers, friends, and mates. Increasingly, women are proud to fight alongside their brothers and as fiercely, in whatever battles their state or cause enlists them. There is nothing in a woman's genetic makeup or history that prevents her from firing a missile or spraying nerve gas over a sleeping village if she desires this or believes it to be her duty.

War is exciting; women, like men, are prey to the excitements of violence and community sacrifice it promises. War offers personal adventure and economic advantage to men and women. It may be, however, that women are especially enlivened by war's opportunities just because they are traditionally confined by domestic expectations in peacetime. Nonetheless, women usually justify their militarism as men do, in terms of loyalty, patriotism, and right. Even peace-loving women, like most men, support organized violence, at least in "emergencies." Like some men, some women are fierce and enthusiastic militarists; others, also like some men, see war as a natural catastrophe but collude with it, delegating to leaders political and military judgments they do not intend to understand. Most women, like most men, believe that violence must be met by violence and that the virtue of a cause justifies the horrors done in its name.

Although women and men support war for reasons that transcend gender, war also excites women in gender-related ways. It is sometimes forgotten that to the extent that it is masculine, war is also distinctly feminine. . . . War offers its own redescription of the work that standpoint theorists celebrate. Doing the wash keeps the home fires burning, a kiss inspires a soldier, and daily child care is suffused with a patrio-erotic glow. Even as it excites its distinctive brand of self-congratulatory heroism in feminine women, war also offers the adventurous—or the same woman in her adventurous moments—real and imagined freedoms from feminine duty. In wartime a woman may lead a charge up palace steps, carry secrets behind the lines, blow up the troop train, free prisoners, or torture them—and thereby enrich the romantic imagination of all women.

Perhaps many women do not succumb to the romance of war and are instead horrified by "giving over living sacrifices in the bodies of male children for the survival of the homeland."[31] Yet war affords even horrified women the opportunity "to engage in deeds that partake of received notions of glory, honor, nobility, civic virtue."[32] Not surprisingly, even regretful mothers often construe their military service in maternal terms. A German munitions maker in the second world war, like many of her counterparts elsewhere, pithily described her war acts as a plausible extension of peacetime love and duty: "Earlier I buttered bread for him, now I paint grenades for him, and think 'this is for him.'"[33] . . .

When war ends, mothers nurse the survivors just as, at first, they painted grenades and then put gold stars in their windows. How could they do otherwise? In a time of crisis, would they foster dissension within a family or community whose connectedness it has been their responsibility to sustain? Having applauded their children's efforts from the first somersault to their latest high school test, would they undermine their resolve when legal force combines with community excitement to draft them for war? If her son is killed while killing, should his mother deny herself the consolation of giving his "sacrifice" a point? For her own sake, for her children and family's sake, isn't it a mother's duty to accept, hopefully, justifications for violence? . . .

It is the same blanket that mothers wrap around a sick child and a wounded killer. A pure maternal peacefulness does not exist and cannot be invented.

THE HOPE

A pure maternal peacefulness does not exist; what does exist is far more complicated: a deep unease with military endeavors not easily disentangled from patriotic and maternal impulses to applaud, connect, and heal; a history of caring labor interwoven with the romance of violence and the parochial self-righteousness on which militarism depends. Nor for all her power to move us is the *mater dolorosa* a reliable instrument of peace. In many Western cultures women are portrayed as strong and brave victims of circumstances over which they have little control.

Their sufferings and sacrifices are expected; they persevere in a violent world—but they bear no responsibility for it. Although she reminds us unrelentingly of war's suffering and the loving connections she persistently sustains, the *mater dolorosa* also equates war to natural catastrophes, like hurricanes, and peace to a normal quietness that catastrophe interrupts. It is the beginning of peace politics to realize that war is an activity for which human beings plan, in which they consciously engage, and in which, therefore, they can anticipate the suffering they later mourn. If it is essential for developing a peace politics to keep one's eye on suffering, it is equally important to identify the actions that knowledge of suffering requires.

The dilemma of women's peacefulness is the dilemma of peace politics itself. Peacemakers must make people look closely and persistently at the myriad horrors of war; peace requires standing in solidarity with war's victims. Yet the victims' part can too easily be the part of despair and apolitical perseverance. It is good to persevere and right to admire those who do. But the peacemaking woman has to become as active, inventive, and angry as an ordinary, harassed, coping mother. Yet unlike that mother she must find a way to see and to resist the organized violence that "befalls" her and her people. She must identify threats to the protectiveness that in an ordinary way she has valued and created, starting with threats to her own children and then including as many other children as her imaginative knowledge allows.

Although mothers are not intrinsically peaceful, maternal practice is a "natural resource" for peace politics. For reasons both deep and banal it matters what mothers say and do. Women, and perhaps especially mothers, have serviced and blessed the violent while denying the character of the violence they serve. A peacemaker's hope is a militarist's fear: that the rhetoric and passion of maternity can turn against the military cause that depends on it. Mothers have supported their boys and their leaders, but in the contradiction of maternal and military aims there is a dangerous source of resistance. Because mothers have played their military parts well, their indifference, their refusal to endorse, could matter now. The question peacemakers face is how the "peacefulness" latent in maternal practice can be realized and then expressed in public action so that a commitment to treasure bodies and minds at risk can be transformed into resistance to the violence that threatens them. . . .

NOTES

4. Thewelweit, *Male Fantasies* (Minneapolis: University of Minnesota Press, 1987), p. 62.
6. Shakespeare, *Othello,* I, iii, 167–68.
7. Tim O'Brien, *If I Die in a Combat Zone* (New York: Dell, 1979), p. 52.
12. Plato, *Republic,* 543a, 521d.
13. The phrase "techno-strategic rationality" is Carol Cohn's, and she has enunciated it in numerous talks. See "Sex and Death in the Rational World of Defense Intellectuals," *Signs,* vol. 12, no. 4, pp. 687–718. The notion of a "language of warriors" comes from Freeman Dyson, *Weapons and Hope* (Princeton: Princeton University Press, 1984). Dyson compares the language of warriors with the language of victims.
14. Jean Bethke Elshtain, "Reflections on War and Political Discourse: Realism, Just War, and Feminism in a Nuclear Age," *Political Theory* (February 1985), pp. 49–50.
18. Virginia Woolf, *Three Guineas* (New York: Harcourt Brace/Harvest, 1938), pp. 105, 109. Woolf, however, did not deny her love for her country. Rather, she said that she would use her patriotism, "this drop of pure, if irrational emotion, to give to England first what she desires of peace and freedom for the whole world."
19. East German Woman, *Radical America* (Jan.–Feb. 1983), p. 40.
21. Helen Caldicott, *War Resister's League Calendar,* 1981.
27. Anna Shaw, speech to Women's Peace Party, 1915.
31. Jean Bethke Elshtain, *Women and War* (New York: Basic Books, 1987), p. 101, Chap. 3.

32. Elshtain, *Women and War,* pp. 101–2.
33. I first read this slogan in Leila Rupp, *Mobilizing Women for War* (Princeton: Princeton University Press, 1978), p. 115. I then learned from Claudia Koonz, *Mothers in the Fatherland: Women, the Family, and Nazi Politics* (New York: St. Martin's Press, 1987), that the phrase is from a recruitment poster and that German women themselves were more reluctant than women of other industrial countries to take up war work.

Discussion Questions

1. Discuss Ruddick's claim that military thinking and maternal thinking are set against each other. How would a liberal feminist and a radical feminist (see Chapter 10) most likely respond to Ruddick?
2. Do you agree with Ruddick's argument that maternal practice is a natural resource for peace politics? Support your answer.
3. What would Ruddick most likely think of the current military policy which has men and women serving in the same capacity? In particular, what would she most likely think of sending mothers of young children into active combat duty? What effect, if any, might this policy have on the politics of war and peace? Support your answers.
4. Lynn Searfoss's son Charles Anderson is stationed with the First Marines in Iraq. Searfoss, like her 80-year-old mother, is opposed to the war. Her opposition takes the form of writing to government representatives, signing antiwar petitions, and being a member of the Veterans Against the Iraq War. However, Searfoss also supports her son and the other troops who are in Iraq. "The public perception that protesters do not support the troops is inaccurate," she says. "We love and support them so much that we are fighting to bring them home safely." Is Searfoss being consistent in supporting the troops while also opposing the war? Discuss how Ruddick and a care ethicist would each most likely respond to Searfoss's position.
5. Relate the myth of the "masculinity of war" to the current "Don't Ask, Don't Tell" policy regarding homosexuals in the military.
6. Elaine Donnelly of The Center for Military Readiness is opposed to the current U.S. policy of allowing women to serve near the front lines, arguing that it "violates the long-standing moral imperative that men must protect women from physical harm."[17] Others oppose giving women combat duty on the grounds that women are not physically strong enough for the demands of combat. Also, women combatants who are captured by the enemy are subject to a high risk of rape. Discuss how Ruddick and a liberal feminist would respond to these arguments.
7. In April 2004 photographs were released to the public of smiling American soldiers sexually abusing and humiliating Iraqi prisoners at Abu Ghraib prison in Baghdad. Three of the seven American soldiers initially implicated were women, one of them 21-year-old PGC Lynndie England who was five months pregnant at the time.[1] Discuss how Sara Ruddick would most likely respond to this incident and what steps she might suggest to prevent further incidents of this type.

---

[1] Claudia Wallis, "Why Did They Do It?" *Time,* May 17, 2004, 38–42.

JONATHAN GRANOFF

Peace and Security

Jonathan Granoff is a Philadelphia lawyer and president of the Global Security Institute. The following speech was presented to the 4th World Summit of Nobel Peace Laureates in Rome on November 28, 2003. In the speech Granoff argues that our collective existence is threatened by the possibility of war and ecological disasters. In order to prevent global nuclear or ecological disaster we, as concerned global citizens, must recognize the interconnectedness of living systems and work to promote ethically responsible public policy.

Critical Reading Questions

1. According to Granoff, what responsibility do we have to future generations and why?
2. What issues in particular do we need to address as global citizens?
3. Why is a belief in Social Darwinism a threat to global security?
4. What does Granoff mean when he says that fear is the twin of ignorance and compassion the twin of wisdom?
5. What is the principle of reciprocity and how does it apply to nuclear weapons policies?
6. On what grounds does Granoff maintain that nuclear weapons "can never be ethically legitimate"?
7. How does Granoff define "security of the people"?
8. Why is it important that we change the current paradigm in which security is pursued through military violence?

We are the first generation making ethical decisions that will determine whether we will be the last generation. Science, technology and sophisticated social organizational skills have gifted us with unprecedented capacities for enrichment or destruction. I believe that there is an ethical responsibility to future generations to ensure we are not passing on a future of horrific wars or ecological catastrophe. As individuals and organizations that have received the Nobel Peace Prize, we, particularly, have a heightened responsibility to encourage and empower ethically informed policies.

Each of us knows that our individual life is precious and fragile. We are now reminded that our collective existence is fragile. This compels us to address, among other issues, ensuring bio-diversity and ending the destruction of thousands of species; reversing the depletion of fishing stocks; controlling ocean dumping; preventing ozone depletion; halting global warming; controlling and eliminating nuclear and other weapons of mass destruction; ending terrorism whether by States or non-State actors; fighting pandemic diseases; ending the tragedy of crushing poverty and lack of clean drinking water; and addressing crises arising from States in chaos. No nation or even a small group of nations can succeed in addressing these issues alone.

"Peace and Security," Presented at the *4th World Summit of Nobel Peace Laureates,* Rome, November 28, 2003.

Some solutions must be universal. Chlorofluorocarbon from a refrigerant in the US or China can harm the ozone in Chile, New Zealand or anywhere. If one country allows oceanic dumping, others will follow. Viruses do not recognize religions, races or borders. Our futures are interconnected in unprecedented ways.

Wise people have been instructing us for millennia to recognize our deeper human unity. But, now necessity alerts us: the galvanizing power of moral leadership cannot be ignored in deference to short-term parochial interests. Our collective challenges require principles that are uplifting, inspiring, affirmative of our highest potential and universal. Hope must overcome fear.

Fear is the twin of ignorance, generating a false realism. Nicolo Machiavelli stated it in *The Prince:* "Where the safety of the country depends upon resolutions to be taken, no consideration of justice or injustice, humanity or cruelty, nor of glory or shame, should be allowed to prevail." This policy of "emergency" can hardly make sense as a norm if we are to be ethical beings living in community. Such so called "realists" invariably assert broadly that power in their own hands is necessary to ensure the security of their individual State.

Overlooking the intricate interconnectedness of living systems, they exalt social Darwinism. Strength is good, ultimate strength is better. In the quest for the ultimate weapon, an absurd result is obtained. The means to security and the pursuit of strength undermine the end of security. Such improved means to an unimproved end is most aptly articulated by nuclear weapons whereby the means of pursuing security undermines the end of security. This is not realistic. This is irresponsible.

They also rely on a rigid world view in which the pursuit of the good and the pursuit of the real are divisible. They say that only what can be measured, predicted and controlled is relevant in policy discussion. What gives our lives meaning, what makes us human, what exalts our lives, is thus not considered. They leave little room in the making of policy for conscience, love, or other immeasurable, formless, human treasures. Not the least of these treasures that give our lives meaning is compassion, the twin of wisdom.

Compassion is essential to our ethical nature and has universally guided every successful culture. It is upon the foundation of ethical principles that policies must become based. Without compassion, law cannot attain justice, and without justice, there is never peace. When kindness and compassion guide our policies, our rules become golden.

Buddhism: "Hurt not others in ways that you yourself would find hurtful." *Udana-Varga, 5:18;* "A state that is not pleasing or delightful to me, how could I inflict that upon another?" *Samyutta Nikaya v. 353.*

Christianity: "All things whatsoever you would that men should do to you, do you even so to them." *Matthew 7:12.*

Confucianism: "Do not unto others what you would not have them do unto you." *Analects 15:23;* "Tsi-kung asked, 'Is there one word that can serve as a principle of conduct for life?' Confucius replied, 'It is the word 'shu'—reciprocity. Do not impose on others what you yourself do not desire.'" Doctrine of the Mean 13.3; "One should not behave towards others in a way which is disagreeable to oneself." Mencius Vii.A.4.

Hinduism: "This is the sum of duty: do not unto others which would cause you pain if done to you." *Mahabharata 5:1517.*

Islam: "No one of you is a believer until he desires for his brother that which he desires for himself." *Hadith.*

Jainism: "A man should journey treating all creatures as he himself would be treated." *Sutrakritanga 1.11.33;* "Therefore, neither does he [a wise person] cause violence to others nor does he make others do so." *Acarangasutra 5.101–2;* "In happiness and suffering, in joy and grief, we should regard all creatures as we regard our own self." *Lord Mahavira, 24th Tirthankara.*

Judaism: ". . . thou shall love thy neighbor as thyself." *Leviticus 19:18;* "What is hateful to you, do not do to your fellow man. That is the law; all the rest is commentary." *Talmud, Shabbat 31a.*

Native American: "Respect for all life is the foundation." *The Great Law of Peace.*

Roman Pagan Religion: "The law imprinted on the hearts of all men is to love the members of society as themselves."

Shinto: "The heart of the person before you is a mirror."

Sikhism: "I am a stranger to no one; and no one is a stranger to me. Indeed, I am a friend to all. *Guru Granth Sahib, p. 1299.* "As thou hast deemed thyself, so deem others."

Taoism: "Regard your neighbor's gain as your own gain, and your neighbor's loss as your own loss." *Tai Shang Kan Ying Pien, 213–218.*

Yoruba Wisdom (Nigeria): "One going to take a pointed stick to pinch a baby bird should first try it on himself to feel how it hurts."

Zoroastrianism: "That nature only is good when it shall not do unto another whatsoever is not good for its own self." *Dadistan-I-Dinik, 94:5.*

Philosopher's statements:

Plato: "May I do to others as I would that they should do unto me." *Greece, 4th Century BCE.*
Socrates: "Do not do to others that which would anger you if others did it to you." *Greece, 5th Century BCE.*
Seneca: "Treat your inferiors as you would be treated by your superiors." *Epistle 47:11 Rome, 1st Century CE.*

This principle of reciprocity is the ethical and moral foundation of all the world's major religions. Multilateralism is the logical political outgrowth of this principle. An international order based on cooperation, equity and the rule of law is its needed expression.

Where this rule of reciprocity is violated, instability follows. The failure of the nuclear weapons states to abide by their pledge, contained in the Nuclear Nonproliferation Treaty, to negotiate the elimination of nuclear weapons is the single greatest stimulus to the proliferation of nuclear weapons. For some to say nuclear weapons are good for them but not for others is simply not sustainable.

The threat to use nuclear weapons on innocent people can never be ethically legitimate. Thus, there is a moral imperative for their abolition.

I would like to add two new rules:

First, the Rule of Nations: **"Treat other nations as you wish your nation to be treated."**

Second, the Rule of the Powerful: **"As one does so shall others do."**

We are faced with a moment of collective truth: the ethical, spiritually based insights of the wise coincide with material physical imperatives for survival. The value of the love of power must give way to the power of love. In today's world, leadership must be guided by the duty to love one's neighbor as oneself. This includes the duty to protect the weakest neighbor. And, today, the whole world is one neighborhood—a moral location, not just a physical one.

What was once an admonition as a personal necessity for inner growth has now become a principle that we must learn to utilize in forming public policies. The rule is offended by ethnic and religious exclusivity and prejudice, nationalistic expansionism, economic injustice and environmental irresponsibility.

How should we view the security of people? May I suggest that Timothy Wirth, when he was United States Under Secretary of State for Global Affairs, was correct when he stated that a productive focus of multilateral security should begin with people:

Security is now understood in the context of human security. Human security is about the 1 billion individuals who live in abject poverty. It is about the 800 million people who go hungry every day—the 240 million malnourished. The 17 million who die each year from easily preventable diseases fall into this definition of security, as do the 1.3 billion people without access to clean water and the more than 2 billion people who do not benefit from safe sanitation.

Failure to change from the flawed paradigm in which security is pursued primarily through violence reinforces the brutality inflicted upon millions of daily lives destroyed by conventional weapons, including small arms and anti personnel land mines. And we cannot overlook the exorbitant economic waste and social costs of militarism—more than ten trillion dollars since the end of the Cold War.

If we do not quickly get over the ridiculous excessive attachment to that which divides us, we will fail to establish effective institutions and policies in our time and we will fail to treat future generations as we would be treated. Such failure cannot be accepted by any parent who has looked into the eyes of their children.

We have developed excessively sophisticated technologies for destruction. For our survival, we require appropriate social and human technologies for cooperation, for disarmament—for our very humanity.

An Eskimo elder at the Millennium World Peace Summit at the United Nations said, "Our history goes back 40,000 years and only now are we finding lakes in the Arctic ice cap. You have technology that is melting the ice. When will we develop a technology to melt the human heart?"

Let our deliberations for peace and security also help develop that technology.

Discussion Questions

1. Granoff argues that a resolution to problems that threaten our collective existence requires moral leadership. What does he mean by this? Discuss what steps you are taking, or could take, to resolve problems that threaten global security.
2. What ethical principles, according to Granoff, are found in the world's major ethical teachings and what is the relevance of these principles to global security?
3. In what ways does a belief in cultural relativism, as opposed to universal morality, threaten our global security? Discuss the extent to which the United States's national security policy is informed by these two opposing moral beliefs two ethical systems.
4. Discuss Granoff's claim that a nation's means of pursuing security can actually undermine global security. Do you agree or disagree with him? Use real-life examples to support your answer.
5. Discuss what Granoff's position would most likely be on the just-war theory. In particular, discuss how Granoff might respond to Elizabeth Anscombe's argument that preemptive nuclear strikes may be justified under limited conditions. Which person presents the stronger argument? Support your answer.
6. Compare and contrast Granoff's position on the permissibility of war or arming for war with Sohail Hashmi's Islamic ethics of war and peace.
7. Discuss what solution Granoff would most likely propose regarding (a) the threat of global terrorism or (b) the conflict between the Palestinians and Israel.

CASE STUDIES

1. ALLIED FIREBOMBING DURING WORLD WAR II

In 1942 Winston Churchill responded to the question "How are you going to win the war?" by saying, "We will shatter Germany by bombing . . . the severe, ruthless bombing of Germany on an ever-increasing scale will not only cripple her war effort . . . but will create conditions intolerable to the mass of the German population." This statement was followed by a campaign of firebombing German cities. Firebombing consisted of dropping large amounts of high explosives on buildings, followed by incendiary devices to ignite them, then more explosives. This created a self-sustaining firestorm with temperatures peaking at over 1,500 degrees centigrade.

Bombers were ordered to attack Berlin, Leipzig, and other German cities in the east to "cause confusion in the evacuation from the east" and "hamper the movements of troops from the west."[18] The evacuation from the east referred to refugees fleeing the Russian army, not retreating soldiers. The firebombing of German cities continued until 1945, culminating in an attack on the city of Dresden, a cultural center with little war-related industry. The city at the time was crowded with refugees fleeing the Red Army.

The firebombing of Dresden, which has been called "the worst single event massacre of all time,"[19] killed 100,000 people, more than those killed by the atomic bomb dropped several months later on Hiroshima, and destroyed 85 percent of the city. Kurt Vonnegut, Jr., who was a prisoner of war in Dresden when it was firebombed, later wrote of the horrors of the event, the grisly deaths, and how the place was turned "into a single column of fire" in his book *Slaughterhouse Five.*

Discussion Questions

1. The bombings of German cities were justified by the British on utilitarian grounds. Does utilitarian thinking allow the killing of noncombatants in these cases? Discuss how Jeremy Bentham and John Stuart Mill would most likely answer this question.
2. Were the bombings justified under the just-war theory? Support your answers.
3. It was only after the bombing of Dresden that Churchill questioned the morality of firebombing, stating "It seems to me that the moment has come when the question of bombing German cities simply for the sake of increasing the terror, though under other pretexts, should be reviewed . . . The destruction of Dresden remains a serious query against the conduct of Allied Bombing."[20] Is the use of terrorism morally acceptable as a means of winning a war?
4. In an August 9th radio speech, aired shortly after a second atomic bomb destroyed Nagasaki, President Truman stated: "If Japan does not surrender, bombs will have to be dropped on her war industries and, unfortunately, thousands of civilian lives will be lost. I urge Japanese civilians to leave industrial cities immediately, and save themselves from destruction."[21] Does warning civilians to leave cities relieve the military of moral responsibility for their deaths? Should the citizens of Dresden have been warned ahead of time or would this have put the bombers and the military operation in too much danger?
5. In his speech to the American people Truman referred to Hiroshima as a "military base" when, in fact, it was a city. Is deception permissible during war as a means of justifying military actions to one's own citizens? How about the deception used to justify the war in Iraq? Is it permissible in order to confuse or mislead the enemy? Support your answers with specific examples.
6. What is a war crime? Should British Air Marshall Arthur Harris, inventor of area firebombing and the officer who ordered the bombing of Dresden, be tried for war crimes? Is the fact that killing civilians was not the intended purpose of the firebombing (principle of double effect) morally relevant? Support your answers.

2. USA PATRIOT ACT AND THE WAR AGAINST TERRORISM

The USA Patriot Act, an acronym for Uniting and Strengthening America by Providing Appropriate Tools Required to Intercept and Obstruct Terrorism, was passed in October 2001 shortly following the September 11 terrorist attacks. The Act permits federal agents to search homes and offices, bank accounts, medical and library records, wiretap phones, and read people's emails without their permission. Shortly after the act was passed, more than 1,000 Arab and Muslim men were arrested as terrorist suspects. Many were held without being told the charges against them.

In 2003 the American Civil Liberties Union filed the first legal challenge against the Patriot Act, arguing that the Act violates the Fourth Amendment of the Constitution, which only permits searches with a warrant. Attorney General John Ashcroft responded in defense of the Act that "The Patriot Act's record demonstrates that we are protecting the American people while honoring the Constitution and preserving the liberties we hold dear. You have not heard of one single case in which a judge has found an abuse of the Patriot Act." Supporters of the Patriot Act point out that it does not make sense to warn possible terrorists that they will be subject to search and seizure.

However, it is the potential for abuse that worries civil libertarians. Americans are concerned about the trade-off of their civil liberties for greater national security. Support for the Patriot Act has been dropping since its passage in October 2002. In a recent survey by Cornell University, about 60 percent of Americans opposed wiretapping and monitoring emails. However, 68 percent supported random checks based on racial profiling of suspected terrorists and 57 percent supported the indefinite detention of suspected terrorists.[22]

More than 150 local governments, including at least three state governments, have passed resolutions condemning the Patriot Act as an infringement on civil rights and, in some instances, prohibiting state law enforcement officials from cooperating with the federal government in enforcing the Act.

Discussion Questions

1. Discuss the moral issues involved in the Patriot Act. In particular discuss whether or not apprehending and deterring terrorists outweighs the temporary loss of rights of innocent people who are suspected of terrorism.
2. Does the Patriot Act pose a threat to our civil liberties or does it work to protect our civil liberties? When is it appropriate for a country to override the rule of law, as explicated by Jonathan Granoff in his readings, in the name of national security? Support your answers.
3. If the fear of future attacks and laws to prevent them, such as the Patriot Act, erode our liberties, does this mean that the September 11 terrorists have to some extent achieved their political goals? Support your answers.
4. Ben Franklin once said that those who would trade liberty for security deserve neither.[23] Do you agree with him? Is his position unrealistic in today's world? Support your answers. Discuss how Thomas Hobbes would most likely respond to Franklin's statement.

5. In response to a question about what would happen if the United States was hit with a weapon of mass destruction that inflicted many casualties, General Tommy Franks replied that the Constitution and our liberty and freedoms would likely be discarded for a military form of government.[24] Do you agree?

---

3. THE ANTIWAR ACTIVIST

In 1968, at the height of the Vietnam War, 20-year-old Robert Poe received a notice to report for induction into the military. At the time college students could get a deferment from being drafted. Poe went to the induction center, took the physical exam, and then told them he was refusing to serve. This was the first time he had ever engaged in any sort of antiwar activity. After signing a statement affirming his refusal, Poe went home. Shortly after that an F.B.I. agent appeared at his home, put handcuffs on him, and escorted him to the Oakland County jail. A few weeks later he was sentenced to 42 months in the Federal Prison in Lompoc, California. There he met several other prisoners who were draft resisters.

Initially Poe had hoped this was just the beginning of a massive effort by war resisters to stop the Vietnam War and that thousands of college students and other young men who were leading antiwar marches and staging sit-ins would also choose prison over induction or leaving the country. However, few members of the antiwar movement joined him in prison. Indeed, some 50,000 draft-age men chose to move to Canada during the Vietnam War era in one of the largest political exoduses from the United States since the Underground Railroad.

Poe believes that the war might have ended earlier and thousands of lives been spared if more college students had refused to take their deferments and engaged in civil disobedience, instead of merely staging legal protests or dodging the draft by going to Canada.

Discussion Questions

1. Did Poe do the right thing by refusing to fight a war he didn't believe in and going to prison for his beliefs? Was his decision more moral than those of the young men who moved to Canada to avoid the draft? Did the state do the morally right thing in sentencing Poe to prison? Support your answers.
2. John Rawls writes ". . . if justified civil disobedience seems to threaten civil concord, the responsibility falls not upon those who protest but upon those whose abuse of authority and power justifies such opposition. For to employ the coercive apparatus of the state in order to maintain manifestly unjust institutions is itself a form of illegitimate force that men in due course have a right to resist."[25] Discuss Rawls's position, relating it to the above case.
3. Senator Edward Kennedy wrote in 1971 in support of the draft: "Although I share with many of my colleagues a deep and abiding respect for the concept of voluntarism in a democratic society, I cannot believe it should be raised above the demands of social justice."[26] Forty years later, in December 2001 "The Universal Military Training and Service Act," H.R. 3598, was proposed to Congress. The bill would reinstate the military draft for all male citizens and residents between the ages of 18 and 22. The only exceptions would be for extreme hardship and severe physical/mental disability.

Discuss the moral issues involved in this bill and in conscription as opposed to voluntarism. If the draft is reinstated what provisions should be made for conscientious objectors? Should women and parents of young children be drafted? Support your answers.

4. The 2001 "No Child Left Behind Act" requires high schools to give military recruiters personal information about students and to allow them into the schools to talk directly to students. Some high schools have refused to comply, arguing that the law violates students' privacy rights. Parents also oppose the strategy, saying it entices their children, especially children from lower socioeconomic families, away from going to college. Discuss the pros and cons of this approach to recruiting young people for the military.
5. Thirty-seven percent of college students surveyed in 2002 said they would attempt to avoid a draft, while only 35 percent said they would be "willing to fight and serve anywhere in the world."[27] What would you do and why?
6. Does acceptance of military service entail a duty to obey one's commanders? Why or why not? Discuss what you would have done had you been in My Lai, Vietnam at the time of the massacre or if you had been a bomber during World War II and ordered to drop fire bombs on Dresden or a nuclear bomb on Nagasaki.

---

4. WAR, OCCUPATION, AND NATION-BUILDING

In 1896 Winston Churchill stated that the purpose of the British Empire "was to give peace to warring tribes, to administer justice where all was violence, to strike the chains off the slave, to plant the seeds of commerce and learning." In March 2002 the United States and Britain invaded Iraq. Part of the purpose of the invasion was to topple Saddam Hussein's regime and replace it with a Western-style democracy.

While some people, including some Iraqis, applaud this effort, others feel that nation-building is simply an extension of the colonial mentality. Paul Ehrlich, professor of Population Studies at Stanford University, writes "All too often in the West, 'spreading democracy' has been code for 'civilizing the natives' and our enthusiasm for providing human rights has often not extended to people who have made the 'wrong' democratic choices."[28] For example, Americans did not want national elections as a means of establishing democracy in Iraq since they do not want the majority Shi'a Muslims, who make up 60 percent of the population and, for the most part, oppose American occupation, to control the government. Radical Muslims also believe that a democracy based on individual expression and openness to outside influences poses a threat to contemporary Islam.

Discussion Questions

1. Compare and contrast Churchill's justification of colonialism and the spread of Christian values with that of nation-building and the spread of democratic values. To what extent do we have the right to impose our values on those of other cultures whose values we regard as destructive? Do the United States and Britain have a right, based on self-defense, to replace the hostile government of Iraq with one that is not a threat to their national security? Support your answers.

2. Does assisting people in their struggle for freedom always violate their right to self-determination? To what extent, if any, do we have a moral obligation to assist people within those cultures who request our assistance in overturning their government? Discuss how John Stuart Mill would most likely answer these questions in light of case 4.
3. Some philosophers argue that when people's right to self-determination is threatened or thwarted, that group has a just cause for the use of violence. Does this argument justify the use of lethal force by Iraqis against the occupying Coalition forces? Does it justify the use of terrorism in the fight against the perceived threat of destruction of Islamic culture and religion by Western globalization.
4. As of December 2003, 53 percent of the American-trained Iraqi police have quit, mainly because their wages of $60 to $100 a month were not enough to support a family. In contrast, American military police serving in Iraq earn many, many times that amount. Is this fair or does the policy violate the equal pay for equal work doctrine? Is it a remnant of colonialism where the conquering Western culture is regarded as morally superior to the "natives"?
5. An estimated 17,500 Iraqi civilians died as a result of the first Gulf War.[29] There is no accurate count of how many civilians died as a result of the second war since the United States interim government in Iraq does not keep track of civilian casualties. Does the interim government have a moral duty to keep track of civilian deaths as it does American military deaths? What obligation, if any, does the American government have to the families of civilians who have been killed in the war and occupation? Discuss your answer in light of the just-war theory and Kant's categorical imperative.
6. War is one of the primary means of nation-building. Do victors in war have a moral right to take over the territory of the defeated, as happened in the United States's acquisition of California, New Mexico, Nevada, and Arizona in the 1846–48 Mexican war and the take-over of the Gaza strip and West Bank by Israel? Does the United States as the victor in the Iraqi war have the moral right to determine the political future of Iraq?
7. Was the United Nations justified in creating Israel after World War II for Jewish refugees from Europe and Russia? Or did this violate the Palestinians right to self-determination? Support your answers.

---

5. WHEN PARENTAL DUTY CONFLICTS WITH MILITARY DUTY

In November 2003, Simone and Vaughn Holcomb took an emergency leave from military duty in Iraq and returned to Fort Carson, Colorado to face a custody battle over two of their seven children, ranging in age from four to twelve years old. The children had been staying with Mr. Holcomb's mother who was no longer able to care for them. Mr. Holcomb's former wife was suing for custody for two of the children from his former marriage. The court mandated that one of the parents must remain in Colorado if the couple was to retain full custody of the children. Otherwise the judge would rule abandonment and turn over custody of the two children to Vaughn's former wife.

The Holcombs decided that Vaughn would return to Iraq and Simone would stay behind. "My children always come first," she told a reporter. However, the Army denied Simone Holcomb's request to be released from active duty, so she remained in Colorado without the army's permission. Simone Holcomb said in justification of her actions, "The Army accepted our applications to be soldiers, they should appreciate our custody problems. I will fight with all my motherly might to protect my children. If both my husband and I are in Iraq together, these children could lose their parents."[30] She also noted that there were other families in the same neighborhood facing similar dilemmas. Holcomb, a six-year veteran, faced dismissal plus possible jail time for her disobedience. In the end the Army gave Mrs. Holcomb a "compassionate reassignment" to the Colorado National Guard so she could be with her children.

Discussion Questions

1. Discuss this case in light of Sara Ruddick's contention that "militarist thinking" is set against "maternal thinking." Does "maternal thinking" and putting one's children first make women who are mothers unreliable soldiers?
2. Did the judge make the morally right ruling in this case? If you had been the judge how would you have ruled? Support your reasoning.
3. Morally speaking, how should the Army have responded to the Holcomb's predicament? Support your answer.
4. Should mothers who are members of the military or parents of young children be required to serve in active duty? Discuss how a liberal feminist and a socialist feminist would each most likely answer this question.
5. If conscription (the draft) is reinstated, should parents of dependent children be exempt? Support your answer.

CHAPTER 12

Nonhuman Animals and the Environment

In the fall of 1995, Lisa Simpson, one of television's most famous cartoon characters, became a vegetarian with a little help from her friends Linda and Paul McCartney. The episode, watched by 10 million Americans, opened with the Simpsons visiting a petting zoo. That evening the family had lamb chops for dinner, and Lisa faced a moral crisis as she made the connection between the lambs she had been petting at the zoo and the meat on her plate. Lisa decided to quit eating meat. She soon discovered, however, that being a vegetarian wasn't all that easy in a society of carnivores. Her brother, Bart, tormented her mercilessly. Lisa faced another crisis when her father, Homer, hosted a pig roast. When Lisa's offer of vegetarian gazpacho as an alternative was rejected, she destroyed the barbecue and fled in disgust at her family's indifference to animal suffering.

Lisa found solace and moral support from her friends the McCartneys, who were visiting Apu, a vegan from India. Lisa confided in Apu that she eats cheese. "You must think I'm a monster," Lisa said. "Indeed I do," Apu responded. "But I have learned long ago to tolerate others rather than forcing my beliefs on them." Lisa realized that one cannot convert others through force but only through reason and example.

THE LEGAL AND MORAL STATUS OF NONHUMAN ANIMALS

Do humans have obligations toward other animals? Do other animals have rights that we ought to respect? Most people, when asked, say that they like animals and disapprove of animal cruelty. They draw the line, however, when it comes to animals having rights. When there is a conflict between animal interests and human interests, no matter how trivial, human interests almost always win out. We eat meat, visit zoos, wear leather shoes, use cosmetics and drugs that have been tested on captive animals, and abandon our dogs and cats at animal shelters when they inconvenience us.

Suggestions that other animals have rights that we ought to respect are generally met with ridicule. When Mary Wollstonecraft first published *A Vindication of the Rights of Woman* in 1792, her ideas were also ridiculed. One critic wrote that if the idea of equality was applied to women, why shouldn't it also hold for "brutes"? Because the idea of granting rights to dogs and cats and other animals is absurd, therefore, the critic concluded, it is also absurd to grant rights to women. Women have since been granted rights under the law, although it took more than a century. "Brutes," however, still have a long way to go.

The animal-rights movement is relatively new. In the past three decades, dozens of books and hundreds of articles have been written on animal rights. There are thousands of animal-rights and vegetarian groups that have also proliferated; most colleges have at least one animal-rights group on campus.

In many Asian countries, such as India, vegetarianism has long been the norm. According to Hindu and Buddhist ethics, meat-eating violates the principle of *ahiṃsa,* or nonviolence. Meat-eating also contributes to a mentality of violence and has negative karmic consequences. With the arrival of Christian and Islam colonists, the moral ideal of vegetarianism began to erode. Nevertheless, much of the inspiration for the current animal-rights movement in the West has come from Eastern philosophy. Gandhi's philosophy, in particular, has had an enormous influence on both the American civil rights movement and the animal-rights movement.

Unlike India, in most Western countries nonhuman animals have only instrumental value and are regarded primarily as commodities, or property. One meat-company manager, for example, described a breeding sow as "a valuable piece of machinery whose function is to pump out baby pigs like a sausage machine."[1] For at least ten months out of the year, the pregnant and nursing breeding sow or "mother machine" is isolated in a narrow pen in which she is unable to turn around. She is impregnated forcefully either by being tethered to a "rape rack" for easy access or through "the surgical transplant of embryos from 'supersows' to ordinary sows."[2]

Although animal-rights groups in England have been somewhat effective in changing attitudes and legislation, this fourteen-year trend reversed in 1991 with the advent of biotechnology, which is revolutionizing agriculture and medicine.[3] Through genetic engineering, scientists can create new forms of animals by introducing genes from one species to another. The ability of humans to create new forms of animal life will very likely lead to the further commodification of nonhuman (and possibly human) animals.

The Animal Welfare Act was enacted in the United States in 1970. The act is not concerned, however, with protecting the welfare of rats, mice, birds, reptiles, frogs, or animals raised for food; nor does it include genetically altered animals. In addition, animal welfare laws are paternalistic at best and do not give animals rights. Under legal welfarism almost all animal interests can be sacrificed to even the most trivial human interest. Concern for animal suffering is based primarily on the concept of "necessary suffering." Suffering is wrong ("unnecessary") only when it does not advance human interests.

Not everyone accepts legal welfarism. Ethical positions regarding public policy can be divided into the abolitionist, reformist, and status quo positions. *Abolitionists* argue that we should stop using animals altogether as a source of food and as tools in scientific experiments. They oppose zoos, circuses, and keeping animals as house pets. Their position is supported by animal-rights activists such as Tom Regan. Although few Western philosophers accept this position, it is more generally accepted in Eastern philosophies such as Hinduism, Buddhism, and Jainism, which are based on respect for all living beings.

Reformists accept meat-eating and animal experimentation, but think that we need to improve these institutions. Unlike abolitionists, who sometimes work outside the law, reformist organizations such as humane societies work within the system, promoting reform and legislative initiatives on behalf of animals. Animal-welfare laws that require certain sized cages for animals in laboratories but do not oppose animal experimentation itself are based on the reformist position.

The *status quo* position maintains that no changes are necessary in the way humans treat other animals. The status quo position is supported by traditional Western philosophies, which regard nonhuman animals as lacking moral value. This philosophical tradition has been one of the most deeply rooted obstacles to any serious consideration of the moral rights of both nonhuman animals and the environment.

THE LEGAL AND MORAL STATUS OF THE ENVIRONMENT

The environmental ethics movement is a relative newcomer on the philosophical scene. Environmental ethics is concerned with the moral basis of environmental responsibility, including the moral value of nonhuman nature, pollution, population control, food production, and preservation of the wilderness and species diversity.

In 1967 history professor Lynn White published an article in *Science* in which he blamed Christian anthropocentric thinking for creating an ecological crisis. According to Judeo-Christian tradition, earth was created by God for the benefit of humans. "By destroying pagan animism," White wrote, "Christianity made it possible to exploit nature in a mood of indifference to the feelings of natural objects."[4] The article created an uproar, especially among religious thinkers.

Philosophers entered the fray in the early 1970s. Their attention was initially focused primarily on Aldo Leopold's essay on land ethics, excerpts of which are included in this chapter. This essay was first published in his 1949 *A Sand County Almanac* but did not become widely available until 1970. In the essay Leopold attacks the anthropocentric relationship between humans and environment that is based on humans as the conquerors of the land. He calls on us to replace the old paradigm with a new ecocentric paradigm in which humans are viewed as members, rather than conquerors, of the greater biotic community.

The *deep ecology* movement began in the mid-1970s. Deep ecology is generally regarded as a *radical environmental ethic.* The central concern of deep ecologists, such as Arne Naess, George Sessions, and Bill Devall, is to cultivate a sense of identification with nature and an awareness of our interconnectedness. The goal of environmental consciousness is self-realization based on unity between self and the world.

Ecofeminism emerged as an important movement in the 1980s. Ecofeminists such as Karen Warren link environmental ethics to feminism and animal rights, arguing that oppression of women, oppression of nonhuman animals, and oppression of nature are all grounded in the same logic of dominance.

As in the animal-rights debate, the *status quo* position, which is presented by Richard Watson in his article at the end of this chapter, is based on an anthropocentric worldview that regards nonhuman nature as a resource for human consumption. Most Americans accept an anthropocentric view of nature. The primary purpose for protecting nonhuman nature, according to this view, is to preserve it for ourselves and future generations. While support for environmental protection varies somewhat according to the strength of the economy, there is increasing public support for it. A 2000 Gallup Poll found that 70 percent of Americans felt that protection of the environment should be given priority over economic growth. This is up from 62 percent in 1995.[5] In 2002, because of opposition from environmentalists, the Senate rejected the proviso in the National Energy Plan which allowed drilling for oil in the Arctic National Wildlife Refuge.

THE PHILOSOPHERS ON THE MORAL VALUE OF NONHUMAN ANIMALS AND THE ENVIRONMENT

Ancient Greek philosophers were divided on the issue of the moral value of nonhuman nature. The Pythagoreans, who were vegetarians, taught that other animals should be treated with respect. Aristotle, on the other hand, thought that other animals had only instrumental moral value. Contemporary views on the moral value of nonhuman animals have been shaped primarily by Aristotle's anthropocentric philosophy.

The split between humans and nonhuman nature in Western thought began with the acceptance of the ancient Greek dualism, which split reality into nonthinking material substances (body) and nonmaterial thinking substances (mind or soul). Aristotle argued that reason is an activity of the soul. Humans have a soul; nonhuman animals don't. Because moral value depends on the ability to reason, only humans have intrinsic moral value. Other animals are inferior beings whom nature has made "for the sake of man." We can use other animals for food, clothing, labor, and entertainment.[6] Likewise, we can use inanimate nature to serve human purposes.

Aristotle's worldview was Christianized by Thomas Aquinas. "Humans," according to Aquinas, "are the highest in the order of material beings, yet the lowest in the order of spiritual beings . . . the progression from the non-living to humans is one of increasing perfection . . . schematically, humans are at the apex of material creation."[7] Aquinas backs up his teaching with biblical scripture. According to Genesis 1:26, "God said, 'let us make man in our image, after our likeness; and let them have dominion over the fish of the sea, and over the birds of the air, and over the cattle . . . and over all the earth.'" The world was created by God for humans. Nature and other animals exist only to the extent that they benefit humans. According to this worldview, humans have a radically different nature that sets us apart from other animals. Humans, as beings created in the image of God, are rational and free and, therefore, have intrinsic moral worth. Nonhuman animals, on the other hand, are irrational, mechanistic, and lack moral worth.

The belief that other humans are separate from, and morally superior to, other animals was affirmed by René Descartes, the "father of modern philosophy." Carrying the hierarchical worldview of his predecessors even further, Descartes concluded that nonhuman animals are merely organic machines, much like clocks, without souls, free will, or consciousness. Because of this, it is not immoral to kill and eat them. French philosopher Voltaire (1694–1778) disagreed. "What a pitiful, what a sorry thing," he wrote of Descartes's philosophy, "to have said that animals are machines bereft of understanding and feeling," arguing that animals have thought, feelings, and souls just like humans.

John Locke based his natural rights theory on the belief that humans are a special and unique creation of God. To base rights on equal consideration for the interests of all living beings, rather than on the so-called special nature of humans, is to deny the "natural" order of creation. Locke's anthropocentric, theologically based worldview of humans not only disallows the possibility of nonhuman beings having rights but grants humans the inalienable right to exploit nonhuman nature with impunity.

Francis Bacon (1561–1626), one of the founders of the scientific method, unquestionably accepted the prevailing philosophical views on nonhuman animals. Bacon enthusiastically advocated vivisection—the dissection of live animals—for the pure joy of learning. Because of the tremendous success of science in generating results and new technologies, few people bothered to question the morality of sacrificing nonhuman animals to achieve some of these successes.

In his lectures on ethics, Immanuel Kant taught that we have no direct duties toward animals because they lack rationality and, hence, are nonpersons. We should, however, "practice kindness towards animals, for he who is cruel to animals becomes hard also in his dealings with men." Cruelty toward animals purely for sport cannot be morally justified because it hardens us. While Kant did not regard other animals or nonhuman nature as having intrinsic worth, he emphasized the importance of the aesthetic experience of nature to human well-being. Just as cruelty toward other animals is wrong because it damages our character, destroying a beautiful area of wilderness is wrong because it damages our human sensibilities. On the other hand, because "animals must be regarded as man's instruments," we can use them for scientific experiments and for food just as we can use plants and the natural environment for justifiable human purposes.

The impassioned battle for equal rights for all groups of humans during the various civil rights movements fueled a similar demand for respect for the rights of other animals as well. Mohandas Gandhi, Mary Wollstonecraft, Susan B. Anthony, Elizabeth Cady Stanton, and Horace Greeley, to name only a few human-rights advocates, also spoke out on behalf of other animals. The utilitarians were among the first advocates for the rights of nonhuman animals. According to Jeremy Bentham, it is not reason but the capacity to suffer that is morally relevant.[8] The utilitarian's concern for the happiness of all sentient beings—regardless of their race, gender, or species—reflects the moral ideal of equality that was so important during the late eighteenth century. This ideal gave rise to both the American and French Revolutions. The utilitarians hoped that this moral ideal would someday be extended to all sentient beings—both human and nonhuman. In the selection from his book *Animal Liberation,* utilitarian Peter Singer maintains that to not grant equal consideration to other animals of equal cognitive ability is to engage in speciesism.

Charles Darwin (1809–1882) also rejected anthropocentricism. Darwin attacked the assumption that only humans are capable of reason. Reason, by definition, involves the ability to form general rules from particular experiences. That other animals are capable of reasoning seemed obvious to Darwin and to many other naturalists of his time. "Only a few persons now dispute that animals possess some power of reasoning," he wrote in *The Descent of Man* (1871). "Animals may constantly be seen to pause, deliberate, and resolve. It is a significant fact, that the more the habits of any particular animals are studied by a naturalist, the more he attributes to reason and the less to unlearnt instincts."[9] But Darwin underestimated the power of tradition. Indeed, his theory of evolution was reinterpreted not only to justify the oppression of non-Western people, but to justify the exploitation of other animals and nature by placing humans at the apex of evolution, thus scientifically legitimating the religious view that humans are a special creation.

Feminist philosophers are divided on the issue of animal rights. Nel Noddings argues that we do not have moral obligations toward nonhuman animals because they are incapable of being in reciprocal caring relationships with humans. Other feminists, such as Karen Warren, argue that the domination of women and the domination of nonhuman animals are part of the same patriarchal paradigm. Women can achieve autonomy only by rejecting the dualistic ideology that allows humans to subordinate other animals.

Not all cultures, as we have already noted, share the Western view of nonhuman animals. Some Native American cultures, as well as the Australian Aborigines, regard the earth and all living beings on earth as a sacred whole. Other animals deserve to be treated with respect; accordingly, we should take no more from nature than we need for our survival. Buddhist philosophers also believe that all life is interconnected and that we have to extend moral respect to all living beings if we are ever to have a peaceful world.

ANIMAL FARMING, ENVIRONMENTAL DEGRADATION, AND VEGETARIANISM

Our eating habits are our most direct interaction with the Earth. Americans are steeped in the Jeffersonian tradition that regards farmers as "the chosen People of God" and as our "most valued citizens."[10] Farming, Jefferson claimed, ennobles humans by keeping them in touch with living nature. However, modern agriculture is not a natural process but a cultural institution shaped by cultural beliefs that prescribe our relationships to the environment. Critics of modern agricultural practices maintain that exploitation of the Earth and other animals through agriculture does not ennoble us, as Kant would hope, but instead disrupts our sense of connection and blunts our feelings, particularly of empathy.[11] That agriculture has become one of the major causes of environmental degradation is not surprising given our culture's degraded view of both the environment and other animal species.

Most people are unaware of the extent to which human practices affect other animals. Each year almost 7 billion animals are killed in the United States in laboratories, for their fur, by sports hunters, and in slaughterhouses. Of these animals, 95 percent are killed for food. According to the U.S. Department of Agriculture, worldwide 45 billion animals, excluding fish, were slaughtered in 2000 for food.[12] The average per-capita consumption of meat in the United States, Canada, and Australia is two hundred pounds per year.[13] On an average day in the United States, 130,000 cattle, 7,000 calves, 360,000 pigs, and 24 million chickens are killed.[14]

The affluence boom that followed World War II was accompanied by an increase in meat-eating, which was regarded as a status symbol. By the early 1970s, rich nations were feeding more grain to their livestock than all the people of China and India (who make up more than two-thirds of the world's population) consumed directly.

Intensive farming of animals also began in the United States shortly after the war. Intensive farming involves raising animals indoors in large, automated "factories." Several thousand chickens or pigs may be housed in one building. Confining animals in buildings requires less land and less labor. Intensive farming also makes it easier to collect the animal products and to dispose of animal waste. The modern factory farm reflects the traditional Western view of nonhuman animals as machines.

The institution of animal agriculture is one of the greatest sources of suffering for nonhuman animals. Animals in the modern factory farm are raised in large buildings in crowded cages or stalls. Today almost all of egg production comes from caged birds in automated factory buildings.[15] Journalist Joy Williams writes:

> Factory farmers are all Cartesians. Animals are no more than machines—milk machines, piglet machines, egg machines—production units converting themselves into profits. . . . The factory farm today is a crowded, stinking bedlam, filled with suffering animals that are quite literally insane, sprayed with pesticides and fattened on a diet of growth stimulants, antibiotics, and drugs. Two hundred and fifty thousand laying hens are confined within a single building. (The high mortality rate caused by overcrowding is economically acceptable; nothing is more worthless than an individual chicken.) [16]

We need to eat to stay alive. We do have a choice, however, in what to eat. Humans do not need meat in their diets. Indeed, heavy reliance on meat is one of the leading causes of disease and obesity in the United States, England, Australia, and Canada.[17] In addition, the caloric intake in the United States has increased by 12 percent since 1985,[18] making Americans one of the most overfed and obese people in the world.

More and more people in these countries are becoming vegetarians. A *vegetarian* is a person who refrains from eating the flesh of animals, although some vegetarians eat fish. *Vegans* abstain from all animal products including eggs and milk. A 1977/78 survey by the U.S. Department of Agriculture found that 1.2 percent of Americans identified themselves as vegetarians. In a 1997 survey, 5 percent of Americans identified themselves as vegetarians. About one-third to one-half of these people are vegans.[19] In a 2003 Harris Poll survey, about 6 percent of all those surveyed, and 10 percent of the 25- to 34-year-olds, said that they never ate meat.[20] Asian Americans are the most likely to be vegetarians and whites the least likely to be vegetarians. Women are twice as likely as men to be vegetarians.[21]

Ethical vegetarians maintain that nonhuman animals have moral value. Although meat-eating might be justified if we needed meat for survival, the human taste for animal flesh does not justify killing and eating animals. Ethical vegetarians also point to the tremendous animal suffering by modern farming methods. Those who believe that animals should be treated with moral respect require us to expand our moral community to include other animals as well as humans. This requires giving up certain practices, such as meat-eating and wearing leather or fur. Those who defend meat-eating, such as Jan Narveson, on the other hand, deny that animals have either moral status or rights that we must respect.

Environmental ethicists do not have a unified position on agriculture. Aldo Leopold did not reject agriculture but instead judged it against a holistic model of its impact on the entire biotic community. While many environmental ethicists advocate for the more humane treatment of nonhuman animals, a few support a move toward intensive farming of "farm" animals, blaming grazing "livestock" for the destruction of wildlife habitat. This has led to criticism that environmentalists who identify nature with the pristine wilderness have created an artificial divide not only between humans and nonhuman nature but between "domestic" and "wild" animals. The increased use of genetic engineering in agriculture may further exacerbate this divide if genetically engineered plants and animals are viewed as legal property of their human creators.

Many people adopt a vegetarian lifestyle primarily out of concern for the environment. Green political parties in Europe and Great Britain advocate a vegetarian diet for environmental and political reasons. Animal farming is tremendously damaging to the environment. If we gave up animal farming, there would be enough food for everyone in the world. Many of the world's environmental problems would also be resolved by the elimination of animal agriculture. A meat-based diet uses three times as much fossil fuel as a vegetarian diet. Much of the water pollution, depletion of topsoil, and deforestation is the result of animal agriculture. In the United States, most of the agricultural land is dedicated to raising beef. One acre of land can produce 40,000 pounds of potatoes or 250 pounds of beef.[22]

POLLUTION AND GLOBAL WARMING

Issues of pollution, global warming, and hazardous waste disposal are of central importance to applied environmental ethics. More than half of Americans polled by Gallup in 2002 said that they worried a great deal about water pollution and soil contamination. Of those, 31 percent also thought that global warming would pose a serious threat to them or their way of life in their lifetime.[23] Some of the substances that contribute to atmospheric pollution, such as gases from volcanic explosions, are not of human origin. However, most of the air pollution that is contributing to global warming and acid rain is of human origin.

Global warming is of particular concern to environmentalists. Based on a one-thousand-year record, the 1990s was the warmest decade and the twentieth century the warmest century.[24] Of the one hundred glaciers in Glacier National Park one hundred have melted in the past one hundred years, with much of the glacial runoff eventually ending up in the already swollen Mississippi River. Areas as large as Connecticut have broken off of the Antarctic ice shelf in the last few years. The melting ice, in turn, contributes to rises in sea levels.

While some areas of the world will experience significant warming, global warming may also alter ocean currents which may, in turn, plunge temperatures in Northern Europe twenty degrees in the next ten years.[25] This, along with the clearing of rain forests for agriculture and timber, has already contributed to the extinction or threatened extinction of hundreds, perhaps even thousands, of species of plants and animals.

Solid waste disposal also contributes to environmental degradation and human disease. While population growth in the Third World has been blamed for many of the environmental problems we are currently facing, in fact, affluent Westerners are responsible for much of this pollution. The average American produces much more household waste and is responsible for more industrial and agricultural pollution than anyone else in the world. Hazardous waste disposal, including the disposal of nuclear waste, is particularly problematic. There are currently over twelve hundred hazardous waste sites in the United States, most of them located in poor, minority neighborhoods and on Native American homelands.

ANIMAL EXPERIMENTATION

An estimated 100 million nonhuman animals are killed every year in scientific experiments in the United States alone and this figure is on the increase. In his reading on "Peace and Security" at the end of Chapter 11, Jonathan Granoff also discusses the negative effects of war on the environment.[26] As with animal agriculture, the practice of animal experimentation is based on an anthropocentric paradigm.

EXPERIMENTS USING NONHUMAN ANIMALS[27]

- **Acute toxicity test.** This test involves force-feeding enormous quantities of a substance to a group of animals, either orally or through a tube. The purpose is to determine the lethal dose at which a given percentage of animals die within two weeks. The tests can cause convulsions, vomiting, diarrhea, paralysis, and rupture of internal organs.
- **Chronic toxicity test.** Animals are force-fed smaller quantities of a substance over time to determine if continuous exposure is lethal.
- **Skin and eye irritation tests.** Animals are immobilized in restraining devices and chemicals are applied to raw skin or sprayed in the eyes.
- **Acute inhalation toxicity test.** Animals are subjected to large amounts of spray from aerosol preparations. They are then killed and their tissues examined.
- **Psychology research.** Animals are used in experiments that include electric shock, "punishment," induced fighting and killing, brain damage, mutilation, drug addiction, maternal deprivation, and overcrowding.
- **Weapons tests.** Animals are used to study the effects of atomic blasts, radiation, chemical warfare, and laser weapons on the body.
- **Biotechnology.** Animals are genetically engineered for use in medical experiments, to produce drugs for human use, and for organ transplants.

The U.S. Food and Drug Administration (FDA) requires that all new chemical products be tested. Most of these tests are performed on nonhuman animals. One of the more common tests is the Draize eye irritancy test, which was developed by J. H. Draize, who worked for the FDA. The Draize test involves placing a rabbit's head in a restraining device and then putting in one of their eyes a substance such as bleach, shampoo, nail polish, chemical cleaning substances, or weed killer. These experiments are extremely painful. Some rabbits snap their necks in their frantic attempts to escape.

The medical field, the defense industry, and universities also make extensive use of nonhuman animals in their research. The different types of animal experiments are outlined above. The biggest increase in the use of animals in experiments has been in biotechnology and genetic engineering. Scientists are using genetic engineering to create "designer" animals for specific purposes. It may not be long before pigs, genetically altered to contain human genes, will be mass produced as drug factories and to provide organ transplants for humans. Those who defend the status quo, such as Carl Cohen, argue that animals have no rights that we are bound to respect. They also point out the benefits that animal experimentation has brought to humans.

On the other hand, the results of experiments on one species do not necessarily carry over to humans. Millions of dollars are wasted every year on pointless or repetitive experiments. Eliminating these types of experiments would rule out some animal experimentation, but it would not rule out all of it. Unlike reformists, abolitionists oppose all animal experimentation, even if it can be shown to greatly benefit humans. We cannot use other animals to advance human interests. In England scientific experimentation on dogs and puppies was outlawed as part of the government's preelection promise to implement a far-reaching ban on animal experimentation.

Both abolitionists and reformists encourage the use of alternatives to animal research. These alternatives include observation of patients, clinical tests, tissue and cell cultures, the use of cadavers, mechanical models, and computer-generated models. Some college students have also refused to participate in dissection and the use of animals in experiments in class.[28]

Although some scientists believe that the advent of biotechnology will increase the demand for animal experimentation, others argue that the completion of the Human Genome Project may render much of animal experimentation obsolete. The new field of pharmogenetics, for example, which studies the effects of genetics on an individual's reactions to drugs, will increase the likelihood that medications will be tailored for each individual based on their particular genome rather than on animal models.[29]

MORAL ISSUES

The Moral Standing of Nonhuman Animals and Nature

To attribute moral standing to a being is to claim that it is worthy of moral respect and protection. A common approach for determining moral standing is to ask if a being has cognitive qualities similar to those of a rational and autonomous human adult. The more the being is like a human adult in these respects, the higher its moral standing. Applying this line of reasoning, traditional philosophers and scientists maintain that other animals lack reason and the ability to be autonomous and, therefore, have little, if any, moral standing. Narveson and Cohen represent this view on the moral standing of nonhuman animals. Singer, on the other hand, argues that some adult mammals are sufficiently like humans in their cognitive abilities to warrant moral consideration.

One of the problems in this approach is in knowing the mental life and intentions, if any, of other animals. Furthermore, although lack of certain cognitive abilities may exclude a being from being a moral agent, it does not logically follow that it should be denied moral standing because of this. Regan, for example, argues that nonhuman animals may not be moral agents, but they can still be moral patients; that is, they have interests, and therefore rights, that we ought to respect. For example, a cat companion may not have any moral duties toward us, but we, as moral agents, have a duty to provide her with food and shelter. According to Regan, both moral agents and moral patients, as beings that are subjects of life, have inherent value.

Utilitarians, such as Singer, maintain that sentience, not reason, is the relevant criterion for moral standing. It is wrong to cause suffering no matter what the cognitive level of the being. Singer employs anthropocentric criteria, however, attributing higher moral standing to those animals, such as adult mammals, that are most like adult humans in their cognitive abilities. Hindu and Buddhist philosophers, on the other hand, cast the net wide enough to include all living beings in the moral community.

The primary divide in the environmental rights movement is between ecocentrism and anthropocentrism. Ecocentrists and biocentrists, such as Leopold, maintain that nature has moral standing and that we have a duty to preserve the integrity of the biotic community. Environmental ethicists such as Watson, on the other hand, maintain that the ecocentric arguments are misguided and possibly even misanthropic. While there are good reasons for preserving nonhuman nature, these reasons are based on human interests. We by necessity operate from a human-centered perspective. Human beings, by their very nature, cannot help but treat nature instrumentally in order to use resources from the natural world. Caring for nature is good, not because nature has intrinsic worth, but because identification with nature expands and humanizes us.

Social Contract Theory

According to social contract theorists, such as Narveson, morality is a type of voluntary contract among people. We have moral obligations only toward those who have entered into this agreement. Because nonhuman animals, plants, and inanimate objects such as mountains cannot enter into a social contract, we have no direct moral obligations toward them. Instead we have direct duties only toward other humans. For example, we ought not to kill or destroy someone else's pet, not because the pet has a right to life, but because we have a duty toward the human not to destroy her property. A pet owner, however, may decide to rid herself of her pet.

The Principle of Utility

What matters, according to utilitarians, is whether animals can feel pain, not whether they can reason. Singer and Regan, in their readings, graphically illustrate the pain and torment caused to nonhuman animals by human practices. The moral duty to minimize pain and maximize pleasure militates against most human use of animals. The pleasure humans may get from the taste of meat does not outweigh the suffering caused to animals by farming.

We also need to weigh the benefits to humans of animal experimentation against the animals' interests in living a pain-free life. On the other hand, if our concern is to benefit humans, it could be argued that it would be preferable to use brain-damaged humans rather than nonhuman animals, because the results would be more accurate. Indeed, the use of certain "nonproductive" groups of humans, such as elderly people and children who are mentally retarded, has been justified on utilitarian grounds by researchers in the past. Most people find this implication of utilitarian reasoning morally repugnant.

Another problem with relying on utilitarian criteria is the definition of "necessary suffering." The concepts of necessary and unnecessary suffering, used by Cohen to justify the use of nonhuman animals in experiments, are notoriously vague as well as biased in favor of human interests. Suffering is generally regarded as unnecessary only when it does not facilitate human ends or well-being. People who torture their dogs are seen as despicable cowards; scientists who conduct painful experiments on dogs are seen as promoting human progress. Furthermore, the suffering caused to one hundred dogs by an experiment might be labeled "necessary," whereas the suffering from performing the same experiment on one severely retarded human would probably be deemed morally unacceptable. Thus, talk of benefits and necessary suffering often serves to mask a view of other animals as property and lack of genuine concern for them. The tremendous disparity in power of scientists and agribusiness also ensures that the interests of humans will always be given greater weight than the interests of other animals. The principle of *ahiṃsā,* in contrast, states that the suffering of nonhuman animals cannot be justified by its benefits to humans.

Many environmental ethicists, including the deep ecologists and ecofeminists, reject both the utilitarian and the stewardship models. They believe that utilitarians define the "common good" too narrowly. While many environmental ethicists embrace a concept of the common good it includes all of nature, not just sentient beings. To use the words of Leopold, "a thing is right when it tends to preserve the stability, integrity, and beauty of the biotic community." In addition, the stewardship model, like Singer's utilitarian theory, is hierarchical, placing more value on beings who are the most sentient. Land and nonhuman nature have value beyond their usefulness to humans.

Rights

One of the weaknesses of utilitarianism is that it does not guarantee that animals—human or nonhuman—cannot be used as a means only. Animal-rights advocates argue that just as we ought to respect humans' intrinsic worth, regardless of their utility, we should also treat other animals as ends-in-themselves. Animals welfarists, while acknowledging that animals have welfare rights such as health care, proper nutrition, and a clean living space, do not generally recognize other animals' liberty rights or right to life. Animal-rights advocates, on the other hand, claim that nonhuman animals have both welfare and liberty rights.

Traditional Western philosophy supports a model of rights based on self-assertion. This position is defended by Cohen. According to the self-assertion model, a right is a claim or potential claim that one being may exercise against another. Rights arise only among beings that can make moral claims against one another. Because nonhuman animals presumably lack the capacity for moral choice, they lack moral rights.

In contrast, the model of rights adopted by animal-rights advocates, such as Regan, is based on interests. The existence of interests is based on the capacity for suffering and for enjoyment. All sentient animals, including humans, have an interest in doing that which brings them pleasure, as well as an interest in avoiding harm and suffering. Under this model of rights, benefits to oneself and others are morally acceptable only if no one else's rights have been violated in achieving these benefits.

On the other hand, advocates of deep ecology have been accused of being eco-fascists. There is concern that ecocentrism may motivate the state to be overly coercive and restrictive of the activities of humans for the sake of the greater environmental good.

Justice, Speciesism, and the Principle of Equality

The principle of equality states that it is unjust to treat beings differently unless we can show that there is a difference between them that is relevant to the differential treatment. Singer claims that "speciesism," which he defines as "a prejudice or attitude of bias in favor of the interests of members of one's own species and against those of members of another species,"[30] violates the principle of equality. His rule of thumb for avoiding speciesism is that "we should give the same respect to the lives of animals as we give to the lives of those humans at a similar mental level." Both Singer and Warren relate discrimination against other animals to discrimination based on racism and sexism.

The moral equality of sentient beings does not entail that human and nonhuman animals have the same rights. Different species have different interests. There are distinctly human rights, such as the right to religious freedom and the right to a formal education, that other animals lack because they have no interest in either organized religion or formal schooling. All sentient animals, however—including humans, cats, mice, and frogs—have an interest in not being tortured, starved, or held captive, not because they are capable of rational thought, but because they have the ability to feel pain.

To most people, speciesism doesn't seem as bad as racism or sexism. In fact, many people find the comparison offensive. Whereas gender or skin color is arbitrary and of no moral importance, they argue, the difference in our treatment of humans and other species is based on morally relevant differences. Only humans, as rational autonomous beings, are able to participate in the moral community.

On the other hand, as Singer points out, there are humans who are neither rational nor autonomous. Including these people in the moral community while excluding other animals of equal or greater cognitive capacity violates the principle of equality because it bases moral treatment on group membership rather than on individual differences. Also, the claim that no other animals are capable of reason seems empirically wrong. There would be no point in using nonhuman animals, such as monkeys and rats, in some learning experiments if they were incapable of reason. Indeed, as Singer points out, the reason why we use other animals in learning and medical experiments is precisely because they are so much like us.

The environmental justice movement emerged in the United States in the 1980s as an outgrowth of the movement for social justice for politically disenfranchised groups of people. Its focus has been on the urban environment rather than on the wilderness. As such this movement has radically redefined the meaning of environment to include the broader framework of economic, racial, and social justice. The movement's primary concerns have been on ending environmental racism and on promoting tighter government regulation of industrial pollution and waste disposal.

Natural Law

Defenders of meat-eating point out that other animals eat meat. The human practice of meat-eating is simply part of the natural order. This argument is also used in support of hunting. But because humans are omnivores, an argument based on nature can go either way and hence is not particularly useful in resolving the question regarding the moral acceptability of meat-eating. Opponents of meat-eating maintain that humans are not physiologically suited for a meat-based diet. Indeed many of our modern ailments are due to our meat-eating habits. This argument also commits the naturalist fallacy: Just because humans can and do eat meat does not mean that they ought to.

CONCLUSION

Gandhi once said that "the greatness of a nation can be judged by the way its animals are treated." Even if we don't accept the claim that other animals have inherent moral worth, we ought to stop and consider the ways in which our lifestyles cause suffering to other animals. The case for vegetarianism, especially when almost all the animals we use for food are now raised on factory farms, is strong whichever position we accept on the moral status of nonhuman animals. Morality requires that we be able to justify actions that affect others. Human beings have the power to exploit or to live in harmony with other species and the environment. It is up to each of us to decide how we want to use this power.

TOM REGAN

The Moral Basis of Vegetarianism

Tom Regan is an animal-rights activist and professor of philosophy and religion at North Carolina State University. In the following selection, Regan provides a rights-based argument for vegetarianism. He begins by responding to traditional philosophical arguments that deny moral value and rights to nonhuman animals. After analyzing and rejecting these arguments, Regan concludes that the current differential treatment of human and nonhuman animals cannot be morally justified. All animals that are experiencing subjects of their own lives have inherent value.

Critical Reading Questions

1. How did Gandhi's life and writings influence Regan's thinking on vegetarianism?
2. On what grounds does Regan reject Descartes's view of nonhuman animals?
3. Why does Regan reject the traditional view that language is necessary for experiencing pain?
4. According to Regan, why is the principle of nonmaleficence morally relevant to our treatment of nonhuman animals?
5. How does Regan respond to the argument that humans have certain natural rights that animals lack?
6. How does Regan respond to the argument that only humans have the ability to reason?
7. How does Regan respond to the argument that animals cannot have rights because they lack the ability to claim them? How does he respond to the argument that granting rights to animals is absurd as they are not capable of making moral decisions?
8. What is Regan's position on the use of "intensive rearing methods"? What is the purpose and result of these modern farming techniques? Who, according to Regan, is morally responsible for their continuation?
9. How does Regan respond to the argument that meat-eating may be justified if the meat is bought from farms where intensive rearing methods are not used?
10. How does Regan respond to the argument that meat-eating would no longer be morally objectionable if we could find ways to raise and kill animals painlessly?
11. On what grounds does Regan reject the natural rights argument that "all and only human beings have an equal right to life"?
12. Why does Regan claim that the burden of justification rests on the shoulders of meat-eaters rather than on vegetarians?
13. Does Regan oppose all taking of the lives of animals? Under what circumstances might it be morally justifiable to take the life of a nonhuman animal?
14. According to Regan, what would be necessary to justify the differential treatment of humans and nonhuman animals?

"The Moral Basis of Vegetarianism," in *All That Dwell Therein: Animal Rights and Environmental Ethics* (Berkeley: University of California Press, 1982), 1–36. Notes have been omitted.

My initial interest in vegetarianism grew out of my study of the life and writings of Mahatma Gandhi. Gandhi, as is well known, was an advocate of nonviolence (ahiṃsā), *not only in political affairs but in the conduct of one's life generally. The extreme pacifistic position he advocated, from which he derived the obligatoriness of vegetarianism, struck me as inadequate, and I sought a less radical moral basis for vegetarianism, one that those of us in the Western world would find more hospitable. Since the leading theories were (and remain) one or another version of utilitarianism, on the one hand, and, on the other, theories that proclaim basic moral rights, it seemed to me that the moral basis of vegetarianism would have to be found somewhere among these options. That such a basis may be provided by a rights-based theory is what "The Moral Basis of Vegetarianism" attempts to show. Both the moral right not to be caused gratuitous suffering and the right to life, I argue, are possessed by the animals we eat if they are possessed by the humans we do not. To cause animals to suffer cannot be defended merely on the grounds that we like the taste of their flesh, and even if animals were raised so that they led generally pleasant lives and were "humanely" slaughtered, that would not insure that their rights, including their right to life, were not violated. Despite the Western custom of supposing that vegetarians must defend their "eccentric" way of life, the essay attempts to shift the burden of proof onto the shoulders of those who should bear it—the nonvegetarians.*

Now, there can be no doubt that animals sometimes appear to be in pain. On this point, even Descartes would agree. In order for us to be rationally entitled to abandon the belief that they actually do experience pain, therefore, especially in view of the close physiological resemblances that often exist between them and us, we are in need of some rationally compelling argument that would demonstrate that this belief is erroneous. Descartes's principle argument in this regard fails to present a compelling case for his view. Essentially, it consists in the claim that, since animals cannot speak or use a language, they do not think, and since they do not think, they have no minds; lacking in these respects, therefore, they have no consciousness either. Thus, since a necessary condition of a creature's being able to experience pain is that it be a conscious being, it follows, given Descartes's reasoning, that animals do not experience pain. . . .

Imagine a person whose vocal chords have been damaged to such an extent that he no longer has the ability to utter words or even make inarticulate sounds, and whose arms have been paralyzed so that he cannot write, but who, when his tooth abscesses, twists and turns on his bed, grimaces and sobs. We do not say, "Ah, if only he could still speak, we could give him something for his pain. As it is, since he cannot speak, there's nothing we need give him. For he feels no pain." We say he is in pain, despite his loss of the ability to say so.

Whether or not a person is experiencing pain, in short, does not depend on his being able to perform one or another linguistic feat. Why, then, should it be any different in the case of animals? It would seem to be the height of human arrogance, rather than of . . . "superstition," to erect a double standard here, requiring that animals meet a standard not set for humans. If humans can experience pain without being logically required to be able to say so, or in any other ways to use a language, then the same standard should apply to animals as well. . . .

Now, an essential part of any enlightened morality is the principle of noninjury. What this principle declares is that we are not to inflict pain on, or otherwise bring about or contribute to the pain in, any being capable of experiencing it. This principle, moreover, is derivable from the more general principle of nonmaleficence, which declares that we are not to do or cause evil, together with the value judgment that pain, considered in itself, is intrinsically evil. . . .

Given the intrinsic evil of pain, and assuming further that pleasure is intrinsically good, it is clear that cases can arise in which the evil (pain) caused to animals is not compensated for by the good (pleasure) caused humans. The classical utilitarians—Bentham, Mill, and Sidgwick—all were aware of this . . .

It has already been pointed out that the pain an animal feels is just as much pain, and just as much an intrinsic evil, as a comparable pain felt by a human being. So, if there is any rational basis for rendering conflicting judgments about the two practices, it must be looked for in some other direction.

The most likely and, on the face of it, the most plausible direction in which to look is in the direction of rights. "Humans," this line of reasoning goes, "have certain natural rights that animals lack, and that is what makes the two practices differ in a morally significant way. For in the case of the practice involving humans, their equal natural right to be spared undeserved pain is being violated, while in the case of the practice involving animals, since animals can have no rights, *their* rights are not being ignored. That is what makes the two cases differ. And that is what makes the practice involving humans an immoral one, while the practice involving animals is not."

Natural though this line of argument is, I do not think it justifies the differential treatment of the animals and humans in question. For on what grounds might it be claimed that the humans, but not the animals, have an equal natural right to be spared undeserved pain? Well, it cannot be, as it is sometimes alleged, that all and only human beings have this right because all and only humans reason, make free choices, or have a concept of their identity. These grounds will not justify the ascription of rights to all humans because some humans—infants and the severely mentally defective, for example—do not meet these conditions. Moreover, even if these conditions did form the grounds for the possession of rights; and even if it were true that all human beings met them; it still would not follow that *only* human beings have them. For on what grounds, precisely, might it be claimed that no animals can reason, make free choices, or form a concept of themselves? What one would want here are detailed analyses of these operative concepts together with rationally compelling empirical data and other arguments that support the view that all nonhuman animals are deficient in these respects. It would be the height of prejudice merely to assume that man is unique in being able to reason. To the extent that these beliefs are not examined in the light of what we know about animals and animal intelligence, the supposition that *only* human beings have these capacities is just that—a supposition, and one that could hardly bear the moral weight placed upon it by the differential treatment of animals and humans. . . .

Two objections should be addressed before proceeding. Both involve difficulties that are supposed to attend the attribution of rights to animals. The first declares that animals cannot have rights because they lack the capacity to *claim* them. Now, this objection seems to be a variant of the view that animals cannot have rights because they cannot speak, and, like this more general view, this one too will not withstand a moment's serious reflection. For there are many human beings who cannot speak or claim their rights—tiny infants, for example—and yet who would not be denied the right in question, assuming, as we are, that it is supposed to be a right possessed by *all* human beings. Thus, if a human being can possess this (or any other right) without being able to demand it, it cannot be reasonable to require that animals be able to do so, if they are to possess this (or any other) right. The second objection is different. It declares that the attribution of rights to animals leads to absurdity. For if, say, a lamb has the natural right to be spared undeserved pain, then the wolf, who devours it unmercifully, without the benefit of anesthetic, should be said to violate the lamb's right. This, it is alleged, is absurd, and so, then, is the attribution of rights to animals. Well, absurd it may be to say that the wolf violates the lamb's right. But even supposing that it is, nothing said here implies that such deeds on the part of the wolf violate the lamb's rights. For the lamb can have rights only against those beings who are capable of taking the interests of the lamb into account and [are] trying to determine, on the basis of its interests, as well as other relevant considerations, what, morally speaking, ought to be done. In other words, the only kind of being against which another being can have rights is a being that can be held to be morally responsible for its actions. Thus, the lamb can have rights against, say, most adult human beings. But a wolf, I think it would be agreed, is not capable of making decisions from the moral point of view; nor is a wolf the kind of being that can be held morally responsible; neither, then, can it make sense to say that the lamb has any rights against the wolf. This situation has its counterpart in human affairs. The severely mentally feeble, for example, lack the requisite powers to act morally; thus, *they* cannot be expected to recognize our rights, nor can *they* be said to violate our rights, even if, for example, they should happen to cause us undeserved pain. For as they are not the kind of being that can be held responsible for what they do, neither can they be said to violate anyone's rights by what they do. . . .

Animals who are raised to be eaten by human beings very often are made to suffer. Nor is it simply that they suffer only when they are being shipped to the slaughterhouse or actually being slaughtered. For what is happening is this: The human appetite for meat has become so great that new methods of raising animals have come into being. Called intensive rearing methods, these methods seek to insure that the largest amount of meat can be produced in the shortest amount of time with the least possible expense. In ever increasing numbers, animals are being subjected to the rigors of these methods. Many are being forced to live in incredibly crowded conditions. Moreover, as a result of these methods, the natural desires of many animals often are being frustrated. In short, both in terms of the physical pain these animals must endure, and in terms of the psychological pain that attends the frustration of their natural inclinations, there can be no reasonable doubt that animals who are raised according to intensive rearing methods experience much nontrivial, undeserved pain. Add to this the gruesome realities of "humane" slaughter and we have, I think, an amount and intensity of suffering that can, with propriety, be called "great."

To the extent, therefore, that we eat the flesh of animals that have been raised under such circumstances, we help create the demand for meat that farmers who use intensive rearing methods endeavor to satisfy. Thus, to the extent that it is known that such methods will bring about much undeserved, nontrivial pain on the part of the animals raised according to these methods, anyone who purchases meat that is a product of these methods—and almost everyone who buys meat at a typical supermarket or restaurant does this—is *causally implicated* in a practice that causes pain that is both nontrivial and undeserved for the animals in question. On this point too, I think there can be no doubt. . . .

Now, there are, as I mentioned earlier, two further objections that might be raised, both of which, I think, uncover important limitations in the argument of this section. The first is that a meat eater might be able to escape the thrust of my argument by the simple expedient of buying meat from farms where the animals are not raised according to intensive rearing methods, a difficult but not impossible task at the present time. For despite the widespread use of these methods, it remains true that there are farms where animals are raised in clean, comfortable quarters, and where the pain they experience is the natural result of the exigencies of animal existence rather than, to use an expression of Hume's, of "human art and contrivance." . . .

The [second] objection that reads thus: "Granted, the amount of pain animals experience in intensive rearing units is deplorable and ought to be eliminated as far as is possible; still, it does not follow that we ought to give up meat altogether or to go to the trouble of hunting or buying it from other farmers. After all, all we need do is get rid of the pain and our moral worries will be over. So, what we should do is this; we should try to figure out how to *desensitize* animals so that they do not feel any pain, even in the most barbarous surroundings. Then, if this could be worked out, there would not be any grounds for worrying about the 'morality' of eating meat. Remove the animals' capacity for feeling pain and you thereby remove the possibility of their experiencing any pain that is gratuitous."

Now, I think it is obvious that nothing that I have said thus far can form a basis for responding to this objection, and though I think there are alternative ways in which one might try to respond to it, the case I try to make against it evolves out of my response to the first objection; I try to show, in other words, that an adequate response to this objection can be based upon the thesis that *it is the killing of animals, and not just their pain, that matters morally.*

. . .

Let us begin, then, with the idea that all humans possess an equal natural right to life. And let us notice, once again, that it is an *equal natural* right that we are speaking of, one that we cannot acquire or have granted to us, and one that we all are supposed to have just because we are human beings. On what basis, then, might it be alleged that all and only human beings possess this right to an equal extent? Well, several familiar possibilities come immediately to mind. It might be argued that all and only human beings have an equal right to life because either (*a*) all and only human beings have the capacity to reason, or (*b*) all and only human beings have the capacity to make free choices, or (*c*) all and only human beings have a concept of "self," or (*d*) all and only human beings have all or some combination of the previously mentioned capacities. And it is easy to imagine how someone might argue that, since animals do not have any of these capacities, *they* do not possess a right to life, least of all one that is equal to the one possessed by humans.

I have already touched upon some of the difficulties such views must inevitably encounter. Briefly, it is not clear, first, that no nonhuman animals satisfy any one (or all) of these conditions, and, second, it is reasonably clear that not all human beings satisfy them. The severely mentally feeble, for example, fail to satisfy them. Accordingly, *if* we want to insist that they have a right to life, then we cannot also maintain that they have it because they satisfy one or another of these conditions. Thus, *if* we want to insist that they have an equal right to life, despite their failure to satisfy these conditions, we cannot consistently maintain that animals, because they fail to satisfy these conditions, therefore lack this right.

Another possible ground is that of sentience, by which I understand the capacity to experience pleasure and pain. But this view, too, must encounter a familiar difficulty—namely, that it could not justify restricting the right *only* to human beings. . . .

The onus of justification lies not on the shoulders of those who are vegetarians but on the shoulders of those who are not. If the argument of the present section is sound, it is the nonvegetarian who must show us how he can be justified in eating meat, when he knows that, to do so, an animal has had to be killed. It is the nonvegetarian who must show us how his manner of life does not contribute to practices that systematically ignore the right to life which animals possess, if humans are supposed to possess it on the basis of the most plausible argument considered here. And it is the nonvegetarian who must do all this while being fully cognizant that he cannot defend his way of life merely by summing up the intrinsic goods—the delicious taste of meat, for example—that come into being as a result of the slaughter of animals.

This is not to say that practices that involve taking the lives of animals cannot possibly be justified. . . . For example, perhaps they are satisfied in the case of the Eskimo's killing of animals and in the case of having a restricted hunting season for such animals as deer. But to say that this is (or may be) true of *some* cases is not to say that it is true of all, and it will remain the task of the nonvegetarian to show that what is true in these cases, assuming that it is true, is also true of any practice that involves killing animals which, by his actions, he supports. . . .

Even if it should turn out that there are no natural rights, that would not put an end to many of the problems discussed here. For even if we do not possess natural rights, we would still object to practices that caused nontrivial, undeserved pain for some human beings if their "justification" was that they brought about this or that amount of pleasure or other forms of intrinsic good for this or that number of people; . . . and we would still object to any practice that involved the killing of human beings, even if killed painlessly, if the practice was supposed to be justified in the same way. But this being so, what clearly would be needed, if we cease to invoke the idea of rights, is some explanation of why practices that are not right, when they involve the treatment of people, can be right (or at least permissible) when they involve the treatment of animals. What clearly would be needed, in short, is what we have found to be needed and wanting all along—namely, the specification of some morally relevant feature of being human which is possessed by *all* human beings and *only* by those beings who are human. Unless or until some such feature can be pointed out, I do not see how the differential treatment of humans and animals can be rationally defended, natural rights or no.

Discussion Questions

1. Do you have a moral obligation to be a vegetarian? Support your argument.
2. Some "vegetarians" eat free-range animals, including fish, especially on holidays such as Thanksgiving, Easter, and Passover. Does eating only free-range animals overcome Regan's objection to meat-eating? Support your answer.
3. Discuss how Regan would stand on the morality of keeping animals in zoos. Do their educational value and protection of endangered species justify the existence of zoos? Support your answer.
4. Regan is opposed to animal experimentation no matter how much it benefits humans. Do you agree with Regan's position? Discuss how Aquinas and Kant might respond to Regan's abolitionist position.
5. Would Regan approve or disapprove of the human practice of keeping pets and, if so, under what conditions? Support your answer. Discuss how Regan might stand on the euthanasia of sick and elderly animal companions.
6. In his 1982 essay, "The Nature and Possibility of an Environmental Ethics,"[31] Regan explores the possibility that there is an "inherent goodness" in natural objects that we should respect. This respect should lead us to adopt a "preservation principle" of "nondestruction and noninterference." Do you agree with Regan? Analyze Regan's premises and conclusion.

JAN NARVESON

Animal Rights Revisited

Jan Narveson is a philosophy professor at the University of Waterloo. Narveson argues that it is not clear that utilitarianism requires us to adopt a vegetarian lifestyle. Furthermore, he argues, under social contract theory, animals, being nonrational and lacking language, are not capable of entering into a contractual agreement. Therefore under the social contract, they have no rights that we are morally bound to respect. Although it may be unfortunate for animals that we make meals out of them, we are morally justified in doing so.

Critical Reading Questions

1. What are the three possible options listed by Narveson regarding our moral obligations to nonhuman animals?
2. What assumptions does Narveson make regarding the utility of nonhuman animals?

"Animal Rights Revisited," in eds. Harlan B. Miller and William H. Williams, *Ethics and Animals* (Clifton, N.J.: Humana Press, 1993), 45–59.

3. Why, according to Narveson, do nonhuman animals have less utility than humans?
4. On what grounds does Narveson argue that raising nonhuman animals for food might actually increase the total utility for that species?
5. According to Narveson's interpretation of contractarian theory, what characteristics must a being have to be included in a social contract?
6. Why, according to Narveson, can't nonhuman animals be included in a social contract?
7. What is the connection between being included in a social contract and having moral rights?
8. According to Narveson, what abilities are required to be eligible for moral consideration?
9. On what grounds does Narveson claim that our dealings with other animals need only be based on our own self-interest?
10. How does Narveson respond to the "marginal cases" objection?

What do we owe to the animals? What, that is to say, do we owe them *qua* animal, rather than in their various possible roles as pets, watchdogs, potential sources of protein, or potential sources of knowledge on various matters of medical interest? Our usual repertoire of moral ideas does not give us a very clear answer to this question, for those ideas have been framed for dealing with our fellow humans, by and large. When we address ourselves to this nonstandard case, then, we must scrutinize those ideas rather closely. . . .

It may be well to begin by trying to assemble the options, though even to do this is assuredly to begin to do moral theory. Here, then, are the main ones as I see it:

(1) The moral status of animals is simply that of things, potentially useful or dangerous in various ways; the proper way to deal with them is simply whatever way is dictated by our interests in such things.

(2) Animals are in the same moral boat as we are: to wit, they have the capacity to suffer or prosper, to be better or worse off, and we ought to attach the same weight to a given degree of well- or ill-being on their part as we do to our own, endeavoring to do the best we can for all concerned.

(3) Animals are in the same moral boat as we are, but it is a different boat: to wit, they have the right to lead their lives as they choose, without interference from us—but also, without *help* from us, if we do not wish to give it.

This list of options is not exhaustive of the logical possibilities, obviously. I have come to suspect, however, that it exhausts all the *interesting* possibilities. And curiously enough, those are the same possibilities that we obtain with respect to our moral dealings with our fellow humans. . . .

What assumptions is it reasonable to make about the utility of animals? It seems very reasonable indeed to suppose that animals can feel pain and pleasure. It seems reasonable to attribute to them some degree of intelligence (but unclear just what we are attributing to them in doing so, nor whether it is a capacity of the same sort we attribute to humans). Does that matter? Mill thought it did. It is tempting to say that he thought that the utility of intelligent beings counts more than the utility of less intelligent ones, but that surely will not do. What we must say instead, and what Mill really does say (I think), is that intelligent beings have a greater capability of utility than less intelligent ones: the satisfaction of a satisfied Socrates (if that is possible) involves a great deal more utility than the satisfaction of a satisfied pig. For that matter, even the satisfactions of a dissatisfied Socrates outweigh those of the pig. One question to worry about is: Is Mill right, or even believable, about that? Another is: What follows if he is? . . .

We do, certainly, make judgments of the form "people would in general be happier if . . . " Although there is a good deal of disagreement about such judgments, it may also be admitted that we are not entirely out in left field in making them. The problem is to make judgments of the form, "people *and animals* would be happier if . . . ," and that is trickier. It is acutely trickier in just the cases we have to worry about in the present paper—all the cases wherein there is a genuine conflict between the interests of us and the animals: namely, if our main interest in animals is realized, then their interest in *whatever* they may be interested in is thwarted, because they end up on our dinner plates. And that is a loss of utility that, in the case of humans, would certainly not be thought to be outweighed by the gourmet's interest in them, however powerful that interest might be. So we would surely be headed for vegetarianism if there were no reason for downrating the animals' utility quite substantially.

Actually, there are two sorts of "downrating." One way is to claim that the utility of animals, although admittedly quite comparable to ours, simply does not count, or that it counts very little: as if, for instance, we were allowed to multiply the animal's utility score by 0.01. The other way is to claim that animals have very little utility, really, at least by comparison with our own. As we have noted, utilitarianism must surely take the latter tack. It is axiomatic, after all, that everyone counts for one and none for more (or less).

What might reasonably (as opposed to just self-interestedly) persuade us that animals *do* have a lesser capacity for utility than we? Many would point to their supposedly lesser intelligence as a justification for treating them as we do. But they may or may not have in mind intelligence as a factor influencing utility. They may instead be thinking of it as an intrinsic good. Can we find a reason for supposing that intellect affects capacity for utility, then?

One thing that has long intrigued me in this connection is the involvement of intelligent beings with their own, or indeed, any futures. We are acutely aware of the future stretching out before us, and of the past in the other direction. We are, indeed, often so involved with time that we might be accused of neglecting our present. And we can at least conjecture that with animals things are different. Perhaps it is still excessively anthropomorphic to think so, but we do seem to think that animal awareness of their own future, indeed of their own identity in general, is rather dim; this despite homing pigeons and whatnot, who certainly seem to have a clear idea where to go next. But we do suppose that they are, as the saying goes, guided by instinct rather than reason. . . .

Still, *why* might this matter? I have suggested that animals might "experience only more or less isolated sensations and uninterpreted feelings. If such beings are killed, all that happens is that a certain series of such feelings which would otherwise have occurred, do not occur . . . When beings having a future are killed, they lose that future; when beings lacking it are killed, they do not. So no interest in continued life is lost in their case."[1] Well, setting aside the critical question of whether some such thing is true of animals, there remains the question just why it might make the kind of difference I supposed it did *on utilitarian grounds*. If two beings, one of whom has and one of whom lacks a future, each had a nonutilitarian-type right to its future, then we could agree that if we painlessly killed each of them, we would have violated one creature's rights, but not the other's. Unfortunately, utilitarians are not entitled to nonutilitarian rights. So if this difference is to make a difference, it must be because beings with futures experience more utility than beings without. . . .

What we need to think, therefore, if we are to remain utilitarians *and* we think that normal humans are much greater in their capacity for utility than animals, is that at each typical moment in the sentient life of a human, he or she is chalking up a much higher utility score than a beast at any typical moment for it. And what the basis of this judgment would be is, again, unclear. There is certainly the danger of anthropocentric bias here . . .

Perhaps this affords some hold on the matter in the following way. If utility is based on preference, then perhaps we could say that if being X is able to have in mind more possible states of affairs over which to exercise preference than Y then X has a greater capacity for utility. As stated, this raises some rather kinky problems about individuating states of affairs so that we can get a fair count; and there is a lingering suspicion that the whole idea is wrong anyway, and utility should not really be thought of as preference at all. But it might offer some explanation of how we manage to account for so great a proportion of the universe's known supply of utility, or at least why we think we do.

If that amount of elitism is accepted, what about vegetarianism? It is axiomatic that some beings may, in principle, be sacrificed for others, on the utilitarian view. But may animals be sacrificed merely in order to enable humans to have a wider variety of gustatory pleasures? In order for it to be so, the marginal increment of such pleasure for humans has to exceed the marginal cost to the animals. Consider, then, the case of Kentucky Fried Chicken. Suppose that one chicken feeds three people for one meal. We might suppose that the cost of this is all the utility that the chicken might have experienced had it been allowed to live to a ripe old age. But wrongly. For that is only the cost to *that* chicken. But it is also reasonable to believe that, under the carnivorous regime we are investigating, this chicken will be replaced by another one which would not have existed at all if its predecessor were not eaten. In fact, the plot is thicker than that, for . . . its predecessor would most likely not have existed either, were it not for the prospect of *its* being eaten. Given that we in fact raise animals to be eaten, it is not unreasonable to believe that the total utility of the animal population is enormously higher than it would be if we did not eat them, because so comparatively few would exist at all otherwise. And if we count that way, then the marginal cost to any given animal is the wrong thing to weigh against the marginal benefit to us of eating it. Viewed globally, those costs are very handily outweighed by the total utility increase in question.

That, of course, is to assume that we can apply "total" rather than average or some other sort of utilitarianism here. If we do not, and insist that it is the average utility of animals that should be our sole concern, the prospects for animal rights are much better, perhaps. Or are they? For now we also must reckon the cost of upkeep and care for the animals, which is born by people. Their cost would certainly not be born, in fact, if the animals were not beneficial to people in this way. Chickens would be raised only to lay eggs, cows for milk; but most would have little if any use. It might be argued that the loss in utility to people from having to care for useless beasts would exceed the loss to the beasts if they were (painlessly) killed. So even on average principles, it is far from clear that maximization would preclude the eating of animals.

Of course, if we do use total utilitarianism, then we have another small matter to contend with. Animals are, in fact, quite an inefficient source of food. If humans ate only vegetarian diets, it would be possible for there to be a great many more of *them*. And if, as has been imagined above, each human is so much larger a source of utility than any animal, it might seem that the tables are turned again, since the large animal population is keeping the human population smaller, and yet the human population is so much more efficient a source of utility than the animal one. But that, in turn, is to assume that the marginal utility change associated with the addition of each further human is in fact positive, and it can be argued that *that* is not so. Perhaps a world with two billion humans would have more total utility than one with ten billions. If so, we would have a global justification of carnivorousness from the above arguments.

I am sure that no one will think me excessively conservative if I conclude with the observation that the situation regarding the ethics of our treatment of animals is not entirely clear if we opt for utilitarianism. This is not exactly a surprise, but it is of some importance that it should be so. The vegetarians do not have things all their way on that theory; and it is, I think, the theory that offers the best prospects for animal rights among those I am considering. . . .

On the contract view of morality, morality is a sort of agreement among rational, independent, self-interested persons, persons who have something to gain from entering into such an agreement. It is of the very essence, on such a theory, that the parties to the agreement know who they are and what they want—what they in particular want, and not just what a certain general class of beings of which they are members generally tend to want. Now, Rawls' theory has his parties constrained by agreements that they would have made if they *did not* know who they were. But if we can have that constraint, why should we not go just a little further and specify that one is not only not to know *which* person he or she is, but also whether he or she will be a person *at all:* reason on the assumption that you might turn out to be an owl, say, or a vermin, or a cow. We may imagine that *that* possibility would make quite a difference . . . (Some proponents of vegetarianism, I believe, are tempted by it, and do extend the veil of ignorance that far.)

The "agreement" of which morality consists is a voluntary undertaking to limit one's behavior in various respects. In a sense, it consists in a renunciation of action on unconstrained self-interest. It is, however, self-interested overall. The idea is to come out ahead in the long run, by refraining, contingently on others' likewise refraining, from certain actions, the general indulgence in which would be worse for all and therefore for oneself. There are well-known problems generated by this characterization, and I do not claim to have solutions for them. I only claim that this is an important and plausible conception of morality, worth investigating in the present context.

A major feature of this view of morality is that it explains why we have it and who is a party to it. We have it for reasons of long-run self-interest, and parties to it include all and only those who have *both* of the following characteristics: (1) they stand to gain by subscribing to it, at least in the long run, compared with not doing so, and (2) they are *capable* of entering into (and keeping) an agreement. Those not capable of it obviously cannot be parties to it, and among those capable of it, there is no reason for them to enter into it if there is nothing to gain for them from it, no matter how much the others might benefit.

Given these requirements, it will be clear why animals do not have rights. For there are evident shortcomings on both scores. On the one hand, humans have nothing generally to gain by voluntarily refraining from (for instance) killing animals or "treating them as mere means." And on the other, animals cannot generally make agreements with us anyway, even if we wanted to have them do so. Both points are worth expanding on briefly.

(1) In saying that humans have "nothing generally to gain" from adopting principled restraints against behavior harmful to animals, I am in one respect certainly overstating the case, for it is possible that animal food, for instance, is bad for us, or that something else about animals, which requires such restraint from us, would be for our long-term benefit. Those are issues I mostly leave on one side here . . .

(2) What about the capability of entering into and keeping such agreements? . . .

There remains a genuine question about the eligibility of animals for morality on the score of their abilities. A very few individuals among some animal species have been enabled, after years of highly specialized work, to communicate in fairly simple ways with people. That does not augur well for animals' entering quite generally into something as apparently sophisticated as an agreement. But of course agreements can be tacit and unwritten, even unspoken. Should we postulate, at some such inexplicit level, an "agreement" among humans, it is largely tacit there. People do not enter into agreements to refrain from killing each other, except in fairly specialized cases; the rule against killing that we (virtually) all acknowledge is one we adopt out of common sense and antecedent inculcation by our mentors. Still, it is reasonable to say that when one person does kill another one, he or she is (among other things) taking *unfair advantage* of the restraint that one's fellows have exercised with regard toward one over many years. But can any such thing be reasonably said of animals? I would think not.

On the whole, therefore, it seems clear that contractarianism leaves animals out of it, so far as rights are concerned. They are, by and large, to be dealt with in terms of our self-interest, unconstrained by the terms of hypothetical agreements with them. Just exactly what our interest in them is may, of course, be matter for debate; but that those are the terms on which we may deal with them is, on this view of morality, overwhelmingly indicated.

There is an evident problem about the treatment of what I have called "marginal cases" on this view, of course: infants, the feeble-minded, and the incapacitated are in varying degrees in the position of the animals in relation to us, are they not? True: but the situation is very different in several ways. For one thing, we generally have very little to gain from treating such people badly, and we often have much to gain from treating them well. For another, marginal humans are invariably members of families, or members of other groupings, which makes them the object of love and interest on the part of other members of those groups. Even if there were an interest in treating a particular marginal person badly, there would be others who have an interest in their being treated well and who are themselves clearly members of the moral community on contractarian premises. Finally, it does have to be pointed out that there is genuine question about the morality of, for instance, euthanasia, and that infanticide has been approved of in various human communities at various times. On the whole, it seems to me not an insurmountable objection to the contractarian account that we grant marginal humans fairly strong rights.

It remains that we may think that suffering is a bad thing, no matter whose. But although we think so, we do not think it is so bad as to require us to become vegetarians. Here by 'we,' of course, I mean most of us. And what most of us think is that, although suffering is too bad and it is unfortunate for animals that they are turned into hamburgers at a tender age, we nevertheless are justified on the whole in eating them. If contractarianism is correct, then these attitudes are not inconsistent. And perhaps it is.

NOTES

1. Jan Narveson, "Animal Rights," *Canadian Journal of Philosophy,* vol. 7 (1977), 161–178.

Discussion Questions

1. Narveson argues that by breeding animals destined for our plates we are increasing their overall utility, as they would not have had any existence otherwise. How might Jeremy Bentham respond to this argument? Could this argument also be used to justify the breeding or cloning of humans for slavery or organ transplants?
2. Narveson admits that the criteria we use for eliminating nonhuman animals from moral consideration also eliminates some humans. How does he overcome this criticism? Are you satisfied with his response? Support your answers.
3. Narveson bases much of his argument against vegetarianism on John Rawls's social contract theory. Rawls said, however, that his was "not a complete contract theory . . . since it would seem to include only our relationship with other persons and to leave out of account how we are to conduct ourselves toward animals and the rest of nature." Because of this, "it does not follow [from social contract theory] that there are no requirements at all in regard to [animals], nor in our relations with the natural order."[32] Has Narveson engaged in fallacious logic in concluding that animals lack rights because they cannot be included in a social contract? Discuss how Rawls might respond to Narveson's argument.
4. Discuss how Regan and an ecocentric environmental ethicist would respond to Narveson's defense of meat-eating. Whose position do you find more convincing from a moral point of view?

PETER SINGER

Animal Liberation

Australian philosopher Peter Singer is Ira W. DeCamp Professor of Bioethics at the University Center for Human Values, Princeton University. He is also actively involved in the animal-liberation movement. Singer argues that utilitarian theory requires that the interests of all sentient beings be given equal weight. The pain humans feel and the pain other animals feel should be given equal moral consideration. To not take the pain and interests of other animals seriously is to engage in what Singer calls "speciesism." Singer compares speciesism to racism and sexism.

Critical Reading Questions

1. What is the principle of equality?
2. What is "speciesism"? Why is speciesism wrong, according to Singer?
3. What criteria does Singer suggest we use to avoid speciesism?
4. According to Singer, what kind of lives have greater moral value than others?
5. Why does Singer claim that most humans are speciesists? What does he mean when he says that speciesism is analogous to racism and sexism?
6. What is the moral significance of sentience, or the ability to feel pain? In what ways do humans inflict suffering on other animals?
7. According to Singer, what is the moral significance of a being's level of cognitive ability? Does his argument make it morally permissible to experiment on humans with low-level cognitive functioning?
8. What do we need to do, according to Singer, to avoid speciesism? Does a rejection of speciesism imply that all lives are of equal worth?
9. Why, according to Singer, has opposition to experimentation on animals made such little headway?
10. Why do psychological experiments that use animals pose a dilemma for researchers who claim that other animals are not like us cognitively?
11. In what ways does a pattern of animal experimentation become self-reinforcing?
12. According to Singer, when, if ever, is animal experimentation morally justified?
13. What question does Singer think experimenters must be able to answer in the affirmative to justify the use of animals?
14. Why does Singer claim that the controversy over the benefits derived from animal experimentation is essentially irrelevant?

Jeremy Bentham, the founder of the reforming utilitarian school of moral philosophy, incorporated the essential basis of moral equality into his system of ethics by means of the formula: "Each to count for one and none for more than one." In other words, the interests of every being affected by an action are to be taken into account and given the same weight as the like interests of any other being. . . .

Animal Liberation (New York: Random House, 1990), 5–94. Notes have been omitted.

It is an implication of this principle of equality that our concern for others and our readiness to consider their interests ought not to depend on what they are like or on what abilities they may possess. Precisely what our concern or consideration requires us to do may vary according to the characteristics of those affected by what we do: concern for the well-being of children growing up in America would require that we teach them to read; concern for the well-being of pigs may require no more than that we leave them with other pigs in a place where there is adequate food and room to run freely. But the basic element—the taking into account of the interests of the being, whatever those interests may be—must, according to the principle of equality, be extended to all beings, black or white, masculine or feminine, human or nonhuman. . . .

It is on this basis that the case against racism and the case against sexism must both ultimately rest; and it is in accordance with this principle that the attitude that we may call "speciesism," by analogy with racism, must also be condemned. Speciesism—the word is not an attractive one, but I can think of no better term—is a prejudice or attitude of bias in favor of the interests of members of one's own species and against those of members of other species. It should be obvious that the fundamental objections to racism and sexism made by Thomas Jefferson and Sojourner Truth apply equally to speciesism. If possessing a higher degree of intelligence does not entitle one human to use another for his or her own ends, how can it entitle humans to exploit nonhumans for the same purpose?

Many philosophers and other writers have proposed the principle of equal consideration of interests, in some form or other, as a basic moral principle; but not many of them have recognized that this principle applies to members of other species as well as to our own. Jeremy Bentham was one of the few who did realize this. In a forward-looking passage written at the time when black slaves had been freed by the French but in the British dominions were still being treated in the way we now treat animals, Bentham wrote:

> The day *may* come when the rest of the animal creation may acquire those rights which never could have been withholden from them but by the hand of tyranny. The French have already discovered that the blackness of the skin is no reason why a human being should be abandoned without redress to the caprice of a tormentor. It may one day come to be recognized that the number of the legs, the villosity of the skin, or the termination of the *os sacrum* are reasons equally insufficient for abandoning a sensitive being to the same fate. What else is it that should trace the insuperable line? Is it the faculty of reason, or perhaps the faculty of discourse? But a full-grown horse or dog is beyond comparison a more rational, as well as a more conversable animal, than an infant of a day or a week or even a month, old. But suppose they were otherwise, what would it avail? The question is not, Can they *reason?* nor Can they *talk?* but, Can they *suffer?*

In this passage Bentham points to the capacity for suffering as the vital characteristic that gives a being the right to equal consideration. The capacity for suffering—or more strictly, for suffering and/or enjoyment or happiness—is not just another characteristic like the capacity for language or higher mathematics. Bentham is not saying that those who try to mark "the insuperable line" that determines whether the interests of a being should be considered happen to have chosen the wrong characteristic. By saying that we must consider the interests of all beings with the capacity for suffering or enjoyment Bentham does not arbitrarily exclude from consideration any interests at all—as those who draw the line with reference to the possession of reason or language do. The capacity for suffering and enjoyment is *a prerequisite for having interests at all,* a condition that must be satisfied before we can speak of interests in a meaningful way. It would be nonsense to say that it was not in the interests of a stone to be kicked along the road by a schoolboy. A stone does not have interests because it cannot suffer. Nothing that we can do to it could possibly make any difference to its welfare. The capacity for suffering and enjoyment is, however, not only necessary, but also sufficient for us to say that a being has interests—at an absolute minimum, an interest in not suffering. A mouse, for example, does have an interest in not being kicked along the road, because it will suffer if it is. . . .

Racists violate the principle of equality by giving greater weight to the interests of members of their own race when there is a clash between their interests and the interests of those of another race. Sexists violate the principle of equality by favoring the interests of their own sex. Similarly, speciesists allow the interests of their own species to override the greater interests of members of other species. The pattern is identical in each case.

Most human beings are speciesists. . . . Ordinary human beings—not a few exceptionally cruel or heartless humans, but the overwhelming majority of humans—take an active part in, acquiesce in, and allow their taxes to pay for practices that require the sacrifice of the most important interests of members of other species in order to promote the most trivial interests of our own species. . . .

Do animals other than humans feel pain? How do we know? Well, how do we know if anyone, human or nonhuman, feels pain? We know that we ourselves can feel pain. We know this from the direct experience of pain that we have when, for instance, somebody presses a lighted cigarette against the back of our hand. But how do we know that anyone else feels pain? We cannot directly experience anyone else's pain, whether that "anyone" is our best friend or a stray dog. Pain is a state of consciousness, a "mental event," and as such it can never be observed. Behavior like writhing, screaming, or drawing one's hand away from the lighted cigarette is not pain itself; nor are the recordings a neurologist might make of activity within the brain observations of pain itself. Pain is something that we feel, and we can only infer that others are feeling it from various external indications.

In theory, we *could* always be mistaken when we assume that other human beings feel pain. It is conceivable that one of our close friends is really a cleverly constructed robot, controlled by a brilliant scientist so as to give all the signs of feeling pain, but really no more sensitive than any other machine. We can never know, with absolute certainty, that this is not the case. But while this might present a puzzle for philosophers, none of us has the slightest real doubt that our close friends feel pain just as we do. This is an inference, but a perfectly reasonable one, based on observations of their behavior in situations in which we would feel pain, and on the fact that we have every reason to assume that our friends are beings like us, with nervous systems like ours that can be assumed to function as ours do and to produce similar feelings in similar circumstances.

If it is justifiable to assume that other human beings feel pain as we do, is there any reason why a similar inference should be unjustifiable in the case of other animals?

Nearly all the external signs that lead us to infer pain in other humans can be seen in other species, especially the species most closely related to us—the species of mammals and birds. The behavioral signs include writhing, facial contortions, moaning, yelping or other forms of calling, attempts to avoid the source of pain, appearance of fear at the prospect of its repetition, and so on. In addition, we know that these animals have nervous systems very like ours, which respond physiologically as ours do when the animal is in circumstances in which we would feel pain: an initial rise of blood pressure, dilated pupils, perspiration, an increased pulse rate, and, if the stimulus continues, a fall in blood pressure. Although human beings have a more developed cerebral cortex than other animals, this part of the brain is concerned with thinking functions rather than with basic impulses, emotions, and feelings. These impulses, emotions, and feelings are located in the diencephalon, which is well developed in many other species of animals, especially mammals and birds.

We also know that the nervous systems of other animals were not artificially constructed—as a robot might be artificially constructed—to mimic the pain behavior of humans. The nervous systems of animals evolved as our own did, and in fact the evolutionary history of human beings and other animals, especially mammals, did not diverge until the central features of our nervous systems were already in existence. A capacity to feel pain obviously enhances a species' prospects of survival, since it causes members of the species to avoid sources of injury. It is surely unreasonable to suppose that nervous systems that are virtually identical physiologically, have a common origin and a common evolutionary function, and result in similar forms of behavior in similar circumstances should actually operate in an entirely different manner on the level of subjective feelings. . . .

Other differences between humans and animals cause other complications. Normal adult human beings have mental capacities that will, in certain circumstances, lead them to suffer more than animals would in the same circumstances. If, for instance, we decided to perform extremely painful or lethal scientific experiments on normal adult humans, kidnapped at random from public parks for this purpose, adults who enjoy strolling in parks would become fearful that they would be kidnapped. The resultant terror would be a form of suffering additional to the pain of the experiment. The same experiments performed on nonhuman animals would cause less suffering since the animals would not have the anticipatory dread of being kidnapped and experimented upon. This does not mean, of course, that it would be *right* to perform the experiment on animals, but only that there is a reason, which is *not* speciesist, for preferring to use animals rather than normal adult human beings, if the experiment is to be done at all. It should be noted, however, that this same argument gives us a reason for preferring to use human infants—orphans perhaps—or severely retarded human beings for experiments, rather than adults, since infants and retarded humans would also have no idea of what was going to happen to them. So far as this argument is concerned nonhuman animals and infants and retarded humans are in the same category; and if we use this argument to justify experiments on nonhuman animals we have to ask ourselves whether we are also prepared to allow experiments on human infants and retarded adults; and if we make a distinction between animals and these humans, on what basis can we do it, other than a bare-faced—and morally indefensible—preference for members of our own species?

There are many matters in which the superior mental powers of normal adult humans make a difference: anticipation, more detailed memory, greater knowledge of what is happening, and so on. Yet these differences do not all point to greater suffering on the part of the normal human being. Sometimes animals may suffer more because of their more limited understanding. If, for instance, we are taking prisoners in wartime we can explain to them that although they must submit to capture, search, and confinement, they will not otherwise be harmed and will be set free at the conclusion of hostilities. If we capture wild animals, however, we cannot explain that we are not threatening their lives. A wild animal cannot distinguish an attempt to overpower and confine from an attempt to kill; the one causes as much terror as the other.

It may be objected that comparisons of the sufferings of different species are impossible to make and that for this reason when the interests of animals and humans clash the principle of equality gives no guidance. It is probably true that comparisons of suffering between members of different species cannot be made precisely, but precision is not essential. Even if we were to prevent the infliction of suffering on animals only when it is quite certain that the interests of humans will not be affected to anything like the extent that animals are affected, we would be forced to make radical changes in our treatment of animals that would involve our diet, the farming methods we use, experimental procedures in many fields of science, our approach to wildlife and to hunting, trapping and the wearing of furs, and areas of entertainment like circuses, rodeos, and zoos. As a result, a vast amount of suffering would be avoided. . . .

Just as most human beings are speciesists in their readiness to cause pain to animals when they would not cause a similar pain to humans for the same reason, so most human beings are speciesists in their readiness to kill other animals when they would not kill human beings. . . .

This does not mean that to avoid speciesism we must hold that it is as wrong to kill a dog as it is to kill a human being in full possession of his or her faculties. The only position that is irredeemably speciesist is the one that tries to make the boundary of the right to life run exactly parallel to the boundary of our own species. Those who hold the sanctity of life view do this, because while distinguishing sharply between human beings and other animals they allow no distinctions to be made within our own species, objecting to the killing of the severely retarded and the hopelessly senile as strongly as they object to the killing of normal adults.

To avoid speciesism we must allow that beings who are similar in all relevant respects have a similar right to life—and mere membership in our own biological species cannot be a morally relevant criterion for this right. Within these limits we could still hold, for instance, that it is worse to kill a normal adult human, with a capacity for self-awareness and the ability to plan for the future and have meaningful relations with others, than it is to kill a mouse, which presumably does not share all of these characteristics; or we might appeal to the close family and other personal ties that humans have but mice do not have to the same degree; or we might think that it is the consequences for other humans, who will be put in fear for their own lives, that makes the crucial difference; or we might think it is some combination of these factors, or other factors altogether.

Whatever criteria we choose, however, we will have to admit that they do not follow precisely the boundary of our own species. We may legitimately hold that there are some features of certain beings that make their lives more valuable than those of other beings; but there will surely be some nonhuman animals whose lives, by any standards, are more valuable than the lives of some humans. A chimpanzee, dog, or pig, for instance, will have a higher degree of self-awareness and a greater capacity for meaningful relations with others than a severely retarded infant or someone in a state of advanced senility. So if we base the right to life on these characteristics we must grant these animals a right to life as good as, or better than, such retarded or senile humans.

This argument cuts both ways. It could be taken as showing that chimpanzees, dogs, and pigs, along with some other species, have a right to life and we commit a grave moral offense whenever we kill them, even when they are old and suffering and our intention is to put them out of their misery. Alternatively one could take the argument as showing that the severely retarded and hopelessly senile have no right to life and may be killed for quite trivial reasons, as we now kill animals. . . .

What we need is some middle position that would avoid speciesim but would not make the lives of the retarded and senile as cheap as the lives of pigs and dogs now are, or make the lives of pigs and dogs so sacrosanct that we think it wrong to put them out of hopeless misery. What we must do is bring nonhuman animals within our sphere of moral concern and cease to treat their lives as expendable for whatever trivial purposes we may have. At the same time, once we realize that the fact that a being is a member of our own species is not in itself enough to make it always wrong to kill that being, we may come to reconsider our policy of preserving human lives at all costs, even when there is no prospect of a meaningful life or of existence without terrible pain.

I conclude, then, that rejection of speciesism does not imply that all lives are of equal worth. While self-awareness, the capacity to think ahead and have hopes and aspirations for the future, the capacity for meaningful relations with others and so on are not relevant to the question of inflicting pain—since pain is pain, whatever other capacities, beyond the capacity to feel pain, the being may have—these capacities are relevant to the question of taking life. It is not arbitrary to hold that the life of a self-aware being, capable of abstract thought, of planning for the future, of complex acts of communication, and so on, is more valuable than the life of a being without these capacities. . . .

The practice of experimenting on nonhuman animals as it exists today throughout the world reveals the consequences of speciesism. Many experiments inflict severe pain without the remotest prospect of significant benefits for human beings or any other animals. Such experiments are not isolated instances, but part of a major industry. In Britain, where experimenters are required to report the number of "scientific procedures" performed on animals, official government figures show that 3.5 million scientific procedures were performed on animals in 1988. In the United States there are no figures of comparable accuracy. . . .

Among the tens of millions of experiments performed, only a few can possibly be regarded as contributing to important medical research. Huge numbers of animals are used in university departments such as forestry and psychology; many more are used for commercial purposes, to test new cosmetics, shampoos, food coloring agents, and other inessential items. All this can happen only because of our prejudice against taking seriously the suffering of a being who is not a member of our own species. Typically, defenders of experiments on animals do not deny that animals suffer. They cannot deny the animals' suffering, because they need to stress the similarities between humans and other animals in order to claim that their experiments may have some relevance for human purposes. The experimenter who forces rats to choose between starvation and electric shock to see if they develop ulcers (which they do) does so because the rat has a nervous system very similar to a human being's, and presumably feels an electric shock in a similar way.

There has been opposition to experimenting on animals for a long time. This opposition has made little headway because experimenters, backed by commercial firms that profit by supplying laboratory animals and equipment, have been able to convince legislators and the public that opposition comes from uninformed fanatics who consider the interests of animals more important than the interests of human beings. But to be opposed to what is going on now it is not necessary to insist that all animal experiments stop immediately. All we need to say is that experiments serving no direct and urgent purpose should stop immediately, and in the remaining fields of research, we should, whenever possible, seek to replace experiments that involve animals with alternative methods that do not. . . .

This attitude is illustrated by the following autobiographical statement . . . [that] appeared in *New Scientist:*

> When fifteen years ago I applied to do a degree course in psychology, a steely-eyed interviewer, himself a psychologist, questioned me closely on my motives and asked me what I believed psychology to be and what was its principal subject matter? Poor naïve simpleton that I was, I replied that it was the study of the mind and that human beings were its raw material. With a glad cry at being able to deflate me so effectively, the interviewer declared that psychologists were not interested in the mind, that rats were the golden focus of study, not people, and then he advised me strongly to trot around to the philosophy department next door. . . .

Perhaps not many psychologists would now proudly state that their work has nothing to do with the human mind. Nevertheless many of the experiments that are performed on rats can only be explained by assuming that the experimenters really are interested in the behavior of the rat for its own sake, without any thought of learning anything about humans. In that case, though, what possible justification can there be for the infliction of so much suffering? It is certainly not for the benefit of the rat.

So the researcher's central dilemma exists in an especially acute form in psychology: either the animal is not like us, in which case there is no reason for performing the experiment; or else the animal is like us, in which case we ought not to perform on the animal an experiment that would be considered outrageous if performed on one of us. . . .

Once a pattern of animal experimentation becomes the accepted mode of research in a particular field, the process is self-reinforcing and difficult to break out of. Not only publications and promotions but also the awards and grants that finance research become geared to animal experiments. A proposal for a new experiment with animals is something that the administrators of research funds will be ready to support, if they have in the past supported other experiments on animals. New methods that do not make use of animals will seem less familiar and will be less likely to receive support.

All this helps to explain why it is not always easy for people outside the universities to understand the rationale for the research carried out under university auspices. Originally, perhaps, scholars and researchers just set out to solve the most important problems and did not allow themselves to be influenced by other considerations. No doubt some are still motivated by these concerns. Too often, though, academic research gets bogged down in petty and insignificant details because the big questions have been studied already and they have either been solved or proven too difficult. So the researchers turn away from the well-plowed fields in search of new territory where whatever they find will be new, although the connection with a major problem may be remote. It is not uncommon, as we have seen, for experimenters to admit that similar experiments have been done many times before, but without this or that minor variation; and the most common ending to a scientific publication is "further research is necessary." . . .

When are experiments on animals justifiable? Upon learning of the nature of many of the experiments carried out, some people react by saying that all experiments on animals should be prohibited immediately. But if we make our demands as absolute as this, the experimenters have a ready reply: Would we be prepared to let thousands of humans die if they could be saved by a single experiment on a single animal?

This question is, of course, purely hypothetical. There has never been and never could be a single experiment that saved thousands of lives. The way to reply to this hypothetical question is to pose another: Would the experimenters be prepared to carry out their experiment on a human orphan under six months old if that were the only way to save thousands of lives?

If the experimenters would not be prepared to use a human infant then their readiness to use nonhuman animals reveals an unjustifiable form of discrimination on the basis of species, since adult apes, monkeys, dogs, cats, rats, and other animals are more aware of what is happening to them, more self-directing, and, so far as we can tell, at least as sensitive to pain as a human infant. (I have specified that the human infant be an orphan, to avoid the complications of the feelings of parents. Specifying the case in this way is, if anything, overgenerous to those defending the use of nonhuman animals in experiments, since mammals intended for experimental use are usually separated from their mothers at an early age, when the separation causes distress for both mother and young.)

So far as we know, human infants possess no morally relevant characteristic to a higher degree than adult nonhuman animals, unless we are to count the infants' potential as a characteristic that makes it wrong to experiment on them. Whether this characteristic should count is controversial—if we count it, we shall have to condemn abortion along with experiments on infants, since the potential of the infant and the fetus is the same. To avoid the complexities of this issue, however, we can alter our original question a little and assume that the infant is one with irreversible brain damage so severe as to rule out any mental development beyond the level of a six-month-old infant. There are, unfortunately, many such human beings, locked away in special wards throughout the country, some of them long since abandoned by their parents and other relatives, and, sadly, sometimes unloved by anyone else. Despite their mental deficiencies, the anatomy and physiology of these infants are in nearly all respects identical with those of normal humans. If, therefore, we were to force-feed them with large quantities of floor polish or drip concentrated solutions of cosmetics into their eyes, we would have a much more reliable indication of the safety of these products for humans than we now get by attempting to extrapolate the results of tests on a variety of other species. The LD50 tests, the Draize eye tests, the radiation experiments, the heatstroke experiments, and many others could have told us more about human reactions to the experimental situation if they had been carried out on severely brain-damaged humans instead of dogs or rabbits.

So whenever experimenters claim that their experiments are important enough to justify the use of animals, we should ask them whether they would be prepared to use a brain-damaged human being at a similar mental level to the animals they are planning to use. I cannot imagine that anyone would seriously propose carrying out the experiments described in this chapter on brain-damaged human beings. Occasionally it has become known that medical experiments have been performed on human beings without their consent; one case did concern institutionalized intellectually disabled children, who were given hepatitis. When such harmful experiments on human beings become known, they usually lead to an outcry against the experimenters, and rightly so. They are, very often, a further example of the arrogance of the research worker who justifies everything on the grounds of increasing knowledge. But if the experimenter claims that the experiment is important enough to justify inflicting suffering on animals, why is it not important enough to justify inflicting suffering on humans at the same mental level? What difference is there between the two? Only that one is a member of our species and the other is not? But to appeal to that difference is to reveal a bias no more defensible than racism or any other form of arbitrary discrimination. . . .

No doubt there are some fields of scientific research that will be hampered by any genuine consideration of the interests of animals used in experimentation. No doubt there have been some advances in knowledge which would not have been attained as easily without using animals. Examples of important discoveries often mentioned by those defending animal experimentation go back as far as Harvey's work on the circulation of blood. They include Banting and Best's discovery of insulin and its role in diabetes; the recognition of poliomyelitis as a virus and the development of a vaccine for it; several discoveries that served to make open heart surgery and coronary artery bypass graft surgery possible; and the understanding of our immune system and ways to overcome rejection of transplanted organs. The claim that animal experimentation was essential in making these discoveries has been denied by some opponents of experimentation. I do not intend to go into the controversy here. We have just seen that any knowledge gained from animal experimentation has made at best a very small contribution to our increased lifespan; its contribution to improving the quality of life is more difficult to estimate. In a more fundamental sense, the controversy over the benefits derived from animal experimentation is essentially unresolvable, because even if valuable discoveries were made using animals, we cannot say how successful medical research would have been if it had been compelled, from the outset, to develop alternative methods of investigation. Some discoveries would probably have been delayed, or perhaps not made at all; but many false leads would also not have been pursued, and it is possible that medicine would have developed in a very different and more efficacious direction, emphasizing healthy living rather than cure.

In any case, the ethical question of the justifiability of animal experimentation cannot be settled by pointing to its benefits for us, no matter how persuasive the evidence in favor of such benefits may be. The ethical principle of equal consideration of interests will rule out some means of obtaining knowledge. There is nothing sacred about the right to pursue knowledge. We already accept many restrictions on scientific enterprise. We do not believe that scientists have a general right to perform painful or lethal experiments on human beings without their consent, although there are many cases in which such experiments would advance knowledge far more rapidly than any other method. Now we need to broaden the scope of this existing restriction on scientific research.

Finally, it is important to realize that the major health problems of the world largely continue to exist, not because we do not know how to prevent disease and keep people healthy, but because no one is putting enough effort and money into doing what we already know how to do. The diseases that ravage Asia, Africa, Latin America, and the pockets of poverty in the industrialized West are diseases that, by and large, we know how to cure. They have been eliminated in communities that have adequate nutrition, sanitation, and health care. . . .

It does not seem likely that any major Western democracy is going to abolish all animal experimentation at a stroke. Governments just do not work like that. Animal experimentation will only be ended when a series of piecemeal reforms have reduced its importance, led to its replacement in many fields, and largely changed the public attitude to animals. The immediate task, then, is to work for these partial goals, which can be seen as milestones on the long march to the elimination of all exploitation of sentient animals. All concerned to end animal suffering can try to make known what is happening at universities and commercial laboratories in their own communities. Consumers can refuse to purchase products that have been tested on animals—especially in cosmetics, alternatives are now available. Students should decline to carry out experiments they consider unethical. Anyone can study the academic journals to find out where painful experiments are being carried out, and then find some way of making the public aware of what is happening. . . .

The exploitation of laboratory animals is part of the larger problem of speciesism and it is unlikely to be eliminated altogether until speciesism itself is eliminated. Surely one day, though, our children's children, reading about what was done in laboratories in the twentieth century, will feel the same sense of horror and incredulity at what otherwise civilized people could do that we now feel when we read about the atrocities of the Roman gladiatorial arenas or the eighteenth-century slave trade.

Discussion Questions

1. Do you agree with Singer that most humans are speciesists? If you are a speciesist, on what grounds do you morally justify it? In what ways does your lifestyle contribute to the suffering of the members of other species?
2. Do you agree with Singer that speciesism is similar to sexism and racism? Support your answer. Discuss how both Adams and Narveson might respond to Singer's claim.
3. Singer wants to seek a "middle position that would avoid speciesism but would not make the lives of the retarded and senile as cheap as the lives of pigs and dogs now are, or make the lives of pigs and dogs so sacrosanct that we think it wrong to put them out of hopeless misery." Can he morally justify drawing the line at this point? Or is this middle point arbitrary? Support your answers.
4. Like Singer, R. G. Frey opposes species membership as the criterion of moral standing. Instead Frey uses the quality of life as the criterion of moral worth. He maintains that the lives of certain cognitively impaired humans are such that they may have a lower moral value than that of many nonhuman animals.[33] Whereas Singer concludes that the principle of equality should preclude experimentation on nonhuman animals whose cognitive capacity is equivalent to that of human infants or cognitively impaired humans, Frey draws the opposite conclusion. Humans with an impoverished cognitive life can be used in experiments in the same way we use animals. Discuss Frey's argument as well as how Singer might respond to him.
5. Is Singer, as a utilitarian, being inconsistent when he argues that the benefits derived from animal experimentation are morally irrelevant? Support your answer. Discuss how Jeremy Bentham or John Stuart Mill might respond to this question.
6. Do the benefits of experimentation ever justify the use of nonconsenting humans or nonhuman animals in experiments? Support your answer.

CARL COHEN

Do Animals Have Rights?

Carl Cohen is a philosophy professor at the University of Michigan. Cohen defends the traditional Kantian view of moral agency and rights. According to Cohen, rights are based on self-assertion rather than on interests. Because only moral agents can assert moral claims, only moral agents have rights. Therefore, we do not violate the rights of nonhuman animals by doing research on them. Cohen also argues that we have a moral obligation to increase the use of nonhuman animals in research because doing so benefits humans.

Critical Reading Questions

1. Why is the question of whether animals have rights of great importance?
2. How does Cohen define the term *right?*
3. What are some of the ways in which experimentation using nonhuman animals has benefited humans?
4. Why does Cohen reject Regan's argument that animals have rights?
5. According to Cohen, what is the relationship between rights and obligations?
6. Why can't nonhuman animals be the bearers of rights? How does Cohen use the example of the baby zebra and the lioness to illustrate his position?
7. How does Cohen interpret Regan's concept of nonhuman animals as being moral patients?
8. According to Cohen, where do human rights come from?
9. How does Cohen respond to the objection that, under his definition, human infants and other cognitively impaired humans don't have rights? How does he support his position that all and only humans have rights?
10. Why does Cohen claim that only humans can commit crimes? How does Cohen use Kant's philosophy to support his position?
11. What fallacy does Cohen accuse Regan of committing in his use of the term *inherent value?* According to Cohen, how does this fallacy invalidate Regan's conclusion that animals have rights?
12. What is Cohen's conclusion regarding the use of nonhuman animals in medical experiments?

Whether animals have rights is a question of great importance because if they do, those rights must be respected, even at the cost of great burdens for human beings. A right (unlike an interest) is a valid claim, or potential claim, made by a moral agent, under principles that govern both the claimant and the target of the claim. Rights are precious; they are dispositive; they count.

You have a right to the return of money you lent me; we both understand that. It may be very

"Do Animals Have Rights?" *Ethics and Behavior* 7, no. 2 (1997): 103–111.

convenient for me to keep the money, and you may have no need of it whatever; but my convenience and your needs are not to the point. You have a *right* to it, and we have courts of law partly to ensure that such rights will be respected.

If you make me a promise, I have a moral right to its fulfillment—even though there may be no law to enforce my right. It may be very much in your interest to break that promise, but your great interests and the silence of the law cut no mustard when your solemn promise—which we both well understood—had been given. Likewise, those holding power may have a great and benevolent interest in denying my rights to travel or to speak freely—but their interests are overridden by my rights.

A great deal was learned about hypothermia by some Nazi doctors who advanced their learning by soaking Jews in cold water and putting them in refrigerators to learn how hypothermia proceeds. We have no difficulty in seeing that they may not advance medicine in that way; the subjects of those atrocious experiments had rights that demanded respect. For those who ignored their rights we have nothing but moral loathing.

Some persons believe that animals have rights as surely as those Jews had rights, and they therefore look on the uses of animals in medical investigations just as we look at the Nazi use of the Jews, with moral loathing. They are consistent in doing so. If animals have rights they certainly have the right not to be killed, even to advance our important interests.

Some may say, "Well, they have rights, but we have rights too, and our rights override theirs." That may be true in some cases, but it will not solve the problem because, although we may have a weighty *interest* in learning, say, how to vaccinate against polio or other diseases, we do not have a *right* to learn such things. Nor could we honestly claim that we kill research animals in self-defense; they did not attack us. If animals have rights, they certainly have the right not to be killed to advance the interests of others, whatever rights those others may have.

In 1952 there were about 58,000 cases of polio reported in the United States, and 3,000 polio deaths; my parents, parents everywhere, trembled in fear for their children at camp or away from home. Polio vaccination became routine in 1955, and cases dropped to about a dozen a year; today polio has been eradicated completely from the Western Hemisphere. The vaccine that achieved this, partly developed and tested only blocks from where I live in Ann Arbor, could have been developed *only* with the substantial use of animals. Polio vaccines had been tried many times earlier, but from those earlier vaccines children had contracted the disease; investigators had become, understandably, exceedingly cautious.

The killer disease for which a vaccine now is needed most desperately is malaria, which kills about 2 million people each year, most of them children. Many vaccines have been tried—not on children, thank God—and have failed. But very recently, after decades of effort, we learned how to make a vaccine that does, with complete success, inoculate mice against malaria. A safe vaccine for humans we do not yet have—but soon we will have it, thanks to the use of those mice, many of whom will have died in the process. To test that vaccine first on children would be an outrage, as it would have been an outrage to do so with the Salk and Sabin polio vaccines years ago. We use mice or monkeys *because there is no other way*. And there never will be another way because untested vaccines are very dangerous; their first use on a living organism is inescapably experimental; there is and will be no way to determine the reliability and safety of new vaccines without repeated tests on live organisms. Therefore, because we certainly may not use human children to test them, we will use mice (or as we develop an AIDS vaccine, primates) *or we will never have such vaccines.*

But if those animals we use in such tests have rights as human children do, what we did and are doing to them is as profoundly wrong as what the Nazis did to those Jews not long ago. Defenders of animal rights need not hold that medical scientists are vicious; they simply believe that what medical investigators are doing with animals is morally wrong. Most biomedical investigations involving animal subjects use rodents: mice and rats. The rat is the animal appropriately considered (and used by the critic) as the exemplar whose moral stature is in dispute here. Tom Regan is a leading defender of the view that rats do have such rights, and may not be used in biomedical investigations. He is an honest man. He sees the consequences of his view and accepts them forthrightly. In *The Case for Animal Rights* (Regan, 1983) he wrote,

> The harms others might face as a result of the dissolution of [some] practice or institution is no defense of allowing it to continue. . . . No one has a right to be protected against being harmed if the protection in question involves violating the rights of others. . . . No one has a right to be protected by the continuation of an unjust practice, one that violates the rights of others. . . . Justice *must* be done, though the . . . heavens fall. (pp. 346–347)

That last line echoes Kant, who borrowed it from an older tradition. Believing that rats have rights as humans do, Regan (1983) was convinced that killing them in medical research was morally intolerable. He wrote,

> On the rights view, [he means, of course, the Regan rights view] we cannot justify harming a single rat *merely* by aggregating "the many human and humane benefits" that flow from doing it. . . . Not even a single rat is to be treated as if that animal's value were reducible to his *possible utility* relative to the interests of others. (p. 384)

If there are some things that we cannot learn because animals have rights, well, as Regan (1983) put it, so be it.

This is the conclusion to which one certainly is driven if one holds that animals have rights. If Regan is correct about the moral standing of rats, we humans can have no right, ever, to kill them—unless perchance a rat attacks a person or a human baby, as rats sometimes do; then our right of self-defense may enter, I suppose. But medical investigations cannot honestly be described as self-defense, and medical investigations commonly require that many mice and rats be killed. Therefore, all medical investigations relying on them, or any other animal subjects—which includes most studies and all the most important studies of certain kinds—will have to stop. Bear in mind that the replacement of animal subjects by computer simulations, or tissue samples, and so on, is in most research a phantasm, a fantasy. Biomedical investigations using animal subjects (and of course all uses of animals as food) will have to stop.

This extraordinary consequence has no argumentative force for Regan and his followers; they are not consequentialists. For Regan the *interests* of humans, their desire to be freed of disease or relieved of pain, simply cannot outweigh the *rights* of a single rat. For him the issue is one of justice, and the use of animals in medical experiments (he believes) is simply not just. But the consequences of his view will give most of us, I submit, good reason to weigh very carefully the arguments he offers to support such far-reaching claims. Do you believe that the work of Drs. Salk and Sabin was morally right? Would you support it now, or support work just like it saving tens of thousands of human children from diphtheria, hepatitis, measles, rabies, rubella, and tetanus (all of which relied essentially on animal subjects)—as well as, now, AIDS, Lyme disease, and malaria? I surely do. If you would join me in this support we must conclude that the defense of animal rights is a gigantic mistake. I next aim to explain why animals *cannot* possess rights.

WHY ANIMALS DO NOT HAVE RIGHTS

Many obligations are owed by humans to animals; few will deny that. But it certainly does not follow from this that animals have rights because it is certainly not true that every obligation of ours arises from the rights of another. Not at all. We need to be clear and careful here. Rights entail obligations. If you have a right to the return of the money I borrowed, I have an obligation to repay it. No issue. If we have the right to speak freely on public policy matters, the community has the obligation to respect our right to do so. But the proposition *all rights entail obligations* does not convert simply, as the logicians say. From the true proposition that all trees are plants, it does not follow that all plants are trees. Similarly, not all obligations are entailed by rights. Some obligations, like mine to repay the money I borrowed from you, do arise out of rights.

But many obligations are owed to persons or other beings who have no rights whatever in the matter.

Obligations may arise from commitments freely made: As a college professor I accept the obligation to comment at length on the papers my students submit, and I do so; but they have not the right to *demand* that I do so. Civil servants and elected officials surely ought to be courteous to members of the public, but that obligation certainly is not grounded in citizens' rights.

Special relations often give rise to obligations: Hosts have the obligation to be cordial to their guests, but the guest has not the right to demand cordiality. Shepherds have obligations to their dogs, and cowboys to their horses, which do not flow from the rights of those dogs or horses. My son, now 5, may someday wish to study veterinary medicine as my father did; I will then have the obligation to help him as I can, and with pride I shall—but he has not the authority to demand such help as a matter of right. My dog has no right to daily exercise and veterinary care, but I do have the obligation to provide those things for her.

One may be obliged to another for a special act of kindness done; one may be obliged to put an animal out of its misery in view of its condition—but neither the beneficiary of that kindness nor that dying animal may have had a claim of right.

Beauchamp and Childress (1994) addressed what they called the "correlativity of rights and obligations" and wrote that they would defend an "untidy" (pp. 73–75) variety of that principle. It would be very untidy indeed. Some of our most important obligations—to members of our family, to the needy, to neighbors, and to sentient creatures of every sort—have no foundation in rights at all. Correlativity appears critical from the perspective of one who holds a right; your right correlates with my obligation to respect it. But the claim that rights and obligations are *reciprocals,* that *every* obligation flows from another's right, is false, plainly inconsistent with our general understanding of the differences between what we think we *ought* to do, and what others can justly *demand* that we do.

I emphasize this because, although animals have no rights, it surely does not follow from this that one is free to treat them with callous disregard. Animals are not stones; they feel. A rat may suffer; surely we have the obligation not to torture it gratuitously, even though it be true that the concept of a right could not possibly apply to it. We humans are obliged to act humanely, that is, being aware of their sentience, to apply to animals the moral principles that govern us regarding the gratuitous imposition of pain and suffering; which is not, of course, to treat animals as the possessors of rights.

Animals cannot be the bearers of rights because the concept of rights is essentially *human;* it is rooted in, and has force within, a human moral world. Humans must deal with rats—all too frequently in some parts of the world—and must be moral in their dealing with them; but a rat can no more be said to have rights than a table can be said to have ambition. To say of a rat that it has rights is to confuse categories, to apply to its world a moral category that has content only in the human moral world.

Try this thought experiment. Imagine, on the Serengeti Plain in East Africa, a lioness hunting for her cubs. A baby zebra, momentarily left unattended by its mother, is the prey; the lioness snatches it, rips open its throat, tears out chunks of its flesh, and departs. The mother zebra is driven nearly out of her wits when she cannot locate her baby; finding its carcass she will not even leave the remains for days. The scene may be thought unpleasant, but it is entirely natural, of course, and extremely common. If the zebra has a right to live, if the prey is just but the predator unjust, we ought to intervene, if we can, on behalf of right. But we do not intervene, of course—as we surely would intervene if we saw the lioness about to attack an unprotected human baby or you. What accounts for the moral difference? We justify different responses to humans and to zebras on the ground (implicit or explicit) that their moral stature is very different. The human has a right not to be eaten alive; it is, after all, a human being. Do you believe the baby zebra has the *right* not to be slaughtered by that lioness? That the lioness has the *right* to kill that baby zebra for her cubs? If you are inclined to say, confronted by such natural rapacity—duplicated with untold variety millions of times each day on planet earth—that neither is right or wrong, that neither has a *right* against the other, I am on your side. Rights are of the highest moral consequence, yes; but zebras and lions and rats are totally amoral; there is no morality for them; they do no wrong, ever. In their world there are no rights.

A contemporary philosopher who has thought a good deal about animals, referring to them as "moral patients," put it this way:

> A moral patient lacks the ability to formulate, let alone bring to bear, moral principles in deliberating about which one among a number of possible acts it would be right or proper to perform. Moral patients, in a word, cannot do what is right, nor can they do what is wrong. . . . Even when a moral patient causes significant harm to another, the moral patient has not done what is wrong. Only moral agents can do what is wrong. (Regan, 1983, pp. 152–153)

Just so. The concepts of wrong and right are totally foreign to animals, not conceivably within their ken or applicable to them, as the author of that passage clearly understands.

When using animals in our research, therefore, we ought indeed be humane—but we can never violate the rights of those animals because, to be blunt, they have none. Rights do not *apply* to them.

But humans do have rights. Where do our rights come from? Why are we not crudely natural creatures like rats and zebras? This question philosophers have struggled to answer from earliest times. A definitive account of the human moral condition I cannot here present, of course. But reflect for a moment on the kinds of answers that have been widely given:

- Some think our moral understanding, with its attendant duties, to be a divine gift. So St. Thomas said: The moral law is binding, and humans have the power, given by God, to grasp its binding character, and must therefore respect the rights that other humans possess. God makes us (Saint Augustine said before him) in his own image, and therefore with a will that is free, and gives us the power to recognize that, and therefore, unlike other creatures, we must choose between good and evil, between right and wrong.
- Many philosophers, distrusting theological justifications of rights and duties, sought the ground of human morality in the membership, by all humans, in a moral community. The English idealist, Bradley, called it an organic moral community; the German idealist, Hegel, called it an objective ethical order. These and like accounts commonly center on human interrelations, on a moral *fabric* within which human agents always act, and within which animals never act and never can possibly act.
- The highly abstract reasoning from which such views emerge has dissatisfied many; you may find more nearly true the convictions of ethical intuitionists and realists who said, as H. A. Prichard, Sir David Ross, and my friend and teacher C. D. Broad, of happy memory, used to say, that there is a direct, underivative, intuitive cognition of rights as possessed by other humans, but not by animals.
- Or perhaps in the end we will return to Kant, and say with him that critical reason reveals at the core of human action a uniquely moral will, and the unique ability to grasp and to lay down moral laws for oneself and for others—an ability that is not conceivably within the capacity of any nonhuman animal whatever.

To be a moral agent (on this view) is to be able to grasp the generality of moral restrictions on our will. Humans understand that some things, which may be in our interest, *must not be willed;* we lay down moral laws for ourselves, and thus exhibit, as no other animal can exhibit, moral autonomy. My dog knows that there are certain things she must not do—but she knows this only as the outcome of her learning about her interests, the pains she may suffer if she does what had been taught forbidden. She does not know, cannot know (as Regan agrees) that any conduct is wrong. The proposition *It would be highly advantageous to act in such-and-such a way, but I may not because it would be wrong* is one that no dog or mouse or rabbit, however sweet and endearing, however loyal or attentive to its young, can ever entertain, or intend, or begin to grasp. Right is not in their world. But right and wrong are the very stuff of human moral life, the ever-present awareness of human beings who can do wrong, and who by seeking (often) to avoid wrong conduct prove themselves members of a moral community in which rights may be exercised and must be respected.

Some respond by saying, "This can't be correct, for human infants (and the comatose and senile, etc.) surely have rights, but they make no moral claims or judgments and can make none—and any view entailing that children can have no rights must be absurd." Objections of this kind miss the point badly. It is not individual persons who qualify (or are disqualified) for the possession of rights because of the presence or absence in them of some special capacity, thus resulting in the award of rights to some but not to others. Rights are universally human; they arise in a *human moral world,* in a moral *sphere.* In the human world moral judgments are pervasive; it is the fact that all humans including infants and the senile are members of that moral community—not the fact that as individuals they have or do not have certain special capacities, or merits—that makes humans bearers of rights. Therefore, it is beside the point to insist that animals have remarkable capacities, that they really have a consciousness of self, or of the future, or make plans, and so on. And the tired response that because infants plainly cannot make moral claims they must have no rights at all, or rats must have them too, we ought forever put aside. Responses like these arise out of a misconception of right itself. They mistakenly suppose that rights are tied to some identifiable individual abilities or sensibilities, and they fail to see that rights arise only in a community of moral beings, and that therefore there are spheres in which rights do apply and spheres in which they do not.

Rationality is not at issue; the capacity to communicate is not at issue. My dog can reason, if rather weakly, and she certainly can communicate. Cognitive criteria for the possession of rights, Beauchamp said, are morally perilous. Indeed they are. Nor is the capacity to suffer here at issue. And, if *autonomy* be understood only as the capacity to choose this course rather than that, autonomy is not to the point either. But *moral autonomy*—that is, *moral self-legislation*—is to the point, because moral autonomy is uniquely human and is for animals out of the question, as we have seen, and as Regan and I agree. In talking about autonomy, therefore, we must be careful and precise.

Because humans do have rights, and these rights can be violated by other humans, we say that some humans commit *crimes.* But whether a crime has been committed depends utterly on the moral state of mind of the actor. If I take your coat, or your book, honestly thinking it was mine, I do not steal it. The *actus reus* (the guilty deed) must be accompanied, in a genuine crime, by a guilty mind, a *mens rea.* That recognition, not just of possible punishment for an act, but of moral duties that govern us, no rat or cow ever can possess. In primitive times humans did sometimes bring cows and horses to the bar of human justice. We chuckle at that practice now, realizing that accusing cows of crimes marks the primitive moral view as inane. Animals never can be criminals because they have no moral state of mind.

Mistakes parallel to this in other spheres may be helpful to think about. In the Third Part of *The Critique of Pure Reason,* Immanuel Kant explained with care the metaphysical blunders into which we are led when we misapply concepts of great human import. In our human experience, for example, the concepts of time and space, the relations of cause and effect, of subject and attribute, and others, are essential, fundamental. But, forgetting that these are concepts arising only within the world of our human experience, we sometimes are misled into asking: Was the world caused, or is it uncaused? Did the world have a beginning in time, or did it not? Kant explained—in one of the most brilliant long passages in all philosophical literature—why *it makes no sense to ask such questions.* Cause applies to phenomena we humans encounter *in* the world, it is a category of our experience and cannot apply to the world as a whole. Time is the condition of our experience, not an absolute container in which the world could have begun. The antinomies of pure reason, and after those the paralogisms of pure reason, Kant patiently exhibited as confusions arising from the misapplication of the categories of experience. His lesson is powerful and deep. The misapplication of concepts leads to error and, sometimes, to nonsense. So it is with rights also. To say that rats have rights is to apply to the world of rats a concept that makes good sense when applied to humans, but which makes no sense at all when applied to rats.

WHY ANIMALS ARE MISTAKENLY BELIEVED TO HAVE RIGHTS

From the foregoing discussion it follows that, if some philosophers believe that they have proved that animals have rights, they must have erred in the alleged proof. Regan is a leader among those who claim to *argue* in defense of the rights of rats; he contends that the best arguments are on his side. I aim next to show how he and others with like views go astray. Bear in mind that Regan's book is long, its argument tortuous and at times convoluted. In what follows I must compress the report of his views, obviously; but I promise to be fair and to hold Regan responsible for nothing that he does not clearly say. We know—if we are agreed that rats are not the holders of rights—that Regan must have got off the track. Examining *The Case for Animal Rights,* let us see if we can find the faulty switch.

Much of Regan's (1983) book is devoted to a general treatment of the nature of ethical thinking and theory, to discussions of animal consciousness and animal awareness, and to detailed critiques of the views of others whom he thinks in error. Regan sought to show, patiently and laboriously, that the common belief that we do have obligations to animals, although they have no rights, has not been defended satisfactorily. That belief cannot be justified, he contended, by direct duty views of which he finds two categories: those depending on the obligation to be kind or not to be cruel, and those depending on any kind of utilitarian calculation.

None of this counterargument could possibly establish his conclusion that animals do have rights, unless Regan had proved that his listing of all alternative conflicting views was exhaustive, which it was not, and unless he had proved conclusively that every such candidate is untenable, which he did not do. . . .

The case is built entirely on the principle that allegedly *carries over* almost everything earlier claimed about human rights to rats and other animals. What principle is that? It is the principle, put in italics but given no name, that equates moral agents with moral patients:

> *The validity of the claim to respectful treatment, and thus the case for the recognition of the right to such treatment, cannot be any stronger or weaker in the case of moral patients than it is in the case of moral agents.* (Regan, p. 279)

But hold on. Why in the world should anyone think this principle to be true? Back where Regan first recounted his view of moral patients, he allowed that some of them are, although capable of experiencing pleasure and pain, lacking in other capacities. But he is interested, he told us there, in those moral patients—those animals—that are like humans in having *inherent value.* This is the key to the argument for animal rights, the possession of inherent value. How that concept functions in the argument becomes absolutely critical. I will say first briefly what will be shown more carefully later: *Inherent value* is an expression used by Regan (and many like him) with two very different senses—in one of which it is reasonable to conclude that those who have inherent value have rights, and in another sense in which that inference is wholly unwarranted. But the phrase *inherent value* has some plausibility in both contexts, and thus by sliding from one sense of inherent value to the other Regan appears to succeed . . . in making the case for animal rights.

The concept of inherent value first entered the discussion in the seventh chapter of Regan's (1983) book, at which point his principle object is to fault and defeat utilitarian arguments. It is not (he argued there) the pleasures or pains that go "into the cup" of humanity that give value, but the "cups" themselves; humans are equal in value because they are humans, having inherent value. So we are, all of us, equal—equal in being moral agents who have this inherent value. This approach to the moral stature of humans is likely to be found quite plausible. Regan called it the "postulate of inherent value"; all humans, "The lonely, forsaken, unwanted, and unloved are no more nor less inherently valuable than those who enjoy a more hospitable relationship with others" (p. 237). And Regan went on to argue for the proposition that all moral agents are "equal in inherent value." Holding some such views we are likely to say, with Kant, that all humans are beyond price. Their inherent value gives them moral dignity, a unique role in the moral world, as agents having the capacity to act morally and make moral judgments. This is inherent value in Sense 1.

The expression *inherent value* has another sense, however, also common and also plausible. My dog has inherent value, and so does every wild animal, every lion and zebra, which is why the senseless killing of animals is so repugnant. Each animal is unique, not replaceable in itself by another animal or by any rocks or clay. Animals, like humans, are not just things; they live, and as unique living creatures they have inherent value. This is an important point, and again likely to be thought plausible; but here, in Sense 2, the phrase *inherent value* means something quite distinct from what was meant in its earlier uses.

Inherent value in Sense 1, possessed by all humans but not by all animals, which warrants the claim of human rights, is very different from inherent value in Sense 2, which warrants no such claim. The uniqueness of animals, their intrinsic worthiness as individual living things, does not ground the possession of rights, has nothing to do with the moral condition in which rights arise. Regan's argument reached its critical objective with almost magical speed because, having argued that beings with inherent value (Sense 1) have rights that must be respected, he quickly asserted (putting it in italics lest the reader be inclined to express doubt) that rats and rabbits also have rights because they, too, have inherent value (Sense 2).

This is an egregious example of the fallacy of equivocation: the informal fallacy in which two or more meanings of the same word or phrase have been confused in the several premises of an argument (Cohen & Copi, 1994, pp. 143–144). Why is this slippage not seen at once? Partly because we know the phrase *inherent value* often is used loosely, so the reader is not prone to quibble about its introduction; partly because the two uses of the phrase relied on are both common, so neither signals danger; partly because inherent value in Sense 2 is indeed shared by those who have it in Sense 1; and partly because the phrase inherent value is woven into accounts of what Regan (1983) elsewhere called the *subject-of-a-life criterion,* a phrase of his own devising for which he can stipulate any meaning he pleases, of course, and which also slides back and forth between the sphere of genuine moral agency and the sphere of animal experience. But perhaps the chief reason the equivocation between these two uses of the phrase *inherent value* is obscured (from the author, I believe, as well as from the reader) is the fact that the assertion that animals have rights appears only indirectly, as the outcome of the application of the principle that moral patients are entitled to the same respect as moral agents—a principle introduced at a point in the book long after the important moral differences between moral patients and moral agents have been recognized, with a good deal of tangled philosophical argument having been injected in between.

I invite readers to trace out this equivocation in detail; my limited space here precludes more extended quotation. But this assurance I will give: there is no argument or set of arguments in *The Case for Animal Rights* that successfully makes the case for animal rights. Indeed, there *could* not be, any more than any book, however long and convoluted, could make the case for the emotions of oak trees, or the criminality of snakes.

Animals do not have rights. Right does not apply in their world. We do have many obligations to animals, of course, and I honor Regan's appreciation of their sensitivities. I also honor his seriousness of purpose, and his always civil and always rational spirit. But he is, I submit, profoundly mistaken. I conclude with the observation that, had his mistaken views about the rights of animals long been accepted, most successful medical therapies recently devised—antibiotics, vaccines, prosthetic devices, and other compounds and instruments on which we now rely for saving and improving human lives and for the protection of our children—could not have been developed; and were his views to become general now (an outcome that is unlikely but possible) the consequences for medical science and for human well-being in the years ahead would be nothing less than catastrophic.

Advances in medicine absolutely require experiments, many of which are dangerous. Dangerous experiments absolutely require living organisms as subjects. Those living organisms (we now agree) certainly may not be human beings. Therefore, most advances in medicine will continue to rely on the use of nonhuman animals, or they will stop. Regan is free to say in response, as he does, "so be it." The rest of us must ask if the argument he presents is so compelling as to force us to accept that dreadful result.

REFERENCES

Beauchamp, T. L., & Childress, J. F. (1994). *Principles of biomedical ethics* (4th ed.). New York: Oxford University Press.

Cohen, C., & Copi, I. M. (1994). *Introduction to logic* (9th ed.). New York: Macmillan.

Regan, T. (1983). *The case for animal rights.* Berkeley: University of California Press.

Discussion Questions

1. Most rights ethicists maintain that rights are correlatives of duties or obligations. Cohen acknowledges that inhumane treatment of nonhuman animals is wrong when we can achieve the same results using alternative methods. Is his claim that researchers have a moral obligation to treat nonhuman animals humanely inconsistent with his claim that animals have no rights? Can we have an obligation to animals if they have no rights? Support your answers.
2. Is Cohen a speciesist? Discuss how Singer might respond to Cohen's claim that all and only humans have rights, even those who lack reason and moral autonomy.
3. Cohen admits that nonhuman animals feel pain and that researchers should not subject them to unnecessary suffering. What does he mean by unnecessary suffering? To what extent does this criterion limit the type of research that is morally permissible? Does this criterion oblige Cohen to limit the type of research that he sanctions? Compare and contrast Cohen's and Singer's positions on the significance of suffering in the moral justification of experiments using nonhuman animals. Who presents the more compelling argument? Support your answers.
4. Does Cohen do an effective job of discrediting Regan's argument that nonhuman animals have rights? Support your answer. Discuss how Regan might respond to Cohen's criticism of his position.
5. Do you agree with Cohen's claim regarding the qualitative gap between humans and other animals? Discuss how Cohen might respond to Singer's argument that scientists who justify using nonhuman animals in psychology and learning experiments on the grounds that they are not like humans find themselves in a moral dilemma, because there would be no point in using them if they were not like us.
6. Discuss whether Cohen's argument supports factory farming and meat-eating.

ALDO LEOPOLD

The Land Ethic

Aldo Leopold (1887–1948) was a forester and wildlife manager with the U.S. Forest Service and a professor of wildlife management at the University of Wisconsin. In his highly influential essay "The Land Ethic," Leopold expresses concern about the detrimental impact of human activities on the environment. He argues that instead of seeing the environment primarily in terms of its value to humans (anthropocentrism), we should see ourselves as part of the natural world (ecocentrism).[34]

Critical Reading Questions

1. What does Leopold mean when he talks of the "extension of ethics"?
2. What is the premise of current ethics?
3. In what ways does a land ethics change the role of humans in the land community?
4. Why does Leopold reject an ethics based on a conservation system?
5. What is the land pyramid? Where are humans in Leopold's land pyramid?
6. What attitudes toward the land are required in order for humans to have an ethical relationship with the land?
7. According to Leopold, how does evolution of species take place?
8. What are some of the obstacles impeding the evolution of a land ethics?
9. What strategies does Leopold suggest for overcoming these obstacles?
10. According to Leopold, what are the fundamental criteria for determining if something is ethically right?

When god-like Odysseus returned from the wars in Troy, he hanged all on one rope a dozen slave-girls of his household whom he suspected of misbehavior during his absence.

This hanging involved no question of propriety. The girls were property. The disposal of property was then, as now, a matter of expediency, not of right and wrong.

Concepts of right and wrong were not lacking from Odysseus' Greece: . . . The ethical structure of that day covered wives, but had not yet been extended to human chattels. During the three thousand years which have since elapsed, ethical criteria have been extended to many fields of conduct, with corresponding shrinkages in those judged by expediency only.

THE ETHICAL SEQUENCE

This extension of ethics, so far studied only by philosophers, is actually a process in ecological evolution. Its sequences may be described in ecological as well as in philosophical terms. An ethic, ecologically, is a limitation on freedom of action in the struggle for existence. An ethic, philosophically, is a

---

Aldo Leopold, "The Land Ethic," from *A Sand County Almanac: And Sketches Here and There* (New York: Oxford University Press, 1949 and 1977), pp. 201–226.

differentiation of social from anti-social conduct. These are two definitions of one thing. The thing has its origin in the tendency of interdependent individuals or groups to evolve modes of co-operation. The ecologist calls these symbioses. . . .

The first ethics dealt with the relation between individuals; the Mosaic Decalogue is an example. Later accretions dealt with the relation between the individual and society. The Golden Rule tries to integrate the individual to society; democracy to integrate social organization to the individual.

There is as yet no ethic dealing with man's relation to land and to the animals and plants which grow upon it. Land, like Odysseus' slave-girls, is still property. The land-relation is still strictly economic, entailing privileges but not obligations.

The extension of ethics to this third element in human environment is, if I read the evidence correctly, an evolutionary possibility and an ecological necessity. . . .

THE COMMUNITY CONCEPT

All ethics so far evolved rest upon a single premise: that the individual is a member of a community of interdependent parts. His instincts prompt him to compete for his place in that community, but his ethics prompt him also to co-operate (perhaps in order that there may be a place to compete for).

The land ethic simply enlarges the boundaries of the community to include soils, waters, plants, and animals, or collectively: the land.

This sounds simple: do we not already sing our love for and obligation to the land of the free and the home of the brave? Yes, but just what and whom do we love? Certainly not the soil, which we are sending helter-skelter downriver. Certainly not the waters, which we assume have no function except to turn the turbines, float barges, and carry off sewage. Certainly not the plants, of which we exterminate whole communities without batting an eye. Certainly not the animals, of which we have already extirpated many of the largest and most beautiful species. A land ethic of course cannot prevent the alteration, management, and use of these "resources," but it does affirm their right to continued existence, and, at least in spots, their continued existence in a natural state.

In short, a land ethic changes the role of *Homo sapiens* from conqueror of the land-community to plain member and citizen of it. It implies respect for his fellow-members, and also respect for the community as such. . . .

SUBSTITUTES FOR A LAND ETHIC

When the logic of history hungers for bread and we hand out a stone, we are at pains to explain how much the stone resembles bread. I now describe some of the stones which serve in lieu of a land ethic.

One basic weakness in a conservation system based wholly on economic motives is that most members of the land community have no economic value. Wildflowers and songbirds are examples. . . .

Lack of economic value is sometimes a character not only of species or groups, but of entire biotic communities: marshes, bogs, dunes, and "deserts" are examples. Our formula in such cases is to relegate their conservation to government as refuges, monuments, or parks. . . .

Industrial landowners and users, especially lumbermen and stockmen, are inclined to wail long and loudly about the extension of government ownership and regulation to land, but (with notable exceptions) they show little disposition to develop the only visible alternative: the voluntary practice of conservation on their own lands.

When the private landowner is asked to perform some unprofitable act for the good of the community, he today assents only with outstretched palm. If the act costs him cash this is fair and proper, but when it costs only forethought, open-mindedness, or time, the issue is at least debatable. The overwhelming growth of land-use subsidies in recent years must be ascribed, in large part, to the government's own agencies for conservation education: the land bureaus, the agricultural colleges, and the extension services. As far as I can detect, no ethical obligation toward land is taught in these institutions.

To sum up: a system of conservation based solely on economic self-interest is hopelessly lopsided. It tends to ignore, and thus eventually to eliminate, many elements in the land community that lack commercial value, but that are (as far as we know) essential to its healthy functioning. It assumes, falsely, I think, that the economic parts of the biotic clock will function without the uneconomic parts. It tends to relegate to government many functions eventually too large, too complex, or too widely dispersed to be performed by government.

An ethical obligation on the part of the private owner is the only visible remedy for these situations.

THE LAND PYRAMID

An ethic to supplement and guide the economic relation to land presupposes the existence of some mental image of land as a biotic mechanism. We can be ethical only in relation to something we can see, feel, understand, love, or otherwise have faith in.

The image commonly employed in conservation education is "the balance of nature." For reasons too lengthy to detail here, this figure of speech fails to describe accurately what little we know about the land mechanism. A much truer image is the one employed in ecology: the biotic pyramid. I shall first sketch the pyramid as a symbol of land, and later develop some of its implications in terms of land-use.

Plants absorb energy from the sun. This energy flows through a circuit called the biota, which may be represented by a pyramid consisting of layers. The bottom layer is the soil. A plant layer rests on the soil, an insect layer on the plants, a bird and rodent layer on the insects, and so on up through various animal groups to the apex layer, which consists of the larger carnivores.

The species of a layer are alike not in where they came from, or in what they look like, but rather in what they eat. Each successive layer depends on those below it for food and often for other services, and each in turn furnishes food and services to those above. Proceeding upward, each successive layer decreases in numerical abundance. Thus, for every carnivore there are hundreds of his prey, thousands of their prey, millions of insects, uncountable plants. The pyramidal form of the system reflects this numerical progression from apex to base. Man shares an intermediate layer with the bears, raccoons, and squirrels which eat both meat and vegetables. . . .

Land, then, is not merely soil; it is a fountain of energy flowing through a circuit of soils, plants, and animals. Food chains are the living channels which conduct energy upward; death and decay return it to the soil. The circuit is not closed; some energy is dissipated in decay, some is added by absorption from the air, some is stored in soils, peats, and long-lived forests; but it is a sustained circuit, like a slowly augmented revolving fund of life. . . .

This interdependence between the complex structure of the land and its smooth functioning as an energy unit is one of its basic attributes.

When a change occurs in one part of the circuit, many other parts must adjust themselves to it. Change does not necessarily obstruct or divert the flow of energy; evolution is a long series of self-induced changes, the net result of which has been to elaborate the flow mechanism and to lengthen the circuit. Evolutionary changes, however, are usually slow and local. Man's invention of tools has enabled him to make changes of unprecedented violence, rapidity, and scope. . . .

THE OUTLOOK

It is inconceivable to me that an ethical relation to land can exist without love, respect, and admiration for land, and a high regard for its value. By value, I of course mean something far broader than mere economic value; I mean value in the philosophical sense.

Perhaps the most serious obstacle impeding the evolution of a land ethic is the fact that our educational and economic system is headed away from, rather than toward, an intense consciousness of land. Your true modern is separated from the land by many middlemen, and by innumerable physical gadgets. He has no vital relation to it; to him it is the space between cities on which crops grow. Turn him loose for a day on the land, and if the spot does not happen to be a golf links or a "scenic" area, he is bored stiff. If crops could be raised by hydroponics instead of farming, it would suit him very well.

Synthetic substitutes for wood, leather, wool, and other natural land products suit him better than the originals. In short, land is something he has "outgrown."

Almost equally serious as an obstacle to a land ethic is the attitude of the farmer for whom the land is still an adversary, or a taskmaster that keeps him in slavery. Theoretically, the mechanization of farming ought to cut the farmer's chains, but whether it really does is debatable. . . .

The case for a land ethic would appear hopeless but for the minority which is in obvious revolt against these "modern" trends.

The "key-log" which must be moved to release the evolutionary process for an ethic is simply this: quit thinking about decent land-use as solely an economic problem. Examine each question in terms of what is ethically and esthetically right, as well as what is economically expedient. A thing is right when it tends to preserve the integrity, stability, and beauty of the biotic community. It is wrong when it tends otherwise.

It of course goes without saying that economic feasibility limits the tether of what can or cannot be done for land. It always has and it always will. The fallacy the economic determinists have tied around our collective neck, and which we now need to cast off, is the belief that economics determines *all* land-use. This is simply not true. An innumerable host of actions and attitudes, comprising perhaps the bulk of all land relations, is determined by the land-users' tastes and predilections, rather than by his purse. The bulk of all land relations hinges on investments of time, forethought, skill, and faith rather than on investments of cash. As a land-user thinketh, so is he. . . .

The evolution of a land ethic is an intellectual as well as emotional process. Conservation is paved with good intentions which prove to be futile, or even dangerous, because they are devoid of critical understanding either of the land, or of economic land-use. I think it is a truism that as the ethical frontier advances from the individual to the community, its intellectual content increases.

The mechanism of operation is the same for any ethic: social approbation for right actions: social disapproval for wrong actions.

By and large, our present problem is one of attitudes and implements. We are remodeling the Alhambra with a steam-shovel, and we are proud of our yardage. We shall hardly relinquish the shovel, which after all has many good points, but we are in need of gentler and more objective criteria for its successful use.

Discussion Questions

1. Discuss Leopold's assumption about the evolution of ethics toward a land ethics. Is it indeed morally desirable, as Leopold claims, to expand our concept of moral community to include the environment? Support your answer.
2. Discuss whether or not Leopold's land ethics is compatible with the Judeo-Christian view of creation and our place as human beings in the universe.
3. What does Leopold mean when he says: "A thing is right when it tends to preserve the integrity, stability, and beauty of the biotic community. It is wrong when it tends otherwise"? Discuss the implications of this statement on your own lifestyle and on public policy regarding the environment.
4. In his essay, "Thinking Like a Mountain," Leopold describes watching the death of a wolf he just shot. "We reached the old wolf in time to watch a fierce green fire dying in her eyes. I realized then, and have known ever since, that there was something new to me in those eyes—something known only to her and to the mountain. I was young then, and full of trigger-itch; I thought that because fewer wolves meant more deer, that no wolves would mean a hunter's paradise. But after seeing the green fire die, I sensed that neither the wolf nor the mountain agreed with such a view." Do you agree

with Leopold? Support your answer. Discuss Leopold's experience in light of your own experience.
5. Discuss how Jonathan Granoff would most likely respond to Leopold's land ethics.
6. Discuss the implications of Leopold's land ethics for our eating habits and the use of nonhuman animals in medical experiments. How would Tom Regan, Peter Singer, Jan Narveson, and Carl Cohen each most likely respond to Leopold's land ethics?

BILL DEVALL AND GEORGE SESSIONS

Deep Ecology

Bill Devall is a sociology professor at Humboldt State University in Arcata, California. George Sessions is a philosophy professor at Sierra College in Rocklin, California. Their book has been called a manifesto for the deep ecology movement. In this selection, the authors present the eight principles of deep ecology, as originally put forth by George Sessions and Norwegian philosopher Arne Naess. They also contrast deep ecology with the dominant worldview.

Critical Reading Questions

1. What is the essence of "deep ecology"?
2. Who is Arne Naess?
3. What is the difference between "deep" and "shallow" ecology?
4. What are the foundations of deep ecology?
5. How does the deep ecology worldview differ from the dominant worldview? What are the implications of both of these worldviews for what it means to be human and our place in nature?
6. What are the two ultimate norms of deep ecological consciousness?
7. What is the deep ecology sense of self, and how can society help nurture this self?
8. What is "biocentric equality" and how is it related to self-actualization?
9. What are the eight basic principles of deep ecology, and what is the meaning of each of these principles?
10. What is a biosphere?
11. According to Devall and Sessions, what are the implications of deep ecology for human population growth and our relationship to nature?

Bill Devall and George Sessions, "Deep Ecology," from *Deep Ecology: Living as if Nature Mattered* (Salt Lake City: Peregrine Smith Books, 1985), pp. 65–73. Notes have been omitted.

The term *deep ecology* was coined by Arne Naess in his 1973 article, "The Shallow and the Deep, Long-Range Ecology Movements." Naess was attempting to describe the deeper, more spiritual approach to Nature exemplified in the writings of Aldo Leopold and Rachel Carson. He thought that this deeper approach resulted from a more sensitive openness to ourselves and nonhuman life around us. The essence of deep ecology is to keep asking more searching questions about human life, society, and Nature as in the Western philosophical tradition of Socrates. As examples of this deep questioning, Naess points out "that we ask why and how, where others do not. For instance, ecology as a science does not ask what kind of a society would be the best for maintaining a particular ecosystem—that is considered a question for value theory, for politics, for ethics." Thus deep ecology goes beyond the so-called factual scientific level to the level of self and Earth wisdom.

Deep ecology goes beyond a limited piecemeal shallow approach to environmental problems and attempts to articulate a comprehensive religious and philosophical worldview. The foundations of deep ecology are the basic intuitions and experiencing of ourselves and Nature which comprise ecological consciousness. Certain outlooks on politics and public policy flow naturally from this consciousness. . . .

Many of these questions are perennial philosophical and religious questions faced by humans in all cultures over the ages. What does it mean to be a unique human individual? How can the individual self maintain and increase its uniqueness while also being an inseparable aspect of the whole system wherein there are no sharp breaks between self and the *other?* An ecological perspective, in this deeper sense, results in what Theodore Roszak calls "an awakening of wholes greater than the sum of their parts. In spirit, the discipline is contemplative and therapeutic."

Ecological consciousness and deep ecology are in sharp contrast with the dominant worldview of technocratic-industrial societies which regards humans as isolated and fundamentally separate from the rest of Nature, as superior to, and in charge of, the rest of creation. But the view of humans as separate and superior to the rest of Nature is only part of larger cultural patterns. For thousands of years, Western culture has become increasingly obsessed with the idea of *dominance:* with dominance of humans over nonhuman Nature, masculine over the feminine, wealthy and powerful over the poor, with the dominance of the West over non-Western cultures. Deep ecological consciousness allows us to see through these erroneous and dangerous illusions.

For deep ecology, the study of our place in the Earth household includes the study of ourselves as part of the organic whole. Going beyond a narrowly materialist scientific understanding of reality, the spiritual and the material aspects of reality fuse together. While the leading intellectuals of the dominant worldview have tended to view religion as "just superstition," and have looked upon ancient spiritual practice and enlightenment, such as found in Zen Buddhism, as essentially subjective, the search for deep ecological consciousness is the search for a more objective consciousness and state of being through an active deep questioning and meditative process and way of life.

Many people have asked these deeper questions and cultivated ecological consciousness within the context of different spiritual traditions—Christianity, Taoism, Buddhism, and Native American rituals, for example. While differing greatly in other regards, many in these traditions agree with the basic principles of deep ecology. . . .

From this most basic insight or characteristic of deep ecological consciousness, Arne Naess has developed two *ultimate norms* or intuitions which are themselves not derivable from other principles or intuitions. They are arrived at by the deep questioning process and reveal the importance of moving to the philosophical and religious level of wisdom. They cannot be validated, of course, by the methodology of modern science based on its usual mechanistic assumptions and its very narrow definition of data. These ultimate norms are *self-realization* and *biocentric equality.*

I. SELF-REALIZATION

In keeping with the spiritual traditions of many of the world's religions, the deep ecology norm of self-realization goes beyond the modern Western *self* which is defined as an isolated ego striving primarily for hedonistic gratification or for a narrow sense of individual salvation in this life or the next. This socially programmed sense of the narrow self or social self dislocates us, and leaves us prey to whatever fad or fashion is prevalent in our society or social reference group. We are thus robbed of beginning the search for our unique spiritual/biological personhood. Spiritual growth, or unfolding, begins when we cease to understand or see ourselves as isolated and narrow competing egos and begin to identify with other humans from our family and friends to, eventually, our species. But the deep ecology sense of self requires a further maturity and growth, an identification which goes beyond humanity to include the nonhuman world. We must see beyond our narrow contemporary cultural assumptions and values, and the conventional wisdom of our time and place, and this is best achieved by the meditative deep questioning process. Only in this way can we hope to attain full mature personhood and uniqueness.

A nurturing nondominating society can help in the "real work" of becoming a whole person. The "real work" can be summarized symbolically as the realization of "self-in-Self" where "Self" stands for organic wholeness. This process of the full unfolding of the self can also be summarized by the phrase, "No one is saved until we are all saved," where the phrase "one" includes not only me, an individual human, but all humans, whales, grizzly bears, whole rain forest ecosystems, mountains and rivers, the tiniest microbes in the soil, and so on.

II. BIOCENTRIC EQUALITY

The intuition of biocentric equality is that all things in the biosphere have an equal right to live and blossom and to reach their own individual forms of unfolding and self-realization within the larger Self-realization. This basic intuition is that all organisms and entities in the ecosphere, as parts of the interrelated whole, are equal in intrinsic worth. Naess suggests that biocentric equality as an intuition is true in principle, although in the process of living, all species use each other as food, shelter, etc. Mutual predation is a biological fact of life, and many of the world's religions have struggled with the spiritual implications of this. Some animal liberationists who attempt to side-step this problem by advocating vegetarianism are forced to say that the entire plant kingdom including rain forests have no right to their own existence. This evasion flies in the face of the basic intuition of equality. Aldo Leopold expressed this intuition when he said humans are "plain citizens" of the biotic community, not lord and master over all other species.

Biocentric equality is intimately related to the all-inclusive Self-realization in the sense that if we harm the rest of Nature then we are harming ourselves. There are no boundaries and everything is interrelated. But insofar as we perceive things as individual organisms or entities, the insight draws us to respect all human and nonhuman individuals in their own right as parts of the whole without feeling the need to set up hierarchies of species with humans at the top.

The practical implications of this intuition or norm suggest that we should live with minimum rather than maximum impact on other species and on the Earth in general. Thus we see another aspect of our guiding principle: "simple in means, rich in ends." . . .

A fuller discussion of the biocentric norm as it unfolds itself in practice begins with the realization that we, as individual humans, and as communities of humans, have vital needs which go beyond such basics as food, water, and shelter to include love, play, creative expression, intimate relationships with a particular landscape (or Nature taken in its entirety) as well as intimate relationships with other humans, and the vital need for spiritual growth, for becoming a mature human being.

Our vital material needs are probably more simple than many realize. In technocratic-industrial societies there is overwhelming propaganda and advertising which encourages false needs and destructive desires designed to foster increased production and consumption of goods. Most of this actually diverts us from facing reality in an objective way and from beginning the "real work" of spiritual growth and maturity.

Many people who do not see themselves as supporters of deep ecology nevertheless recognize an overriding vital human need for a healthy and high-quality natural environment for humans, if not for all life, with minimum intrusion of toxic waste, nuclear radiation from human enterprises, minimum acid rain and smog, and enough free flowing wilderness so humans can get in touch with their sources, the natural rhythms and the flow of time and place.

Drawing from the minority tradition and from the wisdom of many who have offered the insight of interconnectedness, we recognize that deep ecologists can offer suggestions for gaining maturity and encouraging the processes of harmony with Nature, but that there is no grand solution which is guaranteed to save us from ourselves.

The ultimate norms of deep ecology suggest a view of the nature of reality and our place as an individual (many in the one) in the larger scheme of things. They cannot be fully grasped intellectually but are ultimately experiential. . . .

As a brief summary of our position thus far, figure 5-1 summarizes the contrast between the dominant worldview and deep ecology.

III. BASIC PRINCIPLES OF DEEP ECOLOGY

In April 1984, during the advent of spring and John Muir's birthday, George Sessions and Arne Naess summarized fifteen years of thinking on the principles of deep ecology while camping in Death Valley, California. In this great and special place, they articulated these principles in a literal, somewhat neutral way, hoping that they would be understood and accepted by persons coming from different philosophical and religious positions.

Readers are encouraged to elaborate their own versions of deep ecology, clarify key concepts and think through the consequences of acting from these principles.

Basic Principles

1. The well-being and flourishing of human and nonhuman Life on Earth have value in themselves (synonyms: intrinsic value, inherent value). These values are independent of the usefulness of the nonhuman world for human purposes.
2. Richness and diversity of life forms contribute to the realization of these values and are also values in themselves.
3. Humans have no right to reduce this richness and diversity except to satisfy *vital* needs.
4. The flourishing of human life and cultures is compatible with a substantial decrease of the human population. The flourishing of nonhuman life requires such a decrease.
5. Present human interference with the nonhuman world is excessive, and the situation is rapidly worsening.
6. Policies must therefore be changed. These policies affect basic economic, technological, and ideological structures. The resulting state

Figure 5–1

Dominant Worldview	*Deep Ecology*
Dominance over Nature	Harmony with Nature
Natural environment as resource for humans	All nature has intrinsic worth/biospecies equality
Material/economic growth for growing human population	Elegantly simple material needs (material goals serving the larger goal of self-realization)
Belief in ample resource reserves	Earth "supplies" limited
High technological progress and solutions	Appropriate technology; nondominating science
Consumerism	Doing with enough/recycling
National/centralized community	Minority tradition/bioregion

of affairs will be deeply different from the present.

7. The ideological change is mainly that of appreciating *life quality* (dwelling in situations of inherent value) rather than adhering to an increasingly higher standard of living. There will be a profound awareness of the difference between big and great.
8. Those who subscribe to the foregoing points have an obligation directly or indirectly to try to implement the necessary changes.

Naess and Sessions Provide Comments on the Basic Principles:

RE (1). This formulation refers to the biosphere, or more accurately, to the ecosphere as a whole. This includes individuals, species, populations, habitat, as well as human and nonhuman cultures. From our current knowledge of all-pervasive intimate relationships, this implies a fundamental deep concern and respect. . . .

The term "life" is used here in a more comprehensive nontechnical way to refer also to what biologists classify as "nonliving"; rivers (watersheds), landscapes, ecosystems. For supporters of deep ecology, slogans such as "Let the river live" illustrate this broader usage so common in most cultures.

Inherent value as used in (1) is common in deep ecology literature ("The presence of inherent value in a natural object is independent of any awareness, interest, or appreciation of it by a conscious being.")

RE (2). More technically, this is a formulation concerning diversity and complexity. From an ecological standpoint, complexity and symbiosis are conditions for maximizing diversity. So-called simple, lower, or primitive species of plants and animals contribute essentially to the richness and diversity of life. They have value in themselves and are not merely steps toward the so-called higher or rational life forms. The second principle presupposes that life itself, as a process over evolutionary time, implies an increase of diversity and richness. . . .

Complexity, as referred to here, is different from complication. Urban life may be more complicated than life in a natural setting without being more complex in the sense of multifaceted quality.

RE (3). The term "vital need" is left deliberately vague to allow for considerable latitude in judgment. Differences in climate and related factors, together with differences in the structures of societies as they now exist, need to be considered (for some Eskimos, snowmobiles are necessary today to satisfy vital needs).

People in the materially richest countries cannot be expected to reduce their excessive interference with the nonhuman world to a moderate level overnight. . . . But the longer we wait the more drastic will be the measures needed. Until deep changes are made, substantial decreases in richness and diversity are liable to occur: the rate of extinction of species will be ten to one hundred times greater than any other period of earth history.

RE (4). The United Nations Fund for Population Activities in their State of World Population Report (1984) said that high human population growth rates (over 2.0 percent annum) in many developing countries "were diminishing the quality of life for many millions of people." . . .

Most of the nations in the developing world (including India and China) have as their official government policy the goal of reducing the rate of human population increase, but there are debates over the types of measures to take (contraception, abortion, etc.) consistent with human rights and feasibility.

The report concludes that if all governments set specific population targets as public policy to help alleviate poverty and advance the quality of life, the current situation could be improved.

As many ecologists have pointed out, it is also absolutely crucial to curb population growth in the so-called developed (i.e., overdeveloped) industrial societies. Given the tremendous rate of consumption and waste production of individuals in these societies, they represent a much greater threat and impact on the biosphere per capita than individuals in Second and Third World countries.

RE (5). . . . The slogan of "noninterference" does not imply that humans should not modify some ecosystems as do other species. Humans have modified the earth and will probably continue to do so. At issue is the nature and extent of such interference.

The fight to preserve and extend areas of wilderness or near-wilderness should continue and should focus on the general ecological functions of these areas (one such function: large wilderness areas are required in the biosphere to allow for continued evolutionary speciation of animals and plants). Most present designated wilderness areas and game preserves are not large enough to allow for such speciation.

RE (6). Economic growth as conceived and implemented today by the industrial states is incompatible with (1)–(5). There is only a faint resemblance between ideal sustainable forms of economic growth and present policies of the industrial societies. And "sustainable" still means "sustainable in relation to humans."

Present ideology tends to value things because they are scarce and because they have a commodity value. There is prestige in vast consumption and waste (to mention only several relevant factors).

Whereas "self-determination," "local community," and "think globally, act locally," will remain key terms in the ecology of human societies, nevertheless the implementation of deep changes requires increasingly global action—action across borders. . . .

RE (7). Some economists criticize the term "quality of life" because it is supposed to be vague. But on closer inspection, what they consider to be vague is actually the nonquantitative nature of the term. One cannot quantify adequately what is important for the quality of life as discussed here, and there is no need to do so.

RE (8). There is ample room for different opinions about priorities: what should be done first, what next? What is most urgent? What is clearly necessary as opposed to what is highly desirable but not absolutely pressing?

Discussion Questions

1. Discuss Devall and Sessions's claim that biocentric equality is intuitively true. How would Cohen most likely respond to this claim?
2. What does self-realization mean to you? Discuss Devall and Sessions's position that self-realization and spiritual growth are enhanced by going beyond the traditional view of humans to the view espoused by deep ecology. What view of human nature are deep ecologists presupposing in making this claim? Discuss how Kant and Buddha would each most likely respond to the deep ecologist view of human nature and self-realization.
3. Discuss the implications of each of the eight basic principles, both for your lifestyle and for public policy.
4. In his book, *Earth in the Balance,* former vice-president Al Gore argues that modern civilization is dysfunctional because it assumes a radical separation between humans and nature. This dysfunction is manifested in spiritual malaise as well as in our addiction to consuming ever larger quantities of oil, trees, top soil, and other "substances we rip from the crust of the earth."[35] However, Gore rejects deep ecology claiming that it incorrectly portrays humans in the "role of pathogens, a kind of virus giving the earth a rash and a fever, threatening the planet's vital life functions."[36] Gore argues instead that we need to seek a balance between our needs and preservation of the global environment. Our proper role is as God's stewards of the earth. Analyze these two approaches to environmental ethics. Discuss how Devall and Sessions might respond to Gore.

5. People from affluent nations, such as the United States, contribute disproportionately to global warming. Despite this there has been little change in the consumer-oriented lifestyles of Americans. Do we as Americans have a moral obligation to change our lifestyles so we don't continue contributing to global warming? If so, should legislation be passed to enforce lifestyle changes? Support your answers. Discuss how a utilitarian would most likely answer these questions.

RICHARD WATSON

A Critique of Anti-Anthropocentric Ethics

Richard Watson is professor of philosophy at Washington University in St. Louis. Watson maintains that biocentric ethics, as put forth by people such as Aldo Leopold, George Sessions, and Arne Naess is neither egalitarian nor fully biocentric. He concludes that human interest in survival is the best foundation for achieving ecological balance that is good for both humans and the whole biological community.

Critical Reading Questions

1. What is "anthropocentrism"? How does it differ from "biocentrism"?
2. What is Tom Regan's "preservation principle"?
3. What is meant by "hands-off-nature"? Who, according to Watson, supports this view?
4. What is "ecosophy"? Why does Watson reject it?
5. What are the five principles of anti-anthropomorphic biocentrism as delineated by Watson?
6. According to Watson, what are some of the internal contradictions in biocentrism?
7. On what grounds does Watson accuse biocentrists of anthropocentric thinking?
8. According to Watson, what are some of the logical conclusions regarding human activities if we accept biocentrism?
9. On what grounds does Watson reject the biocentrists' claim that humans are too destructive of the environment and that these "destructive" human activities should be limited or curtailed?
10. What does Watson mean when he says that "there are anthropocentric foundations in most environmental and ecosophical literature"?
11. What approach does Watson consider best for preserving a rich and balanced ecology?

Richard Watson, "A Critique of Anti-Anthropocentric Ethics," *Environmental Ethics,* Vol. 5, no. 3, Fall 1983, pp. 245–256. Some notes have been omitted.

I

Anthropocentric is defined specifically as the position "that considers man as the central fact, or final aim, of the universe" and generally "conceiv[es] of everything in the universe in terms of human values."[1] In the literature of environmental ethics, anti-anthropocentric biocentrism is the position that human needs, goals, and desires should not be taken as privileged or overriding in considering the needs, desires, interests, and goals of all members of all biological species taken together, and in general that the Earth as a whole should not be interpreted or managed from a human standpoint. According to this position, birds, trees, and the land itself considered as the biosphere have a right to be and to live out their individual and species' potentials, and that members of the human species have no right to disturb, perturb, or destroy the ecological balance of the planet.

An often quoted statement of this right of natural objects to continue to be as they are found to be occurs in John Rodman's "The Liberation of Nature?":

> To affirm that "natural objects" have "rights" is symbolically to affirm that ALL NATURAL ENTITIES (INCLUDING HUMANS) HAVE INTRINSIC WORTH SIMPLY BY VIRTUE OF BEING AND BEING WHAT THEY ARE.[2]

In "On the Nature and Possibility of an Environmental Ethic," Tom Regan follows an implication of this view by presenting a "preservation principle":

> By the "preservation principle" I mean a principle of nondestruction, noninterference, and, generally, nonmeddling. By characterizing this in terms of a principle, moreover, I am emphasizing that preservation (letting-be) be regarded as a moral imperative.[3]

Support for this hands-off-nature approach is provided by George Sessions in his "Spinoza, Perennial Philosophy, and Deep Ecology," where, among other things, he describes how Aldo Leopold moved from a position considering humans as stewards or managers of nature to one considering humans as "plain members" of the total biotic community.[4] As Leopold himself puts it:

> A thing is right when it tends to preserve the integrity, stability, and beauty of the biotic community. It is wrong when it tends otherwise.[5]

According to Sessions, Leopold reached this position in part as a result of his dawning realization that ecological communities are internally integrated and highly complex. He saw how human activities have disrupted many ecological communities and was himself involved in some unsuccessful attempts to manage communities of animals in the wild. These failures led Leopold to conclude that "the biotic mechanism is so complex that its workings may never be fully understood."[6]

Like many other environmentalists, Sessions associates Leopold's position with Barry Commoner's first law of ecology: "Everything is connected to everything else,"[7] according to which "any major man-made change in a natural system is likely to be *detrimental* to that system."[8] . . .

Sessions, at least, is not naive about some of the problems that arise from these pronouncements. He says that if an environmental ethic is to be derived from ecological principles and concepts, this raises

> the old problem of attempting to derive moral principles and imperatives from supposedly empirical fact (the "is-ought problem"). The attempt to justify ecosystem ethics on conventional utilitarian or "rights and obligations" grounds presents formidable obstacles. And, so far, little headway has been made in finding other acceptable grounds for an ecosystem ethics other than a growing intuitive ecological awareness that *it is right.*[9]

Sessions by no means advocates or thinks possible a simple return to pre-Socratic religion or pantheism. But what, on the basis of ecological principles and concepts, is the underlying motif or guiding ideal today for "a correct understanding of God/Nature"?[10] According to [Arne] Naess, the proper position is an *ecosophy* defined as "a philosophy of ecological harmony or equilibrium."[11] Thus, while deploring the Greek contribution to the present desacralization of nature, these ecosophers do acknowledge the Stoic and Epicurean contributions to the philosophy of balance, harmony, and equilibrium. They present a holistic vision of the Earth circling in dynamic ecological equilibrium as the preferred and proper contemplative object of right-thinking environmental man.

In pursuing a statement of anti-anthropomorphic biocentrism, then, I have exposed five principles of the movement:

(1) The needs, desires, interests, and goals of humans are not privileged.

(2) The human species should not change the ecology of the planet.

(3) The world ecological system is too complex for human beings ever to understand.

(4) The ultimate goal, good, and joy of humankind is contemplative understanding of Nature.

(5) Nature is a holistic system of parts (of which man is merely one among many equals) all of which are internally interrelated in dynamic, harmonious, ecological equilibrium.

The moral imperative derived from this "ecosophy" is that human beings do not have the right to, and should not, alter the equilibrium.

II

I do not intend to challenge the controversial naturalistic assumption that some such environmental ethic can be derived from ecological principles and concepts. Whatever the logical problems of deriving value from fact, it is not (and probably never has been) a practical problem for large numbers of people who base their moral convictions on factual premises.

Nevertheless, it must be obvious to most careful readers that the general position characterized in section 1 suffers from serious internal contradictions. I think they are so serious that the position must be abandoned. In what follows I detail the problems that arise in the system, and then offer an alternative to the call for developing a new ecosophic ethic.

To go immediately to the heart of the matter, I take anti-anthropocentrism more seriously than do any of the ecosophers I have quoted or read. If man is a part of nature, if he is a "plain citizen," if he is just one nonprivileged member of a "biospherical egalitarianism," then the human species should be treated in no way different from any other species. However, the entire tone of the position outlined in section 1 is to set man apart from nature and above all other living species. Naess says that nonhuman animals should be "cared for in part for their own good."[12] Sessions says that humans should curb their technological enthusiasms to preserve ecological equilibrium.[13] Rodman says flatly that man should let nature be.[14]

Now, the posing of man against nature in any way is anthropocentric. Man is a part of nature.[15] Human ways—human culture—and human actions are as natural as are the ways in which any other species of animals behaves. But if we view the state of nature or Nature as being natural, undisturbed, and unperturbed only when human beings are *not* present, or only when human beings are curbing their natural behavior, then we are assuming that human beings are apart from, separate from, different from, removed from, or above nature. It is obvious that the ecosophy described above is based on this position of setting man apart from or above nature. (Do I mean even "sordid" and "perverted" human behavior? Yes, that is natural, too.)

To avoid this separation of man from nature, this special treatment of human beings as other than nature, we must stress that man's works (yes, including H-bombs and gas chanbers) are as natural as those of bower birds and beavers.

But civilized man wreaks such havoc on the environment. We disrupt the ecology of the planet, cause the extinction of myriad other species of living things, and even alter the climate of the Earth. Should we not attempt to curb our behavior to avoid these results? Indeed we should as a matter of prudence if we want to preserve our habitat and guarantee the survival of our species. But this is anthropocentric thinking.

Only if we are thinking anthropocentrically will we set the human species apart as *the* species that is to be thwarted in its natural behavior. Anti-anthropocentric biocentrists suggest that other species are to be allowed to manifest themselves naturally. They are to be allowed to live out their evolutionary potential in interaction with one another. But man is different. Man is *too* powerful, *too* destructive of the environment and other species, *too* successful in reproducing, and so on. What a phenomenon is man! Man is so wonderfully bad that he is not to be allowed to live out his evolutionary potential in egalitarian interaction with all other species.

Why not? The only reason is anthropocentric. We are not treating man as a plain member of the biotic community. We are not treating the human species as an equal among other species. We think of man as being better than other animals, or worse, as the case may be, because man is so powerful.

One reason we think this is that we think in terms of an anthropocentric moral community. All other species are viewed as morally neutral; their behavior is neither good nor bad. But we evaluate human behavior morally. And this sets man apart. If we are to treat man as a part of nature on egalitarian terms with other species, then man's behavior must be treated as morally neutral, too. It is absurd, of course, to suggest the opposite alternative, that we evaluate the behavior of nonhuman animals morally.

Bluntly, if we think there is nothing morally wrong with one species taking over the habitat of another and eventually causing the extinction of the dispossessed species—as has happened millions of times in the history of the Earth—then we should not think that there is anything morally or ecosophically wrong with the human species dispossessing and causing the extinction of other species.

Man's nature, his role, his forte, his glory and ambition has been to propagate and thrive at the expense of many other species and to the disruption—or, neutrally, to the change—of the planet's ecology. I do not want to engage in speculation about the religion of preliterate peoples, or in debates about the interpretation of documented non-Judeo-Christian-Platonic-Aristotelian religions. I am skeptical, however, of the panegyrics about pantheism and harmonious integration with sacred Nature. But these speculations do not matter. The fact is that for about 50,000 years human beings (*Homo sapiens*) have been advancing like wildfire (to use an inflammatory metaphor) to occupy more and more of the planet. A peak of low-energy technology was reached about 35,000 years ago at which time man wiped out many species of large animals. About 10,000 years ago man domesticated plants and animals and started changing the face of the Earth with grazing, farming, deforestation, and desertification. About 200 years ago man started burning fossil fuels with results that will probably change the climate of the planet (at least temporarily) and that have already resulted in the extinction of many species of living things that perhaps might otherwise have survived. In 1945 man entered an atomic age and we now have the ability to desertify large portions of the Earth and perhaps to cause the extinction of most of the higher forms of life.[16]

Human beings do alter things. They cause the extinction of many species, and they change the Earth's ecology. This is what humans do. This is their destiny. If they destroy many other species and themselves in the process, they do no more than has been done by many another species. The human species should be allowed—if any species can be said to have a right—to live out its evolutionary potential, to its own destruction if that is the end result. It is nature's way.

This is not a popular view. But most alternative anti-anthropocentric biocentric arguments for preserving nature are self-contradictory. Man is a part of nature. The only way man will survive is if he uses his brains to save himself. One reason why we should curb human behavior that is destructive of other species and the environment is because in the end it is destructive of the human species as well.[17]

I hope it is human nature to survive because we are smart. But those who appeal for a new ethic or religion or ecosophy based on an intuitive belief that they know what is right not only for other people, but also for the planet as a whole, exhibit the hubris that they themselves say got us in such a mess in the first place.[18] If the ecosphere is so complicated that we may never understand its workings, how is it that so many ecosophers are so sure that they know what is right for us to do now? Beyond the issue of man's right to do whatever he can according to the power-makes-right ecosophic ethic outlined by Naess, we may simply be wrong about what is "good" for the planet. Large numbers of species have been wiped out before, e.g., at the time the dinosaurs became extinct. Perhaps wiping out and renewal is just the way things go. Of course, a lot of genetic material is lost, but presumably all the species that ever existed came out of the same primordial soup, and could again. In situations where genetic material was limited, as in the Galapagos Islands or Australia, evolutionary radiation filled the niches. Even on the basis of our present knowledge about evolution and ecology, we have little ground to worry about the proliferation of life on Earth even if man manages to wipe out most of the species now living. Such a clearing out might be just the thing to allow for variety and diversity. And why is it that we harp about genetic banks today anyway? For one thing, we are worried that disease might wipe out our domesticated grain crops. Then where would *man* be?

Another obvious anthropocentric element in ecosophic thinking is the predilection for ecological communities of great internal variety and complexity. But the barren limestone plateaus that surround the Mediterranean now are just as much in ecological balance as were the forests that grew there before man cut them down. And "dead" Lake Erie is just as much in ecological balance with the life on the land that surrounds it as it was in pre-Columbian times. The notion of a climax situation in ecology is a human invention, based on anthropocentric ideas of variety, completion, wholeness, and balance. A preference for equilibrium rather than change, for forests over deserts, for complexity and variety over simplicity and monoculture, all of these are matters of human economics and aesthetics. What *would* it be, after all, to think like a mountain as Aldo Leopold is said to have recommended?[19] It would be anthropocentric because mountains do not think, but also because mountains are imagined to be thinking about which human interests in their preservation or development they prefer.[20] The anthropocentrism of ecosophers is most obvious in their pronouncements about what is normal and natural. Perhaps it is not natural to remain in equilibrium, to be in ecological balance.

As far as that goes, most of the universe is apparently dead—or at least inanimate—anyway. And as far as we know, the movement of things is toward entropy. By simplifying things, man is on the side of the universe.

And as for making a mess of things, destroying things, disrupting and breaking down things, the best information we have about the origin of the universe is that it is the result of an explosion. If we are going to derive an ethic from our knowledge of nature, is it wrong to suggest that high-technology man might be doing the right thing? . . .

III

[U]nlike many ecosophers, I do not believe that we can return to religion, or that given what we know about the world today we can believe in pantheism or panpsychism, I think it is a mistake to strive for a new environmental ethic based on religious or mystical grounds. And I trust that I have demonstrated both how difficult it is to be fully biocentric, and also how the results of anti-anthropocentric biocentrism go far beyond the limits that ecosophers have drawn. Ecosophers obviously want to avoid the direct implications of treating the human species in the egalitarian and hands-off way they say other species should be treated. It is nice that human survival is compatible with the preservation of a rich planetary ecology, but I think it is a mistake to try to cover up the fact that human survival and the good life for man *is* some part of what we are interested in. There is very good reason for thinking ecologically, and for encouraging human beings to act in such a way as to preserve a rich and balanced planetary ecology: human survival depends on it.[21]

NOTES

1. *Webster's New World Dictionary,* 2nd ed. (Cleveland: William Collins and World Publishing Co., 1976), p. 59.

2. John Rodman, "The Liberation of Nature?" *Inquiry* 20 (1977): 108 (quoted with emphasis in capitals by George Sessions in *Ecophilosophy III,* p. 5a).
3. Tom Regan, "The Nature and Possibility of an Environmental Ethic," *Environmental Ethics* 3 (1981): 31–32.
4. George Sessions, "Spinoza, Perennial Philosophy, and Deep Ecology," unpublished, p. 15.
5. Aldo Leopold, *A Sand County Almanac* (Oxford: Oxford University Press, 1966), p. 240 (quoted by George Sessions in "Spinoza, Perennial Philosophy, and Deep Ecology," unpublished, p. 15).
6. Ibid.
7. Barry Commoner, *The Closing Circle: Nature, Man, and Technology* (New York: Alfred A. Knopf, 1971), p. 33 (quoted by George Sessions in "Panpsychism versus Modern Materialism: Some Implications for an Ecological Ethics," unpublished, p. 35).
8. Ibid., p. 41.
9. George Sessions, "Shallow and Deep Ecology: A Review of the Philosophical Literature," unpublished, p. 16.
10. See note 14.
11. Arne Naess, "The Shallow and the Deep, Long-Range Ecology Movement. A Summary," *Inquiry* 16 (1973): 99.
12. Arne Naess, "Environmental Ethics and Spinoza's Ethics. Comments on Genevieve Lloyd's Article," *Inquiry* 23 (1980): 319.
13. George Sessions, "Spinoza and Jeffers on Man and Nature," *Inquiry* 20 (1977): 482.
14. See note 2.
15. Richard A. Watson and Patty Jo Watson, *Man and Nature: An Anthropological Essay in Human Ecology* (New York: Harcourt Brace and World, 1969).
16. Ibid.
17. Biocentrism does not imply radical anti-anthropocentrism, for what is best for man may also be best for the whole biological community. See, e.g., J. Baird Callicott, "Elements of an Environmental Ethic: Moral Considerability and the Biotic Community," *Environmental Ethics* 1 (1979): 71–81. See also R. and V. Routley, "Against the Inevitability of Human Chauvinism," in K. E. Goodpaster and K. M. Sayre, eds. *Ethics and Problems of the 21st Century* (Notre Dame: University of Notre Dame Press, 1979). Sophisticated arguments in diverse fields support the view that cooperation leading to ecological balance is best for the whole biologic community, see, e.g., Robert Axelrod and William D. Hamilton, "The Evolution of Cooperation," *Science* 211 (1981): 1390–96.
18. See note 9.
19. Susan Flader, *Thinking Like a Mountain: Aldo Leopold and the Evolution of an Ecological Attitude toward Deer, Wolves, and Forests* (Columbia: University of Missouri Press, 1974).
20. Christopher D. Stone, *Should Trees Have Standing? Toward Legal Rights for Natural Objects* (Los Altos, Calif.: William Kaufmann, 1974).
21. See note 17.

Discussion Questions

1. Discuss whether Watson's summary of the five principles of "anti-anthropomorphic biocentrism" are consistent with the eight principles of deep ecology put forth by Naess and Sessions.
2. Discuss how Devall and Sessions would most likely respond to Watson's claim that biocentrism (deep ecology) contains serious internal contradictions.
3. In his article "A Defence of the Deep Ecology Movement,"[37] Arne Naess takes exception to Watson's claim that biocentrists set humans apart from nature by viewing humans as destructive to nature. Naess points out that every species, including humans,

alters ecosystems. However, humans have a special responsibility because of our capacity to pose the problem of long-term consequences. Thus, it is an expression of our human nature to act responsibly in our relationships with the environment. Is this an adequate rebuttal of Watson's argument that biocentrism is anthropocentric? Discuss how Watson might reply to Naess.

4. What would Watson most likely think about the morality of the practice of cutting down rain forests to create grazing land for cattle? Role-play a discussion between Watson, Regan, and Sessions on this issue. Which person presents the best argument? Support your answer.

KAREN J. WARREN

The Power and the Promise of Ecological Feminism

Karen Warren is a philosophy professor at Macalester College in St. Paul, Minnesota. Warren argues that the domination of women and the domination of nature are both grounded in the same logic of domination and value-hierarchy thinking. Therefore, feminism and environmental ethics are conceptually inseparable.

Critical Reading Questions

1. What is "ecological feminism"?
2. What types of issues are "feminist issues"? Which of these issues are conceptual ones?
3. What is a "conceptual framework"?
4. What is an "oppressive conceptual framework"? What are the three significant features of oppressive conceptual frameworks?
5. What is a "logic of domination"? What are the assumptions supporting it?
6. How is a logic of domination used to justify both oppression of women and oppression of nature?
7. What is "naturism"?
8. According to Warren, why is the first-person narrative an effective means of raising important issues in environmental ethics?
9. What is the difference between the "loving eye" and the "arrogant eye"? Which type of perception is compatible with ecofeminism?
10. Why is ecofeminism anti-naturalist?

Karen J. Warren, "The Power and the Promise of Ecological Feminism," *Environmental Ethics,* Vol. 12, No. 2, Summer 1990, pp. 123–146. Some notes have been omitted.

11. What does Warren mean when she says that ecofeminism is a contextualist ethic?
12. What does Warren mean when she says that ecofeminism is pluralistic and inclusivistic?
13. What is the ecofeminist view of what it means to be human and to behave ethically?

Ecological feminism (ecofeminism) has begun to receive a fair amount of attention lately as an alternative feminism and environmental ethic. As I use the term in this paper, ecological feminism is the position that there are important connections—historical, experiential, symbolic, theoretical—between the domination of women and the domination of nature, an understanding of which is crucial to both feminism and environmental ethics. I argue that the promise and power of ecological feminism is that *it provides a distinctive framework both for reconceiving feminism and for developing an environmental ethic which takes seriously connections between the domination of women and the domination of nature.* I do so by discussing the nature of a feminist ethic and the ways in which ecofeminism provides a feminist and environmental ethic. I conclude that any feminist theory *and* any environmental ethic which fails to take seriously the twin and interconnected dominations of women and nature is at best incomplete and at worst simply inadequate.

FEMINISM, ECOLOGICAL FEMINISM, AND CONCEPTUAL FRAMEWORKS

Whatever else it is, feminism is at least the movement to end sexist oppression. It involves the elimination of any and all factors that contribute to the continued and systematic domination or subordination of women. While feminists disagree about the nature of and solutions to the subordination of women, all feminists agree that sexist oppression exists, is wrong, and must be abolished.

A "feminist issue" is any issue that contributes in some way to understanding the oppression of women. Equal rights, comparable pay for comparable work, and food production are feminist issues wherever and whenever an understanding of them contributes to an understanding of the continued exploitation or subjugation of women. . . .

Feminist philosophers claim that some of the most important feminist issues are *conceptual* ones: these issues concern how one conceptualizes such mainstay philosophical notions as reason and rationality, ethics, and what it is to be human. Ecofeminists extend this feminist philosophical concern to nature. They argue that, ultimately, some of the most important connections between the domination of women and the domination of nature are conceptual. To see this, consider the nature of conceptual frameworks.

A *conceptual framework* is a set of *basic* beliefs, values, attitudes, and assumptions which shape and reflect how one views oneself and one's world. It is a socially constructed lens through which we perceive ourselves and others. It is affected by such factors as gender, race, class, age, affectional orientation, nationality, and religious background.

Some conceptual frameworks are oppressive. An *oppressive conceptual framework* is one that explains, justifies, and maintains relationships of domination and subordination. When an oppressive conceptual framework is *patriarchal,* it explains, justifies, and maintains the subordination of women by men.

I have argued elsewhere that there are three significant features of oppressive conceptual frameworks: (1) value-hierarchical thinking, i.e., "up-down" thinking which places higher value, status, or prestige on what is "up" rather than on what is "down"; (2) value dualisms, i.e., disjunctive pairs in which the disjuncts are seen as oppositional (rather than as complementary) and exclusive (rather than as inclusive), and which place higher value (status, prestige) on one disjunct rather than the other (e.g., dualisms which give higher value or status to that which has historically been identified as "mind," "reason," and "male" than to that which has been historically identified as "body," "emotion," and "female"); and (3) logic of domination, i.e., a structure of argumentation which leads to a justification of subordination.

The third feature of oppressive conceptual frameworks is the most significant. A logic of domination is not *just* a logical structure. It also involves a substantive value system, since an ethical premise is needed to permit or sanction the "just" subordination of that which is subordinate. This justification typically is given on grounds of some alleged characteristic (e.g., rationality) which the dominant (e.g., men) have and the subordinate (e.g., women) lack. . . .

For ecofeminism, that a logic of domination is explanatorily basic is important for at least three reasons. First, without a logic of domination, a description of similarities and differences would be just that—a description of similarities and differences. Consider the claim, "Humans are different from plants and rocks in that humans can (and plants and rocks cannot) consciously and radically reshape the communities in which they live; humans are similar to plants and rocks in that they are both members of an ecological community." Even if humans are "better" than plants and rocks with respect to the conscious ability of humans to radically transform communities, one does not *thereby* get any *morally* relevant distinction between humans and nonhumans, or an argument for the domination of plants and rocks by humans. To get *those* conclusions one needs to add at least two powerful assumptions, viz., (A2) and (A4) in argument A below:

(A1) Humans do, and plants and rocks do not, have the capacity to consciously and radically change the community in which they live.

(A2) Whatever has the capacity to consciously and radically change the community in which it lives is morally superior to whatever lacks this capacity.

(A3) Thus, humans are morally superior to plants and rocks.

(A4) For any X and Y, if X is morally superior to Y, then X is morally justified in subordinating Y.

(A5) Thus, humans are morally justified in subordinating plants and rocks.

Without the two assumptions that *humans are morally superior* to (at least some) nonhumans, (A2), and that *superiority justifies subordination,* (A4), all one has is some difference between humans and some nonhumans. This is true *even if* that difference is given in terms of superiority. Thus, it is the logic of domination, (A4), which is the bottom line in ecofeminist discussions of oppression.

Second, ecofeminists argue that, at least in Western societies, the oppressive conceptual framework which sanctions the twin dominations of women and nature is a patriarchal one characterized by all three features of an oppressive conceptual framework. Many ecofeminists claim that, historically, within at least the dominant Western culture, a patriarchal conceptual framework has sanctioned the following argument B:

(B1) Women are identified with nature and the realm of the physical; men are identified with the "human" and the realm of the mental.

(B2) Whatever is identified with nature and the realm of the physical is inferior to ("below") whatever is identified with the "human" and the realm of the mental; or, conversely, the latter is superior to ("above") the former.

(B3) Thus, women are inferior to ("below") men; or, conversly, men are superior to ("above") women.

(B4) For any X and Y, if X is superior to Y, then X is justified in subordinating Y.

(B5) Thus, men are justified in subordinating women.

If sound, argument B establishes *patriarchy,* i.e., the conclusion given at (B5) that the systematic domination of women by men is justified. But according to ecofeminists, (B5) is justified by just those three features of an oppressive conceptual framework identified earlier: value-hierarchical thinking, the assumption at (B2); value dualisms, the assumed dualism of the mental and the physical at (B1) and the assumed inferiority of the physical vis-à-vis the mental at (B2); and a logic of domination, the assumption at (B4), the same as the previous premise (A4). . . .

Ecofeminists insist that the sort of logic of domination used to justify the domination of humans by gender, racial or ethnic, or class status is also used to justify the domination of nature. Because eliminating a logic of domination is part of a feminist critique—whether a critique of patriarchy, white supremacist culture, or imperialism—ecofeminists insist that *naturism* is properly viewed as an integral part of any feminist solidarity movement to end sexist oppression and the logic of domination which conceptually grounds it.

CLIMBING FROM ECOFEMINISM TO ENVIRONMENTAL ETHICS

Many feminists and some environmental ethicists have begun to explore the use of first-person narrative as a way of raising philosophically germane issues in ethics often lost or underplayed in mainstream philosophical ethics. Why is this so? What is it about narrative which makes it a significant resource for theory and practice in feminism and environmental ethics? . . .

Consider the following first-person narrative about rock climbing:

> For my very first rock climbing experience, I chose a somewhat private spot, away from other climbers and on-lookers. After studying "the chimney," I focused all my energy on making it to the top. I climbed with intense determination, using whatever strength and skills I had to accomplish this challenging feat. By midway I was exhausted and anxious. . . . I was determined to make it to the top. With renewed confidence and concentration, I finished the climb to the top.
>
> On my second day of climbing, I rappelled down about 200 feet from the top of the Palisades at Lake Superior to just a few feet above the water level. I could see no one—not my belayer, not the other climbers, no one. I unhooked slowly from the rappel rope and took a deep cleansing breath. I looked all around me—really looked—and listened. I heard a cacophony of voices—birds, trickles of water on the rock before me, waves lapping against the rocks below. I closed my eyes and began to feel the rock with my hands—the cracks and crannies, the raised lichen and mosses, the almost imperceptible nubs that might provide a resting place for my fingers and toes when I began to climb. At that moment I was bathed in serenity. I began to talk to the rock in an almost inaudible, child-like way, as if the rock were my friend. I felt an overwhelming sense of gratitude for what it offered me—a chance to know myself and the rock differently, to appreciate unforeseen miracles like the tiny flowers growing in the even tinier cracks in the rock's surface, and to come to know a sense of *being in relationship* with the natural environment. It felt as if the rock and I were silent conversational partners in a longstanding friendship. I realized then that I had come to care about this cliff which was so different from me, so unmovable and invincible, independent and seemingly indifferent to my presence. I wanted to be with the rock as I climbed. Gone was the determination to conquer the rock, to forcefully impose my will on it; I wanted simply to work respectfully with the rock as I climbed. And as I climbed, that is what I felt. I felt myself *caring* for this rock and feeling thankful that climbing provided the opportunity for me to know it and myself in this new way.

There are at least four reasons why use of such a first-person narrative is important to feminism and environmental ethics. First, such a narrative gives voice to a felt sensitivity often lacking in traditional analytical ethical discourse, viz., a sensitivity to conceiving of oneself as fundamentally "in relationship with" others, including the nonhuman environment. It is a modality which *takes relationships themselves seriously.* It thereby stands in contrast to a strictly reductionist modality that takes relationships seriously only or primarily because of the nature of the *relators* or parties to those relationships (e.g., relators conceived as moral agents, right holders, interest carriers, or sentient beings). . . .

Second, such a first-person narrative gives expression to a variety of ethical attitudes and behaviors often overlooked or underplayed in mainstream Western ethics, e.g., the difference in attitudes and behaviors toward a rock when one is "making it to the top" and when one thinks of oneself as "friends with" or "caring about" the rock one climbs. These different attitudes and behaviors suggest an ethically germane contrast between two different types of relationship humans or climbers may have toward a rock: an imposed conqueror-type relationship, and an emergent caring-type relationship. This contrast grows out of, and is faithful to, felt, lived experience.

The difference between conquering and caring attitudes and behavior in relation to the natural environment provides a third reason why the use of first-person narrative is important to feminism and environmental ethics: it provides a way of conceiving of ethics and ethical meaning as *emerging out of* particular situations moral agents find themselves in, rather than as being *imposed on* those situations (e.g., as a derivation or instantiation of some predetermined abstract principle or rule). . . . As a reflection of and on felt, lived experiences, the use of narrative in ethics provides a stance from which ethical discourse can be held accountable to the historical, material, and social realities in which moral subjects find themselves.

Lastly, and for our purposes perhaps most importantly, the use of narrative has argumentative significance. . . . Narrative has argumentative force by suggesting *what counts* as an appropriate conclusion to an ethical situation. One ethical conclusion suggested by the climbing narrative is that what counts as a proper ethical attitude toward mountains and rocks is an attitude of respect and care (whatever that turns out to be or involve), not one of domination and conquest.

In an essay entitled "In and Out of Harm's Way: Arrogance and Love," feminist philosopher Marilyn Frye distinguishes between "arrogant" and "loving" perception as one way of getting at this difference in the ethical attitudes of care and conquest.[1] Frye writes:

> The loving eye is a contrary of the arrogant eye.
>
> The loving eye knows the independence of the other. It is the eye of a seer who knows that nature is indifferent. It is the eye of one who knows that to know the seen, one must consult something other than one's own will and interests and fears and imagination. One must look at the thing. One must look and listen and check and question.
>
> . . . The loving eye does not make the object of perception into something edible, does not try to assimilate it, does not reduce it to the size of the seer's desire, fear and imagination, and hence does not have to simplify. It knows the complexity of the other as something which will forever present new things to be known. The science of the loving eye presuppose[s] The Endless Interestingness of the Universe.[2]

. . . An ecofeminist perspective about both women and nature involves this shift in attitude from "arrogant perception" to "loving perception" of the nonhuman world. Arrogant perception of nonhumans by humans presupposes and maintains *sameness* in such a way that it expands the moral community to those beings who are thought to resemble (be like, similar to, or the same as) humans in some morally significant way. Any environmental movement or ethic based on arrogant perception builds a moral hierarchy of beings and assumes some common denominator of moral considerability in virtue of which like beings deserve similar treatment or moral consideration and unlike beings do not. Such environmental ethics are or generate a "unity in sameness." In contrast, "loving perception" presupposes and maintains *difference*—a distinction between the self and other, between human and at least some nonhumans—in such a way that perception of the other as other *is* an expression of love for one who/which is recognized at the outset as independent, dissimilar, different. . . .

"Loving perception" of the nonhuman natural world is an attempt to understand what it means *for humans* to care about the nonhuman world, a world *acknowledged* as being independent, different, perhaps even indifferent to humans. Humans *are* different from rocks in important ways, even if they are also both members of some ecological community. A moral community based on loving perception of oneself *in relationship with* a rock, or with the natural environment as a whole, is one which acknowledges and respects difference, whatever "sameness" also exists. . . .

ECOFEMINISM AS A FEMINIST AND ENVIRONMENTAL ETHIC

A feminist ethic involves a twofold commitment to critique male bias in ethics wherever it occurs, and to develop ethics which are not male-biased. Sometimes this involves articulation of values (e.g., values of care, appropriate trust, kinship, friendship) often lost or underplayed in mainstream ethics. Sometimes it involves engaging in theory building by pioneering in new directions or by revamping old theories in gender sensitive ways. What makes the critique of old theories or conceptualizations of new ones "feminist" is that they emerge out of sex-gender analyses and reflect whatever those analyses reveal about gendered experience and gendered social reality.

. . . It is a feminism that critiques male-bias wherever it occurs in ethics (including environmental ethics) and aims at providing an ethic (including an environmental ethic) which is not male biased—and it does so in a way that satisfies the preliminary boundary conditions of a feminist ethic.

First, ecofeminism is quintessentially anti-naturist. Its anti-naturism consists in the rejection of any way of thinking about or acting toward nonhuman nature that reflects a logic, values, or attitude of domination. Its anti-naturist, anti-sexist, anti-racist, anti-classist (and so forth, for all other "isms" of social domination) stance forms the outer boundary of the quilt: nothing gets on the quilt which is naturist, sexist, racist, classist, and so forth.

Second, ecofeminism is a contextualist ethic. It involves a shift *from* a conception of ethics as primarily a matter of rights, rules, or principles predetermined and applied in specific cases to entities viewed as competitors in the contest of moral standing, *to* a conception of ethics as growing out of . . . relationships conceived in some sense as defining who one is. . . .

For an ecofeminist, *how* a moral agent is in relationship to another becomes of central significance, not simply *that* a moral agent is a moral agent or is bound by rights, duties, virtue, or utility to act in a certain way.

Third, ecofeminism is structurally pluralistic in that it presupposes and maintains difference—difference among humans as well as between humans and at least some elements of nonhuman nature. Thus, while ecofeminism denies the "nature/culture" split, it affirms that humans are both members of an ecological community (in some respects) and different from it (in other respects). Ecofeminism's attention to relationships and community is not, therefore, an erasure of difference but a respectful acknowledgment of it.

Fourth, ecofeminism reconceives theory as theory in process. It focuses on patterns of meaning which emerge, for instance, from the storytelling and first-person narratives of women (and others) who deplore the twin dominations of women and nature. The use of narrative is one way to ensure that the content of the ethic—the pattern of the quilt—may/will change over time, as the historical and material realities of women's lives change and as more is learned about women-nature connections and the destruction of the nonhuman world.

Fifth, ecofeminism is inclusivist. It emerges from the voices of women who experience the harmful domination of nature and the way that domination is tied to their domination as women. It emerges from listening to the voices of indigenous peoples such as Native Americans who have been dislocated from their land and have witnessed the attendant undermining of such values as appropriate reciprocity, sharing, and kinship that characterize traditional Indian culture. It emerges from listening to voices of those who, like Nathan Hare, critique traditional approaches to environmental ethics as white and bourgeois, and as failing to address issues of "black ecology" and the "ecology" of the inner city and urban spaces.[3] . . .

Sixth, as a feminism, ecofeminism makes no attempt to provide an "objective" point of view. It is a social ecology. It recognizes the twin dominations of women and nature as social problems rooted both in very concrete, historical, socioeconomic circumstances and in oppressive patriarchal conceptual frameworks which maintain and sanction these circumstances.

Seventh, ecofeminism makes a central place for values of care, love, friendship, trust, and appropriate reciprocity—values that presuppose that our relationships to others are central to our understanding of who we are. . . .

Lastly, an ecofeminist ethic involves a reconception of what it means to be human, and in what human ethical behavior consists. Ecofeminism denies abstract individualism. Humans are who we are in large part by virtue of the historical and social contexts and the relationships we are in, including our relationships with nonhuman nature. . . .

By making visible the interconnections among the dominations of women and nature, ecofeminism shows that both are feminist issues and that explicit acknowledgement of both is vital to any responsible environmental ethic. Feminism *must* embrace ecological feminism if it is to end the domination of women because the domination of women is tied conceptually and historically to the domination of nature.

NOTES

1. Marilyn Frye, "In and Out of Harm's Way: Arrogance and Love," *The Politics of Reality* (Trumansburg, New York: The Crossing Press, 1983), pp. 66–72.
2. Ibid., pp. 75–76.
3. Nathan Hare, "Black Ecology," in *Environmental Ethics,* ed. K. S. Shrader-Frechette (Pacific Grove, Calif.: Boxwood Press, 1981), pp. 229–36.

Discussion Questions

1. Analyze Warren's argument that a logic of domination justifies the oppression of both women and nature. For example, are her premises acceptable? Has she left out any important premises? Does her conclusion logically follow from her premises?
2. Discuss Warren's claim that being a feminist entails being an ecofeminist. How might Leopold and Cohen each respond to this claim?
3. Care ethicist Nel Noddings, in her article at the end of Chapter 1, maintains that we cannot have meaningful caring relationships with nonhuman animals or the environment. How might Warren respond to Noddings? Discuss which person presents the more compelling argument and why.
4. Using the first-person narrative, describe a recent experience you had in the "outdoors." Does the use of the narrative make you aware, or more aware, of your relationship with the environment? Discuss some of the philosophical and ethical issues raised by your narrative.
5. Compare and contrast Warren's concept of naturism with Singer's concept of speciesism. Is naturism a logical extension of speciesism? Discuss how both Warren and Singer might respond to this question.
6. Some ecofeminists criticize deep ecology as being patriarchal or embodying masculine egoism.[38] Do you agree? Support your answer.

CASE STUDIES

1. ANIMAL LIBERATION IN THE SCIENCE LAB

Founded in England in the mid-1970s, the Animal Liberation Front (ALF) is a loose organization of radical animal-rights activists who target science laboratories, slaughterhouses, and the fur industry. On May 24, 1984, five members of the ALF broke into the Experimental Head Injury Lab at the University of Pennsylvania and stole files and videotapes of experiments done in the lab. The videotapes showed gruesome scenes of terrified baboons in vises with their heads being smashed by pistons while the researchers joked around. Operations were shown being performed on primates without regard for their pain or for standard research procedures. After taking the videotapes, the ALF ransacked the lab.

In the controversy that followed the release of the tapes to the public, Dr. Thomas Gennarelli, the director of the lab, defended the research, claiming that the animals had been properly treated. He also accused the ALF of setting back medical research. Both the university and the National Institutes of Health (NIH), which gave the lab a new grant to repair the damage, supported Dr. Gennarelli.

The ALF responded to the accusation by comparing the lab experiments to those conducted by Nazi Dr. Joseph Mengele on Jews in concentration camps. Protesters supported the ALF by staging demonstrations on campuses and at the offices of the NIH. In 1985 the secretary of Health and Human Services stopped federal funding for the head injury program. The university also agreed to pay a fine for violating the Animal Welfare Act and promised to pay more attention to the welfare of the animals used in experiments. The members of the ALF were not prosecuted for their actions.

Discussion Questions

1. Were stealing the tapes and ransacking the lab morally justified? Should the ALF have been punished for its actions? Support your answers. Discuss how a utilitarian, such as Peter Singer, might respond to these questions.
2. Morally speaking, does it make a difference, because of their similarity to humans, that primates were used in the experiments? Support your answer. Discuss how both Singer and Cohen would respond to this question.
3. Discuss how an abolitionist, a reformist, and a status quo person would respond to this case. What solutions would each of them most likely propose?
4. Would the experiments have been morally justified if Dr. Gennarelli had not violated that Animal Welfare Act and if it could be shown that thousands of human lives have been saved as a result of these experiments? Support your answer.
5. Discuss the analogy made by the ALF between Dr. Gennarelli and Dr. Mengele.
6. During the 1993 Christmas season, the ALF protested the selling of furs by planting battery-and-paper-bag incendiary devices in three large Chicago department stores. Although no one was hurt, the FBI reported that it was considering classifying the ALF along with dozens of other animal-rights groups as terrorist organizations. Is the ALF a terrorist organization? Do you agree with the ALF that the selling and wearing of fur and leather clothing is immoral? If so, do clerks employed in stores that sell fur and leather have a moral obligation to protest this practice? Support your answers.

7. The Animal Rights Direct Action Coalition has targeted MacDonald's restaurants. They drive up to a MacDonald's in a pickup truck with a dead cow in the back and a sign reading "Here's your lunch." Discuss the moral implications of these tactics.

---

2. USING ANIMALS FOR XENOTRANSPLANTS

In 2001 there were over 77,000 people in the United States waiting for organ transplants, according to the United Network for Organ Sharing, which oversees organ donations. Of this number about 50,000 are waiting for kidney transplants and another 18,000 for liver transplants. In contrast, in 2001 there were less than 12,000 donors, including in roughly even numbers cadavers and live donors.[39] Consequently, most people awaiting an organ transplant will die before a suitable donor is found. Xenotransplants, the transplanting of organs from one species of animal into another, may offer a solution to this shortage.

The first animal-to-human transplant occurred in 1906, when French physician Mathieu Jaboulay transplanted a kidney from a pig into a woman. Neither the woman nor the pig survived the procedure. Since then several people have received organs from pigs and baboons. Although baboons are genetically closer to humans, many researchers prefer pigs for xenotransplants because pigs are anatomically very similar to humans. They are also healthier, less likely to carry viruses, and easier to breed. At Duke University scientists are genetically engineering pigs with human genes so that their livers will be more compatible with humans.

In 1995 researchers at the University of California at San Francisco injected an AIDS patient with baboon bone marrow. Because baboons are resistant to HIV, it was hoped that the bone marrow would provide a replacement for the patient's damaged immune system. Earlier that year, doctors at Lahey Hitchcock Medical Center in Massachusetts injected cells from fetal pig brains into patients with Parkinson's disease.

In 2001 the Secretary's Advisory Committee on Xenotransplantation (SACX) was formed to advise the U.S. Department of Health and Human Services. Since other animals, such as pigs, carry viruses that are harmless to them but might be lethal to humans, one concern is the risk of inadvertently introducing an infectious disease via a xenotransplant. Another issue of concern is using children in xenotransplant experiments.

Discussion Questions

1. Although many people have ethical qualms about using baboons for xenotransplants, because of their similarity to humans, they have fewer objections to using pigs because pigs are already slaughtered for food. Is the fact that pigs are slaughtered for food morally relevant? Is the fact that pigs are not primates morally relevant, or are we being speciesists in making such a distinction? Support your answers.
2. At what point do animals genetically engineered to have human genes become human, and, as such, deserving of the moral respect we normally give other humans? Support your answer. Discuss how Cohen might respond to this question.
3. Xenotransplants raise the possibility of outbreaks of new infectious diseases. Retroviruses that may be harmless in other species can be potentially deadly in humans. For example, many researchers believe that AIDS was transmitted to humans from

monkeys. If xenotransplants might endanger healthy human populations, should they be banned or more closely regulated? Does the possibility of contracting a disease from another species weaken the anthropocentric argument that humans are a special creation? Support your answers.
4. Weigh the rights, if any, of nonhuman animals such as pigs and baboons against those of humans who need organ transplants. Is it morally acceptable to sacrifice the lives of other animals for humans whose organs have been damaged by their destructive lifestyles, such as heavy drinking or smoking? Support your answer. Discuss how Cohen and Singer might respond to this question.
5. Discuss the pros and cons of using infants and children who need transplants in xenotransplant experiments.

---

3. BRITAIN SAYS "TALLY-NO" TO FOX HUNTING

One of the most colorful images of rural England is the hunters in scarlet-and-black jackets riding through the green patchwork countryside, accompanied by their packs of hounds in pursuit of the elusive fox. All this may soon come to an end. In November 1997 the British Parliament voted overwhelmingly to ban fox and deer hunting with dogs. Under the bill, hunters and people who allow hunting with dogs on their land would be liable to maximum sentences of six months and fines of up to $8,400. The bill is currently being challenged by hunting organizations and legislators.[40]

Labour Party lawmaker Mike Foster, who sponsored the bill, said that the intention of the bill is "to protect wild mammals from cruelty and from the unnecessary pain and suffering inflicted in the name of a so-called sport." Although Foster acknowledges that foxes can be a nuisance, he says that hunting them down in this manner is not the answer.

Those who protest the ban argue that it will bring about the end of twenty-seven thousand rural jobs, such as for gamekeepers and saddle makers, as well as destruction of the twenty thousand hounds that are used for hunting. They also point out that much of England's unique patchwork countryside, with its hedges and woodlands, is maintained specifically for field sports.

Discussion Questions

1. Fox hunting has long had its critics in England. In the 1890s playwright Oscar Wilde called it "the unspeakable in full pursuit of the uneatable." Are fox hunting and other types of hunting justified if it is done for food?
2. Sir Brian Mawhinner, a conservative lawmaker who opposes the ban, argues that "the freedom of the individual to hunt with hounds is no different in principle from the freedom of each individual to or not to: fish, shoot, eat meat, use tobacco, drink, gamble or worship, as he or she chooses." Analyze Mawhinner's argument.
3. Supporters of fox and deer hunting argue that bans are an unjustified restriction on their freedom, because foxes and deer are not part of the social contract. People have the right to pursue their lifestyle activities without hindrance from the government so long as those activities do not restrict the personal freedom of or cause harm to another member of society. Opponents of hunting must show that hunting is contrary to the public interest or that it interferes with the freedom of other members of

society. Antihunting legislation does not meet these requirements and, hence, is a violation of human rights. Do you agree with this argument? Support your answer. Discuss how both Narveson and Regan might respond to the social contract argument for hunting.

4. Tory lawmaker John Gummer argues that the ban on hunting violates that "predatory chain" of nature. "The fox has its own animals which it is a predator of, but we are the predator upon the fox, and we need, therefore, within that predatory chain, to carry out our role."[41] Discuss the merits of Gummer's argument.
5. Fox hunting with hounds is also practiced in Australia, New Zealand, Italy, Portugal, and the United States. In the United States and Australia, hunters pursue foxes but usually do not kill them. Is fox hunting morally justified so long as the fox isn't killed? Discuss how a utilitarian might respond to this question.
6. Oregon was recently outlawed for being inhumane by using dogs to track and tree cougars which are then shot at close range. With more cougar habitat being lost to development and agriculture every year, this has resulted in increased conflicts with humans as more cougars are roaming into residential areas. Do you agree with Oregon voters that sport-hunting tactics that put the animal at such an unfair disadvantage are inhumane? Is it morally justifiable to shoot cougars for killing livestock? For "trespassing" into residential areas? Support your answers.

---

4. THE ABANDONED CAT[42]

David had always wanted a cat but couldn't have one because his father was allergic to them. Although pets were forbidden in his dormitory, shortly after he moved to college David went to the local animal shelter and adopted a young cat which he kept confined in his room. At the end of the year, David moved back home and left the cat to fend for herself.

After several weeks of wandering around campus, the cat was taken in by one of the department secretaries, who took pity on it. By this time the cat was near starvation; she also had a rash that had caused her to lose much of her fur. The secretary knew that one of the professors in the department, Professor Carey, was thinking of getting a cat. Professor Carey agreed to take the cat home.

After the cat's rash did not clear up, Professor Carey took her to the veterinarian. The vet told the professor that the cat had multiple allergies and would have to receive cortisone shots as well as eat a special diet. In addition, the cat had an overactive thyroid that would require an expensive operation or else medication for the rest of her life. The medication would cost approximately $30 a month and would have to be given to the cat three times a day at six-hour intervals. After thinking about it, Professor Carey decided that the expense and inconvenience was not worth it. She asked the veterinarian to euthanize the cat.

Discussion Questions

1. What are the professor's moral obligations, if any, toward the cat? Support your answer.
2. Is it morally acceptable to euthanize the cat? Or does the cat's interest in staying alive outweigh the professor's inconvenience? Are there any conditions under which it is

morally acceptable to have an animal companion euthanized? Support your answers. Discuss how Narveson, Cohen, and Singer might respond to this question.

3. About seventy thousand kittens and puppies are born each day in the United States. More than 70 percent of people who adopt them end up giving them away, abandoning them, or giving them to shelters. More than half of these animals—about 17 million annually—are destroyed.[43] Do dogs and cats have a right to have kittens and puppies? Or, given these statistics, is it morally irresponsible for humans to allow cats and dogs in their care to breed? Support your answers.
4. Was it morally acceptable for David to adopt a cat from the animal shelter, knowing that it was against the rules to keep a cat in the dormitory and knowing that he could not take her home with him once the school year ended? Did he have a moral obligation to find another home for the cat when he moved out of the dormitory? Support your answers.
5. Some animal-rights activists, such as Regan, argue that owning house pets (animals that are kept inside or allowed outside only on a leash or in an enclosure) is a type of slavery. Do you agree? Can having a pet or animal companion be compatible with respect? Support your answers.
6. A lot of animal shelters do not allow college students to adopt cats and dogs. Is this policy a violation of the autonomy of college students? Support your answer.

---

5. ZOOS: PRISONS OR HAVENS?

Zoos are a relatively new phenomenon. The first modern zoos were established in Europe in the nineteenth century. Britain's famous London Zoo was opened in the nineteenth century to house the collection of animals brought back from the British colonies around the world.

In the early 1990s, the London Zoo became mired in a financial crisis because of the mismanagement of funds and a steady drop in attendance. Like other zoos around the world, it had also been under attack by animal-rights activists. One of these groups, Zoo Check, wanted to see zoos closed and the money used for conservation instead.

In 1993 it was announced that the London Zoo would have to close down. A high-profile "Save Our Zoo" campaign, however, raised enough money to keep the zoo going. Supporters of the zoo argued that zoos are often the first contact young people have with "wild animals." They also pointed out the important role that the London Zoo plays in educating people about conservation and in saving endangered species.

Opponents responded by pointing out that watching captive and anguished animals is hardly a good introduction. The use of documentaries of animals in their natural habitat is a more realistic way to educate young people about other animals. They also argued that conservation, including the preservation of endangered species, should take place within the animals' natural habitats. According to Wills Travers of Zoo Check, as many black rhinos in zoo-based captive breeding programs die as are bred.

Discussion Questions

1. Are zoos ever morally justified? If so, under what conditions? What about safari parks, such as Six Flags or Disney's Animal Kingdom, where animals roam free, within limits, and the people remain in their cars? Support your answers.

2. While it may be possible to protect some of these species, such as the black rhino, within their natural habitats, in other cases the habitats have been destroyed by human encroachment. The destruction of the rain forests in Central and South America for agricultural land has already resulted in the extinction of hundreds of species of animals. Does the preservation of endangered species, in these cases, morally justify the continuation of zoos as a means of preserving endangered species? Support your answer. Discuss how Leopold, Devall, and Sessions might each respond to this question.
3. Discuss the institution of zoos in light of Warren's ecofeminist analysis. What would Warren's position on zoos most likely be? In what ways, if any, do zoos, and the continued justification of zoos, illustrate a dualistic, patriarchal ideology? Compare and contrast the institution of zoos to other patriarchal institutions such as colonialism, slavery, sexism, and meat-eating.

---

6. THE "BAMBI BOOM"

The Teneja family were on the way to the College of William and Mary where 19-year-old Baninder Teneja was starting a summer research project. As they exited Interstate 95 on a side trip to nearby Lake Anna, a panicked deer struck and careened off a van ahead of them and came crashing through their front window. Baninder, who was riding in the back seat, was fatally injured when she was struck by the decapitated head of the deer before it smashed through their back window.

This was just one of over four thousand vehicle/deer collisions that occurred in Virginia in 1999, up from six hundred in 1997. In Michigan the state police alone logged in 67,669 deer/vehicle collisions in 1999. According to the National Highway Traffic Safety Administration, there were 182 human fatalities from vehicle/deer collisions in 1998, up from 139 in 1996.[44]

The increase in vehicle/deer accidents is causing concern especially since the deer population in the United States is growing at an unprecedented rate. In many parts of the United States the deer population is two to four times what it was in pre-European times. This population explosion is due to a number of factors, including the milder winters we've had in the last decade and a decline in the number of natural predators such as the wolf.

Humans aren't the only ones being negatively impacted by the "Bambi boom." Some scientists predict that the deer population, if left unchecked, could lead to the catastrophic disintegration of certain biotic communities. Overbrowsing by deer not only damages their own habitat but reduces vegetation that butterflies and songbirds use. Their eating habits are also threatening plant species such as orchids and lilies and eastern hemlock and white cedar trees.

The use of an organic deer contraceptive has had only limited success. Fencing has also been unsuccessful. Many people feel that the only way to control the deer herds is through culling—hunting deer with the goal of thinning out the herds.

Discussion Questions

1. Many animal-rights activists oppose the use of hunting to control deer populations, arguing that hunting is inconsistent with the belief that other animals have inherent

worth. Do you agree? Discuss solutions that Singer and Regan might suggest to the Bambi boom.

2. Discuss how a utilitarian might approach the problem of the growing deer population. Are you satisfied with this solution? Support your answer.
3. Aldo Leopold supported the "harvesting" of deer herds to control their population. If what is right is defined in terms of preserving the "integrity, stability and beauty of the biotic community," would the land ethic also justify the culling of human populations where overpopulation is threatening the integrity of the biotic environment? Support your answer. Discuss how both Leopold and Watson might respond to this question.
4. Discuss how an ecofeminist, such as Karen Warren, might respond to the use of hunting to control the deer population.
5. Working in small groups, develop an ethical public policy for dealing with the Bambi boom.

---

7. BIOTECHNOLOGY AND AGRICULTURE

Biotechnology offers farmers increased food production and reduced unit costs. In particular, it may offer substantial benefits to developing countries in terms of reducing malnutrition, starvation, and poverty.

On the other hand, there are concerns about the safety of genetically modified (GM) food both for humans and the environment. There is the possibility of gene transfer to other closely related natural species through cross-pollination as well as through the buildup of resistance in insects and viruses to the insect-resistant and virus-resistant strains of GM crops. This could prove disastrous to naturally occurring plants. The pollen of genetically engineered plants might also be harmful to species such as the Monarch butterfly.

So far the United States, with 72 percent of the world's GM plantings, is the primary user of GM crops. In 2002, in the United States 66 percent of the agricultural acreage planted was with GM crops, a 20-fold increase in the acreage since 1996. The only other country that has more than 10 percent of its acreage planted with GM crops is Argentina at 33 percent.[45]

There is strong opposition to GM food in the European Union, which has placed severe restrictions on the use of GM crops and imports from the United States containing GM food products. In Asia, only China has significant areas planted with GM crops. India has not approved the use of any GM crops. In Thailand research programs are looking at conventional breeding, rather than using GM seeds, as a way to develop desirable new crop varieties from their own biodiversity.[46]

Discussion Questions

1. Biotechnology has been offered as a solution to increasing food needs in areas where population growth and urbanization have outstripped food production. Is this solution environmentally and morally sound? Discuss how an ecocentric environmental ethicist might respond to this proposed solution.

2. There is concern that biotechnology advances in food production may create a sort of "scientific apartheid" in which the rich countries have access to technological advances that are not available in poorer countries. Discuss this concern from a justice perspective.
3. Genetic engineering is already used in animal agribusiness. In the United States, pigs are bred with an extra human growth hormone. Broiler chickens now grow so fast that their legs can't support their own body weight. Cows are being bred to produce more milk as well as milk that contains therapeutic drugs for human use. These biological alterations place great stress on the animal's bodies. Is it morally acceptable to genetically alter other animals to increase their utility for human consumption? Support your answer. Discuss how both Narveson and Warren might respond to this question.
4. Are genetically modified foods "unnatural"? What criteria should we use to draw the line between what is "natural" and what is "unnatural"? If humans are technologists by nature, should the products of our technology be considered part of the natural world, just as modifications to the environment by animals such as beaver, oak trees, or volcanoes are considered natural? Support your answers. Discuss how Watson and Devall and Sessions might answer these questions.

---

8. ANTARCTICA: PRESERVING PRISTINE NATURE

Antarctica has been called "the world's most pristine environment."[47] And it's no wonder it has remained untouched by human activities for so long. With temperatures as low as 100 degrees below zero, the climate here is so hostile that life—tiny microbes/organisms—take refuge inside the pores of the ancient rock merely inches below the surface where they are safe.

In 1959 twelve nations signed a treaty agreeing to reserve the area south of latitude 60°S just above the Antarctic Circle for peaceful scientific purposes. By 1984 there were thirty-three full-time bases with a population of five thousand in summer and seven hundred who wintered over. In 1985 thirty-two nations agreed to limit access of humans to Antarctica to specific research sites.

Despite the bleak climate and restrictions on their travel, Antarctica is fast becoming a fashionable tourist destination, at least for those who can afford to pay the up to $25,000 for a tour. In 1999–2000, 13,370 tourists visited the continent; 3,500 people visit America's McMurdo Station each year.

Environmentalists are concerned about the effect of humans on Antarctica's unique ecology. Adélie penguins, who are not used to looking upwards, fall over backwards when airplanes fly overhead. The delicate Antarctic lichens, which are only a few millimeters thick, can be destroyed by one carelessly placed boot. While some want to limit tourism, others propose more radical solutions. Scott Base staffer Lana Hastie says that no humans should be allowed in Antarctica; instead, it should be left the way it is.

Discussion Questions

1. The high cost of a tour to Antarctica makes it prohibitive for all but the rich. Given deep ecology's directive that we ought to cultivate a sense of identification and interconnectedness with nature, is it fair that only the rich can visit the most pristine area of nature in the world? Isn't this limiting the nonaffluent's chance for self-realization?

On the other hand, if we make Antarctica and other pristine wilderness areas more accessible to everyone, will we destroy the very reason for visiting them in the first place? Support your answers. Discuss how deep ecologists Devall and Sessions would respond to these questions.

2. Discuss Hastie's proposal that all human visitation, including scientific expeditions and tourism, be stopped. Is the fact that humans are not, as far as we know, native to Antarctica morally relevant? Should migration of other species to new areas be halted as well? Is Hastie's argument consistent with evolutionary theory, or is Hastie adopting an anthropocentric view that places humans outside of nature? Support your answers. Discuss how Watson might answer these questions.
3. Humans do not have to visit the Antarctic to alter its ecology. The ozone hole over the Antarctic is getting bigger each year. Do we have a moral obligation to preserve faraway environments? If so, is this obligation direct or indirect—that is, does our obligation stem from respect for the inherent value of the Antarctic biosphere or because of the indirect effects of global warming on humans? Support your answers.
4. The Antarctic is a massive storehouse of fresh water—containing over 70 percent of the earth's fresh water. Do icebergs have inherent moral worth or only instrumental worth? Discuss the moral implications of harvesting the icebergs for fresh water for human agriculture and drinking water.

9. EARTH'S DWINDLING FORESTS

People, like other animals, need to use nature in order to survive. We use trees for lumber to build our homes, the soil for growing crops, the earth as a source of minerals and energy. However, are there limits to how much we ought to use and, if so, what is the justification for these limits?

Most of the world's forests have been cleared by humans. Tropical rain forests have been bulldozed to create land for cattle grazing, mining operations, hydroelectric dams, and for growing export plants such as coffee. Destruction of the rain forest throughout the world has been implicated in the extinction, or threatened extinction, of thousands of species of animals and plants. In addition to destruction of wildlife habitat, the lifestyles as well as the lives of indigenous people living in the Amazon rain forests have been threatened by the clearing operations and by epidemics such as measles.

The rain forests are not the only forests that are being destroyed at an alarming rate. In the United States, the U.S. Forest Service has long regarded assisting the logging industry as one of its primary roles. There is little wilderness left in our national forests that is not crisscrossed with logging roads. With the exception of 34 million acres designated as wilderness, most accessible tracts of public forests have already been logged. In some cases the logging has threatened bird species with extinction and destroyed recreational areas, creating animosity between environmentalists, and businesses and workers whose livelihood depends on harvesting natural resources.

Discussion Questions

1. Discuss the prevailing attitude and practices regarding using natural resources in light of the ecofeminists concept of the logic of dominance. What policy might Warren suggest for the human use of rain forests and our national forests?

2. Americans drink one-third of the world's coffee.[48] Much of this coffee is grown on land that used to be rain forests. This is because coffee plants grown on bare land are much more productive than coffee plants that are shade-grown. However, some environmentalists are encouraging coffee drinkers to buy only shade-grown coffee, which does not require the destruction of surrounding trees, even though it is more expensive and harder to find at the stores. Discuss whether or not we have a moral obligation either to give up coffee drinking or to drink only shade-grown coffee.
3. Role-play a discussion between Warren and Watson on our current policy of allowing logging in national forests. Which person presents the strongest argument? Support your answer.
4. One of the primary reasons for clearing rain forests is to raise beef for the U.S. market. Discuss your moral obligation, if any, to modify your lifestyle in order to use fewer natural resources. If you do have such an obligation, what is the source of this moral obligation? Discuss how Regan, Narveson, Leopold, and Watson might each answer this question.

Glossary

abolitionists: In the debate over the consumption of animals, abolitionists believe that we should stop using animals altogether as a source of food and as tools in scientific experiments.

abortion: The intentional termination of a pregnancy resulting in the death of the fetus.

absolute pacifism: The belief that all violence is wrong including violence that is done in self-defense.

active euthanasia: Taking direct action to bring about a patient's death.

addiction: A behavioral pattern of drug use characterized by the compulsive use of a drug, the securing of its supply, and a high tendency to relapse after withdrawal.

addiction, disease model of: The theory that addicts are ill, and thus are biologically different from nonaddicts.

addiction, moral model of: The view that addiction is a vice in which individuals freely choose to engage, and that overcoming addiction depends on willpower.

adultery: Consensual sexual intercourse between a married person and someone who is not his or her legal spouse.

affirmative action: Programs designed to encourage increased representation of minorities and women in employment and college admissions.

agape: Unconditional love.

ahimsa: The Buddhist principle of nonhurting.

androgyny: The theory that men and women share the same nature and that the expression of this sameness is a desirable goal.

anthropocentrism: The belief that human beings are the central or most significant entities in the universe.

autonomy: Self-determination or the freedom to make one's own decisions.

beneficence, duty of: The duty to do good acts and to promote happiness.

binge drinking: The consumption of five or more drinks of alcohol in a short period of time.

capital punishment: *See death penalty.*

capitalism, laissez-faire: An economic system based on the pursuit of rational and prudent self-interest, individual freedom, and minimal government interference.

care ethics: The metaethical theory that caring relationships are more important than impartial moral principles such as justice.

categorical imperative: A term introduced by Immanuel Kant to describe moral injunctions that are unconditionally binding on us.

censorship: The controlling or silencing of speech that is deemed offensive, dangerous, or inappropriate by a government or group.

civil disobedience: The refusal, on moral grounds, to obey certain government laws, for the purpose of trying to bring about a change in legislation or government policy.

cloning: The process of producing genetically identical individuals through asexual reproduction.

cohabitation: Unmarried people living together as sexual intimates.

colonialism: The subjection of people in one country to the authority of another country.

color-blind principle: The belief that public policy should not be based on racial considerations.

common good: The idea that each individual member of a community has a moral duty to work to enhance the good of the entire community.

communism: The social theory that property and the means of production in a society should be held in common instead of by private individuals.

competency: In medical ethics, a patient who is rational and capable of making decisions about his or her own care.

conscientious objection: Opposition to war, in any form, based on moral or religious beliefs.

consequentialism: The ethical theory that the consequences of our actions are more important than our intentions.

conservatism: The position that the traditional state of affairs is the best and that there is no need for any alterations.

cultural relativism: A type of ethical relativism that maintains that morality is created collectively by groups of humans and that it differs from culture to culture.

death penalty: Infliction of death by the state as punishment for a crime.

deep ecology: A movement begun in the mid-1970s which cultivates a sense of identification with nature.

deontology: The ethical theory that duty is the basis of morality.

deterrence: In the death penalty debate, the argument that the more severe the punishment for a crime, the more other people are going to be discouraged or deterred from committing that crime.

discrimination: The treatment of others based on their group membership. Unjust discrimination is based on prejudice rather than relevant differences.

distributive justice: The duty to distribute the benefits and burdens of society in a fair manner.

divine command theory: The metaethical theory that something is moral merely because God approves of it.

doctrine of the mean: The doctrine, put forth by both Aristotle and Confucius, that moral virtues, in general, entail moderation or seeking the middle path between excess and deficit.

domestic violence: Violence among intimates or people living in the same household.

double effect, principle of: Principle that where a course of action is likely to have different effects, one morally desirable and the other not, it may be permissible to take that course as long as the desirable effect is intended but not the other.

doublethink: Simultaneously holding two contradictory views and believing both to be true.

drug abuse: Taking a drug for purposes other than those for which the drug was intended, and/or the illicit use of a drug which can cause physical and/or mental harm to oneself and/or others.

drugs: Chemicals that enter the bloodstream and predictably alter the way individuals feel.

ecocentrism: The view that humans are members, rather than conquerors, of the biotic community.

ecofeminism: A movement that links environmental ethics to feminism and animal rights, arguing that oppression of women, nonhuman animals, and nature are all grounded in the same logic of dominance.

ecology: The branch of biology dealing with the interdependent relationship between organisms and their environment.

eightfold path: In Buddhist philosophy the guidelines for leading a moral and virtuous life.

embryo: An unborn human between two weeks and eight weeks gestation.

environmental ethics: An ethic concerned with the moral basis of environmental responsibility, including the moral value of nonhuman nature, pollution, population control, food production, and preservation of the wilderness and species diversity.

equality, principle of: The principle that it is unjust to treat beings differently unless we can show that there is a difference between them that is relevant to the differential treatment.

erotic love: Sexual love.

erotica: Literature and art dealing with sexual love.

ethical relativism: The theory that morality is created by people and that moral systems can be different for different people.

ethical subjectivism: A type of ethical relativism that claims that morality is relative to each individual person.

ethnocentrism: The belief that one's ethnic or cultural group is morally superior.

eugenics: The science of improving the genetic quality of offspring.

euthanasia: The act of painlessly bringing about the death of a person who is suffering from a terminal or incurable disease or condition. *See also: active euthanasia, passive euthanasia, and physician-assisted suicide.*

extraordinary treatment: Medical treatment that provides no reasonable hope of benefiting a patient.

fallacy: An argument that is psychologically or emotionally persuasive but logically incorrect.

feminism: A broad movement that holds a commitment to improving women's position in society.

fetus: An unborn human between eight-weeks gestation, when all the organs are in place, and full-term.

fidelity, duty of: A moral duty that stems from a commitment or promise made in the past.

fighting words: Words that are inherently likely to provoke a violent reaction.

fornication: Consensual sexual intercourse between two unmarried adults.

freedom of speech: The individual right to express opinions without interference from the government or other people.

gay: A male homosexual.

gay gene: Preliminary research suggests that sexual orientation may be partially determined by genetics.

gender essentialism: The belief that men and women have essentially different natures.

genetic engineering: Alteration of genetic material by artificial means.

genetic enhancement: Manipulation of genetic material in order to improve a person's phenotype.

genetic therapy: Introduction of normal or desirable genes into cells to override deleterious genes. *See also: germ line therapy and somatic cell therapy.*

genome: Genetic blueprint or code containing a complete set of chromosomes.

genotype: The genetic blueprint of a particular individual.

germ cells: The ova (egg) and sperm cells.

germ line therapy: Genetic therapy that alters the genetic structure of the sperm and ova so that the genotype of future generations is also altered.

global warming: The increasing temperature of the earth over the past century due, at least in part, to the increase in air pollution.

globalization: The worldwide transmission of Western-style democracy and capitalism.

good will: A will that always acts from a sense of duty and reverence for moral law, without regard for consequences or for immediate inclinations.

gratitude: A duty based on past favors and unearned services.

habituation: A term used by Aristotle to describe the regular practice of virtuous behavior, much as one practices any other skill, until it becomes second nature.

harassment, sexual: Unwanted sexual attention that makes a person feel uncomfortable at work, school, or in social attentions.

hate crime: Criminal behavior that is motivated by hatred or bigotry against a particular group or community of individuals.

hate speech: Speech that is likely to provoke anger, alarm, or resentment in others on the basis of race, color, creed, religion, or gender.

heterosexism: The belief that heterosexuals are morally superior to homosexuals.

heterosexual: A person whose sexual attraction is exclusively, or almost exclusively, toward members of the opposite gender.

homophobia: Fear or hostility toward homosexuals, expressed or unexpressed.

homosexual: A person whose sexual attraction is exclusively, or almost exclusively, toward members of the same gender.

hospice: A setting for terminally ill patients that provides palliative care and companionship so they can live the last days of their lives as fully and painfree as possible.

Human Genome Project: A worldwide cooperative effort to map the entire human genetic code.

in vitro fertilization: Fertilization of an ovum by a sperm outside of the woman's body in a laboratory.

incapacitation: A punishment, such as the death penalty or life imprisonment without parole, which ensures that criminals will never repeat their crimes.

informed consent: Requirement that competent people, who are free to consent, be sufficiently informed to be the principle decision-maker in their own lives.

jihad: An Islamic term often taken to mean "holy war," but more broadly defined as an "effort."

just-war tradition: A framework of theories, guidelines, and beliefs regarding the question of what makes a war just.

justice, duty of: The duty to give each person equal consideration.

juvenile: In U.S. law a person under the age of eighteen.

legitimate interest: In rights ethics, interests that do not prevent others from pursuing similar and equally important interests.

lesbian: A female homosexual.

liberal feminism: The belief that men and women share a common nature and, consequently, that women can achieve liberation through equal access to opportunities and privileges enjoyed by men.

libertarian: A person who is opposed to social or political restraints on individual freedom.

liberty right: The right to be left alone to pursue one's legitimate interests without interference from the government or from others.

Manifest Destiny, doctrine of: The nineteenth-century doctrine that the United States had a divine right to expand its borders from coast to coast.

marginalization: The act of relegating beings or groups to the fringes or margins of the moral community.

Marxism: The doctrine that the dictatorship of the proletariat by the capitalists will eventually be superseded by a classless society.

McCarthyism: An atmosphere of distrust produced by Senator Joseph McCarthy when he used the free speech of individuals as evidence of their communist allegiances. His followers believed that communist ideas should be repressed in order to protect democratic values.

mercy, principle of: The principle based on the duty of

nonmaleficence that we have an obligation not to cause further pain and suffering and also to relieve pain and suffering.

metaethics: The subdivision of ethics concerned with appraising the logical foundations and internal consistencies of ethics systems. Also called theoretical ethics.

minimally decent Samaritan: Term used by Judith Jarvis Thomson to describe a person who subscribes to the minimal standard of decency required by morality.

moral community: The community of all beings who have moral worth in themselves and, as such, deserve the protection and respect of the community.

moral development, stage theory of: Theory that humans move through distinct stages of moral development from egoist to acceptance of universal moral values.

moral dilemma: A situation where there is a conflict between moral values such that no matter what solution is chosen, it will involve doing something that is wrong in order to do what is right.

morning after pill: A high dose of birth control pills taken over the three days following intercourse to prevent the blastocyst from implanting in the uterine wall.

multiculturalists: Individuals who believe that racism is based primarily on individual ignorance and that education can eliminate racism.

natural law ethics: The metaethical theory that morality is grounded in rational human nature.

natural rights ethics: The ethical theory that people's entitlements as members of society are the basis of ethics.

Noble Eightfold Path: *See: Eightfold Path.*

noncombatant: An individual who does not serve as an agent of aggression in war.

nonmaleficence, duty of: The duty to do no harm and to prevent harm.

normative ethics: The study of the values and guidelines by which we live.

objectivist theory: The metaethical theory that morality is discovered by humans and that universal moral truths exist that are true for all humans.

opinion: A statement that is based on feeling rather than on fact.

pacifism: An opposition to war or violence based on principle.

partial-birth abortion: Late-term form of abortion that involves partial delivery of a live fetus.

passive euthanasia: Withholding or withdrawing medical treatment, resulting in a patient's death.

paternalism: Relationship in which an authority, such as the government or a physician, overrides a person's own decision and decides what is best for that person in order to protect him or her.

patriarchy: Social organization in which men hold the positions of authority.

persistent vegetative state: Condition in which the cortical, or higher brain, function is absent due to a lack of oxygen, resulting in an irreversible coma.

persons: Beings who are worthy of respect as valuable in themselves rather than because of their usefulness or value to others; members of the moral community.

phenotype: The physical appearance or make-up of a particular individual.

physician-assisted suicide: A type of active euthanasia in which a physician assists a patient in bringing about his or her death.

political correctness: In academia, subscribing to particular views based on their popularity, rather than their truth, and the suppression of opposing views.

pornography: Material featuring actual or unmistakably immolated or unmistakably threatened violence presented in a sexually explicit fashion with a predominant focus on the sexually explicit violence.

prejudice: Personal judgment that is informed by negative feelings and stereotypes rather than reason.

prima facie duty: A duty that is morally binding unless it conflicts with a more pressing moral duty.

pro-choice: In the abortion debate, the position that a woman should have the right to make her own choice about whether or not to have an abortion at any time during the pregnancy.

pro-life: In the abortion debate, the position that abortion is immoral except when it is used to save the life of the mother.

proportionality: A principle of retributive justice in which the severity of the punishment must be proportionate to the crime.

race: A loose classification of groups of people based on physical characteristics; a social construct that forms an important component of personal identity.

racial profiling: The routine, and often unconscious, practice by police or other law enforcement agents of targeting suspects on the basis of their race or ethnicity.

racism: An ideology or worldview based on the belief that people can be classified based on race and that some races are morally inferior to others.

radical feminism: The theory that men are socialized to be both protectors and sexual predators, and that women are objectified by men as objects for sexual violence.

rape: Nonconsensual sex.

reciprocity, principle of: The moral principle in Confucian ethics that states that we have a moral duty to treat others as we would wish to be treated ourselves.

reductionism: The belief in science and medicine that the human body can be reduced to or described as an elaborate machine.

reparation, duty of: A duty that stems from past harms to others.

restitution: Reparation made by giving a person or group compensation for past harms.

retributive justice: The principle that punishment for wrongdoing should be in proportion to the crime.

retributivism: In the death penalty debate, the belief that those who violate other people's right to life by murdering them in turn forfeit their own right to life.

same-sex marriage: Marriage between two people of the same gender.

satyagraha: In the philosophy of Mohandas "Mahatma" Gandhi, *satyagraha* is the skill of nonviolent resistance.

selective abortion: Abortion performed because a particular fetus, rather than the pregnancy itself, is unwanted, usually because the fetus has a genetic defect or is the "wrong gender."

self-improvement, duty of: The duty to improve our knowledge and virtue.

sentient being: A being with the capacity to experience pain and pleasure.

sexism: The worldview or belief that women are morally inferior to men.

slippery slope argument: Argument that stresses the potentially harmful effects if a particular action is endorsed or undertaken.

social contract: Agreement among individuals to freely give up some of their liberties in exchange for living in a well-ordered and just society.

sociobiology: The branch of biology that applies evolutionary theory to the social sciences.

sociological relativism: The observation that there is disagreement among cultures regarding moral values. Unlike cultural relativism, sociological relativism is neither an argument nor a moral theory. It is merely a descriptive statement about societies.

somatic cell therapy: Genetic therapy in which a normal or desirable gene is introduced into cells to override the effects of deleterious genes. The genetic structure of the germ cells remains unchanged.

speciesism: A term coined by utilitarian Peter Singer to describe a prejudice or bias in favor of the interests of members of one's own species and against those of members of another species.

speech codes: Codes that place restrictions on some forms of speech, such as hate speech, fighting words, or speech that violates civility codes.

state of nature: In Hobbes's philosophy, the hypothetical condition in which people lived before the formation of civil states.

status quo: The existing state of affairs and social structure.

stewardship: Religious doctrine that God has given humans dominion or stewardship over the lives of other animals and the planet.

stimulants: Drugs such as cocaine, caffeine, nicotine, and prescription diet pills that enhance performance, provide alertness, and a sense of power.

supererogatory duty: A duty that exceeds the normal expectations of moral behavior.

surrogate motherhood: Arrangement whereby a woman agrees to gestate a child for another woman.

terrorism: The use of politically motivated violence that targets noncombatants and creates intimidation.

theoretical ethics: *See: metaethics.*

theory: A conceptual framework for explaining a set of facts or concepts.

third world: A term referring to non-industrial or developing nations.

toxicity test: Force-feeding or exposing animals to large quantities of a substance in order to determine the lethal dose at which a given percentage of animals die.

transgenic: Animals and plants with genes introduced from another species.

universalist theories: Metaethical theories that claim there are objective, universal moral principles and values that are true for all human beings.

utilitarianism: The metaethical theory that actions producing the most pleasure are good and those that produce pain are bad.

vegan: A person who abstains from all animal products including eggs and milk.

vegetarian: A person who refrains from eating the flesh of animals, although they may eat fish.

veil of ignorance: A conceptual device used by John Rawls to establish a social contract that is unbiased and based on impartiality.

viability: In the abortion debate, the capacity of the fetus to survive disconnection from the placenta.

vice: A character defect or disposition to act in a manner that harms oneself and others.

virtue: An admirable character trait or disposition to habitually act in a manner that benefits oneself and others.

virtue ethics: The metaethical theory concerned primarily with character and the type of people we should be rather than with our actions.

vivisection: Cutting or operating on a live animal for the sake of scientific research.

war: The use of armed violence between nations or between competing political factions within a nation to achieve a political purpose.

Way, the: In Eastern philosophy, the path of equilibrium and harmony.

weapons of mass destruction (WMD): Nuclear, chemical, and biological weapons. Unlike conventional weapons, WMD target both combatants and noncombatants.

welfare rights: The right to receive primary social goods such as adequate nutrition, housing, education, and police and fire protection.

xenograph: Cross-species tissue transplantation.

Endnotes

CHAPTER 1

1. *Obedience* is available on both film and video.
2. Stanley Milgram, *Obedience to Authority* (New York: Harper & Row, 1969), 6.
3. Elliot Turiel, Carolyn Hildebrandt, and Cecilia Wainryb, "Judging Social Issues: Difficulties, Inconsistencies, and Consistencies," *Monographs of the Society for Research in Child Development* 56, no. 2, 1991.
4. Lawrence Kohlberg, *The Philosophy of Moral Development* (New York: Harper & Row, 1981).
5. This is not to say that religious people are necessarily cultural relativists; many people who are religious believe that morality exists independently of religion; religious teachings confirm, rather than create, morality.
6. Stephen A. Satris, "Student Relativism," *Teaching Philosophy* 9, no. 3 (1986): 193–200.
7. Gontran de Poncins, *Kabloona* (New York: Reynal & Hitchcock, 1941).
8. Nancy L. Jacobs, Alison Landes, and Mark A. Siegd (eds.), *Capital Punishment—Cruel and Unusual* (Wylie, Tex.: Information Plus, 1996), 85.
9. Elliot Turiel et al., "Judging Social Issues."
10. Satris, "Student Relativism," 193–200.
11. Edward O. Wilson, *On Human Nature* (Cambridge, Mass.: Harvard University Press, 1978).
12. Carol Gillian, *In a Different Voice* (Cambridge, Mass.: Harvard University Press, 1982).
13. Adapted from Lawrence Kohlberg, *The Philosophy of Moral Development* (San Francisco: Harper & Row, 1984), 510–511.
14. From Norma Haan, *On Moral Grounds: The Search for Practical Morality* (New York: New York University Press, 1985).
15. Paul M. Valliant, "Personality, Peer Influence, and Use of Alcohol and Drugs by First-Year University Students," *Psychological Reports* 77, no. 2 (1995): 401–402.
16. For more on moral development in college students see Alexander Astin and Gregory Blimling, "Developing Character in College Students," *NASPA Journal* 27, no. 4 (1990): 268; and Dwight Boyd, "The Condition of Sophomoritis and Its Educational Cure," *Journal of Moral Education* 1 (1980): 24–39.
17. Eva Skoe and Rhett Diessner, "Ethic of Care, Justice, Identity, and Gender: An Extension and Replication," *Merrill-Palmer Quarterly* 40, no. 2 (1994): 272–289.
18. Carol Gilligan and Jane Attanucci, "Two Moral Orientations: Gender Differences and Similarities," *Merrill-Palmer Quarterly* 34, no. 3 (1988): 223–227; R. Blotner and D. J. Bearison, "Developmental Consistencies in Socio-Moral Knowledge: Justice Reasoning and Altruistic Behavior," *Merrill-Palmer Quarterly* 30, no. 4, (1984): 349–357; Nancy Stiller and Linda Forrest, "An Extension of Gilligan and Lyon's Investigation of Morality: Gender Differences in College Students," *Journal of College Student Development* 31, no. 1 (1990): 54–63.
19. Children by the age of four, regardless of their culture, recognize the duty of justice, even though they mostly apply it egocentrically, protesting only when they are unjustly treated. William Damon, *The Moral Child* (New York: Free Press, 1993), 36.
20. The film *Obedience* on the Milgram study is an excellent example of this occurring.
21. James Rest, "Research on Moral Development: Implications for Training the Counseling Psychologist," *The Counseling Psychologist* 12, no. 2 (1984): 26.
22. Study by William Damon of Stanford University.
23. Although Confucianism and Buddhism are sometimes included under the rubric of religion, they are philosophies.
24. See Kwame Gyekye, *An Essay on African Philosophical Thought: The Akan Conceptual Scheme* (New York: Cambridge University Press, 1964), 184–185.
25. An exception here is fundamentalist religion, such as fundamentalist Christianity or Islam, in which the

Bible and the Koran are interpreted literally and are regarded as the final word on certain moral issues such as drinking and homosexuality.

26. John Stuart Mill, "Utilitarianism," in *Utilitarianism*, ed. by Mary Warnock (New York: Meridian, 1962), 257.
27. John Rawls, *A Theory of Justice* (Cambridge, Mass.: Belknap Press, 1971), 30.
28. Chang Wing-tsit, *A Source Book in Chinese Philosophy* (Princeton, New Jersey: Princeton University Press, 1963), bk. 3:1.
29. Elliot Turiel et al., "Judging Social Issues."
30. Immanuel Kant, "Duties to Oneself," in *Lectures on Ethics* (Indianapolis: Hackett, 1775–1780/1963), 123.
31. Jeane Kirkpatrick, "Establishing a Viable Human Rights Policy," *World Affairs* (winter 1980/81): 323–334.
32. Confucius, *The Analects*, bk. 2:1.
33. Adapted from Aristotle's *Nicomachean Ethics*, bk. 2.
34. Virginia Held, "The Meshing of Care and Justice," *Hypatia* 10, no. 2 (1995): 128–132.

CHAPTER 2

1. ABC Nightly News, 16 January 1998.
2. Lawrence B. Finer and Stanley K. Henshaw, "Abortion Incidence and Services in the United States in 2000," *Perspectives on Sexual and Reproductive Health*, 35 (1), January/February 2003, 6.
3. Marji Gold, Denis Luks, and Matthew R. Anderson, "Medical Options for Early Pregnancy Termination," *American Family Physician* 56, no. 2 (1997): 533.
4. Gold, et al., "Medical Options," 533.
5. "Abortion Surveillance: Preliminary Data—United States, 1993 (From the Centers for Disease Control and Prevention)," *JAMA, The Journal of the American Medical Association* 275, no. 14 (1996): 1073; and Vrazo Fawn, "Abortions Drop Significantly, Study Reports," *Knight-Ridder/Tribune News Service*, 19 June 1994; "Experts Try to Explain Declining Abortion Rate," *CQ Researcher* 44, no. 44 (1997): 1038.
6. Julia Duin, "'Millennials' Are Coming (Survey about College Freshmen)," *Insight on the News* 15, no. 9, p. 40.
7. Brief of 281 American Historians as *Amici Curiae* Supporting the Appellees in *Webster v. Reproductive Services*, 1988.
8. James C. Mohr, *Doctors and the Law: Medical Jurisprudence in Nineteenth-Century America* (New York: Oxford University Press, 1993): 42–43.
9. Reva Siefel, "Reasoning from the Body: A Historical Perspective on Abortion Regulation and Questions of Sexual Protection," *Stanford Law Review* 44 (1992): 286.
10. Elizabeth Cady Stanton, "Child Murder," *The Revolution* 1, no. 10 (1868): 146–147.
11. Susan B. Anthony, "Marriage and Maternity," *The Revolution* 1, no. 1 (1869): 4.
12. Elizabeth Cady Stanton, "Infanticide," *The Revolution* 1, no. 4 (1868): 57–58.
13. Judith Blake, "Abortion and Public Opinion: The 1960–1970 Decade," *Science* 171 (1971): 540–548.
14. George Gallup, Jr., *The Gallup Poll: Public Opinions 2002,* Scholarly Resources Inc., Wilmington Delaware, 2003, p. 205–206.
15. George Gallup, Jr., *The Gallup Poll: Public Opinions 2002,* Scholarly Resources Inc., Wilmington Delaware, 2003, p. 149.
16. The Gallup Organization (http://www.gallup.com/poll/indicators/indabortion.asp), July 2000.
17. George Gallup, Jr., *The Gallup Poll 1996:* 112–113.
18. "Fewer Doctors Performing Abortions," *Facts on File World News Digest,* 12 October 1995, p. 766–B2.
19. S. K. Henshaw, "Abortion Incidence and Services in the United States, 2000," *Family Planning Perspectives* 35, January/February 2003.
20. For more on the Islamic Perspective, see "Abortion: Religious Traditions," Warren T. Reich, *Encyclopedia of Bioethics,* vol. I (New York: Simon & Schuster; New York: Macmillan, 1995), 38–42.
21. Gold, et al., "Medical Options," 533–539.
22. "Advocate Lied on Late-Term Method," *Facts on File World News Digest,* 20 March 1997, p. 195–F3.
23. Robert J. White, "Partial-Birth Abortion: A Neurosurgeon Speaks," Testimony by U.S. House Committee on the Judiciary, 19 June 1996.
24. For a defense of this definition of personhood, see Baruch Brody, "The Morality of Abortion," in *Abortion and the Sanctity of Human Life: A Philosophical View* (Cambridge, Mass.: MIT Press, 1975).
25. Clifford Grobstein, *Science and the Unborn* (New York: Basic Books, 1988), 109.
26. Sharon R. Edwards, "The Role of Men in Contraceptive Decision-Making: Current Knowledge and Future Implications," *Family Planning Perspectives,* March/April 1994, p. 77.
27. Bernard Dickens, "Prenatal Diagnosis and Female Abortion: A Case Study in Medical Law and Ethics," *Journal of Medical Ethics* 12 (1986): 144.
28. "Ultrasound Effects," *The Economist* 336, no. 7926, (1996): 34(1).
29. "Ultrasound Effects," 34(1).
30. Dorothy Wertz and John Fletcher, "Ethics and Medical Genetics in the United States," *American Journal of Medical Genetics* 29 (April 1988): 815–827.

31. See http://news.bbc.co.uk/1/hi/sci/tech/325979.stm for more on genetic research on a "gay gene."
32. Marc Miringoff, *The Index of Social Health, 1989. Measuring the Social Well-Being of Children* (New York: Fordham Institute for Innovations in Social Policy, Fordham University, 1989), pp. 7–8.
33. Martha Goldsmith, "Researchers Amass Abortion Data," *JAMA* 26 (September 15, 1989), pp. 1431–1432.
34. Mary Benedict, Roger White, and Donald Cornely, "Maternal Perinatal Risk Factors and Child Abuse," *Child Abuse and Neglect* 9 (1985): p. 222.
35. Philip Ney, "Infant Abortion and Child Abuse: Cause and Effect," in the *Psychological Aspects of Abortion,* David Mall and Walter Watts, eds. (Washington D.C., University Publications of America, 1979): p. 26. See also Judith Boss, "Pro-Child, Pro-Choice: An Exercise in Doublethink?" *Public Affairs Quarterly* 7 (1993): pp. 85–91.
36. See Chapter 3 for a summary of the cloning process.
37. "The Right Ear," *Human Events* 53, no. 45 (1997): 24.
38. Deroy Murdock, "United Nations' Social Welfare Produces Scant Results," *Headway* 9, no. 10 (1997): 20.
39. Lawrence B. Finer and Stanley K. Henshaw, "Abortion Incidence and Services in the United States in 2000," *Perspectives on Sexual and Reproductive Health* 35, January/February 2003, p. 6.
40. James M. Humber, "Maternity, Paternity, and Equality," in *Reproduction, Technology, and Rights,* eds. James M. Humber and Robert F. Almeder (Totowa, NJ: 1996): pp. 27–41.
41. Steven D. Hales, "More on Fathers' Rights," *Reproduction, Technology, and Rights,* eds. James M. Humber and Robert F. Almeder (Totowa, NJ: 1996), pp. 43–49.
42. "Ultrasound Effects," 34(1).
43. Paul A. Logli, "Drugs in the Womb: The Newest Battlefield in the War on Drugs," *Criminal Justice Ethics* (winter/spring 1990): 25.
44. http://www.pcrm.org/issues/Ethics_in_Human_Research/ethics_human-birthdefects.html. 9/10/2003.
45. "Supreme Court: Debates Pregnancy Drug Testing Policy," *American Health Line,* 29 February 2000.
46. Katherine Beckett, "Fetal Rights and 'Crack Moms': Pregnant Women in the War on Drugs," *Contemporary Drug Problems* 22, no. 4 (1995): 587–612.
47. Quoted in "A Proposal to Control Fetal Alcohol Hell," *Report,* February 17, 2003, p. 19.
48. J. M. Lawrence, "Police Say Arsonist Set N.H. Abortion Clinic Fire," *Boston Herald,* 30 May 2000, p. 2.
49. S. K. Henshaw, "The Accessibility of Abortion Services in the United States, 2001," *Perspectives on Sexual and Reproductive Health* 35, January/February 2003.
50. "Blasts Probed at Atlanta Family Clinics," *US News & World Report,* 16 January 1997.
51. "Abortion-Related Crime Increased in 1997," *Providence Journal,* 18 January 1998, p. F5.
52. S. K. Henshaw, "The Accessibility of Abortion Services in the United States, 2001," *Perspectives on Sexual and Reproductive Health* 35, January/February 2003, p. 6.
53. "For what reasons are partial-birth abortions usually performed?" www.nric.org/abortion/pba/pbafact10.html.
54. Marianne Lavelle, "When Abortions Come Late in Pregnancy," *U.S. News & World Report,* 19 January 1998, p. 31.

CHAPTER 3

1. Plato, *Republic,* bk. III: 410; bk. IV: 456–461.
2. Robin Marantz Henig, "Pandora's Baby," *Scientific American* 288, no. 6, June 2003, p. 62.
3. In actual fact, as of 2000, about 1% of the human genome remains uncertain; but, for all practical purposes, the genome is "ready for use." See Nicholas Wade, "Researchers Unlock Genetic Code Secrets," *Providence Journal,* 27 June 2000, p. A6.
4. "Gene Testing," Human Genome Project Information, http://www.pcrm.org/issues/Ethics_in_Human_Research/ethics_human-birthdefects.html 9/10/2003.
5. Sheryl Bay Stolberg, "A Small Leap to Designer Babies," *New York Times,* 1 January 2000, p. E7.
6. *Ibid.*
7. Nicholas Wade, "Researchers Unlock Genetic Code Secrets," *The Providence Journal,* 27 June 2000, p. A1.
8. David Stipp, "Speed-Reading Your Genes," *Fortune* 148, no. 4, September 1, 2003, p. 150–152.
9. "Cloning Success Spurs Debate; Other Developments," *Facts on File World News Digest,* 3 April 1997, p. 235-E2.
10. Mitochondria are slender microscopic filaments that provide energy to the cell.
11. *The Opinion of the Advisers to the President of the European Commission on the Ethical Implications of Biotechnology,* 28 May 1997.
12. George Gallup, Jr., *The Gallup Poll: Public Opinions 2002* (Scholarly Resources Inc., Wilmington Delaware, 2003), p. 144.
13. Robin Marantz Henig, "Pandora's Baby," *Scientific American* 288, no. 6, June 2003, pp. 64–66.
14. "Vatican Condemns Birth Technologies," *Facts on File World News Digest,* 13 March 1987, p. 158-F1.
15. Richard A. McCormick, "Blastomere Separation: Some Concerns," *Hastings Center Report* 24, no. 2 (1994): 14–16.

16. Allen Bushanan, Dan W. Brock, Norman Daniels, Daniel Wikler, *From Chance to Choice: Genetics and Justice* (Cambridge, UK: Cambridge University Press, 2000), pp. 160–161.
17. For information on issues related to the Human Genome Project visit their website at http://www.ornal.gov/TechResources/Human_Genome/.
18. Johnathan Marks, "Contemporary Bio-Anthropology," *Anthropology Today* 18, no. 4, August 2002, pp. 6–7.
19. Quoted in Bob Harris, "Second Thoughts about Cloning Humans," *The Humanist* (May/June 1997): 43.
20. Aisling Irwin, "Cloning Can Save Giant Panda, Claim Chinese," *The Daily Telegraph* (London), 7 October 1999, p. 10.
21. Quoted in Charles Marwick, "Put Human Cloning on Hold, Say Bioethicists," *The Journal of the American Medical Association* 278, no. 1 (1997): 14.
22. "The Right to be Beautiful," *Economist* 367, no. 8325, May 24, 2003, p. 9.
23. Terence Chea, "Going Whole Hog for Cloning: Biotech Firm Plans Its Use in Breeding Farm Animals," *The Washington Post,* 5 August 2000, p. E1.
24. "Many U.S. Animals Pregnant with Clones," *Providence Journal,* 28 June 1997, p. A4.
25. John Travis, "Cloning Extends Life of Cells—and Cows?" *Science News,* 29 April 2000, 157, no. 18, p. 279.
26. David Stipp, "Speed-Reading Your Genes," *Fortune* 148, no. 4, September 1, 2003, p. 150.
27. Judith B. Hall, "Mendel Might Get Dizzy," *Canadian Medical Association Journal* 157, no. 12 (1997): 1669–1670.
28. Frederick Hutt, *Animal Genetics* (New York: John Wiley & Sons, 1982), 108.
29. Clive Cookson and David Firn, "Dolly's Creators to End Pig Cloning Project," *Financial Times* (London), 15 August 2000, p. 2.
30. Stephen S. Hall, "The Recycled Generation," *New York Times Magazine,* 30 January 2000. Section 6: p. 30.
31. "Clonaid Claims Birth of First 5 Cloned Babies," http://www.globalchange.com/clonaid.htm.
32. "Rael: No DNA test for Baby Eve," CNN.com.Health, January 3, 2003.
33. "Company Gets Funds to Clone Baby," *Science,* 29 September 2000.
34. "The Moo Two: Any Way You Splice It," *Newsweek,* 2 February 1998, 65.
35. Roger Dobson, "Cloning of Pigs Bring Xenotransplants Closer," *British Medical Journal,* 320, March 2000, p. 826.
36. "Transgenic Animals: The Latest in Anti-Terror Technology," *The Pew Initiative on Food and Biotechnology,* August 26, 2003, http://pewagbiotech.org/newsroom/summaries.
37. This is a fictional case study set in the future.
38. Glenn Zorpette, "Off With Its Head!" *Scientific American,* January 1998, 41.
39. Pierre-André Dubois and Kate McCallie, "Of Mice and Men" *Managing Intellectual Property,* no. 130, June 2003, pp. 32–36.
40. Andrew Blattman, "Patently Animals—Where Does Singapore Sit?" *Managing Intellectual Property,* no. 130, June 2003, p. 56–57.
41. Gloria Goodale, "Mammoth Mystery," *The Christian Science Monitor,* 10 March 2000, p. 17.
42. Ricky James, "Intact Mammoth Cells DNA Reported; Cloning to Begin," *SciScoop,* http://www.sciscoop.com/story/2003/2/6/8840/98171.
43. This is based on correspondence to British geneticist and author Dr. Patrick Dixon, November 1997.

CHAPTER 4

1. Quoted in Sogyal Rinpoche, *The Tibetan Book of Living and Dying* (San Francisco: HarperCollins, 1992), 375.
2. One exception was David Hume who, in his 1783 essay "On Suicide," argued that suicide may sometimes be part of our duty to society.
3. Robert Jay Lifton, *The Nazi Doctors: Medical Killing and the Psychology of Genocide* (New York: Basic Books, 1986), 63.
4. George Gallup, Jr., *The Gallup Poll: Public Opinion 1996* (Wilmington, Del.: Scholarly Resources Inc., 1997), 197.
5. George Gallup, Jr., *The Gallup Poll: Public Opinions 2002* (Wilmington, Del.: Scholarly Resources Inc., 2003), p. 149.
6. Gallup Poll Releases, March 24, 1999; A. Albanese, "A Question of Human Rights," *The Sydney Morning Herald,* 27 September 1996, p. 11.
7. Carol Daniel, "Killing with Kindness," *New Statesman,* 15 August 1997, 16.
8. M. Cuttini et al., "End of Life Decisions in Neonatal Intensive Care: Physician's Self-Reported Practices in Seven European Countries," *The Lancet* 355, no. 9221, p. 2112.
9. Katherine K. Young, "Death: Eastern Thought," *Encyclopedia of Bioethics,* vol. 1, p. 497.
10. Studies cited in Barbara Dority, "The Ultimate Liberty," *The Humanist* 57, no. 4 (1997): 16–20.
11. Sharon Fraser and James Walters, "Death—Whose Decision?" *Journal of Medical Ethics,* April 2000, 26, no. 2, p. 121.

12. Ellen Moskowitz, "The Consensus on Assisted Suicide," *Hastings Center Report,* July-August 2003, p. 46.
13. "Australia Euthanasia Law Faces New Legislative Challenge," *Catholic World News,* September 13, 2003, http://www.cwnews.com/news/viewsotry.cfm?recnum_1701.
14. Wim Weber, "Dutch Proposal for Children's Right to Euthanasia Withdrawn," *The Lancet* 356, no. 9226, 22 July 2000, p. 322.
15. Layne Cameron, "Death Becomes Him," *The American Legion Magazine,* October 1997, 64.
16. Cameron, "Death Becomes Him," 33, 64.
17. Martha L. Twaddle, "Hospice Care," in *Dignity and Dying,* ed. by John F. Kilner, Arlene F. Miller, and Edmund D. Pellegrino (Grand Rapids, Mich.: William B. Eerdmans, 1996), 183.
18. Willamette University College of Medicine, "Recent Developments in Physician-Assisted Suicide," March 2003, http://www.willamette.edu/wucl/pas/pasupdatemarch2003.html.
19. Cicely Saunders, "A Commitment to Care," *Raft, The Journal of Buddhist Hospice Trust* 2 (winter 1989/90): 10.
20. Donna White, "Death on Trial," *US News & World Report,* 25 April 1994, 31–41.
21. Willamette University College of Medicine, "Recent Developments in Physician-Assisted Suicide," March 2003, http://www.willamette.edu/wucl/pas/pasupdatemarch2003.html.
22. Stuart N. Davidson, "Pain and Opiophobia," *Healthcare Forum Journal* (May/June 1997): 64–67.
23. Sarah Ramsay, "Debate Continues on End-of-Life Issues," *The Lancet* 355, no. 9206, 4 March 2000, p. 811.
24. *Ibid.*
25. *Ibid.*
26. Raymond S. Duff, and A. G. M. Campbell, "Moral and Ethical Dilemmas in the Special-Care Nursery," *New England Journal of Medicine* 289 (1973): 890–894.
27. "Dutch, U.S. Doctors' Views on Assisted Suicide Vary," *Star Tribune* (Minneapolis, MN), 23 January 2000, p. 5E.
28. www.efmoody.com/longterm/dying.html.
29. Harry A. Cole and Martha M. Jablow, *One in a Million* (Boston: Little, Brown, 1993).
30. Quoted in Steve Hallock, "Physician-Assisted Suicide: 'Slippery Slope' or Civil Right?" *The Humanist* 56, no. 4 (1996): 7–14.
31. Tom Koch, "Living Versus Dying 'With Dignity': A New Perspective on the Euthanasia Debate," *Cambridge Quarterly Healthcare Ethics* 5, no. 1 (1996): 50–61.
32. Richard Selzer, "A Question of Mercy," *The New York Times Magazine,* 22 September 1991, 32–38.
33. Jack Kevorkian, *Prescription: Medicide* (Buffalo, N.Y.: Prometheus, 1991).
34. Case study adapted from Judith A. Boss, *Perspectives on Ethics* (Mountain View, Calif.: Mayfield Publishing Co., 1997), 312.
35. "Kevorkian Charged in Assisting 3 Suicides," *Patriot Ledger* (Quincy, Mass.), 1 November 1996, p. 11.
36. Doreen Iudica Vigue, "The Top 10 Local News Stories of 1996," *Boston Globe,* 1 January 1997, p. B1.
37. Derek Humphry, "Prisoner of Conscience," Dr. Jack Kevorkian, Prisoner #284797," http://www.finalexit.org/drkframe.html, 29 January 2000.
38. John Stuart Mill, "Utilitarianism," in *Utilitarianism,* ed. by Mary Warnock (New York: Meridian Books, 1962), 308.
39. Kim Murphy, "Graphic How-to Program on Suicide to Air on TV in Oregon, Sparking Debate," *Los Angeles Times,* 1 February 2000, p. A-13.
40. *Ibid.*
41. Sharon Doyle Driedger, "Should Latimer Go Free?" *Maclean's,* 17 November 1997.

CHAPTER 5

1. Amnesty International, "United States Leads World in Juvenile Offender Executions and Ranks Third Worldwide in Total Number of Executions, Newest Statistics Show," April 11, 2003, http://www.amnestyusa.org/news/2003.
2. *Ibid.*
3. Robert F. Drinan, "Catholics and the Death Penalty," *America* 170 (June 1994): 13–15.
4. Amanda Paulson and Abraham McLaughlin, "Despite Reprieves, 3,500 Still on Death Row," *Christian Science Monitor* 95, no. 196, September 4, 2003, p. 4.
5. George Pettinico, "Crime and Punishment: America Changes its Mind," *Public Perspective* (September/October 1994): 29–32.
6. Bureau of Justice Statistics, "Capital Punishment," December 1999, NCJ-179012.
7. Bureau of Justice Statistics, "Capital Punishment Statistics," August 24, 2003, www.ojp.usdoj.gov/bjs/.
8. Kathleen Maguire, Ann L. Pastore, and Timothy J. Flanagen (eds.), *Sourcebook of Criminal Justice Statistics 1992,* U.S. Department of Justice, Bureau of Justice Statistics (Washington, D.C.: USGPO, 1993), 357.
9. George Pettinico, "Crime and Punishment," 29–32.
10. "Criminal Justice American Style," *America* 188, no. 19, June 9, 2003, p. 3.
11. Gallup Poll, (http://www.gallup.com/poll/indicators/inddeath_pen.asp), July 2000.

12. George Gallup, Jr., *The Gallup Poll: Public Opinions 2002* (Scholarly Resources Inc., Wilmington Delaware, 2003), p. 147.
13. *Ibid.*
14. Ernest van den Haag, "The Ultimate Punishment: A Defense," *Harvard Law Review* 99 (1986): 1662–1669.
15. Helen Prejean, *Dead Man Walking* (New York: Random House, 1993), 47.
16. *The Gallup Poll,* 1991 (Wilmington, DE: 1992), pp. 130–131.
17. Bureau of Justice Statistics, "The Proportion of Serious Violent Crimes Committed by Juveniles has Generally Declined Since 1993," August 24, 2003, www.ojp.usdoj.gov/ bjs/.
18. Victor Streib, "The Juvenile Death Penalty Today: Death Sentences and Executions for Juvenile Crimes," January 1, 1973–June 30, 2003. www.law.onu.edu/ faculty/streib/juvdeath/htm.
19. *Ibid.*
20. Margaret Talbot, "The Executioner's I.Q. Test," *The New York Times Magazine,* June 29, 2003.
21. *The World Almanac and Book of Facts 1996* (Mahwah, N.J.: Funk & Wagnalls, 1995), 960.
22. Leah Brumer, "Lethal Objection," *New Physician* (January/February 1997): 52.
23. *Ibid.*
24. *Ibid.*
25. *Ibid.*
26. Tracy Moran, "DNA Tests Should End Capital Punishment," *USA Today,* June 6, 2000. www.usatoday.com/news/opinion/columnists/tmoran/tm8.htm.
27. "Leading Forensic Scientist Calls for Halt to Executions Because of Faulty DNA Testing," *Tallahassee Democrat,* June 15, 2003. http://deathpenaltyinfo.org/article.php?scid&2&did=533.
28. John Locke, *The Second Treatise of Government* (Indianapolis: Bobbs-Merrill, 1952), ch. 2.
29. Jeremy Bentham, *An Introduction to the Principles of Morals and Legislation,* in Mary Warnock (ed.), *Utilitarianism* (Cleveland: Meridian, 1962).
30. John Stuart Mill, "Parliamentary Debate on Capital Punishment Within Prisons Bill," in *Hansard's Parliamentary Debates,* 3d ser. (London: Hansard, 1868).
31. Immanuel Kant, *The Philosophy of Law,* pt. II, trans. by W. Hastie (Edinburgh: T. T. Clark, 1887), 194–198.
32. Prejean, *Dead Man Walking,* 110.
33. *The Death Penalty* (London: Amnesty International Publications, 1987), 18.
34. Ted Gest, "A House Without a Blueprint," *US News & World Report,* 8 July 1996, 41–42.
35. Brian Gilmore, "Spotlight on the Death Penalty," *Progressive* 67, no. 8, August 2003, p. 38.
36. "Researchers Find Prejudice Shapes Support for Death Penalty," Joe Soss, Laura Langbein and Alan Metelko, "Why Do White Americans Support the Death Penalty?" *The Journal of Politics* 397, 2003, p. 65.
37. Stanley Rothman and Stephen Powers, "Execution by Quota," *The Public Interest* 116 (summer 1994): 3–17.
38. Amnesty International, "The Death Penalty Worldwide: Developments in 2002," http://www.amnestyusa.org/news/2003.
39. Eric M. Freedman, "The Case Against the Death Penalty," *USA Today* (magazine), March 1997, 48–50.
40. "Death Penalty Costs Cause Concern in Kansas," June 29, 2003. http://deathpenaltyinfo.org/article.php? scid&2&did=533.
41. Albert Camus, "Reflexions sur la Guillotin," in *Reflexions sur la Peine Capital* (Paris: Calmann-Levy, 1957).
42. "The Needle Paused," *Economist* 366, no. 8316, March 22, 2003, p. 29.
43. "Study Reveals Flaws in U.S. Death Sentences," *Facts On File* 60, no. 3106, 15 June 2000, p. 404.
44. "The Needle Paused," *Economist* 366, no. 8316, March 22, 2003, p. 29.
45. Lawrence Kohlberg, P. Scharf, and J. Hickey, "The Justice Structure of the Prison: A Theory and Intervention," *Prison Journal* 51 (1972): 3–14.
46. Clarence Darrow, *Crime and Criminals* (Charles H. Kerr & Co., 1902).
47. Prejean, *Dead Man Walking,* p. 122.
48. Dan Malone, "Views from Death Row," *Providence Sunday Journal,* 25 May 1997, p. D1.
49. Case study and questions adapted from Judith A. Boss, *Perspectives on Ethics* (Mountain View, Calif.: Mayfield Publishing Co., 1998), 362.
50. Jimmy Moore, "Ashcroft Calls for Expanding Death Penalty to Terrorists," *Talon News,* June 6, 2003.
51. Albert Camus, *Reflections sur la Pein Capital* (Paris: Calmann-Levy, 1957), 199.
52. Jill Smolowe, "Not in My Backyard!" *Time,* 5 September 1994, 59.
53. John Larrabee, "At 21, RI Serial Killer Soon Will Go Free," *USA Today,* 6 June 1994, p. A8.
54. Normal males have one X and one Y chromosome (XY). About one in every one thousand males, however, is born with an extra Y chromosome (XYY).
55. Juan Williams, "Violence, Genes, and Prejudice," *Discover Magazine* (November 1994): 92–101.
56. Patricia B. Sutker, C. E. Moran, and Albert N. Allain, "Assessment of Cognitive Control in Psychopathics

and Normal Prisoners," *Journal of Behavioral Assessment* 5 (1983): 275–287.

57. Malone, "Views from Death Row," p. D5.

CHAPTER 6

1. *Global Health Research, Drugs and Beyond* (Alberta, Canada: Global Health, 1995), 7.
2. Jerome Jaffe's definition, quoted in Francis F. Seeburger, *Addiction and Responsibility* (New York: Crossroad, 1996), 48.
3. Listed are the effects of small or moderate amounts of these drugs. Excessive amounts may be accompanied by other, sometimes harmful, effects.
4. Jean Kinney and Gwen Leaton, *Understanding Alcohol* (St. Louis: Mosby Year Book, 1992), 17.
5. George B. Wood, *A Treatise on Therapeutics, and Pharmacology, or Materia Medica,* 3d ed., vol. 1 (Philadelphia: J. B. Lippincott, 1868), 712.
6. For an excellent history of drug and alcohol use in the United States, see David R. Musto, *The American Disease* (New Haven: Yale University Press, 1973) and his article "Legal Control of Harmful Substances," in the *Encyclopedia of Bioethics,* vol. 5 (New York: Simon & Schuster, 1995), 2439–2443.
7. "Trends in Tobacco Use," American Lung Association Epidemiology and Statistics Unit Research and Scientific Affairs," June 2003, p. 6.
8. "It's Time to Open the Doors of Our Prisons," *Newsweek* 133, no. 16, 19 April 1999, p. 10.
9. Chris Wood, "'This Was Global,' The RCMP Shuts Down a Major Illicit Drug Lab," *Maclean's,* October 1996, 58.
10. Ross Atkins, "Homefront: Keeping Kids 'Clean'," *The Christian Science Monitor,* vol. 95, no. 7, December 4, 2002, p. 11.
11. Barry Stimmel, *Drug Abuse and Social Policy in America* (New York: Haworth, 1996), 3.
12. Ross Atkins, "Homefront: Keeping Kids 'Clean'," *The Christian Science Monitor,* vol. 95, no. 7, December 4, 2002, p. 11.
13. "Trends in Tobacco Use," American Lung Association Epidemiology and Statistics Unit Research and Scientific Affairs, June 2003, p. 1.
14. "Trends in Tobacco Use," American Lung Association Epidemiology and Statistics Unit Research and Scientific Affairs, June 2003, pp. 2–3.
15. "Trends in Tobacco Use," American Lung Association Epidemiology and Statistics Unit Research and Scientific Affairs, June 2003, p. 2.
16. J. B. Treaster, "Drugs Not Just an Urban Problem, Study Finds," *New York Times,* 1 October 1991, p. B1.
17. John Iwasaki, "Forum Tackles Race and Drug Use," *Seattle Post,* December 6, 2002. http://seattlepi.nwsource.com/local/98767_drug06.shtml
18. Stimmel, *Drug Abuse,* 9.
19. Adam Cohen, "Battle of the Binge," *Time,* 8 September 1997, 55.
20. Cohen, "Binge," 55.
21. "Clean up Campuses," *Maclean's,* September 1996, 14.
22. Henry Wechsler et al., "Health and Behavioral Consequences of Binge Drinking in College. A National Survey of Students at 140 Campuses," *The Journal of the American Medical Association* 272 (1994): 1672–1677.
23. Wechsler et al., "Health and Behavioral Consequences," 1672–1677.
24. Mary E. Larimer, Daniel L. Irvine, Jason R. Kilmer, and G. Alan Mariatt, "College Drinking and the Greek System: Examining the Role of Perceived Norms for High-Risk Behavior," *Journal of College Student Development* 38, no. 6 (1997): 587–598.
25. "Surveys: College Binge Drinking Rate 44 Percent; Remains the Same Eight Years Running," News Releases, March 25, 2002. http://www/rwjf.org/newsEvents/medicaRelease.jsp?id=1016047715299.
26. Barbara Reynolds, "Other Voices: Save a Kid; Talk About Drugs," *Detroit Free Press,* June 12, 1998, Section A, p. 11.
27. Nweze Nnakwe, "Anabolic Steroids and Cardiovascular Risk in Athletes," *Nutrition Today* 31, no. 5 (1996): 206–208.
28. Jürgen Rehm et al., "The Relationship of Average volume of Alcohol Consumption and Patterns of Drinking to Burden of Disease: An Overview," *Addiction,* vol. 98, 2003, pp. 1220–1221.
29. Henry Wechsler et al., *Secondary Effects of Binge Drinking on College Campuses* (Newton, Mass.: Higher Education Center for Alcohol and Other Drug Prevention, 1996).
30. Antonia Abbey et al., "Alcohol and Dating Risk Factors for Sexual Assault Among College Women," *Journal of Women Quarterly* 20, no. 1 (1996): 147–169.
31. Sara Markowitz et al., "Substance Use and Suicidal Behaviors among Young Adults," Working Paper 8810, National Bureau of Economic Research, March 2002, p. 2.
32. Kalb, "Drinking and Dying," 69.
33. Keith F. Durkin et al., "College Students' Use of Fraudulent Identification to Obtain Alcohol," *Journal of Alcohol and Drug Education* 41, no. 2 (1996): 92–104.
34. "Picture of Drug Use by Young Is Mixed" *The San Diego Union-Tribune,* 1 September 2000, Page A-6.
35. Jenny Williams et al., "Alcohol and Marijuana Use Among College Students: Economic Complements

or Substitutes?" Working Paper 8401, National Bureau of Economic Research, July 2001, p. 1.

36. "Steroid Cloud Mars Baseball," *Milwaukee Journal Sentinel,* 15 October 2000, p. 1C.

37. "College Athletes and Alcohol and Other Drug Use," *Infofacts,* http://www.edc.org/hec/pubs/factsheets/fact_sheet3.html.

38. See E. M. Jellinek, *The Disease Concept of Alcoholism* (Highland Park, N.J., 1960).

39. Alison M. Goate, "Molecular Biology," *Alcohol Health and Research World* 19, no. 3 (1995): 217–220.

40. Mark Edward Lender and James Kirby Martin, *Drinking in America* (New York: Free Press, 1987), 200–201.

41. Lender and Martin, *Drinking,* 96.

42. Aristotle, *Nicomachean Ethics,* bk. 3, ch. 5.

43. *Encyclopedia of Religion,* vol. 12, ed. Mircea Eliade (New York: Macmillan, 1987), 129.

44. John Stuart Mill, *On Liberty* (Indianapolis: Hackett, 1859/1978), 9.

45. H. Thomas Milhorn, *Drug and Alcohol Abuse* (New York: Plenum, 1994), 3.

46. E. Webb, C. H. Ashton, P. Kelly, and F. Kamali, "Alcohol and Drug Use in UK University Students," *The Lancet* 348, no. 9032 (1996): 922–925.

47. Jean Kinney and Gwen Leaton, *Understanding Alcohol* (St. Louis: Mosby Year Book, 1992), 20.

48. Cohen, "Binge," 54–56.

49. G. Alan Marlatt, "Harm Reduction: Come as You Are," *Addictive Behaviors* 21, no. 6 (1996): 779–788.

50. "Alcohol Illness Cited as Big Cost," *New York Times,* 12 September 1993, A22.

51. Mark S. Gold, "Addiction and Dependence," ed. Warren T. Reich, in *Encyclopedia of Bioethics,* vol. 5 (New York: Simon & Schuster, 1995), 2145.

52. Stimmel, *Drug Abuse,* 14.

53. William W. Latimer, Ken C. Winters, and Randy D. Stinchfield, "Screening for Drug Abuse Among Adolescents in Clinical and Correctional Settings Using the Problem-Oriented Screening Instrumentation for Teenagers," *American Journal of Drug and Alcohol Abuse* 23, no. 1 (1977): 79–98.

54. Stimmel, *Drug Abuse,* 17.

55. For a description of who is eligible to possess marijuana for medical purposes see the Health Canada website: http://www.hc-sc.gc.ca/english/protection/marijuana.html.

56. Gold, "Addiction and Dependence," 2416.

57. Cohen, "Binge," 54–56.

58. H. Wesley Perkins and Henry Wechsler, "Variation in Perceived College Drinking Norms and Its Impact on Alcohol Abuse: A Nationwide Study," *Journal of Drug Issues* 26, no. 4 (1996): 961–974.

59. Clayton L. Thomas, ed., *Taber's Cyclopedic Medical Dictionary,* 16th ed. (Philadelphia: F. A. Davis, 1989), 1045.

60. Alvin H. Moss and Mark Siegler, "Should Alcoholics Compete Equally for Liver Transplants?" *Journal of the American Medical Association* 265, no. 10 (1991): 1295–1297.

61. John Taylor, "Live and Let Die: In Praise of Mickey, Jerry, and the Reckless Life," *Esquire,* December 1995, 120.

62. This case study is based on questions used in a 1995 poll of U.S. Olympians or aspiring Olympians as reported in Michael Bamberger and Don Yaeger, "Over the Edge," *Sports Illustrated,* April 1997, 60–67.

63. Stimmel, *Drug Abuse,* 41.

64. Case study adapted from Judith A. Boss, *Perspectives on Ethics* (Mountain View, Calif.: Mayfield Publishing Co., 1998), 222–223.

65. Drugs and crime are closely connected. The majority of prison inmates are serving time for drug-related crimes. See Ted Gup, "Drugs and Crime," *Cosmopolitan,* July 1996, 180.

66. Peter D. Kramer, *Listening to Prozac* (New York: Viking, 1993), 294.

67. Kramer, *Prozac,* 291.

68. Kramer, *Prozac,* 258.

69. Kramer, *Prozac.*

70. This case study is adapted from "AA Made Me Confess," in Alan Dershowitz, *The Abuse Excuse* (Boston: Little, Brown & Co., 1994), 69–71.

71. Sheryl Magzamen and Stanton Glantz, "The New Battleground: California's Experience with Smoke Free Bars," American Journal of Public Health, Vol. 91, no. 2, February 2001, pp. 245–252.

72. M. Eisner et al., "Bartenders' respiratory health after establishment of smoke-free bars and taverns. *JAMA,* vol. 280, 1998, p. 1909.

73. Sheryl Magzamen and Stanton Glantz, "The New Battleground: California's Experience with Smoke Free Bars," American Journal of Public Health, Vol. 91, no. 2, February 2001, p. 247.

74. This is a fictional case.

75. John Iwasaki, "Forum Tackles Race and Drug Use," *Seattle Post-Intelligence,* Dec. 6, 2002.

CHAPTER 7

1. Hebrews 13:4; Mark 7:21; Ephesians 5:5.

2. Leviticus 18:22–23; Romans 1:26–27.

3. Elizabeth Llorente, "Homosexuals Seek U.S. Political Asylum," *The Report,* 11 August 1996, p A1.
4. Alan Goldman, "Plain Sex," *Philosophy and Public Affairs* 5, Spring 1977, pp. 267–287.
5. Elizabeth Anscombe, "Contraception and Chastity," orthodoxytoday.org/articles/AnscomebeChastity.shtml.
6. Haleh Esfandiari, "The Woman Question," *Wilson Quarterly* 28, Spring 2004, pp. 56–63.
7. Arif Khan, "Marriage between Muslims and Non-Muslims." www.jannah.org/sisters/intermarriage.html.
8. The Vatican, "Declaration on Sexual Ethics," 19 December 1973.
9. Immanuel Kant, *Grounding for the Metaphysics of Morals,* trans. James Ellington (Indianapolis: Hackett, 1981), p. 24.
10. Ralph Wedgewood, "The fundamental argument for same-sex marriage," *The Journal of Political Philosophy* 7, no. 3, September 1999, p. 233.
11. Carolyn A. Kapinus and Michael P. Johnson, "Personal, Moral and Structural Commitment to Marriage: Gender and the Effects of Family Life Cycle Stage," *Sociological Focus* 35, no. 2, May 2002, pp. 189–205.
12. Matthew 19:4–6.
13. Department of Health and Human Services, *Vital and Health Statistics: Cohabitation, Marriage, Divorce and Remarriage in the United States,* Series 23, no. 22, July 2002, pp. 17–19.
14. Steven L. Nock, "Commitment and Dependency in Marriage," *Journal of Marriage and Family* 57, May 1995, p. 513.
15. George Gallup, Jr., *The Gallup Poll Public Opinion 2002* (Wilmington, DE: Scholarly Resources Inc., 2003), p. 149.
16. "Grading Schools on the Treatment of Gays," *USA Today Magazine,* December 1997, p. 11.
17. G. D. Comstock, *Violence Against Lesbians and Gay Men* (New York: Columbia University Press, 1991), pp. 171–172.
18. These include Denmark, Norway, Sweden, France, Hungary, Portugal and Croatia.
19. George Gallup, Jr., *The Gallup Poll: Public Opinion 2002* (Wilmington, DE: Scholarly Resources Inc., 2003), p. 149.
20. Diana West, "Opening the Door: College Romance in the New Century," *Jewish World Review,* August 3, 2001.
21. Department of Health and Human Services, *Vital and Health Statistics: Cohabitation, Marriage, Divorce and Remarriage in the United States,* Series 23, no. 22, July 2002, p. 19.
22. George Gallup, Jr., *The Gallup Poll: Public Opinion 2002* (Wilmington, DE: Scholarly Resources Inc., 2003), p. 240.
23. http://personalwebs.myriad.net/Roland/cohab1.html.
24. http://health.discovery.com/centers/loverelationships/articles/marriage_myths.html.
25. http://health.discovery.com/centers/loverelationships/articles/marriage_myths.html.
26. Immanuel Kant, "Of Duties to the Body in Regard to the Sexual Impulse," *Lectures on Ethics* trans. Louis Infield (New York: Cambridge University Press, 1930), p. 159.
27. Immanuel Kant, "Of Duties to the Body in Regard to the Sexual Impulse," *Lectures on Ethics* trans. Louis Infield (New York: Cambridge University Press, 1930), p. 161.
28. *G.W.F. Legel Philosophy of Right,* trans, T. M. Knox (NY: Oxford Press, 1942).
29. George Gallup, Jr., *The Gallup Poll Public Opinion 2002* (Wilmington, DE: Scholarly Resources Inc., 2003), p. 149.
30. Amanda Orr, "Unfaithfully Yours," *People* 59, no. 19, September 19, 2003, p. 159.
31. http://www.kstatecollegian.com/issues/v101/sp/n133/city-dviolence-dsfritchen.html.
32. http://www.wikipedia.org/wiki/Domestic_violence.
33. "New Law Offers Stronger Weapons Against Domestic Violence," *The Providence Journal,* 29 October 2000, p. A4.
34. Gregory L Greenwood et al., "Battering Victimization Among a Probability-Based Sample of Men Who Have Sex with Men," *American Journal of Public Health* 9, no. 12, December 2002, pp. 1964–1969.
35. http://health.discovery.com/centers/loverelationships/articles/marriage_myths.html.
36. Susan Brownmiller, *Against Our Will; Men Women and Rape* (New York: Simon & Schuster, 1975), 13.
37. Julie Osland, Marguerite Fitch, and Edmond Willis, "Likelihood to Rape in College Males," *Sex Roles* 35, nos. 3 and 4 (1996): 171–175.
38. See Patricia Yancey Martin and Robert A. Hummer, "Fraternities and Rape on Campus," *Gender and Society* 3, no. 4, 1989.
39. Katie Roiphe, "Reckless Eyeballing: Sexual Harassment on Campus," in *The Morning After: Sex, Fear and Feminism on Campus* (Boston: Little Brown and Col., 1993), 85–112.
40. National Institute of Justice, *Extent, Nature and Consequences of Intimate Partner Violence* (Washington, DC: U.S. Department of Justice, 2000).

41. National Institute of Justice, *The Sexual Victimization of College Women* (Washington, DC: U.S. Department of Justice, 2000).
42. "Forced Labor: The Prostitution of Children," (Washington, DC: U.S. Department of Labor, 1996).
43. Kimberly Klinger, "Prostitution Humanism and A Woman's Choice," *Humanist* 63, no. 1, Jan/Feb 2003, pp. 16–19.
44. Catharine MacKinnon, *Toward a Feminist Theory of the State* (Cambridge, MA: Harvard University Press, 1989) p. 245.
45. For a more in-depth discussion of the arguments against homosexuality see Burton Leiser, *Liberty, Justice and Morals: Contemporary Value Conflicts* (New York: Macmillan, 1979), ch. 2.
46. George Gallup, Jr., *The Gallup Poll: Public Opinion 2002* (Wilmington, DE: Scholarly Resources Inc., 2002), p. 83.
47. Elliot Turiel, Carolyn Hildebrandt, and Cecilia Wainryb, "Judging Social Issues: Difficulties, Inconsistencies, and Consistencies," *Monographs of the Society for Research in Child Development* 56, no. 2, 1991.
48. George Gallup, Jr., *The Gallup Poll: Public Opinion 1996* (Wilmington, DE: Scholarly Resources Inc., 1997), 48–49.
49. See Scott Wiener, "Homophobia Cannot Be Tolerated," *Harvard Law Record* (29 April 1994), 11.
50. William Bennett, "Leave Marriage Alone," *Newsweek*, 3 June 1996, 27.
51. "House Passes Gay Marriage Recognition Ban," *Facts on File World News Digest*, 18 July 1996, p. 499-D3.
52. *CNN U.S. News*, 10 September 1996.
53. Gabriel Rotello, "To Have and to Hold: The Case for Gay Marriage," *Nation*, June 1996, 11.
54. Cheshire Calhoun, "Family's Outlaws: Rethinking the Connections between Feminism, Lesbianism, and the Family," *Feminism and Families*, ed. by Hilde Lindermann Nelson (New York: Routledge, 1997), p. 131.
55. M. Around and S. L. Pauker, *The First Year of Marriage* (New York: Basic Books, 1987).
56. R. Berger and M. Hannah, eds. *Preventive Approaches in Couple Therapy* (Philadelphia, PA: Bunner/Mazel, 1999).
57. 10 USCA s. 654(b).
58. See "Don't Ask, Don't Tell: Homosexuals and the Military," *Congressional Digest* 75, no. 11 (1996): 262.
59. "MIT Tries a New Approach in the Battle over ROTC," *Chronicle of Higher Education*, 31 May 1996, p. A23 (1).
60. "Foundation, ROTC Students Defeat Campus Leftists," *Liberatus*, March/April 1996.
61. *Meinhold v U.S. Department of Defense*, 34 F 3d 1469 at 1479 (9th Cir. 1994).
62. For more on legal cases involving sexual orientation and the military, see Robert Wintemute, *Sexual Orientation and Human Rights* (Oxford, England: Clarendon, 1995), 78–83.
63. Bruce Fleming, "Gay Poets, Women, and Other Threats to Group Loyalty at the Naval Academy," *Chronicle of Higher Education*, 30 January 1998, p. B45.
64. Marie Blanchard, "Students Arrested in Alleged Rape Case," *Daily Bruin Online*, 6 June 1996.
65. Patricia Yancey Martin and Robert A. Hummer, "Fraternities and Rape on Campus," *Gender and Society* 3, no. 4, 1989.
66. Naomi B. McCormick, "Fraternity Gang Rape: Sex, Brotherhood, and Privilege on Campus," *Archives of Sexual Behavior* 24, no. 3 (1994): 355–358.
67. Jill Rhynard, Marlene Krebs, and Julie Glover, "Sexual Assault in Dating Relationships," *Journal of School Health* 67, no. 3 (1997): 89–93.
68. George Gallup, Jr., *The Gallup Poll: Public Opinion 2002* (Wilmington, DE: Scholarly Resources Inc., 2002), p. 83.

CHAPTER 8

1. Larry Alexander, "Banning Hate Speech and the Sticks and Stones Defense," *Constitutional Commentary* 13, no. 1 (1996): 71.
2. Burton Leiser, "Truth and Civil Rights," *Intellect*, February 1973, 311.
3. For a history of free speech and the First Amendment, see O. Lee Reed, "Is Commercial Speech Really Less Valuable than Political Speech?" *American Business Journal* 34, no. 1 (1996): 1–37.
4. William F. Buckley, Jr., and L. Brent Bozell, *McCarthy and His Enemies* (Chicago: Henry Regnery, 1954).
5. www.moveon.org/gore/webcast.html.
6. http://gseis.ucla.edu/heri/nomrs-pr_98.html.
7. Russell Weaver, "Free Speech, Crime, and the Challenge of Advancing Technology," *International Review of Law, Computers & Technology* 14, no. 1, March 2000, p. 25.
8. http://www.nua.le/surveys/how_many_online/.
9. L. J. Sax, J. A. Astin, W. S. Korn, and K. N. Mahoney, "The American Freshman: National Norms for 2002." www.gseis.ucla.edu/heri/heri/html.
10. Reid Goldsborough, "Free Speech in Cyberspace—Both a Privilege and a Burden," *Community College Week* 12, no. 1, 23 August 1999, p. 27.
11. Kevin Platt, "With a Click, Chinese Vault Cultural Walls," *Christian Science Monitor* 92, no. 133, 1 June 2000, p. 1.

12. Wendy Grossman, The Spam Wars, *Reason* 35, no. 6, p. 40.

13. See Gloria Steinem, "Erotica and Pornography: A Clear and Present Difference," *Ms.* magazine, November 1978, for a more in-depth discussion of the difference between erotica and pornography.

14. House of Commons, Standing Committee on Justice and Legal Affairs, *Report on Pornography,* no. 18, 22 March 1978, p. 4.

15. Ronald J. Berger, Patricia Searles, and Charles E. Cottle, *Feminism and Pornography* (New York: Praeger, 1991), 4.

16. Cynthia A. Stark, "The War Against Pornography," *Social Theory and Practice* 23, no. 2 (1997): 279. For a critique of some of these studies see Ann Garry, "Pornography and Respect for Women," *Social Theory and Practice,* Spring 1978, vol. 4, pp. 395–421.

17. For more on radical feminism and liberal feminism see Chapter 10.

18. John Leo, "Watch What You Say," *U.S. News & World Report* 128, no. 11, 20 March 2000, p. 18.

19. "Supreme Court Overturns 'Hate-Speech' Law," *Facts on File World News Digest,* 25 June 1992, p. 464–D1.

20. "Free Speech and Europe," *The Economist,* 16 December 1995, 15.

21. Phil Cox, "The Disputation of Hate: Speech Codes, Pluralism, and Academic Freedoms," *Social Theory and Practice* 21, no. 1 (1995): 113.

22. Martin Bentham, "College Guide Bans 'Lady' and 'History' as Offensive Words," *Sunday Telegraph* (London), 11 June 2000, p. 3.

23. John Locke, *The Second Treatise of Government* (New York: Cambridge University Press, 1960), 457.

24. Ayn Rand, "Man's Rights," in *The Virtue of Selfishness* (New York: Penguin, 1964), 114.

25. John Rawls, *A Theory of Justice* (Cambridge, Mass.: Harvard University Press, 1971).

26. John Stuart Mill, "On Liberty," in *Collected Works of John Stuart Mill* (Toronto: University of Toronto Press, 1977), 220.

27. Mill, "On Liberty," 224.

28. For more on this interpretation of Mill's theory of free speech, see Jill Gordon, "John Stuart Mill and the 'Marketplace of Ideas,'" *Social Theory and Practice* 23, no. 2 (1997).

29. "Forbidden Thoughts: A Roundtable on Taboo Research," *The American Enterprise,* January/February 1995, 69.

30. D. F. B. Tucker, *Law, Liberalism and Free Speech* (Totowa, N.J.: Rowman & Allanheld, 1985), 141.

31. Herbert Marcuse, "Repressive Tolerance," in *A Critique of Pure Tolerance,* ed. by Robert Paul Wolff and Herbert Marcuse (Boston: The Beacon Press, 1969).

32. Keith Burgess-Jackson, "Justice and the Distribution of Fear," *The Southern Journal of Philosophy* 32 (1994): 367–388.

33. "Mapplethorpe or 2 Live Crew: 'As Nasty as They Wanna Be'?" *Newsweek,* 15 October 1990, p. 74.

34. Henry Louis Gates Jr., "Let Them Talk: Why Civil Liberties Pose No Threat to Civil Rights," *The New Republic,* 20 September 1993, 37–49.

35. "Hate on the Web," *Maclean's,* October 1997, 25.

36. Quoted by Sarah J. McCarthy, "Pornography, Rape, and the Cult of Macho," in *The Humanist,* September/October 1980, 15.

37. Oliver L. North, "Constitution Rights are Latest Wares Hustled by Hollywood," *Insight on the News,* 24 February 1997, p. 29.

38. "The Real Meaning Behind Horowitz Advertisement," Op-Ed, *The Brown Daily Herald* 139, no. 93. http://www.browndailyherald.com/stories.sep?dbversion+2&storyID+4243.

39. *Doe v University of Michigan,* 721 F. Supp. 852 (E.D.Mich. 1989).

40. *New York Times,* 15 October 1986, p. A27.

41. This is a paraphrase of Samuel Johnson's famous statement, "Patriotism is the first refuge of scoundrels."

42. For a more complete description of this case study, see Christopher McMahon, "Preserving the Bastion: The Case of the *Dartmouth Review,*" in eds. Milton Heumann and Thomas W. Church, *Hate Speech on Campus* (Boston: Northeastern University Press, 1997), 192–212.

43. Jerry Kirkpatrick, *In Defense of Advertising: Arguments from Reason, Ethical Egoism, and Laissez-Faire Capitalism* (Westport, Conn.: Quorum, 1994), 154.

44. See Calvin Reid, "Appeals Court Reviewing 'Hitman' Ruling," *Publishers Weekly,* 19 May 1997, 14.

45. Brandon S. Centerwall, "Exposure to Television as a Cause of Violence," in ed. G. Comstock, *Public Communication and Behavior,* vol. 2 (Orlando: Academic, 1989), 1–58.

46. Richard B. Felson, "Mass Media Effects on Violent Behavior," *Annual Review of Sociology* 22 (1996): 103–128.

47. Kevin Grace, "Eclectia," *Report/Newsmagazine* (Alberta Edition), 27, no. 6, 24 July 2000, p. 33.

48. Joshua Quittner, "Home Pages for Hate: A Campaign to Limit the Voices of White Supremacists on the Internet Has Defenders of the First Amendment Worried," *Time,* 22 January 1996, 69.

49. Alissa Quart, "The Sex Avengers," *Time* 5, no. 5, September 2000.

50. See Sharon Machlis, "University Sues Over Internet Term-Paper Site," *Computerworld,* October 1997, 3; and Julianne Basinger and Kelly McCollum, "Boston U. Sues Companies for Selling Term Papers Over the Internet," *Chronicle of Higher Education,* 31 October 1997, pp. A34–35.
51. Dylan B. Tomlinson and Adam Thompson, "Freedom of Speech: Both Sides of the Prayer Debate in College Sports Point to the First Amendment for Justification," *The Denver Post,* 21 June 2000, Page D-1.

CHAPTER 9

1. George Gallup, Jr., *The Gallup Poll 1995* (Wilmington, DE: Scholarly Resources, Inc., 1996), 265.
2. Mark Whitaker, "White v. Blacks," *Newsweek,* 16 October 1995, p. 28; and "O.J. and Race: Will the Verdict Split America?," *Time,* 9 October 1995.
3. William H. Holcombe, "Characteristics and Capabilities of the Negro Race," *Southern Literary Messenger* vol. 33 (1986): 401–410.
4. See Chapter 8 on "Freedom of Speech."
5. See Jonathan Kozol, *Savage Inequalities: Chidren in America's Schools* (New York: Crown Publishers, Inc., 1991).
6. Barbara Kantrowitz and L. Rosado, "Falling Further Behind: A Generation of Hispanics Isn't Making the Grade," *Newsweek,* 19 August 1991, p. 60.
7. Jonathan Alter, "The Long Shadow of Slavery," *Newsweek,* 8 December 1997, p. 62.
8. Ronald L. Taylor, "Black Males and Social Policy: Breaking the Cycle of Disadvantage," in *The American Black Male: His Present Status and His Future,* eds. Richard G. Majors and Jacob U. Gordon (Chicago: Nelson-Hall Publishers, 1994), 148–166.
9. Melvin Oliver, "American Dream? How Government Initiatives Made Blacks House Poor," *Crisis* 110, no. 5, Sept/Oct 2003, p. 17.
10. George Gallup, Jr., *The Gallup Poll: Public Opinion 2002* (Wilmington, DE: Scholarly Resources Inc., 2003), p. 179.
11. Linda Mizell, *Think About Racism* (New York: Walker & Co., 1992), 156.
12. Kozol, *Savage Inequalities.*
13. Gallup Poll Topics: Race Relations, 24 September–16 November, 1999. http://www.gallup.com/poll/indicators/indrace.asp.
14. Carroll P. Horton and Jessie Carney, eds., *Statistics Record of Black America* (Detroit: Gale Research, 1990).
15. Mizell, *Think About Racism,* 160–161.
16. Lydia Lum, "A Welcome Increase," *Black Issues in Higher Education* 20, no. 18, pp. 36–37.
17. Ben Hammer, "Study: Minority Enrollments Double, But Gaps Still Linger," *Community College Week,* October 27, 2003, p. 10.
18. Nancy E. Carriuolo, "Recruiting and Retaining Women and Minority Faculty," *Journal of Developmental Education* 27, no. 2, Winter 2003, p. 19.
19. *Uniform Crime Reports: Hate Crime—1995,* U.S. Department of Justice, FBI, Criminal Justice Information Services Division.
20. "Hate Springs Eternal," *Harper's Magazine* 3000, no. 1978, March 2000, p. 96.
21. "Burned Churches, Fiery Politics," *Christian Century* (December 1996): 1243–1254.
22. David P. Johnson, Jr., "American Arab Anti-Discrimination Committee Tackles Prejudice in Boston," *Washington Report on Middle East Affairs* 22, no. 6, July/August 2003, p. 43.
23. "World News Briefs," *Maclean's* 116, no. 47, Nov. 24, 2003, p. N.
24. "Time to Tell Hate, 'Not on Our Campus,'" *Black Issues in Higher Education* 16, no. 27, 2 March 2000, p. 48.
25. "Race, Crime and Justice," *Christian Century* 117, no. 11, 5 April 2000, p. 379.
26. Gallup Poll Topics: Race Relations, 24 September–16 November, 1999. http://www.gallup.com/poll/indicators/indrace.asp.
27. Jeffrey Prescott, "New Facts on Racial Profiling," *Christian Science Monitor 92,* no. 118, 10 May 2000, p. 8.
28. *Ibid.*
29. *Ibid.*
30. See Robert H. Bork, "Civil Liberties After 9/11," *Commentary* 116, no. 1, July/August 2003, pp. 29–35; and Sarfraz Mansoor, "I'm a Muslim but I Can Still Fly," *New Statesman* 131, no. 4614, 11/18/2002, pp. 32–33.
31. Michael Isikoff, "A Question of Profiling," *Newsweek* 136, no. 12, 18 September 2000, p. 68.
32. See the Gallup polls.
33. Herbert I. London, "Minority Enrollment Rebounds at California Schools," *Human Events* 56, no. 24, 30 June 2000, p. 24.
34. See David Horowitz, "Ten Reasons Why Reparations for Blacks is a Bad Idea for Blacks—and Racist, Too!" http://www.adversity.net/reparations/anti_reparations_ad.htm.
35. Bernard Boxill, "A Lockean Argument for Black Reparations," *The Journal of Ethics,* vol. 7, 2003, p. 87.
36. Barbara MacKinnon, *Ethics: Theory and Contemporary Issues* (Belmont, Calif.: Wadsworth, 1995), 238.
37. Ayn Rand, "Racism," in *The Virtue of Selfishness* (New York: Penguin, 1964), 147–161.
38. Alan Bloom, *The Closing of the American Mind* (New York: Simon & Schuster, 1987), 95.

39. Michael Levin, "Response to Race Differences in Crime," *Journal of Social Philosophy* 23, no. 1 (1992): 5–29.

40. Kevin Lamb, "IQ and PC," *National Review,* 27 January 1997, pp. 39–42.

41. John J. DiIulio, "State of Grace," *National Review,* 22 December 1997, p. 63.

42. "*Barbara Grutter v. Lee Bollinger et al.,*" U.S. Supreme Court, 2003, p. 4.

43. See *Cheryl Hopper v. The State of Texas,* 78 F.3d 932 (5th Cir. 1996).

44. Quoted in Sophfronia Scott Gregory, "Black Rage: In Defense of a Mass Murderer," *Time,* 6 June 1994, p. 31.

45. Quoted in Alan Dershowitz, *The Abuse Excuse* (Boston: Little, Brown and Company, 1994).

46. Dershowitz, *The Abuse Excuse.*

47. Ward Harkavy, "Left Behind," *Village Voice* 45, no. 19, 16 May 2000, pp. 41–43.

48. George Will, "The Bad Seed of Our Politics," *Newsweek,* 8 October 1990, p. 80.

49. "Environmental Racism: Hispanics Fight a Toxic Waste Incinerator," *Business Week,* 20 May 1991.

CHAPTER 10

1. Betty Friedan, *The Feminine Mystique* (New York: Dell Books, 1963), pp. 370–371.

2. Edward O. Wilson, *On Human Nature* (Cambridge, MA: Harvard University Press, 1978), Chapter 6.

3. See Catharine MacKinnon, *Toward A Feminist Theory of State* (Cambridge, MA: Harvard University Press 1989).

4. Robin Morgan, ed., *Sisterhood is Forever* (New York: Washington Square Press, 2003), p. xli.

5. George Gallup, Jr., *The Gallup Poll: Public Opinion 2002* (Wilmington, DE: Scholarly Resources Inc., 2002), p. 152.

6. See Sidney Callahan, "Abortion and the Sexual Agenda: A Case for Prolife Feminism" in the *Ethics PowerWeb.*

7. John Stuart Mill, *On Liberty* (Indianapolis: Hackett, 1978/1859), 104.

8. Friedrich Engels, *The Origin of the Family, Private Property, and the State* (New York: International Publishers Co., Inc, 1942), pp. 144–145.

9. Sigmund Freud, "Femininity," copyright 1933 by Sigmund Freud. In *New Introductory Lectures on Psychoanalysis* (W.W. Norton & Co., Inc., 1964), p. 184.

10. For an excellent coverage of this issue see Susan Dwyer, *The Problem of Pornography* (Belmont, Calif.: Wadsworth, 1995).

11. See Jeffner Allen, "Motherhood: The Annihilation of Women," in Joyce Trebilcot, "Mothering: Essays in Feminist Theory (Towota, NJ: Rowman & Allanheld, 1984), pp. 315–330.

12. Robin West, "Jurisprudence and Gender," *University of Chicago Law Review,* vol. 1, 1988.

13. Sara Ruddick, *Maternal Thinking: Toward a Politics of Peace* (Boston: Beacon Press, 1989), p. 24.

14. Lena Graber and John Miller, "Economy in Numbers: Wages for Housework: The Movement and the Numbers," *Dollars and Sense,* no. 243, Sept–Oct, 2002, p. 45.

15. Ibid.

16. Margaret Gibelman, "So How Far Have We Come? Pestilent and Persistent Gender Gap in Pay," *Social Work* 48, no. 1, January 2003, p. 23.

17. H. Remick, ed., *Comparable Worth and Wage Discrimination* (Philadelphia, PA: Temple University, 1984), p. ix.

18. D. Kelly Weisberg, ed., *Application of Feminist Legal Theory to Women's Lives* (Philadelphia: Temple University Press, 1996), p. 538.

19. D. Kelly Weisberg, ed., *Application of Feminist Legal Theory to Women's Lives* (Philadelphia: Temple University Press, 1996), p. 354.

20. "The Feminization of Poverty," www.un.org/womenwatch/daw/followup/session/presskit/fs1.htm.

21. Ibid.

22. George Gallup, Jr., *The Gallup Poll: Public Opinion 2002* (Wilmington, DE: Scholarly Resources Inc., 2003), p. 152.

23. N. Bernstein, "Study Finds Equality Eludes Most Women in Law Firms," *New York Times,* January 6, 1996, p. A9.

24. Margaret Gibelman, "So How Far Have We Come? Pestilent and Persistent Gender Gap in Pay," *Social Work,* 48, no. 1, January 2003, p. 23.

25. Lisa Belkin, "The Opt-Out Revolution," *The New York Times Magazine,* October 26, 2003, p. 44.

26. Lisa Vogel, "Debating Difference: Feminism, Pregnancy and the Workplace," *Feminist Studies,* 16, no. 1, Spring 1990, p. 9.

27. See N. Holla, "Blame it on Feminism," *Mother Jones* 16, no. 5, September 1991, pp. 24–29.

28. T. J. Wallis, "Sexual Harassment on the Job," *Career World* 28, no. 5, Feb/March 2000, p. 16.

29. Ronni Sandoff, "Sexual Harassment: The Inside Story," *Working Woman,* June 1992.

30. Hilary M. Lips, "Female Powerlessness: a Case of 'Cultural Preparedness'?" in H. Lorraine Radtke and Henderikus J. Stam, eds., *Power/Gender: Social Relations in Theory and Practice* (London: Sage Publications, 1994), p. 99.

31. Vaughana Macy Feary, "Sexual Harassment: Why the Corporate World Still Doesn't 'Get It'," *Journal of Business Ethics* 13 (1994): 648–662.
32. Davidson, *The Failure of Feminism,* 295–296.
33. F. E. Barcus, "Images of Life on Children's Television: Sex-roles, Minorities, and Families" (New York: Praeger Publishers, 1983), 20–22.
34. E. S. Davidson, A. Yasuna, and A. Toward, "The Effect of Television Cartoons on Sex-Role Stereotyping in Young Girls," *Child Development* 50, no. 2, 1979, pp. 597–600.
35. Kimberly A. Powell and Lori Abels, "Sex-Role Stereotypes in TV Programs Aimed at the Preschool Audience: An Analysis of Teletubbies and Barney and Friends," *Women and Language* 25, no. 1., 2002, pp. 14–22.
36. Mary Daly, *The Church and the Second Sex* (Boston: Beacon Press, 1985).
37. Jennifer Scanlon, "Not Just a Pretty Face," *Women's Review of Books* 19, no. 6, 2002, pp. 18–20.
38. Cynthia Hubert, "Birth of Change," *Sacramento Bee,* November 2, 2003.
39. Peggy Drexler, "Same-sex Parents Spring Open Gender Traps," Women's eNews, August 6, 2003. http:// www.womensenews.org/article.cfm/dyn/aid/1477/context/archive.
40. Peggy Drexler, "Same-sex Parents Spring Open Gender Traps," Women's eNews, August 6, 2003. http:// www.womensenews.org/article.cfm/dyn/aid/1477/context/archive.
41. *Providence Journal,* 2 April 1998, pp. A1, A8.
42. Linda Bird Francke, "The Military Culture of Harassment," in Linda LeMoncheck and James P. Sterba, eds., *Sexual Harassment: Issues and Answers* (New York: Oxford University Press, 2001), pp. 95–102.
43. Randy Shilts, *Conduct Unbecoming: Gays and Lesbians in the U.S. Military* (New York: St. Martin's, 1993), p. 595.
44. "USA: Air Force Academy Survey: Rate of Rape Reported at 12%," *The New York Times,* August 29, 2003.
45. Hilary M. Lips, "Female Powerlessness: A Case of 'Cultural Preparedness'?" in H. Lorraine Radtke and Henderikus J. Stam, eds., *Power/Gender: Social Relations in Theory and Practice* (London: Sage Publications, 1994), p. 99.
46. American Anorexia Bulemia Association, Inc., www.aabainc.org/general.
47. For more on this issue see Susan Bordo, "Anorexia Nervosa: Psychopathology as the Crystallization of Culture," in eds. Ann Garry and Marilyn Pearsall, *Women, Knowledge, and Reality: Explorations in Feminist Philosophy* (New York: Routledge, 1996), 388–418.
48. Cherry Boone O'Neill, *Starving for Attention* (New York: Dell, 1982), 131.

CHAPTER 11

1. Paul W. Williams, "The Twentieth Century and Beyond," *Vital Speeches of the Day* 55, no. 20, 1989, p. 624.
2. Thomas Hobbes, *Leviathan* (New York: Cambridge University Press, 1996), p. 126.
3. C. A. J. Coady, "War and Terrorism," in *A Companion to Applied Ethics,* ed. R. G. Frey and Christopher Heath Wellman (Oxford, UK: Blackwell Publ., 2003), p. 256.
4. Stephen Schwartz, "The Hidden Costs of Our Nuclear Arsenal," Report by The Brookings Institution, Washington, D.C., 1998. The United States military budget is more than the military budgets of the twenty next highest spenders combined.
5. "Israel's Nuclear Programme," BBC News, December 22, 2003.
6. "U.S. Unprepared for Disease Outbreak," *USA Today Magazine* 131, no. 2697, June 2003, p. 16.
7. See Jan Narveson, "Pacifism: A Philosophical Analysis," *Ethics* 75, no. 4 (July 1965).
8. See Cheyney Ryan, "Self-Defense, Pacifism, and the Possibility of Killing," *Ethics* 93, no. 3 (April 1983).
9. Gabriel Packard, "Hundreds of U.S. Soldiers Emerge as Conscientious Objectors," April 15, 2003, InterPress Service. www.commondreams.org/headlines03/0415-11.htm.
10. John Keegan, "Men in Battle," *Human Nature* 1, no. 6, June 1978, p. 36.
11. Gabriel Packard, "Hundreds of U.S. Soldiers Emerge as Conscientious Objectors," April 15, 2003, InterPress Service. www.commondreams.org/headlines03/0415-11.htm.
12. George Gallup, Jr., *The Gallup Poll: Public Opinion 2002* (Wilmington, DE: Scholarly Resources, Inc., 2003), p. 277.
13. World Health Organization, *World Report on Violence and Health,* 2002, http://www.who.int/violence_injury_prevention/violence/world_report/wrvh1/en/.
14. Paul Williams, "The Twentieth Century and Beyond," *Vital Speeches of the Day* 55, no. 20, 1989, p. 624.
15. John Rawls, "Definition and Justification of Civil Disobedience," from *Civil Disobedience in Focus,* ed. Hugo Bedau (London: Routledge, 1991), p. 104.
16. For more on these two positions see John Kelsey, "Suicide Bombers," *Christian Century* 119, no. 17, p. 23.
17. Joseph A. D'Agostino, "Center for Military Readiness," *Human Events* 59, no. 18, May 26, 2003, p. 20.
18. http://en.wikipedia.org/wiki/Bombing_of_Dresden_in_World_War_II.
19. http://www.rense.com/general19/flame.htm.
20. Quoted in Michael Walzer, *Just and Unjust Wars* (New York: Basic Books, 1977), p. 261.

21. *Public Papers of the Presidents of the United States: Harry S. Truman, Containing the Public Messages, Speeches and Statements of the President April 12 to December 31, 1945* (Washington, DC: United States Government Printing Office, 1961), p. 212.
22. Blaine P. Firedlander, Jr., "Americans Support Maintaining Civil Liberties During War on Terror, Cornell Survey Finds," http://www.news.cornell.edu/resleases/Jan03/ConstRights.bpf.html.
23. Randall Hamud, "We're Fighting Terror, But Killing Freedom," *Newsweek,* September 1, 2003, p. 11.
24. "Perspectives," *Newsweek,* December 1, 2003, p. 21
25. John Rawls, "Definition and Justification of Civil Disobedience," from *Civil Disobedience in Focus,* ed. Hugo Bedau (London: Routledge, 1991), p. 121.
26. Quoted in Christopher Glausen, "An Army of One," *American Scholar* 72, Issue no. 4, Autumn 2003, p. 55.
27. Erin Cusnick, "Indicators: Students Don't Want to Right War on Terror," *Yes! A Journal of Positive Futures,* Fall 2002, no. 23, pp. 7–8.
28. Paul R. Ehrlich, "Bioethics: Are Our Priorities Right?" *Bioscience* 53, no. 12, Dec. 2003.
29. Jack Miles, "The Iraq Dead: Respect Must be Paid," *Commonweal,* July 18, 2003, p. 11.
30. Joanne Laurier, "Colorado Woman Faces Charges by Military: Interview with U.S. Soldier Who Refused to Abandon Children and Return to Iraq," *World Socialist Website,* November 7, 2003. http://www. ccmep.org/2003_articles/Iraq/.
31. 10 USCA s. 654(b).
32. See "Don't Ask, Don't Tell: Homosexuals and the Military," *Congressional Digest* 75, no. 11 (1996): 262.
33. "MIT Tries a New Approach in the Battle over ROTC," *Chronicle of Higher Education,* 31 May 1996, p. A23 (1).
34. "Foundation, ROTC Students Defeat Campus Leftists," *Liberatus,* March/April 1996.
35. *Meinhold v U.S. Department of Defense,* 34 F 3d 1469 at 1479 (9th Cir. 1994).
36. For more on legal cases involving sexual orientation and the military, see Robert Wintemute, *Sexual Orientation and Human Rights* (Oxford, England: Clarendon, 1995), 78–83.

CHAPTER 12

1. David Coats, *Old MacDonald's Factory Farm* (New York: Continuum, 1989), 32.
2. Coats, *Factory Farm,* p. 34.
3. The Vegetarian Society, "Gene Genius?" *The Vegetarian,* spring 1993.
4. Lynn White, "The Historical Roots of Our Ecological Crisis, *Science* 155, 10 March 1967, p. 1205.
5. http://www.gallup.com/poll/indicators/inenvironment.asp.
6. Aristotle, "Politics," I, ch. 8. *The Oxford Translation of Aristotle,* trans. by Benjamin Jowett (Oxford: Oxford University Press).
7. Thomas Aquinas, *Summa Contra Gentiles,* bk. III, pt II, ch. CXII, trans. by the English Dominican Father (Chicago: Benziger Brothers, 1928).
8. Jeremy Bentham, *Principles of Morals and Legislation* (London: Clarendon Press, 1907), 1.
9. Charles Darwin, *The Descent of Man,* excerpt from Tom Regan and Peter Singer, eds., *Animal Rights and Human Obligations* (Englewood Cliffs, N.J.: Prentice-Hall, 1989), 30.
10. Thomas Jefferson, *Writings* (New York: Literary Classics of the United States, 1984), pp. 290 and 818.
11. See Judith Boss, "Treading on Harrowed Ground: The Violence of Agriculture," in *Institutional Violence,* eds. Deane Curtin and Robert Litke (Amsterdam: Rodopi, 1999), pp. 263–277.
12. http://www.upc-online.org/slaughter/2000slaughter_stats.html.
13. *Discussing Vegetarianism with a Meat-Eater: A Hindu View* (Kapaa, Hawaii: Himalayan Academy Publications).
14. Joy Williams, "The Inhumanity of the Animal People," *Harper's,* August 1997, p. 65.
15. Jim Mason and Peter Singer, *Animal Factories* (New York: Crown, 1990), 3.
16. Williams, "Inhumanity," p. 61.
17. See John Robbins, *Diet for a New America* (Walpole, N.H.: Stillpoint, 1987).
18. Economic Research Service, "Food Consumption," January 2003. http:www.ers.usda.gov/briefing/consumption/
19. "How Many Vegetarians Are There?" *Vegetarian Journal* 16, no. 5, Sept./Oct. 1997.
20. "How Many Americans are Actually Vegetarian?" http://www.supermarket gurur.com/page.cfm/2244.
21. John Fetto, "It Ain't Easy Eating Greens," *American Demographics* 22, no. 5, May 2000, p. 13.
22. *Discussing Vegetarianism* (Kapaa).
23. George Gallup, Jr., *The Gallup Poll: Public Opinion 2002* (Wilmington, DE: Scholarly Resources, Inc., 2003), p. 90.
24. Andrew Weaver, "Earth, Not Debate, Heating Up," *The Gazette* (Montreal), 8 December 2000, p. B3.
25. Sharon Begley, "The Mercury's Rising," *Newsweek,* 4 December 2000, p. 52.
26. Peter Singer, *Animal Liberation* (New York: Random House, 1990), 37.

27. Adapted from *PETA Factsheet on Animal Experiments,* no. 1.
28. See Rutgers Animals Rights Law Center, *1996 Supplement to Vivisection and Dissection in the Classroom.*
29. "The President of Europeans for Medical Advancement Responds to the Prediction that the Mapping of the Human Genome Will Increase Animal Experimentation," *The Independent* (London), 28 June 2000, p. 2.
30. Singer, *Animal Liberation,* p. 6.
31. Tom Regan, "The Nature and Possibility of an Environmental Ethics," in *All That Dwell Therein: Animals Rights and Environmental Ethics* (Berkeley: University of California Press, 1982).
32. John Rawls, *A Theory of Justice* (Cambridge, Mass.: Harvard University Press, 1971), 17, 512.
33. R. G. Frey, "Moral Community and Animal Research in Medicine," *Ethics and Behavior* 7, no. 2 (1997): 123–136.
34. Aldo Leopold, *A Sand County Almanac* (New York: Ballantine Books, 1982), pp. 138–139.
35. Al Gore, *Earth in the Balance: Ecology and the Human Spirit* (Boston: Houghton Mifflin Co., 1992), p. 221.
36. Al Gore, *Earth in the Balance: Ecology and the Human Spirit,* p. 216.
37. Arne Naess, "A Defence of the Deep Ecology Movement," *Environmental Ethics* 6, no. 3, Fall 1984, pp. 265–270.
38. See Val Plumwood, *Feminism and the Mastery of Nature* (New York: Routledge, 1993).
39. The Donor Foundation. http://www.donorfoundation.org/stats.html.
40. Sir David Goodall, "An Opportunity to Rethink Hunt Bill," *New York Times,* February 26, 2001.
41. Quotes from Robert Barr, "Tally-No! House of Commons Votes to Ban Fox Hunting," *Athens Daily News,* 29 November 1997.
42. This is based on a true story. However, the professor in question—the author—did not have the cat euthanized.
43. "Companion Animals, Pets or Prisoners?" *PETA Factsheet,* no. 19.
44. Sean Paige, "Hunting a Solution to the Bambi Boom," *Insight on News,* 3 July 2000, http://www. findarticles.com.
45. Pew Initiative on Food and Biotechnology, "Genetically Modified Crops in the United States," 2003. http://pewagbiotech.org/resources/factsheets/display.php3?FactsheetID=2
46. Per Pinstrup Andersen, "Biotechnology: A Matter of Life or Starvation," *Bangkok Post,* 26 November 2000.
47. NAAP Bernie, "Rules for Our Slice of the Ice," *The Evening Post* (Wellington, NZ), 5 December 2000, p. 7.
48. Steve La Rue, "More Retailers Warming to Rainforest-Friendly Coffee," *The San Diego Union-Tribune,* 5 November 2000, p. B-1.

Credits

p. 56: Reprinted by permission of the publisher from *A Theory of Justice* by John Rawls, Cambridge, MA: The Belknap Press of Harvard University Press, Copyright © 1971, 1999 by the President and Fellows of Harvard College. **p. 62:** Ayn Rand, "Man's Rights" from *The Virtue of Selfishness* by Ayn Rand. Copyright © 1961, 1964 by Ayn Rand. Used by permission of Dutton Signet, a division of Penguin Putnam Inc. **p. 66:** Nel Noddings, "*Caring: An Approach to Ethics and Moral Education,*" University of California Press, 1984. Copyright © 1984 The Regents of the University of California. Used with permission. **p. 69:** Confucius, *The Analects,* translated by D.C. Lau, Penguin Classics, 1979. Copyright © 1979 D.C. Lau. Reproduced by permission of Penguin Books Ltd. **p. 73:** P. Don Premasiri, "The Relevance of the Noble Eightfold Path to Contemporary Society" from *Buddhist Ethics and Modern Society,* Charles Wei-hsun Fu and Sandra A. Wawrytko, eds. Copyright © 1991. Reproduced with permission of Greenwood Publishing Group, Inc., Westport, CT. **p. 92:** Judith Jarvis Thomson, "A Defense of Abortion," from *Journal of Philosophy and Public Affairs,* Fall 1971, pp. 47–66. Reprinted by permission of Blackwell Publishing Ltd. **p. 102:** Reprinted by permission of the publisher from "An Almost Absolute Value in History," in *The Morality of Abortion: Legal and Historical Perspectives,* by John T. Noonan, Jr., pp. 51–59, Cambridge, MA: Harvard University Press, Copyright © 1970 by the President and Fellows of Harvard College. **p. 107:** Mary Anne Warren, "The Moral Significance of Birth," *Hypatia,* Vol. 4, No. 3, Fall 1989, pp. 46–65. Reprinted with permission from the author. **p. 114:** Don Marquis, "Why Abortion is Immoral" from *The Journal of Philosophy,* LXXXVI, 4, April 1989, pp. 183–202. Reprinted with permission from the publisher and the author. **p. 118:** Steven D. Hales, "Abortion and Fathers' Rights" from *Reproduction, Technology, and Rights,* eds. James M. Humber and Robert F. Almeder. Copyright 1996 by Humana Press. Reprinted by permission of Humana Press. **p. 147:** Matt Ridley, "The New Eugenics" *National Review,* July 31, 2000, pp. 33–37. Reprinted by permission of the publisher. **p. 151:** W. French Anderson, "Genetics and Human Malleability," *Hastings Center Report,* vol. 20, January/February 1990, pp. 21–24. Notes have been omitted. **p. 154:** John A. Robertson, "The Question of Human Cloning," *Hastings Center Report* 24, No. 2, 1994, pp. 6–14. Reprinted with permission from the author. **p. 161:** Excerpted, with the author's permission, from Leon Kass, "The Wisdom of Repugnance" from *The New Republic* 216, No. 22, June 2, 1997, pp. 17–26. **p. 169:** Lori Andrews and Dorothy Nelkin, "Whose Body Is It Anyway? Disputes Over Body Tissue in a Biotechnology Age," *The Lancet,* January 3, 1998, vol. 351, pp. 53–57. Copyright © 1998 by The Lancet Ltd. With permission from the publisher. **p. 195:** James Rachels, "Active and Passive Euthanasia" from *New England Journal of Medicine* Vol. 292, January 9, 1975. Copyright © 1975 Massachusetts Medical Society. All rights reserved. Reprinted with permission. **p. 200:** Margaret Pabst Battin, "The Case for Euthanasia" *Health Care Ethics,* D. VanDeVeer and Tom Regan, eds., Temple University Press, 1987. Reprinted by permission of the author. **p. 209:** Daniel Callahan, "'Aid-in-Dying': The Social Dimension" from *Commonweal,* August 9, 1991. Copyright © 1991 Commonweal Foundation. Reprinted with permission. **p. 213:** John Hardwig, "Is There a Duty to Die?" *Hastings Center Report* 27, no. 2 (1997): 34–42. Reprinted with permission from the publisher and author. Notes have been omitted. **p. 220:** Susan Wolf, "Gender, Feminism, and Death: Physician Assisted Suicide and Euthanasia," *Feminism and Bioethics* 1996. Reprinted with permission from the publisher and the author. **p. 249:** Ernest van den Haag, "The Ultimate Punishment: A Defense of Capital Punishment," *The Harvard Law Review,* Vol. 99, 1986. Copyright © 1986 by the Harvard Law Review Association. Used with permission. **p. 254:** Christopher W. Morris, "Punishment and Loss of Moral Standing," *Canadian Journal of Philosophy,* Vol. 21, No. 1, University of Calgary Press. Used with permission of the publisher. **p. 261:** Hugo Adam Bedau, "Capital Punishment" from *Matters of Life and Death,* Tom Regan, ed., 1993. Reprinted by permission of The McGraw-Hill Companies, Inc. **p. 360:** Jeffrey Reiman, "Why the Death Penalty Should Be Abolished in the United States," in Louis J. Pojman and Jeffrey Reiman, *The Death Penalty: For and Against,* Rowman and Littlefield, 1998. Reprinted with permission from the publisher. **p. 280:** From *Dead Man Walking* by Helen Prejean, copyright © 1993 by Helen Prejean. Used by permission of Random House, Inc. **p. 311:** Thomas Szasz, "The Ethics of Addiction" from *Harper's Magazine* 244, April 1972. Copyright © 1972 by Harper's Magazine. All rights reserved. Reproduced from the April edition by special permission. **p. 319:** James Q. Wilson, "Against the Legalization of Drugs," *Commentary,* 89, No 2, February 1990. Reprinted by permission of the author. **p. 327:** Douglas N. Husak, "A Moral Right to Use Drugs" in *Drugs and Rights,* Cambridge University Press, 1992. Reprinted with the permission of Cambridge University Press. **p. 335:** Thomas H. Murray, "Drugs, Sports, and Ethics," in *Feeling Good and Doing Better: Ethics and Nontherapeutic Drug Use,* T.H. Murray, W. Gaylin, R. Macklin, eds., Humana Press, 1984. Reprinted with permission of the publisher. **p. 364:** The Vatican, *Declaration on Sexual Ethics* (December 29, 1975). Reprinted with permission. **p. 369:** From *Philosophy and Sex, New Revised Edition,* edited by Robert Baker and Frederick Elliston, "Better Sex," by Sara Ruddick. (Amherst, NY: Prometheus Books). Copyright © 1994 by Robert Baker and Frederick Elliston. Reprinted with permission.

p. 379: Michael Ruse, "Is Homosexuality Bad Sexuality?" in *Homosexuality: A Philosophical Inquiry,* Basil Blackwell, 1994. With permission from the author. **p. 386:** John M. Finnis, "Law, Morality, and 'Sexual Orientation,'" Vol. 69, No. 3, *Notre Dame Law Review* (1994) 1049–1076. Reprinted with permission. Copyright by *Notre Dame Law Review,* University of Notre Dame. **p. 393:** Michael Nava and Robert Dawidoff, "The Case For Gay Marriage" in *Created Equal: Why Gay Rights Matter to America.* Copyright © 1994 by Michael Nava and Robert Dawidoff. Reprinted by permission of St. Martin's Press, LLC. **p. 398:** Cheshire Calhoun, "Family's Outlaws: Rethinking the Connections Between Feminism, Lesbianism, and the Family," *Feminism and Families,* Routledge 1997, Hilde Lindmann Nelson, ed. Copyright © 1997 Cheshire Calhoun. Reprinted with permission of the author. **p. 404:** Richard Wasserstrom: "Is Adultery Immoral?" from *Today's Moral Problems,* Richard Wasserstrom, ed. Reprinted by permission of the author. **p. 412:** Lois Pineau, "Date Rape: A Feminist Analysis," *Law and Philosophy* 8, 1989, 217–243. Reprinted with kind permission from Kluwer Academic Publishers. **p. 452:** Catherine Mackinnon, "Pornography, Civil Rights, and Speech" *Feminism Unmodified: Discourse on Life and Law,* Harvard University Press, 1987. Reprinted with permission from the author. **p. 460:** Charles R. Lawrence III, "If He Hollers Let Him Go: Regulating Racist Speech on Campus," *Duke Law Journal* 431, 1990. Used with permission from the author. **p. 469:** Jonathan Rauch, "In Defense of Prejudice: Why Incendiary Speech Must Be Protected," *Harper's Magazine,* May 1995. Copyright © 1995 by Harper's Magazine. All rights reserved. Reproduced from the May issue by special permission. **p. 475:** John Taylor, "Are You Politically Correct?" from *New York Magazine,* January 21, 1991. Edited from the original. Copyright © 1991 New York Magazine. Reprinted with permission from New York Magazine. **p. 482:** Alan Dershowitz, "Political Correctness, Speech Codes, and Diversity," *Harvard Law Record,* September 20, 1991. Reprinted with permission from the publisher. **p. 484:** Cass R. Sunstein, "The First Amendment in Cyberspace." Reprinted by permission of The Yale Law Journal Company and William S. Hein Company from *The Yale Law Journal,* Vol. 104, pp. 1751–1804. **p. 518:** Shelby Steele, "I'm Black, You're White, Who's Innocent?" in *The Content of Our Character: A New Vision of Race in America.* Copyright © 1990 Shelby Steele. Reprinted by permission of St. Martin's Press, LLC. **p. 523:** Jorge Garcia, "The Heart of Racism" *The Journal of Social Philosophy,* Vol 27, No. 1, Spring 1996. Reprinted with permission from the publisher. **p. 535:** Bernard R. Boxill, "The Color-Blind Principle," *Blacks and Social Justice,* Rowman and Littlefield, 1984. Reprinted with permission from the publisher. **p. 542:** Michael Levin, "Race, Biology, and Justice," *Public Affairs Quarterly,* Vol. 8, No. 3, July 1994. Reprinted with permission from the publisher. **p. 551:** Uma Narayan, "Colonialism and Its Others: Considerations on Rights and Care Discourses," *Hypatia,* Vol. 10, No. 2, Spring 1995. Reprinted with permission from the author. **p. 565:** National Organization for Women, *Bill of Rights.* Reprinted by permission. **p. 575:** From *The Second Sex* by Simone De Beauvoir, translated by H.M. Parshley, copyright 1952 and renewed 1980 by Alfred A. Knopf, a division of Random House, Inc. Used by permission of Alfred A. Knopf. **p. 581:** Ruth E. Groenhout, "Essentialist Challenges to Liberal Feminism," originally published in *Social Theory and Practice,* vol. 28, no. 1, January 2002, pp. 51–75. Reprinted by permission. **p. 589:** Christina Hoff Sommers, "Philosophers Against the Family" from *Person to Person,* George Graham and Hugh Lafollette, eds. Reprinted by permission of the author. **p. 599:** Nancy Dowd, "Work and Family: The Gender Paradox and the Limitations of Discrimination Analysis in Restructuring the Workplace," *Harvard Civil Rights Civil Liberties Review,* vol. 79, 1989. Reprinted by permission. **p. 609:** Katie Roiphe, "Reckless Eyeballing: Sexual Harassment on Campus," *The Morning After: Sex, Fear and Feminism on Campus.* Little, Brown and Co., 1993. Copyright © 1993 by Katherine Roiphe. By permission of Little, Brown and Company. **p. 617:** Steve Goldberg, "Male Aggression and the Attainment of Power, Authority, and Status," *The Inevitability of Patriarchy,* William Morrow, 1973. Copyright © 1973 Steven Goldberg. Reprinted by permission from the author. **p. 643:** Elizabeth Anscombe, "War and Murder" in *Nuclear Weapons: A Catholic Response,* Walter Stein, ed. Reprinted by permission of Rowman & Littlefield. **p. 649:** C.A.J. (Tony) Coady, "War and Terrorism" in *A Companion to Applied Ethics,* R.G. Frey and Christopher Heath Wellman, eds. Reprinted by permission of Blackwell Publishing Ltd. **p. 657:** Sohail H. Hashmi, "Interpreting the Islamic Ethics of War and Peace" from *The Ethics of War and Peace,* Terry Nardin, ed. © 1996 Princeton University Press, 1998 paperback edition. Reprinted by permission of Princeton University Press. **p. 666:** Robinson A. Grover: "The New State of Nature and the New Terrorism," from *Public Affairs Quarterly,* Vol. 16, No. 2, April 2002. Reprinted by permission of the author. **p. 676:** Excerpted with permission from Jonathan Granoff's article, "Nuclear Weapons, Ethics, Morals and Law" originally published in the *Brigham Young University Law Review* Volume 2000 Number 4 and available at: <http:www.law2.byu.edu/lawreview/2000_4.htm>. **p. 681:** David Luban, "The War on Terrorism and the End of Human Rights" in *Philosophy & Public Policy Quarterly,* Vol. 22, No. 3, Summer 2002. Reprinted by permission of Rowman & Littlefield. **p. 688:** Sara Ruddick, "Mothers and Men's Wars," from *Maternal Thinking: Toward a Politics of Peace.* Copyright © 1989 by Sara Ruddick. Reprinted by permission of Beacon Press, Boston. **p. 696:** With permission from Jonathan Granoff's speech, "Peace and Security" presented at the 4th World Summit of Nobel Peace Laureates, Rome, November 28, 2003. **p. 720:** Tom Regan, "The Moral Basis of Vegetarianism" in *All That Dwell Therein: Animal Rights and Environmental Ethics,* University of California Press, 1982. Reprinted with permission from the author. **p. 725:** Jan Narveson, "Animal Rights Revisited," *Ethics and Animals,* Harlan B. Miller and William H. Williams, eds., Humana Press, 1983. Reprinted with permission from Humana Press, Inc. **p. 731:** Peter Singer, *Animal Liberation, Second Edition,* Random House, 1990. Copyright © 1990 Peter Singer. Reprinted with permission of the author. **p. 740:** Carl Cohen, "Do Animals Have Rights?" *Ethics and Behavior,* Vol. 7, No. 2, 1997. Copyright © 1997 Carl Cohen. Reprinted with permission of the author. **p. 749:** "The Land Ethic, pp. 201–226.", from *A Sand County Almanac: And Sketches Here and There* by Aldo Leopold, copyright 1949, 1953, 1966, renewed 1977, 1981 by Oxford University Press, Inc. Used by permission of Oxford University Press. **p. 753:** Bill Devall and George Sessions, *Deep Ecology: Living as if Nature Mattered,* Salt Lake City: Peregrine Smith Books (Gibbs Smith, Publisher), 1985. Reprinted with permission from the publisher. **p. 759:** Richard Watson, "A Critique of Anti-Anthropocentric Ethics," *Environmental Ethics,* Vol. 5, No. 3, Fall 1983. Reprinted with permission from the publisher and the author. **p. 765:** Karen J. Warren, excerpted from "The Power and the Promise of Ecological Feminism," *Environmental Ethics,* Vol. 12, No. 2, Summer 1990, pp. 123–146. Reprinted with permission from the publisher and the author.

Index

Dec 10/07

IMPORTANT

HERE IS YOUR REGISTRATION CODE TO ACCESS MCGRAW-HILL PREMIUM CONTENT AND MCGRAW-HILL ONLINE RESOURCES

For key premium online resources you need THIS CODE to gain access. Once the code is entered, you will be able to use the web resources for the length of your course.

Access is provided only if you have purchased a new book.

If the registration code is missing from this book, the registration screen on our website, and within your WebCT or Blackboard course will tell you how to obtain your new code. Your registration code can be used only once to establish access. It is not transferable.

To gain access to these online resources

1. **USE** your web browser to go to: **http://register.dushkin.com**
2. **CLICK** on "First Time User"
3. **ENTER** the Registration Code printed on the tear-off bookmark on the right
4. After you have entered your registration code, click on "Register"
5. **FOLLOW** the instructions to setup your personal UserID and Password
6. **WRITE** your UserID and Password down for future reference. Keep it in a safe place.

If your course is using WebCT or Blackboard, you'll be able to use this code to access the McGraw-Hill content within your instructor's online course.

To gain access to the McGraw-Hill content in your instructor's WebCT or Blackboard course simply log into the course with the user ID and Password provided by your instructor. Enter the registration code exactly as it appears to the right when prompted by the system. You will only need to use this code the first time you click on McGraw-Hill content.

These instructions are specifically for student access. Instructors are not required to register via the above instructions.

The McGraw-Hill Companies

Higher Education

Thank you, and welcome to your McGraw-Hill Online Resources.

978-0-07-297826-1
0-07-297826-0 t/a
Boss
Analyzing Moral Issues, 3/e

98f29-k6eq-bcnn-esv8

REGISTRATION CODE

REGISTRATION CODE

The McGraw-Hill Companies
Mc Graw Hill Higher Education